UNIVERSITY OF WASHINGTON PUBLICATIONS

IN

LANGUAGE AND LITERATURE

Volume 12

May, 1949

A REFERENCE GUIDE TO THE LITERATURE OF TRAVEL

Including Tours, Descriptions, Towns, Histories and Antiquities, Surveys, Ancient and Present State, Gardening, etc.

BY

EDWARD GODFREY COX

VOLUME THREE

GREAT BRITAIN

GREENWOOD PRESS, PUBLISHERS
NEW YORK

Originally published in 1949 and reprinted
with the permission of the University of Washington Press

First Greenwood Reprinting 1969

Library of Congress Catalogue Card Number 70-90492

SBN 8371-2163-9

"If anyone came to the Lords of the Counsell for a License to travaile, hee would first examine him of England: if he found him ignorant, would bid him stay at home and know his owne countrey firste."—Lord High Treasurer Baron Burghley, quoted from Henry Peacham's *Compleat Gentleman*.

PREFACE

John Speed, in the Preface to his *Theatre of the Empire of Great Britain,* endeavored, he says, to give satisfaction to all, without offense to any. If he has failed, he must confess, "This to myself I have gained, that whilst I set all my thought and cogitations hereon, I had small regard for the bewitching pleasures and enticements of this wicked world. Therefore in the sight of the Congregation of the Lord, and the audience of our God, let us keep and seek for all the commandments of the Lord our God, that we may possess this good land, and leave it for an inheritance for our children after us forever."

While my regard for the enticements of this wicked world is less tinged with the color of piety and original sin, I confess to the same deprivation of the social pleasures that my time might be spent in the dull work of typing off references, in prowling through the shelves of libraries, searching through files of periodicals, and reading books of travel, to the end that my name might be read on the back of this volume, while my personal self fades out of recollection under the trappings of a grammarian's funeral.

Speed consoled himself with the vision of the coming generations learning to know and love their land through increasing their awareness of its pride and its glories, its beauties and its shame, and thus enlarging for themselves "the frame of Kingdomes and Commonwealths." The response which he did not live to hear might well be summed up in the memorable words spoken by Johnson when faced with the antiquities of Iona: "Whatever withdraws us from the powers of our senses; whatever makes the past, the distant or the future predominate over the present, advances us in the dignity of thinking beings."

So, in turn, I put my trust in the hope that this compilation of dead men's books, by bringing to light the times and conditions of an England that has been, will enhance the sense of man's long continuity and open up for future students new relations of literature and life.

I had thought that with the completion of this volume I could write *finis* as far as my connections with the work were concerned, and turn my attention to endeavors more creative. But its ever-expanding bulk shut out the discovery of Ireland, which must now be content to wait on volume IV, with which will be combined items that missed printing in the preceding volumes, and even in the present one. Behind the opaque future of this consummation lies the promise of a lasting respite.

In plan the present work follows the course laid down for the first two volumes, with some slight variations in typography and make-up. The prefatory annotations to the various sections attempt to tell somewhat of the lay of the land and to account for the choice of sections and items listed. That the work will turn out to be flawless is a vain expectation. "Nature deviates; and can man do less"? But what I do pray for is that no one consulting the index will fail to find the name sought for under the paging listed.

It remains to express my grateful acknowledgments of help received. The University of Washington Press must naturally be absolved from any "guilt by

association" for mistakes that are my own. Its efforts were directed to as correct a proofreading as could be expected of man. To the proofreaders, then, and particularly to Dr. William M. Read, the Director, who scrutinized meticulously the Latin titles and suggested emendations, I offer my hearty thanks. I wish also to thank Mr. Alexander Davidson, Jr., bookseller of rare Americana in New York, for his kind assistance in looking up imprints and dates in the New York Public Library. To Dr. Francis S. Bourke, of Dublin, who himself is working on a bibliography of tours in Ireland, I am indebted for help in verifying titles and dates. The presses of Columbia University and Princeton University graciously allowed me permission to quote John Alexander Kelly's *England and the Englishman in German Literature of the Eighteenth Century* (Columbia) and *German Visitors to English Theaters in the Eighteenth Century* (Princeton), respectively. And what I owe to the Huntington Library in a three months' sojourn there, both for its magnificent collections and for the ever willing assistance of its staff, is beyond measurement.

In Elizabethan days, criticism was rough and ready. I should like to have the confidence in the perfection of my work that Drayton expressed in his *Polyolbion*, so that I could say to those that take great pride in their ignorance and delight in their folly: "I wish that it may be hereditary from them to their posteritie, that their children may bee beg'd for Fooles to the fift Generation, untill it may be beyond the memory of man to know that there was ever any other of their Families." But such high-flying and full-toned boasting does not become the modern scholar who fears at every turn to meet some specialist fixing him with a critical eye and commanding him to stay. In these days the cause of learning is best advanced by sharing knowledge. Hence I am too appreciative of the corrections I have already received from reviewers and in personal letters to wish my critics anything short of their hearts' desires. And so, echoing Drayton, thus I take my leave.

EDWARD GODFREY COX

Seattle, Washington
April, 1949

Contents of Volume III

ERRATA ET CORRIGENDA

P. 24, 1. 18, *for* Sir Donald Monro *read* Donald Monro (Dean)

P. 50, 1. 27, *for* Edward Calamy *read* Edmund Calamy

P. 56, 1. 21, *for* Rev. J. E. Craven *read* Rev. J. B. Craven

P. 86, 1. 1, *for* Mission *read* Misson

P. 135, 1. 11, *for* Robert Burton *read* William Burton

P. 180, 11. 11, 12, 14, *for* Schnebbelie *read* Schnebberlie

P. 393, 1. 24, *for* John Fantosme *read* Jordan Fantosme

P. 561, 1. 11, *for* Healy *read* Heely

A REFERENCE GUIDE TO THE
LITERATURE OF TRAVEL

I
Tours by Natives

(As Beresford remarks in his Introduction to the *Torrington Diaries,* the history of man is very largely the history of communications, and material progress, morals, and manners depend in great measure on the pathways opened out on the earth, over the seas, and in the air. True it is, but it must be admitted that, in bringing the remote within reach of the general public, men have paid a price: in return for comfort and speed, they have leveled provincial picturesqueness to uniformity, substituted commercialization for pristine charm and hospitality, and smothered adventure with ennui. Travelers have become tourists, and tourism supports the population. It is well then for the rugged soul who yet prefers life in the raw to be reminded that Merry Old England is still his to traverse if he but reach up to the shelf and take down John Leland's *Itinerary* or John Taylor's *The Pennyless Pilgrimage* or Celia Fiennes' *Through England on a Side Saddle* or Martin's *A Late Voyage to St. Kilda* or any or all of the accounts of travel listed below. To such a hardy adventurer England will show many faces. It may be of a wilderness of heath and common, great stretches of unfenced ploughland, thinly dotted with habitations, trackways that never felt the grind of wheeled traffic, and roads that turned to quagmires in a day's rain. It may be of vast reaches of parklands smoothed to a velvet finish by the application of great stone rollers, adorned with artfully arranged clumps of trees, temples of Vesta, Palladian bridges, Roman ruins, and man-made lakes. Some regions will be black with the smoke of new industries, and others rural and innocent enough to pose as "Sweet Auburns." Whatever the mood of the reader, the England of his choice awaits his outstretched hand.

What did these men go out for to see? Many and various things. Much of early travel was undertaken for official purposes, rarely for the zest of the open road. Some were prompted by the search for antiquities and others by the scientific urge to describe and classify the flora of a given region. To report on the trade and manufactures of the country, investigate the conditions of life that depended on mining, fishing, farming, bring the Gospel to benighted regions, observe the manners and customs of people for the edification of mankind, visit show places like gentlemen's seats, enjoy scenery and experience emotion in the presence of the gloomy, the sublime, or the picturesque—such were motives that operated according to the whim of the individual and the prevailing vogue. Some were moved by the unamiable desire to feed their spleen by visiting places and peoples they disliked. And here and there appears the universal and timeless yearning to taste the mere joy of the road. Reasons for traveling are as "plentiful as blackberries," and he who must have them can do no better than look for them in the narratives themselves.)

1549 LELAND, JOHN. The Laboryouse Journey and serche of Johan Leylande, for Englandes Antiquitees, geven of hym as a new yeares gyfte to Kynge Henry VIII., in the XXXVII. yeare of his Reygne, with declaracyons enlarged: by Johan Bale. 12mo. London.

Reprinted in *The Lives of Leland, Hearne, and Wood,* Oxford, 1772 (with some copies printed separately); Leland's *Itinerary* printed by Hearne, 9 vols., Oxford, 1710 (see Leland under 1710-12 below); his *Collectanea* by Hearne, 6 vols., Oxford (see under HISTORY AND ANTIQUITIES), 1715. Portions dealing with various counties printed: Leland's Journey through Wiltshire, A. D. 1540-42, with notes by J. E. Jackson, in *Wiltshire Arch. and Nat. Hist. Mag.,* vol. I, Devizes, 1875; Leland in Somersetshire, by Edward H. Bates, in *Proc. Somersetshire Arch. and Nat. Hist. Soc.,* vol. 33, Taunton; Leland's Itinerary, by Wm. Harrison, in *Trans. Lancashire and Cheshire Antiq. Soc.,* vol. 28, Manchester, 1911; Leland in Devon and Cornwall, by Chope, *Early Tours in Devon and Cornwall,* Exeter, 1918. The best edition is that by Lucy Toulmin Smith, 5 vols., 4to, London, 1907-10. Her introduction is especially valuable for the life and work of Leland.

Gibson, in his *Life of Camden,* says that Leland was the first man to turn the eyes of the kingdom toward English antiquity. From him stems a long and worthy line of English antiquaries. His learning led Henry VIII to appoint him as Keeper of the King's Library and to issue a Commission in 1533 authorizing him to travel over the kingdom with power "to serche after England's Antiquities and to peruse the libraries of all cathedrals, abbyes, priories, colleges, &c. as also all places wherein records, writings and secrets of Antiquity were reposited." These perambulations used up six years. He then retired to the rectory of St. Michael's in le Querne, London, to begin the enormous task of arranging his collections for a history of Britain, with all its shires and families, from the earliest times to his own day. He wrote an account of his project in address to the king in 1546. Neither

the king nor the author lived to see its accomplishment. Henry died in 1547 and Leland became insane in 1550, probably from want of wages as much as from overwork. He died in this state in 1552. His collections passed from hand to hand, lessening in bulk during the process. Finally what was left found a resting place in the Bodleian Library, where they were edited as noted above by Hearne. Leland had the good fortune, which we share through him, of having had access to manuscripts in the monasteries before they were scattered to the winds by the spoilers. Written records and tradition were both checked, however, by personal contact with places as he rode on horseback over the kingdom. One wishes he had been as generous with descriptions of buildings then existing as he was with notations of distances from town to town and the best way of approaching them. But English cosmography can be grateful for the establishment of regional surveying based on personal observation, thus preparing the way for Saxton, Lambard, Norden, and Stow.

1576   LAMBARDE, WILLIAM. Perambulation of Kent. 4to. London.

This work offers rather a perambulation of the reader than a record of the writer's journeys. It is in reality a description of the county, its history and antiquities. For fuller account, see under DESCRIPTIONS.

1577   SETTLE, DIONYSE. A True Reporte of the laste Voyage into the West and Northwest Regions . . . worthily atchieued by Capteine Frobisher of the sayde Voyage . . . . 8vo. London.

A short portion of this work relates to the Orkneys, which were visited en route to the Arctic regions. For this voyage see this date under NORTHWEST PASSAGE, vol. II of this work.

1578   CHURCHYARD, THOMAS. A Discourse of the Queenes Maiesties entertainement in Suffolk and Norfolk: with a description of many thinges then presently seene. Deuised by Thomas Churcheyarde, Gent. with divers shewes of his own inuention sette out at Norwich: and some rehearsal of his Highnesse retourne from Progresse, Whereunto is adioyned a Commendation of Sir Humfrey Gilberts ventrous Iourney. 4to. London.

This presumably refers to the Queen's Progress to Norwich in 1576. There are listed below two more items bearing close resemblance to the above, one dated 1579 and the other without date. Both use Churchyard's name.

1579   CHURCHYARD, THOMAS. The Entertaynement of the Queenes Maiestie into Suffolke and Norfolke. A matter touching upon the Iourney of Sir Humfrey Gilberte, Knight. A Welcome home to Master Martin Frobisher, and all those gentlemen . . . that have been with him in the country called Meta Incognita. 4to. London.

n. d.   Queen Elizabeth's Progress to Norwich 1576, collected by B. G. (B. Goldingham) and T. C. (Thomas Churchyard). Imprinted at London by Bynneman. With a map of Norwich by John Day. 4to. London.
This was also printed in Stow's Supplement to Holinshed, vol. II, and in Blomefield's *History of Norwich.*—Gough, *Anecdotes of Brit. Topog.,* 368.

1585   GIRALDUS DE BARRI (called Cambrensis). Itinerarium Cambriae: seu laboriosae Baldvini Cantuar. Archiepiscopi per Walliam legationis accurata descriptio, Auctore Sil. Giraldo Cambrense. Cum Annotationibus Davidis Poveli, Sacrae Theologiae professoris. 12mo. London.

This makes up the second of the three parts of Ponticus Virunnius, *Britannicae Historiae libri sex,* edited by David Powel; reprinted in Camden, without notes or comment, *Scriptores Historiae Anglicanae,* Frankfort, 1603 (see under HISTORY AND CHRONICLE). For the second treatise of Cambrensis, *Cambriae Descriptio,* sometimes called *De laudabilibus Walliae,* which is the third part of Ponticus, see under DESCRIPTIONS this date. The second book of the latter was also printed by Wharton, *Anglia Sacra,* London, 1691 (see under HISTORY AND CHRONICLE). Reprinted, with text and translation, by Sir Richard Colt Hoare, 2 vols, 4to, London, 1806; this translation, with most if not all of its faults, reprinted in Bohn's Library, together with the Irish treatise, London, 1847-64. The Itinerarium and

Descriptio edited by James F. Dimock, Rolls Series (*Rerum Brit. Medii Aevi Scriptores*) vol. VI, *Opera*, London, 1868.

Powel, Camden, and Wharton were all bad editors. The same may be said of Hoare, despite the voluminous notes on Welsh history, antiquities, and topography. The first three omit or alter without warrant; the last translates loosely and inaccurately. For the history of the MSS, their relations, versions, and future course, see Dimock's Introduction.

The first version of the *Itinerarium* must have appeared in the spring or summer of 1191; the second, with additions and alterations, in about 1197; and the third after the summer of 1213 (the text used by Dimock). Of the three treatises of Cambrensis, the Itinerarium, the Description of Wales, and the Description of Ireland, it is the first that holds top place in value, with the second following after. The first was written in a generous, amiable spirit, and is quite free from the bitter tone, the lies and scandalous assertions often disfiguring the other two. For the weeks he spent traveling through Wales in company with Archbishop Baldwin must have been the happiest of his life. High in favor with Henry II, as he believed, full of confidence in his future, the chosen companion of the Metropolitan of England on an important and solemn mission through his own country, where he could shine as a great man among his friends and princely relatives, he could not do otherwise than paint his progress in a roseate light. His *Description of Wales,* though far more complete and reliable than that of Ireland, at times gives the Welsh a bad name. But so did his friend Walter of Map. It has to be remembered, however, that at this period the Welsh had not as yet become imbued with the sanctity of Roman law; they did not think it necessary to get a Papal dispensation in order to marry their cousins. How these treatises were received by his contemporaries he does not tell us. It is said that his name was not honored by later Welshmen, either bards or chroniclers. But Higden, in his *Polychronicon,* borrowed, with acknowledgements, largely from Cambrensis for both his account of Wales and of Ireland, and probably thus brought Cambrensis to the notice of English historians and antiquaries.

1590 FERRIS, RICHARD. The most dangerous and memorable Adventure of R. Ferris, who undertoke in a small wherry boate to rowe by sea to the Citie of Bristowe. London.

See J. P. Collier, *Illustrations of Early English Popular Literature,* vol. II, London, 1863; reprinted also in Edward Arber, *An Early English Garner,* vol. VI, 154-66, London, 1877.

This was a right venturesome voyage even for a trained seaman, let alone for one who like Ferris was not. To make the trip he had to get a permit from the Lord Chamberlain. The boat, a newly built wherry with oars and sails, was given a great send-off, and after battling winds and tide rips, with enforced anchorages in various coves, and pursuit by a pirate, who was himself taken prisoner, it reached Bristol, where a hearty welcome awaited him. The boat was paraded up the street with flags, trumpet, drums, and fife. Both Ferris and his boat returned to London by land. His object seemingly was to encourage his countrymen to accustom themselves to hazardous undertakings in order better to daunt the Spaniards.

1607 BUSH, M. A True Relation of the Travels of M. Bush, a Gentleman; who with his owne handes without any other mans Helpe made a Pynace, in which hee past by Ayre, Land and Water: from Lamborne, a place in Barkshire, to the Custome-house Key in London, 1607. 4to. London.

The title page has a curious woodcut depicting Mr. Bush being raised in his ship to the top of a church-tower.—Quoted. The account seems to have been written by an A. N.

1609 Old Meg of Herefordshire for a mayd-marian, and Hereford towne for a morris-dance; or twelve Morris-dancers in Herefordshire of 1200 years old. Dedicated to that renowned old Hall, Taberer of Herefordshire, and to his invincible weather-beaten, nut-browne taber, being old and sound thirty years and upwards. 4to. London.

This cryptic title is meant to tell how Serjeant Hopkins, who entertained James I on his Progress here, to show how healthy and long-lived the inhabitants were, assembled these twelve old men and women, whose ages together amounted to above 1200 years, to dance before him.—From Gough, 712.

1614 LITHGOW, WILLIAM. The Totall Discourse of the Rare Aduentures and painfull Peregrinations of long nineteene Yeares Travayles from Scotland to the most Famous Kingdomes in Europe, Asia, and Africa. 4to. London.

> For a fuller account of this 36,000-mile traveler and various editions, see under GENERAL TRAVELS AND DESCRIPTIONS, vol. I of this work.

1617 MORYSON, FYNES. An Itinerary VVritten by Fynes Moryson, Gent. . . . Containing His Ten Yeeres Trauell Through the Twelve Dominions of Germany, Bohmerland, Sweitzerland, Netherland, Denmarke, Poland, Italy, Turky, France, England, Scotland and Ireland, written first in the Latine tongue, and then translated into English. Fol. London.

> For an account of the writer's travels and the various editions of his work, see under CONTINENTAL EUROPE, vol. I of this work. His relation of his travels in the British Isles is contained in the First Part. Much of the Scottish part is printed in Hume Brown, *Early Travellers*, 80-90.
>
> This was the day of doughty travelers. In his ramblings Moryson is to be ranked with Lithgow, Coryate, and Peter Mundy. He set out for Scotland by way of Berwick in April, 1598. Like other visitors he was struck with the number of gentlemen's seats and castles in the neighborhood of Edinburgh. Like others he noticed that the horses are small, and added that the Scotch would give any price for one of the English geldings, except that at this period none could be had without paying a great penalty. The trade of Scotland with England, France, and the Baltic Sea and its imports from abroad received considerable attention from him. But the poverty of the country led to large emigrations to Poland and other countries. He observed no art in cookery nor in furniture and other household conveniences. The visitor was bound to be much inconvenienced by the want of inns, despite the efforts of Scottish kings to encourage their establishment. As usual with other travelers, the climate called for no good words.

1618 TAYLOR, JOHN (the Water Poet). The Pennyles Pilgrimage, or the Moneylesse Perambulation, of Iohn Taylor, Alias the Kings Majesties Water-Poet. How He Traueled on Foot from London to Edinborough in Scotland, not carrying any Money to or fro, neither Begging, Borrowing, or Asking Meate, Drinke or Lodging. With a Description of his Entertainment in all places of his Iourney . . . with a true Report of the unmatchable Hunting in the Braes of Marre and Badenoch in Scotland, etc. 4to. London.

> Reprinted by Charles Hindley in *Old Book Collector's Miscellany*, London, 1871; in Hume Brown, *Early Travellers*, 104-186. A collected edition of his works supervised by Taylor himself, printed in London, 1603 (he continued to publish till his death in 1653). Works reprinted by the Spenser Society, London, 1867-68, 1877-88.
>
> Few accounts of travel are more amusing than the above. This unpredictable itinerant was always on the go, and never failed to turn his wanderings into print, which he used to hawk about himself, and with good financial returns. It was charged that he was prompted to propose this trip by the rumors that Ben Jonson had purposed making a pedestrian tour to Scotland, an intention that raised greater curiosity even than that of Samuel Johnson in 1773. Though Jonson was only forty-five years old, yet his "mountain belly" and "prodigious waist" were a burden that only he could carry. Jonson set out near the beginning of July, 1618; Taylor followed, July 14, and to do Jonson one better pledged himself to start without a penny, neither to beg nor borrow en route, and to return penniless. But he did borrow ten shillings in Edinburgh, though on leaving that city he "discharged his pocket of all the money he had got, so that he might leave as empty of pocket as he entered." He received the utmost civilities while in Scotland from both nobles and gentry, and enjoyed in general good fare at the inns and lodgings, which he describes in good particulars. He visited the coal mines under the sea, ventured into the Highlands, experienced the usual contacts with dirt and vermin, etc. He met Jonson on his return at Leith, and, as he was not a man to repay civility with discourtesy, commemorates his kindness. It has been pointed out that his description of the old Holyrood Palace is the latest we have, for it was destroyed by Cromwell's soldiery, whom lovers of antiquity have good reason to curse. All through his account runs a genial tone and a quaint style.

1620 ———. The Praise of Hempseed. With the Voyage of Mr. Roger Bird and the Writer hereof in a Boat of brown paper from London to Quinborough in Kent (Queensborough). 4to. London.

> Taylor, being a waterman by profession, comes naturally by his propensity to enjoy navigation of the rivers and the coast. But a voyage in a *brown paper* boat caps a' for whimsicality. Naturally the water made short work of the boat but not of Taylor, who managed to scramble safely to shore.

1622 ———. A Verry Merry Wherry-Ferry-Voyage, or Yorke for my Money, sometimes Perilous, sometimes Quarrellous, by John Taylor and Job Pennell. 8vo. London.

1623 ADAMSON, HENRY. The Traveller's Joy; to which is added, The Ark, a Poem. 12mo. London.

> This work is listed here on a hazard that it might have something to do with traveling in England.

TAYLOR, JOHN. A New Discovery by Sea, with a Wherry from London to Salisbury. 8vo. London.

> In verse. This trip was performed in a boat fully found and with a crew of five men. The trip down the Thames ran smoothly enough, and afforded opportunity for descriptions of the seats and sights lining the banks. But on reaching the sea they were plentifully vexed with rough water and hard landings, with running aground on shoals, and with being mistaken for pirates. They made Salisbury, however, and gave this city a well-merited rebuke for not making the river more navigable. Here they gave their boat away and proceeded by land to London. The work contains descriptions of places, of the sea's ravages on the shore line, and of manners of people, some of whom are named.

———. The World runnes on Wheeles or Oddes, betwixt Carts and Coaches. 8vo. London.

1629 JOHNSON, THOMAS. For the tour of this writer in search of plants, see his *Iter Plantarum Investigationis,* under NATURAL HISTORY.

1630 TAYLOR, JOHN. All the Works of John Taylor, the Water Poet. Being Sixty-Three in number. Collected into one Volume by the Author, with sundry new Additions, Corrected, Revised, and newly Imprinted. Woodcuts of the Kings and Queens in the text. First collected edition. Fol. London.

> As is noted above, Taylor did not cease publication with this collected edition.

1635 HERBERT, SIR THOMAS. Travells in Wales. (Place?)

> So cited in Rowlands, *Cambrian Bibliography,* who adds that this well known traveler gave a full account of the Voyage of Madoc ab Owain to America.

1638 BRATHWAITE, RICHARD. Barnabee's Journall, under the Names of Mirtilus and Faustulus Shadowed: for the Travellers Solace lately published, to most apt numbers reduced, and to the old tune of Barnabee, commonly chanted. 16mo. London.

> Numerous editions followed, frequently with additions and some changes in title: 2nd edit., 8vo, London, 1716; 3rd, London, 1723; another, 12mo, London, 1774; again, 1778; with an account of the author and bibliographical history of former editions, London, 1818; again, 1822; edit. by Haslewood, revised by W. Carew Hazlitt, 12mo, London, 1876; Penguin Press, 1932. See below.

The excessively rare first edition was dedicated to his intimate friend, Sir Alexander Radcliffe. The poem is a sprightly record of a tour, in Latin and English doggerel verse. Southey pronounced it to be the best piece of rhymed Latin in modern literature.—Maggs, no. 574.

A waggish, lecherous, but wittily irresponsible scoundrel, who frolicked all his rollicking way over England, and ended up at Stavely, with his neat gilt canister in one hand and his pipe in the other, singing.

But I am chaste as doth become me,
For the country's eyes are on me.—Bookseller's Note.

The modern reader may purse up his lips at some of the lines of this poem, but let him remember that our forefathers had ears that were fairly robust.

1716   BRATHWAITE, RICHARD. Drunken Barnaby's Four Journeys to the North of England, in Latin and English Verse . . . to which is added Bessy Bell. 2 plates. 8vo. London.

An index and some introductory matter were added to this edition. These were reprinted in subsequent ones.

1762   ———. Barnaby's Journal, alternate English and Latin, to which is added, Lucus Chevinus, Chevy Chase, with separate pagination. 12mo. Dublin.

The same title is repeated in the London edition of 1774.

1778   ———. Drunken Barnaby's Four Journies to the North of England. In Latin and English metre. Wittily and merrily (tho' an Hundred Years ago) composed, found among some old musty Books that had lain a long Time in a Corner and now at last made public. Together with Bessy Bell. To which is now added (never before published) the Ancient Ballad of Chevy Chase. In Latin and English verse. London.

1818   ———. Barnabae Itinerarium, or Barnabee's Journal, to which are prefixed an Account of the Author, A Bibliographical History of the former editions of the work, by Joseph Haslewood. Plates. 8vo. London.

TAYLOR, JOHN. Taylors Travels and Perambvlation, through, and by more than thirty times twelve Signes of the Zodiack, of the Famous Cities of London and Westminster . . . With an Alphabeticall Description of all the Taverne Signes in the Cities, Suburbs, and Liberties *aforesaid and significant Epigrams upon the said severall* Signes. London.

Evidently the names of inns ran in favorites, as certain ones are often repeated in various parts of the city.

1639   ———. Part of this Summer's Travels; or, news from Hell, Hull, and Halifax, from York, Linne, Leicester, Chester, Coventry, etc. 12mo. London. (26 leaves.)

In verse and prose. Leicester is noted for clean streets, being free of dung hills, filth, and soil, so that a man may wander all over the town in a pair of slippers and never wet his feet. Coventry still had walls, gates, and posterns. At Nottingham the poor dug their homes out of the rocks. In Derby lead mining was free to any one on payment of a tenth part of the ore dug to the landlord. An account of the famous Halifax gibbet, the precursor of the guillotine, brings out the fact that the owner of the goods stolen must cut the line which lets the knife fall on the thief's neck (see Midgley, under 1708, TOWNS). The Hell mentioned in the title is the high Exchequer bar at Westminster, a good drinking place.

1640   CARVE (CAREW), THOMAS. Itinerarium ex Hibernia per Poloniam, Germaniam, et Bohemiam. Mainz.

The only complete edition of this work is that published in 1859.
A portion of these travels relates to England and Ireland as well as to the continent (see under WEST EUROPE, vol. I of this work).

1641   TAYLOR, JOHN. John Taylor's last Voyage and Adventure, performed from the twentieth of July last 1641 to the tenth of September following. In which he

past, with a Sculler's Boate from the Citie of London, to the Cities and Townes of Oxford, Gloucester, Shrewesbury, Bristoll, Bathe, Monmouth and Hereford, etc. 8vo. London.

In verse and prose. Taylor naturally praises navigable rivers and deplores those that are not. He says he bears a "naturall affection to Portable Rivers and a setled inclination and desire of the preservation and use of them." He obtained money for the journey from friends on promise to repay them with a book on his return. In going up the Thames he was often forced to wade, lead, and haul the boat, and encountered fourteen locks. Sometimes he used wagons to haul the boat over portages. The rivers navigated were the Thames, Isis, Severn, Wye, Teme, Lugge, Loden, Doyre, Monnoes, and Avon. While Camden, Drayton, and Speed declared these rivers on their maps, he alone sought to find their wrongs and discover their remedy. Glimpses are given of the commerce carried on at various places and notice is taken of some of the religious sects encountered, such as the Schismatiques, Brownists, Anabaptists, Familists, Humorists, and Foolists.

1647 CORBET, RICHARD. Iter Boreale. In Poetica Stromata: a Collection of Sundry Pieces in Poetry: Drawne by the known and approved Hand of R. C. 12mo. London.

Another edit., London, 1672.
This work relates the doings of four Oxford dons on a vacation trip. The record is taken up mainly with what they ate and drank, diversified with diatribes against Papists and Puritans and details of what befell them on their journey. The author was Dean of Christ Church and later Bishop of Oxford and Bishop of Norwich. His *jeu d'esprit*, which seems to have been composed in 1621, circulated in manuscript until it was printed as listed above, twelve years after his death.—From Aubin, *Topographical Poetry*.

1648 TAYLOR, JOHN. Taylor's Travels from London to the Isle of Wight: with his Returne and Occasion of his Journey. 4to. London.

Taylor made this trip to see his sovereign and to earn some money wherewith to pay his bills. He instances many cures of the King's evil by the royal touch. The work is in prose and verse printed on six leaves.

1649 ———. John Taylor's Wandering to see the Wonders of the West: How he travelled neere 600 miles from London to the Mount, in Cornwall. 4to. London.

In this work Taylor recounts his meetings with the ravages of war, his experience with inns and drunken hosts, with inns overrun with fleas, with rescues by hospitable gentlemen, etc. His opinion of Mont Saint Michael is not high.

———. What Will You Have? A Calf with a White Face; or, A Relation of his Travailes from England into Ireland, Scotland, Poland, Holland, Amsterdam, and other Places, and is now newly arrived in the Citie of London, where he means to abide. Woodcut on title of a Cavalier, a calf with a white face, and three puritans. 4to. London.

WELDON, SIR ANTHONY. A Perfect Description of the People and Character of Scotland. 12mo. London.

Reprinted with Evelyn's *A Character of England*, London, 1659; an edit., London, 1697; in *North Briton*, no. 13, 1762; in *The Life and Political Writings of John Wilkes*, 12mo, Birmingham, 1769; also in *Edinburgh Weekly Magazine*, 1769; in Hume Brown, *Early Travellers*, 103 ff.
This scurrilous, vituperative libel on the Scotch and Scotland has been attributed to James Howell, of the *Ho-Epistolae* (see under 1645-55, LETTERS, DIARIES, MEMOIRS), but the evidence points otherwise, for apparently it was the work of one who accompanied James I on his visit to Scotland in 1617, the year when Howell had just left the university to take charge of a glasshouse in London. Furthermore it lacks the genial tone of Howell's writings. More probably it was written by Sir Anthony Weldon, who is known to have been one of the company attending James I. The royal visit was unpopular with the

Scotch, who had asked James to defer his coming until the grass had grown for cattle, thereby occasioning Weldon's charge that hay was something neither man nor beast knew the meaning of. As a specimen of his wholesale condemnation of things Scotch may be quoted the following: "They hold their noses if you talk of bearbaiting, and stop their ears if you speak of play; fornication they hold but a pastime, wherein man's ability is approved, and a woman's fertility is discovered; at adultery they shake their heads; theft they rail at; they think it impossible to lose the way to heaven, if they can but leave Rome behind them . . . they go to church in the forenoon to hear the law, and to the crags and mountains in the afternoon to louse themselves." As for trees, he concludes that Judas would find it easier to repent than to find a tree to hang himself on. This pasquinade is not to be taken seriously, for by reading between the lines one will find considerable information on Scotland of that day. It naturally provoked some indignant replies.—From Brown, *op. cit.*

1650   TAYLOR, JOHN. A Late Weary Merry Voyage, from London to Gravesend, to Cambridge. London.

1653   ———. The Certaine Travailes of an uncertain Journey begun on Tuesday the 9th of August, and ended on Saturday the 3rd of September following, 1653. 8vo. London.

In verse. This trip was made on horseback through Sussex into Kent and back by way of Canterbury and Gravesend. Much attention is centered on good eats and drinks, one of which, known as "Eastbourne Rug," was remarkable for its potency. Mine hosts of the inns were still fat and burly. Thus ends the printed records of Taylor's peregrinations, which, if not of the company of the *Urn Burial, Ecclesiastical Polity,* or *Areopagitica,* have contributed generously to the "gaiety of nations."

1656   HEYLYN, PETER. A Survey of the Estate of the Two Islands, Guernsey and Jarsey, with the Isles appending. According to their Politie, and Forme of Government, both Ecclesiastical and Civill. 4to. London.

This is the Second Journey, which was included in his *Survey of the Estate of France,* etc. (for the author and editions, see under WEST EUROPE, vol. I of this work).
These two journeys were published together by Heylyn, because a short time before a false copy had got abroad under the title of France Painted to the Life, stole by one Lek, a bookseller, who fathered it in Stationer-Hall on one Rich. Bignall.—Gough, 611.

1661   The Prince of Tartaria, his Voyage to Cowper in Fife. *He that* will to Cowper, will to Cowper. (Place?)

This is a 4to tract of eight pages, without title, imprint, or date, but printed in 1661, and connected with the newspaper *Mercurious Caledonius.* It is a satirical and humorous description of a jaunt to Cowper [Cupar] in Fife, by a personage entitled Prince of Tartaria, to attend the horse races there. It was reprinted by James Maidment in 1828, forming one of the items that make up his *Reliquiae Scoticae.*—Mitchell, *List of Travels.* The modern version of the saying is, "He that will to Cupar, maun to Cupar."

1670   RAY, DR. JOHN. For his tours over England collecting plants, see his *Catalogus Plantarum,* under NATURAL HISTORY, and also under 1760 below.

1678   WINSTANLEY, WILLIAM. Poor Robins Perambulation, from Saffron-Walden to London, performed this month of July, 1678. 4to. London. (In verse.)

1679   KIRKE, THOMAS. A Modern Account of Scotland by an English Gentleman. London.

Another edit., London, 1699; reprinted in Cleveland's *The Rebel Scot, ca.* 1720; in Hume Brown, *Early Descriptions,* 251-65.
All that is known of the author is printed in Sir Egerton Brydges, *Censuria Literaria,* vol. VI, 373. This work was written in so splenetic a disposition that the author naturally

concealed his name and refused permission for its publication. The name, however, was supplied from the manuscript, which makes it appear that he was Thomas Kirke, of Crookege, Yorkshire. He seems to have been well acquainted with Scotland and reports facts not mentioned by other travelers. His bias was apparently due to his political leanings and to his disgust with the Scotch for their treatment of Charles I and Charles II. In Scotland everything stinks, everybody is lousy, the food rotten, the women sluttish, the men savage, and the towns nasty. Edinburgh is high and dirty; the plentiful supply of stools of repentance in their kirks evinces an equal plentitude of whoremongers and adulterers of both sexes. The practice of the bellman going about announcing the death of so and so is given in broad Scots that is not bad. On the whole, he does not quite come up to Weldon in invective.—From Brown, *op. cit.*

1682 RICHARDS, WILLIAM. Wallography, or, The Briton Described, being a pleasant Relation of a Journey into Wales; wherein are set down several remarkable Passages that occurred in the way thither, and also many choice Observables and notable Commemorations concerning the State and Condition, the Nature and humorous Actions, Manners, Customs, etc. of that Country and People. By William Richards, a mighty Lover of Welsh Travels. 12mo. London.

> See *Athenae Oxon.,* vol. II, 1072, concerning Richards.—Gough, 588.

1688 ADAIR, J. An Account of a Voyage round the Isles of Scotland by King James V. Chart. Fol. Edinburgh.

> See Nicolay under 1583, TOURS BY FOREIGNERS.

1693 LEWKENOR, JOHN. Metellus His Dialogues. The First Part, containing a Relation of a Journey to Tunbridge-Wells. Also a Description of the Wells and Place. With the Fourth Book of Virgil's Aeneids in English. 8vo. London.

1694 FOX, GEORGE. A Journal or Historical Account of the Life of George Fox. Fol. London.

> There followed many later editions of this work.
> Fox visited Scotland in 1657.

FRANCK, RICHARD. Northern Memoirs, calculated for the Meridian of Scotland. Wherein most or all the Cities, Citadels, Sea-Ports, Castles, Forts, Fortresses, Rivers, and Rivulets are compendiously described. Together with Choice Collections of Various Discoveries, Remarkable Observations, . . . To which is added, *The Contemplative and Practical Angler,* by way of Diversion. With a Narrative of that Dextrous and Mysterious Art, experiment in England, and perfected in more remote and solitary Parts of Scotland. Writ in the Year 1658, but not till now made publick. 8vo. London.

> Edit. by Sir Walter Scott, 1821; in Hume Brown, *Early Travellers,* 182 ff.
> This account of travels in Scotland is done in a bombastic Euphuistic style reminiscent of Urquhart's translation of Rabelais. In the portion dealing with angling he makes a vituperative attack on Izaak Walton whom he describes as a "scribling Putationer," and "deficient in Practicks, and indigent in the lineal and plain Tracts of Experience." He denies that from one river one may learn all that is necessary to angle successfully in other rivers. Franck seems to have been especially adept in fishing for salmon in Scotland.

ROGERS, R. (pseudonym). An Historical Account of Mr. Rogers's Three Years Travels over England and Wales, giving a true and exact description of all the chiefest Cities, Towns, and Corporations, etc. 8vo. London.

2nd edit., 8vo, London, 1697.
This was a surreptitious version of Brome's Travels, which was not published under
the rightful name until 1700 (see this date below).

1698   KING, DR. WILLIAM. A Journey to London, in the Year 1698. 8vo. London.

Reprinted, London. 1704.
See under Sorbière, 1664, TOURS BY FOREIGNERS. This was fictitiously attributed to
Sorbière. It was written in ridicule of Dr. Lister's Journey to Paris, 1697, for being full
of impertinences similar to those charged against Sorbière's *Journey to London.*—Gough, 27.

MARTIN, MARTIN. A Late Voyage to St. Kilda, the Remotest of the Hebrides, or
Western Isles of Scotland, giving an Account of the very remarkable Inhabitants of that Place; their Beauty and singular Chastity . . . their Genius for
Poetry, Music, and Dancing; with a History of the Island, Natural, Moral, and
Topographical, wherein is an Account of their Customs, Religion, Fish, Fowl,
etc., to which is added, An Account of Roderick, the late Imposter there, pre-
tending to be sent by John the Baptist with New Revelations . . . Map and
folding plate of birds. 8vo. London.

2nd edit., London, 1716; 3rd, corrected, London, 1749; 4th, with title enlarged, 1753;
again, 1774. Printed in *Misc. Scot.,* vol. 2, Glasgow, 1818; edit. by Donald J. Macleod,
Stirling, 1935. It is also found bound up with some editions of his *Description of the
Western Islands of Scotland* (see under 1703, DESCRIPTIONS). See below.
Johnson said that it was the reading of Martin's account of the Western Islands that
woke in him the desire to visit those regions. Martin was born in Skye, went to Edinburgh University, entered Leyden University in 1710, where he took his M. D. degree, and
lived in London afterwards till his death in 1719. He was interested in visiting personally
the places known to him in legends and traditions. He made the trip to St. Kilda in an
open boat manned by oars and sails. When the weather obscured the view, the flight of
birds was found to be as good as a compass. He gives an interesting account of the ways
of birds, which frequented this island in such large numbers and provided the inhabitants
with food and other things needed. His daily maintenance allotted him by the islanders
was bread, butter, cheese, mutton, fowls, eggs, and also fire, which was provided by each
family in quotas according to the measure of their land. During his three weeks' stay he,
his company, and the factor consumed 6,000 eggs. This island belonged to the Macleods of
Dunvegan, some of whom used it for sequestering wives not wanted. Readers familiar
with the career of Lady Mary Wortley Montague will recall her interest in preventing
Lord Grange from obtaining control of her sister, Lady Mar, during the period of her
lunacy. Probably she feared that her brother-in-law would repeat with Lady Mar his banishment of his own wife to St. Kilda. Within the past few years the natives petitioned
Parliament for removal to the mainland.

1749 MARTIN, MARTIN. A Voyage to St. Kilda, the remotest of all the Hebrides . . .
their Genius for Poetry, Musick, Dancing, Climbing Rocks and Walls of Houses,
Diseases and Cures, Notions of Spirits and Visions, Account of Roderick the
Impostor, his diabolical Inventions, Attempts upon the Women, etc. 3rd edit.
8vo. London.

1699   A Journey to Scotland; giving a Character of that Country, the People, and their
Manners. By an English Gentleman. With a Letter from an Officer there; and
a Poem (by John Cleveland) on the same Subject. London.

1700   BROME, REV. JAMES. Travels over England, Scotland and Wales, 1669, giving a
True and Exact Description of the Chiefest Cities, Towns and Corporations,
with the Antiquities of divers other Places, the most famous Cathedrals and
other Eminent Structures; of several remarkable Caves and Wells, with many
other Diverting Passages never before Published. 8vo. London.

2nd edit., 8vo, London, 1707; another, 1726. The preface refers to a "false edition,"
published in 1694 (see Rogers this date above). Extracts on Scotland in Hume Brown,
op. cit., 241-250. Also published separately by Brown, Edinburgh, 1892.

Brome was rector of Cheriton in Kent and chaplain of the Rt. Hon. the Earl of Romney. He was a fair minded and intelligent observer. His remarks on the caves of Wokey Hole, near Wells, anticipate the Burke Sublime. But neither Snowdown nor any of the Welsh mountains stirred his blood, though he was startled by the passage of Penmaen. Mawr.— Hussey, *The Picturesque.* He left an interesting account of the universities of Glasgow and Edinburgh.

HAYDOCK, ROGER. A Collection of the Christian Writings, Labours, Travels, and Sufferings of that Faithful, and Approved Minister of Jesus Christ, Roger Haydock, To which is added, An Account of his Death and Burial. 8vo. London.

The subject of this account was a Quaker who was fined and imprisoned in 1667 for preaching in Lancashire. He visited Scotland and Ireland in 1680 and Holland in 1681. Subsequently he obtained protection for Quakers in the Isle of Man. His collected writings listed above were edited by J. Field.—*DNB.*

1700-06 (Burlesque Travels.) A Step to Stir-Bitch Fair, 1700; A Trip to North Wales; A Trip to Leverpoole, 1706. London.

The *Trip to North Wales* has been attributed to Ned Ward. The only existing copy known is in the Harvard University Library. It was reprinted by the Facsimile Text Society, Columbia University Press, vol. 7, 1933. It is a coarse vilification of the Welsh people, without wit, written in imitation of Ward's Trips.

1701 BRAND, JOHN. For a short journal of his voyage to the Orkneys, see his *A Brief Description of Orkney,* under DESCRIPTIONS.

SACHEVERELL, WILLIAM. For an account of his voyage to Icolumbkill, see his *An Account of the Isle of Man,* under DESCRIPTIONS.

1702 MORER, THOMAS. For an account of Scotland, see Morer under DESCRIPTIONS.

1703 FULLER, WILLIAM (alias FULLEE, alias FOWLER, alias ELLISON, etc.). William Fuller's Trip to Bridewell, with a True Account of his barbarous Usage in the Pillory, etc., written by his own Hand. 8vo. London.

1704 A Step to Oxford: In which is comprehended an Impartial Account of the University; with a pleasant Relation of such Passages as befel the Author in his Journey. Fol. London (?).

1705 DAVIES, RICHARD. An Account of the Convincement, Exercises, Services, and Travels, of that Ancient Servant of the Lord, Richard Davies, with some Relation of Ancient Friends, and of the spreading of Truths in North Wales. London.

2nd edit., 1752; 3rd, 1765; another, London, 1771.
This friend of Lord Cherbury was a Welsh Quaker who suffered imprisonment in 1660, but who obtained the release of some of his followers on their promising to appear at the Shrewsbury Assizes. He was also excommunicated, but, along with other Quakers, was later restored to former privileges.—*DNB.*

A Trip to Litchfield, with a Character of the French Officers there, by the Author of A Trip to Nottingham. Fol. London. (In verse.)

A Trip to Nottingham, with a Character of Mareschal Tallard and the French-Generals. Fol. London. (In verse.)

17—   Bribery and Corruption: or, The Journey to London; alias, the O***** in Town, at Windmill-College assembled. 4to. London. (A poem.)

> So listed by Bookseller.

1710   D'ARVILLE, NICHOLAS. The Navigation of King James V. round Scotland, The Orkney Isles, and the Hebrides, or Western Isles: under the Conduct of that Excellent Pilot, Alexander Lindsay. Methodized by Nicholas D'Arville, Chief Cosmographer to the French King. London.

> Reprinted 12mo, Perth, 1785; in *Misc. Antiqua*, vol. 3, Glasgow, 1820. It also is bound up with *The Life and Death of King James V . . .* (from the French of 1612), London, 1701, which in turn was reprinted at Edinburgh, 1819. See Nicolay under 1583, TOURS BY FOREIGNERS.
> This is listed here as a journey by a native of Britain. While it is mainly concerned with the flow of tides, good harbors, courses by compass to follow between various points on the east and west coast of Scotland, it does not neglect to describe places of interest. The navigation was undertaken by James V in order to get acquainted at first hand with the rim of his kingdom.

1710   SMITH, J. E. A Tour to Hafod. Views. Fol. London.

1710-12   LELAND, JOHN. Itinerary of John Leland the Antiquary through England and Wales. Published from the Original Manuscript in the Bodleian Library by Thomas Hearne. To which is prefix'd Mr. Leland's New Year's Gift. A Discourse concerning some Antiquities lately found in Yorkshire. 9 vols. 8vo. Oxford.

> 2nd edit., collated and improved from the original MS, with the addition of a general index, 9 vols., 8vo, Oxford, 1744-45; 3rd edit., printed from Hearne's Corrected Copy in the Bodleian Library, 9 vols., 8vo, Oxford, 1767-70. See also Leland under 1549 above.
> After Leland's death his MSS were borrowed and copied in whole or in part many times, and so suffered in the process. Fortunately Stow copied nearly all of the Itinerary, and this was recopied by the painstaking antiquarian of Oxford, Thomas Hearne, which he edited and published as listed above. After his death in 1735, the second edition was prepared from a careful examination of the original MS and corrections made. The third edition is little more than a reprint of the second. Hearne also published the contents of the three folio volumes left by Leland, called *Collectanea,* in 1715 (see Hearne this date under HISTORY AND ANTIQUITIES). Of the two manuscript copies made of the original Itinerary only Stow's remains extant; the other was burnt in the fire of James Wright's library in 1678. —From Lucy Toulmin, Introduction.

1711   Occasional Reflections in a Journey from London to Norwich and Cambridge. 8vo. London.

> This consists of facetious reflections on various happenings in the towns passed through.—Maggs, no. 603.

1714   CHANCEL, A. D. A New Journey over Europe; from France thro' Savoy, Switzerland, Germany, . . . Great Britain, and Ireland. With several Observations on the Laws, Religion, and Government, etc., of each. Together with an Account of the Births and Marriages of all the Kings and Princes of Europe from the Year 1650. 8vo. London.

MACKY, JOHN. A Journey through England. In Familiar Letters from a Gentleman here to a Friend Abroad. 2 vols. 8vo. London.

> 2nd edit., 2 vols., London, 1722-23 (vol. 1 only is of the 2nd edit.); another edit., with Journey through Scotland included, 3 vols., London, 1723-24; a 4th vol., with a Journey

through the Austrian Netherlands added, 1724. Another edit., 3 vols., London, 1732. See below.

The claim was made by the writer that it was published when it was to refute Misson's *Memoirs* (see Misson under 1698, TOURS BY FOREIGNERS).

1732 MACKY, JOHN. A Journey through England: Seats, Diversion and Manners, Gardens, Government, etc. With Journey through Scotland: The Country, Noble Families, their Seats, etc. 3 vols. 8vo. London.

1715 PENNYCUIK, DR. Tweedale. A Poem. Edinburgh.

This physician came to know every corner and nook of the district. He took great pleasure in "beholding shady groves and mountains." Its chief value lies in its botanical observations. Apparently the beauty of scenes about the Tweed made no impression on him. See Myra Reynolds, *Nature in English Poetry*. Also listed under DESCRIPTIONS.

1717 BRERETON, ——. A Day's Journey, from the Vale of Evesham to Oxford, in a Familiar Epistle to N. Griffith, Esq.; to which are added, Two Town Eclogues. 8vo. London (?).

1719 RAMKIN, MAJOR ALEXANDER. For a possible account of travel in Scotland, see his *Memoirs*, under LETTERS, DIARIES, MEMOIRS.

1722 The Comical Pilgrim, or Travels of a Cynick Philosopher thro' the most wicked Parts of the World, namely, England, Wales, Scotland, Ireland, and Holland, etc. 8vo. London.

This is said to be mainly abusive. It has been attributed to Defoe.

DUNCAN, MATTHEW. A Journey through Scotland. (Place?)

It has been thought that Defoe's Travels in Scotland may have originally appeared in this form.—Mitchell, *List of Travels*.

The Wand'ring Spy, or, The Merry Travellers, part II., to which is added, The Contending Candidates; or, The Broom-Staff Battles, dirty Skirmishes and other Comical Humours of the Southwark Election, by the Author of the Cavalcade. 8vo. London.

1723 MACKY, JOHN. A Journey through Scotland. 8vo. London.

2nd edit., London, 1729. See Macky under 1714 above.

1724 The Royal Progress, or, A Historical View of the Journeys or Progresses which several Great Princes have made to Visit their Dominions and acquaint themselves with their People. 8vo. London.

STUKELEY, DR. WILLIAM. Itinerarium Curiosum; or, An Account of the Antiquitys and remarkable Curiositys in Nature and Art, observ'd in Travels thro' Great Britain, Centuria I, 1724. Frontispiece and 100 copperplates of ancient monuments. Fol. London.

2nd edit., with an added volume completing the work, fol., London, 1776; the portion dealing with Devon reprinted by Chope, *Early Tours in Devon and Cornwall*, 137-45. See below.

Stukeley was an outstanding member of the numerous band of ardent antiquaries who have distinguished the 18th century with publications of their researches. In 1718 he became secretary to the Society of Antiquaries, which he helped to found. He won an M.D.

degree in 1719, and turned minister in 1729. In company with Roger Gale, a brother antiquary, he used to make long journeys in search of antiquities, of which the above work is one of the fruits. His views on Stonehenge (1740), as well as on Richard of Cirencester (1757), aroused much controversy. As a preacher he must have been both unpredictable and entertaining. It is recorded that in April of 1764 he put off the services for an hour in order that his congregation might witness the eclipse of the sun. And when, at the age of seventy-six, he preached for the first time wearing spectacles, he chose for his text, "Now we see through a glass darkly" (extracted from Maggs, no. 723). For his antiquarian publications, see various dates under HISTORY AND ANTIQUITIES.

> 1776 STUKELEY, DR. WILLIAM. Itinerarium Curiosum . . . Centuria II, to which is added, The Itinerary of Richard of Cirencester. Over 200 views illustrating ruins, parks, gardens, ancient British camps, dolmens, barrows, ancient towns, etc. 2 vols. Fol. London.

1724-27 DEFOE, DANIEL. A Tour Thro' the Whole Island of Great Britain, divided into Circuits or Journies, giving a particular and diverting Account of whatever is curious and worth Observation. By a Gentleman. 3 vols. 8vo. London.

> Numerous editions followed with constant enlargements, with the result that the original text gets quite submerged in the additions. 3rd edit., 4 vols., 1742; 4th, 1748; 5th, 1753; 6th, 1755; 7th, edit. by Richardson, 4 vols., 1769; 8th, 1778; excerpt in Chope, *op. cit.*, 1918; edited with an Introduction by G. D. H. Cole, 2 vols., London, 1928 (an exact reprint of the original edition). For notes on these various editions, see Mitchell, *List of Travels*.
> Defoe was the sensitive nerve through which Robert Harley received impulses from the nation at large. His numerous travels through England and Scotland to observe the reaction to political and fiscal policies and to note the progress of trade and manufacture gave him the right to speak with authority on the condition of England. Few things escaped his eye, unless it were the scenery of the countryside, though even here he could respond to the beauty of a town's situation. What he preferred to find was, however, towns both populous and full of trade, and what he deplored was the state of those places once flourishing but now decayed through the silting up of harbors and rivers with the consequent loss of navigation. He had no concern for the improvements of art or of nature, and as for antiquities what he remarked on a circle of stones not unlike those at Stonehenge would apply to all such curiosities, namely, that all that could be learned about them was that here they were. The prices of food in the country he found to be much lower than in London. In Devon, for instance, lobsters cost six to eight pence, whereas in London they brought three or three and a half shillings. One would have to look farther back than Defoe's day, however, to find "merry old England."

1725 MANLEY, DELIA DE LA RIVIERE. A Stage-Coach Journey to Exeter . . . To which is added, the Force of Love . . . by Richardson Pack. London. (So cited in Straus, Handlist to *The Unspeakable Curll.*)

1726 GORDON, ALEXANDER. Itinerarium Septentrionale: or, A Journey through most of the Counties of Scotland, and those in the North of England, containing an Account of all the Monuments of Roman Antiquity; also of the Danish Invasions. Folding map and 66 plates. Fol. London.

> A Latin version, with additions and corrections, published in Holland, 1731; these last incorporated in a new edition, London, 1732.
> Gordon was immortalized by Scott in his novel *The Antiquary.* An account of his life is given in *Proc. Soc. Antiq. Scot.*, vol. 10, 363 ff., by Sir Daniel Wilson and David Laing. An estimate of his claims as an antiquary is offered in Sir George Macdonald's *John Horsley, Scholar and Gentleman* (see under GENERAL REFERENCE). A severe censure was passed on him by John Whiston in the words, "He had some learning, some ingenuity, much pride, much deceit, and very little honesty, as everyone who knew him believed" (see Nichols, *Literary Anecdotes*, vol. V, 699). This verdict seems to have been confirmed in part at least by his failure to mention either Cay or Horsley, to whom he was indebted for aid on the Antonine Wall. Horsley, on the other hand, was just to Gordon in his *Britannia Romana* (see under 1732, BRITISH, ROMAN, AND SAXON ANTIQUITIES), correcting him when due and giving him credit when called for. The material for the above work was collected in three expeditions with his patron Sir John Clerk. He published the book at a considerable personal expense. He died in Carolina.

1727 BUCHAN, REV. ALEXANDER. For an account of St. Kilda, see his *A Description of St. Kilda,* under DESCRIPTIONS.

1733 GENT, THOMAS. For travels into various parts of Yorkshire, see his *Antient and Modern History of the Loyal Town of Rippon,* under TOWNS.

1734 A Curious and Diverting Journey through the whole Island of Great Britain. 4to. London.

A Journey from London to Scarborough, in several Letters from a Gentleman there, to his Friend in London . . . With a List of the Nobility, Quality, and Gentry at Scarborough, during the Spaw Season, in the Year 1733. To which is annexed, an Account of the Nature and Use of the Scarborough Spaw-Water, in a Short View of the most celebrated writers on that Subject, interspers'd with some Observations and Remarks. 8vo. London.

This gives a description of the town and its accommodations. A print of Dicky Dickinson, keeper of the wells, is prefixed.—Gough, 571.

1735 BORDE (BOARDE, BOORDE), ANDREW. The Itinerary of England, or Peregrination of Dr. Boorde. London.

This peregrination of Henry VIII's rambling physician was first published by Hearne at the end of his *Benedictus Abbas, de Vita et Gesta Henrici III et Ricardi I,* vol. II, 764-804, from a copy in the handwriting of Lawrence Noel. Wood (*Athenae Oxon.,* vol. II, 57) says that the Doctor intended to publish it himself if Thomas Cromwell, to whom he had lent the manuscript, had not lost it. Norden quotes it to prove that Barrow on the Hill was a market town in Borde's day.—Gough, 21. It has a list of market towns, downs, mountains, rivers and hills, forests and parks, highways from London to Colchester and Orford, the compass of England round about by the towns on the sea coasts, and the isles adjacent. The work may be a part of the lost Itinerary of Europe. See his *Fyrst Boke of the Introduction of Knowledge* (1547), edit. for the E.E.T.S. by Furnivall, Introduction (1870). Borde was an inveterate traveler, visiting the continent four times and spending a year in Scotland in the study and practice of medicine.

1736 VAUGHAN, WILLIAM OWEN GWIN. Voyages, Travels, and Adventures, with the History of his Brother Jonathan. (So cited by Rowlands, *op. cit.*)

1737 TORBUCK, JOHN. A Collection of Welsh Travels and Memoirs of Wales: containing, I. The Briton Described, or a pleasant Relation of D--n S--t's Journey into that Antient Kingdom, and remarkable Passages that occurred on the way: also many choice Observations and notable Commemorations concerning the State and Condition, the Nature, Humours, Manners, Customs, and mighty Actions of that Country and People. II. A Trip to North Wales by a Barrister of the Temple. III. A Funeral Sermon preached by the Parson of Langwillin. IV. The Welsh School-master, by Dr. K--g. V. Muscipula; or the Welsh Mouse-trap, a poem in Latin and English. The Whole collected by J. T., a mighty Lover of Welsh Travels. 12mo. London.

This is listed in *Gent. Mag.,* vol. 7, Oct., 1737. Another edit., 8vo, London, 1742; 8vo, Dublin, 1743; London, 1749, 1752; with added matter, 3 vols., London, 1764-67. See below. Some of the above items are taken from Rowlands, *op. cit.* Dean Swift's name seems to be involved, but that he is the author, as Rowlands asserts, is extremely doubtful.

1764-67 TORBUCK, JOHN. A Collection of Welsh Travels and Memoirs of Wales . . . [with the addition of] The Oxford Sausage, or Select Poetical Pieces written

by the most celebrated Wits of the University of Oxford, 1764 (T. Warton);
Bagatelles (in this collection is reprinted the Fragment of Allen and Olla which
appeared some years since under the title of Colin and Lucy, 1767). **3 vols.**
12mo. London.

1738 MOREAU, S. A Tour to Cheltenham Spa; or, Gloucestershire display'd 3rd
edit. 8vo. Bath.

> 4th edit., Bath, 1789; 8th, 1797.

WEDDELL, ——. A Voyage up the Thames. 8vo. London.

> This facetious production is dedicated to Heidegger. The voyagers got no farther than
> Windsor. In the course of the narrative are introduced accounts of Vauxhall (Ridotto Al
> Fresco), Chelsea, Richmond, Kingston, Hampton Court, Staines and Windsor.—Book-
> seller's Note.

1743 PHILELEUTHERUS BRITANNUS. A Short Trip into Kent, containing the Occurrences of Four Summer Days, calculated as an Antidote against the Gloominess
of the Winter Months, in Hudibrastic Verse. 8vo. Printed for the Author.

1744 "Nimble Nancy."—A Woeful Voyage Indeed! being a Full and Particular Account of the Voyage, Adventures and Distresses of the Crew belonging to the
Nimble Nancy, commanded by Capt. A. Wr—t . . . in their dangerous Voyage
to the Nore. 8vo. London.

> This title reads as if the "Voyage" might have been a yachting cruise.

1745 CAREW, BAMPFYLDE-MOORE. The Life and Adventures of Bampfylde-Moore
Carew, the noted Devonshire Stroller and Dog-Stealer; as related by Himself,
during his Passage to the Plantations in America. Exeter.

> See also Goadby, under 1749 below. An account of this famous bamboozler is given
> under the above title in section ADVENTURES, DISASTERS, SHIPWRECKS, vol. II of this work.
> Lowndes cites an edition of this date with a different title and place of printing. See below.
>
> Few narratives in rogue literature are as absorbing as this one, which relates how this
> "King of Beggars" lived in good estate by sheer audacity of wit. Having once tasted the
> spice of vagabond life, he resisted all efforts of his respectable connections (for the name
> Carew was honored in Devon) to reclaim him. It brings one into intimate relation with
> places, people, and manners of his time.

> 1745 CAREW, BAMPFYLDE-MOORE. The Accomplish'd Vagabond, or Compleat Mumper,
> exemplify'd in the bold Enterprizes, and merry Pranks of Bampfylde Carew. 8vo.
> Oxford.
> Despite the suggestions of the title, this "Mumper" was not a Til Eulenspiegel.

A Trip to Scotland; or, A Hue and Cry after the Young Chevalier. (So listed in
Gent. Mag., vol. 15, Sept.)

1746 Journal of an English Medical Officer who attended the Duke of Cumberland's
Army as far north as Inverness, during the Time of the Rebellion. (Place?)

> Reprinted in *The Contrast, Scotland as it was in the Year 1745 and Scotland in the
> Year 1819,* London, 1825.

A Journey through Part of England and Scotland along with the Army under the
Command of H. R. H. the Duke of Cumberland . . . by a Volunteer, in several Letters to a Friend in London. 4to. London.

3rd edit., 12mo, London, 1747.
There are nine letters in all, but two are numbered as Letter VII, and they are dated from both English and Scottish towns. The manners and customs of the people, especially of the Highlanders, receive due attention.—From Mitchell, *op. cit.*

A Journey to Llandrindod Wells, in Radnorshire; with a particular Description of those Wells, the Places adjacent, the Humours of the Company there, etc., being a faithful Narrative of every Occurrence worth notice, that happened in a Journey to and from those Wells. To which is added, Observations and Information for those who intend visiting Llandrindod: and to which is prefixed the Parson's Tale, a Poem, by a Clergyman. 2nd edit., corrected and amended. London.

The 1st edit. appeared about 1744.—Gough, 600. The author was a lawyer who gave himself great airs there, and afterwards drew caricatures of all the characters he conversed with.

Tom Thumb. The Travels of Tom Thumb over England and Wales, containing Descriptions of whatever is most remarkable in the several Counties, interspersed with many pleasant Adventures. 12mo. London.

The hero of these adventures may have been borrowed from Fielding's farce.

1747 A Short Trip from Harborough to Northampton (in a Letter complaining of bad roads). In *Gent. Mag.*, vol. 17, 233.

Story, Thomas. Journal of the Life of Thomas Story (Quaker) . . . and of his Travels and Labours in the Service of the Gospel. Fol. Newcastle.

In this are records of visits to Scotland in 1692, 1696, 1717, 1728, and 1730. It affords much curious information on the state of religious opinion and feeling.—Mitchell, *op. cit.*

1748 Of Travelling in Britain (in a letter dated from Carlisle, June 9, 1746). In *Gent. Mag.*, vol. 18, Dec.

The traveler set out from Derby, visiting many famous seats en route, such as Chatsworth, one of the show places of Derbyshire. He was much struck with the beauty of Lake Windermere. Some scenes evoke from him the term "romantic."

A Trip to North Wales, being a Description of that Country and People. 12mo. London.

This is probably the item cited in Torbuck's *Collection of Welsh Travels* (see Torbuck under 1737 above).

1749 Goadby, Robert. An Apology for the Life of Mr. Bampfylde-Moore Carew, commonly called the King of the Beggars: being an Impartial Account of his Life, from his leaving Tiverton School, at the age of Fifteen, and entering into a Society of Gypsies, to the Present Time; wherein the Motives of his Conduct will be explain'd and the great Number of Characters and Shapes he has appear'd in through Great Britain, Ireland, and several other Places of Europe, be related; with his Travels twice through great Part of America. Portrait. 12mo. London.

Another edit., London, 1788. A modern edit., by C. H. Wilkinson, 8vo, Oxford, 1931.
This is said to have been dictated by Carew himself. It is a different account from that listed under 1745 above.

RAY, JAMES (of Whitehaven). Volunteer under His Royal Highness the Duke of Cumberland. A Compleat History of the Rebellion, from its first Rise, in 1745, to its total Suppression at the glorious Battle of Culloden, in April 1746 . . . Likewise the Natural History and Antiquities of the several Towns thro' which the Author pass'd with His Majesty's Army; together with the Manners and Customs of the different People, particularly the Highlanders . . . 8vo. York.

> The latter part of this book, from p. 291 on to the end, may be regarded as a tour through Scotland, and a tour of some value. It extended from Edinburgh through Fife, Forfar, and Kincardine to Aberdeen, and thence by old Meldrum, Turriff, Banff, Elgin, Forres, and Nairn to Inverness. There is much that is new in the author's descriptions of the towns he passed through.—From Mitchell, *op. cit.*

1750   MACKENZIE, MURDOCH. Orcades: or, Geographic and Hydrographic Survey of the Orkney and Lewis Islands in eight maps. Also an Account of the Orkney Islands. Fol. London.

> The account was the outcome of much traveling in the north and west of Scotland.— Mitchell, *op. cit.* See under MAPS AND CHARTS.

1751   A Voyage to Shetland, the Orkneys, and the Western Isles of Scotland, giving the Laws, Customs, Antiquities, Natural Curiosities, Fisheries, etc., of those Places, particularly the Herring Fisheries; with the present Methods of catching, curing, packing, etc., the singular Sincerity, Honesty, and Temperance of the Inhabitants; their religious Ceremonies, Superstitions, Charms, Apparitions, and that amazing Faculty of the Second Sight so frequent among them, by which future Events are with Certainty foretold. 8vo. London.

> A meagre compilation made to favor the herring fishery.—Gough, 656.

1753   A Tour through Great Britain. 2 vols. London. (So cited by Rowlands.)

> The same title is listed in Bandinel, *A Catalogue of the Books relating to British Topography*, as of four volumes, which may be an edition of Defoe's Tour.

1754   BURT, CAPTAIN EDWARD. Letters from a Gentleman in the North of Scotland, to his Friend in London, containing the Description of a Capital Town in that Northern Country, with an Account of some uncommon Customs and Manners of the Inhabitants, likewise an Account of the Highlands, with the Customs and Manners of the Highlanders. Plate of bare-legged Highland women. 2 vols. 8vo. London.

> A posthumous printing. Reprinted without plates, Dublin, 1755; 2nd edit., 2 vols., London, 1757; 3rd, London, 1759; in 2 vols., edit. by R. Jamieson, London, 1876. Translated into Dutch, Haarlem, 1758; into German, Hanover, 1760.
> Among descriptions of Scotland this account is a classic. The author, Captain Burt, seems to have been an army engineer who was sent to Scotland, one surmises, in connection with construction work. Making his headquarters at Inverness, of which he gives an ample description, he had occasion to travel over many parts of the Highlands whose poverty stricken condition outweighs the romantic glamor cast over the region, its people, and the clan system by Scott and his readers. His bias as an Englishman constantly shows itself, but it is an objective appreciation after all that he offers us. The period of his stay would seem to have been from about 1728 to 1736, that is, before the break-up of the traditional way of life following the Rising of the '45.

G., S. Journey to Edinburgh. In *Gent. Mag.*, vol. 24, 119.

1756 HANWAY, JONAS. A Journal of Eight Days Journey from Portsmouth to Kings-
      ton-upon-Thames through Southampton, Wiltshire, etc., with Miscellaneous
      Thoughts, Moral and Religious; in a Series of Sixty-four Letters: Addressed
      to two Ladies of the Partie. To which is added, An Essay on Tea, considered
      as pernicious to Health, obstructing Industry, and impoverishing the Nation,
      with the Growth and Consumption in these Kingdoms; also with several Poli-
      tical Reflections; and Thoughts on Public Love, in Twenty-five Letters to the
      same Ladies. By a Gentleman of the Partie. 4to. London.

    2nd edit., 2 vols., London, 1757.
    This was printed for presentation only and was not sold.—*DNB*. According to Austin
    Dobson ("Hanway's Travels," *Eighteenth Century Vignettes*), the Moral and Religious
    Reflections almost entirely swallow up the Travels. Goldsmith, in his review of the book,
    said, "On every occurrence he expatiates and indulges in reflection." His attack upon tea
    aroused Johnson's ire, and the book as a whole led the latter to say, "Jonas acquired some
    reputation by travelling abroad, but lost it all by travelling at home." His more abiding
    reputation reposes in the monument erected to him in Westminster Abbey for his note-
    worthy efforts to alleviate the miseries of the poor and the children.

      LYTTELTON, LORD GEORGE. An Account of a Journey into Wales in two Letters to
      Mr. Bower. 4to. Bristol.

    Reprinted in *Annual Register*, vol. 17, 160-64, 1774.
    This short account is taken up mainly with the varieties in scenery and natural beauty,
    together with his personal experiences.

1757 MAITLAND, WILLIAM. History and Antiquities of Scotland. 2 vols. Fol. London.

    The material for this work was collected from a tour he made over the whole kingdom.
    It is also listed under HISTORY AND ANTIQUITIES.

      PATCHING, RESTA. Four Topographical Letters written in July, 1755, upon a
      Journey thro' Bedfordshire, Northamptonshire, Leicestershire, Nottingham-
      shire, Derby, and Warwick, from a Gentleman of London to his Brother and
      Sister in Town. 8vo. Newcastle-upon-Tyne.

    This is of slight value, but it makes some comments on conditions of people and espe-
    cially on roads.—J. Williams, *Guide to Printed Materials*.

      RICHARDSON, JOHN. An Account of the Life of John Richardson, giving a Rela-
      tion of many of his Trials and Exercises in his Youth and his Services in the
      Work of the Ministry in England, Ireland, America, etc. 8vo. London.

    3rd edit., London, 1774.

      ROVER, WILLIAM. Scapin Triumphant, or, The Journey to Petersfield and Ports-
      mouth. 4to. London (?).

      TUCKER, DEAN (probably Josiah Tucker, Dean of Gloucester). Instructions for
      Travellers, which was "A Plan for improving in the Moral and Political Theory
      of Trade and Taxes by means of Travelling." In *Selected Works*, 223-24.
      London.

1760 HEPBURN, THOMAS. A Letter to a Gentleman (George Paton) from his Friend in
      Orkney, written in 1757, containing the true Causes of the Poverty of that
      Country. 8vo. London. (44 pp.)

RAY, JOHN. Itineraries and Letters (from *Select Remains*) of the learned John Ray, with his Life by W. Derham, D.D., published by G. Scott. 8vo. London.

His Itineraries included in *Memorials of John Ray,* edit. by Edw. Lankester for the Ray Society, London, 1846; the Scottish portion in Hume Brown, *op. cit.,* 230-40.

Ray, the "father of English botany," made his first botanical tour, lasting six weeks, in 1658. In 1661 he traveled to Scotland with Dr. Willoughby, returning by Westmoreland and Cumberland; in 1662, with Willoughby, he explored Wales, and in 1673 the two made a trip to the continent (see Ray and Willoughby under 1673, WEST EUROPE, vol. I of this work). These Itineraries are selections from his original journals, which manifestly were not written for publication, as they were intended to be private jottings on things that interested him. His first concern was naturally botanical phenomena, but anything unusual or famous drew his attention, such as the baths at various spas and the claims and methods of bathing, some of which he tried out. He notes historical features, what happened to places after Cromwell's soldiers took them in hand, and sights that every traveler should notice,—tombs, churches, Stonehenge, religious houses, customs and superstitions, etc. These "simpling voyages," as he called them, furnish entertaining descriptions of manners and places as well as of plants.

1762   ENGLISH, JOHN. Travels through Scotland, containing a curious and entertaining Account of the Manner and Strange Customs of the Inhabitants, with many humorous Anecdotes and natural Discoveries. 12mo. London.

The date given is approximate. The work is a coarse, abusive attack upon the Scotch.

EVANS, ——. A Tour through North Wales. London. (So cited in Pinkerton, vol. XVII. See EVANS under 1800 below.)

1765   PERCY, THOMAS (Bishop of Dromore). A Letter describing the ride to Hulme Abbey from Alnwick. 8vo. n. p. (11 pp.)

1766   Extract of a Letter from a Gentleman to a Lady, giving an Account of his Journey from Lancashire into Scotland. In *Gent. Mag.,* vol. 36, 166-69, 209-12.

This traveler was apparently ready to be pleased with everything he saw. He commends especially the manners and hospitality of the Scotch—a slight offset to the constant abuse heaped on this people by English travelers.

1767   BROWN, DR. JOHN. Letter to Lord Lyttelton. Newcastle.

This Letter was printed as a note to Dr. Dalton's "Poem addressed to two Ladies at their Return from Viewing the Mines near Whitehaven," in Pearch's *Continuation of Dodsley's Collection of Poems* (1768-70). It describes the scenery at Keswick with ardent appreciation and enthusiasm for the varied beauties of the scene. For him Keswick is outstanding in three respects: "beauty, horror, and immensity united." To picture the scene adequately would call for the combined efforts of a Claude, Salvatore, and Poussin. Brown's letter no doubt influenced Young and Gray to visit this spot. In fact, Young practically admits his indebtedness in 1768 and 1769. It was probably written between 1756 and 1760, and appears to have been widely read. See Hussey, *The Picturesque.* Myra Reynolds thinks its date lies between 1748 and 1754. She points out that this letter with John Buncle's account and Dr. Dalton's poem are the three earliest descriptions of the Lake District.—*Nature in English Poetry.*

DERRICK, SAMUEL. Letters written from Leverpoole, Chester, Corke, the Lake of Killarney, Dublin, Tunbridge Wells, Bath. 2 vols. 12mo. Dublin.

K., T. Account of a Journey through North Wales. In *Gent. Mag.,* vol. 37, Dec.

YOUNG, ARTHUR. For his agricultural tours, see his *Farmer's Letters to the People of England,* under AGRICULTURE.

1768 BEAUMONT, GEORGE, ESQ., and CAPT. H. DISNEY. A New Tour through England, performed in 1765, 6, and 7. 8vo. London.

YOUNG, ARTHUR. A Six Weeks' Tour through the Southern Counties of England and Wales, describing the Present State of Agriculture and Manufactures; the different Methods of Cultivating the Soil; the State of the Working Poor in those Counties, wherein the Riots were most remarkable. Plates. 8vo. London.

> 2nd edit., London, 1769, Dublin, 1771; 3rd, London, 1772.
> This agricultural tourist had his eyes open for other things than husbandry. Scenery, antiquities, and gentlemen's seats called forth comment that helps one to understand why he was popular as a traveling companion. See Young under 1770 below.

1769 JACKSON, W. The Beauties of Nature displayed in a Sentimental Ramble through her Luxurious Fields. 8vo. Birmingham.

1770 CRADOCK, JOSEPH. Letters from Snowdon: Descriptive of a Tour through the Northern Counties of Wales, containing the Antiquities, History, and State of the Country; with the Manners and Customs of the Inhabitants. Maps and plates. 8vo. London.

> 2nd edit., to which is added an account of inns and roads, with directions to travelers, 8vo, London, 1777.
> With this work tourism for the purpose of enjoying scenery may be said to have begun.

FORBES, RIGHT REV. ROBERT, M.A. Journals of the Episcopal Visitations of the Right Reverend Robert Forbes, M.A., of the Dioceses of Ross and Caithness, and of the Dioceses of Ross and Argyll, 1762 and 1770. Edit. and compiled by the Rev. J. B. Craven. 8vo. London.

> An interesting account of travel in Scotland.—Mitchell, *op. cit.*

ROBERT, T. For Whitefield's travels in England, Scotland, and Ireland, see under NORTH AMERICA, vol. II of this work.

WHITEFIELD, WILLIAM. A Trip to Scotland. As it is acted at the Theatre Royal in Drury-Lane. 8vo. London. (40 pp.)

> An imaginary trip.—Mitchell, *op. cit.*

YOUNG, ARTHUR. A Six Months' Tour through the North of England. Containing an Account of the present State of Agriculture, Manufactures and Population. Numerous plates. 4 vols. 8vo. London.

> 2nd edit., 4 vols., 8vo, London, 1771; an Abridgement of the Six Weeks' Tour and the Six Months' Tour, 12mo, Dublin, 1771; Extracts, 8vo, London, 1774.

1771 PENNANT, THOMAS. A Tour in Scotland, 1769. 8vo. Chester.

> 2nd edit., 8vo, London, 1772; Supplement, 8vo, Chester, 1772 (reviewed *Gent. Mag.*, vol. 45, April); 3rd, 4to, Warrington, 1774; the additions to the 4to edition and the new appendix reprinted for the purchasers of the 1st and 2nd editions, 8vo, London, 1774; 5th edit., with additions and corrections by Dalrymple, 4to, London, 1790; summary in Mavor, *The British Tourist*, vol. I, 1-60, 12mo, London, 1800; in Pinkerton, vol. III, 1-170, London, 1808-13.
> The confused bibliography of Pennant's various tours is the subject of an article by Dr. L. F. Powell in *The Library*, Sept., 1938. The National Library of Wales is making an extensive bibliographical collection of material by and relating to Pennant. See the

Journal of this association, vol. I, no. 1, Summer, 1939. For an account of his works written by himself, see his *Literary Life* (GENERAL REFERENCE).

Pennant's tour of Scotland preceded Johnson's by four years. Comparisons were inevitable then as they still are now. Wesley, in commenting on this work, says (*Journal*), "Pennant is doubtless a man of sense and learning. Why has he then bad English in almost every page? No man should be above writing correctly." At the same time he praises warmly Johnson's account. With this preference for the latter the modern reader will also agree. His object was to perfect himself in British zoology, on which he published several ponderous works, but he by no means confined himself to this subject. Antiquities, historical associations, and literary reminiscences, with occasional glances at scenery, were duly noticed, not without a display of learning and complete objectivity in observation. Nevertheless his tour was extremely popular. He himself observed that "A candid Account of that country was such a novelty that the impression was instantly bought up, and in the next year (1772) another printed and as soon sold." He had labored, he said, to conciliate the affections of the two nations, and had thereon received many flattering letters. Johnson's comment was, "Pennant is the best traveller I had ever read, he observes more things than anyone else does." Other tours are noted in due course below.

SMOLLETT, TOBIAS. The Expedition of Humphrey Clinker. 3 vols. 12mo. London.

Smollett's Scotch nativity gave him an opportunity to turn the tables on the English tourist—"the egregious Englishman," as a modern Scotchman has called him. And in his role of novelist, Smollett could present his own country as seen through the eyes and temperaments of different characters, such as Jerold, the eager traveler, Winifred Jenkins, ignorant, provincial, and suspicious of anything unfamiliar, and Lydia, gushing and gullible. Jenkins's letters constitute a running parody of the prejudices held by the English against Scotland. The party arrived at Edinburgh via Berwick, made a little excursion to Fifeshire, a journey to Glasgow by Stirling and to Loch Lomond by Dumbarton. Bramble and his nephew Jerold take a trip into Argyllshire and to some of the Islands and thence back to Glasgow, whence all return by Carlisle to England. The novel was loudly applauded in the reviews.

YOUNG, ARTHUR. A Farmer's Tour through the East of England, being the Register of a Journey through various Counties to enquire into the State of Agriculture, Manufactures, etc. 29 folding and other plates of agricultural implements and folding tables. 4 vols. 8vo. London.

This tour investigated also the methods of cultivating the soil, live stock, the condition of the poor, labor, provisions, rents, experiments, etc.

1772 LELAND, JOHN. For an account of Leland's *Laborious Journey in Search of England's Antiquities*, see *The Lives of those Eminent Antiquarians John Leland, Thomas Hearne, and Anthony à Wood*, under GENERAL REFERENCE.

QUINCY, THOMAS. A Short Tour in the Midland Counties of England, performed in the Summer of 1772. In *Gent. Mag.*, vol. 42, 206-09, 253-56, 299-303, 353-56, 410-16. London.

Also published separately with another tour, 8vo, London, 1774. See below.

1774 QUINCY, THOMAS. A Short Tour in the Midland Counties of England, performed in the Summer of 1772. With an Account of a similar Excursion undertaken Sept. 1774. 8vo. London.
This last tour was also printed in *Gent. Mag.*, vol. 46, 325 ff.
The writer is chiefly concerned with curiosities and scenery, though he comments on manufactures and enclosures.

ROBINSON, DR. NICHOLAS. The Triumphs of the Muses; or, The Grand Reception and Entertainment of Queen Elizabeth, at Cambridge, in 1564, and at Oxford, in 1566. London (?).

A résumé is given in *Gent. Mag.*, vol. 42, 451-54, 625; vol. 43, 21-25, 72-73. See also under 1566, UNIVERSITIES. Robinson was chaplain to Archbishop Parker and afterwards bishop of Bangor.

WHITEFIELD, REV. GEORGE. Memoirs of his Life, edit. by Rev. J. Gillies. 8vo. London.

> In the course of his evangelical work, Whitefield made numerous trips to Scotland, but he speaks of little else but his ministry.

1773 GRAY, THOMAS. The Traveller's Companion in a Tour through England and Wales. London.

> This was originally published for private distribution by William Mason. It was printed from notes written by Gray on the blank margins of Kitchin's English Atlas.—Thorp, no. 518. A new edition appeared in 1789. See Gray under 1787 below.

HERRING, BISHOP. An Account of Two Journies into Wales. Bishop Herring to Mr. Duncombe. Written Nov. 3, 1737, and 2nd, Sept. 11, 1739. In *Annual Register*, vol. 16, 200-03. London.

> The writer describes his journey as "a very romantic . . . a most perilous journey."

MURRAY, JAMES. The Travels of the Imagination: A True Journey from Newcastle to London in a Stage Coach, with Observations upon the Metropolis, 1773. 12mo. London.

1774 BANKS, JOSEPH. For his letter to Pennant on Staffa, see the latter's second *Tour of Scotland* under 1774 below. This letter was also printed in the *Annual Register*, vol. 20, 1777, and in Troil's *Letters on Iceland* (see under 1780, NORTH EUROPE, vol. I of this work).

> This letter was written while Banks was en route to Iceland. It may be said to have discovered this famous island of basaltic columns with its Fingal's Cave. Banks was pleased to notice how Nature esthetically vindicated regularity in architecture by her arrangement of these columns in a likeness to those of ancient Greece.

COLLIER, JOEL. Musical Travels through England By Joel Collier, Organist. 8vo. London.

> 2nd edit., with the scarce appendix, London, 1775; 3rd, London, 1775; 4th, 1776; also 1785. See below.
> The writer's real name, according to *DNB*, was George Veal; but according to another notice, it was J. L. Bicknell. At any rate, it was suppressed by the Burney and Bicknell families. It was intended to be a satire on Dr. Burney's *Tour through Germany*, etc., (see Burney under 1773, WEST EUROPE, vol. I of this work). The particular animus held by the author was his dislike of carillons, Burney's praise of Italian music, and the frequent personal references of Burney to his own doings, which are taken to be a token of egotism. The appropriateness of the satire is not very evident. Ridicule is poured on the English taste for Italian singers, the *castrati*, and their shakes and quavers, Italian opera, the teaching of music to young girls in the foreign manner, preferences for Italian airs over good old English songs. Among these songs mentioned is "Yanky Doodle," which he says is more popular in certain parts of America than in England (and this before the opening guns of the American Revolutionary War). The volume purports to recount his travels over England in the guise of a musician, carrying with him a bassoon, fiddle, and cello. Many absurd adventures are related: with pigs that have musical ears, the carillons of bells fastened to sheep, and oddities of other kinds. At Bristol he engages in an amour with the barber's wife, is castrated, and then becomes eligible to join the elect. The humor is decidedly stretched and is marked by a taste for talking of physiological functions of the body.

> 1775 COLLIER, JOEL. Musical Travels through England by the late Joel Collier, licentiate in Music, with an Appendix containing an Authentic Account of the Author's last Illness and Death, by Nat Collier, School-Master. 3rd edit. 8vo. London.
> This includes the story of his conversion to Methodism.

HUTCHINSON, WILLIAM. An Excursion to the Lakes in Westmoreland and Cumberland, August 1773. 8vo. London.

> 2nd edit., with addition of a Tour through part of the Northern Counties, plates, 8vo, London, 1776; a compressed version of this in Mavor, vol. II, 223-286. Reviewed *Gent. Mag.*, vol. 47, 60-61, where it is spoken of as a hasty performance marred by mistakes in facts and names.
>
> Hutchinson made this tour in company with his brother who did the sketches for the plates, and repeated it the next summer after his brother's death to verify the drawings left incomplete. The work evidences esthetic response to the appeal of scenic effects of light and shade as the changes were rung on these by sunrise, sunset, and storms. From the '70's on the vogue of the picturesque drove many visitors to ramble among the lakes and mountains of this district, sometimes to view scenes in their natural arrangement and sometimes to convert them into pictures by means of the Claude Lorrain "glass."—The *Monthly Magazine* in 1778 expressed the opinion that "To make the Tour of the Lakes, to speak in fashionable terms, is the *ton* of the present hour."—Quoted by Hussey, *op. cit.* Hutchinson's antiquarian description of various counties will be found under HISTORY AND ANTIQUITIES.

MONRO, SIR DONALD. For his travels through the Hebrides, see his *Description of the Western Isles of Scotland,* under DESCRIPTIONS.

1774   PENNANT, THOMAS. A Tour in Scotland and Voyage to the Hebrides, 1772. 44 plates. 2 vols. 4to. Chester.

> 3rd vol. added in 1775; reprinted with his *Tour* of 1769, 4to, London, 1776; 5th edit. of this, with additions and corrections by Dalrymple, London, 1790; in Pinkerton, vol. III, 171-569, 1808-13. Translated into German, 2 vols., Leipzig, 1779; abridged in French in *Nouveau Recueil des Voyages au Nord,* tom. 3, Genève, 1786. See below. For his relations with Rev. Charles Cordiner, see the latter under 1780 below.
>
> This second tour was made in company with Rev. Mr. Lightfoot, who supplied the botanical particulars. It completed the circuit of Scotland by passing up the west coast to the Inner Hebrides and thence over to the east coast by the Tay valley and down to Edinburgh and back to Chester. Of Hawkshead, where Wordsworth's school days were spent, he remarks that it stands in a fertile valley but contains nothing worthy of notice. Of Keswick, which excited the enthusiasm of Brown, Young, and Gray, he observes nothing but the topographical features. He quotes parts of Bank's letter on Staffa, which was addressed to him and printed in the *Annual Register.* The alleged gift of second sight to the Highlanders he takes no stock in. In Skye he noted the practice of accompanying work with appropriate songs, and the fact that the basalt line extended from Skye to the Giant's Causeway. The work is highly informative but pedestrian in style, with the barest mention of personal movements. Nevertheless, according to his Preface, since the publication of his first journey to Scotland, that country had been inundated with visitors, an impulsion which spread even to France. French criticism was directed against the want of a philosophical point of view, whereas Johnson's account offered a rich diversity of reflections on the variety of productions of Nature, and the divers states of man and degrees of civilization (*La Gazette littéraire de Deux-Ponts,* 1775, 532). The work naturally excited comment among the English literati. Gough writes to Tyson, March 28, 1772, "Mr. Pennant is setting out to approfondir every corner of Scotland, both by land and sea. I verily believe, where horses and boats fail, he will take unto himself cork jackets, if not wings. We shall thirst after a second edition of his Tour." Tyson replies, "Mr. Pennant is very entertaining; and I wish him an agreeable tour. I wish he would take a good Botanist with him—in that respect Scotland is little known."—Quoted by Nichols, *Literary Anecdotes,* vol. VIII, 586.
>
> 1779   (In German.) Thomas Pennant Reise durch Schottland und die Hebridischen Inseln. Aus dem Englischen übersetzt von J. P. Ebeling. 2 The. 8vo. Leipzig.

1775   BRERETON, OWEN SALUSBURY. Observations in a Tour through South Wales, Shropshire, etc. In *Archaeologia,* vol. 3, 111-17. London.

> This tour was made in the summer of 1771. The traveler started from Stockton in Shropshire and took in South Wales. He was interested mainly in antiquarian matters, particularly ruined castles, many of which he noted were allowed to lapse into decay. The account is matter-of-fact and impersonal, except where questions of antiquarian opinion are called for.

GRAY, THOMAS. Journal of the Lakes. In Mason's *Life and Memoirs of Gray*. London.

> Gray described the Highlands and the Lake District for the enjoyment of his friend Dr. Wharton. These as well as his letters on his tour of France and Italy, which helped to bring the Alps into their own, were published by Mason as stated above. His reactions to the beauties of mountain scenery went far in lifting from such scenes the stigma of being "horrid excrescences" which had been scornfully applied to them by unappreciative travelers. His tour as related in the Journal extended from Oct. 18, 1769, to April 18, 1770. For Gray's omnivorous interest in travel literature, see Powell Jones, *Thomas Gray, Scholar*, chapter "The Road to Cathay" (1937). See also Tovey, *Gray and His Friends*, 260-64; Clark S. Northup, "Addison and Gray," in *Studies in Language and Literature in Honor of J. M. Hart* (1910).

HANWAY, MRS. MARY ANNE. A Journey to the Highlands of Scotland, with Remarks on Dr. Johnson's Tour, by a Lady. 12mo. London.

> Another edit., London, 1777; again, 1800.
> Reviewed *Gent. Mag.*, vol. 48, 37. The statement by the reviewer that these letters were evidently not intended for publication can well be doubted. She liked to parade her intellectual accomplishments by quoting verse on any occasion; she pretends rather too often to the modesty becoming a female of the period; and she complacently demolishes Johnson's narrative of his journey to the Hebrides. She also lards her text with the vocabulary of the picturesque tourist, such as "most romantic views," "ruinous beauties," "horrid gulph," "terrifying noise," "the astonished eye," etc. She describes various gentlemen's seats, the portraits, and the gardens, wherein she exhibits a properly cultivated knowledge. Her accounts of experiences with balky post-horses and bad roads are, however, amusing, as likewise her general assumption of *ton*.

HENDERSON, ANDREW. A Letter to Dr. Samuel Johnson on his Journey to the Western Hebrides. 8vo. London.

JOHNSON, DR. SAMUEL. A Journey to the Western Islands of Scotland, performed in the Year 1773. 8vo. London.

> An edit., 8vo, Dublin, 1775; another, London, 1791; in Mavor, vol. II, 1-164; edit., with Boswell's *Journal of a Tour to the Hebrides*, by R. W. Chapman, map and illustrations, London, 1924 (and many others).
> Reviewed *Gent. Mag.*, vol. 45, 35-38, with an epitome and commendation of the author's powers of observation; Strictures on Dr. Johnson, Mr. Pennant, and Mr. Walpole, by Vindex, in *Gent. Mag.*, vol. 45, which consist of corrections in historical matters and topographical descriptions. Translated literally into French in the *Nouvelle Recueil de Voyages au Nord d'Europe et de l'Asie*, Genève, 1785.
> Few books of travel were more eagerly awaited than Johnson's and few crackled more loudly in the flames of controversy. Some Scotchmen asserted that Johnson waited until the bad weather had set in in order to be more vituperative; others declared that the account was eminently just. However that may be, Johnson came back with a mind much the richer for experience with a different way of life, and a heart much the warmer for the many courtesies he had received from Scotchmen of all degrees. Boswell tells us that he not only praised highly the intelligence and manners of his many hosts but also expressed great solicitude over the proper acknowledgement of his indebtedness. While modern scholarship has upheld his contention that Macpherson was a forger, yet he fell down in his failure to recognize the strength of age-long oral transmission of Ossianic tales and ballads and the existence of a vast quantity of literature likewise preserved. As travelers Johnson and Boswell had little eye for the romantic beauties of Highland scenery. Their interest was chiefly in manners, which to Johnson was the field for the legitimate exercise of observation. (For the weightiest attack upon his book, see MacNicol under 1779 below.)

WYNDHAM, HENRY PENRUDDOCKE. A Gentleman's Tour through Monmouthshire and Wales . . . in the Months of June and July, 1774. 8vo. London.

> 2nd edit., including a journey into Wales in 1777, 4to, Salisbury, 1781; also the same bound up with Lord Lyttelton's Tour into Wales, with continuous pagination, London, 1781; in Mavor, vol. III, 2nd edit., 1800.

1776   A Short Tour in the Midland Counties of England, performed in the Summer of 1772. Together with an Account of a similar Excursion undertaken in Sept. 1774. (Cited in *Gent. Mag.*, vol. 46, July.)

TOPHAM, EDWARD. Letters from Edinburgh, written in the Years 1774, 1775, containing some Observations on the Diversions, Customs, Manners, and Laws of the Scotch Nation, during a Six Months' Residence in Edinburgh. 8vo. Edinburgh.

> Another edit., 2 vols., 8vo, Dublin, 1780. Translated into German, Leipzig, 1777.
> These unsigned letters written in no connected order to real or imaginary correspondents were soon discovered to be the work of Topham, who at the time was twenty-five years old. Those on fashions and the education of young women are addressed to ladies; those on the diversions of the population to an intimate friend; and those on religion and the church to a reverend doctor at Oxford. Edinburgh is presented in a more favorable light than in Johnson's account.

WHEELDON, J. Epistola ad Thomas Pennant armigerum in Scotia Nuperrime sciscitantem, Poetica. 4to. London (?).

1777   BRAY, REV. WILLIAM. Sketch of a Tour into Derbyshire and Yorkshire; including Part of Buckingham, Warwick, Leicester, Northampton, Bedford, and Hertfordshire. 12mo. London.

> 2nd edit., 8vo, London, 1783; again, 1798; in Mavor, vol. II, 287-342; in Pinkerton, vol. II, 336-464.
> Reviewed *Gent. Mag.*, vol. 78, 48, 175. A professed antiquary, Bray gave most attention to historical matter, though he did not neglect the face of the country, which he seemed to have observed rather closely. In his descriptions he displays a partiality for wild scenery and romantic views over trim formal gardens. He also writes up manufactures, architecture, inscriptions, mines, and the trade of the northern districts. Gentlemen's seats, such as Stow and Chatsworth, are duly noticed.

CRADOCK, JOSEPH. An Account of some of the most romantic Parts of North Wales, 1776. 8vo. London.

Description of Keswick Lake in Cumberland. In *Gent. Mag.*, vol. 47, 487-88.

HEELY, JOSEPH. Letters on the Beauties of Hagley, Envil, and the Leasowes. (See under DESCRIPTIONS this date.)

> This work has some elements of a tour in that the author describes the scenes and places he passes by and relates occasionally incidents encountered.

HERRING, DR. THOMAS. Letters from the late Reverend Dr. Thomas Herring. London (?).

> Herring was so impressed (in 1738) by the "magnificence of Nature" as it was presented in a Welsh valley that he feared lest the sight of the garden at Stow would make him smile, and that he would behold with contempt an artificial ruin.—From Hussey, *The Picturesque*, 94.

Poetical Excursions in the Isle of Wight. 4to. London.

1778   BONGOUT, DR. ROBERT. The Journey of Dr. Robert Bongout and his Lady to Bath, Portrait. 12mo. Bath (?).

> Was Dr. "Goodtaste" an assumed name?

HEARD, ——. A Sentimental Journey to Bath, Bristol, and their Environs. (Place?)

HUTCHINSON, WILLIAM. For his excursion to Mailross Abbey in Scotland, see his *View of Northumberland,* under DESCRIPTIONS.

LOCH, DAVID. A Tour through most of the Trading Towns and Villages of Scotland; containing Notes and Observations concerning the Trade, Manufactures, Improvements, etc. Edinburgh.

> A summary of this tour by Sir Arthur Mitchell, in *Proc. Antiq. of Scot.,* 3rd ser., vol. 8, 19-28, Edinburgh, 1898.
> This account was written at the suggestion of the Board of Manufactures, with the object of noting trade and manufactures carried on in Scotch towns. One learns a great deal about the prevalence of certain trades and the variety of fabrics and articles produced. Surprise is expressed at finding a trade in silk stockings and shoes for the London market in so small and distant a town as Huntly. The trade now carried on is centered in large cities and focuses of population, since small home industries have died off in the course of large scale productions.

PENNANT, THOMAS. A Tour in Wales in 1770. Plates. 4to. London.

> Supplemental corrections and additions, together with *A Journey to Snowdon,* 11 plates, 2 vols., 4to, London, 1781; another edit., 8vo, Dublin, 1779; in 3 vols., with additional plates by Moses Griffith, 3 pts. in 2 vols., London, 1784; an edit., 3 vols., 8vo, London, 1810; translated into Welsh, edited by John Rhys, 3 vols., Caernarvon, 1883. Remarks on, *Gent. Mag.,* vol. 47, 71; vol. 48, 506-07; vol. 50, 515. See below.
> After several journeys over the six counties of North Wales, Pennant put his observations together in the above form and published his first volume this date. He was accompanied on his tours by a friend, the Rev. John Lloyd, who was skilled in the Welsh language and antiquities.

> 1883 (In Welsh.) Teithiae yn Nghymru. Translated by Prof. John Rhys. Numerous illustrations. 8vo. Caernarvon.

The Travellers. A Satire. (Cited by Mead in his bibliography to *English Travellers of the Renaissance.*)

WILLIAM OF WORCESTER. Itinerarium, sive liber memorabilium in viaggio de Bristol usque ad montem S. Michaelis. MS 1478. (So cited by Taylor, *Late Tudor and Early Stuart Geography.*)

> His Itinerary through Cornwall, *temp.* Edward IV, mentioned by Chope, *op. cit.*

1779 ₊BURLINGTON, CHARLES. For a tour arranged as a guide, see his *The Modern Universal Traveller,* under AIDS TO TRAVELERS.

KEATE, GEORGE. Sketches from Nature; Taken and Coloured in a Journey to Margate. Published from the Original Designs. 2 vols. 8vo. London.

> This work was popular and ran into several editions; also translated into French. Reviewed *Gent. Mag.,* vol. 49, 313-14. These "Shandean Chapters," as the reviewer called them, were evidently built upon the plan of Sterne's *Sentimental Journey.* Walpole, in a letter to Wm. Cole, May 21, 1779, describes it as being an imitation of Sterne and as possessing a sort of merit, though nothing arriving at originality. Keate, in addition to being an author and a poet, was also a painter.

M'NICHOL, REV. DONALD. Remarks on Dr. Samuel Johnson's Journey to the Hebrides, in which are contained Observations on the Antiquities, Language, Genius and Manners of the Highlanders of Scotland. 8vo. London.

This learned minister of Lismore was the most formidable of those who made forays on Johnson's tour of Scotland. He himself was a good Gaelic scholar and possessed many manuscripts of the Highland Bardic poetry. For an examination and weighing of the charges on both sides, see my article, "The Case of Scotland vs. Dr. Johnson," in *Trans. Gaelic Soc. of Inverness,* vol. 33, 49-79, Inverness, 1932.

(QUEEN ELIZABETH). The Honourable Entertainment gieuen to the Queenes Majestie in Progresses, at Elvetham in Hampshire, by the Rt. Hon. the Earle of Hertford (1591).

This was sent in by "A Constant Reader" to the *Gentleman's Magazine,* where it was reprinted in vol. 49, 81-85; 121-25. It gives interesting details of the preparations and entertainments, such as enlarging the house with additional rooms and increasing the help, the decorations and platforms, the orations and allegories presented, the songs, fireworks, etc. The performance lasted four days and must have cost the Earl many a pretty penny, but in return he was assured of the Queen's favor.

1780 CORDINER, REV. CHARLES. Antiquities and Scenery of the North of Scotland, in a Series of Letters to Thomas Pennant, Esq. 4to. London.

Another edit., 22 plates, London, 1790.
Pennant had asked Cordiner to visit and report on those parts of Scotland he had been unable to reach in his tour. See Pennant under 1774 above.

A Diary kept in an Excursion to Littlehampton near Arundel and Brighthelmston, in Sussex, in 1778 and . . . 1779. 2 vols. 8vo. London.

SULLIVAN, RICHARD. Observations made during a Tour through Parts of England, Scotland, and Wales; in a Series of Letters. 4to. London.

The 1st edit. appeared anonymously; 2nd edit., corrected and enlarged, with author's name, 2 vols., London, 1785; 3rd, 2 vols., 12mo, Dublin, 1785; redacted in Mavor, *British Tourist,* vol. III, 2nd edit., 1800. Translated into German, Leipzig, 1781. See below.
Review of 2nd edit. in *Gent. Mag.,* vol. 56, 47-48. The reviewer comments sarcastically on the veracity and learning of the author, finding the text full of misnomers, which he corrects. The author shows some interest in factories, iron works at Carron, lead, coal, and salt mines. But he seems to be mainly concerned with describing sites and country seats, with their pictures, busts, galleries, curios, grounds, together with the historical associations connected with such spots. The stages of the journey are marked but no mention is made of incidents peculiar to the tour. The romantic wildness and beauty of the Lakes are disposed of with a quotation from Dr. Dalton's poem. Stonehenge, which he visited, he is willing to allow to be a grand temple of the British Druids, in keeping with Stukeley's views. He also believes in the authenticity of Macpherson's version of the Ossianic legends.
1785 (In German.) Bemerkungen auf einer Reise durch verschiedene Theile von England, Schottland, und Wales. Nebst einer Nebenreise in der Hölen von Ingleborough und Settle in Yorkshire by J. H. Aus dem Englischen nebst einigen Anmerkungen Übersetzers. 8vo. Leipzig. (For J. H. see under John Hutton below.)

Tour through the Peak of Derbyshire. In *Gent. Mag.,* vol. 50, 503-04.

A slight descriptive sketch with little attempt to be picturesque. The favorite terms are delightful, pleasant, sublime, lively, agreeable, etc. Such a phrase as "the shrubbery is disposed with taste" indicates the writer's powers of description.

1781 GALE, SAMUEL. For an account of his tours with Dr. Stukeley on antiquarian researches, see his *Reliquiae Galeanae,* under HISTORY AND ANTIQUITIES.

HUTTON, JOHN (Vicar of Burton). A Tour to the Caves in the Environs of Ingleborough and Settle, in the West Riding of Yorkshire. 2nd edit. 8vo. London.

This contains a glossary of local dialect. It was incorporated with the German translation of Sullivan's Tour noted above.

A Journal of First Thoughts, Observations, Characters, Anecdotes, which occurred in a Journey to Scarborough in 1779. 12mo. London.

LYTTELTON, LORD GEORGE. Account of a Journey into Wales. 8vo. London.

> Bound up with Wyndham's *A Gentleman's Tour through Monmouthshire and Wales*
> (see Wyndham under 1775 above).

A Month's Tour in North Wales, Dublin and its Environs. With Observations on
their Manners and Police in the Year 1780. 12mo. London.

> Reviewed *Gent. Mag.*, vol. 51, 430-31. This is written in the form of a diary with the
> necessary adaptation of style and matter, much of which is trivial. His observations are
> not very noteworthy, but they give an amusing account of the inhabitants of Dublin's
> suburbs sitting in the sun and divesting each other of vermin. The writer's defense of the
> legs of Irish ladies must have reference to some previous slighting comment.

PARKER, GEORGE. A View of Society and Manners in High and Low Life: being
the Adventures in England, Ireland, Scotland, Wales, France, etc., of Mr. G.
Parker; in which is comprised a History of the Stage Itinerant. 2 vols. 8vo.
London.

PENNANT, THOMAS. A Journey to Snowdon. 4to. London.

> Reviewed *Gent. Mag.*, vol. 51, 474-75. This is a continuation of his *Tour in Wales* (see
> Pennant under 1778 above). Pennant was an assiduous collector of information on every
> place he came to as naturalist and antiquary. The ascent of Snowdon, with its shifting
> scenes of mist, cloud, storms, and prospects, moved him for once to a degree of enthusiasm.

1782 CALLANDER, J. Deformities of Dr. Johnson. Edinburgh (?).

> So cited in Mitchell, *Scot. Topog.*, vol. II. Mitchell says that this has some relevance to
> Johnson's tour of Scotland.

FORREST, E. An Account of what seemed most remarkable in the Five Days'
Peregrination of the Five Following Persons, viz. Messieurs Tothall, Scott,
Hogarth, Thornhill, and Forrest. Plates by Hogarth and Scott. Fol. London.

> This edit. was printed by R. Livesay on 9 fol. pages, with drawings in facsimile, the
> size of the original aquatints. A few years later Nichols reprinted a few copies of this
> work and also 20 copies of Gostling's rhyming version. These were incorporated in the
> *Works of Hogarth* printed by Nichols and Steevens. The account was reprinted, with a
> slightly different title, London, n.d. (1870's?). See below.
> This tour was begun at midnight in the summer of 1732, surely an unusual hour for
> starting out in those days on a jaunt. The members of the party were a jovial lot of high-
> spirited Englishmen bent on enjoying to the full whatever adventures might befall them.
> Each had his allotted task: Scott and Hogarth to do the illustrating, Tothall to act as
> treasurer and caterer, Thornhill to make the map, and Forrest to write up the journal.
> The account containing their doings was bound, lettered in gilt, and read to the group the
> second night after their return. It was then sent to their friend, the Rev. W. Gostling,
> author of *A Walk in and about Canterbury* (see Gostling under 1774, TOWNS), who was
> moved by the humor of the narrative to rewrite it in Hudibrastic verse, with additions of
> his own. Thackeray describes them as "a jolly party of tradesmen engaged in high jinks."
> As a matter of fact, while they were thorough-going John Bulls, they were not tradesmen.
> Scott was a marine painter, Tothall a seaman and later a shopman with a variety of
> fortunes, Thornhill, Hogarth's brother-in-law, was Serjeant Painter to George II, and
> Forrest an attorney of note. Their expedition took them down the Thames as far as
> Sheerness and included stops at Deptford, Rochester, Queensborough, and Gravesend, all
> of which were viewed in a most unorthodox manner and amid much horseplay. The total
> cost of the trip was £6/6/0.

1870 (?) Hogarth's Frolic: the Five Days' Peregrination by Land and Water 1732 around the Isle of Sheppey of William Hogarth and His Fellow Pilgrims, Scott, Tothall, Thornhill, and Forrest. Sketches in Sepia from the Original Drawings illustrating the Tour by W. Hogarth and Sam. Scott. Sq. 8vo. London.

GILPIN, REV. WILLIAM. Observations on the River Wye, and Several Parts of South Wales, etc., relative chiefly to Picturesque Beauty: Made in the Summer of the Year 1770. London.

> 4th edit., 12mo, London, 1800. Translated into French, Breslau, 1800. See below.
>   With this his earliest work, Gilpin begins publishing his series of tours in search of picturesque beauty. In his Preface addressed to William Mason, he refers to Gray's commendation of his observations, which the poet had seen in manuscript. Gray had made a similar tour but acknowledged that he had kept no journal of his wanderings through Worcestershire, Gloucestershire, Herefordshire, Monmouthshire, and Shropshire, and along the River Wye. Gilpin points out that his little work differs in purpose from other tours by proposing "to examine the face of a country *by the rules of picturesque beauty*: opening the sources of those pleasures which are derived from comparison." And so he tests his theories with observations taken direct from nature. In so doing he transfers the esthetics of composition in painting to landscape scenes. When the party reached Ross they planned their trip down the Wye to Monmouth by boat "navigated by three men," wherein there is little of incident but much discourse of side-screens, front-screens, perspectives, and broken ground. Of Tintern Abbey he complains that the "number of gabelends hurt the eye with their regularity, and disgust it by the vulgarity of their shape. A mallet judiciously used (but who durst use it?) might be of service in fracturing some of them; particularly those of the cross isles, which are both disagreeable in themselves, and confound the perspective." Of personal incident in the whole tour there is little mention.

> 1800 (In French.) Observations pittoresques sur le Cour de la Wye et sur différentes parties du Pays de Galles. Traduit par le Baron de Blumenstein. 17 gravures. Breslau.

PENNANT, THOMAS. Journey from Chester to London. Plates. 4to. London.

> Another edit., 8vo, Dublin, 1783; summarized in Mavor, vol. III, 1800.
>   This account was made up from notes and observations taken on various trips to London. His attention was engaged as usual with information on history, soil, commerce, antiquities, etc.

SHARPE, WILLIAM (Junior). A Ramble from Newport to Cowes, in the Isle of Wight. 4to. (Published in the Isle of Wight.)

Viator, a Poem; or, A Journey, from London to Scarborough, by the way of York. London.

1782-83 HILL, T. F. An Excursion of some Months in the Highlands in the Summer of 1780. Reprinted from the *Gentleman's Magazine*.

> So cited by Mitchell, *Scot Topog.*, vol. II. The trip was made in connection with the Ossianic controversy.

1784 GILLIES, J. (Bookseller of Perth). One Day's Journey to the Highlands of Scotland, March 12, 1784; antiquam exquirite matrem. 4to. Perth.

> So cited by Mitchell, *List of Travels*. Reviewed *Gent. Mag.*, vol. 59, 243. This expedition was undertaken in search of Ossian's grave supposed to have been destroyed by running the military road through the middle of it. There were found remaining the large stone 7½ by 5 feet, and four gray stones near it, which formed a coffin containing burnt bones. It was surrounded by a circular dyke 299 feet in circumference and three feet high.—From the review.

LUNARDI, VINCENT. An Account of the First Aerial Voyage in England, in Letters to his Guardian Chevalier Gherardo Compagni, written under the Impres-

sion of the various Events that affected the Undertaking. Portrait by Bartolozzi after Cosway and 2 plates, with Author's signature on half-title. 8vo. London.

2nd edit., same year.

This is a personal account by the famous aeronaut of the first aerial voyage over England, when on Sept. 15, 1784, Lunardi ascended from the Hon. Artillery Company's ground at Moorfields, in the presence of nearly 200,000 spectators. The balloon, which was 32 feet in diameter, was filled with hydrogen under the direction of Dr. Fordyce. He sailed over London at a great height and descended near Ware in Hertfordshire. The balloon was afterwards placed on exhibition in the great central hall of the Pantheon. For his ascents in Scotland, see under 1786 below. Lunardi was secretary to the Neapolitan Ambassador.

WALPOOLE, GEORGE AUGUSTUS. The New British Traveller, etc. (Though stated, in the title, to be a new tour through England, etc., in reality it is a description, whose chief interest lies in its numerous plates of towns, castles, seats, etc. See under DESCRIPTIONS.)

1784-1809 YOUNG, ARTHUR. In his *Annals of Agriculture* are recorded a number of tours made in the interest of husbandry. See under AGRICULTURE.

1785 ANDERSON, JAMES. For his tour of the Hebrides and the Western Coast of Scotland, see his *An Account of the Present State of the Hebrides,* etc., under ANCIENT AND PRESENT STATE.

BOSWELL, JAMES. The Journal of a Tour to the Hebrides with Samuel Johnson, LL.D., containing Some Poetical Pieces by Dr. Johnson relative to the Tour, and never before published; a Series of his Conversation, Literary Anecdotes, and Opinions of Men and Books: with an Authentick Account of the Distresses and Escape of the Grandson of King James II in the Year 1746. 8vo. London.

2nd edit., corrected and revised, London, 1785; 1st Irish edit., 8vo, Dublin, 1785; reprinted 1807 and 1813; in Everyman's Library, based on the 3rd edit., London and New York, 1909; printed from the original MS, New York, 1936. Translated into German, Lübeck, 1787. See below. Reviewed *Gent. Mag.,* vol. 55, 889-94.

The Irish edition, which is very rare, was issued in a form strikingly similar to the first edition, and, unlike the usual Irish piracy, it was printed on a fine quality of paper, in every respect being worthy of comparison with the genuine first edition. Even Boswell had not heard of it.—From Pottle, quoted by Bookseller.

As a narrative of personal adventures, Boswell's account is to be preferred to Johnson's. Naturally such a work, as was true of everything concerning Dr. Johnson, aroused great interest, which was heightened by Boswell's frankness in expressing opinions about his hosts as well as by his naiveté in relating incidents that did not reflect credit to himself. Consequently numerous attacks, parodies, and defenses followed both in the *Gentleman's Magazine* as well as separately. Some of these are listed below. It is the general consensus of opinion that the original account published by the Literary Guild in 1936, under the editorship of Professor Pottle and Charles H. Bennett, is vastly more entertaining than the first published version, which experienced the excising hand of Malone. Besides it adds to the zest of reading to know that this was the very journal which Johnson used to read over while on the tour.

1787 (In German.) James Boswell, Esq., Tagebuch einer Reise nach den Hebridischen Inseln mit Doktor S. Johnson. 8vo. Lübeck.

1786 A Defence of Mr. Boswell's Journal, in a Letter to the Author of the Remarks on a Journal of a Tour to the Hebrides. 8vo. London.

PINDAR, PETER. A Poetical and Congratulatory Epistle to James Boswell, Esq., on his Journal of a Tour to the Hebrides with the celebrated Dr. Johnson. 8vo. London.

Remarks on a Journal of a Tour to the Hebrides. In a Letter to James Boswell, Esq. 8vo. London.

The Remarker remarked, or, A Parody on the Letter to Mr. Boswell, on his Tour, etc. 8vo. London.

Rowlandson, T. Twenty Humorous Illustrations of Boswell's Tour. 4to. London.

Douglas's Travelling Anecdotes. (So listed in the *Gent. Mag.*, vol. 35, August.)

Hutton, William. A Journey from Birmingham to London. 12mo. London.

2nd edit., London, 1818.
Reviewed *Gent. Mag.*, vol. 55, 979-81. The reviewer is not particularly favorable to this work. But it is not without interest for its descriptions of places and objects of historical associations, for it lets the present day reader know the condition of many venerable remains, such as the ruinous state of Westminster Abbey, at the time of his visit. And his account of a speedily conducted tour through the British Museum is quaintly humorous. For his *History of Birmingham* see under 1781, TOWNS.

Observations on a Tour through the Island of Jersey. Signed M. S. in *Gent. Mag.*, vol. 55, 332-33.

Voyages aux montagnes d'Ecosse et aux Isles Hebrides, de Scilly, d'Anglesey, etc. Traduits de l'Anglais par une Société de Gens de Lettres, avec les notes et les éclaircissements nécessaires. Ouvrage enrichi de cartes et beaucoup de vues et de dessins, gravés par les meilleurs artistes. Tom. I and II of *Nouveau Recueil de Voyages dans le Nord de l'Europe,* 8vo, Genève.

This seems to be drawn from Pennant, Banks, Macaulay, Johnson, and Dalrymple. I cannot identify any one tour that embraces the Highlands and the Scilly Islands.

1786 Gilpin, Rev. William. Observations relative chiefly to Picturesque Beauty, made in the Year 1772, on several Parts of England, particularly the Mountains and Lakes of Cumberland and Westmoreland. Aquatint plates. 2 vols. 8vo. London.

2nd edit., 2 vols., London, 1788; 3rd edit., London, 1792. Translated into French, Paris and London, 1789; again into French, 2 vols., Breslau, 1801. See below.
Gilpin's tours were known in manuscript before they appeared in print. With his entrance on to the scene the picturesque shared with the sublime and the beautiful the field of esthetic speculation, and helped to change the character of English traveling from the philosophic type to the romantic, which gave freer play to the personal equation, wherein the reaction on one's individual self, the cultivation of the proper responses to different facets of a scene, and the esthetic analysis of these reactions into their categories, all became the object of touring. Henceforth with Gilpin's works as handbooks, one could look at Nature and discourse knowingly on background, foreground, and offskip, describe the functions of mountain and lake, valley, wood, and river, broken ground and ruins, as well as point out where Nature had gone wrong in composition and how the error could be righted, and analyze the relations of light and shade, line and mass in their bearing on the picturesque intention struggling to get expressed. Gilpin exerted an enormous influence in furthering the romantic appreciation of nature, though it should be noted that neither Coleridge nor Wordsworth showed much leaning towards the picturesque. He was equally potent in inspiring satires, the best of which is John Wolcot's *Dr. Syntax's Tour in Search of the Picturesque* (especially with Rowlandson's illustrations), 1812. Other tours of Gilpin are noted below.

1789 (In French.) Voyages en différentes parties de l'Angleterre et particulièrement dans les montagnes et sur les lacs du Cumberland et du Westmoreland, contenant des observations relatives à des beautés pittoresques. Traduit de l'anglois par Guédon de Berchere. 2 toms. 8vo. Paris et Londres.

Jeffries, Dr. John. A Narrative of the Two Aerial Voyages of Doctor Jeffries with Mons. Blanchard; with Meteorological Observations and Remarks. The

first Voyage on the thirteenth of November, 1784, from London into Kent; the second on the seventh of January, 1785, from England into France. Engraved portrait of Jeffries in his balloon, and plate of the column erected to commemorate the second flight. 4to. London.

> Jeffries was an American physician, born in Boston and graduated at Harvard in 1763. He took his medical degree at Edinburgh. During the American Revolution he sided with the British and became surgeon major to the royal army in America. In 1780 he resumed the practice of medicine in London. Being interested in atmospheric temperatures, he made the first crossing by air to France.—Maggs, no. 563.

LUNARDI, VINCENT. An Account of Five Aerial Voyages in Scotland, in a Series of Letters to his Guardian, Chevalier Gerardo Compagni, written under the Impression of the various Events that affected the Undertaking. Portrait of author and 2 plates. 8vo. London.

> At the end are Verses "To Mr. Lunardi, on his Successful Aerial Voyages from Edinburgh, Kelso, and Glasgow," by James Tytler, the first British aeronaut, in which the latter gives some interesting details regarding his "Edinburgh Fire Balloon."—Bookseller's Note.

MATTHEW, WILLIAM. The Miscellaneous Companions, being a short Tour of Observation and Sentiment thro' a Part of South Wales: Maxims and Thoughts on Marriage, Our Last Day, Punishment, World of Spirits. 3 vols. Bath.

YOUNG, ARTHUR. A Tour to the West of England. In *Annals of Agriculture,* vol. 6. London.

1787 Extracts from the Publications of Mr. Knox, Dr. Anderson, Mr. Pennant and Dr. Johnson relative to the Northern and North-Western Coasts of Great Britain. 8vo. London. (31 pp.)

GRAY, THOMAS. A Supplement to the Tour through Great Britain, containing a Catalogue of the Antiquities, Houses, Parks, etc., in England and Wales. 12mo. London.

KNOX, JOHN. A Tour through the Highlands of Scotland and the Hebrides, in 1786. 8vo. London.

> Reviewed *Gent. Mag.,* vol. 57, 704. Translated into French, 2 vols., Paris, 1790. See below.
> This Scottish philanthropist was for many years a bookseller of eminence in London and devoted the fortune he acquired in his business to the improvement of his country. He had long been concerned over the wretched condition of the Highlanders and had made as many as sixteen journeys, since 1764, into various parts of the North. He succeeded in arousing the active interest of the London Highland Society in the formation of a British Society for extending the fisheries and improving the sea ports on the coasts. Subscriptions were taken and then he set out on the above recorded tour, for which he was voted a gold medal by the Society. The two principal improvements he advocated were inland navigation, e.g. the Crinan Canal (since accomplished), and the establishment of free villages or fishing stations on the east coast. See his *View of the British Empire* under 1784, ANCIENT AND PRESENT STATE, where he sets forth in detail his plan for encouraging the fisheries.

> 1790 (In French.) Voyages dans les montagnes et dans les Iles Hébrides. 2 vols. Paris.
>> This work served as a good introduction of Scotland to Frenchmen, and is of importance for the story of Ossianism in France. He reproduced some of the arguments of John Smith's *Gaelic Antiquities* (Edinb., 1780) in reply to Johnson's

attacks, whereby Frenchmen became acquainted with some of the theories of Smith and acquired some notion of the Highland bards. Smith himself claimed to have known MacVurich, the "Last of the Bards."—From Bain, *Les Voyageurs Français en Ecosse,* etc.

LEWIS, H. An Excursion to Margate in June, 1786, with Anecdotes of well-known Characters. 3rd edit. 8vo. London.

WEST, J. A Trip to Richmond in Surrey. London.

1788 BLAINE, HENRY. Voyage to Ramsgate, interspersed with Reflections Natural, Moral and Divine. 8vo. London.

DIBDIN, CHARLES. The Musical Tour of Mr. Dibdin, in a Series of 107 Letters; with seven Pieces of Music. 4to. Sheffield.

> Didbin was a dramatist, song-writer, and actor, best remembered for his sea songs, the earliest of which was his "Blow high, blow low." He also composed the music for Garrick's Shakespeare's Jubilee at Stratford in 1769. In addition to plays, farces, and puppet shows, he wrote *A History of the Stage,* 1795, an autobiography and two novels, *Hannah Hewit,* 1792, and the *Younger Brother,* 1793.—From *DNB.*

NEWTE, THOMAS. A Tour in England and Scotland in 1785 by an English Gentleman. 8vo. London.

> A much enlarged edit., London, 1791. See below.
> It has been suggested that the author was a Dr. Wm. Thomson.

> 1791 NEWTE, THOMAS. Prospects and Observations on a Tour in England and Scotland, Natural, Oeconomical, and Literary. Folding map of Scotland and 23 plates. 4to. London.
> > Reviewed *Gent. Mag.,* vol. 61, 748-50 (see vol. 58, 803, for review of first edition). The reviewer says that in this second edition the author has profited by some of the criticisms of the former work, but in some places has made things worse. On the whole, however, it is considerably improved. It contains remarks on settling officers on farms, the sinking fund, the national debt, Aberdeen, etc.

NICHOLS, JOHN. The Progresses and Public Processions of Queen Elizabeth; among which are interspersed other Solemnities, Public Expenditures, and Remarkable Events during the Reign of that illustrious Princess. Now first printed from Original MSS. of the Times; or collected from scarce Pamphlets. Illustrated with historical Notes. Plates. 2 vols. Edinburgh and Perth.

> A 3rd volume was added in 1805. Reviewed *Gent. Mag.,* vol. 58, 425.
> The numerous "Progresses" which the Queen made to various parts of her realm no doubt redounded to her popularity as well as gratified her love of public entertainments, but they left her hosts much the poorer in purse. The idea of collecting these accounts was started by Mr. Tyson, at whose death Nichols took over the work. The progresses here reprinted are: to Cambridge, 1564, 1578; Oxford, 1566, 1592; Kenilworth, 1575; Norwich, 1579; Cowdrey and Elvetham, 1591; Bisham, Sudley, Ricot, 1592; Gray's Inn, 1594; lesser ones from 1559 to 1581 and 1588 to 1602, when she was entertained at the houses of the nobility.

SHAW, REV. STEBBING. A Tour in 1787 from London to the Western Highlands of Scotland, including Excursions to the Lakes of Westmoreland and Cumberland, with minute Descriptions of the principal Seats, Castles, Ruins, etc. 12mo. London.

Reprinted in Pinkerton, vol. II, 172-334.

Published anonymously. Reviewed *Gent. Mag.,* vol. 58, 805-07. The reviewer commends the book as a whole but complains that the practice of not acknowledging authorship puts it out of the power of others to quote from such works as authorities, because the sanction of the author's name cannot be used. The tour is written in the form of a diary and is fairly readable for detailed accounts of movement from place to place and for its description of places still flourishing or in ruins. The author defends, in his write-up of Canons "Timon's Villa" (of Pope's *Moral Epistle,* IV), both the Duke of Chandos and his mansion, and informs us that Pope's "ill-natured prophecy" about the Duke and his seat was too soon fulfilled, in that Chandos died in 1744 and the villa leveled to the ground by its purchaser at public auction in 1747. This purchaser, by the way, was one Hallet, a mere cabinet-maker. Other famous mansions and their contents come in for minute portrayal. Of interest to readers of Burns is his printing of the verses which the poet wrote over the mantelpiece of the inn at Taymouth when on his tour of the Highlands in 1787, verses that Burns did not include in his poetical works until 1793.

STEVENS, GEORGE A. Adventures of a Speculist: or, A Journey through London, with Life and Notes by the Editor. 2 vols. 8vo. London.

THOMSON, WILLIAM. A Tour in England and Scotland in 1785, by an English Gentleman. 6 plates. 8vo. London.

This is the work that is attributed to Thomas Newte (see Newte this date above). Reviewed *Gent. Mag.,* vol. 58, 803-05, where severe strictures are passed upon it for triteness of observations and the many mistakes in fact.

A Tour in England and Wales. 8vo. London (?). (So listed in *Gent. Mag.,* vol. 58, 635, among the new books.)

1789 ATKINSON, FREDERICK, and THOMAS WILSON. The Tour to York. A Circumstantial Account of the Prince of Wales's Visit to that City. 4to. York.

This item may be the same as the one listed below under the title *The Tour to York.*

Description of a Tour through the West of England. Signed S. E. In *Gent. Mag.,* vol. 59, 518-19.

This short narrative gives brief descriptions of Tavistock and Dartmoor. Only thing of interest is its amusing account of Brent-Torr and the small church on top of this steep rock. In the church is inscribed appropriately enough, "Upon this rock will I build my church, and the gates of Hell shall not prevail upon it." In their climb to the church the inhabitants are forced to do weekly penance, for they are compelled to ascend with their bodies bent toward the ground, and in blowy weather the pastor often has to humble himself upon all fours before he is exalted into the pulpit.

Diary of their Majesties' Journey to Weymouth and Plymouth. In *Gent. Mag.,* vol. 59, 951-52; 1046-47; 1142-44; 1202-04.

Printed separately, 8vo. London, 1789.
From this we learn that their Majesties bathed, saw this and that, remarked on so and so, and that is about all. The account is as dull as were their Royal Highnesses.

A Diary of the Royal Tour in June, July, August and September, 1789; interspersed with Anecdotes, Poetry, and Descriptions, Historical, Topographical, etc. To which is added, that of the Prince of Wales and Duke of York; with Character of the King, Prince of Wales, and Duke of York and Clarence. By an Observer of the Times. In *Gent. Mag.,* vol. 59, 1020.

GILPIN, REV. WILLIAM. Observations, relative chiefly to Picturesque Beauty, made in the Year 1776, on Several Parts of Great Britain, particularly the Highlands of Scotland. Many plates in aquatint. 2 vols. 8vo. London.

Later edits. separately and in combination with his other works. Reviewed *Gent. Mag.,* vol. 60, 928-32.

The principles of the picturesque are here applied to Scottish scenery, which offers the author ample opportunity to correct the mistakes of Nature in matters of composition. These principles are most fully set forth in his *Three Essays on Picturesque Beauty.* See also under 1791 below.

————. A Tour in Hampshire, Sussex, and Kent made in the Summer of 1774. London.

MOREAU, SIMEON. A Tour to the Royal Spa at Cheltenham. (Place?)

An edit., Bath, 1873.

The author was master of ceremonies at the Spa, and also the author of the first Cheltenham Guide. He retained his position until his death in 1810.

A Pleasing Narrative of Sunday passed in Westmoreland. Signed Eusebius. In *Gent. Mag.,* vol. 59, 899-901.

The sojourner on this Sunday was a Scotch Presbyterian. He gives an idyllic picture of piety, plenty, and innocent amusements of the villagers, their liberality in religion and absence of anything repressive.

SHAW, REV. STEBBING. A Tour to the West of England in 1788: Middlesex, Bucks, Berks, Oxford, Hereford, Somerset, Devon, etc. 8vo. London.

The portion dealing with Devon reprinted in Chope, *Early Tours in Devon and Cornwall.*

Shaw made this tour to the west because this part of England had been less visited and described. He gazed with delight on "the skeleton of Gothic Architecture, Tintern Abbey." He went back to London by way of the south coast. The improved conditions of the roads in this section of the country enabled him to travel by carriage. On the whole he gets quite close to rural England, except when he describes places with historical and literary associations, such as Woodstock with its memories of Chaucer, Horton and Milton, Windsor Forest and Pope, Beaconsfield and Waller. Being an ecclesiastic, he was naturally interested in churches, but the antiquarian in him must have been weak for he passed up Stonehenge.

STANLEY, SIR JOHN THOMAS. A Voyage to the Orkneys. 4to. (Place?) (So cited in Mitchell, *List of Travels.*)

Tour through various Parts of England and Wales. Signed C. C. In *Gent. Mag.,* vol. 59, 997-99; 1071-74; 1189-91; vol. 60, 21-23.

An uninteresting, matter-of-fact, topographical and antiquarian description.

The Tour to York: a circumstantial Account of the Prince of Wales's Visit to that City, A.D. 1789: with a Description and Engraving of the Gold Box presented him by the Corporation. n. p.

Reviewed *Gent. Mag.,* vol. 59, 1020. The reviewer is caustic and witty in his comments on the writers of these royal tours. As an instance of the intellectual level of the discourse he cites the remark of the Clerk of the Works that in a certain cathedral his Majesty should notice that the center of the church was in the middle of the building.

WARNER, RICHARD. A Companion in a Tour round Lymington, the New Forest, Isle of Wight, Southampton, Christchurch, etc. 12mo. Southampton.

YOUNG, ARTHUR. A Tour in Sussex. In *Annals of Agriculture,* vol. 11. London.

1790   GALE, SAMUEL. Tour through several Parts of England in 1705. Revised by him in 1730. In no. 11, *Bibl. Topog. Brit.*, vol. IV. London.

> This contains a folding plate showing the route from Salisbury to Stonehenge. The brothers Roger and Samuel Gale were close friends of Stukeley, who married their sister.

HASSELL, J. A Tour of the Isle of Wight. 30-aquatints. 2 vols. 8vo. London.

> Extracts printed in Pinkerton, vol. II, 729 ff.
> Hassell is a Gilpin on a less technical scale. He views natural phenomena with an eye for the picturesque, for varying effects of light and shadow as modified by sunrise and sunset.

MACDONALD, JOHN (Cadet of the Family of Keppoch). For an account of his travels in Scotland, see his *Travels in various Parts of Europe*, etc., WEST EUROPE, vol. I of this work.

WIGSHEAD, HENRY, and THOMAS ROWLANDSON. An Excursion to Brighthelmstone, made in the Year 1789. Embellished with 9 engravings from views taken on the Road to, and at that Place. Fol. London.

> The views, which are in sepia, include Sutton, Reigate, Crawley, Cuckfield, The Steine, Saloon at the Marine Pavilion, Bathing Machines, Race Ground.

WILSON, ALEXANDER. The Pack and other Poems, with a Journal of a Tour on Foot in the East of Scotland, in 1789. 8vo. London (?).

> Wilson was a poet and pedlar who started life as a weaver, emigrated to America, where he taught school at several places in 1794, and published a seven volume work on American ornithology, 1803-11, with two more added posthumously.

1791   ELDERTON, JOHN. Tour into the Lower Part of Somersetshire. In *Gent. Mag.*, vol. 61, 229-31.

> This describes mainly gentlemen's seats, among them being Fonthill Abbey and Wardour of Lord Arundel.

GILPIN, REV. WILLIAM. Remarks on Forest Scenery and other Woodland Views, illustrated by the Scenes in the New-Forest in Hampshire. 2 vols. 8vo. London.

> 2nd edit., 2 vols., 40 plates, London, 1794.

TOWNLEY, RICHARD. A Journal kept in the Isle of Man; giving an Account of the Wind and the Weather, and Daily Occurences for upwards of eleven Months; with Observations on the Soil, Clime, and Natural Productions of that Island; also, Antiquities of various kinds now extant there; A Trait of the Manners and Customs, etc.; An Account of their Harbours, etc. Together with a large Appendix containing an Account of the Antient Forms of Government, and mild Administration of Justice under the noble House of Stanley, etc. 2 vols. 8vo. Whitehaven.

> Reviewed *Gent. Mag.*, vol. 61, 840. The journey began on April 30, 1789, and ended April 21, 1790, in which time a complete circuit of the island was made. The account is fuller than that of any other traveler. During a spell of bad weather which confined his movements, he framed his second volume with copious extracts from Seacome's *Memoirs* (see under 1746, HISTORY AND ANTIQUITIES), and from a MS history by a Welsh justice of the last age, which was lent him by a friend. From another MS of Alex. Ross, of Gray's Inn, are extracts on the customs and laws, which form the Appendix. This is the most useful part of the work. The journal itself is dull, full of tedious quotations. It could be condensed to an hundred pages.—From the review.

YOUNG, ARTHUR. A Month's Tour to Northamptonshire. In *Annals of Agriculture,* vol. 16. London.

1792   An Account of a Voyage to the Hebrides, by a Committee of the British Fishery Society, in the Year 1787. In *The Bee,* vol. 8, 81-85; 173-78; 209-17; 280-86; vol. 9, 51-57; 89-95; 118-25. 16mo. Edinburgh.

BUDWORTH, JOSEPH. A Fortnight's Ramble to the Lakes in Westmoreland, Lancashire, and Cumberland. By a Rambler. 8vo. London.

> 2nd edit., 8vo, London, 1795; 3rd, London, 1810.
> The first two editions appeared anonymously. A fire consumed 500 copies of the 1,000 printed in the 2nd edition. The first being full of inaccuracies, the author stopped the sale and *disfigured* the remaining copies.—Nichols, *Literary Anecdotes,* vol. IX, 155-56. Reviewed *Gent. Mag.,* vol. 62, 1114, where it is commended as an "effusion of a young and generous mind." The author was the son of an innkeeper of Manchester, and lieutenant in the Manchester Royal Volunteers, which served at Gibraltar.

CATCOTT, GEORGE SYMES. A Descriptive Account of a Descent made into Pen Park Hole, in the Parish of Westbury, in the County of Gloucester, in the Year 1775, now first published; to which is added, Copper Plate Engravings of that remarkable Cavern; also the Narratives of Captains Sturmy and Collins, containing their Descriptions of the same Place in the Years 1669 and 1682 (the latter published in the *Philos. Trans.,* no. 143).

> Reviewed *Gent. Mag.,* vol. 63, 157. The interest in this Hole arose from the Rev. Newnam's having fallen into the cavern. The author made two surveys of it within a month after the accident. He gives a detailed description of its depth, length, the water at the bottom, etc.—From the review.

DEMPSTER, G. An Account of the Magnetic Fountain of Cannay. Paper read 1787. In *Arch. Scot.,* vol. I, 183. Edinburgh.

GORDON, ALEXANDER (Principal of the Scots College, Paris). Remarks made in a Journey to the Orkney Islands, in 1781. In *Arch. Scot.,* vol. I, 256, Edinburgh.

> The author visited three of the islands. He recorded with some care the physical features, buildings, particularly the churches and the remains from Norse antiquity and from pre-Reformation days, and the stone circles. The population at the time was 35,000. His indignation was aroused at the way the Government allowed the inhabitants to be cheated through false weights and measures. He found that the Orkneys had supplied the navy with more than 2,000 seamen during the last war and with 1,500 at the present time. The people themselves were unsurpassed in patience, docility, boldness, and activity.

A Sketch of a Two Months' Tour in Scotland performed on Horseback in the Summer of 1773. In *Gent. Mag.,* vol. 62, 37-39; 323-24; 406-07; 522-23; 717-18; 911-12; 1007-08; vol. 63, 221-22; 417-18; 512-13; 706-07; 809-10; 894-96; 1003-05; 1093-95; 1194-95.

WALKER, A. Remarks made in a Tour from London to the Lakes of Westmoreland and Cumberland, in the Summer of MDCCXCI, originally published in the Whitehall Evening Post, and now reprinted with additions and corrections. 8vo. London.

> Said to be a lively and "matterfull" book.

WATKINS, REV. THOMAS. The Travels of Rev. Thos. Watkins, Pennoyre. 2 vols. 8vo. (Place?) (So cited in Rowlands.)

1793 BUCHANAN, REV. JOHN. Travels in the Western Hebrides from 1782 to 1790. 8vo. London.

Reviewed *Gent. Mag.,* vol. 63, 927. The author was a missionary minister from the Church of Scotland to the Isles. The shocking pictures he draws of the wretchedness and misery of the population is not to be laid, if true, to Governmental oppression but to the hard-hearted landlords. The inhabitants are so down-trodden that they do not even resent blows from the tacksmen. It would have been different in olden times. He exposes as false some of the incredible tales current, such as that of sewing up the guts of young eaglets so that their continuous screams make their parents think them still hungry, whereupon the constant supply of food brought by their parents can be confiscated by the waiting evil-doers. The Presbyterian church is accused of shamefully abusing its power over the islanders.—This charge may not have been made by Buchanan but by Dr. William Thomson, to whom he had entrusted the publication of his travels, for in his *General View of the Fishery of Great Britain,* Buchanan indignantly disclaimed having criticized the clergy of Scotland.

CLARKE, DR. E. D. A Tour through the South of England, Wales, and Part of Ireland, made during the Summer of 1791. 10 colored illustrations and plan. 8vo. London.

The *Gent. Mag.* calls this a foolish, ill-placed piece of levity. However, it is not so bad.

COZENS, Z. A Tour through the Isle of Thanet, and some other Parts of East Kent, including a particular Description of the Churches in that extensive District, and Çopies of the Monumental Inscriptions. Plates. 4to. London.

Reviewed *Gent. Mag.,* vol. 64, 243-44.

GIBSON, W. Two Months' Tour in Scotland. In *Gent. Mag.,* vol. 63, 706-07; 809-10; 894-96; 1003-05; 1194-95; vol. 64, 221-22; 329-30; 522-23; 610-12.

This traveler was struck with the gloom of so many Highland glens, dusky moors, vast lochs and scowling mountains, often veiled in fog, intersected with defiles and hollows, the roar of torrents and moaning of the wind, the absence of any objects suggestive of sociability as compared with the comfortable cottages, neat farm houses, ornamented seats, cultivated ground, and the sights and sounds of cheerful active life to be found in well populated places. The Highlands are full of sights that are sublime and magnificent, but they pall after repetition.

HERON, ROBERT. Observations made in a Journey through the Western Counties of Scotland in 1792. 2 vols. 8vo. Perth.

To record personal experiences was not the aim of this tour. Rather its object was to note the scenery, antiquities, customs, manners, population, agriculture, manufactures, political conditions, and literature of this part of the country.

MALCOLM, J. P. A Journey from Chesterfield to Matlock (in Derbyshire). In *Gent. Mag.,* vol. 63, 505-06.

Rough and rugged scenes mingled with smooth and domestic aspects; crowds of people swarming over the Torr to witness the funeral of Sir Richard Arkwright; the gloomy clouds and darkened sky in keeping with the occasion; the solemn stillness and dismal tolling of a distant bell—such were the elements in this tour that gave pleasure to his melancholy-seeking soul.

A Meteorologist's Tour from Walton to London. A Journal of the Two Hottest Days in July. In *Gent. Mag.,* vol. 63, 619-21.

What gives this little tour more than ordinary remark is the talk the traveler had with Francis Barber, Johnson's negro servant, who related some anecdotes concerning his master. The testimony to the heat makes up part of the journal. At Manchester the thermometer registered 79 degrees in the shade and 129 in the sun. The author recommends the establishment of a regular meteorological journal. The *Gentleman's Magazine* had for some time, however, been publishing such observations each month.

A Naturalist's Stray from Gosport to London in the Sultry Days of July. In *Gent. Mag.*, vol. 63, 913-16; 1087-89. (Signed A Southern Faunist.)

Before his account was all printed, readers were beginning to complain of the peculiarities of the author's language. He seemed to have no particular field of interest; everything he met received the same amount of notice.

A Tour to Cheltenham Spa, or Gloucestershire display'd. 12mo. Bath.

WORDSWORTH, WILLIAM. An Evening Walk, an Epistle to a Young Lady, from the Lakes of the North of England. London.

This, the opening poem in Wordsworth's collected works, was reviewed in *Gent. Mag.*, vol. 64, 252-53. The reviewer, who signs himself Peregrinator, not only has experienced the charm of those vales, but he was a contemporary of the poet at Cambridge. He wishes to repay the debt he owes to the pleasures afforded him by those regions by recommending this poem to the attention of diverse visitants. He warns readers not to expect descriptions of particular areas, but to look for the general imagery of the country, which is handled with spirit and elegance.

1794   HARVEY, MISS J. A Sentimental Tour through Newcastle. By a Young Lady. 8vo. Newcastle.

LETTICE, JOHN. Letters on a Tour through various Parts of Scotland, in the Year 1792. 8vo. London.

Reviewed *Gent. Mag.*, vol. 64, 348-53, where a pretty full epitome of the book is given. The author proposes to take the reader with him as a companion, and aims to catch the great characteristic features as he goes along as well as to describe particular scenes as they appeared in each day's ride. This account is somewhat more personal than many of the preceding and contemporary tours; yet much generalized description is resorted to. Lettice seems to be well acquainted with the current descriptive language. In addition to scenes he pays attention to progress in commerce, buildings, trade, and mining industries. His route lay along the west coast to Fort William, thence across the Great Glen, and down the east coast.

The Ramble of a Naturalist in the North of England. Signed X. Z. In *Gent. Mag.*, vol. 64, 111-13; 326-27.

This contains his observations on a journey to Kentsands in Westmoreland, in search of natural curiosities, such as ornithology, fishes, flora, etc.

ROBERTSON, DAVID. A Tour through the Isle of Man, to which is subjoined a Review of Manks History. Plates in aquatint. Printed for the Author. 8vo. London.

Another edit., London, 1798. Reviewed *Gent. Mag.*, vol. 63, 1113; in Mavor, vol. V, 87-136, London, 1800; in Pinkerton, vol. II, 785-833. Translated into French, Rouen, An XI. See below. As a Tour the work has merit; as a more particular history of the Island from the earliest times to the latest period, it is wanting. The format of the book—wide margins and slender column of type—is in keeping with what was thought *elegant*. The author's style is pleasing, though a bit affected.—From the review. The work led to the author's imprisonment on account of some violently democratic passages on the last three pages, which were later suppressed. Like most travelers he must note down the historical associations, the antiquities, laws and manners of the people and the place. He advises the inhabitants to take up manufactures to offset their primitiveness and remoteness, but

what the island would and could manufacture he does not make evident, nor does he consider whether the accompaniments of factory economy would prove to be a blessing. He says little about the Manx language, beyond acknowledging that he does not know how far it was in use. According to Campbell (*Political Survey,* vol. I, 538), the Manx tongue was spoken generally by the common people and used by the clergy in their preaching. The author seems to have been bred in an atmosphere of melancholy, sentimental romances.

AN XI   (In French.) Voyages dans l'île de Man, avec des réflexions sur l'histoire des habitans. Traduit de l'Anglois par J.-P. Coignard. 8vo. Rouen.

SOTHEBY, WILLIAM. A Tour through Parts of Wales, Sonnets, Odes, and other Poems. 13 aquatint plates in yellow tints by J. Smith. 4to. London. (In verse.)

WALLIS, ———. A Tour through England and Wales: a New Geographical Pastime. Colored map. 8vo. London.

WYNDHAM, HENRY PENRUDDOCKE. A Picture of the Isle of Wight in 1793. 8vo. London.

1795   HUCK, J. Pedestrian Tour through North Wales, in a Series of Letters. 8vo. London.

> Reviewed by Herbert Wright in *Nineteenth Century*, vol. 99, May, 1926, under title of "The Tour of Coleridge and his Friend Huck in Wales, in 1794."
> The name is sometimes given as Hucks. The author does not mention his three companions by name, which is all the more to be regretted, since Coleridge was one of them; the other two were undergraduates, Brooke and Berdin (?), of Jesus College. Huck's account needs to be supplemented by Coleridge's letters to Southey and to Harry Martin, another Jesus College student. The poet's outspoken democratic leanings were omitted as being too dangerous to put into print at this time.—From Wright. Huck is a thoroughgoing romantic of the picturesque and primitive persuasion. He expects to see emerge in solitary places either the genius of the spot or else banditti "more terrible in aspect than ever Salvatore could ever have painted," to rush upon him from behind a rock. Venerable ruins also have guardian genii. A visit to Mona is *de rigeur* because of its associations with the druids. Ruins of castles provide occasion for pleasing melancholy reflections on mutability tinged with the republican thought of their having been strongholds of tyranny. The account is quite personal in tone in its references to adventures met in an unknown wild country and with an unknown language. Like other travelers of the period, they were much taken with the beauty of the Wye valley and the ruins of Tintern Abbey. And the 18th century association of vice and luxury also comes to the fore. The travelers carried their clothes in a wallet or knapsack, excusing their ungenteel appearance on the ground that they traveled on foot to see, not to be seen.

L., J. A Three Days' Excursion on Dartmoor, July 21, 22, 23, and 24. In *Gent. Mag.*, vol. 65, 910-11; 1008-09; 1080-82; vol. 66, 34-36.

> This tour marks the stages of the journey in a very pedestrian fashion. It notices rocks, natural history, antiquities, boundaries, rivers, cascades, etc. It contains nothing unusual in style or in narrative.

MORGAN, MRS. MARY. A Tour to Milford Haven, in the Year 1791. 8vo. London.

> Noticed briefly in *Gent. Mag.*, vol. 65, 943. The writer chose one of the most public and least picturesque roads in England—that from London to the South of Ireland—and filled up her book with trifling incidents, with now and then a marvellous story.—From the review.

NAISMITH, JOHN. A Tour through the Sheep Pastures in the Southern Parts of Scotland. Observations on the different Breeds of Sheep, and the State of Sheep Farming in the Southern Districts of Scotland; being the Result of a Tour through these Parts, made under the Direction of the Society for Improvement of British Wool. 4to. Edinburgh.

PRATT, SAMUEL JACKSON. Gleanings through Wales, Holland and Westphalia; with Views of Peace and War at Home and Abroad. To which is added, Humanity, or, The Rights of Nature; a Poem; revised and corrected. 4 vols. 8vo. London.

> 2nd edit., London, 1796; another (3rd?), 2 vols., 1797; 5th, 3 vols., 1800.
> Vol. I treats of Wales and vol. IV of England. The work contains descriptions of landscapes, inhabitants, queer and distinguished personalities, Welsh fairies, walking candles, invisible guides, and other superstitions. Pratt was a miscellaneous writer who used the name of Courtney Melmoth. He made an unsuccessful bid as actor in Dublin in 1773, and then tried his hand at writing plays.

RADCLIFFE, ANNE. Observations during a Tour of the Lakes of Lancashire, Westmoreland, and Cumberland (added to her *Journey made in the Summer of 1794, through Holland,* etc. See this latter date under WEST EUROPE, vol. I of this work).

SKRINE, HENRY. Three Successive Tours in the North of England and Great Part of Scotland. Interspersed with Descriptions of the Scenes they Presented and Occasional Observations on the State of Society and the Manners and Customs of the People. Folding map and 23 engraved views after Barret, Nasmyth, etc. 4to. London.

> Reviewed *Gent. Mag.,* vol. 65, 493-94. Apparently the edition reviewed contained no engravings. Unlike many tourists, Skrine openly admits that the object of these tours was publication. The Preface states that the first tour was made many years ago and covered those central parts of England which were too well known to need much description. The second took place in 1787 into Staffordshire and the Lake counties. The third was made in 1793 to the eastern and northern Highlands of Scotland. He apparently owes much to Gray and West, Ainslee's New Map and account of Scotland, and to Pennant, whom he recommends to future travelers in the north of England. He praises the hospitality of the Highlanders but has little good to say of the Lowlanders. The stories of their filth and dirtiness he says are surpassed by the reality.

1796   BUDWORTH, JOSEPH. Picturesque Tours of the Lakes of Westmoreland, Lancashire, and Cumberland. London. (So cited by Pinkerton, vol. XVII.)

CUMBERLAND, GEORGE. An Attempt to describe Hafod (in Wales). 12mo. London.

FERRAR, JOHN. A Tour from Dublin to London in 1795, through the Isle of Anglesea, Bangor, Conway, etc. Dublin.

HOUSMAN, ——. Tour to the Lakes of Cumberland. London. (So cited by Pinkerton, vol. XVII.)

JONES, J. G. A Sketch of a Political Tour through Rochester, Chatham, Maidstone, Gravesend, etc. 8vo. London.

TOMKINS, CHARLES. A Tour to the Isle of Wight. 80 aquatint views by and after Charles Tomkins, in bistre. 2 vols. 8vo. London.

Tour in Rutland. In *Gent. Mag.,* vol. 66, 17-18; 186-87.

YOUNG, ARTHUR. A Farming Tour to the South and West of England, 1796. In *Annals of Agriculture,* vols. 28-41.

1797 AIKIN, ARTHUR. A Journal of a Tour through North Wales and Part of Shropshire; with Observations in Mineralogy and other Branches of Natural History. 8vo. London.

> This mineralogical and geological tour was made in the summer of 1796.

A Collection of Welch Tours, or, A Display of the Beauties of Wales, Selected principally from Celebrated Histories and Popular Tours, with occasional Remarks. 3 aquatints. 12mo. London.

> 2nd edit., 12mo, London, 1797; 3rd, with Tour of the River Wye, 12mo, London, 1798.

A Descriptive Account of the Devil's Bridge, Hafod, Strata Florida Abbey, and other Scenery in that District of Cardiganshire. In an Excursion from Aberystwith; Comprehending the Objects adjoining the River. 2nd edit. Hereford.

MATON, W. G., M.D. Observations relative to the Natural History, Picturesque Scenery, and Antiquities of the Western Counties of England, made in the Years 1794 and 1796, illustrated by a Mineralogical Map and 16 views in Aquatint, by Alken. 2 vols. 8vo. Salisbury.

> Reprinted in Chope, *Early Tours,* 233-278.
> His main interest lies in matters of scientific and technological progress, such as the composition of soils, the export of serges and kerseys from Exeter, variations in the rocks of various districts, the fishing and curing industries, the tin and copper mines, the weaving of carpets at Axminster, the laws of the Stanneries, etc. He adds some antiquarian remarks on the cathedral towers of Exeter, which he mistakenly calls Saxon instead of Norman, and discredits the Arthurian associations with Tintagel and St. Michael's Mount. In general his observations are of a fairly personal nature.

M'NAYR, JAMES. A Guide (i.e. a Tour) from Glasgow to some of the most remarkable Scenes in the Highlands of Scotland; and to the Falls of the Clyde. Glasgow.

PENHOUET, A. B. L. MAUDET DE. Letters describing a Tour through Part of South Wales, by a Pedestrian Traveller. Illustrations. 4to. London.

A Tour to the Isle of Wight. Views. 2 vols. (Place?) (So listed in *Gent. Mag.,* vol. 67, 48.)

WEST, DR. Letters from Dr. West, Ambassador of Henry VIII to Scotland. Quoted in John Pinkerton, *History of Scotland from the Accession of the House of Stuart to that of Mary,* 2 vols., 4to, London.

> This item is cited by Mitchell, *List of Travels,* who says that these letters may be deemed the outcome of personal observation during his travels. In the App. to vol. II, there is a draft of a letter about Scotland from West to Henry VIII.

1798 Description of the Royal Excursion to Weymouth. In *Gent. Mag.,* vol. 68, 804; 986-990; 1076-78; 1111-15.

> This begins as an Intelligence Item, p. 804, and is carried on in diary form. One learns that their Majesties bathed in turn and walked the Esplanade.

FELTHAM, JOHN. A Tour through the Isle of Mann, in 1797 and 1798; comprising Sketches of its Ancient and Modern History, Constitution, Laws, Commerce, etc. Map, pedigree, and 3 plates. 8vo. Bath.

Later edit., London, 1801; and 1861, as vol. 6. of *Publ. Manx Soc.*

Reviewed *Gent. Mag.,* vol. 69, 44-46. The reviewer remarks that pedestrian tours are now all the rage. Feltham traveled two hundred and eight and one-half miles in seven days, and one hundred ninety-eight miles in eight days, going from Salisbury to Liverpool and back again at the expense of only £5/3/2½. His account is written in twelve letters to Dr. Wm. Hawes, whom he wished to introduce to the Humane Society there. Letter V deals with the literal translation of the Bible into Manx and with English and Manx publications on the Island. The letters are followed by a parochial fortnight's tour on foot written to other friends. The narrative is well done, and combines observations, history, and reading happily conjoined.

GILPIN, REV. WILLIAM. Observations on the Western Parts of England, relative chiefly to Picturesque Beauty, to which are added, A Few Remarks on the Picturesque Beauties of the Isle of Wight. 18 plates. 8vo. London.

GRANT, JOHNSON. A London Journal of a Three Weeks' Tour in 1797, through Derbyshire to the Lakes.

In Mavor, vol. V, 1800.
Grant, a student at Oxford, with two companions, sets out for the Lakes by way of Derbyshire, and loses no occasion for describing towns, inns, seats, falls, caves, etc., en route. He becomes quite rapturous over the beauties in the Lake District, and complains of the encroachments of villas, white houses, and other like objects as incongruous with the romantic character of the country. He finds Coniston the most romantic body of water, a term not applied to the other lakes. Other place names, later to be associated with Wordsworth, that are mentioned are Rydal House, Borrowdale, Helvellyn, which he climbed, Ulswater, Skiddaw, and many others. He is much given to melancholy reflections as if to order at the proper place. He knows what emotions are appropriate to a scene, and likes to imagine sinister figures lurking in dark, gloomy spots. He also knows what Poussin and Salvatore stand for in the landscape world, likewise the differences between the picturesque, the beautiful, and the sublime. His eye for scenes that can be painted in words is sure, and he does the pictorial job well.

HALDANE, R. A Journal of a Tour through the Northern Counties of Scotland and the Orkney Isles in the Autumn of 1797; undertaken with a View to promote the Knowledge of the Gospel of Jesus Christ. 12mo. Edinburgh.

2nd edit., 1798. See Rev. Gavin Mitchell under 1799 below.

JAMESON, ROBERT. An Outline of the Mineralogy of the Shetland Islands and of the Island of Arran, with Mineralogical Observations made in a Tour through the Mainland of Scotland, and Dissertations upon Peat, Kelp, and Coal. Map and plates. 8vo. Edinburgh.

Journal of a Tour to Scarborough in the Summer of 1798. 8vo. Wisbech.

MAVOR, WILLIAM. The British Tourist, or Traveller's Pocket Companion. 5 vols. 12mo. London.

2nd edit., 6 vols., 12mo, London, 1800 (the edition quoted in this work).
This is a collection of tours by well known travelers, which are reproduced sometimes complete and sometimes in extracts.

SHEPARD, CHARLES (Jun.). A Tour through Wales and the Central Parts of England. In *Gent. Mag.,* vol. 68, 303-04; 390-92; 486-90; 560-63; vol. 69, 452-56; 755-58; 851-54; 932-35; 1036-40; 1098-1102.

The author sets forth his intention on pp. 303-04, where he briefly reviews a number of tours and points out their shortcomings. For instance, Aikin gives too much natural history, which for itself is good but is poorly written; Wyndham writes with care and elegance but pays

little attention to natural beauties and besides describes too many castles; Huck writes with spirit and enthusiasm but falls too readily into politics; Shaw is too voluble to afford any profitable instruction. The present writer proposes to steer a middle course: to blend the general with the local, the sentimental with the speculative, to avoid sameness, bias, and the prolixity characteristic of others. The trip was begun in the summer of 1795 and was written up in 1796. The ground covered was about 930 miles, and the rate of walking on an average was fourteen miles a day, though for a whole fortnight he made it twenty miles. He starts from London but defers describing anything till he reaches Oxford. He keeps in mind the urge to impart information and indulges in quotations. Of Birmingham he notes that it is no more than a village but outside of London is estimated to have the largest group of buildings. With the account in vol. 69, 755-58, comes a change in the work. The original manuscript written at the time was lost; the author has neither the time nor the inclination to compose a new one. So he writes now from superficial sketches made occasionally during the tour. The last pages bring the traveler back to London. As is fitting, he gives some cursory hints to the tourist. Traveling on foot has its disadvantages, especially in rainy weather and over boggy ground. Accommodations are poor, progress is slow, and the track confined. It is better to go on horseback, for then one has better chance to secure good lodgings and more considerations. A list of places where the inns are good concludes the account. On the whole, it does not make much advance over some of those criticized.

SKRINE, HENRY. Two Successive Tours throughout the Whole of Wales, with several of the adjacent English Counties, so as to form a comprehensive View of the picturesque Beauty, the peculiar Manners, and the fine Remains of Antiquity in that interesting Part of the British Island. 8vo. London.

> Reprinted in Mavor, *op. cit.,* vol. V, 137-98, 1800; 2nd edit., London, 1812.
> This account is combined of several tours taken in different summers. Skrine makes the common error of confusing Saxon architecture with Norman. He is entranced with the ruins of Tintern Abbey, as were likewise Wyndham, Shaw, Gilpin, and others, and gives full play in general to his predilection for Salvatorish scenes. His visit to St. Donats, by calling to mind the name and character of its American buyer, evokes a mournful reflection on the sad fate dealt to historical continuity by unfeeling Time.

THOMPSON, G. A Sentimental Tour collected from a Variety of Occurrences from Newbiggin, near Penrith, Cumberland, to London by way of Cambridge, and from London to Newbiggin by way of Oxford. 8vo. Penrith.

A Tour of the River Wye and its Vicinity. 2 sepia engravings. 8vo. Chester.

WARNER, REV. RICHARD. A Walk through Wales in August, 1797. Bath.

> 2nd edit., Bath, 1798; 3rd, Bath, 1799.
> It is of interest to compare Warner's conclusions on the object of traveling with those of Johnson: "There is something wonderfully inspiriting in the commencement of a journey to a place which we have never before visited. The mind, delighting in novelty, eagerly anticipates the gratification, which scenes that are new to it are found to afford; and the imagination, always alive and active, when its creative powers are not restrained by previous knowledge, is busied on painting fanciful beauties, and forming ideal pleasures, which are never discovered in the real picture, nor experienced in actual enjoyment." Getting down to particulars, he tells how to prepare for a pedestrian tour. One should take a single change of raiment, and have a commodious pocket that sweeps clear across the back to carry articles in. It is also advisable to take along a drinking horn. A new era intervenes between these sentiments and those expressed by Johnson on his tour (1773): "I shall return from an expedition extremely pleasurable, with an increase in humility, an expansion of benevolence, and an enlargement of every better affection."

WOODWARD, G. W. Eccentric Excursions, or Literary and Pictorial Sketches of Countenance, Character and Country. 100 caricature engravings by Cruikshank after Woodward. 4to. London.

1799 Douglas, N. Journal of a Mission to Parts of the Highlands of Scotland in the Summer and Harvest of 1797, by Appointment of the Relief Synod, in a Series of Letters to a Friend; as also an Account of a former Mission, appointed by the Relief Presbytery of Glasgow, to a certain District of the Highlands, at the Request of the late Lady Glenorchy; both designed to show the State of Religion in that Country, and the Claim the Inhabitants have on the Compassion of Fellow Christians. 8vo. Edinburgh.

> This traveler is urged only once to speak of the beauties of the scenery through which he passed (p. 98). Yet apparently he did lift his eyes to look upon some remarkable places, for he regrets (p. 151) his inability to visit Mount-Stuart in Rothesay, and says that he did "take a view" of Dumbarton Castle, and that "several cannon were discharged while he stood on the top." He was tried for sedition, May 26, 1817, and found not guilty. —Mitchell, *List of Travels*.

Heath, C. Excursion down the Wye from Ross to Monmouth, Wilton and Goodrich Castles, New Weir, the Swifts, John Kyrle, etc. 8vo. Monmouth.

> 10th edit., much enlarged, 1827.

Hill, Rev. Rowland, M.A. Journal of a Tour through the North of England and Parts of Scotland, with Remarks on the Present State of the Established Church of Scotland, and the different Secessions therefrom. Together with Reflections on some Party Distinctions in England; showing the Origin of these Disputes, and the Causes of their Separation. Also, some Remarks on the Propriety of what is called Lay and Itinerant Preaching. 8vo. London.

> See John Jamieson below for *Remarks* on this work. The good minister was so taken up with his preaching that he had no eye for the country he had to traverse.

Hutton, William. Remarks in a Tour through Wales. In *Gent. Mag.*, vol. 69 (cont. from vol. 67, 1084), 846-50; 925-28.

> The ascent of Snowdon and the experiences in general are quite personal in tone. The top of Snowdon he finds to be a level circle of about eight feet in diameter, surrounded by a wall two feet high of loose slate stones. The view is described in terms of the eyesight. One should compare Wordsworth's account of his ascent and view in *Prelude*, XI.

Jamieson, John, D.D. Remarks on the Rev. Rowland Hill's Journey, etc., in a Letter to the Author: including Reflections on Itinerant and Lay Preaching. 8vo. Edinburgh.

> This work went through two editions at least.—Mitchell, *op. cit.*

Lipscomb, G. A Journey into Cornwall from Hampshire, through the Counties of Southampton, Wilts, Dorset, Somerset, and Devon: interspersed with Remarks, Moral, Historical, Literary, and Political. 8vo. Warwick.

> The author was chiefly interested in scenery, but he takes time to describe a carpet factory, a prison, and mines.

Mitchell, Rev. Gavin. Remarks upon the "Journal of a Tour in 1797." Aberdeen. (See Haldane under 1798 above.)

Warner, Rev. Richard. A Second Walk through Wales in August and September, 1798. Bath.

> The Reverend continued walking and publishing after the turn of the century.

1800 BINGLEY, REV. WILLIAM. A Tour round North Wales performed during the Summer of 1798, containing a Sketch of the History of the Welsh Bards: an Essay on the Language, the Habitats of above 400 of the more Rare Native Plants, etc. Aquatint plates by Alken. 2 vols. 8vo. London.

> Another edit., 2 vols., 8vo, London, 1804.
> In this work the language, manners, customs, antiquities, and botany are particularly attended to and well described.—Lowndes.

DUNSFORD, M. (Merchant). Miscellaneous Observations in the Course of Two Tours through several Parts of the West of England. Portrait. 8vo. Tiverton.

EVANS, REV. JOHN. A Tour through Part of North Wales in the Year 1798 and at other Times; principally undertaken with a View to Botanical Researches in that Alpine Country, interspersed with Observations on the Scenery, Agriculture, Manufactures, Customs, History, and Antiquities of the Principality. 8vo. London.

> So cited in Pinkerton, vol. XVII. It is listed in bookseller's catalogue as of 1804. This may be another edition.

GARNETT, DR. THOMAS. Observations on a Tour through the Highlands and Part of the Western Isles of Scotland, particularly to Staffa and Icolmkill; to which are added, A Description of the Falls of Clyde, of the Country round Moffat, and an Analysis of its Mineral Waters. Map and 52 illustrations. London.

> Translated into German, 2 vols., 8vo, Lübeck, 1802.
> The plates were drawn on the spot by W. H. Watts, the miniature and landscape painter, who accompanied Garnett on his tour. So much had been written of the north of England that little fresh matter remained for the author to print. He seems to have been conscious of this fact, for he transcribes whole pages from works well known. As he was no picturesque traveler, he preferred to describe nature as it was, not as it should have been. Garnett was a physician and chemist, and lecturer at Glasgow. See the *Beneden Letters,* 242 ff., under LETTERS, DIARIES, MEMOIRS, for more detail about him.

HILL, REV. ROWLAND. Extract of a Journal of a Second Tour from London through the Highlands of Scotland and the North Western Parts of England, with Observations and Remarks. 8vo. London.

HOUSMAN, JOHN. A Descriptive Tour and Guide to the Lakes, Caves, Mountains, and other Natural Curiosities in Cumberland, Westmoreland, Lancashire, and a Part of West Riding of Yorkshire. 8vo. Carlisle.

A Journey from London to the Isle of Wight. London. (So cited in Pinkerton, vol. XVII.)

A Journey to the Western Isles of Scotland. 8vo. Alnwick.

A Rambler's Re-Visit to Buttermere. In *Gent. Mag.,* vol. 70, 18-24.

> The Rambler revisited the Lake District in the winter of 1797-98 to see the Scale-Force waterfall "bound up in icicles." At a dance in the country he met again the maid whom he had celebrated in his poem, "Fortnight's Ramble," and takes the occasion to moralize to her. In his attempt to undo any false pride he feared his praise of her might have engendered, he naively tells her that she was not so handsome as she promised to be five years before. Her reply was that she trusted that she could take care of herself. His

descriptions of the scenery, rustic folk, the clergyman, the old soldier, the country lads and lasses are not without their intrinsic interest, though they are marked by self-consciousness in style. One notes that he employed the term "beautiful" instead of "romantic."

A Tour of Health and Pleasure; or, A Visit to the Principal Sea-bathing Places, and Mineral Waters in England; In a Letter to the Editor. In Mavor, *op. cit.,* vol. VI, 253-80.

> This account is the outcome of a summer's rambling from one watering place to another. It offers brief general descriptions of what each has to offer, with some reference to medical cures.

WARNER, REV. RICHARD. Excursions from Bath: to Stourhead, Wardour Castle and Charlton Park; the Castles and Seats, etc. 8vo. Bath.

> This consists of letters to James Comrie, Esq. Using Bath as a starting point, he proceeds in various directions on the several tours and describes the countryside he passes through. What especially appeals to him are scenes of distress and the sentiments aroused by wild, gloomy scenery. He also gives considerable attention to noting the portraits gracing the galleries of gentlemen's seats, of which the English gentry had made large collections. At Beckford's Fonthill he tells us that the price of two Claudes was 7,000 guineas. He describes Stonehenge but merely mentions Avebury.

———. A Walk through some of the Western Counties of England. 2 plates. 8vo. Bath.

WIGSTEAD, HENRY. Remarks on a Tour to North and South Wales, in the Year 1797. 22 plates from Rowlandson, Pugh, Howitt, etc., in aquatint. London.

1801   STODDART, JOHN. Remarks on Local Scenery and Manners in Scotland, 1799-1800. Numerous aquatint views of Highland and Lowland scenery. 2 vols. 4to. London.

1802   LIPSCOMB, G. A Journey into South Wales, through the Counties of Oxford, Warwick, Worcester, Hereford, Salop, Stafford, Buckingham, and Hertford, in 1799. 8vo. London.

1803   HUTTON, WILLIAM. Remarks upon North Wales, being the Result of Sixteen Tours through that part of the Principality. Plates. 8vo. Birmingham.

> Reviewed *Gent. Mag.,* vol. 74, 41-45, where it is termed a lively piece of writing.

1804   GILPIN, REV. WILLIAM. Observations on the Coasts of Hampshire, Sussex, and Kent, relative chiefly to Picturesque Beauty, made in 1774. 6 plates in aquatints. 8vo. London.

THORNTON, T. A Sporting Tour through the North Parts of England and great Part of Scotland (in 1786). London (?).

> The favorite sport of the writer was falconry.

1805   MANNERS, JOHN HENRY (Duke of Rutland). Journal of Three Years' Travels through different Parts of Great Britain in 1795, 1796, and 1797. 8vo. London. (Privately printed.)

1807 My Pocket Book; or, Hints for a Right Merrie Conceited Tour in Quarto, by Knight Errant. 12mo. London (?).

> This work is included solely on its face value.

1810 PEMBERTON, JOHN. Some Account of the last Journey of John Pemberton to the Highlands and other Parts of Scotland (in 1787), with a Sketch of his Character, by Thomas Wilkinson. London.

> Pemberton was a Quaker. His preaching tour, like others of its kind, mentions people, but pays scant attention to places, objects, or customs.—Mitchell, *List of Travels.*

1810-23 CLARKE, EDWARD DANIEL. Travels in various Countries of Europe, Asia, and Africa. 6 vols. 4to. London.

> These travels took place in 1790-1800 and covered Great Britain as well as other lands.

1813 HEARNE, THOMAS. Journeys to Reading, and to Whaddon Hall, the Seat of Browne Willis, Esq. In John Aubrey, *Letters Written by Eminent Persons in the 17th and 18th Centuries* (see under LETTERS, DIARIES, MEMOIRS).

MANNERS, JOHN HENRY (Duke of Rutland). A Journal of a Tour to the Northern Part of Great Britain. 8vo. London.

> This journey took place in 1796. It is doubtless part of the tour listed under Manners, 1805, above.

RERESBY, SIR JOHN. For observations on England and English ways of life, people and events, see his *The Travels and Memoirs of Sir John Reresby, Bart.*, under LETTERS, DIARIES, MEMOIRS. See also this title under WEST EUROPE, vol. I of this work.

1816 JOHNSON, SAMUEL. A Diary of a Journey into North Wales, in the Year 1774. First printed and elaborately edited by Richard Duppa, with Mrs. Piozzi's Help. 8vo. London.

> This was incorporated in Croker's *Boswell* in vol. V of Birkbeck Hill's *Boswell,* 1885. See Johnson-Thrale under 1910 below.

1818 The North of England and Scotland in 1504. By an unknown Traveller. 16mo. Edinburgh.

> This journal, which fell into the hands of Thomas Johnes, the translator of Froissart, was first published by Blackwood. Nothing is known of the writer, but he seems to have been a Londoner. A long notice of this tour appeared in *Blackwood's Magazine,* vol. 2, 517, Edinburgh, 1815.

1818-19 EVELYN, JOHN. For an intimate and interesting contact with the English scene, events, and personages in the seventeenth century, see his *Diary,* under LETTERS, DIARIES, MEMOIRS. His account of his experiences during the episodes of the plague and fire of London is well known.

1824 TUCKER, THOMAS. Report upon the Settlement of the Revenues of Excise and Custom in Scotland. First printed by the Bannatyne Club, no. 7. Edinburgh.

> Also printed in *Misc. Burgh Records Soc.,* vol. 7, 1824. The part describing Scottish seaports in Hume Brown, *op. cit.*

In 1652 the English Parliament resolved on an Act for Incorporating Scotland into one commonwealth with England. In 1655 Commissioners were appointed to proceed to Scotland to get information and to assist in the project. Tucker was one of these. His duties were "to give his assistance in settling the excise and customs there." The entire report is valuable but the only portions relating to travel are those dealing with the various seaports of Scotland. As an official report it can serve as a check against irresponsible stories of travelers. Tucker thinks that Scotland is favorably situated for trade, but the "barrenesse of the countrey, the poverty of the people, generally afflicted with slothe, and a lazy vagrancy of attending theyr heards up and down in theyr pastorage . . . hath quite banished all trade from the inland parts, and drove her downe to the very sea-side." The description of the ports, harbors, trade, commerce, and situation is probably accurate for the time. —From Hume Brown.

1825 CLARKE, EDWARD DANIEL. Tour in Scotland in the Summer and Autumn of 1797, along with Hon. B. Paget. In *Life and Remains of Edward D. Clarke,* by Rev. W. Otter, 2 vols., London.

> The party visited the Hebrides, the west of Ross, and Argyll, Inverness, Nairn, Aberdeen, Forfar, Perth, etc.—From Mitchell, *Scot. Topog.,* vol. II. Clarke was professor of mineralogy at Cambridge, and a widely traveled man.

1827 ELDER, JOHN (Clerk, a Reddshanke). Letter to Henry VIII of England, 1542 or 1543. In *Bann. Misc.,* vol. 1. Edinburgh.

> Printed also in *Collectanea de Rebus Albanicis,* Iona Club, Edinburgh, 1847.
> This letter seems to be a sort of introduction to a *plot* (i.e., a description or chart) of Scotland, a document now lost. It gives an account of the dress of the "wild Scots," based on personal observations during travels in the islands and on the mainland. The writer was a Caithness man.—Mitchell, *List of Travels.* It had something to do with uniting England and Scotland.

1829 CALAMY, REV. EDWARD, D.D. For an account of his visit to Scotland in 1709 and to the west of England in 1713, see his *Historical Account of my Own Life,* under LETTERS, DIARIES, MEMOIRS.

> Chapter VII, 141-227, tells of his "Journey into North Briton, his reception there, and return thence." He was made a free burgess of Edinburgh and honored with the degree of D.D. from the universities of Edinburgh and Glasgow. He visited Kinghorn, St. Andrews, Dundee, Montrose, Aberdeen, Brechin, Perth, Glasgow, and Hamilton.—From Mitchell, *op. cit.*

KING JOHN. Itinerarium Johannis Regis Angliae. A Table of the Movements of the Court of John, King of England, from his Coronation, May 27, 1199, to the End of his Reign: selected from the Attestations of the Court of Records preserved upon the Rolls in the Tower of London, by Thomas Duffes Hardy, F.S.A. in *Archaeologia,* vol. 22, 124-60. London.

> The introduction explains the value of this table to be that by means of it one can locate King John at any period of his reign. It consists of lists of stopping places in his kingdom, together with the dates by days, months, and years. The Court of Common Pleas had to attend the king wherever he might be. This arrangement obliged suitors to keep following the king's movements. How great an inconvenience it was may be judged from the fact that he moved with celerity remarkable for those days, usually covering as much as thirty-five to forty miles a day and at times even fifty. Complaints led to fixing the sittings of the Court at Westminster.

1830-32 KIRK, THOMAS. An Account of a Tour in Scotland (1677). Printed in Appendix to *Diary and Correspondence of Ralph Thoresby* (see Thoresby under LETTERS, DIARIES, MEMOIRS). London.

> Printed also by Hume Brown, Supplement to *Early Travellers.* See Kirk under 1845 below.

This tour was made before the publication of the coarse, abusive tract (see Kirke under 1679 above), which is attributed to Kirke. The tour occupied more than three months—from 14th May to 29th August—and extended to the Orkneys. Many parts of Scotland were visited and the account of what was seen makes interesting reading.

THORESBY, RALPH. Travel in Scotland in 1681. In *Diary and Correspondence of Ralph Thoresby*. London.

> Printed also in Hume Brown, Supplement to *Early Travellers*.

1831 STUART, DAVID (11th Earl of Buchan). Part of a Letter . . . giving an Account of a Tour through Aberdeenshire, in 1879. In *Arch. Scot.,* vol. 3, 18-21. Edinburgh.

1834 BRAYLER, E. W. A Topographical Excursion in the Year 1634. In *The Graphic and Historical Illustrator,* 319-48. London.

BURNS, ROBERT. For the journals of his Border tour and tour in the Highlands, 1787, see Allan Cunningham, *Life and Works of Robert Burns,* Edinburgh.

> The Border tour was included in all complete editions of Burns after Cunningham. Reproduced correctly by DeLancey Ferguson in *Robert Burns, His Associates and Contemporaries* by Robert T. Fitzhugh, Chapel Hill, N. Carolina, 1943.
> The shortcomings of Cunningham as an editor were exposed by Prof. Ferguson in "Burns's Journal of His Border Tour," *PMLA,* vol. 49, 1934. The original journal of the Highland tour came to light some years back and was printed in facsimile by J. C. Ewing, London, 1927. These journals contain but little description of places; they relate rather his movements and make brief notes on dinners, and comments, often pungent, on individuals. Neither tour produced any great poetry.

The Locklomond Expedition, MDCCXV. Reprinted and Illustrated from Original Documents. 8vo. Glasgow.

> A reprint of a very rare tract, with appendix of original matter relating to the Highlanders.—Bookseller's Note.

1836 BROWNE, SIR THOMAS. Journal of a Tour in Derbyshire in 1662. In *Works of Sir Thomas Browne,* vol. I. Norwich.

1837 HOWEL, JAMES. Satire against Scotland. In *Misc. Abbotsford Club,* vol. 1, no. xviii. Edinburgh.

> No. xix of the same publication contains an *Answer to the Satire against Scotland.*

MELROS, THOMAS, EARL OF. James's Visit to the Western Isles of Scotland. In *State Papers and Miscellaneous Correspondence,* 1599-1625. *Publ. Abbotsford Club,* 2 vols. in 1., vol. 9. 4to. Edinburgh.

1838 TELFORD, THOMAS. For an account of surveys that may be regarded as results of travels, see *Life of Thomas Telford by Himself,* GENERAL REFERENCE.

1838-40 BRUCE, J. (Editor). The History of the Arrivall of Edward IV in England, 1471. *Publ. Camden Soc.,* vol. 1. London.

1840 Journal from Kirkwall to Edinburgh. In *Misc. Maitland Club,* vol. 2. Edinburgh.

> The journal is without date and merely indicates the route and mileage.—Terry, *Catalogue Publications.*

1841   COLMAN, GEORGE (the Younger). For an account of a tour to the north of England in 1775, see *Memoirs of the Colman Family*, vol. I, 345-86, under LETTERS, DIARIES, MEMOIRS.

> The account of the tour was written up by the younger Colman, who with his father set out for the North by way of Oxford, Stratford-upon-Avon, Warwick Castle, Birmingham, Derby, Chatsworth to York and Scarborough, and so on. At Derby's famous cavern he narrowly escaped death by burning and drowning. At York they met with Captain Phipps, later Lord Mulgrave, the Arctic voyager, Joseph Banks, later president of the Royal Society, and the Tahitian youth Omai. With the latter he took his first dip in the ocean, hanging on to Omai's shoulders. The style of the narrative is jocular, sparkling, and somewhat affected, but invariably amusing.

KEMP, WILLIAM. Kemp's Nine Daies Wonder: performed in a Daunce from London to Norwich. Edit. with Introduction and Notes by Rev. Alexander Dyce. *Publ. Camden Soc.*, vol. 11. London.

> This famous feat by the well known Elizabethan comic actor was performed in 1599. To refute the lying ballads in circulation concerning his exploit and to evidence his gratitude for favors received during his "gambols," he published in the following year the curious pamphlet here printed. It was entered in the Stationers' Books 22 April, 1600. On his dance he was attended by his taborer Thomas Slye. Each day's distance and faring were recorded as well as the contests he engaged in en route. Naturally he had no lack of company on the road and took up many challenges to outdance the natives here and there.

1844   BLAKHAL, GILBERT. A Brieffe Narration of the Services done to three Noble Ladyes by Gilbert Blakhal, Priest of the Scots Mission in France, in the Low Countries, and in Scotland, MDCXXXI-MDCXLIX. Edit. by Dr. John Stuart for the Spalding Club, vol. 11, Aberdeen.

> See Hume Brown, *Scotland before 1700*, 303-12. For an account of Blakhal's sojourn in France, see Françisque Michel, *Les Ecossais en France*, vol. II, 340-58.
> Of the priest little is known except what he tells us in his Narration. Ordained a priest at Rome in 1630, he returned to Scotland in 1637, where he became a missionary to the Catholics in Aberdeenshire and Banffshire, acting also as chaplain to Lady Aboyne. On her death he went to France with the object of inducing the Marchioness of Huntly to withdraw her granddaughter from Scotland to that country. The success of his mission is related in the third and longest chapter of his book. The book was extremely popular, for his adventures are curious and his narrative manner so vivid and so simple that the work reads precisely like one of those romances in which the story teller bases his inventions on some long lost manuscript which has come into his hands in some surprising manner. He seems to have loved adventure for its own sake and rises to meet emergencies like any novel hero.—From Brown, *op. cit.* The narrative as a whole relates to the period 1631-49, but the part dealing with his travels is comprised in the years 1643-44. The three noble ladies were Lady Isabel Hay, Sophia, Countess of Aboyne, and Madame de Gordon.

BRERETON, SIR WILLIAM, BART. Notes of a Journey through Durham and Northumberland in the Year 1635. In *Reprints of Rare Tracts and Imprints of Ancient MSS.*, edit. by M. A. Richardson. 8vo. Newcastle.

————. Travels in England, Scotland and Ireland. *Publ. Chetham Soc.*, vol. 1, edited by Edward Hawkins. Manchester.

> This is bound up with his *Travels into Holland*, etc., in 1634. The portion dealing with Scotland in Hume Brown, *Early Travellers*, 132-58; the Journal was printed by the Surtees Society in *North Country Diaries* (see under 1914, LETTERS, DIARIES, MEMOIRS).
> The tour listed above took place in 1635, and included Ireland, Scotland and England. In describing his return from Ireland to England, he gives a good idea of what travel by boat was like and shows off his knowledge of nautical nomenclature. His vessel was "a most dainty, steady" one as long as she was under sail. He had "through God's Mercy a quick, pleasant and dainty passage," which apparently was unusual. As for Scotland, he finds the "sluttishness and nastiness" of the Scotch beyond endurance, and he backs up his

charges with convincing detail. Edinburgh was not noted for its sweetness and cleanliness at any time. Things are washed in "sluttish greasy water." Their linen is "sluttishly and slothfully washed" by women's feet, a long established practice which always excited the wonder of the Sothron. He is frequently forced to hold his nose as he goes through the hall or in bed or abroad. The "houses of office" used by the population are tubs or firkins placed upon end, which they never empty until full, "so the scent thereof annoyeth and offendeth the whole house." Their pewter pots, in which they bring their wine, "are furred at the edges, so that it loathes one to touch them." The government and orders of the church naturally come in for notice, as the discipline of the church was deeply impressed upon the people. After leaving Edinburgh, he journeys to Glasgow, of which he gives some particulars. Thence he moves on to Irvine, Ayr, and Galloway, where he takes boat for Ireland. He cites many curious remedies for various ailments, some of which have a tempting appeal, and names the things he finds hurtful and those that are beneficial. Irish drink was among the former and usquebaugh "with the yolk of an egg first and last" among the latter. One will note some interesting observations on the pronunciation of English by the Scotch and comments on the emigration of some 10,000 Scotch from the west of Scotland to the Ulster plantations. His account, though biased, makes delightful reading.

1845 JAMES, REV. RICHARD. Iter Lancastriense: A Poem, written A. D. 1636, now printed from the Original MSS. in the Bodleian, with Notes and Introduction by Rev. Thos. Corser. *Publ. Chetham Soc.*, vol. 7. 2 colored plates. 4to. Manchester.

The plates consist of representations of the windows of Middleton Church. The work discusses the scenery and local history; the manners, customs, and genealogy of Lancashire. A large folding pedigree of the Heywoods of Heywood forms a portion of the volume.—Bookseller's Note.

KIRK, THOMAS. Journeyings through Northumberland and Durham anno Dom. M.DC.LXXVII. In *Reprints of Rare Tracts and Imprints of Ancient MSS*. 8vo. Newcastle.

This is an extract from his *Tour in Scotland* and is concerned with his travels in the northern counties of England (see under 1830-32 above). The journey begins May 14, 1677, somewhere near Ripon. The travelers visit the sights that have historical interest as well as local fame. They report some curious customs, such as that of people dancing on the green for a wedding. It is evident that they were not averse to enjoying their ale.

SOMERSET, DUKE OF. The Tour of the Duke of Somerset and the Rev. J. H. Michell, through Parts of England, Wales, and Scotland, in the Year 1795. 8vo. London.

WILSON, ALEXANDER. The Poetical Works and also his Miscellaneous Prose Writings, Journals, Letters, Essays, etc., now first collected. Illustrated by critical and explanatory Notes, with an extended Memoir of his Life and a Glossary. 8vo. Belfast.

On pages 321-73 will be found two journals of travel in the south-east and in the county of Fife in Scotland. The author was a weaver, but traveled around as a packman, selling his poems along with the contents of his pack. Afterwards while working as a weaver in Paisley, he wrote a little book in verse called "The Shark," which was regarded as defamatory. He was prosecuted, fined, imprisoned, and made to burn copies of the book publicly. Later he had a distinguished career in America as an ornithologist.—From Mitchell, *List of Travels*.

1846 BORDE (BOORDE), ANDREW. A Letter to Thomas Cromwell, 1536. In Ellis's *Original Letters Illustrative of English History*, 3rd ser., vol. II, 303. London.

This letter is found also in Borde's *Introduction to Knowledge*, E.E.T.S., 1870. In this latter work appears a chapter on Scotland, where the food, the traits of the people, the condition of various parts of the country, and specimens of Scotch speech are described. The writer also states here that he had attended a little university in Scotland named Glasco and there had practiced physic.—From Mitchell, *op. cit.*

1847   THORESBY, RALPH. The Wayfarings of Ralph Thoresby in the North of England. Extracted from the *Diary and Correspondence of Ralph Thoresby,* etc., edit. by Rev. Joseph Hunter. Reprinted in *Reprints of Rare Tracts and Imprints of Antient MSS.,* vol. II, Newcastle.

> See Thoresby under 1830, LETTERS, DIARIES, MEMOIRS. Though brought up to trade, Thoresby turned antiquary and author of researches, the most notable of which being his *Ducatus Leodiensis* (see under 1715, TOWNS). As a woolen draper he had frequent occasions to make journeys into Durham, Northumberland, and Newcastle. These trips began in 1680 and continued to 1703.

1849   A Captain, a Lieutenant, and an Ancient. A Relation of a Short Survey of Twenty-six Counties, briefly describing the Cities and their Scituations . . . Observed in a Seven Weeks' Journey at the City of Norwich. In *Reprints of Rare Tracts,* etc. Newcastle.

> Edit. in its entirety by L. G. W. Legg, 12mo, London, 1904. The second tour, edit. by Legg in *Camden Misc.,* 3rd ser., vol. III, no. 16. See below. A portion in Chope, *op. cit.,* 83-92.
> The year of this journey was 1634. The travelers were evidently Royalists. They went north by the east coast and along the Borders and then down by the west coast. Their remarks on their experiences in Cumberland and Westmoreland indicate that they did not care for mountain scenery.

> 1904   A Relation of a Short Survey of Twenty-Six Counties Observed in a Seven Weeks' Journey begun on August 11, 1634, By a Captain, a Lieutenant, and an Ancient All Three of the Military Company in Norwich. Edit. with Introduction and Notes, by L. G. W. Legg, New College, Oxford. 12mo. London.

1851-52   BURNS, ROBERT. Tour to the South of Scotland; Trip to the West Highlands; Tour to the Highlands and North and East of Scotland (made in 1787). In *Life and Works of Robert Burns,* edit. by Robert Chalmers. 4 vols. 8vo. Edinburgh. (See Burns under 1927 below.)

1854   CAMPBELL, REV. THOMAS. Diary of a Visit to England in 1775 by an Irish Clergyman, and other Papers by the same Hand. Edit. with Notes by Samuel Raymond. 12mo. Sydney.

> Reviewed *Edinburgh Review,* vol. 110, Oct., 1859. Somehow this manuscript had found its way to Australia, but how is not known. It was the diary of an Irish clergyman (Rev. Thomas Campbell), who wrote it seemingly as a private record of incidents he notes on his first visit to London in 1775 and his subsequent one in 1781, with a few memoranda of a trip to Paris. He has been identified as the "Irish Dr. Campbell" of Boswell, who was said to have come from Ireland expressly to see Dr. Johnson. His reception and the impression he made are related in Boswell under Wed., April 25, 1775. He also dined with the Thrales, where he met Baretti and Johnson. His description of Johnson is amusing and brings home the fact that cats may have their opinions of queens. He was not afraid to refute Johnson's vehement outburst against the Irish Volunteers and the Americans.
> Newly edited from the MS, by James L. Clifford, Cambridge, 1947.

1855   WALDEN, LORD. The Progress of my Lord Walden's Journey in Scotland, 1614. In Sir J. Balfour, *Collections,* No. 71, and printed in *Bann. Misc.,* vol. III, xii, no. 19B. Edinburgh.

> The writer is unknown and the narrative contains little of interest or value.—Mitchell, *Scot. Topog.,* vol. II.

1859   TAYLOR, JOHN (The Water Poet). A Short Relation of a Journey through Wales, made in the Year 1652. Edit. by James O. Halliwell. 4to. London. (Only 26 copies printed.)

The Thane of Cawdor's Western Journey, 1591. First printed by Cosmo Innes in the *Book of the Thanes of Cawdor, Publ. Spalding Club.* 4to. Edinburgh.

> Reprinted in Cosmo Innes, *Sketches of Early Scotch History,* 8vo, Edinburgh, 1861. This is a record of the Thane's personal and traveling expenses from 20 Sept. to 7 Nov., 1591. It makes an interesting and instructive account.—Mitchell, *List of Travels.*

1861 CLEPHANE, DR. JOHN. A Journey from Scarborough to Kilravook (in Nairnshire), 1750. In Innes, *Sketches of Early Scottish History.* Edinburgh.

> The writer is mainly concerned with the condition of the roads. He notes the number of country seats near Edinburgh, and the length of the Scottish miles.—Mitchell, *op. cit.*

1862 JONSON, BEN. Ben Jonson in Edinburgh in the Year M.DC.XVIII. By David Laing, *Proc. Soc. of Antiq.,* vol. 3, 206-08. 8vo. Edinburgh.

1864-65 RICHARD THE PRIOR. For the Itinerary of Richard, see *Itinerarium Peregrinorum et Gesta Regis Ricardi,* 1147-92, under HISTORY AND CHRONICLE.

1866 WINDHAM, RT. HON. WILLIAM. Travels in various Parts of Scotland, in 1785, in Company with Mr. Burke. In his *Diary,* edit. by Mrs. H. Baring. 8vo. London.

1868 R———, ALEXANDER. Journal of a Soldier in the Earl of Eglinton's Troop of Horse, 1689. In *Trans. Glasgow Arch. Soc.,* vol. 1, 38. Glasgow.

1869 Narrative of the Journey of an Irish Gentleman through England in the Year 1752. Edit. from a Contemporary Manuscript, with a few Illustrative Notes, by W. C. Hazlitt. 8vo. London. (Only 50 copies printed.)

1870 John Sanders His Book. The Accounts of My Travels with my Mistress. *Records of Buckinghamshire,* vol. 3, 3-98.

> So cited by Fussell, *Exploration of England,* who says that this consists of extracts from a MS and that it furnishes an excellent description of a wedding.

1871 BROUGHAM, LORD. Tour in the Western Isles, including St. Kilda, in 1799. In *Brougham's Life and Times,* vol. I, 99. 8vo. London.

> The account of these travels is given in letters from Islay, Stornoway, and Ullapool to Lord Robertson, one of the judges of the Supreme Court. He was twenty-two years old at the time, and was accompanied by two friends, John Joseph Henry, nephew of Lord Moira, and Charles Stuart, grandson of the 3rd Earl of Bute.—Mitchell, *op. cit.*

1874-76 Diary of a Journey to Glastonbury Thorn (from near Wakefield). In *Reliquary,* vol. 15, 45-51; 73-80; 140-44; 201-06; vol. 16, 19-27. 8vo. London.

> Glastonbury with its ruins and legends drew to itself a goodly number of tourists.

1878 HENRY II. The Court, Household and Itinerary of Henry II.; also the Chief Agents and Adversaries in his Government, Diplomacy, and Strategy. By R. W. Eyton. 4to. London.

1879 LOW, REV. GEORGE. A Tour through the Islands of Orkney and Shetland, containing Hints relative to their Ancient, Modern, and Natural History collected in 1774, with an Introduction by Joseph Anderson. Illus. 8vo. Kirkwall.

> Full of interest.—Mitchell, *op. cit.*

1882-85   CLERK, SIR JOHN. An Account of a Journey to Dalguise in the Highlands, with a Description of the Country and its Inhabitants, 1742. In *The Family Memoirs of the Rev. William Stukeley,* vol. III, 421-25. Surtees Society. Durham.

> For the *Memoirs,* see under LETTERS, DIARIES, MEMOIRS.

GALE, SAMUEL. A Journey to Scotland and Return, 1739. In a Letter to Dr. Stukeley. In *Family Memoirs of the Rev. William Stukeley.* Durham.

> This letter is also listed under the name of Roger Gale, brother of Samuel. Both were antiquaries of note and intimate friends of Stukeley, who often accompanied them on antiquarian tours. The itinerary included a visit to Castle Howard, the work of Vanbrugh, Berwick, Edinburgh, stops at Mavisbank, the seat of Baron Clerk, and at Pennycuik, Moffat and the two famous camps at Burnswork, and return by way of Carlisle.

1884   CALDERWOOD, MRS. (of Polton). Letters and Journals from England, Holland, and the Low Countries in 1756. Edit. by Alex. Ferguson. 5 illus. 8vo. London.

> See under WEST EUROPE, vol. I of this work.

FORBES, DUNCAN. Account of a Visit to Mull, Morvern, Tiree, Coll, etc., in connection with Estate Management; in a Letter to John, Duke of Argyll, 24 Sept., 1757. Printed in *Reports of the Crofter Commission.* Edinburgh (?).

WOODWORTH, JONATHAN. Letters from a Lancashire Student at Glasgow University, during the Rebellion of 1715. Privately printed in 8vo.

> Cited by Mitchell as a work that probably gives some description of Scotland.

1886   CRAVEN, REV. J. E. Journals of the Episcopal Visitations of the Right Rev. R. Forbes (Bishop of Ross), of the Diocese of Ross and Caithness . . . 1762 and 1770; with Memoirs of Bishop R. Forbes. 8vo. London.

> See Forbes under 1895-96 below.

1887   POCOCKE, DR. RICHARD (Bishop of Ossory). Tours in Scotland in 1747, 1750, 1760. Edit. from the original MS. by D. W. Kemp. Illus. *Publ. Scot. Hist. Soc.,* No. 1. Edinburgh.

> The tour of 1760 was edited separately, 1888. See below. These visits included trips to Iona, Kirkwall, Sutherland, Moray, Melrose, etc. His information on St. Kilda was obtained at second hand.

1888   DINELEY, THOMAS. The Account of the Official Progress of . . . Henry, the first Duke of Beaufort . . . through Wales in 1684. Preface by R. W. Banks. 8vo. London.

FIENNES, CELIA. Through England on a Side Saddle, in the Time of William and Mary. Being the Diary of Celia Fiennes, with an Introduction by the Hon. Mrs. Griffiths. 8vo. London.

> New edit., London, 1947. The sections on Devon and Cornwall in Chope, *Early Tours.*
> This famous diary is a much quoted authority on country life in the seventeenth century. See Joan Parkes, *Travel in the Seventeenth Century,* and Chr. Hussey, *The Picturesque,* for uses of this work. The author was the daughter of Col. Nathaniel Fiennes, a Parliamentary officer. She set out on her travels to improve her health by the exercise and the change of scene. She proved to be a keen and original observer of whatever she chanced upon, whether seats, gardens, objects, places, or people. In her time the change from the formal garden to the new so-called natural style was scarcely begun. Her descriptions

of these glories of landscape art, with long avenues of trees, geometrical parterres, canals, fountains, some of which played tricks upon the unsuspecting visitor, make us join in the more enlightened condemnation, occasionally met with in the following century, on Kent, Brown, and other like "improvers." We also learn that roads were execrable, even in the more traveled regions, a condition that was of great Parliamentary concern in the next century as well. How little was the appeal of natural beauty in her time, at least as it was expressed in print, may be gathered from her response to the Lakes, which she enjoyed rather as a novelty, and to waterfalls, which interested her likewise as an oddity and not as a stimulus to the sublime or romantic.

POCOCKE, DR. RICHARD. The Tour of Dr. Richard Pococke, Lord Bishop of Ossory, through Sutherland and Caithness in 1760, with Introduction and Notes by D. W. Kemp. *Publ. Sutherland Assoc.,* vol. 2. 5 plates. 4to. Edinburgh.

1888-89 ———. The Travels through England by Dr. Richard Pococke, successively Bishop of Meath and Ossory, during 1750, 1751, and later Years. Edit. by James Joel Cartwright, M.A., F.S.A. 2 vols. *Publ. Camden Soc.,* vol. 42. London.

> The portion dealing with Devon and Cornwall printed in Chope, *op. cit.*
> The Bishop had a passion for traveling both at home and abroad (see Pococke under 1743, NEAR EAST, vol. I of this work). This journey took him from Dublin into England by way of the Isle of Man, whence he went to Liverpool, where he describes the changes in progress since a former visit; thence into Staffordshire, where he inspected the potteries, to Cheshire, to Keswick and the Lake District, Lancashire, York, Huntingdon, Cambridge, etc., to London. Another trip seems to have taken him from Devonshire into Cornwall and Somerset, closing November, 1750. In May, 1751, he commenced another from London to the Midland counties over to Shropshire and back to Dublin. The second volume of the above covers tours in 1754, 1756, and 1757. These take in Lancaster, Monmouth, Bristol, Marston Moor, Wilton, Fonthill Abbey, the south and east coast, Salisbury, Wales, Southampton, London, and back to Dublin. His interests seem to have been antiquarian and historical, buildings, seats, etc.; there is little of inns and roads, little of how people lived. He made other trips to the Orkneys, and parts of Ireland and England in 1760 and 1764. Much of his information is second hand.

1889 FORBES, DUNCAN. Letter to John M'Farlane, Edinburgh, giving an Account of a Ride from Edinburgh to Culloden, 1715. Printed in App. II to *Major Fraser's Manuscript* (see following item).

FRASER, MAJOR. Major Fraser's Manuscript, 1696-1737, giving his Adventures in Scotland and the Continent, edit. by Lieut.-Col. Alex. Ferguson. 2 vols. 8vo. Edinburgh.

1890 GRAY, THOMAS. An Account of his Journey into Scotland from Rose Castle in Cumberland, in August 1764. In *Works of,* edit. by Gosse, 4 vols., London.

> This account is reprinted in Duncan C. Tovey's *Gray and His Friends,* 260-65. Gray visited Annan, Dumfries, Drumlanrig, Lanark, Hamilton, Glasgow, Loch Lomond, Dumbarton, Stirling, Falkirk, Edinburgh, Melrose, Kelso, etc.

LOVEDAY, JOHN (of Caversham). Diary of a Tour in 1732 through Parts of England, Wales, Ireland and Scotland. Edit. with Introduction and Itinerary, by his Grandson. *Publ. Roxburghe Club.* 4to. London. (Only 75 copies printed.)

> This is a tour of much value and interest. The traveler observed well and recorded accurately and pleasantly.—Mitchell, *op. cit.*

1891 CAVE, SIR T. A Journey to the North of Scotland and back in the Year 1763. In Rev. C. Holme's *History of the Midland Counties.* Rugby.

1893 BASKERVILLE, THOMAS. Journeys in England (*temp.* Car. II), from Notes made by him during his Tours. In *Portland MSS.,* vol. II, 263-314, *Hist. MSS. Comm.* London.

> This consists of a collection of tours: 1. A Journey from Oxford to Cambridge, Yarmouth, Norwich, Ely, etc., in May, 1681. 2. An Account of some remarkable Things in a Journey between London and Dover. 3. Remarks upon the Way from Abingdon to Southampton, and other Places. 4. Remarkable Notes on the Road to several Inland Towns in this Nation (Islip, Buckingham, Towcester, Warwick, Worcester, Hereford, etc.). 5. The Description of Towns on the Roads from Faringdon and Bristow and other Places. 6. An Account of the Way from Morage to Winchcombe and other Places. 7. An Account of a Journey from Bayworth to St. Albans—Wm. Griffith then my Man. 8. A Journey into the North with my Friend Mr. Washborne, a Student of Christ Church, Oxford.
>
> Little is known of the author beyond that he was the son of the antiquary Hannibal Baskerville, and was born 1630, and died 1720. Evidently he was fond of traveling, and his accounts, while pedestrian in style, show a keen eye for the significant in sights to be seen. He usually gives the distance between towns, describes the fare at various inns, the appearance of buildings, schools, and the conditions of the inhabitants. One note of interest is the fact that butchers in Norwich were obliged to get rid of their meat by Thursday night in order that the market might be cleared for the catch of fishermen.

SHARP, JAMES (Archbishop). Journey Chairgis, Edinburgh to St. Androis. In Hume Brown, *Scotland before 1700,* 319-22. Edinburgh.

> Taken from the *Memorandum Book of Archbishop Sharp,* published in *Maitland Miscellany,* vol. 2, pt. ii. The above account consists of notes of the expenses incurred in the journey from Edinburgh to St. Andrews. One of the charges is for the poor, i. e., the beggars who swarmed over the country to an estimated number of 200,000. Gifts to these were regularly entered into expense accounts of well-to-do travelers. The money was here reckoned after the French manner.

Travel along the Roman Wall. In *Portland MSS.,* vol. II, pt. ii, App. 54-57, *Hist. MSS. Comm.* London.

1894 LOWTHER, C., R. FALLOW, PETER MANSON. Our Journall into Scotland, Ano Domini 1629, 5th of November from Lowther. Edit. by Hume Brown. Edinburgh.

> Also printed in 13th Report, *Hist. MSS. Comm.,* App. VII, edit. by J. J. Cartwright.

1895 FERRIER, MAJOR RICHARD. The Journal of Major Richard Ferrier, M.P., while travelling in France in the Year 1687. With a brief Memoir of his Life. Compiled by Richard F. E. Ferrier, and John A. H. Ferrier, two of his lineal Descendants. In *Camden Misc.,* IX, vol. 53, n.s. London.

> This traveler came of a family that had for 200 years supplied mayors to Norwich and bailiffs to Yarmouth. He was M.P. for Yarmouth 1708, 1710, and 1713. The first two and a half pages describe his route from London to Dover and offer good descriptions of the English scene. The remainder of the account deals with France.

WENTWORTH, THOMAS. A Perfect Narrative of the Days and Times of the Earl of Strafforde's first and second Journeys from Ireland to England; as also his Lordship's Journey from London to the North, and so back to London, 1639, 1640. In *Papers relating to Thomas Wentworth, First Earl of Strafford.* Edit. by C. H. Firth. *Camden Misc.,* IX, vol. 53, n.s. London.

> This is no more than a bare itinerary of dates and places, with length of stay.

1895-96 FORBES, ROBERT (Minister at Leith and Bishop of Ross). Journal of a Jaunt to Moffat, to Places near it, and back to Edinburgh by a different Route, 1769. In

The Lyon in Mourning, vol. III, 227-47, *Publ. Scot. Hist. Soc.,* no. 23. Edit. from his MS., with a Preface, by Henry Paton, M. A. Edinburgh.

This trip was made from Moffat to Gray Mare's Tail waterfall in company with Bishop Gordon, of London, Mrs. Forbes, and others. This fall was regarded as the finest in Scotland and was stated with exaggerated enthusiasm to have a 100 fathom drop! The narrative is lively and amusing.

1896 Observations upon a Jaunt to the West Country with Mr. James Robinson, 1781. In *Scot. Antiquary, or Northern Notes and Queries,* vol. 42, 75-83. Edinburgh.

The jaunt occupied five days, from 14th to 18th July. From Edinburgh the two "young men" went to Carron, Stirling, Dumbarton, Luss, Glasgow, Hamilton, and back to Edinburgh.—Mitchell, *List of Travels.*

1896-97 MACRITCHIE, REV. WILLIAM. Diary of a Tour through England in 1795, with Notes by David MacRitchie, F.S.A. Scot. In *Antiquary,* vol. 32, 107-112; 137-42; 175-77; 237-42; 270-74; 301-07; 331-35; vol. 33, 11-15; 44-50. London.

Printed separately, London, 1897.
Beginning with p. 237, the title is changed to Diary of a Visit to London in 1795, and with p. 301, to From London to Edinburgh. The writer is a good companion for a fireside travel. He was minister of the parish of Clunie in Perthshire, and one of the contributors to Sir John Sinclair's *Statistical Account of Scotland* (see under 1791-99, SURVEYS). He was much interested in natural history, especially botany, and made collections of plants which he sent back home. The diary printed here begins with his arrival at Carlisle and departure for London. The portion covering Perthshire to Carlisle was printed in *Antiquary,* Jan. and April, 1896. Generally he traveled on horseback, but from Sheffield to London he took the stage coach. He notes the tendency lamented by other travelers to cut down the trees in the parks of country seats. While in London he lets little escape his eyes. He visits also Cambridge, Castle Howard, and Alnwick Castle, which he describes in good detail, especially the evidences of the new taste in landscape gardening. In general he is effective in description. The diary was written in shorthand.

1897 HOLMES, REV. DR. Oxford to Edinburgh and Back, in 1737. In *Antiquary,* n.s., vol. 33, 207-09, London.

The traveler was president of St. John's College, Oxford. With a companion he journeyed north by way of the western counties and back by a more easterly route. His companion wrote down the notes on the places they visited and the distances they traveled, the houses where they dined, etc. These notes are of a random nature.

The Itinerary of Prince Charles Edward Stuart from his Landing in Scotland, July, 1745, To his Departure in Sept., 1746. Compiled from *The Lyon in Mourning,* supplemented and corrected from other Contemporary Sources. Edit. by Walter Biggar Blaikie. *Publ. Scot. Hist. Soc.,* no. 23. Edinburgh.

This Itinerary is not intended to take the place of a history, but it does serve as an indispensable supplement to a study of the incidents of '45. The movements of the Prince are recorded from day to day with such detail as to make them independently clear. Most of the authorities documenting the record are contemporary.

WILLIS, R. L. Journal of a Tour from London to Elgin made about 1790 in company with Mr. Brodie, Younger, of Brodie, by R. L. W. Printed from the Original Manuscript. Edit. by J. T. 8vo. Edinburgh.

Whether the author was sincere in his declaration that this journal was written up to be circulated in manuscript, at any rate he expected it to be read, otherwise he would not have sprinkled so many literary quotations throughout its pages. Still it makes interesting reading, being free from the priggishness and pedantry of the professional tourist. His travels run from London to Elgin by way of the Lake District, thence across the Lowland Border through Hawick to Edinburgh, whose picturesque setting greatly impressed him. The New Town was then in the midst of a rage for building. He is evidently a socially minded soul, for he recounts with zest the visits to various seats and his mingling with gay company. The account is full of personal reactions.

1898 Notes of a Tour through the Shires of Fife, Forfar, Perth, and Stirling, in 1800. (Place?) (So cited in Mitchell, *Scot. Topog.*, vol. II.)

ROBERTSON, JAMES. Tour through Some of the Western Islands, etc., of Scotland, in 1768. By Sir Arthur Mitchell, in *Proc. Soc. Antiq. of Scotland*, 3rd ser., vol. 8. Edinburgh.

> The above reproduces the substance of a paper that had been read at a meeting of the Society of Antiquaries in 1788. Who Robertson was is unknown. He had been sent on this journey apparently to examine marine plants, which he does for a while, but then turns to the subject of customs, ways of life, superstitions, abodes, diseases and their remedies. Extracts are given from the original on butter making, thatching, dwellings, beds, preserving yeast, whey making, etc. Smallpox was prevalent, though inoculation was in vogue also.

Travels in the Highlands of Scotland in 1750; from MS. 104 in King's Library, Brit. Mus. Edit. by Andrew Lang. Edinburgh and London.

1900 BOWLES, GEORGE. For an account of his journey from Ireland into England in 1761-62, see his *Diary*, under LETTERS, DIARIES, MEMOIRS.

EDWARD I. Itinerary of King Edward the First throughout his Reign, A.D. 1272-1307, exhibiting his Movements from Time to Time, as far as they are recorded. Extracted from the Public Records of England. Edit. and annotated by Henry Gough. 2 vols. 4to. Paisley.

LAUDER, SIR JOHN (of Fountainhall). Notes of Journies in England and Scotland, 1667-70; and of Journies in Scotland, 1671-72. In *Journal of Sir John Lauder*, edit. by Donald Crawford. *Publ. Scot. Hist. Soc.*, no. 36. Edinburgh.

SWETE, REV. JOHN. A Tour across Dartmoor into North Devon, 1789. In *Devon Notes and Queries*, vol. 1, 88-96; 121-26; 169-75. Exeter.

> Published here for the first time with omissions of antiquarian matters. The writer was an antiquary of some local note and assisted in the publication of such works. He started on his tour in September, 1789, with two gentlemen but finished it alone. His account shows appreciation of beautiful scenery and a leaning towards the picturesque school in his criticisms of Nature's arrangement of her elements. He speaks in terms of the painter's art, using such words are foreground, relief, distant parts of the picture, and attempts to reproduce in words the impressions of scenes. He likes to feel the sensations of awe, terror, grandeur, wildness, and the like.

1901 HARLEY, EDWARD (Lord Oxford). Journies and Tours of Edward, Lord Harley, afterwards Earl of Oxford, in the Eastern Counties. In *Portland MSS.*, vol. VI, *Hist. MSS. Comm.* London.

> The following tours are reported: in Kent, 1723, pp.79-80; through Hertfordshire, Lincolnshire, and Notts to the Northern Counties and Scotland, 1725, 81-147; through Suffolk, Norfolk, and Cambridgeshire, 1732, 148-68; in the Eastern Counties, 1737, 64-66; 1738, 168-72; through Hampshire, Wiltshire, and Berkshire, 172-81; in Kent, Sussex, and Hampshire, 1738, 68-69. Some of these are in the Earl's own handwriting, but they were not all written by him. He went to see what was to be seen. The accounts are enlivened with personal observations, and—what is welcome—express no rancour against the Scotch.

OXFORD, LADY. Journey through Hertfordshire, Lincolnshire, and Notts to the Northern Counties of Scotland, in 1725. In *Portland MSS.*, vol. VI, 81 ff., *Hist. MSS. Comm.*; Journey through Yorkshire, Durham, etc., into Scotland, in 1745. *Ibid.*, 182-91. London.

> On the trip of 1725 Lady Oxford accompanied her husband. She herself was not the author of the write-up, which is done in the form of daily entries. It is a decorous account, but it offers a good description of Castle Howard, built by Vanbrugh. In Edinburgh she dined with the Lord Commissioner. Her comment is revealing: "A very fine dinner, the first course fifteen, the second eighteen, and the dessert thirty dishes." The rebellion under Prince Charles Edward Stuart raised its head three months later.

1901-35 NICHOLSON, WILLIAM (Bishop). For his travels in England see his *Diary,* under LETTERS, DIARIES, MEMOIRS.

1903 BARLOW, CAPT. J. Letters from the Hebrides, 1753. Printed from a MS. in Brit. Mus., in Appendix to Mackenzie's *History of the Outer Hebrides.* Paisley.

LEYDEN, DR. JOHN. Journal of a Tour in the Highlands, Western Isles and other Parts of Scotland in 1800. 8vo. Edinburgh.

> This tour extended from July 14 to Oct. 1. His principal objects of interest were, in addition to those of geology and mineralogy, curiosities, such as vitrified forts, remains of bison and elk, a boiling well at Dunstaffnage, a lamp for burning wooden chips, and the Ossianic controversy. He does not neglect, however, descriptions of towns and scenes.

MORYSON, FYNES. Shakespeare's Europe; Unpublished Chapters of Fynes Moryson's Itinerary; being a Survey of the Condition of Europe at the End of the 16th Century, with Introduction and an Account of Fynes Moryson's Career by Charles Hughes. 4to. London.

> Chapters III, IV, V, Bk. II, contain Of the Commonwealth of England, Of Scotland, Of Ireland; chaps. III, IV, V, Bk. V, Of England, Of Scotland, Of Ireland.

TAYLOR, JOSEPH. A Journey to Edenborough in Scotland (1705), by Joseph Taylor, Esq., late of the Inner Temple. Now first printed from the original MS. with Notes by William Cowan. 4to. Edinburgh.

> He and his traveling companions made their way north by Northampton, Derby, where they viewed the "Wonders of the Peak," Chatsworth, Nottingham, York, Newcastle, and Berwick to Edinburgh. The most interesting parts of the narrative are those describing the Scottish districts they passed through. The account of Edinburgh and of the Scotch is tainted with the prejudice rampant among English of the day. At the time of their visit, the negotiations for the Union were under way, and the debates that were taking place are given in some detail.

1903-06 PAUL, SIR JAMES BALFOUR. Royal Pilgrimages in Scotland. In *Publ. Scot. Ecclesiol. Soc.,* vol. 1. 4to. Aberdeen.

1904 COXE, WILLIAM (Archdeacon). Historical Tour through Monmouthshire (1798-99). Numerous illustrations. 4to. London.

J., P. A Scottish Journie, being an Account in Verse of a tour from Edinburgh to Glasgow in 1641. Edit. by C. H. Firth, *Misc. Scot. Hist. Soc.,* vol. 2. Edinburgh.

LEYDEN, DR. JOHN. Journal of a Tour to Gilsland and the Cumberland Lakes, June 1800; and Journal of a Tour to the Eastern Borders, Sept. 1823. Edit. by James Sinton, *Publ. Hawick Arch. Soc.,* vol. 38. 4to. Hawick.

1906   VERULAM, EARL OF (Lord Grimston). A Northern Tour from St. Albans, 1768; a Tour in Wales, 1769. In *Verulam Reports, Hist. MSS. Comm.,* 229-42; 242-83. London.

> The main interests of his Lordship were the country seats, such as Hagley and the Leasowes, of Lord George Lyttelton and the poet Shenstone respectively, and the paintings to be found in them. At the end is an itemized account of expenses, which reveals that his jaunts were not extravagantly costly.

1909-16   WESLEY, JOHN. Journals. Edit. by N. Curnock. 8 vols. London.

> For a description of this work, see Wesley under 1827, LETTERS, DIARIES, MEMOIRS. Much of its interest for the general reader lies in its descriptions of various parts of the world —America, Holland, and Germany—but especially of the British Isles, which he must have criss-crossed in a most bewildering fashion. He made forty-two visits to Ireland, sixteen to Scotland, and almost countless trips up and down England. For a man so wrapped up in his mission, he manifests considerable curiosity about places where he stopped, for many of his descriptions show keen observation. But one wishes he had told more, particularly of the little known districts. Nowhere does he appear to have been touched by the appeal of the romantic, the picturesque, or the sublime; rather his taste inclines toward the controlled forms of art. He likes trim gardens and cultivated lands, landscapes composed of painterly elements, such as those of Hagley and the Leasowes. He admires cathedrals, and while in London he visits museums, the wax works, Chelsea Gardens, etc. He finds much to praise in Scotland and its people. Towns like Edinburgh, Arbroath, places like Roslyn, Monymusk, and Holyrood, and such views as open to the eye like that from Arthur's Seat come in for a good word. What he does not care for—nor did any other man but a native—is the filth and its stench littering High Street in the "Athens of the North." His journeys are said to have measured 3,000 miles a year.

1910   ASTON, JOHN. For an account of his journey to Scotland in the First Bishops' War, 1639, see his *Journal* in *Six North Country Diaries,* under LETTERS, DIARIES, MEMOIRS.

THRALE, MRS. HESTER LYNCH. For an account of her Welsh Tour in 1774, see A. M. Broadley, *Dr. Johnson and Mrs. Thrale,* under LETTERS, DIARIES, MEMOIRS.

1912   SINCLAIR, G. A. The Scottish Progress of James VI. In *Scot. Hist. Rev.,* vol. 10, 21-28. Edinburgh.

1913   ANDERSON, W. (?) A Journal, being an Account of a short Tour or Excursion from Edinburgh: Excursion from the Capital through the Middle Parts of Scotland: Fife, Dumbarton, and Stirlingshire, 1787. 8vo. Nairn.

> This MS book was picked up in Sydney, Australia, by Hon. J. Mackintosh, and sent to Mr. G. Bain, Nairn.—Mitchell, *Scot. Topog.,* vol. II. It has been surmised that W. Anderson was the writer.

1914   BRERETON, SIR WILLIAM. For his tour to the North of England, see his *Journal,* under *North Country Diaries,* LETTERS, DIARIES, MEMOIRS.

Description of Scotland, a Letter *ca.* 1617. In *Harvey Bruce MSS.,* "Various Collections," vol. VII, Report 15, *Hist. MSS. Comm.* London.

This consists of a running diatribe against the land, food, dress, manners, appearance of both men and women, religion, habits of bodily care or lack of such, etc., of the Scotch. Of the ladies it says, "theire flesh naturallie abhoreth cleanes"; "To be chained in marriage with one of them, were to be tied to a dead carcase, and cast into a stinkinge ditch," and more stuff still worse. "The ointment they use is brimstone and butter for theire scabbs, and oils of bayes and stavesaker for theire lise." It is a wonder "that so brave a Prince as King James should be borne in so stinkinge a towne as Edenbrough in lowsie Scotland."

POCOCKE, RICHARD (Bishop). For his tour in the northern counties, see his *Northern Journies* under *North Country Diaries*, LETTERS, DIARIES, MEMOIRS.

1915 DALE, SAMUEL, M.D. Dr. Dale's Visits to Cambridge, 1722-1738. Summarized with Quotations from an unpublished MS. by Prof. T. McKenny Hughes, F.R.S., F.S.A. *Proc. Camb. Antiq. Soc.*, vol. 12, n.s. Cambridge.

The MS of the Doctor is a record of notes in part jotted down on the way and in part later. From the summaries given by the editor, it must be an interesting account and full of information on traveling, the condition of the roads, the routes taken, dykes and other earthworks, Cambridge itself, the Woodwardian Museum, botany, dinners, churches, chapels, libraries, etc.

1916 EEDES, DR. Iter Boreale. See A *Sixteenth Century Journey to Durham,* by Rev. Henry Gee, F.S.A. *Publ. Arch. Aeliana,* vol. 13, 3rd ser. Newcastle.

The above Latin poem of about 600 lines in hexameter was the work of a Dr. Eedes, who became dean of Worcester in 1597 and later one of the board of revisers which issued the Authorized Version of the Bible in 1611. He was also royal chaplain to Queen Elizabeth for a period. But when he wrote the above poem he was a young man at Oxford, a great friend of Toby Matthew, president of St. John's and later dean of Christ Church. In the summer of 1583 the latter was appointed dean of Durham, later bishop, and finally archbishop of York. He persuaded Eedes to go with him on the trip commemorated in the poem, which relates where they stayed on their way to the North, their experiences at various places, and their reception at Durham and stay at other places in the neighborhood. Their return to Oxford is likewise recorded. According to Gee, the narrative makes pleasant reading.

1918 HUTCHESON, CHARLES. Mr. Hutcheson's 'Journal' to Arran in 1783. By W. P. Ker. In *Scot. Hist. Rev.,* vol. 16, Jan. Edinburgh.

This journal has been printed before but not literally, in the *Evening Times,* Jan., 1885; and in the *Kilmarnock Standard,* under the title of A Trip to Arran. Written by a Glasgow Merchant. Of this 25 copies were printed in pamphlet form. In the above transcript the manuscript is followed as exactly as possible. The diarist was a youth born in 1752 in Glasgow, where he became a merchant and member of the Grand Antiquity Society of Glasgow. The island of Arran in the 18th century was a place of holiday resort for the west of Scotland. The diarist journeyed thither in company with a friend and others picked up en route. They were evidently out to enjoy themselves. The style is extremely personal, full of mannerisms, affected perhaps from Sterne, such as dashes, incomplete sentences, exclamations, broken phrases, but it is readable. He makes many observations on towns, places, and the inhabitants. He considers Arran to have made but small progress in civilization. The party loaded up with necessities at Irvine, since the island was not plentifully provided with food and other personal needs. They took with them their "German flutes," which they played on every possible occasion. No comment is made on scenery, evidencing that the writer was not afflicted with the craze for the picturesque.

1919 FARRER, WILLIAM. An Outline Itinerary of King Henry the First. 8vo. London.

1920 A Journey to London in 1698. In *A Miscellany of Wits,* being Select Pieces by William King, D.C.L., John Arbuthnot, M.D., and other Hands (1705-12), with an Introduction by K. N. Colvile. The Scholar's Library. 8vo. London.

1921 ILCHESTER, EARL OF. Queen Elizabeth's Visit to Blackfriars, June 16, 1600. *Publ. Walpole Soc.,* vol. 9, Oxford.

1925 FOX, GEORGE. The Short Journal and Itinerary Journals of George Fox. In Commemoration of the Tercentenary of His Birth (1624-1924). Now first published. Edit. by Norman Penney. With an Introduction by T. E. Harvey. 8vo. New York and Cambridge.

> Hitherto available in MS to only a few Quaker scholars, the important documents which underlie the Great Journal are gathered together into this one volume. The Short Journal was written during the author's long imprisonment in Lancaster Gaol, and describes his sufferings as an evangelist. The Itinerary Journal illuminates the last years of George Fox, in and around London, as the bishop of an active, settled church. The Haistwell Journal is included. The whole is accompanied by numerous Notes, Facsimiles and Index.—From Dauber & Pine, Catalogue no. 307.

MUNDY, PETER. A Petty Progress through England and Wales, and his Tour round the Coast (1639). In his *Travels in Europe and Asia,* Hakluyt Soc., 2nd ser., vol. IV, pp. 1-53. London.

> The five volumes of Peter Mundy's *Travels* make up the most extensive and interesting peregrinations to be found in those days of spacious travels. See Mundy under 1936 below.

1927 BURNS, ROBERT. Journal of a Tour in the Highlands, made in the Year 1787. Reproduced in Facsimile from his original MS. in the possession of Mr. W. K. Bixby. With Introduction and Transcript by J. C. Ewing. Frontispiece and 39 pp. of Facsimilies. 4to. London.

1928 WALPOLE, HORACE. Journal of Visits to Country Seats. In *Publ. Walpole Soc.,* vol. 16. Edit. by P. Toynbee. Oxford.

1930 BROCKBANK, REV. THOMAS. For an entertaining account of a tour from Oxford to London by a student of Oxford, see *The Diary and Letter Book of the Rev. Thomas Brockbank,* under LETTERS, DIARIES, MEMOIRS.

SCOTT, J. B. An Englishman at Home and Abroad, 1792-1828, with some Recollections of Napoleon, being Extracts from the Diaries of J. B. Scott, of Bungay, Suffolk. 8vo. London.

WINDHAM, WILLIAM. For accounts of his tours in England, see the *Early Life and Diaries of William Windham,* under LETTERS, DIARIES, MEMOIRS.

1934-38 BYNG, HON. JOHN (Viscount Torrington). The Torrington Diaries. Containing the Tours through England and Wales of the Hon. John Byng (later fifth Viscount Torrington) between the Years 1781 and 1794. Edit., with an Introduction by C. Bruyn Andrews, and with a Foreword by John Beresford. Illustrated with reproductions of Contemporary Prints. 4 vols. 8vo. London.

> The list of his journeys as they appear in the order printed in the above volumes is:
> Vol. I: Tour to the West. 1781.
>   Tour to North Wales. 1784.
>   Tour in South Wales. 1787.
>   Tour into Sussex.

Vol. II :   Tour in the Midlands. 1789.
            Tour in the Midlands. 1790.
            Tour in Bedfordshire. 1790.
            Tour in Lincolnshire.
Vol. III : Tour to the North of England. 1792.
            Tour to North Wales. 1793.
Vol. IV :   Tour in Bedfordshire. 1794.
            Tour in the Midlands. 1789.
            Tour into Kent. 1790.

These diaries are now printed for the first time. The author did not write with the idea of immediate publication, for he believed that too many travelers rush into print as it was. A hundred years or so later he considered would be the proper interval. We today can rejoice that he did not set the term at two hundred years, for whosoever starts looking into these diaries becomes lost to business, friends, and duties. In the power of absorbing the interest they excel those of Parson Woodforde. Byng was a nephew of the Admiral Byng who was executed for misconduct at sea. He himself had seen service on the Continent. Few men have ever been so possessed with the passion for touring, and as the roads by his time were in a greatly improved condition, which he noted brought disadvantages as well, he found nearly every place accessible, at least on horseback, his usual mode of traveling. At times he went with friends and family, but often he moved about alone. The value of his descriptions lies in their picture of the English countryside, with its loveliness, the habits and manners of the population, the inns, roads, spas, houses of the gentry and cottages of the poor, the prospects, views, ruins, of which he liked the Gothic, entertainments in the towns, the provincial theatres, whose playbills he often reproduces, the modes of travel and changing aspect of the country under the impact of the industrial revolution, the alteration of manners, the boldness and insolence, where formerly innocence and simplicity ruled. Of the numberless incidents and observations tempting one to quotation, only that relating to his visit to Tintern Abbey will be cited. These famous ruins, the property of the Duke of Beaufort who kept them in tolerable repair, usually stirred the ordinary tourist to rapturous description. Byng, whose visit is recorded in vol. I, thoroughly enjoyed them but he proposed to do it in his own way. The old attendant, "who knew nothing," he wished to have along, "as his venerable, grey beard, and locks, added dignity to my thoughts; and I fancied him the hermit of the place." Then to further enhance the enjoyment of the scene and the moment, he would bring wines, cold meat, with corn for the horses, spread the table amid the ruins, and possibly secure a Welsh harper from some nearby place, thus combining the antiquarian with the gourmand. Byng disliked straight roads of the new turnpike kind, and preferred the twisting lanes of the country. He also disliked being boxed up in coaches with disagreeable people and offensive stinks. In all his impressions he reveals an independent and original turn of mind, whether with vogues, traditions, personages, or places. His diaries show us, as do no other works, exactly how 18th century England of the last two decades looked to the traveler.

1936   A Relation of a Short Survey of the Western Counties Made by a Lieutenant of the Military Company in Norwich in 1635. Edit. for the Royal Hist. Soc. by L. G. Wickham Legg, M.A., F.R.H.S. In *Camden Misc.,* vol. 16, lii, 3rd ser. London.

In this relation the author, the Lieutenant of the 1634 trip (see under 1849 above), whose name we learn is Hammond, carries out his promise made in the earlier survey to complete his journey. The present expedition was a short one and was done at a more leisurely pace. He evidently had some legal training, education, and social standing, for he unearthed friends in the suites of great lords and church dignitaries. He seems to have been of amiable character, with strong high church principles and a love for ceremony and antiquities, and a dislike of the Celts. He avoided Wales entirely and spoke contemptuously of the Cornish. He had an eye for beauty in architecture, wherein his taste was neo-classical, but he was chiefly interested in churches, monuments, carvings, sculptures, and painted windows. Though he did little more than catalogue these, yet his descriptions have value for the present day. Apparently he spent every Sunday in a cathedral town. His route ran from Norwich via Yarmouth, Colchester, Tilbury, Gravesend, Rochester, Canterbury, Margate . . . Winchester, Stonehenge, Wilton, Weymouth, Exeter, Taunton, Bath, Glastonbury, Ely, Peterborough, etc., back to Norwich. He arrived home Sept. 17, 1635. His style is inflated and full of puns, but readable and effective in its broad sketches of the places visited.—From the Introduction.

MUNDY, PETER. Travels in South West England and Western India, with a Diary of Events in London (1657-63). In his *Travels in Europe and Asia,* Hakluyt Society, 2nd ser., vol. V. London.

1941   COLE, REV. WILLIAM. A Tour with Walpole, 1763. Printed for the first time in App. 4, *Horace Walpole's Correspondence,* vol. II, Yale Edition. New Haven.

These two antiquaries traveled in a chariot, visiting seats, picture galleries, and antiquities.

II
Tours by Foreigners

(The discovery of Great Britain by continental Europe was accomplished by 1600, though some time was yet to elapse before accounts rid themselves of marvels and fables and cut themselves loose from the authority of Polydore Vergil for England and of Hector Boece for Scotland. By 1600 England had emerged from below the horizon. Henry VIII and his break with Rome, the visits of humanists like Erasmus, the defeat of the Spanish Armada, and the fame of Queen Elizabeth, all served notice that behind the stormy waters of the English Channel lay a country and a race that were to be reckoned with. The early visitors were drawn largely from the ranks of emissaries, diplomats, ambassadors, great noblemen and merchants, who, if they saw nothing else, dutifully made the rounds of the sights of London, such as the palaces of Richmond, Nonesuch, Theobalds, Hampton Court, and Windsor, the universities, the shrine of St. Thomas at Canterbury, and the shipping on the Thames. Not the least sight of all was the Queen herself. The reports sent back home, however, present some odd contradictions. There was a general consensus that the island was fertile and lovely with its well watered green fields, but the climate was damned for its murkiness and fogs. Nor did the inhabitants come off uniformly well. Savorgnano finds the English slothful and grossly in love with food. Jovius, who probably never set foot on the island, finds excuse for their gluttony in the dense air which seemed to generate hunger. Paradin suspects that the rumor of Englishmen being tailed is not true. Perlin, who surpasses all in bilious defamation, declares that the English are great drunkards and reprobates, a people who do not know whether they belong to God or the devil; they belch at their meals without shame, even in the presence of the great. Rozmital advises one not to trust an Englishman "even on his bended knee." But a cloud of witnesses arise to affirm the contrary, whose testimony is voiced by Lemnius to the effect that the race is marked by an incredible courtesy, friendliness, and affability. All agree in saying a good word for the kiss which by custom English ladies bestow on visitors, and in condemning the rudeness of the London mob toward foreigners, in that they were too much given to "fisting strangers." Most interesting of the accounts coming down from this period are those of the Germans, who by all reckoning were inveterate travelers, and much inclined to taking notes. Their diaries fall short of the sharp political observations native to the Italians, but they are richer in their personal reactions. Even in those days the German was methodical in his pursuit of pleasure, in that before setting out on his "Cavalier's Tour," the equivalent of the Englishman's "Grand Tour," he had prepared himself by close study of one of the numerous manuals instructing the traveler how to get profit from his travels.

In the 17th century one will notice an increase in the number of French visitors, particularly during the Stuart rule. The intercourse established between the two nations by the royal exile continued to be maintained by the bond of mutual cultural interests down to the end of the next century. From it arose, among intellectuals at least, a cosmopolitan spirit known neither before nor since that suffered little, if any, diminution even while wars were on foot between them. The 18th century witnessed the rise of an Anglomania that called forth some beautiful exchanges of courtesies between Englishmen and Frenchmen. Naturally there arose protests from more ardent nationalists on both sides. It was the Germans, however, who were stricken more deeply with Anglophilism. Though both the French and German peoples were drawn to England as to a shrine, for where was liberty of conscience, religious toleration, and personal freedom of action so untrammeled, where else were laws so benign and politics so actively the concern of the common man, yet to the Germans who professed themselves disciples of Herder and Lessing, England was the native land of Shakespeare and the English stage the domain of Garrick and Siddons.

Italians still occasionally appear on the scene in this century and a Spaniard or two steps ashore. But the visitors can speak for themselves.)

Ante 322 B.C. PYTHIAS ("the Discoverer of Britain"). This famous Greek navigator made two voyages from Massilia (Marseilles) to the western and northwest coasts of Europe. These two journeys were recorded in his (1) On the Ocean, and (2) Periplus, of which only fragments are preserved in quotations in Strabo, Polybius, Erastothenes, Hipparchus, etc. It is accepted that he visited the coast of Britain and may have traveled over its southern part.—From W. J. Harrison, *Bibliog. of the Great Stone Monuments of Wiltshire.*

1493   SCHEDEL, HARTMANN. Historia Aetatum Mundi. Nürnberg.

This is a Latin chronicle of the world, which was turned into German in 1493. It starts out, as such chronicles were wont to do, with the creation of the world, and gives but general descriptions. The woodcut termed England is used further on to illustrate France. —Clare Williams, *Thomas Platter's Travels in England,* Introd.

1527   GLAREAN (or LORITI), Heinrich. De Geographia. (Place?)

A popular and much used handbook, which notices England but offers nothing new. It compliments the island on her eminent men and "what is rare" the erudition of her monarch.—From Clare Williams, *op. cit.*

1534   FRANCK, SEBASTIAN. Weltbuch, spiegel und Bildtnis der gantzen Erdboden. . . . Tübingen.

Many editions followed. The verbose and spread-eagle title of this work is typical of German scholars of the day. After the manner of the old chroniclers, it gives a generalized description of the appearance and habits of Englishmen. London is full of commerce, the fertile land has more rain than snow, the Scots are proud, choleric, vengeful, and superstitious, and Ireland has no poisonous creatures like spiders, frogs, foxes, and such.—From Clare Williams.

VERGIL, POLYDORE. Historiae Anglicae libri XXVII. Basel.

By the time Vergil was ready to write his history of England he had become an adopted son. Accordingly his accounts of the land and its people are reserved for the section DESCRIPTIONS. See also under HISTORY AND CHRONICLE.

WATT, JOACHIM VON. Epitome trium partium terrae. . . . (Place?)

The author was distinguished in the field of neo-classical learning, but he adds little to the sum of knowledge about Anglia. He quotes Tacitus on her damp climate and cloudy sky and leans on Ptolemy for a description of the shape of the island. His account of the vast superiority in arms of ancient Britain tells nothing of the Britain of Henry VIII. But he does stress her commercial prosperity, her exports, mines, fine wool, the pearls collected on her coasts, etc. Loriti and De Watt may be said to have put England on the map, but not much more.—From Clare Williams, *op. cit.*

1538   DESMONTIERS, JEHAN. Summaire de lorigine description et meruilles Descosse. Auec vne petite cronique des roys du dict pays iusques e ce temps. A tresexcellente et tresillustre dame, Ma dame la Daulphine. On les vends au Palays les boutiques de Iehan andre et Vincent certenas. 1538 auec priuilege . . . . 8vo. Paris.

Privately printed at Bordeaux, 1863, under the supervision of Françisque Michel, with a short Introduction by David Laing (80 copies). There is an essay on this work by A. H. Millar, in *Scot. Hist. Rev.,* vol. 1, Oct. 1903.

The Dauphine was Magdalene de Valois, third daughter of Francis I, and wife of James V and Queen of Scotland for a period of 180 days, of which 49 were spent in Scotland. The one fact that is certified about her is that she died July 7, 1537. The pair had been betrothed to each other "three years before she was born," and threatening severances of this relationship only made them more anxious to carry it out. At that period Scotland was but little known to France and that little was summed up in the idea of a wilderness inhabited by a savage race, illiterate, and unfriendly to its own geniuses. The Duke of Albany, heir presumptive to the throne and regent, was so disgusted with his native land that he forfeited the office of regent rather than remain in Scotland. The Queen-to-be was curious to know something about the country she was to live in and rule over. James had little knowledge of French and the Princess knew neither Latin nor, of course, the Scotch vernacular. In Jehan Desmontiers there was discovered the proper go-between. The latter, who was an important personage and was known to the Duke of Albany, may have visited Scotland. At any rate, he was employed to make a book on the country based on Boece's *Scotorum Historiae,* written in 1500 and published at Paris in 1527, a book which had so pleased James that he had Bellenden turn it into the vernacular, a copy of which James probably took with him to Paris. It was not printed until 1536 at Edinburgh (see Boece

and Bellenden under HISTORY AND CHRONICLE). Desmontiers' version was completed before the marriage, but the Princess died before authority to print was granted. A postscript added tells of her marriage and journey to Scotland. The book begins with a description of Scotland or Albion, repeats the early legendary stories, and in the main follows Boece closely. It is not a mere transcription, however, for inserted are remarks by Desmontiers. In places it differs from Bellenden's account, which repeats Boece faithfully enough.—From Millar's "Essay" cited above.

1545   PARADIN, GUILLAUME. Anglicae Descriptionis compendium, Per Gulielmum Paradinum Cuyselliemsem. Parisiis, apud Vinantium Gaultherot, sub intersignio Sancti Martini, via ad divum Jacobum. 12mo. Paris.

This guide book advocates a "better known Britain." Its material is taken from the writings of learned men, chiefly from Polydore Vergil (see his *Historiae Anglicae* under 1534, HISTORY AND CHRONICLE). Along with generalized descriptions, it contains some "tall tales" current among foreigners, such as the one about the climate being so healthful that men often live to be 120 years old, that shepherds and laborers never sweat, that shepherds never allow their sheep to drink anything but dew. It is to the author's credit, however, that he suspects the stories about tailed Englishmen (for which see Lambard, *Perambulation*, under 1610, TOURS BY NATIVES). Paradin never crossed the Channel himself.

1548   JOVIUS, PAULUS. Descriptio Britanniae, Scotiae, Hyberniae, et Orchadum, ex libro Pavli Iovii, episcopi Nucerae, de imperiis et gentibus cogniti orbis, cum eius operis proemio ad Alexandrum Farnesium. 4to. Venice.

Many editions followed.
This compilation became the standard textbook of his day. It depends largely upon Polydore Vergil's *Historiae Anglicae* but to a less extent than does Paradin's work. The author apparently never visited England in person. He gives London superlative praise, describes the Thames and the places on its banks from Windsor to Greenwich, commends the universities and the youth for their devotion to learning, their mentors—Linacre and Grocyn—and describes in pictorial terms the verdant fields watered by rivers, the mountains upswelling to heaven, but decries the climate as being in the grip of fogs, and the air as murky and humid. Englishmen are noted for their gluttony, luxury, and sloth, etc., which are attributed to the dense air. Harrison, in his *Description of England* (see under 1577, DESCRIPTIONS), finds the same excuse for the appetite of his countrymen.—From Clare Williams. The author was bishop of Nucera, Italy.

1551   AENEAS SYLVIUS PICCOLOMINI (Pope Pius II). Opera Omnia. Basel.

In his works are three accounts of or references to his visit to Scotland, whither he was sent by the Cardinal of Santa Croce in 1435: one in his *Cosmographia de Europa* (*Opera Omnia*, where a map of England, Scotland, and Ireland is found); another in his *Opus Epistolarum*; and a third in his *Commentaria Rerum Memorabilium*.—Mitchell, *List of Travels in Scotland*. The first and third accounts are translated by Hume Brown, *Early Travellers in Scotland*.
"A Gil Blas of the Middle Ages"—such was the character, the easy morals, and equivocal career of him who became Pope Pius II, one of the most distinguished Italian humanists. The accounts of his visit to Scotland do not agree in every respect. In one (*Commentaria*) his object was to effect a reconciliation between King James I and a certain bishop; in another to incite James I to war against England. The accounts of his way of reaching the country differ likewise, but the two agree that it was by sea after a succession of storms. In his extremity he vowed, if he were spared, to make a pilgrimage to the nearest shrine. This he did in the snow, whereby he contracted rheumatism which never left him for the remainder of his life. His mission, whatever it was, failed of success, though James treated him generously. He repeats some of the common fables about Scotland, such as that fruit falling from trees growing on river banks became geese if it dropped into the water. He also notes the treelessness of the country and the scarcity of wood. He made his way back through England disguised as a merchant.—Hume Brown, *op. cit.* Clare Williams speaks of an earlier visit which took him to London, a city he found to be wealthy and populous. His *Cosmographia de Europa,* the outcome of his wanderings, prepared the way for the new descriptive geography.

1556 BEAUGUE, JEAN DE. L'Histoire de la Guerre D'Escosse, Traitant comme le Royaume fut assailly, et en grand partie occupe par les Anglois, et depuis rendu paissable a sa Reyne, et reduit en son ancien estat et dignite. A Monseigneur Messire Francois Montmorency. 8vo. Paris.

Only three imprints are known. A free translation by Dr. Abercrombie, 8vo, Edinburgh, 1707; the French text edit. by Joseph Bain, *Publ. Maitland Club,* vol. 2, Edinburgh, 1830; translated extracts in Hume Brown, *Early Travellers,* 63-70; the French text translated as The French Troops on the Borders of Scotland, Being the Narrative of Jean de Beaugué, by J. B. Brown, *Publ. Hawick Arch. Soc.,* vol. 37, Hawick, 1905.

The disastrous battle of Pinkie, Sept. 10, 1547, and the threatened invasion of Lord Grey led the French king to come to the aid of Mary of Guise with an armed force under André de Montalembert, Sieur d'Essé. The latter was accompanied by his personal friend, Jean de Beaugué, who afterwards published the above account. The thoroughness with which the English ravaged the country and burnt the towns in their path are described, as well as the places in which the author was interested as a member of the expeditionary force. Among the places noticed are Aberdeen, Montrose, Dundee, Dunbar, the Bass Rock, the Isle of May, and Inchkeith. With the aid of this force the Scotch compelled the English to evacuate the country.—From Brown, *op. cit.*

1558 ERASMUS, DESIDERIUS. Epistolae. Fol. Basel.

His *Opera Omnia* edit. by J. Clericus, based on the Basel edition, 10 vols., Leyden, 1703-06; modern edit. of his letters, edited by F. S. and H. M. Allen, 8 vols., Oxford, 1906-34.

His first stay in England was in the years 1499-1500; his second, 1505-06; and his third, 1509-14. On separate occasions he made three more short visits but did not take up residence there again. In a day when letter writing was an art and letters took the place of newspapers, his correspondence exceeded in bulk as it did in value that of any of his contemporaries. To receive a letter from Erasmus became a wide ranging ambition. After 1515 he himself took over the task of superintending their publication in increasingly larger collections. To Erasmus England "was his adopted country, the chosen home of his old age." This hope, however, was not to be realized. His letters contain many kindly descriptions of his English friends and the English way of life.

PERLIN, ESTIENNE. Description des royaulmes d'Angleterre et d'Escosse. 4to. Paris.

This work was dedicated to Marguerite, Duchesse de Berri, sister of Henri II. Reprinted by Gough, 4to, London, 1775; translated and printed by Grose and Astle, *Antiquarian Repertory,* vol. IV, 501 ff., London, 1807-09. See also Rye, *England as Seen by Foreigners,* 190-91, note 26. See below.

Perlin was an ecclesiastic who visited England during the last two years of Edward VI's reign. The bitterness of feeling existing between England and France at this period may be gathered from the violent prejudices displayed by Perlin against the English character. His account of Scotland, to which he gives only twelve pages out of thirty-seven, is more kindly. That he ever visited the latter country has been doubted, because he perpetuates the error of Ptolemy of making Scotland swing toward Denmark. According to his account, it was France that had preserved Scottish independence. The marriage of Mary Queen of Scots to Francis II naturally gave the country a standing in Perlin's eyes. Among the customs he notes is one (confirmed by Fynes Moryson) to the effect that if one will lend a merchant, say, a hundred pounds, the latter will maintain the lender for a whole year at his house and table, and at the end of the year will return the money (a rather high rate of interest).—From Brown, *op. cit.* On the other hand, he berated the English with right hearty cheer. For one thing, they are great drunkards, always pledging one's health; the people are reprobates, and thorough enemies to good manners and letters, for they do not know whether they belong to God or to the Devil. They belch at the table without shame or reserve, even in the presence of the highest dignitaries.—From Rye. They are always feasting on rabbits and hares and other varieties of meat. Furthermore they are neither valiant in war nor faithful in peace. And then they call the French vile names. The whole record of foreign visits offers no equal to this in exacerbated vituperation.

1775 PERLIN, ESTIENNE. Description des Royaumes d'Angleterre et d'Escosse par Estienne Perlin, 1558; Histoire de l'Entrée de La Reine Mere dans la Grande Bretagne, par P. de la Serre, 1639. With English Notes (by Richard Gough). Engravings, including one of a procession in Cheapside. 4to. London.

ROSSE, GUILIO RAVIGLIO. Historia delle Cose Occorse nel Regno D'Inghilterra, in materia del Duca di Nortomberlan dopo la morte di Odoardo VI. 4to. Venice.

The author was an eyewitness to the scenes he relates. After a brief reference to Henry VIII and his Queen, the work takes up the history of the intrigues of the Duke of Northumberland (John Dudley, first Earl of) to place Lady Jane Grey on the throne, reproducing the proclamation of Jane as Queen, and continuing with the execution of the Duke, the coronation of Mary at Westminster, the landing of Philip II of Spain at Southampton, his journey to Winchester, reception in London, etc.—Bookseller's Note.

1561 LEMNIUS, LEVINUS. Levini Lemnii, medici Zirizaei, de habitu et constitutione corporis, quam Graeci κρᾶσιν, Triviales Complexionem [*sic*] vocant, libri duo. Antwerp.

This is said to have been frequently reprinted. Translated into English by Thomas Newton, London, 1581. Extract in Rye, *op. cit.*, 77-80. See below.
The author was a Dutch physician, later a minister of Zierikzee, in Zealand, where he practiced upwards of forty years. He apparently traveled in England during the year 1559. He was greatly charmed with the comforts of life obtaining in England, and was much taken with the incredible courtesy and friendliness in speech and affability of the inhabitants. He did not find that they overdid the business of eating as did Paradin and Van Meteren (see below under 1599). He admired their custom of wetting the pavements and floors and then strewing sedge, as well as their practice of trimming up the parlors with green boughs. For further references to his volume, see Amherst, *History of Gardening in England* (2nd edit., 1896) and Rohde, *Old English Gardening Books*.

> 1581 LEMNIE, LEVINE. The Touchstone of Complexions. Generallye appliable, expedient and profitable for all such as be desirous and carefull of theyr bodily health . . . Fyrst wrytten in Latine by Levine Lemnie, and now Englished by Thomas Newton. London.

1572 BELLEFOREST, FRANCOIS DE. L'Histoire Vniversalle dv Monde, contenant l'entiere description et situation des quatre parties de la terre . . . Nouvellement augmenté. 8vo. Paris.

MUNSTER, SEBASTIAN. Cosmographiae Vniversalis, lib. VI. 8vo. Basileae.

This was first printed at Basel in 1544. Extracts appeared in English as *A Brief Collection and Compendious Extracts,* etc. (see Munster under 1572, GEOGRAPHY, vol. II of this work.
This work had a best-seller vogue during the century. The addition of maps was a great asset. The description of England is largely that of Franck (see under 1542 above). It prints details of the soil's fertility, good pasturage, abundant mineral products, fish, cattle, the general character of the people, and the numbers of pretty women. The past history is related in the stereotyped order, but the immediate present, such as would confront a bona fide traveler in the island, is passed by.

PORCACCHI, T. L'Isole piu famose del Mondo. Fol. Venice.

There were later editions. The map of the Hebrides and the Orkneys measures 4 x 5½ inches, and that of Scotland 5½ x 4.

1572-1618 BRAUN, G., and F. HOGENBERG. Civitates Orbis Terrarum. 6 vols. Fol. Cologne. (See under VIEWS.)

The verbal descriptions of England published so far register little progress, being made up of the familiar stuff from Vergil, Paradin, and Jovius. But the engravings tell a different story. A view plan of London, for example, reproduces existing state of affairs, such as the palaces, Temple Gardens, the bull-baiting rings, playhouses, the outlying suburbs, wharves, the rectangular bend of the River at Lambeth, the playgrounds of London and the marshlands. In volume II is shown a similar plan of Cambridge, with colleges and sights inscribed, a fine view of Windsor, the castle's whole length, and also Oxford; another volume adds Canterbury and other English towns, with a valuable illustration of the famed Nonesuch palace.—From Clare Williams, *op. cit.*

1574   TURLER, HIERONYMUS. De Peregrinatione et Argo Neapolitano libri II, scripti ab Hieronymo Turlero. Omnibus peregrinantibus utiles ac necessarii; ac in eorum gratiam nunc primum editi. 8vo. Argentorati (Strasbourg).

> Translated into English as The Traveiler of Jerome Turler, London, 1575. Extract in Rye, *op. cit.*, 83-84. See also Turler under 1575, DIRECTIONS FOR TRAVELLERS, vol. II of this work.
>
> The author was a Doctor of Laws, born at Leissnig in Saxony in 1550. He was burgomaster of his native place. Of the sights he viewed in London, he admired most Henry VII's tomb.

1577   LEO VON ROZMITAL ET BLATNA. Commentarius brevis et jucundus itineris atque peregrinationis pietatis et religionis causa susceptae ab Illustri et Magnifico Domino, Domino Leone libero Barone de Rosmital et Blatna, Johannae Reginae Bohemiae fratre germano, Proavo illustris et Magnifici Domini Zdenco Leonis liberi Baronis de Rosmital et Blatna, nunc supremi Marchinatus Moraviae Capitanei. Ante centum annos Bohemice conscriptus, et nunc primum in latinam linguam translatus et editus. Ex condensu Reverendissimi Domini, Domini Joannis Olomucensis Episcopi Anno Domini MDLXXVII. Olmütz.

> Of this journey there were two narratives. The original of the above was written in Bohemian by one Schaschek, a gentleman of Bohemia. This redaction was lost but not before it had been translated into Latin by Stanislas Pawlowski, Canon of Olmütz. The other was written in unpolished German by Gabriel Tetzel of Nuremberg, composed from memory after their return from their European journey. The first version is probably the more correct of the two, being the official record of the tour, drawn up on the spot. The second is more quaint and fuller of minute details and likewise of fantastic legends, which were plentifully rife in fifteenth century Europe. The two together give a highly variegated report of the condition of Europe in this century, as the group passed from court to court, from dinners, entertainments, tiltings, pilgrimages to shrines in England, Spain, Italy, and Germany. The Latin account above was reprinted by the *Literarischer Verein* of Stuttgart, 1844; the work was used as the basis of an article by Richard Ford, "Bohemian Embassy to England, Spain, etc., in 1466," in the *Quarterly Review*, pp. 413-44, March, 1852; a brief summary given in Rye, *op. cit.*, xxxix-xl; and summarized at length in Mrs. Henry Cust, *Gentlemen Errant*, 1909. (Most of the above was taken from the Introduction in Mrs. Cust's volume.) The German version by Tetzel was included in the 1844 edition at Stuttgart.
>
> The Baron was received by Edward IV with great distinction. He spent several days in London, visiting the royal treasures, the monuments of the city and the relics of saints. He enjoyed to the full the good things that came his way, such as the feastings, dancings, and merrymakings. He was present at the ceremony of churching Queen Elizabeth Woodville in Westminster Abbey, and attended the banquet in Westminster Hall and the ball that followed. He was greatly taken with the beautiful ladies at court. Notwithstanding the favors received, Schaschek declared the character of the English nation to be "so cunning and faithless, that a foreigner would not be sure of his life among them; and that a Briton was not to be trusted even on his bended knees." From Rye's account, *op. cit.*

1579   BERNARD, JEAN. Un Discours des plus memorables faicts des Roys et Grand Seigneurs d'Angleterre depuis cinq cens ans: Auec les Genealogies des Roynes d'Angleterre, et d'Ecosse. Plus vn traicté de la Guide des chemins, les assiettes et descriptions des principales villes, Chasteaux et Riuieres d'Angleterre. Par Iean Bernard Secretaire de Chambre du Roy. 8vo. Paris.

> 2nd edit., Paris, 1587.
> This is the first English road book, properly so-called. The Guide has 28 pages of text. In addition to the dimensions of England and Wales, it sets forth nine principal lines of communication, distance in miles of the chief towns and stopping-places from one to another, with historical and descriptive comment on the more important events and places connected with the main trunk roads traversed. The descriptive text is of little import, though perhaps it is to be preferred to the time-worn commonplaces on the country. Coventry, for instance, is one of the finest towns after London, Walsingham, once noted

for its vast throngs of pilgrims, is now dead, Salisbury Plain is dangerous because of thieves and brigands, and Shooter's Hill Wood is to be avoided. Bernard probably took his idea from an earlier work of Charles Estienne, *La Guide des Chemins et Fleuves de France*, 1552. See Sir H. G. Fordham, "An Itinerary of the Sixteenth Century," in *Proc. Cambridge Antiq. Soc.*, vol. 14. 8vo. Cambridge.

1583 NEANDER, MICHAEL. Orbis Terrae Partium Succincta Explicatio. Islebii.

> So cited by Clare Williams, *op. cit.* Neander was a Silesian schoolmaster. He retells the familiar fables of the slit pike healed by tenches, the barnacle story of Ireland, the birds reborn at certain times of the year. He informs us that London is the capital of England. For more solid information he sends the reader back to Herodotus and his successors.— Clare Williams.

NICOLAY, NICOLAS DE, SIEUR D'ARFEVILLE. La Navigation dv Roy d'Escosse Iaques Cinquiesme dv Nom, Avtour de son Royaume, & Isles Hebrides, & Orchades, soubz la conduicte d'Alexandre Lyndsay excellent Pilote Escossois. Recueillie & redigee en forme de Description Hydrographique, et representee en Carte Marine, & Routier au Pilotage, pour la Cognoissance particuliere de ce qui est necessaire & considerable a ladicte Navigation. Par Nicolay d'Arfeuille, Seignevr dudict Lieu & de Bel-Air, Dauphinois, premier Cosmographe dv Roy, Commissaire ordinaire de son Artillerie & a la Visitation & Description generalle dv Royaume de France. 37 feuillets et deux Cartes, plus six feuillets de Preliminaires. Folding map and woodcut of the compass. 4to. Paris.

> Translated into English, *Miscellanea Antiqua*, 71-93, London, 1710; same in *Miscellanea Scotica*, vol. III, 100-122, Glasgow, 1819. See below. See also Adair's *An Account of a Voyage*, under 1688, TOURS BY NATIVES.
> The map, which is excessively rare, was drawn by the pilot Lyndsay, who was an excellent navigator and hydrographer. The narrative of this voyage was made by the Frenchman Nicolay, who in his Epistle Dedicatory to the Duke de Joyeuse, told of the circumstances of its publication: that he desired to communicate a little book written in the Scotch language, containing the navigation of King James V. In so doing he had the aid of a Scotchman (John Ferrier) in turning it into French (see Françisque Michel, *Les François en Ecosse*, 439-40). It appears from the same dedication that Nicolay, during his stay in Scotland, had made a map and a memoir, and that he had printed this last, together with a translation of Lyndsay's *Navigation of James V*, at the request of Lord Dudley, Admiral, and afterwards Duke of Northumberland, who was the English Ambassador to France in 1546. James had long meditated the design of making a tour of his realm, and finally realized it under the conduct of the pilot Lyndsay. The map or chart was, in the parlance of the day, a Rutter (see Nicolay under 1583, MAPS AND CHARTS).

> 1710 NICOLAY, NICHOLAS, SIEUR DE ARFEVILLE. The Navigation of King James V. round Scotland, the Orkney Isles, and the Hebrides or Western Isles, under the Conduct of that excellent Pilot Alexander Lyndsay; methodized by N. d'Arfeville, the chief Cosmographer to the French King, etc., done from the French Original, printed at Paris, 1583. 12mo. London.
> Another edit., 12mo, Perth, 1785.

1585 BRUNO, GIORDANO. La Cena de le Ceneri (the Ash Wednesday Supper). Paris.

> Bruno professed to have published this at Paris and other works of his at Venice. But scholars are of the opinion that they were printed at London.
> This famous humanist, who was burned at the stake in Rome, 1600, after seven years' imprisonment by the Inquisition, was in England from 1583 to 1585. In London, under the patronage of the French Ambassador Castelnau, he enjoyed many opportunities to observe English life. Much of this, as well as his impressions of the city, was set forth in the above work, which consists of five dialogues among four speakers, of whom Teofilo represents himself. Here his attitude toward England and Englishmen, his dislike of their preference for Aristotelianism, and his own leanings toward science are expressed with much satiric vigor. He considers the English courtiers to be well bred, but the London rabble to be comparable, in their insolence towards strangers, only with Arabs, Tartars, and cannibals. His description of the difficulties he experienced in finding his way by water and by the

streets to Master Fulke Greville's house is amusing to read but to the author it must have expressed some heartfelt vexations. An excellent unpublished thesis on Bruno and his reactions to England, by Dr. Angelo Pellegrini, is in the library of the University of Washington. See the latter's "Giordano Bruno and Oxford," *Huntington Library Quarterly,* vol. V, no. 3, April, 1942.

CARDANUS, HIERONYMUS. Somniorum Synesiorum libri IIII. 4to. Basel.

At the end of this work is a general characterization of the English nation. His collected works were published in 10 volumes, Lyons, 1663. For his career see Henry Morley, *Jerome Cardan,* 2 vols., London, 1854; see also Sir Henry Yule, *Geographical Magazine,* Sept., 1874, and John Young, "An Early Medical Visitor to Scotland," *Scot. Antiquary,* vol. 17, 157-171, Edinburgh.

A physician and astrologer of Milan, Cardan visited Scotland in 1552 at the invitation of Archbishop Hamilton, whom he is said to have cured of asthma. Among the specifics he used were turtle soup and distilled snails! He took horse for England on the invitation of Edward VI, who was suffering from an affection of the lungs, and was introduced at court by Sir John Cheke, with whom he lodged. The astrologer cast the young king's horoscope and predicted a long life for him, despite which Edward died the following year. But the astrologer, accustomed to such mischances, revised his calculations and corrected his figures, by which he made out that the king had died according to the rules of astrology. See Rye, *op. cit.,* xlviii-xlix. Among his observations on the English nation is the opinion that Englishmen study to imitate the Italians as much as possible. He was much impressed by the fortitude of the Highlanders, who, he says, when led to execution, "take a piper with them; and he, who is himself often one of the condemned, plays them up dancing to their death."

1588   MEDINA, DUKE OF. Orders set down by the Duke of Medina, Lord General of the King's Fleet, to be observed in the Voyage toward England. Translated out of Spanish into English by T. P. 4to. London. (8 leaves.)

Reprinted *Harl. Misc.,* vol. I, 1744.

UBALDINO, PETRUCCIO. Descrittione del Regno di Scotia, et delle Isole sue adiacenti di Petruccio Vbaldini Cittadin Fiorentino. Anversa il di primo di Gennaio M.D.LXXXVIII. Fol. Antwerp.

Reissued, edit. by Andrew Coventry, *Publ. Bann. Club,* no. 32, Edinburgh, 1829.
Ubaldino was an Italian scholar and illuminator, who resided in England from 1545 on at various periods. He says that he drew up his information partly from his own personal observations—and perhaps he did—but it is certain that he borrowed very largely from Boece, *Scotorum Regni Descriptio.*—Mitchell, *op. cit.* Gough thinks that perhaps he translated his book from a Latin MS in the King's Library, 13 A. VIII., in the British Museum, viz., Scotiae descriptio a Deidonensi quodam facto [*sic*], A.D. 1550, & per Petruccium Ubaldinum transcripta A.D. 1576.—*Op. cit.,* 626.

1592   BOTERO, GIOVANNI. Relazioni Universali, etc. Venice.

The complete edition of this work came out in 1595, with other editions following. It was translated as *The Travellers Breviat, or an Historicall Description of the most famous Kingdomes,* etc., London, 1601. See Botero under 1601, GENERAL TRAVELS AND DESCRIPTIONS, vol. I of this work.
In its description of England this book slid back sixty years, being no farther advanced than Polydore Vergil. It repeats the old stuff in the same generalized manner—the climate, humid air, fine pasturage, delicate white wool, main rivers, fisheries, the two archbishoprics and universities, London described in full stringed epithets, etc.—Clare Wliams, *op. cit.*

1597   Kronn und Ausbundt aller Wegweiser. (Place?)

So cited by Clare Williams, *op. cit.,* who adds that this is a German roadbook, which gives teh highways to London and two alternate routes.

1599 METEREN, EMANUEL VAN. Historie der nederlandsche ende haerder Naburen oorlogen en geschiedissen. Delft.

> Later editions, 1614, 1636, etc. That of 1614 was revised under governmental supervision and hence is less trustworthy.—Read, *Bibliog. Brit. History.* Extracts translated into English in Rye, *op. cit.,* 69-73.
> The author was an Antwerp merchant who settled in London and resided there during the whole of Elizabeth's reign. In 1575, in company with his cousin Abraham Ortelius, the renowned geographer, he traveled through the whole of England and Ireland. In 1583 he was appointed Dutch consul for England and held this office till his death in 1612. His *History of the Netherlands* is deservedly esteemed a masterpiece. His account of the English is not altogether flattering. While bold and courageous, they are inconsistent, rash, vainglorious, light and deceiving. Though their words sound eloquent and fair, it will not do to put complete trust in them. However, they are hospitable. They eat a great deal, especially of meat. They are not as industrious as the Dutch or French, preferring for the most part to enjoy an indolent life. In dress they are very desirous of novelties. Their language is "broken German." Their wives are entirely in their husbands' power, but they are not kept in such strict seclusion as obtains among the Spaniards and others. They have the free management of their households. They like to sit out in front of their doors dressed out in their finery to see and be seen. Hence England is called the "Paradise of married women."—From Rye.

1600 EHINGEN, JÖRG VON. Historische Beschreibung weiland Hern Georgen von Ehingen Reisens nach der Ritterschaft vor 150 Jaren in unterschiedliche Koenigreich verbracht. Augsburg.

> Translated and edited by Malcolm Letts, Oxford, 1929, as *The Diary of Jörg von Ehingen.*
> The Diary records his travels as a young man from 1450 to 1460, in his "errantry in search for Knighthood." His travels took him to Rhodes, Jerusalem, Cyprus, the Courts of France, Castile and Portugal, in service against the Moors in Granada and Morocco, where he fought as the Christian champion in single combat against a mighty infidel, his return to Swabia by way of England and Scotland, where he spent some time at the court of James II, and was decorated by Henry VI. Strange to relate, after all this hospitality, he was ungratefully silent about the island and its people.

QUADT, MATTHIAS (of Kinklebach). Europa Universalis (1594) ; Geographisches Handbuch (1600). Cöln am Rhein.

> The above are geographical Handbuchs made up of maps and commentary, which though traditional are enlivened by flashes of personal observation. But the shadow of Polydore Vergil hangs over them. While rejecting some of the hand-me-down marvels, the author admits others just as preposterous. For instance, the fabulous origin of the British people has no standing, but Ireland's barnacle geese and magic wells have a place. The Irish people he condemns as a peasant and inhospitable race, which loves idleness but is also fond of music.

1602 RATHGEB, JACOB. Kurtze und Warhaffte Beschreibung der Badenfahrt: welche der Durchleuchtig Hochgeborn Fürst und Herr, Herr Friderich, Hertzog zu Württemberg unnd Teckh, Grave zu Mümppelgart, Herr zu Heidenheim, Ritter der beeden Uhralten Königlichen Orden, in Franckreich S. Michaels, unnd in Engellandt, etc. In nebst abgeloffenem 1592 Jahr, von Mümppelgart auss, in das weitberümbte Königreich Engellandt, hernach im zurück ziehen durch die Niderland, biss widerumb gehn Mümppelgart, verrichtet hat. Auss I. F. G. gnedigem Bevelch, von dero mitraisendem Cammer-Secretarien (Jacob Rathgeb), auffs kürtzist von tag zu tag verzeichnet. (Follows ten lines of verse.) Getruckt zu Tübingen, bey Erhardo Cellio, anno 1602. 4to. Tübingen.

> The portions dealing with England translated in Rye, *op. cit.,* 3-53, London, 1865.
> This narrative was drawn up by the Duke's secretary, who accompanied him on the journey. The party sailed for England from Emden Aug. 7, 1592, and after a tempestuous trip across the Channel landed at Dover. The wetness of the passage gave rise to the

phrase "Bathing Excursion" used in the title (see Rye, Introd., xc and xcii). The stay in England, which lasted a month, was filled with sight-seeing and entertainments, all of which suited the show-loving Duke right heartily. In one of his interviews with Queen Elizabeth, the Duke got the impression that he had been promised an induction into the Order of the Garter. If so, the Queen took her time about fulfilling her promise, and it was not until James I came on the throne that it was carried out, and then the ceremony took place in Stuttgart. The account gives interesting information on the roads, country seats, palaces, the universities, and London. Whether the Duke served Shakespeare as the prototype of his "Duke de Jamanie" and "Cosen Garmombles," first suggested by Charles Knight in 1838-43, was a question that exercised scholars in the nineteenth century.

> 1865 RATHGEB, JACOB. A True and Faithful Narrative of the Bathing Excursion, which His Serene Highness Frederick, Duke of Wirtemberg, Count Mümppelgart, Knight of the Garter, made a few years ago to the far-famed Kingdom of England; as it was noted down daily in the most concise manner possible at his Highness's gracious Command by his private Secretary, who accompanied him. (Title in Rye's version.)

1603 TASSIS, JUAN DE (Count Villamediana). An Account of his Mission to England in 1603 to congratulate James I and to pave the way for Peace was published this date in Seville. It is referred to by Rye, 270, who mentions also a work by Chifflet *Maison de Tassis,* fol., 1645.

1604 VELASCO, JUAN FERNANDEZ DE (Duke de Frias and Constable of Castile). Relacion de la jornada del Excmo Condestable de Castilla, a las pazes entre Hespana y Inglaterra, etc. 4to. Anvers (Antwerp).

> An abstract of this work was made by Mr. Konig and used by Sir Henry Ellis in his *Original Letters,* 2nd ser., vol. III, 207 ff., 1827. According to Rye, this abstract contains some remarkable mistakes. The portion relating to the banquet is translated by Rye.
> The Duke de Frias was the ambassador sent by Philip III to negotiate and conclude a peace between Spain and England. The rough Channel passage quite undid the Duke so that he had to be carried in a litter when he set out from Dover for London. From Sittingbourne the party was conveyed in twenty-four covered barges up the Thames to the capital. After "swearing the peace," the contracting parties enjoyed a round of entertainments of bull and bear baiting, dancing, etc.. The next day the Constable was laid up with lumbago. The plenipotentiaries left for home by way of Dover and Calais.

1606 The King of Denmarkes Welcome: containing his Arivall, Abode, and Entertainment, both in the Citie and other Places. London.

1610 GRASSER, JOHANN JACOB. Frantzösische und Englische Schatzkammer, etc. 8vo. Basel.

> The notices "Of the beautiful and powerful Kingdom of England" occupy pp. 235-63 of this work.—Rye, *op. cit.* A portion was translated into English in Rye, 127-28.
> The author was a Swiss historian and pastor and professor at Nismes. He traveled into England and returned to his native country about 1608.—Rye.

For the Journal kept of the visit of Prince Lewis Frederick of Wirtemberg, 2nd son of Duke Frederick, see Wurmsser under 1865 below.

1611 HENTZNER, PAUL. Itinerarium Germaniae, Galliae, Angliae, Italiae, cum indice locorum et rerum. Basel.

> The above citation is taken from Pinkerton, vol. XVII. Other printings, which were numerous, are: 4to, Nürnberg, 1612; 12mo, Breslau, 1617; 12mo, Nürnberg, 1629, Translation into English of the portion dealing with England, 12mo, Strawberry Hill, 1757; Dublin, 1762, 1765, 1771; with additions, 8vo, Strawberry Hill, 1797; portions in Rye, 101-13; in *Publ. Aungervyle Soc.,* vol. 2, 1st ser., Edinburgh, 1881. See below. (Apparently no other part of his Itinerary was ever published in English.)

The writer of this account, which is one of the most valuable descriptions by a foreigner of Elizabethan England, was a native of Brandenburg, a jurist by profession, and counsellor to Duke Charles of Münsterberg and Öls. His Latin, which has been highly praised for its purity, shows him to have been a man of great attainments. He visited England in August and September of 1598 as companion or traveling tutor to Christoph Rehdiger, a young Silesian nobleman. The party was augmented by the addition of some more aristocrats from Bohemia. Among the many scenes of past days that could be singled out may be mentioned his description of the Queen and the ceremony attending her appearance from her own apartments, which was extraordinarily elaborate. Her bosom was uncovered, "as all the English ladies have it till they marry." Setting the table for her dinner was a fixed ceremony. As for the English in general—they are grave like the Germans, lovers of show; they excel in dancing and music; they are good sailors and better pirates, cunning, treacherous, and thieving. Above 300 are said to be hanged annually at London. In eating they are more polite than the French, consuming less bread but more meat, which they roast to perfection. They put a great deal of sugar into their drink (which it is alleged accounts for their black teeth). They are vastly fond of loud noises, such as firing of cannon, beating of drums, and the ringing of bells, etc., etc. The travelers seem to have journeyed for the most part on horseback.

1629 HENTZNER, PAUL. Itinerarium Germaniae, Galliae, Angliae, Italiae, cum Indice Locorum, Rerum atque Verborum commemorabilium. Huic libro accessere nova hac editione I. Monita Peregrinatoria duorum doctissimorum Virorum: II. Incerti Auctoris Epitome Praecognitorum Historicorum, antehac nonedita. 12mo. Norimbergae.
　　The third edition, valuable for the additions which it contains of the most curious description extant of Elizabethan England and great Eliza's court.—Bookseller's Note.

1757 ———. A Journey into England in the Year MDXCVIII. 12mo. Strawberry Hill.
　　Of this first edition in English of this portion of Hentzner there were 220 copies printed. It contains the Latin text and a translation by Richard Bentley. Walpole wrote the Introduction. The work is one of the earliest imprints of this press.

1613 ENS, G. Magnae Britanniae deliciae seu Insularum & Regnorum quae M. Britanniae nomine & sereniss. Regis Jacobi, &c. Imperio hodie comprehenduntur Descriptio: ex variis Auctoribus collectae & Reliquarum Europae Nationum jam ante editis deliciis Additae. 12mo. Cologne.

Evidently a mere compilation.—Gough, 24.

1614 EISENBERG, PETER. Itinerarium Galliae et Angliae: Reisenbüchlein. 16mo. Leipzig.
　　Extracts relating to England translated in Rye, 171-73.
　　The author was a Dane whose father was secretary to Frederick II, King of Denmark. His account was compiled as a guidebook for the use of the two sons of Caspar Marckdaner, who were about to travel and to whom Eisenberg had been tutor. Of the curiosities to be observed in England he mentions the mirror of Henry VII, which revealed to the king whatever he wished to see and which broke at his death. Pictures and other rarities are included, such as Queen Elizabeth's draught board adorned with thirty-two beautiful emeralds and other jewels, Drake's ship at Deptford, then nearly derelict, etc.

1615 C., N. D. Joornal der Keyseren en Coningen van Christenryk, etc. Fol. Arnhem. (So cited in Mitchell, *Scot. Topog.*, vol. I.)

SCHEIDT, HIERONYMUS. Reise von Erfurt nach dem Gelobten Land, auch Spanien, Frankreich, Holland, und England. Erfurt.

1616 WECKHERLIN, GEORG RUDOLPH. The Triumphall Shews set forth lately at Stutgart. Written first in German, and now in English, by G. Rodolfe Weckherlin, Secretarie to the Duke of Wirtemberg. 8vo. Stuttgart.
　　The above title, which is incomplete, is taken from Rye, Introduction, cxxvii, where some selections from the work are given.

This German poet was resident in England altogether for a period of about forty years, with one interruption, from 1607 on. He occupied several posts and was sent on missions by both James I and Charles I to Scotland, Ireland, and elsewhere. Despite the esteem which evidently he had won, he often lived in hard straits. From his poems and the above account we are able to glean many curious items about the English and their habits. The occasion for the work cited was the christening of the eldest son of the Duke of Wirtemberg. It also emphasizes the close connection existing between the courts of England and Wirtemberg at this period.—From Rye, cxxiii-cxxxii.

ZINZERLING, JUSTUS (Jodocus Sincerus). Itinerarium Galliae. . . . 16mo. Lugduni (Lyon).

Extracts from the section *Itineris Anglici brevissima delineatio* Englished by Rye, 131-35. The author was a native of Thuringia and doctor of laws at Basel. He published his travels under the name of Jodocus Sincerus, and his work became a favorite guidebook to the countries he visited for nearly half a century. In the English portions he notes the many curiosities to be seen, the libraries and pictures, and the various ceremonies to be observed in washing the feet of the poor and in feeding them.

1618 ARITHMAEUS, VALENTIN. Mausolea Regum, Reginarum, Dynastarum, Nobilium, sumtuosissima, artificiosissima, magnificentissima, Londini Anglorum in occidentali urbis angulo structa; h.e. Eorundem Inscriptiones omnes in lucem reductae, cura Valentis Arithmaei, Prof. Acad. literis et sumtobus Joannis Eichorn. 12mo. Frankfort on the Oder.

This work is briefly described by Rye, 177-78, who quotes author's complaint about the avarice of the English: "No German is admitted to it (St. Paul's steeple), unless he pays his money beforehand, so intense is the avarice of the English, and I don't know whether the reason be not the simplicity of the Germans." He gives as his reason for printing only the Latin inscriptions that "very few persons understand English." The author was doctor of laws at Basel and professor of poetry at Frankfort on the Oder.

1620 NEWMAYR VON RAMSSLA, J. W. Des durchlautigen hochgebornen Fürsten und Herrn, Herrn Johann Ernsten des Jüngern, Hertzogen zu Sachsen, etc., Reise in Frankreich, Engelland und Niederland. 4to. Leipzig.

Reprinted Jena, 1734; portions dealing with England translated by Rye, 149-55. The Duke of Saxe-Weimar stayed in England from Aug. 24 to Oct. 23, 1613. While traveling he assumed the name of Herr von Hornstein. The account here given deals with his visit to King James I at Theobalds. It tells how royal meals were served, relates a hunting expedition with James, who was inordinately fond of such sports, and goes into some detail in his description of two cures for the King's Evil which he witnessed. It also lists pictures and other art works in the royal palaces.

1621 CASTELNAU, MICHEL DE. Mémoires. Paris.

Another edit., with additions relating to Anglo-French and Anglo-Scottish dealings, 3 vols., Paris, 1731; translated into English without the additions, published anonymously, London, 1724.
The memoirs were written in England between 1575-85 by the French Ambassador. It relates many details concerning the part taken by the English in the early French religious wars. The correspondence of La Mothe-Fénélon while ambassador in England and of Castelnau when in the same office is of particular value.—From Read, *Bibliog. Brit. Hist.*

SAGITARII, T. Ulysses Saxonicus, seu Iter Ernesti ducis Saxoniae in Germaniam, Galliam, Angliam, et Belgium. 4to. Breslau. (So cited in Pinkerton, vol. XVII.)

1624 THOMAS, HUBERTUS. Annalium de vita et rebus gestis illustrissimi Principis Friderici II, Elect. Pal., etc. Frankfort.

This account was written in the middle of the 16th century but not published until 1624. A German translation, under the title of *Spiggel des Humors grosser Potentatem*, etc., Leipzig, 1629; done into modern German by Eduard von Bülow, as *Ein Fürstenspiegel*,

etc., (date and place?) ; retold in Mrs. Henry Cust's *Gentlemen Errant*, 1909.

The adventures of this Palgrave among the great folk of the day—Charles V, Francis I, Henry VIII, the Archduke Ferdinand, and the lesser dignitaries of Germany, Flanders, Spain—make up an amazing tale of love, war, and intrigue. It is charmingly rewritten in Mrs. Cust's book. Hubertus was sent on three different missions to England, none of which succeeded, but which resulted for the modern reader in bringing to light many curious matters in customs. Henry VIII received him cordially and took much pleasure in his company, for Hubertus was a skilful diplomat, though being a temperate man, he must have suffered torture in his drinking bout with the English king. On the third trip the Palgrave went along in person. His purpose, which had to do with forwarding his desire to succeed to the Danish crown, whereby he might recuperate his empty treasury, failed to materialize. Among the presents he received was a "toothpicker" from Lady Lisle, who said that she had noticed he had none and she had had hers for seven years.—From Mrs. Cust.

1627 LAET, JOANNES DE. Respublica sive Status Regni Scotiae et Hiberniae. Leyden.

This is borrowed from Buchanan, Camden, Boece, Moryson, Giraldus, and Stanihurst.—*Camb. Bibliog.*

1630 ———. Angliae Chorographica Descriptio. In Thomae Smithi Angli De Republica Anglorum. Leyden.

This matter is borrowed from Camden, Speed, Barclay, and Lambard.—*Camb. Bibliog.*

1631 OTTO, PRINCE OF HESSE. For an account of his visit to England to sue for the hand of Elizabeth, eldest daughter of James I, see Stow, *Annales* (1615 edition) under 1565, HISTORY AND CHRONICLE. See also the account by Rye, 143-45.

In the library at Cassel is a MS narrative of this journey by an unknown hand, some extracts from which were published by Rommell in his *Geschichte von Hesse* (1837), Bd. 6, 327-28. Otto was a suitor for the hand of Elizabeth, daughter of James I, but as history deponeth, returned home unsuccessful. He received, however, some magnificent gifts and attended the King at his ceremony of "touching for the King's evil." He paid a visit to Scotland before he left.—Rye. The visit took place in 1611.

1634 CHASTELLAIN, CHEVALIER GEORGE. Historie du bon Chevalier Messire Jacques de Lalain frere et compagnon de l'ordre de la Toison d'Or: Ecrite par Messire George Chastellain Chevalier Historiographe des Ducs de Bourgougne Philippe le Bon et Charles le Hardi. Brussels.

Used by Hume Brown, *Early Travellers*, 30-38.

This doughty knight had challenged and overcome every opponent of any reputation at jousting, and having heard that James Douglas was a valiant foe worthy of his mettle, he sent him a challenge couched in courteous, high-flown terms, which was accepted in equally gracious and circumlocutory phraseology. Gorgeously equipped he sailed for Scotland, where he and his two chosen companions in combat were well entertained. The combat, with three on each side, was held before King James II at Stirling. When the fortunes of the fight seemed to be going against the Scottish knights, the king threw down his truncheon. The end of the Chevalier's career was not very appropriate for a knight of chivalry, for he was killed at the age of thirty-two by a musket ball. See Hume Brown.

ZEILLER, MARTIN. Itinerarium Magnae Britanniae oder Reisesbeschreibung durch Engell Schott und Irrland colligiert und verfertigt durch Martinum Zeillerum. 2 vols. 12mo. Strasburg.

Another edit., 8vo, London and Paris, 1674 (with the names of the countries spelled out in full). See Mitchell, *List of Travels.*

1637 ABDELLA, ALKAID JAURER BEN. The Arrivall and Intertainements of the Embassador, Alkaid Jaurer Ben Abdella, with his Associate, Mr. Robert Blake. From the High and Mighty Prince, Mulley Mahamed Sheque, Emperor of Morocco,

King of Fesse, and Suss. With the Ambassadors good and applauded Commendation of his royall and noble Entertainments in the Court and City . . . . 4to. London.

> This account tells something of the customs and rites of African nations and the release of 302 English captives from slavery at Sallee.—Britwell Library Catalogue.

1638 SULLY, MAXIMILIAN DE BETHUNE, DUKE OF (Prime Minister of Henry the Great). Mémoires. Amsterdam.

> In Bohn's *French Memoirs,* 5 vols., London, 1856.
> The memoirs were printed at Chateau Sully in 1638 and published at Amsterdam; translated into English sometime in the middle of the 18th century. The embassy to England is found in the second volume of Bohn's edition. The minister displayed great discernment and shrewdness in sizing up the character of James I and his court. He was most favorably impressed by the English nation.

1639 LA SERRE, LE SIEUR J. PUGIN DE. Historie de l'Entrée de la Reigne Mère dans la Grande Bretagne. Fol. London.

> An English version, 8vo, London, 1639; another edit., by Gough, 3 pts., 4to, London, 1756; reprinted in *Antiquarian Repertory,* vol. IV, 520 ff., 4to, London, 1775 (along with Perlin, *Description d'Angleterre,* see under 1558 above). See below.
> The author, historiographer of France, was a miscellaneous writer of somewhat ephemeral books. He was immensely pleased with his visit to England.—Smith, *Foreign Visitors in England.* La Serre's history of the journey of the Queen Mother of France, Mary de Medici, to England and her reception is a pompous folio, with curious prints of towns, seats, and St. James's Palace at that time. Hollar engraved six plates for the work.—Gough, 726. The work does not give us much information on England. After a stormy passage the party had to stay a week at Harwich to recuperate. Charles I and his queen met them at the Castle of de Nulding. Nothing marred the harmony of the visit except perhaps the pregnancy of the queen and the death of the Duke of Savoy.

> 1639 LA SERRE, LE SIEUR J. PUGIN DE. The Mirrour which Flatters Not. Dedicated to their Maiesties of Great Britain, by Le Sieur de la Serre, Historiographer of France. Enriched with Faire Figures. Transcribed English from the French, by T. C. [Thomas Cary], and Devoted to the well-disposed Readers. 8vo. London.

> 1775 ———. The History of the Entry of Mary de Medicis, the Queen Mother of France in to England 1638, translated from the French . . . published anno 1639. In *Antiquarian Repertory,* vol. IV, 520 ff. 4to. London.

1641 DU CHESNE, A. Historie d'Angleterre, d'Escosse, et d'Irlande, contenant les Choses plus dignes de Mémoire auenuës aux Isles et Royaumes de la grande Bretagne, d'Irlande, de Man, et autres adiacentes. Tant sous la Domination des Anciens Bretons et Romains, que durant les Regnes des Anglois, Saxons, Pictes, Escossois, Danois, et Normans. . . . Troisième édition. Fol. Paris. (The date of the first edition is 1614.)

1646 ROHAN, HENRI DUC DE. Voyage du Duc de Rohan, faict en l'an 1600, en Italie, Allemaigne, Pays-Bas Uni, Angleterre, et Escosse. 12mo. Amsterdam.

> In 2 vols., augmented, Paris, 1661; Scottish part Englished in Hume Brown, *op. cit.,* 91-95. See below.
> Rohan was a distinguished Huguenot soldier, who, when the Peace of Vervius (1598) was concluded, decided to improve his time in traveling, which appears to have extended over twenty months. He was received with the greatest cordiality by Queen Elizabeth and by the Scotch. His accounts are disappointing since he was an indifferent observer. Scottish towns possess for him little attraction, for they boast neither remarkable buildings nor antiquities worthy of notice. The crowded condition of Edinburgh and its commercial prosperity strike his attention. Linlithgow, Stirling, and Dunfermline receive some notice because of their association with the births and deaths of the kings of Scotland. He recalls with pride the long alliance between Scotland and France, running it back to

Charlemagne, an alliance recorded by the historians Fordun, Boece, Major, and Buchanan.
—From Brown, *op. cit.*

1661 ROHAN, HENRI DUC DE. Mémoires du Duc de Rohan, sur les choses advenues en France depuis la mort de Henry le Grand jusques à la Paix faite avec les Reformes au mois de Juin 1619. Augmentés d'un quatrième Livre, et de divers Discours Politiques du mesme Auteur cy-devant non priméz. Ensemble le Voyage du mesme Auteur, fait en Italie, Allemagne, Pais-bas-Uni, Angleterre, et Ecosse. Fait en l'an 1600. 2 vols. 12mo. Paris.

1653 LABOULLAYE LE GOUZ, SIEUR FRANCOIS DE. Les Voyages et Observations du Sieur François Laboullaye le Gouz, gentilhomme Angevin, ou sont descrits les religion, gouvernment, et situation des Etats et Royaumes d'Italie, Gréce, Natolie, Syrie, Perse, Palestine, Caraminie, Kaldée, Assyrie, Grand Mogal, Bizapour, Indes-Orientals des Portugais, Arabie, Afrique, Hollande, Grande-Bretagne, Danemarck, Pologne, etc., etc. Avec figures. Paris.

The portion dealing with Ireland edit. by Crofton Croker, with notes, etc., London, 1837. See below.
This far-ranging traveler has been termed an exact and faithful recorder.

1837 LA BOULLAYE LE GOUZ, FRANCOIS DE. Tour of the French Traveller M. de la Boullaye le Gouz in Ireland, A.D. 1644, edit. by T. Crofton Croker, with Notes and Illustrative Extracts contributed by J. Roche, the Rev. F. Mahoney, T. Wright, and the Editor. 12mo. London.

1654 COULON, LOUIS. Le Fidèle Conducteur pour le voyage d'Angleterre. 8vo. Paris.

1659 A Character of England as it was lately presented to a Noble Man of France. London.

1661 HERMANNIDES, RUTGERUS. Britannia Magna Sive Angliae, Scotiae, Hiberniae & adjacentium Insularum Geographico-Historica Descriptio. 12mo. Maps and plates. Amstelodami (Amsterdam).

The author was professor of history in the University of Harderowick in Guelderland.— Gough, 24. The map of London is of interest as it represents the Globe Theater and the bear-garden before their destruction by the Great Fire.—Bookseller's Note. The topographical description is full and minute, and there is some appearance of its being derived from personal observation.—Mitchell, *List of Travels.*

1662 MANDELSLO, J. ALBERT DE. The Voyages and Travels of J. Albert de Mandelslo . . . into the East Indies. Rendered into English by John Davies of Kidwelly. 3 vols. London.

On his return from India, in company with the President at Surat, this German traveler spent three months in England, from the last of December, 1639, to March 20, 1640. He describes his reception and courtesies received from the East India Company, his audience at court, his visits to places of state in London, etc. See Mandelslo under this date, EAST INDIES, vol. I of this work.

1663 CARLTON, MARY. An Historicall Narrative Of The German Princess, Containing All material Passages, from her first Arrivall at Graves-end, the 30th of March last, untill she was discharged from her Imprisonment . . . Written by her Self. . . . 4to. London.

PAYEN, LIEUT.-GEN. DE MEAUX. Les Voyages de Monsieur Payen, avec une description de l'Angleterre, de la Flandre, et du Brabant, dediéz à Monseigneur de Lionne. 12mo. Paris.

Cited in Bastide, *Anglais et Français,* who quotes from him a Table of the Roads, of the Inns, and the expense to be incurred. His work is a guidebook.

1664   SORBIERE, SAMUEL. Relation d'un Voyage en Angleterre, où sont touchées plu-
        sieurs choses, qui regardent l'estat des Sciences, et de la Religion, et autres
        matières curieuses. 8vo. Paris.

> Other French edits., Cologne, 1666, 1669 (this called forth Observations and Replies in
> French); reply by Thomas Sprat, London, 1665; a skit on the voyage and the contro-
> versy by William King, London, 1698; translated into English, with Sprat's Reply, 8vo,
> London, 1709; a résumé entitled "A Journey to England A. D. 1663," by Jusserand in
> *English Essays from a French Pen,* 8vo, London, 1895; an article, "Authour de *La Rela-
> tion* du Voyage de Samuel Sorbière en Angleterre 1663-1664," by Vincent Guilloton, in
> *Smith College Studies in Modern Languages,* vol. 11, no. 4, July, 1930. See below.
> Few books of this sort have aroused such general confutations and refutations, obser-
> vations and replies as did this rather innocent account of England, and still fewer in-
> volved so many diplomatic dispatches and apologies, as well as exchanges between Euro-
> pean courts. The literati on the three sides of the North Sea took up their pens, and, in
> Jusserand's words, "even the gentlemen belonging to the Church wrote in unChristian
> language on the subject." Louis XIV, who was anxious to cultivate English good will,
> sentenced the book to be suppressed with other strictures. All this helped to spread the
> fame of the book, which got translated into other languages, though it availed the author
> little until Charles II interceded for poor Sorbière, who was at last granted amnesty by his
> sovereign. The best known reply is that of Bishop Sprat, the historian of the Royal Society.
> What it was that stirred up wrath is rather hard to guess from the account itself. Perhaps,
> at bottom, it was English distrust of things French and more particularly Sorbière's
> mild criticism of certain traits of Clarendon; and, for Sprat at least, the charge that
> English dramatists did not appreciate the unities. On the whole, the book has much good
> to say of London and Englishmen. It gives a detailed description of London, its chief
> places of interest, of visits to Canterbury, Dover, Gravesend, and Oxford, and of associa-
> tions with learned and prominent men of the day. Sorbière was the chief friend of Hobbes
> abroad, translated some of his works and in general promoted his interests; and while in
> England he was the guest of Hobbes.

> 1665 Observations sur le Voyage de Sorbière. Paris.

> 1675 Réponse aux faussetés et invectives de la Relation de M. Sorbière. Amsterdam.

> 1665 SPRAT, THOMAS. Observations on Monsieur de Sorbier's Voyage into England.
>   Written to Dr. (Christopher) Wren, Professor of Astronomy in Oxford. 8vo.
>   London.

>> This was praised by Addison as "full of just satire and ingenuity," as a defense of
>> England and Englishmen against the attacks of Sorbière. A section of the book
>> states the claims of the English against the French stage.—Bookseller's Note.
>> Sprat had the assistance of Evelyn in composing this biting reply.

> 1698 SORBIERE, SAMUEL DE. A Journey to London, in the Year 1698. 8vo. London.

>> This humorous tract was written by Dr. William King. It long held the reputa-
>> tion of being the real article and was reprinted as such as late as 1832 (see Ap-
>> pendix to *Mirabeau's Letters* under 1832 below).

> 1709 SORBIERE, SAMUEL. A Voyage to England, and containing many things relating to
>   the State of Learning, Religion, and other Curiosities of that Kingdom, as also
>   Observations on the same Voyage, by Thomas Sprat, with a Letter of M. Sor-
>   bière's concerning the War between England and Holland in 1652. To which is
>   prefixed his Life, writ by M. Graverol, done into English from the French. 8vo.
>   London.

>> As several spurious translations had appeared already, this one professed to be
>> the first correct one.

1665   DE MONCONYS, —. Journal du Voyage de Monsieur de Monconys, en Portugal, en
        Provence, en Italie, en Egypte, en Syrie, à Constantinople, en Natolie, en Angle-
        terre, dans les Pays-Bays, en Allemagne, en Espagne, où les savans trouveront
        un nombre infini de nouveautés en machines de mathematiques, expérience de
        physique, curiosités de chimie; outre la description des divers animaux et des
        plantes rares; les ouvrages des peintres fameux, les coutumes et moeurs des

nations, etc. Enrichi de figures, et publié par le Sieur de Lignières, son fils. 3 vols. Lyon.

> A 2nd part in 1666. Another edit., 5 vols., Paris, 1699.
> "The extent of these travels, commenced in 1645, are not exaggerated in the title. Their chief objects are rather the sciences and arts than the descriptions of the countries visited. The travels in the East are said to have been undertaken for the purpose of tracing the remains of the philosophy of Mercurius Trismegistus and Zoroaster."—Pinkerton, vol. XVII.

1666 BASSOMPIERRE, MARECHAL DE. Mémoires. 2 vols. 12mo. Cologne.

> In English, by John Wilson Croker, London, 1819. See below.
> This well known record, though regretably meagre, comes from the pen of a shrewd observer, whose life was spent mostly among courts and fine ladies when not on the battle-field. It deals mainly with his difficulties and dinners with celebrities of the court of Charles I.—From Smith, *Foreign Visitors in England.*

> 1819 (In English.) Memoirs of the Embassy of the Marshall de Bassompièrre to the Court of England in 1626. Translated with Notes (by John Wilson Croker). 8vo. London.

GEORGE, WILHELMUS. Historische Landbeschrivinge van Groot Britannje ofte Engelandt, Schotlant, en Yrlandt. 12mo. Middleburgh.

1667 FRISIUS, B. Dissertatio de imperio Magnae Britanniae hodierno statu. 4to. Wittenberg.

Reise Beschreibung nach Spanien und England. Translated from the French into German, by T. Mackel. 12mo. Frankfort.

1668 CORRERO (or CORRER), MARC ANTONIO. Relation d'Angleterre. Montbeliard.

> Correr, who was sometimes called Cornao and Cornaro, was the Venetian resident "ordinary" or "lieger" Ambassador in England in the time of King James I. He was well spoken of by Sir Henry Wotton, who wrote a letter from Venice, Aug. 16, 1608, recommending to Prince Henry this gentleman and his son, a youth of "so sweet a spirit." Correr returned to Venice in 1611, in which year he presented his Relation of England to the Senate. This work, which is very rare, and hitherto unused, it is believed, by English writers in illustration of the reign of James I, is a translation from the Italian MS descriptive of the country to which the author was accredited. Correr, it seems, was in London again on a diplomatic mission in July, 1626. His dispatches, written from England, are at Venice, and most probably his original Relation.—From Rye, 226, who gives a translation of his description of James I.

1669 CHAPPUZEAU, —. L'Europe vivante. Genève.

> Cited by Edith Philips in "French Interest in Quakers," *PMLA*, vol. 45, Mch., 1930.
> The writer in this work left a record of his impressions of England. He found the state of religion peaceable. Most of the Independents had become Anglicans or Quakers. His account of the latter was the fairest yet given.

1670 Lettres galantes et de Voyages, dans lesquelles on décrit les moeurs, les coutumes, et les intérêts de l'Italie, de la Hongrie, de l'Allemagne, de la Suisse, de la Hollande, de la Flandre, de l'Espagne, et de l'Angleterre. Paris.

PATIN, CHARLES. Relations Historiques et Curieuses des Voyages en Allemagne, Bohéme, Angleterre, Holland et Suisse. Strasburg.

> Other edits., Basel, 1673; Rouen, 1676; Amsterdam, 1695.

1672   Descrittione del nostro veduto in Olando e in Inghilterra. Milano.

ROCHEFORT, JOREVIN DE. Travels in England, Scotland, and Ireland. 3 vols. 12mo. Paris. (So cited in Mitchell, *List of Travels*, where the French title is not given.)

> Reprinted in *Antiquarian Repertory*, vol. IV, 549-622, London, 1809 edition; extract from his narrative of Scotland in Hume Brown, *op. cit.*, 217-29.
> For an account of the true identity of this author, see this date under TOURS, Ireland. His visit to Scotland seems to have taken place shortly after the Restoration. He visited Glasgow, passed over to Edinburgh, which he describes at some length as well as Leith. His eyes were taken with objects rather than with manners. Grose, the editor of the *Antiquarian Repertory*, speaks of him as an indifferent historian but a tolerable topographer.

1673   Two Letters: the One from a Dutchman to his Correspondent in England; the other an Answer from the said Correspondent in which most Things of Note (that relate to this Hostility) are fully handled, with the Present Condition of both Countries. (Place?)

1678   FERDINAND ALBRECHT, HERZOG VON BRAUNSCHWEIG. Wunderliche Begebenheiten und Reise-Beschreibung durch Deutschland, Italien, Malta, Frankreich, und England. 2 vols. 4to. Bevern. (So cited in Pinkerton, vol. XVII.)

1681   LARCHIER, FRANCOIS. Les Voyages d'un homme de qualité faits en Angleterre. . . . Tables. 12mo. Lyon.

> See Laurent under 1685 below.

1682   KIRCHMAIER, J. C. De Anglici regni, genio, moribus, ac dotibus. 4to. Wittemberg. (So cited in Pinkerton, vol. XVII.)

1683   LETI, GREGORIO. Teatro Britannico. Venice (?).

> This work is referred to several times by Darby, *The Draining of the Fens,* 1940. Leti, a Milanese by birth, spent the years 1680-83 in London, where he wrote the above work as a sort of tribute to the friendship of Charles II. Its publication, however, offended the Catholics of England, and led him to retire to Ireland. He was none too orthodox in his attitude toward the Church of Rome. He also published a *Teatro Gallico* in 1691-97.

1685   LAURENT, G. C. Viaggi d'un Huomo qualificato, fatti in Inghilterra, Flandra, Ollanda, Dannemarck, Svezia, Polonia, Venezia, ed el Piemonti, con un indrizzo delle strade e commodita che si trovanno: tradotti del Francese di Laurenti. Turin. (So cited in Pinkerton, vol. XVII.)

Le Voyageur d'Europe en Allemagne, en Pologne, en Danemarck, en Angleterre, et en Suède. Paris.

1689   Das jezt-lebende Engelland, oder eigentliche Beschreibung dess Königreichs Gross-Britannien, und aller darzu gehörigen Insuln. . . . Mit einer Zugabe der vornehmsten Staats-Begebnüssen und Veränderung der Regenten voriger und gegenwärtiger Zeiten. 12mo. Leipzic.

1690   LIMBERG, JOHANN. Denkwürdige Reisebeschreibung durch Teutschland, Italien, Portugal, Engelland, Frankreich und Schweitz. Leipzig.

> Pages 157-74 deal with his visit to England in 1677. His account gives itineraries and

dry descriptions of countries and cities, museums and curiosities. He thinks London is the most beautiful city in the world.—From Kelly, *German Visitors to English Theaters.*

Das Neu-Beharnischte Gross-Britannien, Das ist: Wahre Landes- und Standes-Beschaffenheit derer drey-vereinigten Königreiche Engel- Schott- und Irlande. In Völliger Beschreibung ihrer Provintzen Inseln Städte Schlosser Festungen Fruchten Reichthümer und Regiments-Form Wie nicht weniger des lesswürdig-sten Staats- und Kriegs-Beschichten Bevorab ihrer neulichsten gross wichtig-sten Handlungen, . . . Darzu mit wahren Contrefaiten Landkarten und Abris-sen der fürnehmsten und andern Hierzu füglichen Kupffer-Bildung Beleuchtet. Maps, views, portraits, etc., 4to. Nürnberg.

1691 Lettres Curieuses de Voyage écrite d'Angleterre, d'Italie, d'Hongrie, et d'Alle-magne. 8vo. Paris.

1692 CORNELIUS A BEUGHEM. Polimetria Britannica, dat is, Stedemeting van Groot Britanie, ziinde een korre aenwiizinge hoe wiid, voernamste stede in drie koningriiken van Angleand, Schotland, Yreland, van malkandered leggen. In kooper gesneden. 12mo. Amsterdam.

CORONELLI, PADRE MAESTRO V. Corso geografice universale. Fol. Venetia.

Two maps of Scotland—Scotia parte meridionale and Scotia parte septentrionale, each 16⅞ x 23½ ins.—Cited in Mitchell, *Scot. Topog.*, vol. II.

1693 COLSONI, F. Le Guide de Londres pour les Etrangers. 12mo. London.

3rd edit., 4to, London, 1705.

1693-95 Voyages Historiques de l'Europe. 12mo. Paris.

Tome IV: "qui comprend tout ce qu'il y a de plus curieux dans les Royaumes d'Angle-terre, d'Irlande, & d'Ecosse."

1697 CORONELLI, PADRE MAESTRO V. Viaggi dell' Inghilterra. Venice.

HOCHSTETTER, A. A. Oratio de utilitate peregrinationis Anglicanae. Tübingen.

TORFAEUS, THORMONDUS. Orcades, seu rerum Orcadensium historiae libri iii, quorum primus praeter insularum situm, numerumque, comitum, procerum, in-colarumque origines, familias, gesta & vicissitudines a primis monarchiae Nor-vegicae incunabulis ad A.D. 1222, continua fere serie exhibet. Secundus, primos Orcadum episcopos eorumque successores, &, qui postea vixerunt, comites sub regibus Norvegiae fiduciarios, tum etiam quae de rebus Orcadensibus & Haebudensibus exinde ad an. 1469, annotata, complectitur. Utroque firmiter afferitur regum Norvegiae jus dominii in insulas illas. Tertius, indefessa poten-tissimorum regum Daniae Norvegiaeque studia in jure suo repetendo continet, variis documentis ex archivis regiis asserta. Fol. Hafniae (Copenhagen).

The author, an Icelander by birth, was historiographer royal of Norway. His most famous work was *Historia rerum norvegicarum,* 1711.

1698   MISSON DE VALBOURG, HENRI. Mémoires et Observations faites par un Voyageur en Angleterre, sur ce qu'il y a trouvé de plus remarquable tant à l'égard de la religion, que de la politique, des moeurs, des curiositéz naturelles et quantités de faits historiques. Avec une description particulière de ce qu'il y a de plus curieux dans Londres. Plates. 12mo. Amsterdam.

> Misson's residence of three years in England gave him opportunity and leisure to observe closely and intimately what he describes and relates. His book is a valuable informant on life in England at the close of the 17th century. He was assisted in his composition by his brother Maximilian Misson, who in turn was the author of a delightful *Voyage to Italy* (see under 1695, WEST EUROPE, vol. I of this work).

>> 1719   (In English.) Memoirs and Observations in his Travels over England, with some Account of Scotland and Ireland. Written in French and translated by Mr. Ozell. 8vo. London.
>> John Ozell was a handyman of the bookseller Curll, for whom he did an enormous amount of translation and hackwork.

1699   CASIMIR, JOHN (Duke Palatine of Germany). His stay in England (1579) is reported by Hubert Languet, *Arcana . . . Ep.*, 161-63. (So cited by Clare Williams.)

> Casimir was one of a batch of German visitors to England in the reign of Elizabeth. He was well fêted with entertainment by royalty, nobility, and the city. His preferences were rather for the chase than for pictures and tapestries. He went home laden with gifts, and best of all the Knighthood of the Garter.—From Clare Williams.

Gedenkwaardige Aantekeningen Gedaan door een Reisiger in de Jaaren 1697, en 1698, van geheel Engeland, Schotland, en Yrland. Illustrations. 8vo. Utrecht.

KING, DR. WILLIAM. A Journey to England; with some Account of the Manners and Customs of that Nation. Written at the Command of a Nobleman in France. Made English. 8vo. London.

> Halkett and Laing attribute this book to King. It seems to be a parody on Dr. Lister's Journey to Paris, according to Gough, 27, who says that it was attributed fictitiously to Sorbière (see King under Sorbière, 1664 above). It contains chapters on Ale and Ale Houses, Bowling Greens, Dancing Masters, Spring-Garden, Taverns, etc.

1700   Reisebeschryving door Vrankryk, Spanien, Italien, Deutschland, England, Holland, Moscovien, Mitsgaders de Indien. Leyden.

1702   LE PAYS, RENE. Three Letters reporting on his travels in England and the Low Countries. First printed in English in Tom Brown's *Select Epistles*. London. (Also in *Prose and Verse*, vol. I, 356-70; vol. III, 142-58, 246-60, London, 1702.)

> Le Pays was often called "le singe de Voiture." He represented the decadence of the "precieux" style, mixed buffoonery with *esprit,* and slated gallantry with indecencies. His letters are fresh and vivid and were popular in England. He considered English culture to be coarse in comparison with that of France.—From Boyce, *Tom Brown of Facetious Memory* (1939).

1707   BEEVERELL, JAMES. Les Délices de la Grand' Bretagne et de l'Irlande, où sont exactement décrites les antiquitéz, les provinces, les villes, etc. 235 plates. 8 vols. 8vo. Leyden.

> Another issue of the plates only, 8 vols. in 1, 4to, Leyden; reissued in 8 vols., Leyden, 1727.

Gough says that the plates are the best part of the work. Their value lies also in the fact that they have preserved features that have been erased by time.

MIEGE, GUY. The Present State of Great Britain, etc. 8vo. London.

For this work, its numerous editions, its relation to Chamberlayne's *Angliae Notitia,* see Miege under 1707, ANCIENT AND PRESENT STATE.

1708-13 Nouveau Théâtre de la Grande Bretagne. . . . Tome I. Description exacte de Palais de la Reine et des Maisons les plus considérables des Seigneurs et des Gentilshommes. Tome II. Description exacte des villes, églises, cathédrales, hôpiteaux, ports de mer, etc. 2 vols. Fol. London.

This appeared also in 5 vols., 1724-29.

1710 AA, PIETER VAN DER. Vues des villes, édifices, et autre choses remarquables de l'Ecosse, et de l'Irlande, representées in Taille-douces . . . avec une courte description sous chaque figure. 2 tom. Leide.

1711 ERDEL, CHRISTIANUS HENRICUS. De Itinere Suo Anglicano et Batavo annis 1706 et 1707 facto relatio ad amicam, qua variae ad anatomiam, chirugiam, botanicam et materiam medicam observationes sistuntur. 8vo. Amstelodami.

1711 (In English.) A Relation of a Journey into England and Holland in 1706 and 1707, by a Saxon Physician, in a Letter to his Friend at Dresden, by C. H. E. D. Physician in Ordinary to the King of Poland, translated from the Latin. 8vo. London. This gives a trifling account of London, Oxford, etc.—Gough, 25.

1714 LOCHNERI, J. H. Observationes Anglicae. Bremen. (So cited in Pinkerton, vol. XVII.)

Relation der Reise Königs George I von Hanover nach London. Hamburgh. (So cited in Pinkerton, vol. XVII.)

1715 LE SAGE, G. L. Remarques sur l'état présent d'Angleterre, faites par un voyageur inconnu, dans les années 1713 et 1714. 12mo. Amsterdam.

1716 LEWIS OF ANHALT-GÖTHEN, PRINCE. His poetical Itinerary of his travels was printed by Beckmann in his *Accessiones Historiae Anhaltinae,* fol.—From Rye, cxii.

At the age of seventeen this German prince traveled with his tutors through the Netherlands, England, France, and Italy, and later Malta, returning after an absence of several years. He wrote an account of these wanderings in German verse. Most of his journeys were done on horseback. The year of his visit to England was 1596. He mentions four theaters to be seen in London, which were all on the Bankside.—From Rye.

Das Vereinigte Gross-Britannien, oder Engelland und Schottland, nach dem neuesten Zuständen aller Provintsen, Städte, Seehaven, Schiff- und Fisch-reichen Flüssen, stahende Seen, mineralischen Wassern, unterirrdischen Hölen, Berg-Wercken, Raritäten der Natur und Kunst, Europaisch- Asiatisch- Africanisch- und Americanischen Commercien, und andern Merckwürdigkeiten. Wobey insonderheit eine umständliche Nachricht von der Weltberühmten Haupt-Stadt London; . . . Aus dem bewährtesten Scribenten und neuesten Nachrichten

zusammen getragen; mit einer accuraten Land-Charte, und verschieden Portraits geziert, auch curieusen Beylagen zur Erleuterung der Englischen Historie versehen. 4to. Hamburg.

1717   DESLANDES, FR. BOURREAU. Nouveau Voyage d'Angleterre (in his *Etat présent d'Espagne*). Villefranche.

1718   Voyages historiques de l'Europe, qui comprend tout ce qu'il y a de plus curieux dans les Royaumes d'Angleterre, d'Irlande, et d'Ecosse. 4 tom. 12mo. Amsterdam.

1721   S. G., MONSIEUR DE (Saint-Gellais). Remarques sur l'Angleterre faites en 1715. (So cited in *Camb. Bibliog.*, vol. II.)

1723   EBERT, ADAM PAUL. Reisebeschreibung von Villa Franca der Chur-Brandenburg durch Teutschland und Brabant, England. . . . Frankfurt-an-der-Oder.

> Pages 45-95 are concerned with England. The author was professor of law at Frankfurt, and wrote under the pseudonym of Aulus Apronius. He was in London from Easter to October, 1674. He found little worth seeing in England except London, and London could not compare with Paris.—From Kelly, *German Visitors*.

LA MOTRAYE, AUBRY DE. Travels through Europe, Asia and into Part of Africa . . . Revised by the Author. Translated from the French (the author's manuscript). Maps and copperplates. 2 vols. Fol. London.

> For full title see La Motraye under GENERAL TRAVELS AND DESCRIPTIONS, vol. I of this work. The translation appeared four years ahead of the French publication. The author was considered an accurate observer. He had high praise for Kent, which was called the garden spot of England, inasmuch as this county supplied London with most of its garden produce. He thought that England was superior to the rest of Europe in grain and fruit.

1724   NICOLAS DE BOSC. Le Voyage de Nicolas de Bosc, Evêque de Bayeux, pour negocier la Paix entres les Couronnes de France et d'Angleterre en 1381. 4to. Paris.

1725   MURALT, BEAT LUDWIG. Lettres sur les Anglois et les François, et sur les Voiages. 3 vols. 8vo. Zürich.

> Some of these letters appeared in French in 1712, and the complete edition in 1725; 2nd edit., 1726; at Cologne, 1725; English version, 2 vols., 8vo, London, 1726; modern edit., with notes in English by Gould and Oldham, London, 1933. See below.
> His travels in France and England took place in 1694-95. While in England he picked up some Deistic views which on his return to his native Bern caused his banishment. He then began destroying the letters he had written recording his impressions of France and England, but fortunately most, if not all, of them were rescued and published. Translated into German, they gave a decided stamp to German views. His observations on the English way of life are objective in tone. He was much taken with the pleasant existence of the English country gentleman and his concern for his estate. He found the people as a whole distinguished for their common sense, but he deplored the immorality of London. Like most foreign visitors of this century, he was keenly interested in the stage, but in dramatic matters he was a disciple of Boileau.—From Kelly, *op. cit.*

> 1726   (In English.) Letters describing the Character and Customs of the English and French Nations, with a curious Essay on Travelling and a Criticism on Boileau's Description of Paris (Satyr VI), translated from the French, Remarks on the Letters. . . . 2 vols. 8vo. London.

1726 KNIGHT, SAMUEL. Life of Erasmus, more particularly that part of it which he spent in England, wherein an Account is given of his learned Friends and the State of Religion at that Time in both our Universities, with an Appendix containing several Original Papers. Portrait and plates. 8vo. Cambridge.

KÜCHELBECKER, JOHANN BASIL. Der nach Engelland reisende curieuse Passagier, oder kurtze Beschreibung der Stadt London. Hannover.

> 2nd edit., enlarged and corrected, Hannover, 1736; another volume on England appeared in 1737 as *Allerneueste Nachricht vom Königreich Engelland,* Frankfurt und Leipzig.
> The date of his visit to England is probably around 1717. He was much interested in the world of the theater and the opportunities available for witnessing plays. The English stage he considered to be inferior to the Parisian, but he conceded that the opera excelled all others with both its composition and its singers.—From Kelly, *op. cit.*

1732 BENTHEM, H. L. Neu-eröffneter Engeländischer Kirch- und Schulen-Staat, zum Nutzen, aller nach diesem Königreich Reisenden, auch anderer, insonderheit de Theologie Beflissenen . . . mit vielen . . . Nachrichten . . . von denem berühmtesten Gelehrten dieser Nation. 18 plates. 8vo. Leipzig.

> This is a survey of contemporary England, the Established Church, the state of education and learning.—Bookseller's Note.

CARERI, JOHN FRANCESCO GEMELLI. Travels through Europe in several Letters to the Counsellor Amato Danio (1686). In Churchill's *Collection of Voyages,* vol. VI, 111 ff., fol., London.

> See Careri this date under WEST EUROPE, vol. I of this work. Few individuals brought to the study of any one country a wider experience as a traveler than did Careri. His observations on England are of considerable interest.

LA CROZE, —. Histoire d'un Voyage littéraire fait dans l'année 1732 en France, en Angleterre, et en Holland. La Haye.

> So cited in Pinkerton, vol. XVII, where the same title is listed under the name of C. E. Jourdan and the date 1735. See Jordan under 1736 below.

1734 PÖLLNITZ, KARL LUDWIG, BARON VON. Lettres et Mémoires du Pöllnitz contenant les Observations qu'il a faites dans ses Voyages . . . en Allemagne, en Italie, en France, en Flanders, en Hollande, en Angleterre, etc. 3 vols. Liège.

> In English, 4 vols., 1737; 5 vols., Dublin, 1738; 2nd edit., 4 vols., London, 1739; 3rd, 5 vols., London, 1745.
> The English translator was S. Whatley. The main concern of this soldier of fortune in his travels through cities and courts was political matters. He thoroughly enjoyed, however, the good things that came his way. He was particularly delighted with England, going into raptures over its landscape, and would like nothing better than 1,000 pounds a year to keep him going in England, which he much preferred to Italy or France. London afforded him great pleasure and excitement with its shows, spectacles, and operas, though he found the music of Handel somewhat over his head. The memoirs cover the period of 1729-32.

> > 1737 (In English.) The Memoirs of Charles-Lewis, Baron de Pöllnitz, being the observations he made in his late Travels from Prussia through Germany, Italy, France, Flanders, Holland, England . . . In Letters to his Friend. Discovering not only the present State of the Chief Cities and Towns, but the Characters of the Principal Persons of the Several Courts. 4 vols. 8vo. London.

1735 VOLTAIRE, FRANCOIS AROUET DE. Letters concerning the English Nation. Translated from the French by John Lockman. 12mo. London.

> An edit., the same year, Dublin; so-called 2nd edit., London, 1741; Glasgow, 1752; in 12mo, London, 1760; edit. by Charles Whibley, London, 1929.

This work appeared in its English version before it did in its original tongue. It was received with universal applause. That these letters were written with an ironic eye turned towards France is suggested by the four discourses on the Quakers. That they were the means of introducing the French to Shakespeare is a claim made by Voltaire, though the strictures he passed on the dramatist must have confirmed his countrymen in their belief that French tragedy was much the superior. If Shakespeare had been fortunate enough to have been a contemporary of Addison, he might have learned how to write a drama correctly. Other letters contained appreciations of Bacon, Locke, Newton, Pope and Swift. And he points out to France how to learn from England to pay the honor due a genius before he is interred in the earth.

1736 JORDAN, CH. ET. Histoire d'un Voyage littéraire fait en 1733 en France, en Angleterre, et en Hollande. 8vo. La Haye.

See this title under La Croze, 1732, above. The present item is taken from Lanson, *Manuel Bibliographique,* an infinitely more trustworthy authority than Pinkerton.

MESNAGER, MONSEIGNEUR. Minutes of his Negotiations at the Court of England During the Four Last Years of her Late Majesty Queen Anne, containing many Curious Particulars of those Times. 2nd edit. 8vo. London.

1740 RIPPERDA, DUC DE. Memoirs: Spain, Moors, England, etc. 8vo. London.

The author died in 1737.

SCALIGER, JOSEPH JUSTUS. Visit to Holyrood in 1566 or 1567. In *Scaligerana.* 2 vols. 12mo. Amsterdam.

1744 BRAZEY, MOREAU DE. Le Guide d'Angleterre, ou relation curieuse d'un voyage de M. Brazey, avec une description de Londres, de Tunbridge, et d'Epsom. Amsterdam.

1745 GONZALES, DON MANOEL. The Voyage of Don Manoel Gonzales (late Merchant) of the City of Lisbon in Portugal, To Great-Britain: Containing An Historical, Geographical, Topographical, Political, and Ecclesiastical Account of England and Scotland; with a curious Collection of Things particularly Rare, Both in Nature and Antiquity. Translated from the Portuese Manuscript. In Osborne, *Collection of Voyages,* vol. I, 9-208. London.

Reprinted in Pinkerton, vol. II, 1-171, London, 1808-14.
Osborne's collection of voyages is sometimes called the Harleian and sometimes the Oxford Collection. Gonzales arrived in England, April, 1730 (n.s.). He was advised by the captain of the ship not to travel alone but to take a tutor. This latter in true tutorial style prepared him for his travels by giving him a long historical account of the island, with its geographical features. The prosiness of the preceptor is reflected in the traveler's relation, which dutifully describes places and things, climate, soil, manners, customs, etc., quite by rote.

LE BLANC, ABBE JOHN BERNARD. Lettres d'un François, concernant le gouvernement, la politique et les moeurs des Anglois et des François. 3 vols. 8vo. The Hague.

Another edit., 3 vols., Lyon, 1758; in English, 2 vols., London, 1746. See below.
Reviewed *Gent. Mag.,* vol. 16, Dec., with two letters as samples. These letters were written between 1734-37. The author, who was an historiographer and a member of several learned societies, stayed in England about seven years. His letters were highly praised.

1746 (In English.) Letters on the French and English Nations by Mons. l'Abbé Le Blanc. 2 vols. London.

1746 State of England in 1588; in a Letter from a Priest to the Spanish Ambassador at Paris: Account of our Preparations, Power and Riches, the Armada, Examination of Prisoners, etc. 8vo. London.

> This is a reprint, from what I do not know.

1750 LA BODERIE, ANTOINE LE FEVRE DE. Ambassades en -Angleterre. 5 vols. 12mo. Paris.

> In April, 1606, Henry IV appointed La Boderie ambassador to England, where he remained until 1611. His correspondence was voluminous. The impressions he records of James I and his court are not very favorable.—From Rye, 225.

1752 ALBERTI, GEORG WILHELM. Briefe betreffende [*sic*] den allerneuesten Zustand der Religion und der Wissenschaften in Gross Britannien. 4to. Hanover.

> The author visited England in 1745 as a theological student and remained there until 1747. Like most Germans he was interested in the theater and the opera. His praise of the actors was offset by his condemnation of the immorality of the plays themselves, which he thought must demoralize the youth.—From Kelly, *German Visitors*. He gives considerable space to a description of the country.

1753 ROBERT, —. Le Royaume d'Angleterre, les Sept Royaumes ou Heptarchie des Saxons avec la Principauté de Galles, et subdivisé en Shires ou Contés, par le Sr. Robert. 20 x 19 ins., with boundaries colored.

1753-54 VON UFFENBACH, ZACHARIAS CONRAD. Merkwürdige Reisen durch Niedersachsen, Holland und Engelland. 3 vols. Vol. I, Frankfurt und Leipzig; vols. II and III, Ulm.

> English portion, especially that dealing with Oxford and London, translated and edited by W. H. and W. J. C. Quarrell, 8vo, London, 1928; and London, 1934. See below.
> The author began his travels in 1702, reaching England in 1710, where he stayed five months using his eyes well and satisfying a far-ranging curiosity. Being interested in books, he bought many items and visited all sorts of collectors, generally known in England as Virtuosi, among them Dr. Hans Sloane, whose collection of natural curiosities gathered from many places was bought by the newly founded British Museum. He was attracted to mechanical inventions, for which he admired the English, though he found many of them merely exercises in ingenuity. He experienced the usual rudeness of the London mobs. His eyes and mind noticed many things passed over by the average traveler both native and foreign. His account of his two months' stay at the universities tells us much concerning the libraries and the scholars resident there. His interest extended to the stage and the opera as well.

> 1928 ———. Oxford in 1710, from the Travels of Z. Conrad von Uffenbach, edited by W. H. and W. J. C. Quarrell. 8vo. London.

> 1934 ———. London in 1710, from the Travels of . . . Translated and edited by W. H. Quarrell and Margaret Mare. 8vo. London.

1754 PLUMARD DE DANGEUL. Remarks on the Advantages and Disadvantages of France and Great-Britain with respect to Commerce, and to the other means of encreasing the Wealth and Power of a State. Being a (pretended) Translation from the English, written by Sir J. Nickolls . . . Translated from the French Original. London.

> The comparison runs between the general conditions in both lands, population, money, resources, government, commercial policy, taxation, monopoly, currency, etc. It was the result of a visit to Great Britain, undertaken with a view of securing suggestions for the French.—J. Williams, *Printed Materials*.

WILLIAM LE MARCHANT. Histoire de l'Erection originelle de l'Avancement et Augmentation, du Havre de la Ville de St. Pierre Port à Guernsey, avec quelques Remarques pour justifier la Propriété, ou Domaine utile que les Habitans de la dite Isle de Guernsey ont au dit Havre. 4to. Oxford.

1757   BELLIN, JACQUES NICOLAS. Essai géographique sur les Isles Britanniques, contenant une Description de l'Angleterre, l'Ecosse, et l'Irlande, tant pour le navigation des costes, que pour joindre aux cartes réduites de ces Isles, qui ont été dressés au dépost des cartes, plans, et journaux de la Marine pour le service des vaisseaux du roy, par ordre de Mons. de Machault, garde des sceaux de la France, ministre et secrétaire d'état, ayant le department de la marine, par M. Bellin, ingenieur de la marine et du dépost des plans, censeur royal de l'Academie de Marine, etc. 4to. Paris.

> This work has a general map and three distinct maps of the British Isles and views of various towns, castles, lighthouses, bearings into harbors. Bellin observes that the French maps of England are worth very little; he uses Moll's, 1710, Speed's *Theatre*, Morden, Kitchin, and Jefferys' *Small English Atlas*, 1751, Bowen's maps in the *System of Geography* and Jefferys' six-sheet map, the latest and best, which he says proves the want of exactness in the others.—Gough 29.

1759   EXPILLY, L'ABBE. Description historique et géographique des Isles Britanniques ou des Royaumes d'Angleterre, d'Ecosse et d'Irlande. Cartes géographiques. 12mo. Paris.

> His many fantastic details about Scotland lead one to believe that the Abbé was never in that country.—From Bain, *Les Voyageurs Français en Ecosse*.

1760   BARETTI, GIUSEPPE. Lettere familiari de Giuseppe Baretti ai suoi tre fratelli Filippo, Giovanni et Amadeo. 2 vols. Milan.

> 1770   (In English.) A Journey from London to Genoa, through England, Portugal, Spain, and France. 2 vols. 8vo. London.
> In its English form this book of travels is said by Baretti to be practically a new work. It proved to be very popular and called for several editions the same year. When he set out for Italy, Johnson advised him to keep a diary. While he gives up most space to his adventures in Portugal and Spain, he does not neglect that part of England he traversed on his way to his ship. The serge and tapestry factories at Exeter, the Cornish tin mines, and Eddystone Lighthouse come under his notice. See Baretti under 1770, WEST EUROPE, vol. I of this work.

GRAM, CHRISTEN. Kort Journal eller Reise-Beskrivelse til England. Christiania.

1761   Schottländische Briefe oder merkwürdige Nachrichten von Schottland. (So cited in *Camb. Bibliog.*, vol. II.)

1762   DU BOCAGE, MADAME FIQUET. Lettres sur l'Angleterre, tome III des *Oeuvres,* 1762-74. 2 vols. Paris.

> Letters dealing with her visit to England translated into English, 2 vols., London, 1770. These letters were addressed to Madame Duperron. They are considered still readable, much more so, in fact, than her poetry, for which she was then celebrated. She was popular in England, and her company was much sought after.

VON HERSEL, W. Briefe aus England. Hanover. (So cited in Pinkerton, vol. XVII.)

1763 BIELFIELD, BARON JACOB FRIEDRICH VON. Lettres familières et autres. Le Haye.

> 2nd German edit., as *Freundschaftliche Briefe,* Danzig und Leipzig; in English, London, 1768-70. See below.
> The Baron Bielfield was in London the first half of the year 1741 as a member of the Prussian Embassy, but he had made a visit earlier in 1737. His letters, dedicated to Voltaire, were written to Hagedorn, Pöllnitz, and other Germans interested in English life and culture. What his taste in literature was like may be measured by his praise of the poet Glover of *Leonidas* fame, whom he ranked next to Pope. He noticed the English enjoyment of rough, brutal sports, wherein they resembled the old Romans. He found much pleasure in the theater and the opera, though the latter had fallen off in excellence since the days of Handel's ascendancy.—From Kelly, *German Visitors.*

> 1768-70 (In English.) The Letters of Baron Bielfield, translated from the German by Mr. Hooper. 4 vols. London.

BURKHARDT, JOHANN GOTTLIEB. Bemerkungen auf einer Reise von Leipzig bis London an eine Freundin. Leipzig.

1766 LEROUGE, —. Curiosités de Londres et de l'Angleterre. 12mo. Bordeaux.

A Traveller's Opinion of the English in General. In *Annual Register,* vol. 9, 219-20, 1766.

> The author purports to be a foreigner. He connects the ferocity of the English with their climate and points out contradictions in their character—such as their insolence and rudeness and their generosity and sympathy.

1768(?) Gesichten der steeden London, Canterbury, & Colchester, en andere onleggende plaatzen, met haare voornaamste kirken, palacien, gebouwen, lust huizen en andere aarmerkelyke zaaken. In 82 zeer naauwkeurige prenten afgebeeld, verdeeld in twe deelen. 5 vols. 4to. Amsterdam.

> Cited by Gough, 47, without date. So it must have appeared before 1768.—The 3rd and 4th volumes contain views of colleges, etc., in Oxford and Cambridge after David Loggan; the 5th has views of Scotland.—Gough.

ZIMMERMAN, J. G. Vom Nationalstolze. 4th edit. Zürich.

> Translated into English by Samuel H. Wilcocke as *Essay on National Pride,* New York, 1799.
> This has much to say on the national traits of Englishmen. The work is frequently quoted by Kelly, *England and the Englishman in German Literature of the Eighteenth Century.*

1769-72 DAMIENS DE GOMICOURT, AUGUSTE-PIERRE. L'Observateur français à Londres ou Lettres sur l'état présent de l'Angleterre. 46 vols. in 12. Londres et Paris.

1769-73 BUSCHING, ANTON FRIEDRICH. Neue Erdbeschreibung. 12mo. Hamburg.

> For Great Britain see vol. IV. An earlier edition, translated into English as *A New System of Geography,* 6 vols., London, 1762.—Kelly, *op. cit.*

1770 D., C. (D'ORVILLE, CONTANT). Les Nuits anglaises ou recueil de traits singuliers. 4 pts. in 8. Paris (?). (So cited in Lanson, *op. cit.*)

GROSLEY, PIERRE JEAN. Londres. Folding plan. 3 vols. 12mo. Lausanne.

> Several later editions, among them one with notes by an Englishman, 3 vols., 12mo, Neufchatel; another, 4 vols., Paris, 1788; in English, by Thomas Nugent, 2 vols., 8vo, London, 1772; 3 vols., 12mo, Dublin, 1772. See below.

This work was much esteemed on the continent. It remained the best guide to London for thirty or forty years.—Smith, *Foreign Visitors*. As an account of England and the city of London by a foreigner, it is one of the best.

1772 (In English.) A Tour to London, or New Observations on England and its Inhabitants, by M. Grosley, translated by Thomas Nugent. 2 vols. 8vo. London.

His comment on Swift may be quoted: "The works of Swift are political and theological tracts, varnished over with a satire rather pungent than delicate, where it would be in vain to look for the refined raillery, or the delicacy and ease, of Paschal's Provincial Letters."

1774 GROSLEY, PIERRE JEAN. Londres. Ouvrage d'un François, augmentée dans cette édition des notes d'un Anglois. 3 tom. 12mo. Neufchatel.

RUTLEDGE, JEAN JACQUES, CHEVALIER DE. An Account of the Character and Manners of the French, with occasional Observations on the English. 2 vols. 8vo. London.

1776 (In French.) Essai sur le caractère et les moeurs des François comparés à ceux des Anglais. 12mo. Londres.

TOZE, M. E. The Present State of Europe, translated from the German by Thomas Nugent. 3 vols. London.

The German original appeared in 1767. Toze never was in England himself.

1771 KERGUELEN, TREMAREC DE. Relation d'un Voyage dans la Mer du Nord, aux côtes d'Islande, du Groênland, de Ferro, de Schettland, des Orcades, et de Norvège, fait en 1767 et 1768. Illustrations. 4to. Paris.

English version in Pinkerton, vol. I, 735-803. See this date under ADDENDA to ARCTIC REGIONS, vol. II of this work.

The author borrows largely in his account of the Orkney and Shetland Islands from Bellin's *Essai sur Isles Brittaniques*.—Mitchell, *List of Travels*.

RICHARD, ABBE. Character of the English Nation, drawn by a French pen. Translated from the French. London. (So listed in *Gent. Mag.*, vol. 42, Feb.)

Cited by Pinkerton, vol. XVII, with Richard as the translator.

1773 CHAMPIGNY, COLONEL CHEVALIER DE. Reveries d'un Habitant de Lillyput à Londres, à un de ses compatriotes, dans son Isle. Traduite du Lillyputien en François. 8vo. Londres.

The disbelief expressed by the bishop in the existence of Lilliput may well be transferred to this report.

1774 TAUBE, F. W. VON. Abschilderung der Englischen Manufacturen, Handlung, Schiffahrt, und Kolonien nach ihres jetzigen Beschaffenheit. Wien.

Taube was born in London, where his father, Christian Ernst von Taube, resided as physician to Queen Charlotte.

1774-81 JARS, GABRIEL. Voyages metallurgiques, ou recherches et observations sur les mines et forges de fer, la fabrication de l'acier, cette de ferblanc, et plusieurs mines de charbon de terre, le mines d'or, et d'argent . . . faites depuis l'année 1757 jusques et compris 1769, en Allemagne, Suède, Norvège, Angleterre et Ecosse. . . . 3 vols. 4to. Lyon.

This is an official report by a French expert. which takes up the legal as well as the technical aspects of the mining industry. It is of great value.—J. Williams, *op. cit.*

1775 DUTENS, LOUIS. Itinéraires des routes les plus frequentées, ou Journal de plusieurs voyages sur principales villes de l'Europe. 8vo. Paris.

> 4th edit., 1783; 6th, 1793. See Dutens under 1787 and 1792 below.
> Dutens was a French Huguenot, diplomat, traveler, numismatician, and man of letters who adopted England as his country. He first came to London in 1758, then became chaplain to the English Embassy at Turin, and later chargé-d'affaires in 1762. Having gained the friendship of the Duke of Northumberland, he was appointed curate of Elsdon and tutor to the Duke's second son, with whom he made the Grand Tour. He met Voltaire at Geneva and Frederick the Great at Potsdam, Gustav III of Brunswick, and other famous figures. His extensive travels and varied contacts with the great of his day should have given more lift to his Journal than proved to be the case. In the two earlier issues of his roadbook, the only British roads listed are those from Edinburgh to London, and from London to Dover; but in the 6th edition, in which the Journal extends to 1783, others were added. The road from Edinburgh to Belmont, the seat of Stewart Mackenzie, reminded him of scenes from Macbeth. Evidently he had no eye for the savage grandeur of the Highlands.

GRIMM, JOHANN FRIEDRICH KARL. Bemerkungen eines Reisenden durch Deutschland, Frankreich, England und Holland. 3 vols. Altenburg.

> This work appeared anonymously, but it was ascribed to Grimm in Holzmann & Schatta's *Anonymen-lexicon*. Grimm was in England from March 12 to May 12, 1774, taking special note of the state of hospitals, as he was body-physician to the Duke of Saxe-Gotha. Like other foreign visitors, he was much impressed with the honors paid to men of genius while they were still alive.—From Kelly, *German Visitors*.

1776 FERBER, J. J. Versuch einer Oryktography von Derbyshire in England auf einer Reise dahin. Mittau.

> English version the same year; this reprinted in Pinkerton, vol. I, 465-88, 1808-14. See below.

> 1776 (In English.) An Essay on the Oryctography of Derbyshire, a province of England, by the celebrated M. Ferber. Translated from the German. London.
> > This account gives a list of the principal works which treat of the natural history of England, beginning with 1700.

1776-88 STURZ, HELFERICH PETER. Briefe, im Jahre 1768 auf einer Reise im Gefolge des Königs von Danemark geschrieben. In *Deutsches Museum*. Leipzig.

> These letters tell of his movements while attached to the court of Christian VII of Denmark, and while visiting in London. He belonged to the band of enthusiasts who, like Lessing and Möser, were fighting to free German drama from dependence on the French, and like them helped to turn German dramatists to their own past for subject matter. While in England he became acquainted with notabilities of the stage and the world of art. Naturally he gave whole hearted admiration to his friend Garrick. These *Briefe* are the best comments yet written by any German on England.—From Kelly, *op. cit.*

1777 LACOMBE, FRANCOIS. Observations sur Londres et ses environs par un Atheronne de Berne. Londres.

> Another edit., London, 1784. See below.
> Reviewed *Gent. Mag.*, vol. 65, 381-83, with some strictures on the work.

> 1784 LACOMBE, FRANCOIS. Tableau de Londres, un Précis de la Constitution de l'Angleterre et de sa decadence. Londres.
> > Lacombe asserted that if the war continued three years longer, there would be left only soldiers, beggars, and thieves. London was full of robbers and footpads, with whom the drivers of coaches were in collusion. To avoid being attacked, it was neccessary for two men to go together armed. He praised the English treatment of horses as compared with that of Frenchmen, who were really executioners. He found the English jury system beautiful in theory, but in practice it led innocent men to the gallows. To improve justice he proposed to dissect alive coiners and murderers. Englishmen attached themselves to no one, because they

considered strangers enemies whom they dared not openly offend, though their treatment of foreigners was fair enough. The English character had deteriorated since 1756.

1779   COYER, L'ABBE. Nouvelles Observations sur l'Angleterre. Paris.

> In *Complete Works,* 2 vols., Paris, 1782-83. See below.

> 1782-83 COYER, L'ABBE. Oeuvres Completes, (including) Voyage de Hollande, Histoire Cochinchinoise, Observations sur l'Angleterre. 2 vols. 8vo. Paris.

COUDAR, —. L'Espion français à Londres, ou Observations critiques sur l'Angleterre et les Anglais. Paris (?).

NIVEL, H. Voyage forcé, ou manière de tirer avantage de circonstances, tiré des Mémoires d'un Homme des Lettres qui a fait un long séjour en Angleterre et en a observé les moeurs et les usages. Paris.

1780   Beyträge zur Kentniss Gros-Britanniens vom Jahre 1779. 8vo. Lemgo. (So cited in Anderson, *Book of Brit. Topog.*)

BJÖRNSTÅHL, JACOB JONAS. Resa til Frankrike, Italien, Sweitz, Tyskland, Holland, England, Turkien och Grekeland, beskriven af och efter Jacob Jonas Björnståhl. 5 vols. Stockholm.

> Another edit., 6 vols., Stockholm, 1784; in German, Rostock.
> The chief objects of these travels were public libraries, manuscripts, and scarce books, with the lives of learned men. The traveler lost his life in Macedonia.—Pinkerton, vol. XVII.

CARACCIOLI, MARQUIS. The Travels of Reason in Europe. Translated from the the French of Marquis Caraccioli. 8vo. London.

> Reviewed *Gent. Mag.,* vol. 50, 282-84. Reason, under the name and guise of *Lucidor,* an amiable philosopher, is the Traveller and Observer. He was supposed to have visited Europe in 1769. Beginning with Turkey, he proceeded through Russia, Poland, Sweden, Denmark, Prussia, Germany, and the Netherlands to England. His comments on the English, as given in the review, show them to be not wholly admirable in manners and temper. London he found to be inferior to Paris. Reason also visited Scotland and Ireland. He then journeyed on to Portugal and Spain, Corsica, Sicily, Malta, etc., back to France. The reviewer regards the work as a correct representation of the manners of Europe and as exhibiting the principles of Reason and sound policy without bitterness or animosity. But the translation is termed inadequate.

Die Flucht eines Franzosen nach England, oder Bemerkungen über den Charakter und die Gebräuche der Englischen Nation. 8vo. Frankfort.

GAULANDRI, ANGELO. Lettere odoporiche di Francia, Inghilterra, etc. Venice.

LESCURE, —. Les Amants françois à Londres ou les Délices de l'Angleterre. Paris (?). (So cited in Lanson.)

MARGAROT, M. Histoire du Relation d'une Voyage: L'Angleterre, France, Italie, Alsace, Hollande, etc. Anecdotes et descriptions. 2 vols. 8vo. Londres.

1781   BÜSCHEL, JOHANN GABRIEL BERNHARD. Bemerkungen auf einer Reise durch verschiedene Theile von England, Schottland und Wales, aus dem Englischen, nebst Anmerkungen des Übersetzers. Leipzig.

This is little more than an indiscriminate compilation of quotations from English writers, detailed descriptions of art collections, and excerpts from guide books. It testifies in its matter to the vogue of Sterne in Germany.—From Kelly, *German Visitors*. See Büschel under 1784 below.

1781-82 VOLKMANN, JOHANN JACOB. Neueste Reisen durch England vorzüglich in Absicht auf die Kunstsammlungen, Naturgeschichte, Oekonomie, Manufacturen und Landsitte der Grossen. 4 vols. Leipzig.

Volkmann was in England in 1761.—His book was a mine of information on the constitution, geography, topography, and other aspects of the "queen of the isles." It reads like a work compiled for the use of German travelers to England.—From Clare Williams. His chief interest was in the fine arts, of which the many valuable collections in England furnished good examples. He is frequently quoted by Kelly, *England and the Englishman in German Literature of the Eighteenth Century*.

1781-85 DEICHSEL, JOHANN GOTTLIEB. Reise durch Deutschland nach Holland und England, in den Jahren 1717-19. In Bernoulli, *Archiv*, vol. VIII, pt. iii, "Aufenthalt in England." Berlin.

TITIUS, DR. C. V. Reisejournal von seiner im Jahre 1777 durch Deutschland nach Holland, England und Frankreich angestellten Reise. In Bernoulli, *Archiv*, vols. IX-XI.

ULRICH VON VERDUN. Neueste Reisen durch Engelland, Dennemark, und Schweden (1670-77). In Bernoulli, *Archiv*, vol. VI.

1782 ÖDER, JOHANN LUDWIG. Beyträge zur Oekonomie, Kameral- und Polizeywissenschaft aus den Berichten eines deutschen Kameralisten von seinen Reisen nach der Schweiz, Frankreich, Holland und England im Jahre 1759 und 1763. Dessau.

1783 FORSTER, JOHANN REINHOLD. Tableau d'Angleterre pour l'année 1780 continué par l'Editeur jusqu'à l'année 1783. 8vo. Dessau.

Through his long association with Captain James Cook as naturalist on Cook's second circumnavigation (1772-75), his lengthy residence in England, and his own scientific abilities, Forster was well known to the English public. He cherished a grudge against the English, however, from a feeling that his merits had not been properly recognized and left for Halle in 1783. His book shows his anti-bias, but even without this trait, it has little value. He charges the English with encouraging the arts and sciences merely out of whim, with being uncritical and inartistic. Even their music is not their own, being entirely in the hands of foreigners, such as Bach, Abel, Fischer, Cramer, etc.—From Kelly, *German Visitors*.

GÜNDERODE, FRIEDRICH JUSTINIAN, FREIHERR VON. Beschreibung einer Reise aus Teutschland durch einen Theil von Frankreich, England und Holland. 2 vols. in 1. Breslau.

The author began his travels in 1774 and continued on the move till the summer of 1775. Being a South German, he was drawn rather to the French than to the English, though he regarded England as more enlightened than France. London he found to be cleaner than Paris but the Parisians to be more friendly and hospitable. Like many other foreign visitors, he commented on the English tendency to suicide, especially in November, the "hanging month." He did not approve of English drama though he enjoyed the scenic realism of the settings. Garrick was for him the supreme actor.—From Kelly, *op. cit.*

MORITZ, KARL PHILIP. Reisen eines Deutschen in England im Jahre 1782. Berlin.

Translated into English, London, 1795; reviewed *Gent. Mag.*, vol. 65, 750; in Pinkerton, vol. II, 489-573, 1808-14; in Cassell's National Library, 1887; in Oxford Misc. series, Oxford,

1926. It has been suggested that the translator of the 1795 edition may have been one of the two daughters of Charles Godfrey Woide, a native of Poland but domiciled as a preacher in London. See below.

This naive yet sensible travel book is one of the most entertaining accounts of England by a foreigner that has been published. Long remembered will be his account of a drinking bout at Oxford, his unpleasant experiences as a foot traveler, his perilous ride in the basket at the back of a coach, etc. His electing to be modern and see the country on foot exposed him to much suspicion and disagreeable encounters at inns and on the road. His visit ran from the end of May to the middle of July. He belonged to the group of German enthusiasts who advocated absolute freedom of personal expression. His novel *Anton Reise,* which is a veiled autobiography, is an expression of the *Sturm und Drang* movement in Germany.

1795   MORITZ, CARL PHILIP. Travels on Foot, etc., translated from the German by a Lady. London.

> The reviewer in the *Gentleman's Magazine* comments adversely on this work. How could one expect, he asks, a correct account of England by a foreigner who rambled on foot? It is a dull farrago of blunders, misadventures, commonplace observations, and low humour. This charge, however, the modern reader is not inclined to accept.

1784   BÜSCHEL, J. C. B. Neue Reisen eines Deutschen nach und in England im Jahre 1783. Ein Pendant zu des Herrn Professor Moritz' Reisen. Berlin.

> See Büschel under 1781 above. This work apparently arose out of the sensation created in Germany by Moritz's book. It has been denied that he ever was in England, but no authority is quoted for the statement. The author was a playwright and critic, but little is known of him beyond the fact that he was a native of Leipzig, where he lived many years as a pensioned regiment quartermaster. The above travel book is in the form of a diary, whose first entry on England is dated June 10, 1783. He goes beyond all others in eulogizing England, "whose very name is music to German ears." He has little to say of the theaters, which were closed during his stay; he notices, however, the unruly conduct of the riff-raff, which knew no bounds.—Quoted.

FABRICIUS, JOHANN CHRISTIAN. Briefe aus London vermischten Inhalts. Dessau und Leipzig.

> This writer visited England first in 1767-78, and several times later. He was as full of enthusiasm for the country as was any of his contemporaries, but he points out many of the evils darkening the English scene—the poverty, vice, immorality, robberies, etc. Offsetting the seamy side of the national life is his tribute to the positive virtues of English character, such as the animated stir of London, the quiet beauty of the country, and the constant display of hospitality, and what all foreigners admired—the freedom of speech and action. He notes the intellectual insularity of Englishmen, their ignorance of continental literature and scholarship. But he admits their superiority in science. He gives a full account of the decline of the English stage after the death of Garrick as well as a good critical estimate of theatrical life during this period.—From Kelly, *op. cit.*

————. Mineralogische und technologische Bemerkungen auf einer Reise durch verschiedene Provinzen in England und Schottland, von J. C. Fabricius, mit Anmerkungen und Zulagen von J. J. Ferber. Dessau und Leipzig. (So cited in Pinkerton, vol. XVII.)

LINDEMANN, CHRISTOPH FRIEDRICH HEINRICH. Reisebeschreibungen über einen Theil von Italien, Frankreich und Engelland. Celle.

> This is signed "C. F. H. L.," identified as Lindemann in Holzmann & Bohatta. Lindemann visited England in the summer of 1782. In his account of his visit he departs from the pattern of the average description, in that the more he saw of other peoples the more highly he thought of his own. Since he was in London after the two chief theaters were closed for the summer, he missed opportunities of seeing Shakespeare played. He did get the chance to see the *Beggar's Opera,* which greatly delighted him. He thought that comedy was done better in France but admitted that the English excelled in tragedy.—From Kelly, *op. cit.*

VOLKMANN, J. J. Neueste Reisen durch Schottland und Irland. Leipzig.

1784-88 WENDEBORN, GEBHARD FRIEDRICH AUGUST. Der Zustand des Staats der Religion, der Gelehrsamkeit und der Kunst in Grossbritannien gegen das Ende des achtzehnten Jahrhunderts. 4 vols. Berlin.

> This is an expansion of an earlier work—*Beiträge zur Kenntnis Grossbritanniens vom Jahre 1779,* hrsg. von Georg Forster, Lemgo, 1780; English version, 2 vols., London, 1791. See below and also Wendeborn under 1793 below.
> His residence in England from 1768 to 1790 as pastor of the newly formed German church in Ludgate gave Wendeborn unexcelled opportunities to get acquainted with the land and its people. He helped the English in turn toward a knowledge of things German by publishing in 1774 his *Elements of the German Language.* And his connection with the *Hamburger Correspondent* as the London correspondent from 1779 to 1792 provided Germans with additional information on England. He was quite a severe critic of the faults of the British and by 1790 was of the opinion that the country was deteriorating. His remarks on Shakespearean performances are of much interest. Mrs. Siddons he thought had been overrated.—From Kelly, *op. cit.*

> 1791 (In English.) A View of England Towards the Close of the Eighteenth Century. 2 vols. London.
> > This translation was made under the author's supervision. There is listed an edition in English, Dublin, 1790. Reviewed *Gent. Mag.,* vol. 61, 256-58. Here the work is spoken of as "the production of a man of learning," and the author is lauded for adhering to his motto from Shakespeare—"Speak of me as I am."

1785 ARCHENHOLZ, WILHELM VON. England und Italien. 2 vols. Leipzig.

> Another edit., 5 Teile, Leipzig, 1787; in French, 3 vols., Paris (Pinkerton, vol. XVII), Bruxelles; in English, 2 vols., London, 1789; Dublin, 1791 (from the French); London, 1797. See below.
> The original work was so popular that Archenholz was moved to make a continuation of it in 20 vols., to which he gave the title: *Annalen der Brittischen Geschichte des Jahres* [*sic*] *1788-96.* Also during his editorship of *Minerva, ein Journal historischen und politischen Inhalts,* from 1792 to 1812, he gave England a prominent place.

> 1788 (In French.) Tableau de l'Angleterre et de l'Italie . . . Traduit de l'Allemand. 3 vols. Gotha (also Paris and Bruxelles and, according to another listing, Carlsruhe).

> 1789 (In English.) A Picture of England. 2 vols. London.
> > This is translated from that part of his *England und Italien* which deals with England. Archenholz did more than any other man to present a complete picture of England to Germans. His fifteen years of study and travel well qualified him as an observer of different peoples and their manners, and his views of England served Germany for a quarter of a century as their chief source of information. He greatly admired English freedom, which he judged to be based on trial by jury, habeas corpus act, parliamentary representation, and the liberty of the press. Industry and commerce, science and literature all interested him. He was in England for six years.—From Kelly, *op. cit.*

> 1791 (In English.) A Picture of England, containing a Description of the Laws, Customs and Manners of England, interspersed with Curious and Interesting Anecdotes of the King of Denmark, Prince of Wales, Louis XV, Lord North, Mr. Fox, Mr. Pitt, Lord Thurlow, Lord Chatham, Mr. Luttrell, Mr. Wilkes, Mr. Horne Tooke, Lord Clive, Mrs. Siddons, etc., translated from the French. 8vo. Dublin.
> > Frequent references to the views of this traveler occur also in Kelly, *England and the Englishman in German Literature.*

H., COMTE F. DE. Lettres sur la France, l'Angleterre, et l'Italie. Genève.

LENZEN, JOACHIM FRIEDRICH. Anmerkungen und Erinnungen über Herrn Professor Moritzens Briefe aus England, von einem Deutschen, der auch einmal in England gewesen ist, an Herrn L. G—e in Berlin. Göttingen.

Moritz's book reminded Lenzen of happy days he had spent in England, and awoke in him a desire to emend Moritz and put England in the right. He reproached the latter for his subjectivity, which was in bad taste, and corrected his slips in the language. His aim thus avowed denied him any opportunity for regular description of the country. He also commented on the wretched translations from English which Germans have to put up with. —From Kelly, *German Visitors*.

Reisen und Begebenheiten in Frankreich, Italien, Deutschland und Engelland, eines Cavaliers im Dienst Gustav Adolphs König in Schweden, und Karl I. König in England. 2 vols. Leipzig.

1785-86 MEYER, J. H. L. Bemerkungen auf einer Reise durch Holland, England und Norddeutschland im Jahre 1771 und 1774. In Fabri, *Neues geographisches Magazin,* vol. I, pt. 1, 89-102; vol. II, pt. 1, 48-71. Halle.

The author visited England in the fall of 1771. His observations are rather trivial. He finds traveling conditions in England superior, and gives such advice as to make his work something of a tourist guidebook. His attitude is one of admiration.—From Kelly, *op. cit.*

1786 BRANDES, ERNST. Bemerkungen über das Londoner, Parizer und Wiener Theatre. Göttingen.

Brandes spent the period of 1784-85 in England. There he became acquainted with Burke and submitted himself to the philosophical and political ideas of the English statesman, and in turn used them to stem the enthusiasm in Germany for revolutionary France. His discussion of the English theater is the fullest so far given by German visitors and should be included in the reading of any student of eighteenth century dramatic history.— From Kelly, *op. cit.*

BÜSCH, JOHANN GEORG. Bemerkungen auf einer Reise durch einen Theil der Vereinigten Niederlande und Englands. Hamburg.

Büsch spent part of a ten weeks' summer vacation in England in 1777. His impressions of the Dutch were far more favorable than of the English who, he admits, did excel in commerce and industry, a subject of which he was a student.—From Kelly. *op. cit.*

CORDES, FERDINAND (a frequent contributor to *Deutsches Museum.*) *Schreiben aus London,* May 5, 1786; Sept., 1786. (Cited in Kelly, *op. cit.,* Appendix.)

HARTIG, FRANZ PAULA, GRAF VON. Lettres sur la France, l'Angleterre et l'Italie. Genève.

In German as *Interessante Briefe über Frankreich, England und Italien,* Eisenach. These letters were written during the years 1775-76. Hartig was a gifted young man, advanced in the diplomatic service and a favorite of Maria Theresa and Joseph II, and thoroughly French in his culture. Being well conversant with English, he was enabled to make much of his stay in England. He greatly admired English women, English liberty and English laws. His command of the language qualified him to judge critically of English drama and the actors. Garrick, whom he knew personally, he greatly admired for his intellectual capacities. His appreciation of English dramatic achievements was conditioned by his French predilections, which led him to condemn the mixture of low and lofty diction in English plays.—From Kelly, *op. cit.*

LA COSTE, —. Voyage philosophique d'Angleterre fait en 1783 et 1784. 2 vols. Paris.

RIESCH, BARON J. W. DE. Lettres sur un voyage dans quelques Provincez meridionales d'Angleterre. Dresden.

WATZDORF, HEINRICH MAXIMILIAN FRIEDRICH VON. Briefe zur Charakteristik von England gehörig, geschrieben auf einer Reise im Jahre 1784. Leipzig.

Watzdorf was a Saxon, who had served as an officer in the Saxon army and apparently had traveled in Italy before coming to England. His account in the form of travel letters shows the influence of Moritz and Sterne. The fact that he felt called upon to defend England and the English shows that by now German *Schwärmerei* for England had begun to wane. He found the Englishman more gay than the Frenchman, more polite and amiable. He could not help deplore the national addiction to alcohol, which was only too obvious in eighteenth century England. The refusal to learn foreign languages came in for censure also. His accounts of the theater are very informing in their descriptions of scenery and setting used, lighting effects, dramatic ability of the performers, whom he finds superior to both the German and French. He was delighted with English folk music, such as was performed at Bowling Green and Priesthood Common, and contradicts the common opinion that the English language was not suitable to vocal performance. The English organ which he heard at Vauxhall impressed him with its sweet and soft tone. He had little fault to find with the behaviour of audiences at public performances.—From Kelly, *op. cit.*

1787 DUTENS, LOUIS. L'Ami des étrangers qui voyagent en Angleterre. 12mo. Paris.

Another edit., 12mo, Londres, 1789; again, 1794.

Eenige Berichten omtrens Groot Britanie en Yrlonde. 8vo. 's Graavenhaage.

MYLIUS, CHRISTLOB. Tagebuch seiner Reise nach England. In Bernoulli, *Archiv*, vol. V, 85-176; vol. VI, 39-140; vol. VII. Leipzig.

Mylius, who was a cousin of Lessing, had a rather shady reputation because of adventures of a dubious character. One of these had something to do with the break between Voltaire and Frederick the Great. He started the first German periodical devoted entirely to the theater. He set out for England and America to engage in scientific research, reaching London, Aug. 22, 1753, where he died March 7, 1754. He prepared under Hogarth's supervision a translation of the latter's *Analysis of Beauty*, published 1754 as *Zergliederung der Schönheit*. The theater naturally engaged much of his attention and was the subject of many of his discussions. He disliked *Romeo and Juliet* but admired *Volpone*. The quality of his taste in drama may be gauged by his praise of Glover's *Boadicea*.—From Kelly, *op. cit.*

1788 BORUWLASKI, JOSEPH. Memoirs of the celebrated Dwarf, Joseph Boruwlaski, a Polish Gentleman, containing a faithful and curious account of his Birth, Education, Marriage, Travels and Voyages, written by himself, translated from the French by M. des Carrières. 8vo. London.

For an account of this object of curiosity while in England, see under this date, CONTINENTAL EUROPE, vol. I of this work. He remained in England till his death (1837), living mainly on what he took in from concerts.

CAMBRY, J. Promenades d'Automne en Angleterre. 8vo. Paris.

Gemälde von London. 8vo. (Place?)

L., M. D. S. D. Londres et ses environs, ou guide des voyageurs curieux, etc. 2 vols. Paris. (See De Serre this date below.)

2nd edit., Paris, 1790.

POORTEN, —. Bemerkungen einer Reise durch England. In the *Geographical Journal*, vol. 10. (So cited in Pinkerton, vol. XVII.)

ROCHE, SOPHIE VON LA. Tagebuch einer Reise durch Holland und England von der Verfasserin von Rosaliens Briefen. Offenbach.

> Translated into English by Clare Williams, London, 1933. See below.
> Sophie was the representative woman of culture in Germany, full of enthusiasm for all intellectual movements, and widely acquainted with the literati of Germany. While her stay in England extended only to forty days in all, she managed to fill a good sized volume of diary. And in this period (1786) she got to know a wide circle of eminent people, and contrived to see a great deal of the amusement places.—From Kelly. Her account of London especially is a parade of names familiar to a reader in 18th century life and literature. And her diary provides a serviceable guide to the places one should visit as well as detailed information on the contents of museums. At Bedlam she sees Mrs. Nicholson; she talks with Lord George Gordon of the Gordon riots fame; she has much to say of Warren Hastings, John Wesley, Sir George Saville, William Herschel, the astronomer, Angelica Kaufmann, painter, etc. At any time she is likely to break out into sentimental raptures. She herself is mentioned in quite a variety of works in German literature.— From Clare Williams (translator).

> 1933   (In English.) Sophie in London, being the Diary of Sophie von la Roche. Translated from the German, with an Introductory Essay by Clare Williams. With a Foreword by G. M. Trevelyan. 8vo. London.
> The Introduction gives an animated account of the English scene as viewed by Sophie.

DE SERRE DE LA TOUR. Londres et ses environs, ou guide des voyageurs curieux. 2 tom. 12mo. Paris.

WIMPFEN, BARON VON. Souvenirs d'un voyageur. Paris.

> Translated into German, Darmstadt, 1814.
> Wimpfen was chamberlain to her Highness, the Duchess of Wirtemberg. His education was French and service in the French army had advanced him to the rank of general. He was well read in French literature and acquainted with the chief English writers of the century. He made several visits to England, the first of a few weeks' extent in 1788 or earlier, again for seven months in 1793, and for nearly two years in 1795-97, and once more from August, 1799, to April, 1800. His *Souvenirs* or *Briefe* date mainly from his first visit. He found the English amiable enough as a people, but he notes as a fault the action of the British government against the city of Boston, and on the stage, the practice of representing Frenchmen as coxcombs, whereas the latter invariably show the English to be men of worth. He dislikes the mixture of high and low language in English drama and the tendency to cater to the vulgar. His distinction between Shakespeare as dramatist and Shakespeare as poet is, as Kelly points out, a symptom of the coming romantic attitude.—From Kelly, *op. cit.*

1789   DECREMPS, H. Le Parisien à Londres. Amsterdam.

REILLY, F. J. J. VON. Schauplatz der fünf Thiele der Welt. 3 vols. Fol. Wien.

> Das Königreich Scotland: 10½ × 7¾ ins.; Das Königreich Scotland: Nördlicher Theil und Südlicher Theil, each 7⅜ × 10 ins.

SPRITTER, REV. Reise über Holland nach England; in *Die Reisenden fur Länder- und Völkerkunde*, von zwein Gelehrten hrsg., vol. III, 36-191. Nürnberg.

> This anonymous work seems to be largely based on guidebooks. The reasons for attributing it to Spritter are given by Kelly (p. 88). It is an uninspired work, exhibiting personal feeling chiefly in its description of the miseries of crossing the Channel, which generally turned out to be an unwelcome experience. His impressions of England are on the whole favorable.—From Kelly, *op. cit.*

Voyage au Pays de Bambouk, suivi de notions intéressantes sur les castes Indiennes, sur l'Angieterre, et sur la Hollande. Paris.

1790 ANGIOLINI, IL CAVALIERE. Lettere sopra l'Inghilterra, Scozia e Olanda. 2 vols. 8vo. Firenze.

> Translated into English in *Scots. Mag. and Edinburgh Lit. Misc.*, vol. 72, Edinburgh, 1810. The author visited Paisley, Glasgow, Edinburgh, and the Highlands. He discusses costume, mountains, state of learning, eminent Scotchmen, industrial progress, and character of the natives.—Mitchell, *List of Travels*. Part of the work treats of manufactures, politics, law, punishment, Quakers, education, banking, canals, etc.—J. Williams.

SAINT FOND, FAUJAS DE. Voyage en Angleterre, en Ecosse et aux Iles Hébrides, ayant pour objet les sciences, les arts, l'histoire naturelle et les moeurs. 8vo. Paris.

> Translated into English, 2 vols., 8vo, London, 1799; modern edition, Glasgow, 1907. See below.
> Some of his countrymen who visited Scotland later complained of his lack of interest in the picturesque, finding his account too dry. But while not romantically inclined, he was sympathetic and tried to understand the life, manners, and culture of the Scotch. He understood and spoke English, had read accounts of the country, and was a learned and respected geologist. He tried to combine in his account his scientific interests and his experiences as a traveler, the one purely objective and the other personal and subjective. But the geologist usually takes the place of the picturesque traveler. He visited the chief men of science, Banks, president of the Royal Society, Herschel at his observatory, the city of Birmingham with its advanced application of technical knowledge. His great interest was the discovery of basaltic rocks, which he found occasionally where they were not, except, of course, at Staffa, where he reveled in their profusion. His account of a bagpipe competition in the Highlands is extremely amusing. His book came out at a time when France was much excited over Ossianic Scotland. His work offers much information on the use of applied science in English industries. His visit was made in 1784.

> 1799 (In English.) Travels in England, Scotland and the Hebrides, Undertaken for the purpose of examining the State of the Arts, The Sciences, Natural History and Manners, translated from the French of B. Faujas Saint-Fond. 7 engravings. 2 vols. 8vo. London.
> The edition of 1907 was edited by the well known Scotch geologist Arch. Geikie, who points out both the accuracies and inaccuracies of the original.

Tournée faite dans la Grande-Bretagne par un Français parlant la langue Anglaise. 8vo. Paris.

> This was written in the form of letters to a friend in France during a trip of ten days in 1788. The recital is simple and natural but he sees things as a tourist and man of affairs. He passes from a rapturous description of Loch Lomond to a talk on the cotton factories at Dumbarton.—Bain, *Les Voyageurs Français en Ecosse*.

1790-91 BAHRDT, KARL FRIEDRICH. Reise nach London, Pt. 3 of Geschichte seines Lebens, von ihm selbst geschrieben. Pt. 1, Frankfurt à Main, 1790; pts. 2-4, Berlin, 1791.

> Bahrdt was a theological adventurer, beginning as an orthodox clergyman and ending as a founder of a school of naturalistic religion of his own. His visit to England in 1777-78 was for the purpose of obtaining adherents for his Institute at Oppenheim, which was to reform the world, and to better his financial condition, which was at a low ebb. His efforts met with little encouragement. Despite his ignorance of English, he managed to get much enjoyment out of his stay, and came to regard the people as "the most perfect nation" he knew.—From Kelly, *op. cit.*

1791 FORSTER, JOHANN GEORG. Voyage philosophique et pittoresque en Angleterre et en France fait en 1790. Paris.

> See Forster under 1791-94 below.

HAYDN, JOSEPH. Journal of London Observations.

> Haydn made a visit to London in 1791. Whether the above is a printed account of his experiences in London I have not been able to discover.

MEISTER, JACQUES HENRI. Souvenirs d'un voyage en Angleterre. 12mo. Paris.
See Meister under 1795 below.

1791-94 FORSTER, JOHANN GEORG ADAM. Ansichten vom Niederrhein, von Brabant,
Flandern, Holland, England und Frankreich, im April, Mai und Junius 1790.
3 Theile. Berlin.

> Modern German edition, Halle, 1893. See below.
> Forster and his father, Johann Reinhold Forster, had been associated with Captain
> James Cook on his second voyage round the world (1772-75). Through their long asso-
> ciation with England and the English, both father and son were qualified to give a tem-
> perate estimate of the island and its people, provided one discounts the bias generated in
> their friction with the Admiralty Office. Forster left England in 1788 but returned in 1790
> accompanied by one who was to be greatest among German scientists, Alexander von
> Humboldt, then a young man of twenty-one. His descriptions of England do not form a
> consistent whole, but they furnish an adequate representation of the face of England. His
> work is regarded as one of the most satisfying treatments of the subject yet written by
> Germans. His views are justly balanced between what is commendable and what is not.
> He looked upon England as the home of political freedom, and as a land where class
> distinctions did not obtrude so noticeably as in other countries. See Kelly, *op. cit.*

> 1893 FORSTER, JOHANN GEORG. Briefe und Tagebücher Georg Forsters von seiner Reise am
> Niederrhein, in England und Frankreich im Frühjahr 1790. Hrsg. von. A. Leitz-
> mann. Halle.

1791-96 KÜTTNER, KARL GOTTLIEB. Beyträge zur Kenntnis vorzüglich des Innern von
England und seiner Einwohner. 16 vols. Leipzig.

> Küttner was also the author of *Briefe über Irland*, 1785, and of articles on English cul-
> ture in the *Hallische Zeitung* and *Allgemeine Deutsche Bibliothek*. His letters in his mag-
> num opus date back to 1783. His personal preferences are not clearly visible, but they do
> indicate a belief in England's superiority to other lands. Much of his material is taken
> from other German travelers and the whole seems to have been intended as a guidebook.
> His account of the stage is valuable, expecially of the provincial theater, such as that at
> Manchester, where he spent the winter of 1783-84. This theater was reckoned as being
> next to those of London. He had ample opportunity of witnessing Shakespearean repre-
> sentations, which were given almost every week. Here, as in other English tragedies,
> realism was carried to a revolting extreme. His descriptions of the manner of acting,
> stage properties, and costuming make interesting and informative reading.—From Kelly,
> *op. cit.*

1792 CHANTREAU, PIERRE NICOLAS. Voyage dans les trois royaumes d'Angleterre,
d'Ecosse et d'Irlande, fait en 1788 et 1789; ouvrage où l'on trouve tout ce qu'il y
a de plus intéressant dans les moeurs des habitants de la Grande-Bretagne, leur
population, leurs opinions religieuses, leurs préjuces, leurs usages, leur constitution politique, leur forces de terre et de mer, les progrés qu'ils ont faits dans les
arts et dans les sciences, avec des anecdotes aussi piquantes que philosophiques:
par le Citoyen Chantreau. Avec trois cartes et dix gravures. 3 vols. 8vo. Paris.

> This traveler had read up previously on his subject but he depended rather more on
> his personal observations for his judgments. His trip was an extended one. He visited
> Edinburgh, where he discreetly mocks at the false portraits of Scottish kings exhibited in
> Holyrood Palace, Glasgow, St. Andrews, Aberdeen, where his party embarked for the
> Orkneys and Shetlands, and later the Hebrides. He passes in review of his personal
> opinion everything he met with in Scotch manners, costumes, festivals, marriages, funerals,
> song, music, etc. Naturally the question of Ossian was much in evidence. What was
> unusual in a Frenchman was his appreciation of national aspects of Scotch music.—From
> Bain, *op. cit.* He gives a tolerably fair statement of the political constitution, religious
> opinions, manners, prejudices, state of the arts and sciences, etc., of Great Britain.—
> Lowndes, vol. II.

DUTENS, LOUIS. Le guide, moral, physique, et politique des étrangers qui voyagent
en Angleterre. 12mo. Londres.

HASSELL, FRIEDRICH WILHELM VON. Briefe aus England. Hanover.

Hassell was an officer in the Hanoverian forces who was called to England in 1790 to be tutor to an English prince (evidently William Frederick, son of the Duke of Gloucester). This position offered him many chances to become acquainted with men in the highest stations in English life. He was of an enthusiastic disposition, finding many occasions to go into raptures, which culminated in the general blessing he pronounced on England at the conclusion of his ten months' stay. He was tremendously moved by the acting of Mrs. Siddons, especially in the role of Jane Shore and that of the Grecian Princess. The tears shed by the audience and their audible sobbing, also commented on by Sophie von la Roche, testify to the dramatic abilities of this great actress.—From Kelly, *op. cit.*

SCHÜTZ, FRIEDRICH WILHELM VON. Briefe über London, ein Gegenstück zu des Herrn Archenholz' England und Italien. Hamburg.

Schütz's short visit took place apparently in 1791, for he mentions seeing at the Pantheon the opera *Idolide,* the first performance of which was given on April 30, 1791. He was chiefly interested in dramatic criticism, having done some reviewing of current plays while a student and later having edited a *Theaterzeitung* in Hamburg. He intended his picture of England to be a corrective of the extreme partiality shown by Germans, and especially by Archenholz, towards England and things English. And he does quite a thorough job of fault-finding. Their boasted freedom was but a delusion, as any one would discover who had to pass through the hands of their customs officials. He did find the Handel festival at Westminster Abbey very impressive and the Quakers not so bad as they had been made out to be. But generally in the theatrical world, the English lagged far behind the Germans.—From Kelly, *op. cit.*

1793 PANZANI, GREGORIO. The Memoirs of, giving an Account of his Agency in England in the Years 1634-36, with an Introduction and Supplement, exhibiting the State of the English Catholic Church . . . translated from the Italian Original by Rev. J. Berington. 8vo. Birmingham.

WENDEBORN, GEBHARD FRIEDRICH AUGUST. Reise durch einige westliche und südliche Provinzen Englands. 2 vols. Hamburg.

See Wendeborn under 1784-88 above. See also *Cornhill Magazine,* Dec., 1928, for an article by Matheson on Wendeborn's *Grammar for English Learners.* This sight-seeing tour listed above called forth miscellaneous observations.

1794 SCHAEFFER, JACOB CHRISTIAN GOTTLIEB. Briefe auf einer Reise durch Frankreich, England, Holland und Italien in den Jahren 1787 und 1788 geschrieben. 2 vols. Regensburg.

Schaeffer was a Bavarian physician who attracted some notice as a writer on children's diseases and other medical subjects. These letters were written to a Nürnberg physician at the request of the latter and were in part published by him before they appeared in volume form. The author's travels in the interest of his profession led him to investigate not only medical progress but also medical institutional care. France and Italy he found to be lagging far behind in organized care for the sick. He arrived in England in the spring of 1788. His stay must have been pleasant, for he left with deep regret. His judgments on the English stand midway between the enthusiasm of Archenholz and the fault-finding of Wendeborn. He desired to disabuse his countrymen of the notion that the English people are morose, melancholy, and given to suicide, for he discovered the very opposite to be the case.—From Kelly, *op. cit.*

SNEDORF, F. Samlede Skrifter. 4 vols. Copenhagen.

The first volume contains letters written during a tour of Germany, France, Sweden, and England, which are replete with curious and able observations. The traveler met his death in the last named country through the indiscretion of a coachman.—From Pinkerton, vol. XVII.

1795   Kleine Reisen durch einen Theil von Italien, Frankreich und England. Halberstadt. (So cited in Pinkerton, vol. XVII.)

LA TOCNAYE, CHEVALIER DE. Promenade autour de la Grande-Bretagne, précédé de quelques détails sur la compagne du Duc de Brunswick. Par un Officier Français Emigré. 8vo. Edinburgh.

> In German, Riga, 1797; in English, Dublin, 1797; also at Dublin, 2 vols., including his Irish tour, 1797. See Lenotre, "L'Inventeur du Voyage à Pied," *Histoire étrangers qui sont arrivées,* in *Lectures pour Tous,* Paris, 1920.
> This émigré made the most of his exile. After a stay of four months in London learning English, he proceeded to Scotland (1793), where he made himself perfectly at home. He accustomed himself to the fare of oatcakes and even to the Scotch Sunday, which permitted one only "to drink, yawn, and sleep." He visited Edinburgh, Glasgow, Stirling, Ben Lomond, Perth, Dundee, Aberdeen, Banff, Nairn, Elgin; thence by Culloden he went to Inverness, to Fort William, where he took the road for the Lowlands and arrived at Dreghorn Castle. Here he stayed a year or more writing under the eye of his host the narrative of his travels. In addition to his own experiences in traveling, he had as background the reading of Johnson's Journey to the Hebrides and Scotch histories. His impressions are fresh and naive. Feeling lonesome in Scotland, he left for London. But becoming dissatisfied with a sedentary life there, he set out for Ireland, which served him as an occasion for another volume of travels (1797). Later on he passed over to the Scandinavian countries. It needs to be mentioned that he traveled on foot.

> 1797   LA TOCNAYE, CHEVALIER DE. Meine Füssreise durch die drey brittischen Königreiche. Voran einige Nachrichten von dem Feldzüge in Champagne. Von einem Französischen Offizier. 8vo. Riga.

MEISTER, JACQUES HENRI. Souvenirs de mes voyages en Angleterre. 2 vols. 8vo. Zürich.

> Translated into English, London, 1799. See below.
> For Meister's account of his first trip to England in 1789, see under 1791 above. That stay lasted but a fortnight; his second in 1792 was extended to six months. His travel experiences were recounted in letter form, some of which were published in French and some in German in Archenholz's *Minerva.* He was greatly struck at first with the differences which England presented to a European in cleanliness, prosperity, and security. The food he found much to his taste; English women appealed to him as more beautiful than the French; and English liberty and the Constitution won from him high praise. He thought English drama was remarkable for its sweep, variety, and passion, and Shakespeare supreme as a poet if not as a dramatist. As would be expected from one who was thoroughly indoctrinated with French culture, he considered English comedy inferior to French. The usual charge of immoral tendencies in English comedy finds a place. For instance, the *Beggar's Opera* he rated highly for its "verve and esprit," yet he knew of no other work so dangerous and immoral in its effect upon the youth.—From Kelly.

> 1799   (In English.) Letters written during a Residence in England: Manners, Government, Theatres, etc. 8vo. London.

1799   BAERT, F. B. DE P. DE. Tableau de la Grande-Bretagne, de l'Irlande et des possessions anglaises dans les quatre parties du monde. 'La partie de l'ouvrage qui regarde l'Ecosse et l'Irlande a été redigée sur les lieux en 1787.' Maps and illustrations. 4 vols. 8vo. Paris.

> Baert resided in England two years. His style of writing up a country is marked by a total absence of the personal note. He had read widely what had been written about Scotland before 1786, and he compared on the spot what had been observed by Johnson, Pennant, Banks, Martin, Macaulay, and Dalrymple with what he noticed himself. He treated the Highlands, the Hebrides, and the Lowlands under general headings, such as the situation, physical aspect, state of culture, habitations, manners, economic life, and character. These materials for his *Tableau* he collected in 1787 and 1788. The outbreak of the French Revolution found him in Spain but he returned to France to become a Deputy to the Assembly in 1792. Later he was obliged to flee to America, where he busied himself with arranging his material, which he published in Paris.—From Bain, *op. cit.*

Londres et ses environs avec des planches. 12mo. Paris.

This is probably another edition of the work listed under 1788 above.

1800 LESCALIER, D. Voyage en Angleterre, en Russie et en Suède en 1773. 2 vols. Paris.

NEMNICH, PHILIP ANDREAS. Beschreibung einer im Sommer 1799 von Hamburg nach und durch England geschehenen Reise. Tübingen.

This work is valuable for its account of industry, statistics, cities, and small towns.—J. Williams. Another tour was undertaken later, which was published at Tübingen in 1807. See below.

1807 NEMNICH, PHILIP ANDREAS. Neueste Reisen durch England, Schottland, und Irland, hauptsächlich in Bezug auf Produkte, Fabriken und Handlung. Tübingen.

ROLAND DE LA PLATIERE, JEAN MARIE (née Phlipon). Oeuvres de J. M. Phlipon Roland . . . contenant: les mémoires . . . Sa correspondance et ses voyages . . . . 3 tom. Paris (An VIII).

1800 (In English.) The Works of . . . containing her Philosophical and Literary Essays written previous to her Marriage; her Correspondence and her Travels . . . . 8vo. London.
Included in the above is a trip to England in 1784.

TARDY, —. Manuel du voyageur à Londres, ou recueil de toutes les instructions nécessaires. 12mo. Londres.

1800-01 THAER, ALBRECHT DANIEL. Einleitung zur Kenntnis der englischen Land-wirthschaft und ihrer neueren praktischen und theoretischen Fortschritte in Rückseit auf Vervollkommung deutscher Landwirthe und Cameralisten. 2 vols. Hanover.

This is made up of information collected during a sojourn in England, and treats of drainage, buildings, rotation of crops, social classes, history of the corn laws, the work of Young, Sinclair, and other agriculturalists.—J. Williams.

1801 SALADIN, C. L'Angleterre en 1800. Cologne.

[WILL, PETER.] Sittengemälde von London. Hrsg. von H. Gotha.

The authorship of this work is in doubt, some attributing it to Hüttner, who more likely was the editor. For the evidence see Kelly, *German Visitors*, note, 158. Will is known to have been pastor of the German church in the Savoy. Some good features are allowed the English way of life, but on the whole the judgments passed are hostile. Music is culti-vated as a fad, the stage has sunk to a low level, pandering to the taste of the rabble is rampant, German plays receive little attention and are badly translated, and comedies ap-plauded in England would be hissed off the stage in Germany.—Kelly.

1802 PICTET, MARC-AUGUSTE. Voyage de trois mois en Angleterre, en Ecosse et en Irlande pendant l'été de l'an IX. 8vo. Genève.

1802-04 HARMES, EMILIA. Caledonia. Von der Verfasserin der Sommerstunden. 4 vols. 8vo. Hamburg.

This tour, which was an extensive one over the Highlands, took place in 1800.

1806 DUTENS, LOUIS. Mémoires d'un voyageur qui se repose. 3 vols. 8vo. Paris.

This gives an account of a brief sojourn in Scotland. The fact that Dutens was so widely acquainted with the notabilities of Britain would lead one to expect a narrative of great interest. Yet it is said to possess little merit.

1810 ABU TALEB KHAN. Travels of Abu Taleb Khan (commonly called the Persian Prince) in Asia, Africa, and Europe, during the Years 1799, 1800, 1801, and 1802. Written by Himself in the Persian Language and Translated by Charles Stewart, Esq. Portrait of Author. 2 vols. 8vo. London.

> Reviewed at length in *Quarterly Review*, vol. 4, pp. 86 ff., 1810. "A bona fide Mahommedan has produced a tour." Deprived of an appointment held under the East India Company in India, he took advantage of his leisure to go on a tour, which he hoped would bring about his death. But he survived and arrived in the British Isles, where he visited parts of Ireland and England, thence went to France, Italy, Constantinople, Busserah, and back to India, where he was again appointed Collector. He was amazed and delighted with Ireland, and no less pleased with the 10,000 oriental MSS at the Bodleian. The curiosities at the British Museum received careful attention as well. He notes with disapproval the fact that in London prostitutes lived on streets with such virtuous names as Providence Street, Modest Court, St. Paul's Churchyard, etc. He greatly admired England's progress in manufactures.—From the review.

1817 BRETSCHNEIDER, HEINRICH GOTTFRIED VON. Reise nach London und Paris nebst Auszügen aus seinen Briefen an Herrn F. Nicolai. Hrsg. von L. C. F. Gockingk. Berlin und Stettin.

> His notes on his visit to England, which took place in 1773 (?), are fragmentary. He was personally acquainted with Garrick and Sir John Fielding but he tells us nothing about them. He may be regarded as the first traveler to write an *Empfindsame Reise*, an offspring of the vogue of Sterne's *Sentimental Journey*.—From Kelly, *op. cit.*

1820 DUC DE BERRY. On his stay in Scotland, see Chateaubriand, *Mémoires, letters et pièces authentiques touchant le vie et la mort de S. A. R. CH. F. d'Artois, fils de France, duc de Berry*. 8vo. Paris.

1821 COSMO THE THIRD. Travels of Cosmo the Third, Grand Duke of Tuscany, through England, during the Reign of Charles II. Translated from the Italian MS. in the Laurentian Library at Florence, with a Memoir of his Life. Portrait and 30 tinted views of London, cities, and seats, as delineated at that time by artists in the suite of the Duke. 4to. London.

> The portion of his travels through Devon reprinted in Chope, *Early Tours in Devon and Cornwall*, 92-111.
> The narrator of these travels was Count Lorenzo Magalotti, one of the most learned and eminent men of the court of Ferdinand II, and secretary to the Academy del Cimento. He enjoyed the friendship of numerous scholars in Europe, among them Sir Isaac Newton. Dissatisfied with the narrow type of education the mother was providing Cosmo, his father Ferdinand, who was interested in the literary, philosophical, and scientific movements of the day, contracted for him what he thought would be a corrective, i. e., a marriage with the eldest daughter of Gaston, Duke of Orleans. Vivacious, beautiful, and well educated, she had set her heart on Prince Charles of Lorrain. Her aversion to her new home and the people developed into rancor for her husband. Cosmo was then sent out on journeys to escape scenes and to help drive from his heart his attachment to his wife. These travels ranged through Spain, Portugal, England, and Holland, and terminated at Florence in 1669. They failed dismally in their purpose. The trip from Corunna to England was difficult. Instead of landing in England, they made port in Ireland. The description of the population at Kinsale, their way of living, and their poverty, especially that of the Catholic element, bespeaks the neglected and desolated condition of Ireland after Cromwell had done his work. On the road from Plymouth to London, plenteous detail is given of the productions of the country, towns, gentlemen's seats, forts, Stonehenge, Salisbury Cathedral, etc. He tried to enter London incognito, but on his arrival he was visited by the notabilities as if he were an expected guest. His tour continued through various other counties, the sights of which are duly described, and took him to the homes of scientists as well as to curiosities. Little that is personal or anecdotal is furnished us, but the account tells much of the English scene.

MORRELLET, L'ABBE. Mémoires sur le XVIIIe siècle et sur la Révolution. 2 vols. 8vo. Paris.

Morrellet traveled in England in 1772 and retained some pleasant memories of his experiences. One incident he records is rather unusual—that of meeting some young girls near Plymouth who sang to him some Scotch songs, which greatly delighted him. Later he translated into French a Scotch song that had pleased his friend Benjamin Franklin.

1825 BERTEVILLE, LE SIEUR. Récit de l'Expédition en Ecosse, l'an MDXLVI (should be MDXLVII), et de la Battayle de Muscleburgh. Par le Sieur Berteville au Roy Edouard VI. With facsimile of a contemporary plan of the battle of Pinkie. *Publ. Bann. Club,* no. 10. Edinburgh.

Berteville took part in the expedition as a retainer of Warwick.

1827 BONSTETTEN, KARL VICTOR VON. Briefe von Bonstetten an Matthisson, hrsg. von H. H. Füssli. Zürich.

Bonstetten was in England in 1769-70. The earliest letters in this collection were written in 1795.—Kelly.

MICHELE, SIGNOR GIOVANNI. Report of the Signor Giovanni Michele on his Return from England, A.D. 1557 (from his Embassy). Translated in Ellis, *Original Letters,* 2nd ser., vol. II, 218-42. London.

This Relation is full of interesting and valuable detail concerning the wealth, forces, revenues, dress, the royal family, etc. Queen Mary is represented in quite an attractive light but as subject to her hatred for Elizabeth, whom, were it not for the influence of the King of Spain, she would "bastardize."

MIRZA, ITESA MODEEN. Travels in Great Britain and France (1763). Translated from the Persian by J. E. Alexander. 8vo. London. (Cited in Mitchell, *Scot. Topog.,* vol. II.)

The genuineness of this work has been doubted.

1830 DE LARA, DON MANRIQUE (Duke de Najera). Narrative of the Visit of the Duke de Najera to England in the Year 1543-44: written by his Secretary Pedro de Gante; communicated in a Letter by Frederick Madden, F.S.A. In *Archaeologia,* vol. 23, 344-57. London.

This account was taken from a folio MS in the British Museum and translated by Madden. The Duke was a Spanish nobleman whose family was one of the most ancient and powerful in Castile. He visited England to pay his respects to Henry VIII. The narrative of his tour was written by his secretary and relates his reception by King Henry, the dancing of the various members of the household, the sights of London, the sport of bear-baiting, etc. London is described as having 250 parish churches. The author was delighted with the Thames, its fine bridge with houses upon it, and the swarms of swans on the river. He notes, as did Erasmus before him and others after him, the habit of English ladies bestowing kisses on distinguished guests. He describes the Princess Mary as possessing a "pleasing countenance and person. She is so much beloved throughout the kingdom that she is almost adored." His stay in London lasted eight days. He then traveled to Plymouth and sailed from there home.

1832 MIRABEAU, COUNT DE. Mirabeau's Letters during his Residence in England (1784-85). Now first translated from the original MSS. To which is prefixed an Introductory Notice on the Life, Conduct, and Character of the Author. 2 vols. 8vo. London.

The letters range over many things and call attention to matters that are passed over by the native traveler or inhabitant as being too well known. They contain a most enlightening account of a trial which Mirabeau instituted against a baker who stole his shirts, in which all the legal procedures governing English trials are detailed.

1835   Louis de Bruges (Seigneur de la Gruthuyse). Narrative of the Arrival of Louis
       de Bruges, Seigneur de la Gruthuyse, in England, and of his Creation as Earl of
       Winchester in 1472. Communicated in a Letter from Sir Frederick Madden.
       In *Archaeologia,* vol. 26, 265-88. London.

> This narrative is taken from ADD. MS. No. 6113 and describes in the words of a
> herald, who must have been an eye-witness of the scene, the reception of the Seigneur in
> England, and the ceremonial of his creation as Earl of Winchester. On the flight of Ed-
> ward IV from England to Holland in 1470, Louis de Bruges had been the means of prac-
> tically saving the king's life. When Gruthuyse arrived in London on a mission from his
> master the Duke of Burgundy, Edward returned the favor by making him Earl of Win-
> chester. The account is simply told but it is evident that the ceremony was imposing.

1836   D'Amour, Matthias. Memoir of Matthias d'Amour, edit. by Paul Rodgers. Por-
       trait. 12mo. London.

> This includes the author's travels in Scotland in 1782-85, during which he visited Raasay,
> Skye, Edinburgh, Gordon Castle, Peterhead, etc. They are interesting and curious.—
> Mitchell, *List of Travels.*

1837   Otto von Schwerin. Briefe aus England über die Zeit von 1674 bis 1678 . . .
       hrsg. von Leopold von Orlich. 8vo. Berlin.

1840   Alberi, Eugenio. Relazioni degli Ambasciatori Veneti. Firenze.

> This is a collection of the Relations sent by Venetian Ambassadors to the Senate at
> home from their various stations. A number of these emanating from England will ap-
> pear in items listed below. See Emma Gurney Salter, *Tudor England through Venetian
> Eyes,* London, 1930, for a detailed account of the regulations imposed upon the am-
> bassadors in making their reports and despatches, particularly in the period between 1496
> and 1558, viz., what they were instructed to observe and how to communicate their obser-
> vations. This work of Salter gives an excellent exposition of the ups and downs of Eng-
> lish and Venetian commercial and diplomatic interactions and summarizes the views of
> these emissaries on Tudor England. See also the Introduction to C. A. Sneyd, *A Relation
> of the Island of England,* under 1847 below. Most of the English Relations have been
> edited and translated in the *Calendar of State Papers.*

1841   Nucius, Nicander. The Second Book of the Travels of Nicander Nucius, of
       Corcyra. Edit. from the original MS. in the Bodleian Library, with an English
       Translation, by the Rev. J. A. Cramer, D.D. *Publ. Camden Soc.,* vol. 17. London.

> The author, a Greek exile in Venice, became attached to the suite of Gerard Veltvick,
> a minister of Charles V, and in his train went to England when Gerard was dispatched
> thither on a mission. His stay there lasted from about the middle of 1545 to the spring of
> 1546. His account of his visit is short but it brings to light some new material on the sup-
> pression of the monasteries by Henry VIII. It describes London Bridge and the river with
> its traffic, the houses lining its banks, the commercial interests of London, and comments
> on the familiar freedom allowed English women as well as the equally familiar greeting
> with a kiss from English ladies.

1841   Smith, Abigail (Adams). Journal and Correspondence of Miss Adams, Daugh-
       ter of John Adams, . . . Written in France and England in 1785. Edited by
       her Daughter. New York.

1842   Curwen, Samuel. Journal and Letters of Samuel Curwen, an American Refugee
       in England from 1775 to 1784, comprising Remarks on the prominent Men and
       Measures of that Period. To which are added Biographical Notices of many
       American Loyalists and other eminent Persons. Edit. by G. A. Ward. 8vo.
       London.

VAN SHAACK, H. C. The Life of Peter van Shaack, an American Loyalist in England, 1778-85. New York.

1843 MÖSER, JUSTUS. Sämmtliche Werke. 10 vols. Berlin.

Scattered throughout these volumes are letters and comments on the English stage, plays, actors, and operas, with which Möser became acquainted during his stay in England of seven months at the close of the Seven Years' War. While he warmly espoused the efforts of his compatriots to liberate the German stage from French formalism and to effect a closer adherence to the freedom of English drama and stage, yet he found little to please him either in the actors or the repertory. A city of the size of London should have more than two theaters.—From Kelly.

1845 FOLKERZHEIMER, HERMAN. Letter to Josiah Simler (dated at Salisbury, Aug. 13, 1562). In *Zürich Letters,* vol. 23, 2nd ser., 377, published by the Parker Society. Cambridge.

This letter was written while he was the guest of the Bishop of Salisbury. The passage across the Bay of Biscay to Southampton took eight days, the food was terrible, the ship stunk, the wine gave out and a mixture of vinegar and water was substituted. Some description is given of life at the episcopal palace and table, of hunting, and especially of a trip to Stonehenge, which he considers to have been a monument erected by the Romans as a trophy.

NIEBUHR, BARTHOLD GEORG. For his residence and tour in Scotland during 1798 and 1799, see *Tait's Edinburgh Magazine,* for Jan., Feb., and April. Edinburgh.

See also *Die Briefe Barthold Georg Niebuhrs,* hrsg. von D. Gerhard und W. Norvin, vol. I, Berlin, 1926. (Cited by Kelly.)

1847 TREVISANO, ANDREA. A Relation, or rather a True Account of the Island of England, with sundry Particulars of the Customs of these People, and of the Royal Revenues under Henry VII, about the year 1500. Translated from the Italian with Notes by Charlotte Augusta Sneyd. *Publ. Camden Soc.,* vol. 37.

Neither the author nor the precise date (1497) was known to Miss Sneyd; these were supplied by Rawdon Brown in his work, *Giustinian's Four Years at the Court of Henry VIII* (see under 1854 below). This Relation became the pattern of all subsequent reports sent from England by the Italians down to the accession of Elizabeth. Its form takes the following shape: amounts of royal revenues and expenditures, descriptions of the ruling house and persons of eminence attached to it, alterations in parliamentary or city jurisdiction, position and form of England, details of physical geography, natural products and raw materials, a short discourse on Scotland and Wales, their character and customs, a survey of the capital and its government, the armed forces, etc. The vague descriptions of the country and the position of the island suggest that the Italian ambassadors did not venture far into the interior. For his description of Scotland Trevisan depended directly on Don Pedro de Ayala (see under 1862 below). See also Hume Brown, *Early Travels,* 50-54, for Trevisan's account of Scotland.

1854 GIUSTINIAN, SEBASTIAN. Four Years at the Court of Henry VIII. A Selection of Despatches written by the Venetian Ambassador, Sebastian Giustinian, and addressed to the Signory of Venice, Jan. 12, 1515, to July 26, 1519. Translated by Rawdon Brown. London.

Brown used in the above work a very rare printed narrative written by a former ambassador, Piero Pasquaglio, while on a diplomatic mission to Henry VIII.

1856 BAROZZI, NICHOLO, e GUIGLIELMO BERCHET. Le relazioni degli stati Europei lette al senato dagli ambasciatori Veneziani nel secolo decimosettimo. Serie IV. Inghilterra. Edit. by Nicholo Barozzi and Guiglielmo Berchet. 8vo. Venezia.

These Relations cover the whole century.—Fussell, *The Exploration of England.*

DUC DE SULLY. Memoirs of the Duc de Sully; Prime Minister to Henry the Great. Translated by Mrs. Lennon. 4 vols. 8vo. London.

> Vol. II, 340-422, contains an account of the Duke's embassy to England in 1603.

WATSON, ELKANAH. Journal of a Visit to England (1782-84). In *Men and Times of the Revolution,* edit. by W. C. Watson. London. (See under LETTERS, DIARIES, MEMOIRS.)

1857   BUSIONO, ORAZIO. Diaries and Dispatches of the Venetian Embassy at the Court of King James I in the Years 1617, 1618. Translated by Rawdon Brown. London.

> Résumé printed in *Quarterly Review,* vol. 204, Oct., 1857. See also *Calendar State Papers, Venetian,* 1617-19.
> Busiono was chaplain to the Venetian Ambassador Contarine in England and Spain, 1617-18. The part of his report referring to England was translated by Brown.

1859   EYB, LUDWIG VON (the Younger). Geschichten und Taten Wilwolts von Schaumburg, hrsg. von Keller. In *Bibliothek des litterarischer Verein in Stuttgart.* Stuttgart.

> So cited by Mrs. Cust, *Gentlemen Errant,* Bibliography. She also refers to a study of this chronicler's report by Ullman called "Der unbekannte Verfasser der Geschichten und Thaten Wilwolts von Schaumburg," in Sybel's *Histor. Zeit.,* Bd. III.
> The chronicle of this Captain of the Landsknechts, who served under some of the most famous princes of Germany, loses nothing in its retelling by Mrs. Cust (*op. cit.*). Wilwolts was sent on an embassy in 1489 to Henry VII of England. Its real object is obscure but it may have had something to do with the question of the homely Anne of Brittany and the sudden change in Maximilian's French policy, with fears ensuing of the loss of Calais. The crossing of the Channel proved, as usual, very trying to the ambassadors from Philip of Burgundy and the King of the Romans, but they finally made London. Here they remained three days and visited the royal ordnance and other sights of the city whose opulence struck them with wonder. They were received in a royal audience with much splendor and were entertained with dances and so many other honors that they could not guess what could possibly have been overlooked. They returned by way of Canterbury to Dover and so on to the French coast. What the embassy accomplished remains in the dark. But one is thankful for the chance to read this tale of jousts, battles, miseries of warfare, and mutinous landsknechts as it is related by Mrs. Cust in the chapter called "A Master of War."

1861-65   SWAVE, PETER. Diary (of his visit to Scotland *temp.* James V). Written in Latin. Published in *State Papers,* vol. III, from the Archives of Copenhagen. Edit. by C. F. Wegener. London.

> Extract in Hume Brown, *Early Travellers,* 55-58. Swave visited Scotland in 1535 to gain the support of James V for Christian II against the citizens of Lübeck, who had cast off his authority. The greater part of the diary is taken up with his efforts to accomplish his mission. But the author does not neglect to recount the well-worn marvels of Scotland, such as the famous fasting John Scott, who left a beautiful wife to live as a hermit, the tree that produces birds from its fruit, the serpents near the Abbey of Dundee which have no sting or venom, the habit of the gannet of hatching its one egg under its foot while in a standing position, the floating island in Loch Lomond.—From Brown.

1862   AYALA, DON PEDRO DE. Letter from Don Pedro de Ayala, 25th July 1498, to Ferdinand and Isabella. In *Cal. of Letters,* etc., *relating to England and Spain.* London.

> Reproduced in Hume Brown, *op. cit.,* 39-49.
> Don Pedro was the ambassador from Ferdinand and Isabella at the court of James IV. By his lightheartedness and geniality, he completely won over the Scottish king, who consulted him on every occasion, and he in turn gave James the highest character to his

royal master. The letter, which is taken from the *Simancas Papers*, edit. by Bergenroth, is dated 25th of July, 1498. At this time James IV was twenty-five years old, with an agreeable address, versed in many languages, even that of Gaelic, "the language of the savages who live in some parts of Scotland." While the young king was a pious and God-fearing humane man, yet he loved war so much that Ayala feared that the peace with England would not last much longer. His tragic, mysterious death at Flodden Field one will remember from Scott's *Marmion*. The Ambassador finds the Scotch so hospitable that they vie with one another as to who shall have the honor of treating a foreigner as his guest. His conception of Scottish geography exhibits some curious errors, showing that the country was but little known at that period. Notable is his statement that Scotland is nearer to Spain than is London.

1863 BREUNING VON BUCHENBACH, H. J. Relation über seine Sendung nach England im Jahre 1595. Mitgetheilt von August Schlossberger. In *Bibliothek des litterarischen Verein in Stuttgart*, vol. LXXXII. Stuttgart.

This is an account of the mission to England to solicit fulfillment of the alleged promise made by Queen Elizabeth to bestow the Order of the Garter on his master, the Duke of Wirtemberg, referred to under Rathgeb, 1602, above.

1865 KIECHEL, SAMUEL. Journal of his Travels. See Rye, 87-90, for a brief account with some quotations.

The journal was edited for the *Bibliothek des litt. Ver. in Stuttgart*, vol. LXXXVI, 1866. The date of his visit to England is here given as 1586.
This wealthy young merchant of Ulm traveled extensively over Europe and the Holy Land as well as in England and Scotland. He set foot on English soil at Dover on Sept. 9, 1586, and on the 11th arrived in London, where he stayed for two months, putting up at the "White Bear," an inn mentioned by most other German travelers. The ceremonies of swearing in of the Lord Mayor he describes in detail. According to Rye, these are precisely the same as those which still prevail. He notes that for hanging the English have no regular executioner, but use for this business a butcher. Friends and acquaintances hasten the approach of merciful death by pulling at the victim's legs. On his departure from England in November, the news arrived of the capture by Drake of a Spanish ship which was said to have in its hold ingots of uncoined gold and silver besides coins worth in our day $2,500,000.

WURMSSER, HANS JACOB. A Relation of the Journey which I, in company with his Serene Highness the Duke Lewis Frederick of Wirtemberg, have with God's help undertaken and happily accomplished, through Part of the Rhine Country, Holland, Zealand, England, Scotland, Friesland, likewise part of Germany; and which has been penned in the French Language by me, Hans Jacob Wurmsser von Vendenheym (1610). Translated from the French MS. by Rye, 57-66.

The journal contains nothing about Scotland. The Prince was the second son of the Duke Frederick of Wirtemberg. He was sent by his brother John Frederick, the reigning duke, on a mission to England and France in behalf of the United Protestant League. This first trip took place in 1608. The second journey, which is the one recorded by Wurmsser, was undertaken in 1610, and was again concerned with the affairs of the League of Protestant Princes opposing the League of Catholic Princes. James was finally induced to send 4,000 troops to be employed in their service. It is to be remembered that the Thirty Years' War was in the offing. The journal is written in a matter-of-fact style, and contains many interesting allusions to places and persons visited by the travelers during their brief sojourn in England. One notable fact recorded is their visit to the Globe Theater, Monday, April 30th, 1610, to see *Othello* acted.—From Rye.

1868 CHIERICATI, FRANCESCO. One Letter concerning Ireland and three on England by Chiericati printed in *Quattro Documenti d'Inghilterra ed uno di Spagna dell' Archivo Gonzago di Mantova*, edit. by Attilio Portioli. Mantua. (So cited in Bates, *Touring in 1600*.)

1871   FALIER, LODOVICO. Report of England made to the Senate by Lodovico Falier
Nov. 10, 1531. In *Cal. State Papers, Venetian*, vol. 4, 292-301. London.

> This report gives high praise to Henry VIII and his Queen, crediting him with amiable
> qualities of address and excellent scholarly attainments. The fact that Henry wore a beard
> is noticed as being contrary to English habit. After a general description of England, its
> products, and its damp climate, there follows an account of London, its courts of law, its
> government, the revenues of the crown, and a brief biography of Wolsey.

SAVORGNANO, MARIO. Tour in England. In *Cal. State Papers, Venetian*, vol. 4,
285-89. London.

> The date is Aug. 25, 1531. The writer bestows many compliments on Henry VIII for
> his appearance, learning, and accomplishments. In his description of London, he says,
> "the population is immense, and comprises many artificers. The houses are in very great
> number but ugly and half the materials of wood, nor are the streets wide." He considers
> the women to be extremely handsome. Englishmen drink heavily but less than the Germans;
> they are an idle race and spend much time in archery. They are gross in their love of food,
> eating five or six times a day and consuming huge quantities of meat, which is supplied
> by a plenteous number of butchers in London. All in all, England is "paradise inhabited
> by devils." One anecdote he relates, apparently a traditional one, is worth passing on, that
> of an Englishman forced to blush because he had to acknowledge that none of his
> ancestors had been hanged.—See Clare Williams, *op. cit.*

1874   MIRABEAU, LE COMTE DE. On his travels in Scotland, see *The Life and Letters of
Sir Gilbert Elliot*, 3 vols., 8vo. London.

1875   EWALD, JOHANN JOACHIM. Briefe an Ramler, in *Archiv für Litteratur Geschichte*, vol. IV, 281-89, Leipzig; Briefe an Kleist, *ibid.*, 445-52; Bisher un-
gedrückte Briefe an von Brandt, Gleim und Nicolai, *ibid.*, vol. XIII, 448-84;
vol. XIV, 250-80. (So cited by Kelly.)

> Here is recorded Ewald's impressions of England, where he spent five months in 1757.
> In these letters he gives rapturous praise to everything English.—Kelly, *op. cit.*

1877   HARDENBERG, KARL AUGUST, FÜRST VON. Denkwürdigkeiten des Staatskanzlers
Fürsten von Hardenberg bis zum Jahre 1806, von Leopold von Ranke. Leipzig.

> Ein zweites kleineres Tagebuch liegt vor, in welchem Hardenberg die Reise beschreibt,
> die er über Holland nach England unternahm. Er hat sie am 31. Juli 1773 angestellt und
> ist erst am Anfang des folgenden Jahrs nach Hannover zurückgekommen. (Vol. I, p. 37.)
> —Quoted by Kelly, Appendix, *op. cit.*

1877   MUNOZ, ANDRES. Viage de Felipe II en Inglaterra. Saragossa, 1554. By Pascual
de Gayangos. *Sociedad de Bibliofilos Españoles*, no. 15. Madrid.

> Munoz was an inmate of the royal household and accompanied Philip II to Corunna.
> The rest of the story he got from letters and reports sent back to him.—Read, *Bibliog.
> Brit. Hist., Tudor Period*.

1880   Summaire de L'origine Description et mervveilles Descosse, avec une petite cronique des roys dudict pays jusques a ce tempts, 1538. 8vo. (Reprint, so cited by
John Grant, Catalogue, March, 1942.)

> The date of publication here given is approximate.

1883   HALLER, ALBRECHT VON. Tagebücher seiner Reise nach Deutschland, Holland
und England, 1723-27. Hrsg. von L. Hirzel. Leipzig.

> This is the first publication of his diary. Haller was the first German of importance in
> the field of letters to visit England. This famous Swiss scholar and scientist spent a few

weeks in England in the summer of 1727, dividing his time between London and Oxford. At that time he did not possess the thorough knowledge of English he acquired later. He was greatly taken with the English political system but he failed to perceive the greatness of English literature, particularly the drama.—From Kelly, *op. cit.*

1883 A Description of England sent to Philip II of Spain. Communicated to the *Antiquary*, vol. 8, 151-53. London.

This account was written by one of Philip's agents two or three years before the Armada was launched against England, and it probably influenced the King to attempt the enterprise. The letter, of which a literal translation is given here, was among the Spanish MS letters in the British Museum, without name or date. It alludes to the year 28 Eliz. as the one in which it was written. It was composed in bad Italian, with a Spanish translation appended. Perhaps it was sent by some French-speaking merchant, possibly from Flanders. It describes the various divisions of land, the ports and seacoasts, pointing out how few the ports were and what vessels they could serve. The forts are accounted of no value. Lists of Catholics are given as well as of those who are considered so and those who are safe. It estimates the numbers of infantry and horse, which apparently were not deemed formidable. It sets forth the revenues of the Queen and the part played by piracy in maintaining the country. The open country should offer little obstacle to Philip's cavalry. It could be overrun in a month once the troops were landed. In case war is determined upon, Philip should provide himself and the Spanish with certain necessities, which he enumerates.

1884 DOISY DE VILLARGENNES, A. J. Reminiscences of Army Life under Napoleon Bonaparte. 8vo. Cincinnati.

This is a detailed account of the life of a French army officer who spent his years as a prisoner of war in Selkirk, Scotland.

London in 1669. Communicated by Theodore Bent to the *Antiquary*, vol. 10, 62-64. London.

The account printed here is undated and unsigned, but it alludes to the Great Fire of London as a recent event. It is written in excellent Italian. The evidence points to the Florentine Ambassador resident in London in 1669, the year of the visit of Cosmo III to London, one Antelminelli, who, if not actually born there, had spent the greater part of his life in London. The narrative shows an excellent knowledge of English affairs. It gives valuable information on how one lived in the city after the Fire, what the effect was upon transportation, the equipages used, and the efforts at rebuilding. It reports on the eating and drinking places in the city, the differences between ordinaries and taverns, the two theaters for comedies and the three companies of actors, the infinite number of beer shops, the amusements, tennis courts, bowls, the bear- and bull-baiting courts, cock fights, the places where one may walk with ladies, etc.

1891 MELLE, J. VON, und H. POSTEL. Beschreibung einer Reise durch das nordwestliche Deutschland nach den Niederland und England, 1683. 4to. Lübeck.

SCHÖN, THEODOR VON. Studienreise eines jungen Staatsmanns in England am Schlusse des vorigen Jahrhunderts. Berlin.

Schön was a Prussian statesman whose education had early been formed by the political and economic thought of the school of Adam Smith. Naturally he turned to England for the study of its ways and people. With a traveling companion he arrived in London in the spring of 1798, and after a few weeks' sojourn in the capital he made a tour of England and Scotland, coming back to London in October and remaining the rest of the winter. His comments in his diary show him to have been open-minded towards England's faults as well as towards her virtues. His conclusion that the English were inhospitable and interested only in themselves is at variance with that of the enthusiasts. But he credits them with integrity and above all patriotism. He had a passion for the theater and attended performances everywhere, thus adding sensibly to our knowledge of the stage in the period when Kotzebue was beginning his invasion. His observations on the liberties taken with the originals need surprise no one familiar with the principles of translation in vogue during the 18th century. His account of various plays presented and of their performers makes a useful addition to the history of the 18th century stage. See Kelly, *op. cit.*

1892   GUARAS, ANTONIO DE. The Accession of Queen Mary, being the contemporary Narrative of Antonio de Guaras, a Spanish Merchant Resident in London; edit., with Introduction, Translation and Notes and an Appendix of Documents, by Richard Garnett. London.

PHILIP JULIUS, DUKE OF STETTIN-POMERANIA. Diary of the Journey of . . . through England in the Year 1602. Edit. by Dr. Gottfried von Bülow, assisted by Wilfred Powell. In *Trans. Roy. Hist. Soc.*, 2nd ser., vol. 6, 1-67. London.

> This trip to England of a prince and his tutor was part of the education that was comprised in the Grand Tour, the purpose of which was to form character and to increase knowledge. The diary kept by the tutor, Frederic Gerschow, is here for the first time printed (limited to the portion dealing with England). It records day by day whatever was seen or heard in the various places visited. Gerschow put down his observations in the form of notes with the intention of bringing them into better shape at his leisure. Part of the MS notes were lost and part spoiled by rain, but they were rewritten from memory. The diary is a matter-of-fact piece of writing, giving distances from place to place but preserving for us some curious facts in the lives of our ancestors, such as the habit of ringing bells when one was sick and, in fact, on any occasion that offered. They visited Whitehall, museums, the Tower, the great seats like Oatlands, Theobalds, Windsor, etc., Oxford and Cambridge, and in general the sights usually sought out by foreigners.

1893   KALM, PETER. Account of his Visit to England on his way to America in 1748, translated (from the Swedish) by Joseph Lucas. 2 maps and several illustrations. 8vo. London.

> For the account of Kalm's visit to America, see under 1770-71, NORTH AMERICA, vol. II of this work. Being particularly interested in botany, he notes carefully in his journal on England the progress made by English farmers and vegetable gardeners, especially in Kent, from whose fields came so much of the produce consumed by Londoners.

WINDECKE, EBERHARD. Denkwürdigkeiten des Eberhard Windecke. Edit. by Wilhelm Altmann. Berlin.

> This chronicler to Sigismund of Bohemia came to England in the time of Henry IV. When the party arrived at London, they were royally received by an escort sent out to meet them and by citizens "most magnificently clad." But the chronicler offers no intimate revelations on the London of Prince Hal's day.—From Clare Williams, *op. cit.*

1894   REPAS, DENIS DE. Letter to Sir Edward Harley, 13 Sept. 1672. In Portland MSS., vol. 3, 326-33, *Hist. MSS. Comm.*, 14th Report.

> This records a journey in Scotland 200 miles beyond Edinburgh. The writer was a traveling merchant, who made three visits to Scotland, in addition to tours of Holland, France, Germany, and Italy. He found nothing good in Scotland nor in the Scotch people, whom he condemned for their laziness and their vile food (like their horses they live on oatmeal). He wondered why they did not comport themselves like Englishmen. In fact, he "never saw a nation in general, more nasty, lazy, and less ingenious in matter of manufacture."

1895   BEAUMONT, ELIE DE. Un Voyageur français en Angleterre en 1764. In *Revue Britannique*, Sept., Oct., and Nov. (So cited in *Camb. Bibliog.*)

REGNAULT, GERARD (Knight). A Journey to Scotland in the Year 1435. In Jusserand, *English Essays from a French Pen.* 8vo. London.

> This Relation, which Jusserand gives in résumé, deals with the mission of Regnault to Scotland for the purpose of bringing back to France the Lady Margaret, daughter of James I, who had been affianced to the Dauphin Louis (Louis XI to be). She was then three years old and he five. Regnault much disliked the trip and tried in vain to buy his way out. After encountering severe storms, the party landed on the west coast of Scotland.

James, who was very unwilling to part with his daughter, contrived many delays, during one of which he advised Regnault, who was getting bored, to travel about the country. Accordingly he visited several "among the good towns of the kingdom" and recorded something of what he saw in these trips. The voyage back to France turned out to be more comfortable, and favored by good weather the party landed safely in France. The life of the princess as wife of the heartless, unloving Louis XI was a sadly neglected one. She died childless and heart-broken at the age of twenty. Jusserand notes that this French MS was being prepared for publication by Andrew Lang for the Roxburghe Club.

WEDEL, LEOPOLD VON. Journey through England and Scotland made by Leopold von Wedel in the Years 1584 and 1585. Translated from the original MS. by Gottfried von Bülow. In *Trans. Roy. Hist. Soc.*, n.s., vol. 9. 8vo. London.

> An account of Wedel's wanderings and of his life is given in Klarwill, *Queen Elizabeth and Some Foreigners*. The author came of a roaming set of ancestors and was himself incurably given to making journeys. He fought in numerous wars for various sides, and visited the Holy Land, Egypt, Spain, France, England, and Scotland. His stay in Britain lasted from Aug. 17, 1584, to April, 1585. He tells a good deal of the festivities in London, of the Queen with whom he was greatly taken, describes one of the public meals, how served, the gentlemen present, the dancing, a mass hanging of fourteen persons, the Lord Mayor's procession, a bear-baiting, Westminster, the convening of the House of Parliament, etc. The absence of fortified towns greatly surprised him. The countryside gets but a perfunctory description. See Klarwill.

1898 BELL, JAMES. A Narrative of the Journey of Cecilia, Princess of Sweden, to the Court of Queen Elizabeth. Edit. by M. Morrison. In *Trans. Roy. Hist. Soc.*, n.s., vol. 12. London.

> Edit. by Ethel Seaton, London, 1926.
> This high-spirited and beautiful princess sought distraction from an unfortunate love adventure by taking this trip to England (1565-66), though her father, Gustavus Vasa of Sweden, had opposed it as he had done with the journey made by her brother Eric, who had lately returned home from an unsuccessful venture to win the hand of the youthful Elizabeth. But the good time Eric had enjoyed in England led him to suggest a similar voyage to his sister. The account, which was written by James Bell and presented to Queen Elizabeth, concerns itself wholly with the sea voyage, which was diversified by danger after danger until it seemed that death was inescapable. Reports are added to this account from the Spanish Ambassador to Philip, together with the letters exchanged between Cecil and Elizabeth, Cecilia and Elizabeth, and others of high note. The welcome the princess received from Elizabeth did not remain unmarred, for her husband, the Marquis of Baden, was detained in prison, and both owed 15,000 crowns. Cecilia was finally successful in getting out of the country. Her later career was one of extravagance and restless travel.

Estat et puissance du royaulme d'Ecosse. In *Cal. State Papers,* Scottish Series, vol. 1, 205.

> This describes the situation of the country, its strength, government, power of the French in the affairs of Scotland, dearness of grain, want of horses, etc.

1899 BISONI, BERNARDO. Aventures d'un grand seigneur Italian (Marquis Vicenzio Giustano) à Travers l'Europe. Paraphrased into French (as in the above title) by Emmanuel Rodocanachi. 18mo. Paris.

> Bisoni accompanied Vicenzio Giustano in his travels through Germany, the Low Countries, England, and France in 1606. His MS is in the Vatican Library.—From Bates, *Touring in 1600.*

1901 CAULIER, JEAN DE. For a Frenchman's impression of London and the English countryside (1779-80), see *The Beneden Letters,* bk. II, 154-78, under LETTERS, DIARIES, MEMOIRS.

LICHTENBERG, GEORG CHRISTOPH. Briefe, hrsg. von Albert Leitzmann und Carl Schuddekopf. 3 vols. Leipzig.

See also his *Vermischte Schriften,* 8 vols., Göttingen, 1844; *Gedanken, Satiren, Fragmente,* hrsg. von W. Herzog, 2 vols., Jena., 1907; and *Briefe aus Lichtenberg's englischen Freundeskreis,* edit. by Hans Hecht, Göttingen, 1925. An English version of his letters describing England, translated and annotated by Margaret L. Mare and W. H. Quarrell, Oxford, 1938. See below.

The author was a famous physicist and professor at Göttingen. He presents no comprehensive account of the English scene, but he offers much of interest in scattered descriptions throughout his works. His first visit to England was of a few weeks' duration in 1770; his second, in 1784, lasted fifteen months. He wrote at length on the theater and particularly on the acting of Garrick, who is the subject of extended eulogies in his *Briefe aus London.* His distaste for sentimentalism led to great esteem for Fielding and Hogarth, and he was no less behind in his admiration for Shakespeare. He saw the *Beggar's Opera* but he left no comment on it.

1938 LICHTENBERG, GEORG CHRISTOPH. Lichtenberg's Visits to England as described in his Letters and Diaries. Translated and annotated by Margaret L. Mare and W. H. Quarrell. Oxford.

This contains a most readable Introduction on the author's life and interests. It touches upon his relations with George II and the king's interest in Hanover, together with the Queen's intellectual occupations. Free as Hanover was considered to be, England surpassed that country in freedom, for here it was guaranteed by the Constitution itself. Lichtenberg became the interpreter to Germany of every branch of English art.—From the Introduction.

VERNON, J. J. The French Prisoners of War in Selkirk; being the Reminiscences of Sub-Lieutenant Adelbert J. Doisy. Selkirk.

So cited by Mitchell, *Scot. Topog.,* vol. I, without date. The date assigned above is a guess.

1902 KIELMANNSEGGE, FRIEDRICH GRAF VON. Diary of a Journey to England in the Years, 1761-62. Translated from the MS. by Countess Kielmannsegge. 4 portraits. 8vo. London.

This German nobleman crossed over to England in 1761 to witness the coronation of George III. During his stay of seven months he made himself well acquainted with the English stage, which he regarded as superior to all others in acting, number of people cast, the settings, and accessories.

SAUSSURE, CESAR DE. A Foreign View of England in the Reigns of George I and George II. The Letters of Monsieur Cesar de Saussure, translated by Madame van Muyden. Map and illustrations. 8vo. London.

These letters are printed here for the first time. The author was a Swiss who left home in 1725 to be on the road for eleven years, during which time he took in Europe and Constantinople. His first visit to England took place in 1726-29; his second in 1738. The customs examination at Dover was held on board ship and was exercised five or six times, apparently with the expectation, not unfulfilled, of a round of drinks at the captain's expense. He did the sights of London right thoroughly; he witnessed the coronation of George II, the futile act of the King's champion throwing down his gauntlet and challenging any one to deny the King's legitimacy, etc. His book is a mine of information on England for the period covered.

1903 MONTAIGNE, MICHEL EYQUEM DE. The Journal of Montaigne's Travels, 1580-81. Translated and edited by W. G. Waters. London.

1905 ZETZNER, JOHANN EBERHARD. Londres et l'Angleterre en 1700, écrites par un commis-negociant strasbourgeois: Jean-Everard Zetner. In *Revue d'Alsace,* n.s., vol. XVI, 561-91. Colmar.

This was also issued separately, 8vo, Strasbourg, 1905; a German account, edit., by Rudolf Reuss, Strasbourg, 1913. See below.

Zetzner left an autobiography, consisting largely of narratives of his journeys in Germany, along the coasts of the Baltic, in England, Scotland, France, and Spain. Paraphrases of the more interesting parts were printed in three installments in French in the above *Revue*, 1905-07, and reissued separately.—From Bates, *op. cit.*

1913 ZETZNER, JOHANN EBERHARD. Aus dem Leben eines Strasburger Kaufmans des XVII und XVIII Jahrhunderts. Reiss-Journal und Glücks und Unglückfalls von Landes und Volkeskunde von Elsass-Lothringen und dem angrenzenden Gebieten. Hrsg. von Rudolf Reuss. Vol. XLIII. Strassburg.

The portion dealing with England is found in chapters vi-viii.—Fussell, *Exploration of England*.

1907 CONSTANT, BENJAMIN. For accounts of his stay in Edinburgh in July, 1783-April, 1785, see his *Le Cahier Rouge*, 16mo, Paris.

Further information on his residence in Edinburgh is contained in his letters. He enjoyed his experiences as a student at Edinburgh and in his *Le Cahier Rouge* he speaks of his stay there as the most agreeable episode of his life. He became sufficiently at home in English to take part in the debates. See Bain, *Les Voyageurs Français en Ecosse*.

1908 D'ARTOIS, COMTE. For the story of his residence in Holyrood, Edinburgh, see A. F. Steuart, *The Exiled Bourbons in Scotland*. 8vo. London.

The Count had an apartment on the first floor of the principal wing of the old palace. As most of the building was uninhabitable, the rest of his entourage housed themselves nearby. His circle included a large number of the nobility and a crowd of obscure refugees, who took their residence there because of the presence of Monsieur. Since the Count was more nearly related to the royal line of Scotland than to the reigning house of France, Scotland took kindly to his Highness, for he reminded the people of their former glories. His court affairs were attended by the Scotch aristocracy, and he in turn visited some of the families of Edinburgh. Sir John Sinclair tried to interest him in agriculture, but that was going a little too strong for the royal émigré. During his exile he stayed at times in London or at Blair Castle, or at Bothwell Castle, returning once more to Holyrood. He remained here until 1814. Of the group the Duc d'Angoulême was shy and unsociable and had little to do with his Scottish neighbors. The Duc de Berri, on the contrary, profited by his stay to indulge in trips to England and through Scotland. None of the princely exiles was interested in Scotch litertaure.—From Bain, *op. cit.* See also J. Lucas Dubreton, *Le Comte d'Artois, Charles X, le Prince, l'Emigré, le Roi*, Paris, 1927.

BRYCE, W. M. A French Mission to Scotland in 1543. In *Proc. Soc. Antiquaries of Scotland*, vol. 42, 243-52.

COLLINS, J. CHURTON. Voltaire, Montesquieu, and Rousseau in England. Portraits and illustrations. 8vo. London.

1910 DANLOUX, H. P. For his visit to Holyrood, see Le Baron Roger de Portalis, *H. P. Danloux et son Journal pendant l'Emigration*. Fol. Paris.

1911 ROUSSEAU, JEAN-JACQUES. For an account of his residence in England, 1766-67, see L. J. Courtois, *Rousseau en Angleterre*, under GENERAL REFERENCE.

1912 PETRY, LE CITOYEN. On his stay in Glasgow, see H. W. Meikle, "A French Spy in Glasgow in 1793," in *Glasgow Herald*, Aug. 24, 1912.—Bain, *op. cit.*

1914 BALDENSPERGER, F. Le Touriste de l'Emigrations française; le chevalier de La Tocnaye et ses promenades dans l'Europe du Nord. *Bibl. Universelle et Revue Suisse*, tome LXXIV, 225-57, May, 1914. (So cited in Bain, *op. cit.*)

This gives an account of La Tocnaye's peregrinations, which are listed under 1795 above.

1923   CASANOVA, GIACOMO. Casanova in England. Being the Account of the Visit to London in 1763-64 of Giacomo Casanova, Chevalier de Seingalt, his Schemes, Enterprises and amorous Adventures. With a Description of the Nobility, Gentry and fashionable Courtesans whom he encountered, as told by himself. Edit. by Horace Bleakley. 17 plates, chiefly portraits. 8vo. London.

> Casanova in England is no better nor worse than Casanova in Venice or Paris. He lets the light shine more clearly perhaps on persons and places that thrive best in the dark. His experiences with Mrs. Cornelys and her Assemblies are an instance.

SALTER, GURNEY. Tudor England through Venetian Eyes. In *Fortn. Rev.*, n.s., vol. 114, 144-53. London.

1926   ROE, F. C. French Travellers in Britain, 1800-1926. Impressions and Reflections collected and edited by F. C. Roe, M.A. 12mo. *Modern Studies Series.* New York.

1928   KLARWILL, VICTOR VON. Queen Elizabeth and Some Foreigners. Being a Series of hitherto unpublished Letters from the Archives of the Hapsburg Family. Edit. with Introductions by Victor von Klarwill. Authorized translation by Professor T. H. Nash. Illustrations from contemporary sources. London.

> This gives the texts of letters, most of which deal with the question of marriage. The chief characters are the Emperor Maximilian, Archduke Charles, Emperor Ferdinand, Baron Breuner, the Duke of Wirtemberg. Some of the travelers' relations are printed in a more or less full redaction. The Introduction provides a useful survey of England as seen through the eyes of German wayfarers.

1929   PLATTER, THOMAS. Thomas Platters des Jüngeren Englandfahrt im Jahre 1599. Hrsg. von Hans Hecht. Halle.

> An English version, edit. by Clare Williams. London, 1937. See below.
> Platter was an eager traveler, observant and serious but dull and tedious, and unable to distinguish between relevant and irrelevant details. Since he knew no English, he had recourse to Latin and French, and then found difficulty even among the dons and students. At Eton he addressed the boys in Latin, and the boys responded with pointing to their mouths with their fingers and shaking their heads. In other ways the insularity of the English comes to the top in his contacts with the natives. He spent his five weeks to good purpose in sight-seeing. He may have brushed by Shakespeare while in London but the sight of Elizabeth on a state parade or a lunch with the Lord Mayor would have counted far more with him. Like others he was greatly impressed with the three chief distinctions of London—the shipping in the river, the wealth of the city, and the civic pomp. His completed diary is full of stuff lifted from Wirtemberg or Braun and Hogenberg. The borrowings from Munster were intended to meet a demand of German readers for information on England. After his travels he settled down to practice medicine at home.—From Introduction of Williams.

> 1937   (In English.) Thomas Platter's Travels in England, 1599. Rendered into English from the German, and with introductory matter by Clare Williams. 8vo. London.

1930   PREVOST, ABBE. Adventures of a Man of Quality, translated from the French, with an Introduction, by Mysie E. I. Robertson, M.A. 4 plates. 8vo. London. (Broadway Library of Eighteenth Century French Literature.)

> The author of *Manon Lescaut* landed in England in 1728. His adventures here are related in this volume.—Bookseller's Note.

1931   DE MAISSE, SIEUR (ANDRE HURAULT). A Journal of all that was accomplished by Monsieur de Maisse Ambassador in England from Henri IV to Queen Eliza-

beth Anno Domini 1597. Translated from the French, and edited with an Introduction by C. B. Harrison and R. A. Jones. 8vo. London.

The mission of De Maisse was to learn whether Elizabeth would be willing to join in peace negotiations with Spain or whether she intended to prosecute the war further, and if so on what conditions. Henri and Elizabeth had each agreed not to make peace without the consent of the other in the war against the Spaniards. It wås later learned, however, that Henri had secretly made a separate peace with Spain. As a description of England, the account lacks breadth, but it gives a vivid picture of the court and the person of the Queen. His best descriptions are of the audiences with Elizabeth, her fantastic dress, vanity and shrewdness, her scholarly accomplishments, love of music and dancing. Apart from his commendation of Westminster Abbey, he has little eye for the scene.—From Introduction.

1932 COMENIUS (JAN AMOS KOMENSKY). Comenius in England. The Visit of Jan Amos Komensky the Czech Philosopher and Educationalist to London in 1641-42 . . . as described in contemporary Documents. Edit. by R. F. Young. Illustrations. 4to. Oxford.

1933 ROCHEFOUCAULD, FRANCOIS DE LA. A Frenchman in England 1784, Being the *Mélanges sur l'Angleterre* of François de la Rochefoucauld. Now edited from the MS. with an Introduction by Jean Marchand, Archiviste-palëographie, Bibliothécaire à la Chambre des Députés. Paris. Translated with Notes by S. C. Roberts, Fellow of Pembroke College. 4 plates, 1 page from MS and maps on end papers. 8vo. Cambridge.

Rochefoucauld was the author of a number of important memoirs on England. One was a series of impressions of English life, manners and customs with certain personal reminiscences and a record of two journeys in Suffolk and Norfolk; the other was a more extensive diary of a tour through the English counties. The above work contains the first of these, now edited for the first time from the original MS. Readers of Arthur Young's Tour in France will remember the author's father, the Duc de Liancourt, who greatly desired Young's advice on the economic management of his estate. To complete his son's education the Duc de Liancourt sent François to England. With a Polish companion and two servants the son settled at Bury St. Edmunds to learn the language and to study agricultural methods. Suffolk and Norfolk were the scenes of advanced agricultural experiments and so provided the visitors with the best lessons to be had in Europe on scientific husbandry. His remarks illuminate for the English reader the passion of the inhabitants for their land, their practice of returning profits back to the soil, and their freedom from governmental interference—a condition that accounted to him for their success. Much information on methods of traveling in vogue during the period comes to light. Gentlemen traveled mainly by post chaise. In Bury there were 15 horses available for the service of post chaises and diligences, some fifty hacks let out as saddle horses or for cabriolets. The author brings us fairly close to the domestic life of a small town, with its assemblies, social contacts, meals, and attitude towards foreigners.

1937 DE HEERE, LUCAS. Beschrijving der Britsche Eilanded door Lucas De Heere. Een Geillustreed Geschrift uit Zijn Engelsche Ballingschap met een Inleidung, Aanteekening en Glossarium door Dr. Th. M. Chotzen en Dr. A. M. E. Draak, with Summary in English. 8vo. Amsterdam.

The artist Lucas de Heere lived as an exile in England from 1567 to 1577. What is extant of his sojourn in England remains in an illuminated MS in the British Museum (Add. MS. 28.330), which contains two compilations, one treating of the chorography of the British Isles (with a digression on Scottish history), the other dealing with English history. He wrote his descriptions of Britain for his fellow refugees, who were supposed to need a guidebook on contemporary English and London law, municipal and corporation government and commercial possibilities. Some of his information he furnishes at first hand. He displays a sympathetic but not uncritical appreciation of English character. He became well acquainted with London and English worthies.—From the Summary. See also Lionel Cust, "Notice of the Life and Works of Lucas d'Heere," in *Archaeologia*, vol. 54. London, 1894.

1938   ROUSSEAU, JEAN-JACQUES. For an account of Rousseau's visit to England, see R. B. Mowat, *Jean-Jacques Rousseau.*

ADDENDA—PSEUDO-FOREIGN

(Here are listed some of the more notable criticisms of English social, political, and religious life under the guise of observations made by a foreigner sojourning in England. No doubt the number of such publications is much larger than is represented here, for the 18th century readily fell in with the vogue of "spy" and "letter" accounts that seemed to stem from Montesquieu.)

1706   Man Unmask'd: being a Wonderful Discovery lately made in the Island of Japan; written in the Japonese Language by the Spirit of Contradiction, and Translated into English for the Benefit of the Publick, by Sir Tristan Nerebegood, both of them Eye-Witnesses to the Whole Affair. 4to. London.

   A very scarce fictitious narrative setting forth the vices of London in a Japanese setting. —Maggs, no. 739.

1715   HADGI, ALI MUHAMMED. A Brief and Merry History of Great Britain: Containing an Account of the Religions, Customs, Manners, Humours, Characters, Caprices, Contrasts, Foibles, Factions, etc., of the People. Written originally in Arabick, by Ali Mohammed Hadgi, Physician to his Excellency Cossem Hojah, late Envoy from the Government of Tripoli, in South-Barbary, to this Court. Faithfully render'd into English by Mr. Anthony Hilliard, Translator of the Oriental Languages. 8vo. London. (Dating approximate.)

1720   Royal Remarks: or, The Indian King's Observations on the Most Fashionable Follies Now Reigning in the Kingdom of Great Britain. London. (Dating approximate.)

1725   A View of London and Westminster: or, The Town Spy, containing Merry Characters of the Trades People; Customs, Tempers, Manners, Policies of the People in the several most noted Parishes; wherein the Follies and Vices of the English, Welch, Scotch, French, and Irish Inhabitants are exposed; a List of Kept Mistresses; their Places of Abode, etc. By a German Gentleman. 2 pts. 8vo. London.

   Another edit., 2 pts., 8vo, London, 1728.
   It may be hazarded that the German Gentleman is "smoke in the eye."

1735   LYTTELTON, SIR GEORGE. Letters from a Persian in England to his Friend at Ispahan. 8vo. London.

   These letters were inspired by the *Persian Letters* of Montesquieu, but they fall far short of the Frenchman's in acumen and wit.

1736   A Letter from a Moor at London to his Friend at Tunis; containing an Account of his Journey through England, with his Observations of the Laws, Customs, Religion and Manners of the English Nation. London.

   This is so listed in "Books Received," *Gent. Mag.,* vol. 6, July. See under 1740 below.

Remarks of a Persian Traveller on the principal Courts of Europe, with a Dissertation upon that of England, the Nation in general and the Prime Minister. Written in the Persian Language Originally, and translated into English and French. London. (So listed in *Gent. Mag.,* vol. 66, Jan.)

1739 BOYER, JEAN BAPTISTE DE (Marquis d'Argens). Chinese Letters. London.

A Letter from a Spaniard in London to his Friend at Madrid. London. (So listed in *Gent. Mag.,* vol. 9, April.)

1740 Letters from a Moor at London. Edit. by Lloyd. London.

1744 BOYER, JEAN BAPTISTE DE (Marquis d'Argens). The Jewish Spy. London.

1748 GRAFFIGNY, MADAME D. Lettres d'une Peruvienne. Amsterdam.

1748 (In English.) Letters written by a Peruvian Princess. London.

1755 ANGELONI, BATISTA. Letters on the English Nation; by Batista Angeloni, a Jesuit who resided many Years in London. Translated from the Italian by the Author of *The Marriage Act,* a Novel. 2 vols. 8vo. London.

2nd edit., with corrections, 2 vols., 8vo, London, 1756.
"A libellous work by Shebbeare," says Lowndes, "under the feigned name of a Jesuit." Boswell met Shebbeare through Gen. Oglethorpe and praised him as a man of more than ordinary knowledge and abilities, and deserving "to be remembered as a respectable name in literature, were it only for his admirable Letters on the English Nation, under the name of Battista Angeloni, a Jesuit." Johnson also thought well of him. But Fanny Burney, in her *Early Diary,* speaks of him disparagingly and gives specimens of his lame repartee and thrusts against the Scotch. For his *Letters to the English People,* attacking the policy of the Administration on American affairs, see under 1756-57, NORTH AMERICA, vol. II of this work.

1757 Letters from an Armenian in Ireland to his Friends at Trebisond, &c. Translated in the year 1756. London.

The names Edmond Pery and Robert Hellen have been associated with this work. See this title and date under TOURS, Ireland.

WALPOLE, HORACE. A Letter from Xo Ho, a Chinese Philosopher at London, to his Friend Lien Chi at Peking. Fol. London.

This satirical *jeu d'esprit* ran through five editions in a fortnight. Its suggestion to Goldsmith for his Chinese philosopher is well known. See following item.

1762 GOLDSMITH, OLIVER. The Citizen of the World; or, Letters from a Chinese Philosopher, Residing in London, to his Friends in the East. 2 vols. 8vo. London.

These letters were first published in the *Public Ledger,* commencing on Jan. 24, 1760. When printed in collected form they took the name by which they are best known, *The Citizen of the World.* However much Goldsmith may have owed to Montesquieu's *Persian Letters,* or the *Lettres d'une Peruvienne,* and the like, he probably took his cue more directly from Walpole's *Letter,* which was briefly noticed in the May issue of the *Monthly Magazine,* for which Goldsmith was working at the time. When his own letters began to appear in the *Public Ledger* the next year, he gave his Oriental the name of Lien Chi Altangi, one of Walpole's imaginary correspondents. Goldsmith said in his Preface that all the metaphors and images were taken from the East. He probably adopted materials from Du Halde and LeComte. But after all, it was Goldsmith who was commenting on the communal life of London in these informal essays.

1765   The Chinese Spy, or, Emissary from the Court of Pekin, Commissioned to examine into the Present State of Europe. 6 vols. 12mo. London.

>   Vols. IV and V contain letters written from London. Very little good is found in England, the English people, dress, appearance, amusements, theaters, gardens, streets, country manners, morals, or customs. The account constitutes one unbroken diatribe, which, if vitriolic, is amusing.

1775   JOHNSTON, CHARLES. The Pilgrim: or, A Picture of Life. In a Series of Letters, written mostly from London by a Chinese Philosopher to his Friend at Quang-Tong. Containing Remarks upon the Laws, Customs, and Manners of the English and other Nations. Illustrated by a Variety of curious and interesting Anecdotes, and Characters drawn from real life. 2 vols. in 1. 8vo. Dublin.

1781   Anticipation: or, The Voyage of an American to England in the Year 1899, in Letters humourously describing the supposed Situation of this Kingdom at that Period. 12mo. London.

>   How far this forecast squared with the recorded history of 1899 would be a curious matter.

1788   Arabian Letters from Abdallah, a Native of Arabia, to his Friend at Moca. 8vo. London.

>   Reviewed *Gent. Mag.*, vol. 58, 816-18. The review gives some idea of the contents of this work, such as remarks on enclosures, physicians, observance of Sunday, educational methods at the universities, confederacy against the African pirates, exclusive trade, absurd orthography, game laws, etc. It was purported to have been written in Arabic and found in a chest of drawers in a lodging room which a native of Mocha had just quitted.

III

Descriptions

(The practical temper of the English people has naturally inclined them toward useful information and generalized knowledge. This bias manifested itself with growing strength from the latter half of the 17th century on through the 18th and accounts for the welcome given such publications as *Political Survey of Great Britain,* the *Modern Universal History,* the *Biographica Britannia,* the *Lives of the Admirals,* and many like historical and statistical works. It likewise determined the character of descriptions, which, as will be observed from the following titles, tended toward the general, such as the face of the country in its more commonly observed features, the varieties of soil and its products, the state of manufactures, the population, the roads, etc., with something added from the history and antiquities, from which the past and present state of affairs might be deduced. It will be noticed that description of some kind enters into almost every division of this work. Tours, histories, chronicles, antiquities, surveys, maps, and views—all help to carry the load. A large number of the publications listed below plainly state in their titles that they are descriptions, that is, impersonal accounts of what meets the eye, whether in its physical aspect or in its manners and customs. And in the greater part of the remainder, the intention is signified in phrases like observations, accounts of, wonders of, a character of, etc.)

1480   The Description of England, Wales and Scotland. Folio tract, finished by Caxton, 18 Aug. 1480. 20 Edward IV. London.

> So cited by Gough, *Anecdotes of British Topography,* 13, where it is stated that the work consists of twenty-nine chapters printed from Trevisa's translation of Higden's *Polychronicon* (see Higden under 1482, HISTORY AND CHRONICLE). Of the original seven books of Higden, the first is a description of Britain, which Caxton regarded as so important that he issued it again as an independent work. Numerous editions followed down to 1528, among which were printings by Pynson, Wynkyn de Worde, and Julian Notary. See below.

> > 1504   The descrypcyon of Englonda, Walys, Scotlond, and Irlong; speaking of the noblesse and worthynesse of the same. Fol. London. (Julian Notary.)

1521   MAJOR, JOHN. De Britanniae Descriptione. From Book I of the *Historia Majoris Britanniae.* 4to. Paris.

> The Scottish part printed in Hume Brown, *Scotland before 1700,* Edinburgh, 1893. See Major under HISTORY AND CHRONICLE. See below.

> > 1893   MAJOR, JOHN. Of the Boundaries of Scotland, its Cities, Towns, and Villages; of its Customs in War, and in the Church; of its Abundance of Fish, its Harbours, Woods, Islands, etc. In Hume Brown, *op. cit.,* Edinburgh.
> > The translation used here is that by Archibald Constable for the Scottish History Society. Major's descriptions are of interest for the view they give of 16th century life and people in Scotland. This is particularly true of those accounts that were the result of personal observation, but most of his facts were more fully and accurately related by other chroniclers. We learn that the harp was the favorite instrument among "the wild Scots," and that the strings were made of brass and not of animal gut, and that on this "they make most pleasing melody."—From Brown.

1525   FROISSART, SIR JOHN. For some pictures of England and English life, see his *Cronycles of . . . translated oute of the Frenche* by John Bourchier (Lord Berners), under HISTORY AND CHRONICLE.

> Froissart passed many years of his life in England during the reigns of Edward III and Richard II, but his glimpses of England are fleeting. When he lands at Dover, after twenty-eight years' absence, he notices that the place has changed. Children have become men and the houses are no longer the same. The Wat Tyler riots lead to some account

of local scenes, but there is no recognition of uniqueness in his handling of what is local. Like other foreigners he finds sad treatment at the hands of the London mob. Englishmen are, he says, "the peryloust people of the worlde, and the most outragyoust if they be up, and specially the Londoners" (cap. ccxlii). Further in cap. xxxix, "the Englysshemen were so prowde, that they set nothynge by ony nacyon but by their owne."—Quoted by Rye, *England as Seen by Foreigners,* note, pp. xxxvii-xxxviii.

1527   BOECE, HECTOR. For his description of Scotland, see his *Scotorum Historiae a prima gentis origine,* under HISTORY AND CHRONICLE.

    Boece, like other early chroniclers, prefixed geographical descriptions of the country to his history. He professed to pay great attention to natural history, but his extravagant stories, which were copied by nearly all succeeding chroniclers, gave rise to the many credulities long associated with Scotland.

1530   CAESAR, GAIUS JULIUS. For his description of Britain, see his *Commentaryes,* translated by Tiptoft, under HISTORY AND CHRONICLE.

1534   VERGIL, POLYDORE. For his description of Britain, see his *Anglicae Historiae libri viginti septem,* under HISTORY AND CHRONICLE.

    The first book contains a general description of England that is far more valuable than any so far written. In manner it resembles the practice of the times in that it deals with general topographical features, such as rivers, borders, divisions of Britain, shape, climate, etc. But in matter it is much fuller and more personal. Certain wonders and peculiarities cited by him are repeated by Paradin, Munster, Jovius, and others down to Harrison. However, his Scotchmen are flesh and blood human beings and not Calibans. The division of the population into Highlanders and Lowlanders is noted. Wales becomes a land with actual physical features instead of a veiled region of romance. Many details given indicate personal observation, such as the height of Englishmen, their appearance, and their character. The dislike of the baser sort for foreigners is also in evidence.

1536   BELLENDEN, JOHN. For his cosmography and description of Scotland, see his *History and Croniklis of Scotland,* under HISTORY AND CHRONICLE.

    As noted elsewhere, this is a translation into Scots of Boece and therefore is not original.

1542   HALL, EDWARD. For material on the life, manners, and customs of England from the reign of Henry IV to the end of that of Henry VIII, see his *Union of the Two Noble and Illustre Families of York and Lancastre,* under HISTORY AND CHRONICLE.

1543   HARDYNG, JOHN. For an account of Scotland, see his *The Chronicle of John Hardynge,* under HISTORY AND CHRONICLE.

    His Topography, from a MS of his Chronicle, was reproduced in folio, Southampton, 1870; his Itinerary in Hume Brown, *Early Travellers,* 16-23, Edinburgh, 1891.
    The account he gives of Scotland, unlike the majority of descriptions in those days, is favorable. The date of his visit, which lasted three and a half years, was probably early in the reign of Henry V. His object was to obtain certain documents proving or confirming admissions of the feudal subordination of Scottish kings to the English crown. These he obtained after difficulties, dangers, and bodily injuries. These documents have now been proved to be forgeries, but that fact does not affect the veracity of his description of the country, which gives the impression of settled industry and a fair amount of comfort throughout the greater part of the nation.—From Brown. In his Itinerary Hardyng sets forth the distances from town to town and offers descriptions of what he met with.

1545   LELAND, JOHN. ΚΥΚΝΕΙΟΝ ΑΣΜΑ, Cygnea Cantio. Commentarii in Cygneam. 4to. London.

Reprinted in Hearne's edition of the *Itinerary*, Oxford, 1710.
This is a Latin poem dedicated to Henry VIII, "whose exploits are celebrated in the song of a swan swimming between Oxford and Greenwich." It is furnished with elaborate notes in Latin on the places mentioned in the song. See this item under LONDON.

1547 BORDE (BOORDE, BOARDE), ANDREW. For descriptions of England, Wales, Scotland, and Ireland, see his *The Fyrst Boke of the Introduction of Knowledge*. London.

> 2nd edit., 1562; printed by the E.E.T.S., edit. by J. Furnivall, London, 1870.
> This work was dedicated to the Princess Mary, afterwards Queen Mary, May 3, 1542. It is an amusing, quaint work. His account of the British Isles, the characters of the different races, the specimens of their languages as set forth in the guidebook questions and answers, all show an inquiring mind and a keen eye for distinctions. Borde was a great traveler. He left England for the continent at least four times. After his return from the trip of 1535, he obtained through Cromwell release from his monastic vows, and set out for Scotland to study and practice medicine. There he stayed a year, *ca.* 1536-37, and then returned to England. This was followed by another journey to the continent from which he came back probably in 1542. The latter days of his life were spent in the Fleet prison, where he had been confined on the charges of lecherous commerce with three different women. The same charge had been brought against him earlier, and his own comments on the weakness of the flesh make it possible that he was not as pure as Galahad. He died in prison, 1549.

1557-59 BALE, JOHN. Descriptiones Angliae, Scotiae, Hyberniae. In his *Scriptorum Illustrium majoris Brytanniae, Catalogus*. Basel.

> This is made up of matter taken from Jovius, George Lily, John Leland and Polydore Vergil.—*Cambridge Bibliography*.

1558 LYNDSAY, SIR DAVID. The Description of the Realme of Scotland. In his works printed at Paris.

> An edition of his works, 4to, Edinburgh, 1568; numerous later editions.

1572 LLWYD, HUMPHREY. For a description of England, Scotland and Wales, see his *Commentarioli Britannicae Descriptionis Fragmentvm* (Englished as *The Breuiary of Britayne*, by Thomas Twyne, London, 1573), under HISTORY AND CHRONICLE.

1576 LAMBARDE, WILLIAM. A Perambulation of Kent: containing the Description, Hystorie, and Customes of the Shyre, Collected and written (for the most part) in the Yeere 1570, and now increased by the addition of some Things which the Authour him selfe hath observed since that time. Map. 4to. London.

> 2nd edit., "increased and altered after the Author's owne last Copie," 4to, London, 1596 (issued with this was the "Carde of the Beacons in Kent"); 3rd edit. (undated), London, [1636]; 4th, a "remainder" issue of the 3rd, with the Charters of the Cinque Ports added, London, 1656; 5th, same text and date. Another edit., 1826.
> The 1st edition contains "The Names of suche of the Nobilitie and Gentrie as the Heralds recorded in their Visitation, 1574," a section which was omitted in later editions. With this work we meet the first of those county histories which were to issue from the press in greatly increasing numbers.
> Lambard was the son of an alderman and sheriff of London. He was admitted to Lincoln's Inn, where he made considerable progress in the law, which combined with his antiquarian leanings led him to the study of Anglo-Saxon law. This he brought to a head in his publication (1568) of a collection of Anglo-Saxon laws begun by Laurence Nowell, dean of Lichfield, under the title of *Archaionomia,* with the text in Old English and a parallel Latin translation. In his shire history, Lambard made extensive use of Old English documents, quoting rather largely from the *Textus Roffensis,* which he found in the library of Rochester Cathedral. Furthermore, in his office of Record Keeper of the Tower of London, he had unusual opportunities for gathering materials. He had planned a history

similar to Camden's *Britannia* (see under 1586 below), but withheld it. It was published in 1730, when it appeared as *Dictionarium Angliae Topographicum et Historicum*. For Lambard's accomplishments in Old English studies see Adams, *Old English Scholarship in England*.

1577   HARRISON, WILLIAM. An Historicall Description of the Iland of Britaine with a briefe rehersall of the Nature and Qualities of the People of England. In Holinshed, *The Chronicles of England, Scotlande, and Irelande*. See Holinshed under HISTORY AND CHRONICLE.

> The editions of the *Description* in the main accompany those of the *Chronicle*. Edit. by Henry Ellis, 4to, London, 1807; edit., with slightly different title, by F. J. Furnivall, 3 vols., London, 1877-1904; edit. by Lothrop Withington, 8vo, London, 1877. (In content the last two are limited to England.)
>
> The part relating to Scotland is "a simple translation" made by Harrison from Hector Boece (see under 1527 above); that relating to Ireland, by Stanyhurst and Campion; and that relating to England, by Harrison, who relied on Higden, Leland, Camden, and Stow, but transmuted their researches into something of his own. This is one of the most important sources extant for the sociological historian, besides being a work of distinction in itself. The author leaves little untouched—cities and towns, universities, churches, fairs and markets, gardens and orchards, parks and warrens, food, diet, and apparel of the people, furnishing of the houses, provision for the poor, air, soil, cattle and fowls, beasts and vermin, fish, quarries of stone, production of wine in England, minerals and metals, etc. He modeled the first book of his description on his predecessors, but in later books he becomes expansive on the social history, providing us with rich morsels after the dry crusts of the chroniclers. Where the latter repeated statements that were commonplaces, Harrison tried to render English life and institutions with truth. "If the chronicles are the base, Leland is the keystone, Harrison the corner, and Camden, Stow, and Saxton form the finished edifice."—From Clare Williams, *Thomas Platter in England*, Introduction.

> 1877   HARRISON, WILLIAM. Elizabethan England, from "A Description of England" by William Harrison. Edit. by Lothrop Withington, with Introduction by F. J. Furnivall. 8vo. London.

1578   LESLIE, JOHN. For a description of the country and an account of the people of Scotland, see his *De Origine, Moribus, et Rebus Gestis Scotorum*, under HISTORY AND CHRONICLE.

> Translated into Scots (but not published) by James Dalrymple, religious of Regensburg, 1596. This translation published by the Scot. Text Soc., 2 vols., Edinburgh, 1888 and 1895. Sections in Hume Brown, *Scotland before 1700*, 113-83.
>
> This is a more serious performance than that of Boece, though the author is hardly less credulous than the latter. He adorns his narrative with all sorts of strange stories of the sort readers wanted to believe. His description of Scotland has historical value.

1579   CHALONER, SIR THOMAS. De Republica Anglorum instauranda libri decem. Accessit Panegyricus Henrici VIII. Epigrammata, etc. London.

> In this extensive Latin poem Chaloner sets out his precepts for a better and greater England. It contains much important matter on education, agriculture, horse breeding, and a hundred other subjects of Tudor times. Chaloner had been employed in many embassies by Henry VIII and Edward VI, and so had opportunities to see much of the whole of Europe. In 1561 he was ambassador to Spain. The first edition was dedicated to Lord Burghley.

CHAMBERS (or CHALMERS), DAVID. La recherche des singularites plus remarquables concernant l'estat d'Ecosse. 8vo. Paris.

> This was dedicated to Mary, Queen of Scots. For his stay in France see Françisque Michel, *Les Ecossais en France-Les Français en Ecosse*, vol. II, 211. See also Chambers under HISTORY AND CHRONICLE, 1579.

1580   CHURCHYARD, THOMAS. The Wonders of Wiltshire and the Earthquake of Kent. 8vo. London. (So cited in Gough.)

LYLY, JOHN. Euphues and his England . . . the Description of the Country, the Court, the Manners of that Island, etc. London.

Numerous later editions: see the one edited by Morris W. Croll and Henry Clemons, London, 1916.

Euphues has at length arrived in London, and according to the author was as long in viewing it as he was in coming to it. His description of the shape of the Island, the character of the English people, the sights of London, and the universities follows the well known pattern. Of the English he says, "It is the nature of that country to sift strangers. Everyone that shaketh thee by the hand is not joined to thee in heart." "Nothing in England is more constant than the inconsistency of attire,"—a trait noted by other travelers. There is comment on the laws, beasts, vermin, and much on ladies, who "have long ears and short tongues, broad eyes and light fingers, ready to espy and apt to strike." "The Kentish men are most civilized." And so on.

1582 BUCHANAN, GEORGE. For his description of Scotland, see his *Rerum Scoticarum Historia*, under HISTORY AND CHRONICLE.

A selection in Hume Brown, *Scotland before 1700*, 218-35.

The extract given in Brown is from the translation by Thomas Aikman, which appeared in 1821. Like his predecessors, Major, Boece, and Leslie, Buchanan opens up his history with a general description of Scotland. These descriptions took the place of maps, of which there were no satisfactory ones extant. Buchanan was conscious that he was writing for the literati of Europe as well as for his own countrymen, and consequently avoided unnecessary details by making his description shorter than those done before. He corrected some of the errors of Boece and also his too ready acceptance of incredible tales. Though Buchanan made some mistakes in topography, he generally took pains to inform himself directly of what he was describing. As a masterly survey of Scotland his work can hardly be surpassed. Its organization, its subordination of parts, and its selection of details reveal the same artistry that made his history comparable to the best models of antiquity.—From Brown, *op. cit.* The first two books are taken up with the description of the several provinces, while the third is a collection of the Roman accounts of Scotland. This description was turned into verse by Andrew Melvin, in his *Scotiae Topographia*, prefixed to the edition of Pont's Maps, 1655.—From Gough, 624.

1584 PRICE, SIR JOHN. A Description of Cambria, now called Wales, wrote by Sir John Price, Knt. (1559), prefixed to the Historie of Cambria, now called Wales; a part of the most famous Yland of Brytaine, written in the Brytish Language aboue two hundreth yeares past; translated into English by H. Lloyd, Gentleman: Corrected, augmented, and continued out of Records and best approoued Authors, by Dauid Powel, Doctor in Diuinitie. 8vo. London.

Newly edit. by William Wynne, 8vo, London, 1697; five later editions.

See Caradoc of Llancarvon, under HISTORY AND CHRONICLE. The Description of Cambria was reprinted at Oxford, 1663, in two 4to sheets and a half, under the title of A Description of Wales, but so much altered and disguised that many have thought it a different piece.—Gough, 583.

1585 GIRALDUS DE BARRI (Cambrensis). Cambriae Descriptio: Avctore Sil. Giraldo Cambrense. Cum Annotationibus David Poveli Sacrae Theologiae professoris. 8vo. London.

This makes up the third of the three parts of Ponticus Virunnius, *Britannicae Historiae libri sex*, edit. by David Powel (see annotation under TOURS BY NATIVES this date). A 2nd edit., fol., edited by Camden, 1602, is cited in Rowlands, *Cambrian Bibliography* (the reference is to Camden's *Scriptores Historiae Anglicanae*, Frankfurt). To this was annexed the first book of the *Cambriae Descriptio*, with notes by the editor. This is generally called *De laudabilibus Walliae*. The second book was published by Wharton, *Anglia Sacra*, 1691, vol. II, 447 ff., entitled *Giraldi Cambrensis liber secundus de descriptione Walliae, seu liber de laudabilibus Walliae*; divided into ten heads or chapters.—Gough, 581. This treatise and the *Itinerary* reprinted from Wharton and Camden by Sir Richard Hoare, both Latin and translation, 2 vols., fol., London, 1806. Both were again edited by James F. Dimock, Rolls Series, vol. VI, *Opera*, London, 1868 (see under 1858-1911, HISTORY AND CHRONICLE).

There is apparently no early recension of the first version extant. Up to the 16th century, if one may judge by the number of MSS remaining from an earlier date, the *Descrip-*

tion would seem to have been little valued in comparison with the *Itinerary*. Yet the treatise is of much value, though it often gives the Welsh a bad reputation. Higden used it freely and, unlike the majority of chroniclers, recognized fully its authority.

CHURCHYARD, THOMAS. Chips concerning Scotland. London.

An edition by Chalmers, London, 1817. See below.

1817   CHURCHYARD, THOMAS. Chips concerning Scotland; a Collection of His Pieces Relative to that Country. With Historical Notices and Life by G. Chalmers. 8vo. London.

STUBBES, PHILIP. The Anatomie of Abuses: Contayning A Discourse or Briefe Summarie of such Notable Vices and Imperfections, as now raigne in many Christian Countreyes of the Worlde: but (especiallie) in a verie famous Ilande called Ailgna: Together, with most fearfull Examples of God's Iudgementes, executed vpon the wicked for the same, as well in Ailgna of late, as in other places elsewhere. Made dialogue-wise by Philip Stubbes. London.

5th edit., London, 1595; edit. by Furnivall, New Shakespeare Soc., 1877-82, London. This castigation of the English nation arises out of the charges that they dress too flashily, that harlots paint their faces, horrible whoredom is indulged in too freely, Sabbath breaking, gaming, dicing, cockfighting are too prevalent, the poor are neglected, dancing, music, stage plays are too much frequented, and so on through the range of "Imperfections" that spot the features of any civilized Christian land.

1586   CAMDEN, WILLIAM. Britannia, sive Florentissimorum Regnorum Angliae, Scotiae, Hiberniae, et Insularum adiacentium ex intima Antiquitate Chorographica Descriptio. Map by Mercator. 8vo. London.

2nd edit., enlarged, 12mo, London, 1587; 3rd, "nunc tertio recognita, & magna accessione adaucta," 4to, London, 1590, the same year at Frankfurt; 4th, "nunc quarto recognita, & magna accessione post Germanicam editionem adaucta," 4to, London, 1594; 5th, with reply to Brooke's attack (see below), 4to, London, 1600; 6th (the last under Camden's hand), much augmented and corrected, with maps of the counties engraved from surveys of Norden, Saxton, and Owen, by Hole and Kip with Latin text on their backs, fol., London, 1607. 1st English edition by Philemon Holland, maps and plates, fol., London, 1610; again 1625 and 1637; newly translated by Bishop Edmund Gibson, with 50 maps, most of them bearing the name of Morden, and with large additions and improvements, fol., London, 1695; again, with colored reprints on thin paper, and changes of maps, 1722; with uncolored reprints of maps issued in 1722 edition, 1753; 4th edit., of Gibson, portrait and maps, 2 vols., fol., 1772; translated from the 1607 edition, enlarged with the latest discoveries, by Richard Gough, maps, etc., 3 vols., fol., London, 1789.
Abridgements: Latin edition, 1599; Amsterdam, 1617; by Regnerus Vitellius Zirizaeus, Amsterdam, 1639, which was translated into English and published wth maps, 8vo, London, 1626; English text, with portrait and 61 maps, 2 vols., 8vo, London, 1701.
The original was printed by Blaeu, 8vo, Leyden, 1639, and again much altered and interpolated, with Speed's maps, in vol. V of Blaeu's *Theatrum Orbis* (see Blaeu under 1662, MAPS AND CHARTS), Amsterdam, 1662. Translated into French by Salabert and Sorbière, and printed in the *Grand Atlas*. A separate edition of the description of Scotland, by Sir James Dalrymple, Edinburgh, 1695. An index to the work, fol., London, 1616.
The *Britannia* was first dedicated to Lord Burghley; and the 1600 edition to Queen Elizabeth. The latter contained the corrections to the errors pointed out by Brooke accompanied with a polite reply which showed that Camden had very little esteem for the York Herald. During his confinement of nine months in 1607 from an injury to his leg in falling from a horse, Camden gave himself up to enlarging and improving the edition of 1607. And as late as 1621 he was still making researches for another edition, the completion of which was denied him. He assisted Holland in preparing the English edition of 1610, which contained some new matter by way of a little ornithology. To the 1722 edition Samuel Pepys contributed "the Account of the Arsenals for the Royal Navy in Kent, with Additions to Portsmouth, so far as they relate to the Royal Navy," and John Ray drew up the "Catalogues of Plants at the end of each County." The 1789 edition of Richard Gough took seven years in translating and enlarging, and nine more in printing, exclusive of twenty years in journeying (according to Nichols, *Literary Anecdotes*, vol. IX, 52). It was supplemented by the addition of 311 old views by Buck, Kip, Hollar, and

Gough, including maps in color. Before this labor of love could be got ready for the press, Gough had quarreled with the publisher, John Nichols, and withdrew from any further connection with it. This edition was reprinted with additions and corrections to the first volume—the only one Gough superintended—in 1805.

The numerous editions and innumerable references and borrowings give evidence that Camden's countrymen looked upon the *Britannia* as something of a bible. The tribute paid to Camden by the learned of his day may best be summed up in Bishop Nicolson's words: "The common sun, whereat our modern, writers have lighted their little torches." For a description of his labors and qualifications as an antiquary, see his *Remains concerning Britaine,* under 1604, HISTORY AND ANTIQUITIES.

1616   Indexes to Camden's Description of Britain, giving singularly full References to the Principal Old Families living in each County, the Latin Names of the Villages, Towns, Views, etc., of England, also their English Equivalents. Fol. London.

1695   CAMDEN, WILLIAM. Description of Scotland. 2nd edit. by Sir James Dalrymple. 8vo. Edinburgh.

This contains a supplement to the list of those peers or lords of parliament who were mentioned in the first edition, and an account of those since raised to and further advanced in the degree of peerage, until the year 1694. Camden professed only to have run over Scotland. His account of it was altered in different editions as he acquired information. It was published separately from his *Britannia* as listed above.

1587   CHURCHYARD, THOMAS. The Worthyness of Wales, wherein are more than 1000 things rehearsed, set out in Prose and Verse, and enterlarded with many Wonders, etc. 4to. London.

Reprinted, 12mo, London, 1776; in facsimile by the Spenser Society, London, 1871. See below.

This is a long chorographical poem of much antiquarian and historical interest. Churchyard was born of a good family, as he himself says, and was highly esteemed by Henry VIII, Edward VI, Mary, and Elizabeth.

1776   CHURCHYARD, THOMAS. The Worthines of Wales, A Poem. A True Note of the Auncient Castles, famous Monuments, goodly Rivers, faire Bridges, fine Townes, and courteous People, that I have seen in the noble Countrie of Wales, And Now Set Forth by Thomas Churchyard. 8vo. London.

1589   A Comparison of the English and Spanish Nations. Translated out of French by Master Rashley. London.

1590   TWYNE, THOMAS (Editor). De Rebus Albionicis, Britannicis, atque Anglicis: by John Twyne. London (?).

VALLANS, WILLIAM. A Tale of Two Swannes, wherein is comprehended the Original and Increase of the River Lee, commonly called the Ware River: Together with the Antiquities of Sundrie Places and Townes seated upon the same. Pleasant to be read, and not altogether unprofitable to be understood. 4to. London.

Reprinted by Hearne in vol. V of his edition of Leland's *Itinerary,* 1710-12 (see under TOURS BY NATIVES).

This is an imitation of Leland's *Cygnea Cantio* (see under 1545 above), and was published by Hearne from a copy among Rawlinson's books, and prefixed to vol. V of Leland's *Itinerary.*—Gough, 197. It deals with the county of Hertford and is written in unrhymed hexameters.

1593   NORDEN, JOHN. Speculum Britanniae. The firste parte. An historicall and chorographicall description of Middlesex, wherein are also alphabeticallie sett downe the Names of the Cyties, Townes, Parishes, Hamletes, Howses of Name, etc.,

with Directions spedelie to find anie place desired in the Mappe and the Distance between place and place, without compasses. By the Travaile and View of Iohn Norden. Illustrated with maps and the arms of the principal persons interred in the county, engraved by Peter Vanden Keere. 4to. London.

This, the first fruit of his labors, was reprinted, with the Hertfordshire description, London, 1637 and 1723. His other surveys, which included Essex, Northampton, Cornwall, Kent, and Surrey, were published at various later dates. His *Preparatiue* came out in 1596. See below.

Norden's intention was to compose a series of county histories, but lack of money intervened to prevent the completion of this design. According to Hearne and other antiquaries, he certainly left behind him many unpublished manuscripts. As a map maker he probably ranks next to Saxton. Both he and the latter had a common aim in attempting a complete survey of the counties of England, Saxton by means of maps and Norden by descriptions supplemented by maps. In both instances the undertakings had authorization from Lord Burghley and the Queen herself. For an account of his work in cartography, see under this date, MAPS AND CHARTS.

1596 NORDEN, JOHN. A Preparatiue to his Speculum Britanniae. London.
    Being in financial difficulties, Norden here takes occasion to state the object of his work and the hindrances to his undertaking, as well as to silence criticism.

1598 ———. Speculi Britanniae Pars, the Description of Hartfordshire. Engraved map and three leaves, viz., an engraved title-page, dedication D. Edwardo-Seamor militi, Baroni Beauchamp Comiti Hartfordiae. "To Gentlemen well affected to this travaile," "Thinges to be considered in the use of this booke and Mappe," and Corrections. 4to. London.

1720 ———. Speculi Britanniae pars Altera, or a Delineation of Northamptonshire, being a brief Historicall and Chorographicall Description of that County, wherein are alphabetically set down, the Names of Cyties, Townes, Parishes, Hamlets, Houses of Note, and other Remarkables, by the Travayle of John Norden, in the year MDCX. 4to. London.
    This is the most superficial of all Master Norden's surveys, except in a few towns; nor were the map and plans of Peterborough and Northampton referred to in it ever engraved.—Gough, 377.

1728 ———. Speculi Britanniae pars: a Topographical and Historical Description of Cornwall, with a map of the County, and each Hundred; in which are contained the names and seats of the several Gentlemen then Inhabitants; as also thirteen Views of the most remarkable Curiosities in that County. By the Perambulation, View, and Delineation of John Norden. To which are added, The West Prospect of the sometime conventual Church of St. German's, and a Table of the Distances of the Towns from each other; with some Account of the Author. 4to. London.
    This survey was made about 1584. It was edited by Christopher Bateman.

1840 ———. Speculi Britanniae pars. An Historical and Chorographical Description of the County of Essex. Edit. from the original Manuscript by Sir Henry Ellis, *Publ. Camden Soc.,* vol. 9. London.
    This contains map, short descriptions of general produce in various hundreds, boundaries, alphabetical table of the towns, parishes, and hamlets, which are located in the map by means of letters and figures in the margin so coordinated as to make easily found any town. There is a table of houses having special names, with their present occupiers, and a table of halls in Essex which bear the names of their owners.

1938 ———. The Chorography of Norfolk. An Historical and Chorographical Description of Norffolck. Edit. by Christabel M. Hood. Transcribed by Mary A. Blyth. 8vo. Norwich.
    The manuscript is judged from evidence of handwriting and internal details to be one of the completed but unpublished surveys of John Norden.

1594 A Short Description of the Western Iles of Scotland, lying in the Deucalian Sea, being above 300. Also the Iles of Orkney and Shetland or Hethland. London.

This tract was reprinted in *Certayne Matters concerning the Realme of Scotland* (see under 1603 below).

WALDEGRAVE, R. Genealogie of the Kings of Scotland, and List of Nobilitie, etc., with Description of Scotland. 4to. Edinburgh.

1595 Topographical Miscellanies, containing Old History and Descriptions of Mansions, Churches, Families, etc. Numerous plates, including a large folding plate of Blackfriars, Canterbury, by T. Langton, 1595. 4to. (Place?)

> This reads rather like an 18th century title. The work is so cited in Daniell and Feild, *Manual of Brit. Topog.* 1595 may be the date of the engraving.

1596 SYMONSON, PHILIP. A New Description of Kent. Map. London (?).

1600 BROOKE, RALPH. A Discouerie Of Certaine Errours . . . In the much commended Britannia. 1594. Very preiudiciall to the discentes and successions of the auncient Nobilitie of this Realme. By Yorke Herault. 4to. London.

> Reprinted with Camden's answer, 4to, London, 1723. Another title includes Brooke's second reply, London, 1724. See below.
> Quite a full account of the controversy between the two is to be found in Gough, 16-18. Brooke accused Camden not only of being ignorant of the subject of heraldry but also of lifting "not onely handfulls, but whole sheaues" from other collections. Brooke was a man of violent temper who stuck at nothing to win his point. He did not resent so much Camden's getting the position of Clarencieux Herald from him as his pretending to heraldic knowledge. No doubt jealousy was at the bottom of his pique. Camden had touched but lightly in his first three editions on genealogies, but in the fourth he gave a list of nearly 250 families, in which he apparently committed some errors. Though he corrected his mistakes in the fifth edition, he still treated his knowledge of heraldry rather lightly. The discussion stirred up a number of attacks and replies from others.

> 1724 BROOKE, RALPH. A Discoverie of certaine Errours . . . To which are added, Mr. Camden's Answer and Mr. Brooke's Reply. Now first published from an Original MS. 4to. London.

1601 SMITH, SIR THOMAS. The Common-wealth of England, and manner of gouernment thereof. London.

1603 HOWE, EDWARD. For a description of England, Scotland, Wales and Cornwall, see his *Chronicles,* under HISTORY AND CHRONICLE.

MONIPENNIE, JOHN. Certayne Matters concerning the Realme of Scotland, composed together. The Genealogie of the Kings of Scotland, etc.; the Description of the Whole of Scotland, with the Isles and Names thereof. The most rare and wonderfull Things in Scotland as they were about 1597. Edinburgh.

> *Camb. Bibl.* cites place and date of 1st edit., Edinburgh, 1594 (?).

OWEN, GEORGE. The Description of Pembrokeshire. London (?).

> Modern edit., 1892-1906. See below.
> Owen was the author of a number of works, mostly historical and antiquarian. He gave Camden some assistance in the preparation of the *Britannia.*

> 1892-1906 OWEN, GEORGE. The Description of Pembrokeshire by George Owen of Henlyss, Lord of Kemes. Edit. by Harry Owen. *Publ. Cymmrodorion Record Soc.,* no. 2, 3 pts. London.
> Part III contains the Dialogue of the Government of Wales, Cruell Laws against Welshmen, A Treatise of Lordshipps Marchers in Wales, and the Description of Wales.

1608   The Mansion of Magnanimitie, or the Strength of this Realm in respect of Situation, pleasantness of Ayre, etc. London.

1610   SPEED, JOHN. For brief descriptions of shires and towns by way of maps, see his *The Theatre of the Empire of Great Britain,* under MAPS AND CHARTS.

1612   MONIPENNIE, JOHN. For a description of Scotland, see his *Abridgement or Summarie of the Scots Chronicle,* under HISTORY AND CHRONICLE.

1613   DRAYTON, MICHAEL. Poly-Olbion. Or a Chorographical Description of Tracts, Riuers, Mountaines, Forests, and other Parts of this renowned Isle of Great Britaine, with Intermixture of the most Remarquable Stories, Antiquities, Wonders, Rarityes, Pleasures and Commodities of the same: Digested in a Poem. With a Table added, for the direction of those Occurrences of Story and Antiquitie, whereunto the Course of the Volume easily leades not. Portrait and maps. Fol. London.

   2nd and complete edit., fol., London, 1622; the whole reprinted, fol., 1748; 8vo, 4 vols., 1753. Reproduced for the Spenser Society, 1890; whole works edit. by J. William Hebel, Tercentenary Edition, 5 vols., Oxford, 1933. See below.
   The 1st edition appeared with eighteen songs, to each of which were appended copious annotations full of antiquarian learning by John Selden. The 2nd and complete edition included twelve more songs. The Address to the Reader found in the second part contains his anathema on those who spoke ill of the work: "I wish their folly may be hereditary from them to their posteritie, that their children may be beg'd for fools to the fifth generation, until it may be beyond the memory of man to know that there was any other of their families." The book was commended by even such meticulous scholars as Hearne and Wood, and is said to contain many features not noticed by Camden. It is rich in allusions to remote traditions, remarkable facts and personages, curious genealogies of rivers, and adorned with fantastic maps, one to each song, which provide the key to his excursions through the counties of England and Wales. These maps are drawn to include complete courses of rivers without reference to county boundaries.

   1622   DRAYTON, MICHAEL. Poly-Olbion; or, A Chorographical Description of Tracts, Rivers, Mountaines, . . . The Second Part, or, A Continuance of Poly-Olbion from the Eighteenth Song, containing all the Tracts, Rivers, Mountaines, etc., of the East and Northern Parts of this Isle, lying betwixt the two Famous Rivers of Thames and Tweed. 2 vols. in 1. Fol. London.

1615   A Geographical and Statistical Description of all the Counties of England and Wales, in alphabetical Order. 8vo. London.

1616   FENNOR, WILLIAM. Descriptions. (So cited by Rye, *England as Seen by Foreigners,* note, p. 216.)

   Rye says that this "Description" makes evident that it was customary to sell books at the theater before the play began. I have met with this work nowhere else.

1618   ADAMSON, JOHN. Τὰ Τῶν Μουσῶν Εἰσόδια: The Muses Welcome To . . . Iames Of Great Britaine . . . At His Majesties happie Returne to his . . . natiue Kingdome of Scotland, after 14 yeeres Absence, In Anno 1617 . . . . By I. A. Edinburgh. Also Τὰ Τῶν Μουσῶν 'Εξόδια. Planctus, & vota Musarum In . . . Iacobi . . . Regis, etc. Recessu e Scotia in Angliam, Augusti 4 Anno 1617 . . . . 2 vols. in 1. Fol. Edinburgh.

   The editor, John Adamson, was principal of Edinburgh University and a bosom friend of Andrew Melville. Nearly all his famous contemporaries, e. g., David and Alexander Hume, Drummond of Hawthorndon, David Wedderburn, David Primrose and Dr. Robt.

Boyd, contributed poems and speeches. The gem of the collection is Drummond's "Forth Feasting. A Panegyricke to the King," which contains his enumeration of the rivers of Scotland, done with a picturesqueness and felicity of characterization not inferior to Michael Drayton.—From *DNB,* quoted by Bookseller.

GAINSFORD, THOMAS. The Glory of England, or, A True Description of the many excellent Prerogatives and remarkable Blessings whereby She Triumpheth over all Nations of the World: With a justifiable Comparison betweene the eminent Kingdomes of the Earth and Herselfe; plainely manifesting the Defects of them all in regard of her Sufficiencie and Fulnesse of Happinesse. London.

Revised edit., London, 1619; reissued 1620.

1622 BURTON, ROBERT. The Description of Leicestershire, containing Matters of Antiquity, Historye, Armorye, and Genealogy. Portrait, map by Kip, and numerous cuts of arms accompanying pedigrees. Fol. London.

2nd edit., enlarged and corrected, with large folding map, fol., Lynn, 1777.
At first Burton confined himself professedly to the history of property. He left large improvements and additions in MSS.—Gough, 241. Burton was one of our earliest topographical writers, and his work must be compared, not with the elaborate performance of a later age, but with such works as Lambarde's *Kent,* Carew's *Cornwall,* and Norden's *Surveys.*—From *DNB,* quoted by Bookseller.

1629 PLUMPTRE, HUNTINGDON. Castri Nottinghamiensis descriptio. Included in *Epigrammaton opusculum duobus libellis distinctum,* etc., authore Huntingdono Plumptre, A.M. Cantab. 8vo. London.

1630 BUCHANAN AND CAMDEN. Respublica sive status Regni Scotiae et Hiberniae diversorum autorum. 24mo. Lugduni Batavorum.

Another edit., Lugduni Batavorum, 1637.

1633 LITHGOW, WILLIAM. Scotland's Welcome To Her Native Sonne, And Soveraigne Lord, King Charles Wherein is also contained, the Maner of His Coronation, and Convocation of Parliament; The whole Grievance . . . of this Kingdome, with diverse other relations, never heretofore published. 4to. Edinburgh.

In Hume Brown, *Early Descriptions,* 291-95.
This is the most interesting of Lithgow's poems. It gives a very curious picture of North Britain: the decay of education and of football, the runaway marriages to England, the taking of snuff by the ladies, and the immodesty of plaids.—F. Hindes Groome, quoted by Bookseller. This view of Scotland, if true, would surely justify the jibes of travelers like Kirke (see Kirke under 1679, TOURS BY NATIVES) and others. But Lithgow was a slave to his own magniloquence, and he gives it full rein when he takes to verse. However, the poem informs us of matters not mentioned elsewhere. In ridiculous pretension of style Lithgow fairly surpasses Franck, the Cromwellian trooper who left a curious account of his travels in Scotland (see Franck under 1694, TOURS BY NATIVES). He gives the gentry their due for their learning, which he attributes to their having been brought up in France or Italy. Lithgow states that he had completed a Surveigh of Scotland, in which he asserts he had described the country "in all parts and places, besides ports and rivers," but no trace of this has been found.—From Hume Brown. For his chief performance, the *Painful Peregrinations,* see Lithgow under 1614, GENERAL TRAVELS AND DESCRIPTIONS, vol. I of this work.

1636 GORDON, JAMES. Description of Scotland (in *Opuscula tria, chronologicum, historicum, geographicum,* etc.). 12mo. Cologne.

HOBBES, THOMAS (of Malmesbury). De mirabilibus Pecci. London.

Other edits., 4to, London, 1666; 8vo, London, 1678; 12mo, London, 1683. See below. See also Cotton under 1681 below.

These Latin verses were addressed to William Earl of Derby. These wonders of the Peak, which drew visitors in a constant stream down through the 18th century, were known as the Seven Wonders. They consisted of Castleton Cavern, Mam Tor, Elden Hole, Poole's Hole, St. Anne's Well, and the hot and cold springs. The limestone caves around Buxton and Castleton were the central attractions. The curiously carved rocks and pinnacles and the watering places of Buxton and Matlock were also popular resorts.

1678 HOBBES, THOMAS. De Mirabilibus Pecci, being the Wonders of the Peak in Derbyshire, commonly called "the Devil's Arse of Peak." In English and Latine, the Latine by Thomas Hobbes, the English by a Person of Quality. 8vo. London.

1638 ADAMSON, H. The Muses Threnodie: or, Mirthful Mournings on the Death of Mr. Gall: Containing a variety of pleasant Poetical Descriptions, Moral Instructions, Historical Narratives, and Divine Observations, with the most remarkable Antiquities of Scotland, especially of Perth. Edinburgh.

2nd edit., 2 vols., 8vo, Perth, 1774. See below.

The verses on Gall are largely made up of an account of places and objects in and around Perth, which were the outcome of personal visits. They are useful and interesting, and Cant's notes to the 1774 edition increase their value.—Mitchell, *List of Travels.*

1774 ADAMSON, H. The Muses Threnodie, . . . New Edition: to which are added explanatory Notes and Observations: King James's Charter of Confirmation; an Account of Gowrie's Conspiracy; a List of the Magistrates of Perth, with Notes; a List of the Subscribers of a Free Gift for building the New Bridge; and an Account of the two remarkable Inundations which endangered the Town of Perth in 1210 and 1621, etc. Compiled from authentic Records. By James Cant. 2 vols. 8vo. Perth.

1640 Vox Borealis, or The Northern Discoverie: By way of Dialogue between Jamie and Willie. 4to. Amidst the Babylonians, Printed by Margery Mar-Prelat, in Thwackcoat-lane, at the Signe of the Crab-tree Cudgell, without any priviledge of the Cater-Caps, the year coming on, 1641. [Amsterdam, Jan Evertsz Cloppenburg, 1640.]

Written in prose and verse. This tract forms one of a series of books printed at Amsterdam by Cloppenburg, or his successors, all of them printed in the year 1640, and most of them relating to the situations existing between England and Scotland in that year. The authorship has been attributed to Sir John Suckling, the poet. Although he did accompany Charles I to Scotland in 1639, his authorship is extremely improbable. The work has been also attributed to Sir John Mennis and reprinted under his name. The description of life both in London and Scotland at this time is valuable and most diverting. No explanation is needed as to why it was printed abroad.—From A. Rosenthal Ltd., Catalogue V.

1641 PRYNNE, WILLIAM. Movnt-Orgveil, or, Divine and Profitable Meditations raised from the Contemplation of these Three Leaves of Nature's Volume: 1. Rockes; 2. Seas; 3. Gardens; digested into Three Distinct Poems; to which is prefixed a Poeticall Description of Mount-Orgueil Castle in the Isle of Jersey. Portrait. 4to. London.

1644 The Kingdome of England and Principality of Wales, Exactly Described with euery Sheere and the small Townes in euery one of them, in Six Mappes, Portable for euery Mans Pocket. Vsefull to all Commanders for Quarterings of Souldiers . . . Described by one that trauailed throughout the whole Kingdome, for its purpose. 8vo. London.

1646   Forresta de Windsor, in Com. Surrey. The Meers, Meets, Limits, and Bounds of the Forest of Windsor in the County of Surrey. 4to. London.

A Prospect of the most Famovs Parts of the World; viz. Asia, Africa, Europe, America . . . [England, Wales, Scotland, and Ireland are described]. London.

1647   EVELYN, JOHN. A Character of England as it was lately presented in a Letter to a Noble Man of France. 12mo. London.

> 3rd edit., with added matter, 3 vols., 12mo, London, 1659. See below.

>> 1659 EVELYN, JOHN. A Character of England as it was lately presented in a Letter to a Noble Man of France, with Reflexions upon Gallus Castratus; a Perfect Description of the People and Country of Scotland; Brief Character of the Low-Countries under the States. 3 vols. in 1. 12mo. London.
>> Gallus Castratus replied with *An Answer to a slanderous Pamphlet called the Character of England.*

1649   WELDON, SIR ANTHONY. For a description of the inhabitants and country of Scotland, see his *Perfect Description,* under TOURS BY NATIVES.

1650   GORDON, SIR ROBERT (of Straloch). Description of the Inland Provinces of Scotland lying between Tay River and Murra Fyrth, contayning Braid-Allaban, Athol, Brae of Mar, Badenoch, Strath-Spey, Lochaber and the West. Map 16½ x 21 ins. (Probably done for Blaeu's *Theatrum orbis terrarum,* which see under 1634-35, together with Gordon's *Scotia antiqua* under 1653, MAPS AND CHARTS.)

> The date 1650 is approximate.

1652   For poetical descriptions of the Orkneys, see Maidment, *Reprints,* under 1835 below.

1654-62   GORDON, SIR ROBERT. Adnotata ad descriptionem duarum praefecturarum Aberdoniae et Banfiae in Scotia ultra-montana. In Scottish volume of Blaeu's *Atlas,* after the first issue of 1654. Fol. Amsterdam, 1662.

> Reprinted in *Collections for a History of the Shires of Aberdeen and Banff, Publ. Spalding Club,* vol. 9, Aberdeen, 1843; also in MacFarlane, *Geog. Coll.* (with translation into English), vol. II, Edinburgh, 1906-08.

1656   CHALONER, JAMES. For a description of the Isle of Man, see App. under the item following:

SMITH, WILLIAM (Rouge Dragon Herald), and WILLIAM WEBB. The Vale-Royall of England: or, The County Palatine of Chester illustrated, wherein is contained a Geographical and Historical Description, with Coats of Arms belonging to every individual Family of the whole County, an Exact Chronology of its Rulers and Governors . . . also an excellent Discourse of the Island of Man, the Inhabitants, Trade, etc. (by Chaloner). Maps and views by Hollar and 11 plates of arms. Fol. London.

> Originally "performed" by Smith and Webb in 1585. This was expanded and reissued from time to time by different editors. See Bell, under 1830 below. The work is often associated with the name of Daniel King, who, however, did only the dedication and the engravings after the manner of Hollar. Of King, Anthony à Wood said that he was not

able to write one word of true English, being "a most ignorant, silly fellow," and more-over "an arrant knave."—Bookseller's Note. The book is full of foolish theories, misplaced learning and blunders, but the importance of its plans and details, despite inaccuracies, is generally recognized by antiquaries.—*DNB*.

1658 HAWKINS, RICHARD. A Discourse of the Nationall Excellencies of England. London.

1659 KILBOURNE, R. For a topographical account of Kent, see his *A Topographie or Survey of the County of Kent,* under SURVEYS.

LEIGH, EDWARD. England described, or, The several Counties and Shires thereof briefly handled, some things also promised to set forth the Glory of this Nation. 12mo. London.

> Mostly copied from Camden.—Gough, 24.

PHILIPOT, THOMAS. For a description of Kent, see his *Villare Cantianum,* under SURVEYS.

1661 ENDERBIE, PERCY. For a description of Wales, see his *Cambria Triumphans,* under HISTORY AND ANTIQUITIES.

1662 FULLER, THOMAS. The History of the Worthies of England. Fol. London.

> A trifling abridgement and continuation of this appeared under the title of *Anglorum Speculum* by G. S., 8vo, London, 1684 (see George Sandys under 1684 below). An edit., 3 vols., London, 1862. Sometimes the 18th century Index is bound up with various later editions.
> This work is planned on an alphabetical arrangement of counties. In the Dedication to Charles II, by the "Author's Orphan," John Fuller, it is stated that "The matter of this Work, for the most part, is the description of such native and peculiar Commodities as the several Counties of Your Kingdom afford, with a revival of the Memories of such Persons which have in each County been eminent for Parts of Learning." Each county is prefaced with an account of its chorography, its boundaries, extent, productivity, the medicinal herbs, the wonders, buildings, local proverbs, the finny and feathered tribes, etc. Then follow the biographies and lists of gentry and sheriffs.

MELVILLE, ANDREW. Scotiae Topographia. Amsterdam.

> This is a metrical version of Buchanan's first two chapters describing the several provinces of Scotland (see Buchanan, *Rerum Scoticarum Historia,* under 1582, HISTORY AND CHRONICLE). Melville is ranked by Izaac Walton next to Buchanan as a poet. This noted Presbyterian scholar and divine had a varied career in church and state. The above work was first printed in Blaeu's *Atlas Major,* vol. VI (see under MAPS AND CHARTS).

SMITH, CAPTAIN JOHN. For a description of the Orkney and Shetland Islands, see his *Trade and Fishing of Great Britain,* under ANCIENT AND PRESENT STATE.

1670 A Modern Account of Scotland: being an exact Description of the Country, and a true Character of the People and their Manners. Written from thence by an English Gentleman. 4to. London.

> Reprinted in *Harl. Misc.,* vol. VII, 121, 1744-46.
> Is this satirical account the same as that waggish one by Thomas Kirke of Crookege (see Kirke under 1679, TOURS BY NATIVES)?

1673 BLOME, RICHARD. Britannia: or, A Geographical Description of the Kingdoms of England, Scotland, and Ireland, with the Isles and Territories thereto belong-

ing. . . . An Alphabetical Table of the Names, Titles, and Seats of the Nobility and Gentry that each County of England and Wales is, or lately, was, ennobled with. Illustrated with a Map of each County of England, besides several general ones. The like never before published. Fol. London.

The fifty maps by Blome are poorly drawn, in addition to being too sketchy.—Chubb, *The Printed Maps.* A most notorious piece of plagiarism on which Thomas Blount, author of the ancient tenures, wrote animadversions; but whether they were printed Wood could not tell.—Gough, 24.

News from the Channel: or, The Discovery and Perfect Description of the Isle of Serke, appertaining to the English Crown, and never before publickly discoursed of, truly setting forth the notable Stratagem whereby it was first taken, the Nature of the Place and People; their Government, Customs, Manufactures, and other Particulars, no less necessary than pleasant to be known. In a Letter from a Gentleman, now inhabiting there, to his Kinsman in London. 4to. London.

Reprinted in *Harl. Misc.,* vol. III, 480, 1744-46.

1674 The Western Wonder; or, O Brazeel, an inchanted Island, discovered; with a Relation of two Shipwrecks in a dreadful seastorm in that Discovery. To which is added, A Description of a Place called Montecapernia, relating to the Nature of the People, their Qualities, Humours, Fashions, Religions, etc. 4to. London.

A burlesque description of Wales.—Gough, 587. See following item.

1675 O Brazeel, or, The Inchanted Island: being a Particular Relation of the late Discovery and wonderful Disenchantment of an Island on the North of Ireland: with an Account of the Riches and Commodities thereof. Communicated by a Letter from Londonderry to a Friend in London. 4to. London.

The relationship of these items is unknown to me. Someone else may have picked up the idea and spun it out further. The name, O Brazeel, is suggestive of the name given at times by the Irish to their Land of the Ever Young, situated far out to sea.

1676 England's Remarques. A View of all the Counties of England and Wales, with their Growth and Manufactures; the Number of all the Bishops, Dukes, Marquesses, Earls, Viscounts, Barons, Parliament-men, Hundreds, Market-towns, and Parishes, in each County, the Length, Bredth, and Circumference of the same, and to what Diocese it belongs, also the Names of all the chief Cities or Towns of every County, and the Distances of the same from London. And likewise the Names of all Market-towns, and upon what Dayes they are kept. London.

Other edits., 12mo, 1678 and 1682.

1680 MORDEN, ROBERT. For a brief description of England and Wales, see his *Pocket Book of all the Counties of England and Wales,* under AIDS TO TRAVELERS.

1681 COTTON, CHARLES. The Wonders of the Peak. 4to. London.

This was reprinted in all the editions of his works from 1709 to 1765, with miserable views of Chatsworth and the Devil's Arse. Bagford was told he first wrote it in the dialect of the county, and make a glossary to it, but what became of it [Bagford] had not heard. —Gough, 134. Cotton also published burlesques of Vergil (1664) and Lucian (1675); a

"second part" of Walton's *Complete Angler;* and a standard translation of Montaigne's *Essays* (1685). His poems were collected in 1689 and his works in 1715.—*DNB.* See Hobbes under 1636 above.

PATERSON, JAMES. For a geographical description of Scotland, with the fairs, see his *Geographical Description of Scotland,* under AIDS TO TRAVELERS.

1682   BURTON, RICHARD (pseud. of Nathaniel Crouch). Admirable Curiosities, Rarities, and Wonders, in England, Scotland, and Ireland; or, An Account of many remarkable Persons, and Places; and the likewise of the Battels, Sieges, Earthquakes, Tempests, Inundations, Thunders, Fires, Murders, and other Occurrences and Accidents, for many hundred Years past. 8vo. London.

> 2nd edit., 12mo, London, 1683; 8th, 12mo, 1718; 10th, 12mo, 1737; later, 1811.
> The name of the author is also given as Robert Burton. The work reads like a "chamber of horrors."

1683   SIBBALD, SIR ROBERT. Nuncius Scoto-Britannus, sive admonitio de Atlante Scotico seu descriptio Scotiae antiquae et modernae. Fol. Edinburgh.

> This appeared also in English under the title of An Account of the Scottish Atlas, or the Description of Scotland antient and modern, fol., Edinburgh.
> His design was to have published the ancient state of the country, including that of Britain in general, in Latin. The second part of the volume was to have been written in English and to treat of the present government, manners, natural productions, antiquities, etc. His discourse on the Thule of the Ancients, which was not published until it appeared in Wallace's *Description of the Isles of Orkney* (it was printed in Gibson's edition of Camden's *Britannia* also), was to have made a part of the work in a greatly enlarged form. Sibbald answered some attacks on his book in his *Vindiciae Scotiae illustratae,* 1710. See also Sibbald under 1711 below.

1684   [SANDYS, GEORGE.] Anglorum Speculum, or, The Worthies of England in Church and State, Alphabetically digested. Wherein are the Lives and Characters of the most eminent Persons since the Conquest; also the Commodities and Trade of each County, and their most flourishing Cities. 8vo. London.

> George Sandys is the expansion of the G. S. referred to under Fuller (1662 above).

1693   WALLACE, REV. JAMES (Prebendary of St. Magnus, Kirkwall). A Description of the Isles of Orkney . . . published after his Death by his Son James, M.D., F.R.S., to which is added an Essay concerning the Thule of the Ancients. 3 folding plates, one a map. 16mo. Edinburgh.

> Another edit., with additions by the author's son, Edinburgh, 1700; reprinted, Edinburgh, 1883. See below.
> The Essay concerning the Thule of the Ancients was written by Sibbald. Wallace was a loyal Episcopalian, who was deprived of his living by the Council at the Revolution of 1688, the year the description was written. He died in September of that year.
>
> > 1883   WALLACE, REV. JAMES. A Description of the Isles of Orkney. Reprint with illustrative Notes from an interleaved Copy in the Edinburgh University Library, and Additions made by the Author's Son in the Edition of 1700, edited by John Small. Facsimiles of the plates. 8vo. Edinburgh.

1694   FALLE, PHILIP. An Account of the Isle of Jersey, the greatest of those Islands that are now the only Remainder of the English Dominions in France; with a new and accurate Map of the Island. By Philip Falle, M.A., Rector of St. Saviour, and late Deputy from the States of the said Island to their Majesties. 12mo. London.

2nd edit., with additions, 8vo, London, 1734; again, 4to, London, 1797. See below.
This book was freely quoted by Bishop Gibson. The map by Lempriere was made from a survey of Philip Dumaresq, and was published separately in 1755.—Gough, 611-12.

1734 FALLE, PHILIP. Caesarea: or, An Account of Jersey, the greatest of the Islands round the Coast of England, or the ancient Dutchy of Normandy. With an Appendix of Records, etc., and accurate Map of the Island, and a Prospect of Elizabeth Castle. The 2nd edition revised and much augmented. To which are added in a Letter to the Author, Remarks on the 19th Chapter of the 2nd Book of Mr. Selden's Mare Clausum. By Philip Morant, M.A. 8vo. London.

1695 SELLER, J. For a description of England and Wales, see his *Anglia Contracta,* under MAPS AND CHARTS.

1697 MARTIN, MARTIN. Several Observations on the North Islands of Scotland. In *Philos. Trans.,* vol. 19, no. 6, Oct. London. (2 pp.)

This consists of remarks on some peculiar habits of the inhabitants and on certain individuals. See Martin under 1703 below.

1698 SPELMAN, SIR HENRY. Icenia sive Norfolciae descriptio topographica. Oxford.

This is a slight sketch of a survey intended of this county. It was printed among that learned antiquary's *Reliquiae,* Oxford, 1698 and 1727, by Gibson, who made use of it and of Dr. Tanner's *Observations* in his edition of Camden's *Britannia.*—Gough, 368.

1699 DUNSTAR, SAMUEL. Anglia Rediviva, being a full Description of all the Shires, Cities, Principal Towns and Rivers in England. 8vo. London.

1701 BRAND, JOHN. A Brief Description of Orkney, Zetland, Pightland, and Caithness. Wherein after a short Journal of the Author's Voyage hither, these Northern Places are first more generally described. Then a particular View is given of the several Isles thereto belonging. 8vo. Edinburgh.

Another edit. (or new work?), 8vo, Edinburgh, 1703; in Pinkerton, vol. III, 731-810, 1808-14; reprinted verbatim, Edinburgh, 1883. See below.
The first part of the book gives an account of travel in 1700. Brand was one of a commission sent by the General Assembly to inquire into the situation in those northern islands. Consequently he examines closely into heathenish and popish rites, charms and superstitions used in curing diseases. He also discourses on the usual subjects of manners and customs, products of the islands, etc.

1703 BRAND, JOHN. A New Decription of Orkney, Zetland, Pightland-Firth, and Caithness. 8vo. Edinburgh.
This contains numerous references to birds, and a six-page dedication in which the abject author grovels on his wame before James, Duke of Hamilton.—Quoted.

The New Description and State of England; containing the Maps of the Counties of England and Wales in 53 Copper-plates, newly design'd, exactly drawn and engraven by the best Artists. The Several Counties describ'd; their ancient and modern Names, Extent, Soil, former and present Inhabitants; their Number, Rarities, Market-Towns, and the Market Days, etc. 8vo. London.

2nd edit., 4to and 8vo, plates newly designed by Robt. Morden, London, 1704.
The full title as recorded in Arber, *Term Catalogues,* indicates that the book is a sort of World's Almanack description or survey comparable to Chamberlayne's *Anglia Notitia* (see Chamberlayne under 1668, ANCIENT AND PRESENT STATE).

SACHEVERELL, WILLIAM. An Account of the Isle of Man, its Inhabitants, Language, Soil, remarkable Curiosities, the Succession of its Kings and Bishops, with a Voyage to I-Columb-kill. 8vo. London.

Reprinted 12mo, London, 1702; again, edit. with notes by J. G. Cumming, *Publ. Manx Soc.,* vol. 1, Douglas, 1859. See below.

The voyage to I-Columb-kill took place in 1688 and included the north of Ireland and the Island of Mull. It contains many things of interest. Boswell refers to it in ch. XLIII of *Johnson's Life.*—Sacheverell was late governor of the Isle of Man, who really acted as editor to the papers of an anonymous gentleman. He pretends to no further share than rewording and reforming some mistakes, which a stranger would naturally make.—From Gough, 610.

1702 SACHEVERELL, WILLIAM. An Account of the Isle of Man . . . By William Sacheverell, late Governor of Man. To which is added, A Dissertation about the Mona of Caesar and Tacitus, and an Account of the antient Druids, etc. By Mr. Thomas Brown, addressed in a Letter to his learned Friend Mr. A. Sellers. 12mo. London.

Scotland Characteriz'd, in a Letter written to a Young Gentleman, to dissuade him from an intended Journey thither, by the Author of *The Trip to North Wales.* Fol. London.

Reprinted in *Ruddiman's Weekly Magazine,* 229-32, 1781.

This tract gives a very unflattering account of the life and manners of the Scottish people.—Bookseller's Note.

The State of that Part of Yorkshire, adjacent to the Level of Hatfield Chase. 4to. York.

1702 MORER, REV. THOMAS. A Short Account of Scotland, being a Description of the Nature of that Kingdom, and what the Constitution of it is in Church and State, wherein also some Notice is taken of their chief Cities and royal Boroughs. Appendices. 8vo. London.

Reprinted, 8vo, London, 1706; again, 12mo, London, 1715; extracts in Hume Brown, *Early Travellers,* 266-90.

The author was minister of St. Ann's within Aldersgate, and chaplain to a Scottish regiment. Brown estimates this account as one of the most valuable historically that has been given of Scotland. Breadth of interests, intelligence, and justness of mind, all rank him high among English travelers. After reading the diatribes of Weldon and Kirke, it is refreshing to come upon so fair and informative account of that country, its people, language, food, produce, cities, etc., as is this one by Morer. There is nothing in it that even the most perfervid Scot could take amiss.

1703 ADAIR, JOHN. The Description of the Sea Coast and Islands of Scotland, with large and exact Maps for the Use of Seamen. Fol. Edinburgh.

A collection of papers relative to the geographical description, maps, and charts of Scotland by Adair, who was Geographer for the Kingdom of Scotland, was published in vol. II, *Bann. Misc.,* no. xv, vol. 19 of *Publ. Bann. Club, Edinburgh,* 1836.

Adair traveled extensively in preparing this work. The papers published in the *Bann. Misc.* contain a facsimile, from the copy published at Paris in 1583, of the hydrographical description or chart, made in the voyage of King James V around Scotland in 1540 (see Nicolay under 1583, TOURS BY FOREIGNERS).—Mitchell, *List of Travels.*

MARTIN, MARTIN. A Description of the Western Islands of Scotland; containing a full Account of their Situation, Extent, Soils, Product, Harbours, Bays, Tides, Anchoring-places, and Fisheries, the antient and modern Government; religion and customs of the Inhabitants, particularly of their Druids, heathen Temples, Monasteries, Churches, Chappels, Antiquities, Monuments, Forts, Caves, and other Curiosities of Art and Nature. Of their admirable and expeditious way of curing most diseases by Simples of their own Product. A particular Account of the Second Sight, or Faculty of foreseeing Things to come, by way of Visions, so common among them. A Brief Hint of Methods to improve

Trade in that Country, both by Sea and Land. With a new Map of the Whole, describing the Harbours, Anchoring-places, and dangerous Rocks, for the Benefit of Sailors. To which is added, A Brief Description of the Isles of Orkney and Schetland. 8vo. London.

> Although the title page bears the date of 1698, the work was not issued until 1703. 2nd edit., 8vo, London, 1716; this edit. in Pinkerton, vol. 3, 572-699; 3rd, Glasgow, 1884; modern reprint, with additions, London, 1934. See below.
> It is a matter of common knowledge that the reading of this book stirred up in Johnson a desire to visit these distant regions. Except for Dean Monro's work written 150 years earlier (but not published till 1774), Martin's is the earliest account of the Western Islands we have, and the only lengthy, detailed account before the era of modern changes. So it has much value as a document on a way of life long vanished. The folklore, the superstitions that were in the texture of their lives, the names of places, the social customs, the descriptions of families, seats, privileges, population, all of which have changed beyond recognition, bring home the remoteness of the Hebrides, and even add to the sense of magic, mystery, and loneliness of those far-off islands. Celtic Scotland on its outermost fringes, the spelling of Gaelic place names, the life of the fishermen and the cotters are all of intriguing interest. It is not Martin, however, but the reader who imposes the romance on the days and scenes of long ago, for Martin is as prosaic and matter-of-fact as any dry-as-dust antiquary. His distinguishing quality is that, whereas earlier writers who had published accounts of the islands had never visited them in person, he himself had taken down on the spot full and detailed notes on the islands and the inhabitants.

> 1934 MARTIN, MARTIN. A Description of the Western Islands of Scotland, *circa* 1695, including a Voyage to St. Kilda by the same Author, and a Description of the Western Isles of Scotland by Sir Donald Monro, edited with Introduction by Donald J. Macleod, D.B.E. Map and illustrations. 8vo. London.
> For the *Voyage to St. Kilda,* see Martin under 1698, TOURS BY NATIVES, and for Monro, see under 1774 below.

1705 B., E. A Description of Scotland and its Inhabitants. 4to. London.

1707 ROBINSON, NICHOLAS. The Hertforshire Spy, etc. 4to. London.

SIBBALD, SIR ROBERT. History and Description of Stirlingshire, Ancient and Modern. 4to. Edinburgh.

> Reprinted, 8vo, Stirling, 1892. See Sibbald under this date, HISTORY AND ANTIQUITIES.

1709 Britannia Fortior, Or The New State of Great Britain and Ireland under our Sovereign Queen Anne. Containing a Description of the several Counties; of the Original, Temper, Genius, Trade, Laws, and Religion, of the People . . . N.B. The Supplement to "The New State of England," containing an Accurate Description of Scotland and Ireland . . . will be sold by itself, to supply those that have bought the Former Editions of "The New State of England." London.

> See under 1701 above for *The New State.* This may be the work of Guy Miege (see under 1690, *The Present State,* 1707 issue, ANCIENT AND PRESENT STATE).

Hoglandiae Descriptio. 8vo. London. (A mock-heroic description of Hampshire, in Latin verse.)

> Another edit. the same year.

1710 CRAWFURD, GEORGE. A Genealogical History of the Stewarts, from the Year 1034 to the Year 1710. To which are prefixed, A Description of the Shire of Renfrew, and a Deduction of the Noble and Ancient Families Proprietors there for upwards of 400 Years. Fol. Edinburgh.

With altered title and continuation by Wm. Semple, 4to, Paisley, 1782; again, with continuation by Geo. Robertson, 4to, Paisley, 1818.

1711   SIBBALD, SIR ROBERT. The Description of the Isles of Orkney and Zetland; with the Mapps of them, done from the accurate Observation of the most learned who lived in these Isles. Fol. Edinburgh.

> Reprinted from the edition of 1711, 8vo, Edinburgh, 1845.
> This was done from a MS of Sir Robert Monteith, laird of Eglisha and Gairsa, dated Kirkwall, Sept. 29, 1633.—Gough, 654-55.

1712   WALLIS, S. A Topographical Description of Gloucestershire, containing a Compendious Account of its Dimensions, Bounds, Air, Soil, and Commodities, etc. Gloucester.

> Gough (173) calls it a trifling affair; very few copies got abroad. The work deals with towns and villages, with their churches, schools, hospitals, markets, and fairs.

1714   RISDON, TRISTRAM. The Chorographical Description or Survey of the County of Devon, with the City and County of Exeter, containing Matter of History, Antiquity, Chronology, and a Nature of the Country, Commodities, and Government thereof, etc. With a Continuation. 2 vols. 8vo. London.

> The manuscript being dispersed into various hands, and each copy differing from the other, was collated with the best belonging to John Prince, vicar of Berry Pomeroy, and some others, and printed. Republished in the same size, 2 vols., 1723, the 2nd volume using a completer MS in Prince's possession. Risdon worked on it twenty-five years.—Gough, 138.

1715   PENNECUIK, ALEXANDER. Geographical Historical Description of the Shire of Tweeddale, with Miscellany and Curious Collection of Scottish Poems. 4to. Edinburgh.

> The value of his verses lies in the picture they give of the rural life of the time.—*DNB*.

1720-31   COX, REV. THOMAS. For much descriptive matter on the counties of England, see his *Magna Britannia & Hibernia*, under SURVEYS.

1722   FORDUN, JOHN OF. For a description of Scotland, see his *Scotichronicon*, under HISTORY AND CHRONICLE.

> Extract from the Skene edition of 1871 in Hume Brown, *Scotland before 1700*, 8-15.
> In bk. II, chs. 7-11, there is a description of Scotland "which savoureth of the rudeness and driness of the writers of that age."—Sibbald, quoted by Gough, 624. Fordun, like other early Scottish historians, was misled in assigning the Wall to Severus instead of to Hadrian (one exception was Buchanan). He describes the islands of Scotland in much greater detail than the mainland, and so he must at some time have made them a visit. He took pains to inform himself of most of what he wrote about and of the places he described. Since he actually visited England and Ireland to secure materials for his history, we may infer that in his description of Scotland he is drawing on his own impressions, and not reproducing the statements of others.—From Brown. His history was written about 1380.

GALE, ROGER. Registrum Honoris de Richmond, exhibens terrarum & villarum quae quondam fuerant Edwini comitis infra Richmondshire descriptionem: ex libro Domesday, in thesauria domini regis: nec non varias extentas, feoda militum, relevia, fines & wardas, inquisitiones, compotos, clamea, chartasque ad Richmondiae comitatum spectantes. Omnis juxta exemplar antiquum in bibli-

otheca Cottoniana asservatum exarata. Adjiciuntur in appendice chartae aliae, observationes, plurimae genealogiae & indices ad opus illustrandum necessarii. Fol. London.

This account is made up of materials collected by Roger Gale, and published after his death.—Gough, 564. Roger Gale was an enthusiastic antiquary, and a constant friend of the celebrated Dr. Stukeley. He wrote many papers for the *Philosophical Transactions*. His brother Samuel Gale was equally assiduous in the study of antiquities.

1723 LEWIS, REV. JOHN. Description of the Isle of Thanet, and particularly of the Town of Margate. (See Lewis under this date, HISTORY AND ANTIQUITIES.)

1724 MOLL, HERMAN. A New Description of England and Wales, With the Adjacent Islands. Wherein are contained, Diverse useful Observations and Discoveries In respect to Natural History, Antiquities, Customs, Honours, Privileges, . . . To which is added, A New and correct Set of Maps of each County, their Roads and Distances; and, to render 'em the more acceptable to the Curious, their Margins are adorned with great Variety of very remarkable Antiquities. . . . Fol. London.

This contains 50 colored maps of the counties of England and Wales. Other edits. in 1736, 1739, 1753.
Moll was a prolific producer of maps. He is noticed by Swift in *Gulliver's Travels*.

1727 BUCHAN, REV. ALEXANDER. A Description of St. Kilda, the most remote Western Isle of Scotland, giving an Account of its Situation, Extent, Soil, Product, Bay and Adjacent Islands or Rocks, the Ancient and Modern Government, Religion, and Customs of the Inhabitants, and other Curiosities of Art and Nature, also their late Reformation. 12mo. Edinburgh.

2nd edit., 12mo, Edinburgh, 1732; another, 8vo, Edinburgh, 1741; reprinted, edit. by the author's daughter, Miss Jean Buchan, Edinburgh, 1774. Also in Monro's *Description of the Western Isles*, Edinburgh, 1774; and in *Misc. Scotica*, Glasgow, 1818.

P., W. A Description of all the Counties in England and Wales. 2nd edit. 12mo. London.

Another edit., 1752.

1730 LAMBARDE, WILLIAM. Dictionarium Angliae Topographicum et Historicum: An Alphabetical Description of the Chief Places in England and Wales; with an Accounte of the most memorable Events which have distinguished them . . . Now first published from a Manuscript under the Author's own Hand. With the Effigies of the Author curiously engraven by Mr. Vertue. 4to. London.

This, as the author tells us, was meant to be enlarged like his *Perambulation of Kent* (see under 1576, TOURS BY NATIVES), which was for the most part drawn out of the above work, after which sort also the rest of the shires might be described. It is a kind of commonplace of extracts from our historians, etc., under each article, and many curious particulars not selected by other antiquaries in it.—Gough, 31-32. Lambard abandoned his design upon learning that his friend Camden was engaged on a similar undertaking.

1731 WALDRON, GEORGE. A Description of the Isle of Man, with some useful Reflections on the Laws, Customs, and Manners of the Inhabitants. An Appendix to the Complete Works of Geo. Waldron. Fol. Oxford.

First separate edition, 12mo, London, 1744; edit. with Notes and Introduction by W. Harrison, London, 1865. See below.

Sir Walter Scott used this work for his *Peveril of the Peak.*

    1744 WALDRON, GEORGE. The History and Description of the Isle of Man: viz. Its Antiquity, History, Law, Trade, Customs, Religion, and Manners of the Inhabitants; Animals, Minerals, Husbandry, etc., and whatever else is memorable relating to that Country and People: wherein are inserted many surprising and entertaining Stories of Apparitions, Fairies, Giants, etc., believed by the Inhabitants as their Gospel. Collected from original Papers and personal Knowledge during near twenty Years Residence there. 2nd edit. 12mo. London.

1735 GURDON, THORNHAUGH. A Description of the Diocese of Norwich, or, The Present State of Norfolk and Suffolk; giving an Account of the Situation, Extent, Trade, and Customs of Norwich in particular, and the several Market Towns in those two Counties, according to Alphabetical Order. By a Gentleman of the Inner-Temple and Native of the Diocese of Norwich. 8vo. London.

    Very slight and trifling.—Gough, 367.

1737 PACKE, DR. CHRISTOPHER. A Dissertation upon the Surface of the Earth, as delineated in a Specimen of a Philosophico-chorographical Chart of East Kent.

    This was presented to the Royal Society and received with approbation, 1738; described as containing a graphical delineation of the County fifteen or sixteen miles round Canterbury; wherein are described the progress of the valleys, the directions and elevations of the hills, and whatever is curious in both art and nature, that diversifies and adorns the face of the earth. It was to be printed on four sheets of atlas paper, and published in November following, for one guinea: but nothing more came out than the specimen on one sheet accompanied with an essay called Ἀγκογραφία sive convallium descriptio, which was apparently printed again, Canterbury, 1743. See below.

    1743 PACKE, DR. CHRISTOPHER. Ἀγκογραφία, sive Convallium Descriptio. In which are briefly, but fully, expounded, the Origin, Course and Insertion; Extent, Elevation, and Congruity, of all the Vallies and Hills, Brooks and Rivers (as an explanation of a new Philosophico-Chorographical Chart) of East Kent. Occasionally are interspersed some transient Remarks that relate to the Natural History of the Country and to the Military Marks and Signs of Caesar's Route through it, to his decisive Battle in Kent. 4to. Canterbury.

1738 FEARON, S., and C. EYES. A Description of the Sea-coast of England and Wales, from Black Comb in Cumberland to the Point of Linus in Anglesea, with proper Directions to avoid all Dangers and sail into any Harbour . . . . Fol. London.

1739-75 BLOMEFIELD, F., and C. PARKIN. A Topographical History of Norfolk: a Description of the Towns, Villages and Hamlets . . . . 5 vols. Fol. London.

    As this deals largely with antiquities, it is relegated to the section HISTORY AND ANTIQUITIES (see under 1736-45).

1740 An Irregular Dissertation, Occasioned by the Reading of Father Du Halde's Description of China. Which may be read at any Time, except in the present Year 1740. 12mo. London.

    A very clever and well-written little work, comparing the manners and customs of China with those of Europe, and particularly of England. From a remark made on p. 106 it appears that the writer's name was Roberts, which may be the same as that of the publisher J. Roberts; or, on the other hand, the reference may be to Robert Walpole, the Prime Minister.—Maggs, no. 719. (For Du Halde see under 1736, FAR EAST, vol. I of this work.)

FRANSHAM, JOHN. Scotland (in his *The World in Miniature: or, The Entertaining Traveller,* vol. II). London.

> For this title see Fransham this date under GENERAL TRAVELS AND DESCRIPTIONS, vol. I of this work.

1741 R., R. [Dr. Richard Rawlinson?] A New Description of all the Counties in England and Wales. 5th edit. 12mo. London.

> 6th edit., 12mo, London, 1752.

1743-54 BICKHAM, GEORGE (Senior). The British Monarchy: Or, A New Chorographical Description of all the Dominions Subject to the King of Great Britain. Comprehending the British Isles, the American Colonies, the Electoral States, . . . And enlarging more particularly on the respective Counties of England and Wales. To which are added, Alphabets to all the Hands made use of in this Book. Illustrated with maps and tables. Fol. London.

> The title page is dated 1743, the colophon 1749, and the county views 1750 to 1754. Another edit., 1796. See below.
> This work contains 188 copperplates of historical notes and 43 plates of idealized bird's-eye views of the counties of England, and North and South Wales, beautifully engraved on one side of the paper, 58 coats of arms of the county towns, six views, and numerous engravings of antiquarian remains found in the various counties.—Chubb, *Printed Maps.*

> 1796 BICKHAM, GEORGE. A Curious Antique Collection of Bird's-Eye Views of the several Counties of England and Wales; exhibiting a pleasing landscape of Each County; with a Variety of Rustic Figures, Ruins, etc., and the Names of the Principal Towns and Villages, interspersed according to their apparent situation. 46 plates. 8vo. London.
> These are reprints of the bird's-eye views of the Counties of England and North and South Wales.—Chubb, *op. cit.*

MILNE, REV. ADAM. A Description of the Parish of Melrose; in answer to Mr. Maitland's Queries, sent to each Parish of the Kingdom. 8vo. Edinburgh.

> 2nd edit., corrected, 8vo, Edinburgh, 1748; another edit., 1769; 12mo, Kelso, 1782; 12mo, Edinburgh, 1794.

1744 DODSLEY, ROBERT. England Illustrated, or, A Compendium of the Natural History, Geography, Topography, and Antiquities, Ecclesiastical and Civil, of England and Wales; with Maps of the several Counties, and engravings of many Remains of Antiquities, remarkable Buildings, and principal Towns. 2 vols. 4to. London.

> Another edit., with an Appendix descriptive of the Isle of Man, 2 vols., 4to, London, 1764.
> Gough said that this was put out by Dodsley on a pretended new plan, but in reality it was nothing more than an abridgement of Camden, on a different method, with all his errors adopted, and many new ones committed. Furthermore, the views were those of Messrs. Buck, and the maps were of little value. But the edition of 1764 advertises that the maps contained therein were done by Thomas Kitchin and the views and plates by John Ryland, B. Green, and W. Ryland. To quote from the bookseller's notice of this edition: "The illustrative copperplates to this work form what is probably the finest picturization of 18th century England that ever appeared in contemporary print. They were engraved by John Ryland, to whom Blake was taken for apprenticeship as a youth, and who was hung for forgery not so many years after."

PRESTON, CAPTAIN T. An Account of the Island of Shetland, in Letters. In *Philos. Trans.*, Abr. IX, 44. London.

1746 ROCQUE, JOHN. The English Traveller: giving a Description of those Parts of Great-Britain called England and Wales. Maps. 3 vols. 8vo. London.

> The 54 maps of Rocque were reissued in his *The Small British Atlas* (see Rocque under 1753, MAPS AND CHARTS). The above work is also listed under 1749 with the name of Read, who may have been the editor.

SEACOMBE, JOHN. For a "full Description of the Isle of Man," see his *Memoirs,* etc., under HISTORY AND ANTIQUITIES.

SIMPSON, JOHN. The Agreeable Historian, or, The Compleat English Traveller; giving a Geographical Description of every County in that Part of Great Britain, call'd England . . . With a Map of every County . . . after the Designs of Herman Moll and others. 3 vols. 41 maps. 8vo. London.

> The maps precede the accounts of the counties. Gough calls the work a wretched compilation.—*Op. cit.,* 26.

1747 Remarks on the People and Government of Scotland, particularly the Highlanders; their Original Customs, Manners, etc.; with a genuine Account of the Highland Regiment that was decoyed to London. 4to. Edinburgh.

1748 MORRIS, LEWIS. Observations on the Coasts and Harbours of Wales. London (?).

> Morris was a native of Anglesey, who had many collections towards a Natural History of this country. His computations are for 1747, and shew a mighty augmentation in the value of property.—From Campbell, *Political Survey,* vol. I, 495.

NEALE, THOMAS. The Ruinous State of the Parish of Manea in the Isle of Ely. 8vo. London.

OWEN, HENRY. A History of Anglesea, with a Distinct Description of the Towns, Harbours, Villages, etc., as a Supplement to Rowlands; with Memoirs of Owen Glyndwr. (So cited by Rowlands, *Cambrian Bibliog.*)

1749 A New Description of Berkshire, Bucks, Cambridgeshire, Cheshire, Cornwall, Derbyshire, Devon, Dorset, Durham, and Essex, containing an Account of the Market-Towns, Villages, Rivers, Seats, Fairs, Trade, Commerce of each County; with the Rarities both Natural and Artificial. 8vo. London (?).

ROLT, RICHARD. Cambria. A Poem. In Three Books. Illustrated with Notes Historical, Critical, and Explanatory. Humbly inscribed to his Royal Highness Prince George. 4to. London.

1749-55 BOWEN, EMANUEL, and THOMAS KITCHIN. For a description of each county, see their *Large English Atlas,* under MAPS AND CHARTS.

1750 A Brief Description of England and Wales; containing a particular Description of each County, Distance of each Market-Town from London, very useful to Travellers and others, and very proper for Schools. Map of each county. 16mo. London.

> The maps are a reissue of Morden's maps of 1750.—Thorp, Catalogue.

For a description of all the counties and principal towns of England, see *The Present State of England,* under ANCIENT AND PRESENT STATE.

The Curiosities, Natural and Artificial, of Great Britain; What is most remarkable in Nature and Art; with an Account of the Rebellion of 1745. 59 engravings. 6 vols. 8vo. London. (Date approximate.)

> There is a work with the same title dated approximately as of 1776, 6 vols., 8vo, London; and an edition of this entitled *Britannica Curiosa,* 1777.

HEATH, CAPTAIN ROBERT. A Natural and Historical Description of the Islands of Scilly; describing their Situation, Number, Extent, Soil, Culture, Produce, etc., their Importance to the British Trade and Navigation, their Improvement they are capable of, and Directions for all Ships to avoid the Danger of the Rocks. Illustrated with a New and Correct Draught of those Isles from an actual Survey in the Year 1744, including the neighbouring Seas and Sea-Coasts next the Land's End of Cornwall. To which are added, The Tradition of a Tract of Land called Lioness, devoured by the Sea, formerly joining those Isles and Cornwall: of the Cause, Rise, and Disappearance of some Islands; and, lastly, a general Account of Cornwall. 8vo. London.

> The author was an officer in the forces garrisoned at Scilly. His accounts of the wildfowl and seafowl are said to have been taken from Carew (see his *Survey of Cornwall* under 1602, SURVEYS).

1751 CAMPBELL, JOHN. A full Description of the Highlands of Scotland, with a Scheme for making the most disaffected among them become zealously affected to his reigning Majesty. 8vo. London.

> Reprinted, 1752 and 1753.

1753 A True and Exact Description of the Island of Shetland, containing an Account of its Situation, Trade, Produce, and Inhabitants, together with an Account of the great white Herring Fishery, Methods the Dutch use in catching, curing, and disposing of the Herrings they catch there, prodigious Advantages Britain may receive from thence, with many curious Particulars. 2nd edit. 8vo. London.

1755 P[ATCHING], R[ESTA]. Four Topographical Letters, written in July 1755. 8vo. Newcastle-upon-Tyne.

> An edit., London, 1757.
> These were written on a journey through the counties of Bedford, Northants, etc. Gough says this account has "some unborrowed Particulars."—*Op. cit.*

1757 County Curiosities: or, a Description of Gloucestershire. 12mo. (Place?)

A Description of the Counties of Belford, Northampton, Leicester, Nottingham, Derby, Warwick, etc. (So listed in *Gent. Mag.,* vol. 27, April.)

> This may be the same work listed under 1755 above.

STUKELEY, DR. WILLIAM. For his edition of *De Situ Britanniae* by Richard of Cirencester, see under BRITISH, ROMAN, AND SAXON ANTIQUITIES.

1760 For a description of the Orkneys and other Isles of Scotland, see *A History of the Whole Realm of Scotland,* under HISTORY AND CHRONICLE.

1761 A Description of England. (So cited by Hoare, *A Catalogue of Books.*)

A Description of the Parish of Muirkirk. In *Edinb. Mag.,* vol. 62, Edinburgh.

"Pastor." An Account of Ingleborough, a remarkable Mountain. In *Gent. Mag.,* vol. 31, 126-28.

This was continued by another hand in the June number of the same, 148-49; and further by A. B. in November, 500-01.

1762 A Description of the Parish of Bromborough in Cheshire. Signed Ingenuus. In *Gent. Mag.,* vol. 32, Supplementary vol., 616.

SCOTT, MRS. GEORGE. A Description of Millenium Hall, and the Country adjacent; together with Characters of the Inhabitants, and such historical Anecdotes and Reflections, as may excite in the Reader, proper Sentiments of Humanity, and lead the Mind to the Love of Virtue, by a Gentleman on his Travels. 8vo. London.

2nd edit., London, 1764; 3rd, 8vo, London, 1767.
This has been ascribed to Goldsmith. But Prior says that it was merely revised by Goldsmith. Walpole, in a note in the copy of the second edition in the British Museum, maintained that the authors of the book were "Lady Barbara Montagu (5th sister of George Montagu Dunk, Earl of Halifax) and Mrs. Scott, wife of George Scott, Esq., sub-Preceptor of George III, when Prince of Wales."—Sarah Scott, *History of Mecklenburgh.* See Iola Williams, *Seven Eighteenth Century Bibliographies,* 127. The work is a fictitious creation.

TOLDERVEY, WILLIAM. England and Wales described in a Series of Letters; with plates. 8vo. London.

It was proposed to publish this in three volumes, by weekly numbers, of which only nine came out, which had nothing to recommend them but tolerable cuts.—Gough, 25.

1763 CORYATE, GEORGE. Descriptio Angliae et descriptio Londini; being two Poems in Latin Verse, supposed to be written in XV & XVI Century. London.

According to Gough, these may be part of a poem by George Coryat (father of "Tom the mad traveller") called Descriptio Angliae, Scotiae, & Hiberniae, dedicated to Queen Elizabeth. The mention of only fifteen colleges at Oxford fixes the date before 1571.—*Op. cit.,* 21-22. The editor was James Lumley Kingston of Dorchester, F.S.A.

A Description of the Isle of Thanet and particularly of the Town of Margate; with an Account . . . of Bathing-in-the-Sea and Machines for that purpose, the Assemblies, Amusements and Diversions, public and private, etc. Map of the Isle of Thanet and frontispiece of the Bathing Machines. 8vo. London.

Another edit., 12mo, London, 1765.
This was said to have been compiled from Rev. John Lewis, *The History and Antiquities of the Isle of Thanet,* for which see under 1723, HISTORY AND ANTIQUITIES.

Some Account of the Parish of Dorking and its Environs (in Surrey). In *Gent. Mag.,* vol. 33, 220-23.

1764 MACAULAY, KENNETH. The History of St. Kilda: containing a Description of this remarkable Island; the Manners and Customs of the Inhabitants; the religious and pagan Antiquities there found; with many other curious and interesting Particulars. By Kenneth Macaulay, Minister of Ardnamurchan, Missionary to the Island, from the Society for Promoting Christian Knowledge. Map. 8vo. London.

> 2nd edit., 12mo, Dublin, 1765; translated into French, Paris, 1782. See below. Noticed in the *Journal de Littérature, des Sciences et des Arts,* tome IV, 81-95, 1782.
> The doubt expressed by Johnson on Macaulay's authorship is the subject of an article by L. F. Powell, *Rev. Engl. Stud.,* vol. 16, no. 61, Jan., 1940. The conclusion reached here is that his friend the Rev. John Macpherson, of Sleat, contributed the antiquarian (and dull) parts and Macaulay the description and topography (the interesting parts). Macaulay knew St. Kilda at first hand as missionary there in 1759.
>
> 1782 (In French.) Histoire de Saint-Kilda, imprimée en 1764, traduite de l'anglois, contenant la description de cette isle remarquable. Les moeurs et les coutumes de ses habitants, les antiquités religieuses et payennes qu'on y trouvées, avec plusieurs autres particularités curieuses et intéressantes. 12mo. Paris.

A Sketch of Peaks Hole, commonly called the Devil's Arse,—a Peak in Derbyshire. In *Gent. Mag.,* vol. 34, 570-72.

1765 A Description of the Country of Wales. Map and 2 plates. 4to. London (?).

A Geographic Description of England and Wales. Map. London.

1766 Particulars of the Manor of Dolgelly, with the Freehold Estates of Hugh Vaughan, Esq., the Seat called Hengwrt. (So cited by Rowlands, without place or date.)

1768 GOUGH, RICHARD. For his historical survey of descriptions of the topography and antiquities of Great Britain and Ireland, see under HISTORY AND ANTIQUITIES.

Rural Elegance Display'd in the Description of four Western Counties: Cornwall, Devonshire, Dorsetshire and Somersetshire, with additional Remarks. Map and frontispiece. 12mo. London.

SYMONDSON, PHILIP. A New Description of the County of Kent, divided into its Laths, Bailywicks and Hundreds, comprehending all the Cities, Market Towns, Parishes and Post Towns, the Seats of the Nobility and Gentry, and the Nature of the Soil, whether plain, hilly, or woody, is more particularly observed; with a View of Dover and Rye.

> This is cited by Gough, 231, without place or date. Hence its publication is prior to 1768.

1769 A Description of England and Wales, containing a Particular Account of each County, with its Antiquities, Curiosities, Mineral Waters, Caverns, Agriculture, Trade, Cities, Towns, Markets, Battles, Sieges, etc., with the Lives of the Illustrious Men of each County. 240 copperplates of palaces, castles, cathedrals, ruins of Roman and Saxon buildings, abbeys, monasteries, etc. 10 vols. 8vo. London.

> 2nd edit., 10 vols., London, 1775.
> It has been suggested that Goldsmith contributed towards the production of this work. —Bookseller's Note. These universalized accounts generally called for the services of numerous hacks, among whom Goldsmith may well have been numbered.

FRAME, R. Lanarkshire. 8vo. Glasgow.

RUSSELL, P., and OWEN PRICE. England Displayed. Being A New, Complete, and Accurate Survey and Description of the Kingdom of England and Principality of Wales . . . By a Society of Gentlemen: each of whom has undertaken that Part for which his Study and Inclination has more immediately qualified him. The particulars respecting England, revised, corrected, and improved. By P. Russell, Esq.: and those relating to Wales, By Mr. Owen Price. 2 vols. Fol. London.

> The counties are arranged in alphabetical order and the towns and villages are discussed as they lie on the principal roads. The work treats of the natural history, agriculture, manufactures, history, biographies, etc.—J. Williams, *Printed Materials*. Thirty-three of the county maps are taken from *The Small British Atlas* by Rocque, 1753; ten are by Thos. Kitchin, originally issued in the *London Magazine*, 1747-60; four are by Rollos, and one by Bowen.—Chubb, *Printed Maps*.

A View of England, Scotland, and Wales. London.

1770 WYNN, SIR JOHN. The History of the Gwydir Family. Edit. by Daines Barrington. 8vo. London.

> Another edit. in *Miscellanies*, by Barrington, 4to, 1781. Later editions, Ruthin, 1827 and 1878.
> This was written by the first Baronet of Gwydir (1553-1626). It is especially valuable for its picture of social conditions in North Wales about 1600.—Davies, *Bibliog. Brit. Hist., Stuart Period*.

1771 SPENCER, NATHANIEL. The Complete English Traveller: or, A New Survey and Description of England and Wales. Containing a full Account of whatever is curious and entertaining in the several Counties of England and Wales, the Isles of Man, Jersey, Guernsey, and other Islands adjoining to, and dependent on the Crown of Great Britain. . . . To which is added, A Concise and Accurate Description of that Part of Great Britain called Scotland. Its ancient and present State, Antiquities and Natural Curiosities; together with the Manners and Customs of the Inhabitants, etc. Folding maps and numerous engraved plates. Fol. London.

> This is also dated 1772 and 1773.
> The real name of the compiler was Robert Saunders. The work describes agriculture, manufactures, commerce, natural history, fairs, buildings, parks, charities, etc., with biographies.—From J. Williams, *op. cit.*

1772 BEATNIFFE, RICHARD. For a description of noblemen's and gentlemen's seats, see his *Norfolk Tour*, under AIDS TO TRAVELERS.

FERGUSON, JAMES. Mr. Ferguson's Description of the Devil's Cave, at Castleton, in the Peak of Derbyshire. In *Gent. Mag.*, vol. 42, 518-19.

MUILMAN, PETER. An Essay for a New Description of England and Wales, as a Continuation and Illustration of Camden. 12mo. London.

A New Display of the Beauties of England. 2 vols. Numerous plates. 8vo. London.

Another edit., 2 vols., 8vo, London, 1776; revised and enlarged, 1787. There may have been an edition in between the 1772 and the 1776 publications. See below.

1776 A New Display of the Beauties of England: or, A Description of the most Elegant or Magnificent Public Edifices, Royal Palaces, Noblemen's and Gentlemen's Seats. 2 vols. 8vo. London.

1774 ENTICK, JOHN, and JAMES WEBSTER. An Historical and Geographical Description of the British Empire; containing a State of the Kingdoms . . . commercial, civil, and military Establishments, dependent upon the Crown of Great-Britain, in every Part of the World, also the Particulars of the Counties in Great Britain, their Antiquities, Gentlemen's Seats, Products, Extent, Trade, etc. 4 vols. London.

> The object of this work was to present a comprehensive plan or a political chart of the British Empire. It is a manual of information about Great Britain and the Empire, including some history. After a volume of generalities, separate treatment is given to the government, trade, manufactures, manners, religion, navy, army, laws, revenues, customs, of every county and colony. It illustrates the great advantages Great Britain possesses over all the rest of the earth.—J. Williams, *op. cit.*

MONRO, DONALD (Dean of the Isles). Description of the Western Isles, called Hybrides, by Mr. Donald Monro, High Dean of the Isles, Who travelled through most of them in the Year 1549; with the Genealogy of the chief Clans. 12mo. Edinburgh.

> Included in *Misc. Scot.,* vol. 2, pt. 1, Glasgow, 1818; also 8vo, Edinburgh, 1884; in Hume Brown, *Scotland before 1700,* 236-72.
> Little is known of the author beyond that he traveled through the Hebrides in 1549 on a pastoral tour of inspection. The fact that he knew little if any Gaelic did not seem to count against his fitness for the position he held. Much of his description consists of merely placing the islands in their contiguous relation to each other, sometimes with mention of churches found in them and their produce. There is some value, however, in his comments on the social and economic situation of the islands, and in his spelling of place names.

1775 For an account of the Isle of Wight, see *The Portsmouth Guide,* under AIDS TO TRAVELERS.

A Description of the County of Middlesex; containing A Circumstantial Account of its Public Buildings, Seats of the Nobility and Gentry, Places of Resort and Entertainment, Curiosities of Nature and Art (including those of London and Westminster). The Whole forming a Complete Guide to those who may Visit the Metropolis, Or make a Tour through the County. Copperplates. 8vo. London.

> While rather indiscriminate in its eulogies, this description is on the whole quite absorbing reading and informing on what London and the environs had to offer the visitor of the day. Especially interesting is its account of the contents of the British Museum—its books, MSS, exhibits of natural history, fossils, antiques, etc.

WILLIAMS, WILLIAM. The Head of the Rock, a Welsh Landskip, being a Prospect near Abergwily Palace. 12mo. London.

ZETLANDICUS. A Description of the State of the Zetland Islands, 24th March, 1775. In *Ruddiman's Edinb. Weekly Mag.,* June, 1775.

17— The Counties of Leicester and Rutland, divided into their respective Hundreds, with Historical Extracts relative to Natural History, Trade, Manufactures, etc.

Title within Chippendale border and emblematical designs, engraved by E. Bowen. Printed for Laurie and Whittle. 28 × 22 ins. London.

> The date of this and others of like content is merely a guess. There was a mezzotinter of this period by the name of Laurie, and Bowen was a contemporary. The fact that other counties, viz., Lincolnshire, Monmouth, Northampton, are listed with the same title suggests that the entire country was so described either in a series or in separate issues.

1777 An Account of the most Romantic Parts of North Wales. London. (So cited in Pinkerton, vol. XVII, and in Rowlands, *op. cit.*)

BEATTIE, DR. JAMES. A Description of the Highlands of Scotland and Remarks on the Second Sight of the Inhabitants. In *Annual Register,* vol. 20, 82-84. London.

> The author of *The Minstrel* did not find sufficient evidence to support veracity of the tradition.

1778 HUTCHINSON, WILLIAM. A View of Northumberland, with an Excursion to the Abbey of Mailros in Scotland (1776), and A State of the Churches under the Archdeaconry of Northumberland, and in Hexham, peculiar Jurisdiction with the Succession of Incumbents extracted from the MSS. of Thomas Randal, also Ancient Customs which prevail in the County of Northumberland with Conjectures thereon. 2 vols. Numerous copperplates. 4to. Newcastle.

> Reviewed *Gent. Mag.,* vol. 48, 373-74. The reviewer is caustic in his comments on the fashionable rage of "excursion-making, touring, sketching, journeying, topographizing, or whatever name belongs to this mode of writing." The author confesses that his work was the result of yielding to the temptation of "collecting in one view the observations and opinions of former writers on the history and antiquities of Northumberland." The sight of anything mentioned sets him off into a strain of moralizing and sentimentalizing in language reeking with the "sublime." Some credit is allowed his description of Mailros (Melrose), and his plates, with some exceptions, are good.—From the review.

1779 BEATTIE, JAMES. In his *Essays on Poetry and Music* (3rd edit., London), are some descriptions of Highland scenery and its effect upon the mind. He finds the mood of sadness is induced by the mountains of the Scotch Highlands.

JONES, EDMUND. A Geographical, Historical, and Religious Account of the Parish of Aberystruth; in the County of Monmouth. To which are added, Memoirs of several Persons of Note, who lived in the said Parish. Trevecka.

1780 A Brief Description of England and Wales, containing a particular Account of each County; with its Antiquities, etc. 12mo. London. (Date approximate.)

COOKE, G. A. Topographical and Statistical Descriptions of the Counties of Norfolk, Suffolk, Lancaster, Gloucester, Nottingham, Derby, Wilts, Stafford, and Worcester. Manufactures, Agriculture, Antiquities, etc. Maps. 9 vols. 12mo. London.

> The date is approximate. Other counties singly and in groups are similarly listed. An edition complete in 43 volumes is dated *ca.* 1800. See below.

> 1800 COOKE, G. A. Topographical and Statistical Descriptions of the Counties of England and Scotland; with travelling Guides, forming complete County Itineraries, and Indexes, Maps, and Engravings. 43 vols. 12mo. London.

DALTON, W. H. The New and Complete English Traveller. Numerous engravings and maps. Fol. London.

STURCH, JOHN. A View of the Isle of Wight, in four Letters, containing not only a Description of its Form and Principal Productions, but the most Authentic and Material Articles of its Natural, Political and Commercial History. Folding map. Printed for and sold by the Author in Newport.

   4th edit., Newport, 1791; 5th, corrected and enlarged, Newport, 1794. In German, Leipzig, 1781. See below.

   1781   (In German.) Johann Sturch's Nachricht von der Insel Wight. 8vo. Leipzig.

1782   DOUGLAS, FRANCIS. A General Description of the East Coast of Scotland, from Edinburgh to Cullen. Including a brief Account of the Universities of St. Andrews and Aberdeen, of the Trade and Manufactures carried on in the large Towns, and the Improvement of the Country. In a Series of Letters. 8vo. Paisley.

   Reprinted, Aberdeen, 1826.
   The account is instructive but rather dull.

An Historical, Descriptive, and Biographical Survey of the County of Suffolk. Fol. London.

1783   NICHOLS, JOHN. A Short Account of Holyhead. No. 10 of *Bibl. Topog. Brit.* 4to. London.

1784   HURTLEY, THOMAS. A Concise Account of some Natural Curiosities in the Environs of Malham-in-Craven. London (?).

WALPOOLE, GEORGE AUGUSTUS. The New British Traveller; or, A Complete Modern Universal Display of Great-Britain and Ireland . . . Being really the Result of an Actual and Late Survey, accurately made by a Society of Gentlemen . . . including a valuable Collection of Landscapes, Views, County-Maps, etc. . . . The Whole published under the immediate Inspection of George Augustus Walpoole, Esq. Assisted by . . . . Fol. London.

   Another edit., with slight difference in title, London, 1794.
   In addition to the maps, this work has the roads of England, North and South Wales, Scotland, and Ireland; with 17 plates showing the counties of England in groups of two, three, and four on a plate. There are numerous views of towns, residences, churches, etc., throughout the work. These views make up the most important part of the volume.

1785   CHAPPLE, WILLIAM. A Review of Part of Risdon's Survey of Devon, containing the general Description of that County, with Corrections, Annotations, and Additions. 4to. Exeter.

   See Risdon under 1714 above.

1786   BOSWELL, HENRY. Historical Descriptions of New and Elegant Picturesque Views of the Antiquities of England and Wales, Scotland, and Ireland. Maps and hundreds of views of churches, castles, abbeys, seats, ruins, etc. Fol. London. (See under VIEWS.)

GIFFORD, THOMAS. An Historical Description of the Zetland Islands. No. **37** of
Bibl. Topog. Brit. 4to. London.

> Reprinted, with an appendix of illustrative documents, 8vo, Edinburgh, 1879; also in
> *Old-Lore Misc. of Orkney, Shetland, Caithness, and Sutherland,* vol. 4, 8vo, London.
> The description belongs to the year 1733. "An authentic account of the most distant
> part of his Britannic Majesty's dominions, by a very respectable native and resident . . . .
> He has done his subject justice, and given an ample description of Zetland, both as to its
> geography and civil and ecclesiastical history, both ancient and modern."—Gough, in
> *Gent. Mag.,* vol. 56, 424.

NICHOLS, JOHN. Some Account of the Parish of Lambeth. 4to. London.

1787   CLARKE, JAMES. For a topographical account of the Lake District, see his *Survey*
of the Lakes of Cumberland, under SURVEYS.

Extracts from Publications of Knox, Anderson, Pennant, and Dr. Johnson, relative to the North and North-west Coasts of Britain. 8vo. London.

TUNNICLIFF, WILLIAM. For a topographical description of Staffordshire,
Cheshire, and Lancaster, see his *Topographical Survey of the Counties of,* etc.,
under SURVEYS.

1788   AIKIN, DR. JOHN. England Delineated; or, a Geographical Description of every
County in England and Wales; with a concise Account of its most important
Products, natural and artificial, for the Use of Young Persons. 8vo. London.

> 2nd edit., with 43 maps of England, North and South Wales, and the 40 English coun-
> ties (in outline only), 8vo, London, 1790; 3rd edit., 1795; 4th, 1800.
> Reviewed *Gent. Mag.,* vol. 59, 828-29. In his Sketch of his plan the author tells what he
> emphasized and what he passed over. The omissions include antiquities, family history,
> noblemen's and gentlemen's seats, pleasure grounds, prospects, and the like. The geographical
> descriptions are purposely diffuse, as well as is the state of cultivation, trade, and manufac-
> tures.—From the review.

A Description of the High Peak, etc. 12mo. London.

England Described; or, The Traveller's Companion . . . to which is added, as an
Appendix, A Brief Account of Wales, etc. 8vo. London.

A Perfect Description of the People of Scotland. Listed in *Gent. Mag.,* vol. 58,
635.
> This may have some relation to Weldon's *A Perfect Description of the People and
> Character of Scotland* (see under 1649, TOURS BY NATIVES).

1789-91   BRYDGES, SIR E., and REV. H. S. SHAW. The Topographer, containing a Variety of Original Articles, illustrative of the Local History and Antiquities of
England. 42 plates. 4 vols. 4to. London.

1790   For an account of the islands of Scotland and the fisheries, see *A Comprehensive
History of Scotland,* under HISTORY AND CHRONICLE.

1791   GILPIN, REV. WILLIAM. Remarks on Forest Scenery and other Woodland Views,
relative chiefly to Picturesque Beauty. Illustrated by the Scenes of the New
Forest in Hampshire. Plates. 2 vols. 8vo. London.

2nd edit., 2 vols., London, 1794. This is listed as an Addenda to the first edition of W. Gilpin's *Observations on Forest Scenery,* by a friend of the Author.

HERON, ROBERT. Scotland Delineated; or, A Geographical Description of every Shire in Scotland, including the Northern and Western Isles: with some Account of the Curiosities, Antiquities, and Present State of the Country. For the Use of Young Persons. Map. 8vo. Edinburgh.

> Later editions followed.
> Reviewed *Gent. Mag.,* vol. 61, 1210. This work is recommended as a companion volume to Aikin's *England Delineated.*—The vogue of reducing learned matter to the comprehension of the young was well on its way by this date.

LUCKOMBE, PHILIP. The Beauties of England and Wales. 3rd edit. Map. 2 vols. London.

POLE, SIR WILLIAM. Collections toward a Description of the County of Devon; now first printed from the Author's Autograph MS. in the Possession of his lineal Descendant Sir John William de la Pole, Bart. of Shute, etc., in Devonshire. 4to. London.

> Reviewed *Gent. Mag.,* vol. 62, 50-51. Sir William Pole, the original compiler, began collecting his materials in 1604, but died (1635) before he could finish the work. The several volumes of manuscripts showed tremendous industry. His son, Sir John, made additions to the Description of Devon, which all miscarried during the Civil Wars.— From review. "This now very scarce volume (of which only 250 copies were printed) contains the whole of the Collections towards the History of Devonshire, so often quoted by Risdon and Prince, which that eminent and sedulous Antiquary, Sir W. Pole, Knt., began so early as 1604, but was prevented by death from perfecting the extensive work he meditated."—Quoted by Nichols, *Literary Anecdotes,* vol. IX, 96.

ROOKE, H., F.S.A. The Descriptions and Sketches of some remarkable Oakes in the Park at Welbeck, in the County of Nottingham, a Seat of his Grace the Duke of Portland. Plates. (Place?)

> So listed and reviewed *Gent. Mag.,* vol. 70, 140. Major Rooke used his leisure in the examination of ancient trees. The oaks in this park are among the largest in Nottinghamshire, and excel most others in height and stateliness.—From the review.

SINCLAIR, SIR JOHN. For much descriptive material on Scotland, see his *Statistical Account of Scotland,* under SURVEYS.

1792 BARCLAY, GEORGE. An Account of the Parish of Haddington. In *Soc. Antiq. Arch. Scotica,* vol. 1, 40-121, 4to. Edinburgh.

ERSKINE, DAVID STUART (Earl of Buchan). An Account of the Island of Icolumkill. 1 plate. In *Soc. Antiq. Arch. Scotica,* vol. 1, 234-41. Edinburgh.

OWEN, N. Caernarvonshire. A Sketch of its History, Antiquities, Mountains, and Productions. 8vo. London.

Sketches of Description: taken on sailing from Newport, in the Isle of Wight, to Lymington, with a Return by Southampton to Cowes. 8vo. Newport.

Topographical Miscellanies; containing Antient Histories and Modern Descriptions of Mansions, Churches, and Monuments, and Families, with many Engravings, particularly of antient Architecture throughout England. 4to. London.

> This is a continuation of the *Topographer* (see under Brydges, 1789-91 above). Reviewed *Gent. Mag.*, vol. 62, 441. This is made up of seven numbers, larger in size than the *Topographer*. It preserves some old churches for our view, compares their present state, and adds new notes. The plates were engraved by Ravenhill. It is a worthy work.—From the review.

WHYTE, REV. T. An Account of the Parish of Liberton in Mid-Lothian or County of Edinburgh. Paper read 1789. In *Arch. Scot.*, vol. 1, 292-338. 4to. Edinburgh.

> This follows up the fortunes of various prominent families, the history of places and the events connected with them, descriptions of certain houses and their grounds, etc.

1792-96 LYSONS, DANIEL. For an account of Surrey, see vol. I of his *The Environs of London*, under LONDON.

1793 DUNDONALD, 9TH EARL OF. A Description of the Estate and Abbey of Culross. 8vo. Edinburgh.

EDWARD, REV. ROBERT. A Description of the County of Angus, translated (by James Trail) from the original Latin of Robert Edward, Minister of Murroes, written in 1678. 8vo. Dundee.

> Reprint of Trail's edition, with facs. of the rare map, 4to, Edinburgh, 1883.

LOVE, JOHN. The Picturesque Beauties in the County of Dorset. 4to. Weymouth.

WARNER, REV. RICHARD. Topographical Remarks Relating to the South Western Parts of Hampshire, with copies of various Charters, Leases, Grants, etc. 2 vols. in 1. 8vo. London.

> This is a descriptive poem. Reviewed *Gent. Mag.*, vol. 63, 742. Warner continues to be inaccurate, misspelling words and names, and misusing words. His failure to cite his authorities so the facts can be checked again shows itself. He starts off with a trite history of the development of man from the state of savagery. Besides he is shaky in his antiquarian knowledge. Why does he say "fidicinal and wind instruments" in place of "stringed and wind instruments"?—From the review. For Warner's Tours in Wales, etc., see under 1798 and 1799, TOURS BY NATIVES.

1794 DALTON, W. H. The New and Complete English Traveller, or, a New Historical Survey and Modern Description of England and Wales, containing a full Account of whatever is curious and entertaining in the several Counties, Cities, Boroughs, Market Towns, Parishes, etc., of England and Wales, with an Accurate Description of Scotland. 70 plates of views and maps. Fol. London.

HERON, ROBERT. A General View of the Natural Circumstances of those Isles . . . which are distinguished by the common Name of Hebridae, or Hebrides. 4to. Edinburgh.

1795 AIKIN, DR. JOHN. A Description of the Country from Thirty to Forty Miles round Manchester, containing its Geography, Principal Productions, River and

Canal Navigations, a Particular Account of its Towns and Villages, their History, Population, Commerce and Manufactures, Buildings, and Governments, etc. 73 plates. 4to. London.

> Another edit., London, 1797. Noticed in *Gent. Mag.*, vol. 66, 500.
> This work gained a well established reputation. Aikin was a physician and a Unitarian. At his house some of the most noted liberal thinkers of the day, such as Priestly, Darwin, and Howard, used to foregather.

HEATH, JOHN. Descriptive Account of Persfield and Chepstow (in Monmouthshire), including Canvent, and the Passages on the Road to Bristol and Gloucester; interspersed with local and interesting Particulars, selected from the most admired Writers, viz., Young, Wyndham, Wheatley, Shaw, Grose, etc., being the Continuation of a Design for publishing in this Manner, An Account of the most interesting Places in the County. London.

> Noticed in *Gent. Mag.*, vol. 65, 411.

HOLT, JOHN. Lancashire. From the Communications of John Holt. Map and 5 plates. London.

MACNEILL, H. The Links o' Forth, or a Parting Peep at the Carse of Stirling. 8vo. Edinburgh.

A Short Account of the Parish of Waterbeach in the Diocese of Ely. By a late Vicar. 8vo. (Place?)

WYNTOUN, ANDREW OF. For his description of Scotland, see his *De Orygnale Cronykil of Scotland,* under HISTORY AND CHRONICLE.

> Extract from Book I, ch. xv, in Hume Brown, *Scotland before 1700,* 16-18.
> These descriptions add no detail of interest to those of Fordun (see under 1722 above), and they do not even apply exclusively to Scotland. It is clear, however, from the accent of real feeling in the opening lines, that it is as a patriotic Scot he writes. And these lines have a literary interest as an unsophisticated prelude of the many glowing descriptions of their native country in which the Scottish poets have always been at their best.—From Brown, *op. cit.*

1796 CUMBERLAND, GEORGE. An Attempt to describe Hafod, and the neighbouring Scenes over the Funack, commonly called the Devil's Bridge, in the County of Cardigan, an antient Seat, belonging to Thomas Johnes, Esq., Member for the County of Radnor. (Place?)

> Noticed in *Gent. Mag.*, vol. 66, 941-42. The work is approved of as being a useful guide to one making the Welsh circuit. The author seems to be very familiar with the scenes he describes, and is enthusiastic in his descriptions.—From the review.

HUNTER, R. E. A Short Description of the Isle of Thanet. Map. 12mo. London.

KENT, NATHANIEL. A General View of the County of Norfolk: with Observations for the Means of its Improvement. Folding map and illustrations. 8vo. Norwich.

Montgomery, or Scenes in Wales. 2 vols. 12mo. London (?). (So cited in Rowlands, *op. cit.*)

PENNANT, THOMAS. The Parishes of Whiteford and Holywell. Plates. 4to. London.

1797 HERON, ROBERT. Scotland Described : or, A Topographical Description of all the Counties of Scotland: with the Northern and Western Isles belonging to it. Containing an Account of the Extent of each County; of its Mountains, Rivers, Vales, and general Aspect; of its Fossils, Woods, and Animals; of the rural Industry and the Manners of its Peasantry; of its Mansion-houses, Pleasure-grounds; of the eminent Men by whom it has been illustrated. 12mo. Edinburgh.

> 2nd edit., Edinburgh, 1799.
> Heron says, "I have had occasion to traverse in various journeys, in the course of these last ten years, a considerable proportion of the territory of Scotland."

MATON, W. G. Observations relative chiefly to the Natural History, picturesque Scenery, and Antiquities of the Western Counties of England, made in the Years 1794 and 1796. Mineralogical map and 16 plates in aquatint. 2 vols. 8vo. Salisbury.

1798 MIDDLETON, J. Middlesex. Map. 8vo. London.

1799 A Description of the High Peak of Derbyshire, together with an Account of . . . other remarkable Places, hitherto called the Wonders of that Country, etc. 8vo. Manchester.

MURRAY, THE HON. MRS. For a description of Scotland, see her *A Companion and Useful Guide to the Beauties of Scotland,* under AIDS TO TRAVELERS.

1800 HOUSMAN, JOHN. A Topographical Description of Cumberland, Westmoreland, Lancashire, and a Part of the West Riding of Yorkshire. Map and illustrations. 8vo. Carlisle.

> This contains a descriptive tour and guide to the lakes, caves, mountains, and other natural curiosities in these districts. To his own observations the author adds remarks from several popular writers he had read.

1808 BEN, JO. Descriptio Insularum Orchadiarum. Anno 1529 per me Joannem Ben. ibidem Colentem. In Rev. Dr. Barry's *History of Orkney.*

> Translated into English in Macfarlane, *Geographical Collections,* vol. III, with an account of the MSS and guesses at the name, Edinburgh, 1906-08.
> There are two MSS in the Advocates' Library. Jo Ben's MS appears to have been lost. The work is of interest because it is the earliest topographical description of Scotland. Its only rival is that of Dean Monro in 1549 (see Monro under 1774 above). The richest and fullest is Timothy Pont's (see Pont under 1608, MAPS AND CHARTS).—From Macfarlane's Preface to Jo Ben.

MACKAILE, MATTHEW. A Short Relation of the most considerable Things in Orkney. In Appendix to Barry's *History of Orkney,* London.

> Also printed in Macfarlane, *Geog. Coll.,* vol. III, 1-10, Edinburgh, 1908.
> The date of Mackaile's visit is 1664.

1809 MACKENZIE, SIR GEORGE (of Tarbat). An Account of Hirta and Rona; given to Sir Robert Sibbald, *ca.* 1682. In Pinkerton, vol. III, 730.

Also in *Misc. Scotica,* vol. 2, Glasgow, 1818; in Macfarlane, *op. cit.,* vol. III.
On Rona there were five families of about thirty persons. If any family exceeded its quota of children, the additional child was brought up by one with less. Extras were sent to the Isle of Lewis.

RICHARD OF CIRENCESTER. The Description of Britain, translated from Richard of Cirencester (by H. Hatcher); with the original Treatise *De Situ Britanniae* (the forgery by Bertram) : and a Commentary on the Itinerary (by T. Leman). Map. 8vo. London.

> Edit. by Dr. Giles, with another work, London, 1841. See below.
> For this forgery see under Stukeley, 1757, BRITISH, ROMAN, AND SAXON ANTIQUITIES. Richard was no phantom himself, being a chronicler of the 14th century, who wrote a work called *Speculum Historiale de Gestis Regum Angliae* (see under 1858-1911, no. 30, HISTORY AND CHRONICLE).

> 1841 Richard of Devizes Concerning Richard I, and Richard of Cirencester's Description of Britain. Translated and edited by J. A. Giles. 8vo. London.

1813 GORDON, SIR ROBERT. The Description of the Province of Sutherland, with the Commodities thereof (1632). In his *Genealogical History of the Earldom of Sutherland.* Edit. by Henry Ellis. Fol. Edinburgh.

> Also in John Henderson's *General View of the Agriculture of the County of Sutherland,* 159-166, London, 1815.

1818 A Brief Description of the Burrough and Town of Preston, and its Government and Guild. Originally composed between the years 1682 and 1686. With occasional Notes by John Taylor. 8vo. Preston.

1823 SYMSON, ANDREW. A Large Description of Galloway, 1684; with Appendix containing original Papers from the Sibbald and Macfarlane MSS. (edit. by Thomas Maitland, Lord Dundrennan). 8vo. Edinburgh.

1824 MAKGILL, JACQUES, and IEAN BELLENDEN. Discours particulier d'Escosse: escrit par commandement et ordannance de la Royne Dovariere et Regente, par Messires Iacques Makgill Clerc du Registre, et Iean Bellenden Clerc de la Iustice, XI Ianvier MDLIX. In *Publ. Bann. Club,* no. 5. Edinburgh.

> The discourse is an unofficial report on the state of Scotland transmitted to Mary Stuart in France.

1825 PEPYS, SAMUEL. For descriptions of London and neighborhood, see his Memoirs or Diary under LETTERS, DIARIES, MEMOIRS.

> One who has not perambulated London of the Restoration with Pepys has something yet to live for.

1830-53 BELL, J. G. Collection of Twenty-One Reprints and Original Tracts on Topography, Genealogy, Dialects, etc. Numerous woodcuts by Bewick, etc. 2 vols. 8vo. London.

> This includes:—The Howdy and Upgetting, related by Thos. Bewick; Queene's Majesties' Entertaynemente in Suffolke and Norfolke, devised by Thos. Churchyarde (1579); Earle of Huntingdon's Commission for the Cayre and Defens of the Borders; Taking of Gateshead Hill (1644); Glossary of Essex Provincial Words; Ditto of Gloucester, with Proverbs; Ditto of Dorset; Ditto of Cumberland; Ditto of Berkshire; Trial of Janet Preston of Gisburne (1612) for Practising devilish and wicked Arts called Witchcraft; Praise of St. David's Day; Pedigree of the Family of Scott of Stokoe; Hughes' Vale

Royal of England; St. George's Heraldic Visitation of Westmoreland, made 1615; Pulman's Rhymes on Angling; Wyrley's True Use of Armorie (1592); and other Tracts. (Only 60 copies of each tract were printed.)

1831   HAMILTON, WILLIAM (of Wishaw). Descriptions of the Sheriffdoms of Lanark and Renfrew, compiled about MDCCX, by William Hamilton, of Wishaw. With illustrative Notes and Appendices (by John Dillon and John Fullarton). *Publ. Maitland Club,* vol. 12. 4to. Edinburgh.

> This was also edited by William Motherwell, Edinburgh (?), 1832; in *Publ. New Club,* vol. 3, Paisley, 1878.

1834   An Account of Medairloch, Bernera, and I Callim Kill, 1701; from the Wodrow Correspondence, vol. II. In *Analecta Scotica,* vol. 2, 114. 12mo. Edinburgh.

1835   MAIDMENT, JOHN. Poetical Description of Orkney, 1652, From a volume of Miscellaneous MS. Poems in the Advocates' Library (one of three reprints made by James Maidment in 1 vol.). 4to. Edinburgh.

> Only 35 copies printed. The author of the Orkney poem is possibly J. Emerson. Maidment calls the poem "coarse but clever."—From Mitchell, *List of Travels.*

1840   NORDEN, JOHN. Speculi Britanniae Pars: An Historical and Chorographical Description of the County of Essex. Edit. by Sir Henry Ellis for the Camden Society. London.

> This is dated 1594; here first published.

1843   ROBERTSON, JOSEPH (Editor). Collections for a History of the Shires of Aberdeen and Banff. In *Publ.* (Old) *Spalding Club,* vol. 9. Aberdeen.

> 1. Praefecturarum Aberdoniensis et Banfiensis in Scotia ultramontana nova descriptio, auctore Roberto Gordono (of Straloch), 1651-1660.
> 2. Description of Aberdeen, by Samuel Forbes of Foveran, 1716-17.
> 3. A View of the Diocese of Aberdeen, 1732, by H. Keith.

1844   ERDESWICKE, SAMPSON. Certaine verie rare Observations of Cumberlande, Northumberland, verie orderlie and labouriouslie gathered together. London (?).

> MS dated 1574 by Taylor, *Late Tudor and Early Stuart Geography.*

OCHTERLONY, JOHN (of Guynd). An Account of the Shire of Forfar; or, Information anent the Shire of Forfar, 1682-1722. Edit. by James Maidment. In *Spottiswoode Soc. Misc.,* vol. 1, 311. 8vo. Edinburgh.

> Also edit. by Sir Arthur Mitchell, in Macfarlane's *Geog. Coll.,* vol. II, 21; vol. III, 244, Edinburgh, 1907-08.

1845   An Account of the Lewis and some other of the Western Isles, from the Collections of Macfarlane of that Ilk. In *Spottiswoode Soc. Misc.,* vol. 2, no. 3. Edinburgh.

Illustrative Matter relative to Perth Ministers, ancient Festivals, St. John's Church, the Hospital, the Cross, Inundations of the Tay, Perth Bridge, and the Gowrie Conspiracy. In *Spottiswoode Soc. Misc.,* vol. 2, no. 3. Edinburgh.

WESTCOTE, THOMAS. A View of Devonshire in 1630, with a Pedigree of most of its Gentry. Edit. by G. Oliver and F. Jones. 4to. Exeter.

1846 MEYRICK, S. R. (Editor). Heraldic Visitations of Wales and Part of the Marches between the Years 1586 and 1613, transcribed from the original Manuscripts, with numerous explanatory Notes. 2 vols. Llandovery.

1847 Brevis descriptio regni Scotiae, *ca.* A.D. 1296. In *Misc. Maitland Club,* vol. 4, pt. 1, no. ii. Glasgow.

These notes were written by an Englishman towards the end of the thirteenth century, probably between the years of 1292 and 1296. They describe the northern part of the kingdom, and in particular detail the barrier of "The Mounth."—From Terry, *Cat. Publ. Scot. Hist. Clubs.*

CAMPBELL, DIONESS. Observations of Mr. Dioness Campbell, Deane of Limerick, on the West Isles of Scotland, A.D. 1596. In *Publ. Maitland Club,* vol. 4, pt. 1, no. iii. Glasgow.

This report was written for the information of Sir Robert Cecil, with a view to the employment of the Clans to quell Tyrone's rebellion in Ireland. The negotiations of Dennis or Dionysius Campbell to that end led to no results.—Terry, *op. cit.*

For descriptions of the parishes of Aberdeen and Banff, see *Topography and Antiquities of Aberdeen and Banff, Publ.* (Old) *Spalding Club,* vol. 2. Aberdeen. (For the list, arranged alphabetically, see following:)

Parish of Aberlour, 1775. Reprinted from the *History of the Province of Moray,* by L. Shaw.
Parish of Aboyne, 1725, by W. Robertson; also in Macfarlane, *Geog. Coll.,* vol. I.
Parish of Banff and Inverboyndie (or Boyndie), 1724, by W. Ogilvy.
Parish of Birse, 1761.
Parish of Boharm, 1775. Reprinted from the *History of the Province of Moray,* by L. Shaw.
Parish of Cairnie, *ca.* 1726.
Parish of Cluny, 1722, by Mr. Jaffray.
Parish of Coul, 1725.
Parish of Crathie and Kindroghit, 1736.
Parish of Deskford, 1724, by W. Ogilvy.
Parish of Fordyce, 1724, by W. Ogilvy.
Parish of Forgue, 1761.
Parish of Gartly, *ca.* 1726.
Parish of Glenmuick, Tullich, and Glengairn, 1736.
Parish of Glentanar, 1725, by W. Robertson; also in Macfarlane, *Geog. Coll.,* vol. I.
Parish of Inveraven, 1775. Reprinted from *History of the Province of Moray,* by L. Shaw.
Parish of Keith, *ca.* 1726; 1742.
Parish of Kirkmichael, 1775. Repr. from the *History of the Province of Moray.*
Parish of Mortlach, 1775. Repr. as preceding.
Parish of Murthlac, *ca.* 1726.
Parish of Kincardin o'Neil, 1725, by W. Robertson; also in Macfarlane, vol. I.
Parish of Ordequhil, 1724, by W. Ogilvy.
Parish of Rothiemay, *ca.* 1726.

1852 STUART, J. (Editor). Documents relating to Orkney and Shetland, 1438-1563. In *Misc.* (Old) *Spalding Club,* vol. 5. Aberdeen.

1858 PONT, TIMOTHY. Topographical Account of the District of Cunningham, Ayrshire. Compiled about the Year 1600 (1604?), by Mr. Timothy Pont. With Notes and an Appendix. Edit. by John Fullarton. Map. In *Publ. Maitland Club,* vol. 74. Glasgow.

Another edit., Glasgow, 1876. See below.

1876 PONT, TIMOTHY. Cuninghame Topographized, 1604-08, with Continuations and Illustrative Notices by Jas. Dobbie of Crummock, F.S.A., Scot., edited by his Son, John Shedden Crummock, with facsimile of Pont's Map from Blaeu's Atlas. 6 plates on copper and wood engravings. 4to. Glasgow.

> For the work of Pont as mapper and topographer, see under 1608, MAPS AND CHARTS.—The above appears to have been printed from a MS in the Advocates' Library in the handwriting of Sir James Balfour, probably a transcript for Pont's own MS. Pont left a large quantity of notes in writing, as well as maps, which were used by Sir Robert Gordon of Straloch in preparing the Scottish volume of Blaeu's great Atlas, but the notes have disappeared. A volume of the original maps is in the Advocates' Library (Edinburgh). Pont seems to have visited in person every place he surveyed and made many notes of the situation and antiquities. He visited the islands also, though he knew no Gaelic, traveled on foot, was often robbed and harshly treated. He has few equals in the extensiveness and thoroughness of his travels and surveys.—From Mitchell, *List of Travels*.

1862 AUBREY, JOHN. Topographical Collections for Wiltshire, A.D. 1659-70; corrected and enlarged by John Edward Jackson, M.A., F.S.A. *Publ. Wiltshire Arch. and Nat. Hist. Soc.* 4to. Devizes.

> This deals largely with churches, houses, remarks upon families, monuments, seals, armory.

1863 FORBES, J. The Social Condition of Scotland during the 15th and 16th Centuries; illustrated by Extracts from the Burgh Records of the City of Aberdeen. In *Publ. Social Science Assoc.* 8vo. Aberdeen.

1871 STARKEY, THOMAS. England in the Reign of Henry the Eighth. A Dialogue between Cardinal Pole and Thomas Lupset. Edit. with Preface, Notes, and Glossary by J. M. Cowper. 8vo. London.

> Also edit. by Sidney J. Herrtog for the E.E.T.S., ex. ser., vol. 12. London.
> The long introduction of the E.E.T.S. edition gives a detailed account of Starkey's relations with Henry VIII and Cardinal Pole, and an analysis of this lengthy dialogue with its discussions on the decay of England. Starkey was chaplain to Henry VIII and the Countess of Salisbury.

1876-77 BLUNDELL, WILLIAM. Historicall Description of ye Island of Man. *Publ. Manx Soc.*, vols. 25 and 27. Douglas.

> This was printed from a MS of the 17th century. According to a letter (inserted in the above) from William Harrison, founder of the Manx Society, only four other copies of Blundell's History are known to exist. The work was never published before the above date.—From Bookseller's Note.

1879 SMITH, WILLIAM (Rouge Dragon Herald). The Particular Description of England, with the Portratures of Certaine of the Cheifest Cities and Townes, 1588; from the original MS. in the British Museum, edit., with an Introduction, By Henry B. Wheatley, F.S.A., and Edmund W. Ashbee, F.S.A. 28 plates. 4to. London.

> The MS came into the possession of the British Museum through its purchase of the Hans Sloane Collection. It is strange that a work containing carefully drawn views of London, Cambridge, Bristol, Bath, etc., made in the days of Elizabeth, should have lain so long neglected. The date of the title page is 1588, but internal evidence reveals that it was not completed until the reign of James I. Smith early became interested in heraldry and genealogy and in 1597 won a position in the College of Arms as Rouge Dragon Pursuivant. The numerous armorial bearings attest his skill in drawing as do the profile and bird's-eye views of cities. His text starts out with old familiar matter about Brutus and other legendary founders along with some topical history. What is of more account is the

comprehensive summary of the sights of the metropolis, such as buildings, views, the distances between the chief cities, and their distinguishing features. He adds London as the eighth wonder of England.

1882 FLEMING, SIR DANIEL (of Rydal). The Description of the County of Westmoreland . . . A.D. 1671, edit. by Sir R. F. Duckett, Bart. In *Cumberland and Westmoreland Antiq. Soc. Tracts,* ser. no. 1. 8vo. London.

1885 SIBBALD, SIR ROBERT. An Advertisement and general Queries for the Description of Scotland, 1682. In *Misc. Bann. Club,* vol. III. 4to. Edinburgh.

1889 FLEMING, SIR DANIEL. The Description of the County of Cumberland . . . A.D. 1671, edit. by W. S. Ferguson. In *Cumberland and Westmoreland Antiq. Soc. Tracts,* ser. no. 3. 8vo. Kendal.

1893 BROWN, HUME.

> Listed below are accounts of Scotland printed by Brown (*Scotland before 1700,* Edinburgh) but not referred to elsewhere in this present work:

> The Habits of the People, 285-90. Extracts taken from the Privy Council Records, vol. IX.—These extracts bear out certain stinging criticisms of Scottish manners and customs made by travelers in the 16th and 17th centuries. Their habits in drinking merit fully the charges directed against them.

> New Trades and Industries of Scotland, 273-84. A Selection of Letters addressed to James I by the Privy Council of Scotland, from the Collection entitled *The Melros Papers,* which was published by the Abbotsford Club in 1837.—This collection consists of two large volumes and, with exceptions, was compiled from the Balfour MSS in the Advocates' Library. The majority of these papers are purely political, but certain of them deal with topics which tell of the beginning of two great Scottish industries. Those enumerated are the export of timber; the curing of herring, foreign merchant vessels, magistrates and their robes, the new manufacture of textiles, and the export of grain. As the acts of Parliament show, the export and import of grain was a long-standing problem in Scotland.

> Social Legislation of the Seventeenth Century, 344-53. Taken from the Acts of Parliament.—It will be seen from these Acts that the spirit which inspired the earlier legislators included in Brown was the same that prevailed in the nineteenth century. Restrictive measures with regard to foreign goods and State regulation of trades at home were the double means by which they sought to develop the national resources. Fines were directed against noblemen who sent their sons and tutors out of the country to be educated without the bishop's consent. Legislation was enacted for "preserving the said town of Edinburgh, Canongate, and the suburbs thereof, from the nastiness of the streets, wynds, closes, and other places of the said burgh, and for freeing and purging the same of those numerous beggars which repair to and about the said burgh." Bodies were to be buried in Scots linen (1686). It is to be noted that England passed an act in 1678 which held good until 1815 prescribing burial in woolen.

> Social Legislation of the Fifteenth Century, 19-32. Taken from the Acts of Parliament passed mainly during the Fifteenth Cenutry.—These Acts give an impression of an energetic community, fully alive to its own interests, enjoying a fair degree of prosperity, and already plagued with parasitic growths which inevitably inhere to the progressive social organism. In those days the Scottish Estates did not hesitate to interfere with private contracts, rearing of crops, rates of charge, and the like.

> Address to the Merchantis of Edinburgh (from the poet Dunbar), 109-12.—This describes a spectacle which Dunbar must have experienced daily: the sights, sounds, and smells disfiguring street life, which he thinks it shameful for the citizens to present to the senses of strangers. (In verse.)

> Entries from the Accounts of the Lord High Treasurer, 1515-1542, 35-40.—These afford a glimpse into the life of the Scottish kings and court during the first half of the sixteenth century.

Proceedings of the Justice—Aire of Jedburgh, 1510, 65-67. From Pitcairn, *Criminal Trials,* vol. I, pt. 1.—The long catalogues of crimes testify to the rudeness of the times; yet their very length and minuteness of detail are in themselves the intimation of a society with well-defined aims and complex activities.

Sports and Pastimes of the Scottish People, 1440-1565, 184-96. Taken from a paper in the *Analecta Scotica,* 2nd ser., 1837, entitled "Municipal Statutes regulating the Sports, Pastimes, and Processions in the City of Aberdeen, from the Year 1440 to the Year 1565."—From the regulations reprinted here we see what sports were in favor and to what extent they exceeded the bounds of what was regarded as decent and orderly. It was apparent that the city felt that the ancient amusements had served their day and that more rational forms of diversions were required in keeping with the growth of civic consciousness. The Scottish reformers were also active in suppressing what was considered as detrimental to the interests of decency and morality.

Trade Regulations, 1529-1531, 197-200. Taken from the Book of the Statutes to the Burgh of Edinburgh, between the dates of 1529 to 1531. The collection published in the *Misc. Maitland Club,* vol. 2.—These illustrate the deliberate way in which the authorities of public weal interfered in matters which are now left to adjust themselves by the "natural laws of supply and demand" (quotes mine). They set the price of ale, the weight of bread, the quality of candles, the proper furnishing of stables by stablers, the need of merchants of fair booths to have axes ready to keep the public order, the forbidding lepers to mingle with clean folk, etc.

A Trial of Witchcraft, 1576, 207-17. From Pitcairn, *Criminal Trials,* vol. I, pt. 2.—The individual under trial for witchcraft was Elizabeth or Bessie Dunlop, "spous to Andro Jak in Lyne." The Scottish reformers were no laggards in following the trail of witchhunting, although this nation had the cleanest record in decreeing death for religion's sake. The Reformed Church of Scotland was established in 1563; three years later an act of Parliament was passed which brought about the long series of executions for witchcraft, closing with the death of an old woman at Dornoch as late as 1722. The above case well illustrates the procedure followed in such cases.

1894   Letter from an English or Cromwellian Soldier in Scotland. See Letters and Papers illustrating the Relation between Charles II and Scotland in 1650. Edit. by S. R. Gardiner, in *Publ. Scot. Hist. Soc.,* no. 17, 134-40. Edinburgh.

The writer, being a Cromwellian, naturally comments on the excessive cursing indulged in by the Scotch and the variety of imprecations. "The Deele fa me," "the Deele blaw me blind," "God's curse light on me," etc., are some samples. Other comments inform us that the beds were "nasty and greazie, ful of lops (fleas)," that "whoredome and fornication is the common darling sin of the nation."—From Mitchell, *List of Travels.*

1898   LANG, ANDREW (Editor). The Highlands of Scotland, 1750. From a MS. in King's Library, Brit. Mus. 8vo. Edinburgh.

1899-1901   WALKER, JOHN ("Late Professor of Natural History in the University of Edinburgh"). An Oeconomical History of the Hebrides or Western Islands of Scotland (*ca.* 1765). *Trans. Gaelic Soc. Inverness,* vol. 24, 120-39. Inverness.

This is taken from the Brit. Mus. King's MS. 105. The Introduction of the article states that the work was printed in 2 vols., 1808 (Edinburgh?). The portion printed above includes Lewis and Harris. Walker had received a commission from the General Assembly of the Church of Scotland to inquire into the state of religion in the Highlands, along with other matters, and at the same time a commission from H. M. Commissioners of the Annexed Estates to examine into the natural history of those regions, their population, the state of agriculture, manufactures and fisheries, etc.—From the Introduction.

1900   GERARD, THOMAS. The Particular Description of the County of Somerset drawn up by Thomas Gerard of Trent, 1633. Edit. by E. H. Bates in *Publ. Somerset Record Soc.,* vol. 15. 4to. London.

1900-01 HOOKER (HOKER, VOWELL), JOHN. A Discourse of Devonshire: A Discussion of the MS. (Harl. MSS., No. 5827). Concluded by him in 1599. In *Devon Notes and Queries,* vol. I, 184 ff. Exeter.

> The title of the MS is: A Discourse of Devonshire and Cornwall, the Blazon of Arms, etc., the Bishops of Exeter, the revenews of the Deneries and parsonages, and other Gentlemen. Risdon writing in 1630 made large use of this MS and printed one document— List of Places privileged and free from Tax and Toll (edit. of 1811, App. 17). (See Risdon's *Survey of Devon* under 1714 above.) The original has never before been printed. It enumerates the number of market towns, parks, forests, number of the "sweete waters," and points out the abundance of fish. It describes the commodities, nature of the four degrees of the people—the gentleman, the merchant, the yeoman, and the laborer. Other descriptions take care of Dartmoor, and other places; armory, Exeter trading companies, charters of various sorts, valuations of parishes, market towns in Devon, etc. It also points out that the country "is evill to be travelled." See Vowell under 1575, TOWNS.

1902 Breviary of Suffolk. London (?).

> MS dated 1618 by Taylor, *Late Tudor and Early Stuart Geography.*

1903 BARLOW, CAPTAIN J. Letters from the Hebrides, 1753, from MS. in British Museum (Add. MSS., 35891). Printed in Appendix to Mackenzie's *History of the Outer Hebrides.* Paisley.

DYMES, CAPTAIN JOHN. Description of Lewis, 1630. In Mackenzie's *History of the Outer Hebrides,* 591-95. Paisley.

1906-08 MACFARLANE, WALTER. For numerous descriptions of parishes, counties, and larger regions, see his *Geographical Collections,* edited by Sir Arthur Mitchell, 3 vols., nos. 51-53 of *Publ. Scot. Hist. Soc.,* Edinburgh, under GENERAL REFERENCE.

1907 BUCHANAN, DAVID. Provinciae Edinburgiae Descriptio. Edit. by Sir A. Mitchell for the Scot. Hist. Soc. Edinburgh.

> This was written about 1647.

Ane Description of certain Pairts of the Highlands of Scotland. Edinburgh (?).

> MS dated *ca.* 1630 by Taylor, *Late Tudor and Early Stuart Geography.*

1910 POWELL, EDGAR (Editor). A Suffolk Hundred in the Year 1283. 8vo. Cambridge.

1912-13 BRUCE, R. STUART. Glimpses of Shetland Life, 1718-1753. In *Old-Lore Misc. Orkney, Shetland, Caithness, and Sutherland Soc.,* vol. 5, 156-59; vol. 6, 31-37, 92-101, 129-35. 8vo. London.

1938 DONALDSON, JOHN E. Caithness in the Eighteenth Century. London.

> This is based on the family papers and letters of the Sinclairs of May in Caithness. It is a remarkable collection, the existence of which has hitherto been unknown to students of Scottish history. Another useful source is the unpublished manuscript, "A Short History of Caithness, 1735, by Aneas Bayn."—Heffer & Sons Ltd., Catalogue.

IV

Views

(The primary business of topographical and antiquarian illustration was to supply a clear-cut and adequate representation of visual fact, that is, to show things as they stood at the time. This requirement did not prevent the reader from drawing upon his own store of associations to throw a coloring of mind over the object. Nor, where the relation of house to grounds was designed as a landscape composition, as was frequently the intention of the eighteenth century, did the illustrator neglect the opportunity of making his work approach the status of art, especially after the aquatint process and the search for picturesque design came into vogue. Certainly many charming engravings of this sort are prized for their own sake. Since landscape gardening was fondly believed to reproduce on the canvas of nature the "prospects" of Claude Lorrain and Salvatore Rosa, so it may well be that the popularity of engraved views of gentlemen's seats stimulated the emergence of land-scape painting into a branch of art whose end was itself. On the other hand, views of the remains of antiquity, such as abbeys, cathedrals, castles, Roman and Saxon finds, tended to adhere more strictly to the professional viewpoint of the antiquary, who was mainly interested in recording the past. Antiquarian curiosity, however, overflowed into the ornamental, as is evidenced by the fashion of erecting Roman and Gothic ruins as adorn-ments to the landscape, though the practice may have owed as much to the love of novelty as to the influence of the historic past.

The following list of references is limited chiefly to collections and to such individual views as are noteworthy for their subject, artist, or period. Views and panoramic plans of London and the two university towns are to be found in the sections LONDON and UNIVERSITIES.)

1572-1618 BRAUN, GEORG, and FRANZ HOGENBERG. Civitates orbis terrarum. 6 vols. Fol. Cologne.

For this noble work Braun did the text and Hogenberg and Hoefnagel the maps and plans. It appeared in six "Folianta," in which the title varied with each volume. The first volume was dedicated to Maximilian II and was published in 1572. The remaining volumes came out in 1575-1618. This work holds first place in early topographical publications. Hogenberg was in England with his brother around 1560; and while there worked for several booksellers. The items following, attributed to Hoefnagel, are very likely excerpts from the *Civitates orbis terrarum.*

1575 HOEFNAGEL, JORIS. Edinburgium, Scotiae Metropolis. Engraved pictorial plan of the city in contemporary coloring, with the figures of two ladies and two gentlemen of the period, in the foreground. 18 × 13½ ins. Cologne.

———. Nordovicum Angliae Civitas. Engraved bird's-eye pictorial plan of Norwich in bright contemporary coloring. Decorated with two coats-of-arms at the top, a gentleman and his lady in the foreground and a list of the principal sites in English. Latin description on reverse. 16½ × 11½ ins. Cologne.

1580 ———. Canterbury. Engraved in colors. A highly decorated plan of the town and surrounding country, with armorial arms and figures in the foreground showing the costume of the period. 12¾ × 17 ins. Cologne.

———. Chester. Engraved in colors. A highly decorated plan showing the arms of the city and a key to the places of interest. 12¾ × 17 ins. Cologne.

———. Windsor Castle. Engraved in colors. 12¾ × 17 ins. Cologne.

1582 ———. Palatium regium in Angliae regno appellatum Nonciutz [Nonesuch], hoc est, nunquam simile; effigiavit Georgius Hogenbachius, 1582. 12½ × 17½ ins. Cologne.
This seems to represent the back front, a wall running before the entrance. In the foreground is the Queen in a calash, and a prince or nobleman following her in another. At the bottom of the plate are figures portraying the women's dress of that age.—From Gough, *Anecdotes of British Topography,* 506.

1618   ——. Civitas Exoniae (vulgo Excester), urbs primaris in Comitatu Devoniae. Engraved bird's-eye plan of the city in contemporary colors, with Latin description on the reverse. 16 × 12½ ins. Cologne.

——. Shrewsbury, Lancaster, and Richmond. Engraved colored plate, containing three bird's-eye plans and a view of Richmond Palace, Surrey. Along the left side are four colored engravings of an ancient Briton, Roman, Saxon, and Dane; and down the opposite side, a similar series of colored engravings, with two figures in each, King and Queen (apparently James I and Queen Elizabeth), English nobles, citizens, and rustics. 17 × 12½ ins. Cologne.

1577   DRURY, SIR WILLIAM. Plan (bird's-eye view) of Edinburgh, 1573. 15¼ x 10¾ ins. London.

1638   Libellus Novus Politicus Emblematicus Civitatum. Obl. 4to. (Place—Germany? Printed for P. Furst.)

336 engraved views of cities mostly from series E, F, G, and H, including views of Edinburgh, Oxford, Carlisle, Norwich, Windsor, Hull, and many towns in Europe, Arabia, and Africa.

1647   GORDON, JAMES. Bird's-eye View of Edinburgh. 16½ × 41½ ins. Amsterdam.

Engraved by Andrew Johnson, London, 1719; facsimile by Kirkwood, Edinburgh, *ca.* 1824; re-engraved by W. and A. W. Johnston, Edinburgh, 1865, with historical and explanatory notice by David Laing.

James Gordon assisted his father, Sir Robert Gordon of Straloch, in preparing the maps for the Scottish section of Blaeu's *Atlas*. He is known as the first person to have preserved views of particular places and buildings in Scotland. On the above date he executed a large survey of Edinburgh which was engraved by DeWitt at Amsterdam. It was also published in the *Bann. Misc.*, vol. II, with a description of the city by David Buchanan. It is pictorial in design, showing considerable skill and finish.—*DNB.*

1676   WINSTANLEY, HENRY. Plans, Elevations, and Particular Prospects of Audley End. 24 engravings. Fol. London.

These were also issued in 1690, with 21 of the 24 plates.

Winstanley was Clerk of the Works for Charles II at Audley End; he likewise furnished the design for Eddystone Lighthouse in 1696, and while engaged on the building was captured by a French privateer. He lost his life in the great storm of 1703 which destroyed the structure. Of the above engravings Lowndes says, "Copies of these 24 prints were likewise made and engraved by Winstanley, about the same period, in 4to size, but which are so scarce that a perfect set is unknown." The 1690 volume also contains engravings of Eddystone Lighthouse, with other details.—From Bookseller's Note.

1687   A Prospect of the Royal Palace and Castle at Windsor. On a large sheet of paper. (Place?)

1693   SLEZER, CAPTAIN JOHN. Theatrum Scotiae; containing the Prospects of their Majesties Castles and Palaces; together with those of the most considerable Towns and Colleges; the Ruins of many Ancient Abbeys, Churches, Monasteries, and Convents, within the said Kingdom; all curiously engraved on Copper Plates, with a short Description of each Place [by Sir Robert Sibbald]. 57 plates. Fol. London.

2nd edit., London, 1718; 3rd, with large additions, author unknown, 1718; 4th, abridged text of the descriptions, with descriptions wanting where plates are missing, 1719. Reprinted, with additional text and life of Slezer, by John Jamieson, fol., Edinburgh, 1874. See also *Bann. Club Misc.*, vol. II, xiv, no. 19a, 1836, and *Edinb. Bibliog. Soc.*, vol. 3, 141, 1899.

The survey was made in 1673 and engraved on plates 19 × 12 ins. The descriptions drawn up by Sir Robert Sibbald were intended to be published in Latin, but were trans-

lated inaccurately by Slezer into English without leave or acknowledgement. Slezer planned to do prospects of all the considerable places in Scotland, which were to appear in several volumes. But he seemed to have failed of the proper encouragement. Slezer, a Dutchman, attached to the House of Orange, probably came over to England in the time of Charles II. In 1690 he was made Captain of the Artillery Company and Surveyor of his Majesty's Magazines in Scotland. When he went to Scotland is not known. He said he was encouraged by Charles II and James, then Duke of York, and by many of the nobility and gentry of Scotland to make a collection of the most remarkable public and private buildings of that country. The Scottish Parliament was so pleased with what they saw of the work that they levied a tax on the tonnage of all foreign ships trading to Scotland. He seems to have enjoyed more promises than pay, and died deeply in debt. The title used by Slezer for the first part of the work was apparently suggested by that of the Description of Scotland, in Blaeu's *Atlas*. The second part was designed to have the title *Scotia Illustrata* or *North Britain Illustrated*. The various descriptions of individual places were dedicated to different noblemen, whose coats-of-arms appear at the top. The plates, while not the best examples of the art of engraving, are valuable for their pictures of ruins, which were then much more extensive. They also show a countryside unspoiled by industry and extending right up against the towns. Costumes and activities of figures in typical attitudes appear on the plates.

1708 Kip, Johannes, and Leonard Knyff. Nouveau Théatre de la Grande Bretagne, ou Description exacte de Palais de la Reine, et des Maisons les plus considérables des Seigneurs et des Gentilshommes de la Grande Bretagne. 80 double-page engraved bird's-eye views of famous mansions. Fol. London.

Appeared as *Britannia Illustrata*, London, 1709; a 2nd vol. was added to the edition with the French title in 1713; the English title again in 1714; the French title in 1715; seemingly the English title in 1717; the French title in 1724. A series of Seats of the Nobility and Gentry of Great Britain advertised in 1707. The succession of editions is not very clear. See below.

Many of these plates were engraved earlier than the date of publication. Knyff made the drawings and Kip the engravings. Though the latter are indifferently done, they are precious for showing us the layout of mansions and grounds before the formal garden gave way to the new style of the "natural garden," celebrated by Pope and Addison. In the decades to come most of these places suffered revolutionary changes under the guidance of Kent and "Capability" Brown. The book was sponsored by four publishers, Mortier, Midwinter, Overton, and Smith, who designed to publish a series of elaborate, double-page plates in folio, illustrating the great country seats of England at the close of the 17th century. Neither of the artists was of great merit.

1709 ——. Britannia Illustrata, or, Views of the Queen's Palaces; as also of the Principal Seats of the Nobility and Gentry of Great Britain; curiously engraven on 80 Copper Plates. Fol. London.

1708-13 ——. Nouveau Théatre de la Grande Bretagne. . . . Tom I. Description exacte de Palais de la Reine. . . . Tom II. Description exacte des villes, églises, cathédrales, hospiteaux, ports de mer. . . . 147 engravings. 2 vols. Fol. London.

1714 ——. Britannia Illustrata: or Views of several of the Queen's Palaces, and principal Seats of the Nobility and Gentry of Great Britain. Fol. London.
A 2nd vol. was published the year after, with the same number of plates and above 300 coats-of-arms, the views of which were both drawn and engraved by Kip. Both volumes republished with French title in 1724. The 1st contained 80 and the 2nd 68 plates. 2 more vols. were later added by Badeslade in 1736.

1715 ——. Nouveau Théatre de la Grande Bretagne. . . . 4 vols. Fol. London.
2nd vol. contains views of towns and churches; the 3rd, views of castles in Scotland, and a series of maps. In 5 vols., 1724-29.

1717-25 Campbell, Colin. Vitruvius Britannicus: or, The British Architect; containing the Plans, Elevations, and Sections of the Regular Buildings, both Publick and Private, in Great Britain, with a Variety of New Designs. 3 vols. Fol. London.

To this was added a 4th vol. in continuation, by C. J. Woolfe and James Gandon, 1767-71.

The architect Campbell was brought to public attention less by his ability than by the patronage of Lord Burlington, the Maecenas of the century, who paid the expenses of this publication. In putting out this work he was following the fashion of architects, who called notice to their own work by including specimens of their designs with those of their illustrious predecessors. And naturally they selected patrons with heavy purses. Campbell's volumes do not enhance the credit of either his taste or his judgment, since he perpetuated some insignificant names and omitted more deserving ones. They do preserve, however, the elevations and ground plans of many principal buildings in England, many of which have since disappeared. His own best-known work is Houghton Hall, the seat of Sir Robert Walpole. (See Ripley under 1760 below.)

1719 KIP, JOHANNES, ―――― COLLINS (and others). Views of all the Cathedrals in England and Wales, the Collegiate Churches of Westminster and Southwark, and the Chapel Royal, Windsor. 41 double folding copperplates. Descriptions in English and French. Fol. London.

1720 BADESLADE, THOMAS. Views. London.

These were apparently made from Harris's *History of Kent* (see Harris under 1719, HISTORY AND ANTIQUITIES), but were also published separately.

1721 BUCK, SAMUEL and NATHANIEL. Engravings of Castles, Abbeys, etc. London.

With this date the Bucks began their work of issuing series of engravings of towns, ruined abbeys, castles, views, etc., which took up many years and numbered over 500 views. See under 1727 below for further detail.

1724 Britannia Illustrata: Views of all the Palaces, several Seats, and other Publick Buildings of England. 21 views.—Prospects of Palaces and other Publick Buildings in France, Italy, Spain, etc. 15 views. In 1 vol. Obl. 4to. London.

These are interesting old views, most of which display the architectural features from the main 'viewpoint of the building; others give extensive views of the seat, with its gardens, such as Hampton Court, the Palaces of Versailles, etc.—Bookseller's Note.

1726 BUCK, SAMUEL. Engraved Views of Places of Interest in Nottinghamshire. A series of six views.

1727-40 BUCK, SAMUEL and NATHANIEL. Buck's Antiquities; or, Venerable Remains of above Four Hundred Castles, Monasteries, Palaces, etc., in England and Wales. With near 100 views of Cities and Chief Towns. 2 vols. in 3. Fol. London.

Another issue in 2 vols., with a 3rd vol. of cities and towns.
The work was first issued in 17 sets of about 24 plates each, priced at 2 guineas a set. They were also sold in smaller groups, at various dates between 1727 and 1774. The 1774 volumes were published as a new edition. The Bucks spent over thirty years and made numerous tours over England in gathering material for their *Remains*. Unlike Kip and Loggan, who published vast bird's-eye views of mansions and gardens, these later artists went in for views of ruins, castles, abbeys, etc., which displayed remarkably pictorial effect and also such accuracy that they could be used as the bases for restorations. The Bucks were also skilful in the management of light and shade, mass and line, and sky and foliage. Better than most of their contemporaries, they revealed knowledge of the principles of Gothic architecture.

1774 BUCK, SAMUEL and NATHANIEL. Antiquities; or, Venerable Remains of above Four Hundred Castles, Monasteries, Palaces, etc. Map, mezzotint portrait of the two brothers, and 428 engraved views, some large and folding. 2 vols. fol. Perspective Views of Cities and Chief Towns in England and Wales, with Historical Accounts. 83 extra large plates. 1 vol. Obl. fol. Together 3 vols. London.
Vol. 3 is of larger size.—Lowndes.

1731   HAYNES, JOHN. The South-west Prospect of the Antient City of York, with the Platform of Knavesmire; whereon his Majesty King George II's Hundred Guineas was run for Aug. 10, 1731. York (?).

1735   A Collection of Miscellaneous Prints, etc., chiefly illustrating North Wales, including an early View of Penmaenmawr, a Playbill of the Cambro-Britons, and a large engraving of Chirk Castle.

> So cited in Rowlands, *Cambrian Bibliog.*

WARE, ISAAC. The Plans, Elevations, and Sections: Chimney-pieces, and Ceilings of Houghton in Norfolk, the Seat of the Right Hon. Sir Robert Walpole. Fol. London.

> For Houghton see Colin Campbell under 1717-25 above and Ripley under 1760 below. Ware was a prominent architect of the 18th century and author of several works on architecture.

1738   PRIEST, T. Views of Chelsea, Wandsworth, Battersea, Fulham, Chiswick, Mortlock, and Isleworth. Drawn and engraved by T. Priest. Fol. London.

READ, MATTHEW. East Prospect of Whitehaven, Cumberland. Large engraved view by R. Parr, after Matthew Read. 29 × 43 ins.

1741   MENAGEOTT, A., and CHRISTOPHER SETON. A View and Plan of the Camp in the Isle of Wight. (Place?)

1742   BICKHAM, GEORGE. Deliciae Britannicae, or, The Curiosities of Hampton Court and Windsor Castle delineated. 3 copperplates. 12mo. London.

1743   LANGLEY, BATTY. The Plan of Windsor Castle. Obl. 4to. London.

> 5 plates, the first of which contains also "a short historical Account of Windsor Castle, abstracted from Lambert," etc.—Anderson, *Bibliog. of Brit. Topog.* Batty Langley is known as the architect who tried to reduce Gothic design to the bounds of the "five orders."

1744   Kensington Palace: Perspective View of Part of the Serpentine River, with the Queen's Temple, and a distant View of the Palace of Kensington; with costume figures in foreground. Etching by T. Tinney, after Highmore. 14 × 18½ ins.

> Here follows a series of views of this palace variously dated.

> 1744   ———. Perspective View of the South Front of Kensington Palace, taken from the End of the Slope by the Verges of the Great Walk. Etching by T. Tinney, after Highmore. 14 × 18½ ins.

> 1751   ———. Front View of the Royal Palace of Kensington, showing many persons of fashion promenading. Etching by and after Parr. 10 × 15¼ ins.

> 1753   ———. View of the Ornamental Water, with its Grecian structure, swans, a man and a dog on the bank. Original drawing in pen and ink.

> 1787   ———. A Scene in Kensington Gardens; with a gentleman (said to be George III) embracing a lady, who has an extraordinarily large head-dress and hat. Mezzotint. 14 × 9¾ ins.

1747   Vetusta Monumenta: For views of various antiquarian objects, such as abbeys, churches, castles, ecclesiastical monuments, lamps, vases, bronzes, etc., see this title under HISTORY AND ANTIQUITIES.

1748 KIRBY, JOSHUA. An Historical Account of the Twelve Prints of Monasteries, Castles, Antient Churches, and Monuments, in the County of Suffolk, which were drawn by Joshua Kirby, Painter in Ipswich, and published by him, March 26, 1748. Ipswich.

These were engraved by Wood. Among the views are Sudbury priory, Christ Hospital, Ipswich; Blithburgh church and priory; Bungay church and priory, and castle; Clare priory and castle; Lavenham church, and monuments of some of the Howard families.

1749 Green Park: A Description of the Machine for the Fireworks, with all its Ornaments, and a Detail of the Manner in which they are to be exhibited in St. James's Park, April 27, 1749, on account of the General Peace of Aix-la-Chapelle concluded in Oct., 1748. 4to. 16 pp.—Perspective View of the Building for the Fireworks in the Green Park, taken from the Reservoir. Line engraving by Angier, after Brookes ($10\frac{1}{2}$ × 17 ins.).—Perspective of the Magnificent Structure, erected in the Green Park for the Royal Fire Works, exhibited on the 27th of April, 1749, on account of the General Peace; colored line-engraving, showing Buckingham Palace, with surrounding houses and country (10 × $15\frac{1}{2}$ ins.).—View of the Great Fire Works on account of ye General Peace; Exhibiting the Curious Piece of Architecture, erected on that Occasion, the 3 Fire Suns, the middle-most 22 feet, the others 10 feet in Diameter, 12 Fire Trees, and that particular Grand Scene of the Fire Works, called the Girandola, which is the firing at once 6000 Rockets. Etching 14 × 10 ins. Etc.

These prints acknowledged an occasion that was as grandiloquent in its conception as it was humiliating in its execution. The Peace of Aix-la-Chapelle of October, 1748, was to be commemorated by order of George II. Handel was sent for and commanded to prepare some music, and in the center of Green Park was to be built an enormous structure with wings extending on each side and crowned with a great bas-relief representing George II handing out peace to Britannia. At the top, on a tall pole was pictured a vast sun. The fireworks were under the direction of an Italian named Chevalier Servandoli. To admit the crowds that assembled to view the exhibition a large section of the wall surrounding the garden had to be broken down. Handel's *Firework Music,* which at its rehearsal at Vauxhall was attended by a crowd almost as large, a crowd that stopped traffic on London Bridge and witnessed fights between duchesses and charwomen to get seats, was what saved the day, or rather the night, for his Majesty, for the fireworks failed to perform until repeated lightings by workmen, who had to climb the scaffolding to keep touching them off, made them burst into flame that illuminated the Park as though it were day. In the midst of the fiery spectacle, the blazing sun toppled over showering sparks everywhere, and George and Britannia went down with it. An amusing account of the whole performance is to be found in Newman Flower's *Life of Handel* (1923).

1750 ADAMS, W. Vitruvius Scoticus: a Collection of Plans, Elevations, and Sections of Public Buildings, Noblemen's and Gentlemen's Houses in Scotland. 179 plates. Fol. Edinburgh.

BOYDELL, J. View of Erith looking up the Thames. A picture of contemporary life, showing the river bank lined with houses, and an animated assembly in launches, others bathing, etc., in foreground, ships at anchor in distance. Line engraving by and after J. Boydell. $9\frac{1}{2}$ × $16\frac{1}{4}$ ins. London.

————. Wales: 3 Copperplate Views: Rhaidder Fawr, near Penmaen Mawr; View of Penmaen Mawr; Gaunant Mawr. 20 × 14 ins. London.

MAURER, ——. Mansion House: Exterior View. Showing figures, vehicles, etc., in the neighboring streets. Line engraving by Maurer. $9\frac{1}{2}$ × $14\frac{3}{4}$ ins. London.

NICHOLLS, N. Buckingham Palace, in St. James Park. Line engraving by N. Nicholls. 13 × 18 ins. London.

Windsor: a colored engraving of the Royal Palace of Windsor. 16 × 11 ins. London.

1751 PAYNE, JAMES. Elevations, Sections, and other Ornaments of the Mansion House belonging to the Corporation of Doncaster. Engraved by Rooker. Fol. London.

See Paine under 1767 below.

1752 BOYDELL, J. View of Gravesend: view from the Thames, which is shown busy with sailing craft, etc. Line engraving by and after J. Boydell. London.

————. View of Hammersmith, looking down the Thames. Showing numerous craft on the river, houses, trees, etc., along the bank. Line engraving. 9½ × 16¼ ins. London.

————. View of Northfleet. Showing an expanse of the Thames, with houses, gardens, etc., sailing craft on the river. Line engraving by and after J. Boydell. 9¼ × 16 ins. London.

Boydell issued many sets of engravings of landscapes and views of London. He set many artists to work doing paintings to illustrate Shakespeare, which were engraved and published in an 1802 edition of Shakespeare.

1755 SCOTIN, G. A View of the Town and Harbour of Portsmouth, with his Majesty's Fleet under Sail. Line engraving by Scotin after Menageott. 11⅞ × 17⅞ ins.

1757 The Beauties of England, or, A Comprehensive View of the Public Structures. Numerous plates. 8vo. London.

2nd edit., 8vo, London, 1764; another, 12mo, London, 1767; listed in the *Gent. Mag.* is another for 1785. See also *The Beauties of England, a New Display,* etc., under 1772 below, which may be a close relative to the above.

1767 The Beauties of England, or, A Comprehensive View of the Chief Villages, Market Towns, and Cities, etc. 12mo. London.

1760 RIPLEY, THOMAS. The Plans, Elevations, and Sections: Chimney-pieces, and Ceilings of Houghton in Norfolk; Built by the Rt. Honourable Sir Robert Walpole . . . The Whole designed by T. Ripley, Delineated by J. Ware, and W. Kent, and most elegantly engraved by the Ingenious Mr. Fourdrinier. With a Description of the House and of the Elegant Collection of Pictures. 28 plates on 35 leaves. Fol. London.

Houghton Hall was designed on a magnificent scale, with a great central block flanked by symmetrical extended wings. Its interior was still more impressive, with its enormous state rooms, marble stair case, and all the Renaissance renderings of Greek columns, pediments, niches, cartouches, etc., all of which constituted a setting somewhat incongruous with the taste of its owner, who was more of a bluff country squire than a gentleman.

A View of Pekham in Kent. Colored line engraving, with a water scene, showing anglers, swans, and other figures. 7 × 10½ ins. London.

WOOLLETT, W. Coombank, near Sevenoaks. Line engraving by and after W. Woollett. View of the house and gardens, in which are trees, arbors, stone ornaments, etc., figures, cattle, a three-horsed vehicle in the foreground. 13 ¼ 20 ins. London.

——. Foots-Cray Place. Line engraving by and after W. Woollett. Extensive view of the house and the country beyond, showing figures, a six-horsed carriage, stags, etc., in the grounds; in the immediate foreground, a group of persons of fashion viewing the scene through a telescope, which rests on a table; two figures fishing in a rail-enclosed pond. 13 × 20¼ ins. London.

1761 BRETTINGHAM, MATTHEW (the Elder). The Plans and Elevations of the late Earl of Leicester's House at Holkham. Engraved and published by Brettingham, Architect. Fol. London.

> This famous mansion was designed by the architect Kent, who had Brettingham for a pupil. In this work Brettingham takes to himself more credit than was his due. Thomas Coke was one of the most enlightened landowners in England. His successful experiments with sheep breeding brought interested farmers to his place from all over the kingdom.

CARDROSS, LORD. A South East View of the Cathedral of Icolmkill, drawn on the spot and etched by Lord Cardross. (Place?)

1763 CHAMBERS, SIR WILLIAM. Plans, Elevations, Sections, and Perspective Views of the Gardens and Buildings at Kew, the Seat of her Royal Highness, the Princess Dowager of Wales. Designed by Wm. Chambers, Architect to his Majesty, and elegantly engraved on 46 large folio Copperplates by Grignion, Major, Rooker, Woollett, etc. Fol. London.

> Though his architectural works, which attempted to stay the decline of Palladianism proper, were numerous, Chambers is more commonly associated with the introduction into England of the "Chinese style" of gardening. Having made a trip to China, he set himself up as an authority on a style that became the rage in France rather than in England. His pagoda in Kew Gardens was deservedly satirized.

1764 For numerous views of towns, etc., see *England Illustrated* this date, under DESCRIPTIONS.

1767 PAINE, JAMES. Plans of Noblemen and Gentlemen's Residences executed in various Counties; also of Stabling, Bridges, Public and Private Temples, and other Garden Buildings. 74 plates. Fol. London.

> 2nd edit., 2 vols., fol., London, 1783, with 175 plates. See below.
> Gough speaks of Paine's being at work on these engravings, and planning to add the name of each proprietor, a description of the several situations, and an account of the time when they were begun and finished.—*Anecdotes of Topography,* 47. Paine built a large number of houses, the most notable of which were Kedleston and Worksop Manor. The former was begun by Brettingham and completed by Robert Adam. Both were constructed on the grandiose scale of a central block in Palladian design, with symmetrical wings. Unlike many of his fellow architects, Paine paid some regard to the conveniences of living.

> 1783 PAINE, JAMES. Plans, Elevations, and Sections of Noblemen and Gentlemen's Houses . . . executed in the Counties of Derby, Durham, Northumberland, Nottingham, and York. 2nd edit. 2 vols. Fol. London.

1768   STENT, —. Engraved Views of Whitehall, Wansted, Oatlands, Hampton-Court, Theobalds, Westminster, Windsor, Greenwich, Eltham, Woodstock, and Basinghouse.

> Cited by Gough, 506, who states that these views are all extremely scarce, and all the more valuable, as many of the edifices themselves no longer exist.

1770   RYLAND, I. Series of 22 Views of English Towns by and after I. Ryland, on copper, each being an expansive bird's-eye view. 5 × 7½ ins.

View of the City of Glasgow. Expansive view looking over the city in line engraving. 6¾ × 11 ins.

1774   HUTCHINS, JOHN. Views of the Principal Towns, Seats, Antiquities, and other Remarkable Particulars in Dorset. Compiled from Mr. Hutchins's History of the County. Folding plans of the town and castle of Corfe. 4to. London.

> See Hutchins's *History and Antiquities of Dorset* this date under HISTORY AND ANTIQUITIES.

1776   SANDBY, PAUL. Twelve Views in North Wales. The series of aquatint views after Paul Sandby, in brown, depicting the scenery of the shires of Denbigh, Merioneth and Carnarvon, with anglers and other figures, coach, cattle, etc.; illustrating the rural life of the time. 9½ × 12¼ ins. London.

1777   SANDBY, PAUL. A Collection of Landscapes. 32 copperplate views by M. A. Rooker and W. Watts, after Paul Sandby. London.

————. A Series of Twelve Aquatint Views after Paul Sandby, in brown, depicting the scenery of various parts of Wales, with figures, cattle, vehicles, etc., illustrating the life and manners of the day. 8¼ × 11½ ins. Oxford.

1778   ————. The Virtuosi's Museum, containing Select Views in England, Scotland, and Ireland, drawn by Paul Sandby, including copperplate views of Shrewsbury Castle, Glendalough, Luton Tower, Cashel, Milton Haven, Conway, Cardiff Castle, Dromana, Caernarvon Church, Inniskillen, Antrim, Chiswick House, etc. Obl. 4to. London.

> A series of works illustrating this subject was issued from 1777 on into the 19th century. The artists employed in the project were among the best of the day, including Paul Sandby, Samuel Ireland, Claude Nates, Charles Heath, Thomas Girtin, F. Wheatley, Thomas Malton, E. Dayes, W. Orme, W. Watts, W. Angus, T. Medland, J. Farington, and J. Turner. This work was completed in 24 numbers, each number containing 3 plates.

————. A View of Worcester, in aquatint, engraved by Paul Sandby, showing the pottery to the left, the river with boats to the right foreground, a carrier's cart and figures, and in the background the cathedral and town. 14¼ × 21 ins. London (?).

1779   KEATE, GEORGE. Sketches from Nature, Taken and Coloured, in a Journey to Margate, published from the original Designs. 2 vols. 8vo. London.

> 2nd edit., 2 vols., 12mo, London, 1779; 3rd, 12mo, London, 1782; 4th, 2 vols., 12mo, London, 1790. See this work under TOURS BY NATIVES.

WATTS, WILLIAM. Seats of the Nobility and Gentry, in a Collection of the most interesting and picturesque Views, from Drawings by the most eminent Artists. 84 views on copperplates after Paul Sandby, C. Nates, T. Hearne, etc., and the engraver. 2 vols. London.

> This work appeared in parts. The descriptions which accompany each view are invariably complimentary to the mansions and their owners. Watts was a pupil of Sandby.

1781 MERCIER, P. L. Six Views of Edinburgh. Edinburgh (?).

1782 SANDBY, PAUL. A Collection of 150 Views in England, Wales, Scotland and Ireland, with Descriptions in English and French. Drawn by Paul Sandby. London.

> Issued again, 2 vols., fol., London, 1783.

1783-87 GROSE, FRANCIS. For numerous views of antiquities, see his *Antiquities of England and Wales,* under HISTORY AND ANTIQUITIES; also the supplementary volumes on Scotland and Ireland, 1797. These contain hundreds of views of ruins, castles, abbeys, churches, etc.

1784 MIDDIMAN, SAMUEL. Select Views in Great Britain, from Pictures and Drawings by the most eminent Artists; with Descriptions in English and French. Fol. London.

> Issued again, obl. 8vo, London, 1784-85.

WALPOOLE, GEORGE AUGUSTUS. For numerous Views of towns, residences, etc., see his *New British Traveller,* under DESCRIPTIONS.

1785-1806 WOOD, J. G. The County of Kent, a Collection of 36 large coloured Aquatint Views of the principal Seats of the Nobility and Gentry of Kent (originally published in parts). 24 × 18 ins. Obl. fol. London.

1786 BOSWELL, HENRY. Historical Descriptions of New and Elegant Picturesque Views of the Antiquities of England and Wales: being a grand Copperplate Repository of Elegance, Taste, and Entertainment. Containing a new and complete Collection of superb Views of all the most Remarkable Ruins, and Antient Buildings, such as Abbeys, Castles, Monasteries, Priories, Cathedrals, Towers, Gates, Arches, Walls, Hospitals, Colleges, Palaces, Monuments, etc., to which is added, Picturesque Views of the principal Seats of the Nobility and Gentry; also a complete Set of County Maps. Together with an authentic Account of Doomsday-Book. Fol. London.

> Another edit., fol., London, 1800.
> An interesting work, most profusely illustrated, but prosy and pedantic in its text, with 50 maps. According to Chubb, those of England, with the exception of Yorkshire, which was done by Kitchin, appeared originally in the *London Magazine,* from 1747-1760. All traces of their connection with the magazine were removed.—*Printed Maps.*

HARRISON, —. Harrison's Picturesque Views of the Principal Seats of the Nobility and Gentry in England and Wales, by the most Eminent British Artists, with a brief Description of each Seat. 100 engraved plates after Corbould, Metz, Malton, Evans, Watts, etc. 8vo. London.

> This work is found also under dates 1787 and 1788.

HEARNE, THOMAS, and W. BYRNE. Antiquities of Great Britain Illustrated in Views of Monasteries, Castles, and Churches now existing; with Descriptions in English and in French. 50 large engravings (the figures by Bartolozzi and others) by Byrne after drawings by Hearne. London.

> Reissued, 2 vols., London, 1807.
> During the extensive tours throughout Great Britain which the work necessitated, Hearne studied Nature with care, investing his topographical drawings with effects of light and atmosphere seldom attempted by previous draughtsmen in water-colors. He may thus be said to have done much to revive attention to Gothic architecture, and to have been one of the founders of the English school of water-colours. His art much influenced Girtin and Turner.—Cosmo Monkhouse, quoted by Bookseller.

WELLS, J. View of Margate, with the Bathing-Place. Aquatint in color by J. Wells, after T. Smith. 10¾ × 18 ins.

1786-93   CARTER, JOHN. Views of Ancient Buildings in England, drawn in different Tours and engraved. 120 etched views on 119 plates, with text. 6 vols. in 2. 32mo. London.

> These brilliant little views of Westminster, Canterbury, and many other well-known and out-of-the-way places are highly valuable records of English medieval architecture. They include many most interesting remains now destroyed.—Bookseller's Note. Carter was an ardent Gothicist, possessed of real knowledge of Gothic architecture. He combatted vigorously the ignorant restorations going on in the last decade of the 18th century.

1787   ANGUS, W. Seats of the Nobility and Gentry in Great Britain and Wales, in a Collection of Select Views engraved by W. Angus, from Pictures and Drawings by the most Eminent Artists, with Descriptions of each View. 63 plates. Obl. 4to. London.

> Reissued at various dates.

1788   CARDONELL, ADAM DE. Picturesque Antiquities of Scotland. Pts. I and II. 50 vignette etchings of ruins, etc. Descriptive text beneath each view. 4to. London.

> Two more parts published in 1793.
> Reviewed *Gent. Mag.*, vol. 58, 48-50, which states that the introduction gives an accurate list of religious houses in Scotland. The etchings of these views show much improvement over those of Slezer, and are preferable to Cordiner's and Pennant's, whose buildings sometimes looked as though they had just been erected.

Picturesque Views of the Principal Seats of the Nobility and Gentry in England and Wales, by the most Eminent British Artists, with a Description of each Seat. 100 copperplate views by Walker, Middiman, Fittler, Heath, and others after Malton, Dayes, Corbould, Metz, and others. London.

1788-95   CORDINER, REV. CHARLES, and P. MAZWELL. Remarkable Ruins and Romantic Prospects of North Britain, with Ancient Monuments, and Singular Subjects of Natural History. 97 plates. 2 vols. in 1. 4to. London.

1789   FARINGTON, JOSEPH. Views of the Lakes of Cumberland and Westmoreland. 20 large copperplate engravings of scenes in Keswick, Borrowdale, Skiddaw, Grasmere, Rydal Mere, Ulswater, Ambleside, and a topographical survey of the environs of Keswick. Descriptions in English and French. Obl. 8vo. London.

> Another issue of the same date gives the size of atlas folio.
> Farington, who was elected R.A. in 1785, exhibited almost yearly from 1765 to 1813. He is regarded as an inferior painter. See his *Diary* under LETTERS, DIARIES, MEMOIRS.

GRANT, A. Picturesque Scenery of Scotland, drawn by A. Grant and etched by J. Wells; with Descriptions. 8 views. Fol. London.

THROSBY, JOHN. Select Views of Leicestershire, from Original Drawings, containing Seats of Nobility and Gentry, Town Views, and Ruins, with Descriptive and Historical Relations. 4to. London.

> A supplementary volume containing a Series of Excursions was published in 1790. For his *History and Antiquities of the Ancient Town of Leicester,* see under 1777, HISTORY AND ANTIQUITIES. The above work was reviewed in *Gent. Mag.,* vol. 59, 927, where it was stated that it was to appear in numbers, one a month. The drawings and engravings by Walker were praised as having been beautifully done. In a review of 1791, there was a mention of sixteen numbers.

1790-93 BARROW, J. C. Picturesque Views of Churches in the Neighbourhood of London; with Descriptions. 16 plates. Fol. London.

BOYDELL, JOHN. A Collection of Views in England and Wales, drawn and engraved by J. Boydell. Fol. London.

> A 2nd set of 36 plates appeared in 1794.
> Boydell was better known as a publisher of prints than as an original artist. Throughout his life he allowed his activities as a publisher to be affected by his love of scenery. He was the first artist to paint in Wales.—Reynolds, *The Treatment of Nature in English Poetry,* ch. IV.

The Copper-Plate Magazine: or, Monthly Cabinet of Picturesque Prints, consisting of Sublime and Interesting Views in Great Britain and Ireland, engraved by the most Eminent Artists from Paintings and Drawings of the first Masters, including J. Walker, T. Medland, after W. Watts, W. Orme, P. Sandby, Corbould, and others. Vols. I-IV, obl. 4to. In 2 vols. London.

> This appeared in series, with various dates and number of vols.: 1792-94; 1792-1802. The complete series contained 250 prints.

FARINGTON, JOSEPH. Views of Cities and Towns in England and Wales, drawn by J. Farington; with Letter-press Descriptions in English and French. Fol. London.

NIXON, F. R. A Series of Views in Scotland, drawn by F. R. Nixon. 10 plates. Obl. 4to. London. (Date conjectural.)

1791 BIRCH, WILLIAM. Délices de la Grande Bretagne et d'Irlande. Engraved by W. Birch. 36 colored views with descriptions. London.

> Two of the views are after Rowlandson, and one is after Gainsborough. Rare with the plates colored.—Bookseller's Note.

BOYDELL, J. and J. (Publishers). Thirty-six Views in Scotland, chiefly from Drawings by J. C., Esq. (i. e., John Clark, of Eldin; but see Caley below), with Descriptions. London.

> 2nd set of 36 views, 1794.

CALEY, JOHN. Views in Scotland. 36 copperplates. Obl. 4to. London. (Boydell publisher.)

> This may be the same set as that listed immediately above.

LYSONS, SAMUEL. 74 Etchings of Views and Antiquities in the County of Gloucester, hitherto imperfectly, or never engraved. With Descriptive Letter-press. Fol. London. (Some of later date.)

> This work was planned to appear about every three months. The editor was supposed to be the Rev. Samuel Lysons.

MOORE, JAMES. Monastic Remains and Ancient Castles in England and Wales; drawn on the Spot by James Moore; finished and etched by J. Schnebbelie, Draughtsman to the Society of Antiquaries of London; aqua-tinted by J. G. Perkyns. London.

> Reviewed *Gent. Mag.*, vol. 61, 743. It is praised as being superior to others of this kind. Schnebbelie continued his work as draughtsman in the *Antiquaries Museum* (see below).

SCHNEBBELIE, JACOB. The Antiquaries Museum. No. II noticed in the *Gent. Mag.*, vol. 61, 743.

> Nos. III-IV appeared in 1792. The artist Schnebbelie having died, the work was taken over by John Nichols.

1791-95   SMITH, JOHN, and — MERIGOT. Views of the Lakes. 14 large engravings of Windermere, Paterdale, Borrodale, Ulls-water, Grasmere, etc. Plates 22 × 16 ins. Obl. atlas fol. London.

1792   FARINGTON, JOSEPH. Aquatint View of the Forth, including Queensferry, Hopetoun House, Blackness Castle, Garvie Island and distant View of the Grampian Mountains, after J. Farington, by Edy & Jukes. 18 × 25 ins. n.p.

HOLLAND, P. Select Views of the Lakes in Cumberland, Westmoreland, and Lancashire. From Drawings by P. Holland. 21 plates followed by a short description of each of them, printed on the opposite page. Liverpool.

IRELAND, SAMUEL. Picturesque Views on the River Thames, from its Source to the Nore, with Observations on the Public Buildings and other Works of Art in its Vicinity. 53 aquatints in brown, woodcuts, and maps. 2 vols. in 1. 8vo. London.

> Printed again in 1799.

WITTON, P. H. Views (eight in aquatint), after P. H. Witton, Jun., by W. Ellis, of the Ruins of the Principal Houses destroyed during the Riots of Birmingham, 1791, with Letter-press Descriptions in English and French. Obl. 4to. London.

1792-98   WALMSLEY, T., F. JUKES (and others). A volume containing 18 plates of views of the Lake District, comprising 4 plain aquatints after Walmsley and Jukes, and 14 copperplate engravings after J. Smith and Merigot. In 1 vol. Atlas fol. London (?).

1792-1806   HOARE, SIR RICHARD COLT. A Collection of Forty-Eight Views of Noblemen's and Gentlemen's Seats, Towns, Castles, Churches, Monasteries and Romantic Places in North and South Wales, principally from drawings by Sir Richard Colt Hoare, and engraved by the Most Eminent Artists. Descriptive text. Obl. fol. London.

1793 ASHMORE, —. Ashmore's Picturesque Scenery of the Highlands of Scotland, being 24 interesting early views from original Drawings by Mr. Ashmore, of Perth, engraved in aquatint by Jukes; views:—Dochart Castle, Inverary, Ardgarton, Seat of Clan Macfarlane, Moncrieff House. Obl. 4to. Perth.

IRELAND, SAMUEL. Picturesque Views on the River Medway, from the Nore to the Vicinity of its Source in Sussex; with Observations on the Public Buildings and other Works of Art in its Neighbourhood. 29 aquatint engravings. Fol. London.

POLWHELE, RICHARD. Historical Views of Devonshire. Vol. I (all published), the British Period. 4to. Exeter.

For his *History of Devonshire* see Polwhele, under 1794, HISTORY AND ANTIQUITIES.

1794 GILPIN, REV. WILLIAM. Forest Scenery and Woodland Views in the New Forest, Hampshire, England. Illustrated with oval engraved plates in aquatint. 3 vols. 8vo. London.

Gilpin became known as the chief authority on what constituted picturesque scenery. Under TOURS BY NATIVES will be found a number of his publications dealing with the subject.

MOORE, JAMES. Selection of Views in Scotland; 25 Views in the Southern Part of Scotland, from a Collection of Drawings by James Moore, F.A.S., in the Year 1792, engraved by and under the Direction of John Landseer. Edinburgh (?).

Reviewed *Gent. Mag.*, vol. 65, 410-11, which states that this publication is being conducted in a manner similar to that of the *Monastic Remains* (see under 1791 above). The reviewer queries whether the last-named work is to be superseded by this or was it temporarily laid aside? No more of it has appeared than Nos. XI and XII of the 2nd volume. But the monastic remains and castles of Scotland were intended to follow those of England and Wales and to form a 3rd and 4th volume.

RATHBONE, J. Rathbone's Views of the Lakes of Cumberland, etc., a series of 12 aquatint plates by Hassell, after paintings by J. Rathbone. Obl. 4to. London (?).

ROBERTSON, SCOTT (and others). Views in Scotland; a second set comprising 36 copperplates by Robertson, Scott, etc., with descriptions. Obl. 8vo. London (?).

TURNER, JOHN. This celebrated painter spent the summer of 1794 making a tour of the Midland Counties of England. His sketches of this journey, as well as those of the following years, were published in the *Copper Plate Magazine* and in the *Pocket Magazine*.

WALKER, G. Select Views of Picturesque Scenery in Scotland; including the Seats of the Nobility and Gentry; engraved in aquatint, from Original Drawings; accompanied with Topographical and Historical Descriptions. No. 1 (all published). Fol. London.

This work was also issued with text and title in French.

WYNDHAM, HENRY PENRUDDOCKE. A Picture of the Isle of Wight, delineated upon the Spot in the Year 1793. London.

Noticed briefly in *Gent. Mag.*, vol. 64, 1026. Wyndham had already proved his ability by his engravings for his Tour through Monmouth, 1781 (see Wyndham this date, under TOURS BY NATIVES). Here he marks out a three days' route for the curious observer to follow.

1794-96   COMBE, DR. WILLIAM. Views and Scenery on the River Thames and Parts adjacent from its Source, and continued to the Sea. With a Map in two sections, dedication, and 76 colored plates after J. Farington, by J. C. Stadler, of the various picturesque scenes and notable residences along the banks, etc. 2 vols. Fol. London.

This work is frequently called Boydell's Thames. The first volume had two titles, the general title reading as stated above, and the subtitle reading The History of the River Thames.—Bookseller's Note.

1795   IRELAND, SAMUEL. Picturesque Views of the Upper, or Warwickshire Avon, from its Source at Naseby to its Junction with the Severn at Tewkesbury; with Observations on the Public Buildings, and other Works of Art in its Vicinity. 31 full-page engravings in sepia, by the Author. 4to. London.

RIDDELL, R. A. A Collection of 12 Views in Scotland. London.

1796   BICKHAM, GEORGE (Junior). A Curious Collection of Bird's-Eye Views of the several Counties in England and Wales; exhibiting a pleasing Landscape of each County; with a Variety of Rustic Figures, Ruins, etc. 46 engraved plates. 4to. London.

BONNOR, THOMAS. Perspective Itinerary, or Pocket-Portfolio. 8vo. London.

This is No. 1 of the series, which contains "The Beauties of Gloucester Cathedral." More illustrations appeared in 1799. Bonnor engraved plates for a number of county histories.

GREEN, WILLIAM. A Description of a Series of Picturesque Views in the North of England. Drawn from Nature and engraved by William Green. Manchester.

ROGERS, B. Views in Westmoreland and Cumberland, engraved by A. Alken, from Designs by B. Rogers. 6 plates. Obl. 4to. Stafford.

WALLACE, GEORGE. Prospects from the Hills in Fife. 8vo. Edinburgh.

WILSON, A. Twelve Views of Edinburgh and its Vicinity. Engraved by R. Scott from Drawings by A. Wilson. With letter-press descriptions. Obl. 4to. Edinburgh.

1797   HOWLETT, BARTHOLOMEW. A Selection of Views in the County of Lincoln, comprising the Principal Towns and Churches, etc., with Topographical and Historical Accounts. 4to. London (?).

IRELAND, SAMUEL. Picturesque Views on the River Wye, from its Source at Plinlimmon Hill, to its Junction with the Severn below Chepstow. With Observations on the Public Buildings and other Works of Art in its Vicinity. 31 aquatints in brown. 8vo. London.

Noel, Amelia. Views in Kent; a series of 17 coloured aquatint views of various places of beauty and interest in the County of Kent, drawn and etched by Amelia Noel. London (?).

Miss Noel was drawing mistress to the Royal Family.—Bookseller's Note.

Views of the Principal Towns, Castles, Abbeys, etc., in Scotland. London.

1798 Broughton, B. Four Picturesque Views in North Wales; engraved by Alken in aquatint from Drawings made on the Spot by B. Broughton. London.

MacPherson, A. E. Edina Delineata, or Picturesque Perspective Views in or near Edinburgh. 13 plates. 4to. Edinburgh.

Rowlandson, Thomas. Comforts of Bath. 12 plates, 8¾ × 6¼ ins. London (?).

1799 Walker, J. The Itinerant; a Select Collection of interesting and picturesque Views in Great Britain and Ireland; engraved by J. Walker after Paintings and Drawings by Eminent Artists. 180 plates. London.

1800 A Sketch of the most Remarkable Scenery near Callander of Monteith, particularly the Trossachs. 12mo. Stirling.

Scott, R. Scenery in Scotland; a Series of 66 Engravings by R. Scott. Edinburgh.

Wood, J. G. Views in Kent, a Collection of 36 large coloured Views of Gentlemen's Seats in the County of Kent, drawn by J. G. Wood and engraved by W. Green. Fol. London.

1825 Clerk, John. Etchings, chiefly of Views in Scotland. By John Clerk, Esq. of Edinburgh. 1773-79. 28 plates. In *Publ. Bann. Club.*, no. 8. Fol. Edinburgh.

See also no. 98, 1855, for reproductions of these views, with additional etchings and facsimiles from his drawings. 58 plates. Edit. by David Laing. Fol. Edinburgh.

1864 Henderson, Dr. E. Dunfermline in the Olden Time; from a Pen-and-Ink Sketch of 1748. Fol. Edinburgh.

1880 Sime, Rev. J. Edinburgh in the Olden Times; a Series of 63 Drawings of Streets, old Houses, etc., in the City of Edinburgh, its Suburbs, and Leith, 1717-1828. Collected by Rev. John Sime, Chaplain to the Trinity College Hospital, and bequeathed by his widow in 1869 to the Governors of James Gillespie's Hospital. Reproduced in facsimile, with descriptive letter-press by T. G. Stevenson. Fol. Edinburgh.

1908 English Houses and Gardens in the 17th and 18th Centuries: a series of Bird's Eye Views reproduced from contemporary Engravings by Kip, Badeslade, Harris, and others, with descriptive Notes by Mervyn Macartney. 61 plates. Obl. 8vo. London.

1919 The Early Views and Maps of Edinburgh, 1544-1852. 11 maps and 21 illustrations. 8vo. Edinburgh (?).

V

Towns, Castles, Seats

(The dominating motive in the account of towns seems to be that of recording their history and describing their antiquities. Publications bearing evidence of this interest appear in increasing number down to the end of the 18th century, and are to be regarded as part of the passion for such studies that characterize the discussions of Britain as a whole. Occasionally one senses a feeling of affection as an addition to the desire to impart information, e.g., in Gostling's *Walk through Canterbury*, where the historian is so deeply in love with his subject that he wishes others to share his pleasure. Again the promptings of local pride manifest themselves, as in the case of Bristol, which took comfort in its independence of London., to which for a long time it was next in size and importance. The accidents of time brought forward both old and new towns, like Bath and Tunbridge Wells, which competed for popularity as amusement and healing resorts. Some accounts are of the nature of defenses against attacks, as, for instance, Halifax whose famous Gibbet-Law had brought it notoriety. The histories of Edinburgh may have served to justify its claim as the "Athens of the North" by calling attention to its respectable antiquity. Gentlemen's seats and gardens with their art collections as show places needed guides. But through it all it is difficult to trace anything like an evolution in purpose or method. Titles and treatment run monotonously in the same mould from the beginning to the end.

Maps and plans of towns and the more restricted areas are included in this section. But where towns are combined with counties in titles like "The History and Antiquities of," the items are placed under HISTORY AND ANTIQUITIES. The descriptions of towns which are the subject of guides are to be found under AIDS TO TRAVELERS.)

1521 BRADSHAW, HENRY. De Antiquitate et Magnificentia Urbis Cestriae. 4to. London.

> The author, a Benedictine monk of Chester, also wrote a Chronicon and a Life of the Glorious Virgin St. Werbergh in verse. Gough states that he was called by William Webb, antiquary and architect, their best antiquary and has quoted him largely.—*Anecdotes of British Topography*, 121.

1550 ALESIUS, ALEXANDER. Edinburgi Regiae Scotorum Urbis Descriptio, per Alexandrum Alesium Scotum, S.T.D. Basel.

> The original Latin text reprinted in *Bann. Misc.*, vol. I of no. 19, Edinburgh, 1827; in translation in Hume Brown, *Scotland before 1700*.
> This description of Edinburgh was written for Sebastian Munster's *Cosmographia*, published at Basel in 1550. By the beginning of the 16th century, Edinburgh had become the acknowledged center of national life in Scotland. From the description and the map accompanying it, it is evident that the city was small and compact. The account states that the houses were built of stone, not of brick; the churches, palaces, hospitals, etc., are named and located, and the Castle Rock described. The author remembers having nearly lost his life on the Rock when a child. He repeats names that are of the very essence of Edinburgh: Canongate, Cowgate, Holyrood, St. Giles, etc. Alesius or Alane was a Scottish theologian and reformer, who having adopted Lutheranism was forced to leave the country. He betook himself to Germany, where he finally settled down as a professor of theology at Leipzig. His description of Edinburgh is the first in prose that is known, and must apply to the period not later than 1529, the year in which he left Scotland never to return.—From Brown, *op. cit.* See Alex. F. Mitchell, *The Scottish Reformation*, Ch. XI.

1559 CUNNINGHAM, WILLIAM, M.D. For "an accurate Map of the excellent City of Norwich, as the Form of it is 1558," see his *Cosmographical Glasse*, etc., under GEOGRAPHY, vol. II of this work. This map contains many alphabetical references to an explanation of the places at the bottom.—Gough, 40.

1561 BELL, H. The Ground Plat of King's Lyn. (So cited by Taylor, *Tudor and Stuart Geography*.)

1575 LANEHAM, ROBERT. A Letter Vntoo My Good Freend, Master Humfrey Martin, Mercer, whearin, part of the Entertainment untoo the Queenz Majesty, at Killingworth Castl, in Warwik Sheer, in this soomerz progress, 1575, is signified: from a Freend Officer Attendant in the Coourt. 8vo. London.

> Reprinted by the Ballad Society in *Ballads from Manuscripts*, vol. II, Hertford, 1874; edit. by Furnivall, London, 1907. See below.
> This gives an account of Kenilworth Castle and the reception of Queen Elizabeth there. The entertainment lasted from July 9 to July 27. Captain Cox, of the famous "Collection of Ballads," took a prominent part in the performance.

> 1907 Robert Laneham's Letter; Describing a Part of the Entertainment Unto Queen Elizabeth at the Castle of Kenilworth in 1575; edit. with Introduction by F. J. Furnivall. 8vo. London.

NEVILLE, ALEXANDER. For a description of Norwich, see his *De Furoribus Norfolciensium Ketto duce*, under HISTORY AND ANTIQUITIES.

VOWELL, JOHN (pseud. for Hooker). The description of the Citie of Excester. London.

> The date of the 1st edition is in doubt; reprinted by Andrew Brice, Exeter, 1765 (said to be a careless piece of work); an edition of 1775 is cited in *Camb. Bibliog.*, vol. I; parts 2 and 3 edit. by W. J. Harte, J. W. Schopp, H. Tapley-Soper, 2 vols., *Publ. Devon and Cornwall Record Soc.*, 1919.
> This work is a series of extracts from the mass of unpublished records of the city collected by this 16th century chamberlain of Exeter.—Read, *Bibliog. Brit. Hist.*, *Tudor Period*. Hooker was one of the chief editors of the 2nd edition of Holinshed's *Chronicles*.

1578 GARTER, BERNARD. The Ioyfull Receyuing of the Queenes most excellent Maiestie into hir Highnesse Citie of Norvvich: The things done in the time of hir abode there: and the dolor of the Citie at her departure. Wherein are set downe diuers Orations . . . pronounced . . . by Sir Robert Wood . . . now Maior of the same Citie, and others. . . . 4to. London.

> Apparently the 1st edition and extremely rare. It was probably printed in 1578, as it was licensed on 30 Aug. in that year. There was another edition, possibly of the same year, which may be distinguished by the spelling of the name Henry in the imprint as "Henrie." One of the chief interests of this book is the Masque and other poetry which it contains. The Masque, which is usually attributed to Garter, was written in great part, if not, as is most probable, entirely, by Goldingham, who signs it "Finis, Goldingham." . . . Queen Elizabeth's visit to Norwich was part of her Progress through Norfolk and Suffolk, and she entered the Famous City on Saturday, 16 Aug., 1578; her stay continued until "The Frowning Friday folowed, which called hir Maiestie thence. . . ."—From Quaritch, no. 623.

1591 The honourable Entertainment given to the Queen's Majestie in Progress at Elvetham in Hampshire by the Earl of Hertford in 1591. London.

> This has the family arms prefixed, a map, and a description of the great pond at Elvetham and the properties it contained, in colors. The only copy Wanley ever saw was in the public library at Cambridge.—Gough, 139. (See this date under TOURS BY NATIVES.)

1599 NASH, THOMAS. Nashes Lenten Stuffe, Containing, The Description and first Procreation and Increase of the towne of Great Yarmouth in Norffolke: With a new Play neuer played before, of the praise of the Red-Herring. Fitte of all clerkes of Nobelmens kitchins to be read and not unnecessary by all seruing men that have short Boord-wages, to be remembered. 4to. London.

> Reprinted in *Harl. Misc.*, vol. VI, London, 1744; in *The Old Book Collector's Miscellany*, pt. I, 1871; in vol. III of *Works of Thomas Nashe*, edit. by Ronald B. McKerron, 4 vols., London, 1910.

After his banishment from London on account of his play "The Isle of Dogs," Nash betook himself to Yarmouth, where he was hospitably treated, and in return wrote this eulogy of the town, giving lavish praise of its chief commodity.

1613 DRAYTON, MICHAEL. For a work that is very rich in antiquarian particulars of almost every town and village in England, see his *Polyolbion,* under DESCRIPTIONS.

1615 THORNES, EDWARD. Encomium Salopiae, Or the Description of the Pleasant Situation of the ancient and famous Towne of Shrowesbury (in verse). (For *Encomia,* see Johnston under 1642 below.)

1616 MATHEWS, OLIVER. The Scituation, Foundation and Ancient Names of the Famous Towne of Sallop. 8vo. London (?).

Cited by Daniell, *Manual of Brit. Topography,* who says it was reprinted, but where or when is not stated.

1631 BEDWELL, WILHELM. A Brief Description of the Towne of Tottenham High-Cross, in Middlesex; together with an historical Account of such memorable Things as are to be seene and observed there, collected, digested, and written by Wilhelm Bedwell, at this present Pastour of the Parish. To which is added, The Turnament of Tottenham, or, The Wooing, Winning and Wedding of Tibbe, the Reeu's Daughter there. Written long since in verse by Gilbert Pilkington, Taken out of an Ancient Manuscript and published by W. Bedwell. 4to. London.

Reprinted, 8vo, London, 1718, with Survey and Antiquity of Stamford in Lincoln added. The Tournament is inserted in *Reliques* of Percy, who thinks it is a satire on tournaments. Hearne believes it belongs to the time of Henry V or VI or Edward IV. Gough says it is a humorous relation of a country wedding, and the rustic sports connected with it. Its style and versification, Gough believes, fix it in the age of Skelton, whose "Tunning of Eleanor Rumminge" it much resembles.

1638 ADAMSON, HENRY. For a description of Perth, see his *The Muses Threnodie,* under HISTORY AND ANTIQUITIES.

1640 SOMNER, WILLIAM. The Antiquities of Canterbury, or, a Survey of that Antient Citie, with the Suburbs, and Cathedrall; containing principally Matters of Antiquity in them all; Collected chiefly from old Manuscripts, Leiger-Bookes, and other like Records, for the most part never as yet printed. With an Appendix here annexed, wherein (for better satisfaction to the learned) the Manuscripts and Records are faithfully exhibited, all for the Honour of that Antient Metropolis. Map and 2 plates. 4to. London.

A new title page was printed 1662 but not a new edit.; republished, with additions, fol., London, 1703. See below.
Somner was one of the early Anglo-Saxon scholars, or "Saxonists," as they were called. His *Dictionarium Saxonico-Latino-Anglicum* was published in 1659. He was educated at the free school in Canterbury, became clerk to his father, the registrar, and eventually auditor of Christ Church, Canterbury. His printed books and MSS are preserved in the cathedral archives.—The very large additions said by Bishop Kennett to be left by Somner in his copy of Antiquities of Canterbury in the church library, are little more than corrections of the press and some transpositions, and are all inserted in Batteley's edition (1703), in which the views and plans are by Hollar and Kip; the few monuments are wretchedly executed. . . . The Saxon Annals are a transcription of a Cottonian MS intitled, Chronica Saxonica Abingdoniae ad an. 1066.—Gough, 713.

1703 SOMNER, WILLIAM. The Antiquities of Canterbury, in Two Parts: The First Part, The Antiquities of Canterbury, or, A Survey of that Ancient City . . . revised and enlarged by Nicholas Batteley, M.A., second Edition; Also Mr. Somner's Discourse, called Chartham News, or a Relation of some strange Bones found at Chartham in Kent. To which is added, Some Observations concerning the Roman Antiquities of Canterbury, etc. The Second Part, Cantuaria Sacra, or the Antiquities. I. Of the Cathedrall and metropolitical Church. II. Of the Archbishoprick. III. Of the late Priory of Christ Church; and of the present Collegiate Church founded by King Henry VIII. IV. Of the Archdeaconry of Canterbury. V. Of the Monastery of St. Augustine; enquired into by Nicholas Batteley, Vicar of Beaksborn. Illustrated and adorned with severall useful and fair sculptures. Fol. London.

Many of Somner's collections relating to this city and other towns and churches in Kent were published in Thorn's *Chronicle of the Abbey from the Coming of Austin down to 1375*, from Twysden's *Decem Scriptores* (see under 1652, HISTORY AND CHRONICLE); his extracts out of this Chronicle, the obituary, and other registers of this and Rochester Church, and the Saxon annals, in Wharton's *Anglia Sacra* (see under 1691, HISTORY AND CHRONICLE).—Gough, 214-15.

1642 JOHNSTON, ARTHUR. Encomia Urbium. Middleburg.

These first appeared in the Middleburg edition of Johnston's Poems. Reprinted by Skene in his *Succinct Survey of the famous City of Aberdeen* 1685; reprinted by Sir Wm. Geddes, in his *Musa Latina Aberdoniensis, Publ. New Spaulding Club*, vol. 11, 255-87, 1893.

This work consists of poems in praise of Scotch towns. It is all but certain that Johnston visited many, if not all, of the towns singled out in order to make his descriptions correct. Among the towns besung are Edinburgh, Leith, Linlithgow, Stirling, Perth, Glasgow, Dumfries, Ayr, Haddington, coast towns in Fifeshire, Dundee, Forfar, Brechin, Montrose, New Aberdeen, Old Aberdeen, Banff, Inverness, etc.—From Mitchell, *List of Travels*. Johnston was a writer of Latin verse who obtained his degree of M.D. at Padua in 1610. When he returned to Scotland after twenty-four years' absence, he won the favor of Archbishop Laud, who preferred him to George Buchanan. He became rector of King's College, Aberdeen, in 1637. These Encomia Urbium were a form of literary exercise inherited from the Middle Ages, which in turn derived them from the rhetorical schools of ancient days. A famous example of this type is Alcuin's long Latin poem written *ca.* 780-82 in praise of the city and church of York. An example in Old English is the description of Durham and the relics preserved there, written in the early years of the 12th century (for text and annotations, see *The Anglo-Saxon Minor Poems*, edit. by Elliott Van Kirk Dobbie, 1942). See also Margaret Schlauch, "An Old English Encomium Urbis," *Journal of English and Germanic Philology*, vol. 40, 14-28, 1941.

1643 MAY, THOMAS. A True Relation from Hull of the Present State and Condition it is in: as was written in a Letter from [Thomas May]. 4to. London.

1645 HOWELL, JAMES. For a description of Edinburgh in 1639, see his *Epistolae Ho-Elianae*, under WEST EUROPE, vol. I of this work.

The letter describing Edinburgh in Hume Brown, *Early Travellers*, 159-61.

It is regrettable that there were no more letters on Scotland from so experienced a traveler as Howell. He arrived in the Scotch capital in time to see the National Assembly and a Parliament in session. He remarked on the stiff resistance the Scotch put up against having Episcopacy forced on them. In 1638 the Covenant had been renewed amid the enthusiasm of all classes. In consequence the word bishop was fallen into disrepute beyond repair. Wine he noticed was cheaper in Scotland as well as unadulterated, as the law exacted a heavy penalty for such a practice, in contrast with England, where it was permitted. He considered High Street to be one of the fairest streets he had ever seen. —From Brown, *op. cit.*

1646 BUTCHER, RICHARD. The Survey and Antiquitie of the Towne of Stamford, in the County of Lincoln, with its Ancient Foundation, Grants, Priviledges, and severall Donations thereunto belonging; also a List of Aldermens Names, and the Time when they were chosen. With the Names of Ten Lord Mayors (of the Hon. City of London), borne in the aforesaid County of Lincolne, Written by Richard

Butcher Gent. sometime Towne Clerke of the same Towne. Colored coats of arms of Stamford, with the story of this Scutcheon. 4to. London.

> Reprinted, with revisions and additions, by Butcher, 8vo, London, 1717; again, with Notes by Francis Peck, at the end of his *Academia Tertia Anglicana* (see Peck under 1727 below), fol., London, 1727. See below.
> It was planned to republish this work with additions by Mr. Foster, rector of St. Clements Danes, who had begun to revise it in 1706 but was unable to complete his design. All that was found among his papers was a letter to Dr. Tanner, proving that there was neither a British nor a Roman town at that place. The new edition finally came out in 1717. After Butcher's death, about 1635, his son promised to see to its republication, which promise Francis Peck fulfilled by attaching it to his *Academia* (1727). For Howgrave's part in the history of publishing the annals of Stamford, see Howgrave under 1726 below. See also Gough, 246-48.

> 1727   BUTCHER, RICHARD. The Survey and Antiquitie of the Towne of Stamford, with its Antient Foundation, etc., and Two Letters about the Original and Antiquities of the Town of Stamford, by Rev. W. Forster. Large folding plate by Vander Gucht and numerous other plates. Fol. London.
> The name given by Gough is Foster.

1649   GREY, WILLIAM. Chorographia: or, a Survey of Newcastle-upon-Tine, the Estate of this County under the Romans, the Building of the famous Wall of the Picts by the Romans, the Ancient Town of Pandon. A Briefe Description of the Town, Walls, Wards, Churches, religious Houses, Streets, Markets, Fairs, Rivers, and Commodities; with the Suburbs. The ancient and present Government of the Town: as also a Relation of the County of Northumberland; which was the Bulwark of England against the Scots: their many Castles and Towers; their ancient Families and Names. Of the Tenure in Cornage; of Cheviot Hills, of Tinedale, and Reedsdale, with their Inhabitants. 4to. Newcastle.

> Reprinted in *Harl. Misc.,* vol. III, 1744; again at Newcastle, 1813.

SPELMAN, SIR HENRY. Villare Anglicanum, or, a View of the Townes of England. Collected by Appointment of Sir Henry Spelman, Kt. 4to. London.

> Reprinted, with alterations in title and additions, 8vo, London, 1678. It is also inserted in Gibson's edition of Spelman's Works, 1698 and 1727, under its original title. See below.
> Nicolson says it was ascribed to Spelman and Dodsworth jointly; but he thinks it was chiefly drawn out of Speed's Tables on the backs of his maps.—Gough, 30.

> 1678   SPELMAN, SIR HENRY. Villare Anglicanum, or, a View of all the Cities, Towns, and Villages, in England. Alphabetically composed, so that, naming any Town or Place you may readily find in what Shire, Hundred, Rape, Wapentake, etc., it is in. Collected, etc. To which is added, the Bishopricks, and Counties under their several Jurisdictions; Number of Parishes in each Diocese and County; with the several Places that send Members to Parliament, and the Number each sends. 2nd edition, corrected and amended. 8vo. London.

1656   WEBB, WILLIAM. Description of the City of Chester, and of the County Palatine. (Place?) (So cited by Taylor, *Late Tudor and Early Stuart Geography.*)

1661   GORDON, REV. JAMES (of Rothiemay). Abredoniae Novae et veteris Descriptio: A Description bird's-eye plan, of New and Old Aberdeen, with the Places nearest adjacent. (Place?)

> Reproduced by the Spalding Club, Edinburgh, 1842; reprinted, *ca.* 1880. See below.

> 1842   GORDON, REV. JAMES. Abredoniae utriusque Descriptio: A Description of both Touns of Aberdeen. By James Gordon, Parson of Rothiemay; with a Selection of the Charters of the Burgh. 4 plates and a map. *Publ. Spalding Club,* vol. 5. Edit. by Cosmo Innes. 4to. Edinburgh.

1880 GORDON, JAMES (of Rothiemay). Description of New and Old Aberdeen. Inset view
of Aberdeen and King's College, 1661. 23 × 29 ins. Reprint. (Place?)

SOMNER, WILLIAM. The most Accurate History of the Ancient City and Famous
Cathedral of Canterbury . . . together with the Lives of all the Arch-Bishops of
that See. Map and 3 plates. 4to. London.

See Somner under 1640 above.

1664 HILDYARD, CHRISTOPHER. A List, or Catalogue of all the Mayors, and Bayliffs,
Lord-Mayors, and Sheriffs, of the most Ancient, Honourable, Noble, and Loyall
City of Yorke, from the Time of Edward the First, untill this Present Year,
1664; being the 16th Year of the most happy Reign of our most gracious Sov-
ereign King Charles the Second. Together with many, and sundry remarkable
Passages, which happen'd in their severall Years. Published by a True Lover of
Antiquity, and a Well-wisher to the Prosperity of the City; together with his
hearty Desire of the Restoration of its Glory, Splendour, and Magnificence. 4to.
York.

His preface contains more of the antiquities of York than his whole book. The work
was copied by James Torr, who made some additions of his own from Camden and others.
A copy of this or the original transcript fell into the hands of the bookseller, Francis
Hildyard, who dressed it up for the press with a pompous title page, and injudiciously
put his name to it, without informing the public that it was a copy of his illustrious name-
sake's printed book, with a few additions by Mr. Torr. This procedure brought some re-
criminations between the son of Hildyard and the bookseller. By this mistake "a lean catalogue" (as Bp. Nicolson justly calls it) of our mayors and sheriffs, published long ago
by another hand, is crept into the world, with the name of James Torr, under the title of
The Antiquities of York City, etc.—Gough, 547-48. See Torr and Hildyard under 1719 below.

1671 MILLERD, J. An Exact Delineation of the Famous Cittie of Bristol and Suburbs
thereof composed by a Scale and Ichnographically described. Colored plan showing the Armes of ye See and Armes of the Cittie. 8¾ × 7½ ins. London (?).

Another edit., London, 1673; again, 1710. See below.
This plan marks with great clearness the ancient walls and gates shortly after the
destruction of the castle, as also the High Cross, the Temple and St. Peter's Crosses, the
"Red Lodge," etc. No map of Bristol in the 17th century is so valuable as this. It is "the
second authentic plan of Bristol." The twenty marginal views depicted by Millerd portray
architectural subjects of the century not recorded elsewhere.—Thorp, no. 523. Bristol was
a compactly built city whose primary concern was commerce and trade. Under the favor-
ing patronage of the crown during the medieval period it had expanded into the chief
port for the south of Ireland, Gascony, and Brittany. Later it became the focus of trade
with the West Indies. But by 1776 its commercial supremacy was seriously threatened by
the new port of Liverpool, which unlike Bristol founded much of its wealth on the slave
trade.

1673 MILLERD, J. An Exact Delineation of the Famous Citty of Bristoll and Suburbs
thereof; together with all the High Wayes, Thorough-fares, Streets, Lanes, etc.
33 × 30 ins. London.

1672 DAVIES, JOHN (of Kidwelly). Antiquities of Durham. London.

1675 P., E. The State of Northampton from the Beginning of the Fire, September 20,
1675, to November 5, represented in a Letter to a Friend in London. 4to. London.

1676 GUIDOTT, THOMAS, M. D. For an account of Bath see his *Discourse of Bathe,* under
SPAS.

SPEED, JOHN. Map of the Bishopric and City of Durham. Outline colored. 15 × 20 ins. London.

> Later issue, 15 × 20 ins., London, *ca.* 1710.

1677 IZACKE, RICHARD. Remarkable Antiquities of the City of Exeter. Collected by Richard Izacke, Esquire, Chamberlain thereof. Map of the city and woodcuts of arms. 8vo. London.

> Other edits., with title enlarged and additions, 8vo, London, 1681; 1724, 1734, 1741, etc. See below.
> A trivial account of the city, more like an historical register than an antiquarian essay, often reprinted, but never in the least improved.—Gough, 141.

>> 1724 IZACKE, RICHARD. Remarkable Antiquities of the City of Exeter, giving an Account of the Laws and Customs, the Offices, Court of Judicature, Gates, Walls, Rivers, Churches, etc., with a Catalogue of all the Bishops, Mayors, and Sheriffs, 1049-1677. 2nd edit., now very much enlarged and continued to 1723, by Samuel Izacke. Coats of arms, map, view of cathedral. 8vo. London.

1685 PHILOPOLITEIUS (Alexander Skene). Memorialls for the Government of the Royall-Burghs in Scotland: with a succinct Survey of the Famous City of Aberdeen, with its Situation, Description, Antiquity, Fidelity, and Loyalty to their Sovereigns: as also the gracious Rewards conferred thereon: and the signal Evidences of Honour put upon many chief Magistrates thereof; with a Catalogue of them since the City was burned for Loyalty about the Year 1330. (With the epigrams of A. Johnston upon some of the chief burghs, translated into English by T. B[arclay].)

> Johnston's epigrams are cited under 1640 above.—Bishop Nicolson says that there is in this small book a deal of curious remarks in a decent and nervous style. The author was Alexander Skene. Having briefly explained the nature and constitution of these burghs, as distinct from burghs of barony and regality, he treats of the offices and qualifications of the magistrates, deans of gilds, recorders, etc., and gives abstracts of some of the laws, but he writes more like a divine or moralist than a man of laws or business.—Gough, 639.

1686 GUNTON, SIMON (Editor). The History of Peterborough. With a Supplement by Patrick. (Place?)

> Gunton was vicar of Peterborough 1660-66, and Patrick bishop of Chichester 1689-91, and of Ely 1691-1707. Note in Walpole *Correspondence,* vol. I, 16 (Yale Edition).

1693 ADAIR, JOHN. Towne and Water of Montross, with the neighbouring Country and Coast. 18 × 13 ins.

1694 GILMORE, J. Map of Bath, with Historical Descriptions. 4to. Bath.

> Reproduced, Bath, 1888.

1697 HORSLEY, BENEDICT. Ichnography and Ground Plot of the City of Yorke, surveyed by Benedict Horsley, of the City of Yorke. York (?).

> Gough thinks that this furnished a model for Drake's improved plan.

PEIRCE, ROBERT, M. D. For a history and memoir of Bath, see his *Bath Memoirs,* under SPAS.

1700 RALEIGH, SIR WALTER. A Discourse of the Sea Ports: principally of the Port and Haven of Dover, written and addressed to Queen Elizabeth: with useful Remarks

on that Subject, by the Command of his Late Majesty King Charles the Second. 4to. London.

> Reprinted in *Harl. Misc.,* vol. 10, 1808-13.

A Step to the Bath, with a Character of the Place. (Place?)

> A six penny pamphlet, which gives a graphic description of the place. Quoted at length in Ashton's *Social Life in the Reign of Queen Anne,* 330-32.

1703 BAKER, THOMAS. Tunbridge Walks. London. (Cited frequently in Ashton, *op. cit.*)

1704 BRADY, ROBERT. Historical Treatise of Cities, Burghs or Boroughs, shewing their Original, and whence and from whom they received Liberties, Privileges and Immunities. 2nd edit. Fol. London.

> His historical works are laborious, and are based on original authorities; they are marked by the author's desire to uphold the royal prerogative.—Quoted by Sotheran.

1708 MIDGLEY, DR. SAMUEL. Halifax and its Gibbet Law, placed in a true Light. Together with a Description of the Town, the Nature of the Soil, the Temper and Disposition of the People, the Antiquity of its Customary Law, and the Reasonableness thereof; with an Account of the Gentry, and other Eminent Persons born and inhabiting within the said Town, and the Liberties thereof ... To which are added, The Unparalleled Tragedies committed by Sir John Eland of Eland and his grand Antagonists. 12mo. London.

> A duplicate of the above, with a new title page, 12mo, Halifax, 1712; another edit., 8vo, Halifax, 1761, and again 1789; a facsimile edit., Halifax (?), 1886. See below. For a reply to this work, see Wright, under 1738 below.
> The author is supposed to have written this book while he was in jail for debt. Being too poor to get it published himself, he had to leave it unprinted. After his death in 1695, John Bentley, parish clerk of Halifax, issued it under his own name as author. The Gibbett Law had its origin presumably in the desire of the merchants to protect their woolen cloth trade. It gave the inhabitants the power of executing any one taken within the liberties of Halifax who when tried by a jury of sixteen of the frith-burgesses was found guilty of stealing goods of the value of more than thirteen pence. Executions took place on market days on a hill outside the town, and were carried out by means of a gibbet resembling a guillotine. The first recorded execution took place in 1541; the last in 1650.

> 1712 MIDGLEY, SAMUEL. The History of the Famous Town of Hallifax in Yorkshire, being a Description thereof, their Manufactures and Trade, of the Nobility, Gentry and other eminent Persons, with a True Account of their antient Odd Customary Gibbet-Law, etc., also Revenge upon Revenge [Eland Tragedy]. Frontispiece of the Gibbet. 12mo. Halifax.

1711 TOLAND, JOHN. The Description of Epsom, with the Humours and Politicks of the Place, in a Letter to Eudoxa, with a Translation of Four Letters out of Pliny. 8vo. London.

> This was inserted in his *Posthumous Works,* vol. II, 60-119, but so much corrected, enlarged, and explained that it is almost a new work; for which reason he called it *A New Description of Epsom.*—Gough, 501.

1714 DAWSON, T. Memoirs of St. George the English Patron; and of the most Noble Order of the Garter. Being an Introduction to an intended History of the Antiquities of the Castle, Town and Borough of Windsor, with the Parts adjacent, in the County of Berks. Portrait of George I. 8vo. London.

> This is only an abridgement of Ashmole (see Ashmole, *Institution . . . of the Order of the Garter,* 1693, under HISTORY AND ANTIQUITIES); the account of the Patron was taken from Selden's *Titles of Honour.*—Gough, 83.

1715   HERBERT, SIR THOMAS. The History of York and Southwell. Printed in Latin and English in Leland's *Collectanea*. Oxford.

> Herbert was a great collector of ancient MSS, a singular lover of antiquities, and assistant to Dugdale in compiling the third volume of the *Monasticon* (Dugdale under 1655, ECCLESIASTICAL HISTORY AND ANTIQUITIES).—Gough, 558.

RAWLINSON, RICHARD. History and Antiquities of Winchester. 8vo. London.

> Another edit., London, 1730 (?), with "Some Account of Hyde Abbey" by Browne Willis.

THORESBY, RALPH. Ducatus Leodiensis: or, The Topography of the ancient and populous Town and Parish of Leedes, and Parts adjacent, in the West-Riding of the County of York; with the Pedigrees of many of the Nobility and Gentry, and other matters relating to those Parts; extracted from Records, Original Evidences, and MSS. To which is added, at the Request of several Learned Pᵣ ᵣons. A Catalogue of his Museum; with the Curiosities, Natural and Artificial, ...d the Antiquities; particularly the Roman, British, Saxon, Danish   nan, and Scotch coins, with modern Medals. Also a Catalogue of MSS., ι   ːious Editions of the Bible, and of Books published in the Infancy of the Art of Printing; with an Account of some unusual Accidents that have attended some Persons, attempted after the Manner of Dr. Plott. Fol. London.

> To this book is prefixed the most complete map that ever was engraved of these parts, and the first of any part in the north of England, drawn after the new method for twenty miles round Leeds, like those for the like distances from London, Oxford, and Cambridge, and engraved by Sutton Nichols. The historical part of the treatise, giving a view of the state of the northern parts of the kingdom under the Britons, Romans, and Saxons, brought down almost to the end of the 6th century, being left ready for the press, is published in the *Biographia Britannica.*—Gough, 556-57, and note. For his *Diary* see Thoresby, 1830, under LETTERS, DIARIES, MEMOIRS.

1717   BLUNDEL, H. The City of Bristol engraved by Kip. 35 × 20 ins.

> An interesting view of the city. All the landmarks are entirely out of proportion, but it is pleasant to think that our ancestors visited the city in such a glorious state, and as regards the river, the shipping is most fascinating, whilst the church towers and the glass house cones are strongly in evidence.—Thorp, no. 523.

Historia, Antiquitates et Athenae Etonenses; or, The History, Antiquities, etc., of the Famous College of St. Mary, near Eton, from its first Foundation, 1440, to the Present Time; Monuments and Grave-stones formerly in the College Chapel; with an exact Account of all the Persons who have been educated at Eton; and thence to King's College in Cambridge; as also of the Provosts, Fellows, and Schoolmasters, representing the Births, Fortunes . . . of all those Authors. With an Appendix consisting of Original Charters, etc. (Place?)

> This constitutes the "Proposals" for the intended History.

RAWLINSON, RICHARD. For the history and antiquities of Hereford, see his *History and Antiquities of the City and Cathedral Church of Hereford*, under ECCLESIASTICAL HISTORY AND ANTIQUITIES.

1718   The History of the City of Norwich. To which is added, Norfolk's Furies; or, A View of Kett's Camp. 2 pts. 8vo. Norwich.

> See Neville under 1575 above, and Norwich under 1728 below. The latter may be another edition of the above work.

1719   ASHMOLE, ELIAS. For a description of the Castle, College, and Town of Windsor, see his *Antiquities of Berkshire,* under HISTORY AND ANTIQUITIES.

HILDYARD, CHRISTOPHER. The Antiquities of York City, and the Civil Government thereof; with a List of all the Mayors and Bayliffs, Lord-Mayors and Sheriffs, from the Time of King Edward I to this Present Year 1719. Collected from the Papers of Christopher Hildyard,' Esq. with Notes and Observations and the Addition of ancient Inscriptions, and Coates of Arms, from Grave-Stones and Church Windows. By James Torr, Gent. and since continued to this Year present 1719. With an Appendix of the Dimensions of York Minster, the Names of the Founders, Repairers, and Benefactors; a Catalogue of all the Religious Houses, Chappels and Churches, that have been, and at present are, in the said City. As also the Gifts and Legacies to the Charity Schools, with the Names of the first Promoters and Founders thereof. 8vo. York.

> See Hildyard under 1664 above.—Torr's application and exactness in ecclesiastical antiquities and family descents were prodigious. One of his MSS dealing with the ecclesiastical antiquities of York contains no less than 1255 columns in folio, for the most part closely writ, in a very small but legible hand, with a complete index. There are others which were all given to the library of the dean and chapter of Archb. Sharp's executors. 1500 pounds were offered for them to be printed; and the greatest part of them are included in Burton's *Monasticon.*—Gough, 548.

1722   EYSTON, CHARLES. For a description of Glastonbury, see his *History and Antiquities of Glastonbury,* especially Rawlinson's *A Little Monument,* etc., under ECCLESIASTICAL HISTORY AND ANTIQUITIES.

1723   LEWIS, REV. JOHN. For an account of the town of Margate, see his *History and Antiquities of the Isle of Tenet,* under TOURS BY NATIVES.

1724-26   DEFOE, DANIEL. For descriptions of many towns, especially of their trade, see his *Tour through England,* under TOURS BY NATIVES.

1725   CHAPMAN, HENRY. Thermae Redivivae; or, The City of Bath described. 8vo. London. (Bound up with Guidott, *A Collection of Treatises relating to the City and Waters of Bath,* under SPAS.)

GUIDOTT, THOMAS, M.D. For a description of Bath, see his *A Collection of Treatises,* etc., under SPAS.

RASTRICK, WILLIAM. Ichnographia Burgi perantiqui Lennae Regis in agro Norfolciensi accurate delineata a Gulielmo Rastrick. Views of Exchange, market-house, etc. (Place?)

> Cited by Gough, 372. The author was a preacher at King's Lynn, where he succeeded his father John Rastrick. Both were nonconformists.

1726   ELLISON, DR. A most Pleasant Description of Benwel Village in the County of Northumberland, intermix'd with several diverting Incidents both serious and comical, by Q. Z., late Commoner of Oxon. 12mo. Newcastle upon Tyne. (In verse.)

> A poem of 2,290 six-line stanzas. A most extraordinary production, and very curious in places.—Bookseller's Note.

GILMORE, J. Plan of Bath, with a View of Bath. Bath.

HOWGRAVE, FRANCIS. An Essay of the Antient and Present State of Stamford; its Situation, Erection, Dissolution, and Re-edification; antient and present Sports, Endowments, Benefactions, Churches, Monuments, and other Curiosities; Monasteries, Colleges, Schools, and Hospitals: some Account of a Monastic Life, when the Monks first appeared in the World, what Orders of them settled here, and the Time of their Coming into England. The Whole gathered from the printed Accounts as well as original Manuscripts, particularly the Registers of Durham and Peterborough, the Rolls in the Tower and Cotton Library, old Writings belonging to Brown's Hospital, etc. 4to. Stamford.

> In the Preface to this superficial compendium is a long detail of what passed between the author and Peck, who thought it was intended to prejudice his performance, and is most unmercifully handled by Howgrave.—Gough, 248.

1727   PECK, FRANCIS. Academia Tertia Anglicana: or, The Antiquarian Annals of Stanford [*sic*] in Lincoln, Rutland and Northampton Shires, in XIV Books. Large folding view of the town by Van der Gucht, after Tillemans, and numerous other plates. Fol. London.

> Stamford is named the Third Academy owing to its having been for some time in the 13th and 14th centuries the seat of a university with several colleges, and a serious rival to Oxford and Cambridge. Reprinted at the end is Richard Butcher's *Survey and Antiquitie of the Towne of Stamford,* first published in 1646 (see this date above).—Bookseller's Note. Tillemans was a painter who did country seats and sporting subjects.—*DNB.* This work included a draught of Stamford by Speed.

1728   A Compleat History of the Famous City of Norwich, from the earliest Accounts to this present Year 1728, with a large Chronology of Occurrences in and near the City, an Exact List of the Bishops, Mayors, and Sheriffs, . . . and of the Posts and Carriers; also of the present Bishops and Deans in England, and of the Judges; to which is annexed, an Exact Map; published at the Request of several ingenious Gentlemen and other curious Persons. 8vo. Norwich.

> Bound in the same volume is the following: An Appendix to the Chronological History of the Famous City of Norwich . . . To which is added, An Abridgement of Neville's Furies of Norfolk.

DOUGLAS, WILLIAM. Some Historical Remarks on the City of St. Andrews in North Britain; with a particular Account of the ruinous Condition of the Harbour in that Place; and of what Importance the Repairing of it will be to all concerned in Trade and Navigation. 8vo. London.

GAIRDNER, ANDREW. An Historical Account of the Old Peoples Hospital, commonly called, the Trinity Hospital, in Edinburgh. 8vo. Edinburgh.

> Another edit., Edinburgh, 1734.

GURDON, THORNHAUGH. An Essay on the Antiquity of the Castle of Norwich; its Founders, and Government from the Kings of the East Engles down to modern Times. 8vo. Norwich.

JEAKE, SAMUEL. Charters of the Cinque Ports, Two Antient Towns, and their Members, translated into English, with Annotations historical and critical thereupon; wherein divers old Words are explained, and some of their antient Customs and Privileges observed. Fol. London.

1730 DALE, SAMUEL. The History and Antiquities of Harwich and Dovercourt, topographical, dynastical, and political; first collected by S. Taylor, alias Domville, Gent., Keeper of the King's Stores there, and now much enlarged in all its Parts with Notes and Observations relating to Natural History: illustrated with many Copperplates. 4to. London.

> Reprinted, with an Appendix, 4to, London, 1732.
> This was based on the work of Silas Taylor (alias for Domville), 1676, and published by Dr. Dale with additions and comments. For Taylor, see *DNB*.

G., T. (Thomas Gent). The Antient and Modern History of the Famous City of York; and in a particular Manner of its magnificent Cathedral, commonly called York-minster; as also an Account of St. Mary's Abbey, and other antient Religious Houses and Churches . . . with a Description of those Churches now in Use, of their curiously painted Windows, the Inscriptions carefully collected, and many of them translated: the Lives of the Archbishops of this See; the Government of the northern Parts of the Romans . . . of the Kings of England, and other illustrious Persons, who have honoured York with their Presence, and Account of the Mayors and Bayliffs . . . To which is added, A Description of the most noted Towns in Yorkshire, with their antient Buildings that have been therein, alphabetically digested for the Delight of the Reader . . . The Whole diligently collected by T. G. Folding plate and other illustrations. 12mo. York.

> Another edit., 3 vols., 12mo, York, 1785.
> A useful compendium, the work of an industrious printer, containing some things not in larger histories.—Gough, 550.

1731 GAMBARINI, C. A Description of the Earl of Pembroke's Pictures at Wilton House. Now published by C. Gambarini of Lucca, being an Introduction to his Design. 8vo. Westminster.

> Gambarini had proposed to engrave the most celebrated pictures in English collections. —Gough, 528.

1732 BICKHAM, GEORGE. The Gardens at Stowe of the Right Honourable Ld. Viscount Cobham. A Poem addressed to Mr. Pope. London.

> Another work, with a similar title, which may be another edition of the above, 1747. Many descriptions of Stow were published both in poetry and prose in the succeeding decades. The most popular was that of Seeley (see under 1744 below).
> Pope's famous line on Stow, "A work to wonder at—perhaps a STOW," is found in his Fourth Epistle (to Lord Burlington). Sir Richard Temple, who died in 1697, commenced rebuilding the house at Stow, and his son, Lord Cobham, continued the work and began the gardens, which were constantly expanded till 1755. By that time the grounds covered an extent of 500 acres. Bridgeman was the first designer and Kent the next. Vanbrugh constructed several of the temples and monuments. Stow was considered to be the ideal landscape garden of the century, and was much visited and written up in handbooks and traveler's accounts. It was also the subject of numerous engravings.

1733   GENT, THOMAS. The Antient and Modern History of the Loyal Town of Rippon: (introduced by a poem on the surprising Beauties of Studley Park, with a description of the venerable Ruins of Fountains Abbey, written by Peter Aram, and another on the Pleasures of a Country Life by a Reverend young Gentleman). Adorned with many Cuts, preceded by a South-West Prospect (and a new Plan) of Rippon. Besides are added, Travels into other Parts of Yorkshire. 1. Beverly; an Account of its Minster: the Seal of St. John: the Beauties of St. Mary's: and a List of the Mayors of the Town since incorporated. 2. Remarks on Pontefract. 3. Of the Church at Wakefield. 4. Those of Leeds: with a Visit to Kirkstal and Kirkham. 5. An Account of Keighley. 6. State of Skipton Castle. 7. Knaresborough: of the Church and its Monuments, St. Robert's Chapel, etc. 8. Towns near York: as Tadcaster, Bilbrough, Bolton-Percy, Howlden, Selby, Wistow, Cawood Church and Castle, Acaster and Bishop's Thorpe, Acomb, Nunmonkton, and Skelton, etc., with their Antiquities and Inscriptions. Faithfully and painfully collected by Thomas Gent of York. 8vo. York.

The Happiness of Retirement, in an Epistle from Lancashire to a Friend at Court, to which is added, An Encomium of the Town of Preston (Lancashire). London.

1734   A Description of Bath: a Poem, humbly inscribed to H.R.H. the Princess Amelia. Fol. (Place?)

1735   DENNE, ARCHDEACON. The State of Bromley College in Kent. Fol. (So cited by Gough, 715.)

A Description of the Diocese of Norwich; or, The Present State of Norfolk and Suffolk with respect to the Situation, Extent, Trade, and Customs of Norwich, etc. By a Gentleman of the Inner-Temple. 8vo. London.

   Gough calls this piece a very slight and trifling composition.—*Op. cit.,* 367.

FULLER, THOMAS. For a history of the town of Waltham, see his *History of the Antient Town and once Famous Abbey of Waltham,* under ECCLESIASTICAL HISTORY AND ANTIQUITIES.

GENT, THOMAS. Annales Regioduni Hullini: or, The History of the Royal and beautiful Town of Kingston-upon-Hul, from the Original of it, through the Means of the illustrious Founder King Edward I, etc., till this present Year 1735: in which are included all the most remarkable Transactions ecclesiastical, civil, and military: the Erection of the Churches, Convents, Monasteries, with the Names of their Founders and Benefactors: also a succinct Relation of De la Pole's Family, from the first Mayor of that Name to his Successors who were advanced to be Earls and Dukes of Suffolk: the Monuments, Inscriptions, etc., in the Churches of Holy Trinity and St. Mary: the Names of the Mayors, Sheriffs, and Chamberlains, with what remarkable Accidents have befallen them in the Course of their Lives: interspersed with a Compendium of British History, etc. Adorned with Cuts; as likewise various Curiosities in Antiquity, History, Travels, etc. Also a necessary and compleat Index to the Whole. Together

with several Letters containing some Accounts of the Antiquities of Bridlington, Scarborough, Whitby, etc., for the Entertainment of the curious Traveller who visits the North-East Part of Yorkshire. Faithfully collected, etc. 8vo. York.

> Reprinted in facsimile, with notices of the life and works of the author, by G. Ohlson, 8vo, Hull, 1869.

The Rarities of Richmond: Being exact Descriptions of the Royal Hermitage and Merlin's Cave, in the Gardens there. 8vo. London.

> 2nd edit., with the Life and Prophecies of Merlin, 8vo, London, 1736.
> Merlin's Cave was a celebrated edifice, which drew large crowds.

1736 BOURNE, HENRY. The History of Newcastle-upon-Tyne; or, The Ancient and Present State of that Town. Large folding map. Fol. Newcastle.

> This, the first regular history of the town, was utilized by Brand in his work of 1789 (see under HISTORY AND ANTIQUITIES).

Bristol. The City Charters: containing the Original Institution of Mayors, Recorders, Sheriffs, Town-Clerks, and all other Officers whatsoever, as also of a Common-Council, and the ancient Laws and Customs of the City: diligently compared with, and corrected according to the Latin Originals. To which is added, The Bounds of the City, by Land, with the exact Distances from Stone to Stone, all round the City. 4to. Bristol.

CHANDLER, MRS. MARY. The Description of Bath: a Poem; to which are added several Poems by the same Author. 8vo. London (?).

> 8th edit., with additions, 8vo (place?), 1767.

DRAKE, FRANCIS. Eboracum: or, The History and Antiquities of the City of York, from its Original to the Present Times, Together with the History of the Cathedral Church, and Lives of the Archbishops of that See, from the first Introduction of Christianity into the Northern Parts of this Island, to the present State and Condition of that Magnificent Fabrick. Collected from Authentick Manuscripts, Publick Records, Ancient Chronicles, and Modern Historians; illustrated with many finely engraved Plates by Isaac Basire, Maps, etc. In Two Books. Fol. London.

> Other edits., 3 vols., 8vo, York; 2 vols. in 1, York.
> The author was a surgeon of York as well as a highly esteemed antiquary.—This is the best account of York. Besides the assistance derived from the collections of Johnson, Widdrington, Gale, and Torr, Drake acknowledges some in a heraldic way from those of Henry Keepe, who began an account of York about 1684, and who was very particular in his description of arms in the windows of the several churches. The law part is chiefly taken from the collections of Mr. Hopkinson, clerk of the peace to the West Riding of York about 1670, many of whose MSS there is reason to expect were embezzled.—Gough, 550-51.

M'URE, JOHN (*alias* CAMPBELL). A View of the City of Glasgow: or, An Account of its Origin, Rise, and Progress, with a more particular Description thereof than has hitherto been known. Containing the Foundation of the Episcopal See, with the Succession of the Bishops and Archbishops from the Year 1122 to the late happy Revolution; the Erection of the Town into a Royal Burgh, with the

subsequent Grants from the Crown thereto; the Account of the Cathedral Church, as well as the other Churches of the City, the Hospitals, Halls, Streets, Lanes, Markets, Fairs, the several Incorporations, the Sett of the Merchants . . . the Rise, Growth, and Progress of Trade, the several Benefactors to the City, the University, Gardens, and Walks here . . . Collected from many antient Records, Charters, and other antient Vouchers, and from the best Historians and private MSS. 8vo. Glasgow.

> Reprinted, with additions and illustrations, edit. by J. F. S. Gordon, 2 vols, 8vo, Glasgow, 1873.

A New and Correct Plan of the City of Bath, from the Survey of Mr. J. Wood of Bath. Engravings. So listed in *Gent. Mag.*, vol. 6, November.

The Records of Norwich, containing the Monuments in the Cathedral, the Bishops, the Plagues, Fires, Martyrs, Hospitals, etc. In Two Parts. 8vo. Norwich.

1737 BEARCROFT, PHILIP. An Historical Account of Thomas Sutton, Esq., and of his Foundation in Charter House. Portrait and folding plate of Charterhouse. 8vo. London.

1738 ELDRIDGE, THOMAS. The Authentick History of the Ancient City of Norwich. 12mo. Norwich.

> At this time Norwich was the principal city of eastern England, rivaled only, outside of London, by Bristol in the southwest. It must have been a much more pleasant town than the latter, being widespread in area and possessing gardens and fruit trees attached to many houses within its bounds. It was to go down later before the more energetic cities of the West Riding of York when the industrialization of the North got under way.

MACKERELL, BENJAMIN. The History and Antiquities of the flourishing Corporation of King's-Lynn; containing whatever is or has been curious and remarkable in every respect in this Town: a particular Account of whatever is contained in each Parish Church or Chapel, etc., with a particular Description and Account of King John's Sword and Cup. Cuts. 8vo. London.

> 2nd edit., London, 1768.
> In addition this contains accounts of the Charters, Catalogue of all the Mayors of Lynn, and an alphabetical description of every individual Person or Thing that is treated of in this book.—Bookseller's Note.

A Short Account of the Town's Hospital in Glasgow. 8vo. Edinburgh.

> Reprinted Edinburgh, 1742.

WRIGHT, REV. THOMAS. The Antiquities of the Town of Halifax in Yorkshire. Wherein is given an Account of the Town, Church, and Twelve Chapels, the Free Grammar School; a List of Vicars and School Masters; the Ancient and Customary Law, called Halifax Gibbet-Law, with the Names of the Persons that suffered thereby, and the Times when; the public Charities to Church and Poor; the Men of Learning . . . together with the most remarkable Epitaphs and Inscriptions in the Church and Church Yard. The whole faithfully collected from printed Authors, Rolls of Courts, Registers, Old Wills, and other authentic Writings. Portrait and views. 12mo. Leeds.

This is said to have been directed against Midgley's account of Halifax. See Midgley, under 1708 above.

1739 BLOMEFIELD, REV. FRANCIS. History of the Ancient City and Burgh of Thetford. 4to. Fersfield.

>   This work is inserted in the author's first volume of his History of Norfolk (see Blomefield, *Essay towardes the Topographical History of County of Norfolk,* under 1736-45, HISTORY AND ANTIQUITIES).—Lowndes:

A Letter from a Gentleman in Town to his Friend in the Country, relating to the Royal Infirmary of Edinburgh. 4to. Edinburgh.

1740 ROCQUE, J. Plan of ye Garden and Plantation of Drumlangrig in Scotland, the Seat of the Duke of Queensbury. With inset views of the North, South and West Fronts of the House and view of the Cascade. 26½ × 22 ins. (Place?)

1741 NEWTON, WILLIAM. The History and Antiquities of Maidstone, the County-Town of Kent, from the Manuscript Collections of William Newton, Minister in Wingham. 8vo. London.

1741-42 GENT, THOMAS. For an account of Pontefract, see his *Historia Compendiosa Anglicana,* under HISTORY AND ANTIQUITIES.

1742 BICKHAM, GEORGE. Deliciae Britannicae, or The Curiosities of Kensington, Hampton Court, and Windsor Castle delineated. Engravings. 8vo. London.

>   2nd edit., with additions, 12mo, London, 1742.

ROCQUE, JOHN. Plan of the City of Bristol, engraved by J. Pine. 26 ins. to the mile. (Place?)

>   Pine was one of the foremost engravers of his time, and Rocque in the front line of surveyors.

THORPE, THOMAS. An Actual Survey of the City of Bath, in the County of Somerset, and of five Miles round. Wherein are laid down all the Villages, Gentlemen's Seats, Farm Houses, Roads, Highways, Rivers, Water Courses, and all Things worthy of Observation. Engraved map. 40 × 40 ins. Bath (?).

1742-43 WOOD, JOHN (Architect). An Essay towards a Description of the City of Bath. In Two Parts. Wherein its Antiquity is ascertained: its Situation, Mineral Waters, and British Works described: the antient Works in its Neighbourhood, the Gods, Places of Worship . . . occasionally considered; the Devastations committed by the Romans at Bath; their Encamping on the Hot Waters, and their Turning their Camp into a City, fully set forth: and the Works of the Saxons and their Successors briefly related. Illustrated with 13 octavo plates, engraved by Mr. Pine. Bath.

>   2nd edit., corrected and enlarged, 2 vols., 8vo, London, 1749; 3rd, 2 vols., 8vo, London, 1765; another, 2 vols., 8vo, London, 1769.
>   The 2nd part deals with the public buildings, streets, etc. Wood was the architect who gave the city its Palladian aspect.

1743   D., H. (Heneage Dering). Reliquiae Eboracenses. Per H. D. 4to. Eboraci. (In
       verse, with notes.)

>   Translated into English verse by Thomas Gent as *Historical Antiquities,* 8vo, York,
>   1771.

PHILALETHES. Belvidere; or, Admiral Lahe's Villa at Greenwich. Fol. London.
(8 pp.)

1744   SAVAGE, RICHARD. London and Bristol Compared; a Satire by the late Richard
       Savage, Esq. Fol. London.

>   Savage has become better known through Johnson's essay than through the merits of
>   his own works.

SEELEY, B. A Description of the Gardens of Lord Viscount Cobham at Stow. 8vo.
Northampton.

>   Other editions, 1745; 3rd, 1746; 4th, 1747; 5th, 1748. See Seeley under 1749-50 below.

1745   SAVAUX, ALEXANDER DE. Plan of the City and Castle of Chester, survey'd and
       drawn by Alexander de Savaux, Engineer. A large folding plan, drawn to the
       scale of 100 yards to one inch. 25 × 37 ins.

SERLE, J. A Plan of Mr. Pope's Garden as it was left at his Death; with a Plan and
Perspective View of the Grotto, all taken by J. Serle, his Gardener; with an
Account of all the Gems, Minerals, Spars, and Ores of which it is composed,
and from whom and whence they were sent: to which is added, A Character of
his Writings. From Thompson's Poem on Sickness; also R. Dodsley's Cave of
Pope. Plates. 4to. London.

>   Pope was vastly fond of his grotto at Twickenham and of the various minerals and
>   rocks which he collected from friends all over England.

WOOD, JOHN. A Description of the Exchange of Bristol: wherein the Ceremony of
laying the first Stone of that Structure: together with that of opening the
Building for the Publick Use is particularly recited. 8vo. Bath.

1746   PATERSON, G. and W. A Survey of Old and New Aberdeen, with the adjacent
       Country between the Rivers Dee and Don. London.

1747   WALPOLE, HORACE. Aedes Walpolianae; or, A Description of the Collection of Pic-
       tures at Houghton-Hall in Norfolk. 4to. London.

>   2nd edit., with additions, 4to, London, 1752; 3rd, 1767.
>   Though Sir Robert Walpole was notoriously ill at ease in the world of art, he never-
>   theless must act the part of a country gentleman by filling his gallery at Houghton with
>   pictures. Their disposal by sale was the subject of considerable correspondence between
>   Horace Walpole and the Rev. Wm. Cole.

1748   HOOKE, ANDREW. A Dissertation on the Antiquity of Bristol; wherein Mr. Cam-
       den's Opinion of the late Rise of that antient City is shewn to be not only con-
       tradictory to general Tradition, and the Opinion of all the Antiquaries before
       him; but also inconsistent with his own Authorities, as well as other positive
       and authentic Testimonies. 8vo. London.

This Dissertation was to be prefixed to an ambitious work called Bristolia: or Memoirs of Bristol, etc. Gough says that only the Dissertation and another Number were published.—*Op. cit.*, 473.

MORANT, REV. PHILIP. The History and Antiquities of Colchester, in Three Books, collected chiefly from MSS., with Appendix of Records and Original Papers. Folding map, copperplate views. Fol. London.

2nd edit., fol., London, 1768. See his *History of Essex,* under 1768, HISTORY AND ANTIQUITIES.
The author was a learned and indefatigable antiquary.—Nichols, *Anecdotes,* vol. II.

West Newbiggin (Co. Durham), Plan of, belonging to Robt. Fenwick, colored on linen, large sheet.

WILKINS, ROBERT. The Borough: being a faithful, tho' humorous Description of one of the strongest Garrisons and Sea-Port Towns in Great Britain. 8vo. London. See Wilkins under 1768 below.

1749 A Dialogue upon the Gardens of Viscount Cobham, at Stow in Buckinghamshire. 8vo. London.

POTE, JOSEPH. The History and Antiquities of Windsor Castle, and the Royal College, and Chapel of St. George; with the Institution, Laws, and Ceremonies of the Most Noble Order of the Garter; including the several Foundations in the Castle, from their First Establishment to the Present Time. With an Account of the Town and Corporation of Windsor; the Royal Apartments, and Paintings in the Castle; the Ceremonies of the Installation of a Knight of the Garter; also an Account of the First Founders, and their Successors Knights-Companions, to the present Time, with their several Stiles or Titles, at large, from their Plates in the Choir of St. George's Chapel; the Succession of the Deans and Prebends of Windsor; the Alms-Knights; the Monumental and Ancient Inscriptions; with other Particulars not mentioned by any Author. Numerous plates. 4to. Eton.

An Appendix to Pote's *History of Windsor* was published in 1762, continuing the knights to the last installation, with an alphabetical index of them from the first installation and of the plates or arms.—Gough, 704.
Pote was a bookseller at Eton. In the Preface he states that "necessity, not choice, obliged the Bookseller to act himself in the double capacity of Author and Printer." He had previously acknowledged that it was compiled from Ashmole's *History of the Order of the Garter,* together with the Monumental Inscriptions collected by a Mr. Mapletoft, who felt that he had not received his share of credit.

1749-50 SEELEY, B. Stow: the Gardens of the Rt. Hon. Lord Viscount Cobham, containing: I. Forty Views of the Temples and other Ornamental Buildings in the said Gardens; II. A Description of all the Buildings, copies of the Inscriptions, and Translations of them; III. A Dialogue upon the said Gardens. 42 views. 8vo. London.

The same title, London, 1751; an edit., London, 1756; an edit. called "a new edition," 8vo, Buckingham, 1763; again, with additions, London, 1769; London, 1777; "a new edition," Buckingham, 1780; again (place?), 1783; Buckingham, 1788, 1797. See below.

1769 SEELEY, B. A Description of the Magnificent House and Gardens of the Right Honourable Richard Grenville Temple, Earl of Temple, Viscount and Baron Cobham.

Embellished with a General Plan of the Gardens, and also a separate Plan of each Building, with Perspective Views of the same. New edition, with all the Alterations and Improvements that have been made therein, to the present Time. 8vo. London.

1750   CHASSEREAU, PETER. A Plan of York, surveyed by Peter Chassereau, with Improvements, published by John Rocque. Adorned with views of the city-house, county hospital, west view of the cathedral, Archbishop Bowet's monument, map of the county with Roman roads, gaol, section of the assembly room, Clifford's Tower, Thursday Market cross, and the church of All-hallows pavement. 17 × 25¾ ins. London.

A Compleat and Authentical History of the Town and Abbey of Glastonbury . . . giving an Account of its first Founders, the Means whereby it rose to so much Glory, the high Veneration, etc., the immense Riches, etc., the Holy Men who lived in it, and many other curious Particulars collected from Sir Wm. Dugdale, Bishop Usher, Bishop Godwin, Mr. Hearne, Bishop Tanner, and other learned Men. To which is added, An Accurate Account of the Properties and Uses of the Mineral Waters there, confirmed by proper Experiments; with some Observations how they should be made use of, so as to be most serviceable, and an Authentick Account of many remarkable Cures performed by them, with Remarks. By a Physician. 2nd edition, corrected. 8vo. London (?).

   This is a meager compilation written to recommend the aforesaid water discovered by the dream of one Matthew Chancellor, 1750.—Gough, 479. The success of these cures is testified to in a pamphlet *Wilt Thou be Made Whole.* (See under 1751, SPAS.)

ROCQUE, JOHN. A Geometrical Plan of the City and Suburbs of Bristol, with the Arms of the City and Merchant Venturers and Five Views on either side, with descriptions. 28 × 20½ ins.

WARTON, THOMAS. A Description of the City, College, and Cathedral of Winchester, exhibiting a complete and comprehensive Detail of the Antiquities and Present State: the Whole illustrated with several curious and authentic Particulars collected from a MS. of Anthony Wood, preserved in the Ashmolean Museum at Oxford, the College and Cathedral Registers, and other Original Authorities, never before published. London.

   Gough cites this, with the name spelled Wharton, as having been published "about six years ago," which would place it *ca.* 1762.—*Op. cit.*, 181. But it is given in Anderson, *British Topography,* dated as above. Gough calls it a very useful short description. See Warton under 1773 below.

1751   BRADFORD, SAMUEL. A Plan of Birmingham surveyed in 1750. With inserts of the churches of St. Martin and St. Philip and new canals indicated in water color. London.

COWDRY, RICHARD. Description of the Pictures, Statues, Bustos, Bass Relievos, and other Curiosities at Wilton House. 8vo. London.

   2nd edit., London, 1752. See Kennedy, *New Description,* under 1758 below, and Gambarini, under 1731 above.
   In this collection of antiques are contained the whole of Cardinal Richelieu's and Cardinal Mazarin's antiquities, and the greatest part of the Earl of Arundel's; besides several particular pieces purchased at different times.—Gough, 528-29. This famous seat of Wilton House was designed and built by Inigo Jones in the newly arrived Palladian style.

DEERING, CHARLES. Nottinghamia Vetus et Nova, or, An Historical Account of Nottingham, gathered from MSS., and divers other Curious Papers. Numerous plans and plates. 4to. Nottingham.

1752 DOIDGE, W. and H. A Plan of the Antient City of Canterbury, shewing the several Precincts and Liberties within the said City which are exempt from its Juris- diction, together with the Remains of St. Austin's Monastery, carefully sur- veyed and delineated by W. and H. Doidge, Land Surveyors, April 1752. J. Hilton, sculp.

1753 BICKHAM, GEORGE. The Beauties of Stow . . . Copperplate views. 8vo. London.

CARTER, EDMUND. For an account of the town of Cambridge, see his *History of the County of Cambridge,* under HISTORY AND ANTIQUITIES.

MAITLAND, WILLIAM. The History of Edinburgh from its Foundation to the Pres- ent Time 1753, containing a Faithful Relation of the Publick Transactions of the Citizens, Account of the Several Parishes, Government, Civil, Ecclesiastical, and Military, Incorporations of Trades, and Manufactures, Courts of Justice, State of Learning, etc. 20 engravings of the principal buildings. Fol. Edinburgh.

1754 DAVIS, DR. JOHN. Origines Divisianae: or, The Antiquities of the Devizes: in some Familiar Letters to a Friend, wrote in the Years 1750 and 1751. 8vo. London.

A satire on antiquaries, particularly Dr. Stukeley.—Gough, 527. "I have catched at everything relating to the town."—Bookseller's Note.

GARDNER, THOMAS. An Historical Account of Dunwich, antiently a City, now a Borough; Blithburgh, formerly a Town of Note, now a Village; Southwold, once a Village, now a Town corporate; with Remarks on some Places contigu- ous thereto; principally extracted from several antient Records, MSS., etc., which were never before made public. Copperplates. 4to. London.

1755 POTE, JOSEPH. Les Délices de Windsor; or, A Description of Windsor Castle and the Country adjacent, to which is added, An Appendix containing the Cere- monies of Installation of a Knight of the Garter. Plates. 12mo. Eton.

2nd edit., 1763; 3rd, 1771; others, 1778, 1782, 1784.
Th's reads like a revamping of his volume of 1749 above.

WILLIS, BROWNE. For an account of the town of Buckingham, see his *History and Antiquities of the Town, Hundred,* etc., *of Buckingham,* under HISTORY AND ANTIQUITIES.

1756 Alnwich Described. In *Gent. Mag.,* vol. 26, 73-76. (Customs, antiquities, seats, and curiosities.)

BAUR, F. W. (Engineer). A Correct Plan of the City of Winchester, and the ad- jacent Parts with the Hessian Camp, by Order of Count Isenburg. (Place?)

1758 CLUBBE, REV. JOHN. The History and Antiquities of the Ancient Villa of Wheatfield in the County of Suffolk. 4to. London.

> Résumé in *Gent. Mag.,* vol. 28, 303-05. A ludicrous burlesque upon accounts of antiquities in general and in particular on Morant's *Antiquities of Colchester* (1748 above). At least three editions were printed: Dublin, 1762; London, 1765; 3rd edit., 8vo, London, 1771.

KENNEDY, JAMES. A New Description of the Pictures, Statues, Bustos . . . and other Curiosities in the Earl of Pembroke's House at Wilton. 8vo. Salisbury.

> Other edits., 1769, 1771, 1774. See below.

> 1769 KENNEDY, JAMES. A Description of the Antiquities and Curiosities in Wilton-House, with Anecdotes and Remarks of Thomas, Earl of Pembroke, who collected these Antiquities. 25 engravings of busts, statues, relievos, etc. Salisbury (?).

1759 BAYLIES, WILLIAM, M.D. An Historical Account of the Rise, Progress, and Management of the General Hospital or Infirmary in the City of Bath: with some Queries to the Principal Conductors of that Charity. 8vo. London.

> This was answered in: A Short Answer to a Set of Queries annexed to Pamphlet . . . pretending to be an Historical Account of the Rise . . . of the General Hospital, etc. By a Governour of the said Charity. 8vo. London.
> Dr. Baylies came back with: A Full Reply to, etc. 8vo. London.

RELHAN, ANTHONY. A Short History of Brighthelmston, with Remarks on its Air and an Analysis of its Waters, particularly of the uncommon Mineral one, long discovered though but lately used. 12mo. London.

> Another edit., 8vo, London, 1761. A partial summary of this is given in *Gent. Mag.,* vol. 31, 249-51.

1760 The City (Edinburgh) Cleaned and Country Improved. Edinburgh.

PYE, MRS. ROBERT HAMDON. A Short Account of the Principal Seats and Gardens in and about Twickenham. 16mo. Twickenham. (Privately printed.)

> This appeared again as *A Short View,* 4to, London, 1767; and as *A Peep into the Principal Seats,* etc., By a Lady of Distinction, in the Republic of Letters, 12mo, London, 1775.
> Horace Walpole, in a letter to Rev. Wm. Cole, April 25, 1775, describes this as "a silly little book, of which a few copies were printed some years ago for presents and which now sets up for itself as a vendible book. Inaccurate, superficial blundering account of Twickenham, by a Jewess, turned Christian, poetess and author."

1761 GROVE, JOSEPH. Dialogue between Woolsey and Ximines.

> In this is included a short historical account of Ipswich, and a plan of the streets through which the procession passed from Cardinal College to Our Lady of Ipswich; with uprights of St. Laurence, Nicholas, Stephens, and Peter's churches and the college gates.—Gough 492.

1762 GOLDSMITH, OLIVER. For an account of Bath as a watering place, see his *Life of Richard Nash of Bath, Esq.* London.

PARKIN, CHARLES. The Topography of Freebridge Hundred and Half, in the County of Norfolk, containing the History and Antiquities of the Borough of King's Lynn, etc. (With prints, drawings, etc., collected, and partly executed by W. Taylor.) Fol. Lynn.

1763   A Description of Canterbury, its Cathedral, etc. In *Gent. Mag.,* vol. 33, 587-91. London.

> In 1763 and 1764 a number of descriptions of various towns and local places were printed in the *Gentleman's Magazine* signed Novus, Ingenuus, Verax, etc. Some of these are listed below.

E., J. The Humours of Harrogate described, in a Letter to a Friend, by J. E. with Notes descriptive, historical, explanatory, critical, and hypercritical, by Mart. Scriblerus. 4to. London.

> A local performance, without wit or humour.—Gough, 572.

For a description of the town of Margate, see *A Description of the Isle of Thanet,* under DESCRIPTIONS.

A Description of Shrewsbury. By Verax. In *Gent. Mag.,* vol. 33, 481-82.

1764   DODSLEY, ROBERT. A Description of the Leasowes by Dodsley is inserted in his *Works,* vol. II, with a plan, and in Woodhall's *Poems.*—Gough, 456.

GREEN, VALENTINE. A Survey of the City of Worcester; containing the Ecclesiastical and Civil Government thereof, as originally founded, and the Present Administration as since reformed: comprehending also the most material Parts of its History, from its Foundation to the Present Time; extracted from the best Authorities: together with an Account of whatever is most remarkable for Grandeur, Elegance, Curiosity, or Use, in this antient City. The Whole embellished with 16 copperplates of perspective Views of the public Buildings, etc., engraved from original Drawings taken on purpose for this Work. 8vo. Worcester.

> This is a correct as well as judicious and entertaining account.—Gough, 540. See his more mature work on this city under 1796 below.

A Description of the City of Hereford. By Ingenuus. In *Gent. Mag.,* vol. 34, 11-12.

A Description of the Town of Bridgnorth (on the Severn). By Paliopolis. In *Gent. Mag.,* vol. 34, 262.

A Description of the City of Chester. By Philo-Cestriensis. In *Gent. Mag.,* vol. 34, 409-10.

Further Account of the City of Chester. By Vestus. In *Gent. Mag.,* vol. 34, 510-11.

A Description of the City of York. In *Gent. Mag.,* vol. 34, 461-64.

MEIN, ROBERT. The Edinburgh Paradise Regain'd; or, The City set at Liberty, to propagate and improve her Trade and Commerce, being a curious Dissertation thereon, and Discovery of the Disease that obstructs the Growth and Progress thereof, and an effectual Remedy and Cure therefor, by redressing and removing her Grievances. Plan. 8vo. Edinburgh (?).

A Natural History of Liverpool. By Novus. In *Gent. Mag.*, vol. 34, 278-79.

ROCQUE, JOHN. A Collection of the Plans of the Principal Cities of Great Britain and Ireland, drawn from the most accurate Surveys, in particular those taken by the late Mr. J. Rocque. 22 colored maps and plans. Obl. 8vo. London.

1765   The Ancient History and Description of Exeter. An Account of St. Peter's Cathedral. Catalogue of all the Bishops of Tawnton, Crediton, and Exeter, and Memoirs of their Lives, with the Offices and Duties (as of old) of the sworn Officers of the City. Compiled from the Works of Hooker, Izacke, and others. 8vo. Exeter.

A Description of the Queen's Cross, near Northampton [one of those erected by Edward I marking the places the body of Queen Eleanor rested]. In *Gent. Mag.*, vol. 35, March.

DONN, BENJAMIN. For a map of the city and county of Exeter, see his *A Map of the County of Devon,* under MAPS AND CHARTS.

DUGDALE, SIR WILLIAM. The Antiquities of Coventre, Illustrated from Records, Leidger-Books, Manuscripts, Charters, Evidences, Tombes and Armes. Map, 7 plates, and numerous coats of arms. Fol. Coventry.

EDGAR, W. Plan of the City and Castle of Edinburgh. 27 × 14 ins.

EYES, JOHN. A Correct Plan of Liverpool, on one sheet of imperial Atlas Paper; shewing all the Streets, Lanes, and Allies, with the Docks and Basons, and a short historical Account of the Town. This survey was taken by order of the Corporation in June 1765, by J. Eyes and engraved by Thomas Kitchin.

Some Account of the City of Oxford. By Publicus. In *Gent. Mag.*, vol. 35, 73-75. London.

Theobalds. The Society of Antiquaries published this year a folio plate of a view of Theobalds, the famous palace formerly owned by Burghley, where Queen Elizabeth was entertained twelve times, at the expense of 3000 pounds each visit. It was traded in 1607 for the equally fine palace of Hatfield to James I, who made it his favorite resort. It was here he died in 1625. Charles I occasionally resided at Theobalds. In 1649, on the sale of the crown lands, notwithstanding the recommendations of the Commissioners to the Rebel Parliament to save it from destruction, it was pulled down and the money divided among the soldiers. Not a stone remains now.—From Rye, *England as Seen by Foreigners.*

WOOD, JOHN. A Description of Bath, wherein the Antiquity of the City as well as the Eminence of its Founder, its Magnitude, Situation, Soil, Mineral Waters, etc., are respectively treated. 2nd edit. corrected and enlarged. Portrait and 22 copper plates. 2 vols. 8vo. London.

See Wood, under 1742-43 above.

1766 ANSTEY, CHRISTOPHER. The New Bath Guide, or, Memoirs of the B-n-r-d Family, in a Series of Poetical Epistles.

> 2nd edit., 8vo, Cambridge, 1766; 14th edit., 12mo, 1791; other editions kept appearing, even into the next century.
>
> This popular book was not a guide but a satire on Bath society and its foibles. It was first published anonymously but was later acknowledged by its author. It is now chiefly remembered for being one of the sources of *Humphrey Clinker*. It contains an account of Lady Huntingdon's chapel, whose owner was a great admirer of the evangelist George Whitefield.

BURR, THOMAS BENGE. The History of Tunbridge Wells (with an Appendix: Of the Interest of the Inhabitants of Tunbridge Wells; Of the Improvements that may be made at Tunbridge Wells; Observations on . . . the Mineral Springs . . .). 8vo. London.

CARACCIOLI, CHARLES J. Antiquities of Arundel; the Peculiar Privilege of its Castle and Lordship; with an Abstract of the Lives of the Earls of Arundel, from the Conquest to this Time. By the Master of the Grammar School at Arundel. 8vo. London.

> The account of the town and castle is comprised in 20 pp., charters of religious foundations take up 20 more; the remaining 226 contain the lives of the earls, most awkwardly compiled from printed books. The church antiquities are slightly passed over. —Gough, 510.

EDMONDSON, JOSEPH. Historical and Genealogical Account of the noble Family of Greville . . . including . . . some Account of Warwick Castle. 10 plates, including a view of Warwick Castle, and numerous engravings in the text. 8vo. London.

The English Connoisseur, or, An Account of whatever is curious in Painting, Sculpture, etc., in the Palaces and Seats of the English Nobility and Gentry. 2 vols. 12mo. London.

> This work was designed on the plan of the *Apelles Britannicus*, which was advertised to be a New and Ample Description of all the most valuable paintings, statues, bustos, and other curiosities of the royal places of Hampton Court, Windsor, Richmond, Kensington, St. James', Whitehall, and Somerset House, with the seats of the nobility and gentry, and all the other most remarkable public edifices throughout Great Britain. With the History of the subjects, etc., and the Lives of the most eminent painters, sculptors, architects, and other artists, with the dates of their performances. The whole was to have been illustrated with a great variety of large copper plates, exactly drawn from the capital and most valuable originals in each building by Henry Gravelot and other celebrated hands. But only a few numbers are said to have come out. When and where this work was to have been published I have been unable to find out.

For an account of Norwich, see *History of the City and County of Norwich*, under HISTORY AND ANTIQUITIES.

KING, SAMUEL. A New and Accurate Plan of the City of Norwich, shewing the exact length and breadth of all the Streets and Lanes, with their Bearings, Bendings, and proper Names, ornamented with the Prospects of several publick Buildings in the said City, from an actual Survey taken by Samuel King, Land-Surveyor, and laid down by a Scale of three chains (or 66 yards) in an inch.

TICKELL, REV. J. For the history of the town of Kingston-upon-Hull, see his *History of the Town and County of*, etc., under HISTORY AND ANTIQUITIES.

1767   CRAIG, JAMES. Plan of the New Streets and Squares intended for the City of Edinburgh. 26 × 16 ins. Edinburgh.

> A facsimile in Wilson's *Memorials of Edinburgh*, 1846, reprinted 1872.

GOUGH, RICHARD. An Account of the Ancient Royal Palace of Placentia in East Greenwich. In *Vetusta Monumenta*. Fol. London.

HANBURY, REV. WM. The History of the Rise and Progress of the Charitable Foundations at Church-Langton: together with the different Deeds of Trust of that Establishment. 8vo. London (?).

> The rector of this town, with a firmness of mind equal to the benevolence of his heart, seems to have brought to the utmost degree of maturity and stability human affairs are capable of this singular undertaking of raising from a plantation of all the various trees, plants, etc., the world produces, a yearly fund of nearly 10,000 pounds, sufficient to relieve the distressed, instruct the ignorant, assist the curious, adorn the parish, and benefit this and the neighbouring County of Rutland, as long as integrity and public spirit subsist in Britain, or dare defy singularity and censure. This generous design claims a place here on a double account. We antiquarians have great obligation to this liberal founder, who has appropriated part of this fund to the compiling and publishing a history of every county of England by a professor appointed on purpose. *An Essay on Planting*, Oxford, 1758, was his first publication. He proposes speedily to publish, for the benefit of charity, *A Complete Body of Planting and Gardening*, in 2 vols., Folio. Price 4 guineas.—Gough, 717-18. This work appeared in 1770-71.

LAYARD, —. An Account of Somersham Water (in Huntingdon). *B.T.* vol. 3. (So cited by Hoare.)

1768   AWSITER, JOHN. Thoughts on Brighthelmston, concerning Sea-Bathing and drinking Sea-Water. 4to. London. (Also under SPAS.)

The Borough; being a Faithful though Humourous Description of one of the strongest Garrison and Sea Port Towns in Great Britain; with an Account of the Temper and Commerce of the Inhabitants: left by a Native of the Place, who was lost in the *Victory* Man of War, and now published for the Benefit of the Gentlemen of the Navy, and the Entertainment of the rest of Mankind, by Robert Wilkins.

> Cited by Gough without date, *op. cit.*, 187. It has to do with Portsmouth. See Wilkins under 1748 above.

Description of the Ancient and Present State of the Town and Abbey of Bury St. Edmunds in Suffolk, containing an Account of its Monastery, etc., with their Founders; also a List of Abbots, etc.; to which is also added, a List of the Post and Stage Coaches, etc., to and from Bury. Bury St. Edmunds.

> 2nd edit., 8vo, Bury St. Edmunds, 1771; 3rd edit., 8vo, Bury, 1782 (reviewed *Gent. Mag.*, vol. 53, Jan.) ; again, 1787.

SETTERINGTON, JOHN. The Town, Harbour, and Spaw of Scarborough. 2 sheets. (So cited by Gough without date, 734.)

Windsor and its Environs, Curiosities of the Town, Palaces, and Seats. 2 plates. 12mo. London.

1769 HARGROVE, ELY. The History of the Castle and Town of Knaresbrough, with Remarks on Spofforth, Rippon, Aldborough, Boroughbridge, Ribston, etc. 12mo. Knaresborough.

> See Hargrove under 1775 below.

Plan of the City of Bath, with Key Buildings and Sites marked for "intended new streets." 18 × 14½ ins. Bath.

> Another issue, with Post Time-Table added, 18½ × 15 ins. Bath, *ca.* 1770.

WHELER, R. B. History and Antiquities of Stratford-upon-Avon. with the Life of Shakespeare and an Account of the Jubilee. 8 aquatint engravings. 8vo. Stratford.

> This refers to the celebrated Shakespeare Jubilee, which took place this year under the management of Garrick. It lasted several days and was signalized by pageants, plays, and concerts. Boswell appeared in the procession dressed in Corsican costume. He wrote an account of it for the London papers. The weather was very unpropitious for the bard.

1770 A Description of the Royal Gardens at Richmond, in Surrey. 8vo. Richmond.

HOLLAR, W. A. A True Mapp and Description of the Town of Plymouth, 1643. 10½ × 14¾ ins.

The Regulations and Establishment of the Household of Henry Algernon fifth Earl of Northumberland, at his Castles of Wresil and Leckinfield in Yorkshire, begun 1512, edit. by Thomas Percy, Bishop of Dromore. 8vo. (Not printed for sale.)

> Reprinted by Pickering, 1827.
> This work marks a new departure. It stands chronologically at the head of a long series of household regulations and accounts whose publication has rendered the knowledge of old English life minute and exact.—*DNB*, quoted by Bookseller.

1771 ANDREWS, J. Engraved Plans of the Chief Cities of the World. 42 engraved plates, with numbered references to streets, buildings, etc. 2 vols. Obl. 8vo. London.

City of Bath from a Survey by Thomas Thorpe. 16 × 16 ins.

> See Thorpe's Survey under 1742 above.

A General Account of Tunbridge Wells and its Environs, Historical and Descriptive. 12mo. London.

LEDWICH, EDWARD. Antiquitates Sarisburnienses, containing:—I. A Dissertation on the Ancient Coins found at Sarum; II. The Salisbury Ballad (by Walter Pope); III. The History of Old Sarum; IV. Historical Memoirs, relative to the City of New Sarum; V. Bishops of Old and New Sarum; VI. Lives of Eminent Men, Natives of Salisbury. 2 plates. 8vo. Salisbury.

> Another edit., 8vo, Salisbury, 1777.

The Life and Extraordinary Adventures, the Perils and Critical Escapes of Timothy Ginnadrake, that Child of Checquer'd Fortune. 2 portraits. 3 vols. 12mo. Bath.

> Vol. 3 contains a Concise Account of the City of Bath, 1670-1770.—Bookseller's Note.
> The author is named F. Fleming in *Camb. Bibliog.*

MUSCIPULA (pseud. JOHN COLLIER). Curious Remarks on the History of Manchester. By Muscipula Sen. 8vo. Manchester.

> Reprinted by John Heywood, Manchester, 1864.
> Its author was John Collier (Tim Bobbin), or perhaps, as the author of the "Manchester School Register" puts it—"Tim Bobbin supplied the jokes, and his neighbour, Colonel Rownley of Bellfield Hall, the learning."—Fishwick, *The Lancashire Library.*
> The work was a criticism of Whitaker's *History of Manchester* (see following item).

WHITAKER, JOHN. The History and Antiquities of Manchester. 4to. London.

> 2nd edit. (so-called), 2 vols., 8vo, London, 1773, being merely a reprint, with corrections, of the single volume edit.; another edit. (the real 2nd edit.), with added matter, 2 vols., 4to, London, 1775.
> Reviewed *Gent. Mag.*, vol. 45, 184. This work, which extends no farther than the Roman-British period, was never finished. It was highly praised, however. Nichols speaks of it as "a work which, for acuteness of research, bold imagination, independent sentiment, and correct information, has scarcely its parallel in the Literature of this country . . . being perhaps the book in which the truth of our Island History has best been elucidated by the hand of a master."—*Literary Anecdotes*, vol. III.

1772 ASTLE, THOMAS. A Discourse of Sherburne Castell and Mannor, written in the Year 1670. From the Original Manuscript in the Possession of Thomas Astle, Esq. Extract in *Annual Register,* vol. 15, 143-44. London.

DENNE, REV. SAMUEL. The History and Antiquities of Rochester and its Environs; to which is added, A Description of the Towns, Villages, Gentlemen's Seats, and Ancient Buildings, Situate on or near the Road from London to Margate, Deal, and Dover. Map and views on copper. 8vo. Rochester.

> Another edit., Rochester, 1777.
> This work was begun by William Shrubsole, and completed with much added matter by Denne.—Bookseller's Note.

GOUGH, RICHARD. Observations on the Round Tower at Brechin, in Scotland. In *Misc. Coll.* of the Darlington Press; also in *Archaeologia,* vol. 2. London.

An Historical Account of Sturbridge, Bury and the most Famous Fairs in Europe and America, with curious Anecdotes, and on the Origin, Progress and Decline of all the Marts in this Kingdom. 8vo. Cambridge.

> The dating of this work is pure guess. My source merely prints 17—.

PARKIN, CHARLES. For a history of various towns in the county of Norfolk, see his *A Topographical History of Freebridge Hundred,* under HISTORY AND ANTIQUITIES.

SWINDEN, HENRY. The History and Antiquities of the Ancient Burgh of Great Yarmouth in the County of Norfolk, collected from the Corporation Charters, Records, and Evidences, and most authentic Materials. 4to. Norwich.

1773　Curiosities at the Seat of Ashton Lever, Esq. (near Manchester). In *Gent. Mag.*, vol. 43, 219-21.

> This treats of natural history, antiquities, fossils, etc.

DONN, BENJAMIN. A Plan of the City of Bristol, delineated from an Actual Survey. 19 × 13 ins.

> This is a detailed map with references in the margins. It was dedicated to the booksellers of Bristol and Bath.—Thorp, no. 523. A number of such plans following Donn continued to appear as late as 1800.

ENFIELD, WILLIAM. The History of Leverpool, drawn up by the Papers left by Mr. George Perry, and from other Materials since collected. Chart of the harbor, 2 maps of the environs, and 9 views of the principal public buildings. Fol. Warrington.

> 2nd edit., fol., with title *An Essay Towards the History,* etc., 1774.
> This work is regarded as a standard history of Liverpool. Reviewed *Gent. Mag.*, vol. 44, 475-77, where it is stated that the whole was designed and executed by the late Mr. George Perry, and edited by Dr. Enfield. The chart of the harbor and map of the environs seem to have been published separately.

GOUGH, RICHARD. The History and Antiquities of Winchester. 2 vols. 13 plates. 12mo. Winchester. (See Warton this date below.)

TAYLOR, G. A Plan of the City of Aberdeen, the Old Town, and the adjacent Country, made out from an Accurate Survey. 37 × 34¼ ins; about 8 Scotch Chains. Aberdeen.

WARTON, THOMAS. The History and Antiquities of Winchester, together with the Charters, Laws, Customs, Rights, Liberties and Privileges of that ancient City. Engravings. 2 vols. 12mo. Winton.

> Another edit., 2 vols., 12mo, Winton, 1783.
> This Professor of Poetry at Oxford was also interested in antiquities. See under 1750 above.

WOOD, ANTHONY A. The Antient and Present State of the City of Oxford, containing an Account of its Foundation, Antiquities . . . Churches, Mayors, Members of Parliament. Folding plans, and other engravings. 4to. London.

> Published in 3 vols. by the Oxford History Society, vols. 15, 17, 37, Oxford, 1889-99.
> Reviewed *Gent. Mag.*, vol. 45, May. The work contains the history of Oxford, its antiquities, situation, suburbs, division by wards, castle, fairs, religious houses, inscriptions, etc., a profusion of elaborate materials, collected by "that industrious but rude artificer, Wood, and not much polished or well digested by this reverend Baronet, though a son of Isis."—From the review. The materials for this work were collected by Wood in 1661-66.

1774　BATTELEY, JOHN (Archdeacon of Canterbury). The Antiquities of Richborough and Reculver translated and abridged from the Latin of Mr. Archdeacon Batteley by J. Duncombe. 8vo. London.

> Reviewed *Gent. Mag.*, vol. 44, 373-75. This work was begun with a Latin dissertation on the antiquities of Richborough, composed with more elegance of style than accuracy of sentiment.—Gough. See Batteley under 1711, ECCLESIASTICAL HISTORY AND ANTIQUITIES.

An Engraved Plan of Newcastle, showing streets, markets, and buildings. 12¾ × 16 ins.

GOSTLING, REV. WILLIAM. A Walk in and about the City of Canterbury, with many Observations not to be found in any Description hitherto published. Plates. 8vo. Canterbury.

> 2nd edit., with additions and corrections, 8vo, Canterbury, 1777; 3rd, Canterbury, 1779; again, 1796; modern edit., 8vo, Canterbury, 1925.
> In the preface to the fourth edition is this delineation of the author: "This book is indeed a true characteristic of the excellent disposition of the author, who, at all periods of his life, during his residence within the precincts of the Cathedral, found the greatest satisfaction, in rendering this City and its environs worthy the attention of the Traveller . . . When no longer able to do the friendly office of attending upon strangers in their Walk round the City, being many years before his death confined to his chamber, he gave to the Printers this little, though copious Tour, undertaken by him from no other motive, but that of information to the curious and inquisitive traveller."—Quoted by Nichols, *Anecdotes*, vol. IX, 348. The work was reviewed in *Gent. Mag.*, vol. 44, 483-86. "Exceptions" and "Observations" appeared in succeeding issues of this periodical, together with "Replies" by Gostling.

An Historical Account of the Town and Parish of Nantwich: with a particular Relation of the remarkable Siege it sustained in the Rebellion of 1643. 8vo. Shrewsbury.

HUTCHINS, REV. JONATHAN. View of the Principal Towns, Seats, Antiquities and other remarkable Particulars in Dorset. Compiled from Mr. Hutchins's History of that County. Folding plan of the town and castle of Corfe. 4to. London.

JACOB, EDWARD, F.S.A. The History of the Town and Port of Faversham, in the County of Kent. Copperplates. 8vo. London.

> Reviewed with epitome *Gent. Mag.*, vol. 44, 521-23.

WALPOLE, HORACE. A Description of the Villa of Horace Walpole at Strawberry Hill, near Twickenham. Strawberry Hill.

> An undated abridged edition, for the use of servants showing the house, was printed apparently the same year; 3rd edit., with additions, 1784.
> The first two volumes of Walpole's Correspondence with the Rev. Wm. Cole (Yale Edition) contain much material on the growth of this "singular mansion" toward completion. Its interior must have presented an heterogeneous aspect with its odds and ends picked, bought, and donated from all over England.

1775   An Account of the Hospitals, Alms-Houses, and Public Schools in Bristol. 4to. Bristol.

BARRY, —. Map of Glasgow, Gorbals, Caltoun, and Environs. Glasgow.

HARGROVE, ELY. The History of the Castle, Town and Forest of Knaresborough, with Harrogate and its Medicinal Waters. Engraved frontispiece of the Castle. 8vo. York.

> 3rd edit., 12mo, 1782; 4th, 8vo, York, 1789 (reviewed *Gent. Mag.*, vol. 59, 438-39); 5th, 1798. See also Hargrove under 1769 above. See below.
> The review of the fourth edition considers this to be a superior work, evincing both accuracy and knowledge in its handling of antiquities.

> 1789 HARGROVE, ELY. The History of the Castle, Town, and Forest of Knaresborough, with Harrogate, and its medicinal Waters, including an Account of the most remarkable Places in the Neighbourhood. The Curious Remains of Antiquity, elegant Buildings, ornamental Grounds, and other Singular Productions of Nature and Art. 4th edit. 12mo. York.

1776 COPLAND, JOHN. Saint Andrews: or, A Sentimental Evening Walk near the Ruins of that Ancient City; a poem in Three Parts, written in Autumn, 1775. 4to. Edinburgh.

PARKIN, CHARLES. The History of Great Yarmouth, collected from Antient Records and other Authentic Materials. 8vo. Lynn.

This is a reprint of his account of Yarmouth from the folio *Topographical History of Norfolk* (1775). See Blomefield under 1739, HISTORY AND ANTIQUITIES.

SEYMOUR, CHARLES. A Topographical, Historical, and Commercial Survey of the Cities, Towns, and Villages of Kent. 8vo. Canterbury.

1777 Bath, its Beauties and Amusements. (So cited in *Gent. Mag.*, vol. 47, March.)

A Concise History and Description of Kenilworth Castle: from its Foundation to the Present Time. Folding Plan. 8vo. Kenilworth.

2nd edit., Coventry, 1781; 3rd, 12mo, Birmingham, 1790; again, 1798 and 1800.

GIBSON, JOHN. The History of Glasgow from the Earliest Accounts to the Present Time; with an Account of the Rise, Progress, and Present State of . . . the Commerce and Manufactures now carried on in the City. With Appendix. Folding plan. 8vo. Glasgow.

HEELY, JOSEPH. Letters on the Beauties of Hagley, Envil, and the Leasowes. With Critical Remarks: and Observations on the Modern Taste in Gardening. 2 vols. 12mo. London.

Throughout the following decades there appeared a number of titles closely resembling the above.

From the author's preface it appears that he had published some time before a concise description of Hagley, Envil, and Leasowes, "merely as a companion to the visitors of those celebrated recesses." Finding it had been copied and generally received, he resolved on a more extensive description. This work is in part a tour, but it is chiefly turned to a description of these famous estates converted into landscape scenes: Hagley, the seat of Lord Lyttelton, the patron of the poet James Thomson; Envil, the seat of the Earl of Stamford, and Leasowes, the seat of the poet Shenstone and the model to all England for the small *ferme ornée*. These three gardens the author regards as forming a school of taste, "where you are taught, whatever be the genius of your grounds, how the pencil should be guided—where the cascade should gush—where the tower, the obelisk, the temple, or the grot best become their situations—it will teach you where woods, groves, and lawns should intermingle to grace each other—where water should be secluded, and where visible—where light and shade have the best, and most agreeable effect, and where the solemn and the gloomy more happily contrast the sprightly and gay." Heely was well versed in the theories of the Rev. Wm. Gilpin on the picturesque and in the vogue of the painters Claude, Poussin, and Salvatore, whose influence was directed towards making the ground conform to the painterly idea of landscape scenery; in the ideas of the sublime as analyzed by Burke, and in the Brown principle of sheets of water in the foreground, the trees in clumps, obelisks crowning the hill top, hidden sounds of running water, etc., etc. He also describes the art objects within the mansions, medals, vases, intaglios, portraits, the works of the Dutch and Italian masters—all of which point to the gentleman of taste. The center of reference is always Nature as the directress of all effort.

————. A Description of Hagley Park. By the Author of Letters on the Beauties of Hagley, Envil, and the Leasowes. 12mo. London.

This and the following work may be separate reprints of the two volume edition above. See also *The Description of Hagley*, etc., under 1800 below.

A Description of the Leasowes. 12mo. London.

The History of Guildford, the County Town of Surrey . . . with some Account of the Country Three Miles round. 8vo. Guildford.
    2nd edit., 1800.

RYMER, JAMES. A Sketch of Great Yarmouth, in the County of Norfolk, with Reflections on Cold Bathing. 12mo. Norwich.

THROSBY, JOHN. For an account of the town of Leicester, see his *Memoirs of the Town and County of Leicester,* under HISTORY AND ANTIQUITIES. See also Throsby under 1790 below.

1778   A Plan of Edinburgh. In a Collection of Six Maps, 1741. (See under MAPS, 1741.)

1779   ARNOT, HUGO. The History of Edinburgh, from the Earliest Accounts to the Present Time. 4to. Edinburgh.
    2nd edit., 4to, Edinburgh, 1789.
    Reviewed *Gent. Mag.,* vol. 49, 502-03. The reviewer concedes that the author has done a good job in assembling his material so as to show the city interwoven in the affairs of the nation and in exhibiting interesting and instructive views of manners at different periods.

CHARLTON, LIONEL. The History of Whitby, and of Whitby Abbey, collected from the Original Records of the Abbey, and other Authentic Memoirs. Plates and folding plan. 4to. York.

MARTIN, THOMAS, F.S.A. The History of the Town of Thetford, in the County of Norfolk and Suffolk, from the Earliest Accounts to the Present Time. Plates by Francis Grose. 4to. London.
    Reviewed *Gent. Mag.,* vol. 49, 411. The work is commended for its solidity and for offering to view what rich materials for the antiquary this town and its history exhibit here.

PHILLIPS, T. The History and Antiquities of Shrewsbury, from its First Foundation to the Present Time. With Appendix on Castles, Monasteries, etc., in Shropshire. 14 plates. 4to. Shrewsbury.
    Phillips's history was not written by him, but by Mr. Bowens, an amanuensis of the late W. Mytton, Esq., of Halston. The MS was lent to Cheney Hort, Esq., who unwittingy allowed Phillips to copy it. The latter subsequently printed it with some alterations.— Lowndes.

1780   A Description of Brighthelmstone and the adjacent Country. 12mo. London.
    Another edit., 12mo, Brighthelmston, 1788; another, 8vo, London, 1792; again, 12mo, Brighton, 1800.

The History and Antiquities of Cirencester, with some Account of the Abbey and Abbots. 8vo. Cirencester.

MORES, EDWARD ROWE. The History and Antiquities of Tunstall in Kent, by the later Mr. Edward Rowe Mores. 4to. London.

> This is No. 1 of *Bibliotheca Topographica Britannica*, edited by John Nichols, 1780-90. This work contains many accounts of towns and castles. For its purpose, see Nichols under 1780, HISTORY AND ANTIQUITIES.

Plan of Manchester and Salford. (By Bancks, who was interested in editing the Directory of Manchester.)

SAUNDERS, SAMUEL. A Short Description of the Curiosities of Glastonbury, in Somersetshire. 8vo. London.

1781   ARMSTRONG, MOSTYN JOHN. For an account of Norwich, see his *History and Antiquities of the County of Norfolk*, under HISTORY AND ANTIQUITIES.

HUTTON, WILLIAM. An History of Birmingham to the end of 1780. Map, plan, and engravings. 8vo. Birmingham.

> 2nd edit., with considerable additions, 8vo, Birmingham, 1783; 3rd much augmented, 8vo, 1795.
> Hutton is a rare instance of a man who in the 18th century rose from extreme poverty to a comfortable fortune. Beginning life as a poor boy in the silk mills, he became a prosperous owner of a paper warehouse.—From Nichols, *Anecdotes*, vol. IX, 98 ff. He lost a thousand pounds' worth of books in the Birmingham riots of July, 1791. See Hutton under 1786, TOURS BY NATIVES, and also his *Memoirs*, under LETTERS, DIARIES, MEMOIRS.

RUDDER, SAMUEL. (Matter relating to the town of Gloucester was reprinted from his *New History and Antiquities of Gloucestershire*, 1779. Cirencester.)

TOPHAM, JOHN. A Description of an Antient Picture in Windsor Castle, representing the Embarkation of Henry VIII at Dover, May 31st, 1520, preparatory to his Interview with the French King Francis I. Plan of Dover town and harbor, and folding plate of the ship "Hary Grace a Dieu" [*sic*]. 4to. London. (42 pp.)

1782   GREENE, RICHARD. A Particular and Descriptive Catalogue of the Natural and Artificial Rarities, in the Lichfield Museum. 12mo. Lichfield.

> For Johnson's visit to this museum, see his letter to Boswell, Oct. 22, 1779.

KING, EDWARD. Observations on Ancient Castles. 4to. London.

> For a sequel, see below. Reviewed *Gent. Mag.*, vol. 53, 237-39, where it is stated that the Observations were published in four volumes in 1777. If so, it has not come to my knowledge from any other source. King contributed many papers to *Archaeologia*, some of which were published separately between 1774 and 1782. His great work was *Munimenta Antiqua, or, Observations on Ancient Castles*, etc. See King this date under HISTORY AND ANTIQUITIES.

> 1783   KING, EDWARD. Sequel to the Observations on Ancient Castles. In *Archaeologia*, vol. 6. London.

OREM, WILLIAM. A Description of the Chanonry in Old Aberdeen, in the Years 1724-25. By William Orem, Town-Clerk of Aberdeen. No. 3 of *Bibl. Topog. Brit.* London.

Reprinted, 12mo, Aberdeen, 1791.
The Chanonry was the College of Canons, founded by Edward, fifth Bishop of the See. The work includes a history of the foundation of the university.—*Gent. Mag.*, vol. 52, 86.

1783   DUCAREL, ANDREW COLTEC. Some Account of the Town, Church and Archiepiscopal Palace of Croydon, in Surrey. No. 12 of *Bibl. Topog. Brit.*

NICHOLS, JOHN. The History and Antiquities of Hinckley, in the County of Leicester. With a large Appendix containing some Particulars of the Ancient Abbey of Lira in Normandy; Astronomical Remarks . . . Biographical Memoirs. No. 7 of *Bibl. Topog. Brit.*

OGDEN, JAMES. A Description of Manchester, giving an Historical Account of those Limits in which the Town was formerly included; some Observations upon its Public Edifices, present Extent, and late Alterations; with a succinct History of its former original Manufactories, and their gradual Advancement to the Present State of Perfection at which they are arrived. By a Native of the Town. 8vo. London.

> Reprinted by John Heywood, Manchester, 1849; reprinted, 1860 and 1887.
> Ogden, born in 1718, was by trade a fustian shearer, and afterwards a schoolmaster. He published some poetical effusions, one of which was called "The Revolution, an Epic Poem." He is said to have collected much material that was used by Dr. Aikin in his *History of Manchester.*—Fishwick, *op. cit.*

PARKIN, CHARLES. The History and Antiquities of the City of Norwich, collected from Ancient Records, and other authentic Materials. 8vo. Lynn.

1784   CULLUM, SIR J. The History and Antiquities of Hawsted, in Suffolk. No. 23 of *Bibl. Topog. Brit.*

> This work was mentioned by Arthur Young, the agriculturist, in his *Autobiography.*

MOSS, W. A Familiar Medical Survey of Liverpool. 12mo. Liverpool. For fuller title see under 1784, SPAS.

PEGGE, SAMUEL. The History and Antiquities of Eccleshal Manor and Castle; and of Lichfield House, London. No. 21 of *Bibl. Topog. Brit.*

RODENHURST, T. A Description of Hawkstone, the Seat of Sir Richard Hill, Bart. 12mo. Shrewsbury.

1785   COMBE, WILLIAM. The History and Antiquities of the City of York, from its Origin to the Present Time. 22 copperplates. 3 vols. 12mo. York.

> 1788   COMBE, WILLIAM. Eboracum: or, The History and Antiquities of the City of York, from its Origin to this Time. Together with an Account of the Ainsty, or County of the same, and a Description of the Cathedral Church. 2 vols. 8vo. York.

DUNCOMBE, J. and N. BATTELEY. The History and Antiquities of the Three Archiepiscopal Hospitals and other Charitable Foundations at and near Canterbury. No. 30 of *Bibl. Topog. Brit.*

HARROD, W. The Antiquities of Stamford and St. Martin's, compiled chiefly from the Annals of the Rev. Francis Peck; with Notes. To which is added, Their Present State, including Burghley. 2 vols. 12mo. Stamford.

See Peck under 1732-35, HISTORY AND ANTIQUITIES. Reviewed *Gent. Mag.*, vol. 56, 598. The first volume is an epitome of Peck's folio volume. The second deals with modern history of the places mentioned, including the epitaphs. The notes were furnished mainly by Mr. Lowe, surgeon of Stamford.

The History of Chichester. 12mo. Chichester.

HUTCHINSON, WILLIAM. For the antiquities of the town of Durham, see his *History and Antiquities of the County Palatine of Durham,* under HISTORY AND ANTIQUITIES.

PEGGE, REV. SAMUEL. Sketch of the History of Bolsover and Peak Castles, in the County of Derby. In a Letter to the Duke of Portland. Illustrated with drawings by Hayman Rooke. No. 32 of *Bibl. Topog. Brit.*

1786 BARRETT, WILLIAM. Plan of Mr. Barrett's Intended History of Bristol. Letter in *Gent. Mag.*, vol. 56, 544-45.

See the published work under 1789 below. The plan includes the history, descriptions, present state, government, trade and navigation, parochial history, annals of each year, etc.

CRAIG, J. A Plan for Improving the City of Edinburgh. Illustrated with folded engravings. 4to. Edinburgh.

DARRELL, WILLIAM. The History of Dover Castle. Illustrated with ten views and a plan of the Castle (translated from the Latin by A. Campbell). 4to. London.

Another edit., 4to, London, 1797.
Darrell, at one time chaplain to Queen Elizabeth, was an antiquary of some note. He wrote a Latin treatise, "Castra in Campo Cantiano ab antiquo," etc., of which the part concerning Dover Castle was translated as listed above.

A Description of the Gardens and Buildings at Kew, in Surrey; with the Engravings belonging thereto, in Perspective: To which is added, A Short Account of the Principal Seats and Gardens in and about Richmond and Kew. 8vo. Brentford.

The date assigned to this work is a guess. It was published in this decade.

DUGDALE, SIR WILLIAM. The Antiquities of Warwick and Warwick Castle, extracted from Dugdale's Warwickshire, with Queen Elizabeth's Visit in 1572; the Gilds, the Blackfriars, etc. Folding plate of St. Mary's Church. 8vo. Warwick.

For his *Warwickshire,* see under 1656, HISTORY AND ANTIQUITIES.

H., S. Description of Hatfield Peverill, in Essex. In *Gent. Mag.*, vol. 56, 664-65.

This contribution is mainly concerned with the old priory at the place.

The History and Antiquities of Barnwell Abbey, and of Sturbridge Fair, in the County of Cambridge. No. 38 of *Bibl. Topog. Brit.*

KENNEDY, J. A Description of the Antiquities and Curiosities in Wilton House, with the Anecdotes and Remarks of the Earl of Pembroke. Plates. 4to. Sarum.

> This fair, which dates from the time of King John, was originally designed to benefit lepers. The present method of handling business by wholesale dealers, however, has greatly shortened the time required for people from different parts of the Kingdom to meet, and now the fair is little more than a jubilee for the country folk and the academics remaining for the long vacation.—From the review, *Gent. Mag.,* vol. 56, 681.

HURTLEY, —. Hurtley's Curiosities of Craven, etc. Listed in *Gent. Mag.,* vol. 56, 599.

> In 1647 the south front of this famed mansion was destroyed by fire, and rebuilt after designs by Inigo Jones, with Webb acting as Superintendent of the Works. Jones was responsible for the famous Double Cube Room, with its splendid chimney piece. This room has been called the most beautiful room of any house in the kingdom, and the great Banqueting Hall, similar in shape, with dimensions of 110 by 55 feet, was not far behind in fame. The owner was the eccentric 4th Earl of Pembroke, who was, according to Anthony Wood, so illiterate that he could scarcely write his name. This house represents the finest example of Jones's domestic work.

LAURIE, J. A Plan of Edinburgh and the County adjacent, from an Actual Survey. Edinburgh.

A Topographical Description of Aukborough and Clifton Manbank. In *Gent. Mag.,* vol. 56, 475-77.

1787 A Brief History of Dover Castle. 12mo. Canterbury.

DENNE, REV. SAMUEL. Observations on the Archiepiscopal Palace of Mayfield, in Sussex. No. 45 of *Bibl. Topog. Brit.*

Eastbourne; being a Description of that Village, in the County of Sussex, and its Environs; addressed by Permission to H.R.H. Prince Edward, and the Princess Elizabeth and Sophia. Map, view of Beachy Head, and Newhaven Bridge. 8vo. London.

> 2nd edit., 12mo, London, 1799.

The Former and Present State of Glasgow contrasted, a Dream, etc. Glasgow.

> Reprinted in *Trans. Glasgow Arch. Soc.,* vol. 2, 151-72.
> A very rare pamphlet, which gives a curious glimpse of the social life of the city at the end of the 18th century.—Black, *List of Works on Scotland.*

KINCAID, ALEXANDER. The History of Edinburgh from the Earliest Account to the Present Time, with a Plan of the Town and Suburbs, and a Map of the Environs. 8vo. Edinburgh.

MAVOR, REV. WILLIAM. A New Description of Blenheim, the Seat of the Duke of Marlborough. To which is prefixed, Blenheim, a Poem. Plates and plans. 8vo. London.

> Of this there were numerous editions: one in 8vo, 1789; 4th, 8vo, 1797; another, 12mo, 1800. Translated into French, London (date?). See below.
> The connection of Sir John Vanbrugh with the building of Blenheim, the gift of the nation, or perhaps more exactly the gift of Queen Anne, to the celebrated conqueror of

the French, is well known, as is also his bitter experience with the imperious Duchess, or, as he called her, "that . . . the Duchess of Marlborough." His financial difficulties were complicated by the uncertain temper of Parliament and the refusal of the Duke to settle the debt lest he become personally involved. Vanbrugh's Blenheim is the best example in England of the baroque in architecture, with his Castle Howard running a close second. Being a national monument, as well as a personal one, its construction neglected comfort and convenience for the display of pride of place and power, and occasioned the lines attributed to Pope,

> . . . 'tis very fine,
> But where d'ye sleep, where d'ye dine?
> I find, by all you have been telling,
> That 'tis a house, but not a dwelling.

The scandal connected with its erection is well told in Disraeli's *Curiosities of Literature.*

1800 MAVOR, REV. WILLIAM. A New Description of Blenheim, the Seat of his Grace the Duke of Marlborough. Containing a full and accurate Account of the Paintings, Tapistry, and Furniture: a picturesque Tour of the Gardens and Park; and a general Description of the China Gallery, etc., with a Preliminary Essay on Landscape Gardening. Map. 12mo. London.

(In French.) Nouvelle Description de Blenheim, le Palais magnifique, dans la Province d'Oxford. Ornée d'un Plan du Parc, Jardins, etc. London.

NICHOLS, JOHN. The History and Antiquities of Aston Flamville and Birbach, including the Hamlets of Sketchley and Smockington, and the Granges of Leicester and Horeston, in the Counties of Leicester and Warwick. With a large Appendix to the History of Hinckley. No. 43 of *Bibl. Topog. Brit.*

This production sets a pattern for future work of this kind.—*Gent. Mag.,* vol. 58, 139.

———. The History and Antiquities of the Town, College, and Castle of Fotheringay, in the County of Northumberland. No. 43 of *Bibl. Topog. Brit.*

Fotheringay has a romantic interest as being the scene of the closing hours in the life of Mary Queen of Scots. Her execution and funeral are discussed at large in the Appendix, taken from new and hitherto unpublished materials. There are views of the church, ruins, the Duke of York's palace, etc.—From *Gent. Mag.,* vol. 57, 165.

RASTALL, WILLIAM DICKINSON. The History of the Antiquities of the Town and Church of Southwell. Portrait, plates of architecture, antiquities, etc. 4to. London. (Privately printed for the author.)

1788 An Account of New Hall in Essex. 2 plates with 7 pp. of description. In *Vet. Mon.*

New Hall was acquired by Henry VIII in 1517 and given the name of Beau Lieu, which, however, never came into general use.—Bookseller's Note.

The Case of the Inhabitants of Croydon, 1673; with an Appendix to the History of that Town. 2. A List of the Manorial Houses which formerly belonged to the See of Canterbury. 3. A Description of Trimly Hospital, Guildford; and of Albury House. 4. Brief Notes on Battersea, Chelsham, Nutfall, and Tatsfield, in the County of Surrey. No. 46 of *Bibl. Topog. Brit.*

The case of the inhabitants of Croydon against their vicar was that he was given to extortion and oppression, that he pulled down the parsonage house and sold the materials, that he was inefficient in preaching, that he preached *printed* sermons and nonsense, got drunk and kept a woman, all of which was a little excessive even for an 18th century clergyman.

Collections for a History of Sandwich. Pt. I. 4to. London.

> Reviewed *Gent. Mag.,* vol. 58, 619. This is accounted a valuable addition to antiquarian knowledge. The part published contains a description of the hospitals of St. Bartholomew, St. John, St. Thomas, and the Carmelite Friary, the Chantries, the Free Grammar School founded by Sir Roger Manwood, Knt., 1563. The second part will begin with churches and parishes.

CROFTES, RICHARD. Particulars of the Manor of Little Saxham, in the County of Suffolk. Fol. Bury St. Edmunds.

HADLEY, GEORGE. A New and Complete History of the Town of Kingston-upon-Hull. With a cursory Review of, and Observations on, the Ancient Legend, from its original Foundation in A.D. 1296 by Edward the First, to the Present Period. 4to. Hull.

History of the Town and Parish of Halifax, Account of the Gentry, Eminent Persons, its Ancient Customs, also the Tragedies committed by Sir John Eland, with the Lives and Deaths of Wilkin Lockwood, and Adam Beaumont, Esqs. Folding plates. 8vo. Halifax.

> See a similar title under Nelson, 1789, below.

HUTCHINS, REV. JOHN. For an account of the town of Poole, see his *History of the Town and County of Poole,* under HISTORY AND ANTIQUITIES.

NICHOLS, JOHN. The History and Antiquities of Canonbury, with some Account of the Parish of Islington. No. 49 of *Bibl. Topog. Brit.*

> This tract was in substance incorporated by Mr. Nelson in his *Islington.*—Nichols, *Anecdotes,* vol. IX, 40.

SOANE, SIR JOHN. Plans, Elevations, and Sections of Buildings erected in the Counties of Norfolk, Suffolk, Yorkshire, Staffordshire, Warwickshire, Hertfordshire, etc. Fol. London.

> Soane was the architect who erected the Bank of England, by which he gained much fame.

1789 BARRETT, WILLIAM. The History and Antiquities of the City of Bristol, compiled from Original Records and Authentic MSS. in Public Offices or Private Hands. Numerous copperplates. 4to. Bristol.

> Reviewed *Gent. Mag.,* vol. 59, 921-24. The reviewer considered this to be a readable book but lacking in what is called scholarship, because his looseness of reference makes it difficult to check him; his etymologies are full of errors, e.g., his equation of Caer Brito with the British "the Painted." He accepts too readily Chatterton and Rowlie as authorities. He makes many mistakes in facts, and he translates Latin originals instead of giving us the original text itself.

BRAND, JOHN. For an account of the town of Newcastle-upon-Tyne, see his *History and Antiquities of the Town and County of,* etc., under HISTORY AND ANTIQUITIES.

A Brief Account of Cranbrook, the Capital Town in the Weald of Kent. 12mo. Cranbrook.

A Companion to the Leasowes, Hagley, and Enville, with a Sketch of Fisherwick; to which is prefixed, The Present State of Birmingham. Birmingham.

COOKE, JOHN. An Historical Account of the Royal Hospital for Seamen at Greenwich. Plates. 4to. London.

> See under 1790 below for a title very similar to the above.

A Descriptive Sketch of Wyddiall, in Hertfordshire. 8vo. (Place?)

HUTTON, WILLIAM. A Description of Blackpool, in Lancashire, frequented for Sea-Bathing. 8vo. Birmingham.

> Reviewed *Gent. Mag.*, vol. 59, 1020. The impression got from Hutton's description is that Blackpool must have been a dreary place. It was later to become the favorite resort of Bank Holiday trippers.

LAZARUS, EBENEZER. A Particular Description of the Town of Kelso, with a plain and undisguiséd Account of its admirable and delightful Situation. 12mo. Kelso.

MORANT, PHILIP. History and Antiquities of Colchester, selected from the most approved Authors, with Broadside List of Borough Members. London.

> This work came out originally in 1748. See Morant under this date above.

NELSON, REV. A History of the Town and Parish of Halifax, with an Account of its Ancient Customs, etc., also the Unparalleled Tragedies committed by Sir John Eland of Eland and his Grand Antagonists; Revenge upon Revenge; or, An Historical Narrative of the Tragical Practices of Sir John Eland of Eland. 2 vols. in 1. Plates. 8vo. Halifax.

> For Halifax and its Gibbet Law and Sir John Eland, see Midgley, under 1708 above.

SHIERCLIFF, E. For descriptive accounts of Bristol and adjacent places, see his *Bristol and Hot-Well Guide,* under AIDS TO TRAVELERS.

1790 A Concise Description of the Royal Hospital for Seamen at Greenwich. 8vo. London.

> Another edit., Greenwich, 1793. Translated into French, 12mo, 1793. See below.
>
> 1793 Description abrégée de Hôpital par Madame W. Charron. 12mo. (Place?)

A Description of Buxton and the Adjacent Country. 8vo. Manchester.

Description of a Highland Village, with a View of Leneivilg. In *Literary Magazine and British Review.* (*Ca.* 1790.)

DUNSFORD, MARTIN. Historical Memoirs of the Town and Parish of Tiverton, in the County of Devon. Map and plates, with observations. 4to. Exeter.

> This traces the history of the textile manufactures there from 1753 to 1761. Other current affairs are mentioned.—J. Williams, *Guide to Printed Materials.* Reviewed *Gent. Mag.*, vol. 62, 925-27. The work is commended for its effective increase of information on national antiquities.

DYDE, WILLIAM. The History and Antiquities of Tewkesbury from the Earliest Periods to the Present Time; with an Account (by James Johnstone) of the Medicinal Water, near Tewkesbury; with Thoughts on the Use and Diseases of the Lymphatic Glands (2nd edit.). 2 vols. Folding frontispice and plates. 8vo. Tewkesbury.

> 2nd edit., with considerable additions, 8vo, Tewkesbury, 1798.

GILLINGWATER, EDMUND. An Historical Account of the Ancient Town of Lowestoft, in the County of Suffolk. To which is added, Some Cursory Remarks on the adjoining parishes, and a General Account of the Island of Lothingland. 4to. London.

> Reviewed *Gent. Mag.,* vol. 61, 548-51. The reviewer is impressed with the evidence of a general spirit of investigation of national history and antiquities all over Great Britain. The author was an inhabitant of the decaying town of Lowestoft and the island, now become a peninsula, of Lothingland. He has caught the spirit of the place, aided generously by his countrymen and neighbours. The work deals with the island and the origin of Lowestoft, the fisheries, church and chapels, religious sects, naval and military affairs, etc. Lothingland had always been a royal demesne. Its history is in large part the history of the sea's encroachment on the island and the land. It had varied fortunes, being ravaged sixteen times by the plague and suffering in Kett's Rebellion, Parliamentarian wars, and the wars with the Dutch. George II landed there in 1736, being brought ashore in his barge with all his attendants by the sailors. The herring fishery is supposed to have originated there, later being transferred to Yarmouth. The quarrels between the two towns were not settled until 1576. At present its herring fishery is in a flourishing condition.— From the review.

GOUGH, RICHARD. Description of the Hospital of St. Mary Magdalen, near Winchester, from Drawings taken by Mr. Schnebbelie, August, 1788. 3 plates and 17 pp. of text. From *Vet. Mon.*

MACAULAY, REV. AULAY. The History and Antiquities of Claybrook, in the County of Leicester, including the Chapelries of Wibtoft and Little Wigston, and the Hamlets of Bittesby and Ullesthorpe. 8vo. London.

> Reviewed *Gent. Mag.,* vol. 61, 360. The work is praised for disproving to idlers and scholars that the writing of local parish histories cannot be made interesting.

NICHOLS, JOHN. For an account of the town of Leicester, see his *Collections towards the History and Antiquities of the Town and County of Leicester,* under HISTORY AND ANTIQUITIES.

———. Collections towards the History and Antiquities of Elmeswell and Campsey Ann, in the County of Suffolk. No. 52 of *Bibl. Topog. Brit.*

OLDFIELD, H. G., and R. R. DYSON. For an account of the town of Tottenham High Cross, see their *History and Antiquities of the Parish of Tottenham High Cross,* under HISTORY AND ANTIQUITIES.

THROSBY, JOHN. The History and Antiquities of the Ancient Town of Leicester. 4to. London.

> Another edit., 4to, London, 1797. See Throsby under 1777 above.

1791 For a History of Chester, see the *History of the County and City of Chester,* under HISTORY AND ANTIQUITIES.

HUTTON, WILLIAM. The History of Derby; from the Remote Ages of Antiquity to the Year MDCCXCI. Describing its Situation, Air, Soil, Water, Streets, Buildings, and Government. With the Illustrious Families that have inherited its Honours. Also the Ecclesiastical History, the Trade, Amusements, Remarkable Occurrences, the Eminent Men, with the adjacent Seats of the Gentry. Plates. 8vo. London.

> 2nd edit., with considerable additions, 1793; 3rd, much augmented, 1795; 4th, with many embellishments, "is now in contemplation."—Nichols, *Anecdotes,* vol. IX, 100.
> Reviewed *Gent. Mag.,* vol. 63, 150-52, where the work is commended for its lively and entertaining reading and for its minute descriptions and attention to detail. It also gives some account of the silk and porcelain manufactures which helped to make Derby famous.

LANGDALE, THOMAS. The History of North-Allerton, with a Description of the Castle-Hills by Miss A. Crosfield. 8vo. North-Allerton.

A Slight Descriptive Sketch of Edinburgh, when viewed as a picturesque Object. 1 plate. In *The Bee,* vol. 2, 241-47. 16mo. Edinburgh.

TOULMIN, JOSHUA. The History of the Town of Taunton in the County of Somerset. Folding map and engravings. 4to. Taunton.

> Reviewed *Gent. Mag.,* vol. 62, 241. The book offers an historical account of the fortunes of the town—its ancient state, charter, manors, religious houses, public buildings, civil constitution, trade, manufactures, political transactions, etc.

WILLYAMS, REV. COOPER. The History of Sudeley Castle. Aquatint view of the castle ruins. Fol. (Place?)

> An advertisement pasted inside of the front cover expresses regret at the long delay in the publication of the work on account of "a Want of a proper Kind of Paper"—a curious apology for so small a work.—Bookseller's Note. The castle is in Gloucestershire.

1792 BOYS, WILLIAM. Collections for an History of Sandwich, with Notices of the other Cinque Ports and Members, and of Richborough. 52 copperplates, mostly of views and plans, seals, and pedigrees. 4to. Canterbury.

CREECH, WILLIAM. Letters respecting the Mode of Living, Trade, Manners and Literature of Edinburgh in 1763 and the Present Period. 8vo. Edinburgh.

> The only letter which is signed bears the name of William Creech and the date of 1792. —Bookseller's Note.

GARDENSTONE, LORD. Travelling Memorandum, made in a Tour upon the Continent of Europe, in the Years 1786, 1787, and 1788. Edinburgh.

> The author, who was one of the Scotch judges or Lords of the Session, concludes his travel account with a narrative of the rise and progress of the village Laurence-kirk, in Kincardinshire, between Perth and Aberdeen, a development that was due entirely to his own generosity.

MARTIN, REV. JOHN (Vicar of Naseby). The History and Antiquities of Naseby, in the County of Northamptonshire. Folding plan of troops drawn up preparatory to the battle of Naseby. 8vo. Cambridge.

A brief notice of the work in *Gent. Mag.,* vol. 63, 147. The parish is one large common field, twenty miles round, and contains near 6,000 acres. Its situation is elevated, and is supposed to be the highest ground in England, from which three rivers rise, and from which forty churches may be seen on a clear day. Scarcely a recollection of the battle fought there remains.—From the review.

OLDFIELD, T. H. B. The Entire History, Political and Personal, of the Boroughs of Great Britain; together with the Cinque Ports; to which is now first added, The History of the Original Constitution of Parliaments, from the Times of the Ancient Britons to the Present Day, with a State of the Representation and an Account of Contested Elections. New edit., corrected. 3 vols. 8vo. London.

ROBERTSON, ARCHIBALD. For descriptions of towns, villages, and seats on the Great Road from London to Bath and Bristol, see under AIDS TO TRAVELERS.

TYTLER, WILLIAM. On the fashionable Amusements and Entertainments in Edinburgh in the last Century, with a Plan of a Grand Concert of Music on St. Cecilia's Day, 1675. In *Arch. Scotica,* vol. 11, 499-510. 4to. Edinburgh.

WATKINS, JOHN. An Essay towards a History of Bideford, in the County of Devon. 8vo. Exeter.

Reviewed *Gent. Mag.,* vol. 63, 1029-30. The author intended at first to make this a contribution towards the History of Devonshire, but was persuaded by friends to publish it separately. It discourses on residences, historical personages, events, local anecdotes, etc.

1793 BLORE, THOMAS. The History of the Manor and Manor House of South Winfield. 4 plates of views, 1 of seals, and 2 folding engraved pedigrees. *Bibl. Topog. Brit.* (no. not cited).

Reviewed *Gent. Mag.,* vol. 64, 150. This is a specimen of a projected History and Antiquities of the County of Derby, which has been hitherto neglected by topographers. Blore shows himself well versed in the requirements of a county historian.—From the review.

BROWN, T., and J. WATSON. Plan of the City of Edinburgh, including all the latest Improvements, with List of Names of Closes, etc., etc. 24 × 18 ins. Edinburgh.

HEATH, CHARLES. Descriptive Accounts of Persfield and Chepstow, including Caerwent and the Passages; also the Road to Bristol and Gloucester. 8vo. Monmouth.

An Historical Account of Lincoln and the Cathedral. 8vo. Lincoln.

LAING, REV. W. An Account of Peterhead, its Mineral Well, Air, and Neighbourhood. 8vo. London, Edinburgh, and Aberdeen.

ROBINSON, T. An Historical Narrative of that Renowned Piece of Antiquity, the Jewry-Wall in Leicester. 8vo. Leicester.

SMALL, ROBERT. A Statistical Account of the Parish and Town of Dundee in 1792. Notes, additions, and a plan of the town and suburbs. 8vo. Dundee.

1794   HEATH, GEORGE. The New History, Survey, and Description of the City and
Suburbs of Bristol . . . together with Matthews' New Bristol Directory for
the Year 1793-94. Portrait and folding plan. 8vo. Bristol.

> 2nd edit., corrected, improved, and much enlarged, 12mo, Bristol, 1797.
> In addition to being a general guide, with emphasis upon churches, this gives an
> account of the business carried on in Bristol.

> 1797   HEATH, GEORGE. The History, Antiquities, Survey and Description of the City and
> Suburbs of Bristol, or complete Guide, etc. To which are added, Descriptions of
> the Towns . . . in the Vicinity, and of the Cities of Bath and Wells. 12mo.
> Bristol.

The History and Antiquities of Glastonbury, collected from various Authors. To
which is added, An Account of the Mineral Waters, and of the Glastonbury
Thorn. 16mo. Bath.

HODGES, W. An Historical Account of Ludlow Castle; the Ancient Palace of the
Princes of Wales. 8vo. Ludlow.

> Ludlow Castle was the scene of the performance of Milton's "Comus."

MATTHEWS, —. A New and Correct Plan of the City and Suburbs of the City of
Bristol, including the Hotwells and Clifton and the New Buildings down to the
Year 1794. Bristol.

PAYTON, J. An Authentic History and Description of the Castle and Priory of
Dudley, chiefly compiled from the Works of Leland, Erdeswicke, Plott, Grose,
etc. 8vo. Dudley.

SUTHERLAND, CAPT. A General History of Stirling, containing a Description of
the Town, and Origin of Castle and Burgh. 12mo. Stirling.

1795   The Antient and Modern History of Lewes and Brighthelmstone; in which are
comprehended the most interesting Events of the County at large, under the
Regusan, Roman, Saxon and Norman Settlements. (Place?)

> Reviewed *Gent. Mag.*, vol. 66, 1100. This work is above the common run of compilations
> in merit. It recounts the history of Lewes, its situation, etymology, its state under various
> ruling groups, trade, etc. The history of Brighthelmstone is more compressed.

BROWN, ANDREW. The History of Glasgow; and of Paisley, Greenock, and Port-
Glasgow, etc. 2 vols. 8vo. Glasgow.

Grove-Hill, an Horticultural Sketch. London.

> Reviewed *Gent. Mag.*, vol. 65, 671. Included in a survey of the road from London to
> Brighthelmstone, made three years ago, was a description of the gentlemen's seats in the
> vicinity. In this was inserted an account of Grove-Hill, which was copied in periodicals.
> Requests from abroad that it be printed separately led to making a few imprints in the
> form of a little pamphlet. Grove-Hill is in the Parish of Camberwell, and is the spot where
> George Barnwell (in Lillo's *London Merchant*) murdered his uncle. On the place is a
> house and gardens occupied by Dr. Lettsom (well known physician and naturalist). 4
> plates engraved by Midland and J. Edwards, after Samuel.—From the review.

JACKSON, JOHN (Junior). The History of the City and County of Lichfield. 8vo.
Lichfield.

2nd edit., 8vo, Lichfield, 1796; another, 1800.
Reviewed *Gent. Mag.*, vol. 65, 681. This work was compiled chiefly from ancient authorities, MSS, and other works of eminent authors. The writer is still a young man under
twenty, the son of a bookseller and printer at Lichfield. The book contains several particulars not found in other publications on this subject. A second part describing the
cathedral is expected to follow. There is a curious account of a court held annually at
Green-hill, in the city of Lichfield on Whit Monday, in a temporary stand of wood,
erected for the occasion, amid a grove of trees, surrounded by booths, shows, etc., as at
fairs.—From the review.

LEE, WILLIAM. Ancient and Modern History of Lewes, and Brighthelmston. 8vo.
Lewes.

PRICE, J. An Historical and Topographical Account of Leominster and its Vicinity. Folding and other plates. 8vo. Ludlow.

PYE, C. Plan of Birmingham. 4to.

RICHARDSON, T. Map of the Town of Glasgow and Country Seven Miles round,
from Actual Survey. 24½ × 31½ ins. Edinburgh.

Sarum. An Authentic Account of Old and New Sarum, the Cathedral and other
Public Buildings. 8vo. Salisbury.

THROSBY, J. For an account of Nottingham, see his *History and Antiquities of the
Town and County of Nottingham*, under HISTORY AND ANTIQUITIES.

WALLACE, J. A General and Descriptive History of Antient and Present State of
the Town of Liverpool . . . its Government, Police, Antiquities, and modern
Improvements . . . its extensive African Trade. Map. Liverpool.

2nd edit., Liverpool, 1797.
Regarded as a valuable account. Its findings were based on original manuscripts,
records, and other warranted authority.

1796 BREWSTER, REV. JOHN. The Parochial History and Antiquities of Stockton-upon-
Tees; including an Account of the Trade of the Town, the Navigation of the
River, and of such Parts of the Neighbourhood as have been connected with
that Place. Illustrations and map. Stockton.

Noticed *Gent. Mag.*, vol. 66, 1034. The author has adopted the form of familiar letters
as a variation on the usual way of writing local history. It is said to be a very painstaking
and loyal work. Joseph Ritson, the critic and scholar, contributed from his stores of local
knowledge on the town of his youth. Stockton was virtually a seaport and sent out many
enterprising sailors and adventurers.

CARNEGIE, MRS. (of Pitterrow). Dunnotar Castle, by the Rev. James Walker. In
Aberdeen Mag. for 1796; also printed separately, 12mo. Aberdeen.

CUMBERLAND, GEORGE. An Attempt to describe Hafod and Neighboring Scenes
about the Bridge over the Funack, commonly called the Devil's Bridge, in
Cardigan, an Ancient Seat belonging to Th. Johnes. Folding map. 8vo. London.

A Description of Alnwick Castle, and Warkworth Hermitage, Northumberland.
24mo. Alnwick.

Another edit., 12mo, Alnwick, 1800.

GOUGH, RICHARD. An Account of Lord Montagu's House at Cowdry. 5 plates and 13 pp. of descriptive text. From *Vet. Mon.*

GREEN, VALENTINE. The History and Antiquities of the City and Suburbs of Worcester. Portrait, plan and plates. 2 vols. 4to. London.

> Reviewed *Gent. Mag.*, vol. 67, 138-39. In 1764 Green put out a juvenile performance called A Survey of the City of Worcester, etc., compiled during his residence there; he did the plates and a clergyman friend the history, with equal modesty and skill. Green well deserved for his ability in plates the rank of mezzotinto engraver to his Majesty, and of associate member of the Royal Academy. But in this work, for which he wrote the text, he was not so fortunate, for the narrative is not equal to the plates.—From the review. Green engraved about 400 plates during his career of upwards of forty years. All show great mastery of his art and originality of style.—*DNB*. See Green under 1764 above.

H., D. Pennant's and Jackson's Accounts of Lichfield. In *Gent. Mag.*, vol. 66, 293-97.

> This article finds many inaccuracies in Jackson (see under 1795 above).

The History and Antiquities of Milton Abbas (from Hutchins' *History of Dorset*). View, portrait, and plates. Fol. London. (See Hutchins under 1774, HISTORY AND ANTIQUITIES.)

HUTCHINSON, WILLIAM. The History and Antiquities of the City of Carlisle and its Vicinity. Plan and plates. 4to. Carlisle.

JACKSON, JOHN. Historical Description of the Castle and Priory of Tutbury with an Account of the Borough and Abbey of Burton-upon-Trent (in Staffordshire). 8vo. London.

KING, EDWARD, F.R.S., F.S.A. Vestiges of Oxford Castle; or, A Small Fragment of a Work, intended to be published speedily, on the History of Antient Castles, and on the Progress of Architecture. Fol. London.

> Reviewed *Gent Mag.*, vol. 66, 759. The part on architecture was done by Harris, and is commended for its skill as is also the account by King, in that it gives an accurate story of the castle.

MAJENDIE, —. An Account of Hedingham Castle. Plates. Fol. London (?).

PRICE, JOHN. An Historical Account of the City of Hereford, with some Remarks on the River Wye, and the Natural and Artificial Beauties contiguous to its Banks from Brobery to Wilton. 7 plates of views, plans, etc. 8vo. Hereford.

> Price was the author of a Ludlow Guide and a Worcester Guide. The present work is of a kind with his *Topographical Description of Leominster*, though the subject is more copious. He intended it to be a general history of the county, but laid that project aside to see whether this one met with encouragement. The design deserves to be carried out.— *Gent. Mag.*, vol. 67, 951.

1796-1838 LYSONS, REV. DANIEL. An Historical Account of the Towns, Villages and Hamlets in the County of Kent within Twelve Miles of London. 4to. London.

1797 A Brief History of Birmingham. 8vo. Birmingham.

DENHOLM, J. The History of the City of Glasgow and Suburbs; containing an Account of its Origin and Antiquity, its Ecclesiastical History . . . its Civil History, and Present State; the Situation and Description of it and of the Neighbouring Villages, etc. Illus. 12mo. Glasgow.

Numerous later editions. See below.

1798 DENHOLM, J. The History of Glasgow . . . with a Sketch of a Tour to Loch Lomond and the Falls of Clyde. 13 engravings. 8vo. Glasgow.

A Description of Greenwich Hospital (bound up with Moss's *Liverpool Guide* and other items). See Moss under this date, AIDS TO TRAVELERS.

A Description of Nuneham Courtenay, in the County of Oxford. 12mo. Oxford.

GROSE, FRANCIS. The History of Dover Castle. Copperplates. London.

HEATH, CHARLES. Historical and Descriptive Accounts of the Ancient and Present State of Ragland Castle. 8vo. London.

A History of Leeds. Compiled from various Authors. To which is added, A History of Kirkstall Abbey. 8vo. Leeds.

HORNE, J. A History or Description, General and Circumstantial, of Burghley House, the Seat of the Right Hon. the Earl of Essex. 8vo. Shrewsbury.

IRONSIDE, EDWARD. The History and Antiquities of Twickenham; being the First Part of Parochial Collections for the County of Middlesex. 4to. London.

Reviewed *Gent. Mag.,* vol. 67, 1033. The work of which this is a part is a resumption by John Nichols of the plan of the *Bibliotheca Topographica Britannica,* begun in 1780, taken up again in 1791; Nichols is now engaged in printing a series of parochial collections for the county of Middlesex. Lysons had limited his region to within a certain number of miles around London, and had omitted Twickenham (see Lysons, *The Environs of London,* under 1792-96, LONDON). Three of the eight plates are concerned with Pope's house and grotto.—From the review.

A New Description of Blenheim. (Place?)

POCOCK, R. The History of the Incorporated Towns and Parishes of Gravesend and Milton, in the County of Kent selected with Accuracy from Topographical Writers, and enriched from MSS. hitherto unnoticed, recording every Event that has occurred in the aforesaid Towns and Parishes, from the Norman Conquest to the Present Time. Printed by R. Pocock. 4 plates. 4to. Gravesend.

Brief notice in *Gent. Mag.,* vol. 68, 966.

Ross, A. An Account of the Antiquity of the City of Aberdeen, with the Price of Grain and Cattle from 1435 to 1591. (Taken from *Memorialls of the Royal Burghs,* and from Orem's *Chanonry in Old Aberdeen*). 8vo. Edinburgh.

A View of the Village of Hampton, from Noulsey Hurst. With an original "Lancashire Collier Girl." (Place?)

Noticed in *Gent. Mag.,* vol. 67, 419, where the author is discovered to be an old correspondent to the *Magazine,* who signs himself "The Rambler." Here he commemorates Garrick's numerous benefices to the poor of Hampton and the affection in which he was held by the villagers.

WILSON, THOMAS. An Accurate Description of Bromley. 12mo. London.

1798 ELLIS, HENRY. The History and Antiquities of the Parish of Saint Leonard, Shoreditch, and Norton Folgate. 8 plates. 4to. London. Also listed under 1799, LONDON, with note.

HAWES, ROBERT. The History of Framlingham, in the County of Suffolk; including brief Notices of the Masters and Fellows of Pembroke Hall in Cambridge, from the Foundation to the Present Time; begun by Robert Hawes, Gent. Steward to the Manors of Framlingham and Saxted; with considerable Additions and Notes by Robert Loder. 10 copperplates. 4to. London.

HINDERWELL, T. The History and Antiquities of Scarborough and the Vicinity. Folding plans and 14 plates. 4to. York.

M'ARTHUR, JOSEPH D. The Ruins of Linlithgow, with selected Notes in Vindication of the Character of Mary Queen of Scots. 8vo. Glasgow.

MILNER, JOHN. The History, Civil and Ecclesiastical, and Survey of the Antiquities of Winchester. Engravings. 2 vols. 4to. Winchester.

ROOKE, HAYMAN. A Description of the Great Oak in Salcey Forest, in the County of Northampton. 2 views. 8vo. Nottingham.

TICKELL, JOHN. History of the Town and County of Kingston upon Hull, from its Foundation in the Reign of Edward the First to the Present Time. Plan of town and engraved views of public buildings and antiquities. 4to. Hull.

1799 A Brief Account of Stratford upon Avon; with a Particular Description and Survey of the Collegiate Church, the Mausoleum of Shakespeare, containing all the Armorial Bearings and Monumental Inscriptions there. To which is added, by way of Appendix, Some Account of the Lives of the Three eminent Prelates who derive their Surnames from Stratford, the Place of their Nativity. 12mo. Stratford.

Reviewed *Gent. Mag.,* vol. 69, 960. This is called a useful pocket companion to travelers visiting the place.

FULLER, JOHN, M.D. The History of Berwick upon Tweed, including a Short Account of the Villages of Tweedmouth and Spittal. Plan and engravings. 8vo. Edinburgh.

HASTED, EDWARD. The History of the Antient and Metropolitical City of Canterbury, Civil and Ecclesiastical; of the Cathedral and Priory of Christ Church,

and of the Bishopric . . . collected from Public Records and other good Authorities. Maps, charts, and engravings. Fol. Canterbury.

> See Hasted, *History and Topographical Survey of Kent,* under 1778-99, HISTORY AND ANTIQUITIES.

Old Edinburgh and Modern Edinburgh; a .Historical Sketch of the Ancient Metropolis of Scotland. 12mo. Edinburgh.

ROOKE, HAYMAN. A Sketch of the Ancient and Present State of Sherwood Forest, in the County of Nottingham. 4 plates. 8vo. Nottingham.

1800   An Account of Certain Antiquities and other Curiosities in Saint Edmundsbury, from an Ancient MS. found in the Ruins of the Cloacinium of the Abbey. 4to. Bury St. Edmund's. (11 pp.)

The Ancient and Modern History of Portsmouth, Portsea, Gosport, and their Environs. 12mo. Gosport.

BARTELL, EDMUND. Observations upon the Town of Cromer, considered as a Watering Place. 8vo. Holt.

BISSETT, J. A. A Poetic Survey round Birmingham, with a Brief Description of the different Curiosities and Manufactures of the Place; accompanied by a Magnificent Directory, containing the Names of upwards of 300 Professional Gentlemen, Merchants, Bankers, Tradesmen, Manufacturers, etc. Plan and 27 engraved plates emblematic of the different trades, etc. 8vo. Birmingham.

BOTT, W. Description of Buxton. 8vo. Manchester.

CAPPE, C. An Account of Two Charity Schools for the Education of Girls; and of a Female Friendly Society in York. 8vo. York.

A Descripiton of Hagley, Envil, and the Leasowes. Wherein all the Latin Inscriptions are Translated, and every Particular Beauty described. 12mo. Birmingham.

A Description of the House and Gardens at Stourhead, Wilts, the Seat of Sir R. C. Hoare, Bart. 12mo. Salisbury.

HEDINGER, J. M. A Short Description of Castleton in Derbyshire, its Natural Curiosities and Mineral Productions. 8vo. Derby.

The History of the Antient Town of Cirencester, Pt. I., Antient State; Pt. II., Modern and Present State. 2nd edit. Plan and plates. 8vo. London.

Letters on Malvern, Descriptive and Historical: containing an Account of its Waters and Accomodations, etc. 12mo. Worcester.

Memorandum of Kingswood, in the County of Wilts. In *Gent. Mag.,* vol. 70, 36-39. London.

MOUNTAIN, JAMES. The History of Selby, Ancient and Modern; folding plan and view of the Church; History of Cawood, its Castle and Church. 2 vols. 12mo. York.

A New History of the City of Edinburgh from the Earliest Periods to the Present Time, with a Description of all the Principal Public Buildings. Illustrations. 8vo. Edinburgh. (This is listed as the 4th edit. See Arnot under 1779 above.)

A Sketch of the Town and Trade of Liverpool. 12mo. Liverpool.

1809 TAYLOR, JOHN (of York)? Chorographia: or, A Survey of Newcastle-upon-Tine. 1649. In *Harl. Misc.,* vol. III, 267-84. 4to. London.

1817 KIRKWOOD, R. (Publisher). Plan of the City and Suburb of Edinburgh, from the Earliest Period to the Present Time. Fol. Edinburgh.

1834 Sum Notabill Thinges, Excerptit frome the Auld Recordes of the Honorabill Citie of Aberdeene, 1565-1635. With Notes. Edinburgh.

1836 BUCHANAN, DAVID. Urbis Edinburgi Descriptio per Davidem Buchananum (*ca.* 1648). In *Bann Misc.,* vol. II, no. xvi, *Publ. Bann. Club.* Edinburgh.

Again in Hume Brown, *Scotland before 1700,* 313 ff., Edinburgh, 1893. See below.

> 1893 BUCHANAN, DAVID. A Description of Edinburgh (1647-52). Edinburgh.
> This Latin description was written to accompany a plan of the city prepared by the Rev. James Gordon of Rothiemay, but remained in MS till it was published by the Bannatyne Club, 1836, though part of it had been translated for Chambers' *Reekiana.* According to Chambers, it must have been written between 1647 and 1652. Buchanan was born about 1595, resided some years in France, and returned to Scotland before 1644 engaging himself in literary work until his death in 1653. He was the editor of John Knox's *History of the Reformation,* but in that capacity he did himself some damage by his handling of the original text. He points out the narrowness of the streets, the crowding of people into the houses, which makes the city small in area, though extremely populous. He also calls attention to the great length of time the kings of Scotland have used the city as a royal seat.—From Brown.

A Survey of the Castle and Town of Edinburgh, January, 1573.—Journal of the Siege of the Castle of Edinburgh, April and May, 1573. In *Bann. Misc.,* vol. II, no. 19a of *Publ. Bann. Club.* 4to. Edinburgh.

> The survey was done by Rowland Johnson before the English made their attack upon the Castle, and no doubt involved personal inspection. It was accompanied by a Platte (map), which was probably copied in Holinshed's *Chronicle* (1577). It gives a bird's-eye view of the town and castle of Edinburgh at the time of the siege. The journal is probably the work of Thomas Churchyard, the poet, who was present at the time. This journal is reprinted in the *Book of the Old Edinburgh Club,* vol. XVI. 1928. See Black, *A List of Works on Scotland.* See also Churchyard under 1817, EXPEDITIONS.

1839 HOLLINGWORTH, RICHARD. Mancuniensis, or, An History of the Towne of Manchester, and what is most interesting concerning it. 8vo. Manchester.

> Hollingsworth, who died in 1656, left behind this unfinished manuscript.

1843 Register of Vestments, Jewels, and Books for the Choir, etc., belonging to the College of St. Salvator in the University of St. Andrews (*circa* A.D. MCCCCL). In *Misc. of the Maitland Club,* vol. 3, no. xi. Edinburgh.

1844 Documents relative to the Palace of Linlithgow, 1540-1648. In *Misc. of the Spottiswoode Soc.,* vol. 1, no. xix of No. 3. Edinburgh.

1845-50 GASTRELL, REV. FRANCIS, D.D. (Bishop of Chester). Notitia Cestriensis, or Historical Notices of the Diocese of Chester. Now just printed from the original Manuscript, with illustrative and explanatory Notes. By the Rev. F. R. Raines, M.S., F.S.A., and Rural Dean of Rochdale. *Publ. Chetham Soc.,* vols. 8, 19, 21, and 22. Manchester.

1846 MOUNSEY, GEORGE GILL. Carlisle in 1745. Authentic Account of the Occupation of Carlisle in 1745, by Prince Charles Edward Stuart. Edit. by George Gill Mounsey, from the Narrative of Rev. John Waugh and others. Plan and 5 plates. 8vo. London.

A Relation of a short Survey of the Cities, Castles and chief Scytuations in the Northerne Counties of England . . . begun at the Citie of Norwich, August 11th, 1634. (Place?)

1853 BROOKE, RICHARD. Liverpool as it was during the last Quarter of the Eighteenth Century, 1775-1800. 6 plates and 3 woodcuts. 8vo. Liverpool.

1854-56 MANSHIP, HENRY. The History of Great Yarmouth (completed in 1619), edit. by Charles J. Palmer, together with Palmer's Continuation of the History. 2 vols. 4to. Great Yarmouth.

1866-67 Collectanea relating to Manchester and its Neighbourhood, at various Periods, edit. by John Harland. 2 vols. *Publ. Chetham Soc.,* vols. 68 and 72. Manchester.

1870 M'URE (alias CAMPBELL), —. Glasgow Facies: a View of the City of Glasgow: or, Origin, Rise and Progress. Glasgow, *ca.* 1736. Edit. by J. F. S. Gordon. Illustrations. 2 vols. 8vo. Glasgow.

> Scarce reprint, with additions, of this compilation of "every observation from ancient records, vouchers, private MSS, etc."—Bookseller's Note.

1874 BRIERLEY, SAMUEL. Rochdale in 1745 and 1746. By an Old Inhabitant (Samuel Brierley). 8vo. Rochdale.

> This is an interesting episode in the history of Rochdale.—Fishwick, *op. cit.*

1885 FAWKES, FRANCIS, A.M. A Description of May. From Gawin Douglas, Bishop of Dunkeld. In *Publ. Aungervyle Soc.,* vol. 23, 3rd ser. Edinburgh.

1888 HOGG, JANE D. Glimpses of Old Stirling from the Town Council Records. *Publ. Stirling Nat. Hist. and Arch. Soc.,* vol. 10. 8vo. Stirling.

1891 Charters and Documents illustrating the History of the Cathedral City and Diocese of Salisbury in the Twelfth and Thirteenth Centuries. Edit. by Rev. W. Rich-Jones and Rev. W. D. Macray. Salisbury (?).

1893 LATIMER, JOHN. The Annals of Bristol in the Eighteenth Century. Privately printed.

1899 MOORE, SIR EDWARD. Liverpool in King Charles II. Time, written in the Year 1667-68, edit. by W. F. Irvine. Plates and maps. 4to. London.

1908 PEET, HENRY (Editor). Liverpool in the Reign of Queen Anne, 1705 and 1708, from a Rate Assessment Book of the Town and Parish, with an Appendix containing Inscriptions from the Monuments and Windows of the Parish Churches, and Abstracts of several Wills, transcribed and edited by Henry Peet. 2 folding maps and 2 plates. 8vo. Liverpool.

1919 The Early Views and Maps of Edinburgh, 1554-1852, published by the Committee to form a National Collection. 11 maps and 21 illustrations. 8vo. Edinburgh.

1929-31 Leicestershire Medieval Village Notes, with Introduction by A. H. Thompson. 5 vols. Privately printed.

VI
London

(The growth of London from settlements of huts grouped together on the north and south sides of the Thames to its present amorphous state, described by Frederick Harrison as "the most organic mass of habitations that ever cumbered the planet," has no lack of qualified historians, many of whom are listed in the section GENERAL REFERENCE. What is attempted here is to relate its history, map its expansion, and delineate its character by passing in chronological review its celebrants with their titles, like banners, telling us of its institutions, ceremonial life, pageants, pleasures, buildings, wealth, commerce, turbulence, rogues, the misery of its poor, its inhumanity toward unprotected and unwanted children, and its awakening conscience. From them we can read also of the loyalty and enthusiasm of the Londoner for his city, his jealousy of its liberties confirmed by charter after charter, his independence of pressure from the crown, the church and judiciary, and his strong corporate sense of belonging to a living entity which derived its strength from a long continuity. What London was like in British, Roman, and Saxon times no contemporary voice was raised to tell us. It was omitted from the Domesday survey, probably because the information being sought was not there forthcoming. In Plantagenet times, 1183 to be exact, we meet with the first direct description of London, the *Libellum de situ et nobilitate Londini* of William FitzStephen, a highly colored panegyric, which first saw print in the 1603 edition of Stow's *Survey of London*. Facts and personages begin to emerge with increasing clearness and interest in the city chronicles of the 15th and 16th centuries. By the close of this period there burst forth full blown, as if by magic conjured, a description of London which for enthusiasm, research, and completeness has never been surpassed—the *Survey of London* by John Stow (1598). In the 17th century we should choose for our informants and companions those delightful diarists Evelyn and Pepys, who casually and intimately would lead us into the heart of Cavalier London. London of the Age of Reason grows more complex and calls for a larger variety of guides. For cultural interests one could employ Addison and Steele, for peeps into its murky depths Tom Brown and Ned Ward, and for its trade and commerce Daniel Defoe. For the mid-century who would serve better than Boswell, and for the close the purposeful traveler Pennant?

In addition to these accounts and surveys by the native born, the narratives of foreign visitors, who naturally made for London first and stayed there at greater length, necessarily complete this outline history, in that they bring to light features and facts regarded by the home folk as too ordinary and commonplace to mention.)

1502 ARNOLD, RICHARD. Arnold's London Chronicle (so-called) contains a list of mayors and sheriffs, with brief historical notes, 1189-1502, and a collection of charters, municipal regulations, and other documents relating chiefly to London in the 14th and 15th centuries, together with much miscellaneous information, such as the necessary ingredients for brewing beer and instructions for planting and grafting fruit trees. See this Chronicle under HISTORY AND CHRONICLE.

1516 FABYAN, ROBERT. For valuable material on London, see his Cronycle, under HISTORY AND CHRONICLE.

1545 LELAND, JOHN. Leland's Cygnea Cantio, or, A Voyage of a principal Swan and six others on the Thames from Oxford to Greenwich, describing poetically the several Places they pass by, which are further illustrated by the Author's Commentary at the end in Alphabetical Order by their Antient Names, was first printed in the Author's Life. 4to. London.

Reprinted, by the care of Selden, or Lamphire, Camden's professor at Oxford, London, 1658; again by Hearne in *Leland's Itinerary,* vol. IX, Oxford, 1745.—Gough, *Anecdotes of Brit. Topog.,* 349.

1550   WYNGAERDE, VAN DEN. View of London.

> This panorama view map is usually attributed to Wyngaerde; the date is generally set at 1550, though it may be as early as 1543 or 1544. It was published in facsimile by the London Topographical Society, with notes by H. B. Wheatley, 1881-82. For a type classification of London maps from Wyngaerde to the Great Fire, see William Martin, "The Early Maps of London," *Trans. London and Middlesex Arch. Soc.*, vols. 3-4, 1917-18. The above map is Class I. This article makes the reader acquainted with the extent and variety of London maps, their value as faithful records of topography, buildings, streets, etc., the changes of London in its growth and the changes in style of mapping.—These early city maps are, strictly speaking, hardly maps at all; rather they are panoramas or bird's-eye plans, which have the advantage of showing architectural details. Such city plans were the last to be freed from the illustrator, navigator, and theologian, and to pass from the realm of the cartographer's art to that of the photographer.—From Jervis, *The World in Maps.* For a short list of early London maps, see Brett-James, *The Growth of Stuart London,* App. I. See also G. E. Mitton, *Maps of Old London.*

1553   The Ordre of the Hospital of St. Bartholomewes, in W. Smythefielde, in London, erected for the Benefit of the Sore, and the Diseased: and Revenue of 100 Marks; and that the Citizens should add hundred Marks by the Year; which they received with Thanks. 12mo. London.

1558   The Passage of Our Most Drad Soverigne Lady Quene Elyzabeth through the Citie of London to Westminster, the Daye before her Coronation. Anno 1558. 4to. London.

> This gives a full description of the decorations and five pageants of welcome on the occasion of the Queen's entry into London for her coronation.—Maggs, no. 550. The early pageants in London were exhibited when the Black Prince made his entry with his royal prisoners, 1357. Another was presented when his son Richard II passed along Cheapside, 1392. A third when Henry V made his entry, 1415, after the Battle of Agincourt. A fourth when Henry VIII received the emperor Charles V, 1522. A fifth when Henry VIII and Anne Boleyn passed through the city to her coronation, 1532. In the days of Elizabeth and James I, London was to feast its eyes many times on pageants and processions, as these Majesties indulged to the full their passion for such spectacles.

1563   The Burnyinge of Paule's Church in the Yeare 1561, the 4th and 5th day of June, by Lightenynge, at 3 of the Clock Afternoon; which continued terrible and helpless until night. 12mo. London.

> Visitation by fire seems to have been in the cards for St. Paul's.—The sexton, before he died, confessed that this accident was not caused by lightning. Bagford mentions additions to this book, with an Apology for the Cause of the burning of St. Paul's church, with a confirmation for the same, 1563.—Gough, 307.

1572   BRAUN, G., and F. HOGENBERG. Map of London, in their Atlas *Civitates Orbis Terrarum.* 6 vols. Fol. Cologne.

> This is less of a perspective drawing and more of a map and therefore more accurate than others of its kind. It is still laid down on the bird's-eye view plan. It was probably drawn between 1554 and 1558, certainly not later than 1561.—Brett-James, *op. cit.* It is probably the basis of the map by Agas. Other authorities place it as likely of a little later date. See Agas under 1592 below. These view plans differ from descriptions in that they show the existing state of affairs, such as palaces, Temple Gardens, the bull baiting rings, playhouses, the outlying suburbs, wharves, the rectangular bend of the river at Lambeth, the playgrounds of London, and the marshlands. In volume II of the *Civitates,* is shown a similar plan of Cambridge, with colleges and sights inscribed, a fine view of Windsor, etc.; another volume adds Canterbury, etc., and a valuable illustration of the far-famed Nonesuch Palace.—Clare Williams, *Thomas Platter in England.*

1585   BRAUN, G. Plan of London. 16 × 21 ins.

> This shows London on both sides of the Thames, with a group of figures in contemporary costume in the foreground. The date is tentative.

1592 AGAS, RALPH (or RADULPHUS). Civitas Londinum. Plan of London and Westminster.

> According to Gough, *op. cit.,* 354, this was republished in 1618, with the arms of James I
> (England, France, and Scotland) substituted for those of Elizabeth; this plan, which
> measured 6 feet 3 ins. by 2 feet 4 ins. on 6 sheets and 2 one-half sheets, was re-engraved by
> Vertue (see his *Memoirs*) in 1737; another reproduction 40½ ins. ✕ 15 ins., London, *ca.*
> 1780; accurately reproduced by W. H. Overall, London, 1874. See below.
> The original probably dates from 1560 or 1561. The earliest known copies belong to the
> time of James I.—From Brett-James.—The "Agas" group dates earlier than 1561. This
> bird's-eye view map is attributed by Vertue to Agas, who died 1621. It shows old St. Paul's
> with its spire; so possibly it was executed before the destruction of the spire in 1561. Agas
> had probably nothing to do with the map. It and the Hogenberg view may be descended
> from the same original, or it may be a degraded edition of the Braun Atlas map.—Martin,
> "The Early Maps of London." This plan shows the extent of London and Westminster
> as it was near the beginning of Elizabeth's reign. It abounds in fascinating details, such as
> men and horses in the water filling casks, pens for bull and bear baiting, pleasure grounds,
> and the archery grounds at Spitalfields. According to Gough, Agas says in his *Oxonia
> Antiqua,* published 1578, that near ten years past he was in doubt whether to print or lay
> this work aside until he first had London platted out.—*Op. cit.,* 354-55.

> 1874 AGAS, RALPH. Civitas Londinum. A Survey of the Cities of London and West-
> minster, the Borough of Southwark and Parts adjacent, in the Reign of Queen
> Elizabeth. Published in Facsimile from the Original in the Guildhall Library.
> With a Biographical Account of Ralph Agas and a Critical and Historical Exam-
> ination of the Several so-called Reproductions by Vertue and others, by W. H.
> Overall. The Facsimile by E. J. Francis. The Map 70 ✕ 30 ins. folded to 4to.
> London.

1593 NORDEN, JOHN. Speculi Britanniae Pars. The firste Parte. An Historicall and
Chorographical Description of Middlesex. 4to. London.

> This contains two well-known maps of London and Westminster, 8 ✕ 6 ins. and 6 ✕ 9½
> ins. respectively. These have the legend Johannes Norden Anglus descripsit, anno 1593,
> and Pieter Vanden Keere fecit 1593. They give a clear indication of the extent of London
> and Westminster.—From Brett-James, *op. cit.* The date of this map makes it the most
> satisfactory one for illustrating Shakespeare's London. Its peculiar value lies in the large
> number of references to names of familiar places. This map was frequently reproduced,
> sometimes with the title, *A Guide for Countrymen in the famous Cittey of London,* etc.,
> under the dates 1613, 1653, etc. See H. B. Wheatley, "Notes on Norden and his Map of
> London," in *London Topographical Record,* vol. II, 1903. The map has the arms of the
> twelve companies of London at the sides. It extends from St. Catherines east to Leicester
> House west, which was without Temple Bar, and contains a description of all the out-
> lets or ways into the fields. In the hands of Peter Stent there were added the names of
> churches, streets, lanes, etc., with letters and figures for reference, which were inserted
> in the last edition of the book, 1723, and were copied into the map of Middlesex, 1611, by
> Speed. Norden published another view of London in eight sheets, having at bottom a rep-
> resentation of the lord mayor's show, all on horseback and the aldermen in round caps.—
> From Gough, 355-56. In design Norden's map is a bird's-eye view, but it approaches
> more nearly to a true plan than do those of his predecessors. The same views of London and
> Westminster were published by Speed in his *Theatrum* (see under 1610, MAPS AND CHARTS).

1598 STOW, JOHN. A Survay of London. Contayning the Originall, Antiquity, Increase, Moderne Estate, and Description of that Citie, written in the Yeare
1598. 4to. London.

> 2nd edit., enlarged, London, 1599; another, sometimes called the 2nd, the fullest and
> most authoritative edition, 1603; continued and augmented by Anthony Munday, 1618;
> this enlarged by Henry Dyson, fol., London, 1633; again enlarged, corrected, and brought
> down to date, by John Strype, 2 vols., fol., London, 1720 (known as Strype's edition);
> a version issued by Robert Seymour (pseud. John Mottley), 2 vols., fol.; 1733 and 1754;
> reprint of 1603 edit., by W. J. Thomas, London, 1842; this again, 8vo, 1876; a reprint of
> the 1598 edit., by H. Morley, 8vo, 1890; a new critical edit. of the 1603 publication, by
> C. L. Kingsford, 2 vols., Oxford, 1908; edit. by H. B. Wheatley, Everyman's Library,
> London, 1912. See below.
> From its first issue in 1598 this survey has taken rank as the first authority on the
> history of London, but this very fame has been the cause of some injury to the unity of

the work, owing to the additions of successive editors, whose own words have often been quoted as if they had been written by Stow himself, although often referring to events that happened long after Stow's death.—From Wheatley's Introduction. As Thomas Hearne remarked of Strype's edition, "Stow should have been simply reprinted as a venerable original, and the additions given a different character." Not until 1842 was the original 1603 edition reprinted in its integrity. Stow tells us that the idea of his survey was suggested by Lambard's *Perambulation of Kent* (see under 1576, DESCRIPTIONS). He was the first to attempt a regular and particular description of London, in preparation for which he spent eight years. But he had begun his delvings into antiquities with his *Annals* about 1560, which led to his many journeys over the kingdom, mostly on foot, perusing and buying innumerable early books, parchments, charters, and manuscripts; transcribing in full or making extracts from the mass of stuff that was being dispersed after the dissolution of the monasteries. When his benefactor Archbishop Parker died, he became exceedingly reduced in circumstances and had to face the spectre of indigence the rest of his days. The only relief afforded him was the license granted him by James I to receive at church doors good-will offerings from the well disposed. He died in 1605, as Gough says, of poverty, the gout, and the stone. For his *Survay of London* he made a careful perambulation of the city, exploring the wards, the gates, the suburbs, taking notes of everything of historical, topographical, and antiquarian value. With a passion for factual accuracy, he reproduced with loving fidelity the London he knew as it lived its life in the time of Shakespeare and Ben Jonson. See the Address by Charles W. F. Goss, F.S.A., in the *Trans. London and Middlesex Society,* vol. 7, which was delivered at the John Stow Commemoration.

1603 STOW, JOHN. A Survey of London. . . . Also an Apologie i.e., Defense against the Opinion of some Men, concerning that Citie, the Greatnesse thereof. 4to. London.

1633 ———. The Survey of London: contayning the Originall, Increase, Moderne Estate, and Government, inlarged by the care and Diligence of A[nthony] M[unday], in 1618, and now completely finished by the Study and Labour of A. M., H[enry] D[yson], and others, with Additions and diverse alphabeticall Tables. Numerous coats of arms. Fol. London.

1720 ———. A Survey of the Cities of London and Westminster, written at first in 1598, by John Stow, now corrected and very much enlarged, and the Survey and History brought down to the present Time, by John Strype, with a Life of the Author and a Perambulation to the Parish Churches. 2 vols. Fol. London.

1754 ———. A Survey of the Cities of London and Westminster, and the Borough of Southwark. Containing the Original, Antiquity, Increase, Present State and Government of those Cities, written at first in the Year 1598, corrected and enlarged in 1720 by John Strype, with exact Maps of the City and Suburbs, Wards, Out-Parishes of London and Westminster, and the Country ten miles round; Parish Churches, Monuments of the Dead, . . . with Appendix of certain Tracts, Discourses, & Remarks on the State of the City of London, and a Large Index of the Whole Work. 6th edit. Large folding plan of the county and borough, and 131 engravings by Kip and others. 2 vols. Fol. London.

1908 ———. Survey of London, etc. Edit. from the 1603 edition by C. L. Kingsford. 2 vols. Oxford.

This is the standard edition of Stow's work. It contains valuable bibliographical material in the Introduction.

1600 Londinum: vulgo London (Plan).

Reprinted 1635 as A Plan of London, Westminster and Southwark.

1603 FITZSTEPHEN, WILLIAM. Libellum de situ et nobilitate Londini. Printed (in English) in the Appendix to Stow's *Survey of London,* 1603 edition. London.

Gough says that the English version was printed in the folio editions of Stow and the original Latin in the 4to editions. Republished, with observations and notes at the end of Leland's *Itinerary,* vol. VIII, from a more correct MS given by Dr. Marshall to Hearne (Hearne published the *Itinerary* in 9 vols., Oxford, 1710): the English version in the *Annual Register,* vol. 7, 179-83; newly translated, 4to, London, 1772. See below.

The Latin title given by Gough (*op. cit.,* 281) runs Descriptio nobilissimae civitatis Londiniae. The author was a native of London and a monk of Canterbury. He died 1191. The

account praises London for its reputation abroad, its rich fields and pastures, its schools which were kept at the three principal churches, St. Paul's, the Holy Trinity, and St. Martin's.

> 1772 FITZ-STEPHEN, WILLIAM. Descriptions of the City of London, newly translated from the Latin Original, with a necessary Commentary. A Dissertation on the Author, ascertaining the Exact Year of its Production, is prefixed; and to the whole is subjoined, A Correct Edition of the Original, with the various Readings, and some useful Annotations. By an Antiquary. 4to. London.
>
>   This learned Antiquary was the venerable Dr. Samuel Pegge.—Nichols, *Anecdotes,* vol. III.

1604 DEKKER, THOMAS. The whole Magnificent Entertainment given to King James, Queen Anne his wife, and Henry Frederick the Prince, upon the Day of his Majesties Triumphant Passage (from the Tower) through his Honorable Citie (and Chamber) of London, the 15 of March 1603, as well by the English as by Strangers, with the Speeches and Songs delivered in the several Pageants; and those Speeches that were before published in Latin, now newly set forth in English, by Tho. Dekker. 4to. London.

1604 HARRISON, STEPHEN. The Archs Of Triumph Erected in honer of the High and mighty prince Iames the first of that name King of England and the sixt of Scotland at his Maiesties Entrance and passage through his Honorable Citty & chamber of London vpon the 15th day of march 1603. Invented and published by Stephen Harrison . . . and graven by William Kip. Engraved plates. Fol. London.

> The text is frequently missing in copies of this work. The plates comprise some of the finest specimens of engraving which had appeared in England up to that time, and are besides of extreme interest to the collector of works on ornament.—Quaritch.

1606 ROBERTS, HENRY. The Most royall and honourable Entertainment, of the famous and renowned King, Christiern the fourth, King of Denmarke . . . With a relation of his Meeting, by our royall King . . . the Pleasures sundry times shewed, for his gracious Welcome and most famous and admirable Entertainment at Theobalds, VVith the royall passage . . . thorough the Citty of London . . . . 4to. London.

> Extremely rare. It was reprinted in vol. II of Nichols' *Progresses of James I,* and in vol. IX of the *Harleian Miscellany.* The author, who was attached to the court of James I, was an eyewitness of the festivities, which he here describes in great detail.—Bookseller's Note.

1608 The Great Frost. Cold Doings in London, except it be at the Lottery: with Newes out of the Country. A familiar Talk between a Countryman and a Citizen, touching this terrible Frost, and the great Lottery, and the effect of them. The Description of the Thames frozen over. 4to. London.

> In front is a wooden print of the citizens at their sport on the frozen river; the prizes in this lottery were all of plate; the highest 150 pounds and the tickets one shilling apiece. —Gough, 349.

1609 DEKKER, THOMAS. The Gull's Horn Book. 4to. London.

> No other edition appeared in Dekker's lifetime. Reprinted, London, 1674; reissued and brought up to date by Samuel Vincent, London, 1676; edited by R. B. McKerrow, King's Classics, London, 1905.
>
>   Dekker began his satires on contemporary life in 1606 with his *Seven Deadly Sins of London* and *The Bellman of London.* Other familiar exposures of rogues and vagabonds

are Greene's *Coney-Catching* and Harman's *Caveat for Cursitors*. The *Horn Book* was based on Dedikind's *Grobianus* (*ca.* 1525-28), a poem in Latin elegiac verse which became very popular on the Continent but remained less known in England.—McKerrow, Introduction. By bringing an unlicked countryman to town and exhorting him to do as the city gallants did, Dekker ridicules the vices of London life.

1610 SPEED, JOHN. The Theatre of the Empire of Great Britain. Fol. London. (See under MAPS AND CHARTS.)

His map of Great Britain carries as an inset on ornamental plates a bird's-eye view of London and Southwark from the Surrey side. The original of this inset, which presents distinctive characteristics, is unknown. It shows on Bankside, Southwark, a cylindrical-like structure beflagged with a basal enlargement and near it a polygonal tower-like building, also beflagged. These may represent the Bear Garden, also maybe the Globe Playhouse. This type of map was little used in the 17th century. It does reappear, however, in that of Samuel Tolle, printed 1667, where it is apparently intended to show the fire of London.—From Martin, "The Early Maps of London."

1611 MUNDAY, ANTHONY. Chryso Triumphans; the Triumph of Gold at the Inauguration of Sir James Pemberton to the Dignity of Lord Mayor of London, Fryday 29 Oct. 1611, at the charge of the Worshipfull and Antient Company of Goldsmiths, divised and written by A. Munday. London.

Cited by Gough, who gives quite a list of the successive pageants for lord mayors at the charges of various gilds.—*Op. cit.,* 339 ff.

PEACHAM, HENRY. Among the poems prefixed to *Coryat's Crudities,* is one by Peacham describing the sights and exhibitions in London. It is also to be found in Rye, *England as Seen by Foreigners,* 139-40. It lists in a facetious manner the improbabilities in the way of wonders and marvels.

See Peacham under 1642 below.

1614 The Charter-House; with the last Will and Testament of Thomas Sutton, Esq.; taken out of the Prerogative-Court, according to the true Original. 4to. London.

Reprinted, with another title, 4to, London, 1646; again in *Domus Carthusiana,* 1677. See below.

1646 Sutton's Hospital; with the Names of sixteen Mannors, many thousand Acres of Land, Meadows, Pastures, and Woods; with the Rents and Hereditaments thereunto belonging; the Governors thereof, and Number of Scholars, and others, that are maintained therewith: as also the last Will and Testament of Thomas Sutton, Esq. London.
These two pieces are included also in the following work:

1677 Domus Carthusiana: or, An Account of the most Noble Foundation of the Charter-House, near Smithfield, in London, both before and since the Reformation; with the Life and Death of Thomas Sutton, Esq.; the Founder thereof, and his last Will and Testament. To which are added, Several Prayers, etc. By Samuel Herne, Fellow of Clare-Hall, in Cambridge. 8vo. (Place?)

H[OLLAND], H[UGH]. Monumenta Sepulchraria Sancti Pauli: the Monuments, Inscriptions, and Epitaphs of Kings, Nobles, Bishops, and others, buried in the Cathedral Church of St. Paul, London, until the Present Yeere of Grace 1614. Together with the Foundation of the Church; and a Catalogue of all the Bishops of London, from the Beginning to the Present. Never before, now with authoritie, published. By H. H. 4to. London.

2nd edit., London, 1634, where is added a catalogue of all the archbishops, also of the deans of the same church, and the monuments continued until that year, a copy of the Pope's pardon to Sir Gervais Braybrook 1390; together with a preface touching the decays, and for the repairing of this famous church.—Gough, 305-06.

1616 VISSCHER, NICOLAUS JOHN. View of London.

> A facsimile reproduction of this map was issued in 4 sheets by the Topographical Society of London, 1886. An account of it was also printed in vol. VI of the publications of this same Society.
>
> The original is in the King's Library, Brit. Mus. It measures 7 feet 1 in. by 1 foot 4½ ins. All copies or issues are referable to this one known edition, which was evidently the first. At the base of this picturesque and well designed panorama is engraved a Latin description of London, which is taken, with some variations, from Camden's *Britannia*. This is far more of a picture than a map. It gives a clear detail of churches and houses of the city as they existed towards the closing years of Shakespeare's life. See Martin, "Early Maps of London."

1617 JOHNSON, RICHARD. The Pleasant Walks of Moorfields, the Gift of two Sisters, now beautified, to the continued Fame of this worthy City. Compiled by Richard Johnson, and dedicated to the Right Worshipfull the Knights and Aldermen of the honourable City of London. A Dialogue between a Gentleman and a Citizen. (Bagford.)

> Stow mentions a map or plan of Moorfields as intended to be laid out by one Leate, a citizen, which he was to have inserted in his book.—Gough, 344.

1618 EICHORN, JOANNES. Mausolea Regum, Reginarum, Dynastarum, Nobilium sumptuosissima, artificiosissima, magnificentissima, Londini Anglorum, in occidentali urbis angulo structa, h.e. eorundem inscriptiones omnes in lucem reductae cura Valentis Arithmaei professoris academici. Literis & sumptibus Joannis Eichorn. Francos. Marchion. 12mo. (Place?)

1623 NORDEN, JOHN. A Guide to Countrey-men in the famous City of London, by the help of which Plot they may be able to know how far it is to any Street, as also how to go to the same without further Trouble. London.

> This is an adaptation of Norden's Map of 1593, engraved by Peter Keer, described by Bagford.—From Taylor, *Late Tudor and Early Stuart Geography*, Bibliog.

1624 GUNTER, EDMUND. The Description and Use of his Majesty's Dial in Whitehall-Garden. 4to. London.

> Gunter's dials were placed on a stone block about four feet and a half square; arranged five on the upper part, viz., one at each corner, and the great horizontal concave one in the middle, and four more on the four sides. He made them by order of Charles I, when Prince of Wales, and wrote this account at the King's command. The stone was but lately removed; but the dials had mostly been defaced by the drunken frolics of a nobleman in Charles II's time.—Gough, 275-76.

Monuments of Honour derived frcm Antiquitie and celebrated in the honourable Citie of London. 4to. London.

1631 Coach and Car Sedan disputing for Place and Precedence, the Brewer's Cart being the Moderator. (Cited by Brett-James.)

1632 LUPTON, DONALD. London and the Countrey Carbonadoed, and Quartered into seuerall Characters. London.

> Reprinted in *Publ. Aungervyle Soc.*, vol. 10, 2nd ser., Edinburgh, 1883.

1636 TAYLOR, JOHN. J. Taylor, the Water Poet's Travels through London, to visit all the Taverns in the City and Suburbs, alphabetically disposed, with the Names of all the Vintners at that time. 8vo. London.

16— Ames, Richard. This author made a perambulation through London, after the manner of John Taylor above, in a search for claret. It was printed in two parts for H. Newman, 4to, London. (Cited by Gough, 344.)

1636 Wenceslaus, Clement. Venceslai Clementis a Libeo-montis Trinobantiados Augustae, sive Londini civitatis libri vi. quibus urbis nobilissimae antiquitas, ortus, progressus, gloriae famaeque incrementa, tanquam in sciographia luculenter exprimuntur, praetori, regi, senatui populoque. 1636, 1673. 4to. London (?).

> The date is expressed in this quaint legend: Ne CoLLVCtentVr TrInobantIaDopoLItanI IntestabILIbus soLLIcItVDInIbus.—Gough, 347.

1637 Lithgow, William. The Present Surveigh of London . . . with the several Fortifications thereof. 4to. London.

> This pamphlet was reprinted, London, 1643. See below.

> 1643 Lithgow, William. The Present Surveigh of London and England's State. Containing a topographical Description of all the particular Forts, Redoubts . . . on both sides of the River, etc. 4to. London.

Taylor, John. The Carriers Cosmographie. Or A Briefe Relation of the Innes, Ordinaries, Hostelries, and other lodgings in, and neere London, where the Carriers, Waggons, Footeposts and Higglers, doe usually come, from any parts, townes, shires and countries, of the Kingdomes of England . . . Wales . . . Scotland, and Ireland. As also, Where the Ships, Hoighs, Barkes, Tiltboats, Barges and Wherries, do usually attend to Carry Passengers, and Goods to the coast Townes of England. 4to. London. (12 leaves.)

> Reprinted as no. 11 of "Mr. Ashbee's Occasional Reprints," London, 1869.
> This is a good directory for the traveler, with the names of inns, days of setting out and returning, etc.

1638 Merion, M. Map of London.

> This map first appeared in the 3rd edition of Gottfried's *Neuwe Archontologia Cosmica,* 1638, in which the maps were executed by Merion. The map is sometimes called Hollar's map, presumably by reason of an edition which was engraved by him. Howell, in his *Londonopolis* (see under 1657 below), reproduced this map as a frontispiece. At its base is a reference key which sets out the names of 43 important places. Maps of this group are recognized by the delineation of Bankside, Southwark, of three polygonal towers in proximity and of a similar one to the west, in Privy Garden.—From Martin, *op. cit.*

Taylor, John. Taylors Travels and Perambvlations, through, and by more than thirty times twelve Signes of the Zodiack, of the Famous Cities of London and Westminster . . . with an Alphabeticall Description, of all the Tavern Signes in the Cities, Suburbs, and Liberties aforesaid and significant Epigrams upon the said severall Signes. London. (31 leaves.)

> Evidently the names of inns ran in favorites, for certain ones are often repeated in various parts of the city.

1639 Heywood, Thomas. Londini Status Pacatus; or, London's Peaceable Estate Exprest in sundry Triumphs, Pageants, and Shewes, at the Initiation of . . . H. Garway into the Mayoralty of . . . London. 4to. London.

1640   The Cittie of London: the Country-man's or Strangers ready Helpe. Map. London.

1642   CALTHORPE, SIR HENRY. The Liberties, Usages, and Customes of the City of London; confirmed by speciall Acts of Parliament, with the time of their Confirmation. 4to. London.

> Reprinted, 4to, London, 1674; also printed in *Somers' Collection of Tracts*. It is a sort of alphabetical index to the *Liber Albus.*—Lowndes. It deals with "Bakers and Millers," "Custome Paid," "Hunting," "Liberties and Franchises," "Markets," "Tower of London," "Wines and Victuals," etc.—Maggs, no. 670.

P[EACHAM], H. The Art of Living in London: or, A Caution how Gentlemen, Countreymen and Strangers, drawn by Occasion of Businesse, should dispose of Themselves in the thriftiest Way: not only in the Citie, but in all other populous Places. As also, a Direction to the poorer Sort, that come thither to seeke their Fortunes. London.

> Reprinted in *Harl. Misc.,* 1808-13; also in the selections edited by Henry Savage, London, 1924.
> This contains advice of the expected kind—what dangers to avoid and what temptations to beware of. It offers as a universal rule of conduct, "To serve God, avoid idleness, to keep your money, and to beware of ill company."

1642-43   EYRE, CAPT. JOHN. Views of the Fortifications round London. 22 etched views of the new walls, bastions, etc., including a general plan and a large panoramic prospect from the north, also etched portrait by himself and letter press sheet (with arms) on the Eyre family; five similar plates at the end. Fol. London.

> The author, a captain of Cromwell's regiment, was killed at Marston Moor. He was a friend of the artist Hollar, who "was pleased with my poor work in drawing." The impressions are to be dated about 1850. It contains some additional plates.—Bookseller's Note.

1643   LITHGOW, WILLIAM. The present Surveigh of London and Englands State: Containing a topographical Description of all the . . . Forts . . . and Trenches round about the Citie, . . . London.

1647   HOLLAR, WENCELAUS. The Hollar group of views and plans of London date from 1647. A great number of engravings bear Hollar's name. Many of his views are more closely allied to pictures than to maps.—From Martin, *op. cit.*

1648   B., C. Sion College, what it is and doth; together with a Vindication of that Society from the slanderous Defamation of the two fell and fiery Satyrs, the one called, Sion College Visited, the other, The Pulpit Incendiary. Also a little Tast by the way, of a little Thing of Mr. Goodwin's running about with the Shell on the Head before it is all hatcht, under the Name of the Youngling Elder. By C. B. who accounts it an honor to be a member of Sion College. 4to. London.

> This book gives an account of the foundation and use of this college, intended for the London divines.—Gough, 329.

1651   Ancient Customs of Stebbunheath and Hackney. London. (So cited by Brett-James.)

1657 HOWELL, JAMES. Londinopolis: An Historical Discourse or Perlustration of the City of London, The Imperial Chamber, and chief Emporium of Great Britain: Whereunto is added another of the City of Westminster, with the Courts of Justice, Antiquities, and new Buildings thereunto belonging. Full length portrait of the author and folding plate of London by Hollar. Fol. London.

The folding plate is rarely found in copies of this work. It shows the city before the Great Fire, with the old playhouses and theatres, old St. Paul's, London Bridge with the houses on it, etc.—Bookseller's Note. The work is chiefly interesting as a panegyric, the historical part being borrowed from Stow's *Survey*.—Davies, *Bibliog. Brit. Hist., Stuart Period.*

1658 DUGDALE, SIR WILLIAM. The History of St. Paul's Cathedrall in London, from its Foundation. Fol. London.

For a fuller account of this work, see under ECCLESIASTICAL HISTORY AND ANTIQUITIES.

NEWCOURT, RICHARD. An Exact Delineation of the Cities of London and Westminster and the Suburbs, together with the Borough of Southwark, and all the Thorough-Fares, Highways, Streets, Lanes, and Common Alleys within the same: composed with a Scale, and ichnographically described by Richard Newcourt, in the County of Somerset, Gent.; with a Genealogy from Brute, A Chronology, with the Arms of London, the several Churches within the Walls, St. Paul's and Westminster Abbey; also six Windmills (for so many there were at that time) in 8 sheets, engraven by Wm. Faithorne. London.

1659 JOHNSON, M. Ludgate what it is, not what it was; or, A Full and Clear Discovery and Description of the Nature and Quality, Orders and Government, Duties of Officers, Benefits and Privileges, Fees and Charges, of that Prison; also an Exact Catalogue of the several Donors, and the Persons appointed to pay them; very useful and profitable to all sorts of Persons, especially in London, whether Creditors or Debtors. Humbly presented to the Rt. Hon. Thomas Allen, Lord Mayor of this honourable City, by M. Johnson, typograph, a late prisoner there. 24mo. London.

Bagford dates this 1657.—Gough, 335.

1660 PORTER, T. View of London and Westminster, including Southwark and Lambeth.

The title of this view is somewhat misleading, for his map is seen to be based on an earlier issue, of which it is but a variant. The map is of a composite character, with the marginal portions apparently an afterthought. Suggestions of its dependence on the Ryther map are apparent. The buildings depicted are drawn in a highly conventionalized fashion. Editions of this group of maps as issued in the 18th century incorporate outlying areas that were absent from earlier printings.—Martin, *op. cit.*

1661 EVELYN, JOHN. Fumifugium: or, The Inconveniency of the Air and Smoke of London, dissipated; together with some Remedies, humbly proposed; to his sacred Majesty, and to the Parliament now assembled. Published by his Majesty's Command. 4to. London.

2nd edit., 4to, London, 1772.
Stow records in his *Annals* that Edward I, upon the complaint of the nobility and gentry that they could not go to London on account of the noisome smell and thick air, issued a proclamation forbidding the use of sea coal in the suburbs, on the pain of a fine

and the loss of their furnace.—Quoted by Gough, 297, note. This work gives a curious account of the "hellish and dismal cloude of sea-coale" which makes London unhealthy, and suggests the expulsion of noxious trades and the planting of flowers in the suburbs.—Bookseller's Note.

GRAUNT, JOHN. Natural and Political Observations, mentioned in the following Index, and made upon the Bills of Mortality, with reference to the Government, Religion, Trade, Growth, Ayre, Diseases, and the several Changes of the said City. Folding sheets of tables, including "Table of Casualties re Plague," Wolf, Excessive Drinking, Murdered, Starved, Teeth, Stitch Worms, Lunatique, King's Evil, Cut of the Stone, Burials in Westminster, Islington, Lambeth, Stepney, Burials and Christenings in London. 4to. London.

> 2nd edit., 4to, London, 1662 (admits authorship); 3rd, much enlarged, 8vo, 1665; two other edits. followed, 5th, 1676.
> In the second edition the author styles himself citizen of London; in the third, Captain John Graunt, F.R.S. This edition was published by order of the Royal Society; the fifth published after his death by Sir Wm. Petty, who referred to it as his own, and was followed in this by Burnet (*History of his Own Times*). Burnet's charge that Graunt was a papist and that he stopped the New River at the Fire of London has been repudiated in the *Biographia Britannica.*—From Gough, 293. The work contains particulars of burials and christenings, and totals of deaths by plague in the time of Shakespeare.—Bookseller's Note.

OGILBY, JOHN. The Relation of His Majesties Entertainment passing through the City of London to His Coronation. With a Description of the Triumphall Arches, and Solemnity. 4to. London. (See next item.)

> Reprinted, Edinburgh (date?).
> John Ogilby (1600-1676) laid the foundation to his fortunes by putting his savings into the lottery for the advancement of Virginia. At the Restoration he made himself acceptable to Charles II and his Court, and was appointed by the commissioners for the coronation of Charles II to prepare the "poetical part" of the ceremony. He drew up first a relation of it and a description of the arches, designed by Sir Balthazer Gerbier, in ten sheets, enlarged afterwards as above by the king's command.—Gough, 343. This is the earlier of the two publications upon the subject. The device which he exhibited over the triumphal arch in Leadhall Street was much applauded, and is referred to by Dryden.—Robinson, no. 73.

1662 OGILBY, JOHN. The Entertainment of His most Excellent Majestie Charles II in his Passage through the City of London to His Coronation: containing an exact Account of the whole Solemnity; the Triumphal Arches, and Cavalcade, delineated in Sculpture; the Speeches and Impresses illustrated from Antiquity. To these is added, a Brief Narrative of His Majestie's Solemn Coronation: with His Magnificent Proceeding, and Royal Feast in Westminster-Hall. Frontispiece of the Royal Arms and 7 folding plates of the Royal Procession, the Coronation, etc., by Hollar, plates of the 4 Triumphal Arches by Loggan, a folding plate of Roman trophies, vignettes of medals, etc. Fol. London.

TATHAM, J., Gent. The Entertainment of the King and Queen by the City of London on the Thames, exprest and set forth in several Shews and Pageants, the 3rd of April. London.

1664 HOLLAR, WENCELAUS. South Prospect of London, in 6 sheets, and etched by Robert Precke [or Pricke].

> There is nothing extant that so exactly shews the buildings of old London before the fire.—Gough, 358. No engravings of London in the time of Charles II are so precious as

those of this Bohemian artist, especially the later ones dating from the fire. In 1665 he engraved a small view of London from over the water, chiefly below and as far as St. Paul's, and two views of London by Islington; the next year, 1666, he made a map or ground-plot of the city and suburbs within the jurisdiction of the lord mayor; shewing the present condition since the last sad accident of fire, the blank space indicating the burnt area, and where the houses are expressed yet standing: with a general map or ground-plot of the whole city of London and Westminster, and all the suburbs (in a little compartment below) by which may be computed the proportion of what is burnt with what yet stands, in a small sheet. Also a true and exact Prospect of the city from over a steeple in Southwark, in its flourishing condition before the fire, in a view about ¾ yard long, and underneath another prospect of the city, taken from the same place as it appeared after the calamity and destruction by fire in 1666.—From Gough, 358-59. See Hollar under 1675 below.

SORBIERE, SAMUEL DE. For a description of London, see his *Voyage en Angleterre*, under TOURS BY FOREIGNERS.

1665   London's Lords Have Mercy upon us. A True Relation of Seven Modern Plagues. or Visitations in London, with the Number of those that were buried of all Diseases: viz. the 1st in the Year of Queen Elizabeth An. 1592: the 2nd in the Year 1603: the 3rd in (that never to be forgotten year) 1625: the 4th in An. 1630: the 5th in the Year 1636: the 6th in the Years 1637 and 1638: the 7th this Present Year 1665. London.

   Reprinted in *Somers' Tracts*, 2nd coll., vol. III, 53.—Gough, 298.

1666   KNIGHT, —. A New Model for Rebuilding the City of London with Houses, Streets, and Wharfs, to be forthwith set forth by his Majesty's and City's Surveyors, with the Advantages that will accrue by building the same accordingly. London.

   This project was designed by one Knight, who was committed to prison by order of Parliament. Sir John Evelyn presented to the king a week after the fire two plans, with a discourse now in the paper-office: the plans were engraved by the Antiquarian Society in 1748: one of them contains only 25 churches, reserved on their old foundations, with all the principal streets almost in the same part they formerly were, and spaces for the rest of the houses, lanes and alleys of note, according to the dimensions thus expressed; though by reason of the narrowness of the plan, the measures are not exact.—Gough, 303. The magnificent plan laid out by Wren later was unfortunately for the city not carried out.

1667   LEAKE, JOHN. An Exact Surveigh of the Streets, Lanes, and Churches contained within the Ruines of the City of London, first described in six Plates by John Leake, John Jennings, William Marr, William Leybourn, Thomas Streete, Richard Shortgrave, in December Anno 1666, by Order of the Lord Mayor, Aldermen, and Common Council of the City, reduced here into one intire Plat by John Leake, the City Wall being added, as also the Places where the Halls stood are expressed by the Coats of Arms, and all the Wards divided by Jonas Moor and Ralph Graterix, Surveyors. W. Hollar sec. Published, with a description of the Wards, by the care, industry, and charge of N. Brooke, Stationer. In 2 sheets; at top a view of the fire from Southwark. London.

   Republished by Vertue, with views of old buildings, fol., London, 1727.

ROLLES, —. A Relation of the late dreadful Fire in London, as it was reported to the Committee in Parliament. 8vo. London.

SINCERA, REGE. Observations both Historical and Moral on the Burning of London, September 1666, with an Account of the Losses: and a most Remarkable Parallel between London and Moscow, both as to the Plague and Fire. Also an Essay touching the easterly Wind. Written by way of Narrative, for Satisfaction of the Present and Future Ages. 8vo. London.

> Reprinted in *Harl. Misc.,* vol. III, 282, 1744.
> The booksellers had put their wares in a subterranean church under St. Paul's, which was so strongly propped up that it was thought the fire could never harm it. But the flames licked in by way of the windows, and sucked the moisture out of the mortar that bound the stones together, with the result that it was calcined into sand. When the top of the cathedral fell upon it, it was beaten flat, and everything was set on fire. It was estimated that the loss of books in Stationers' Hall, in the above vault, public libraries, and private houses, could amount to no less than 150,000 pounds. 12,000 houses were thought to be burnt, about 100,000 boats and barges, 1,000 cartloads of goods, besides the churches and public buildings, but few persons.—From Sincera, quoted by Gough, 300, note.

A True and Faithful Account of the several Informations exhibited to the Honourable Committee appointed by the Parliament to enquire into the late dreadfull Burning of London, together with other Informations touching the Insolency of the Popish Priests and Jesuits, and the Increase of Popery, brought to the Honourable Committee appointed by the Parliament for that Purpose. London.

> Reprinted in *Somers' Tracts,* vol. XIV.
> The moralists and Puritans found this occasion a field day for exercising their ingenuity in discovering the causes of the fire. God's wrath against the wickedness of the times and popery rank high in the list. The number of accounts reporting the disaster, both in prose and verse, would make a respectable bibliography in itself. For poems dealing with the fire see Robt. A. Aubin, *London in Flames, London in Glory,* New Brunswick, 1943.

1668 FISHER, PAYNE. A Catalogue of the most Memorable Tombs, Grave-Stones, Plates, Escutcheons or Atchievements in the Demolisht or yet extant Churches in London, from St. Katherine's beyond the Tower to Temple-Bar, the outparishes being included. 4to. London.

> Another edit., 4to, London, 1670.
> Wood says this was compiled mostly from Stow by Payne Fisher, the Toldervey of the last century, and is a confused piece, mentioning neither the dates of the epitaphs, nor the churches where they stood.—Gough, 303-04.

PRIMATT, S. The City and Countrey Purchaser and Builder. Shewing Value of any ground lying in the Ruines of the City of London; Exact Computation of the charge of Building in any plan thereof; Platforms for all sorts of Edifices; Inspections into Materials, and all Artificers incident thereunto; Rules to determine all Differences between Landlord and Tenant; Whereunto is added, The Art of Surveying; Value of all lands in England, all Mines, Leases, etc.; Easie method to measure any Superficies, and Solids. 8vo. London.

1672 Great Britain's Glory; or, A Brief Description of the Splendor and Magnificence of the Royal Exchange: with some remarkable Passages relating to the Present Engagement. Humbly presented to the several Merchants of the City of London, who daily meet to traffick and converse in the said place. 4to. London. (In verse—Lowndes.)

Proposals modestly offered for the full Peopling and Inhabiting the City of London; and to restore the same to her ancient flourishing Trade; which will suit with her Splendid Structure. 4to. London.

1673   Remarques on the Humours and Conversations of the Town. Written in a Letter to Sr. T. L. 12mo. London.

1675   HOLLAR, WENCELAUS. A New Map or Ground-Plot of the Cities of London and Westminster and the Borough of Southwark, with the Suburbs; shewing the Streets, Lanes, Alleys, Courts, with the other Remarks, as they are now truly and carefully delineated; the Prospect of London, as it was flourishing before the Destruction by Fire. London.

> Hollar, born in Prague in 1607, was taken into the service of the Earl of Arundel, and went to England in 1637. From the very first he was fascinated with the architectural, topographical, and scenic characteristics of the city and its suburbs, as well as with the river and the views from it. It was the spirited view rather than the mood of the scene, the deliberate study of fact and its plain statement in picturesque terms that he aimed to reproduce. The Great Fire offered him ample opportunities which he fully exercised by sketching among the ruins. Through him we can see what a vast area was laid low by the flames. Despite his talents, his life was one of vicissitudes. He died in 1677. See Hind, *Wencelaus Hollar*, under GENERAL REFERENCE.

1676   BRYDALL, J. Camera Regis; or, A Short View of London, containing the Antiquity, Fame, Walls, Bridge, River, Gates, Tower, Cathedral, Officers, Courts, Customs, Franchises, etc. 8vo. London.

> Another edit., 8vo, London, 1678.
> This makes copious references to Coke, whose Fourth Institute has an important section on the subject, and to other legal writers, statutes, and law reports.—Davies, *op. cit.* The author, a law-writer, was secretary to the Master of the Rolls.—*DNB*.

A New Map of the City of London, as it is newly built; very plainly shewing the Streets, Lanes, Alleys, Courts, Churches, Halls, and other remarkable Places; together with the Situation of their Houses, their Yards, Gardens, and Back-Sides. Published by J. C., in one sheet of large paper . . . with Descriptions. London. (See Ogilby under 1677 below.)

1677   ADAMS, JOHN. The Renowned City of London; surveyed and illustrated in a Latine Poem, translated into English by W. F., of Gray's Inn. 4to. London.

A Collection of the Names of the Merchants living in and about the City of London . . . directing . . . to the Place of their Abode. (Hereunto is added an Addition of all the Goldsmiths that keep running Cashes.) 12mo. London. (Referred to later as The Little London Directory.)

> Reprinted, 8vo, London, 1863; again, 12mo, London, 1878. See below.

> 1863   The Little London Directory of 1677. The Oldest Printed List of the Merchants and Bankers of London, reprinted from the Exceedingly Rare Original. With an Introduction by J. C. Hotten. 8vo. London.

HERNE, SAMUEL (of Clare Hall, Cambridge). Domus Carthusiana: or, An Account of the most noble Foundation of the Charter-House near Smithfield, in London. Both before and since the Reformation, with the Life and Death of Thomas Sutton, the Founder. Engraved frontispiece. 8vo. London.

OGILBY, JOHN, and WILLIAM MORGAN. London surveyed, with an Explanation of the same; giving a particular Account of the Streets, and Lanes in the City and Liberty, with the Courts, Yards, Alleys, Churches, Halls and Houses of Note in every Street and Lane, and Directions to find them in the Map, with the Names and Marks of the Wards, Parishes, and Precincts therein described; with a Map of London, Westminster, and Southwark, at one mile in an inch. Etched by Hollar. London.

WALLIS, RICHARD. London's Armory accurately delineated in a Graphical Display of all the Arms, Crests, Supporters, Mantles & Mottos of every distinct Company and Corporate Societie in the Honourable City of London. Royal coat of arms, Arms of the city of London, 25 plates of Arms, and the Arms of the Artillery Company; 5 ll. of text. Fol. London. (Printed for the author.)

1681   BURTON, RICHARD (or ROBERT). Historical Remarques and Observations of the Ancient and Present State of London and Westminster. Engraved copperplates of the most considerable matters, with the arms of 66 Companies of London and the time of their incorporating. 12mo. London.

> 2nd edit., 8vo, London, 1683; 3rd, enlarged, 12mo, London, 1684; other edits., 12mo, 1703; 4to, 1710; 12mo, 1730. See below.
> Richard or Robert Burton was the pseudonym of Nathaniel Crouch, a miscellaneous writer. See Burton, *Admirable Curiosities,* under 1682, DESCRIPTIONS.

> > 1684   BURTON, RICHARD. Historical Remarques . . . of London and Westminster, shewing the Foundation, Walls, Gates, Towers, etc., with an Account of the Most remarkable Accidents as to Wars, Fires, Plagues, and other Occurrences till 1681. 3rd edit., enlarged. 12mo. London.

DE LAUNE, T. The Present State of London, or, Memorials comprehending a full and succinct Account of the Antient and Modern State thereof. 12 plates and several illustrations of coats of arms. 12mo. London.

> 2nd edit., entitled, Angliae Metropolis, "continued to this year by a careful hand," 12mo, London, 1690.
> The views of the gates and principal buildings omitted in the second edition.—Gough, 286. The work is mainly descriptive, with a good deal of miscellaneous information; e.g., pp. 345-59 deal with the Post Office and the Penny Post.—Davies, *Bibliog. Brit. History.*
> The work cost the author his ears in the pillory.

1682   GOUGH, WILLIAM. Londinum Triumphans, or, An Historical Account of the Grand Influences the Actions of the City of London have had upon the Affairs of the Nation for many Ages past, shewing the Antiquity, Honour, Glory and Renown of the Famous City, the Grounds of her Rights, Priviledges and Franchises, the Foundation of her Charts, etc. 8vo. London.

KEEPE, HENRY. Monumenta Westmonasteriensis; or, An Historical Account of the Original, Increase, and Present State of St. Peter's, or the Abbey Church of Westminster. With all the Epitaphs, Inscriptions, Coats of Arms, and Atchievements of Honour belonging to the Tombs and Grave-Stones; with the Monuments themselves, faithfully described and set forth. 8vo. London.

MORDEN, ROBERT, and PHILIP LEA. Plan of London, Westminster, and Southwark. On scale of 300 feet to an inch. London.

> Republished, with additions bringing it up to date, by Morden and Lea (after whom it is erroneously named), London, 1732; facsimile edit., by the London Topographical Society, 1904.
> This plan was based on a survey made by John Ogilby, who died in 1676, and William Morgan subsequent to the great fire of 1666. It was the first survey of London worked out on scientific lines and was the basis of the series of Parish and Ward plans, made by Richard Blome, some of which were first published in Strype's edition of Stow's *Survey of London,* of 1720 and 1754-55. It also shows us the London of Evelyn and Pepys and allows us to follow the footsteps of the two diarists about London, through references in their diaries to buildings shown. Up to the time of the fire, all plans of the city had been represented as bird's-eye views of prospects, which were of interest for their picturesqueness but lacking in accurate topographical detail. The fire necessitated a more scientific survey and a more correct system of delineating the streets and properties destroyed in order that the city might be properly rebuilt. Right after the fire, the Corporation appointed Ogilby and Morgan, sworn surveyors, to plot out the disputed areas. Later they surveyed the whole city and prepared a plan on the scale of 100 feet to an inch, showing every street, court, and building very accurately. This plan was published by Morgan in 1677, portions of the plate being engraved by Hollar. In 1682 Morgan published the plan set forth in the title above and on the scale mentioned.—From Spiers, "Morden and Lea's Plan of London, 1682," in the *London Topographical Record,* vol. 5, 1908.

PETTY, SIR WILLIAM. An Essay in Political Arithmetic concerning the Growth of the City of London, with the Measures, Periods, Causes, and Consequences thereof. 4to. London.

> Republished, 8vo, London, 1686.

The Privileges of the Citizens of London, contained in the Charters, granted them by the several Kings of the Realm, and confirmed by Parliaments. 4to. London.

1683 HAWORTH, SAMUEL, M.D. A Description of the Duke's (of York) Bagnio (in Long-acre), and of the Mineral Bath, and New Spaw thereunto belonging; with an Account of the Use of Sweating, Rubbing, Bathing, and the Medicinal Vertues of the Spaw. 12mo. London.

1684 An Exact and Lively Map, or Representation, of the Booths and Varieties of Shows and Humours upon the Ice on the River of Thames by London, during that Memorable Frost in the 35th Year of the Reign of his Sacred Majesty, King Charles the Second, in 1683. With an Alphabetical Explanation of the most remarkable Figures. London.

FISHER, PAYNE. The Tombs, Monuments, and Sepulchral Inscriptions, late visible in St. Paul's Cathedral and in St. Faith's under it; completely rendered in Latin and English; with several historical Discourses on sundry Persons intombed therein. A Work never yet performed by any Order, Old or New. By P. F. Student in Antiquities, Batchelor of Arts, and heretofore one of his late Majesty's Majors of Foot to the late Honourable Sir Patricius Curwen, C. Cumb. Baronet . . . and properly presented to the kind Encouragers of so worthy a Work. 4to. London.

> This is mostly stolen from Dugdale. All his connections with relatives, etc., could not keep Cromwell's laureat and historiographer out of the Fleet.—Gough, 306-07. As the inscriptions recorded were destroyed by the Great Fire, the book is of considerable archaeological interest. The funeral epitaphs include those of Sir Philip Sidney, John of Gaunt, John Donne, etc.— Robinson, no. 61.

Great Britain's Wonder; or, London's Admiration. Being a true Representation of a prodigious Frost, which began about the Beginning of December, 1683, . . . Sheet fol. London.

An Historical Account of the late Great Frost. 12mo. London.

LEYBOURNE, WILLIAM. History of Stepney. (So cited in Brett-James.)

NAIR, WILLIAM. Surveys of Stepney. (So cited in Brett-James.)

1685 JONES, DR., and JOHN CONYERS. The London Spaw, giving an Account of the Water and its Properties. Half a sheet fol. London.

A New Map of the Cities of London and Westminster, with the Borough of South- wark, and all the Suburbs; shewing the several Streets, Lanes, Alleys, Thorow- fares: being a ready Guide for all Strangers how they may find any Street without enquiring. In three large Sheets of Paper. London.

1687 PETTY, SIR WILLIAM. Observations on the Cities of London and Rome. 8vo. London. (3 leaves.)

————. Two Essays in Political Arithmetic, concerning the People, Housing, Hospitals, etc., of London and Paris, the first tending to prove that London hath more People and Housing than the Cities of Paris and Rouen put together: the 2nd tending to prove that in the Hospital called L'Hotel Dieu at Paris there die above 3000 per annum by reason of ill Accomodations. 8vo. London.

Trans. into German, Dantzig, 1687(?). See below.

1687(?) PETTY, SIR WILLIAM. Handgreiffliche Demonstration, dass die Stadt London, . . . mit ihren Vorstädten allein viel mächtiger . . . sey als die Städte Parise . . . Rouen, etc. 4to. Dantzig.

A Prospect of Bow Church and Steeple in Cheapside; whose Height is from the Ground 225 Foot. Printed on a sheet and a half of Royal Paper. London.

SANDFORD, FRANCIS. The History of the Coronation of James II . . . and of His Royal Consort Queen Mary: solemnized in the Collegiate Church of St. Peter in the City of Westminster on Thursday the 23 April. With an Exact Account of the several Preparations in Order thereunto, Their Majesties most splendid Processions and their Royal and Magnificent Feast in Westminster Hall. 30 double-page engravings depicting the Ceremonies and Processions, etc. Fol. London.

1689 STILLINGFLEET, BISHOP EDWARD. Discourse of the true Antiquity of London, and its State in Roman Times. In 2nd Part of his Ecclesiastical Cases. London.

The above data are furnished by Gough, 286. In *DNB* it is stated that this work was published after his death (1699). It "shows him also an antiquary of wide learning." Be- sides being a popular preacher, he was an ardent antiquarian, a great book collector, and owned a very large library of MSS and rare works.—*DNB*.

TAUBMAN, MATTHEW. London's Great Jubilee Restored and performed on Tuesday, October the 29th, 1689, for the Entertainment of the Right Hon. Sir Tho. Pilkington, Kt. Lord Mayor of the City of London; containing a Description of the several Pageants, and Speeches, together with a Song for the Entertainment of their Majesties, who with their Royal Highnesses the Prince and Princess of Denmark honoured his Lordship this Year with their Presence. All set forth at the proper Cost and Charge of the Right Worshipful the Company of Skinners. London.

Reprinted in *Somers' Tracts,* 2nd Coll., vol. III, 33.

1690 D'URFEY, THOMAS. Collin's Walk through London and Westminster, a Poem in Burlesque, written by T. D., Gent. 8vo. London.

HALL, THOMAS. An Account of New Inventions and Improvements now necessary in England for the Improvements of Rivers. 8vo. London.

This gives a large account of the Thames and the rivers and brooks running into it.—Gough, 350.

1691 PITT, MOSES. The Cry of the Oppressed. Being a True and Tragical Account of the Unparallel'd Sufferings of Multitudes of Poor Imprisoned Debtors, in most of the Gaols in England. Together with the Case of the Publisher. Plates. 12mo. London.

"This contains a remarkable account of the actual condition of prisoners for debt, not in London alone, but in many other towns, as Pitt conducted a large correspondence with fellow sufferers throughout the country. It is full of personal details, and is useful for the topographical history of Westminster, where Pitt built, besides other houses, one which he let to Jeffreys (the tool of James II), in what is now Delaney Street."—*DNB,* quoted by Maggs, no. 569. Pitt was arrested and confined in the Fleet after the pecuniary failure of the *English Atlas* (see under 1680-83, MAPS AND CHARTS).

1692 The Orders, Rules, and Ordinances ordained, devised, and made by the Master and Keepers or Wardens and Commonalty of the Mystery or Art of Stationers of the City of London, for the well-governing of the Society. 4to. London.

1693 COLSONI, F. For his guide to London, see his *Le guide de Londres,* under TOURS BY FOREIGNERS.

1694 MERITON, G. A Guide to the Surveyors of London. (So cited in Brett-James.)

1697 KIP, J. Prospectus interior templi Dano-Norwegici Londinensis.

Cited by Gough, who adds that Cibber built this church.—*Op. cit.,* 312.

1698-1703 WARD, EDWARD. The London Spy: The Vanities and Vices of the Town Exposed to View. (Issued in parts.) London.

Complete in 18 parts, London, 1703; edit. by Ralph Straus, London, 1924; an expurgated edit. by A. L. Hayward, London, 1927.
The above began to appear in monthly numbers in 1698. It conducts the London visitor through a variety of low-life dens and dives of the metropolis. It apparently unloosed in the decades following a host of similar excursions or "Trips" and "Tricks." A good part of its appeal lay in its vulgarity and obscenity.

1699   A Companion for Debtors and Prisoners, with a Description of Newgate, the Marshalsea, the two Counters, Ludgate, the Fleet, and King's-bench Prison. 8vo. London.

PETTY, SIR WILLIAM. Five Essays in Political Arithmetic, viz. 1. Objections from the City of Rey in Persia by the Author of the Republique des Lettres and from Mons. Auzout in his Letters from Rome against two former Essays answered; and that London hath as many People as Paris, Rome, Rouen put together. 2. A Comparison between London and Paris in Fourteen Particulars. 3. Proofs that at London within its 134 Parishes named in the Bills of Mortality there live about 696,000 People. 4. An Estimate of the People in London, Paris, Amsterdam, Venice, Rome, Dublin, Bristol, and Rouen, with several Observations upon the same. 5. Concerning Holland and the Rest of the United Provinces. In French and English. (Published with the Essays before recited and others in Political Arithmetic.) 8vo. London.

> Petty supposes that London doubles in forty and England in 360 years: that in 1682 there were about 670,000 souls in London, and in England and Wales about 7 millions 400,000 to about 28 millions of acres of profitable land: that the growth of London must be at its greatest height in 1800, and will stop before 1842, when it will be eight times more than in 1682, with above 4 millions for the service of the country and ports: that the assessment of London is about 1/11 of all England and Wales: that in 1849 there will be in London 10 millions 718,889, and in the whole kingdom only 10 millions 917,389. Then he proposes how to make London invincible, and to establish an uniformity of religion therein. He supposed in 1682 that there were upon the face of the earth 320 millions of souls, and in the next 200 years the world would be so fully peopled, that there should be one head for every two acres in the habitable part, and then the Scripture predictions of great wars and slaughters would be fulfilled.—Gough, 294-95.

S—CY, ED. The Country Gentlemen's Vade Mecum, or, His Companion to the Town, in eighteen Letters from a Gentleman in London to his Friend in the Country; wherein he passionately dissuades him against coming to London, and represents to him the Advantages of a Country Life, in Opposition to the Follies and Vices of the Town, by Ed. S—cy. 8vo. London.

> A rare and interesting book, containing chapters on the humours, customs and tricks of the play-house, tennis-courts, bowling-greens, gaming houses, lotteries, cockers, and cock-matches, etc.—Bookseller's Note.

1700   A Book of the Prospects of the remarkable Places in and about the City of London. Obl. 4to. London.

BROWN, TOM. Amusements Serious and Comical. Calculated for the Meridian of London. London.

> Edit. by A. L. Hayward, London, 1927.
> Brown, "of facetious memory," was one of the best known about-town satirists, who was continuously skirting close to the libelous and the obscene. He and Ned Ward ran a close race in turning out skits upon the town.

COX, REV. THOMAS. A Topographical, Ecclesiastical and Natural History of Middlesex, especially London; together with Pedigrees of all the Noble Families and Gentry, a Table of the Towns, Villages and Hamlets and the Value of the Churches in the King's Books. 4to. London.

1702   BOHUN, WILLIAM. Privilegia Londini: or, The Laws, Customs, and Priviledges of the City of London. Wherein are set forth all the Charters . . . Customs . . . The Nature of By-Laws . . . and how pleadable . . . Together with the Practice of all the Courts . . . . 8vo. London.

> 3rd edit., with large additions, 8vo, London, 1723; another, 12mo, London, 1765. See below.

> 1723   BOHUN, WILLIAM. Privilegia Londini, or, The Rights, Liberties, Priviledges, Laws, and Customs of the City of London; wherein are contained, 1. The several Charters granted to the said City from King William the First to the Present Time. 2. The Magistrates and Officers thereof, with their respective Creations, Elections, Rights, Duties, and Authorities. 3. The Laws and Customs of the City, as the same relate either to the Persons or Estates of the Citizens, viz. of Freemen's Wills Feme Sole, Merchants, Orphans, Apprentices, etc. 4. The Nature, Jurisdiction, Practice and Proceedings of the several Courts thereof, with Tables of Fees relating thereto. 5. The several Statutes concerning the said City and Citizens alphabetically digested. 3rd edit., with large additions. 8vo. London.

    GRIBELIN, S. (Sculp.). Ecclesiae Cathedralis Sancti Pauli, Lond. ab occidente descriptio orthographica, ex autographo architecti. S. Gribelin Sculp.

> Gribelin engraved Rafael's cartoons, portraits, and paintings.

1706   The Freemen of London's Necessary and Useful Companion: or, The Citizen's Birth-Right, with the Foreigners and Aliens Best Instructor; treating of the City's Antiquity, Grandeur, Magistracy, Customs, Priviledges, Trade, and the Advantages thereof, etc. 12mo. London.

    OVERTON, JOHN. Mapp of the City of London. Folded to 4to size. London.

17—   The New London Spy, or, A Twenty-Four Hours Ramble through the Bills of Mortality . . . Modern, High and Low Life . . . Covent Garden, Theatres, Jelly-Houses, Gaming-Houses, Night-Houses, Public Gardens, Motherly Matrons, and their Obliging Daughters, Mock-milliners, Pimps, Panders, Parasites, Decrepit Watchmen, etc. 8vo. London.

> The date of the above publication is no more definite than is here given. Evidently it was subsequent to Ward's *London Spy* and reads as if it were swimming in the wake of the latter.

1708   Les Environs de Londres, ou se trouve toutes les Villes, Villages, Maisons, Chemins, Rivieres, à vinct Milles autour de Londres. Colored engraved map, 22 × 19½ ins. Amsterdam.

> The date is approximate. The map is divided up and colored according to the boundaries of the various Liberties and Hundreds.—Maggs, no. 739.

1708   HATTON, EDWARD. A New View of London, Or, An Ample Account of that City. In Two Volumes, or Eight Sections. Being a more particular Description thereof than has hitherto been known to be published of any City in the World. I. Containing the Names of the Streets, Squares, Lanes, Markets . . . in London, Westminster, and Southwark; shewing the Derivations thereof; Quality of Buildings and Inhabitants; Dimensions, Bearing and Distance from Charing Cross, St. Paul's Cathedral, or the Tower of London. II. Of the Churches; their Names, Foundations . . . III. Of the several Companies; their Nature,

Halls, Armorial Ensigns . . . IV. Of the Nobility; Houses of Lords and Commons; Tower of London, and things Remarkable therein, . . . V. Colleges, Libraries, Museums . . . VI. The Hospitals, Prisons, Work-Houses and Charity Schools . . . VII. Of Fountains, Bridges, Conduits, Ferries, Docks . . . VIII. An Account of about Ninety publick Statues . . . To which is added, An Explanation of the Terms of Art used in this Treatise; also A Supplement. And to the Whole is prefixed, An Introduction concerning London in General . . . Illustrated with Two Plans, viz. 1. Of London, as in Queen Elizabeth's Time. 2. As it is at present. . . . A Book useful, not only for Strangers but the Inhabitants, and for Lovers of Antiquity, History, Poesy, Statuary, Painting, Sculpture, Mathematicks, Architecture, and Heraldry. 2 vols. 8vo. London.

> The complete title of this work as given in Arber, *Term Catalogues,* vol. III, 591, would seem to be well nigh equivalent to the text.—Very erroneous in monumental inscriptions, many of which are abridged and many omitted. Gough takes this to be the book mentioned by Bagford (Letter to Hearne) as a "modern treatise set forth by a gentleman of the Fire-office, wherein he gives an account of churches new built, with all the terms of architecture, in two volumes, 8vo, the map of which is taken from Braun and Hogenbergius, which is copied from the first wooden one done in Holland: there are neither alterations nor additions in it, but if compared together it will be found to be only contracted into a sheet: the plate was bought in Holland by Mr. Lee and used in the above work."—Gough, 284.

1708-10 NEWCOURT, RICHARD. Repertorium Ecclesiasticum Parochiale Londinense: Ecclesiastical Parochial History of the Diocese of London, with an Account of all the Bishops, Deans, Archdeacons, Dignitaries, and Prebendaries from the Conquest, and of the several Parish Churches, of their Patrons and Incumbents, and also the Endowments of several Vicarages, and likewise of the several Religious Houses, continued to 1700 in Alphabetical Order. Portraits and plates by Sturt, and map. 2 vols. Fol. London.

> "Invaluable."—*DNB.* London Diocese included all Middlesex and Essex, with parts of Hertfordshire and Buckinghamshire, and the Bishop drove about the more social portions of it in a coach and four.—Bookseller's Note. The author was a notary public, one of the four procurators-general of the Arches-court of Canterbury.—Gough, 304.

1709 WARD, EDWARD. The History of the London Clubs, or, The Citizen's Pastime, particularly the Lying Club, the Yorkshire Club, the Thieves Club, the Beggar's Club, the Basket Women's Club. London.

1710 DE SOULIGNE, ——. Old Rome and London Compared; the First in its full Glory, and the Last in its Present State; by which it plainly appears, that Lipsius and Vossius are egregiously mistaken, in their overstretched, fulsom, and hyperbolical Account of Old Rome; and that London, as it is at present, exceeds it much, in its Extent, Populousness, and many other Advantages. To which is added, A Comparison between the Beauties, etc. of Old Rome and London. By a Person of Quality [De Souligne, grandson to Mr. Du Plessis Mornay]. 8vo. London.

> Gough says that the addition was first published in 1706.—*Op. cit.,* 295.

KIP, JOHANNES. A Prospect of London and Westminster. 12 sheets.

> Reissued, 1726.
> Kip was a Dutch engraver who moved to London shortly after 1686. His work is of great antiquarian value though not so marked with artistic merit. See Kip, *Britannia Illustrata,* under 1708, VIEWS.

NICHOLLS, SUTTON. Charterhouse Square. Bird's-eye view, showing the Square, with its diagonal avenue of trees in foreground, houses surrounding it, with Bow Church on the left, St. Paul's Cathedral on the right. Line engraving by and after Sutton Nicholls. 12¾ × 18 ins.

————. Fishmonger's Hall. Front elevation, with costume figures. Line engraving by Sutton Nicholls. 12¾ × 17¼ ins.

A List of the Stage Coaches and Carriers, and the Places and Times they come in and go out. 12mo. London.

WOODWARD, JOHN, M.D. Account of some Roman Urns, and other Antiquities, lately digged up near Bishopsgate; with Reflections upon the Antient and Present State of London, in a Letter to Sir Christopher Wren. (Published by Hearne at the end of vol. VIII of Leland's *Itinerary*.)

> Reprinted, with a letter from the author to the editor, 8vo, London, 1713; and in *Somers' Tracts*, vol. IV, 15, 1723.
> Woodward printed this at the desire of Wren, whose observations have since appeared in the *Parentalia*. Wren could not be persuaded that the temple of Diana stood on the site of St. Paul's, though Woodward had prepared a dissertation on her image dug up near that cathedral, and an account of the Roman antiquities in his collection, found in several parts of England, but chiefly about London; but these were never published.—Gough, 315.

1711 TEMPEST, P. The Cryes of the City of London drawne after the Life. Engraved on 74 copperplates after M. Laroon. 4to. London.

> Many of the prints illustrate Granger and Noble's *History of England.*—Bookseller's Note.

17— The Midnight Rambler, or, Nocturnal Spy . . . Modern Transactions of London and Westminster, from 9 p.m. to 6 a.m., Midnight Scenes and Adventures in real Life, serious and comic, from the Dutchess to the Oyster Woman, Votaries of Bacchus and Venus, Bucks, Bloods, Filles de Joye, Round-House Keepers, etc. 8vo. London.

1713 CRULL, JOHN. The Antiquities . . . of Westminster. With a Supplement by Charles Taylor, Gent. 8vo. London.

> This "New Edition," as it was optimistically called, was being advertised as "The Second Edition" in 1715; A so-called second edition of this is announced in the *Post Boy* "to the Death of Queene Anne." The price remains the same, but there may have been a further or revised supplement; 3rd edit., 2 vols., 8vo, 1721 (dated 1722).—Straus, Handlist (*The Unspeakable Curll*).

For "Curiosities in Nature and Art" in London, see *British Curiosities in Nature and Art*, under NATURAL HISTORY.

1714 BARLOW, DR. THOMAS. The Case concerning the Setting up of Images or Paintings of them in Churches, written by Dr. Thomas Barlow, late Bishop of Lincoln, upon his Suffering such Images to be defaced in his Diocese, wherein 'tis disapproved and condemned by the Statutes and ecclesiastical Laws of this

Kingdom, and the Book of Homilies. Published upon Occasion of a Painting set up in Whitechapel Church. 8vo. London.

> First printed in Barlow's *Cases of Conscience*, 8vo, London, 1692.—Quoted.

FITZ-STEPHEN, WILLIAM. Description of the City of London, newly translated from the Latin Original. 4to. London. (See Fitzstephen, under 1603 above.)

The History of the Vestry of St. Dunstan's in the West. 8vo. London.

PATERSON, JAMES. Pietas Londinensis: or, The Present Ecclesiastical State of London; containing an Account of all the Churches, and Chapels of Ease, in and about the Cities of London and Westminster; of the set Times of their publick Prayers, Sacraments, and Sermons, both Ordinary and Extraordinary, with the Names of the Present Dignitaries, Ministers, and Lecturers; with Historical Observations of their Foundation, Situations, Antient and Present Structure, Dedication, and several other Things worthy of Remark. To which is added, A Postscript, recommending the Duty of Publick Prayer. 8vo. London.

> This gives interesting details of the rebuilding of Churches after the Great Fire.— Maggs, no. 610.

WARD, EDWARD. The Field-Spy or the Walking Observer. London.

1715 Antiquities of St. Peter's, or, the Abbey-Church of Westminster. Plates, including Shadwell's, Killigrew's, Isaac Casaubon's, and Drayton's monuments. 8vo. London.

> A Supplement was published with date of 1713 given in bookseller's catalogue, which must be a misprint.

BOWLES, JOHN. A Plan of London as in the Queen Elizabeth's Days. With a view of London after the Great Fire, and Views of Old Buildings in Fleet Street, Baynard's Castle, Old St. Paul's, Cheapside and the Cross, and Inside the Royal Exchange. $14\frac{1}{2} \times 21\frac{1}{2}$ ins. London.

1716 GAY, JOHN. Trivia: or, The Art of Walking the Streets of London. 8vo. London.

> Modern edit., with portrait, map, illustrations, introduction and notes, 8vo, London, 1922. Gay, with the assistance of Swift, began this poem as a burlesque of the "Arts" but becoming fascinated with the subject itself, developed it into an original poem with its own justification.

1717 The Inscriptions upon the Tombs, Grave Stones, etc., in the Dissenters' Burial Ground, near Bunhill-Fields. 8vo. London.

A Walk from St. James's to Covent Garden, the back Way, through the Meuse [Mews]: in Imitation of Mr. Gay's Journey to Exeter, in a Letter to a Friend. London.

1719 PETTY, SIR WILLIAM. Computations on the Increase of London. (So cited in Brett-James.)

1720   An Account of the Burning of the City of London, as it was published by the special Authority of the King and Council in the Year 1666. To which is added, The opinion of Dr. Kennett, the Present Bishop of Peterborough, as publish'd by his Lordship's Order, and that of Dr. Eachard, relating thereunto. With a Faithful Relation of the Prophecy of Thomas Ebbit, a Quaker, who publickly foretold the Burning of said City. From all which it plainly appears, that the Papists had no Hand in that dreadful Conflagration. Very useful for those who keep the annual solemn Fast on that Occasion. 8vo. London.

SENEX, JOHN. A Plan of the Cities of London, Westminster and Borough of Southwark, with the new Additional Buildings, Anno 1720. Revised by Jno. Senex, S. Parker Delin. et Sculpt. Wide double-folio. 20 × 24 ins. London.

    This has splendid detail, showing every street, and all important buildings and Gardens, numerous boats on the Thames, 16 public buildings and 95 churches identified.—Bookseller's Note.

STRYPE, JOHN. For his edition of *Stow's Survey of London,* see under Stow, 1598 above.

A View of the Monument, showing the houses and shops in the immediate vicinity, costume figures, etc., in the foreground. Line engraving 17½ × 13 ins.

1722   BAILEY, N. The Antiquities of London and Westminster, being an Account of whatsoever is Ancient, Curious or Remarkable as to Palaces, Towers, Castles, Walls, etc. 12mo. London.

    2nd edit., 12mo, London, 1726; 3rd edit., 12mo, 1734.

BURRIDGE, R. A New Review of London: being an Exact Survey, lately taken, of every Street, Lane, Court, Ally, etc., within the Cities, Liberties, or Suburbs of London, Westminster and the Borough of Southwark, so that letters from the General and Penny-Post Offices cannot miscarry for the future, by shewing in what Part Places bearing the same Names are situated . . . with the Rates of domestick and foreign Letters, and a List of all the Stage Coaches, Waggons and Carriers, etc., alphabetically digested. 8vo. London.

    3rd edit., 8vo, London, 1728. A Supplement appeared in 1722. See below.

    1722   A Supplement to the Review of London; in an Historical Account of all the Cathedrals, Churches, and Chapels of the Metropolis. 8vo. London.

DEFOE, DANIEL. A Journal of the Plague Year. London.

    Attention is called to this famous fiction as a mere matter of form.

HAYES, R. Rules for the Port of London. (So cited in Brett-James.)

Oliver's Pocket Looking Glass, new framed and clean'd, to give a clear View of the great Modern Colossus. 4th edit., with Supplement and Postscript. 8vo. London.

Reasons against Building a Bridge from Lambeth to Westminster, shewing the Inconveniences of the same to the City of London, and Borough of Southwark. 8vo. London.

STOW, WILLIAM. Remarks on London: being an Exact Survey of the Cities of London and Westminster, Borough of Southwark, and the Suburbs and Liberties contiguous to them, by shewing where every Street . . . is situated in the most Famous Metropolis; so that Letters from the General and Penny-Post Offices cannot Miscarry for the future . . . with many curious Observations, Places to which Penny-Post Letters and Parcels are carried, with Lists of Fairs and Markets . . . The Rates of Coachmen, Chairmen, Carmen and Watermen . . . all Alphabetically digested; and very useful for all Gentlemen, Ladies, Merchants, Tradesmen . . . The like never before extant. 18mo. London.

This reads very much like Burridge's *New Review of London* above.

1723 DART, JOHN. Westmonasterium: the History and Antiquities of the Abbey Church of St. Peter's, Westminster. An Account of its Buildings, Chapels, Relics, Customs, Forms of Government, Ancient Saxon Charters & Writings, etc. Survey of the Church, Monuments, etc., to which is added, Westminster Abbey, a Poem by the Author. Mezzotint portrait by Faber and over 130 full-page engravings by Cole. 2 vols. Fol. London.

Poor Mr. Dart, who began life as an unexemplary attorney, is horribly crabbed by *DNB*, which admits virtue only in his engravings.—From Bookseller's Note. Gough is equally hard upon him; see *op. cit.*, 270, where he states that "for this pompous but very inaccurate work Dart had assistance from the Cotton Library, the church records, and the papers of Mr. Charles Batteley."

The History of the Sherifdom of London and Middlesex, containing the Original Method of Election, etc. 8vo. London.

1724 KIP, JOHANNES. St. James's House, expansive bird's-eye view showing the City beyond; etching by Kip after Knyff. 13 × 18½ ins.

L., B. A Trip through Newgate, with the Rights, Privileges, Allowances, Fees, Dues, and Customs thereof; written for the public Good, by B. L. of Twickenham. London.

READING, WILLIAM. Bibliothecae Cleri Londinensis in Collegio Sionensi Catalogus, etc. (The History of the ancient and present state of Sion College.) 2 pts. Fol. London.

Several Prospects of the most noted Publick Buildings in and about the City of London, with a Short Historical Account relating to the same. 21 plates only. Obl. 4to. London.

This contains views of Bethlem, St. Paul's, College of Physicians, St. Thomas's Hospital, London Bridge, Banquetting House at Whitehall, St. James's Palace, St. Paul's School, St. Peter's, Old Bailey, Guild Hall, Charter House, Tower of London, Aske's Hospital, Navy Office, Christ's Hospital, Custom House, Royal Exchange, St. Bartholomew's Hospital, etc.—Bookseller's Note.

WARD, EDWARD. The Wandring Spy: or, The Merry Observator. Consisting of the Following Familiar Poems, viz. I. The Compleat Vintner. II. The Merry Travellers. III. The Return from Bromley. IV. The Southwark Election. V. The Parish Guttlers. VI. The Garden House Intrigue. VII. The Dancing Devils. Being the Sixth Volume of Miscellanies by Edward Ward. 8vo. London.

Each of Ward's volumes of Miscellanies is complete in itself.

1724-26 DEFOE, DANIEL. For a description of London, see Letters V and VI of his *Tour through the Whole Island of Great Britain,* under TOURS BY NATIVES.

This portion edit., with annotations, by Sir Mayson M. Beeton and E. Beresford Chancellor from the text of the original edition, fol., London, 1929. See below.

1929 DEFOE, DANIEL. A Tour thro' London about the Year 1725, being Letter V and parts of Letter VI of "A Tour thro' the Whole Island of Great Britain." Containing a Description of the City of London, as taking in the City of Westminster, Borough of Southwark and Parts of Middlesex. Reprinted from the text of the Original Edition (1724-26). Edit. and annotated by Sir Mayson M. Beeton, K.B.E., and E. Beresford Chancellor, M.A., illustrated with maps, specially drawn to delineate London of Defoe's day and reproductions of drawings, maps and prints mostly contemporary with the period of his Life. Fol. London.

1726 A New Guide to London; or, Directions to Strangers. 8vo. London.

Other edits., 1740, 1752, 1762.
This consists only of short abstracts, lists of streets, etc., and is on a par with Bailey (see under 1722 above).—Quoted.

1728 A Trip through London, containing Observations on Men and Things. 4th edit., with additions. 8vo. London.

Frequently reprinted and continued. See under 1730 and 1747 below.
This contains an Account of the Vast Number of Foreigners Yearly Imported; a Description of the Coffee-Houses about White-Hall; a Merry Dissertation upon News-Papers, Authors, Printers, and Publishers; an Account of the Surprizing Revolution at the Theatre in the Hay-Market, etc. Two differing accounts of authorship lie to hand in Paul Bunyan Anderson's article, "Thomas Gordon and John Mottley, A Trip through London, 1728," in *Phil. Quart.,* vol. 19, 244 ff. (1940), and John Robert Moore's article, "Defoe and the Eighteenth Century Pamphlets on London," *Phil. Quart.,* vol. 20 (1941). The former identifies Gordon and Mottley as the authors, with the matter taken chiefly from Gordon's collected essays, *The Humourist* (1720, 1724); whereas the latter insists that Gordon was not the joint editor of *A Trip through London,* and that there is no proof that Mottley had any share in the compilation. The part attributed to Gordon, on the contrary, was stolen from one of the most characteristic works of Defoe, *The Great Law of Subordination.* Anderson further states that the above pamphlet, together with *Tricks of the Town laid Open* (1747) and *A Trip through the Town* (1735), was printed by Ralph Straus as *The Tricks of the Town,* 1927.

1729 The Foreigner's Guide; or, A Necessary and Instructive Companion both for the Foreigner and Native in their Tour through the Cities of London and Westminster. Parallel English and French texts. 8vo. London.

Other edits., 8vo, 1740; 8vo, 1752; 12mo, 1760; 8vo, 1763.

Hell upon Earth, or, The Town in an Uproar. London.

MORETON, —. The Way to make London the most Flourishing City in the Universe. 8vo. London.

1730 BRYDALL, JOHN. The Tricks of London laid open: being a True Caution to both Sexes in Town and Country. 7th edit., with considerable Improvements. 8vo. London.

> This deals with cock-fighting, horse racing, gaming, etc.—Maggs, no. 574.

Cox, REV. THOMAS. A Compleat History of Middlesex; to which is added, A Particular Description of the Cities of London and Westminster. Map. 4to. London. (See Cox under SURVEYS.)

PINE, JOHN. The Procession and Ceremonies observed at the Time of the Installation of the Knights Companions of the Most Honourable Military Order of the Bath, June 17th, 1725; with the Arms, Names, Titles, etc., of the Knights Companions, and of their Esquires, as they are Fix'd up in Henry VIIth's Chapel in Westminster Abbey. 21 large copperplates (mostly double size), by Highmore, after drawings and portraits by the Author. Fol. London.

A Trip through the Town, containing Observations on the Customs and Manners of the Age, a Description of London in general, the Humours of Newgate and Tyburn on the Day of Execution, Description of a City-Prison for Debtors, etc. 8vo. London.

> 4th edit., 8vo, London, 1735. See A Trip through London, under 1728 above. See below.

> 1735 A Trip through the Town, containing Observations on the Humours and Manners of the Age, Reflections on London in General, The Art of Walking in St. James Park, Beaus and Blockheads; together with Coffee-House Politicians exposed, The Craft of Town Beggars and the Monstrous Pride and Insolencies of Women Servants, Causes of the Debaucheries practis'd upon the Fair Sex. 4th edit. 8vo. London.
> Reprinted, with other tracts on London, with Introduction, by Ralph Straus, London, 1927.

1731 BOWLES, JOHN. A New and Exact Plan of ye City of London and Suburbs thereof, with the Addition of the New Buildings, Churches, etc. to this Present Year 1731 (Not extant in any other). Laid down in such a Method that in an Instant, may easily be found any Place contain'd therein. With an Alphabetical Table of all the Places contained in the Map. Engraved Map, outlined in color. 24 × 77 ins. London.

GORDON, ALEXANDER. Urbis Londini, fluvii Thamesis, templi, palatii, viridarii Grenovicensis ab austro conspectus; qualem delineavit, illustrissimoq. dom. Archb. Grant, eq. bar. d. Cl. du Bosc. Sc. (So cited in Gough, 361.)

MORGAN, J. Phoenix Britannicus; a Miscellaneous Collection of Scarce and Curious Tracts: London during the Plague, 1603; Nedham's History of the Rebellion, 1661; Lithgow's Description of Ireland, Rawleigh's Ghost, etc. Parts 1 to 4 complete. 4to. London.

> A periodical of great merit.—DNB.

RALPH, JAMES. The Taste of the Town, or, A Guide to all Public Diversions—viz., of Musick, Operas, and Plays, . . . of Poetry; of Dancing, religious and

dramatical; of the Mimes, Pantomimes, and Choruses of the Antients; of Audiences; of Masquerades; of . . . athletic Sports of the Antients; of Cock-Fighting, Puppet-Shows, Mountebanks, and Auctions. Dedication signed, A Primcock. 12mo. London.

> A reissue of *Essays on Reigning Diversions of the Town,* 1728.—Morgan, *Bibliog. of Brit. Hist.*

A View of the Town, or Memoirs of London, in which is contained a Diverting Account of the Humours, Follies, Vices, and what not? of that famous Metropolis . . . here is, in short, as much Sing-Song as in the *Beggar's Opera,* and more new Whims than in the *Orator's Advertisements.* 8vo. London.

1732 The British Spy's Tour through London and Westminster. (So listed in *Gent. Mag.,* vol. 2, Jan.)

JACOB, GILES. City-Liberties, or, The Rights and Privileges of Freemen, being a Concise Abridgement of all the Laws, Charters, By-Laws, and Customs of London down to this Time. 8vo. London.

New Remarks of London, or, A Survey of the Cities of London and Westminster, of Southwark, and Part of Middlesex and Surrey, within the Circumference of the Bills of Mortality. Collected by the Company of Parish-Clerks. 12mo. London.

1733 SEYMOUR, ROBERT (pseud. John Mottley). Survey of the Cities of London and Westminster, Borough of Southwark, and Parts Adjacent. Early engraved folding map and views of London. 2 vols. Fol. London.

> This is a revised version of Stow's *Survey,* reprinted, 2 vols., 1735; in one vol., fol., London, 1736; again, 1754.
> Mottley was the compiler of "Joe Miller's Jests."—Upcott, *Bibliog. Account.*

> 1735 SEYMOUR, ROBERT. A Survey of the Cities of London and Westminster, Borough of Southwark, and parts Adjacent: containing, 1. The Original Foundation, and the Antient and Modern States thereof. 2. An Exact Description of all the Wards and Parishes, Parish-Churches, Palaces, Halls, Hospitals, Publick Offices, Edifices, and Monuments of any Account. 3. A Particular Account of the Government of London, its Charters, Liberties, Privileges, and Customs; and of all the Companies, with their Coats of Arms, etc. The Whole being an Improvement of Mr. Stowe's and other Surveys, by adopting whatever Alterations have happened in the said Cities, etc., to the Present Year. Illustrated with several copperplates. 2 vols. Fol. London.

1734 RALPH, JAMES. A Critical Review of the Public Buildings, Statues, and Ornaments in and about London and Westminster: to which is prefixed the Dimensions of St. Peter's Church at Rome and St. Paul's Cathedral at London. 8vo. London. (This work criticized in the following item.)

> 2nd edit., enlarged with some reflections on the use of sepulchral monuments; a preface, being an Essay on Taste; and Appendix, containing a dispute between the Weekly Miscellany and the author; and a complete alphabetical Index, 12mo, London, 1736. Reprinted with large additions, 1783. See Gough, 313.
> Ralph is contemptuously referred to by Thomas Davies in his *Memoirs of the Life of David Garrick* (2 vols., new edit., 1780) as one who had an itch for writing plays and poems. His quarrel with Garrick and his ungracious attacks upon the actor despite many favors shown him led Garrick to refuse to attend any gathering at which Ralph was present. He became, however, an influential political writer.

Remarks on a Pamphlet, entitled, A Critical Review of the Publick Buildings, Statues, and Ornaments in and about London and Westminster. In *Gent. Mag.,* vol. 4, May, 245.

> This article defends the clergy against some alleged disparagement.

A View of London; in a Letter to the Rev. Mr. ———, A.M. of ——— College Oxon. In *Gent. Mag.,* vol. 4, April.

> This contains a general description of fashions, the trees, professions, etc., taken from the *Universal Spectator,* Apr. 20, No. 289, and printed as above. It was continued in the May number of *Gent. Mag.*

1736   A Design of the Bridge at New Palace-Yard, Westminster, composed of Nine Arches independent of each other, whose Nature is such, that the greatest Weight possible cannot break them down, admitting 880 feet Water-way of the Flux and Reflux of Tides, by which an Expence of 24,172 pounds is saved, and the Building stronger. London.

HAWKSMOOR, NICHOLAS. A Short Historical Account of London Bridge, with a Proposition for a New Stone Bridge at Westminster, with Designs engrav'd on Copper-Plate. Very useful for Artificers, in a Letter to a Member of Parliament for the City and Liberties of Westminster. 4to. London.

> This gives also an account of some remarkable stone bridges abroad and what the best authors have said and directed concerning them. Hawksmoor had numerous engagements as architect, at times with Wren at Chelsea Hospital, with Vanbrugh at Castle Howard and Blenheim, and at times as clerk of the works, as deputy surveyor, and as designer on his own account.

A Sketch of the Situation of a Palace at Whitehall, the better to settle that of a Bridge and the Road to it. (So listed in *Gent. Mag.* vol. 6, March.)

1736-38   The Directory, containing Names and Places of Abode of . . . Persons in Business. 8vo. London.

> Continued as: *Kent's Directory,* 8vo, London, 1754-(1810), and on into the nineteenth century.

1736-39   Perspective Views of all the Ancient Churches, and other Buildings in the Cities of London and Westminster, and Parts Adjacent. 2 pts. Obl. fol. London.

1737   BEARCROFT, PHILIP. An Historical Account of Thomas Sutton, Esq., and of his Foundation in Charterhouse. 8vo. London.

> The most correct and complete piece on the subject.—Gough, 320.

Civitas Londinum Anno Domini circiter 1560. Plan of London and Westminster . . . near the Beginning of the Reign of Queen Elizabeth . . . (by R. Agas), re-ingrav'd. Fol. London. (See Agas under 1592 above.)

LEDIARD, THOMAS. Some Observations on the Scheme, offered by Mess. Cotton and Lediard, for Opening the Streets and Passages to and from the Intended Bridge at Westminster, in a Letter from one of the Commissioners to Mr. Lediard, and his Answer. With the Scheme and Plan prefixed: to which is

added, A Plan of the lower Parts of the Parishes of St. Margaret and St. John the Evangelist, from the Horse Ferry to Whitehall; wherein several farther Improvements are delineated, and a Proposal for Establishing a Perpetual Fund, to defray the Expences of Paving, Watching, and Lighting the said Bridge, and Keeping it in Repair. 4to. London.

This, the second bridge to be built over the Thames at London, was the occasion of many pamphlets. See Labelye under 1751 below.

1738 JOHNSON, SAMUEL. London: A Poem In Imitation of the Third Satire of Juvenal. 4to. London.

This poem, which brought Johnson into notice as a coming literary figure, is too well known to call for comment.

A Ramble through London, containing Observations on Men and Things, *viz.*, some Account of the vast Number of Foreigners and their Behaviour; a Merry Description of the Court-End of the Town, and of the City; Female Conversation described; Jests from St. James's, etc., etc. By a True-Born Englishman. 8vo. London.

A Walk in Kensington Gardens. (So listed in *Gent. Mag.*, vol. 8, Aug.)

1739 A Compleat Guide to London Traders. (So listed in *Gent. Mag.*, vol. 9, Aug.)

Fourteen Views of London Churches not destroyed by the Great Fire were drawn by R. West 1736, engraved by W. H. Toms, and published 1739, with accounts of them at the bottom.—Gough, 312.

GLOVER, RICHARD. London, or, The Progress of Commerce: a Poem. 4to. London.

MAITLAND, WILLIAM. The History of London from its Foundation by the Romans to the Present Time. Containing a faithful Relation of the Public Transactions of the Citizens; Accounts of the several Parishes; Parallels between London and other Great Cities; its Governments, Civil, Ecclesiastical and Military; Commerce, State of Learning, Charitable Foundations, etc. With the several Accounts of Westminster, Middlesex, Southwark, and other Parts within the Bills of Mortality. In Nine Books. The whole illustrated with a variety of Cuts. Compleat Index. Fol. London.

2nd edit., 2 vols., fol., 1756; 3rd, 2 vols., 1769; 3 vols., fol., 1772; new edit., continued by the Rev. J. Entick, 2 vols., fol., 1775. These different editions are probably brought down to the date of publication.
This is regarded as a very useful work. It contains plans of London before the Fire, in its ruins, and as rebuilt, and delineations of localities no longer extant or else much altered.

English Architecture: or the Public Buildings of London and Westminster, with Plans of the Streets and Squares, represented in 123 folio plates, with a succinct Review of their History; and a candid Examination of their Perfections and Defects. Fol. London.

Gough says this is made up of the plates from Maitland's *History of London*, dressed up by the Bookseller's art.—*Op. cit.*, 313. No date is given.

PINE, JOHN (Engraver), and PHILIP MORANT (Historian). The Tapestry Hanging of the House of Lords, representing the several Engagements between the English and Spanish Fleets MDLXXXVIII, with the Portraits of the Lord High Admiral, and the other Noble Commanders, taken from the Life. To this is added, from a Book intitled: Expeditionis Hispanorum in Angliam vera Descriptio, A.D. 1588, done, as is supposed, for the said Tapestry to be worked after, Ten Charts of the Sea-Coasts of England, and a general one of England, Scotland, Ireland, France, Holland, shewing the Places of Action between the two Fleets; ornamented with a Medal struck upon that Occasion, and other suitable Devices. Also an Historical Account of each Day's Action, collected from the most authentic MSS. and Writers (by Philip Morant). By John Pine Engraver. Fol. London.

> Gough supposes the charts or representations to be those of the several actions while the Armada was on the English coast, drawn and engraved by Robert Adams, and published by August Ryther, 1588. They are mentioned by Walpole, *Catalogue of Engravers.* —*Op. cit.,* 273. This work, by the celebrated engraver of "Pine's Horace" is of very great historical and artistic value, as it delineates the splendid series of tapestries which were specially executed by H. C. Vroom to commemorate the defeat of the Armada. They were unhappily destroyed at the burning of the old Palace of Westminster.—Bookseller's Note.

1740   A Complete Guide to all Persons who have any Trade or Concern with the City of London and Parts Adjacent, containing the Names of all the Streets, Squares, . . . Stage-Coaches, Rates of Watermen, Hackney Coachmen, and Places of Abode of Merchants and Traders . . . . 8vo. London.

> The 1st edit. of Osborn's Directory; later edits., 1744, 1749, 1752, 1755, 1757, 1760, 1763, 1765; continued as Baldwin's New Complete Guide for 1768-70; as The New Complete Guide for 1772, 1777, 1783.

The Horse Guards: the Prospect of Whitehall, from the Park of St. James, showing carriages, sedans, etc., with people watching military exercises. Etching, 8¼ × 3 ins.

1741   (London and the Home Counties). "Regionis quae est circa Londinum." Engraved colored map. 23 × 20 ins. Nürnberg.

> This was published by Homann's Heirs, with interesting engraved view of London along the foot.—Maggs, no. 739.

SMART, JOHN. To the Deputies and Common Council, etc. (A short account of the wards, precincts, parishes in London.) 8vo. London.

1742   The Antiquities of St. Peter's, or, the Abbey-Church of Westminster, containing Inscriptions and Epitaphs upon the Tombs and Grave-Stones, with the Lives, Marriages, and Issue of the most Eminent Personages therein Reposited, and their Coats of Arms truly Emblazoned. Many folding and other copperplates. 2 vols. 8vo. London.

BICKHAM, GEORGE. The Curiosities of Hampton-Court and Windsor-Castle, Delineated; with occasional Reflections; And embellish'd with Copper-Plates. Plates by Bickham. 8vo. London.

A New and Complete Survey of London in ten parts; including all the Public Transactions and Memorable Events that have happened from its Foundation, a Description of its Wards, an Historical Account of the Commerce of the City and the Incorporations of the Arts and Mysteries of the Citizens, etc., etc. By a Citizen and Native of London. Folding plan. 2 vols. 8vo. London.

1743 CHARLES, GEORGE, LL.D. A Catalogue of all the Books in the Library of St. Paul's School, London, with the Names of the Benefactors, as given in by George Charles, LL.D. High Master in the Time of John Nodes, Esq: Surveyor, accomptant of the said School. Dated the 2nd Day of March, 1743.

This collection was begun 1670.—Gough, 318.

The Present State of Westminster Bridge, containing a Description of the Bridge, with a True Account of the Time already employed in the Building, etc. 2nd edit. corrected. 8vo. London.

1744 FIELDING, SARAH. The Adventures of David Simple: containing an Account of his Travels through the Cities of London and Westminster in the Search of a real Friend. By a Lady. 2 vols. 8vo. London.

2nd edit., revised and corrected, with a preface by Henry Fielding, 2 vols., 1744; 3rd vol. added, in which his History is concluded, 1753.

FOURDRINIER, PAUL. Plan of the City of London after the Great Fire of 1666, with the Modell of the New City according to the Design of Sir Christopher Wren. Engraved by Fourdrinier. 19 × 27 ins. London.

MOREAU DE BRASEY. For his description of London, see his *Le Guide d'Angleterre,* under TOURS BY FOREIGNERS.

ROCQUE, JOHN. Accurata Descriptio Urbium Londinensis Westmonasteriensis, nec non Municipii Southwarkiensis et Universae Regionis ad decem fere undique Millia Passuum, incepta anno 1741 et absoluta anno 1745, a Johanne Rocquis Topographo. (This title on the first sheet. The 2nd and 3rd sheets have title in English—see below. The 4th sheet has title in French.)

An Exact Survey of the Cities of London and Westminster, and Borough of Southwark, and the Country ten miles round; begun 1741, ended 1745. Surveyed by Rocque and engraved by Farr.

This map of sixteen sheets was reprinted in 1751 and 1754.
The Proposals offer the following account of the use of this map: "It is universally allowed that such a Map will be of great use to all Directors of Insurance Offices, and Commissioners of Turnpikes, to all Church Wardens and Overseers, to all persons who have occasion to travel round this Metropolis for business, health, or pleasure; and lastly to curious persons at home or abroad." There is no account of Rocque in *DNB*, though he was a man of note; nor does Gough enlighten us with any details of his life, though he refers frequently to his maps. He seems to have been a Frenchman by birth, who after emigrating to England was appointed Chorographer to Frederick, Prince of Wales, and later to George, Prince of Wales, afterwards George III. There is an article on him and his plan of London by Henry B. Wheatley, in *London Topographical Record,* vol. 9, 1914.

A Trip from St. James's to the Royal Exchange, with Remarks, Serious and Diverting, on the Manners, Customs and Amusements of the Inhabitants of London and Westminster. 8vo. London.

1746   GRIFFITHS, THOMAS ROGER. An Essay to prove that the Jurisdiction and Conservancy of the River of Thames, etc., is committed to the Lord Mayor and City of London, both in point of Right and Usage, by Prescription, Charters, Acts of Parliament, Decrees upon Hearing before the King, Letters Patent, etc. To which is added, A Brief Description of those Fish, with their Spawning-Time, that are caught in the Thames or sold in London; with some few Observations on the Nature, Element, Cloathing, Numbers, Passage, Wars, and Sensations peculiar to Fish in general; and also of the Water-Carriage on the River Thames to the several Parts of the Kingdom; with a History of the Keys, Wharfs, Docks adjoining to the same. 8vo. London.

The author was a water bailiff on the Thames.

ROCQUE, JOHN. A Plan of the Cities of London and Westminster, and Borough of Southwark; with the contiguous Buildings; From an Actual Survey taken by John Rocque, Land Surveyor, and engraved by John Pine. . . . This work was begun in 1737 and Published in October 1746. In 24 sheets. (As a companion to this plan there was published the next year An Alphabetical Index of the Streets, Squares, Lanes, Alleys, . . . with references for the easy finding the said Places.) Atlas fol. London.

Later edits. of the Index, 1749, 1753; they have this addition to the title-page: Adapted likewise to a contracted Copy of the above mentioned Plan, printed on eight sheets of Paper. *Note.* Both these Plans have all the additions and Alterations to the Present Year.

The Alphabetical Index of Places in the Plan is divided into several Alphabets, forming a classification of thoroughfares, buildings, etc. It is a useful aid to the study of the history and peculiarities of London nomenclature. From these lists one may note a careful and accurate presentation of the large amount of open spaces existing at this time in the outskirts of London. The number of farms around the town was considerable. Some of the lanes in the suburbs have disparaging names: Melancholy Walk, Dirty Lane, Rogue's Lane, six Love Lanes. The West End squares are of later growth but the Index lists 52. —From Wheatley, *London Topog. Soc.* Westward London terminates at Tyburn Lane (now Park Lane) and eastward at Whitechapel. The only Thames bridges are the London and Westminster Bridges, but at Lambeth there is the Horse Ferry. Off Chelsea Road is a large lake like the Serpentine.—Maggs, no. 693.

1747   CAMPBELL, R. London Tradesman: Being a Compendious View of all the Trades, Professions, Arts, both Liberal and Mechanic, now practiced in the Cities of London and Westminster. 8vo. London.

3rd edit., 8vo, London, 1757.

FISHER, JOHN. A Survey and Ground Plot of the Royal Palace of Whitehall . . . A.D. 1680. Surveyed by John Fisher, drawn and published by G. Virtue. Fol. London.

Vertue was a prolific engraver, not only of antiquarian objects but also of portraits. His collections for the history of art in England were utilized by Horace Walpole in his *Anecdotes of Painting.*

The Tricks of the Town laid open, or, A Companion for Country Gentlemen: being the Substance of Seventeen Letters, from a Gentleman at London to his

Friend in the Country, to dissuade him from coming to Town. 8vo. London.

Reprinted as the 16th edit., 12mo, London, n.d. but *ca.* 1800; reprinted with two other tracts, edited by Ralph Straus, 8vo, London, 1927. See below. See also *A Trip through London,* under 1728 above, and S——cy under 1699 above.

1800 The Tricks of London Laid Open, Being a True Caution to both Sexes, in Town and Country. Containing I. A General Reflection on the Town . . . II. The Humours, Customs, and Tricks of the Play-House . . . III. The Tricks of Pro-curers and Procuresses, Bawds, Whores, and Jilts, with a Description of a Bawdy-House. IV. The Character of a Bully . . . V. The Characters of Gamesters . . . VI. The Villany of Money and Ring Froppers . . . VII. The Tricks of Cockers, Cock Matches, and the Cheats of Tennis Courts . . . VIII. The Cheats of Duffers, Kidnappers, Mock Auctioneers, Fortune Tellers, etc. The Sixteenth edition. 12mo. London. (n.d.)

1927 STRAUS, RALPH. (Editor.) Eighteenth Century Diversions: Tricks of the Town; being Reprints of Three Eighteenth Century Tracts, with Introduction by Ralph Straus. 8 illus. 8vo. London.

Reprints of I. The Tricks of the Town (1747). II. A Trip through the Town (1735). III. A Trip from St. James's to the Royal Exchange (1744). The first is a 1747 edition of a 1699 publication, slightly amended and shortened and published as a new edition. Ned Ward with his *London Spy* (1698-1709) had been a great success, and had turned loose a spawn of exposures of vice and corruptions of the Town. The other two are really editions of the same work, or rather they are made up from a common stock, with additions and emendations suited to the particular year of their appearance. This common stock, whose basic term was the *Trip,* existed for more than half a century. There is evident much borrowing from new satires, newspaper articles, etc. All of them lay open the vices of London. Apparently no one was to be trusted.

1747-1770 An interesting collection of 28 Old Coloured Views of London. These are all fairly large views in contemporary colouring and mainly published by Bowles or Sayer from about 1747 to 1770. It forms an interesting record of London in the middle of the eighteenth century.—Bookseller.

1748 LANGLEY, BATTY (Architect). A Survey of Westminster-Bridge, as it is now sinking into Ruin; wherein the Cause of the Foundation's giving way under the sinking Pier, and its dislocated Arches, is not only accounted for, but also that the whole Structure is likewise subject to the same immediate, if not unavoid-able Ruin: with Remarks on the Piratical Methods used for Building the Piers, and a just Estimate of the Expence for which all the Foundation might have been made secure with Piles until every Stone, with which the Bridge is built, was torn into Atoms by the hungry Teeth of devouring Time. 8vo. London.

The author claimed that the Swiss architect employed had pirated his plans published 1736. See *Philos. Trans. of the Royal Soc.,* no. 483.

ROCQUE, JOHN. A New and Accurate Survey of the Cities of London and West-minster, the Borough of Southwark, with the Country 60 miles about it, for 19 miles in Length and 13 in Depth; in which is contained an Exact Description of St. James's Kensington, Richmond, and Hampton Court Palaces, all the Main and Cross Roads, Lanes and Paths, Bye-ways, Walls, Hedges, Hills, Vallies, Rivers, Bridges, Ferries, Brooks, Springs, Ponds, Woods, Heaths, Commons, Parks, Avenues, Churches, Houses, Gardens, etc., etc. In 16 sheets. Atlas Fol. London.

Reprinted, 1751; reduced to one sheet, 1763.
This survey has evidently something to do with the one listed under 1744 above.

1749   BUCK, SAMUEL and NATHANIEL. The Bucks engraved this year five large views
       of London and Westminster, to be united into one, extending from Millbank to
       the Tower. See the Bucks under 1727, VIEWS.

       GWYNN, JOHN. Wren's "Plan for rebuilding the City of London after the Great
       Fire in 1666," and also a Plan of St. Paul's and other works. London.

       > Gwynn was an architect who was assisted by Johnson in several of his writings. The
       > latter also urged Gwynn's plan for Blackfriar's Bridge, the third to be built over the
       > Thames (begun 1760 and finished 1770) after designs by Robt. Milne. The handsome
       > Magdalen Bridge at Oxford was built from his plans as was also the "English" Bridge at
       > Shrewsbury (finished 1774), and the Worcester Bridge (finished 1780).

       WARBURTON, JOHN (Somerset Herald). London and Middlesex Illustrated: By a
       True and Explicit Account of the Names, Residence, Genealogy, and Coat
       Armour of the Nobility, Principal Merchants, and other Eminent Families,
       Trading within the Precincts of this most opulent City and County. 8vo. London.

1750   For an account of the state of London, see A New Present State of England, un-
       der ANCIENT AND PRESENT STATE.

       CHATELAIN, M. Views of Churches, Villages, etc., adjacent to London. 50 plates
       engraved by J. Roberts after Chatelain. Obl. 8vo. London.

       Cheapside. Prospectus Platae Reglae Mercatorum Londini: showing Cheapside
       with its many signs, the Royal Exchange, numerous vehicles, figures, etc.
       Coloured line engraving 11 × 16 ins.

       A Correct List of all the Stage Coaches and Carriers; with the Places where
       they inn, and the Days they set out from London. Single sheet, fol. London.

       An Historical Account of the Tower of London and its Curiosities. 12mo. Lon-
       don.
       > Other edits., 1754, 1755, 1759, 1762, 1768, 1778, 1796, 1800, etc.

       The Pocket Remembrancer; or, A Concise History of the City of London. 12mo.
       London. (The dating is dubious.)

       SHORT, THOMAS, M.D. Observations, Natural, Moral, Civil, Political and Medi-
       cal on City, Town and Country Bills of Mortality. To which are added, Large
       and Clear Abstracts of the best Authors who have wrote on that Subject, with
       an Appendix on the Weather and Meteors. 8vo. London.

1751   DRAPER, W. H. The Morning Walk, or, City Encompassed, a Poem in Blank
       Verse. 8vo. London.
       > This poem gives a rather lively picture of what might be seen and heard in the districts
       > around London in the early hours of the morning, at the time when it was written.—Book-
       > seller's Note.

Gephyralogia. An Historical Account of Bridges, Antient and Modern, from the most early Mention of them by Authors down to the Present Time. Including a More Particular History and Description of the New Bridge at Westminster, and an Abstract of the Rules of Bridge-Building, by the most Eminent Architects: with Remarks, Comparative and Critical, deduced both from the History and the Rules, and applied to the Construction of Westminster-Bridge. To which is added, by way of Appendix, An Abridgment of all the Laws relating thereto. Folding engraved view of Westminster Bridge. 8vo. London.

LABELYE, CHARLES. A Description of Westminster-Bridge; to which are added, An Account of the Methods made use of in laying the Foundations of its Piers, and an Answer to the chief Objections that have been made thereto; with an Appendix, containing several Particulars relating to the said Bridge, or to the History of the Building thereof; as also geometrical Plans, and the Elevation of one of the Fronts as it is finished, correctly engraved on two large copper-plates: drawn up and published by Order of the Commissioners. 8vo. London.

> This contains the Prospectus of 1744 by way of an Appendix. The two engraved plates called for on the title page were never issued.—Maggs, no. 603. An illustration of the bridge is printed in *Gent. Mag.,* vol. 20, 586. Labelye's appointment as architect was supported by Henry Herbert, Earl of Pembroke, who laid the first stone in 1739; the last was put in place in 1747. Its cost was 389,500 pounds, which was made up in part from Parliamentary grants. The high balustrades, which met with considerable criticism, were assumed by Grosley, the French traveler, to be designed to discourage the English propensity to suicide. The bridge was 1,223 feet in length, 45 wide, with 14 arches, the center one of which was 76 feet in width. Labelye was the Swiss architect whom Langley accused of stealing designs from him. See Langley under 1748 above.

MORRIS, CORBYN. Observations on the Past Growth and the Present State of the City of London. To which are annexed, A Complete Table of the Christenings and Burials within this City from 1601 to 1750, both Years inclusive; together with a Table of the Numbers which annually died of each Disease from 1675 to the Present Time, and also a further Table representing the respective Numbers which have annually died of each age from 1728 to this Year: from which is particularly attempted to be shewn the increasing Destruction of Infants and adults in this City; and consequent thereto the excessive Drain which it continually makes upon all the Provinces of this Kingdom for Recruits: to which is added, Some Proposals for a better Regulation of the Police of this Metropolis. By the Author of a Letter from a Bystander [Corbyn Morris, Esq.]. Fol. London.

> For a dismal picture of childhood life in the metropolis, see Dorothy George, *London in the Eighteenth Century.*

1752 A Concise History of the City of London. (So cited in *Gent. Mag.,* vol. 22, Dec.)

Low-Life: or, One Half of the World knows not how the other Half Live. A Critical Account of what is transacted . . . in the 24 Hours between Saturday-Night and Sunday-Morning, calculated for June 21. With an Address to Mr. Hogarth. Printed for the Author. 2nd edit., with "very large Additions of nearly HALF the Work. London.

> 3rd edit., 8vo, London, 1764.
> Minutely detailed description of London life of a Sunday hour by hour, by one who felt the insufficiency of Hogarth's presentation.—Bookseller's Note.

The Monument of London in Remembrance of the Dreadfull Fire in 1666. Showing Fish Street crowded with figures, vehicles, cattle, etc.: line engraving by Bowles. 9¼ × 15¾ ins. London.

1753   The Historical Description of St. Paul's Church. 12mo. London.

> This contains, besides the history of the old Cathedral, an account of the manner of proceeding in taking down its vast ruins, with the discoveries and observations made upon the spot by Sir Christopher Wren; and a full description of the building of the present structure: with observations on its beauties and defects. To which are added, a description of the Monument; some conjectures concerning London-Stone, and other Roman relics; and a review of the antient wall and gates about the city.—Gough, 307.

1754   An Essay on the Many Advantages accruing from the superior Neatness, Conveniences, etc., of Capital Cities, particularly apply'd to London. 8vo. London.

Golden Square. Line engraving after Sutton Nicholls, 12⅞ × 18 ins., with margins. Published according to Act of Parliament 1754 for Stowe's Survey. London.

London in Miniature, being a Concise and Comprehensive Description of the Cities of London and Westminster and Parts adjacent, for forty Miles round, in which the many publick Buildings, Statues, Ornaments, Royal Palaces, etc., are accurately display'd. With an alphabetical List of all the Streets, etc., intended as a Complete Guide for Foreigners. 12mo. London.

> This same title is listed as of 1755 also. It is said to have been collected from Stow, Maitland, and other large works, with several new and curious particulars.

ROCQUE, JOHN. A Plan of London on the same Scale as that of Paris: In order to ascertain the Difference of the Extent of these two Rivals, the Abbé de la Grive's Plan of Paris and that of London by J. Rocque have been divided into equal Squares where London contains 39 and Paris but 29. So that the Superficie of London is to that of Paris as 39 to 29, or as 5455 Acres to 4028. London therefore exceeds Paris by 1427 Acres, the former being 8½ square miles and Paris 6⅓, . . .

> The companion plan of Paris by the Abbé de la Grive was published the same year.—Wheatley, *op. cit.*

1754-78   Tower of London: a Series of 10 original drawings in sepia and color, of Elevations and Plans of the Tower of London, of various dates. All have at the foot explanations and references, the general plan of the Tower and district, made in 1760, being particularly interesting in this respect.—Bookseller's item.

1755   ROCQUE, JOHN. An Alphabetical Index of the Streets, Squares, Lanes, Alleys, etc., contained in the Plan of the Cities of London and Westminster, and Borough of Southwark, with the contiguous Buildings. Engraved by Pine, and published on 24 sheets. 4to. London. (See 1746 above and following item.)

————. A Plan of London and Westminster, and Borough of Southwark, and the contiguous Buildings; with all the new Roads that have been made on account

of Westminster Bridge; and the new Buildings and Alterations to the Present
Year 1755: engraved from an actual Survey by J. Rocque, in 24 sheets, 13 feet
by 6¾ by J. Pine. London.

> This plan extends from east to west near six miles, and from north to south a little
> more than three, and contains about 11,500 acres of ground and is laid down by a scale of
> 200 feet to an inch.—Gough, 362.

Saint James's Palace: an expansive bird's-eye view, showing the city beyond;
etching from Stow's *Survey*, 8½ × 13 ins. (See Cole 1760 below.)

1755-56 The Devil upon Crutches in England, or, Night Scenes in London, a satirical
Work, written upon the Plan of the celebrated Diable Boiteux of Monsieur Le
Sage, by a Gentleman of Oxford. In 2 pts. 8vo. London.

> 2nd edit., 1756; 4th, 12mo, London, 1759.
> Among the topics taken up are A Short view of the Theatres of Drury-Lane and
> Covent Garden; a View of the Academy of Newgate; from Newgate to Bedlam; Survey
> of the City; Whores, Pickpockets and Authors; the Foundling Hospital, etc.—Bookseller's
> Note.

1757 Old Plan, containing The Ichnography of the Cities of London and Westminster
and the Borough of Southwark. 15 × 10 ins.

Reasons offered for the Reformation of the House of Correction in Clerken-
well; shewing, I. The Present State of this Gaol, the Debauchery of the Prisoners, and the miserable Condition they are in from the Want of a Sufficiency
of Food, etc. II. Proposals in what manner these Evils may be prevented for the
Future; humbly submitted to the Consideration of the Magistrates and Inhabitants of the County of Middlesex. To which is prefixed, A Plan of the said
Prison engraved on Copper, with References describing the Manner in which
this Gaol should be altered for the Purposes proposed, with a Calculation of the
expence thereof. 8vo. London.

1758 BINNELL, ROBERT. A Description of the River Thames, etc. With the City of London's Jurisdiction and Conservancy thereof proved, both in Point of Right and
Usage, by Prescriptions, Charters, Acts of Parliament, Decrees, etc., to which
is added, A Brief Description of those Fish, with their Seasons, Spawning
Time, etc. 8vo. London.

CANOT, P. C. View of Westminster Bridge, with Parts adjacent in 1747, showing sailing barges and rowing boats in foreground and houses on the bank;
engraving by P. C. Canot, after Samuel Scott. 13 × 22 ins.

ENTICK, REV. JOHN. A New and Accurate History and Survey of London, Westminster, Southwark, and Places adjacent: containing whatever is most worthy
of Notice in their Ancient and Present State; illustrated with a Variety of
Heads, Views, Plans, and Maps.

> Gough says, "there is now publishing in monthly numbers" by the Rev. John Entick a
> work (with the above title). Perhaps he is referring to the edition in 1766 in four
> volumes, 8vo. The date 1758 I cannot guarantee.

The History of London Bridge from its First Foundation in the Year 994, to the Destruction of the Temporary Bridge by Fire . . . 1758 . . . To which is added, A Brief Description of the several Bridges built over the River Thames within the Memory of Man. Illus. London.

This includes Westminster, Hampton-Court, Blackfriars, Kew bridges.—J. Williams.

The Plan of the Magdalen-House for the Reception of Penitent Prostitutes. By Order of the Governors. 4to. London.

This gives accounts of the rise, progress, and present state of this charity, with the rules, and list of subscribers, and a print of one of the women prefixed. These accounts are printed yearly for the benefit of the house.—Gough, 323.

1760   COLE, B. St. James's Palace and Parts adjacent. An expansive bird's-eye view, including the city beyond. Etching by B. Cole. 8 × 13 ins.

This is doubtless identical with *St. James's Palace,* listed under 1755 above.

St. Thomas's and St. George's Hospitals compared.

A single folio sheet.—Gough, 319.

South View of Cheswick (i.e., Chiswick), looking from the opposite bank, with costume figures, rowing-boats, etc. Line engraving, 9¼ × 15 ins.

A View of the British Museum, or, A Regular Account of what is most remarkable there. 8vo. London. (See following item.)

1761   The General Contents of the British Museum, with Remarks, serving as a Directory in viewing that noble Cabinet. 8vo. London.

2nd edit., enlarged, 8vo, 1762.
A superficial account.—Gough, 333.

GURNEY, SAMUEL. London and its Environs Described, containing an Account of whatever is most remarkable for Grandeur, Elegance, Curiosity, or Use in the City and in the Country twenty Miles round it, comprehending also whatever is most material in the History and Antiquities of this great Metropolis. Maps and plans, and 70 engraved plates. 6 vols. 8vo. London.

The Rise and Progress of the Foundling Hospital Considered; and the Reasons for putting a Stop to the general Reception of all Children. 8vo. London.

This refers to the Foundling Hospital which was established by the benevolent Captain Coram (see Austin Dobson, *Vignettes of the Eighteenth Century,* 1st ser.). Considerable criticism arose over the operation of the hospital.

1762   A Description of Buckingham-House, just purchased by the King for a Palace for the Queen's Majesty. In *Gent. Mag.,* vol. 32, 221-22.

A Description of Ranelagh Rotundo, and Gardens. 12mo. London.

A Description of Vaux-Hall Gardens. 12mo. London.

These two famous pleasure resorts of 18th century London have been so well memorialized by novelists, letter writers, diarists, and travelers of the period that they can be

visualized without the aid of the numerous prints which advertised their attractions. One needs but refer to *Humphrey Clinker, Evalina,* Boswell, and Horace Walpole's correspondence. See also Chancellor, *The Eighteenth Century in London* and his *The Pleasure Haunts of London.*

1763 CHAMBERS, SIR WILLIAM. For views of the gardens at Kew, see his *Plans, Elevations, and Sections of the Gardens at Kew,* under VIEWS.

CORYATE, GEORGE. Descriptio Angliae, et descriptio Londini, being two Poems in Latin Verse, supposed to be written in the XVth Century. 4to. London. (See this date under DESCRIPTIONS.)

A Description of the Gardens and Buildings at Kew, in Surrey. 2 pts. 8vo. Brentford.

REEVES, GEORGE. A New History of London and Westminster, by Question and Answer. 12mo. London.

A title very similar under the same name for the date of 1764 follows below:

1764 REEVES, GEORGE. A New History of London, from its Foundation to the Present Year. . . . Folding map and engravings. 8vo. London.
2nd edit. the same year.

ROCQUE, JOHN. The Environs of London. Reduced from an actual Survey in 16 sheets by the late John Rocque, Topographer to His Majesty, with new Improvements to the Year 1763. London.

This evidently goes back to the Plan of 1746 cited above.

1764 EFFORD, WILLIAM. A Scheme for the better Supplying this Metropolis with Sweet and Wholesome Water from the River Coln, most humbly offered for the Consideration of Parliament, the Nobility, Gentry, and Inhabitants of the West End of the Town in particular. Map of the river from Denham to the Thames. 4to. London.

1765 A Description of Vaux-Hall Gardens. In *Gent. Mag.,* vol. 35, 353-56. London.

TYLER, ARTHUR. The History and Antiquities of St. Saviour's; containing Annals from the First Founding, to the Present Time: Lists of the Priors and Benefactors: a particular Description of the Building, Ornaments, Monuments, remarkable Places, etc. with Notes. 12mo. London.

A superficial compilation.—Gough, 352.

1766 GWYNN, JOHN. London and Westminster Improved, Illustrated by Plans. To which is prefixed A Discourse on Publick Magnificence; with Observations on the State of Arts and Artists in this Kingdom, wherein the Study of the Polite Arts is recommended as necessary to a Liberal Education: Concluded by some Proposals relative to Places not laid down in the Plans. 4 large folding plates. 4to. London.

Dr. Johnson wrote the Dedication to the King prefixed to this work. The book sums up Gwynn's views on art training, and his plans for improvement have gained for him almost a prophetic reputation.—Maggs, no. 559.

LEROUGE, —. For his account of the curiosities of London, see his *Curiosités de Londres,* etc., under TOURS BY FOREIGNERS.

1767   An Account of the Principal Buildings, Streets, etc., in London, Westminster, with their Antiquity, Derivation, etc., extracted from Stow, Speed, Maitland, etc. Extracts in *Gent. Mag.,* vol. 37, 536-40.

1768   BLAKE, —. The State and Case of a Design for the better Education of thousands of Parish Children successively in the Vast Western Suburb of London vindicated; and humbly dedicated to all the Honourable and Pious Persons that have been or may be inclined to be Favourers and Encouragers of it. 4to. London.

> This hospital at Highgate, called the Ladies' Charity-School, was erected by one Blake, a woolen-draper in Covent-Garden, who purchased Dorchester-House, and having fooled away his estate in building was thrown into prison, whence he wrote this account, to which prospects of Dorchester-House and the hospital are fixed.—Gough, who gives no date, 321.

CHATELAIN, J. B. Fifty Views in the Vicinity of London. London.

GROSLEY, PIERRE JEAN. For one of the best known foreign accounts of London, see his *Londres,* under TOURS BY FOREIGNERS.

A Guide through the Cities and Suburbs of London and Westminster, containing an Account of the Government, Manners of the Inhabitants, their Trade, Arts and Sciences, etc., with an Alphabetical List of all the Streets, Squares, Courts, Lanes and Alleys. 12mo. London.

Plagues of London. For a list of publications on this subject, see Gough, 299-303.

SMITH, JAMES. The Art of Living in London. London. (See Peacham under 1642 above.)

For a list of published views of London, see Gough, 353-363.

1769   The City Remembrancer, being Historical Narratives of the Great Plague 1665, Great Fire 1666, and Great Storm 1703, collected from Papers originally compiled by Dr. Harvey. 2 vols. 8vo. London.

An Historical Account of the Curiosities of London and Westminster, in three parts. 8vo. London.

> This points out the well-known sights the visitor would generally want to see, such as the Tower of London, Westminster Abbey, St. Paul's, etc.

The London Directory for 1769. Containing an Alphabetical List of the Names and Places of Abode of the Merchants and Principal Traders of the Cities of London and Westminster, the Borough of Southwark, and their Environs, etc. Large folding map of London. 8vo. London.

> This was reissued many times down to 1799.

1769-70 CHAMBERLAIN, HENRY. The History and Survey of the Cities of London and Westminster, the Borough of Southwark, and Parts adjacent, by a Society of Gentlemen; revised, etc., by Henry Chamberlain. Plates. Fol. London.

An inaccurate compilation, published in numbers by Cooke.—Lowndes.

1769-72 DAMIENS DE GOMICOURT. For an account of London, see his *L'Observateur français,* under TOURS BY FOREIGNERS.

1770 Present State of London and the Outports. (Cited in Campbell's *Survey,* without date, but before 1774.)

A Sunday Ramble, or, Modern Sabbath-Day's Journey in and about London and Westminster. London.

2nd edit., 12mo, 1776.
This work is cited by Chancellor, *The Eighteenth Century in London.* It is a guidebook to the charms or amusements of the city and the characteristic pleasure furnished by each. A number of such little books were published for the benefit of the sight-seer.

WHITE, J. The College of Arms, or Herald's Office, 1768; view from the quadrangle. Line engraving by J. White after T. Malton, within a broad border containing arms and shields engraved by W. Sherwin, 14 × 19 ins.

1771 STUART, JAMES (Athenian). Critical Observations on the Buildings and Improvements of London. With a caricature print of the Duke of Cumberland's statue in Cavendish Square. 4to and 8vo. London.

This has been attributed also to John Gwynn the architect.

1772 HUMPHRY, OZIAS. The Pantheon in Oxford Street; view showing dandies and their ladies, dressed in the extreme of fashion, flirting over coffee-cups; visitors in gallery in rear; mezzotint by Humphry after Edwards. 13 × 9¾, with verse beneath.

The New London Spy; or, A Twenty-Four Hours Ramble through the Bills of Mortality; containing a true Picture of Modern High and Low Life, from the splendid Mansions in St. James's to the subterranean Habitations of St. Giles's . . . the whole exhibiting a striking Portrait of London as it appears in the Present Year 1772. Frontispiece with 20 additional curious and facetious engravings. 8vo. London.

This may be another edition of the work with this title cited under 17— above.

Probable Conjecture on the Use of London-Stone (standing close under the wall of St. Swithin's Church). Signed Investigator. In *Gent. Mag.,* vol. 42, 126.

1773 HANWAY, JONAS. The State of Young Chimney Sweepers Apprentices. London.

This philanthropist well deserved the monument that was erected to his memory in Westminster Abbey. He was very active in reforming abuses and ameliorating the lot of the unfortunate.

The London Companion, or, An Account of the Fares of Hackney Coachmen, Chairmen, and Watermen, with the Rates of Carmen and Porters plying in London, Westminster, and Southwark. 12mo. London.

NOORTHOUCK, JOHN. A New History of London, including Westminster and Southwark. To which is added, A General Survey of the Whole, describing the Public Buildings, late Improvements, etc. 42 folding plates of maps, views, arms, etc. 4to. London.

> Scattered information of value.—J. Williams.

1774   The Ambulator, or, The Stranger's Companion in a Tour round London; within a Circuit of Twenty-Five Miles; describing whatever is remarkable, either for Grandeur, Use, or Curiosity; and comprehending Catalogues of the Pictures by Eminent Artists. To which is prefixed, A Concise Description of London, Southwark and Westminster. 12mo. London.

> Other edits., usually enlarged, 1782, 1783, 1793, 1796, and 1800.

London Unmask'd; or, The New Town Spy: a Complete Picture of the Metropolis and its Inhabitants, the gay Circles, Theatres, etc., by the Man in the Moon. Frontispiece. 8vo. London.

WILLIAMS, J. Laws and Customs of London. London. (So cited in Brett-James.)

1775   For a Guide to London, see *A Description of the County of Middlesex*, under DESCRIPTIONS.

TOMLINS, T. List of the Livery of London, with their Places of Abodes and Incomes. Fol. London.

1776   COGAN, THOMAS. John Buncle Junior, Gentleman. Sketch of London, Anecdotes, Learned Ladies, Politicians, etc. 2 vols. 8vo. London.

> The author was a physician trained in Holland, who also wrote novels, accounts of travels, translations from the Dutch, and treatises on the passions.—From *DNB*.

Curiosities of London and Westminster. 8vo. London.

FIELDING, SIR JOHN. A Brief Description of the Cities of London and Westminster, the public Buildings, Palaces, Gardens, Squares, etc. 12mo. London.

HARRISON, WALTER. A New and Universal History, Description, and Survey of the Cities of London and Westminster, the Borough of Southwark, and Parts adjacent. Numerous copperplate engravings, maps, plans, etc. Fol. London.

> Some of these views were published separately. See following item.

A Series of 13 interesting old Copper-Plate Views of the River Thames, engraved for Walter Harrison's History of London, giving picturesque views of the chief places along the Thames between Windsor and Greenwich, each 6 × 10½ ins.

> This work was begun in 1775.

The London Directory; or, An Account of the Stage Coaches and Carriers, from London to the different Towns in Great Britain. Describing the Number of Miles, Fares, and the Days and Hours of setting out, etc. 8vo. London.

SMITH, WILLIAM, M.D. The State of the Gaols in London, Westminster, and Borough of Southwark. London.

> The author, a physician, had been appointed by the Westminster Charity to attend sick prisoners. His account reveals frightful conditions prevailing and offers wise remedial suggestions.—J. Williams.

1777 ANDREWS, J. Environs of London, 2nd Part—Essex, drawn and engraved by J. Andrews (extent, Dunmow, Rayleigh, Malden, Epping), on a scale of 1⅞ ins. to a mile. Size 26 × 20 ins. on canvas. London.

LACOMBE, FRANCOIS. For his Observations on London, see his *Observations de Londres,* under TOURS BY FOREIGNERS.

Squire Randal's Excursion round London, or, A Week's Frolic in the Year 1776, with the Remarks of John Trusty, in a Series of Letters to their Friends and Bottle Companions in the Country. 8vo. London.

A Survey of the Mansion House, Amphitheatre, Gardens and Lands belonging to the Proprietors of Ranelagh, in the County of Middlesex. Large plan, 26 × 20 ins. London.

1778 An Historical Description of the Tower of London, and its Curiosities . . . Written chiefly to direct the Attention of Spectators to what is most curious in this Repository, and to enable them afterwards to relate what they have seen. 8vo. London.

Kent's Directory for the Year 1778, containing an Alphabetical List of the Names and Places of Abode of the Directors of Companies, Persons in Public Business, Merchants, etc., in the Cities of London and Westminster. 8vo. London.

1780 BOWLES, C. A New Pocket Plan of the Cities of London and Westminster, with the Borough of Southwark, exhibiting the new Buildings to the Year 1780. Map measuring 21½ × 16½ ins. London.

> A reduced plan of the above, exhibiting the New Buildings to the Year 1785, was published in 21 x 15 ins. size, 1785.

A Collection of Plans of London, viz: 15 Plans of Wards: 7 plans of Wards engraved for Thornton's *History of London and Westminster,* fol.; Wren's Plan for rebuilding the City after the Great Fire; Evelyn's Plan for rebuilding the City; Plan of London as fortified in 1642-3; Plan of Baynard's Castle and other Wards. London.

DUGDALE, SIR WILLIAM. The History and Antiquities of the Four Inns of Court, of the Nine Inns of Chancery; also of Serjeant's Inn and Scroop's Inn. 8vo. London.

LETTSOM, J. C. A Morning Walk in the Metropolis. In *Gent. Mag.,* vol. 50, 25-26. London.

> This account is taken up entirely with the scenes of distress, poverty, and misery to be observed in London. Not many tourists looked for such. The author was the well-known physician.

Nine Plans of the Wards of Aldgate, Billingsgate, Cripplegate, Faringdon, Broad Street, etc. London.

Poems by a Young Nobleman . . . particularly the State of England and the once flourishing City of London, in a Letter from an American Traveller dated from the Ruinous Portico of St. Paul's in the Year, 2199, to a Friend settled in Boston, the Metropolis of the Western Empire, . . . 4to. London.

> The author must have felt pretty safe in placing the date so far in the future. Had he had real prevision he might have selected 1940. So far as I know, this must be the earliest of such "Looking Forwards."

1781 TURNER, SAMUEL. A Short History of the Westminster Forum. 2 vols. 8vo. London.

1782 ANDREWS, —. Andrews' New and Accurate Map of the Country Thirty Miles round London from an Actual Survey . . . including Turnpike and Most Cross Roads. Scale 2½ miles to 1 in., size 25 × 27 ins. London.

DUCAREL, A. C. The History of the Royal Hospital and Collegiate Church of St. Katherine, near the Tower of London, from its Foundation in the Year 1273 to the Present Time. In vol. V of *Bibl. Topog. Brit.* 4to. London.

An Historical Account of the Curiosities of London and Westminster. Pt. I. Containing a full Description of the Tower of London. Pt. II. The History of Westminster Abbey. Pt. III. . . . treats of the Old Cathedral of St. Paul's, and the New, etc. 3 pts. 8vo. London.

> This may be another edition of the work listed under 1776. A work with the same title was published in 4 vols., 1786.

A New and Correct Plan of London, Westminster and Southwark. 16 × 27 ins. London.

> Later edit., with hackney coach fares, 16 × 20 ins., 1786.

1783 BOWEN, THOMAS. An Historical Account of the Origin, Progress, and Present State of Bethlehem Hospital, founded by Henry VIII, for the Care of Lunatics, and enlarged by subsequent Benefactors, for the Reception and Maintenance of Incurables. 4to. London.

> Reviewed *Gent. Mag.,* vol. 53, 866-68. The volume was not printed for sale but for distribution to the governors of the hospital and to members of Parliament. Bedlam was one of the few hospitals that escaped destruction at the dissolution of the monasteries, when it was refounded and put into secular hands. The building was designed after the Chateau de Tuilleries by the famous mathematician Robert Hooke, who was in addition a natural philosopher and an architect. This fact so vexed Louis XIV that he ordered a building for inferior offices to be built upon the plan of St. James's in London. A Frenchman who visited Bedlam in 1697 remarked that "all the mad folk of London are not in this hospital."

C<small>ARY</small>, J<small>OHN</small>. Cary's New Survey of the Country round London: Roads, Rivers, Parks, etc., within Twenty Miles of the City. 22 × 25 ins.

For an account of this great surveyor and map maker, who is unnoticed in *DNB,* see under 1787, M<small>APS AND CHARTS</small>.

Ralph's Critical Review of the Public Buildings, Statues, and Ornaments in and about London and Westminster, with additions and Comments. 12mo. London. (See Ralph under 1737 above.)

1784 B<small>AILEY</small>, J<small>OHN</small>. Bailey's British Directory; or, Merchant's and Trader's useful Companion for the Year 1784. 4 vols. 8vo. London.

B<small>OWLES</small>, C. Bowles' New London Guide; being an Alphabetical Index to all the Streets, Squares, Lanes, Courts, Alleys, Docks, Wharfs, Keys, Stairs, etc., Churches, Chapels, and other Places of Worship, Villages, Hamlets, Hospitals and Public Buildings of every Denomination, in and within Five Miles of the Metropolis. 8vo. London. (Date is approximate.)

T<small>HORNTON</small>, W. The History, Description, Survey of the Cities of London and Westminster, and Parts adjacent, and likewise Parishes, Villages, etc., above Twenty Miles round, Original, Antiquities, Companies, Law Courts, etc. Over 100 copperplates, plans, maps, written and compiled by a Society of Gentlemen, and revised by Wm. Thornton, assisted by G. Smith. Fol. London.

1785 C<small>ARY</small>, J<small>OHN</small>. Cary's New Pocket Plan of London, Westminster, and Southwark. (Date is a guess.)

D<small>UCAREL</small>, A<small>NDREW</small> C<small>OLTEC</small>. The History and Antiquities of the Archiepiscopal Palace of Lambeth, from its Foundation to the Present Time. Frontispiece and 9 plates. 4to. London.

The English and French Guide through London. (So listed in *Gent. Mag.,* vol. 55, July.)

K<small>ENT</small>, —. Kent's Directory for the Year 1785, containing an Alphabetical List of the Names and Places of Abode of the Directors of Companies, Persons in Public Business, Merchants, and Traders in the Cities of London and Westminster and Borough of Southwark, also Lists of the Lord Mayors, Aldermen, Lists of Bankers, etc. 8vo. London.

This is probably one of the several editions of the work with the same title listed under 1778 above.

S<small>AYER</small>, R<small>OBERT</small>. A New Pocket Map of London. London.

1786 B<small>OWLES</small>, C<small>ARINGTON</small>. Bowles's New London Guide and Hackney Coach Directory, etc. 8vo. London.

CAREY, —. Survey of Richmond and Hampton Court. (So listed in *Gent. Mag.,* vol. 56, 981.)

CARY, JOHN. An Actual Survey of the Country Fifteen Miles Round London, on a Scale of one inch to a mile; wherein the Roads, Rivers, Woods and Commons, as well as every Market Town, Village, etc., are distinguished. Double page general map and 50 section maps, with Index of Names. 8vo. London.

DORNFORD, JOSIAH. Nine Letters to the . . . Lord Mayor . . . of London, on the State of the Prisons and Prisoners within their Jurisdiction . . . London.

> This work reveals shocking conditions: lack of infirmaries, proper food, medicine, beds and bedding, etc. It recommends better plans for new buildings, regulations, abolition of fees to the keepers, etc. Many instances of neglect are cited.—From J. Williams.

DUCAREL, ANDREW COLTEC. The History and Antiquities of the Parish of Lambeth, in the County of Surrey. Including Biographical Anecdotes of several eminent Persons. 20 plates. No. 39 of *Bibl. Topog. Brit.*

FIELDING, SIR JOHN. Fielding's Hackney Coach Rates. 8vo. London.

GROSE, FRANCIS. A Treatise on Ancient Armour and Weapons in the Tower of London. Plates. 2 vols. London.

> For the chief works of this famous antiquary, see under 1786 and later, HISTORY AND ANTIQUITIES.

Historical Description of the Tower of London. 12mo. London.

TRUSLER, REV. DR. JOHN. The London Adviser and Guide, containing every Instruction and Information useful and necessary to Persons living in London and coming to reside there. 8vo. London.

> Another edition, 12mo, London, 1790.
> Dr. Trusler will be remembered for his moral guide to Hogarth's prints.

1787   KEARSLEY, G. Kearsley's London Register, containing Lists of the Lord Mayors, Aldermen, Sheriffs, Recorders, Chamberlains, Comptrollers, Town-Clerks, and other Officers, from the Year 1660 to the Present Time: The Court of Aldermen at the Time of the Revolution in 1688; and of the Aldermen and Members of Parliament since that Period. To which is added, An Account of the several Wards, Precincts, and Parishes. Also, the Rules and Orders of my Lord-Mayor, the Aldermen, and Sheriffs, for their various Meetings and Wearirg of their Apparel through the Whole Year, etc. London.

> Noticed briefly in *Gent. Mag.,* vol. 57, 909-10.

POLLARD, R. Highbury: A West View of Highbury Place, showing a stretch of open and hilly country, with a row of houses on right, farm buildings, etc., in center, and cattle in immediate foreground; mezzotint by R. Pollard after R. Dodd. 14¼ × 20¼ ins.

POLLARD, R., and F. JUKES. Hanover Square: View looking towards St. George's Church, showing in immediate foreground an "inversable" phaeton-and-four, an assemblage of fashion, mounted and on foot, also street types. Aquatint in sepia by R. Pollard and F. Jukes after E. Dayes. 14¾ × 21 ins.

1788 BOWLES, CARINGTON. Bowles' New Pocket Plan of London for the Year 1788. Colored plan. London.

DENNE, SAMUEL. On the Stone Seats in Maidstone Church. 4to. London. (Bound up with Nichols, *History of Canonbury House, Islington;* see under TOWNS.)

Panoramic View of London, from the New Bridge at Westminster to London Bridge. Contemporary colored engraving, 13 feet by 1 foot. London.

This depicts all the notable buildings, places, and bridges. It was taken from the south side of London.

1789 A Companion to all the principal Places of Curiosity and Amusement in and about London and Westminster . . . details of Programmes at Astley's, Ranelagh, Sadler's Wells, etc. 12mo. London.

FORES, S. W. Fores' New Guide for Foreigners, containing the most complete Description of the Cities of London and Westminster, and their Environs . . . including an Account of all the Palaces, Seats, Villas, . . . and Villages within . . . 25 Miles round the Metropolis. In English and French. 8vo. London.

Historical Account of the Royal Hospital for Seamen at Greenwich. Plates. 4to. London.

PICKETT, WILLIAM. Public Improvement; or, A Plan for making a convenient and handsome Communication between the Cities of London and Westminster. 4to. London.

WAKEFIELD, —. Wakefield's Merchant and Tradesman's General Directory for London, Westminster, Borough of Southwark, and Twenty-two Miles circular from St. Paul's for the Year 1790. London.

1790 The Art of Living in London: a Poem. With a correct map of London, Westminster, and Southwark. Descriptions by W. Green. 8vo. London.

See Smith under 1768 above for a similar title.

FARINGTON, JOSEPH. View of London Bridge from the river, showing the Church of St. Magnus, the Monument, etc., in background, boats, figures, etc., in foreground. Colored aquatint. 14¾ × 19⅜ ins.

The London Companion, or Citizen and Stranger's Guide. 12mo. London.

MALTON, T. The Adelphi: John street, showing costume figures, etc. Aquatint, 12 × 9 ins.

> This famous structure, which was said to have arisen to the sound of the bagpipes, was designed and erected by the Adam brothers, Scotch architects, who had to fight not only national prejudice, but also labor troubles, local hostilities, and financial difficulties. The last named they overcame by promoting a huge lottery, and the labor squabbles by supplanting the Scotch with Irish workmen. The Adelphi has been the home of many a celebrated figure in English literature. Recent expansion of business and building in London decreed its destruction.

————. Charing Cross: view showing Northumberland House, Charles I's Statue, costume figures, carriages, etc. In aquatint. 8½ × 12 ins.

The Midnight Rambler; or, New Nocturnal Spy, for the Present Year, containing a Complete Description of the Modern Transactions of London and Westminster, from the Hours of Nine in the Evening, till Six in the Morning . . . Illustrated with Real Characters, and Whimsical Anecdotes, of several Votaries of Bacchus and Venus, from the First-rate Bucks, Bloods and Filles de Joye, down to those in more Humble Stations; as well as those in more Deplorable Conditions, whose Utmost Prospects are through the Bars of a Prison. 12mo. London.

A Modern Sabbath (in London). London.

A New Plan of London, Westminster, and Southwark, with the New Buildings and Alterations in 1790. 19 × 36 ins. London.

PENNANT, THOMAS. An Account of London. Engraved plates. 4to. London.

> 2nd edit., with many additions and more plates, 4to, London, 1791; 3rd edit., 4to, London, 1793; Dublin, 8vo, 1793; translated into German, Nürnberg, 179–. See below.
> Reviewed *Gent. Mag.,* vol. 60, 522. This work is the result of many rambles through London by Pennant, who used to jot down in a notebook countless scraps of information on buildings, sights, and antiquities. The book aroused much interest among Londoners, who furnished in various ways corrections which Pennant utilized in later editions.

> 1790   Critical Observations on Mr. Pennant's London. Signed Londinensis. In *Gent. Mag.,* vol. 60, 611-12.

> 179-   (In German.) Thomas Pennant's Beschreibung von London, vorzüglich im Rücksicht auf ältere Geschichte, etc. 8vo. Nürnberg.

WALLIS, JOHN. London: or, An Abridgement of Mr. Pennant's Description of the British Capital. 4 folding plates. 12mo. London

Westminster Bridge: View, showing the Abbey Towers above the house-tops in background, and figures and vehicles in foreground. Aquatint by T. Malton. 8½ × 12 ins.

1791   GUYOT, —. View of the Poudre Magasin in Hyde Park; colored aquatint, 5¾ × 7½ ins.

> A choice example of an interesting English subject by a very famous French engraver. —Bookseller's Note.

SMITH, JOHN THOMAS. Antiquities of London, and its Environs, engraved by T. Smith; containing many curious Houses, Monuments, and Statues never before published, and also from Original Drawings, communicated by several Members of the Antiquarian Society: with Remarks and References to the much admired Works of Messrs. Pennant, Stowe, Weever, Camden, Maillard, etc. 97 engravings. Fol. London.

Reviewed *Gent. Mag.*, vol. 61, 157. This was intended to appear in numbers, which must have run up to the year 1800. The reviewer states that the work is not as good as it might be but that the young artist should be encouraged to improve. Many of the views present objects no longer existing.

1792 LYSONS, DANIEL. The Environs of London: being an Historical Account of the Towns, Villages, and Hamlets, within Twelve Miles of that Capital; interspersed with Biographical Anecdotes. Numerous engraved views and portraits. 4to. London.

The first edition was completed in 1796 in 4 vols. To the ground already covered was added An Historical Account of those Parishes in the County of Middlesex, which are not described in the Environs of London, making six vols., and running to the year 1800. The first four included the counties of Surrey, Middlesex, Herts, Essex, and Kent; the fifth, Middlesex parishes not included in the former; and the sixth a Supplement. Vol. I was reviewed in *Gent. Mag.*, vol. 63, 440-44. Here it is stated that Lysons attempted to make good the neglect with which local historians have passed by the counties adjacent to London. He well fulfills what is required of a local historian, but it is regretted that he seemingly confines himself to districts. It is local to the extreme yet most entertaining and useful.—He gives interesting facts on the state of market gardening near London in olden times and in his own day. He calculates that about 5000 acres within twelve miles of London are constantly cultivated for the supply of the London markets with garden vegetables, and about 800 acres of fruits, and 1700 for potatoes, and 1200 with various garden vegetables for food for cattle, principally cows. The average rent of such ground is "now 4 per acre."—Hazlitt, *Gleanings in Old Garden Literature*.

MALTON, THOMAS. A Picturesque Tour through the Cities of London and Westminster, illustrated with the Most interesting Views executed in Aqua-tint. 2 vols. Fol. London.

Malton had the reputation of drawing with extreme accuracy.

————. St. Mary-le-Strand: view showing Somerset House, and the street life of the period; aquatint in brown, 8½ × 12 ins.

1793 BARFOOT, PETER, and JOHN WILKES. The Universal British Directory of Trade, Commerce, and Manufacture, etc. 8vo. London.

It is also a directory to the nobility, gentry, and families of distinction in London and Westminster.

KEARSLEY, G., and C. Kearsley's Stranger's Guide, or Companion through London and Westminster and the Country round. Containing a Description of the Situation, Antiquity, and Curiosities of every Place within the Circuit of Fourteen Miles, etc. 12mo. London. (Date is approximate.)

MAZZINGHI, —. The History of London, Westminster, and Southwark, in French and English. 12mo. London. (So cited in Gray, *Reference Catalogue of Brit. Topography*.)

1794 MALTON, THOMAS. Privy Garden (now Whitehall Gardens); aquatint, 10 ×
12 ins.

Representations of Monuments, Stained Windows, Brasses, and other Antiquities, in different Churches in the Environs of London, hitherto not engraved.
London.

> Noticed briefly in Gent. Mag., vol. 64, 1025. This is No. 1. Each number is to have four
> plates, and in size to agree with Lysons' Environs of London, to which it is to form an
> appendix. Simco or his artist is advised by the reviewer that they will have to mend their
> ways if they are to keep company with Lysons.

VANDERSTEGEN, WILLIAM. The Present State of the Thames considered. 8vo.
London.

1794-99 HORWOOD, R. Plan of the Cities of London and Westminster, the Borough of
Southwark, and Parts adjoining, showing every House. 32 large sheets. Imp.
fol. London.

> Horwood's map is the most important record of London since Rocque's Survey in 1746.
> It takes in the Metropolis from Lisson Grove in the North-West to Deptford in the South-
> East. Regent's Park still appears as open fields, the New (Marylebone) Road is just
> made. Lord's Cricket Ground shows on the side of Dorset Square, the Westbourne from
> Hyde Park to Chelsea is still an open ditch. Pimlico is unbuilt, Stepney is still a country
> village. In fact it shows London before the great building movement, which started in
> the Nineteenth Century. Before this map was executed—at the expense of the Phoenix
> Fire Office—the houses in the main thoroughfares only were numbered; after its publica-
> tion every house was numbered, and is so indicated upon the map, which makes it a most
> important document from a legal and antiquarian point of view.—Sotheran, Catalogue.
> The map was reissued from 1799 to 1802.

1795 CONCANEN, M., and A. MORGAN. The History and Antiquities of the Parish of
St. Saviour's Southwark. Plates and plan. 8vo. London.

> Reviewed Gent. Mag., vol. 65, 944. The opinion is expressed that the author shows
> himself too unpracticed for such work. He goes into too much detail where it is uncalled
> for.

The Country Twenty-Five Miles round London. Large colored map, in 3 sections.

DENNE, REV. SAMUEL. Historical Particulars of Lambeth Parish. No. 5, vol. X,
of Bibl. Topog. Brit.

A Fortnight's Ramble through London, or, A Complete Display of all the Cheats
and Frauds practiced in that great Metropolis, with the best Methods for
eluding them: being a pleasing Narrative of the Adventures of a Farmer's Son,
published at his Request for the benefit of his country. 8vo. London.

> This seems to be a belated "Tricks of the Town" item.

Hints for a New Edition of Mr. Pennant's London. In Gent. Mag., vol. 65, 268-70.

> This contains corrections of facts and expresses a desire to see Pennant improve his
> style.

Remarks on Lysons' Environs of London. In Gent. Mag., vol. 65, 453-54. (Deals
with vol. II.)

View of Fish Street Hill, from Grace Church Street, representing the Monument and the Church of St. Magnus, London Bridge. Portraying contemporary street life, crowded with costume figures on horse and foot, vehicles, and incidents of every description with the Monument and the tower of St. Magnus dominating the scene, and showing a glimpse of London Bridge at the foot of the Hill. Line engraving by T. Morris after W. Marlow, 20 × 16 ins. Twickenham.

1795-1800   Select Views in London and Westminster. Obl. 4to. London.

1796   BOYLE, —. Boyle's New Fashionable Court and Country Guide and Town Visiting Directory for 1796. 12mo. London. (In progress.)

The First Guide to the Tower of London—an Historical Description of the Tower and its Curiosities. 8vo. London.

GIBSON, —. A Short Account of Several Gardens near London, with Remarks on some Particulars wherein they excel or are Deficient, upon a View of them in December, 1691. Paper read July 3, 1794. Communicated to the Society of Antiquaries by the Rev. Dr. Hamilton, Vice-President, from an original Manuscript in his Possession. Printed in *Archaeologia,* vol. 12. London.

This deals with produce gardens in the main; references to orange trees, to the Chelsea Physick Gardens, Kensington Gardens, Sir William Temple's gardens at Shean, etc.

J., W. Two Plans of the London Dock, with some Observations respecting the River immediately connected with the Docks, etc., the Improvement of Navigation. London.

Noticed briefly in *Gent. Mag.,* vol. 66, 853. The plans are those which were first suggested to the Committee of Merchants, 1794, and printed for private circulation, and now made public. Five pages of brief Remarks are added by the editor, William James.

KENT, —. Kent's Directory for the Year 1796; also The Shopkeeper's and Tradesman's Assistant, being a New and Correct Alphabetical List of all the Stage Coaches, Carriers, Coasting Vessels, containing an Account of the Inns in London, where the Coaches put up and go out from, also the Rates of Hackney Coaches, also Rates of Postage of the General Postoffice. 8vo. London.

See Kent under 1778 and 1785 above.

The London Guide and Merchant's Directory for the Year 1796: containing Names and Residences of Merchants, Manufacturers, and Traders, Directors of the South Sea, Hudson's Bay, etc., Companies of the Cities of London, Westminster, and Borough of Southwark. Map and Plan. (Bound up with this is also Guide to Stage Coaches, Mails, Boats, etc., which carry Passengers and Merchandise from London.) 2 vols. in 1. 8vo. London.

There were later editions of this work.

1797   LYSONS, DANIEL. The Environs of London. Vol. IV. London.

Reviewed *Gent. Mag.,* vol. 67, 143-44. (Vols. I came out in 1792, II and III in 1795.) The fourth contains, among other things, "A general View of the former and present State of Market Gardens, and of the Quantity of Land now occupied for that Purpose, within twelve Miles of London," a curious and interesting article.—From the review.

MALCOLM, J. P. A Series of Prints to illustrate Mr. Lysons' "Environs of London," drawn and engraved by J. P. Malcolm.

> Noticed in *Gent. Mag.,* vol. 67, 144. Two numbers of this work only have appeared and their merit deserves encouragement.—From the review.

Report of a Committee of West-India Planters and Merchants on the Subject of a Bill pending in Parliament for forming Wet-Docks, etc., at the Port of London. (49 pp.)

> This urges the establishment of a canal, entrance-basin, and two wet-docks with warehouses, at the Isle of Dogs. These are designed to receive the whole of the West-India trade. It opposes Wapping docks.—J. Williams.

1798 DODD, RALPH. Letters to a Merchant, on the Improvement of the Port of London . . . without making Wet Docks, or any additional Burdens being laid on Shipping . . . . 8vo. London. (18 pp.)

> This offers a plan for altering London Bridge to allow the passage of vessels, the building of quays and warehouses between it and Blackfriar's Bridge, and dredging. A free harbor for 1,000 ships could thus be formed.—J. Williams.

EDEN, SIR WILLIAM. Porto-Bello; or, A Plan for the Improvement of the Port and City of London. 4 folding plates. 8vo. London.

> This describes existing conditions and considers plans for improvement.—J. Williams.

MALCOLM, J. P. Views near London. Nos. IV and V. London.

> Favorably reviewed *Gent. Mag.,* vol. 68, 48-49.

WALLIS, —. Wallis's New Plan of London and Westminster; a folding plan in color, dissected, mounted on canvas, folding into an 8vo postcard case. London.

1799 ELLIS, HENRY. The History and Antiquities of the Parish of St. Leonard's, Shoreditch, and Liberty of Norton Folgate, in the Suburbs of London. London.

> Reviewed *Gent. Mag.,* vol. 69, 588. This is an excellent specimen of industrious research. The parish is a good subject, with its many interesting memorials of natural history. Norton Folgate Manor belongs from the Conquest to the Dean and Chapter of St. Paul's. Here is a girls' school and a free school for boys, the second of its kind in London.

HOLDEN, —. Holden's Triennial Directory, 1799. London.

> This appeared several times up to 1812; then it was continued as the Triennial Directory of London, Westminster, Southwark (for 1817-19, 1822-24). 2 vols. London.

1800 CARY, JOHN. Actual Survey of the Country Fifteen Miles round London, on a Scale of one Inch to a Mile, wherein the Roads, Rivers, Woods, and Commons, as well as every Market Town, Village, etc., are distinguished, and every Seat shown with the Name of the Possessor, with Index of Names. New edit. Index map, and 50 divisional maps, with the roads, commons, and open parks colored. With Index. 4to. London (for the author).

A Collection of Select Views of London and Westminster. Engraved by Watts, Medland, etc. 4to. London.

DANCE, GEORGE. Perspective Sketch of the Proposed Improvements of the Port of London, designed by George Dance; an expansive view showing in foreground a highly original scheme embodying two bridges, each having a central drawbridge somewhat in the manner of the present-day Tower Bridge, the bridge-heads on either bank being joined by imposing crescents of new buildings, with obelisks, etc., the river crowded with shipping; colored aquatint, by William Daniell, 12¾ × 24½ ins. London.

The architect was George Dance the Younger, who designed Newgate Prison in 1770.

An Exact Account of all the Streets, Lanes, Courts, Allies, etc., of London and Westminster. 8vo. London.

FADEN, W. A Topographical Map of the Country Twenty Miles round London. Scale 2 miles to 1 in. Size 24 × 24½ ins. London.

IRELAND, SAMUEL. Picturesque Views, with an Historical Account of the Inns of Court, in London and Westminster; 21 exterior views of the various inns, printed in bistre. 8vo. London.

London Bridge. The Several Plans and Drawings referred to in the Third Report from the Select Committee upon the Improvement of the Port of London. Fol. London.

This consists of 24 large engraved plates including one in colored aquatint and several tinted, of views of bridges suggested by various architects to replace London Bridge, and of improvements to the Pool and the docks. Included are a number of finely conceived designs by Mylne, Dodd, Wilson, Telford and Douglas, Dance, Jessop, Sir Christopher Wren, and Black, for new bridges or for improvements to the Port of London. Wren's plan was for the reconstruction and lay-out of the destroyed area of the city after the great fire of 1666. Telford's plans are of cast iron bridges. The majority of the others are of stone. Probably the most striking design is one of a double bridge, half of which could always be in use, with a large open space on each side of the Thames between the bridges, that on the north containing in the center the Monument to the Great Fire, and that on the south side a large obelisk similar to Cleopatra's needle, and with a triumphal stairway descending to the river on either side.—From Maggs, no. 742. See under Dance this date above.

METCALFE, R. London Tower; colored plan, engraved by R. Metcalfe, showing proposed improvements of Tower Embankment, St. Catherine's Dock, and the area Between Lower Thames St. and Great Tower St., with street-plan of the neighborhood from Cornhill to East Smithfield, also inset of a proposed floating dock of 102 acres for the Isle of Dogs. 19½ × 23½ ins. London.

The New Annual Directory for 1800. 12mo. London. (Continued as The Post-Office Annual Directory for 1801, etc.)

The New Cheats of London Exposed, or the Frauds and Tricks of the Town laid open to both Sexes, . . . Iniquitous Practices of the Metropolis. 8vo. London.

PENNANT, THOMAS. Tour of London. In Mavor, *The British Tourist*, vol. VI, 1-152. London.

A compressed account in the 3rd person of his *Account of London* (see Pennant under 1792 above). It starts out with the history of London, and passes on to the antiquities and historical associations connected with almost every street, building, and sight referred to. It was apparently intended to serve as a real guidebook, informing the traveler of what is to be seen and of what is of interest in the scene.

SMITH, JOHN THOMAS. Views in London. Vol. VII. London.

> This is mentioned in the *Gent. Mag.*, vol. 70, 971. Vols. XI and XII noticed in vol. 70, 1272. These last complete Smith's project.

Views of Hampton Court Palace (with a description from Lysons' *Middlesex Parishes*). Fol. London.

1809 GRAFTON, RICHARD. For his table of bailiffs, sheriffs, and mayors of London for the years 1189-1558 inclusive, see *Grafton's Chronicle,* 1809 edition, under Grafton, 1562, HISTORY AND CHRONICLE.

1815 SMITH, J. S. Antient Topography of London; Specimens of Sacred, Public and Domestic Architecture to 1665. With an Account of Places and Customs unknown or Overlooked. 32 large engraved plates. 4to. London.

1827 Chronicles of London, from 1089 to 1483, written in the 15th Century and for the First Time printed from MSS. in the British Museum, to which are added numerous contemporary Illustrations, consisting of Royal Letters, Poems, and other Articles Descriptive of the Manners and Customs of the Metropolis. Edit. by Sir N. H. Nicolas. 4to. London.

1844 Croniques de London depuis l'an 44 Henry III. jusqu' à l'an 17 Edward III. Edit. from a MS. in the Cottonian Library by George James Aungier. *Publ. Camden Soc.,* vol. 28. London.

> This chronicle gives the names of the mayors and sheriffs of London at the commencement of each year. The Introduction to the volume relates the history of the disputes between the Londoners and the Barons and the Kings, the attitudes of Henry III, Edward I, II, and III; and a descripion of London topography in the 14th century, the various guilds, etc. The text is well supplemented with notes. The MS is in Norman French, and from the handwriting it appears to have been compiled about the middle of the 14th century. The author is unknown.

1852 Chronicle of the Grey Friars of London. Edit. by John G. Nichols. *Publ. Camden Soc.,* vol. 53. London.

> Another (and better) edit. for the Rolls Series, 1858-82.
> Up to the publication of this chronicle, it remained almost unnoticed. Though forming a portion of the register book of the Grey Friars, the chronicle is not a religious but a civic production. As with other London chronicles, this one reckoned the years according to the annual succession of chief magistrates. Here the period of time included in each year commences with the London mayoralty at the end of October, and the king's year has to be fitted in. Properly then this is a London chronicle. It was usual for London chronicles to begin with the reign of Richard I, the date from which the roll of chief magistrates, at first called bailiffs, has been preserved. This one resembles Arnold's Chronicle, in detailing the same events, though not quite so fully, down to the 17th Henry VII, A.D. 1502. After this year, the two London chronicles are wholly different in their contents. Towards the end of Henry VIII's reign this chronicle began to take on a character entirely its own. The writer watched the religious turn of events very closely, particularly as they affected London and the metropolitan church of St. Paul's. The entries are very matter-of-fact in their nature. One is impressed with the numerous notices of victims being led from the Tower to Tyburn for execution, hanging and quartering. He mentions the "sweating sickness" of June, 1551. The account closes with Sept., 1555.—From the Introduction.

1859 A London Chronicle during the Reigns of Henry VII and Henry VIII. Edit. by Clarence Hopper. In *Camden Misc.* IV, vol. 73, of *Publ. Camden Soc.* London.

> The writer was a London citizen, who records under each mayoralty year particulars of the city, notes the Progresses of the Royal Family, arrival of famous visitors to London, the paving of Chancery, Fetter, and Shoe Lanes, the outrages of the London "prentices," the state of the weather, the health of the city in general, the principal fires, the destruction of monastic relics, and the gradual changes in religious worship, etc.—From the Introduction.

1860 COOKE, ROBERT. Visitation of London, taken by Robert Cooke (Clarenceaux King of Arms) A.D. 1568, and since augmented with Descents and Arms (Harl. MS. no. 1463), edit. by J. J. Howard and J. G. Nichols. 4to. London. (Date approximate.)

1861 Liber Albus: the White Book of the City of London, compiled A.D. 1419 by John Carpenter and Richard Whittington, translated from the original Latin by H. T. Riley. 8vo. London.

1865 NORDEN, JOHN. Notes on London and Westminster, 1592. From his *Description of Middlesex*, Brit. Mus. Harl. MS. No. 570. In Rye, *England as Seen by Foreigners,* 93-100. London.

> In a note, Rye says that this description was omitted in the printed edition of Norden's *Middlesex,* as well as in subsequent editions. His account is introduced here as affording an appropriate illustration to the Journal of the Duke Frederick of Wirtemberg of the same year. See Rathgeb, under 1602, TOURS BY FOREIGNERS.

RYE, WILLIAM B. For various accounts of London, see his *England as Seen by Foreigners in the Days of Elizabeth and James I,* under GENERAL REFERENCE.

1868 RILEY, H. T. (Editor). Memorials of London and London Life in the 13th, 14th, and 15th Centuries, being a Series of Extracts from the Early Archives of the City of London, A.D. 1276-1419, selected, translated, and edited. 8vo. London.

1873 OVERALL, WILLIAM H. In the *Proceedings of the Society of Antiquaries* for this year, are some particulars on the early maps of London, and more especially on the map attributed to Ralph Agas. 8vo. London.

1874 AGAS, RALPH. Civitas Londinum. A Survey of the Cities of London and Westminster, The Borough of Southwark and Parts Adjacent In the Reign of Queen Elizabeth. Published in Facsimile from the Original in the Guildhall Library with a Bibliographical Account of Ralph Agas and a Critical and Historical Examination of the Work and of the Several so-called Reproductions of it by Vertue and Others. 4to. London.

1876 Historical Collections of a Citizen of London in the Fifteenth Century. Containing, I. John Page's Poem on the Siege of Rouen. II. Lydgate's Verses on the Kings of England. III. William Gregory's Chronicle of London. Edited by James Gairdner. *Publ. Camden Soc.,* vol. 17, n.s. London.

> All of the matter in the MS seems to have been written by the same hand. William Gregory of the Skinner's Company, born 1410 and died 1452, was Mayor of London 1451-52. The stuff of the chronicle is probably not wholly original, for it was the practice to transcribe the work of other writers. It is a city chronicle of the kind of which Fabyan's

is the best example. It begins with Richard I, 1189-94 and runs to 1469. It relates historic events and items of city interest, such as the coronation of Henry VI, 1429, and the various sittings of Parliament. There are but few glimpses of intimate London doings.—From the Introduction.

1878   CRACE, J. G. (Editor). A Catalogue of Maps, Plans and Views of London and Southwark, collected and arranged by F. Crace. 8vo. London.

This collection was acquired by the British Museum in 1880. On the whole it is the best bibliography on the subject.—Davies, *Bibliog. Brit. Hist.*

1879   HARRIS, ALEXANDER. The Oeconomy of the Fleete; or, An Apologeticall Answeare of Alexander Harris (Late Warden there) unto XIX Articles sett forth against him by the Prisoners. Edit. from original MSS. . . . by Augustus Jessopp, D.D. *Publ. Camden Soc.,* n.s., vol. 25. London.

The Introduction gives an absorbing history of one of the oldest institutions of England, which had existed on the same spot for 800 to 1000 years—the prison for the detention of debtors. In the reign of Richard II (1391) the Fleet was a prison for any one short of a capital charge. First mention of extortion charges against the wardens was made in about 1400. One learns also of the duties of a warden, the source of his profits, the hereditary nature of his job, which was saleable property on which a mortgage could be raised, the relation of debtor, creditor, and warden and why the first could be held as a prisoner. Men could not be fastened with irons in the Fleet as in Newgate. There were various levels of decency in the wards, descending to the dungeon and down to the lowest, the Beggar's ward, where the prisoner was left to his fate. Even in the early years of the 17th century, the prison seems to have been marked by frightful crowding, vermin and filth, brawls, robberies, and murders, for in July, 1619, there occurred a sudden and spontaneous outbreak of passion, which became downright mutiny, against the prevailing conditions. This was aggravated in October, 1619, by the murder of Sir John Whitbrooke, who was stabbed to death. The prisoners drew up a list of charges against the warden Harris, which he attempted to refute in the above pamphlet.

1884   London in 1669. Communicated by Theodore Bent. In *Antiquary,* vol. 10, 62-64. (For this account see under TOURS BY FOREIGNERS.)

1886   Londini quod reliquum, or, London Remains (*ca.* 1550). Seven sheets. Published by the Topog. Soc. of London. (See under 1550 above.)

1887   FRESHFIELD, E. A Discourse on some unpublished Records of the City of London. 4to. London.

This lays open the general character of London Parochial Records, and the extent to which they include material for the history not only of London but also of England, in the 17th century. Davies, *Bibliog. Brit. History.*

1889   Early Maps and Views of London. In *Antiquary,* vol. 20, 63-67. London.

Here is discussed the work of Agas, Braun, Hogenburg, Wyngaerde, and Visscher.

1904-05   GOMME, G. L. (Editor). Topographical History of London. Part of a *Classified Collection of the Chief Contents of the Gentleman's Magazine,* from 1731-1868. 3 vols. 8vo. London. (For this collection see Gomme under GENERAL REFERENCE.)

1905   KINGSFORD, CHARLES LETHBRIDGE. The Chronicles of London. Edit. with Introduction and Notes. 8vo. Oxford.

The book is illustrated by a map of the city of London done by Ryther, 1604. The Chronicles edited are I. Julius B II, which ends 1435. II. Cleopatra C IV, which ends 1443. III. Vitellus A XVI, which ends 1443. The Introduction traces the development of the

Chronicles of London during the 15th century, and the dependence of later historians and chroniclers on them, and the progress of these of London toward their "present form" as given in the text as well as the sources from which they were derived. The close agreement of all the versions of the Chronicles of London down to the close of the 14th century, whether Latin or English, is evidence that by that time there had been put into shape a popular but short chronicle arranged according to the Mayoral years. They began, no doubt, with official records, such as the Liber de Antiquis Legibus, which were supplemented by matter from general chronicles, like the Flores Historiarum, as in the case of the semiofficial Annales Londonienses and their continuations. Aungier's French Chronicle of London evidences that in the middle of the 14th century unofficial records of a similar form were in circulation. From such sources, some of the matter of the existing English chronicles were derived.—From Introduction.

1923 CASANOVA, GIACOMO. For London as the scene of Casanova's exploits, see this date under TOURS BY FOREIGNERS.

1925 KINGSFORD, CHARLES L. The Early History of Piccadilly, Leicester Square, Soho, and their Neighbourhood, based on a Plan drawn in 1585. Illus. 8vo. Cambridge.

1929 DEFOE, DANIEL. A Tour thro' London about the Year 1725, Being Letter V and parts of Letter VI of "A Tour thro' the Whole Island of Great Britain" containing a Description of the City of London, as taking in the City of Westminster, Borough of Southwark, and parts of Middlesex, edited and annotated by Sir Mayson Beeton and E. Beresford Chancellor. Illustrated with Maps, reproductions of Drawings, and Prints mostly contemporary with the Period of his Life, 1659-1731. Fol. London.

1931 DALE, T. C. (Editor). The Inhabitants of London in 1638. Edit. from MS. 272 in the Lambeth Palace Library by the Rev. T. C. Dale. 2 vols. in 1. 8vo. London.

This work contains a list of the householders (about 13,500 in 93 out of the 107 parishes in the City of London).—Bookseller's Note.

1933 KIRK, REV. ROBERT. London in 1689-90. From a MS. Volume Transcribed by Dr. Donald MacLean. In *Trans. London and Middlesex Arch. Soc.*, vol. 6. London.

The Introduction gives an account of Kirk's main endeavors in the work of the Church. He is to be remembered for having put the Irish Bible of Bedell and Donellan into Roman type for the use of the Highlanders. He took his MSS with him to London, an adventurous undertaking just after the Revolution. He remained a stout Episcopalian even while living in the midst of a Presbyterian community in the Highlands, but he was never molested by the inhabitants of neighboring parishes. The story that he was spirited away by the fairies instead of dying a natural death Scott utilized in his *Rob Roy*, and in the *Legend of Montrose*. While in London, Kirk met many people of interest, especially among the divines, and made himself acquainted with the historic sites of the city. His experiences in the metropolis he wrote down in a small commonplace book, preserved in the Edinburgh University Library. His descriptions of London are of great interest as showing the scene before the dawn of the new century. His viewpoint is that of an onlooker who is intrigued by the social and religious life of the place rather than by its physical appearance. His visit to Gresham College with its many rarities, many of which he enumerates, provoked no comment beyond the statement that such things were there.

1935 YEOMAN, JOHN. The Diary of the Visits of John Yeoman to London (1774-75). Edit. by M. Yearsley. (So cited in the *Camb. Bibliog.*)

1941 LEWIS, W. S. (Editor). Three Tours through London in the Years 1748-1776-1797. Illustrations. New Haven.

These imaginary tours, based upon contemporary documents, make delightful reading.

VII

The Universities—Oxford and Cambridge

(This section is limited in the main to the two universities, and includes histories, descriptions, guides, views, plans, etc., of them as a whole as well as of the various colleges. The first accounts dealing with them appear to be pieces concerning their respective priority in antiquity. According to Gough, *Anecdotes of British Topography,* 99-101, 403, the dispute was begun by Nicholas Cantelupe (3rd Baron, died 1355, the only one mentioned in *DNB*), who is supposed to have drawn up the *Historiola* (printed by Hearne at the end of Sprott's *Chronicle,* see Hearne under 1719 below) in the Black Book and was answered by John Ross in a piece now lost. Gough adds in a note that Bale ascribed the piece to Cantelupe or Thomas Aulaby, of whom nothing is said in Tanner's *Bibl. Brit.* The dispute was revived in 1564 when Queen Elizabeth visited Cambridge. The claims and counterclaims called into engagement no less than 380 writers on the side of Oxford and 110 on that of Cambridge. With such literature the titles of this section begin.)

1568 CAIUS, JOHN. De Antiquitate Cantabrigiensis academiae, libri duo, in quorum secundo de Oxoniensis quoque gymnasii antiquitate disseritur, et Cantabrigiensis longe eo antiquius esse definitur, Londiniensi authore: adjunximus assertionem antiquitatis Oxoniensis academiae ab Oxoniensi quodam annis jam elapsis duobus ad reginam conscriptam, in qua docere conatur, Oxoniense gymnasium Cantabrigiensi antiquius esse: ut ex collatione facile intelligas, utra sit antiquior. Excusam Londini, A.D. 1568, mense Augusto, per Henricum Bynneman. 12mo. London.

This piece by John Caius of Cambridge is a reply to the *Assertio* (in MS) by Thomas Caius, of Oxford, of a prior antiquity, and includes the first printing of the *Assertio.* As soon as this book came to the notice of Thomas Caius, he drew up a defense of his position, intending to have it printed in the form of notes with an appendix of animadversions on his opponent's work; but dying in 1572, he left his observations in MS till Hearne printed them in his *Vindiciae,* 1730. John Caius died the following year. In 1574 appeared under Archbishop Parker's patronage a new edition of the *Assertio,* with large additions left by the author, including the printed account by John Caius. This last was reprinted by Henry R. Plomer in *The Library,* vol. 7, no. 3, 4th ser., Dec., 1926. It is said to have a bewildered style but at the same time to exhibit the many-sided erudition of its author.

On the occasion of the Queen's visit to Cambridge in 1564, the public orator, with the like of whom she was frequently to be bored, happened to extol the superior antiquity of Cambridge over that of Oxford. Thomas Caius, master of University College, Oxford, drew up a reply (the *Assertio*) in which he carried the foundation of his own university back to Greek professors who accompanied Brut to Britain, and its restoration to Alfred about 870. The manuscript came into the hands of John Caius, the founder of Caius College, or All Souls, Cambridge, who proved that his university was founded by Cantaber 394 years before Christ, and so was 1267 years older than Oxford. See Gough, *loc. cit.*

1574 CAIUS, THOMAS. Assertio antiquitatis Oxoniensis academiae incerto authore ejusdem gymnasii: ad illustrissimam reginam anno 1566. Jam nuper ad verbum cum priore edita; cum fragmento Oxoniensis historiolae. Additis castigationibus authoris marginalibus ad asteriscum positis. Inter quas libri titulus est, qui ante castigationem (quam editionem secundam dicimus) nullus erat. Omnia prout ab ipsis authoris exemplaribus accepimus, bona fide commissa formulis. 4to. London.

Included is the additional title: Historiae Cantabrigiensis academiae ab urbe condita, libri duo, authore Johanne Caio Anglo. 4to. London. 1574.

1730 ————. Thomae Caii vindiciae antiquitatis academiae Oxoniensis contra Joannem Caium, Cantabrigiensem. 2 vols. 8vo. Oxford. (Edit. by Thomas Hearne.)

This edition comprehends all that both disputants wrote on the subject. Hearne, an Oxford man, makes much of the clear, nervous style of the Oxford advocate, and imagines that the Cambridge adversary broke his heart when he found what a formidable antagonist was facing him.—Gough.

1575 HOEFNAGEL, JORIS. Oxonium, nobile Angliae oppidum. Vindesorium, celeberrimum Angliae Castrum locum amoenissimum: aedificia magnifica; Artificiosa Regum sepulchra; & illustris Garetteriorum equitum Societas memorabile reddunt. Latin description on the reverse. Each of the two engravings 19¼ × 7 ins. Cologne.

> This consists of a pair of engraved views on one sheet in contemporary coloring. That of Oxford includes the arms of the city and in the foreground a Professor and his student. In the Windsor view is depicted a hunting scene, with two ladies in the foreground and four gentlemen with a hound.—Maggs, no. 693.

1578 AGGAS (AGAS), RALPH. Celeberrimae Oxoniensis academiae, aularum & collegiorum aedificibus totius Europae magnificentissimis, cum antiquissima civitate conjunctae elegans simul & accurata descriptio. Radulpho Agaso authore. London (?).

> Engraved on two sheets, with copies of Bereblock's views introduced into the margin, 1728.
> This, the oldest plan of the university and city of Oxford, was engraved by Ralph Agas on a scale of three by four feet. At the bottom of the 1724 reproduction is "Augustinus Ryther, Anglus, delineavit 1588"—the same who engraved the interesting series of charts of the Spanish Armada.—Rye, England as Seen by Foreigners, 208.

1592(?) BIBEUS, SIMON. Brief and circumstantial Account of the University of Oxford in England, as well as of Foundations and the Colleges at present appertaining to it: together with their Arms and the number of Students who derive their maintenance out of the common revenues. Dedicated to the most worshipful lord and father in God, John Whitgift, Archbishop of Canterbury.

> This was written in Latin by Bibeus, an Englishman. The title as given above is the one cited in Rathgeb's account of the visit of the Duke of Wirtemberg to England in 1592. See Rathgeb under 1602, TOURS BY FOREIGNERS.

1602 FITZHERBERT, NICHOLAS. Nicolai Fierberti Oxoniensis in Anglia academiae descriptio ad perillustrem & Reverendissimum D.D. Bernardum Paulinum, S.D.N. Clementis VII. datarium. 12mo. Romae.

> Reprinted in Hearne, Leland's Itinerary, vol. IX, Oxford, 1710; also by Charles Plummer in Elizabethan Oxford Reprints of Rare Tracts, Oxford, 1887.
> The work is scarce and contains many circumstances not to be met with elsewhere.— Gough, 405. Fitzherbert was a member of Exeter College, in 1570, and soon afterwards became a Catholic. His work was the first separate publication descriptive of Oxford. After a Latin epigram on England, "Anglia terra ferax," etc., the book begins with an interesting account of Elizabethan England—then deals with Oxford, its buildings and methods of study, chief officers and assemblies of the University, and great scholars of England and especially of Oxford. The work concludes with exhortations to embrace Roman Catholicism and cites New College as having sent out 32 eminent Roman Catholics in the previous 40 years.—From A. Rosenthal Ltd., Catalogue V.

1605 GENTILIS, ALBERICUS. Laudes academiae Parisiensis & Oxoniensis. 8vo. Hanover.

> The author was an Italian refugee and professor of law at Oxford.

JAMES, THOMAS. Catalogus librorum bibliothecae publicae quam vir ornatissssimus Thomas Bodleius, eq. aur. in academia Oxoniensi nuper instituit; continet autem libros alphabetice dispositos secundum quatuor facultates: cum quadruplice elencho expositorum S. Scripturae, Aristotelis, juris utriusque & principum medicinae, ad usum almae academiae Oxoniensis. 4to. Oxford.

Reprinted under a slightly different title, 4to, Oxford.

James was fellow of New College and an industrious writer against popery. When he could not prevail on the convocation to collate the MSS of the fathers published by the Papists, in order to detect their forgeries, he set about it himself.—Gough, 418, note. For a later catalogue of books see Hyde under 1764 below.

1607   Rex Platonicus, sive de potentissimi principis Jacobi Britanniarum regis ad illustrissimam academiam Oxoniensem adventu Aug. 27, 1605, narratio ab Isaaco Wake publico academiae ejusdem oratore tunc temporis conscripta. 4to. Oxford.

6th edit., 12mo, Oxford, 1663.

This gives an account of the entertainment provided James I on the occasion of his visit there. The work contains several remarkable observations on the ancient and present state of the university.—Gough, 405.

1608   TWYNE, BRIAN. Antiquitatis academiae Oxoniensis apologia. In tres libros divisa. 4to. Oxford.

Twyne intended to put out a second edition, with large additions, but his interleaved copy is supposed to have been lost during the civil confusions. He was the first writer to treat the affairs of this university in a professional antiquarian fashion, for which he was rewarded with the place of keeper of the archives.—Gough, 406. Walpole mentions his valuable collections and antiquities relating to Oxford.—*Corr.*, vol. II, 347 (Yale Edition).

1633   FLETCHER, PHINEAS. De literis antiquae Britanniae legibus, praesertim qui doctrina claruerunt, quique collegia Cantabrigiae fundarunt. 12mo. Cantabrigiae. (So cited by Gough.)

This deals with the university in general.—Gough, 99, note.

1638   TURNER, DR. PETER (Translator). Statuta selecta e corpore statutorum universitatis Oxoniensis ut in promptu, & ad manum sint, quae magis ad usum (precipue juniorum) facere videntur. 12mo. Oxford.

The university statutes printed on vellum are placed in each of the college libraries. The body of statutes confirmed by a charter of Charles I, 1636, was collected by Brian Twyne, and translated as above by Turner, Savilian professor.—Gough, 429. This was reprinted in various editions.

1648   BOBART, JACOB. Catalogus plantarum horti medici Oxoniensis, scil. Latino-Anglicus & Anglico-Latinus. 8vo. Oxford.

This was augmented in a *Catalogus horti botanici Oxoniensis,* etc., by Philip Stephen, M.D., and William Brown, 12mo, Oxford, 1758.

1651   LANGBAINE, GERARD (the Elder). The Foundation of the University of Cambridge, with a Catalogue of the principal Founders, and special Benefactors of all the Colleges, and total Number of Students, Magistrates, and Officers therein being; and how the Revenues thereof are and have been increased from time to time, and by whom, with Buildings, Books, and Revenues, as no Universitie in ·the World can in all points parallel. 4to. London.

Langbaine did the same service to Oxford University this same year. He succeeded Twyne as keeper of the archives. According to Gough, 103-04, the above work was derived principally from a MS in the hands of Thomas Rawlinson, entitled "The Foundation of the University of Cambridge, etc., collected by John Scot, A.D. 1621," which was printed by Hearne in his edition of *Leland's Collectanea*, vol. V, 1715 (see under HISTORY AND ANTIQUITIES).

1655 FULLER, THOMAS. The History of the University of Cambridge, since the Conquest. Fol. Cambridge.

An edit., by M. Prickett and T. Wright, with illustrative notes and two plans, 8vo, Cambridge (?), 1840.

1665 FULMAN, WILLIAM. Notitia Oxoniensis Academiae. 4to. London.

Another edition, very much corrected and augmented, 4to, London, 1675.
The later edition of Fulman's concise guidebook to the University of Oxford was made possible by the appearance of Wood's *Historia Univ. Oxon.*, published in 1674 (see under this date below). It is in larger type than the 1665 edition and adds many new names of writers, etc., educated at Oxford. "A general account of the University is followed by a description of its Officers, Institutions and Professorships, with the names of the staff at the time. Then for each College and Hall is given a succinct description of its history, numbers and distinguished alumni, and finally a list of great men who have passed through the University."—From A. Rosenthal Ltd., Catalogue V.

1668 SAVAGE, HENRY (Master of Balliol). Balliofergus, or, a Commentary upon the Foundation, Founders, and Affairs, of Balliol College, gathered out of the Records and other Antiquities, with a Catalogue of all the Heads of the Colleges. Folding pedigree. 4to. Oxford.

This possesses considerable value, in spite of its inaccuracies, as the first attempt to construct the history of an Oxford college on the basis of authentic records and deeds.—*DNB.*

1672 The Foundation of the University of Cambridge, With a Catalogue of the Principal Founders, and Special Benefactours of all the Colleges; and totall number of Students, Magistrates and Officers therein being. Anno 1672. London.

This was printed on the recto of two large oblong folio sheets, divided into sections, each devoted to a college, and bearing in the margin the Arms of the college represented. —Quoted.

1674 WOOD, ANTHONY A. Historia & antiquitates universitatis Oxoniensis duobus voluminibus comprehensae. Fol. Oxon. (See under 1786 below.)

First English version, with a continuation to his time, by John Gutch, 2 vols., 4to, Oxford, 1786; again 1792.
This work was written by Wood in English but Bishop Fell, of the "I do not like you Dr. Fell" epigram, employed two men by name of Wase and Peers to translate it into Latin, with the design of making it available to foreign readers. Wood, in his *Athenae*, complains bitterly of the liberties taken in this rendering, which was modelled entirely by the Bishop, who not only corrected it and almost composed it, but inserted and left out passages as he pleased, so that Wood was almost obliged to disclaim the whole and to resolve to publish the work just as he wrote it. The first volume contained the antiquities of the university in chronological order to 1648; the second, those of the colleges. Having committed himself to furnish to the delegates of the printing house transcripts of the original charters and the very words of the authors cited by him, as well as the lives of the writers belonging to their respective houses, and the history of all the religious houses and fraternities in Oxford, Wood was sitting on the sharp edge of anxiety all the while the translation was under way. The opinion of Henry Wharton at the time was that the original was far more pleasing to read. Bishop Barlow pointed out some gross mistakes in both the original and the translation. And the learned Wm. Fulman sent the author his additions, emendations, and expurgations. For additional troubles attendant upon Wood's work as editor, see his *Athenae Oxonienses,* under 1692 below.

1675 LOGGAN, DAVID. Oxonia Illustrata, sive omnium celeberrimae istius Universitatis Collegiorum Aularum, Bibliothecae Bodleianae, Scholarum Publicarum, Theatri Sheldoniani; nec non Urbis totius Scenographia Delineavit et Sculpsit Dav. Loggan Univ. Oxon. Chalcographus. 40 double-page engravings (including plan of the city and views of college buildings). Fol. Oxford.

This is praised as a magnificent work. The plates consist of two general views of Oxford (occupying a single plate), a plan of the city, a plate of academical costumes, and thirty-seven views of colleges, halls, and public buildings. The extraordinary amount of accurate detail in these views and equally extraordinary expenditure of time in preparing for their publication can hardly be imagined.—Maggs, no. 577. Every detail of the buildings is said to be realized so that one can walk into the quadrangles of the colleges and discover their style of architecture. The book was evidently intended as a companion to Wood's *History and Antiquities of the University of Oxford* (described above), for the table of contents gives opposite to each plate a reference to the page of that work where the history of the building represented is to be found.—Quoted. Loggan was born of Scotch ancestry in Danzig and came to England in 1653. Something drew him to Oxford, where Wood was then collecting materials for his history. There he was noticed by the authorities who found in him the man for making a permanent record of the colleges, and by Wood who probably suggested to him the idea of furnishing a pictorial supplement to his own project. After leaving Oxford he set up in London and became a sought-after portrait painter. He died in 1700. For his *Cantabrigia Illustrata*, see under 1688-90 below.

1676 PRIDEAUX, HUMPHREY. Marmora Oxoniensia ex Arundellianis, Seldenianis, aliisque constata, recensuit & perpetuo commentario explicavit Humphredus Prideaux aedis Christi alumnus, appositis . . . nonnullis Seldeni & Lydiati annotationibus. Accessit Sertorii Ursati Patavani de notis Romanorum commentarius. Fol. Oxon.

  A corrected edit. by Mattaire, fol., London, 1732; another *Marmora Oxoniensia*, embodying later marbles and inscriptions, fol., Oxford, 1763. See below.
  The ingratitude displayed towards the Arundels, father and son, and the disasters at Oxford make sad reading. For a detailed account of the fortunes of ancient works of art collected by this famous family and others, see Gough, 420-25.
  When it appeared that the above book was becoming scarce, Mr. Pearce of Edmund Hall undertook to reprint it in 1726, with permission of the author, who was growing old. Prideaux proposed to him to correct its many errors, but on his declining this, Dr. David Wilkins undertook the job in 1726, intending to add the Pomfret and Pembroke collections. Mattaire performed the first part in 1732, inserting the conjectures and corrections of various learned men, but never consulting the marbles themselves, and totally omitting Wheeler's monuments. The statues belonging to the Pomfret collection were in time given to the University of Oxford. These, with the ancient inscriptions collected by Sir George Wheeler and Messrs. Dawkins, Bovery, and Robert Wood during their travels (see Wood under 1753, NEAR EAST, vol. I of this work), and various fragments of native antiquities, have all been brought together and engraved by Miller at the expense of the university in the *Marmora Oxoniensia*, a design that will immortalize the university, the nation, and the age. It were to be wished as much could be said for the execution of the engravings.—Gough, 424.

    1732 PRIDEAUX, HUMPHREY. Marmorum Arundelianorum, Seldenianorum aliorumque academiae Oxoniensi donatorum, una cum commentariis & indice. Editio secunda. Fol. London.
      This was edited by Mattaire.

1688 LOGGAN, DAVID. Cantabrigia Illustrata, sive Omnium Celeberrimae istius Universitatis Collegiorum, Aularum, Bibliothecae Academicae Scholarum Publicarum . . . Ichnographia. Engraved title, dedication to the reader, list of plates, and 30 engraved views of Colleges, Halls, etc. Fol. Cambridge.

  Modern edit. by J. W. Clark, fol., Cambridge, 1905.

    1905 LOGGAN, DAVID. Cantabrigia Illustrata. A Series of Views of the University & Colleges and of Eton College, edited with a Life of Loggan, an Introduction and Historical & Descriptive Notes by J. W. Clark. A Reproduction in folio with plates averaging 11 × 9 ins., with the scarce portrait of the Duke of Somerset in photogravure, the center section of Hammond's Map of 1592. Cambridge.

1691-92 WOOD, ANTHONY A. Athenae Oxonienses: an exact History of all the Writers and Bishops who have had their Education in the most famous University of Oxford, from the 15th Year of Henry VII A.D. 1500, to the end of the Year 1690;

representing the Birth, Fortune, Preferment, and the Death of all those Authors and Prelates; the great Accidents of their Lives, and the Fate and Character of their Writings: To which are added, the Fasti or Annals of the said University for the same Time. 2 vols. Fol. London.

Reprinted with continuations, 2 vols., fol., London, 1721.

This historiographer spared neither friend nor foe. With unwearied industry he has thrown together, though not in the best method or most agreeable style, a useful system of English biography. To vol. I is prefixed the author's account of himself, with his head in a border at the top inserted in a very few copies, and those mostly presents from himself. In 1692 the University proceeded against him for insinuations of corruption and bribery against their chancellor, Edward, Earl of Clarendon, when he was chancellor of the kingdom. His defense not proving satisfactory, they condemned him with a fine of thirty-five pounds and banishment as a disturber of the peace, and publicly burned his second volume, where these insinuations were to be found. In the 1721 edition, the *Athenae* were continued down to Wood's death in 1695, from the copy in which he had with his own hand inserted a great number of additions and amendments, together with 500 new lives. These were communicated to the editors by Bishop Tanner, to whom Wood, on his death bed, had bequeathed them. The corrections relative to the Welsh bishops, communicated by Dr. Humphreys, Bishop of Bangor, were printed at the end of *Caii Vindiciae*, 605-678, by Hearne, who received them from Mr. Baker, and he from Bishop Kennett. Dr. Rawlinson bequeathed to the University, on condition the trunks were not opened till seven years after his death (1755), his own collections for a continuation of the *Athenae* and *History of Oxford*. As a collector Wood deserves highly of posterity; but his narrowness of mind and furious prejudices are unpardonable, and correctness both of judgment and of style is also wanting in his works.—Gough, 413.

1705   Rustica academiae Oxoniensis nuper reformatae descriptio: una cum comitiis ibidem 1648, habitis, in Visitatione Fanatica. London.

Reprinted with an English translation, 8vo, London, 1717.

This is assigned to Dr. John Allibond, master of the free school near Magdalen College, and rector of Bradwell, Gloucestershire. Edward Ward's name is associated with the English edition.

1717   Seasonable Sketch of an Oxford Reformation, written originally in Latin by John Allibond, and now reprinted, with an English version. 8vo. London.
A secondary title runs: Rustical Description of the University of Oxford.

1710   The Present State of Trinity College (Cambridge), in a Letter from Dr. Bentley, Master of the said College, to the Right Rev. John Lord Bishop of Ely. Published for general Information by a Gentleman of the Temple. 8vo. London.

This was animadverted upon in the following:

1710   Some Remarks upon a Letter, intitled, The Present State of Trinity College, written by Richard Bentley, D.D., now Master of said College, to the Right Rev. John Lord Bishop of Ely. With some Remarks also upon the Preface, pretended to be written and published together with the Letter, by a Gentleman of the Temple. 8vo. London.

These two pamphlets are samples of a long controversy occasioned by certain regulations promulgated by Dr. Bentley, when master of Trinity college, which gave offense to the Fellows. Complaints and protests poured in upon the Bishop of Ely, who was visitor to the college, but Bentley let the bishop know that he had no business to interfere. The dispute is set forth at some length in Gough, 114-17. In the long run Bentley won out.

1711-47   Oxford. Almanacs. A Series of 31 of the Engraved Views of the Colleges, etc., published with the Oxford Almanac for the Years 1711-40 and 1747 (the plates for 1711-33 do not contain the Calendars). Fol. Oxford (?).

1713   For an account of the curiosities housed by the two universities, see *British Curiosities in Nature and Art,* under NATURAL HISTORY.

Collegium Scholarumque publicarum academiae Oxoniensis topographica delineatio per Thomam Nelum. Oxford (?).

> This was published by Hearne from a Bodleian MS entitled, "Dialogus in adventum reginae serenissimae dominae Elizabethae gratulatorius, inter eandem reginam & dominum Rob. Dudleium comitem Lecestriae & Oxon. acad. cancellarium," written in Latin verse, and presented to the Queen on her visit to the university (1566). It contains views of all the colleges before 1590 (in which year the author died) drawn by Bereblock; those of the old schools were engraved in the notes of Hearne's edition of Fierbert (see 1602 above). Some part of this delineation was written by Miles Wyndsor, M.D.—Gough, 404.

1714 AYLIFFE, JOHN, LL.D. The Antient and Present State of the University of Oxford, containing an Account of its Antiquity, Past Government, and Sufferings from the Danes; an Account of its Colleges, Halls, and Publick Buildings;
an Account of the Laws, Statutes and Privileges of the University, etc., and
with an Appendix and Index to the Whole. 2 vols. 8vo. London.

> Reprinted, 2 vols., 8vo, London, 1723.
> This was compiled from Wood (see under 1674 above). The many misrepresentations and aspersions he indulged in brought about his degradation and expulsion, against which he published a vindication of himself, London, 1716. His transports of passion turned this rather into a satire on himself than on those towards whom his resentment was directed. —Gough, 415. In the above volumes Ayliffe showed, among other things, what was required by the statutes for each degree. These regulations are presented in outline by Birkbeck Hill in his *Dr. Johnson and His Friends and Critics,* London, 1878.

> 1716 AYLIFFE, JOHN. The Case of Dr. Ayliffe at Oxford, Giving an Account of the Unjust and Malicious Prosecution of Him for Writing a Book entituled, The Ancient and Present State of the University of Oxford. 8vo. London.

1715 PARKER, REV. RICHARD. Σκελετός Cantabrigiensis, sive collegiorum umbratilis delineatio, cum suis fundatoribus & benefactoribus plurimis; in qua etiam habes
hospitia academiae antiqua; a tergo vero episcopos, qui ex hac academia pro-
dierunt supra annum abhinc centenarium. Published by Hearne in his *Leland's
Collectanea,* vol. V, 185 (see under 1715, HISTORY AND ANTIQUITIES). Oxford.

> This piece was written in 1622 but not published until 1715. The translation of 1721 indicates that it utilized the *Historiola* of Cantelupe mentioned in the Introduction to this section.
> Parker was an excellent herald, historian, and antiquary. Fuller says the bare bones of his *Skeletos* are fleshed with much matter, and were of great use to him in his history of this university from the Conquest on.—Gough, 103-04. See below.

> 1721 PARKER, REV. RICHARD. The History and Antiquities of the University of Cambridge, in Two Parts. 1. Of its Original and Progress in remote Ages, written above 300 Years ago by Nicholas Cantelupe. 2. A Description of the Present Colleges, their Founders and Benefactors, as also of former Halls and Inns, by Richard Parker in 1622, with Charters granted to the Colleges; an Account of the Authors above-mentioned; as also a Catalogue of the Chancellors, and a Summary of all the Privileges granted to this Seminary of Learning by the English Monarchs; from a MS. in the Cotton Library. 8vo. London.
> For Cantelupe's original title, see under 1719 below. The above work is referred to in *Walpole Corr.,* vol. I, 148, note (Yale Edition).

1717 MILLER, EDMUND. An Account of the University of Cambridge, and the Colleges
there, being a plain Relation of many of their Oaths, Statutes, and Charters, etc.
8vo. London.

> 2nd edit., 8vo, London, 1717.
> This Miller may be the one who was concerned in the Bentley controversy cited above under 1710.

1719   CANTELUPE, NICHOLAS. Historiola de antiquitate & origine universitatis Cantabrigiensis. Praemittuntur bullae quedam papales, aliaque ad universitatis ejusdem historiam spectantia. Published by Hearne at the end of his *Thomae
Sprotti Chronica.* Oxford.

1720   HUTTEN, DR. LEONARD. A Discourse on the Antiquities of the University of Oxford, by way of a "Letter to a Friend." Printed by Hearne in his edition of *Textus
Roffensis* (see under ECCLESIASTICAL HISTORY AND ANTIQUITIES). Oxford.

> This gives an account of the city and university, but not of the colleges particularly.
> In the appendix, no. VII, 392, is an account of the author from Wood, who charges him
> with stealing from Twyne, against which Hearne defends him.—Gough, 405.

1726   AMHERST, NICHOLAS. Terrae Filius; or, the Secret History of the University of
Oxford; in several Essays. To which are added, Remarks upon a late Book,
intitled, University Education, by R. Newton, D.D., Principal of Hart-Hall. 2
vols. 12mo. London.

> This is a reprint of the 50 numbers which appeared between Jan. 11, 1721, and July 6
> of the same year, conducted by Amherst, who had been expelled from St. John's College
> for his irregularities. He vented his resentment on the university in general in a poem
> called "Oculus Britanniae" (1724), and in the two prose volumes cited above. The "Re-
> marks," partly serious, partly ludicrous, were made by an unknown hand on the first
> edition of the book and answered in the second.—Gough, 450. "It was an ancient custom
> at Oxford, in the public acts, for some person, who was called 'Terrae Filius,' to mount
> the rostrum and divert a large crowd from all parts with a merry oration, interspersed
> with secret history, raillery and sarcasm, as the occasion of the times supplied him with
> matter."—Halkett and Laing, quoted by Sotheran.

1729   BEREBLOCK, JOHN. This draughtsman, an M.A. of Oxford (1565), drew some
views of Oxford at the time of Queen Elizabeth's visit in 1566 which he presented to her. He also wrote an account of the royal visit, which was published
by Hearne in 1729. So cited in Rye, *England as Seen by Foreigners,* 208.

1730   CAIUS, THOMAS. For the *Thomae Caii Vindiciae,* edit. by Hearne, see John Caius
under 1568 above.

The Present State of the New Buildings of Queen's College, Oxford. 4to. Oxford.

1732-33   WILLIAMS, WILLIAM. Oxonia Depicta sive Collegiorum et Aularum in Inclyta
Academia Oxoniensi Ichnographica, Orthographica, & Scenographica Delineatio LXV. Tabulis aenis expressa a Guil. Williams cui accedit Unius cujusque
Collegii Aulaeque Notitia. 65 engraved plates of the colleges, etc. Fol. London (?).

> This work is said to offer more architectural detail than Loggan's.

1744   A Pocket Companion for Oxford, containing an accurate Description of the public Edifices. 12mo. Oxford.

> New edit., Oxford, 1768.

SALMON, THOMAS. The Present State of the Universities, and of the Five adjacent Counties of Cambridge, Huntingdon, Bedford, Bucks, and Oxford. Vol.
I (all published). The County and City of Oxford. 8vo. Oxford (?).

> The countryside gets only a few notes.

1747   The Gentleman and Lady's Pocket-Companion through the Universities of Cambridge and Oxford. 12mo. Oxford (?).

> Gough says this was stolen by the booksellers from Salmon's account of 1744.

GIBBS, JAMES (Architect). Bibliotheca Radcliffeiana, or, A Short Description of the Radcliffe Library at Oxford, containing its several Plans, Parts, Sections, and Ornaments, in 23 copper plates, with an explication to each. Fol. London.

> Gibbs designed this Library and a number of London churches.

1748   SALMON, THOMAS. The Foreigner's Companion through the Two Universities. 12mo. London.

> This is called a flimsy production.

1749   POINTER, JOHN, M.D. Oxoniensis Academia: or, the Antiquities and Curiosities of the University of Oxford. 12mo. London.

> In this account Pointer had degraded the famous mallard into a goose and thereby provoked a number of replies which restored the bird to the status of mallard. For two of these see below. The work contains also a list of the curiosities in the Museum Pointerianum, which he had given to St. John's College.

> 1750   A Complete Vindication of the Mallard of All-Souls College against the injurious Suggestions of the Rev. Mr. Pointer. 8vo. London (?).

> At the end of this work was advertised as to be speedily published:

> An Apology for the Conduct of the Rev. J. S. John Swinton, M.A., wherein the Reasons and particular Circumstances, which provoked him to make use of some unguarded and unjustifiable Expressions (highly reflecting on the Mallard of All-Souls and the Author of the Vindication) in a Sermon preached before the University of Oxford at St. Mary's on Sunday, Dec. 16, 1750, will be fully explained, and submitted to the Candour of the Publick.

1750   BLOMEFIELD, REV. FRANCIS. Collectanea Cantabrigiensia, or, Collections relating to Cambridge University, Town and County, containing the Monumental Inscriptions in all the Chapels of the Several Colleges and Parish Churches, List of Mayors, Charters of the Town, etc., etc. 4to. Norwich.

1752   PESHALL, SIR JOHN. The History of the University of Oxford, to the Death of William the Conqueror. 8vo. Oxford.

1753   CARTER, EDMUND. For a history of the University of Cambridge, see his *History of the County of Cambridge,* under HISTORY AND ANTIQUITIES.

1753-55   MASTERS, ROBERT. The History of the College of Corpus Christi and the B. Virgin Mary (commonly called Benet) in the University of Cambridge, from its Foundation, with Appendix, List of Members, etc. Portrait, elevation and plan, plates of arms. 4to. Printed for the Author. Cambridge.

1759   The New Oxford Guide; or, Companion through the University. 8vo. Oxford.

> Later edits. numerous: 1763, 1765, 1768, 1777, 1789, etc., with probably some in between. See below.

> 1769   The New Oxford Guide: or, Companion through the University. Exhibiting every Particular worthy of the Observations of the Curious in each of the Public Build-

ings, Colleges, Halls, &c., To which is added, A Tour to Blenheim, Ditchley, Hey-thorp, Nuneham, and Stow (the seats of the Duke of Marlborough, Earl of Litch-field, Earl of Shrewsbury, Earl Harcourt, and Earl Temple). Containing an accurate Description of their Tapestry, Paintings, Sculptures, Temples, Gardens, and other Curiosities. By a Gentleman of Oxford. Corrected and enlarged. Oxford.

Oxford contained at the time, exclusive of the University, a population of 8292 inhabitants.

Observations on the Present State of the English Universities. (So cited in *Gent. Mag.*, vol. 29, April.)

1760 WARTON, THOMAS. A Companion to the Guide, and Guide to the Companion, be-ing a compleat Supplement to all the Accounts of Oxford hitherto published; containing an accurate Description of the Several Halls, Libraries, Schools, Public Edifices, Busts, Statues, Antiquities, Hieroglyphics, Seats, Gardens, and other Curiosities omitted or misrepresented by Wood, Hearne, Salmon, Prince, Pointer, and other eminent Topographers, Chronologers, Antiquarians, and Historians. The Whole interspersed with original Anecdotes and interesting Discoveries, occasionally resulting from the Subject: and Embellished with perspective Views and Elevations neatly engraved. 12mo. London.

2nd edit., corrected and enlarged, London, 1762 (?); another, 12mo, London, 1780.
This was published anonymously, but it was known at the time to be a work of "local facetiae" by the genial author of the *History of English Poetry*. It was intended to ridicule all such Guides and Companions.

1763 Cantabrigia Depicta: a Concise and accurate Description of the University and Town of Cambridge, and its Environs, etc. 12mo. Cambridge.

Another edit. the same year; other edits., 1776, 1785, and 1790. See below.
Gough calls this a worthless piece, being a very inaccurate compilation of the Cam-bridge booksellers.

1776 Cantabrigia Depicta: A Concise and Accurate Description of the University and Town and its Environs. A History of the Colleges and Public Buildings, their Founders and Benefactors. List of University Officers. An invariable Rule for the Beginnings and Endings of Terms, etc. Folding map and plates. 8vo. Cam-bridge.

A Description of the University, Town, and County of Cambridge. Map and Plates. 12mo. Cambridge.

1769 MALDEN, H. An Account of King's College Chapel, including a Character of Henry VI, and Short History of the Foundation of his Two Colleges King's and Eton. 2 illus. 8vo. London.

1771 An Act for amending certain of the Mile-ways leading to Oxford . . . for re-pairing Magdalen Bridge . . . for making commodious Roads through the University and City, etc. Fol.

See Manning, *Survey and Tokens*, under 1923, TOWNS.

1773 TATHAM, EDWARD. Oxonia Explicata et Ornata: Proposals for Disengaging and Beautifying the University and City of Oxford. 4to. London.

This pamphlet is of interest to the student of the history of Oxford, as it contains the earliest proposal for a Martyr's Memorial.—Bookseller's Note.

1775   Marmora Oxoniensia, published under the Care of Mr. Chandler. In *Gent. Mag.,* vol. 45, 227-29. (Contains strictures on his editing.)

1776   SOONE (ZOONE) WILLIAM. A Description of Cambridge in the 16th Century. With Plan. By Wm. Soone or Zoone (a member of the University, 1561). In *Gent. Mag.,* vol. 46, 201-03. London.

> This was sent to George Braun, compiler of a concise description of the several cities of the known world, with plans. The plan in Braun is the second oldest one of Cambridge. The above article includes a translation of John Major's account of the University. Major the historian died in 1530. Braun was associated with Hogenberg in publishing the *Civitates Orbis Terrarum* (see under 1572-1618, VIEWS).

1780   A Collection of 24 Engraved Plates by Grignion after Huddesford and Taylor, of Costumes of the various Degrees of Oxford University. 8vo. n.p. (The date is approximate.)

Observations on the University of Oxford. In *Gent. Mag.,* vol. 50, 119-20; 277-78. London.

> The university comes in for criticism for its obsolete methods of teaching that in themselves are futile and for its obsolete and antiquated forms of disputation. This criticism is borne out by Godley, *Oxford in the Eighteenth Century* (see under GENERAL REFERENCE).

1781   GUTCH, JOHN. For tracts relating to the universities of Oxford and Cambridge, see his *Collectanea Curiosa,* under HISTORY AND ANTIQUITIES.

1786-96   WOOD, ANTHONY A. The History and Antiquities of the several Colleges and Halls in the University of Oxford. Now first published, in English, from the Original Manuscript in the Bodleian Library; with a Continuation to the Present Time, by the Editor, John Gutch, M.A., Chaplain of All-Souls College. 4to. Oxford.

> The separate parts are listed here:
> 1790   WOOD, ANTHONY A. Appendix to the Historical Account of the Colleges and Halls in the University of Oxford; containing Fasti Oxonienses: or, a Commentary of the Supreme Magistrates of the University: By Anthony Wood: Now first published in English . . . with a Continuation to the Present Time; also, Additions and Corrections to each College and Hall, and Indexes to the whole. By the Editor John Gutch. 4to. Oxford.
>
> 1792-96   WOOD, ANTHONY A. The History and Antiquities of the University of Oxford; now first published in English from the Original Manuscript in the Bodleian Library. By John Gutch. 2 vols. 4to. Oxford.
> This was published first in Latin, 2 vols., fol., 1674 (see Wood this date above). Because of the liberties taken with his text by the student translators, Wood began to revise and transcribe the whole of the English copy, with continuations and improvements, and on his death bequeathed it to the University, where it remained as manuscript till Gutch printed it as above. The Annals are here brought down to 1661, at which time a second visitation reinstated those whom the preceding parliamentarian visitation in 1648 had ejected. The work was reviewed in progress in *Gent. Mag.,* vols. 56, 973-74; 63, 439; 64, 1116; 66, 858.

1788   BEVERLEY, JOHN. An Account of the different Ceremonies observed in the Senate House of the University of Cambridge, throughout the Year. 8vo. Cambridge.

1789   JUNG, P. Guide d'Oxford. 12mo. Oxford.

1790(?) KILNER, S. An Account of Pythagoras's School in Cambridge. 9 folding and other plates. Cambridge (?).

> Only a few copies of this curious book were printed by the author, who was a senior fellow of Merton College, Oxford. It contains much valuable information respecting Merton College and its founder.—Daniell, *Manual of British Topography.*

1794 SIBTHORP, JOHN. Flora Oxoniensis, exhibens .plantas in agro Oxoniensi sponte crescentes. 8vo. Oxonii.

1800 DALLAWAY, JAMES. Anecdotes of the Arts in England; or comparative Remarks on Architecture, Sculpture, and Painting, chiefly illustrated by Specimens at Oxford. 8vo. London.

MAVOR, WILLIAM. Tour of the University of Cambridge, by a Student, in a Letter to a Friend. In *British Tourist,* vol. VI, 217-52 (2nd edit.). London.

> This describes after the manner of a guidebook the various colleges, their endowments and founders, halls, etc. It is a twin book to the one following on Oxford.

MAVOR, WILLIAM. Tour of the University of Oxford, by the Editor. In *British Tourist,* vol. VI, 153-215. London.

> This is strictly a guidebook designed purely for information.

WALKER, JOHN. Oxoniana. 4 vols. in 2. 8vo. London.

> An edit., 1807 (cited by *Camb. Bibliog.*).
> So many curious and interesting scarce titles make up the contents of this work that a listing of them seems justifiable. Many of them belong to MSS in the Bodleian Library. Among other articles are:—Antiquity of Oxford; University Degrees; State of Learning in the University at the end of Thirteenth Century and beginning of Sixteenth Century; Jews numerous in Oxford; Story of Friar Bacon and Cambridge Scholars; Franciscans and Roger Bacon; Poeta Laureatus; Univ. Discipline in time of Henry VIII; Devastations committed by Visitors in Reign of Edward VI and Anecdotes relative to the Scarcity of Books in 14th and 15th Centuries; Glossed MSS; Cranmer, Ridley, and Latimer; State of Music in Oxford; Oxford Riots in Thirteenth Century; James Ist at Oxford; Price of Provisions in Oxford; Origin and Progress of Newspapers previous to the Gazette; Oxford Almanacks; Religious Houses in Oxford before the Reformation; Balliol College Library; Prices of Books in Merton College Library; William of Wykeham; Bees of Ludovicus Vives; Classical Literature particularly insisted upon by the Founder of Trinity College; Players at Oxford; Exact Account of the whole numbers of Scholars and Students in the University of Oxford, taken anno 1612, in the Long Vacation; Bodleian Library and Selden's Library added; The Theatre; Letters from Originals in Bodleian; Collier tortured in New College; Original Charters in New College; Memoirs of Leland, Twyne, Wood & Aubrey; Walter Mapes; Parliament in Oxford; etc., etc.— From Bookseller's Catalogue.

1868 Munimenta Academica, or, Documents illustrative of Academical Life and Studies at Oxford. Edit. by Bishop Stubbs for the Rolls Series. London.

1876 DUDLEY, D. Cambridge of 1776, with a Diary of Dorothy Dudley, Cambridge. Illus. n.p.

1887 PLUMMER, CHARLES (Editor). Elizabethan Oxford. Reprints of Rare Tracts. *Publ. Oxford History Society,* vol. 8. Oxford.

> The contents of this collection are listed below:
>
> I.   Nicolai Fierberti Oxoniensis Academiae Descriptio. Romae, 1602. (See under this date above.)
> II. Leonard Hutten on the Antiquities of Oxford. (See under 1720 above.)

III. Queen Elizabeth at Oxford, 1566.
    A. Johannis Berebloci Commentarii (in Hearne's *History, Life,* etc., *of Richard II by a Monk of Evesham,* Oxford, 1729).
    B. Academiae Oxoniensis Topographica Delineatio per Thomam Nelum. (See under 1713 above.)
    C. Of the Actis Done at Oxford by Nicholas Robinson.
    D. A Brief Rehearsal By Richard Stephens.
IV. Queen Elizabeth at Oxford, 1592.
V. Appolonis et Musarum Eidyllia, Per Joannem Sanfordum, 1592.
    If the Queen put her subjects to vast expenditures on her "progresses," she in turn had to endure many dreary hours listening to orations, dialogues, and verses, some of which manifestly bored her to distraction. She did not always stay them out, and even stipulated that she would listen "so that it were not too long."

1896 Old Plans of Oxford, by Agas, Hollar, and Loggan. A Portfolio of Reproductions of 15 Plans. In *Publ. Oxford Hist. Soc.,* vol. 38. Fol. Oxford.

1898 Epistolae Academicae Oxon., a Collection of Letters and other Documents Illustrative of Oxford in the 15th Century. Edit. by Rev. H. Anstey, M.A. Illustrations. Part I. *Publ. Oxford Hist. Soc.,* vol. 35. Oxford.

1911 MAYOR, J. E. B. Cambridge under Queen Anne. Illustrated by a Memoir of Ambrose Bonwick, and Diaries of Francis Burman and Zacharias von Uffenbach. Preface by M. R. James. *Publ. Cambridge Antiq. Soc.,* vol. 25. Cambridge.

1913 For an account of the University of Oxford, see *A Step to Oxford,* under TOWNS.

1921 Old Plans of Cambridge, 1574-1798; by Richard Lyne, George Braun, John Hamond, Thomas Fuller, David Loggan, and W. Custance; comprising 7 plans on 17 sheets reproduced in facsimile in a portfolio, with a volume of descriptive text (with 33 illustrations), by J. Willis Clarke, M.A., and Arthur Gray, M.A., 2 vols. 1 8vo and 1 imp. fol. Cambridge.

1923 MANNING, PERCY. Sport and Pastimes in Stuart Oxford. In *Surveys and Tokens. Publ. Oxford Hist. Soc.,* vol. 75. Oxford.

    This concerns the play activities of both town and university and describes sports lawful and otherwise, shows, coffee houses, drinking, gambling, and sinning generally, visits of royalty, etc., all collected from various sources both contemporary and later. Stuart Oxford was not distinguished for gravity and decorum. An interesting fact noted is that the town possessed no playhouse but had to improvise stages here and there as opportunity offered.

1928 UFFENBACH, ZACHARIAS CONRAD VON. Oxford in 1710: from the Travels of Zacharias Conrad von Uffenbach, edit. by W. H. Quarrell. 8vo. London.

    This is an extract from the traveler's account that dealt with Oxford. The author is rather caustic in his remarks on the difficulty of access to the books. Librarians apparently at that time did not attend to their business very assiduously.

1931 HOLBERG, LUDWIG. For material dealing with his stay at Oxford in 1706, see his *Memoirs,* under LETTERS, DIARIES, MEMOIRS.

1935 GRAY, THOMAS. For numerous references to Cambridge, see his *Correspondence,* edit. by Toynbee and Whibley, under 1900, LETTERS, DIARIES, MEMOIRS.

VIII

Spas

(The history of watering places in England during the seventeenth and eighteenth centuries records the growth of an interest in ailments and the development of a new life of fashion. The popularity of these resorts, particularly in the eighteenth century, brought together all classes of people, which were forced to mingle rather indiscriminately irrespective of their social distinctions. Though still visited for cures in this period, resorts were sought out more for the pleasures they afforded. After the middle of the century, bathing in the sea and drinking sea water came into vogue bringing great influxes of tourists to such places as Brighton, for instance, which in 1724 was described by Defoe as a poor fishing village, and in 1781 by George Byng, Viscount Torrington, as a dull, garish place, though it was often the scene of the solemn dips of George III. In the following items one will notice the recurring claims of newly discovered springs, and the growing interest in their chemical analyses, which often appear to have been performed solely to see what happened. For a general account of watering places and mineral waters, see John Campbell's *Political Survey of Great Britain,* vol. I, ch. v [under 1774, SURVEYS].)

1562 TURNER, WILLIAM, M.D. A Booke of the Natures and Properties, as well of the Bathes in England as of other Bathes in Germanye and Italye, very necessarye for all syck Persons that can not be healed without the Helpe of Natural Bathes: gathered by William Turner, Doctor in Physicke. Fol. Cologne.

> The Preface was dated 1557. 2nd edit., "lately oversene and enlarged," fol., Collen, 1568. (So cited in Gough.)
> The author was educated at Pembroke-Hall, Cambridge, where he took orders, and was imprisoned for preaching the Reformation doctrines; but winning release he retired to Italy, and took a degree at Ferrara. During the reign of Henry VIII he resided in Germany, but came home in Edward VI's time, and got the deanery of Wells in 1550. At about the same time he proceeded M.D. at Oxford, and was appointed physician to the Lord Protector, Edward Duke of Somerset, to whose son, Edward Earl of Hertford, he dedicated the first edition of his book. This is the first physical examination of these baths.—Gough, *Anecdotes of British Topography,* 459-60.

1572 JONES, JOHN, M.D. The Benefit of the Auntient Bathes of Buckstones, which cureth most greevous Sicknesses, never before published, compiled by John Jones, Phisition at the King's Mede, nigh Derby, Anno Salutis 1572. 4to. London.

> Jones appeared to have repaired, for the purpose of practice, to Bath and Buxton during the seasons, and to have been patronized by Henry Herbert, second Earl of Pembroke, and George Talbot, Earl of Shrewsbury.—Bookseller's Note.

——————. The Bathes of Bathes Ayde. Compendiously compiled by John Jones, Phisition. 4to. London.

> This title runs more intelligently as *The Bathes Ayde of Bathe.*

1573 WILLES, RICHARD. De Thermis Buckstonis (Poematum Liber). London (?).

1580 SKENE, DR. GILBERT (Medicinar to His Majesty). Ane breif Descriptioun of the Qualiteis and Effectis of the Well of the Woman Hill, besyde Abirdene. 4to. Edinburgh.

> Reprinted, with another tract called *Ane breve Descriptioun of the Pest,* by the Bannatyne Club, no. 108, Edinburgh, 1860, edit. by W. F. Skene. Reprinted with facsimiles, with introduction by A. K. Kemlo, 4to, Aberdeen, 1884.

The Pest was the earliest medical work published in Scotland, and the *Well* the earliest topographical tract connected with Scotland.—Bookseller's Note. Gough notices the *Well* and refers to Ames's *History of Printing*. See Gough, 586.

1582 BAILEY, WALTER, M.D. A Briefe Discours of certaine Bathes or Mineral Waters in the Countie of Warwick, neare vnto a Village called Newennam Regis. London.

> Another edit., 8vo, York, 1654; again, 8vo, Leeds, 1736. See below.
> The author was "Professor of Physick" at Oxford, and chief physician to Queen Elizabeth.

> 1587 BAILEY, WALTER. A Briefe Discours of certaine Bathes or medicinall Waters in the Countie of Warwicke, neere vnto a Village called Newnam Regis. 12mo.
> > Cited in Madan, *Early Oxford Press*, where it is stated that this work was probably not printed at Oxford but at London, though ascribed to the former place in the British Museum Catalogue.

1600 W., G. Newes out of Cheshire of the new founde Well. (Place?)

1615 BARCLAY, DR. WILLIAM. Callirhoe, commonly called the Well of the Spa or the Nymph of Aberdene. 18mo. Aberdeen.

> So cited in Gough, 639. Another edit., Aberdeen, 1670. Reprinted, 8vo, Aberdeen, 1799. See below.

> 1670 BARCLAY, DR. WILLIAM. Callirhoe, commonly called the Well of Spa or the Nymph of Aberdene, resuscitat by W. Barclay; what diseases may be cured by drinking of the Well of Spa, and what is the true Use thereof. As it was printed by Andro Hart, 1615, and now reprinted at Aberdene.

1618 ANDERSON, P. The Colde Spring of Kinghorne Craig, his admirable and new tryed Properties, so far foorth as yet found true by Experience. 4to. Edinburgh.

BARCLAY, WILLIAM. The Nature and Effects of the New Found Well at Kinghorne, declared by William Barclay. 12mo. Edinburgh.

1626 DEANE, EDMUND. Spadacrene Anglica: or, the English Spaw-Fountain: being a Briefe Treatise of the Acide or tart Fountaine in the Forest of Knaresborow. 4to. London.

> Another edit., 8vo, York, 1654; again, 8vo, Leeds, 1736. See below.

> 1736 DEAN, DR. EDMUND. Spadacrene Anglica: or, the English Spaw, being an Account of the Situation, Nature, physical Use and admirable Cures performed by the Waters of Harrowgate, by Dr. Dean of York, and also the observations of Dr. Stanhope. 8vo. Leeds.

STANHOPE, MICHAEL. Newes out of York-shire; or, an Account of a Journey in the true Discovery of a Sovereigne Minerall, Medicinall Water, in the West-Riding of York-shire, neere an Ancient Town called Knaresborough. 4to. London.

1628 VENNER, THOMAS, M.D. The Baths of Bathe: or a necessary compendious Treatise concerning the Nature, the Use, and efficacies of those famous hot Waters. Published for the Benefit of all such as yeerely, for their Health resort to those Baths, with an Advertisement of the great Utility that cometh to Man's Body, by the Taking of the Physick in the Spring, Inferred upon a Question moved,

concerning the Frequencie of Sicknesse and Death of People more in that Season than in any other: Whereunto is also annexed, a Censure concerning the Water of St. Vincent's Rocks, neere Bristoll, which is in great Request and Use against the Stone. 4to. London.

Annexed to his *Via Recta ad Vitam Longam* (first printed, 1622), 1637 and 1650, and since reprinted in the *Harl. Misc.*, vol. II, 1809; 4th edit., London, 1660. See below.
Wood says his great eminence and practice at Bath was owing to the last of these useful and popular treatises.—Gough, 462.

1650 VENNER, THOMAS. Via recta ad Vitam Longam . . . whereunto is annexed by the same Author, a very necessary and compendious Treatise of the famous Baths of Bathe. 4to. London.

1631 JORDAN, EDWARD, M.D. A Discourse of Naturall Bathes and Minerall Waters . . . and lastly, of the Nature and Vses of Bathes, but especially of our Bathes at Bathe in Somersetshire (with a collection of other items dealing with 17th century science, etc.). 4to. Oxford (London also given).

Republished, 1633; again, with an Appendix by Guidott, 1669; 4th edit., 8vo, London, 1673. See below.

1673 JORDAN, EDWARD, M.D. A Discourse of Natural Bathes and Mineral Waters . . . with an Appendix by Thomas Guidott; A Treatise concerning Bath, wherein the Antiquity both of the Bath and the City is discussed, with a brief Account of the Nature and Virtues of the Hot Waters there. 8vo. London.

1632 ROWZEE, LODOWICK, M.D. (at Ashford). The Queenes Welles; that is, A Treatise of the Nature and Vertues of Tunbridge Welles. . . . 12mo. London.

Reprinted 1658, 1670, 1671; also in *Harl. Misc.*, vol. VIII, 316. See below.
Tunbridge mineral waters were discovered in 1632 by Lord North and their virtues celebrated the same year by Dr. Rowzee. The name Queen's Wells was given them from the fact that Henrietta Maria, consort of Charles I, spent nine weeks there after the birth of Prince Charles.—Gough, 284.

1670 ROWZEE, LODWICK (Doctor of Physick, practicing at Ashford in Kent). The Queens Welles, that is, a Treatise of the Nature and Vertues of Tunbridge Water; together with an Enumeration of the chiefest Diseases which it is good for, and against which it may be used, and the Manners and Order of taking it. 12mo. London.

STANHOPE, MICHAEL, M.D. Cures without Care: or, A Summons to all such as Find little or no Help by the Use of Physick, to repair to the Northern Spa; wherein by many Precedents of a few late Years it is proved to the World, that Infirmities of their own Nature desperate and of long Continuance have received perfect Cure by Virtue of Mineral Waters near Knaresborough, in the West Riding of Yorkshire. (London?)

1634 JOHNSON, THOMAS, M.D. Thermae Bathonicae, sive earum Descriptio, Vires, utendi tempus, modus, . . . (printed at the end of his *Mercurius Britannicus*). 8vo. London.

1636 MURE, ANDREW, M.D. Πίδαξ Πετρεία: or, The Discovery of St. Peter's Well at Peterhead, shewing the admirable Vertues thereof. 12mo. Edinburgh.

Reprinted, Aberdeen, 1680; also in *Aberdeen Magazine*, 1790, and in *Peterhead Sentinel*, July 7, 1900. See below.

1680 MURE, ANDREW, M.D. Πηγίαμα, or the Vertues and Way how to use the Minerall and Medicinall Water at Peterhead, . . . Aberdeen. (Broadsheet.)

1649 TAYLOR, JOHN (Apothecary of York). Spadacrene Angliae, the English Spaw, or the Glory of Knaresborough. 4to. London.

1652 FRENCH, JOHN. The Yorkshire Spaw, Or A Treatise Of four Famous Medicinal Wells, viz. the Spaw, or Vitrioline-Well; the stinking, or Sulphur-Well; the Dropping, or Petrifying-Well; and S. Mungus-Well, near Knaresborow in Yorkshire. Together with the causes, vertues, and use thereof. . . . 8vo. London.

1659 MACKAILE, MATTHEW. Fons Moffetensis seu Descriptio Topographico-spagyrica Fontium mineralium Moffetensium in Annandia Scotiae. 12mo. Edinburgh.
> Another edit., Edinburgh, 1664.

> 1664 MACKAILE, MATTHEW. A Topographico-Spagyricall Description of the Mineral Wells at Moffat in Annandale, translated and much enlarged by the author, Matthew Mackaile, Chyurgo-Medicene; also the Oyly-Well, or a Topographico-Spagyricall Description of the Well at St. Catherine's Chapel, in the Parish of Liberton, near Edinburgh; also The Character of Mr. Culpeper, Chyurgo, with Mr. Culpeper's Ghost, and a Monstrous Child, born and living in Caithness. 8vo. Edinburgh.
> Mackaile was a practicing physician in Aberdeen. He was much incensed at Culpeper, who was something of a braggart theologian and empiric. But by the time Mackaile had launched this bitter attack upon him, he was dead. It is to be regretted that Culpeper was not alive to answer back, for he had a nimble pen.—From Davis & Orioli, Booksellers.

1660 WITTIE, ROBERT, M.D. Scarbrough Spaw, or a Description of the Nature and Vertues of the Spaw at Scarbrough in Yorkshire, also A Treatise of the Nature and Use of Water in general, and the Several Sorts thereof, as Sea, Rain, Snow, Pond, Lake, Spring, and River Water, with their Original Causes and Qualities. 12mo. London (?).
> Another edit., 12mo, York, 1667, followed by others, and a Latin version in 1678. See below.
> This work gave rise to a paper war which extended over many years and involved a number of antagonists, chief of whom were Dr. Wm. Simpson and Dr. George Tonstal. The dispute was carried on in the true spirit of controversy, each discovering within himself plenteous argument and in his opponent a want of judgment, knowledge, and sufficient proof, but, on the other hand, no lack of impudence, arrogance, and ignorance. Wittie, an excellent practical physician, was prejudiced in favor of his spa, which brought to him much advantage; Simpson, a bigoted adherent of the Paracelsian system and of hot regimens, desired to disgrace Wittie and succeed to his place; and Tonstal, disappointed in his efforts to monopolize these waters for his own advantage, grew peevish and abusive, decried them, and set up Harrogate against them. A partial list of these publications follows.

> 1667 WITTIE, ROBERT, M.D. Scarborough Spaw; or, a Description of the Nature and Vertues of the Spaw at Scarborough, Yorkshire. Also a Treatise of the Nature and Use of Sea, Rain, Dew, Snow, . . . and River-Waters, Where more largely the Controversie among learned Writers, about the Original of Springs is discussed. To which is added a Short Discourse concerning Mineral-Waters. Corrected and Augmented throughout the whole, together with an Historical Relation of Cures done by the Waters. 12mo. York.

> 1669 SIMPSON, WILLIAM, M.D. Hydrologia Chymica: or, the Chymical Anatomy of the Scarbrough and other Spaws in Yorkshire. Wherein are interspersed some animadversions upon Dr. Wittie's lately published Treatise of the Scarbrough Spaw. Also a short Description of the Spaws at Malton and Knarsbrough. . . . Also a Vindication of Chymical Physick; where a probable Way is propounded for the Improvement of experimental Philosophy. . . . 8vo. London.

> WITTIE, ROBERT. Pyrologia Mimica: or, an Answer to Hydrologia Chymica of William Simpson, philo-chimico-medicus, in Defense of Scarbrough Spaw, . . . Also a Vindication of the Rational Method and Practice of Physick, called

Galenical; and a Reconciliation betwixt that and the Chymical. Likewise a further Discourse about the Original of Springs. 8vo. London.

1670 SIMPSON, WILLIAM. Hydrological Essays: or, A Vindication of Hydrologia Chymica: being a farther Discovery of Scarbrough Spaw, and of the Right Use thereof. And of the Sweet Spaw, and Sulphur Well at Knarsbrough, with a brief Account of the Allom-Works at Whitby. Together with a Return to some Queries propounded by the ingenious Dr. Daniel Foot, concerning Mineral Waters. To which is annexed, an Answer to Dr. Tunstal's Book concerning the Scarbrough Spaw. . . . 8vo. London.

1672 TONSTAL, GEORGE, M.D. Scarbrough Spaw Spagirically anatomized: . . . 8vo. London.

> Here Tonstal charges Wittie with ignorance of the nature of the waters, want of judgment to try them, inconclusive arguments and unjust observations. He upbraids Simpson for his presumption before he had laid in a sufficient stock of learning.

WITTIE, ROBERT. Scarbrough's Spagyrical Anatomizer Dissected: or, An Answer to all that Dr. Tonstall hath objected in his Book against Scarbrough Spaw. . . . 12mo. London.

> With this Wittie withdrew from the controversy. Tonstal came back quickly with an ill-natured reply, dedicated to the Royal Society, to which he appeals for a decision. In no. 52 of the *Philosophical Transactions,* Dr. Daniel Foot attacked Wittie on the cause of the sudden loss of virtues of mineral waters. In no. 56, Dr. Highmore published a Letter relating to "Dr. Wittie's Defence of Scarbrough Spaw." To both of these Wittie returned a reply in no. 60.

1678 ————. Fons Scarburgensis: sive Tractatus de omnis Aquarum Generis Origine ac Usu; particulariter de Fonte minerali apud Scarbrough in Comitatu Eboracensi Angliae. . . . Item Dissertationes variae tam philosophicae quam medicinales. 12mo. London.

> This is a Latin version of the original work which appeared in 1660. It stirred Simpson to another reply.

1679 SIMPSON, WILLIAM. The History of the Scarbrough Spaw; or, A Further Discovery of the excellent Vertues thereof, in the Cure of Scurvy, Hypochondria, Agues, Jaundice, Dropsie, Womens Diseases, &c. by many remarkable Instances, . . . Also a Discourse of an artificial Sulphur-bath, and Bath of Sea-Water, with the Uses thereof in the Cure of many Diseases: . . . 12mo. London.

> Silence seems to have settled over Scarbrough Spa till 1682, when Dr. Martin Lister published a treatise on the medicinal waters of England, the title of which I have not seen. An impartial review of the whole affair is contained in Dr. T. Short's *History of Mineral Waters* (see Short under 1734 below), from which *via* Gough, 567-71, the above annotations are drawn.

1661 A Brief Account of the Virtues of the Famous Well of Astrop, not far from Oxford, of late so much frequented by the Nobility and Gentry. 8vo. London (?).

1672 BORLASE, EDMUND, M.S. Latham Spaw in Lancashire, with some Remarkable Cases and Cures effected by it. 12mo. London.

> 2nd edit., 1672. See below.
> Borlase was an eminent physician of Chester, where he died in 1682.

1672 BORLASE, EDMUND. Latham Spaw in Lancashire, with some remarkable Cases and Cures effected by it; together with a farther Account of it, as may conduce to the Publick Advantage with Ease and little Expence. Frontis. 8vo. London.

CLAREMONT, CHARLES, M.D. Caroli Claromontii Doct. Medici, nob. Lotharing. de aere, locis, & aquis terrae Angliae, deque morbis Anglorum vernaculis. Cum Observationibus, Ratiocinatione & curandi modo illustratis. 12mo. London. (So cited by Gough.)

> At the end are Observations medicae Cambro-Britannicae. Twenty-six cases are reported for his two years' practice in South Wales.—Gough, 704.

1673 CHAPMAN, HENRY. Thermae Redivivae: The City of Bath described: with Some Observations on those Soveraign Waters, both as to the Bathing in, and Drinking of Them, Now so much in Use. Plan of the City. 4to. London.

GUIDOTT, THOMAS, M.D. A Quaere concerning Drinking Bath Water at Bath resolved. 8vo. London.

> Two sheets, published under the name of Eugenius Philander. Guidott, a physician who practiced about Oxford and later at Bath and London, revived the use of the waters at Bath. His practice was eminently successful as long as he could refrain from abuse and impertinence. He left several treatises relating to the place and its waters.—Gough, 463.

1674 —————. A Letter concerning some Observations lately made at Bathe, written to his much honoured Friend Sir E. G. Knight and Baronet, M.D., in London. 4to. London(?).

1675 SIMPSON, WILLIAM, M.D. A Discourse of the Sulphur-Bath at Knaresborough, in Yorkshire. 8vo. London.

WILSON, EDWARD, M.D. Spadacrene Dunelmensis: or, A Short Treatise of an Ancient Medicinal Fountain, or Vitrioline Spaw, near the City of Durham. Together with the constituent Principles, Virtues, and Use thereof. 12mo. London.

1676 GILBERT, SAMUEL. Fons Sanitatis: or, The Healing Spring at Willow-Bridge in Staffordshire; found out by the Right Hon. the Lady Jane Gerard, Baroness of Bromley: published for the Common Good by Samuel Gilbert, Chaplain to Her Honour, and Rector of Quat. 12mo. London.

GUIDOTT, THOMAS, M.D. A Discourse of Bathe, and the Hot Waters there. Also some Enquiries of the Water of St. Vincent's Rock near Bristol; and that of Castle-Cary. To which is added, A Century of Observations, more fully declaring the Nature, Property, and Distinction of the Baths: with an Account of the Lives and Characters of the Physicians of Bathe. Plan of Bath, and plates of Roman antiquities, etc. 12mo. London.

PUGH, ROBERT. Bathoniensium & Aquisgranensium Thermarum comparatio variis adjunctis illustrata. Epistola ad illustrissimum virum Rogerum Castlemaini Comitem. 12mo. London.

> Pugh was a native of Caernarvonshire, and confessor to Henrietta Maria, queen mother. He died in Newgate, where he was confined for complicity in Titus Oates's plot.—Gough, 463.

1681 PETER, JOHN, M.D. A Treatise of Lewisham (but vulgarly called Dulwich) Wells, in Kent, shewing the Time and Manner of their Discovery, the Mineralls with which they are impregnated, the severall Diseases Experience hath found them good for, with Directions for the Use of them. 12mo. London.

1683 HAWORTH, SAMUEL, M.D. A Description of the Duke of York's Bagnio, and of the Mineral Bath and New Spaw thereunto belonging. With an Account of the

Use of Sweating, Rubbing, Bathing, and the Medicinal Vertues of the Spaw. 12mo. London.

1684 GUIDOTT, THOMAS, M.D. A True and Exact Account of Sadler's Wells: or, The New Mineral Water lately found out at Islington; treating of its Nature and Virtues. Together with an Enumeration of the chiefest Diseases which it is good for, and against which it may be used, and the manner and order of taking it. 4to. London. (Tract of 4 leaves.)

1685 DERHAM, SAMUEL. Hydrologia Philosophica: or, An Account of Ilmington Waters, in Warwickshire; with Directions for the Drinking of the same. Together with some Experimental Observations touching the Original of Compound Bodies. 8vo. Oxford.

JONES, DR., and JOHN CONYERS. For an account of the London Spaw, see Jones under LONDON.

1687 BYFEILD, T., M.D. A Short and Plain Account of the late found Balsamic Wells at Hoxdon, and of their excellent Virtues above other Mineral Waters; which make them effectually cure most Diseases, both inward and outward. With Directions how to use them. 12mo. London.

MADAN, P. A Philosophical and Medical Essay of the Waters of Tunbridge Wells. 4to. London.
> Reprinted in *Harl. Misc.*, vol. I.

1691 GUIDOTT, THOMAS, M.D. Thomae Guidotti Anglo-Britanni de Thermis Britannicis Tractatus, accesserunt Observationes hydrostaticae, chromaticae, & Miscellaneae unius cujusque Balnei apud Bathoniam Naturam, Proprietatem, & Distinctionem curatus exhibentes. Experientiae diuturnioris Opus, & Plurium Annorum Pensum cum Indicibus necessariis ad Regale Collegium Medicorum Londinensium. 4to. London.

1694 ————. The Register of Bath, or two hundred Observations, containing an Account of Cures performed, and Benefit received, by the Use of the Famous Hot Waters of Bath, in the County of Somerset, as they, for the most part, came under the Observation and Knowledge of Thomas Guidott, Physician there. Being the great Part of his Experience of the Effects of the Baths of Bath, for 27 Years last past. 12mo. London.

————. Epistolarum Medicarum Specimen de Thermarum Bathoniensium Effectis ad Clarissimos Medicos D. Bate, Fraser, Wedderburne, etc. 4to. London.

1695 GREW, NEHEMIA, M.D. Tractatus de Salis Cathartici in Aquis Ebesharlensibus & hujusmodi aliis contenti Natura & Usu, Authore Nehemia Grew, M.D. utriusque Regiae Societatis Socio. 12mo. London.

In English, London, 1697.

1697   GREW, NEHEMIA, M.D. A Treatise of the Nature and Use of the bitter purging Salt, contained in Epsom and such other Waters. 8vo. London.

1697   FLOYER, SIR JOHN. An Enquiry into the Right Use and Abuses of the Hot, Cold, and Temperate Baths in England. . . . To which is added, An Extract of Dr. Jones's Treaty on Buxton; A Letter from Dr. Clayton of Lincolnshire, concerning St. Mungus Well; an Abstract of some Cures perform'd by the Bath at Buxton. 8vo. London.

See Jones's tract under 1572 above.

PEIRCE, ROBERT, M.D. Bath Memoirs: or, Observations in the Three and Forty Years Practice at the Bath; what Cures have been there wrought both by Bathing and Drinking these Waters from 1653 to 1697. 2 pts. Folding plan. 8vo. Bristol.

Another edit., 8vo, London, 1713. See below.
Peirce is probably the first English writer who noted the now well-known occurrence of acute rheumatism as a sequel to scarlet fever.—Quoted.

1713   PEIRCE, ROBERT, M.D. The History and Memoirs of the Bath: containing Observations on what Cures have been there wrought, both by Bathing and Drinking those Waters. An Account of King Bladud, said to be the first Founder of the Baths: with a philosophical Preface, of several Experiments and Remarks relating to the Origin, Quality, and Nature of Baths in general, and of these in particular. 8vo. London.
First published in Philos. Trans., no. 169.—Gough, 465.

1699   ALLEN, BENJAMIN. Natural History of the Chalybeat and Purging Waters of England, with their particular Essays and Uses, with some Observations on the Bath Waters in Somersetshire. 8vo. London.

Another edit., 8vo, London, 1711.

1703   UNDERHILL, JOHN. Johannis Subtermontani Thermologia Bristoliensis: or, Underhill's Short Account of the Bristol Hot Well Water: its Uses and historical Cures. 8vo. Bristol.

A Hot Well at Bristol was known as far back as 1480, when it was mentioned by William Wurcestre. It originally issued at low water from the rocks on the right bank of the Avon, but owing to recent widening of the channel of the river, it cannot now be approached. In 1695 a pump room had been built which was resorted to by the fashionable folk of London. The spring was mentioned in Humphrey Clinker and in Evelina. A rival spring known as the New Hotwell is noticed in 1702. Because it seemed to have cured John Wesley of a consumptive attack in 1754, it received quite an access of visitors for a while, but its popularity did not last.—From notes by the editor of the Torrington Diaries, vol. I, 381.

1705   GUIDOTT, THOMAS, M.D. An Apology for the Bath: being an Answer to a late Enquiry into the right Use and Abuses of the Baths in England, so far as may concern the Hot Waters of the Bath in the County of Somerset. Engraving. 8vo. London.

Another edit., 8vo, London, 1708.

1708   GUIDOTT, THOMAS, M.D. An Apology for the Bath. Being an Answer to a late Enquiry into the right Use and Abuses of the Baths in England, so far as may concern the Hot Waters of the Bath in the County of Somerset. With some Reflections on fresh Cold-Bathing, Bathing in Sea-Water, and Dipping in Baptism. By the Author of the Latin Tract De Thermis Britannicis. 8vo. London.
These two tracts, with the others of his and Chapman's description of Bath, were reprinted together in one volume by Leake at Bath, 8vo, 1725. See Guidott, 1725, below.

1707   ALEXANDER, J. Tituli Fontium Abredonensium; the Titles of Aberdeen's Wells. Aberdeen.

> Partly reprinted in *Scot. Notes & Queries,* vol. 8, 87, from a unique copy in the Bodleian.—Mitchell, *Scot. Top.,* vol. I.

OLIVER, WILLIAM, M.D. A Practical Dissertation on Bath-Waters . . . design'd for the Use of the Nobility, Gentry, etc., who resort to the Bath. 8vo. London.

> Other edits., 1716; 12mo, 1719; 1747; 5th edit., 1764. See below.
> Oliver was a physician who had seen service under Monmouth in Poland, and came to England with William of Orange. He became physician to the Fleet, to Chatham Hospital, and Greenwich Hospital. His *Practical Essay on Fevers,* 1704, and the above work were his chief publications. He was a friend of Pope, for whom he obtained from Borlase the minerals which decorated Pope's Grotto at Twickenham.

> 1719 OLIVER, WILLIAM, M.D. A Practical Dissertation on Bath-Waters. Treating of the Antiquity of Bath: and its Waters. Of the Original of Springs. Of the Cause of the Heat of Bath-Waters; and of their Ingredients. Of drinking Bath-waters. Of Bathing. Of the City of Bath, its Situation, Baths, etc. To which is added, A Relation of an extraordinary Sleepy Person at Tinsbury, near Bath. Designed for the Use of the Nobility, Gentry, etc., who resort to the Bath. 12mo. London.
>   The addition was first subjoined to Oliver's treatise of fevers.—Gough, 465. This sleepy person was "one Samuel Chilton," a laborer who "happen'd without any visible cause or evident Sign, to fall into a very profound Sleep; out of which, no Art used by those that were near him, could rouse him."—Quoted.

1717   Hydro-Sidereon, or, A Treatise of Ferrugineous Waters, especially the Ipswich Spaw; being an excellent Spring of that Nature, there lately discovered; with the vast Difference of such Medicinal Waters, their proper medical.Uses in various Diseases, grounded on several curious Experiments and nice Observations never before made; with a plain Demonstration also of the great Vanity and Folly in buying and Cheat in selling German Spaw Water in England. 8vo. London.

1720   CHEYNE, GEORGE, M.D., F.R.S. Observations concerning the Nature and due Method of treating the Gout, for the Use of my Worthy Friend Richard Tennison, Esq.: together with an Account of the Nature and Quality of Bath-Waters. London.

> 6th edit., revised, corrected, and enlarged to more than double the former, called: An Essay on the true Nature, etc., 1724.—Gough, 466.

1723.   An Historical Account of the Cures done by the Mineral Waters at Holt, with some short Observations concerning its Nature, Virtues, and the Method of using it. 12mo. Sold at the Old Mineral-Well in Holt. (16 pp.)

1725   GUIDOTT, THOMAS, M.D. A Collection of Treatises relating to the City and Waters of Bath, all written by the learned Th. Guidott, M.D., to which is added, Thermae Redivivae: or the City of Bath described, by Henry Chapman, Gent. 8vo. London.

MERRICK, DR. JOHN. Heliocrene: a Poem in Latin and English, on the Chalybeate Well at Sunninghill. Reading.

ROUSE, LEWIS, M.D. Tunbridge Wells: or, A Directory for the Drinking of those Waters. Shewing, 1. Their Nature and Virtues. 2. The Diseases in which they

are most beneficial. 3. The Time, Manner, and Order of drinking them. 4. The Preparation of the Body required. 5. The Diet proper to be used by all Mineral-Water Drinkers. To which are annexed two Tracts. I. Mr. Boyle's Observations upon Tunbridge and other Mineral Waters. II. A Physico-mechanical Dissertation on Water in general, proving it to be the best Specifick for the Cure of all Diseases, with a particular Account of all the Virtues of the German Waters. Made English from the Latin Original. 12mo. London.

WYNTER, JOHN, M.B. (e Coll. Christi, Cantab.) Cyclus metasyncriticus: or, An Essay on Chronical Diseases; the Methods of Cure; and herein, more fully, of the Medicinal Waters of Bath and Bristol, their several Virtues and Differences. 8vo. London.

1728 —————. Of Bathing in the Hot Baths, at Bathe: chiefly with regard to the Palsie, and Some Diseases in Women. In a Letter, addressed to a Friend. 8vo. London.

1730 MEDLEY, JOHN, M.D. Tentamen Hydrologicum, or, An Essay upon Matlock Bath in Derbyshire. Whereto are prefixed, Three Short Preliminary Dissertations, upon, 1. Water in general. 2. The tactile Qualities (so-called). 3. Minerals. Further demonstrating, from the fundamental Principles of Philosophy and Physick, the excellent Qualities of these Waters, in the Cure of several Diseases incident to the Human Body. 8vo. Nottingham.

1731 EYRE, HENRY. A Brief Account of the Holt Waters, containing the one hundred and twelve eminent Cures, performed by the Use of the famous Mineral Waters at Holt (near Bath) in Wiltshire. Being faithfully collected by Henry Eyre, sworn Purveyor to Her Majesty for all Mineral Waters. To which are added, Directions for drinking the Holt Waters, and some Experimental Observations on the several Wells. 12mo. London.

MILLIGAN, G. An Account of the Virtues of the Mineral Waters near Moffat. *Edinb. Med. Essays.* Edinburgh.

WILLIAMS, STEPHEN, M.B. An Experimental History of Road Water in Wiltshire, with a short mechanical Account of its Virtues, and of chronical Distempers, in a Letter to the Rev. Dr. Durham. 8vo. London.

1733 EYRE, HENRY. Account of the Mineral Waters of Spa, commonly called German Spaw. Folding plate by Fourdrinier (cuts of the vendor's seals impressed on bottles of water). 12mo. London (?).

QUINCY, JOHN, M.D. A Treatise of Warm Bath Water, and of Cures made lately at Bath, in Somersetshire: particularly proving that it is more probable to cure Diseases by drinking warm Mineral Waters and Bathing in them than in Cold Mineral Waters (vol. I). A Treatise of Warm Bath Water: in which is more

than 200 Cures made at Bath in Somersetshire, by Bathing, Pumping, and Drinking the Waters. With a Philosophical Account of the Elements, subterraneous Fires, and Fermentation of Metals, Minerals, etc. Taken from Sir Isaac Newton, Jones, Baccius, Guidott, Boerhave, Miller, Lister, Cheney, Oliver, Wynter, Willis, Floyer and Baynard, Quincy, Sydenham, Lodwick, Rowzee, and many others (vol. II). 4to. Oxford.

1734 SHAW, PETER, M.D. An Enquiry into the Contents, Virtues, and Uses of the Scarborough Spaw Water, with the Method of examining any other Mineral Water. 8vo. London.

SHORT, THOMAS, M.D. The Natural, Experimental, and Medicinal History of the Mineral Waters of Derbyshire, Lincolnshire and Yorkshire, particularly those of Scarborough, with the Natural History of the Earth's Minerals and Fossils; to which are added Notes. 4 folding plates of crystals. 4to. London.

> A 2nd vol. was added as a continuation in 1740.

> 1740 SHORT, THOMAS, M.D. Essay towards a Natural History of the principal Mineral Waters, etc. 4to. Sheffield.
> This work is still held in esteem for its account of older writers and their publications on mineral waters.

SOAME, JOHN, M.D. Hampstead Wells: or, Directions for the Drinking of those Waters, . . . With an Appendix relating to the Original of Springs in general; with Some Experiments on the Hampstead Waters, and Histories of Cures. 8vo. London.

1735 A Dissertation on the Contents, Virtues, and Uses of Cold and Hot Mineral Springs, particularly those of Scarborough. In a Letter to Robert Toninson, Esq. Recorder of that Corporation. (Listed in *Gent. Mag.,* vol. 5, May.)

1736 NEALE, GEORGE, M.D. (of Leedes). Spadacrene Eboracensis: or, The Yorkshire Spaws, near Knaresburgh: being a Description of five Famous Medicinal Wells, viz. The Sweet Spa. 2. The Sulphur or Stinking-Well. 3. The Dropping Well. 4. The Black Spring, found out by the Author. 5. St. Magnus's or St. Mungo's Well. All which Wells, with their Situation, Operation, Virtues, etc., are described, together with the Hot and Cold Baths; as likewise fume Baths.

> This is an unfinished piece which was inserted in Short's *History of Mineral Waters,* 286-93, Notes.—Gough, 566. See Short under 1734 above. Gough adds that no more of the many curious observations left by the doctor, who died in 1681, could be found by his son, Dr. John Neale of Doncaster.

SHORT, THOMAS, M.D. History of the Mineral Waters of England. London.

> Whether this is another edition of the 1734 work I have been unable to ascertain.—It contains the most accurate and particular description of the three caverns in the district of the Peak (in Derbyshire).—Gough, 134.

1737 ANDREE, JOHN, M.D. An Account of the Tilbury Water; containing a Narrative of the Discovery of the medicinal Qualities of this Spring, Experiments on the Water, Observations on the Experiments; the Vertues of the Water, inter-

spersed with various Cases; the Manner of drinking it; and lastly, several re-markable Cures. 8vo. London.

2nd edit., London, 1737; 3rd, with additions, London, 1764.

ATKINS, JOHN (Surgeon). A Compendious Treatise on the Contents, Virtues, and Uses of Cold and Hot Mineral Springs in general, particularly the cele-brated Hot Waters of Scarborough; with Observations on their Quality and proper Directions in drinking them. The Whole consisting of what is chiefly useful in the Works of the most celebrated Authors who have wrote on this Subject. To which are annexed the Opinion of Sir John Floyer and Dr. Bay-nard, on the great Use and Effect of Bathing in the Sea. 8vo. London.

KING, JOHN. An Essay on Hot and Cold Bathing, with some Observations on the Mineral Waters at Bungay in Suffolk. (Listed in *Gent. Mag.,* vol. 7, Aug.)

TAVERNER, JAMES, M.B. An Essay upon the Whitman Spa in Essex. 8vo. London.

1739 KEIR, P., M.D. An Enquiry into the Nature and Virtues of the Medicinal Waters of Bristol, and their Use in the Cure of Chronical Distempers. 8vo. London.

1740 SHEBBEARE, JOHN (Chemist). A New Analysis of the Bristol Water, together with the Cause of the Diabetes, and Hectic; and their Cure, as it results from those Waters, experimentally considered. 8vo. London.

This was written in refutation of Keir (see above).—Gough, 476.

1742 A Discourse of the Virtues and Uses of Nevile Holt Water. 8vo. London.

1749 The Contents, Virtues, and Uses of Nevil Holt Spaw Water further proved, illus-trated, and explained from Experiments and Reason. With some Histories of its signal Effects in various Diseases. Collected by several Hands. Also Rules and Directions for its more easy Use and greater Success. 2nd edit. with several emendations and great additions. 8vo. London. (With a postscript printed 1750.)

HILLARY, WILLIAM, M.D. Inquiry into the Contents and Medicinal Virtues of Lincomb Spaw Water near Bath. Frontis. 8vo. London.

The frontispiece illustrates chemical experiments on the waters. Hillary was a pupil of Boerhave.—Bookseller's Note.

1744 PERRY, CHARLES, M.D. An Account of an Analysis made on the Stratford Min-eral Water, comprehending nearly thirty different Experiments, with Observa-tions thereon, and Conclusions drawn from the Whole. In this Work the min-eral or medicinal Contents of that excellent Water are faithfully and accurately set forth: its wonderful Virtues and Properties are proved as well from its Contents as its Effects, and the great Cures it has performed are accounted for upon the Principles of Mechanical Reasoning; and lastly it is judicially con-sidered, and directed to such Diseases for which it is peculiarly proper and good. 8vo. Northampton.

1745 BAYLIES, WILLIAM. Short Remarks on Dr. Perry's Analysis made on the Strat-ford Mineral Water, with a Short Essay, by way of Appendix, towards a more perfect Examination into the same Waters. 8vo. Stratford upon Avon.

RANDOLPH, GEORGE, M.D. An Enquiry into the Medicinal Virtues of Bristol Water, and the Indications of the Cures which it answers. (Place?)

The *Gent. Mag.,* vol. 20, March, lists Randolph, G., *Of Bristol Waters*, 1750.

1746 MANNING, M. Aquae Minerales omnibus morbis chronicis medentur. . . . Accedit Aquarum Sitomagensium (vulgo Thetfordiensium) Analysis, etc. 4to. Londini.

1748 LINDEN, DIEDERICK WESSELS, M.D. A Treatise on . . . Chalybeate Waters, and Natural Hot Baths. With a Physico-chemical Analysis, and medicinal Description of the Mineral Waters at Tunbridge, etc. 8vo. London.

1750 For an account praising the waters of Glastonbury for cures, see *A Compleat and Authentic History of the Town and Abbey of Glastonbury,* under TOWNS.

1751 HOME, FRANCIS, M.D. An Essay on the Contents and Virtues of Dunse Spa (Berwickshire), in a Letter to my Lord —————. 8vo. Edinburgh.

LINDEN, DIEDERICK WESSELS, M.D. An Experimental Dissertation on the . . . Hyde Saline Purging Water, commonly called the Hyde Spaw, near Cheltenham, in Gloucestershire. 8vo. London.

SMITH, HUGH. Experimental Observations on the Water of the Mineral Spring near Islington, commonly called New Tunbridge Wells. 8vo. London.

5th edit., much enlarged, London, 1773.

1773 SMITH, HUGH. Experimental Observations on the Water of Mineral Spring near Islington, commonly called New Tunbridge Wells . . . with an Account of its Medicinal Virtues and Use. (Seemingly bound with it by the same author is: A Treatise of the Mineral Spring at the New Tunbridge Well near Islington, with Rules for drinking the Waters.) 8vo. London.

Wilt Thou be made Whole? Or the Virtues and Efficacy of the Water of Glastonbury in the County of Somerset, illustrated in above twenty remarkable Cases faithfully described, of Persons who by the Use of that Water have been cured of Disorders of the most obstinate and deplorable Kinds; such as Asthma, Rheumatism, Dropsy, King's-evil, Deafness, Blindness, Wens, Cancers, Ulcers, Old Swellings, Leprosy, etc., etc., by the Attestations of the Ministers, and Church-Wardens, etc., or by credible and impartial Witnesses, etc. Collected by an Inhabitant of Bath. 8vo. London.

The weight of ministers' testimony should win credence to this loyal booster.

1752 RANDOLPH, GEORGE, M.D. An Enquiry into the Medicinal Virtues of Bath Waters, and the Indications of Cures which it answers. London.

1754 CHARLTON, RICE, M.B., F.R.S. A Treatise on the Bath Waters, wherein are discovered the several Principles of which they are composed, the Causes of their Heat, and the Manners of their Production. 8vo. London.

HORSEBURG, WILLIAM, M.D. Experiments and Observations upon the Hartfell Spaw, made at Moffet 1750; and an Account of its Medicinal Virtues so far as they have been hitherto discovered from Experience. Edinburgh.

> This is article xii of *Essays and Observations, Physical and Literary,* read before a society in Edinburgh, and published by them. Vol. I. 8vo.—Gough, 642.

OWEN, EDWARD. For observations on the Hot Well at Bristol, see his *Observations,* this date, under NATURAL HISTORY.

1755   LINDEN, DIEDERICK WESSELS, M.D. A Treatise on the Medicinal Mineral Water at Llandrindod, in Radnorshire, South Wales; with some Remarks on Mineral and Fossil Mixtures in their native Veins and Beds, at least as far as respects their Influence on Water. 8vo. London.

1756   REYNOLDS, THOMAS (Surgeon). Some Experiments on the Chalybeate Waters lately discovered near the Palace of the Lord Bishop of Rochester at Bromley, in Kent. With Observations on Chalybeate Waters in general, and the most successful method of drinking them: . . . with some plain and easy Directions to make artificial Chalybeate Waters, and to distinguish with absolute Certainty the factitious from the native. To which are added some Directions for discovering the unwholesome Contents of Common Water, and some Method of correcting them, . . . 8vo. London.

1757   BAYLIES, WILLIAM, M.D. Practical Reflections on the Uses and Abuses of Bath Waters, made from actual Experiments and Observations: to which is added, by way of Appendix, a Narrative of Facts relative to the physical Confederacy in Bath in the Year 1757. 8vo. London.

RUTTER, JONATHAN, M.D. (Quaker). A Methodical and Medieval Synopsis of Mineral Waters. Hard and Soft Waters, Nitrous, Saline, Chalybeate, Alcaline, Calcareous, Sulphureous, etc., and on Mineral Baths. 4to. London.

WALL, JOHN. Experiments and Observations on the Malvern Waters, 2nd edit., with Appendix containing some farther Particulars. 8vo. Worcester.

> 3rd edit., Worcester, 1763.

1758   STEVENS, J. N., M.D. A Treatise on the Mineral Qualities of Bath Waters: in Three Parts. By J. N. Stevens, M.D. of Bath, and Fellow of the Royal Academy of Sciences. 8vo. London.

SUTHERLAND, A., M.D. The Nature and Qualities of Bristol Waters, illustrated with Experiments and Observations; with Practical Reflections on Bath Waters occasionally interspersed. 8vo. Bristol.

1759   RELHAN, ANTHONY. For an analysis of the air and waters at Brighthelmstone, see his *A Short History of Brighthelmstone,* under TOWNS.

1760 An Account of the Remarkable Well near Settle in Yorkshire. In *Gent. Mag.,* vol. 30, July, 315-16.

BEVIS, JOHN. An Experimental Enquiry concerning the Contents, Qualities, and Medicinal Virtues of the two Mineral Waters lately discovered at Bagnigge Wells near London; with Directions for drinking them, and Some Account of their Success in obstinate Cases. 8vo. London.

> 2nd edit., with additions, 8vo, London, 1767.
> The author was Fellow of the Royal Academy of Sciences at Berlin.

1761 A Treatise on the Nature and Virtues of Buxton Waters, with a Preliminary Account of the External and Internal Use of Natural and Artificial warm Waters among the Antients: By a Physician. 8vo. London.

> 3rd edit., by A. H. Hunter, M.D., 8vo, London, 1773.

1763 SUTHERLAND, ALEXANDER, M.D. Attempts to revive Antient Medical Doctrines: 1. Of Waters in general. 2. Of Bath and Bristol Waters in particular. 3. Of Sea Voyages. 4. Of Local Remedies. 5. Of the Non-Naturals: with an Appendix on Plaistering in the Small-Pox. The Whole confirmed by Histories of Facts. 8vo. London.

> Part of this work was reprinted under the title:
>
> 1764 SUTHERLAND, ALEXANDER, M.D. An Attempt to ascertain, as well as to extend, the Virtues of Bath and Bristol Waters by Experiments and Cases. 2nd edit., new modelled and improved. 8vo. London.

1764 LUCAS, C., M.D. Cursory Remarks on the Method of Investigating the Principles and Properties of Bath and Bristol Waters: set forth in attempting to revive Ancient Medical Doctrines, etc.: Both by Alexander Sutherland, . . . by C. Lucas, Doctor of Physic of Rheims, Leyden, and Dublin, and Member of the Royal College of Physicians in London. 8vo. London.

> The medical question involved here was taken up by others.

1766 BURR, THOMAS. For observations on the mineral springs of Tunbridge Wells, see his *History of Tunbridge Wells,* under TOWNS.

1767 LAYARD, DANIEL PETER, M.D. Account of the Somersham Water (in Huntingdonshire). 8vo. London (?).

> This pamphlet contains only some history, list of subscribers, rules and directions for drinking the waters.—Gough, 713.

LINDEN, DIEDERICK WESSELS, M.D. An Experimental and Practical Enquiry into the Ophthalmic, Antiscrophulous, and Nervous Properties of the Mineral Waters of Llangbi, in Carnarvonshire. To which is annexed, An Essay on the Prize Question, proposed by the Royal Academy of Bourdeaux, for the Year 1767, on the Subject of Analizing Mineral Waters. London.

1768 AWSITER, J. Thoughts on Brighthelmstone concerning Sea Bathing and drinking Sea Water. London.

LINDEN, DIEDERICK WESSELS, M.D. A Medicinal and Experimental History and Analysis of the Hanly's Spa, Saline, Purging, and Chalybeate Waters, near Shrewsbury. 8vo. London.

1769   Directions for the Use of Harrogate Waters. London.

> Date is not given; but it is later than 1767.

A Treatise on Buxton Waters. London.

> Date is not given; but it is later than 1767. See under 1761 above.

1770   Cocks Lodge Water Analyzed. Newcastle.

Observations on the Mineral Water at Horwood Well near Wincanton, Somerset. (Place?)

1771   Pre-eminence of Marget as a Bathing Place. Signed Philomaris. In *Gent. Mag.,* vol. 41, 166-68.

1772   FALCONER, WILLIAM. An Essay on the Bath Waters, in Four Parts: containing a Prefatory Introduction on the Study of Mineral Waters in general. Part I. An Account of their possible Impregnations. Part II. The most approved Means to be used for the Discovery of their Contents. Part III. Experiments on the Bath Waters, with an Application of the foregoing Rules to a Discovery of their Contents. Part IV. Of the Effects of the Bath Waters on the Human Body, and the Propriety of their Use in Medicine, with an Application of the Experiments to Medicine and Pharmacy. 8vo. London.

MONRO, DONALD, M.D. An Account of the Sulphureous Mineral Waters of Castle-Loed and Fairburn, in the County of Ross; and of the Salt Purging Water of Perkeathly in the City of Perth, in Scotland. In *Philos. Trans.,* vol. 62, 15-32.

> This article contains an analysis of the water and its behavior when combined with various substances. Many of the experiments seemed to get nowhere. There is adduced testimony certifying cures, particularly in cutaneous disorders.

PERCIVAL, THOMAS, M.D. Experiments and Observations on the Waters of Buxton and Matlock, in Darbyshire. In *Philos. Trans.,* vol. 62, 455.

> This contains the usual analysis of contents and behavior. These waters were believed to stimulate the pulse to a strong degree.

1773   Experiments with a new Well-water discovered at Epsom, and compared with Harrogate; shewing their Affinity, and ascertaining their Contents. N.B. Well was first sunk in 1767, depth, 39 feet; contains about 26 feet of Water. In *Gent Mag.,* vol. 43, 125-26.

> The two wells are compared in taste, color, smell, specific gravity, effects on metals, oil of tartar, etc.

1774   BLENKINSOP, J., M.D. An Account of the Medicinal Waters at Llanwrtyd in Breconshire. In *Gent. Mag.,* vol. 44, 469-71.

CHARLETON, RICE, M.D. Three Tracts on Bath Water: I., A Chymical Analysis of Bath Water; II., Inquiry into the Efficacy of Bath Water in Palsies; III., Histories of Hospital Cases under the Care of Dr. Oliver. Plate. 8vo. Bath.

1775 HARGROVE, ELY. For an account of the medicinal waters of Harrogate, see his *History of the Castle, . . . of Knaresborough,* under TOWNS.

1776 SMITH, HUGH. A Treatise on the Use and Abuse of Mineral Waters: also Rules to be observed by Invalids who visit Chalybeate Springs of Old and New Tunbridge Wells. 8vo. London.

1780 Adams Well (Speldhurst, near Tunbridge Wells), a History of its Original . . . a drinking . . . salutary Effects on various Cases and Disorders. 8vo. London. (30 pp.)

THICKNESSE, PHILIP. The Valetudinarian's Bath Guide: or, the Means of obtaining long Life and Health. Dedicated to the Earl Shelburne. London (?)

> Reviewed *Gent. Mag.,* vol. 50, 136-38, from which the following summary is taken. The author thinks that a chemical analysis of the waters at Bath should be made, for those who prescribe them are ignorant of their contents. The work treats of the waters; of apothecaries whose ethics are questionable; of physicians at Bath, of whom he had a low opinion; when to bathe and when not to; of long life; of surgeons, who have his respect; of bilious disorders, of which he knew something; of antiquity and ancient baths of the city; of wine and overdrinking; of promiscuous bathing of both sexes, etc. The reviewer commends the work as being serviceable to prospective visitors, despite its waggishness. The travels of Thicknesse are recorded in vols. I and II of this present work. See Index to vol. II.

1781 ELLIOT, JOHN, M.D. An Account of the Nature and Medicinal Virtues of the principal Mineral Waters of Great Britain and Ireland, and . . . on the Continent, with Directions for Impregnating Waters with Fixed Air . . . a Description of Dr. Booth's Apparatus . . . and a Method of impregnating Water with Sulphureous Air. Folding copperplate of apparatus. 8vo. London.

1783 TRINDER, W. MARTIN. An Enquiry, by Experiments, into the Properties and Effects of the Medicinal Waters in the County of Essex. 8vo. London.

1784 Moss, W. A Familiar Medical Survey of Liverpool: addressed to the Inhabitants at Large. Containing Observations on the Situation of the Town; the Qualities and Influence of the Air; the Employments and Manner of Living of the Inhabitants; the Water; and other Natural and Occasional Circumstances whereby the Health of the Inhabitants is liable to be particularly affected. With an Account of the Diseases most peculiar to the Town; and the rules to be observed for their Prevention and Cure; Including Observations on the Cure of Consumption. 8vo. Liverpool.

PEARSON, GEORGE (?), M.D. Pearson's Observations and Experiments for Investigating the Chymical History of the Tepid Springs of Buxton. 2 vols. 8vo. London (?).

WALKER, J., M.D. Essay on the Waters of Harrogate and Thorp-Arch in Yorkshire, containing some Directions for their Use in Diseases; to which are prefixed Observations on Mineral Waters in general. London.

1786   RICHARD, LORD BISHOP OF LANDAFF. Observations on the Sulphur Wells at Harrogate, made in July and August, 1785, by the Rt. Rev. Richard Lord Bishop of Landaff. In *Philos. Trans.,* vol. 76, 171-88.

> By 1735 three wells were known at Harrogate. A fourth was brought to light by some person digging for minerals in the Forest of Knaresborough. Evidently he intended to dig for coal on the spot of the three wells. The innkeeper and others interested in the wells became alarmed at the prospect of losing custom and compromised with him for 100 pounds. An Act of Parliament of 1770 enclosing Knaresborough Forest made it unlawful to sink any pit or dig any quarry or mine that would injure the medicinal springs or waters at Harrogate. The bog at several places near Harrogate yielded sulphur water upon digging. The water was got to the houses where visitors lodged by being carried in casks—a mode of delivery that was recognized as being inconvenient.

1787   JOHNSTON, JAMES, M.D. Some Account of the Walton Water, near Tewkesbury; with Thoughts on the Use and Diseases of the Lymphatic Glands. In a Letter from James Johnston, M.D., Physician of the General Infirmary at Worcester, to J. C. Lettsom. 8vo. Worcester.

> 2nd edit., Tewkesbury, 1790.
> Reviewed *Gent. Mag.,* vol. 58, 810 (1788). The author thinks that the water in its chemical composition is similar to that at Cheltenham (then much frequented). The reviewer believes that much of the efficacy of these "bitter, saline, salino-sulphureous, and chalybeate kind" could be traced to the regular habits of life practiced at such places and the absence of continuous rounds of amusements.

1790   FALCONER, WILLIAM, F.R.S. A Practical Dissertation on the Medicinal Effects of the Bath Waters. 8vo. Bath.

> 2nd edit., with additions, 8vo, Bath, 1798. See Falconer under 1772 above.

GARNETT, THOMAS, M.D. Experiments and Observations on the Horley-Green Spaw, near Halifax. To which is added, A Short Account of Two other Mineral Waters in Yorkshire. 8vo. Bradford.

> Reviewed *Gent. Mag.,* vol. 62, 447-48. Chemical analysis showed that this water contained of earth of iron 1 cwt.; of vitriolated iron 3 and 8.8 cwt.; alum 2 and 9.2 cwt.; of vitriolated lime or selenite 1 and 13. cwt.; dephlogisticated martial vitriol 0 and 14. cwt.; aerial acid of fixed air 18 cubic inches. Its temperature exposed to air was 49 degrees Fahr. Its composition makes it a good tonic; and an excellent remedy in "atonic gout," hemorrhages, and in some consumptive complaints. This is a characteristic analysis of this period.

RYALL, J. For an account of the mineral springs at Weymouth, see his *New Weymouth Guide,* under AIDS TO TRAVELERS.

TAYLOR, J., M.D. St. Bernard's Well, Edinburgh; Treatise on the Virtues, Qualities, and Mode of using its Mineral Waters; Historical Account, etc. Illus. Edinburgh.

1791   GARNETT, THOMAS, M.D. Experiments and Observations on the Crescent Water at Harrogate. 8vo. Leeds.

1792 An Analysis of the Medicinal Waters of Tunbridge Wells. (Listed in *Gent. Mag.*, vol. 62, 447, with an extract.)

> The question had been raised whether the marble dome erected over one of the basins, by excluding air, would cause the water to lose some of its essential constituents. Experiments proved the fear to be groundless as long as some air was admitted. The only effect registered was on its cleanliness. The work contains also an account of attempts to make accurate analyses of the waters.

GARNETT, THOMAS, M.D. A Treatise on the Mineral Waters of Harrogate. Containing the History of these Waters, their Chemical Analysis, Medicinal Properties, and Plain Directions for their Use. 8vo. Bradford.

> Another edit., 1798.

SCHMEISSER, JOHANN GODFR. Description of Kilburn Wells, and Analysis of their Water. In *Philos. Trans.*, vol. 82, pt. i, 115-27.

> These waters were located about two miles from London. The account reports changes in the water when experimented on with various substances.

1793 LAING, REV. W. For an account of the mineral well at Peterhead, see his *An Account of Peterhead*, under TOWNS.

1794 DENMAN, JOSEPH, M.D. Observations on the Effects of Buxton Water. (Listed and reviewed in *Gent. Mag.*, vol. 64, 647.)

> Most of this essay is concerned with the history, situation, and climate, structure of the earth, and the use of springs and analysis of mineral waters in general and these in particular. The author found that these waters seldom failed to give relief in stomach and bowel troubles and in tonic gout, but not in palsy; in nervous cases, the water and air of Buxton operated with some benefit. The author was a physician of forty years' practice.

For an account of the mineral waters at Glastonbury, see *The History and Antiquities of Glastonbury*, under TOWNS.

1795 ANDERSON, JOHN. A Preliminary Introduction to the Act of Sea-Bathing; wherein is shewn its Nature, Power, and Importance; with some necessary Hints for the Attention of Visitors, at the watering Places, previous to, and during a Course of Bathing. 8vo. Margate.

> John Anderson, M.D., was physician to, and director of, the General Sea-Bathing Infirmary at Margate.—Bookseller's Note.

WHITE, THOMAS. Saint Guerdun's Well, a poem written in 1789. 8vo. Dumfries.

1797 CARRICK, —. Dissertation of the Bristol Hot Wells Water. 8vo. Bristol.

1798 SMITH, JOHN, M.D. Observations on the Nature, Use and Abuse of the Cheltenham Waters. New edit., with Additions. 8vo. Cheltenham.

1799 CAREY, G. S. The Balnes, or, An Impartial Description of all the popular Watering Places in England. 12mo. London.

1800 BARTELL, EDMUND. Observations upon the Town of Cromer considered as a Watering Place. 8vo. London.

A Companion to the Watering and Bathing Places of England, to which are added, A Medical Analysis of their Mineral Waters, etc. 12mo. London.

GARNETT, THOMAS, M.S. Observations on Moffat and its Mineral Waters. 2 aquatint views. 4to. Printed for the Author.

GIBBES, SIR GEORGE SMITH. A Treatise on Bath Waters. 8vo. Bath.

An Historical Description of St. Winefred's Well, at Holywell, in Flintshire. Woodcut. 4to. Holywell.

Inquiry into the Nature and Quality of the New Saline Mineral Spa Water at the Tennis Court near Bristol. (Date and place?)

For an account of the waters of Malvern, see *Letters on Malvern,* under TOWNS.

SAUNDERS, WILLIAM, M.D. Treatise on the Chemical History and Medical Powers of some of the most celebrated Mineral Waters, with Observations on the Use of Cold and Warm Bathing. 8vo. London.

TAYLOR, J., M.D. The Virtue of the Firhill Well, Aberdeen. Aberdeen.

IX

Canals, Rivers, Fen Drainage

(The wretched condition of the roads in England for a long time greatly hindered communication between towns and thus hampered trade, until the development of a network of canals and the improvements in river navigation, particularly in the last half of the eighteenth century, provided safer and cheaper routes. Some few efforts towards bettering such communications were made during the sixteenth century, but not until the latter part of the seventeenth century, when Parliament passed some acts to improve the navigability of rivers, was any real progress made. Where possible and necessary, channels were straightened and deepened, especially near the mouths of rivers. The greatest advance made in canals came in the seventeenth century, with the opening of the Aire and Calder rivers, the first modern canal with locks. But the real stimulus to canal building on an extensive scale began with the construction of the Duke of Bridgewater's Canal, opened in 1761, to carry coal from Worsley to Manchester. Thereafter freight resorted very rapidly to this means of carriage. Josiah Wedgwood, of pottery fame, became very active in promoting such movements for safer transportation of his wares. Canals continued to grow in numbers and popularity till the advent of the railroad. Part of the interest toward draining the Great Level of the Fens, the Bedford Level, which extended into several counties on the east coast, was prompted by the need of navigable canals. Then, as now, towns that were fearful of losing their commercial supremacy often exerted great pressure to render such improvements impossible. Another deterrent was the excessive cost of building a canal, estimated sometimes at a thousand pounds a mile. Some of these were projected on a grand scale, such as that of Earl Gower, for instance, which was to be twelve feet wide at the bottom and three feet deep on the average, except at fords, where thirty inches was thought to suffice. The boats were to be seventy feet in length, six in width, and about thirty inches in depth. Such vessels would carry about twenty tons of freight, and were so designed that by shifting the rudder they could be sailed either end foremost. Operating these barges called for a man, a boy, and a horse. For a detailed account of these projects, see John Campbell, *Political Survey of Great Britain,* vol. II, 259-67 [under 1774, SURVEYS]. See also T. Willan under 1938 below.)

1580 SPENSER, EDMUND. Epithalamion Thamesis. London.

1606 HAYWARD, W. A Plan and Description of the Fenns . . . survey'd by W. Hayward. . . . 1604. London (?).

1613 Lamentable News out of Lincolnshire of the overflowing of Waters. (Place?)

1614 The leeses of the New River lately brought from Amwell to London by Master Hugh Middleton. London (?).

1618 GAINSFORD, THOMAS. The Glory of England. 4to. London.

Cited by Campbell, *Political Survey,* vol. I, 157. This work discusses the advantages of navigable rivers as a means of improving the prosperity of the country.

1629 C., H. A Discoverie concerning the Drayning of Fennes and surrounded Grounds in the Sixe Counties of Norfolke, Suffolke, Cambridge with the Isle of Ely, Huntingdon, Northampton and Lincolne. London.

1632 HONDIUS, HENRICUS. General Plot and Description of the Fennes and surrounded Grounds, etc. London.

TAYLOR, JOHN (the Water Poet). Taylor on Thame Isis: or, The Description of the two Famous Riuers of Thame and Isis who being conioyned or combined together are called Thamisis, or Thames, With all the Flats, Shoares, Sheules, Sands, Weares, Stops, Riuers . . . As also a Discouery of the Hindrances which doe impeach the Passage of Boats and Barges, betwixt the famous Vniuersity of Oxford and the City of London. London. (14 leaves.)

1641 FORD, HENRY. A Design for bringing a Navigable River from Rickmansworth in Hartfordshire to S. Gyles in the Fields near London: the Benefits of it declared, and the Objections Answered. 4to. London.

> This was followed by *An Answer to the Whole*. London. Both were reprinted, 8vo, London, 1720.
> Ford, who under Cromwell's patronage had laid the Thames water into the streets of London by pipes and erected the great waterworks by Somerset-House for supplying the neighborhood, projected and published this useful design. Its revival has been attempted in our own day.—Gough, *Anecdotes of British Topography*, 263.

A Strange Wonder, or, the Cities Amazement: being A Relation occasioned by a Wonderful and Unusuall Accident in the River of Thames . . . there flowing Two Tydes at London Bridge, within the Short Space of an Houre and a Halfe. 4to. London.

1642 BURRELL, ANDREWS. A Briefe Relation. Discovering Plainely the true Causes why the Great Levell of Fenns in the severall Counties of Norfolk, Suffolk, Cambridge, Huntington, Northampton and Lincolnshire; Being Three Hundred and Seven Thousand Acres of Lowlands, have been drowned, and made Unfruitfull for many Yeares past. And as briefly how they may be drained, and preserved from Inundation in the Times to come. Humbly presented to the Honourable House of Commons assembled in Parliament. 4to. London. (22 pp.)

VERMUIDEN, SIR CORNELIUS. A Discourse touching the Drayning the great Fennes, lying within the severall Counties of Lincolne, Northampton, etc. 4to. London.

> The estate of Hatfield Chace, the largest in England, containing within its limits above 180,000 acres, one half of which was yearly drowned and surrounded with water, Charles I had sold to Vermuiden, without the consent of the commissioners and tenants, to dischace, drain, and cultivate, which he, to the general surprise and advantage, succeeded in effecting at the expense of about 400,000 pounds. Questions were raised in Parliament about the lawfulness of taking away certain portions from 370 persons in the query whether they were bound, or ought, to be deprived of their ancient right of common in the 7400 acres in question.—Gough, 251-52. This called forth replies.

1656 MATHEW, FRANCIS. To His Highness Oliver, Lord Protector, is presented a Mediterranean Passage by Water between Lynn and Yarmouth, upon two Rivers, the Little Owse and Waveny. 4to. London.

1658 SCOTCHER, RICHARD. Representation of Richard Scotcher, of Guildford, with respect to making the River Wye Navigable. 4to. London.

1660 A Short Demonstration that Navigation to Bedford is for the Benefit of Bedfordshire. Fol. London.

1662 DUGDALE, SIR WILLIAM. The History of Imbanking and Drayning of divers Fens and Marshes, both in Foreign Parts, and in this Kingdom, and of the Improvements thereby. Fol. London.

> 2nd edit., revised and corrected by C. N. Cole, fol., London, 1772. See below.
>
> "The scarcest of all Dugdale's works. It was published at the instance of Lord Gorges and others, who were the principal adventurers in that costly and laudable undertaking for draining the Great Level, extending into a considerable part of the counties of Cambridge, Huntingdon, Northampton, Norfolk, and Suffolk."—Anthony à Wood, quoted by Bookseller. 500 copies of the 1662 edition having been destroyed by the Fire of London, the volume became so scarce that a copy of it fetched ten pounds and 10 shillings when in 1772 it was reissued, with the spelling modernised, at the expense of the corporation of the Bedford Level, and edited by its registrant, C. N. Cole, partly from the copy used by Dugdale himself.—*DNB,* quoted by Bookseller.

> 1772 DUGDALE, SIR WILLIAM. The History of the Imbanking and Draining of divers Fens and Marshes, both in Foreign Parts and in this Kingdom, and of the Improvements thereby, extracted from Records, MSS., and other authentic Testimonies. 2nd edit., revised and corrected by Charles Nelson Cole. 11 folding plates and maps. Fol. London.

POWEL, SIR NATHANIEL. A Summary Relation of the Past and Present Condition of the Upper Levels, lying in the Counties of Kent and Sussex: . . . (Date and place?)

> This was answered in the following item:

> 1663 HERLACKENDEN, THOMAS. Animadversions on severall Material Passages in a Book written by Sir. N. P. Bart. Together with a more exact Narration of the State of those Levels. 4to. London.

1665 DODSON, COL. WILLIAM. The Designe for the perfect Draining of the Great Level of the Fens (called Bedford Level) lying in Norfolk, Suffolk, Cambridgeshire, Huntingdonshire, Northamptonshire, Lincolnshire, and the Isle of Ely, as it was delivered to the Honourable Corporation for the Draining of the said Great Level the 4th of June 1664: as also several Objections answered since the Delivery of the said Designe; with Objections to the Designe now in Agitation, and as for the new Works intended in this Designe appears in the annexed Maps: and the Charge of the Whole calculated. London.

> The draining of this vast tract of fenland baffled for over two centuries the best designs of technicians and engineers. When the sea was expelled from one district, it took possession of another hitherto under cultivation; when a river was made to flow to the sea in one instance, in another it flowed landward. The problem called forth innumerable publications.

1670 MATHEW, FRANCIS. To the King's Most Excellent Majesty, and the Honourable Houses of Parliament, is presented, A Mediterranean Passage by Water, from London to Bristol, and from Lynne to Yarmouth, and so consequently to the City of York; for the great Advancement of Trade and Traffique. 4to. London.

1672 CUSTIS, EDMOND. A Brief Relation and Exact Map of the Harbour of Newcastle, near Tinmouth Barre, since December, 1672, when Eight Ships were overwhelmed by the Freshet. Fol. London. (Single sheet.)

HELY, JAMES. A Modest Representation of the Benefits and Advantages of making the River Avon Navigable from Christ Church to the City of Sarum.

Humbly submitted to the Consideration of the City aforementioned and the Counties bordering upon the said River, and to all other Persons that are or may be concerned therein, for their Incouragement jointly to carry on so noble a Work. By J. H., a real Well Wisher both to the City and County. 4to. London.

1675 S., R. Avona: or, A Transient View of the Benefit of making Rivers in this Kingdom Navigable. Occasioned by observing the Situation of the City of Salisbury upon the Avon, and Consequence of opening that River to the City; communicated by a Letter to a Friend at London. 8vo. London.

1685 MOORE, SIR JONAS. The History or Narrative of the Great Level of the Fens, called Bedford-Level. Witth a large Map of the said Level, as Drained, Surveyed, and Described by Sir Jonas Moore, Knight, His Late Majesty's Surveyor-general of His Ordnance. 12mo. London.

> The survey and map were made in the previous year. It is an elaborate work in sixteen sheets and measures six feet four inches in width by four feet and seven inches in height, giving the whole drainage system as it then existed in great detail.—Fordham. This map was published separately, and is to be found in reduced form in Cox's *Magna Britannia* (see under 1720, SURVEYS) and elsewhere. Moore was an eminent mathematician employed by Charles I, 1647, to teach the Duke of York arithmetic, geography, etc., till the latter's escape from St. James's, 1648; he was sent to Tangier in 1663; on his return he was appointed Surveyor of the Ordnance, and knighted by Charles II. He became Fellow of the Royal Society in 1674, and helped Flamsteed, the first astronomer royal.—Gough, 93-94.

1700 A New and Easy Project, of making the Water of Leith Navigable; whereby Ships may pass into the North-Lough. The Water to be deepened as far as Inverleith, then a cut made to the North-Lough, which could be deepened, with Estimate of Cost. 4to. Edinburgh. (4 leaves.)

1714 Ports of North Britain, with their Members and Creeks. 8vo. Edinburgh.

1717 CONGREVE, DR. THOMAS. A Scheme or Proposal for making a Navigable Communication between the Rivers of Trent and Severn, in the County of Stafford, with Observations on the Rivers between Oxford and Bath, and a Map. 8vo. London.

> This was bound up with Erdeswicke's *Survey of Staffordshire* (see this date under SURVEYS). Reprinted 1753.

1720 KINDERLEY, NATHANIEL. The Present State of the Navigation of the Towns of Lyn, Wisbech, Spalding, and Boston. The Rivers that pass through those Places, and the Counties that border thereupon, truly, faithfully, and impartially Represented, and humbly Proposed to the Consideration of the Inhabitants of those Places and Counties, and to the Corporation of Adventurers for draining the vast Level of the Fens. 8vo. Bury St. Edmunds.

> 2nd edit., 8vo, London, 1751.

1723 The Methods Proposed for Making the River Dunn Navigable, and the Objections to it answered: with an Account of the Petitioner's Behaviour to the Land Owners, To which is annexed, A Mapp of the River, and the Reasons lately printed for making it Navigable, with the Advantages of it. 4to. London.

1724 BRIDGEMAN, CHARLES. A Report of the Present State of the Great Level of the Fens, called Bedford Level, and of the Port of Lynn; and of the Rivers Ouse and Nean, the two great Sewers of that Country. With Considerations on the Scheme Proposed by the Corporation of Lynn for draining the said Fens, and reinstating that Harbour. And also a Scheme humbly proposed for the effectual Draining those Fens, and reinstating that Harbour or Port: from a Survey thereof made in August 1724. On the opposite Pages is printed An Answer, paragraph by paragraph, to the Report and Scheme, drawn from Authentic Testimonies of the State of that Level, Harbour and River, before and since Denver Dam and Sluices were built, etc., and from a Survey made in the Years 1723, 1724. To the whole is annexed, Col. Armstrong's Report, with Proposals for draining the Fens, and amending the Harbour of Lynn. Maps of the Fens, cuts, and new proposed rivers, surveys of the Humber, Ouse, and Thames, from their sources to the sea. Fol. (Place?)

1725 ARMSTRONG, COLONEL JOHN (Chief Engineer of England). History of the Navigation of the Port of King's-Lyn and of Cambridge, and the Rest of the Trading Towns in those Parts, and of the Navigable Rivers that have their Course through the Bedford Level. Fol. London.

> Reissued in 1766, with new title, preface, contents page, and an addition of "An Abstract of the Navigation and of Draining the Fens," etc. See below.

> 1766 ARMSTRONG, COLONEL JOHN. History of the Ancient and Present State of the Navigation of the Port of King's Lyn and of Cambridge: and the rest of the Trading Towns, in those Parts, and of Navigable Rivers that have their course through the Great Level of the Fens, called the Bedford Level. Also the History of the Ancient and Present State of Draining that Level, from Authentick Records and Manuscripts. 7 maps and plates. Fol. London.

BADESLADE, THOMAS. A Scheme for Draining the Great Level of the Fenns, called Bedford-Level; and for improving the Navigation of Lyn-Regis: founded upon self-evident Principles in Experimental Philosophy and Practical Mathematicks, and upon Historical Facts; and further demonstrated by comparing the River Ouse with the River Thames, &c. and Lyn-Harbour with the Harbour of Rye. With Reflections upon all the Schemes hitherto proposed. Map. Fol. London.

> This was also reprinted and bound up with the 1766 edition of Col. Armstrong's work listed just above. Fourteen Acts of Parliament were passed between 1725 and 1794 dealing with the improvement of and making navigable the Rivers Dun, Dee, Medway, Tamar, Loyne, Mersey, Irwell, etc., and the Proposals for a Manchester Ship Canal. These were collected in a folio volume.

1733 The Intended Navigation of the River Chelmer, briefly considered. 8vo. London.

SCRIBO, J. The Present Bad State of the River Witham, between the City of Lincoln and the Borough of Boston. (Place?)

WHITTENBERG, WILLIAM. Extracts from the Books of the Mayor and Aldermen of Hertford, together with Copies of Papers relating to the Navigation of the River Lea between Hertford and Ware. Map of the river between the tollbridges of each town. 4to. (Place?)

1735   BADESLADE, THOMAS. Reasons Humbly Offer'd to the Consideration of the Publick; Shewing how the Works now executing by Virtue of an Act of Parliament to recover and preserve the Navigation of the River Dee, will destroy the
Navigation; and occasion the Drowning of all the Low Lands adjacent to the
said River. From Observations made on the Spot; and from Instances of the
ruinous Effects like Works have had at the Ports of Lyn, Rye, Wisbech, and
Spalding. With an Appendix. Map of each of those rivers, to compare with a
map of the River Dee, all drawn by hand. Fol. Chester.

    A 2nd edit. was issued with the same title, but where or when I have not seen.

1736   ——————. The New-cut Canal, Intended for Improving the Navigation of the
City of Chester, with the low Lands adjacent to the River Dee, compared with
the Welland, alias Spaulding River, now silted up, and Deeping Fens adjacent,
now drowned . . . also Experiments and Reasons agreeing with Sir I. Newton's Theory of the Tides, relating to the Practice of taking a Level by the
high-water Mark of a Spring-Tide. Fol. Chester.

1737   Plan of the River Wear from Newbridge to Sunderland Barr, including part of
Sunderland and inset Tables of Landed Proprietors, "coal and cynder staiths,"
etc. Engraved by J. Tinney after Burleigh and Thompson. 19 × 82 ins.

1739   BROWN, JOHN. An Exact Survey of the River Medway from Maidstone up to
Penshurst, in the County of Kent, and also of the Stream falling thereinto from
Forrestrow, Sussex. Tunbridge.

1741   An Essay on the Ways and Means of Improving Inland Navigation. In *Gent.
Mag.,* vol. 11, Jan.

1742   ELSTOBB, WILLIAM. Some Thoughts on Mr. Rosewell's and other Schemes now
proposed for amending Lynn Channel and Harbour. 4to. Lynn.

1744   GRUNDY, JOHN. A Scheme for Restoring and Making Perfect the Navigation of
the River Witham from Boston to Lincoln, etc. 4to. London.

    See Grundy (and others) under 1761 below.

1745   An Essay on Joining the Thames and the Severn; a Description of the Country
involved. By Agricola. In *Gent. Mag.,* vol. 15, 147-48.

      LABELYE, CHARLES (Engineer). The Result of a View of the Great Level of the
Fens, taken at the Desire of the Duke of Bedford, &c. Governor and the Gentle-
men of the Corporation of the Fens in July 1745. With Moore's Map. 4to.
London.

    Another issue, London, 1748.

      Reasons for and against making a Harbour at Sandwich [advocates Ramsey in-
stead]. In *Gent. Mag.,* vol. 15, 95-6; in same volume is a proposal for using
Christ Church, Hamptonshire, 96-7. For discussions of Ramsey as a harbor,
see under 1755-56 below.

1749   An Actual Survey of the North Level, Part of the Great Level of the Fenns, commonly called Bedford Level, also of Crowland, Great Porsand, and part of South Holland, in the County of Lincoln, and of Wisbeach, north side of the Isle of Ely, and County of Cambridge; wherein is described the several Drains, Sewers, Sluices, etc., by which the Lands contained in this Survey drain to their Outfalls at Sea. Taken Aug. 1749, by John Wing, Nathaniel Hill, etc. (Place?)

EDWARDS, RICHARD. Observations on the Decay of the Outfalls or Loss of the Channels of divers weak Rivers, particularly of the River Neen, otherwise Wisbech River, and Shire-drain, humbly offered to the Consideration of the Hon. Corporation of Adventurers, and of all Gentlemen, Merchants, and others interested in the preserving the Navigation of the said River, etc., with a Scheme to recover the said Navigation, and drain the said Lands effectually. To which is added, The Form of a Reservoir lately invented for the scouring the Sands out of the Mouths of any weak Rivers. 8vo. London.

1750   COLLINS, CAPT. G. The River Avon from the Severn to the Citty of Bristol, with boats, decorations, and a plan of Bristol. 35 × 18 ins.

1755   DALLAWAY, JOHN. A Scheme to make the River Stroudwater Navigable, etc. 4to. Gloucester.

1755-56   Ramsgate Harbour. The project of building a harbor at Ramsgate called forth a number of pamphlets:

A Brief Account of the Proceedings of the Trustees appointed by Act of Parliament for building a Harbour at Ramsgate, together with some Considerations in Vindication of the Safety and Usefullness of the Harbour on their Present Plan. 8vo.

A True State of Facts relating to Ramsgate Harbour. 4to.

A Seaman's Plain Answer to every Thing that may seem material in the Landsman's Pamphlett relating to the contracting Ramsgate Harbour. 8vo.

State of the Expence of building Ramsgate Harbour on the contracted Plan. Fol. (One sheet.)

Narrative of Facts and Observations thereon which induced many Trustees to be against contracting Ramsgate Harbour, and against taking up Works built agreeable to the Direction of the Board of Trustees. Fol. (Sheet.)

Report, and Estimate subjoined, relating to the Harbour of Ramsgate. An. 1755-56. Fol.

A Plan of the Pier and Harbour, with the Additions proposed to enlarge it.

1758 For a description of the River Thames within the City of London's jurisdiction, see *Description of the River Thames,* under LONDON.

PERRY, G. A Description of the Severn with its Navigation. In *Gent. Mag.,* vol. 28, 277-78.

SMEATON, J. From a Survey of the River Calder from Wakefield in Brooksmouth, and from thence to Salter-Hebble Bridge, near Halifax, taken in . . . 1757. Fol. (Place?)

1759 The Case of the Undertakers for Making Navigable the Rivers Aire and Calder, in the County of York. Fol. London.

A Cursory View of a Proposed Canal from Kendal to the Duke of Bridgewater's Canal, leading to . . . Manchester by the several Towns of Milnthrop, Lancaster. 8vo. Manchester.

> This deals with the need of a survey and the estimates of population to be served, tonnage expected, etc.—J. Williams, *Printed Materials.*

A Plain Disquisition on the Indispensible Necessity of fortifying and improving Milford Haven (Pembrokeshire); containing likewise an Attempt to demonstrate the Advantages that will arise from it to this Nation, with some Hints on the Prosecuting Scheme. To which is annexed, An Exact Map of the Harbour, drawn after a very late Survey. Addressed to a Patriot Member of Parliament. 8vo. London.

A Short Historical Account of Bristol Bridge. With a Proposition for a New Stone Bridge, . . . some Bridges of Note in England . . . By . . . a Citizen. Bristol.

> This points out the defects in the old bridge, and recommends improvements and the building of an additional suspension bridge.—J. Williams, *op. cit.*

WATT, J. The River Clyde, surveyed in 1736. Edinburgh.

1760 STRATFORD, FERDINAND. Remarks on a Paper, entitled Improvements and Savings on Inland Navigation, etc., by the Dean of Gloucester. In *Gent. Mag.,* vol. 30, 263-64. (See next item.)

TUCKER, JOSEPH. The Improvements and Savings in Inland Navigations exemplified on the River Stroud, in the County of Gloucester. In *Gent. Mag.,* vol. 30, 167-68.

1762 An Act for draining and preserving certain Low Lands called the Fens lying on both Sides of the River Witham, in the County of Lincoln, and for restoring and maintaining the Navigation of the said River, from the High Bridge in the City of Lincoln, through the Borough of Boston to the Sea. Fol. (Place?)

GRUNDY, JOHN, LANGLEY EDWARDS, and JOHN SMEATON. The Report of Messrs. John Grundy, etc., Engineers, concerning the Present Ruinous State and Con-

dition of the River Witham, and the Navigation thereof, from Lincoln through Boston, to its Outfall into the Sea; and of the Fen Lands on both Sides the said River. Together with Proposals and Schemes for restoring, improving, and preserving the said River and Navigation, and also for effecting the Drainings of the said Fen Lands. To which is annexed, A Plan and Proper Estimates of the Expences in performing the several Works recommended for those Purposes. 4to. Lincoln.

1763 VALLANCEY, CHARLES (Engineer). A Treatise on Inland Navigation; or, The Art of Making Rivers Navigable, of making Canals in all Sorts of Soils, and of Constructing Locks and Sluices, extracted from the Works of Guglielmini, Micheline, Castellus, Belidor, and others, with Observations and Remarks. 24 folding plans. 4to. Dublin.

1764 BURTON, JOHN. The Present State of Navigation on the Thames considered, and certain Regulations proposed, by a Commissioner. 4to. Oxford.

1765 A Plan for Making the River Chelmer Navigable. (Place?) (So cited by Gough, 170.)

A View of the Advantages of Inland Navigations; with a Plan of a Navigable Canal, intended for Communication between the Ports of Liverpool and Hull. 8vo. London.

> This contains a plan from a survey by Brindley, engineer to the Duke of Bridgewater, drawn by Hugh Henshall and engraved by Kitchin. For this canal and its interest for Wedgwood see Meteyard, *Life of Wedgwood* (under GENERAL REFERENCE). The canals promoted by the Duke of Bridgewater and by Earl Gower, in Staffordshire, Cheshire, and Derbyshire, were absorbing popular attention at this time.

1766 BRINDLEY, JAMES. The History of Inland Navigation, particularly those of the Duke of Bridgewater, in Lancashire and Cheshire; and the intended one promoted by Earl Gower and other Persons of Distinction in Staffordshire, Cheshire, and Derbyshire. In Two Parts. 2 folding plates. 8vo. London.

> 2nd edit., of Part 1, with additions, London, 1769; 3rd edit., London, 1779. See below. This work contains little more than various accounts of the Duke of Bridgewater's canal, with answers to several objections that had been made to it and discussions of plans.

> 1779 BRINDLEY, JAMES. The History of Inland Navigation, particularly that of the Duke of Bridgewater, shewing the Counties and Townships through which these Navigations are carried, the Whole Shewing the Utility and Importance of Inland Navigation. 2 folding plans. 8vo. London.

An Entertaining Description of the Duke of Bridgewater's surprising Navigable Canal, near Manchester. Plate. In *Gent. Mag.*, vol. 36, 31-33.

HARRISON, JOHN. A New Method of Making the Banks of the Fens almost impregnable, so as in time to resist the Force of Rivers in the most impetuous Floods, and prevent all Future Inundations; with a New but Certain Method of preparing the Lands for the Growth of our most valuable Timber, viz. Oak, Elm, Ash, etc., particularly those extensive Tracts of Land in the Counties of

Cambridge and Lincoln. Also, Some Observations on the River Cam; how to confine its Bounds and improve its Navigation; which may serve as a Plan for any other Inland River, etc. Cambridge (?).

> Harrison was a botanist and nurseryman in Cambridge.

Seasonable Considerations on a Navigable Canal intended to be cut from the River Trent . . . to the River Mersey. Maps. (Place?)

> This is a criticism of the intended project in favor of a shorter route.—J. Williams.

WHITWORTH, R. Advantages of Inland Navigation; or Some Observations offered to the Public, to shew that an Inland Navigation may be easily effected between Bristol, Liverpool, and Hull; together with a Plan for Executing Same. Folding portrait of the Duke of Bridgewater. 8vo. London.

1767   Considerations upon the Intended Navigable Communication between the Firths of Forth and Clyde. In a Letter to the Lord Provost of Edinburgh, Preses of the General Convention of the Royal Boroughs of Scotland, from a Member of the Convention. 4to. (Edinburgh?)

> This enlarges the plan described under Smeaton, 1767, below.

SMEATON, JOHN. The Report of John Smeaton, Engineer, concerning the Practicability and Expence of Joining the Rivers Forth and Clyde by a Navigable Canal, and thereby to join the East Sea and the West. Addressed to the Hon. Trustees for Fisheries, Manufactures, and Improvements in Scotland, at whose Desire the Survey was made; with a Map of the Country, and a Plan of the Canal. 4to. Edinburgh.

> This report was followed by a second, and the two printed together, Edinburgh, 1768. Variations from the plan were reported by Brindley and others, Edinburgh, 1768. See below.
>
> The expense of Smeaton's plan, amounting to 80,000 pounds, was not encouraged by the government; then some merchants of Glasgow and Carron subscribed for a smaller canal, for which a bill was passed in Parliament. The greater utility of the larger cut was vindicated by Smeaton, without success, in "Considerations upon the Intended Navigable Communications," 1767.—Gough, 641. Smeaton will be remembered for his great engineering feat, the construction of Eddystone Lighthouse. See Smeaton under 1791 below.

WHITWORTH, ROBERT. Plan of an Intended Canal from Birmingham to Aldersley. Engraved by Westwood after Whitworth. 9⅜ × 21 ins.

1768   BRINTON, JAMES, THOMAS YEOMAN, and JOHN GOLBORNE. Reports of James Brinton, Engineer, Thomas Yeoman, F.R.S., and John Golborne, Engineer, relative to a Navigable Communication betwixt the Firths of Forth and Clyde. Map. Edinburgh.

> This suggested some variations from Smeaton's plan. It was followed by another defense from Smeaton, 1768. See following:

SMEATON, JOHN. Review of Several Matters relative to the Forth and Clyde Navigation, as now settled by the Act of Parliament, with Observations on the Reports of Brindley, Yeoman, and Golborne. 4to. Edinburgh. (34 pp.)

> These reports by Brindley, Smeaton, and Golborne, together with a Letter to Pulteney on the Canal, were collected in 5 vols., London, 1768.

1769 BRINDLEY, JAMES. Plan of the Navigable Canals for opening a Communication to the Ports of London, Bristol, Liverpool and Hull. 20 × 33 ins.

SMEATON, JOHN. Report upon the Harbour of Dover. Fol. London.

1770 BRINDLEY, JAMES. Plan of the Intended Canal from Chesterfield, by Retford, to the River Trent proposed by Brindley, with the suggested Alterations. 11½ × 30 ins.

KITCHIN, THOMAS. A Plan of the Navigable Canals which communicate with Liverpool, and of a proposed one from Wigan to that Port. 21 × 17 ins.

Survey of the River Thames from Boulter's Lock to Mortlake. Fol. London.
This may have been the work of Brindley. See Brindley under 1775 below.

1774 For a history of the Fens Drainage, see John Campbell, *Political Survey*, vol. II, 274 ff., where the story of the various attempts, the acts passed by Parliament from Elizabeth's time on, and the actual entering upon the enterprise in Charles II's time are related.

SHARP, JAMES. Extracts from Mr. Young's "Six Months' Tour through the North of England" on the Subject of Canal Navigation. 12mo. London.

WHITWORTH, ROBERT. A Report and Survey of the Canal Proposed to be made on one Level from Waltham-Abbey to Moorfields, also Report and Survey of a Line which may be continued from Marylebone to the said proposed Canal, in Case any future Design of Navigation from the River Thames or Coln should ever take place, with an Address to the Lord Mayor, etc., of the City of London on the Importance of Canals in General. 2 large folding maps. Fol. London. (18 pp.)
In *Gent. Mag.*, vol. 44, 121-22, is a communication as follows:

> 1774 An Account of an Intended Canal Navigation from Waltham Abbey to Moorfields; a noble Improvement projected and promoted by Mr. James Sharp, for the Advantage and Ornament of the City of London.
> The argument ran that it would pass through land easy to turn into a canal; it would be ornamental; it would furnish cheap transportation of meats and vegetables to London; and of people from Waltham Abbey to the city. For the "small fare of threepence will be of great consequence to passengers in general." The article contains some descriptions of the region concerned and a plan.

1775 BRINDLEY, JAMES. Plan of the River Thames from Boulter's Lock to Mortlake, by James Brindley, continued to London Bridge in 1774 by R. Whitworth. 25 × 26 ins.

PAGE, SIR THOMAS, F.R.S. Observations on the Present State of the South Level of the Fens, with a proposed Method for the better Drainage of that Country, made at the Desire of Viscount Townshend, and the Corporation of Bedford Level. 4to. London.
Reprinted, 1793.

WATT, JOHN. The River Clyde (from Hamilton to the Ayrshire Coast) and Firth of Clyde (showing Kintyre, Arran, Jura, Islay, etc.). Engraved after Watt by T. Phinn. 20 × 29 ins.

1777   An Account of a Navigable Canal now making from the several Coal-Mines in the Neighbourhood of Stourbridge and Dudley, to communicate with the Great Canal from the Trent to the Severn, near Stourton, in the County of Stafford. In *Gent. Mag.*, vol. 47, 313. Plan.

Observations on the Means of better Draining the Middle and South Levels of the Fenns, by two Gentlemen who have taken a View thereof. 4to. London.

A Sketch of the Difficulties that have attended the Navigation now making from the Town of Stroud in Gloucestershire, to the River Severn. With plan. In *Gent. Mag.*, vol. 47, 272.

> The obstructions were chiefly the unwillingness of some land owners to part with their land and of the mill owners on the river to do the same.

1779   ELSTOBB, WILLIAM. The Report of William Elstobb, . . . on the State of the Navigation between Clayhithe and Denver Sluice. Plan. Cambridge.

> An elaborate report describing the course of the Cambridge-Lynn canal and proposed changes.—J. Williams.

1780   ERSKINE, R. Dissertation on Rivers and Tides, intended to demonstrate the Effect of Bridges, Cuttings, Removing of Shoals and Imbankments; in particular of the River Thames. London.

1781   MYLNE, ROBERT. Mr. Mylne's Report on his Survey of the Harbour, etc., of Wells, in Norfolk. Fol. London.

> See Smeaton's report, 1782, below.

1782   Considerations on the Idea of Uniting the Rivers Thames and Severn through Cirencester. 4to. London.

SMEATON, JOHN. Mr. Smeaton's Report on the State of Wells Harbour. Fol. London.

1783   HOLME, EDMOND. An Account of the Measurement of the Public Bridges within the Hundred of Salford, in the County Palatine of Lancashire. 8vo. London.

> Holme was a bridge master.

1784   PAGE, SIR THOMAS. Considerations upon the State of Dover-Harbour, with its relative Consequence to the Navy of Great Britain. . . . Canterbury. (29 pp.)

> This makes a plea for restoring the harbor to its pre-Roman form, thus making a deep-water shelter.—J. Williams.

1785   PHILLIPS, J. Treatise on Inland Navigation; illustrated with a whole-sheet Plan delineating the Course of an intended Navigable Canal from London to Norwich and Lynn, through the Counties of Essex, Suffolk and Norfolk . . . and

a Plan for extending the Navigation from Bishop Stortford to Cambridge. Large folding map and frontispiece. 4to. (Place?)

1786   Manley on the Navigation of the River Dee. Listed in *Gent. Mag.,* 56, 981.

Plan of all the English Canals. Listed in *Gent. Mag.,* vol. 56, 694.

1788   Tracts on the Worcester Canal. I. Observations on the Comparative Merits of the Eastern and Western Canals, folding map. II. A Short Reply to a Pamphlet "Observations on a Design for Improving the Navigation of the Severn." III. Observations on the Bill for a Canal from Birmingham to Worcester, map. IV. Brief Replies to the Birmingham and Worcester Canal Bill. V. Observations on the intended Worcester Canal, map. In 1 vol. 8vo. (Place?)

A Treatise on Inland Navigation. Salisbury. (44 pp.)
   A discussion of the advantages to manufactures and agriculture as outweighing the disadvantages.—J Williams.

1790   Some Account of the Bay and Harbour of Fishguard in Pembrokeshire, and of the Proposed Pier to be constructed there for the Safety of Vessels navigating the Irish Channel. (So cited in Rowland's *Cambrian Bibliography* without place.)

1791   Considerations on the Present State of the Navigation of the River Thames, from Maidenhead to Isleworth; and also on the Utility of a Navigable Canal, from Boulter's Lock, near Maidenhead to Isleworth; proposed by the Corporation of the City of London, and the Commissioners of the Upper District, in the Year 1770, agreeable to the Survey of Messieurs Brindley and Whitworth. London. (29 pp.)

JESSOP, W. The Report of W. Jessop, Engineer, on the Practicability and Expence of making a Navigable Communication between the River Witham and the Town of Horncastle. 8vo. Horncastle.

————. Reports of the Engineers appointed by Commission of the Navigation of the Rivers Thames and Isis. 8vo. London.

LEACH, THOMAS. A Treatise of Universal Inland Navigation, and the Use of all Sorts of Mines. 8vo. London.
   A scheme fcr canal building with inclined planes instead of locks.—J. Williams.

MYLNE, ROBERT. Report the Second on the Navigation of the River Thames between Lechlade and Whitechurch. 8vo. London.

Reflections on the General Utility of Inland Navigation to the Commerce and Landed Interests of England: with Observations on the Intended Canal from Birmingham to Worcester; and some Strictures upon the Opposition given to it by the Proprietors of the Staffordshire Canal. 8vo. London.

Inland navigation at this time was looming as large as turnpike roads.

SMEATON, JOHN. A Narrative of the Building and a Description of the Construction of the Eddystone Lighthouse with Stone; to which is subjoined, An Appendix, giving some Account of the Lighthouse on the Spurn Point, built upon a Sand. 23 plates. Fol. London.

> 2nd edit., fol., London, 1793. See below.
> The first lighthouse on this rock was erected by Henry Winstanley, of Littlebury, in 1696. This was blown down in the great storm of 1703, killing its builder in its fall. A second was raised by John Rudyard, an engineer of no great ability, in 1708. This was burned down in 1755. Smeaton, who was one of the most distinguished engineers of his day, built the third.

> 1793 SMEATON, JOHN, F.R.S. A Narrative of the Building, and a Description of the Construction of the Eddystone Lighthouse with Stone; to which is subjoined, An Appendix, giving an Account of the Lighthouse on Spurn Point, built upon a Sand. 2nd edit., corrected, with 22 large engraved plates of details, etc. Fol. London.

——————. An Historical Report on Ramsgate Harbour; written by Order of and addressed to the Trustees. 2 folding plates. 8vo. London.

> 2nd edit. same year.
> The report tells of the progress made, the difficulties overcome in sluicing the harbor, the piers built out and the large number of ships that now can be received. In 1780 twenty-nine vessels took shelter there; in 1790 the number was 387. In the last seventeen months more than 600 ships of sail and vessels put into the harbor, of which above 300 were from and to the Port of London.—From *Gent. Mag.*, vol. 61, 745.

WATTE, JOHN. The Report of John Watte for the better Drainage of the South and Middle Levels of the Fens. 4to. Wisbeach.

1791-96 BOYDELL, JOHN. An History of the River Thames. Plates. Fol. London.

> Cited again as of 1794-96. See below.

> 1794-96 BOYDELL, JOHN and JOSIAH. An History of the River Thames. 2 vols. Frontispiece, large folding map, and 76 large, coloured plates after J. Farington by J. C. Stadler. Fol. London.
> The plates reproduce various picturesque scenes and notable residences along the bank, etc., from the source to the sea.

1792 HODSKINSON, JOSEPH. Report on the probable Effect which a New Cut now in Contemplation, from Eau-Brink to a little above Lynn will have on the Harbour and Navigation of Lynn; with a Plan for improving the Present Channel. 4to. Lynn.

MYLNE, ROBERT. Report on the Proposed Improvement of the Drainage and Navigation of the River Ouse, executing a Straight Cut from Eau-Brink to King's Lynn. 4to. Lynn (?).

> This cut, one of the great engineering designs of Mylne, was intended to improve the fen drainage. After much opposition, it was carried out by Rennie in 1817.

PHILLIPS, JOHN. A General History of Inland Navigation, Foreign and Domestic; containing a complete Account of the Canals already executed in England, with Considerations on those projected. Large folding colored map and 4 plates. London.

Another edit., with Addenda, 4to, London, 1793; again, 1795.

An important work, which describes canals with reference to the country through which they pass, the products to be carried, the advantages of such means of conveyance, with some pages on American canals.—Quoted.

1793   Eau-Brink Cut: Letter to Sir Thomas Hyde Page in Answer to his Letter on the Subject of the Eau-Brink Cut. 8vo. London (?).

ELSTOBB, WILLIAM. An Historical Account of the Great Level of the Fens, called Bedford Level, and other Fens, Marshes and Lowlands. 8vo. Lynn.

MYLNE, ROBERT. Report on a Survey of the River Thames from Boulter's Lock to the City Stone, near Staines, and on the best Method of improving the Navigation of the said River. . . . 8vo. London.

RENNIE, JOHN. Plan of the Proposed Crinan Canal, between the Lochs of Crinan and Gilp in the County of Argyll; surveyed at the expense of the Duke of Argyll and the Earl of Breadalbane in the Year 1792. 19⅝ × 25⅜ ins. 1 inch equals ⅖ mile. London.

This canal provides a short route between Glasgow and the Outer Isles, besides doing away with the trip around the stormy Mull of Cantyre. Rennie was highly esteemed as a builder of canals, bridges, docks, and harbors. Among the bridges he designed is Waterloo Bridge, London.

1794   An History of the Principal Rivers of Great Britain. (An History of the River Thames [by W. Combes]). Illustrated with colored plates. 2 vols. Fol. London.

Only the River Thames is considered.—Anderson, *Brit. Topog.*

RENNIE, JOHN. Estimate of the Expense for carrying into Execution the Plan of Embankment for the Improvement of the Drainage of the South and Middle Levels, and other Lands having their Drainage through the River Ouse, and for the Improvement of its Navigation, etc. Folding map. 8vo. London.

————. Report of a Survey of the River Thames, between Reading and Isleworth: and of the several Lines of Canals projected to be made between those Places: with Observations on their comparative Eligibility. London. (55 pp.)

This report recommends many important improvements to be made if the Thames is to continue to be used, and explains the best route for a canal otherwise.—J. Williams.

VANDERSTEGAN, WILLIAM. The Present State of the Thames Considered; and a Comparative View of Canal and River Navigation. London.

This defends the plan of the Commissioners for the Thames Navigation for improving the river as against a canal.—J. Williams. Father Thames appeared to be threatened with desertion and even with being drained for the benefit of canals. The tendency of John Bull to stick to a thing even at the risk of ruin is exemplified in the danger of being overwhelmed in numbers and expense of canals.—*Gent. Mag.,* vol. 64, 835.

1795   AIKIN, JOHN. For an account of canals and river navigation, see his *A Description of the Country . . . round Manchester,* under DESCRIPTIONS.

This contains material relative to canal and river navigation on the Irwell and Mersey, Weaver, Douglas, Aire, Calder and Dun, Sankey Canal; Duke of Bridgewater's Canals; Trent and Mersey communication; Grand Trunk Canal; Huddersfield, Langley Bridge;

Manchester, Bolton, and Bury; Ashton-under-Lyne, Oldham; Rochdale; Huddersfield canal to Ashton, Peak Forest Canal; Cromford, Lancaster, Ellesmere, and other canals, with maps.

CARY, JOHN. Inland Navigation; or, Select Plans of the several Navigable Canals throughout Great Britain. Maps. 4to. London. (See under MAPS AND CHARTS.)

DODD, RALPH. Report of the various Improvements, Civil and Military, that might be made in the Haven or Harbour of Hartlepool; as surveyed, at the Request of the Corporation. Newcastle-upon-Tyne. (17 pp.)

> No better harbor for a naval base is to be found in England. Deep water, if dredged, high shores, protected roadstead are all to be had there.—J. Williams.

————————. Report on the First Part of the Line of Inland Navigation from the East to the West Sea by way of Newcastle and Carlisle. Folding map of the country. 8vo. Newcastle.

> Very general, from Greece to America.—J. Williams.

1796　FULTON, ROBERT. A Treatise on the Improvement of Canal Navigation: exhibiting the numerous Advantages to be derived from Small Canals. And Boats containing from two to five Tons Burthen. With a Description of the Machinery for facilitating Conveyance by Locks and Aqueducts: including Observations on the great Importance of Water Communications, with Thoughts on, Designs for, Aqueducts and Bridges of Iron and Wood. 17 plates. 4to. London.

> This treats of the origin, construction of boats, navigations, crossing of rivers, cast-iron rails, iron bridges, and a scheme for avoiding a lock system to save water.—J. Williams.

HIBBARD, JOHN. Thoughts on the Great Utility of a circular and other Inland, etc. Canal Navigation, and Drainage . . . . 2nd edit. London.

> This deals with a plan to construct a canal that would circle about England.

1797　CHAPMAN, WILLIAM. Observations on the various Systems of Canal Navigation . . . in which Mr. Fulton's Plan of Wheel Boats and the Utility of subterraneous and of Small Canals are particularly investigated. London.

> Although Fulton was not the first to apply steam to propulsion of boats, he was the first who did it successfully.

RENNIE, JOHN. Report concerning the different Lines surveyed . . . for a Canal proposed to be made between the Cities of Edinburgh and Glasgow. 4to. Edinburgh.

1798　TATHAM, WILLIAM. Remarks on Inland Canals, the Small System of Interior Navigation, various Uses of the Inclined Plane, etc., in a Letter from William Tatham. . . . London. (20 pp.)

> He describes his own inclined-plane sytem, which he considers superior to Fulton's.—J. Williams.

1799　CLARKE, CHARLES. Observations on the Intended Tunnel b e n e a t h the River Thames. 4to. Gravesend.

DODD, JAMES. Report on the proposed Canal Navigation, forming a Junction of the Rivers Thames and Medway. London. (14 pp.)

This canal would run from Gravesend to Stroud.

1800 CHAPMAN, WILLIAM. Report on the Harbour of Scarborough, and on the Means for its Improvement. Scarborough. (32 pp.)

COLQUHOUN, PATRICK. A Treatise on the Commerce and Police of the River Thames, with a Map of the Port of London and of the Thames from London Bridge to Sheerness. 8vo. London.

DODD, RALPH. Report on the Intended Grand Surrey Canal Navigation. London. (17 pp.)

This canal would connect Deptford and Epsom.

RENNIE, JOHN. Report concerning the Drainage of Wildmore Fen, and of the East and West Fens. Fol. London.

T., J. Different Plans for Improving the Harbour of Bristol, impartially examined: and a Mode pointed out for embracing all the Advantages, without the Risk of affecting the Health of the Inhabitants, or injuring their Property. Plan. Bristol.

This writer criticizes the plans of Smeaton, 1765, and of William Champion, 1767, for dams. He prefers a dock in Canon's Marsh.—J. Williams.

1801 SKRINE, HENRY. Rivers of Note in Great Britain, with a Minute Description of the Thames. Emblematical plate of the Thames and river maps. 8vo. London.

This treats of their courses, peculiar characters, and countries through which they flow.

1884 BAKES, ERNEST A. True Report of Certain Wonderful Overflowings of Waters in Somerset, Norfolk, and other Parts of England, A.D. 1607. Edit. by Ernest A. Bakes. 4to. Weston-super-Mare.

1938 WILLAN, T. S., M.A., Ph.D. River Navigation and Trade from Witham to the Yare, 1600-1750. In *Norfolk Archaeology* of the Norfolk and Norwich Archaeological Society, vol. 26. Norwich.

The network of streams flowing into the Wash formed in the seventeenth century the most complete system of river navigation in England. These rivers ran through one of the richest grain producing areas of the country, and were radically affected by fen drainage, around which developed a constant conflict of interests. The nucleus of the system was that "goodly fayr River," the Great Ouse itself, on which navigation never actually ceased, but was often impeded. The Bedford Level scheme in 1649 initiated that conflict between the interests of drainage and those of navigation, which lasted for a century. Acts of Parliament of various kinds indicate the shifting power of one side or the other to obtain redress. The harbors at mouths of rivers were affected by dams in the upper reaches, and floods in regions where the carry-off was insufficient distressed the farmers. The importance of a place like Great Yarmouth depended on its ability to ship goods to and from the back country by water. Defoe boasted that by the river system of the Wash, the merchants of Lynn supplied "about six Counties wholly, and three Counties in part, with their goods." Chief cargoes up the river were coal and wine. The downward freight was almost wholly agricultural produce, especially down the Great Ouse itself. Cambridge shipped down the river great quantities of hops, which went north to Hull, York, Newcastle, and Scotland. Upon the river and sea trade the prosperity of the East Anglian counties depended. The river system south of the Wash was centered on Great Yarmouth —the Yare, the Bure, or North River, and the Waveny, of which the Yare was the most important.—From the Article.

X

Ancient and Present State

(The items in this section are linked together by the controlling idea residing in the title printed above. That this control sits lightly upon the contents of works admitted here is evidenced by the variety of aspects treated. These include historical accounts, antiquities, descriptions, financial status, economic changes, trade, arts, customs, population, government, and the like. Purely economic treatises have been omitted as not contributing to the traveler's interests. The overlapping of divisions resulting from the mixture of subject matter makes difficult the proper ordering of many a title.)

1591 [NELSON, THOMAS.] The Blessed State of England . . . wherein is shewed how greatly foraine Nations do admire and wonder thereat. . . . 4to. London.

Apparently unique. An hitherto unknown Elizabethan pamphlet. Not in *STC* or any bibliography or library catalogue. Thomas Nelson was an Elizabethan printer and ballad writer.—From Robinson, no. 74.

1614 TOBIAS, — (Gentleman). Englands VVay to VVin Wealth, and to employ Ships and Mariners: or, A Plaine Description what great Profite, it will bring vnto the Common-wealth of England, by the Erecting, Building, and aduenturing of Busses, to Sea, a fishing. With a true Relation of the inestimable Wealth that is yearely taken out of his Maiesties Seas, by the Hollanders, by their great numbers of Busses, Pinkes, and Line-boates: And Also A Discourse of the Sea-coast Townes of England, and the most fit and commodious places, and Harbours that wee haue for Busses, and of the small number of our Fishermen, and also the true Valuation, and whole charge, of Building, and Furnishing, to Sea Busses, and Pinks, after the Holland Manner. By Tobias Gentleman, Fisherman and Marriner. London.

1626 CARY, WALTER. The Present State of England expressed in this Paradox, our Fathers were very rich with little, and wee poore with much. 4to. London.

Reprinted in *Harl. Misc.*, vol. III, London, 1809.

1630 DODRIDGE, SIR JOHN. The History of the Ancient and Modern Estate of the Principality of Wales, Dutchy of Cornewall and Earldome of Chester. Collected out of the Records of the Tower of London, and diuers ancient Authours. By Sir Iohn Dodridge Knight, late one of his Maiesties Iudges in the Kings Bench. And by himself Dedicated to King Iames of euer blessed memory. 4to. London.

2nd edit., 8vo, London, 1714. See below.
In this treatise Sir John, with a great deal of industry and exactness, calculates the ancient and present revenues of the palatinate.—Bookseller's Note. This was written by Dodridge in the early part of the reign of James I to urge the revival of the principality.—Davies, *Bibliog. of Brit. Hist., Stuart Period.*

1714 DODRIDGE, SIR JOHN. Historical Account of the Ancient and Modern State of the Principality of Wales, Dutchy of Cornwall and Earldom of Chester, Collected out of the Records of the Tower of London, and divers Ancient Authors, to which is added his Royal Highness the Prince of Wales Patent, also an Account of his Dignity, Privileges, Arms, Rank, and Titles, and of his Sons and Daughters. 8vo. London.

1643 GREVILLE, SIR FOULKE. The Five Yeares of King James; or, The Condition of the State of England, and the Relation it had to other Provinces. 4to. London.

1645 BUCHANAN, D. A Short View of the Present Condition of Scotland. 4to. London.

1661 ENDERBIE, PERCY. For the Antient and Modern Estate of Wales, see his *Cambria Triumphans* under HISTORY AND ANTIQUITIES.

1662 SMITH, CAPTAIN JOHN. The Trade and Fishing of Great Britain Displayed; with a Description of the Islands of Orkney and Shetland. 4to. London.

> This was incorporated with his *England's Improvement Reviv'd*, 1670 (see Smith this date below).

1668 CHAMBERLAYNE, EDWARD. Angliae Notitia, or, The Present State of England; together with divers Reflections upon the Ancient State thereof. 12mo. London.

> 2nd edit., corrected and much augmented, 12mo, London, 1669, and from then on numerous editions, reaching the 22nd by 1707, and under the title of *Magnae Britanniae Notitia*, to the 38th and last by 1755. From 1704 on it was edited by his son John Chamberlayne. Translated into French, Amsterdam, 1669; reprinted and augmented, 1692 and 1728. Abridged translation into Latin, Oxford, 1686, and Leyden, 1688. For some of these see below.
> With the passage of years this work grew in bulk until it came to represent the modern equivalent of an annual encyclopedia on government, revenues, politics, statistics, etc. Its popularity led Guy Miege to issue a rival publication, *The New State of England*, London, 1683, with a change in title after 1707 to *The Present State of Great Britain*.

> 1669 (In French.) L'Estat Present de l'Angleterre. 12mo. Amsterdam.

> 1686 (In Latin.) Angliae Notitia, sive praesens Status Angliae succincte enucleatus (abridged and translated into Latin by T. Wood). 12mo. Oxonii.

> 1704 CHAMBERLAYNE, EDWARD and JOHN. Angliae Notitia; or, The Present State of England, with divers Remarks upon the Ancient State thereof. By Edward Chamberlayne and continued by his Son, John Chamberlayne. Engraved portrait. 8vo. London.

> 1708 CHAMBERLAYNE, JOHN. Magnae Britanniae Notitia, or, The Present State of Great Britain, etc. 8vo. London.
> The 22nd edit. of the English part and the 1st of the Scottish.

> 1755 ————. Magnae Britanniae Notitia; or, the Present State of Great Britain. 38th edit. 2 pts. 8vo. London.
> Described are the climate, soil, religion, trade, government, institutions, lists of officials in various capacities, etc.

1670 SMITH, CAPTAIN JOHN. England's Improvement Reviv'd; Digested into Six Books. 4to. London.

> Another edit., London, 1673. See below.
> This is Smith's most elaborate work. It includes his earlier work on the trade and fishing, etc. (See Smith under 1662 above). Here he gives most attention to forestry, with some practical discussion on live stock and reclamation of waste land.—From Maggs, no. 594.

> 1673 SMITH, CAPTAIN JOHN. England's Improvement Reviv'd: in a Treatise of all Manner of Husbandry and Trade, by Land and Sea. 4to. London.

1672 PHILALETHES, THEOPHILUS. Great Britain's Glory, or, A Brief Description of the present State, Splendor, and Magnificence of the Royal Exchange, with some Remarkable Passages relating to the present Engagement, humbly pre-

sented to the several Merchants of the City of London, who daily Meet, Traffique, and Converse in the said Place, by Theophilus Philalethes. 4to. London.

This poem contains a description of the Great Fire of London, "also a small hint of the Present Engagement between His Majesty of Gt. Britain, and the States General of the United Provinces . . . also how Queen Elizabeth (of ever blessed memory) with all her Nobles and Princely Train did come to this stately structure."—Bookseller's Note.

1679 REYNEL, CAREW. The True English Interest; or, An Account of the Chief National Improvements; in some Political Observations, Demonstrating an Infallible Advance of this Nation to Infinite Wealth and Greatness, Trade and Populacy, with Imployment, and Preferment for all Persons. 8vo. London.

This contains a chapter on tobacco, which advocates its cultivation in England.—Maggs, no. 594.

1681 YARRANTON, ANDREW. England's Improvement by Sea and Land; its Situation, Growths, and Manufactures; the Benefits and Necessity of a Voluntary Register; a Method for improving the Royal Navy, lessening the Growing Power of France; and obtaining the Fishery; Proposals for Fortifying and Securing Tangier, so that no Enemy shall be able to Attaque it; Advantageous Proposals for the City of London, for the Preventing of Fires and Massacres therein, . . . the Way to make Newhaven in Sussex, fit to receive Ships of Burthen; Discourses of the Tinn, Iron, Linen, and Woollen Trades. Folding copperplates. 4to. London.

Yarranton has been regarded as the father of English political economy. It needed the enterprise of the Brighton Railway to make Newhaven fit to receive ships of burden.—Bookseller's Note. His interest was much taken up with projects of cutting canals and making rivers navigable. He published numerous works on manufacturing and commercial enterprises.

The Present State of England, set forth in a Dialogue between John and Jeroboam. 4to. London.

1682 MUDIE (or MOODIE), A. (Philopatris). Scotiae Indiculum, or, The Present State of Scotland; together with divers Reflections upon the Ancient State thereof; with List of the Professors of Glasgow College. 12mo. London.

1683 The Present State of England, Part III and Part IV; containing I. An Account of the Riches, Strength, Magnificence, Natural Production, Manufactures, of this Island; with an exact Catalogue of the Nobility, and their Seats, etc. II. The Trade and Commerce within itself, and all Countries traded to by the English, as at this day established; and all other Matters relating to Inland and Marine Affairs. Supplying what is omitted in the two former Parts: useful for Natives and Foreigners.

Parts I and II seem to have escaped my notice. This work may be the rival publication issued by Miege referred to in the note on Chamberlayne, under 1668. See Miege under 1690 below.

1684 Britannia Reflorescens, in a Prospect of the Ancient and Flourishing State of Great Britain, wherein a Description of the Island, Air, Soil, and Commodities is contained, a full Account of the Inhabitants, etc. 12mo. London.

Medulla Historicae Scoticae; being a Comprehensive History of the Lives and Reigns of the Kings of Scotland . . . To which is added, A Brief Account of the Present State of Scotland; the Names of the Nobility and Principal Ministers. . . . 8vo. London.

1689 A Discourse of the Growth of England in Populousness and Trade since the Reformation. Of the Clerical Revenue; of the Numbers of People of England . . . Of the Bills of Mortality and Political Observations thereon . . . Of the Advancement of the Linnen Manufacture; with an Account of the Linnen Cloaths, Canvas, Linnen-Yarn, Hemp, Flax, and Cordage, imported into the Port of London from Holland, Flanders, Germany, France, East-Land, Russia, Scotland, East Indies, from Michaelmas 1688 to Michaelmas 1689. With various political Remarks and Calculations relating to most parts of Christendom. Shewing likewise, from Natural Causes, the Impossibility of the Advancement of Popery. . . . Fol. London.

1690 Britanniae Speculum, or, A Short View of the Ancient and Modern State of Great Britain, and the Adjacent Isles, and of all other Dominions and Territories now in the actual possession of his present sacred Majesty King Charles II., the first part treating of Britain in general. Portrait. 12mo. Thomas Milburn for Christopher Hussey, at the Flower-de-Luce in Little Britain. London.

MIEGE, GUY. The New State of England under their Majesties King William and Queen Mary, in Three Parts: containing, 1. A Geographical Description of England in general, and of every County in particular; with useful and cautious Remarks. 2. An Account of the Inhabitants, their Original, Genius, Customs, Laws, Religion, and Government; of their present Majesties, their Court, Power, Revenues, etc. 3. A Description of the several Courts of Judicature, viz. the Parliament, Privy Council, etc. With a Catalogue of the present Officers in Church and State. 12mo. London.

2nd edit., London, 1693, with a 3rd part added in 1696; 4th, with great improvements, 8vo, 1702; and so on till 1707, when the title was changed to *The Present State of Great Britain*; the 2nd edit. of this version, 1711, included Ireland; 11th edit., 2 pts., 1748. Translated into French, Amsterdam (date?).
This work ran along the lines of the *Angliae Notitia* by Chamberlayne (see under 1668). Though expanded in later editions, it received no great alterations. See below.

1699 MIEGE, GUY. The New State of England, under our present Monarch, King William; in Three Parts. 1. A General Account of England; with a particular Description of its several Counties, Cities, Universities, Market and Borough Towns; and a Survey of Wales. 2. Of the original Temper, Genius, Language, Trade, Religion, Government, of the English; of the King's Prerogative, Power, Court, . . . Of the Nobility, Gentry, . . . With a succinct History of the Kings and Queens of England to this time; . . . 3rd edit., with Great Improvements. 4to. London.

1707 ————. The Present State of Great Britain, under the Auspicious Government of Her Most Sacred Majesty, Queen Anne: containing, 1. A General Description of England, Scotland and Wales. . . . 8vo. London.

1711 ————. The Present State of Great Britain and Ireland, being a . . . Treatise of their several Inhabitants, their Religion, Policy, Manufactures, etc. 2nd edit. of the new title.

1728 ————. The Present State of Great Britain and Ireland. In Three Parts: I. Of South Britain; II. Of North Britain; III. Of Ireland. Containing an accurate and

impartial Account of these Famous Islands . . . Of the vast, populous, and opulent City of London . . . and of the two celebrated Universities, Oxford and Cambridge. Of the Britons Original, Language, Temper. . . . Engraved portrait. 8vo. London.

1695   CARY, JOHN. An Essay on the State of England, in relation to its Trade, its Poor, and its Taxes, for carrying on the present War against France. 8vo. Bristol.

A Discourse concerning the Fishery within the British Seas, and other His Majesties Dominions, and more especially as it relates to the Trade of the Company of the Royal Fishery of England. 4to. London.

1711   BATTELEY, REV. JOHN. Ancient State of the Isle of Thanet. London (?).
The author was prebendary of Canterbury and master of King's Bridge Hospital in 1688.

1712   ATKYNS, SIR ROBERT. The Ancient and Present State of Glostershire. Portrait, map, and 8 plates containing 320 coats-of-arms, and 64 views by Kip. Fol. London.

> 2nd edit., fol., London, 1768. See below.
> This work was published by his executors. Sir Robert, having once conceived the use of such a history, thought himself obliged to carry it on, and pursued it with unremitting attention. Some have imagined that there is a larger proportion of merit due elsewhere than has been acknowledged. This large work was very expensive to the undertaker, who printed it in a pompous manner, adorning it with a variety of views and prospects of the gentry and nobility, with their arms. It were to be wished that more authorities had been given, and the charters and grants published in the original language. The Transcripts of all these were collected by Parsons.—From Gough, *Anecdotes of British Topography*, 173. In the fire of Jan. 29, 1712, the printing office of W. Bowyer was burned to the ground. Among the articles which perished "was by far the greater number of Sir Robert Atkyns's valuable 'History of Gloucestershire'; a few copies of it only were snatched from the flames, of which they still retain indelible marks."—Nichols, *Literary Anecdotes of the Eighteenth Century*, vol. I, 55.

> 1768   ATKYNS, SIR ROBERT. The Ancient and Present State of Gloucestershire. 2nd edit. 73 copperplates, map of the county, plan and prospect of the city, view of the cathedral, 61 seats and 320 coats-of-arms. Fol. London.
> This edition was republished from the 1st by William Herbert, editor of Ames's *Typographical Antiquities*. Gough says that only the literal errors were corrected in this edition.

1719   HOWELL, JAMES. The Ancient and Present State of England, being a compendious History of all its Monarchs from the Time of Julius Caesar. . . . 7th edit. Illus. with Sculptures. 8vo. London.

1720   The Ancient State of Great Britain—Customs, Manners, Ways of Living; of English, Saxon, Danish, Norman Names, etc. London.

Britain's Golden Mines Discover'd; or, The Fishery Trade considered, under these Three Heads: I. What Benefit Britain may reap by it. II. Which is the most probable Way of recovering it. III. The Three Great Fishing Trades, viz., That upon our own Coasts, that upon the Coasts of Greenland, and that upon the Coasts of Newfoundland, particularly examined. In a Letter from Sally Fisher, at Paris, to Mally Loverus, at London. 8vo. London.

The Present State of the British Court, or, An Account of the Civil and Military Establishments of England. 8vo. London.

1727   His Majesty's (George II) Patent for Improving Fisheries and Manufactures in Scotland. 8vo. Edinburgh.

1729   GEE, JOSHUA. The Trade and Navigation of Great Britain Considered: shewing that the surest Way for a Nation to increase in Riches, is to prevent the Importation of such Foreign Commodities as may be rais'd at Home. That this Kingdom is capable of raising within itself, and its Colonies, Materials for employing all our Poor in those Manufactures, which we now import from such of our Neighbours who refuse Admission of ours. Some Account of the Commodities each Country we trade with takes from us, and what we take from them; with Observations of the Balance. 8vo. London.

   4th edit., 1738.

   SPEARMAN, JOHN. An Inquiry into the Antient and Present State of the County Palatine of Durham, wherein are shewn the Oppressions which attend the Subjects of this County by the Maleadministration of the present Ministers and Officers of the said County Palatine; with some Reasons humbly offered to the Freeholders, Leaseholders, and Copyholders of the said County to consider of Ways and Means to remedy the said Abuses. (Place?)

   HALL, A. Magna Britannia, or, An Account of the Ancient State of Britain. 4to. London.

   This consists of only the Introduction.—Bandinel, *Catalogue of Books Relating to British Topography.*

1733   LINDESAY, PATRICK. The Interest of Scotland Considered, with Regard to its Police in imploying the Poor, its Agriculture, its Trade, its Manufactures, and Fisheries. 8vo. Edinburgh.

   Another edit., Edinburgh, 1736.

   LOGAN, WILLIAM. A View of the Present State of Scotland, in Regard to the Tenures and Slavish Dependencies of the Subjects of that Part of North Britain. In a Memorial drawn up by William Logan, Esq. a Scottish Gentleman. 8vo. London.

   New edit., London, 1737.

1734   The British Fishery recommended to Parliament, shewing the great Importance of it, to the Trade and Navigation of this Kingdom: what has been formerly done, and what is still wanting for its Encouragement: Why it has hitherto miscarry'd, and how we may succeed in it beyond all other Nations, with an Exact Map of the Coasts of Great-Britain; in which, all the Fishing Stations, and those parts where the Dutch Fleets fish for Herrings, are describ'd. Folding map dedicated to George II. 8vo. London. (44 pp.)

1737   FLETCHER, ANDREW (of Saltoun). Political Works: Discourse on Government, Affairs of Scotland, 1698, State of the Nation, 1701, etc. 8vo. Edinburgh (?).

1738   SYMPSON, M. The Present State of Scotland. Enlarged and amended. 8vo. London.

1739 SIBBALD, SIR ROBERT. A Collection of several Treatises concerning Scotland. Concerning Scotland, as it was of Old, and also in later Times. Fol. Edinburgh.

These were separately published, dated respectively 1707, 1710, 1711.

1740 BACON, FRANCIS. Of the true Greatness of the Kingdom of Britain. London.

MS dated approximately 1617 by Taylor, *Late Tudor and Early Stuart Geography*.

1741 State of the Society in Scotland for Propagating Christian Knowledge; giving a Brief Account of the Condition of the Highlands and the Islands of Scotland, and of the Attempts for the Reformation of those Parts. Together with some Account of this Society's Missionaries for converting the Natives of America. 8vo. (Place?)

1743 A Short History of the Highland Regiments, interspersed with some Occasional Observations as to the Present State of the Country, Inhabitants, and Government of Scotland. 8vo. London.

1744 FORBES, DUNCAN. Some Considerations on the Present State of Scotland, in a Letter to the Commissioners and Trustees for Improving Fisheries and Manufactures. To which is subjoined, A Letter from the Annual Committee of the Convention of Royal Boroughs to the General Boroughs of Scotland, for preventing the pernitious Practice of Smuggling. 1 plate. 8vo. Edinburgh.

1747 Remarks on the People and Government of Scotland, particularly the Highlanders; their Original, Customs, Manners, etc.; with a Genuine Account of the Highland Regiment that was decoyed to London. 4to. Edinburgh.

A General Description of all Trades, digested in Alphabetical Order: by which Parents, Guardians, and Trustees, may, with greater Ease and Certainty, make Choice of the Trades agreeable to the Capacity, Education, Inclination, Strength and Fortune of the Youth under their Care. To which is prefixed, An Essay on Divinity, Law, and Physic. 12mo. London.

An interesting book with chapters on numerous trades, dealing with hours of work, wages, cost of apprenticeships, customs of the trade, amount necessary to set up in business.—Bookseller's Note.

1750 A Letter to a Member of Parliament, concerning the Free British Fisheries, with Draughts of a Herring Buss and Nets, and of the Town and Harbour of Peterhead. Plates. 8vo. London (?).

A New Present State of England. Containing a concise History of its Situation, Extent, . . . Buildings, Government, Roads, a History of the Inhabitants, Manners, Customs, and Trade. . . . 2 vols. London.

A collection of miscellaneous information. It includes 90 pp. on London.

The Present State of England, containing a Description of all the Counties and Principal Towns, etc. 2 vols. 8vo. London.

Shetland Islands. An Exact and Authentic Account of the Greatest White-Herring-Fishery in Scotland, carried on yearly in the Island of Zetland, by the Dutch only. 8vo. London.

1751 POSTLETHWAYT, MALACHY. Universal Dictionary of Trade and Commerce, with large Additions and Improvements. 2 vols. 4to. London.

> Another edit., 1757; 4th edit., 1774.
> This was a translation from the French, with large additions, of J. Savary des Brulons. The translator was a writer on economics, who spent twenty years in preparation of this work.—*DNB.*

1756 BORLASE, WILLIAM, M.A., F.R.S. Observations on the Antient and Present State of the Islands of Scilly, and their Importance to the Trade of Great Britain. In a Letter to the Rev. Charles Lyttelton, Dean of Exeter, F.R.S. With Charts and Drawings of what is most remarkable. 4to. Oxford.

> This was an extension of a paper that had been read before the Royal Society, Feb. 8, 1753. At the request of Dr. Lyttelton, it was enlarged into a treatise, entitled, "An Account of the great Alterations which the islands of Scilly have undergone, since the Time of the Antients who mention them, as to their Number, Extent, and Position."—Nichols, *Literary Anecdotes,* vol. V, 296. Favorably reviewed by Samuel Johnson in the *Literary Magazine.*

1758 WALLACE, ROBERT. Characteristics of the Present Political State of Great Britain. 2nd edit., with corrections and additions, by the Author. 8vo. London (?).

1759 An Account of the Constitution and Present State of Great Britain, together with a View of its Trade, Policy, and Interest, respecting other Nations; and of the Principal Curiosities of Great Britain and Ireland. 12mo. London.

> Another edit., 32mo, London, 1770; again, 12mo, 1779.

1760 HEPBURN, THOMAS. A Letter to a Gentleman (George Paton), from his Friend in Orkney, written in 1757, containing the True Causes of the Poverty of that Country. 8vo. London. (44 pp.)

HYNDMAN, DR., DR. DICK (and others). Report of Doctors Hyndman, Dick, etc., appointed by the General Assembly, 1760, to visit the Highlands and Islands: Details of the Places of Worship, Population, Parishes, Catechisers, Schoolmasters, etc. Fol. (Place?)

1762 State of the Process of Valuation of the Forfeited Estates of Lochiel, against the Duke of Gordon, the Duke of Argyle, etc. (Place?)

> Cameron of Lochiel was "out in the '45" on the side of Prince Charles; the Duke of Argyle was an ardent Hanoverian.

1764 ANDERSON, ADAM. An Historical and Chronological Deduction of the Origin of Commerce, from the Earliest Accounts to the Present Time. Containing, An History of the great Commercial Interests of the British Empire, with an Introduction, exhibiting a View of the Ancient and Modern State of Europe; of the Importance of our Colonies; and of the Commerce, Shipping, Manufactures, Fisheries, etc., of Great Britain and Ireland, etc. Folding maps. 2 vols. Fol. London.

A justly celebrated and valuable work, replete with useful information.—Bookseller's Note.

1766   A General View of England (said to be translated from the French), respecting its Policy, Commerce, Taxes, etc.

Cited in Campbell, *Political Survey of Great Britain,* vol. II, 15.

1767   A Short View of the Present State of the Isle of Man: humbly submitted to the Rt. Hon. the Lords of his Majesty's Board of Treasury. By an Impartial Hand. 8vo. London (?).

This is a proposal to redress the grievances of its civil institutions to strangers, and those of its ecclesiastical government to natives. These causes for complaint arose after the transfer of the Island to the crown of Great Britain.—Gough, 611.

1769   KNOX, WILLIAM. The Present State of the Nation: particularly with respect to its Trade, Finances, etc. 8vo. London.

1770   The New Present State of the Climate, Divisions, Soil, Natural Productions, Trade, and Manufactures of Great Britain; Power and Revenues of the King, Privileges of Parliament, Trading and other Companies. 8vo. London.

1771   An Authentic Narrative of the Oppressions of the Islanders of Jersey; to which is prefixed a Succinct History of the Military Actions, Constitution, Laws, Customs and Commerce of that Island. 8vo. London.

1772   Letters concerning the Present State of England, particularly respecting the Politics, Arts, Manners, and Literature of the Times. 8vo. London.

An optimistic survey of England's condition. The writer prefers a slower development of manufactures.—J. Williams, *Guide to the Printed Materials.* Walpole criticizes this work and its author for his disparagement of Gray's Odes, and for other remarks, in a letter to Cole, Jan. 28, 1772.

The Present State of Scotland considered: and its sinking Condition charged upon the Conduct of the Landed Gentry. Edinburgh.

WALKER, JOHN. Dr. John Walker's Report concerning the State of the Highlands and Islands, to the General Assembly, 1772, *Scots Magazine,* vol. 34, 289-93. 8vo. Edinburgh.

See Walker under 1899-1901, DESCRIPTIONS, for a fuller statement of his report.

1774   LOCH, DAVID. Essays upon the Trade, Commerce, Manufacture, and Fisheries of Scotland, containing many curious and interesting Articles never before published. 8vo. Edinburgh.

An edit., 3 vols., 12mo, Edinburgh, 1778.

1775   FEA, JAMES (Surgeon). The Present State of the Orkney Islands considered, with their Situation, Trade, etc., calculated to shew by what Means their Usefulness to the British Empire, and the Happiness of their own Inhabitants may be increased. 8vo. Edinburgh.

Reprinted, Edinburgh, 1884.

1777 ANDERSON, JAMES. Observations on the Means of Exciting a Spirit of National Industry; Chiefly Intended to Promote the Agriculture, Commerce, Manufactures, and Fisheries of Scotland. 4to. London.

HOWARD, JOHN. The State of the Prisons in England and Wales. 4to. Warrington.

> 2nd and 3rd edits., with additions, Warrington, 1780 and 1784. His subsequent volume, *An Account of the Principal Lazzarettos in Europe,* Warrington, 1789. For an account of this great humanitarian, see Howard this date, under WEST EUROPE, vol. I of this work.

1783 BOSWELL, JAMES. A Letter to the People of Scotland, on the Present State of the Nation. 8vo. Edinburgh. (43 pp.)

1784 KNOX, JOHN. A View of the British Empire, more especially of Scotland, with some Proposals for the Improvement of that Country, Extension of its Fisheries, and Relief of the People. 4to. London.

> In 2 vols., 8vo, 1785; again, 1789.
> This work was reviewed *Gent. Mag.,* vol. 54, 610-11; 844-47. Knox was greatly distressed over the miseries of the population, which were steadily growing worse. In 1782 he arranged the various memoranda collected during a series of years and evolved plans for mitigating the popular distresses, such as improving the country for agriculture, which was then largely in a state of nature, and extending the fisheries and nurseries for seamen. This book was called a "Truly patriotic publication." See Knox under 1787, TOURS BY NATIVES.

1785 ANDERSON, JAMES. An Account of the Present State of the Hebrides and Western Coasts of Scotland . . . being the Substance of a Report to the Lords of Treasury, etc. 8vo. Edinburgh.

> Another edit., 8vo, Dublin, 1786. Translated into German, Berlin, 1785 (?). See below. See also under TOURS BY NATIVES.

> 1785(?) (In German.) Nachrichten von dem gegenwärtigen Zustands der Hebridischen Inseln. Aus dem Englischen übersetzt. 8vo. Berlin.

1786 KNOX, JOHN. A Discourse on the Expediency of Establishing Fishing Stations, or Small Towns, in the Highlands of Scotland and the Hebride Islands. 4to. London.

> Knox followed for many years the trade of a bookseller in the Strand, London, retired with a large fortune and from 1764 until his death devoted himself to the improvements of the fisheries and manufactures of Scotland. . . . Among other suggestions he recommended the formation of three canals in Scotland . . . all have since been constructed. —*DNB.*

1787 FEA, JAMES. Considerations on the Fisheries in the Scotch Islands; to which is prefixed a general Account elucidating the History, Soil, Productions, Curiosities, etc., of the same, the Manners of the Inhabitants, etc. 2 pts. in 1 vol. Map. 8vo. London.

WRAXALL, SIR NATHANIEL W. A Short Review of the Political State of Great Britain at the Commencement of 1787. 7th edit., with additions. 8vo. London.

1788 EUNSON, G. The Ancient and Present State of Orkney, particularly the Capital and Borough of Kirkwall. 12mo. Newcastle-upon-Tyne.

1789   DEMPSTER, G. A Discourse containing the Proceedings of the Society for Extending the Fisheries and Improving the Coasts of Great Britain since 1788; and
Thoughts on Emigration from the Highlands. 8vo. London.

PILKINGTON, JAMES. A View of the Present State of Derbyshire, with an Account of its most Remarkable Antiquities. Map and plates. 8vo. Derby.

> This includes mines, canals, agriculture, manufacture, trade, customs, etc., and accounts
> of particular towns.—J. Williams, *Guide to Printed Materials.*

1789-90   M'CULLOCH, L. Observations on the Herring Fisheries upon the North and
East Coasts of Scotland. 2 pts. 8vo. London.

1790   MACKENZIE, A. A View of the Political State of Scotland at the late General
Election. 8vo. Edinburgh.

1791   WHITE, PATRICK. Observations upon the Present State of the Scotch Fisheries,
and the Improvement of the Interior Parts of the Highlands. 12mo. Edinburgh.

1792   BELL, H. Observations upon Scotch Fisheries, Emigration,.and the Means of Improving the Highlands and Isles. 8vo. Edinburgh.

STOKES, ANTHONY. Desultory Observations on the Situation, Extent, Climate,
Population, Manners, Customs, Commerce, Constitution, Government, . . .
of Great Britain: occasionally contrasted with those of other Countries. . . .
London.

> This was directed against America to prevent emigration.—J. Williams.

1793   CREECH, WILLIAM. Letters addressed to Sir J. Sinclair, Bart. respecting the Mode
of Living, Arts, Commerce, Literature, Manners, etc., of Edinburgh in 1763,
and since that Period. 8vo. Edinburgh.

WEDDERBURN, ALEXANDER (Lord Loughborough). Observations on the English
Prisons, and the Means of improving them; communicated to the Rev. Henry
Zouch, a Justice of the Peace. . . . London. (31 pp.)

> A brief sketch of the history of prisons, Howard's work, and the efforts of his follow-
> ers, together with further needs.—J. Williams.

1794   BUCHANAN, JOHN LANNE. A General View of the Fishery of Great Britain,
drawn up for the Consideration of the North British Fishing. 8vo. London.

> This criticizes the plan of a company, especially for setting up establishments where
> fishing was poor.—J. Williams.

HERON, ROBERT. General View of the Natural Circumstances of the Hebudae or
Hebrides, and the Means to contribute to their Improvement. 4to. Edinburgh.

WOOD, JOHN PHILIP. The Antient and Modern State of the Parish of Cramond, to
which are added biographical and genealogical Collections respecting some of
the most considerable Families and Individuals connected with that District,

comprehending a Sketch of the Life and Projects of John Law of Lauriston, Comptroller-General of the Finances of France. Engravings and genealogical tables. Maps. Edinburgh.

> Reviewed *Gent. Mag.,* vol. 65, 319. This is the first parochial history attempted in Scotland on the detailed plan used in England. It is one of the most exact and elegant topographical works ever published. Engravings by Scott are well done. The account of John Law is ample and clear, and is published in separate form, 1791. The sections dealing with cultivation and products are compiled chiefly from the communications of the most extensive practical farmer in the district.—From the review.

1796 TROUTBECK, J. A Survey of the Antient and Present State of the Scilly Islands, describing their Situation, Towns, Fort, Produce, Government, Customs, Antiquities, Number of Churches, Harbours, Language, etc. Carefully extracted and compiled not only from the most esteemed Historians extant, but from the Observations of the most skilful Pilots and other intelligent Inhabitants, etc. 8vo. London.

> Noticed in *Gent. Mag.,* vol. 67, 952. It would seem that Borlase (see Borlase under 1756 above) had exhausted all the information on these islands, but the author, who is minister of St. Mary's Church, has found ample material to justify his lengthy title.—From the Review.

1797 KEITH, GEORGE SKENE. An Impartial and Comprehensive View of the Present State of Great Britain; containing, I. The Advantage which we enjoy. . . II. The Disadvantages which we labour under. . . III. Methods of removing . . . our Disadvantages. . . . London.

> A general discussion of factors, from physical to economic and moral, affecting the situation. Has suggestions for improvement.—J. Williams.

1799 ROOKE, MAJOR H., F.S.A. A Sketch of the Antient and Present State of Sherwood Forest, in the County of Nottingham. London (?).

> Reviewed *Gent. Mag.,* vol. 69, 600-01. The history of the Forest is illustrated from the time of the Romans to the present. The initials of King John and of King William III have been cut in oak trees there.—From the Review.

WILLIAMS, J. On Promoting and Improving the Fisheries upon the Coasts of the Highlands and Isles. *Trans. High. Soc.,* vol. 1, 250. 8vo. Edinburgh.

1810 KING, G. Natural and Political Observations and Conclusions upon the State and Condition of England, 1696. Edit. by G. Chalmers. 8vo. London.

1825 The Contrast; or, Scotland as it was in the Year 1745 and Scotland in the Year 1819. 8vo. London.

> Part I. Journal of an English Medical Officer who attended the Duke of Cumberland's Army, as far north as Inverness, during the time of the Rebellion. Part II. Letters from Professor Garscombe, of New York, descriptive of Society, Manners, Arts, Sciences, and Manufactures in Scotland in 1819. See under 1746, EXPEDITIONS.

1835 Reports of the State of certain Parishes in Scotland, made to His Majesty's Commissioners for Plantation of Kirks, etc., in pursuance of their Ordinance dated April XII, MDCXXVII. From the Originals preserved in His Majesty's General Register House. *Publ. Maitland Club,* vol 34. Edinburgh.

1836   SLEZER, CAPTAIN JOHN. Collection of Papers relating to the *Theatrum Scotiae,* and *History and Present State of Scotland,* by Captain John Slezer, 1693-1707. In *Bann. Misc.,* vol. II, no. xiv, *Publ. Bann. Club,* No. 19. Edinburgh. (See Slezer under 1693, VIEWS.)

1847   GREGORY, DONALD. Documents Illustrative of the History of the Fisheries in the West Highlands and Isles, 1566-1635. *Publ. Iona Club,* vol. I, no. viii. Edinburgh.

1859   Oppressions of the Sixteenth Century in the Islands of Orkney and Zetland; from Original Documents, edit. by David Balfour. *Publ. Maitland Club,* vol 75. 4to. Edinburgh.

> Contents: I. Articles and Informations by the Inhabitants of Orkney and Zetland, of the Oppressions committed by Lord Robert Stuart, Dec. 1575. II. The Complayntis of the Commownis and Inhabitants of Zetland, and Probatiounis led thair upoun, Feb. 1576. III. The Commission by James VI. to the Chancellor and others to try Lord Robert Stuart for Oppression, 1587. IV. A Supplication to Parliament by Lawrence Bruce and others, against Patrick Earl of Orkney, 1592. V. Appendices.
> This was published also in *Publ. Abbotsford Club,* vol. 31, 1859.

1861   Register containing the State and Condition of every Burgh within the Kingdom of Scotland, in the Year 1692. In *Misc. Scot. Burgh Records Soc.,* 49-157. 4to. Edinburgh.

1915   STEUART, BAILIE JOHN (Merchant of Inverness). Letter-Book, 1715-52. West Coast Meal Trade, Fish Trade, Import of Coal, Shipbuilding, Smuggling, etc. Introd. by Wm. Mackay. *Publ. Scot. History Soc.,* 2nd ser., no. 9. Edinburgh.

1936   WILSON, THOMAS. The State of England Anno Dom. 1600. Edited from the MSS. among the State Papers in the Public Record Office by F. J. Fisher, M.A. *Camden Soc. Misc.,* vol. 52, no. xvi, 3rd ser. London.

> The author, who was born a cadet about 1560, had to depend on his wits for a living and was led thereby into a great variety of experiences as author, translator, judge, diplomat, publisher, politician, public agent for Robert Cecil, archivist, and perhaps spy. His view of England shows him to have been a realist in economics and a snob in class distinctions, in that he regards the yeomanry as becoming too forward through their purchasing land at low prices and selling it at high profit. He records with evident pleasure, however, that the gentry are becoming more efficient in the management of their estates, though he thinks that the nobility are spending too much money on building for themselves stately mansions and palaces. Castles, he believes, make for prolonged wars, whereas their absence forces people to depend on their own courage. Towns are no longer fortified because cannon have rendered walls useless, and walls make for weak hearts. He notes that no one is allowed to leave the country without a license from the Queen or the Privy Council; and that all letters are opened before they are carried out of the country. Altogether his observations provide much interesting information on the state of affairs in England during the reign of Elizabeth.—From the Introduction by the editor.

XI

Surveys

(Surveys have to do primarily with boundaries, the rights and succession of property, the objects of "visitations," family pedigrees, and the like, but they greatly extended their limits to include within their investigations statistical information, industrial and economic conditions, historical and antiquarian matters, natural history and descriptions. Consequently one will find the term combined with titles printed in other sections. Sometimes a work listed as a survey turns out to be simply a map or map with text on natural history, trade and manufactures; at other times its chief burden seems to be recording the history and antiquities of a county, parish, or town.)

1602 CAREW, RICHARD. The Survey of Cornwall. 4to. London.

> 2nd edit., with added material, 4to, London, 1723; a new edit. of the 2nd, London, 1769; best edit., London, 1811. See below.
> Carew was highly esteemed by his contemporaries for his scholarship, his liberality and eloquence. Camden acknowledges him to be his "guide" through Cornwall. Others, like Spelman, called him "another Maro." His own country gave him many honors. He dedicated his book, which is regarded as a masterpiece of early topographical literature, to Raleigh, to whose son Carew he was probably godfather. Gough speaks of him as a person who was extremely capable of describing the history and monuments of his country, if the infancy of those studies at that time had afforded him light and material.—*Anecdotes of British Topography*, 123.

> 1723 CAREW, RICHARD. The Survey of Cornwall, and Epistle concerning the Excellencies of the English Tongue, with Life by H[ugh] C[arew]. 4to. London.

> 1811 ————. The Survey of Cornwall, etc. With copious Notes illustrative of its History and Antiquities, by Thomas Tonkin, now first published from the original MSS. by Francis [Basset] Lord de Dunstanville. Portrait by W. Evans. 4to. London.

1646 Forresta de Windsor, in Com. Surrey. The Meers, Meets, Limits, and Bounds of the Forest of Windsor, in the County of Surrey, as the same are found, set out, limited, and bounded by Inquisition; taken by Vertue of his Majesties Commission, in pursuance of one Act, made in the Parliament begun at Westminster, in the 16th Year of the Reign of our Sovereign Lord, King Charles, intitled, An Act for the Certainty of Forrests, and of the Meets, . . . as the same now remains upon Record, in his Majesties High Court of Chancery. 4to. London.

1651 HEYLYN, PETER. A Survey of the Estate of France, . . . The Second Journey, containing a Survey of the Estate of the two Ilands Guernzey and Jersey, with the Isles appending, according to their Politie and Formes of Government, both Ecclesiasticall and Civill. 4to. London.

> The date of 1656 is cited for the Survey of the two Islands by Taylor, *Late Tudor and Early Stuart Geography*.

1657 KILBURNE, RICHARD. A Brief Survey of the County Kent, viz., the Names of the Parishes in the same; in what Bailywick, Hundred, Lath, Division of the County, and Division of the Justices, every one of the said Parishes is; what Liberties do claim in the same; the Day on which any Market or Fair is kept therein; the Antient Names of the Parish Churches; in what Hundred or what

Township every one of the said Churches doth stand; and in what Diocesse every one of the said Parishes was. Obl. form in various columns. London.

Another edit., with corrections and enlargements, 4to, London, 1659. See below.

1659 KILBURNE, RICHARD. A Topographie, or Survey of the County of Kent, with some Chronological, Historicall, and other Matters touching the same: and the Parishes and Places therein. 4to. London.

1659 PHILIPOTT, THOMAS. Villare Cantianum: or, Kent Surveyed and Illustrated. An exact Description of all the Parishes, Burroughs, Villages, and other respective Mannors in Kent, and the Original and Intermedial Possessors of them, even until these Times, drawn out of Charters, Escheat Rolls, Fines, and other Public Evidences, but especially out of Gentleman's Private Deeds and Muniments; . . . by Thomas Philipott. With an Historical Catalogue of the High-Sheriffs of Kent, collected by John Philipott, Father to the Authour. Large colored folding map by W. Hollar after P. Symonson, including views of Rye and Dover. Fol. London.

Reprinted, 1664; a 2nd edit., corrected, fol., Lynn, 1776; reviewed *Gent. Mag.*, vol. 48, 590-91.
Bishop Kennet speaks very slightingly of Philipott, and calls both him and Kilburne modern and superficial, and says the whole was the work of John Philipott, father to the author.—Gough, 209. Apparently Thomas did try to palm off this work of his father as his own.

1714 RISDON, TRISTAM. For a Survey of the County of Devon, see his *Chorographical Description or Survey of the County of Devon,* under DESCRIPTIONS.

1717 ERDESWICKE, SAMPSON. A Survey of Staffordshire. Containing the Antiquities of that County, and a Description of Beeston Castle in Cheshire. Publish'd from Sir Wm. Dugdale's Transcript of the Author's original Copy, to which is added, Observations on Monastery-Lands in Staffordshire by Sir Simon Degge, and Anthony Wood's Note on the Author. 8vo. London.

Reprinted, 8vo, London, 1723.
Erdeswicke worked many years collecting the antiquities of this county, but he died (1603) before he had a chance to publish it. The MS passed into the hands of a Walter Chetwynd, of Ingestree, who was long engaged in the same enterprise. Afterwards it reached the hands of Sir Simon Degge, who added the letter annexed to the printed edition. Only the latter part was printed from Dugdale's copy, the other from a MS in Thoresby's Museum, no. 144. Among the MSS in the Harleian Collection, no. 1990, is a very correct copy of this survey, with many considerable additions, which deserves a new edition. Gough speaks of the above as a most incorrect edition.—*Op. cit.,* 185.

1720-31 COX, REV. THOMAS. Magna Britannia & Hibernia antiqua & nova, or, A New Survey of Great Britain, wherein to the Topographical Account given by Mr. Camden and the late editors of his Britannia, is added a more large History, not only of the Cities, Boroughs, Towns, and Parishes, mentioned by them, but also of many other Places of Note and Antiquities since discovered; together with the Chronology of the most Remarkable Actions of the Britons, Romans, Saxons, Danes, and Normans: the Lives and Constitutions of the Bishops of all our Sees; Founders and Benefactors to our Universities and Monasteries; the Sufferings of Martyrs; and many other ecclesiastical Matters; the Acts and Laws of our Parliaments, with the Place of their Meeting; a Character of such eminent Statesmen and Churchmen as have signalized themselves by their wise Conduct and Writings, and the Pedigrees of all our noble Families and Gentry,

both Antient and modern, according to the best Relations extant. Collected and composed by an impartial Hand. 6 vols. 4to. London.

This work was first published in monthly numbers as a supplement to Europe in the *Atlas Geographicus,* and afterwards collected into these six volumes, of which the 1st and 2nd came out in 1720; the 3rd in 1724; the 4th in 1727; the 5th in 1730; the 6th in 1731. According to Morgan, *Bibliog. of British History,* vol. III, there is another edition, with 29 extra maps, 1720-38. Although Ireland is mentioned in the title, neither that country nor Scotland is included. The surveys of various counties were also sold separately.

Considered as a compilation from the best original histories and surveys of England, it has a great deal of merit. To each county is prefixed a map; besides which there are some indifferent cuts of ancient British habits, etc. Gough ranks it after Camden, as a kind of supplement to his imperfections, though itself not completed.—*Op. cit.,* 20-21.

1725 HAYWARD, WILLIAM. Survey of Lynn Haven and the Ouse. (Place?)

MS dated 1604 by Taylor, *Late Tudor and Early Stuart Geography.*

1728 NORDEN, JOHN. Survey of Cornwall. London.

Norden finished this survey about 1584; it was intended to be a part of his *Speculi Britanniae Pars.* For this survey and others of Norden, see under DESCRIPTIONS.

SALMON, NATHANIEL. A New Survey of England; wherein the Defects of Camden are supplied. 2 vols. 8vo. London.

Reissued with a new title page, 2 vols., 8vo, London, 1731. See below.

For his relation to the antiquary Horsley and his indebtedness for help, see R. C. Bosanquet, "John Horsley and his Times," *Arch. Aeliana,* vol. 10, 4th ser., 1933.

1731 SALMON, NATHANIEL. New Survey of England, in which the Defects of Camden are supplied, and the Errors of his Followers remarked: the Opinions of our Antiquaries compared: the Roman Military Ways traced; and the Stations settled according to the Itinerary, without altering the Figures: with some Natural History of each County. 2 vols. 8vo. London.

1732 COKER, REV. JOHN. A Survey of Dorsetshire, with the Antiquities, Natural History, and copious Genealogical Account of 300 of the principal Families of that County. Folding map and 6 plates, containing 295 arms. Fol. London.

The author died about 1635. The above account is said to have been published from the original MS. It was probably compiled between 1617 and 1633. It has also been attributed to Thomas Gerard of Trent.

1736 KIRBY, JOHN. Survey of the County of Suffolk. London.

This was contracted to half its scale in 1737 and engraved by Bashire. Kirby published another survey still smaller, which was since inserted in the last edition of his *Suffolk Traveller.*—Gough, 498. This is a survey map.

1738 Magna Britannia; or, A Survey of the Antient and Present State of Great Britain; being more comprehensive and instructive than Camden, or any other Author on this Subject. Maps. London.

This item was taken from Ponton's Catalogue. It may be another edition of Cox's *Magna Britannia,* referred to by Morgan. See note to Cox, 1720-31 above.

1756 BLAGDON, RICHARD. A Survey of the County of Essex. (Cited in *Gent. Mag.,* vol. 26, April.)

WEBB, P. C. A Short Account of some Particulars Concerning Domesday Book, with a View to Promote its being Published. Folding plate. 4to. Privately published.

1760   Cumberland and Westmoreland divided into their respective Wards, from the best Surveys, with historical Extracts relative to Natural History, Trade, and Manufactures, etc. Title within a Chippendale design. 28 × 22 ins. London.

1761   ROCQUE, J. Topographical Survey of the County of Berks, in 18 Sheets, with the Royal Palace of Windsor, Seats, Towns, Villages, Main and Cross Roads, Commons, Greens, etc. Fol. London.

1774   CAMPBELL, JOHN, LL.D. A Political Survey of Britain: Being a Series of Reflections on the Situations, Lands, Inhabitants, Revenues, Colonies, and Commerce of this Island: Intended to shew That we have not as yet approached near the Summit of Improvement, but that it will afford Employment to many Generations before they push to their utmost Extent the natural Advantages of Great Britain. 2 vols. 4to. London.

> This voluminous work includes an examination of the topography, geography, and hydrography of England, Scotland, and Ireland, showing how nature has blessed this region with advantages: the harbors, coast-line, rivers, navigation possibilities, the uses of river and canal navigation, in fact, all the matters that relate to transportation which make for prosperity; the soils, what they are fit for and what has been done with them, the mineral resources, the agricultural products, etc.; the history of Great Britain. All is done in a spirit of optimism. The text is bolstered up with an imposing array of references, classical and modern. His notes are frequently of more interest than his text, being far more particular in their reference. Campbell was a prolific writer. To have read all the authorities he cites—if he did—and to have compiled besides two such bulky volumes in so ambitious a sweep is the life work of any one man; but, in addition, he wrote many more volumes, such as the *Lives of the British Admirals*, etc. Apparently the above work was indifferently received. His friend Dr. Johnson thought that its lack of success killed him.

SHARPE, GLANVILLE. Account of the Ancient Division of the English Nation into Hundreds and Tithings. 8vo. London.

SPYERS, JOHN. A Survey of the Estate at Laleham in the County of Middlesex, belonging to Sir James Lowther, together with the Land at Hengrove and Staines, and Rights and Privileges in Laleham Borough; Meadows and Enclosures, with the Field commonly called Laleham South Common Field, and Laleham Borough; a series of 15 large scale water color drawings. Fol. London.

> Of the author Walpole says that he was equally unamiable in public and private life (*Memoirs of George III*). He was the subject of Peter Pindar's satire in "A Commisserating Epistle to Lord Lonsdale," and in "An Ode to Lord Lonsdale," and his political influence was celebrated in *The Rolliad.*—Bookseller's Note.

1776   SEYMOUR, C. A Topographical Survey of the County of Kent. 8vo. Canterbury. (See Seymour under 1782 below.)

1777   An Actual Survey and Plan of the Processional Boundaries of the Parish of Ealing, taken in 1777 (bound up with Rocque, *A New and Accurate Survey of the Cities of London and Westminster, 1751*).

17—   BOWEN, EMANUEL. Bedford divided into its Hundreds, drawn from a late Survey, with historical Extracts relating to its Produce, Trade, etc. With emblematical border around title engraved by E. Bowen. 28 × 22 ins. Printed for Bowles and Carver. n.d.

> Since Bowen, who was map engraver to George II, flourished around 1752, it is probable that his engravings, and possibly maps, were done in the middle of the century. Seem-

ingly a whole series of county surveys were engraved and published at about the same time. Nearly all of them have some engraving executed by Bowen; others bear the name of Kitchin. They were put out by a variety of publishers. As the dates 1777 and 1778 appear on a few, I have assumed that they belong to this decade. All carry about the same text. The description of Bedford above will serve as a sample of the general run.

1782 An Historical, Descriptive, and Biographical Survey of the County of Suffolk. Fol. London. (Date approximate.)

SEYMOUR, C. A New Topographical, Historical, and Commercial Survey of the Cities, Towns, Villages of the County of Kent, arranged in Alphabetical Order . . . The ancient and obscure Terms of the Feudal Law, and the obsolete Tenures and Customs relative to it, are all explained. 8vo. Canterbury.

1783-1816 Domesday Book: seu Liber Censualis Wilhelmi primi Regis Angliae inter Archivos, regni in domo capitulari Westmonasterii Asservatus, Indices. Accessit Dissertatio Generalis de ratione hujusce Libri Additamenta ex codic. Antiquiss., Exon. Domesday, Inquistro Eliensis, Liber Winton. Boldon Book (edited by Sir Henry Ellis). 4 vols. Fol. London.

> *A Photo-Zincograph Facsimile of the Original Domesday Book in the Public Record Office,* in 2 volumes, was published in 1862. This is a complete set of the Domesday Facsimiles, which were issued in separate counties by the Ordnance Survey Office. Sir Henry Ellis's Introduction to Domesday Book is listed below.

> 1833 ELLIS, SIR HENRY. General Introduction to Domesday Book, accompanied by Indexes of the Tenants in Chief, and Under Tenants at the Time of the Survey, as well as of the Holders of Lands mentioned in Domesday Anterior to the Formation of that Record, with an Abstract of the Population of England at the Close of the Reign of William the Conqueror, illustrated by Notes and Comments. 2 vols. 8vo. London.

> The literature on the Domesday Book is too vast for an attempt to survey it here. As representative of the eighteenth century knowledge of the work, the following account by Gough is summarized. It was begun in 1080 and finished in six years, for the universal establishment of tenures; . . . it contains a general survey of the greatest part of the kingdom, divided into counties, rapes, lathes, and hundreds, and subdivided into cities, towns, villages, etc., each man's proportion of arable, pasture, meadow, and wood land, with their extent and value, the number and condition of men in each town, etc. The first volume, a large folio, finely written on 382 double pages of vellum, in a small but plain character and double columns, contains 31 counties. The other in 4to, written on 450 such pages in single columns, and a fair but large hand, contained Essex, Norfolk, and Suffolk, . . . Northumberland, Cumberland, and Durham had suffered so much from the ravages of war that no survey could be taken of them. In the orthography of place names the Norman scribes made many mistakes, seldom copying them from other writings, but setting them down from Saxon pronunciation, which they depraved and contracted.—Gough, 12. See Edward Dove under GENERAL REFERENCE.

1787 CLARKE, JAMES. Survey of the Lakes of Cumberland, Westmoreland, and Lancashire; together with an Account, Historical, Topographical, and Descriptive, of the Adjacent Country. To which is added, A Sketch of the Border Laws and Customs. 21 large views of the Lakes engraved from drawings made by J. Farington, together with 12 large folding maps. Fol. London.

> 2nd edit., fol., London, 1789.
> Reviewed *Gent. Mag.,* vol. 60, 57. In his introduction to these views the author describes manners and customs, dialects, and scenery, and passes the usual strictures on his predecessor tour writers and describers, such as Gray, Young, Pennant, West, Hutchinson, Gilpin, etc. The plates show the roads to the Lakes, with the adjacent country. The work is mentioned in Wordsworth's "Evening Walk."

PLAYFAIR, WILLIAM. The Commercial and Political Atlas, which represents at a Single View, by Means of Copper Plate Charts, the most important Public Accounts of Revenues, Expenditures, Debts, and Commerce of England. 40 copperplates. London.

> This includes charts and descriptions for Exports and Imports to and from the West Indies; to and from North America for eighty years; to and from the U.S.A., Spanish West Indies, Greenland, Bermuda; Chart of the National Debt from the Accession of William III until the end of the War with America; Navy and Army expenses, etc.— Maggs, no. 442.

TUNNICLIFF, WILLIAM. A Topographical Survey of the Counties of Stafford, Chester, and Lancaster; containing a new engraved Map of each County, with a complete description of the Great, Direct, and Cross Roads. 16 plates of arms. 8vo. Nantwich.

> For further surveys by Tunnicliff, see under 1789 and 1791 below.

1788   Survey of the Province of Moray. Aberdeen.

WYNDHAM, HENRY PENRUDDOCKE. Domesday Book of Wiltshire, to which is added a Translation of the Original Latin into English, with an Index, in which are adapted the modern Names of the Antient, and with a Preface, in which is included a Plan for a General History of the County. 8vo. Salisbury.

1789   DONALD, T. An Actual Topographical Survey of the Environs of Keswick, engraved by J. Haywood. On one sheet, 19 × 13 ins. London.

TUNNICLIFF, WILLIAM. A Topographical Survey of Somerset, Worcester, Gloucester, Stafford, Chester, and Lancaster, with Direction and Survey of Great Roads, Names and Seats of the Nobility and Gentry, Directory, etc. Folding maps and numerous plates of arms. 8vo. Bath.

1791-99   SINCLAIR, SIR JOHN. A (Old) Statistical Account of Scotland: consisting of the Topography, Geology, Land Owners, Parochial Registers, Celebrated Characters, Population, and Industries of every Parish in Scotland, drawn up from the Communications of the Ministers of the different Parishes, and edited by Sir John Sinclair, Bart. 21 vols. Maps and illustrations. 8vo. Edinburgh.

> The Prospectus and an analysis of this work were published in French, London, 1792.
> Sir John Sinclair circulated among the ministers of the Church of Scotland a prospectus containing a list of queries as a guide for their inquiry and research and as a model for their completed report. These queries dealt with topography, climates, diseases, number of proprietors, husbandry in all its various details, soil, fisheries, prices, wages, manufactures, towns and villages, churches, stipends, livings, the poor, state of morality, habits and customs, mineral springs, roads, antiquities, miscellaneous observations, etc. The ministers responded nobly and earned for themselves a well deserved tribute for zeal and learning. From the extracts given in the *Gentleman's Magazine,* as it followed the course of publication of the work, one gains the impression that the reading of any report will be entertaining and curious. It has been termed the most valuable repertory of statistics, topography, agriculture and commerce at the command of any country in Europe at the period. It is well indexed: vol. 20, index of parishes, and vol. 21, index of topics, persons, and places. This work is called the "Old Statistical Account" as distinguished from the "New Statistical Account" published in London, 1845.

> > 1792   SINCLAIR, SIR JOHN. Sir John Sinclair's Prospectus d'un Ouvrage intitulé: Analyse de L'Etat Politique D'Ecosse, d'après les rapports des Ministres de chaque Paroisse; Contenant la Situation Présente de ce Royaume et les moyens de la rendre plus florissant, par le Chevalier Sinclair, Bart. 8vo. Londres.

TUNNICLIFF, WILLIAM. A Topographical Survey of the Counties of Hants, Wilts, Dorset, Somerset, Devon and Cornwall, commonly called the Western Circuit, containing an accurate and comprehensive Description of all the Principal Direct and Cross Roads in each respective County. Colored folding maps and plates of arms. 8vo. Salisbury.

1792 ARMSTRONG, M. J. (Land Surveyor). An Essay on the Contour of the Coast of Norfolk, but more particularly as it relates to the Marium-banks and Sea-breaches, so loudly and so justly complained of. Read to the Society for the Participation of Useful Knowledge, Oct. 20, 1789, in Norwich. Norwich.

> Reviewed *Gent. Mag.,* vol. 62, 455. The Postscript to the published paper adds that the author had not satisfactorily examined the subject until after this little memoir went to press. Nor could he do so even then because of floods. Marshall, in his *Rural Oeconomy of Norfolk,* had anticipated Armstrong in the account of the bank cast up against the sea, and in proposing further remedies.—From the review.

1794 BARCLAY, REV. DR. GEORGE. Statistical Account of Haddington, County and Presbytery Synod of Lothian and Tweeddale. 8vo. Edinburgh.

> The above was taken from Vol. I of *The Transactions of the Society of Antiquaries in Scotland.*

1796 SCOTT, JAMES. Statistical Accounts of the Town and Parish of Perth and Parish of Kinnoul in the Years 1794 and 1795. 8vo. Perth.

1798 AIKIN, JOHN. A Survey of the Counties of Lancashire, Cheshire, Derby, West Riding of Yorkshire, and the Northern Part of Staffordshire, Describing the Rivers, Lakes, Soil, Manure, Climate, Production, Morals, Property, Civil and Ecclesiastical Divisions; with a general Account of the River and Canal Navigation within those Districts. London.

> Reviewed *Gent. Mag.,* vol. 68, 42. This is an extract from Dr. Aikin's *Description of the Country round Manchester,* to enable those to buy who could not afford the original work. Several of the canals have been completed since these pages were printed off. The title is grossly inaccurate, as the work by no means covers the territory mentioned.—From the review. For the original work by Aikin see under 1796, DESCRIPTIONS.

GRANT, REV. J., and REV. W. LESLIE. A Survey of the Province of Moray, Historical, Geographical, and Political. Map. 8vo. Aberdeen (but published by Forsyth of Elgin).

SHAW, L. A Survey of the Province of Moray, Historical, Geographical, and Political (with additions). 8vo. Aberdeen.

> This may be a republication of the preceding item.

1799 HENSHALL, SAMUEL, and J. WILKINSON. Domesday; or, An Actual Survey of South-Britain . . . 1086 . . . faithfully translated, with an Introduction, Notes, and Illustrations. Kent, Sussex, Surrey. Map. 4to. London. (See under 1783-1816 above.)

1799-1801 MUDGE, CAPTAIN W., and ISAAC DALBY. Trigonometrical Survey of England and Wales, carried on in 1784 to the end of 1796. 2 vols. Plates. London.

1809   Domesday Book: Dom Boc, A Translation of the Record called Domesday, so far
       as Relates to the County of York, including also Amounderness, Lonsdale, and
       Furness, in Lancashire, and such parts as Westmoreland and Cumberland are
       Contained in the Survey, also the Counties of Derby, Nottingham, Rutland, and
       Lincoln, with an Introduction, Glossary, and Indexes, by the Rev. William
       Bawden. 4to. Doncaster.

1845   WESTCOTE, THOMAS. A View of Devonshire in 1630, with a Pedigree of Most of
       its Gentry, by Thomas Westcote, Gent. Edited by the Rev. George Oliver and
       Pitman Jones. 4to. Exeter.

1849   Visitation of the County of Huntington, 1613. 4to. *Publ. Camden Soc.,* vol. 43.
       London.

1859   HALLIWELL, J. O. (Editor). An Ancient Survey of Penmaen Mawr, North Wales,
       of the Time of Charles I, containing notices of Priestholme, Aber, Penmaen-
       mawr, and the ancient Ruins, Conway, etc. London.
           Later edit., 8vo, ed. by W. B. Lowe, Llanfairfechan, 1906.

1862   Domesday Book: Photo-Zincograph Facsimile of the Original Domesday Book
       in the Public Record Office. 2 vols. Large and small 4to. London.
           See under 1783-1816 above. Separate issues of counties and combinations of counties,
       and others which may be independent studies, were published in the following years.

1868   HARLAND, JOHN, F.S.A. (Editor). Three Lancashire Documents of the Four-
       teenth and Fifteenth Centuries. Comprising, I. The Great De Lacy Inquisition,
       Feb. 16, 1311. II. The Survey of 1320-46. III. Custom Roll and Rental of the
       Manor of Ashton-under-Lyne, Nov. 11, 1422. *Publ. Chetham Soc.,* vol. 74.
       Manchester.

1870   LOWER, MARK ANTHONY. A Survey of the Coast of Sussex, made in 1587, with a
       View to its Defence against Foreign Invasion, and especially against the Span-
       ish Armada. Obl. fol. Leses (?).

1870-1922   Visitation Series, published by the Harleian Society. 8vo.
           The following list is doubtless partial: Leicestershire in 1619. 1870.—Cornwall in 1620.
       1874.—Essex in 1552. Pt. 1, 1878.—Bedfordshire in 1566, 1582, and 1634. 1884.—Dorset in
       1623. 1885.—Hertfordshire in 1572 and 1634. 1886.—Norfolk in 1563, 1589, and 1613. 1891.—
       Surrey in 1530, 1572, and 1623. 1899.—Sussex in 1530 and 1633-34. 1905.—Berkshire in
       1532, 1566, 1623, 1665-66. 1907. Buckinghamshire in 1634. 1909.—Rutland in 1681-82. 1922.

1882   Visitations of Suffolk, made by Hervey, 1561, Cooke, 1577, and Raven, 1612,
       with Notes and Appendix of additional Suffolk Pedigrees. Edit. by Walter C.
       Metcalfe. 8vo. Privately printed, Exeter.

1888-91   Domesday Commemoration, 1086-1886. Domesday Studies: being the Papers
       used at the Meeting of the Domesday Commemoration, 1886, with a Bibliog-
       raphy of Domesday Books and Accounts of the MSS and Printed Books ex-
       hibited. Edit. by P. Edward Dove. Map. 2 vols. 4to. London.
           This is a work that richly rewards reading. See Dove under GENERAL REFERENCE.

1891   A Survey of the Debateable and Border Lands adjoining the realm of Scotland, and belonging to the Crown of England. (Place?)

> MS dated 1604 by Taylor, *Late Tudor and Early Stuart Geography*.

1893-99   HABINGTON, THOMAS. A Survey of Worcestershire. Edit. by J. Amphlett. 2 vols. *Publ. Worcestershire Hist. Soc.*, vols. 2-3. Worcester.

> A survey, parish by parish, made between 1560 and 1647.—Read, *Bibliog. Brit. Hist.* This was printed from a MS in the possession of the Society of Antiquaries. It is largely an historical description of the ownership of land, armorial bearings, church buildings, etc. There are some descriptive passages of land and countryside.—Fussell, *Exploration of England*.

1897   Domesday of Inclosures, 1517-18. Being the Extant Returns to Chancery for Berkshire, Buckinghamshire, Cheshire, Essex, Leicestershire, Lincolnshire, Northants, Oxfordshire, and Warwickshire in 1517, and for Bedfordshire in 1518. Edit. with Notes and Tables, by I. S. Leadam. 2 vols. London.

1901   CASH, C. G. The First Topographical Survey of Scotland. (An Account of the preparation of the maps that appeared in Blaeu's *Atlas of Scotland*, 1654.) In *Scot. Geog. Mag.*, vol. 17, 399-414. 4to. Edinburgh.

1903   OWEN, HENRY. A Survey of the Lordship of Haverford in 1577. In *Arch. Camb.*, vol. 3, 39-55, 6th ser. London.

1923   Survey of Oxford in 1772. In *Surveys and Tokens*, edit. by Rev. H. E. Salter, M.A. *Publ. Oxford Hist. Soc.*, vol. 75. Oxford.

> This has to do with the survey of the city called for by the "Milesway Act," which purposed to widen and repair the approaches to the city, make new roads, take down some of the gates, repair or pull down bridges, and buy land for a new market place. The money was to be raised by erecting turnpike gates at the entrance to the city, levying rates on houses on certain streets, and by borrowing. All tenements having frontage on the streets were to pay for the lighting and cleaning of the streets at so much a yard of frontage. The cost of paving was to be met by the houses on the streets so benefited. With this project the middle ages come to an end in Oxford topographically. With the exception of Blue Boar Lane, no new road had been made since the days of William the Conqueror up to the years 1770-1771, when the aforenamed road was constructed. In the medieval period a street was never widened or straightened because such a need was not sufficiently realized and because there existed no power of compulsory purchase until the passage of this act of 1771, whose result was the obliteration of the ancient boundaries of Oxford.—From the Account.

1927   SINCLAIR, SIR JOHN. The Orkney Parishes: Statistical Account of Orkney, 1795-98. With Introduction and Notice of each Parish by J. S. Clouston. 4to. Kirkwall.

XII

Geography

(In the section GEOGRAPHY, vol. II of this work, there are listed many titles which include geographical descriptions of the British Isles. The present section, with few exceptions, is limited to works dealing specifically with Great Britain. Of the various terms, geography, chorography, and topography, none seemed to have stayed within its bounds. For Ptolemy, geography meant a description of a limited area. Later writers recognized no such restriction but indiscriminately mingled descriptions of countries with their manners and customs, their products and manufactures. The 18th century used the term much as it pleased. In the 19th century there emerged the concept of regional geography, which displaced the divisions based on political affiliations. In the present century geographers are largely concerned with man's attempts to relate his physical environment to his activities in making a living. In all, English geographers were slow in arriving at a philosophy of geography.)

1462 PTOLEMY, CLAUDIUS. Geographia. Maps. Bologna.

> This, the first printed edition, was in Latin. The Greek text, edited by Erasmus, was printed at Basel in 1533. Since that time more than fifty editions have appeared. Modern edit., fol., New York, 1933 (see below). For details on the date, the work, and its map of Britain, see under MAPS AND CHARTS.

> 1933 PTOLEMY, CLAUDIUS. The Geography of Claudius Ptolemy. Translated into English and edited by Edward Luther Stevenson. Based upon Greek and Latin Manuscripts and important late Fifteenth and Sixteenth Century Editions, including Reproductions of the Map from the Ebner Manuscript, *ca.* 1460. With an Introduction by Professor Joseph Fischer. Fol. With collotype reproductions of 27 maps from the Ebner MS and 2 early printed world maps showing America (Ruysch, 1508, and Lorenze Fries, 1522). New York.

1472 STRABO. Geographia. Fol. Venice.

> This, the second edition of this great geographer, was translated into Latin by Guarino de Verona and Gregorius Tiphernas and edited by Jo. Andreae. It was modeled on the *editio princeps* of Sweynheym and Pannartz of 1469. Strabo was translated into English by Hamilton and Falconer, Bohn Series, 3 vols., London, 1854-57. The work contains geographical descriptions of Britain. Strabo put no faith in Pytheas' account of his visit to Britain.

1590 B., W. Geographical Playing Cards, with County Maps. London.

1600(?) BARCLAY, WILLIAM. Gul. Barclaii ex Vita Julii Agricolae, Auctore Genero, Praemetia. (Place?)

> This work is cited by Gough, *Anecdotes of British Topography*, 618, in his opening paragraph of Roman Geography of Scotland. Agricola's progress as described by Tacitus throws much light on the ancient geography of Britain. The historian's narrative of his father-in-law's exploits takes in so large a detail of Roman transactions in Scotland that Gough places it at the head of a list of topographical writings on Scotland. So far Gough is probably correct. But he is wrong in identifying Barclay with the Scotch professor of law at Pont-a-Mousson in Lorrain, and in stating that Lipsius studied under him. It must have been William Barclay, the physician, who was a student under Lipsius and who added the commentary to his master's edition of Tacitus. This latter Barclay took his degree in medicine at Louvain, taught at Paris, returned to Scotland to practice, and then went back to Nantes. He is known for his work in praise of tobacco called *Nepenthe, or the Vertues of Tobacco*, 1614. Tacitus was also translated by Savile in 1581.

1614 SPEED, JOHN. For the geography of England, Scotland, and Ireland, and the adjoining isles, see his *Theatre of the Empire of Great Britain*, under MAPS AND CHARTS.

1667 GORE, THOMAS. Nomenclator Geographicus Latino-Anglicus & Anglico-Latinus Alphabetice digestus, complectens plerorumque omnium Magnae Britanniae &

Hiberniae Regionum, Comitatum, Episcopatum, Oppidorum, Fluviorum, etc.
Nomina & Appelationes (quae scilicet apud Scriptores occurrunt Latinos) ex
Libris qua MSS quam Typis excusis, Chartis Geographicis aliisque rei an-
tiquariae Monumentis summa Diligentia Collectas. 12mo. Oxford.

1673 BLOME, RICHARD. Britannia, or, A Geographical Description of England, Scotland, and Ireland, and the Isles and Territories thereto belonging. Maps and
plan of London before the Fire by Hollar. Fol. London.

> "A most entire piece of theft out of Camden and Speed."—Bishop Nicolson, quoted
> by Lowndes.

1676 Recreative Pastime by Card-Play; Geographical, Chronological, and Historiog-
raphical, of England and Wales; shewing the Commodities and Rarities of each
Country. Very useful for all Travellers; especially those whose concerns tend
to the commodities of our English Nation. By a long Student in the Mathematicks. London.

> 2nd edit., 1691.
> This is a gazetteer with descriptive notes.—Fussell, *Exploration of England.*

The Chorography of Britain. By the anonymous Ravennas. 8vo. Paris.

> The title and data of this work are taken from Gough, 4. It was found by Father
> Porcheron as he was making a catalogue of the King of France's MSS. It was written
> probably in the 7th century by an anonymous monk of Ravenna, and has been ascribed to
> Gallio of Ravenna, the last Roman commander in Britain. Salmon, who proposed this
> conjecture, did not take into consideration that this work was only a small part of a larger
> geographical project in five books, where Britain receives, along with other islands, a
> limited attention at the end.

1701-21 COLLIER, JEREMY. A Great Historical, Geographical, Genealogical and Poetical Dictionary: A Miscellany of Sacred and Prophane History. With Lives of
the Families of the English, Scotch, and Irish Nobility, etc. 4 vols. Fol. London.

> 2nd edit., 4 vols., same date. Another edit., with Supplement, 3 vols., fol., dated 1701-27
> *DNB* gives the date as 1705-21, and states that it was adapted from Louis Moreri. Its
> omnibus character makes difficult its listing.

1730 LAMBARDE, WILLIAM. For his *Topographical Dictionarie,* see under DESCRIPTIONS.

1743 MARTIN, B. A Course of Lectures in Natural and Experimental Philosophy,
Geography and Astronomy: in which the Properties, Affections, and Phae-
nomena of Natural Bodies, hitherto discover'd are exhibited and explain'd on
the Principles of the Newtonian Philosophy. 10 folding plates. 4to. Reading.

1744 A Complete System of Geography (that part which relates to Great Britain and
Ireland). Fol. London.

DODSLEY, ROBERT, and J. COWLEY. The Geography of England: Done in the Manner of Gordon's Geographical Grammar, . . . To each County is Prefix'd a
compleat Mapp from the Latest and Best Observations, shewing the Chief
Towns, Parks, Rivers and Roads, both direct and across. Also a Separate Mapp
of England, of the Roads, of the Channel, and a Plan of London. . . . 55 engraved maps. 8vo. London.

Another edit., with a change of title and without maps, London, 1765. See below.
The introduction gives a view of the constitution of England, and of every branch of legislature.

1765   DODSLEY, ROBERT. The Geography and History of England, done in the Manner of Gordon's and Salmon's Geographical and Historical Grammars. London.

1744-47   BOWEN, EMANUEL. A Complete System of Geography, being a Description of all the Countries, Islands, Cities, . . . of the known World. Maps of Great Britain, Ireland and Scotland. 2 vols. Fol. London.

Other editions followed. Vol. I contains description of Great Britain and Ireland that is better than usual with such works.—Gough, 27.

1759   The Philosophical Geography of Scotland. (Place?)

1765   PINKERTON, —. The Geography of England. 8vo. London.

I am unable to identify this Pinkerton. The John Pinkerton associated with Scottish Ballads and the Collection of Voyages was born in 1758.

1780   GOUGH, RICHARD. An Essay on the Rise and Progress of Geography in Great Britain and Ireland, illustrated with Specimens of our oldest Maps. 4to. London.

The Geographer of Ravenna. In a collection of tracts entitled *Antiquities,* listed under HISTORY AND ANTIQUITIES.

1786   PTOLEMY. British Topography by Ptolemy. In a collection of tracts entitled *Antiquities,* listed under HISTORY AND ANTIQUITIES.

1797   MACPHERSON, DAVID. Geographical Illustrations of Scottish History, containing the Names and Places mentioned in Chronicles, Histories, Records, etc., with Corrections of the difficult disputed Points in the Historical Geography of Scotland; the Names being alphabetically arranged, with Reference to their Position in the Historical Map of Scotland, which accompanies this work; together with a Compendious Chronology of the Battles to the Year 1603; collected from the Best of Authorities, Historical and Geographical. London.

Reviewed *Gent. Mag.,* vol. 67, 48-49. Scotland has had no Camden to illustrate her antiquities and historical geography with such illumination as has favored England. The design of this work is laudable, but a better undertaking would have been to improve Camden's account in the new edition of his work.—From the review.

1876   THOMAS, FREDERICK WM. L. An Analysis of the Ptolemaic Geography of Scotland. 1 plate. In *Proc. Soc. Antiq. Scot.,* vol. 2, 198-225. Edinburgh.

1885   BRADLEY, HENRY. Ptolemy's Geography of the British Isles. In *Archaeologia,* vol. 48, 379-96. London. (See under MAPS AND CHARTS.)

WEBSTER, H. A. What has been done for the Geography of Scotland, and What remains to be done. Paper read at the Brit. Assoc., Aberdeen, 1885. In *Scot. Geog. Mag.,* vol. 1, 487. Edinburgh.

1894   MACBAIN, ALEXANDER. Ptolemy's Geography of Scotland. Map. In *Trans. Gaelic Soc. of Inverness,* vol. 6, 267-88. Inverness.

XIII

Expeditions

(Those who took part in foreign forays were more likely to be struck with the peculiarities of the countryside, with the appearance of cities, with the differences in ways of life than were those to whom these things were the natural environment. If they do nothing else, at least they record itineraries.)

1523 FROISSART, JEAN. The Cronycles of Sir John Froissart, translated oute of the Frenche by John Bourchier Knyghte, Lord Berners. London.

> This work gives accounts of French military expeditions to Scotland. Extracts recording these are printed in Hume Brown's *Early Travellers in Scotland*. See below. For more detail on Froissart see under HISTORY AND CHRONICLE.

> 1891 FROISSART, JEAN. Extracts from his Chronicles dealing with Scottish Matters. From vols. I, ch. 17, and II, chs. 2 and 3. *Early Travellers in Scotland*, 7-15. Edinburgh.
> These selections treat of the Scotch on their military expeditions and of a French army in Scotland in the time of Robert II. The opinion of the country and its people held by Froissart, as well as by the French knights, was pretty low. The latter were much put out by the kind of accommodations purveyed them while in the country, and no wonder, for they nearly starved. The independent behavior of the Scotch peasantry, they noted, was in marked contrast with the servility of the French "jacques." The troops left Scotland cursing loud and full.

1544 HERTFORD, EARL OF. The Late Expedicion in Scotlande made by the Kynges Highnys Armye, under the Conduct of the Ryght Honourable the Erle of Hertforde, the Yere of our Lorde God 1544. 8vo. London.

> This narrative was largely incorporated in Grafton's *Chronicle*, 1563. Reprinted in Dalyell, *Fragments of Scottish History*, Edinburgh, 1798. Also in *Rare and Curious Collections of Historical Tracts and Pamphlets*, Edinburgh, 1886. In *Tudor Tracts* (*An English Garner*), edit. by A. F. Pollard, Westminster, 1903.
> This expedition was a manifesto to Scotland that England could be a more uncomfortable enemy than France, and also a species of revenge for Scotland's repudiation of Henry VIII's treaty. The account deals mainly with the progress of the army, its burnings and battles, but it offers some information on conditions in oft beleaguered Scotland.

1548 PATTEN, WILLIAM. The Expedicion into Scotlande of the most woorthely fortunate Prince Edward, Duke of Soomerset, vncle vnto our most noble Souereign . . . Edvvard VI, Goovernour of hys Hyghnes Persons, and Protectour of hys Graces Realmes, Dominions and Subiectes: made in the first Yere of hys Maiesties most prosperous Reign, and set out by way of Diarie, by W. Patten, Londoner. Woodcut initials and 3 full page view maps. 8vo. London.

> Patten's narrative was quoted by Holinshed almost verbatim, 1577; it was followed by Sir John Hayward in his *Life and Reign of Edward VI*, 1630. Reprinted in Dalyell *Fragments of Scottish History*, 1798; in Arber's *English Garner*, 1880; in *Tudor Tracts*, 1903. A French account was given in J. B. A. Teulet's *Papiers d'Etat . . . relatifs à l'histoire de l'Ecosses*, vol. I, Paris 1852.
> This expedition was a renewal of the attempt by Protector Somerset to effect the union of Scotland and England by a marriage between Queen Mary and Edward VI. Though the Scots suffered a most disastrous defeat at Musselburgh (1548), the English failed to gain their object. Patten was an important personage whom the Earl of Warwick made one of the judges to administer martial law in the provost marshal's court. He accompanied the expedition into Scotland as did also William Cecil, afterwards Lord Burghley. In his account he obtained some aid from Cecil's notes.

1556 BEAUGUE, JEAN DE. For an account of an expedition to Scotland, see his *Histoire de la Guerre d'Ecosse*, under TOURS BY FOREIGNERS.

1589 ADAMS, ROBERT. Expeditionis Hispanorum in Angliam vera Descriptio. Anno
      Do.; MDLXXXVIII. London.

> Cited in Fordham's *Carto-Bibliography*. It contains very interesting and artistic maps
> showing the English and Spanish fleets and their engagements in the Channel, followed by
> a chart of the whole course of the Armada round the British Isles. A good specimen of
> native work.—Fordham. See this same under MAPS AND CHARTS.

1660 MANLEY, T. Iter Carolinum; being a Succinct Relation of the necessitated
      Marches, Retreats, and Sufferings of his Majesty Charles the First (Jan. 1642-
      49). London.

> Reprinted in Gutch's *Collectanea Curiosa* (see under 1781, HISTORY AND ANTIQUITIES);
> in *Somers' Tracts*, vol. V, edit. by Scott, 1809-15; and (down to 1647) from the original
> MS in Hereford Library, in *Royal Revelations*, by H. S. Wheatley-Crowe, London, 1922.
> This gives the places where Charles stayed and the length of time he spent in each.

      WILD, ROBERT. Iter Boreale. Attempting Something upon the Successful and
      Matchless March of the Lord General George Monck, from Scotland to Lon-
      don, by a Rural Pen. 4to. London.

> Another edit., 4to, London, 1660; with additional poems, 12mo, 1665; again 12mo, Lon-
> don, 1668. See below.
> This poem received high praise from contemporaries, among them Dryden and Pepys.
> —From Maggs, no. 598.

> 1605 (for 1665) WILD, ROBERT. Iter Boreale. Together with some Select Poems, not here-
> tofore printed. 12mo. London.

1723 SKINNER, THOMAS. Life of General Monk, from an Original Manuscript of
      Thomas Skinner in which is a very Particular Account of that most Memorable
      March, from Coldstream to London, etc.; with an Account of the Manuscript
      and some Observations in Vindication of General Monk's Conduct, by William
      Webster. 8vo. London.

> 2nd edit., corrected, 8vo, London, 1724.

1746 Journal of an English Medical Officer who attended the Duke of Cumberland's
      Army as far north as Inverness, during the Time of the Rebellion. London (?).

> Reprinted in *The Contrast*: etc., 8vo, London, 1825. See below.

> 1825 The Contrast: Scotland as it was in the Year 1745 and Scotland in the Year 1819.
> 8vo. London. (See under 1825, SURVEYS.)

174– Ascanius, or the Young Adventurer, a True History. Translated from a Manu-
      script privately handed about at the Court of Versailles. Containing a Particular
      Account of all that happened to a certain Person, during his Wanderings in the
      North. . . . 8vo. London.

> Another edition (?), 24mo, Edinburgh, 1802. See below.

> 1802 Ascanius, or the Young Adventurer; containing an Impartial History of the Re-
> bellion in Scotland, in the Years 1745-46. To which is added, A Journal of the
> Miraculous Adventures and Escapes of the Young Chevalier, after the Battle of
> Culloden. 1 plate and portrait. 24mo. Edinburgh.
> For a host of beautiful Scotch songs inspired by the adventures and glamorous
> person of the Young Chevalier, Prince Charles Edward Stuart, see Hogg's
> *Jacobite Relics*, 2 vols., 1819.

1747 A Journey through Part of England and Scotland along with the Army, under
      the Command of His Royal Highness the Duke of Cumberland; wherein the

Proceedings of the Army and the Happy Suppression of the Rebellion in the Year 1746 are particularly described, by a Volunteer, in several Letters to a Friend. 3rd edition. 12mo. London.

1749 RAY, JAMES. For an account of the expedition of the Duke of Cumberland against the Highlanders at Culloden, see his *A Compleat History of the Rebellion,* under TOURS BY NATIVES.

1789 CARTER, MATTHEW. A True Relation of the Expedition of Kent, Essex, and Colchester, in 1648. 2nd edition. (Bound up with Morant, *History and Antiquities of Colchester.* See under TOWNS, this date.)

1817 CHURCHYARD, THOMAS. The Siege of Edenbrough Castell in ye xv. Yeere of the Raygne of our Soueraigne Lady Queene Elizabeth, at which Seruice Sir William Drury, Knight, was Generall. . . . In Churchyard's *Chips concerning Scotland,* edit., by George Chalmers. 8vo. London.

Also in *Bann. Misc.,* vol. II, no. 19a, *Publ. Bann. Club,* Edinburgh, 1836. See Churchyard under 1585, DESCRIPTIONS.

1820 GRAHAM, JOHN (of Deuchrie). An Account of the Expedition of William the ninth Earl of Glencairn . . . in the Highlands of Scotland in the Years 1653 and 1654. 12mo. Glasgow.

Extracted from *Miscellanea Scotica,* vol. 4, Glasgow.

1822 GWYNNE, JOHN. Memories of the Civil War of the Expedition into the Highlands of Scotland, 1653-54, under the Earl of Glencairn, by an Eye-Witness. 4to. London.

1827 A Narrative of the Progress of King Edward I. in his Invasion of Scotland in the Year 1296. Communicated with some Observations thereon by Nicholas Harris Nicolas, Esq., F.S.A. In *Archaeologia,* vol. 23, 478-98. London.

Also in *Bann. Misc.,* vol. I, pt. ii, 263-82, Edinburgh, 1827; as an appendix to Tytler's *History of Scotland,* vol. I, 1828-43; in Hume Brown's *Early Travellers in Scotland,* 1891. For a variant title see the *Bann. Misc.* printing below.
The above account appears in several MSS, some in Latin, some in Norman French, and three in English. The Cottonian MS used by Nicolas seems to have been originally written in Norman French by one who accompanied the King. The account is mainly a list of the halting places of the army. Edward passed the Tweed on March 28, 1296, with an army estimated at 30,000 foot and 4,000 horse, and returned to Berwick after two weeks. Where he went, where and how long he stayed, the days of the events noted, and notices of sieges and submissions make up the record. The editor examines the dates, distances, agreement of names of places in MS with documents in the *Foedera,* the agreement of events mentioned in the MS with contemporary narratives, all with the idea of testing the veracity of the narrative.

1827 Diary of Edward the First (his) Journey into Scotland, in the Time of John, Kinge of Scottis, Anno regni 24, 1296. *Or otherwise*—The Voyage of Kinge Edward into Scotland with all his Lodgyngs expressed. In *Bann. Misc.,* vol. I, pt. ii. With introductory Note by Patrick F. Tytler. Edinburgh.

1829 TURNER, SIR JAMES. For an account of the expedition into Scotland in 1645 under Hamilton, see *Memoirs of his own Life and Times,* under LETTERS, DIARIES, MEMOIRS.

1830   ASHBURNHAM, JOHN. Narrative of his Attendance on King Charles The First
       from Oxford to the Scotch Army, and from Hampton-Court to the Isle of
       Wight: Never before Printed. To which is prefixed a Vindication of his Char-
       acter and Conduct from the Misrepresentations of Lord Clarendon. 2 vols. 8vo.
       London.

1839   Letter giving an Account of an Expedition of Edward III. (1336) to relieve the
       Beleaguered Countess of Athole and her Garrison in the Castle of Lochindorb.
       In Preface to *Ferrerii Historia Abbatum de Kynlos,* in *Publ. Bann. Club,* no.
       63. Edinburgh.

> Printed also in Stuart's *Records of the Monastery of Kinloss.* Edinburgh, 1872.
> This document gives an account of the king's route from Friday, July 7, 1336, when he
> set out from Perth by Blair Athole, to Glen Feshie and Kincardine in Strathspey, from
> which he crossed the moors to Lochindorb and raised the siege, thence to Kinloss, Forres,
> Elgin, Cullen, Fyvie, Aberdeen, and Dunottar to Forfar, which he reached July 21.—
> From Mitchell, *List of Travels.*

1841   MAXWELL, JAMES. A Narrative of Charles Prince of Wales's Expedition to Scot-
       land in the Year 1745. In *Publ. Maitland Club,* vol. 53. Edinburgh.

> Maxwell took part in the expedition.

1858   Edward I. of England in the North of Scotland: Being a Narrative of his Pro-
       ceedings in that Part of the Kingdom, with Historical and Topographical Re-
       marks. By a Member of the Literary and Scientific Association of Elgin. In
       Publ. of the Literary and Scientific Association of Elgin. Elgin.

1859   SYMONDS, RICHARD. For marches of the Royal Army during the Civil War, see
       Symond's *Diary,* under LETTERS, DIARIES, MEMOIRS.

1864   DINELEY, T. The Official Progress of . . . Henry . . . Duke of Beaufort through
       Wales in 1684. Edit. by C. Baker. 4to. London.

> Later edit., edited by R. W. Banks, 4to, London, 1888, with Dineley's MS reproduced in
> photolithography.
> Beaufort was Lord President of Wales from 1672 to 1689.

1868   Journal of a Soldier in the Earl of Eglinton's Troop of Horse, Anno 1689. In
       Publ. of the Glasgow Arch. Soc., vol. 1. Glasgow.

> This account illustrates military events in Scotland in 1689-90.

1893   A Military Expedition, 1568. In Hume Brown's *Scotland before 1700.* 8vo. Edin-
       burgh.

> A contemporary account, though still more brief, is to be found in Lord Herries'
> *Historical Memoirs of the Reign of Mary Queen of Scots,* Publ. of Abbotsford Club,
> vol. 6, Edinburgh, 1836; also published in *Bann. Misc.,* vol. II, no. 19, Publ. Bann. Club,
> Edinburgh, 1836.
> This account relates the progress, with interesting topographical details, made by the
> Regent Moray into the southern counties of Scotland, immediately after the Battle of
> Langside (June, 1568), to crush the Lords Herries, Maxwell, Fleming, and other sup-
> porters of Queen Mary who refused to acknowledge the new government.—Brown,
> *Scotland before 1700.* The expedition left in its progress the usual quantum of burnings
> and destruction.

1897   Itinerary of Prince Charles Edward Stuart from his Landing in Scotland, July
       1745, to his Departure in September 1746. Compiled from *The Lyon in Mourn-*

ing, supplemented and corrected from other contemporary Sources by Walter Bigger Blaikie. Map and 2 plates. *Publ. Scot. Hist. Soc.,* no. 23. 4to. Edinburgh.

1904   Narratives illustrating the Duke of Hamilton's Expeditions to England, 1648. *Misc. Scot. Hist. Soc.,* no. 44. Edinburgh.

1907   BRUCE, GAINSFORD. The English Expedition into Scotland in 1542. In *Arch. Aeliana,* vol. 3, 3rd ser., 191-212. Newcastle.

1910   ASTON, JOHN. For an account of his expedition to Scotland in the First Bishop's War, 1639, see his *Journal* under *Six North Country Diaries,* under LETTERS, DIARIES, MEMOIRS.

WHEELER, ADAM. Iter Bellicosum Adam Wheeler His Account of 1685. Edit. by Henry Elliot Malden, M.A. *Misc., Publ. Camden Soc.,* vol. 18, 3rd ser. London.

Wheeler took part in the campaign that put down Monmouth's Rebellion. He records the marches of the army of which he was a drummer in a regiment of foot, under the command of Col. John Windham. His title tells his story in outline: Iter Bellicosum, or a Perfect Relation of his Majesties Truely Loyal Subject and Magnanimous Souldier Colonel John Windham, Esq. With his Regiment of Foote into the Western Parts of England for the Suppressing of James Scot and his Accomplices in Theire Rebelious Insurrection, etc. Faithfully set down by Adam Wheeler, one of the Drums of his Honour's own Company. Anno Christo 1685. He begins his story at New Sarum, June 16, 1685, and from then on records the marches to the battlefield of Sedgemoor. His matter-of-fact narrative is now and then touched with suggestive incidents, such as his writing down names of prisoners on his drumhead as they passed by. He seems to have possessed some education, for he quotes Latin passages. He also gives some detail of the wounded prisoners and of the hanging of others.

XIV

History and Chronicle

(The development of the chronicle into history is the story of the English people awakening to a consciousness of their existence as a nation. In her *Caxton Mirrour of Fifteenth Century Letters,* Nellie Slayton Aurner has pointed out how the increasing interest in secular affairs and the rise of large religious foundations encouraged local and national historians, and led the way from the bare notation of dates and facts to the richly embroidered narratives of chroniclers like Geoffrey of Monmouth. The further shift of the chronicle from monastic hands, which were not above fabricating if it benefited some particular house, to secular historians more bent on glorifying royal figures and the life of cities, such as flowered so profusely in Tudor times, were indicative also of the spread of education and the growing power of the commercial classes. This interest was expanded by Caxton when he printed his two editions of the *Chronicles of England, A Description of Britain,* and Trevisa's translation of Higden's *Polychronicon,* with continuations of his own down to 1460. As faithful records of events, the chronicles are dubious; they reveal great industry, but indiscriminate credulity as well. Yet they are precious. For the historian they have preserved transactions and names of actors which might otherwise have sunk into the limbo of the forgotten; for the antiquary, names of places which have long since vanished from remembrance or become changed beyond recognition, and manners and customs of folk long laid to rest; and for the topographer, descriptions of lands and boundaries, together with cities and their buildings. The numerous histories succeeding the chronicles from the 16th century on gradually diverged, in their trend toward continuity and interpretation, from the pattern discernible in these chronicles, and in consequence have generally been omitted. The regional histories, such as those of counties and parishes, being more concerned with antiquities, genealogies of prominent families, records, and the like, and less with recounting transactions of the passing hour, have been considered as legitimate claimants to entries. As a rule, the latter are more likely to have occasioned a certain amount of travel on the part of the writer, though they exhibit little evidence of personal reactions.)

1475 (?) BEDE. Historia Ecclesiastica Gentis Anglorum. Strasburg.

An edit., Antwerp, 1565 (sometimes called the 1st edit.); translated into English by Thomas Stapleton, Antwerp, 1565; Latin text edit. by J. Commelin, *Rerum Britannicarum,* Heidelberg, 1587 (see this date below); edit., with the Alfredian version, by A. Whelock, 2 vols., Cambridge, 1643-44; by J. Smith, also with Alfredian version, Cambridge, 1722 ("a monument of learning and scholarship"); by Jos. Stevenson, Eng. Hist. Soc., 2 vols., London, 1841; by J. A. Giles, with translation, *Patres Ecclesiae Anglicanae,* London, 1843-44; translated by Giles, *Bohn's Antiquarian Library,* London, 1847; Latin edit. by Charles Plummer, 2 vols., Oxford, 1896; Alfredian version by T. Miller, E.E.T.S., London, 1890-98; reprint of Stapleton's translation by P. Hereford, Oxford, 1930. A Middle Irish version of the first two books edit. by Osborn Bergin, *Anecdota from Irish MSS.,* vol. III, Dublin, 1910; this edit. with translation, notes, and glossary by Edward G. Cox, *Studies in Language and Literature in Honor of J. M. Hart,* New York, 1910.

It seems fitting that the Venerable Bede, the "father of English history," with whose version by Alfred so many students begin their study of Old English, should head this list. This history, completed 731, tells the story of the conversion to Christianity of the Saxon tribes and the struggle between the Roman and Irish forms of church ritual. Its account of British history is derived from Gildas' *De Excidio* and other native writers. But the best parts are his own.

1643 BEDE. Historiae Ecclesiasticae Gentis Anglorum Libri V. A Venerabili Beda Presbytero scripti; tribus praecipue MSS. Latinis, a mendis haud paucis repurgati: Ab Augustissimo veterum Anglo-Saxonum Rege Aluredo (sive Alfredo) examinati . . . . Ecclesiae Anglicanae Homiliis . . . E Bibliotheca Publica Cantabrigiensi, edit. A. Whelock. Fol. Cantabrigiae.

1930 BEDE. The History of the Church of Englande. Compiled by Venerable Bede, Englishman. Translated out of Latin into English by Thomas Stapleton. First printed in Antwerp by John Laet anno 1565. Edit. P. Hereford. Newly printed at the Shakespeare Head Press. 4to. Oxford.

1480 Chronicles of England. Printed by Caxton. London.

> Edit. for E.E.T.S. by Fr. Brie, orig. ser., vols. 131, 136. London, 1906-08.
> This is also known as Caxton's Chronicle. Its popularity is attested by the thirteen editions that appeared between 1480 and 1528. It calls for notice by the fact that it was written in English for the ordinary layman by some one who was totally unrelated to a monastery or university (C. L. Kingsford, *The First English History of Henry V*). It is an English version of the *Brut,* a history of Britain from mythical times. The original French text is in two recensions, the longer of which ends 1333. Towards the end of the 14th century it was turned into English, with a continuation to 1377, which in turn was extended in two more continuations, the first to 1419, and the second to 1460. The latter was the one taken up by Caxton.—Nellie Slayton Aurner, *Caxton Mirrour of Fifteenth Century Letters.*

ROLEWINCK, W. Chronica que dicit[ur] Fasciculus Temporum edita et [per] quenda[m] carthusiensem. Nunc secundo emendata cum quibusdam additionibus usque ad hoc nostra tempora. Woodcut views of towns (Venice, Antioch, Britannia, Byzantium, Syracuse, etc.). Fol. Venetiis impressa cura impensisque Erhardi Ratdolt de Augusta.

> This interesting and very scarce volume is one of the principal books from which Caxton borrowed his materials for his Polychronicon. Rolewinck was a Carthusian monk who first brought this chronicle down to 1470, and afterwards to 1484.—Bookseller's Note.

1482 HIGDEN, RANULPH. Polychronicon [sive historia polycratica, ab initio mundi usque ad mortem regis Edwardi III]. Printed by Caxton. Fol. London.

> 2nd edit., printed by Wynkyn de Worde, fol., London, 1495; 3rd edit., printed by Peter Treveris, fol., London, 1527; the Latin text, edit. by Thomas Gale, in *Historiae Britannicae, Saxonicae, . . . scriptores XV,* fol., London, 1691 (see Gale this date below); the Latin text and Trevisa's translation, and one by an unknown writer of the 15th century, in Rolls Series, edit. by C. Babington and J. R. Lumby, 9 vols., 8vo, London, 1865-86. See below.
> Higden was a monk of the monastery of St. Werberg in Chester, who died before 1360. His chronicle was compiled from a Latin work, with many additions, by Roger, a monk of the same monastery. Like the majority of such histories, it gives a universal account of the world, but its English portions are important for their presentation of the historical, geographical, and scientific knowledge of the times and their pictures of social conditions. It was turned into English in 1387 by John of Trevisa, chaplain to the Earl of Berkeley. Caxton added another book, bringing the story down to 1460, at the same time rewriting the whole work to make it more attractive to readers. His preface, omitted in the Rolls edition, is a dialogue between a lord and a clerk on the need of translations into the vernacular. The lord insists on a prose version rather than a poetical one, "for communly prose is moore cleere than rhyme."

> 1495 HIGDEN, RANULPH. Polichronicon. A translacion of Ranulphus of Chestres bokes of Cronycles in to our Englysshe tongue by Johan Trevysa chapelayn unto Lorde Thomas of Barkley. Emprented by me Wynkyn de Worde and lytell embelysshed from tholde makynge. Fol. London.
> De Worde's addition to the work proper was the music on folio 101 (the earliest English example of music printing).—Quaritch, no. 592.

> 1527 ————. Polychronicon [in whiche Boke ben comprysed bryefly many Wonderfull Hystoryes. Fyrste ye descrypcyon of ye Unyuersal Worlde, as well in length as in brede . . . also the Hystorycal Actes and Wonderful Dedes syth ye fyrst makynge of Heuen and Erthe unto the begynnunge of Kynge Henry the Seventhe, etc., Englysshed by one John de Trevisa, Vycarye of Barkley, whiche at requeste of one Syr Thomas Lord Barkley, translated this sayd Booke]. Woodcuts. Imprinted in Southwerke by me Peter Treueris at ye expences of John Reynes. Fol. London.
> A page-for-page reprint of Wynkyn de Worde's edition of 1495, with illustrations added, which makes it the first illustrated edition. It contains also the specimens of music found in the second edition.—Bookseller's Notes.

1502 ARNOLD, RICHARD. Arnold's London Chronicle. In this booke is Conteyned the names of ye baylifs Custos mairs and sherefs of the cite of london from the tyme of king richard the furst. and also thartycles of the Chartur and libarties

of the same Cyte. And of the chartur and Liberties off England wyth odur dyuers mat's good and necessary for euery Citezen to vndir stond and knowe. . . . Fol. Antwerp.

2nd edit., printed by Pynson with additions, London, 1521; an edit. reprinted from the first one, edited by Francis Douce, London, 1811.

This work was first called Arnold's "Chronicle" by Thomas Hearne, but it has little claim to that title. It contains a list of mayors and sheriffs, with brief historical notes, 1189-1502, and a collection of charters, municipal regulations, and other documents relating chiefly to London in the 14th and 15th centuries, with also miscellaneous information on a large variety of subjects. Every mention of the work unfailingly refers to the fact that it contains the famous ballad of "The Nutbrown Maid," of unknown authorship. The book was probably printed by Adrian van Berghen.—Bookseller's Note.

1811 ARNOLD, RICHARD. The Customs of London, containing, among Divers Other Matters, the Original of the Celebrated Poem of the Nut-Brown Maid. Reprinted from the First Edition (edited by Francis Douce). 4to. London.

1508 GEOFFREY OF MONMOUTH. Historia Britonum Britanniae utriusque regum et principum Origo et gesta insignia. Ab Galfrido Monumetensi ex antiquissimis Britannici sermonis monumentis in latinum sermonem traducta: et ab Ascensio cura impendio magistri Iuonis Cauellati in lucem edita. 4to. Paris.

Printed again, Paris, 1517; edit. by J. Commelin, *Rerum Britannicarum,* Heidelberg, 1587; translated into English by Aaron Turner, 8vo, London, 1718; edit. by J. A. Giles in facsimile, London, 1842; translated by Giles in *Six Old English Chronicles,* London, 1848; edit., with a translation of a Welsh text, by A. Griscom and R. E. Jones, 8vo, London, 1929. See below.

This most famous of the early chronicles is a Latin prose work based upon material drawn from Nennius and other native British, English, and Latin authors, knit together with weavings from the author's own observations and fertile imagination. As a popularizer of the "Matter of Britain," that is, the Arthurian legends, it is the most significant production of medieval times. In less than fifty years after its appearance, the age had come to know of Lancelot, Percival, the Holy Grail, the Round Table, Tristan, Merlin, the Forest of Broceliande, Modred, the guilty love of Guinevere, etc. It also exercised a powerful influence in unifying the English peoples through the legend of a common origin of Briton, French, and Teuton. The *Historia* was turned into Anglo-Norman verse by Geoffrey Gaimar; freely paraphrased by Robert Wace, and, much enlarged, made over into English by Layamon. Geoffrey's life spanned the years 1100-1155.

1718 GEOFFREY OF MONMOUTH. The British History, translated into English from the Latin of Jephrey of Monmouth. With a large Preface concerning the Authority of the History. By Aaron Turner. London.

1929 ————. The Historia Regum Britanniae, with Contributions to the Study of its Place in Early British History, by Acton Griscom, together with a literal Translation of the Welsh MS. No. LXI, of Jesus College, Oxford, by R. E. Jones. 16 photographs of MSS. 8vo. London.

The opening chapters of this volume give a spacious account of MSS, the Welsh texts, and Geoffrey's position in English history, all of which are fortified with the critical apparatus of modern scholarship. The work is distinguished by (1) presenting the first accurate Latin text of the MSS; (2) giving the first literal translation of one of the surviving Welsh chronicles dealing with the same early history; and (3) discussing Geoffrey's claim to have had and translated an ancient British book. The editor points out that the charges against Geoffrey, such as romancing, inventing, making fictions, falling back upon an active imagination, have held too long, and have delayed the true appreciation of the many historic details wherein he was faithful to events. One reason for this lies in the fact that up to now there has been no reasonably critical or accurate text of the *Historia* printed. The MSS number 190, located in more than 49 different libraries and private collections of 11 countries. None of the existing Welsh MSS represents exactly, or perhaps even closely, the *vetustissimus liber* itself. Of the 58 such MSS, only three have been printed and only one translated.—The Latin text used here is from a MS in the University Library, Cambridge, No. 1706, old number II. i. 14.—From the Introduction.

1516   FABYAN, ROBERT. Fabyan's Cronycle, which he nameth the concordance of histories, newly prynted with the Cronycle, Actes and Dedes done in the Tyme of
. . . Henry VII. . . . Printed by Pynson. Fol. London.

> Other edits., in 1533, 1542, and 1559. Edit. by Henry Ellis, 4to, London, 1811. See below.
> From the accession of Richard I this work takes the form of a London chronicle, and as
> such it has considerable importance. His account of the reigns of Edward IV and Richard
> III is not without value, but it is chiefly as a forerunner of Hall and Holinshed that his
> work deserves recognition.—Maggs, no. 670. The history had its usual continuations by
> other hands. Fabyan, a well-to-do London citizen, was sheriff of the city in 1493.

> 1559   FABYAN, ROBERT. The Chronicle of Fabian, whiche he nameth the concordaunce of
> histories, newly perused. And continued from the beginnyng of Kyng Henry the
> seuenth, to thende of Queene Mary, 1559. 2 vols. in 1. Fol. London.

> 1811   ————. The New Chronicles of England and France, in Two Parts; by Robert
> Fabyan. Named by himself the Concordance of Histories. Reprinted from Pyn-
> son's Edition of 1516. The First Part collated with the editions of 1533, 1542, and
> 1559; and the Second with a Manuscript in the author's own time, as well as the
> subsequent editions; including the different continuations. To which are added a
> Biographical and Literary Preface, and an Index, by Henry Ellis. 4to. London.

1521   MAJOR, JOHN. Historia Maioris Britanniae, tam Angliae quam Scotiae, per Ion-
nem Maiorem nomine quidem Scotum professione autem theologum e veterum
monumentis concinnata. Venundatur J. B. Ascensio. 4to. Paris.

> An edit., Edinburgh, 1740; translated into English by A. Constable, *Publ. Scot. Hist.
> Soc.*, no. 10, Edinburgh, 1892.
> For an estimate of his descriptions, see Major this date under DESCRIPTIONS. Major
> lectured at the Sorbonne on scholastic divinity, 1505; on philosophy and logic at St. An-
> drews University, 1522. He returned to Paris, where he taught six years, and then went
> back to St. Andrews in 1531.

1523-25   FROISSART, JOHN. The Cronycles of Sir John Froissart, translated oute of the
Frenche by John Bourchier Knyghte, Lorde Berners. London.

> French original, 4 vols. in 3, fol., Paris, 1514. A reprint of the 1525 edi:., 2 vols., 4to,
> London, 1812; translated with variations and additions, by Thomas Johne;, 2 vols., 8vo,
> London, 1857; another issue, 2 vols., 1868; in Tudor Translations, 6 vols., London, 1801;
> Shakespeare Head Press, 8 vols., Oxford, 1927; Everyman's Library, London, 1906. See
> below.
> This work deals principally with events from 1326 to 1400 in France, England, and
> Flanders, though it presents also much information of value on other parts of Europe.
> Lord Berners' translation was undertaken at the suggestion of Henry VIII and was dedi-
> cated to him. Its style is remarkably vivid and clear, and, although Berners introduces
> French words here and there, he has adhered so closely to the English idiom as to give the
> work the character of an original English product. It set going the taste for historical
> reading and composition, by which the later literature of the century is characterized.
> Fabian, Hall, and Holinshed were all indebted to him.—Maggs, no. 636. Froissart was first
> heard of in England as secretary to Philippa of Hainault; he was introduced to the court
> of David II of Scotland in 1364; in 1368 he was present at the nuptials of Lionel Duke of
> Clarence. A copy of his Chronicle intended for a son of Edward III was intercepted by
> the Duke of Anjou. He finished the second volume in 1388. In 1390 he was in Flanders,
> where apparently he was at work rewriting his history. He revisited England in 1394. In
> 1399 he had occasion to mourn the death of his benefactor Richard II. He himself died
> in 1410 or 1420. See Froissart under DESCRIPTIONS for further account.

> 1812   FROISSART, JOHN. Chronicles of England, France, Spain, Portugal, Scotland, Brit-
> tany, Flanders, and the Adjoining Countries; translated from the original French,
> at the Command of King Henry the Eighth, by John Bouchier, Lord Berners.
> Reprinted from Pynson's Edition of 1523 and 1525; With the Names of Places
> and Persons Carefully Corrected. To which are added A Memoir of the Trans-
> lator, and a Copious Index to the Work. 2 vols. 4to. London.

> 1514   (French Original.) Chroniques. Le premier volume de froissart De:, croniques de
> france, dangleterre, descoce, despaigne, de bretagne, de gascongne, de flandres et
> lieux circonuoisins. 4 vols. in 3. Fol. Paris.

1525   GILDAS. De Excidio et Conquestu Britanniae. 8vo. London.

This first edition printed by Polydore Vergil; another by John Josseline, 8vo, London, 1569 (said to be more accurate); edit. by the "Heidelberg Writers" in *Rerum Britannicarum,* fol., Heidelberg, 1587; reprint of 1st edit., Paris, 1610; 1st English translation by Habington, London, 1638; the English version again, 12mo, London, 1652; edit. by Thomas Gale, in *Historiae Britanniae,* fol., London, 1691 (said to be the most accurate so far); by the English Hist. Soc., London, 1838 (said to be the worst); translated by J. A. Giles, London, 1841; edit. by Petrie and Sharpe (based on Gale's edition and collated with two other MSS), under direction of Monumenta Historica Britannica, London, 1848; edit. by Hadden and Stubbs in the series *Councils and Ecclesiastical Documents,* London, 1869; by Theodore Mommsen in *Monumenta Germanica Historica,* 1894; by Professor Williams, *Cymmrodorion Record Series,* London, 1899. See below.

The dates of birth and death of this first British historian are in doubt. The date of the *Excidio* is placed tentatively at 547. In "Notes on the Excidio Britonum," *Celtic Review,* vol. I, no. 4 (1905), A. W. Wade-Evans argues that the *Excidio,* which is generally prefixed to the *Epistolae,* was not the work of Gildas, but is to be dated *ca.* 700. This view is not generally held, I believe. The historical value of this book "depends upon the absence of better authorities." The only MSS extant are two in the University Library, Cambridge. His account of the triumph of the Saxons and his deeply rooted conviction of the weakness of his countrymen reveal irritation and sadness. He seems to have retired to Brittany and there to have written his book, which is full of religious harrangues and tirades. See Harrison, *Bibliography of the Great Stone Monuments of Wiltshire.*

1568   GILDAS. Gildae, cui cognomentum est Sapientis, de Excidio et Conquestu Britanniae, ac flebili castigatione in reges, principe et sacerdotes epistola, vetustissimorum exemplariorum auxilio non solum a mendis plurimis vindicata, sed etiam accessione eorum quae in prima editione a Polydoro Vergilio resecta erant, multipliciter aucta. 8vo. London.

The editor of this edition, which is more complete and more accurate than that of Vergil, was John Josseline, secretary to Archbishop Parker.

1638   ————. The Epistle of Gildas the most ancient British Author: who flourished in the Yeere of our Lord, A.D. 546. And who by his great Erudition, Sanctitie, and Wisdome, acquired the Name of Sapiens. Faithfully translated out of the Original Latin. 12mo. London.

The translator was Thomas Habington, who was imprisoned for complicity in Babington's plot, 1586. His translation was reprinted in 1641.

1652   ————. A Description of the State of Great Britain, written eleven hundred Yeares since. 12mo. London.

What relation this version bears to Habington's I have not been able to discover.

1527   BOECE, HECTOR. Scotorum Historiae a prima gentis origine, cum aliarum & rerum & gentium illustratione non vulgari: praemissa epistola nuncupatoria, tabellisque amplissimis, & non poenitenda Isagogue quae ab huius tergo explicabuntur diffusius. Quae omnia impressa quidem sunt Iodici Badii Ascensi typis & opera: impensis autem Nobilis & praedocti viri Hectoris Boethii Deidonani: a quo sunt & condita & edita. Fol. Paris.

Reprinted with augmentation of two more books (XVIII and XIX) by John Ferrier, fol., Paris, 1574 (probably 2nd edit.); translated into Scots by John Bellenden, fol., Edinburgh, 1536, an English version by Wm. Harrison (completed by Thynne) of the description of Scotland, in Holinshed's *Chronicles,* fol., London, 1577; used by Leslie, *De Origine Scotorum* (see below), Rome, 1578; a metrical version by Wm. Stewart, *ca.* 1530, edit. by W. B. Turnbull, under another title, 3 vols., 8vo, in Rolls Series, London, 1858. Translated into Italian by Petruccio Ubaldini, Antwerp (or London?), 1588. Selections in Hume Brown, *Scotland before 1700,* Edinburgh, 1893. See below.

The dedication of this work to James V is dated 1st April, 1526. Boece was a disciple of the new learning. His concern was to present his subject in the most attractive style of which it was capable. His literary conscience shows itself not so much under the pressure to ascertain and relate facts as they were, but as under the desire to adapt his narrative to what he knew to be the tastes and prepossessions of his readers, with whom he seems to be in perfect accord even when relating his most incredible stories. He wanted to show that Scotland and its people had a history that was not below that of any other nation in point of interest and antiquity. As a result he is responsible for the extraordinary notions regarding Scotland which were current in England and on the continent till at least the close of the 17th century. In England he was made known through the description by Har-

rison included in Holinshed. And it was from Boece, as presented in Holinshed, that Shakespeare drew the plot for *Macbeth* as well as those vivid touches of local color found in that tragedy. Through the translation into French by Nicholas d'Arfeville, the work found wide currency on the continent.

1574 BOECE, HECTOR. Scotorvm Historiae a prima gentis origine, cum Aliarum et rerum et gentium illustratione non vulgari Libri XIX. Duo postremi huius Historiae libri nunc primum emittuntur in lucem. Accessit et huiĉ editioni eiusdem Scotorum Historiae continuatio, per Ionnannem Ferrium. Fol. Paris.

1858 ———. The Buik of the Chroniclis of Scotland; or a Metrical Version of the History of Hector Boece, by W. Stewart, edit. by W. B. Turnbull. Rolls Series. 3 vols. London.
   This is the first printing of this version.

1529 RASTELL, JOHN. The pastyme of People. The Cronycles of dyuers realmys and most specyally of the realme of England. Briefly compiled, and imprinted in Cheapside by John Rastell. Full-page woodcuts, and numerous small cuts in the text and margins. Fol. London.

   Reprinted, London, 1811.
   A most interesting and important book in the history of English printing and illustration. The work is best known for the eighteen full-page woodcuts of English kings from William the Conqueror to Richard III. These cuts, which must have been done especially for the book, are executed with particularly bold lines both for outline and shading, and are, we believe, unique in style. The book is extremely rare.—Quaritch, no. 562.

1530 CAESAR, JULIUS. Julius Caesar's Commentaryes. Newly translated owte of laten into Englyshe, as much as concerneth thys realme of England sumtyme callys Brytayne: which is the eldest hystoryer of all other that can be found, that euer wrote of thys realme of England. *Colophon,* Here endyth the commentarye of Julius Cesar as towchynge Brytayne now callys Englande. Cum privilegio. Fol. London.

   This translation was made by John Tiptoft, Earl of Worcester, and the impression is attributed to John Rastell.—Britwell Catalogue. The original text is printed on each side of the page. The eight books of the Commentaries were translated by Arthur Golding in 1565. The Latin text was printed 1585, followed by later editions. Several translations were done in the seventeenth century. Books IV and V describe his two expeditions to Britain and give many particulars about the inhabitants.

1534 VERGIL, POLYDORE. Historiae Anglicae libri viginti septem. Basel.

   2nd edit., bringing the history down to 1509, Basel, 1546; 3rd edit., bringing the history down to 1538, Basel, 1555; another, Basel, 1556; 5th edit., 2 vols., Ghent, 1556-57; 6th, Basel, 1570; 7th, 8vo, edit. by Thysius (who forgot the reign of Henry VIII, and then prefixed it to the whole with an apology), 8vo, Lyon, 1651; with additions, Leyden, 1751; 3 books (Henry VI, Edward IV, and Richard III), edit. by Sir Henry Ellis, *Publ. Camden Soc.,* vol. 29, London, 1844; 3 more vols. were proposed by Ellis bringing the history up to where the 1844 volume began, but only the first covering the Anglo-Saxon period was printed, *Publ. Camden Soc.,* vol. 36, 1846.—
   Vergil attempted to live up to his ideal—"an History is a full rehearsal and declaration of things done, not a guess or divination," and produced an honest book, though he was abused by his contemporaries as "a disparager of English antiquities," probably because he divested Wales and its legends of romance. Like other chroniclers, he opens up with a description of England and Scotland, but he exhibits a more personal observation. He cannot forego all the wonders and marvels which made up the stock in trade of previous writers on England and Scotland, and which appear as late as Harrison's Description (in Holinshed, *Chronicles,* 1577). He rejects the exploits of Arthur, of Brennus, and of Brutus as fabulous, as well as much of the account by Geoffrey. His Scotchmen are flesh and blood, not brutes. He distinguishes between the Highlander and Lowlander; he praises English sheep for their wool; he finds plenty of game, though he doubts whether camels and elephants are to be included. The flavor of English meat is delightful, the beef is unexcelled. Englishmen are hospitable, fond of entertaining, valiant in war, and skillful in shooting. But the baser sort are rude enough in their treatment of foreigners.
   Vergil was sent by Pope Alexander VI to England in 1501 as subcollector of the tribute.

He was recommended to Henry VII, who requested him to do the history of England. He won the favor of many men of learning and rank within the court, and became naturalized in 1510. He died at Urbino, his native place, in 1555. See Introduction to the *Publ. Camden Soc.,* vol. 29, 1844.

1536 BELLENDEN, JOHN. Heir beginnis the hystory and Croniklis of Scotland, with the Cosmography & dyscription thairof. Compilit by the noble clerk maister Hector Boece channon of Aberdene. Translatit laitly in our vulgar and commoun langage be maister Johne Bellenden Archdene of Murray: And Imprentit in Edinburgh, be me Thomas Dauidson, prenter to the Kyngis nobyll grace. Com Privilegio. Fol. Edinburgh.

   Reprinted, Edinburgh, 1541 and 1585; in 2 vols, 4to, Edinburgh, 1821; edit. by R. W. Chambers and Edith C. Batho, *Scot. Text Soc.,* Edinburgh, 1938 (from the MS belonging to Pierpont Morgan, said to be the most accurate and primitive).
   Bellenden's Boece is extant in two versions. The first, best represented by the Auchinleck MS, shows the translation as it was presented to King James V in 1531. The printed edition differs in almost every sentence from the earlier version. It claims to be "newly correckit" by Boece himself, and some of the corrections do appear to have been made by the latter. It is evident also that Bellenden had a hand in the revision, and he seems to have been rewarded by the king for the presentation of a revised MS. Bellenden's Boece is one of the two or three most noteworthy examples of the noble Scottish prose of the 16th century uncontaminated by Southern English influence. See R. W. Chambers and Walter W. Seton, "Bellenden's Translation of the History of Hector Boece," *Scottish Historical Review,* vol. 17, Oct., 1919.

1543 HARDYNG, JOHN. The Chronicle of Ihon Hardyng, from the firste begynnyng of Englande, vnto the reigne of kyng Edward the fourth . . . And . . . a continuacion of the storie in prose to this our tyme, now first imprinted, gathered out of diuerse . . . autours . . . Londini Ex officina Richardi Graftoni. 4to. London.

   2nd edit., 1543; an edit. by Henry Ellis, London, 1812 (containing both Hardyng's version and Grafton's continuation); the part relating to Scotland in Hume Brown, *Early Travels,* taken from Ellis.
   Folio V contained the remark about Edward IV, "for the kyng was a man that loued both to see and feele a fayre woman," which was suppressed in the second and subsequent editions. The chronicle in its original form (Lancastrian) ended 1436; the version presented to Edward IV (Yorkist) extended to 1461. The Grafton form, which is in prose, goes on to 1543. The versions of the latter varied from these two original forms and from each other. The chronicle is said to be of little value.

1548 HALL, EDWARD. The Union of the two noble and illustrate Famelies of Lancastre & Yorke beeyng long in continual discension for the Croune of this noble Realme, with all the Actes done in bothe of the Tymes of the Princes, both of the one Linage and of the other, beginnyng at the Tyme of King Henry the Fowerth, the first Aucthor of this devision, and so successively proceadyng to the Reigne of the high and prudent King Henry the Eighth, the undubitate Flower and very Heire of the sayde Linages. London.

   The 1st edition of Hall was printed in 1542, but having been burnt by order of Queen Mary, only fragments survive. It was reprinted by Grafton as above in 1548 and 1550. Not reprinted until Henry Ellis brought out his edition, 4to, London, 1809; modern edit. by Charles Whibley, 2 vols., London, 1904. See below.
   The earlier portion of this chronicle is said to have been derived from Polydore Vergil. With Henry VIII it entered on familiar ground and reads like the record of an eye-witness.

   1809 HALL, EDWARD. Hall's Chronicle, containing the History of England, during the Reign of Henry the Fourth, and the succeeding Monarchs, to the end of the Reign of Henry the Eighth, in which are particularly described the manners and Customs of those Periods, carefully collated with the Editions of 1548 and 1550. 4to. London.

1904 —————. The Life of Henry the Eighth. Reprinted with Introduction by Charles Whibley. 2 vols. London.

1549 LANQUET, THOMAS. Cooper's Chronicle, conteynynge the whole discourse of the hystoreis as well of thys realme, as well as other countreis, with the Succession of theyr kynges, the tyme of theyr raigne, and what notable actes were done by them. London.

> This title is taken from the 1565 edition. The above work was left unfinished by Lanquet on his death in 1545, and was completed by Cooper and first printed in 1549. Another edition surreptitiously issued with additions by a third hand in 1559; Cooper published two more editions, under the title *Cooper's Chronicle,* 4to, 1560 and 1565.
> Lanquet was engaged on a general history, which he had brought down to A.D. 17. Cooper undertook to carry it on to the reign of Edward VI. His part was about three times as long as Lanquet's. Cooper started out in life as a tailor and ended up as Bishop of Lincoln. His great literary work was the *Thesaurus Linguae Romannicae et Britannicae . . . accessit Dictionarium Historicum et Poeticum,* known as *Cooper's Dictionary,* London, 1565.

1562 GRAFTON, RICHARD. An Abridgement of the Chronicles of England, gathered by Richard Grafton, Citizen of London. London.

> Other edits., London, 1563, 1564, 1570, and 1572. See below and also Grafton under 1565 and 1568 below.

> 1572 GRAFTON, RICHARD. An Abridgement of the Chronicles of Englande, newely corrected and augmented, to thys present Yere of our Lord, 1572. 8vo. London.
> This contains a list of the fairs and highways.

1565 GOLDING, ARTHUR (Translator). The Eight Books of Julius Caesar . . . with Exposition of the old Names of the Countries, Cities, etc. London.

GRAFTON, RICHARD. A Manuell of the Chronicles of England to this Yere 1565. London.

> Note the following title:

> 1566 GRAFTON, RICHARD. A Manuell of the Chronicles of England from the Creacion of the Worlde to this Yere of our Lorde, 1566. London.

STOW, JOHN. A Summarie of Englyshe Chronicles, conteyning the true Accompt of Yeres, wherein every Kyng of thei Realme of England began theyr Reygnes, how long they reigned, and what notable Thyngs have beene done durynge theyr Reygnes. London.

> Later edits., 1566, 1570, 1574, 1590.
> Stow's chronicles fall into three groups, each of which appeared in numerous editions. First, the *Summary,* as titled above; second, the *Abridgement of the Summary;* third, the *Chronicles* and *Annals.* For a description of these titles and editions of these groups, see Conyers Read, *Bibliography of British History,* p. 24.

> 1566 STOW, JOHN. The Summary of the Englyshe Chronicles abridged. London.
> Later edits., 1567, 1573, 1584, 1587, 1598, 1604, 1607, 1611, 1618. These later editions continued the history down to the year of publication.

> 1580 —————. The Chronicles of England, from Brute unto this Present Yeare of Christ, collected out of the most authenticall Authors, Records and other Monuments of Antiquitie, from the first Inhabitation untill this Present Yeare 1581. London.
> Rearranged as the *Annales of England,* London, 1592. Other edits., 1601, 1605; re-edited, with augmentation, by Edmond Howes, fol., London, 1615 and 1631.

> 1601 —————. Flores Historiarum, or Annals of England. 8vo. London.

1615 —————. The Annales, or, General Chronicle of England, begyn first by maister John Stow and after him continued and augmented with matters forreyne, and domestique auncient and moderne, unto the ende of this Present Yeere 1614, by Edmond Howes. Fol. London.

> A finely appreciative account of Stow's labors and sterling qualities and his struggles with poverty of such a nature that he had to become a licensed beggar, even after his great work had made him famous, is to be found in the "Stow Commemoration," *Trans. London and Middlesex Soc.*, n.s., vol. 7, 452 ff. The address was made by Charles W. F. Goss, F.S.A. Stow bought and collected, as far as he could, early printed books, parchments, charters, and manuscripts. Others he transcribed in full or copied in extensive extracts, thus attempting to salvage before it was too late materials for the history of England, which the dispersal of books resulting from the dissolution of the monasteries was threatening to overwhelm. His travels, which took him all over the country, were made on foot. His great ambition to compile the English chronicles *in extenso* was not to be realized. At his death the manuscript was ready in his desk. The fate and final disposal of that work as well as of other manuscripts have been lost to sight. For his survey of London, see under 1598, LONDON.

1567 MATTHEW OF WESTMINSTER. Flores Historiarum. Edit. by Stow. London.

> An edit., with added matter, Frankfurt, 1601; parts relating to affairs of Britain translated by C. D. Yonge, 2 vols., London, 1853; edit. by H. R. Luard for the Rolls Series, 3 vols., London, 1890.
> This author is a product of the imagination, to whom was assigned in a 15th century MS the above chronicle, which was in reality compiled by various writers at the abbeys of St. Albans and Westminster.—*DNB*. See below.

1601 MATTHEW OF WESTMINSTER. Flores Historiarum . . . praecipue de Rebus Britannicis ab exordio mundi usque ad annum 1307; et Chronicon ex Chronicis ab initio mundi ad 1118 auctore Florentio Wigorniensi, cui accessit continuatio ad annum 1141. Fol. Frankfurt.

1567-74 PARKER, MATTHEW (Archbishop, Editor). Chronicles. 4 vols. London.

> The chronicles edited are: Asser's *Alfred*; *Matthew Paris*; *Matthew of Westminster*; *Thomas Walsingham*. See below.

1571 PARIS, MATTHEW. Historia Major. Edit. by Archbishop Parker. London.

> An edit., fol., Zürich, 1589; again, 1606; edit. by Wm. Wats, with additions, fol., London, 1640; this last reprinted, Paris, 1644, and London, 1684; translated into French by A. H. Breholles, 9 vols., Paris, 1840-41; into English by J. A. Giles, London, 1849-53; edit. by H. R. Luard for the Rolls Series, London, 1866-69. See below.
> For the intricate relations of MSS, the respective shares of Roger of Wendover, Matthew Paris, and the reputed Matthew of Westminster as authors, see the Introduction by Luard to vol. I of his edition. Matthew Paris is regarded as one of the best of medieval historians for his vigor and integrity of mind that led him to a remarkable independence in his handling of delicate questions. In addition, his contacts with the leading personages of the day opened up to him the heart of historical and ecclesiastical transactions. His history covers the period from the Creation down to 1253. For his *Historia Minor*, see no. 44 of the Rolls Series under 1858 below.

1606 —————. Historia Major a Guilielmo Conquaestore, ad ultimum annum Henrici tertii. Fol. Tiguri (Zürich).

1640 —————. Matthaei Paris (Monachi Albanensis) Angli, Historia Major juxta exemplar Londinense, 1571, verbatim recusa et cum Rogeri Wendoveri, Willielmi Rishangeri, Authorisque Majori Minorique Historiis, Chronicisque fideliter collata . . . editore Willielmo Wats. Glossary and Index. Fol. London.

1568 GRAFTON, RICHARD. A Chronicle at large and meere History of the Affayres of Englande and Kinges of the same, deduced from the Creation of the Worlde, vnto the first Habitation of thys Islande; and so by contynuance vnto the first yere of the Reigne of our most deere and souereigne Lady Queene Elizabeth: collected out of sundry Aucthors. Fol. London.

> Reprinted in *A Collection of Reprints of Famous Chronicles*, edit. by Henry Ellis and others, 4to, London, 1807-12.

1572 LLWYD, HUMPHREY. Commentarioli Britannicae descriptionis fragmentum, auctore Humfredo Lhuyd, Denbyghiense, Cambro-Britanno. Hujus auctoris diligentiam et judicium lector admirabitur. 8vo. Coloniae Agrippinae.

> The original Latin edition of Llwyd's book was so full of errors that it was hardly intelligible. A new edition of it was published by the learned Moses Williams, with the pieces *De Mona Insula* and *De Britannica Arce,* which had been annexed to Sir John Price's *A Description of Cambria, now called Wales.*—Gough, *Anecdotes of British Topography,* 582-83. The above work was reprinted with separate title page at the end of John Lewis' *History of Great Britain,* fol., 1729.
> Llwyd, physician and antiquary, had retired to Denbigh in 1563 to practice medicine and study music and the arts. His fellow townsman Richard Clough, who had long resided in Antwerp, made him acquainted with the great geographer Ortelius, to whom, on his death bed, Llwyd sent the manuscript of the *Commentarioli* along with his maps of England and Wales. Ortelius describes Llwyd, in his *Theatrum Orbis Terrarum,* as "nobilis et eruditus vir." This work formed for Ortelius the chief source of his information on the British Isles, which he later utilized in the *Theatrum.* Llwyd died Aug. 3, 1568.

> 1573 LHUYD, HUMFREY. The Breuiary of Britayne, as this most noble, and renowned Iland, was of auncient time deuided into three Kingdomes, England, Scotland and Wales, Contaynyng a learned discourse of the variable state, and alteration thereof, vnder diuers, as wel natural, as forren princes, and Conquerors. Together with the Geographicall Description of the same, such as neither by elder, nor later Writers, the like hath been set foorth before. Written in Latin by Humfrey Lhuyd of Denbigh, a Cambre Britayne, and lately Englished by Thomas Twyne, Gentleman. 12mo. London.

> 1731 LLWYD, HUMPHREY. Britannicae Descriptionis commentariolum. Necnon de Mona Insula, et de Britannica Arce, sive Armamentario Romano disceptatio epistolaris. (Latin and Welsh.) 4to. London.

1573 PRICE, SIR JOHN. Historiae Britannicae Defensio. London.

> Later edits., 1697, 1702, 1774, and 1812.
> This work was written in 1553 and published by the author's son Richard in 1573. In part it was a protest against Polydore Vergil's history of England, which had tended to deflate Welsh romance. Price entered the Inns of Court and became one of Cromwell's agents in the Visitation of 1535. For his *Description of Cambria,* see under 1584, DESCRIPTIONS.

1574 WALSINGHAM, THOMAS. Chronicon Angliae, ab Anno Domino 1328 usque ad Annum 1388, auctore monacho quodam Sancti Albani. Edit. by Stow. London.

> Edit. by Camden, *Anglica, Normannica . . . Scripta,* Frankfort, 1602 and 1603; edit. by Sir E. M. Thompson for the Rolls Series, London, 1874. See below.
> This monk and historian, contemporary with Chaucer, was precentor and superintendent of the scriptorium of St. Albans Abbey. His other works include *Ypodigma Neustriae,* a record of events in Normandy, completed in 1419, and perhaps *Historia Anglicana* from 1272 to 1422. He is our chief authority for Richard II, Henry IV, and Henry V.—*DNB.* The earlier portion of the above work was compiled from other chroniclers, mainly from Hemingburgh, Higden, etc. The contemporary years of 1377-1422 have original value, especially for the career of Wyclif, Wat Tyler's rebellion, and other events of the reign of Richard II.—Gross, *The Sources and Literature of English History.*

> 1602 WALSINGHAM, THOMAS. Historia brevis ab Edwardo I ad Henricum V. Edit. by Camden. Frankfort.

1577 HOLINSHED, RAPHAEL. The Chronicles of England, Scotland, and Ireland. Conteyning the Description and Chronicles of England, from the first inhabiting unto the Conquest. Until this present time 1577. The Description and Chronicles of Scotland, from the first Originall of the Scottes Nation, till the yeare of our Lorde 1571. The description and Chronicles of Yreland, like wise from the firste Originall of that Nation, vntil the yeare 1547. Faithfully gathered and set forth, by Raphaell Holinshed. Numerous woodcuts. 2 vols. Fol. London.

2nd edit., augmented and continued, 3 vols. in 2, fol., London, 1587; a poor reprint, 2 vols., 4to, Arbroath (date?); in 6 vols., 4to, London, 1807-08 (said to be good as a working copy in a library). The different volumes were printed separately. See below.

This is the best known set of chronicles for the English student. It excels its rivals in range of matter and is backed up by an extensive list of authorities. Hence it is of great value as a repertory of historical information. And its use as a source of plots for the Elizabethan dramatists is a commonplace of knowledge. Holinshed employed a staff of writers to assist him, assigning particular fields to each. He himself compiled the Historie of England drawing upon the usual sources. The Description of Scotland is "a simple Translation" made by Harrison from Hector Boece. The Historie of Scotland was made up from Boece, Major, and Jovius, and others. The Description of Ireland was entrusted to two Jesuits, Stanyhurst and Campion. Hooker provided the translation of Giraldus Cambrensis, which served as a chronicle for Ireland.—*Camb. Hist. Eng. Lit.,* vol. III. See this date under HISTORY AND ANNALS.

> 1587 HOLINSHED, RAPHAEL. [Chronicles.] The First and Second [and Third] Volumes of Chronicles, comprising: 1, The Description and Historie of England; 2, The Description and Historie of Ireland; 3, The Description and Historie of Scotland. First collected and published by Raphaell Holinshed, William Harrison, and others, now newlie augmented and continued (with manifold matters of singular note and worthie memory) to the yeare 1586 by Iohn Hooker alias Vowell, Gent., and others, . . . 3 vols. in 2 (the usual format). Fol. London.
>
> This revision of Holinshed was one of the chief labors of Hooker alias Vowell, who was also assisted by Francis Thynne. Many of the additions aroused the wrath of Elizabeth and resulted in a generous "castration" of passages. These passages were collected and issued in a separate volume in 1728. Stow likewise had a hand in the editing of this edition. Thynne has received notice for the material he collected for the edition of Chaucer which he left to Spight, printed in 1602.

1578 LESLIE, JOHN (Bishop). De origine, moribus et rebus gestis Scotorum libri decem, accessit nova et accurata regionum et insularum Scotiae, cum ejusdem tabula topographica, descriptio. Engraved map of Scotland, engraved plate with portrait of Mary Queen of Scots and her son James, and numerous other plates, containing genealogical portraits of Scottish kings. 4to. Rome.

> Another edit., 4to, Rome, 1675; English version, edit. by Thomas Thomson, *Publ. Bann. Club,* no. 38, Edinburgh, 1830; English version edit. by E. G. Cody and W. Murison, from Father James Dalrymple's translation of 1596, now first printed for Scot. Text Soc., 2 vols., Edinburgh, 1888-95. Selections printed by Hume Brown, *Scotland before 1700.* See below.
>
> Originally Leslie intended his history to be a supplement to that of Boece, who stopped short at the death of James I. The first part of the work to be written was his account of the period from the death of James I to the year 1562. This portion was done in the Scots tongue in 1570 during his residence in England in connection with the imprisonment of Queen Mary. While in exile on the continent he published the completed history in Latin, of which the first seven books were, in the main, an epitome of Boece, and the last three his original sketch composed in Latin. The translation by Father Dalrymple, a monk at Ratisbon, gives a harsh rendering of the Latin, but it has interest that a modern translation would lack. —Brown, *op. cit.* Leslie aimed by his history to bolster up the cause of Mary and to maintain the Catholic faith in Scotland. He was the chief Catholic historian of Scotland.

> 1675 LESLIE, JOHN. De Origine, Moribus, et Rebus gestis Scotorum Libri Decem, e quibus septem veterum Scotorum Res in primis Memorabiles Contractius, Reliqui vero tres posteriorum Regum ad nostra tempora Historiam, quae huc usque desiderabatur, fusius explicant. Romae, in Aedibus Populi Romani, 1578. Nunc denuo recus. Anno Domini, 1675.

1579 CHAMBRE (CHAMBERS), DAVID. Histoire Abbregee De Tous Les Roys De France, Angleterre Et Escosse mise en ordre par forme d'Harmonie contenant aussi vn brief discours de l'ancienne alliance, & mutuel secours entre la France & l'Escosse . . . auec le recherche tant des singularitez plus remarquable concernant l'estat d'Escosse—Discours de la legitime succession des Femmes aux biens & gouuernement des Empires & Royaumes. Par Dauid Chambre Escos-

sois conseiller en la cour de Parlement a Edinbourg. . . . 3 parts in 1 vol.
8vo. Paris.

Chambers was a Scotch judge, one of the goodly number of Scotch scholars who either
sought refuge in France or taught or studied there in the 16th century. He was privy to
Darnley's murder and a partisan of Mary Queen of Scots. Being attainted in 1568, he left
for France, published his *Abbregée,* a summary of European history, and returned to
Scotland in 1582. His attainder was reversed in 1584. He became Lord of the Sessions
1586-92.—*DNB.*

1581 TACITUS, CORNELIUS. Histories of Tacitus: Life of Agricola (with account of
Britain). Translated by Sir Henry Savile. London.

Sir Henry Savile established the Savilian chairs of geometry and astronomy at Oxford,
which were open to mathematicians from any part of Europe (1619). He is regarded as
the most learned Englishman in the profane literature of Elizabeth's reign. For his
Rerum Anglicarum Scriptores, see under 1619 below.

1582 BUCHANAN, GEORGE. Rerum Scoticarum Historia . . . Ad Jacobum VI Scotorum. 4to. Edinburgh.

Reprinted at Geneva, 1583; 8vo, Frankfurt, 1584; Francofurti ad Moenum, 8vo, 1594;
Trajecti ad Rhenum, 8vo, 1697; editio novissima, 2 pt., 12mo, Edinburgh, 1727; 8vo, Aberdeen, 1762. Translated into English, fol., London, 1690; 2nd edit., revised and corrected
from the Latin original by Bond, 2 vols., 8vo, London, 1722; again, London, 1733; 5th
edit., 2 vols., 8vo, Edinburgh, 1762; 7th, 2 vols., 8vo, Glasgow, 1799; translated by James
Aidman, Glasgow, 1827.
Owing to its wide circulation on the continent, this work served as the chief source of
information to foreigners on Scotland. Buchanan began his history late in life and to it
he entrusted his fame. His aim was to provide information about the country for the use
of King James VI, to whom he had been tutor, and to secure for its history more ample
justice than was to be had in the histories of his predecessors, Fordun, Boece, or Major.
By writing it in Latin he curtailed its circulation among his own countrymen, but he made
the story of Scotland accessible to Europe, by whom it was widely read up to the beginning of the 18th century. The first twenty books were considered to be the best. Here he
describes in detail and from careful observation the physical condition of the country and
the manners and habits of the people, especially of the Western Isles. The value of the
later portion lies in his close acquaintance with many of the leading characters of the
period. Being a humanist rather than a scientist, he naturally followed the ancients in his
conception of history, which was to give a clear narrative of events and not to probe
causes or to discover motives and explain the meaning of the tangled web of national life.
However, it did open the public mind to questions of constitutional government. See D.
Macmillan, *George Buchanan* (1906).

1584 [CARADOG OF LLANCARVAN]. The Historie of Cambria, now called Wales: a part
of the famous Yland of Brytaine, written in the Brytish language aboue two
hundreth yeares past [by Caradog]: translated into English by H. Lhoyd,
Gentleman: Corrected, augmented, and continued out of Records and best approued Authors, by Dauid Powel, Doctor in diuinitie. Wood engraved title page
and woodcut portraits of the kings, queens, princes and chiefs. 4to. London.

Many editions followed. Some are headed by the name of Powel, who continued and
corrected Llwyd's MS translation and included Sir John Price's *Description of Cambria*
(see this date under DESCRIPTIONS). New edit., augmented by W. Wynne, 8vo, London,
1697; 6th edit., greatly "improved" and enlarged, London, 1784; an edit., London, 1811.
The supposed original Welsh chronicle, the *Brut Y Twysogion,* was edited and translated
by Rev. J. Williams ab Ithel for the Rolls Series, London, 1860.
Humphrey Llwyd left in MS an English version of the Welsh Chronicles of the
Princes, commonly known as the Chronicles of Caradog of Llancarvan. This, at the request of Sir Henry Sidney, David Powel published with corrections and additions such as
to make it a practically new work. To it he prefixed Sir John Price's *Description of Cambria.* Caradog, to whom the *Brut y Twysogion* was erroneously attributed, was a friend
of Geoffrey of Monmouth, who writes at the end of his History, "The princes who afterwards ruled in Wales I committed to Caradog for he was my contemporary. And to him
I gave the materials to write that book." The above work was then a sort of continuation
of Geoffrey's fictions and in its original form is not now extant. Some Welsh chronicles

exist, however, which continue to much later times and yet profess to be derived from Caradog.—In part from Sotheran Catalogue.

> 1697 CARADOC. The History of Wales, comprehending the Lives and Succession of the Princes of Wales, etc. Written originally in British by Caradoc, of Llancarfan, and formerly published by Dr. Powel; now newly augmented by W. Wynne. Enlarged with pedigrees of families. 8vo. London.

1585 PONTICUS VIRUNNIUS. Pontici Virunni viri doctissimi Britannicae Historiae libri sex, magna et fide et diligentia conscripti; ad Britannici codicis fidem correcti & ab infinitis mendis liberati; quibus praefixus est catalogus Regum Britanniae: per Davidem Pouelem. 3 pts. in 1 vol. 8vo. London.

> The three parts have each their own separate title pages, the second has "Giraldus Cambrensis. Itinerarium Cambriae," the third "Giraldus Cambrensis. Cambriae Descriptio." See this date under TOURS BY NATIVES and DESCRIPTIONS.

1586 WARNER, WILLIAM. Albion's England. London.

> Continuation, 4to, London, 1602; a further continuation, 4to, London, 1606; complete edit., 1612. Five edits. had appeared by 1602. See below.
> This was Warner's chief work and his earliest experiment in writing in verse. It was a long episodic poem in fourteen-syllable lines, treating of legendary or imaginary incidents in British history from the days of Noah till the arrival in England of William the Conqueror. The continuations carried the history down to James I. The work was eulogized in Meres and by Drayton.

> 1602 WARNER, WILLIAM. Albion's England: a Continued Historie of the same Kingdome, from the originals of the first Inhabitants thereof: with most of the chiefe Alterations and Accidents theare hapning, unto, and in the happie Raigne of our most gracious Soueraigne Queene Elizabeth: revised and newly inlarged by the same Author; whereunto is also newly added an Epitome of the whole Historie of England. 4to. London.

1587 Rerum Britannicarum, id est Angliae, Scotiae, vicinarumque insularum ac regionum Scriptores vetustiores ac praecipui. Fol. Heidelberg.

> For contents see following:
> 1. Galfredi Monumetensis, cognomento Arturi, de Origine et Gestis Regum Britanniae libri xii. See under 1508 above.
> 2. Pontici Virunii Britannicae Historiae libri vi. See under 1585 above.
> 3. Gildae Sapientis de Excidio et Conquestu Britanniae Epistola. See under 1525 above.
> 4. Bedae Anglo-Saxonis Historiae Ecclesiasticae Gentis Anglorum libri v. See under 1475 above.
> 5. Continuatio eiusdem Historiae, incerto auctore, libris tribus comprehensa.
> 6. Gulielmi Newbricensis de Rebus Anglicis libri vi. See below.
> 7. Joannis Frossardi Historiarum Epitome. See under 1525 above.
> This is the earliest collection of British historians and chroniclers. It is usually referred to as the "Heidelberg Writers."

> WILLIAM OF NEWBURGH. Historia Rerum Anglicarum. Heidelberg.
> Edit. by Hearne, 3 vols., 8vo, Oxford, 1719; edit. by R. Howlett, vol. III of *Chronicles of the Reigns of Stephen, Henry II, and Richard I,* for the Rolls Series, London, 1884-90. This chronicle, written *ca.* 1198, covers the period 1066 to 1198. It is the finest historical work extant by an Englishman of the 12th century.—*DNB.* While regarded as often inaccurate, it is said to be marked by clarity, impartiality, and a critical spirit.

1588 LYTE, HENRY. The Light of Britayne; a Recorde of the honourable Originall and Antiquitie of Britaine. London.

> Reprinted, 8vo, London, 1814.

1592 FLORENCE OF WORCESTER. Florentii Wigorniensis, Monachi. Chronicon ex Chronicis, ab initio mundi vsque ad Annum M.C.XVII. London.

> Edit. by Benj. Thorpe for the English Historical Society, 2 vols., London, 1848-49;

English version for the Bohn Library, London, 1847; another by T. Forester, 12mo, London, 1854. See below.

This chronicle extends from the Creation to 1117. It derives its material as far as 1030 from the work of Marianus Scotus. From 1117 on, it is continued till 1295 by other hands. It is said to be accurate but uninteresting.

1854 FLORENCE OF WORCESTER. The Chronicle of Florence of Worcester, with the two Continuations. Comprising Annals of English History, from the Departure of the Romans to the Reign of Edward I. Translated from the Latin, with Notes, by T. Forester. 12mo. London.

1595-99 DANIEL, SAMUEL. The Civill Wars between the Two Houses of Lancaster and York. 5 Books. London. (In verse.)

The first four books appeared in 1595 and the fifth in 1599. An edit., fol., London, 1601; the five books redistributed and made into seven and an eighth added, 1609.

The 1609 edition called from Ben Jonson, with whom Daniel was "at jealousies," the remark that "Daniel wrote 'Civil Wars' and yet hath not a battle in all his book." In 1612-17 Daniel published a history of England in prose.

1596 SAVILE, SIR HENRY (Editor). Rerum Anglicarum Scriptores post Bedam praecipui ex vetustissimis Cod. MSS. nunc primum in lucem editi. Fol. London.

Reprinted, Frankfort, 1601.

This contains the first editions of the Chronicles of William of Malmesbury, Henry of Huntingdon, Roger of Hoveden, Ethelwerd and Ingulph. See the following listings:

HENRY OF HUNTINGDON. Historia Anglorum. Fol. London.

Translated and edited by Thomas Forester for the Bohn Series, London, 1853; edit., by T. Arnold for the Rolls Series, London, 1879.

The latest form of this chronicle carries the history down from A.D. 55 to 1154. The earlier parts are a compilation from Bede and Anglo-Saxon Chronicles, but when the writer approaches his own time, he assumes the character of an eyewitness of the events he narrates, and establishes himself as among the earliest of British national historians as distinguished from mere chroniclers. For the first time, perhaps, form and proportion take mastery of the material. Like later historians he opens up with a description of Britain.

INGULF. Historia Croylandensis. London.

Edit. by William Fulman, *Rerum Anglicarum Scriptores,* Oxford, 1684 (see below, this date); edit. by W. de Gray Birch, Wisbech, 1883 (inferior to Fulman's edition and less complete); English version (as far as 1091) by Jos. Stevenson, and by H. T. Petrie (to 1486), London, 1854.

The period covered runs from 626 to 1091, with continuations by different groups of years to 1486. Ingulf was abbot of Croyland and one of the secretaries or chancery clerks of William the Conqueror. The chronicle gives a history of the abbey, bolstering up its claims with many spurious charters, as well as many particulars concerning the affairs of the kingdom. It used to be regarded as possessing great historical value, but now it is known to be a forgery designed probably to forward certain interests of the abbey. This discovery "necessitated revision of every standard book on early English history."— Stubbs, quoted by Gross, *The Sources and Literature of English History.*

WILLIAM OF MALMESBURY. De Gestis Pontificum Anglorum; de Gestis Regum Anglorum. London.

Edit. by Thomas Gale, Oxford, 1691 (see Gale, this date, below); by Thomas D. Hardy for the English Hist. Soc., 2 vols., London, 1840; the *Gestis Pontificum* edit. by N. E. S. A. Hamilton, London, 1870; the *Gestis Regum Anglorum* and the *Historiae Novellae* by Bishop Stubbs for the Rolls Series, 2 vols., London, 1887-89. English version of the *Kings of England* by Rev. John Sharpe, 4to, London, 1815; by Giles, London, 1847.

"William of Malmesbury is the chief of your historians," says Archbishop Ussher. He completed his *History of the Kings of Britain* and *Of the Prelates* in 1125. This was followed by his *Historiae Novellae.* A considerable portion of his work had been printed by the Heidelberg Writers as a continuation of Bede (see under 1587 above), but it was Savile who produced the two histories complete. The historian was a careful writer, spending much time correcting his works. He endeavored to give a clear and connected account of every event he dealt with, and he was no less particular in his delineation of character. In the use of anecdote to arouse interest, he was very effective. But to arrive at the truth, which he insisted must rest upon the author, was his great aim.

1603   CAMDEN, WILLIAM (Editor). Anglica, Normannica, Hibernica, Cambrica, a vet-
       eribus Scripta. Frankfort.

> For contents see the following:
> Asser de Rebus gestis Aelfridi Regis.
> Fragmentum de Gulielmo Conquestore.
> Chronica Thomae Walsingham quondam monachi S. Albani.
> Ypodigma Neustriae, per Th. de Walsingham.
> Vita et Mors Edwardi II. Regis Angliae.
> Wilhelmus Gemeticensis de Ducum Normannorum gestis.
> Topographia Hiberniae, auctore Giraldo Cambrense.
> Expugnatio Hiberniae, sive Historia Vaticinalis Silbestris Giraldi Cambrensis.
> Itinerarium Cambriae, seu Laboriosae Balduini Cantuariensis Archiepiscopi per William
>   Legationis accurata descriptio, auctore Sil. Giraldo Cambrense.
> Cambriae Descriptio, auctore Sil. Giraldo Cambrense.
> These chronicles were some of his early collections for his *Britannia* (see under 1586,
> DESCRIPTIONS).

       HOWE, EDWARD. Chronicles. 12mo. London. (The date is approximate.)

> This contains a Description of England, Scotland, Wales and Cornwall. A Summarie
> of English Chronicles to James I, of the Universities in England and Colleges in the
> Same. How a Man may journey from any notable Towne in England to the Citie of
> London, or from London to any notable Towne in the Realme. The principall Faires in
> England.

1606   The Historie of Great Britaine, declaring the Successe of Times and Affaires in
       that Island, from the Romans' first entrance, with Account of the Warres upon
       the Ancient Inhabitants of South and North Wales, the Overthrowe of Carac-
       tacus, their Captaine, the Subdueing of the Isle of Anglesey, the Doctrine and
       Manners of the religious Druids, etc. 4to. London. (So cited in Rowlands,
       Cambrian Bibliog.)

1611   SPEED, JOHN. The Historie of Great Britaine under the Conquests of the Romans,
       Saxons, Danes & Normans. Their Originals, Manners, Habits, Warres, Coines,
       Seales: With the Successions, Lives, Acts, & Issues of the English Monarchs
       from Julius Caesar. London.

> 2nd edit., London, 1623; 3rd, fol., London, 1632; another, with numerous engravings,
> fol., London, 1650.
> Speed published this history to form an accompaniment to his *Theatre of the Empire of
> Great Britaine* (see this date under MAPS AND CHARTS), making the paging in the two
> volumes continuous. This was no doubt suggested to him by the alliance between Saxton's
> *Atlas* and Holinshed's *Chronicles*. Speed's fondness for rhetorical utterance led him to
> attempt an elevated style for his history. He backed up his narrative, however, by a more
> frequent reliance on unpublished documents than was true of the majority of historians.
> His praise of England was unstinted.

1612   MONIPENNIE, JOHN. The Abridgement, or Summarie of the Scots Chronicles,
       with a short Description of their Originall. With a true Description of the whole
       Realme of Scotland, and of the principall Cities, Townes, Abbies, Fortes,
       Castles, etc., and of the Commodities in every part thereof, and of the Isles in
       general; with a Memoriall of the most rare and wonderfull Things in Scotland.
       4to. London.

> An edit., corrected and augmented, 12mo, Edinburgh, 1633; an edit., with an account
> of the Western Isles added, Edinburgh, 1756; reprinted in *Misc. Scotica,* Edinburgh, 1818;
> the same, Glasgow, 1820.
> The descriptive part consists of the enumerations of names of places, gentlemen's seats,
> rivers, lochs, etc., with occasional curious explanations and traditions, amusing to the
> modern reader at times for the unusual phraseology. The Western Isles receive a special
> description, in which he often uses old names that are Latin in texture. For instance, he
> mentions Iona under the name of Columbaria instead of Icolmkill. The forty-eight Scot-
> tish kings and the eight kings of Norway buried there come in for their notice.—Quoted.

1612-17   Daniel, Samuel. The History of England. London.

> 1st complete edit., fol., London, 1618; 4th edit., revised and corrected, fol., London, 1641. A continuation by John Trussell, making 2 vols., London, 1650.
> His history does not possess the interest of the chronicles. He was also an historian of the "Civill Warres" (between York and Lancaster), 1609. He is best known for his poetry and dramas, and for his defense of rhyme in English poetry.

1615   Camden, William. Annales Rerum Anglicarum et Hibernicarum Regnante Elizabetha, ad Annum Salutis. . . . Fol. London.

> The above contains only part I, which comes down to 1588; reprinted, Francofurti ad Moenum, 1616; pts. I and II (down to 1603), Leyden, 1625; pt. II, London, 1627; pts. I and II, Leyden, 1639; again, Amsterdam, 1677; edit. by Thomas Hearne, 3 vols., (standard edit.), Oxford, 1717; pt. I translated into English by W. Darcie from French version by Paul de Bellegent (pt. I, 1624, pt. II, 1627, Paris), London, 1625; pt. II (English) by T. Browne, London, 1629; both pts. (English) by H. Norton, London, 1630, 1635; again in English, London, 1675, 1688; in White Kennett, *Complete History*, vol. II, 1706. See below.
> This is regarded as the best Elizabethan chronicle in print; it reveals keen insight into political affairs and is thoroughly independent of other chronicles. It is better proportioned and more carefully related to perspective. It was Lord Burghley who suggested to Camden that he write a work on the Queen's life and reign. The numerous editions and translations attest its popularity.

> 1625   Camden, William. The True and Royall History of the famous Empresse Elizabeth, Queene of England, France, and Ireland . . . True Faith's Defendress of Divine Renowne and happy Memory. London.
> > This is the translation made of pt. I by Darcie from the French version (see below).

> 1675   ————. The History of the Renowned and Victorious Princess Elizabeth, Late Queen of England. Revised and compared with the Original, whereby many gross Faults are amended. . . . Fol. London.
> > This is called the 3rd edit. Presumably it is based on Norton's complete edition.

> 1624-27   (In French.) Histoire d'Elizabeth royne d'Angleterre, comprenant ce qui s'est passé de plus memorables és Royaumes d'Angleterre, Escosse, et Irlande, depuis . . . 1588 a sa mort, en l'année 1603, traduit du Latin par M. Paul de Bellegent. Portrait. Paris.

1618   Bolton, E. Hypercritica. London.

> Reprinted in Spingarn, *Critical Essays of the Seventeenth Century*, Oxford, 1908.
> This essay makes caustic comments on the chroniclers Camden, Speed, Stow, and others, and on the practice of leaving those "vast, vulgar tomes" to be put out by printers instead of royal authorities.

1622   Dempster, Thomas. Apparatus ad Historiam Scotorum. Fol. Bononia (Bologna).

1627   ————. Historia Ecclesiastica Gentis Scotorum. (Place?)

> Dempster also published an Autobiography, which is regarded as untrustworthy. For an interesting account of his activities in France, see Françisque Michel, *Les Ecossais en France*, vol. II, ch. xxx. For a later edition see below.

> 1829   Dempster, Thomas. Thomae Dempsteri Historia Ecclesiastica Gentis Scotorum; sive, De Scriptoribus Scoticis. Editio altera. 2 vols. Edit. by David Irving. In *Publ. Bann. Club*, no. 21. Edinburgh.

Respublica, sive status regni Scotiae et Hiberniae, diversorum auctorum (Buchanan, Camden, Boece, etc.). 12mo. Leyden.

1630   Dodridge, Sir John. The History of the Ancient and Moderne Estate of the Principality of Wales, Dutchy of Cornwall, and Earldom of Chester. Collected

out of the Recordes of the Tower of London, and divers Ancient Authors. Dedicated to King James of ever blessed Memory. 4to. London.

2nd edit., with added matter, 8vo, London, 1714. See below.

> 1714 DODRIDGE, SIR JOHN. An Historical Account of . . . To which is added, His Royal Highness the Prince of Wales's Patent both in Latin and in English; also an Account of his Dignity, Privileges, Arms, Rank and Titles, and of his Sons and Daughters. 8vo. London.

GODWIN, FRANCIS (Bishop of Hereford). Annales of England. Containing the Reignes of Henry the Eighth, Edward the Sixt, Queene Mary. Written in Latin. This Englished, corrected and inlarged with the Author's consent by [his son] Morgan Godwyn [Archbishop of Salop]. 3 portraits of T. Cecil. Fol. London.

> In his dedication to Lord Scudamore the translator declares that "no one has written either so largely or so freely as this Author."—Sotheran, no. 869.

1640 HABINGTON, WILLIAM. The Historie of Edward The Fourth, King of England. Fol. London.

> This is the first of Habington's only two prose works. It was published at the instigation of Charles I, from materials collected by Habington's father, the well-known antiquary. —Quaritch.

1652 TWYSDEN, SIR ROGER. Historiae Anglicanae Scriptores X . . . Ex vetustis Manuscriptis nunc primum in lucem editi. 1 vol. in 2. Fol. London.

> For contents see following:
> Aelred of Rievaulx.
> Brompton.
> Gervase of Canterbury.
> John of Hexham.
> Knighton.
> Ralph Diceto.
> Richard of Hexham.
> Simeon of Durham.
> Thomas Stubbes, Chronica pontificum Ebor'.
> William Thornton, De rebus abbatum Cant'.
> Three of these chronicles have been separately edited in the Rolls Series, and in each case the editor has referred to Twysden with respect. The work entitles him to rank with Camden, Selden, and Savile as a pioneer in the study of medieval history. "Even the Puritans themselves," says Hearne, "affecting to be Maecenases with Cromwell at their head, displayed something like a patriotic ardour in purchasing copies of this work as soon as it appeared."—Quoted by Robinson, no. 72.

> SIMEON OF DURHAM. Historia Dunelmensis ecclesiae (635-1096, with two continuations to 1154). London.
> Edit. by Thomas Bedford, London, 1732; for two other editions see under this comment.
> This chronicle was written between 1104 and 1108. In the main it is a history of the church of Durham, but it provides useful information on secular affairs in the north of England, especially for the 9th century. The earlier portion is derived from Bede.— Gross, *op. cit.*

> ————. Historia Regum, or Historia de regibus Anglorum et Danorum (616-1129). London.
> In his *Opera et Collectanea,* edit. by J. H. Hinde, for the Surtees Soc., Durham, 1868; in *Opera Omnia,* edit. by Arnold, 2 vols., for the Rolls Series, London, 1882-85. A translation of the historical works of Simeon made by Jos. Stevenson, for the Church Historians of England Series, vol. III, pt. ii, London, 1855.
> This was derived in part from a Durham compilation based in portions on the lost Northumbrian Annals and on Asser. The passages from the lost Annals are of value. For 1119-24 the work is an independent authority. Simeon was a monk and precentor of the church of Durham.—Gross, *op. cit.*

1655 DRUMMOND, WILLIAM. The History of Scotland from the Year 1423 until the Year 1542. London.

> Another edit., Edinburgh, 1711.

SPOTTISWOODE, JOHN (Archbishop). The History of the Church and State of Scotland from the Year 203 to the End of the Reign of King James VI, 1625. London.

> Reprinted, London, 1677; again in 3 vols., by the Spottiswoode Society, Edinburgh, 1847. This work is said to be highly partisan. It contains a description of the magnificence of the city of St. Andrews in the time of Cardinal Beaton and Archbishop Hamilton.

1670 MILTON, JOHN. The History of Britain, That part especially now call'd England. From the first Traditional Beginning, continu'd to the Norman Conquest. Collected . . . by John Milton. Portrait of Milton by Faithorne. 4to. London.

> 2nd issue of the 1st edit., 4to, London, 1671.
> "It is written with great simplicity . . . and is the better for it. But he sometimes rises into a surprising grandeur in the sentiments and expressions, as at the end of the second book."—Bishop Warburton, quoted by Quaritch.

1684 FULMAN, WILLIAM. Rerum Anglicarum Scriptores veteres. Tom. I. Fol. Oxford.

> This collection was made under the auspices of Bishop John Fell (often ascribed to him). It is usually called vol. I of Thomas Gale's collection, though the two are entirely distinct. For contents see the following:
> 1. Ingulfi Croylandensis Historia. (See under Savile, 1596 above.)
> 2. Petri Blesensis Continuatio.
> 3. Chronica de Mailros.
> 4. Annales Burtonenses.
> 5. Historiae Croylandensis Continuatio.
>
> Chronica de Mailros. Oxford.
> Edit. by Jos. Stevenson for the Bann. Club, Edinburgh, 1835; English version by Jos. Stevenson for the Church Historians of England Series, London, 1856.
> The part down to 1129 was mainly derived from Simeon of Durham. From 1150 on, the chronicle is an original authority, and much of the information is contemporaneous. It has value for its notices of Scotland and northern England, especially during the reign of Henry III. It was compiled soon after 1236 by a monk of Melrose and continued by others.—Gross.

1687 GALE, THOMAS. Historiae Anglicanae Scriptores Quinque. Oxford.

> For chronicles edited see following:
> Annals of Margan.
> Annales Waverleienses.
> Itinerary of Richard I.
> Chronicon Thomae Wykes.
> Walteri Hemingford Historia de Rebus Gestis Edwardi I, II, et III.
>
> Annales Waverleienses, 1066-1291. Oxford.
> These were first published from a MS in the Cotton Library, Vesp. A. xvi. 14. They begin at the year 1066, though the abbey was not founded (at Lambeth) till 1128, and end 1291.—Gough, 502.

1691 GALE, THOMAS. Historiae Britannicae, Saxonicae, Anglo-Danicae, Scriptores XV., ex vetustis codd. MSS. editi Opera Thomae Gale, Th. Pr. Praefatio ostendit Ordinem, Accessit Rerum & Verborum Index locupletissimus. Fol. Oxford.

> Gale calls this collection vol. I and the *Quinque* vol. II. But it is usually numbered vol. III in combination with Fulman's collection. For contents see following:
> Alcuin, De Pontificibus Ebor'.
> Chronicon fani S. Neoti.
> Eddi, Vita S. Wilfridi.

Fordun, Scotichronicon (see below).
Gildas, De Excidio (see under 1525 above).
Higden, Polychronicon (see under 1482 above).
Historia Eliensis, Bks. I-II.
Historia Ramesiensis.
Nennius, Historia Britonum (see below).
Ralph of Diceto, Historia de regibus Britonum.
John of Wallingford.
William of Malmesbury, De Glastonia; De Pontificibus.
   For these seventeenth-century editors and these chronicles, see David C. Douglas, *English Authors.*

JOHN OF FORDUN. Chronica gentis Scotorum (Scotchicronicon). Oxford.
   This chronicle runs from Noah to 1388, although in Gale's edition it stops with 1066. Edit. by Hearne, with Walter Brown's continuation to 1437, 5 vols., Oxford, 1722; edit., with the same continuation, by Walter Goodall, 2 vols., Edinburgh, 1759; edit. and translated, with Introduction and Notes, by W. Skene, 2 vols., for Historians of Scotland Series, Edinburgh, 1871.
   This is the first attempt at a complete history of Scotland. The work was composed during the years 1363-84. Fordun was probably a chantry priest in the cathedral of Aberdeen. He compiled also "Gesta Annalia" in continuation of the history.

NENNIUS. Historia Britonum. Oxford.
   Edit. with English version by William Gunn, London, 1819; edit. by Jos. Stevenson for the Eng. Hist. Soc., 8vo, London, 1838; translated from the Latin by J. A. Giles, London, 1841, 1848. Irish version, edit. by J. H. Todd and Hon. Algernon Herbert for the Irish Arch. Soc., 4to, Dublin, 1848. The Irish Nennius from *Lebor na Huidhre*, edit. by Rev. Edmund Hogan, text and translation, the Todd Lecture Series, vol. VI, Dublin, 1895.
   This work is known through thirty manuscripts, the earliest of which cannot be dated before 1000, and all are defaced by interpolations. Zimmer, in his *Nennius Vindicatus* (1893), traced the history of the work, stripping off later accretions from the original nucleus. Only that part can be regarded as of historical importance which is known as Genealogiae Saxonum (sections 57-65), which is a recension of a work composed about 679 by a Briton of Strathclyde. The date usually assigned to the *Historia* is *ca.* 796. Nennius is the first writer to relate the legend so inveterately associated with Stonehenge, viz., the massacre of the British nobles by Hengist at a feast to which they had been invited, and the story of the wondrous boy Ambrose (Ambrosius Aurelius) who had no mortal father. He does not allude to Stonehenge itself. He is also credited with being the first to mention Arthur by name. The Irish version was compiled by Gille Coemgin *ca.* 1071.

WHARTON, HENRY. Anglia sacra, sive collectio historiarum de archiepiscopis et episcopis Angliae ad annum 1540. 2 vols. London.
   This contains, among other things, lives of the bishops, Giraldus Cambrensis, Historia Eliensis, Robert Graystanes, History of the Church of Durham. Wharton, who died at the age of thirty, was considered a marvel of a scholar.

1692 GIBSON, EDMUND. Chronicon Saxonicum, seu Annales rerum in Anglia praecipue Gestarum a Christo nato ad Annum MCLIV. deducti, ac jam demum Latinitate donati. Cum Indice rerum Chronologico. Accedunt Regulae ad Investigandas Nominum Locorum Origines et Nominum Locorum ac virorum in Chronico Memoratorum Explicatio. Opera & Studio Edmundi Gibson. Map. 4to. Oxford.
   This contains two of the Saxon Chronicles, with supplementary extracts from others. Of this most famous of our chronicles, there are six recensions, of which the Parker Chronicle (or A-text) and the Peterborough Chronicle (or E-text) are the most important. These two have been edited by Charles Plummer (with supplementary extracts from the others) in 2 vols., text and translation, London, 1892.

1694 B[URTON], R[OBERT]. The History of the Principality of Wales: In Three Parts: Containing I. A Brief Account of the Antient Kings and Princes of Brittain and Wales till the final Extinguishing of the Royal British Line. II. Remarks upon the Lives of all the Princes of Wales, of the Royal Families of England, from King Edward the First to this Time. III. Remarkable Observations on the most Memorable Persons and Places in Wales, and of many considerable

Transactions and Passages that have happened therein for many hundred Years Past. Together with Natural and Artificial Rarities and Wonders in the several Counties of the Principality. 24mo. London.

> 2nd edit., 12mo, London, 1730.
> For his *Admirable Curiosities,* see under 1682, DESCRIPTIONS. The author's first name is sometimes given as Richard, and the whole name was a pseudonym for Nathaniel Crouch.

1706 BALFOUR, SIR JAMES. The History of the Picts, containing an Account of the original Language, Manners, Government, Religion, Bounds and Limits of their Kingdom. Also, their most Memorable Battles with the Brittains, Romans, Scots, etc., until their final Overthrow and Extirpation. With a Catalogue of their Kings, and of the Roman Governors who fought against them and the Scots. And at the End is added a Clavis, explaining the proper Names and difficult Words of the History. 12mo. Edinburgh.

> This has also been attributed to Henry Maule of Melgum, and is believed to have been written about 1650.—Mitchell, *List of Travels.*

SIBBALD, SIR ROBERT. Introductio ad historiam rerum a Romanis gestarum in ea borealis Britanniae parte quae ultra murum Picticum est; in qua veterum in hac plaga incolarum nomina et sedes explicantur. Cum tabula aenea Britanniae integrae et Hiberniae, et una hujus plagae borealis juxta rectum ejus situm, et figurae castri Romani Iernensis. Fol. Edinburgh.

> To this is annexed: Specimen glossari, de populis et locis Britanniae borealis in explicatione locorum quorundam difficilium apud scriptores veteres. In 9 sections, with an appendix of ancient historians, and another of some places in Buchanan. The author intended to continue this glossary to the times succeeding the Romans and speaks of copperplates in it, which, however, do not appear.—Gough, 619.

1708-14 COLLIER, JEREMY. Ecclesiastical History of Great Britain . . . to the End of the Reign of Charles II. Fol. London.

> This is a learned work which Hearne at first thought to be of little account, but which later he came to regard highly. It was, with the exception of Fuller's *Worthies,* the first of its kind.—*DNB.*

1709 HEYLYN, PETER. A Help to English History, containing a Succession of all the Kings, Dukes, Marquesses, Earls, with a Description of the Places from whence they had their Titles, etc. Numerous coats of arms. 12mo. London.

1715 TORFAEUS, THORMODUS. Orcades seu Rerum Orcadensium Historiae Libri tres. Fol. Copenhagen. (See under TOURS BY NATIVES.)

1716-35 HEARNE, THOMAS (Editor). Chronicles and Records. Oxford.

> Below is a selected list of those that are pertinent to this work:
> 1716 Aluredi Beverlacensis Annales.
> Titi Livii Foro-Juliensis Vita Henrici Quinti.
> Joannis Rossi Antiquarii Warwicensis Historia Regum Angliae. 2nd edit., 1745.
> Guilielmi Camdeni Annales rerum Anglicarum et Hibernicarum, 3 vols.
> 1719 Guilielmi Neubrigensis Historia, 3 vols.
> Thomae Sprotti Chronica.
> 1720 Textus Roffensis.
> Roberti de Avesbury Historia de Mirabilibus gestis Edvardi.
> 1722 Joannis de Fordon Scotichronicon Genuinum, 5 vols.
> History and Antiquities of Glastonbury.
> 1723 Heningi Chartularium Ecclesiae Wigorniensis, 2 vols.
> 1724 Robert of Gloucester's Chronicle, 2 vols.
> 1725 Peter Langtoft's Chronicle, 2 vols.

1727   Thomae de Elmham Vita et Gesta Henrici V.
       Adami de Donnerham Historia de Rebus Gestis Glastoniensibus, 2 vols. Editio
       altera, 1774.
1729   Historia Vitae et Regni Ricardi II.
       Johannis de Trokelowe Annales Edvardi II.
1731   Walteri Hemingford Historia de Rebus Gestis Edwardi I, II, et III, 2 vols.
1732   Duo Rerum Anglicarum Scriptores Veteres, viz., Thomas Otterbourne et J. Wheth-
       amstede, 2 vols.
1733   Chronicon sive Annales Prioratus de Dunstaple, 2 vols.
1735   Benedictus Abbas Petroburgensis de Vita et Gestis Henrici II et Ricardi I, 2 vols.

A few of these are singled out for commentary. For their dates see above.

LANGTOFT, PETER. Chronicle (as illustrated and improved by Robert Brunne), from the death
    of Cadwallader to the End of King Edward the First's Reign. Transcribed and now first
    published, from a MS. in the Inner-Temple Library, by Thomas Hearne. To which are
    added, besides a Glossary and other curious Papers, A Roll concerning Stone-henge. 2
    vols. Oxford.
       This chronicle was written in French verse. It was edited by Thomas Wright for the
    Rolls Series, 2 vols., London, 1866-68.

ROBERT OF GLOUCESTER. Chronicle. Transcribed and now first published from a MS. in the
    Harleian Library by Thomas Hearne. To which is added, besides a Glossary and other
    Improvements, A Continuation (by the author himself) of this Chronicle from a MS. in
    the Cottonian Library. 2 vols. Oxford.
       Reprinted, Oxford, 1812; edit. by W. A. Wright for the Rolls Series, 2 vols., London,
    1887. Translated by Jos. Stevenson for the Church Historians of England Series, 1853-58.
       The date of this metrical chronicle is placed at about 1300. It runs from the coming of
    Brutus to England to 1272. Its peculiar verse form is regarded as important in the develop-
    ment of English poetical practice, and its language as a transition stage before the appear-
    ance of Chaucer.

ADAM OF DONNERHAM. Historia de rebus gestis Glastoniensibus. E codice MS. perantiquo in
    bib. coll. S. Trinitatis Cantabrigiae descripsit primusque in lucem protulit Tho. Hearnius.
    Qui (praeter alia, in quibus dissertatio de inscriptione pervetere Romana Cicestriae nuper
    reperta) Gulielmi Malmesburiensis librum de antiquitate ecclesiae Glastoniensis, & Ed-
    mundi Archeri excerpta aliquam multa satis egregia e registris Wellensibus, praemisit.
    2 vols. Oxford.
       This author lived about the middle of the 13th century. The history is merely a continua-
    tion of William of Malmesbury's, which was printed by Gale very incorrectly (Oxford,
    1691). Hearne republished it with large additions.—Gough, 477.

JOHANNIS, confratris & monachi Glastoniensis, Chronica, sive historia de rebus Glastoniensi-
    bus. E codice MS. membraneo antiquo descripsit ediditque Tho. Hearnius. Qui & ex eodem
    codice historiolam de antiquitate & augmentatione vetustae ecclesiae S. Mariae Glastoni-
    ensis praemisit, multaque excerpta e Richardi Beere (abbatis Glastoniensis) terrario
    hujus caenobii subjecit. Accedunt quaedam, eodem spectantia, ex egregio MS. nobiscum ab
    amicis eruditis Cantabrigiensibus communicato, ut & appendix, in qua, inter alia, de S.
    Ignatii epistolarum codice Medicaeo, & de Johannis Dee mathematici celeberimmi, vita
    atque scriptis agitur. 2 vols. Oxford.
       Hearne published this chronicle from a MS belonging to Lord Charles Bruce, collated
    with another in the Ashmolean Library. The history reaches from the foundation of the
    abbey to 1400, continuing Donnerham, who leaves off at 1290.—Gough, 478.

1719   MUSGRAVE, DR. WILLIAM. Belgium Britannicum. Illus. 8vo. Exeter.

       The author gives the name of "Belga" to a district extending from the Solent to Hen-
    ley, Bath, and Cirencester.—Harrison, *Bibliography of the Great Stone Monuments of
    Wiltshire.*

1723   SPARKE, JOSEPH. Historiae Anglicanae Scriptores Varii. 2 vols. London.

       This collection contains, among others, the following chronicles:
    John of Peterborough, Chronicles.
    Fitzstephen, Life of Becket.
    Hugo Candidus, Histories of Peterborough Abbey.
    Robert Swapham.
    Walter of Whitlesey.

1728 LINDSAY, ROBERT (of Pitscottie). The History of Scotland from 21 Feb. 1436 to March 1565. . . . To which is added, a Continuation by another Hand, till Aug. 1604. Fol. Edinburgh.

> Edit. by John G. Dalyell, 2 vols., 12mo, Edinburgh, 1814; edit. by Aeneas J. G. Mackay for the Scot. Text Society, 3 vols., Edinburgh, 1899-1911. See below.
> This chronicle is a continuation of Bellenden's translation of Boece (see Bellenden under 1536 above). It is an important Renaissance history written in the vernacular of the day. It covers a period of Scottish history—from the death of James I to that of James III —of which very little is known.

> 1899-1911 LINDSAY, ROBERT (of Pitscottie). History and Cronicles of Scotland from the Slauchter of King James the First to the Ane thousande fyve hundreith thrie scoir fyftein zeir, being a continuation of the Translation of the Chronicles written by Hector Boece, and translated by John Bellenden. Written and collected by Robert Lindesay of Pitscottie. Edit. by Aeneas J. G. Mackay. 3 vols. *Publ. Scot. Text Soc.*, nos. 42, 43, 60. Edinburgh.

1729 LEWIS, JOHN. The History of Great Britain from the first Inhabitant thereof, till the Death of Cadwalader, last King of the Britains; and of the Kings of Scotland to Eugene V. as also a short account of the Kings, Dukes, and Earles of Bretagne, till the Dukedom was united to the Crown of France, ending with the Year of our Lord 68; in which are several Pieces of Talieson, an antient British Poet, and a Defence of the Antiquity of the Scotish Nation: with many other Antiquities never before published in the English Tongue. By John Lewis, Esq. Barrester at Law; now first published from his original MS. Fol. London.

1740 FANTOSME, JOHN. Chronicle of the War between the English and Scots, 1173-74. Text, translation, and Notes by F. Michel. 8vo. London.

> Printed in the *Chronicles of the Reigns of Stephen, Henry II, and Richard I,* no. 82 of the Rolls Series, London, 1884-90.

1747 RAY, JAMES. A Compleat History of the Rebellion. London (?).

> Another edit., Bristol, 1752.
> The author speaks of the depressing effect of the barren mountain scenery of the High-lands upon the English soldiers stationed near Loch Ness, which he describes as "these hideous mountains and the noisy ding of the great falls of water." To overcome the mood of hypochondry induced by such surroundings, games and races were instituted. The soldiers were delighted to be released.—Birkbeck Hill, *Footsteps of Dr. Johnson.*

1749 DUFF, WILLIAM. A New and Full, Critical and Biographical, and Geographical History of Scotland. Containing the History of the Succession of their Kings, from Robert Bruce, to the Present Time. With an impartial Account of their Constitution, Genius, Manners, and Customs . . . Together with an Appendix. By an Impartial Hand. 4 plates. Fol. London.

1757 BERTRAM, CAROLUS. Britannicarum gentium historiae antiquae tres: Ricardus Corinensis, Gildas Badonicus, et Nennius Banchorensis. 8vo. Havniae (Copenhagen).

1759 ROBERTSON, WILLIAM. History of Scotland. London.

> 2nd edit., London, 1760; collective edit., 8 vols., Oxford, 1825.
> This history met with enormous success and was one of the most highly paid productions of the pen in the 18th century. The author augmented his fame and his income with his *History of Charles V* and his *History of North America.*

1760 ROBERTSON (etc.). A History of the Whole Realm of Scotland, Civil, Natural, and Ecclesiastical; comprehending an Account of all its Kings and remarkable Events . . . and likewise a Description of the Orkneys and other Isles. Maps and plates. 8vo. Edinburgh.

1774 LELAND, JOHN. Johannis Lelandi Antiquarii de Rebus Britannicis Collectanea. Cum Thomae Hearnii Praefatione Notis et Indice ad Editionem primam. Editio altera. 5 plates. 6 vols. 8vo. Oxford.

1776 HAILES, LORD (Sir David Dalrymple). The Annals of Scotland from the Accession of Malcolm Kenmore to the Death of James V. Edinburgh.

> Another edit., 3 vols., 8vo, Edinburgh, 1797. See below.
> On May 12, 1774, Boswell wrote to Johnson that Lord Hailes desired to have the benefit of his criticism on the Annals. Johnson sent in his revisions on July 4 following, stating that he found little to criticize.

> 1797 HAILES, LORD. The Annals of Scotland from the Accession of Malcolm III, 1057, to the Accession of the House of Stewart, 1371, to which are added Tracts relative to the History and Antiquities of Scotland. 3 vols. 8vo. Edinburgh.

1779 LANGHORNE, DANIEL. Chronicon Regum Anglorum, Insignia Omnia eorum Gesta, tum Ecclesiastica, ab Hingisto Rege Primo, etc. Una, cum Regum Catalogia, Schematibus genealogicis cupro incisis. 8vo. London.

> The author was an antiquary of the 17th century. See under 1673, BRITISH, ROMAN, AND SAXON ANTIQUITIES.

STRUTT, JOSEPH. Chronicles of England, or a Complete History of Ancient Britons and Saxons, Manners, Customs, Arts, etc. Copperplates. 2 vols. 4to. London.

> Translated into French, 2 vols., 4to, Paris, 1789.

YORKE, PHILIP. The Royal Tribes of Wales. Wrexham (?).

> Another edit., 4to, Wrexham, 1799; edit. by R. Williams, Liverpool, 1887.
> A valuable account of the five regal tribes.—DNB.

1786 JOHNSTONE, J. Antiquitates Celto-Normannicae, containing the Chronicles of Man and the Isles, abridged from Camden, and now first published complete from the Original Manuscript in the British Museum, with an English Translation and Notes. To which are added, Extracts from the Annals of Ulster and Sir James Ware's Antiquities of Ireland, British Topography by Ptolemy, Richard of Cirencester, the Geographer of Ravenna, and Andrew, Bishop of Caithness: together with accurate Catalogues of the Pictish and Scottish Kings, by the Rev. James Johnstone, Rector of Mogher-Cross, and Member of the Royal Societies of Edinburgh and Copenhagen. 4to. London.

> Copenhagen has also been listed as the place of publication. Reviewed Gent. Mag., vol. 56, 1061. Strictures are passed upon the editor's conduct for not giving the check number of the MS in the British Museum which he used. His chronology is at variance with Camden's use of the MS, as are the dates. Camden's copy of the Chronicon Regum Mannias dates Edward the Confessor's death 1065; but here it is given as 1047. The MSS he refers to are not listed by numbers, so that it is difficult to check them. Johnstone was also the editor of works on northern literature.

WARRINGTON, REV. WILLIAM. The History of Wales, with an Appendix. 2 folding maps. 4to. London.

> 2nd edit., 2 vols., 8vo, London, 1788; again, London, 1791.
> This is spoken of as a valuable work.

1790 A Comprehensive History of Scotland, with an Account of the Islands and Fisheries. 8vo. Edinburgh.

1792 OLDFIELD, THOMAS H. B. An Entire and Complete History, Political and Personal, of the Boroughs of Great Britain together with the Cinque Ports, and a Sketch of Constitutional Rights, from the earliest Period. 3 vols. 8vo. London.

> Another edit., 2 vols., London, 1794.

1795 ANDREW OF WYNTOUN. De Orygynale Cronykill of Scotland, by Andrew of Wyntoun, Prisner of Sanct Serfis Ynche in Loch Levyn, now first published, with Notes, Glossary, etc., by David Macpherson. 2 vols. London.

> Edit. by David Laing for the Historians of Scotland Series, 3 vols., 8vo, Edinburgh; edit., with Introduction, Notes, and Glossary, by F. J. Amours for the Scot. Text. Soc., 6 vols., Edinburgh, 1903-14. See below.
> Wyntoun was Prior of St. Serf's Inch in Loch Leven, where he probably wrote his chronicle, a vernacular history of Scotland from the beginning of the world to the accession of James I, 1406. His purpose was to justify the claim of Scotland to an independent nationality by an appeal to the authority of antiquity, by a recital of the history of the Scotch nation, from the earliest dawn of tradition. It is written in octosyllabic couplets, but can lay no claim to poetic merit.—See Henderson, *Scottish Vernacular History*.

> 1903-14 ANDREW OF WYNTOUN. The Original Chronicle of Andrew of Wyntoun, printed on parallel pages from the Cottonian and Wemyss MSS., with the Variants of the other Texts. Edit., with Introduction, Notes, and Glossary, by F. J. Amours. 6 vols. *Publ. Scot. Text Soc.*, nos. 39-44, Edinburgh.
> The first volume was published last (1914). Wyntoun aimed to write a world chronicle and to fit Scotland into the chronology. He was much indebted to Barbour's *Bruce* for the metrical form and purpose.—From the Introduction.

1796 MACPHERSON, D. Geographical Illustrations of Scottish History, containing the Names of Places mentioned in Chronicles, Histories, Records, etc.; with Corrections of the corrupted Names and Explanations of the difficult and disputed Points in the historical Geography of Scotland, with a Chronology of the Battles to 1603. 4to. London.

1798 DALYELL, SIR J. G. Fragments of Scottish History, viz., I. The Diary of Robert Birrel, 1532-1605. II. An Account of the Expedition into Scotland, under the Earl of Hereford, 1544. III. Patten's Account of the Expedition in Scotland under the Duke of Somerset, 1547. Edit., with Desultory Reflections on the State of Ancient Scotland, etc. 4to. Edinburgh.

> The two expeditions mentioned here are listed under EXPEDITIONS.

1801 Brut y Twysogion (Welsh text A.D. 660-1282), edit. by Owen Jones, in *Myvyrian Archaeology of Wales*, vol. II. London.

> The part 681-1066 edit., with translation, by Aneurin Owen, in Petrie, *Monumenta*, London, 1848; the Brut, or the Chronicle of Princes (681-1282), edit. and translated by Rev. J. Williams ab Ithel for the Rolls Series, London, 1860; the Brut, the Gwentian Chronicle of Caradog of Llancarvan (660-1196), edit. by Aneurin Owen, in *Cambrian Arch. Assoc.*, London, 1863; best edition of the Welsh text (680-1282) edit. by John Rhys and J. G. Evans, in *Red Book of Hergist*, vol. II; the text of the Brut from the *Red Book*, Oxford, 1890. See Caradog of Llancarvan under 1584 above.

This, the chief authority for Welsh history down to 1120, seems to be a Welsh translation of the lost Latin chronicle compiled by Caradog (died *ca.* 1250). The earlier portion, to 954, was probably based on the *Annales Cambriae*. From *ca.* 1100 on, the work seems to be contemporaneous with the events narrated.—Gross. See the *Annales Cambriae* under no. 20, Rolls Series, 1858-1911 below.

1807-12   A Collection of Reprints of Famous Chronicles, mostly from the old Folio Editions, edit. by Henry Ellis, E. V. Utterson, R. H. Evans, F. Douce, and others. 15 vols. in 14. 4to. London.

> For contents of this collection, see following:
> Holinshed (see under 1577 above), 6 vols.
> Hall (see under 1548 above).
> Hardyng (see under 1543 above), 2 vols.
> Grafton (see under 1568 above), 2 vols.
> Fabyan (see under 1516 above).
> Froissart (see under 1525 above), 2 vols.
> Arnold's Chronicle (see under 1502 above), together with
> Rastell's Pastimes (see under 1529 above).
> In the reprint of Holinshed the castrated passages are included, many chronological errors corrected, and a copious index furnished.—Thorp, Bookseller.

1821   Chronicle of the Kings of England, from William the Norman to George III, written after the manner of the Jewish Historians, with Notes. London (?).

> Did this work set going the vogue of the facetious style of writing beginning "And so it came to pass that"?

1828   Chronicon coenobii Sanctae Crucis Edinburgensis, iterum in lucem editum. *Publ. Bann. Club,* no. 20, Edinburgh.

> Presented by Robert Pitcairn. The Chronicle of Holyrood ends abruptly at the year 1163. The foundation charter of the House is printed in the same volume.

1829   AMYOT, THOMAS (Editor). Transcript of a Chronicle, entitled An Historical Relation of Certain Passages about the End of Edward III and of his Death. In *Archaeologia,* vol. 22, 204-84, for the Soc. Antiq. London. London.

> Edit. by E. M. Thompson Ross, London, 1874.
> This chronicle covers the period 1328-88, of which only the years 1376-77 were edited by Amyot. It had been transcribed by Stow. The account of the period 1376-77 is full of valuable detail, compiled probably by a contemporary monk of St. Albans. Certain parts may have been the work of Thomas Walsingham (see under Camden, 1603 above). It makes a bitter attack upon the Duke of Lancaster and the Lollards.—Gross.

1838-56   ENGLISH HISTORICAL SOCIETY. A Set of the Chronicles printed under the auspices of the English Historical Society. 29 vols. Numerous facsimilies. 8vo. London.

> For contents see following. A few are singled out for detailed mention.
> 1838   Bede, Historia Ecclesiastica Gentis Anglorum.
>   Gildas, De Excidio et Conquestu Britanniae.
>   Nennius, Historia Britonum.
>   Richard of Devizes, Chronicon de Rebus Gestis Ricardi I.
> 1840   William of Malmesbury, De Gestis Regum Anglorum, 2 vols.
> 1841   Bede, Opera Historica Minora.
> 1841-44   Roger of Wendover, Chronica, 5 vols.
> 1845   Nicholas of Trivet, Annales Sex Regum Angliae.
> 1845-48   Codex Diplomaticus Aevi Saxonici, 6 vols.
> 1846   Adam of Murimuth, Chronica.
>   Gesta Stephani, Regis Anglorum et Ducis Normannorum.
>   Chronique de la Traison et Mort de Ric. II.
> 1848-49   Florence of Worcester, Chronicon ex Chronicis, 2 vols.
>   Walter of Hemingburgh, 2 vols.
> 1850   Henrici V. Gesta.
>   W. Parvi, Historia Rerum Anglicarum, 2 vols.

1838 RICHARD OF DEVIZES. Chronicon Ricardi Divisiensis de Rebus Gestis Ricardi Primi, Regis Angliae. Nunc primum Typis mandatum, curante Josepho Stevenson. London.

> Translated and edit. by J. A. Giles, London, 1841; translated by Jos. Stevenson for Church Historians of England Series, London, 1858; edit. by R. Howlett for the Rolls Series, London, 1884-90.
>
> The date of the compilation is probably 1193. The Introduction of the Rolls edition states that it is one of the most amusing products of the Middle Ages with its "classical quotations, bombastic speeches, and keen gibes mixed up with valuable historical facts." It supplies information available nowhere else on conditions and affairs in England during the early years of Richard I. The author was a monk of St. Swithins, Winchester. He was still alive in 1202.

1841-44 ROGER OF WENDOVER. Chronica, sive Flores Historiarum. Nunc primum edidit Henricus O. Coxe. With Appendix . . . in qua Lectionum varietas additionesque quibus Chronicon istud ampliavit et instruxit Matthaeus Pariensis. 5 vols. London.

> Edit. by H. G. Hewlett for the Rolls Series, 3 vols., London, 1886-89.
>
> The chronicle begins with the Creation and comes down to 1154, the first year of the reign of Henry II. For the relation of this chronicle to that of Matthew Paris, see the Introduction by Luard (Rolls edition of the latter work, 1872-84). For Matthew Paris, see Matthew Parker under 1567-74 above.

1839 Chronicon de Lanercost MCCI. MCCCXLVI. E codice Cottoniano nunc primum typis mandatum. Edit. by Jos. Stevenson. *Publ. Bann. Club,* no. 65. Edinburgh.

> Also *Publ. Maitland Club,* vol. 46, Edinburgh; translated with Notes by Sir Herbert Maxwell, London, 1913.
>
> This contains a general history of affairs in England and Scotland, with references to continental events, 1201-1346.

WARKWORTH, JOHN. Chronicle of the First Thirteen Years of the Reign of King Edward the Fourth. Edit. from the MS. now in the Library of St. Peter's College, Cambridge, by J. O. Halliwell. *Publ. Camden Soc.,* vol. 10. London.

1840 JOCELIN DE BRAKELONDA. Chronica Joselini de Brakelonda. De Rebus Gestis Samsonis Abbatis Monasterii Sancti Edmundi. Nunc primum typis mandata. Curante Gage Rokewode. *Publ. Camden Soc.,* vol. 13. London.

> The Latin text, which is complete in only one MS—Harl. MS. 1005, British Museum— is here printed for the first time. It was edited for the Rolls Series (No. 96) by Thomas Arnold. Translated into English by Thomas Edlyne Tomlins, London, 1844. A modern version in the King's Classics, London, 1907. See below.
>
> This record by a monk of the establishment has been made familiar by Carlisle in his *Past and Present.* It gives a vivid picture of monastic community life as regulated by the abbey, particularly during the rule of the strong-minded Abbot Samson, to whom Jocelin was secretary. The style is pleasing in its humor and naiveté and for its spirited sketches of characters and incidents. It covers the reigns of Henry II and Richard I. The chronicle breaks off abruptly.

1844 TOMLINS, THOMAS EDLYNE. Monastic and Social Life in the Twelfth Century, as exemplified in the Chronicle of Jocelin of Brakelond. London.

1907 JOCELIN OF BRAKELOND. Chronicle of Jocelin of Brakelond. Monk of St. Edmundsbury. Newly translated and edited by L. C. Jane; Introduction by Abbot Gasquet. In King's Classics Series. London.

1842 ROW, JOHN. The History of the Kirk of Scotland from 1558 to 1637; with a Continuation to July, 1639, by his Son. *Publ. Wodrow Soc.,* vol. 4. 8vo. Edinburgh.

1842-45 GILES, J. A. (Translator). Scriptores Monastici. 6 vols. London.

> For contents see following:
> Bede, Works.
> Chronicle of the White Rose (*temp.* Edward IV).

Geoffrey of Monmouth.
Gildas and Nennius.
Richard of Devizes, Chronicle, together with
Richard of Cirencester, Description of England.

1843-48   GILES, J. A. (Editor). Patres ecclesiae Anglicanae. 35 vols. Oxford.

For contents see following:
Aldhelm, Opera.
Arnulf of Lisieux, Epistolae.
Becket, Epistolae et Vita, 4 vols.
Bede, Opera, 12 vols.
Boniface, Opera, 2 vols.
Foliot, Epistolae, 2 vols.
Herbert of Bosham, Opera, 2 vols.
John of Salisbury, Opera, 5 vols.
Lanfranc, Opera, 2 vols.
Peter of Blois, Opera, 4 vols.

1844   For a chronicle of London from the 44th year of Henry III to the 17th year of Edward III, see under LONDON.

1844-51   CAXTON SOCIETY PUBLICATIONS. 16 vols. London.

For contents see following:
Alani Tewkesberiensis Scripta.
Benedicti Petriburgensis De Vita S. Thomae Canterburiensis.
Chronicon Petriburgense.
Chronicon Henrici de Silgrave.
Epistolae Herbert de Lonsinga.
Gaimar, Chronicle.
Galfridi Monumetensis Historia.
Galfridi le Baker Chronicon.
Radulphi Nigri Chronica.
Revolte du Conte de Warwick.
Scriptores rerum Wilhelmi Conquestoris.
Vita quorundam Anglo-Saxonum.
Walteri Dervensis Epistolae.

1845   Chronicles of the White Rose of York: a Series of Historical Fragments, Proclamations, Letters, and other Contemporary Documents relating to the Reign of King Edward the Fourth, with Notes and Illustrations, and a Copious Index. 8vo. London.

1847   Collectanea de rebus Albanicis, consisting of Original Papers and Documents relating to the History of the Highlands and Islands of Scotland. *Publ. Iona Club,* vol. I (all published). 8vo. Edinburgh. (The following item is no. xvii.)

SKENE, WILLIAM F. Extracts from the Irish Annalists, illustrative of the Highlands of Scotland. With early History. A literal Translation. Edinburgh.

1847-64   BOHN'S ANTIQUARIAN LIBRARY. A Series of Translations. 41 vols. London.

For contents see following:
Bede's Ecclesiastical History and Anglo-Saxon Chronicles.
Chronicles of the Crusades; Richard of Devizes; Itinerary of Richard I.
Florence of Worcester.
Giraldus Cambrensis.
Henry of Huntingdon and Acts of King Stephen.
Ingulf, Croyland.
Matthew of Westminster.
Matthew Paris.
Ordericus Vitalis.
Roger of Hovenden.

Roger of Wendover.
Six Old English Chronicles: Ethelwerd, Chronicle; Asser, Life of Alfred; Geoffrey of Monmouth, British History; Gildas, De Excidio; Nennius, History of Britain, and Richard of Cirencester, Speculum Historiale.
William of Malmesbury, Chronicle of the Kings.
    This set contains works other than chronicles. A new edit. 34 vols., London, 1890. For Richard of Cirencester see below.

RICHARD OF CIRENCESTER. Speculum Historiale de Gestis Regum Angliae. London.
    Another edit., by J. E. B. Mayor, for the Rolls Series, 2 vols., London, 1863-69.
    Richard was a monk attached to St. Peter's, Westminster. After a visit to Jerusalem in 1391 he returned to the Abbey, where he compiled this Speculum, which covers the period 447-1066. He composed other works as well. Charles Bertram fathered on him the forgery *De Situ Britanniae* (see Stukeley under 1757, BRITISH, ROMAN, AND SAXON ANTIQUITIES).

1848   Monumenta Historica Britannica, or Materials for the History of Britain, from the Earliest Period, vol. I (extending to the Norman Conquest). 27 plates of Saxon coins, charters, etc. Fol. London. (All published.)

1849   Chronicon Petriburgense, Nunc primum Typis Mandatum, curante Thomas Stapleton. Introduction by John Powell. *Publ. Camden Soc.,* vol. 47. London.

    This was compiled by an unknown monk in the ancient abbey of Peterborough. It begins with the year 1122, making but brief entries for the first hundred years and more minute ones for the next fifty, specifically with regard to Peterborough. But after 1273 it assumes an important character. The Introduction provides a good history of the fortunes of the abbey, its internal life, and the litigations in which it was involved after the death of the abbot Robert de Sutton, 1273.

1852   For the Chronicle of the Grey Friars of London, see under LONDON.

1853   ORDERICUS VITALIS. Ecclesiastical History of England and Normandy. 4 vols. 8vo. London.

1853-58   The Church Historians of England. A series of translations edit. by Rev. Jos. Stevenson. 5 vols. London.

    For contents see following:
Vol. I.   Bede's Historical Works.
Vol. II.   Anglo-Saxon Chronicles; Florence of Worcester; Asser, Book of Hyde; Ethelwerd, Chronicles; Geoffrey Gaimar; Ingulf; John of Wallingford.
Vol. III.   William of Malmesbury, History of the Kings and History of his own Times; Simeon of Durham, Historical Works.
Vol. IV.   Chronicle of Holyrood; Chronicle of Melrose; Chronicle of Winchester and Canterbury; John and Richard of Hexham; Jordan Fantosme; Robert de Monte, Chronicles; William of Newburgh.
Vol. V.   Acts of Stephen; Chronicle of the Isle of Man; Gervase of Canterbury, Archbishops of Canterbury; Giraldus Cambrensis, Instruction of Princes; Richard of Devizes; Robert of Gloucester (excerpts); Robert de Monte, History of Henry I.

1856   An English Chronicle of the Reigns of Richard II, Henry IV, Henry V, and Henry VI. Written before the Year 1471. With an Appendix and Supplementary Additions from the Cotton MS. Chronicle called "Eulogium." Edit. by Rev. John S. Davies, M.A. *Publ. Camden Soc.,* vol. 64. London.

    This is a version of the English Chronicle called the Brut. This text follows it with but little variation as far as Edward III. From Richard II on, the matter becomes more valuable, and there are large and curious additions, though the text of the Brut still serves as the thread of the narrative. This portion of the history is printed for the first time. It had passed through Stow's hands and also Speed's. The author is unknown.—From the Introduction. It relates some curious incidents, such as the attempt in 1440 to encompass the death of King Henry VI by necromancy, and how it was to be accomplished. One gathers that witches were of much concern at the time, and that sorties, sallies, and expeditions were the order of the day.

1858   CHAMBERS, ROBERT. Domestic Annals of Scotland from the Reformation to the Revolution. 3 vols. 8vo. London and Edinburgh.

These annals consist of excerpts from contemporary records arranged chronologically but not fashioned into a continuous narrative, though they are linked together by a running comment from the editor. Different aspects of the same subject are grouped together, such as political passages, religious questions, economic changes, deeds of violence, calamities, storms, etc. These volumes give the impression that to survive in Scotland in those days one had to be tough.

1858-1911   Rerum Britannicarum Medii Aevi Scriptores; or, Chronicles and Memorials of Great Britain and Ireland during the Middle Ages. Published by Authority of H. M.'s Treasury under the Direction of the Master of the Rolls. 99 nos. 8vo. London.

This collection is generally known as the Rolls Series, and as such has been used as reference in this work. The listings to follow omit some of the numbers published, but aim to include all such titles as seem to bear on the purposes of the work in hand. A few of them are singled out for comment. At the conclusion the chronological order of other items is resumed.

No. 1.   CAPGRAVE, J. The Chronicle of England. Edit. by F. C. Hingston. 1858.
This extends from the creation to the year 1417. As a record of the language spoken in Norfolk, it is of considerable value.—Quaritch.

No. 2.   Chronicon Monasterii de Abingdon. Edit. by Rev. J. Stevenson. 2 vols. 1858.

No. 3.   Lives of Edward the Confessor. (La Estoire de Seint Aedward le Rei. Vita Beati Edvardi Regis et Confessoris. Vita Eduardi qui apud Westmonasterium requiescit.) Edit. and trans. by H. R. Luard. 1858.

No. 4.   Monumenta Franciscana. (I. Thomas de Eccleston de Adventu Fratrum Minorum in Angliam. Adae de Marisco Epistolae. Registrum Fratrum Minorum Londoniae. II. A further Collection of original Documents respecting Franciscans in England.) 2 vols. Edit. by Rev. J. S. Brewer and R. Howlett. 1858-82.

No. 6.   The Buik of the Chroniclis of Scotland; or, Metrical version of the History of Hector Boece by Wm. Stewart. Edit. by W. B. Turnbull. 3 vols. 1858.

No. 7.   CAPGRAVE, J. Liber de Illustribus Henricis. Edit. by Rev. F. C. Hingston. 1858.

No. 8.   THOMAS OF ELMHAM. Historia Monasteri S. Augustini Cantueriensis. Edit. by C. Hardwick. 1858.

No. 9.   Eulogium Historiarum sive Temporis. Chronicon ab Orbe condito usque ad A.D. M.CCC.LXVI., a Monacho quodam Malmesburiensi exaratum. Edit. by F. S. Haydon. 3 vols. 1858-63.

No. 10.   Historia Regis Henrici Septimi; a Bernardo Andrea Tholosate conscripta; necnon alia quaedam ad eundem Regem spectantia. Edit. by J. Gairdner. 1858.

No. 11.   HENRY V. Memorials. (Vita Henrici Quinti, Roberto Redmanno auctore. Versus Rhythmici in Laudem Regis Henrici Quinti. Elmhami Liber Metricus de Henrico Quinto.) Edit. by C. A. Cole. 1858.

No. 12.   Munimenta Goldhallae Londoniensis. Liber Albus, Liber Custumarum et Liber Horn. 3 vols. in 4. Edit. and translated by H. T. Riley. 1859-62.

No. 13.   OXNEDES, or OXNEAD (John de). Chronica. Edit. by Sir. H. Ellis. 1859.
The reputed author of the above chronicle, which was in reality written by a monk of St. Benet's, Hulme, Norfolk, died about 1293. The chronicle covers the period from Alfred to 1293. It is particularly valuable for notices of events in the eastern part of the realm, which are not to be obtained elsewhere, and for some curious facts relative to the floods in that part of England, which are confirmed in the Friesland Chronicle of Anthony Heinrich, pastor of the Island of Mohr.—Quaritch.

No. 16.   COTTON, B. DE. Historia Anglicana (A.D. 449-1298). Necnon ejusdem Liber de Archiepiscopis et Episcopis Angliae. Edit. by Rev. H. R. Luard. 1859.

No. 17.   Brut y Twysogion; or, The Chronicle of the Princes of Wales. Edit. and translated by Rev. J. Williams ab Ithel. 1860. (See under 1801 above.)

No. 18.   HENRY IV. Royal and Historical Letters during the Reign of Henry IV. Vol. I, 1399-1404. Edit. by Rev. F. C. Hingston. 1860.
A 2nd volume was printed but was withdrawn from publication.—Quaritch.

No. 20.   Annales Cambriae. Edit. by Rev. J. Williams ab Ithel. 1860.
A fundamental document in research into early Welsh history, especially the oldest of the extant MSS—that printed in Y Cymmrodor, vol. 9, London, 1888. The Brut listed above belongs to the latter part of the 10th century or beginning of the 11th. It is found without title or introduction in the body of a MS by Camden.

No. 21.   GIRALDUS CAMBRENSIS. Opera. Edit. by Rev. J. S. Brewer, James F. Dimock, and G. F. Warner. 8 vols. 1861-91.

No. 23. Anglo-Saxon Chronicle, according to the several original Authorities. Edit. by
         Benj. Thorpe. 2 vols. 1861.
No. 24. RICHARD III and HENRY VII. Letters and Papers illustrative of their Reigns.
         Edit. by J. Gairdner. 2 vols. 1861-63.
No. 25. GROSSETESTE, R. Epistolae. (Illustrating the social Condition of his Time.) Edit.
         by Rev. H. R. Luard. 1861.
No. 26. Descriptive Catalogue of Materials relating to the History of Great Britain and
         Ireland to the End of the Reign of Henry VII. Edit. by Sir T. D. Hardy. 3 vols.
         in 4. 1862-71.
No. 27. HENRY III. Royal and other Historical Letters illustrative of the Reign of
         Henry III. Edit. by Rev. W. W. Shirley. 2 vols. 1862-66.
No. 28. Chronica Monasterii S. Albani. (Thomae Walsingham, 2 vols. Willhelmi
         Rishanger. Johannis de Trokelowe et Henrici de Blaneforde. Gesta Abbatum
         Monasterii S. Albani a Thomas Walsingham, 3 vols. Johannis Amundesham,
         2 vols. Saeculo XVmo floruere, 2 vols. Ypodigma Neustriae a Thomas Wal-
         singham.) Edit. by H. T. Riley. 12 vols. 1863-76.
No. 29. Chronicon Evesham Abbey. Edit. by Rev. W. D. Macray. 1863.
No. 30. RICHARD OF CIRENCESTER. Speculum Historiale de Gestis Regum Angliae. Edit.
         by J. E. B. Mayor. 2 vols. 1863-69. (See under 1847-64 above.)
No. 31. Year Books. Edward I. Years 20-35. Edit. by A. J. Horwood. 5 vols.—Edward
         III. Years 11-20. Edit. by A. J. Horwood and L. O. Pike. 15 vols. 1866-1911.
No. 33. Historia et Cartularum Monasterii Gloucestriae. Edit. by W. H. Hart. 3 vols.
         1863-67.
No. 36. Annales Monastici. (De Margan, Theokesberia et Burton. De Wintonia et
         Waverleia. De Dunstaplia et Bermundeseia. De Oseneia Chronicon Thomae
         Wykes et de Wigornia.) Edit. by Rev. H. R. Luard. 5 vols. 1864-69.
No. 38. RICHARD I. Chronicles and Memorials of the Reign of Richard I. Edit. by Bishop
         Stubbs. 2 vols. 1864-69.
No. 39. WAURIN, J. DE. Recueil des Croniques et Anchiennes Istoires de la Grant
         Bretaigne. Edit. by Sir W. Hardy and E. Hardy. 5 vols. 1864-91.
No. 40. ————. Translation of the above. 3 vols. 1864-91.
No. 41. HIGDEN, R. Polychronicon, together with the English Translation of John of
         Trevisa, and of an unknown Writer in the 15th century. Edit. by Rev. J. R.
         Lumby. 9 vols. 1865-96. (See under 1482 above.)
No. 43. Chronica Monasterii de Melsa. Edit. by E. A. Bond. 3 vols. 1866-68.
No. 44. MATTHEW PARIS. Historia Anglorum, sive ut vulgo dicitur, Historia Minor. Edit.
         by Sir Frederic Madden. 3 vols. 1866-69.
             This is an abridgement and to some extent a continuation of his *Chronica
         Majora*. (For the latter see under 1567-74 above.)
No. 45. Liber Monasterii de Hyda. Edit. by E. Edwards. 1866.
No. 47. LANGTOFT, PETER DE. Chronicle (in French verse). Edit. with Translation by T.
         Wright. 2 vols. 1866-68. (See under 1716-35 above.)
No. 49. HENRY II. Gesta Regis Henrici Secundi Benedicti Abbatis. The Chronicle of the
         Reigns of Henry II and Richard I, A.D. 1169-1192; known commonly under
         the name of Benedict of Peterborough. Edit. by Bishop Stubbs. 2 vols. 1867.
No. 50. Munimenta Academica, or, Documents illustrative of Academical Life and
         Studies at Oxford. Edit. by Rev. H. Anstey. 2 vols. 1868.
No. 51. ROGER OF HOVEDEN. Chronica. Edit. by Bishop Stubbs. 4 vols. 1868-71.
             Hoveden or Howden was envoy of Henry II to the chiefs of Galloway,
         1174. His chronicle deals with the years 732-1201. It was first printed by
         Savile (see under 1596 and 1838-56 above).
No. 52. WILLIAM OF MALMESBURY. De Gestis Pontificum Anglorum libri quinque. Edit.
         N. E. S. A. Hamilton. 1870. (See under 1596 above.)
No. 56. HENRY VI. Memorials of the Reign of Henry VI. Official Correspondence of
         Thomas Bekynton. 2 vols. 1872.
No. 57. MATTHEW PARIS. Chronica Majora. Edit. by Rev. H. R. Luard. 7 vols. 1872-84.
         (See under 1567-74 above.)
No. 58. WALTER OF COVENTRY. Memoriale Fratris Walteris de Coventria. Edit. by Bishop
         Stubbs. 2 vols. 1872-73.
No. 60. HENRY VII. Materials for a History of the Reign. Edit. by Rev. W. Campbell.
         2 vols. 1873-77.
No. 61. Historical Papers and Letters from the Northern Registers. Edit. by Rev. J.
         Raine. 1873.
No. 63. DUNSTAN, SAINT (Archbishop of Canterbury). Memorials of St. Dunstan. Edit.
         by Bishop Stubbs. 1874.
No. 64. Chronicon Angliae, ab Anno Domini 1328 usque ad Annum 1388, Auctore
         Monacho quodam Sancti Albani. Edit. by E. M. Thompson. 1874.
No. 65. BECKET, THOMAS (Archbishop of Canterbury). Thomas Saga Erkibyskups: a
         Life of Thomas Becket in Icelandic. Edit. and translated by M. E. Magnusson.
         2 vols. 1875-88.
No. 66. COGGESHALL, RALPH OF. Chronicon Anglicanum. Edit. by Rev. J. Stevenson. 1875.

No. 67. BECKET, THOMAS. Materials for the History of. Edit. by J. C. Robertson and J. B. Sheppard. 7 vols. 1875-85.

No. 68. DICETO, RALPH DE. Opera Historica. Edit. by Bishop Stubbs. 2 vols. 1876.

No. 71. The Historians of the Church of York and its Archbishops. Edit. by J. Raine. 3 vols. 1879-94.

No. 73. GERVASE OF CANTERBURY. Historical Works. The Chronicle of the Reigns of Stephen, Henry II, and Richard I. Edit. by Bishop Stubbs. 2 vols. (in Latin). 1879-80.

No. 74. HENRY OF HUNTINGDON. Historia Anglorum (A.D. 55 to 1154). Edit. by T. Arnold. 1879. (See under 1652 above.)

No. 75. SYMEON OF DURHAM. Opera Omnia. Edit. by T. Arnold. 2 vols. 1882-85. (See under 1596 above.)

No. 76. EDWARD I and II. Chronicles of the Reigns of Edward I and Edward II. (Annales Londoniensis and Annales Paulini. Commendatio Lamentabilis, etc.). Edit. by Bishop Stubbs. 2 vols. 1882-83.

No. 79. Cartularum Monasterii de Ramesia. Edit. by Rev. W. H. Hart and Rev. A. P. Lyon. 3 vols. 1884-94.

No. 81. EADMER (the Monk). Eadmeri Historia Novorum in Anglia et Opuscula duo de Vita Sancti Anselmi et quibusdam miraculis ejus. Edit. by Rev. M. Rule. 1884.
The first recension of this work is dated 1112; it was completed 1124. The early portion deals with Lanfranc's career. The last two books are a history of the see of Canterbury, 1110-22. For unity of plan and treatment, this work has no equal among the great histories of the 12th century. Eadmer was a monk of Christ Church, Canterbury, and confidential advisor to Anselm.—Gross.

No. 82. STEPHEN, HENRY II, and RICHARD I. Chronicles of the Reigns of Stephen, Henry II, and Richard I. (William of Newburgh, Historia Rerum Anglicarum, bks. I-IV. William of Newburgh, Historia, bk. V. A continuation of the same to 1298. The Draco Normanicus of Etienne de Rouen. The Gesta Stephani Regis Anglorum. The Chronicle of Richard Prior of Hexham. The Relation de Standardo of St. Aelred Abbot of Rivaulx. The metrical Chronicle of Jordan Fantosme. The Chronicle of Richard of Devizes. Chronicle of Robert of Torigni.) Edit. by R. Howlett. 4 vols. 1884-90.

No. 83. Ramsey Abbey. Chronicon, a Saeculo X usque ad Annum circiter 1200. Edit. by Rev. W. D. Macray. 1886.

No. 84. ROGER OF WENDOVER. Chronica. Liber qui dicitur Flores Historiarum ab Anno Domini MCLIV, annoque Henrici Anglorum Regis Secundi primo. Edit. by H. G. Hewlett. 3 vols. 1886-89.

No. 85. The Letter-Books of the Monastery of Christ Church, Canterbury. Edit. and (partly) translated by Rev. J. B. Sheppard. 3 vols. 1887-89.

No. 86. ROBERT OF GLOUCESTER. Metrical Chronicle. Edit. by W. A. Wright. 2 vols. 1887. (See under 1716-35 above.)

No. 87. MANNING, ROBERT (of Brunne). The Story of England. Edit. by F. J. Furnival. 2 vols. 1887.

No. 88. Icelandic Sagas and other Historical Documents relating to the Settlements and Descents of the Northmen on the British Isles. Edit. by G. Vigfusson and translated by Sir G. W. Dasent. 4 vols. 1887-95.

No. 90. WILLIAM OF MALMESBURY. De Gestis Regum Anglorum libri V, et Historiae Novellae, libri III. Edit. by Bishop Stubbs. 2 vols. 1887-89. (See under 1596 above.)

No. 91. GAIMAR, GEOFFREY. Lestoire des Engles solum . . . Maistre Geffrei Gaimar, with Gesta Herewardi. Edit. by Sir T. D. Hardy and C. T. Martin. 2 vols. 1888-89. (Text and translation.)

No. 92. KNIGHTON (or Cnitthon), H. Chronicon. Edit. by Rev. J. R. Lumby. 2 vols. 1889-95.

No. 93. ADAM OF MURIMUTH. Adae Murimuth continuatio chronicarum. Robertus de Avesbury de Gestis Mirabilibus Regis Edwardi Tertii. Edit. by Sir. E. M. Thompson. 1889.

No. 95. MATTHEW OF WESTMINSTER. Flores Historiarum. Edit. by Rev. H. R. Luard. 3 vols. 1890. (See under 1567 above.)

No. 96. Memorials of St. Edmund's Abbey. Edit. by T. Arnold. 3 vols. 1890-96.

No. 97. Charters and Documents illustrating the History of the Cathedral City, and Diocese of Salisbury in the 12th and 13th Centuries. Edit. by Rev. W. Rich-Jones and Rev. W. D. Macray. 1891.

1867 SKENE, WILLIAM F. (Editor). The Chronicle of the Picts, the Chronicle of the Scots and other early Memorials of Scottish History. Edinburgh.

1870-89 BARBOUR, JOHN. The Bruce, or the Books of the most excellent and Noble Prince Robert de Broyas King of the Scots. Compiled by Master John Barbour,

Archdeacon of Aberdeen A.D. 1375. Edit., with Preface, Notes, and Glossarial Index, by Rev. Walter Skeat. 2 vols. E.E.T.S. London.

Reprinted with revisions by Skeat, *Publ. Scot. Text Soc.,* nos. 22-23, Edinburgh, 1894.

1871-80 THE HISTORIANS OF SCOTLAND. Edit. by Skene, Laing, Forbes, etc., from the Original MSS. With Facsimiles and Notes. 10 vols. 8vo. Edinburgh.

This contains: John of Fordun; Andrew of Wyntoun; Lives of Ninian and Kentigern; St. Columba; the Book of Pluscarden; Ancient Inhabitants of Scotland by Innes.

1875 WRIOTHESLEY, CHARLES (Herald). A Chronicle of England During the Reigns of the Tudors, from A.D. 1485 to 1559. Edit. from a MS. by William D. Hamilton, F.S.A. 2 vols. *Publ. Camden Soc.,* vols. 11 and 20, n.s. London.

The author was born in London and passed his life there. His familiarity with the changing face of the city is apparent in his chronicle. He came of a literary-minded family, his immediate forbears having collected MSS, charters, Royal Charters, etc. The many books he probably inherited from his father Stow says he "kept too long from the sight of the learned ᵥ(1561)." He adopted the latter part of Arnold's Chronicle as the starting point of his own, repeating the same blunders. From the eleventh year of Henry VIII, he seems to have depended on his own observations and becomes an independent authority. He notes that Stow and Holinshed were the chief rivals of each other.

1876 ADAM OF USK. Chronicon Adae de Usk, 1377-1421, edit. with Translation and Notes by Sir E. Maunde Thompson. 8vo. London.

2nd edit., Royal Soc. of Literature, London, 1904.
The author was a lawyer, who entered the church. He joined Henry IV's party in the revolution of 1399. Later he was banished to Rome for criticism of the king's government. —DNB.

1877 TACITUS. Annales et Historiae (A.D. 97). Translated for the Bohn Series. 2 vols. London.

This contains numerous references to Britain and the Britons.

1880 STOW, JOHN. Three Fifteen-Century Chronicles, with Historical Memoranda by John Stow. Edit. by James Gairdner. *Publ. Camden Soc.,* vol. 28. London.

This consists of contemporary occurrences written down by Stow.

1909 THOMAS OF ECCLESTON. Chronicle. Introduction and Notes by Father Cuthbert. 8vo. London.

The author was a Franciscan monk, who studied at Oxford. He wrote "De Adventu Fratrum Minorum in Angliam," ca. 1250. This was first printed in the Rolls Series, 1858 (see No. 4 above).

1925 PYNCEBEKE, WALTER. The Pinchbeck Register, etc. Edit. by Lord Francis Hervey. 2 vols. 4to. London.

This comprises the Register of the Abbey of St. Edmunds compiled by Walter Pyncebeke, of Pinchbeck, in Lincolnshire, who was a monk of Bury St. Edmunds. Begun in 1333, it records the disputes between the abbot and the town, papal bulls and privileges, fees and services of knights holding the honor of St. Edmund, and privileges, legal terms, wages, dues. sundry ancient customs, townsmen's customs, Domesday of all the manors and lands of the feudatories, various legal proceedings, maintenance of monks and abbots and servants, etc.—Quoted from Bookseller's Note.

XV
History and Antiquities

("What antiquaries suffer from the neglect of the public is a small thing compared to what they suffer at the hands of one another." This feeling complaint expresses not only the rancor too often found within the group but stands likewise as an apt description of what awaited the labors of this much derided breed of scholars. One could cite additional ill fortune. Many of them saw the work of a lifetime pass into the hands of another for publication, because "amorous Death" would wait no longer. Others were denied even posthumous fame because their property was appropriated by a brother antiquary, and even by an unfilial son, and passed off as his own. Some spent a fortune in gathering their material and died in poverty. And others found themselves in their closing days with palsied hands and dimmed eyesight. The rewards, outside of satisfying an immediate urge, were, in many instances, pitiful indeed. Historians accused them of ignoring method, meaning, and continuity of history; of failing to base their work on any philosophical principle and to give any interpretation of facts, forgetting apparently that they themselves were open to the same charges until the middle of the 18th century. Yet to these men, who took up where the chroniclers left off, is due a large share of the efflorescence of racial pride and national consciousness such as Shakespeare put into the mouth of John of Gaunt. And what later historians owed to the assiduity of these unwearied collectors and transcribers of countless manuscripts, charters, wills, deeds, cartularies, and like records can hardly be estimated. To them later generations of readers are likewise in debt for curious information on the face of the country over which they traveled at the cost of much physical discomfort. They have been sneered at for having produced "folios of tremendous corpulence and dull enough to read;" much of their work has been undone by later scholarship. Yet they ploughed the ground and we reap the harvest. And they deserve the brief resurrection to light that the following pages can achieve for them.

Early in the 18th century, the natural consanguinity of antiquities and county histories thrust itself forward. The fellowship thus struck up remained fairly constant through the period following. The county historian, however, was restricted to definite boundaries, both physical and intellectual. Hence he was less inclined to indulge a personal viewpoint. If his labors proved to be more dull and pedantic, his learning was less liable to be misplaced. Not only the field of history was affected by the study of antiquities, but well nigh every cultural trend that engaged the English gentleman of this century—numismatics; medals; British, Roman, and Saxon finds; architecture; landscape gardening; pottery; furniture; poetry; and the novel.

While this section lists the chief antiquaries and their works, supplementary references will be found in TOURS, DESCRIPTIONS, SURVEYS, HISTORY AND CHRONICLE, etc.

1549 LELAND, JOHN. For an account of England's antiquities, see *The Laboryouse Journey*, under TOURS BY NATIVES.

1575 NEVILLE, ALEXANDER. Alexandri Nevylli de Furoribus Norfolciensium Ketto duce. Liber unus. Eiusdem Norvicus. 4to. London.

> Another edit. at the end of Ocland's *Anglorum praelia, ab anno domini 1327 usque ad annum 1558,* London, 1582; in English by R. W[ood], 12mo, London, 1615; English edit., 4to, London, 1615; again, 1623 and 1650; again in 1750. See below.
> The edition of 1582 contains the first printed account of the city of Norwich. It includes also an engraved map of the descent of the British and Saxon kings.—From Gough, *Anecdotes of Brit. Topog.,* 368. The work ·is a history of the rebellion in Norfolk, in the year 1549, conducted by R. Kett.

> > 1615 NEVILLE, ALEXANDER. Norfolk's Furies, or, A Review of Kett's Camp, with a Table of the Mayors and Sheriffs of Norwich, etc., done out of Latin by R. W[ood]. 4to. London.

> > 1623 ————. The Norfolk Furies and their Foyle under Kett their accursed Captain; with a Description of the famous City of Norwich, englisht by Rich. Wood, Minister of Fretnam, out of the Latin of Alex. Nevil. London.

> > 1650 ————. Norfolke Furies, And their Foyle. Vnder Kett, their accursed Captaine. With a Description of the famous Citie of Norwich, and a Catalogue of the seuerall Gouernors thereof from the Dayes of King Edred, with the Succession

of Bishops there . . . with other memorable Accidents. Englished by Rich. Wood, Minister of Fretnam, out of the Latine Copie of Alexander Neuill. 4to. London.

1587   CHURCHYARD, THOMAS. For antiquarian matters relating to Scotland, see his *Chips Concerning Scotland,* under DESCRIPTIONS.

————. For antiquarian matters relating to Wales, see his *The Worthyness of Wales,* under DESCRIPTIONS.

1602   CAREW, RICHARD. For a history of Cornwall, see his *Survey of Cornwall,* under SURVEYS.

1605   CAMDEN, WILLIAM. Remaines of a Greater Worke Concerning Britaine, the Inhabitants thereof, their Language, Names, Surnames, Empresses, Wise Speeches, Poesies, and Epitaphs. 4to. London.

> 2nd edit., 4to, London, 1614; 3rd, enlarged, 4to, 1623; 4to, 1629; with additions, 4to, 1636; 6th edit., 4to, 1647; again, 1657; 7th impression, 8vo, 1674; Gibson's edit., 1722; 8vo, 1870.
> This miscellaneous collection of antiquities may be considered as left-overs from his *Britannia* (see under 1586, DESCRIPTIONS).

> 1674   CAMDEN, WILLIAM. Remains concerning Britain, their Languages, Names, Armories, Moneys, Impresses, Apparel, Artillerie, Proverbs, Poesies, etc. 7th impression, much amended, with many rare Antiquities never before imprinted, by the Industry and Care of J. Philpot and W. D. 8vo. London.

VERSTEGAN, RICHARD (pseud. for RICHARD ROWLANDS). A Restitution of Decayed Intelligence: In antiquities, Concerning the most noble and renowned English Nation. By the studie and travell of R[ichard] V[erstegan]. Numerous illustrations. 4to. Antwerp.

> 2nd edit., 4to, London, 1628; again in 1634 and 1655.
> Rowlands had assumed his grandfather's name of Verstegan. Later he was imprisoned for publishing while at Paris a work protesting against Queen Elizabeth's treatment of Roman Catholics in England. The above work contains the first printed collection of the meanings and etymologies of Old English words arranged alphabetically. It contains further discourses on the etymologies of Old English proper names, as well as those of Danish and Norman families; on the antiquity of the English tongue and its Teutonic origin; the arrival of the Saxons, Danes, and Normans; and ancient titles of honor, dignity, and office. It relates also an early version of the Pied Piper of Hamelin: ". . . the pied piper with a shrill pipe went piping thorow the streets, and forthwith the Rats came all running out of the Houses in great numbers." See Adams, *Old English Scholarship in England.*

1629   SELDEN, JOHN. Marmora Arundelliana. London.

> Though these remains of antiquity are not English, yet the work is included here because they were one of the sights that Englishmen traveled to see. It is an account of the ancient remains of art in the collection of Thomas Howard, 2nd Earl of Arundel. In the volume was included a chronicle called the *Parian Chronicle,* deciphered from the Marmor Parium, documents relative to the treaty between the people of Smyrna and of Magnes, followed by versions in modern Greek and Latin. This Chronicle is listed as a publication in *Gent. Mag.,* vol. 58, Feb. Selden's book had a rapid sale.—*DNB.*

1631   WEEVER, JOHN. For ecclesiastical antiquities see his *Funeral Monuments,* under ECCLESIASTICAL HISTORY AND ANTIQUITIES.

1639   ADAMSON, HENRY. For a poetical description of the antiquities of Scotland and of Perth, see his *Muses Threnodie,* under DESCRIPTIONS.

1654   Boxhorn, M. S. Origines Gallicae in quibus Gallorum origines, antiquitates, mores, lingua, etc., illustrantur; cui accedunt Antiquae Linguae Brittanicae Lexicon Britannico-Latinum, et Proverbia Druidum. 4to. Amsterdam.

1656   Dugdale, Sir William. The Antiquities of Warwickshire Illustrated, from Records, Leiger-Books, Manuscripts, Charters, Evidences, Tombes and Armes, beautified with Maps, Prospects, and Portraitures. Numerous maps and copperplate engravings by Hollar, etc. Fol. London.

> 2nd edit., corrected by the author, revised, augmented, and continued by Dr. Wm. Thomas, rector of Exhall, 2 vols., fol., London, 1730; original edit. reprinted by a bookseller at Coventry, with Hollar's plates (but carelessly done), 1765; in extracts, 8vo, London, 1786.
> Perhaps to few county histories is such constant reference made by lawyers, antiquarians, or other writers, as to Dugdale's *Warwickshire.* "This celebrated county history, the result of twenty years' indefatigable research, is not only considered the *chef d'œuvre* of Sir William, but in the words of Mr. Gough, 'it must stand at the head of all our county histories.' "—Quoted by Bookseller. Dugdale is said to have been the first county historian to include church notes and to have impressed the practice on all of his successors, with the exception of Hasted. This work is further distinguished by its print of the first engraved monumental portrait of Shakespeare—that of the bust in Stratford Church. There are also some notices of Shakespeare, his daughter, and his son-in-law, John Hall.—Robinson, no. 373.

> > 1730   Dugdale, Sir William. Antiquities of Warwickshire . . . continued by Dr. Wm. Thomas, Rector of Exhall in this County, with complete Lists of the Members of Parliament and Sheriffs, from the original Records, an alphabetical Index and blazonry of the Arms on the several Plates . . . and several additional Prospects of Seats, Churches, Tombs, and new and correct Maps of the County, and several Hundreds from an actual Survey by Henry Leighton, F.R.S. 2 vols. Fol. London.

Finett, Sir John (Master of the Ceremonies). Finnett Philoxenia: Observations touching the Reception, Precedence, Audience, Punctillios, etc., of forren Ambassadors in England. With the Dedication of James Howell. 8vo. London.

1661—Enderbie, Percy. Cambria Triumphans, or, Britain in its Perfect Lustre, shewing the Origin and Antiquity of that Illustrious Nation. The Succession of their Kings and Princes, from the First, to King Charles of Happy Memory. The Description of the Countrey: the History of the Antient and Moderne Estate. The Manner of the Investure of Princes, with the Coats of Arms of the Nobility. Engraved plates of Coats of Arms of the Welsh Nobility. Fol. London.

> An early 19th century reprint, 2 vols., fol., London, 1812.
> The history and description are copied, if not verbally transcribed, from Powel (see under 1584, HISTORY AND CHRONICLE); but the history has authorities noted in the margins, and comes down no later than 1281. The first book of volume II contains the early part of the Welsh history, and a description of Wales; the 3rd is the history continued; the 4th contains a list of the princes of Wales of English blood, their investiture, jurisdiction, etc. Wood calls this work justly enough a scribble from late authorities.—Gough, 584.

1662   Vaughan, Robert. British Antiquities Revived; or, A Friendly Contest touching the Soveraignty Of the Three Princes of Wales in antient Times, managed with certain Arguments, whereunto are Answers applied . . . To which is added, The Pedigree of the Right Hon. the Earl of Carberry, Lord President of Wales: with a Short Account of the Five Royal Tribes of Cambria; by the same Author. 4to. Oxford.

> Dr. Nicolson says that this contains "a great many very pretty remarks and discoveries." The author was patronized by Ussher, to whom he sent his translation of the Annals of Wales into English for his opinion on whether they were worth printing. His researches and collections intended for the new edition of Powel's history passed into the hands of

Thomas Ellis of Jesus College, Oxford, who began to print Powel's work with his own and Vaughan's, but completed no more than 128 pp., 4to, dated 1663, most of which was sold for waste paper. Vaughan's collections were accessible to Edward Lhuyd, who succeeded Dr. Plot as keeper of the Ashmolean Museum (see Lhuyd under 1707 below).— Gough, 584-85.

1666 DUGDALE, SIR WILLIAM. Origines Juridiciales, or, Historical Memorials of the English Laws, Courts of Justice, Forms of Tryal, Punishment in Cases Criminal, Law Writers, Law Books, Grants and Settlements of Estates, Degree of Serjeants, Innes of Court and Chancery: also a Chronologie of the Lord-Chancellors, and Keepers of the Great Seal, Lord-Treasurers, Justices Itinerant, Justices of the King's-Bench and Common-Pleas, Barons of the Exchequer, Masters of the Rolls, King's Attorneys and Sollicitors, and Serjeants at Law. Copperplates of several halls, the portraits of the then judges, etc., by Hollar. Fol. London.

> This was abridged and continued in *Chronica Juridicialia*, 8vo, 1685 and 1739.—Gough, 333-34.

1672 Antiquities of Durham. Published by J. Davies, of Kidwelly. London.

HOWELL, JAMES. Divers Choice Pieces of that Renouned Antiquary Sir Robert Cotton, preserved from the Injury of Time and Exposed to Publick Light for the Benefit of Posterity. 12mo. London.

1673 LEYCESTER, SIR PETER. Historical Antiquities, in two Books: the first treating in general of Great-Britain and Ireland; the second containing particular Remarks concerning Cheshire, faithfully collected out of authentick Histories, old Deeds, Records, and Evidences. Whereunto is annexed, A Transcript of Doomsday-Book, so far as it concerneth Cheshire, taken out of the original Record. Folding plan and woodcuts of arms. Fol. London.

> A copy dated 1683 was advertised for sale in a book catalogue.
> The second part is divided into four: of which the first three relate to the county in general; but the fourth treats only of the antiquities of Bucklow hundred. Sir Peter having impeached the legitimacy of Amicia, daughter of Hugh Cyveliock, Earl of Chester, an historical contest was begun between him and his cousin Sir Thomas Mainwaring, which ended not until the death of the former. Some eleven pieces refuting and counter-refuting passed between them. The quarrel was ridiculed in a ballad of the time.—Gough, 117-19. These tracts were edited in three volumes by William Beaumont, *Publ. Chetham Soc.*, vols. 78-80, 1869.

1675 Magna et antiqua charta quinque portuum domini regis et membrorum eorundem. 8vo. Cantabrigia.

1677 THOROTON, ROBERT. Antiquities of Nottinghamshire, extracted from Records, Original Evidences, Leiger Books, other MSS. and Authentick Authorities. Maps, numerous portraits, views, plates of antiquities, etc., on copper by W. Hollar. Fol. London.

> 2nd edit., 3 vols., 4to, London, 1790; 3 vols., 4to, London, 1797.
> The second edition received large additions from John Throsby. Thoroton commenced his Antiquities in 1667. He first worked on some transcript notes from Domesday Book. . . . He did not conduct all his researches personally, but employed paid assistants at great expense to himself. His industry was mainly exercised among family archives, registers, estate conveyances, monumental heraldry, and epitaphs.—From *DNB*. His model is said to have been Burton's *Leicestershire* (see under 1622, DESCRIPTIONS).

1679   B[LOUNT], T. Fragmenta Antiquitatis. Antient Tenures of Land, and Jocular Customs of some Mannors, made publick for the Diversion of some, and Instruction of others. 8vo. London.

1684   WRIGHT, JAMES (Barrister). The History and Antiquities of the County of Rutland; collected from Records, antient MSS., Monuments on the Place, and other Authorities: illustrated with Sculptures. Fol. London.

> 10 pp. of additions were printed in 1687; new edit., parts I and II (all printed), Stamford, 1788.
> The author owed much to the collections which Sir Wingfield of Ryhall, an eminent antiquary, made during his confinement in the Tower in the Civil War out of Dodsworth's papers. But his book is far from perfect.—Gough, 452.

1685   JOHNSTON, DR. NATHANIEL. Enquiries for Information towards the Illustrating and Compleating the Antiquities of Yorkshire. Single sheet fol. London.

> The author of this prospectus was a Yorkshire antiquary. His collections for a topographical account of the county, which he spent over thirty years in gathering, he intended to publish in ten volumes, but he died (1705) before he completed his design. His handwriting was said to be so atrocious that no amount of practice availed in deciphering some of the names. He fell into obscurity in his later days and seemingly passed away without attracting any notice.

1693   ASHMOLE, ELIAS. Institution, Laws, and Ceremonies of the Order of the Garter. The History of its Foundation, Windsor Castle, and College, etc. Engravings and portrait of Charles II. Fol. London.

> Another edit., 8vo, London, 1715.
> Ashmole's name is perpetuated in the Ashmolean Museum at Oxford. He later bequeathed his library to the university.

1695   KENNETT, WHITE (Bishop of Peterborough). Parochial Antiquities attempted in the History of Ambrosden, Burcester, and adjacent Parts in the Counties of Oxford and Bucks., with extensive Glossary of Obsolete Terms. 9 plates of views of seats and churches by M. Burghers, several displaying the costume of the period, and landscape gardens, etc. 4to. Oxford.

> New edit., greatly enlarged from the author's own MS notes, 2 vols., 4to, Oxford, 1818.
> This work will be duly valued as long as ecclesiastical history bears any repute amongst us.—Bishop Nicolson, quoted by Bookseller. Kennett was one of the original members of the Society for Propagating the Gospel in Foreign Parts. For an estimate of his scholarly abilities, see David Douglas, *English Scholars*.

1698   SPELMAN, SIR HENRY. Posthumous Works of Sir Henry Spelman, relating to the Laws and Antiquities of England, publish'd from Original Manuscripts with Life of the Author. Portrait and pedigree. Fol. Oxford.

> This was republished with additional works and a revised Life, fol., Oxford, 1723; and again, edit. by Bishop Edmund Gibson, fol., London, 1727.
> Spelman was a great collector of MSS, a member of the Society of Antiquaries, the founder of a (short-lived) "Saxon" lectureship at Cambridge. He was a laborious student of the Old English language, and an extensive editor of his own researches. His *Archaeologus*, published at London, 1626, marks an important stage in the study of Old English. See Adams, *Old English Scholarship in England*.

1700   CHAUNCY, SIR HENRY. The Historical Antiquities of Hertfordshire, with the Original of Counties, Hundreds or Wapentakes, Boroughs, Corporations, Towns, Parishes, Villages, and Hamlets, the Foundation and Origin of Monasteries, Churches, Rectories, etc., in General, describing those of this County

in Particular, as also the several Honors, Mannors, Castles, etc., of the Nobility and Gentry, etc., also the Characters of the Abbotts of St. Albans. Portrait and engravings, map of the county. Fol. London.

Another edit., fol., London, 1703.
It were to be wished that more care had been taken with the engravings. The author had by him considerable additions and continuations, which afterwards came into the hands of N. Salmon, and became the chief foundation of his *History of Hertfordshire* (see under 1728 below).—Gough, 196. It is not so much to the credit of Chauncy that he had a witch arrested in 1712.

Cox, Rev. Thomas. A Topographical, Ecclesiastical, and Natural History of Buckinghamshire. Map. 4to. London.

Other counties, perhaps all, were similarly treated and under the same date.

1704 Brady, Robert, M.D. Historical Treatise of Cities, Boroughs, shewing their Original, and whence and from whom they received their Liberties, Privileges and Immunities. 2nd edit. Fol. London.

His historical works are laborious, and are based on original authorities; they are marked by the author's desire to uphold the royal prerogative.—Quoted by Sotheran, no. 869.

1705 Bowack, John. The Antiquities of Middlesex; being a Collection of the several Church Monuments in that County: also an Historical Account of each Church and Parish; with the Seats, Villages, and Names of the most Eminent Inhabitants, etc. Part I. beginning with Chelsea and Kensington. Now in the Press. Part II. will also contain the Parishes of Fulham, Hammersmith, Chiswick, and Acton. Fol. London.

Arber, *Term Catalogues*, vol. III, 464, gives the name as Bowback. No more was published.

1705-10 Blomefield, Rev. Francis. An Essay towards a Topographical History of the County of Norfolk, continued by the Rev. Charles Parkin. 2nd edit. Portrait, pedigrees, engravings. 11 vols. 4to. London.

Blomefield began to issue his *History of Norfolk* in numbers in 1639. He died before he got the third volume published. See Blomefield under 1736 below for continuation of this work.

1707 Lhuyd, Edward. Archaeologia Britannica, giving some Account, additional to what has been hitherto publish'd, of the Languages, Histories and Customs of the Original Inhabitants of Great Britain; from Collections and Observations in Travels through Wales, Cornwall, Bas-Bretagne, Ireland and Scotland. Vol. I, Glossography (all published). Fol. Oxford.

Volume II was never published, owing to ravages by fire at different times and places. The volume printed contains a Comparative Vocabulary of the Original Languages of Britain and Ireland; Cornish Grammar; Irish-English Dictionary; Armoric Grammar, etc. —Maggs, no. 715. The author was keeper of the Ashmolean Museum, and a very industrious antiquary. He traveled over Wales, Cornwall, Scotland, Ireland, Armoric Bretagne several times, compared their antiquities, and made observations on the whole. Before he had opportunity to digest them into proper form he died (1709), as was the fate of many another laborer in this field. Many of his observations he communicated to Bishop Gibson, who revised Camden's *Britannia*.—Gough, 585-86.

Sibbald, Sir Robert. The History, Ancient and Modern, of the Sheriffdoms of Linlithgow and Stirling; in which there is an Account of the royal Seats and

Castles, and of the royal Burghs, and the Ports, and of the Religious Houses, and Hospitals, and of the most remarkable Houses of the Nobility and Gentry, with an Account of the Natural Products of the Land and Water. Fol. Edinburgh.

Reprinted, Edinburgh, 1892.

1707-08   The Phenix; or, A Revival of Scarce and Valuable Pieces from the Remotest Antiquity down to the Present Time. 2 vols. 8vo. London.

1708   The Monthly Miscellany, or, Memoirs for the Curious. Vol. II. Reprinted at the end of Leland's *Itinerary* (Hearne's edition), vol. I. Oxford.

This is so cited by Gough, 79, who adds that it contains a letter giving an account of some antiquities lying between Windsor and Oxford. See Hearne under 1725 below.

ROGERS, N. Memoirs of Monmouthshire, anciently called Gwent, and by the Saxons, Gwentland; shewing when this County was subdued by the Romans, but never by the Saxons or Danes, nor by the Normans, till King Henry II. That this was the first Place in Great Britain in which Christianity was planted. That a College of 200 Philosophers was first of all founded at Caer-Leon, the Station of the Roman Chief Legion in this Island, called Augusta Secunda: and that the first Academy in Britain was at Caer-Went, the Venta Silurum of the Ancients. With an Historical Account of the most important Affairs there transacted; the several Rarities of Nature in this County, of its several Kings and Princes, and other eminent Men born and bred therein; and that the Kings of England and Scotland, since Henry VII. derive themselves from this County. With an Appendix, of the Case of Wentwood, with the severe Usage and Suffering of the Tenants in the late Reigns for defending their Rights. 12mo. London.

This is all that has been printed about this county, and it is very superficial.—Gough, 364.

1710   SIBBALD, SIR ROBERT. The History, Ancient and Modern, of the Sheriffdoms of Fife and Kinross; with the Description of both, and of the Firths of Forth and Tay, and the Islands in them; in which there is an Account of the royal Seats and Castles; and of the royal Burghs and the Ports; and of the Religious Houses and Schools; and of the most remarkable Houses of the Nobility and Gentry: with an Account of the Natural Products of the Land and Water. Fol. Edinburgh.

Republished in a *Collection of Several Treatises,* fol., Edinburgh, 1739; also separately, Cupar-Fife, 1803.

——————. Miscellanea quaedam eruditae antiquitatis quae ad Borealem Britanniae majoris partem pertinent, in quibus loci quidam historicorum, variaque monumenta antiqua illustrantur. Cura Rob. Sibbaldi, M.D., eq. aur. Fol. Edinburgh.

This contains also an appendix on the friths Bodotria and Tay, and their islands. Of the eleven sections of this very miscellaneous work the two first relate to the history of Orrok, and the antiquities found there and in other places, with three cuts; the third treats of Caesar's root called *Chara,* the *Karemile* of the Highlands; the fourth, the elogiis medicinae indigenae; the fifth, of fossils, represented in plate 2; the sixth of magis, and the druids; the seventh of marine animals; the eighth of the Nautilus; in the ninth Sir R. Gordon clears up the vulgar error about the Barnacles; the tenth and eleventh are

medical exercitations; the twelfth [*sic*] is an essay on the antient temples, followed by another eleventh on medical subjects.—Gough, 619.

1711   SALMON, NATHANIEL. The History of Essex. Fol. London.

>   The publication of this work was described by Gough as "his last shift to live." See under 1739-40 below.

1712   MORTON, JOHN. For an account of the antiquities of Northamptonshire, see his *Natural History of Northamptonshire,* under NATURAL HISTORY.

1713   ILLIDGE, SAMUEL. British Curiosities in Art and Nature, exhibiting an Account of natural and artificial Rarities both Antient and Modern. 12mo. London.

>   Another edit., 8vo, London, 1721; again, with author's name, 12mo, London, 1728. See below.
>   There is some doubt whether the above is the work of Illidge. His name appears only with the edition of 1728. The first edition contains a scheme of twenty-two columns of things to be observed by strangers. For a work with a similar title see Burton under 1682, DESCRIPTIONS.

>>   1721   ILLIDGE, SAMUEL. British Curiosities in Art and Nature, giving an Account of Rarities both Ancient and Modern—viz., Monuments, Monasteries, Walls, Roman Camps, Coins, Temples, Palaces, Caverns, Flowers, Birds, etc.; likewise an Account of the Posts, Markets and Fair-Towns; to which is added, A very useful Scheme, containing a Brief Account of each County in England, printed on a Sheet. 8vo. London.
>>   This contains an account of Stratford-on-Avon, with mention of Shakespeare, 70-71.—Bookseller's Note.

1715   LELAND, JOHN. De Rebus Britannics Collectanea. Edit. by Thomas Hearne. 6 vols. Oxford.

>   Another edit., 6 vols., 1774.

      WILLIS, BROWNE. Notitia Parliamentaria, or, A History of the Counties, Cities, and Boroughs in England and Wales, who they return, Antiquities, Charters, Lords, Monasteries, etc., Roman Towns, Nobility, etc. 8vo. London.

>   A 2nd vol. appeared in 1716. Another edit. of the 1st vol., London, 1730. A 3rd vol. was added in 1750.

1716-23   MACKENZIE, SIR G. Works, on the Antiquities of Scotland, Laws, Science of Heraldry, with Etymologies of hard Words. Portraits and coats of arms. 2 vols. Fol. Edinburgh.

1717   ERDESWICKE, SAMPSON. For the antiquities of Staffordshire, see his *Survey of Staffordshire,* under SURVEYS.

1718-19   AUBREY, JOHN. The Natural History and Antiquities of the County of Surrey, begun in the Year 1673, and continued to the Present Times. Illustrated with sculptures. 5 vols. 8vo. London.

>   Another edit., 5 vols., 8vo, London, 1730.
>   Aubrey, who may be called a general Boswell for his short but vivid accounts of some of the great men of his time, began his topographical tours through the county in 1673, and in the course of his peregrinations made copious collections, which were revised, corrected, and published by Dr. Rawlinson.—The following letter was addressed to the author: "Sir. Something I would contribute to your natural history of Surrey, if it were possible; but your performance is so accurate, that you left nothing almost for those who shall come after you. . . ."—John Evelyn, quoted by Nichols, *Literary Anecdotes,* vol. I.

1719   Ashmole, Elias. The Antiquities of Berkshire, with a large Appendix of valuable Papers, Pedigrees of the most considerable Families in the County, and a particular Account of the Castle, College, and Town of Windsor. Portrait by Van de Gucht, folding map by Hollar, folding pedigrees, plates of antiquities and the arms of John Latton. 3 vols. 8vo. London.

> Another edit., 3 vols., 8vo, London (date?) ; again, fol., Reading (date?).
> Ashmole was Windsor Herald and son-in-law to Sir William Dugdale. He has left an enduring monument to his name in the collection of curios and the library he donated to Oxford.

Harris, Dr. John. The History of Kent, in five Parts, containing an exact Topography of the County, its Civil, Ecclesiastical, and Natural History, and the History of the Royal Navy of England, Vol. I (all published), with List of Subscribers, etc., portrait by Vertue, and numerous double-page bird's-eye views of seats by J. Kip, and maps. Fol. London.

> Harris died before he had completed more than half of his design, so that not quite three parts were published out of the five. The second volume was to have contained the history of Rochester Cathedral, an account of the eminent persons of the county, the religious foundations, and the history of the royal navy. The materials for all these heads were got ready, and a good part of them transcribed before the author's death, which happened before the publication of the first volume. He was only eight years compiling this work from the former description of Kent, with little alteration, and few continuations of families. The author experienced no small opposition and lack of proper assistance from those who had materials in their hands. What is published has barely merit enough to make the second volume regretted. Most of the plates were engraved by Kip, except a few by Harris, and all were drawn by Badeslade.—Gough, 211. He died an absolute pauper on Sept. 7, 1719.

1720   Hearne, Thomas. A Collection of Curious Discourses, written by Eminent Antiquaries upon several Heads in our English Antiquities. 8vo. Oxford.

> Another edit., with added matter, 2 vols., 8vo, London, 1775.
> These discourses were the unpublished papers of the Society of Antiquaries, dissolved by King James I in 1604, in his fear that some of the members might be subversively inclined, although they had pledged themselves to take no notice of state affairs. Dr. Thomas Smith made transcripts of these papers with the intention of publishing them, but dying before he could complete the work, he passed them on to Hearne. The above edition contained 48 of the papers; that of 1775 added a number omitted by Hearne, but includes the preface and appendix dealing with the lives of the members printed in the first edition. The range of the subjects is extensive—Ancient Britons, Etymology, Duelling, Money, Epitaphs, etc.

Rawlinson, Dr. Richard. The English Topographer : or, An Historical Account (from Printed Books and MSS) of all the Pieces that have been written relating to the Antiquities, Natural History, or Topographical Description of any Part of England. Alphabetically digested. By an Impartial Hand. 8vo. London.

> Another edit., 8vo, London, 1729.
> The plan of this work was utilized in a much broader and improved way by Richard Gough in the second edition of his *British Topography*, 1780 (see Gough under 1768 below). Rawlinson was a great antiquary for his day and left behind him much published and unpublished work. He assisted in bringing to light many county descriptions and histories. For his parochial collections see under 1920 below. The introductory portion of the above work lists all general topographical undertakings from Morden on.

1723   Lewis, Rev. John. The History and Antiquities, Ecclesiastical and Civil of the Isle of Tenet (Thanet), in Kent, with Appendix of Papers, Records, etc. Engravings. 4to. London.

> 2nd edit., 2 vols. in 1, 4to, London.
> The author is chiefly known by his biographies of Wycliffe, Caxton, and others.— Bookseller's Note.

Memoirs of the Antiquities of Great-Britain, relating to the Reformation, etc., containing the first Institution of the Order of the Grey-Friars, some Remarks upon Wolsey, Cromwell, etc. Plates. 12mo. London.

ROWLANDS, REV. HENRY (Vicar of Llanidan). Mona Antiqua Restaurata, an Archaeological Discourse on the Antiquities, Natural and Historical, of the Isle of Anglesey, the antient Seat of the British Druids. In two Essays. With an Appendix, containing a comparative Table of Primitive Words, and the Derivatives of them in several of the Tongues of Europe; with Remarks upon them. Together with some Letters, and three Catalogues added thereunto. 1. Of the Members of Parliament for the County of Anglesey. 2. Of the High Sheriffs; and, 3. Of the beneficed Clergy thereof. 8 full-paged plates, 2 portraits, engraved initial letters and tail-pieces. 4to. Dublin.

> 2nd edit., by Dr. Owen of St. Olave's, corrected both in language and matter, with additions of notes by Lewis Morris, London. 1766.
> The second edition clears up some difficulties in the first, which was very incorrectly printed, and which came out after the author's death. At the end of both editions are some letters between the author and E. Lluyd on grammatical subjects.—Gough, 607-08. The work contains interesting particulars respecting the aboriginal Britons, druids, etc.

1724 STUKELEY, WILLIAM. For an account of antiquities and curiosities in nature and art, see his *Itinerarium Curiosum,* under TOURS BY NATIVES.

1725 BOURNE, H. Antiquitates Vulgares, or, The Antiquities of the Common People, giving an Account of their several Opinions and Ceremonies. 8vo. Newcastle.

HEARNE, THOMAS. Letter containing an Account of some Antiquities between Windsor and Oxford, with List of Pictures in the School-Gallery, Bodleian Library. 8vo. Oxford.

> This is a reprint of an item included in the *Monthly Miscellany* (see this work under 1708 above).

1726 MADOX, T. (His Majesty's Historiographer). Firmi Burgi, or, An Historical Essay concerning the Cities, Towns and Boroughs of England, taken from Records. Fol. London.

A Treatise of Gavelkind, both Name and Thing, shewing the true Etymologie and Derivation of the One, the Nature, Antiquity, and Original of the Other, with sundry emergent Observations pleasant to be known of Kentish-Men; corrected, with the Life of the Author, by the Bishop of Peterborough (White Kennett), with frontispiece. 4to. London.

> The standard work on this Kentish tenure.—Bookseller's Note.

1728 SALMON, NATHANIEL. The History of Hertfordshire, describing the County and its Ancient Monuments, particularly the Roman, with the Character of those that have been the Chief Possessors of the Lands. Map. Fol. London.

> "Extracted and epitomized, though he says but very poorly and injudiciously, from Sir Henry Chauncy. Yet I think it better done than Mr. Willis's own performances, I mean where he has been left to himself."—Hearne, *Remains,* vol. III, 18.

1729 INNES, THOMAS. For his essay on the ancient Picts, the Romans, etc., in Britain, see his *Critical Essay on the Ancient Inhabitants of the Northern Parts of Britain*, under BRITISH, ROMAN, AND SAXON ANTIQUITIES.

1730 A Compleat History of Essex, containing a Geographical Description, Ecclesiastical, Civil and Literary History, Antiquities, etc. Folding map. 4to. London.

History of Berkshire, containing Geographical Description, Ecclesiastical, Civil, Natural and Literary History, Antiquities, etc. Folding map by Morden. 4to. London.

1732 COKER, JOHN. For the antiquities of Dorsetshire, see his *Survey of Dorsetshire*, under SURVEYS.

MORGAN, J. Phoenix Britannicus, being a miscellaneous Collection of Scarce and Curious Tracts . . . collected by J. Morgan. 4to. London.
See The *Phenix* under 1707-08 above.

TINDAL, REV. NICHOLAS. The History of Essex: Containing 1. Doomsday of Essex; 2. History of the Manours, etc.; 3. Antiquities, etc.; with a large Introduction, containing the State of the County from Julius Caesar's Invasion to the Present Time, digested and improved by N. Tindal, Vicar of Great Waltham, from Materials collected by T. Jekyl, of Broking, J. Ousley, late Rector of Pamfield, and particularly by W. Holman, late of Hasted, who spent 20 Years in making Collections for their work. Parts I-II (all published). Folding map of the Hundred of Hinckford. 4to. London.

1732-35 PECK, FRANCIS. Desiderata Curiosa: or, A Collection of Divers Scarce and Curious Pieces relating chiefly to Matters of English History; consisting of Choice Tracts, Memoirs, Letters, Wills, Epitaphs, etc. 2 vols. 4to. London.
Issued again by T. Evans, 2 vols., 4to, London, 1779.
Volume I and book i of volume II deal with Elizabeth's reign. The work is a mixed collection of pieces on English history and personages, and of scattered out-of-the-way facts. The author was rector of Goadby and later prebendary of Lincoln. The second edition has some memoirs of the life and writings of Peck. The following item is selected from among the pieces for separate listing:

The History and Antiquities of the Isle of Man. By James Stanley Earl of Derby and Lord of Man, beheaded at Bolton, Apr. 1, 1651, with an Account of his many Troubles and Losses in the Civil War, and of his own Proceedings in the Isle of Man during his Residence there in 1643: interspersed with large and excellent advices to his Son Charles Lord Strange upon many curious Points.
From the original MS all in his own handwriting, divided into chapters and illustrated with contents and notes, introduction and appendix by the editor.—Gough, 609. For Stanley and the fate of the Isle of Man, see Seacombe under 1746 below.

1732-47 HOME, HENRY (Lord Kames). Essays upon British Antiquities: Introduction of Feudal Law into Scotland, Succession, etc. Also Essays upon Law, Jus Tertii, Vinco Vincentem, etc. 2 vols. 8vo. Edinburgh.

1736   SALMON, NATHANIEL. The Antiquities of Surrey, collected from the most antient Records. With some Account of the Present State and Natural History of the County. 8vo. London.

1736-45   BLOMEFIELD, FRANCIS. Essay towards a Topographical History of the County of Norfolk. 2 vols. Fol. Fersfield (vol. I) and Norwich (vol. II).

> Nos. 1 to 21 were issued in parts, running to p. 604 of vol. I (nearly complete), beginning with 1736 and completed in 1739. Vol. II in 1745. Continued by Rev. Charles Parkin, after Blomefield's death (1752), and completed by a hack writer, 5 vols., fol., Lynn, 1775; the whole republished, 11 vols., 8vo, London, 1805-10. A Supplement was added in 4to, 1929. See below.
> Blomefield set up his own press in 1736 and began issuing this work in numbers. He died before he had completed vol. III, which was taken up by Parkin, "a Most incompetent man," who likewise died before he had finished the task. It was ultimately brought to its end by some hack writer in the employ of the bookseller Wittingham of Lynn, where the third volume was published. The two remaining volumes were put out at Lynn. An Index of the names in the edition of 1805-10 was published by J. N. Chadwick at King's Lynn, 1862.—Vol. I contained matter relating to Thetford and vol. II the history of Norwich. Blomefield made use of the materials collected by Peter le Neve who had left behind him much material on the history of this county, as well as the collection of Norroy, who had spent above forty years in amassing the greatest fund of antiquities for his native county that was ever collected for any single county in the kingdom. These MSS passed into the hands of that industrious antiquary Thomas Martin, and later into the possession of Blomefield. He was also greatly assisted by Bishop Tanner, who had been chancellor of that diocese and was well acquainted with innumerable records dealing with the county. Tanner also died before the completion of the work. Other valuable materials were amassed by J. Kirkpatrick, merchant in Norwich, a judicious antiquarian, and an intimate friend of le Neve. Parkin had drawn up accounts of certain deaneries for parts left unfinished.—Gough, 366. The *DNB* characterizes the work as full of errors, scanty in its descriptions of buildings, ridiculous in its etymologies, wanting in critical acumen, yet an enduring monument of hard work and truly a labor of love. Like so many of his brother searchers in antiquities Blomefield died in hard circumstances.

> 1739-75   BLOMEFIELD, FRANCIS, and PARKIN, CHARLES. An Essay towards a Topographical History of the County of Norfolk, containing a Description of the Towns, Villages, Hamlets, with the Foundations of Monasteries, Churches, Chapels and other Religious Buildings, etc., likewise an Account of the Castles, Seats and Manors, with their Present and Antient Owners. Numerous views of ancient monuments, churches, etc., folding pedigrees and coats of arms. 5 vols. Fol. Fersfield, Norwich, Lynn.

> 1929   A Supplement to Blomefield's Norfolk, being a Series of Articles on the Antiquities of the County, contributed by many distinguished Antiquarians, and profusely illustrated with about sixty plates in full colour, selected and reproduced from the collection of water colour drawings made during the last century by the Rev. S. C. Neville-Rolfe. With an Introduction by Christopher Hussey. 4to. London.

1737   BRIDGES, JOHN. The History and Antiquities of the County of Northampton. The first Part (164 pp. in folio). London.

> This valuable work was first projected and begun in the year 1719 by John Bridges, Esq. and F.S.A., a man in the highest degree qualified to direct such an undertaking, being of sound judgment, various and extensive learning, and equal skill and diligence in the investigation of Antiquities; who properly commenced his career by a personal visitation of every parish in the County.—Nichols, *Literary Anecdotes*, vol. II.

1738   MALCOMBE, DAVID. An Essay on the Antiquities of Great Britain and Ireland: Wherein they are placed in a clearer Light than hitherto. Designed as an Introduction to a larger Work, especially an Attempt to shew an Affinity betwixt the Language, etc., of the ancient Britons, and the Americans of the Isthmus of Darien. In Answer to an Objection against revealed Religion. 8vo. Edinburgh.

> Another edit., 8vo, London (?), 1744.
> This contains Letters, Essays and other Tracts illustrating the antiquities of Great Britain and Ireland. The last piece, "Irish-English Dictionary," is imperfect, having pp. 1 to 16 only.—From Bookseller's Note.

Tracts on the English, Welsh, and Irish. (So cited in Rowlands, *Cambrian Bibliography,* without place or other identification.)

1739   PROBUS BRITANNICUS. Marmor Norfolciense; or, An Essay on an Ancient Prophetical Inscription, in monkish Rhyme, lately discover'd near Lynn in Norfolk. By Probus Britannicus (i. e., Dr. Samuel Johnson). 8vo. London.

> Another edit., with notes and a Dedication to S. Johnson, LL.D., by Tribunus. 8vo, London, 1775.

1739-40   SALMON, NATHANIEL. The History and Antiquities of Essex, from the Collections of Mr. Strangeman; with Notes and Illustrations by Nathaniel Salmon. Fol. London.

> This was begun in Nov. 1739; and the nineteenth number, with title page and subscribers' names appeared in Feb. 1740/1. The author's death put a stop to the work, when he had gone through about two-thirds of the county.—Nichols, *op. cit.,* vol. II. Another notice of the work states that he had drawn upon the collection of T. Jekyll, the papers of Mr. Ouseley, and Mr. Holman. Gough says of it that, despite its extravagances, it was the best history of the county then extant.

1741-42   GENT, THOMAS. Historia Compendiosa Anglicana: or, A Compendious History of England, with an Appendix relating to York, an Historical Account of Pontefract, etc.; with which is bound up "Judas Iscariot," by Thomas Gent. 3 vols. in 2. 8vo. York.

> Whether Gent wrote the History is not certain from the listing. But see his *The Antient and Modern History of . . . York,* under 1730, TOWNS.

1742   A Compleat History of Somersetshire, etc., to which is added, A Scheme of all the Market-Towns, etc. Fol. Sherborne.

1743   Memoirs of the Antiquities of Great Britain relating to the Reformation. 12mo. London.

1743-52   STUKELEY, DR. WILLIAM. Palaeographia Britannica, or, Discourses on Antiquities in Britain. 3 nos. 4to. London and Stamford.

> 1743   No. 1. Origines Roystonianae, or An Account of the Oratory of Lady Roisia, Foundress of Royston, discovered in August, 1742. 4to. London.
> Another edit., with change in phrasing, 8vo, Cambridge. This brought forth an attack from Charles Parkin, as follows:
>
> 1744   PARKIN, CHARLES. An Answer to, or Remarks upon Dr. Stukeley's Origines Roystonianae; wherein the Antiquity and Imagery of the Oratory lately discovered at Royston in Hertfordshire are truly stated and accounted for. 4to. London.
> Parkin affirms the oratory to have belonged to a hermitage long before Lady Roisia's time (*ca.* 1167), and that her ladyship was not buried there as Stukeley had asserted. This was answered by Stukeley, as follows:
>
> 1746   No. 2. Origines Roystonianae, or A Defence of Lady Roisia de Vere, Foundress of Roiston, against the Calumny of Mr. Parkin, Rector of Oxburgh: wherein his pretended Answer is refuted; the former Opinion further confirmed and illustrated. To which occasionally are added, many curious Matters in Antiquity: and six copperplates. 4to. Stamford.
> Parkin countered with:
>
> 1748   PARKIN, CHARLES. A Reply to the Peevish, Weak, and Malevolent Objections brought by Dr. Stukeley, in his Origines Roystonianae No. 2, against an Answer to, or Remarks upon, his Origines Roystonianae No. 1, wherein the said answer is maintained; Royston proved to be an old Saxon Town, its Derivation and

Original: and the History of Lady Roisia shewn to be a meer fable and figment. 4to. Norwich.

Stukeley closed the controversy with a No. 3 of *Palaeographia Britannica*, London, 1752.

1744-46 The Harleian Miscellany, or, A Collection of Scarce, Curious and Entertaining Pamphlets and Tracts found in the late Earl of Oxford's Library, with Historical, Political and Critical Notes and an Index. 8 vols. 4to. London.

The bookseller Thomas Osborne acquired from the widow of Edward Harley, 2nd Earl of Oxford, the books, pamphlets, and tracts belonging to the famous library of Robert Harley. Urged to publish a selection of the rarer tracts and pamphlets, he employed the antiquary Wm. Addys to supervise the text and Samuel Johnson to write the Preface and Proposals. The Introduction was reprinted separately. This is said to be Johnson's first attempt to write a literary history.

1745 TRAIN, J. An Historical and Statistical Account of the Isle of Man, from the earliest Times, etc., with a View of the Ancient Laws, Customs, and Superstitions. 2 vols. in 1. Douglas.

1746 SEACOMBE, JOHN. Memoirs containing Genealogical and Historical Account of the House of Stanley, from the Conquest to the Death of James, Earl of Derby, in 1735, with a full Description of the Isle of Man, etc. 4to. Liverpool.

An edit., 4to, Manchester, 1767; another, London (?), 1793.

This ill printed, ill spelt, ill written, confused book seems partly taken out of Bishop Rutter's MSS who was tutor to Lord Strange and chaplain in the family at the siege of Latham House, of which he wrote an account.—Gough, 610. The relation of the Isle of Man to the Crown was a peculiar one. By a formal deed in 1290 the Manx had placed themselves under the protection of Edward I. Succeeding kings of England granted the island to various favorites until 1406, when it was granted in perpetuity to Sir John Stanley, to be held of the crown of England, by rendering to the king, his heirs, and successors, a cast of falcons at their coronation. This family afterwards became the House of Derby, which continued to rule as kings of Man till 1651, when the style Lord was adopted. The island passed by default of issue to James, 2nd Duke of Athol. In 1765 the Athol family sold the island to the British government, retaining certain rights and privileges. In 1829 these were likewise sold. The total sum received by the Athol family in 1765 and 1829 amounted to 493,000 pounds.—From an article by the Rev. T. E. Brown in *Chambers' Encyclopedia*, quoted by David MacRitchie, in his paper, "Notes on Manx Language and Folklore," *Trans. Gaelic Society of Inverness*, vol. 30, 218-19, 1919-1922. For more details on the island see Waldron, *A Description of the Isle of Man*, under 1731, DESCRIPTIONS.

1747-1904 Vetusta Monumenta quae ad rerum Britannicarum memoriam conservandam [pertinent] Societas Antiquariorum Londini sumptu suo edenda curavit. Volumen primum. His accessit sodalium societatis ab anno MDCCXVII catalogus. Fol. London.

This was issued at intervals with the English title of Ancient Monuments Illustrative of the History and Antiquities of Great Britain. Long intervals separated the appearance of the various volumes. The third came out in 1796; the fifth in 1835; the sixth in 1842; and part four of the seventh in 1904.

The Society of Antiquaries, which was founded toward the close of Elizabeth's reign and suppressed by that timid pedant James I, was again incorporated by George II in 1751. The above volumes consist of prints engraved at their expense. The set of 1904 contains 352 finely engraved plates of views of churches, castles, monuments, seals, plans, lamps, vases, bronzes, portraits, etc., with accounts of different antiquities.

1750(?) HALS, W. The Compleat History of Cornwall. Part II. Being the Parochial History (of 72 parishes). Fol. Exeter.

Part I was never published.

HEATH, CAPTAIN ROBERT. For an historical account of Cornwall, see his *Natural and Historical Account of the Islands of Scilly,* under DESCRIPTIONS.

1751   DICEY, THOMAS. An Historical Account of Guernsey from its First Settlement, with Remarks on Jersey and other Channel Islands. 8vo. London.

      Another edit., London, 1798.

     KENNEDY, DR. A Discourse on Oriuna. 4to. London. (So cited in Bandinel.)

     MORRIS, LEWIS. A Short History of the Crown Manor of Creuthyn, in the County of Cardigan, South Wales. (Place?) (So cited in Rowlands, *Cambrian Bibliog.*)

     Two Historical Accounts of the Making of the New Forest in Hampshire by King William the Conqueror, and Richmond Park . . . by Charles the First. 8vo. London.

1752   JACKSON, —. Chronological Antiquities. (Place?) (So cited in Ponton's Catalogue.)

1753   CARTER, EDMUND. The History of the County of Cambridge, from the Earliest Account to the Present Time, 1753; and also a particular Account of the Antient and Modern Cambridge, with the City of Ely, and the Parishes therein; and an Account of the several Towns and Villages, in an Alphabetical Order: The History of the University of Cambridge from its Original to the Year 1752, in which a particular Account is given of each College and Hall, etc. 2 vols. 8vo. Cambridge.

      The author was a schoolmaster in Cambridge. Under each parish are set forth the particulars of the ravages committed in the churches by W. Dowling, employed by the Government (1643) to destroy all the ancient monuments, etc., as ministering to superstition, of which ravages he kept a detailed account, published by Dr. Grey in 1739. Bishop Hall saved the windows in his chapel at Norwich from destruction by taking out the heads of the figures; and this is the reason we see so many faces in church windows supplied with white glass.—Gough, 93.

1754   BORLASE, WILLIAM. Observations on the Antiquities, Historical and Monumental, of the County of Cornwall, consisting of several Essays on the first Inhabitants, Druid Superstitions, Customs, and Remains of the most remote Antiquity in Britain and the British Isles, exemplified and proved by Monuments now extant in Cornwall and the Scilly Islands, faithfully drawn on the Spot, and engraved according to their Scales annexed, with a Summary of the Religious, Civil, and Military State of Cornwall before the Norman Conquest: illustrated by the Plans and Elevations of several antient Castles, . . . and a Vocabulary of the Cornu-British Language. Fol. Oxford.

      2nd edit., with revisions and additions by the author, to which is added a map of Cornwall and 8 new plates, fol., London, 1769.

      This is the best and completest account of Cornwall . . . and contains the most consistent and satisfactory relation of Druidism, supported by the best vouchers, the remains of which are scattered up and down this county, where it seems to have subsisted in its greatest purity and splendor as well as to have maintained its empire longest.—Gough, 124. This work was largely consulted by Buckle for his *History of Civilization.*—Bookseller's Note. For his *Natural History of Cornwall,* see under 1758, NATURAL HISTORY.

Queries proposed to Gentlemen in the several Parts of Great Britain in the Hope of obtaining a better Knowledge of its Antiquities and Natural History. 8vo. London.

Queries similar in form and wording are to be found in the *Gentleman's Magazine*, vol. 25, 157-59.

1755 WILLIS, BROWNE. The History and Antiquities of the Town, Hundred, and Deanery of Buckingham: containing a Description of the Town, Villages, Hamlets, Monasteries, Churches, Chapels, Chantries, Seats, Manors; their ancient and present Owners; together with the Epitaphs, Inscriptions, and Arms in all the Parish Churches; and State of the Rectories, Vicarages, Donatives; their Patrons, and Incumbents, Terriers, and Valuations in the King's Books. Also some Account of the Earls and Dukes of Buckingham, and High-Sheriffs of the County. With a Transcript of Domesday-Book, and the Translation thereof into English. Map. 4to. London.

This was the result of many years of labor initiated by the circulating of queries dated Apr. 8, 1712.—Gough, 89.

1757 BUSWELL, JOHN. An Historical Account of the Knights of the most Noble Order of the Garter, from its first Institution in the Year 1360 to the Present Time, by John Buswell, one of the Gentlemen of his Majesty's Chapel Royal and of his Majesty's Free Chapel of St. George at Windsor. London.

MAITLAND, WILLIAM. The History and Antiquities of Scotland from the Earliest Account of Time to the Death of James I, A.D. 1437, and continued from that Period to the Accession of James VI to the Crown of England, A.D. 1603. 2 vols. Fol. London (or Edinburgh?).

This was written in a most uncouth style. The author was self-conceited, knew little, and wrote worse.—Gough, *British Topog.*, quoted by Nichols, *Anecdotes*, vol. V. Later criticism is to the effect that the work is of particular interest and value for the light it throws on early Celtic Scotland, its times, manners, and inhabitants. The continuation was by another hand.—Dr. Thomas Granger.

1759 GOODALL, W. An Introduction to the History and Antiquities of Scotland, containing many curious Particulars either little known or entirely overlooked by other Writers. 2 vols. Fol. Edinburgh.

This was first issued in Latin, prefixed to Fordun's *Scotichronicon*. Reprinted, 8vo, London, 1769 and 1773; again at Edinburgh, 1782.

On a Stone Coffin found at Litchfield. Conjectures concerning the Person buried in it. To Mr. Green at Litchfield. In *Gent. Mag.*, vol. 29, 65-8. London.

1762 PARKIN, CHARLES. A Topographical History of Freebridge Hundred and Half, containing the History and Antiquities of the Borough of King's Lynn, with a Description of the Towns, Villages and Hamlets, etc. Plans and 2 plates. Fol. Lynn.

Also dated 1772, perhaps another edition.

1764 The Beauties of England, or, A Comprehensive View of the Antiquities, Seats of the Nobility, Chief Villages, Market-Towns and Cities, etc. 12mo. London.

1766   The History of the City and County of Norwich, from the Earliest Accounts to
       the Present Time. Folding plan and engravings. 2 vols. 8vo. Norwich (?).

>   The same title is given for 1768.

MORANT, PHILIP. The History and Antiquities of the County of Essex: compiled
from the best and most ancient Historians; from the Domesday-Book, Inquisitiones post Mortem, and other the most valuable Records and MSS., etc., particularly from the Collections, and the great Improvements of the late most
accurate Mr. John Booth. The Whole digested, improved, perfected, and
brought down to the Present Time. Fol. London.

>   Another edit., 2 vols., fol., with maps and views, London, 1768.
>   The three numbers that were published making up the first volume comprise only
>   certain hundreds, with maps of each and views of certain seats. The collections of N.
>   Salmon, who published about 1739 nineteen numbers of a history of this county, with those
>   of Samuel Dale, Richard Symons, H. Wanley, Smart Lethieullier, were put into the hands
>   of Morant, rector of St. Mary's, Colchester, and form the basis of this work.—Gough, 161.

TICKELL, REV. JOHN. The History of the Town and County of Kingston-upon-
Hull, from its Foundation in the Reign of Edward the First to the Present
Time. Folding and other plates. 4to. London.

>   Another edit., 4to, Hull, 1798.

1768   Antiquities in Dorsetshire. In *Gent. Mag.*, vol. 38, 109-13. London.

FEILDE, REV. THOMAS, M.A. A General History of Staffordshire; comprehending its Antiquities, Natural History, Historical Accounts of Families, Present
State of Manufactures, Public Works, Produce, etc. Illustrated with Views of
the Public Buildings, Principal Seats of the Nobility and Gentry, some Remains
of Antiquity and the Subjects of Natural History, and an improved map of the
County. Compiled from the MS. of the late learned and ingenious Dr. Wilkes,
of Willenhall, in the said County, with considerable Additions by the Rev.
Thomas Feilde, Head Master of the Free Grammar-School at Brewood, in the
same County. (Place?)

>   Gough states that proposals for this work were being circulated. Query: was it ever
>   printed?

GOUGH, RICHARD. Anecdotes of British Topography; or, An Historical Account
of what has been done for illustrating the Topographical Antiquities of Great
Britain and Ireland. 4to. London.

>   2nd edit., corrected and enlarged, and brought down to 1779, 2 vols., 4to, London, 1780.
>   Gough left a third edition ready for the press, with many considerable additions, the
>   printing of which was begun in 1806, to be interrupted by a great fire and the declining
>   health of the author. A corrected copy and plates were left to John Nichols, who pro-
>   fessed himself ready to "relinquish his right, if the respectable Curators of the Oxford
>   Press think proper to undertake a new edition."—Nichols, *Literary Anecdotes*, vol. VI, 273.
>   Gough was a tireless student of topography and antiquities. His edition of Camden's
>   *Britannia*, which came out in 1789, took seven years to translate and nine to print. For
>   the good opinion held of his *Anecdotes* by his contemporaries, see the review in *Gent. Mag.*,
>   vol. 38, 377-80; 530-31. How much this present work owes to this volume, both in listing
>   of titles and in annotations, will become evident to one who works through it.

RUDDER, SAMUEL. The History of the Parish and Abbey of Hayles in Gloucestershire. Fol. Cirencester.

1769 FORDUN (John of). An Introduction to the History and Antiquities of Scotland, translated from the Original Latin. London.

>   See Fordun under 1722, HISTORY AND CHRONICLE.

TETLOW, RICHARD JOHN. An Historical Account of the Borough of Pontefract, in the County of York. 8vo. Leeds.

WALLIS, JOHN. For the antiquities of Northumberland and part of Durham, see his *The Natural History and Antiquities of Northumberland,* under NATURAL HISTORY.

1770 Archaeologia: For this journal published by the Society of Antiquaries, see under GENERAL REFERENCE.

KNIGHT, —. Knight's Old England, a Pictorial Museum of Regal, Ecclesiastical, Baronial, Municipal, and Popular Antiquities. Numerous colored plates and 2,546 engravings of remains, churches, cathedrals, mansions, monuments, portraits, arms, coins, medals, autographs, costumes, etc. 2 vols. London. (The date is approximate.)

A New and Complete History of Essex, from a late Survey, compared with most celebrated Historians, containing a Natural and Pleasing Description of the several Divisions of the County, with their Products and Curiosities of every Kind both Ancient and Modern, and a Review of the most remarkable Events and Revolutions there, from the Earliest Era down to 1769, by a Gentleman, dedicated to Peter Muilman of Kirby Hall. Folding plates and maps. 6 vols. 8vo. Chelmsford.

1771 GOWER, FOOTE. Sketch of the Materials for a New History of Cheshire: with some Accounts of the Genius and Manners of its Inhabitants, and of some local Customs peculiar to that distinguished County: in a Letter to Thomas Falconer, of Chester. 4to. Chester.

>   2nd edit., with a new preface, Chester (?), 1773; 3rd edit., London, 1800.

A Letter pointing out some Mistakes in Harris's History of Kent. In *Gent. Mag.,* vol. 41, 448. London.

1772 HEARNE, THOMAS. Liber Niger; or, Black Book; containing Papers relative to the History and Antiquities of England. 2 vols. Oxford (?). (So cited in Ponton's Catalogue.)

WALPOLE, HORACE. Miscellaneous Antiquities; or, A Collection of Curious Papers, either republished from Scarce Tracts, or now first published from Original MSS. 4to. Strawberry-Hill.

1773 IVES, JOHN. Select Papers chiefly relating to English Antiquities published from the Originals in the Possession of John Ives. 4to. London.

Low, G. An Account of Antiquities in Stromness. In *Archaeologia,* vol. 3. 4to. London.

STRUTT, JOSEPH. Regal and Ecclesiastical Antiquities of England from Edward the Confessor to Henry VIII. 50 etched plates. 4to. London.

> Another edit., with additions, 4to, London, 1777; again, London, 1787 and 1793. See below.

> 1777 STRUTT, JOSEPH. The Regal and Ecclesiastical Antiquities of England: containing the Representations of all the English Monarchs, from Edward the Confessor to Henry VIII; together with many of the Great Persons that were eminent under their several Reigns. The Whole carefully collected from antient MSS. 60 plates. 4to. London.

1773-77   GROSE, FRANCIS. The Antiquities of England and Wales. 4 vols. and 2 vols. added as supplement. Numerous plates. 4to. London.

> Another edit., likewise with hundreds of plates, fol., London, 1784-87. Several times republished with the *Antiquities of Scotland* (see under 1789 below) and *Antiquities of Ireland* (1791).
> These volumes gain immensely from the very fine views of cathedrals, churches, abbeys, castles, and ancient remains. The 52 maps of the counties of England and Wales have historical accounts at the bottom which are continued on the back. The total number of views of England and Wales, and the Islands of Guernsey and Jersey amounts to 589, besides 40 plans, the headpieces, and other plates illustrative of his prefatory dissertations on monastic institutions, castles and military subjects, Gothic architecture, and druidical and sepulchral remains. In the summer of 1789 he set out on a tour of Scotland for the purpose of collecting material to illustrate the antiquities of that country. Before he had concluded his researches there, he moved over to Ireland to round out the design of illustrating the whole kingdom. He died in Dublin in 1791.

1774   HUTCHINS, JONATHAN. History and Antiquities of Dorset, with a Copy of Domesday Book and Inquisitio Gheldi for the County. Map and plates. 2 vols. Fol. London.

> 2nd edit., 4 vols., edited by Gough, 1796-1815; modern edit., by W. Shipp and J. W. Hodgson, 4 vols., Westminster, 1861-70. See below.
> Reviewed *Gent. Mag.,* vol. 44, 583-85; 621-22; the first volume of the 2nd edition reviewed *Gent. Mag.,* vol. 67, 771. The author's house was burned along with almost the whole town of Wareham, July 25, 1762. The MSS were saved by Mrs. Hutchins at the risk of her own life. After the work appeared, the value of the book advanced far beyond the subscription price. It was remarked in a review of the time, "With respect to the ornaments of style and diction, they will not be much sought for in works of this sort."— Nichols, *Lit. Anec.,* vol. VI, 418. The work contains good descriptions of the camps, barrows, and plans which line the ridges and crown the hilltops of the chalk ranges. The great dykes, Roman and Vicinal Ways, the White Horse of the hillside, and the gigantic human figure which at Cerne Abbas occupies a similar position are also depicted.—From Harrison, *Bibliog. of the Great Stone Monuments of Wiltshire.* The views published in this *History* were printed separately as well.

> 1769-1815 HUTCHINS, JONATHAN. History and Antiquities of Dorset; compiled from the most antient Historians, Inquisitiones post Mortem and other valuable Records, and MSS. in the Public Offices, and Libraries, and in Private Hands, with a Copy of Domesday Book, and the Inquisitio Gheldi for the County; interspersed with some remarkable Particulars of Natural History, and adorned with a correct Map of the County, and Views of Antiquity, Seats of the Nobility and Gentry, etc. 2nd edit., corrected, augmented, and improved. 4 vols. Fol. London.
> This was brought out under difficulties, as the whole impression was burnt in a fire, with the exception of one copy of the third volume, that occurred at Nichols' printing office in 1808. The third volume was delivered to subscribers in 1812 and the fourth in 1814. An Appendix of additions and corrections appeared soon after. —This is the second instance of a second edition of a County History getting into print. The first was Dugdale's *Warwickshire,* which Hutchins took for his model —From the review.

URQUHART, SIR THOMAS. Tracts of the Learned and celebrated Antiquarian; with Pedigrees of the Urquharts. 8vo. Edinburgh.

1774-76 STRUTT, JOSEPH. Horda Angel-Cynnan: A Compleat View of the Manners, Customs, Arms, Habits, etc., of the Inhabitants of England, from the Saxons' Arrival to the Reign of Henry VIII, with a Short Account of the Britons during the Government of the Romans. 157 plates. 3 vols. 4to. London.

> The first two vols. translated into French by Boulard, 2 vols., 12mo, Paris, 1789. See below.

> 1789 (In French.) Angleterre Ancienne, ou tableau des moeurs, usages, armes . . . des anciens habitans de l'Angleterre. (Translated by A. M. H. Boulard.) 2 vols. 12mo. Paris.
> According to Lowndes, Strutt lent the plates to the French translator, who never returned them, and they were said to be lost. For this reason Henry G. Bohn was unable to reprint this with the author's other works.—Bookseller's Note.

1775 OWEN, REV. NICHOLAS. A History of the Island of Anglesey, from its first Invasion by the Romans, until finally acceded to the Crown of England: together with a Description of the Towns, Harbours, Villages, and other Remarkable Places in it; and of several Antiquities relating thereto never before made public. Serving as a Supplement to Rowland's Mona Antiqua Restaurata. To which are also added, Memoirs of Owen Glendowr: . . . Translated from a MS. in the Library of Jesus College, Oxford: To which are subjoined, Notices Historical and Illustrative. The Whole collected from authentic Remains. 4to. London.

> Priodolir y gwaith hwn i'r Parch. Henry Owen, M.D., golygydd yr ail Argraffiad o'r 'Mona Antiqua.' Y mae gwyneblen arall i Memoirs of Owen Glendowr: . . . Originally written by Mr. Thomas Ellis, Rector of Dolgelle, in Merionethshire; and now faithfully copied out of a MS. in the Library of Jesus College in Oxford.—Rowlands, *Cambrian Bibliog.*

SHAW, REV. L. The History of the Province of Moray, including Part of Banffshire, the Whole of the Shires of Nairn and Moray, and Part of Invernesshire, before they were directed into Counties. Edinburgh.

WATSON, JOHN. The History and Antiquities of the Parish of Halifax. Etched portrait, plans, and copperplates of antiquities, druidical remains, etc. 4to. London.

> 2nd edit., with additions and corrections by F. A. Leyland, 4 parts (all published), fol., London, 1869.

1775-84 The Antiquarian Repertory, a Miscellany intended to preserve and illustrate several valuable Remains of Old Times. 4 vols. 4to. London. (Compiled by Grose, Astle, and others.)

> Vol. I reviewed *Gent. Mag.*, vol. 46, 560, where it is called "a valuable treasure collected from fragments of antiquity." Besides numerous plates, it contains historical notes on manners, customs, antiquities, laws of England, etc. The review of 1785 (vol. 55, 301) says that it did not stand up in the execution of the plates.

1776 BORTHWICK, WILLIAM. Remarks on British Antiquities, etc. 8vo. Edinburgh.

RIDPATH, REV. GEORGE. The Border History of England and Scotland, deduced from the earliest Times to the Union of the two Crowns; comprehending a par-

ticular Detail of the Transactions of the two Nations with one another, Account of remarkable Antiquities, and a Variety of interesting Anecdotes of the most considerable Families and distinguished Characters in both Kingdoms. 4to. London.

Revised edit. by Ph. Ridpath, Berwick, 1848.

1777　BRAND, JOHN. Observations on Popular Antiquities: including the Whole of Mr. Bourne's Antiquitates Vulgares. With Additions to every Chapter of that Work; as also an Appendix containing such Articles on the Subject as have been omitted by that Author. 8vo. Newcastle-upon-Tyne.

Edited by Henry Ellis, 2 vols., 4to, London, 1813; also in Knight's *Miscellanies*, London, 1840-42; in Bohn's Antiquarian Library, 1849; edited by W. C. Hazlitt, 3 vols., 1870.
Reviewed *Gent. Mag.*, vol. 47, 383-85. The *Antiquitates Vulgares* was originally published in 1725. Among the matters presented are proposals to regulate popular customs, which, though apparently harmless, are really sinful, and most of them superstitions originating in ancient heathenism or modern monkery.—From the review.

Britannia Curiosa: or, a Description of the most remarkable Curiosities of the Island of Great Britain. 6 vols. Plates. 8vo. London.

NICOLSON, J., and R. BURN. The History and Antiquities of the Counties of Westmorland and Cumberland. 2 folding maps by Kitchin. 2 vols. 4to. London.

An Index, Kendal, 1934. See below.
Reviewed *Gent. Mag.*, vol. 48, 272-74. Burn was a well-known lawyer and magistrate, and Nicolson the nephew of Bishop Nicolson of Carlisle. Compared with other histories of the counties, this one is not very interesting, being mainly a history of manors, tithes, and genealogies, under particular parishes.—From the review. This work was based on a large MS collection for the histories of the two counties left by William Nicolson, Bishop of Carlisle, and uncle of the first named author.

1934　NICOLSON, JOSEPH, and RICHARD BURN. Index to Nicolson's and Burn's History and Antiquities of the Counties of Westmorland and Cumberland. Abridged and revised from the MS. of the late Daniel Scott. Edit. by Henry H. Strickland. *Publ. Cumberland and Westmoreland Antiquarian and Archaeological Soc.*, vol. 17, extra ser. Kendal.

NIMMO, REV. WILLIAM. General History of Stirlingshire; its ancient Monuments, and most important and curious Transactions, since the Roman Invasion, with the Natural History of the Shire. Large folding map. 8vo. Edinburgh.

2nd edit., by Rev. W. Macgregor, 2 vols., 1817; again, edit. by R. Gillespie, London and Glasgow, 1880; 4th, 1895.
The work contains a reference to the decrease of birds, owing to the progress of factories in Scotland. The beginning of the book has much to say about the Antonine Wall and other Roman remains.—Bookseller's Note.

OWEN, REV. NICHOLAS. British Remains; or, A Collection of Antiquities relating to the Britons: Comprehending, i. A Concise History of the Lord Marchers; their Origin, Power, and Conquests in Wales. ii. The Arms of the Ancient Nobility and Gentry of North Wales. iii. A Letter of Dr. Lloyd, Bishop of St. Asaph's, concerning Jephrey of Monmouth's History. iv. An Account of the Discovery of America, by the Welsh, more than 300 Years before the Voyage of Columbus. v. A Celebrated Poem of Taliesin, translated into Sapphic Verse. The Whole selected from original MSS. and authentic Records. To which are also added, Memoirs of Edward Llwyd, Antiquary. Transcribed from a MS. in the Museum, Oxford. 8vo. London.

THROSBY, JOHN. The Memoirs of the Town and County of Leicester. 6 vols. 12mo. Leicester.

WILLIAMS, JOHN. An Account of some remarkable ancient Ruins, lately discovered in the Highlands and northern Parts of Scotland. 8vo. Edinburgh.

> See the same in *Annual Register,* vol. 20, 146-53. This deals largely with "vitrified forts."

1778 The History of Cheshire, containing King's Vale-Royal, with Extracts from Leycester's Antiquities of Cheshire, and the Observations of later Writers, particularly Pennant, Grose, etc. The Whole forming a complete Description of the County, with all its Hundreds, etc. 2 vols. 8vo. Chester.

> Reviewed *Gent. Mag.,* vol. 49, 411. The reviewer makes sarcastic remarks on the loud-mouthed promises made eight years ago by the present editors of this work, which finally were realized in this meagre republication of old materials, eked out with a little new criticism by a Chester bookseller.

Museum Britannicum, being an Exhibition of a great Variety of Antiquarian and Natural Curiosities belonging to that Cabinet, illustrated with Prints, by John and Andrew Rymsdyk. Fol. London.

1778-99 HASTED, EDWARD. The History and Topographical Survey of Kent, containing the Antient and Present State of it, Civil and Ecclesiastical, from Public Records and other the best Authorities. 168 views of seats, etc., maps, besides engravings in the text. 4 vols. Fol. Canterbury.

> This well-known work underwent various enlargements, to as high as fifteen volumes, by means of extra insertions or illustrations, totaling as many as three thousand. A 2nd edit., improved, corrected, and continued, with maps, plates, etc., 12 vols., 8vo, Canterbury, 1797; this edition also includes his *History of Canterbury.* Another revised edit. by Henry H. Drake, with additions from other MS sources, Part I (all published), London (?), 1886.
> Hasted spent forty years in writing up this history of his native county. For it he copied all the Kent wills in the Prerogative Court of Canterbury, carried on researches in the public records and libraries, and finally brought it out as listed above. It is said to be more remarkable for its research than for its literary merit, and in some respects is very defective; but it forms an admirable record of the history and genealogy of the principal families. He has been charged with having become slovenly towards the end of the work, but this was excused on the grounds that he was short of money. He is described by Sir Egerton Brydges as a good topographical antiquary but imprudent and eccentric.—From Walters, *The English Antiquaries.*

1779 ANDERSON, JAMES. An Account of ancient Monuments and Fortifications in the Highlands of Scotland. In *Archaeologia,* vol. 5, 24-266. 4to. London.

COLLINSON, REV. JOHN. The Beauties of British Antiquity: selected from the Writings of esteemed Antiquaries with Notes and Observations. 8vo. London.

> Concerning Stonehenge, he prudently observes that "We have not history to determine at what time, or on what occasion, Stonehenge was erected."—Harrison, *A Bibliography of the Great Stone Monuments of Wiltshire.*

GARDEN, JAMES. A Letter to John Aubrey, on the circular Stone Monuments in Scotland. *Publ. Soc. Antiquaries,* vols. 1-2, 314-21. 4to. London.

JONES, EDMUND. A Geographical, Historical, and Religious Account of the Parish of Aberystwith: to which are added, Memoirs of several Persons of Note who lived in the said Parish. 8vo. Trevecke.

POPE, REV. A. A Description of the Dune of Dornadilla in Sutherlandshire. In *Archaeologia Scotica,* vol. 5, 216. 4to. Edinburgh.

RUDDER, SAMUEL. A New History of Gloucestershire, comprising the Topography, Antiquities, Curiosities, Produce, Trade, and Manufactures of that County; Foundation Charters and Endowments of Abbies and other religious Houses, Bishoprick, Patrons and Incumbents, Charters, Seats, Manors, Genealogies, Monumental Inscriptions, etc. Map and plates. Fol. Cirencester.

> Another edit., 8vo, Cirencester, 1781. According to Halkett and Laing, it is "partly based on the work of Sir Robert Atkyns (see under 1712, SURVEYS), but with supplementary material added from other sources, or supplied by the editor and printer, Samuel Rudder."

1780   CORDINER, REV. CHARLES. For the antiquities of the North of Scotland, see under TOURS BY NATIVES.

MORES, EDWARD ROWE. 1. Queries for the better illustrating the Antiquities and Natural History of Great Britain. 2. The History and Antiquities of Tunstall in Kent. No. 1 of *Bibliotheca Topographica Britannica* (see next item). 4to. London.

1780-1800   NICHOLS, JOHN (Editor). Bibliotheca Topographica Britannica. 10 vols. 4to. London.

> The first eight volumes of this extensive collection of articles on antiquities and descriptions of parishes, towns, abbies, etc., were issued in parts from 1780 to 1790. The two remaining volumes appeared in continuation under the title of *Miscellaneous Antiquities* from 1790 to 1800. The eight volumes are to be met with commonly enough, but the other two are very rare because of a fire that destroyed the stock. The editor Nichols was assisted by the antiquary John Gough and others. The design was to publish papers separately and at irregular intervals with no attempt to maintain the same size or the same price. One part was to consist of reprints of scarce and curious tracts, the other of manuscript papers. The researches were regulated by the plan of the "Queries" listed just above. The contributions sent in are listed below according to name of author and date of printing. Some will be found under other sections—TOWNS, ECCLESIASTICAL ANTIQUITIES, DESCRIPTIONS, etc.

1781   ARMSTRONG, CAPTAIN MOSTYN JOHN. The History and Antiquities of the County of Norfolk and the City of Norwich. Engravings of churches, houses, views, portraits, and maps. 8vo. Norwich.

> This was mostly compiled from Blomefield (see under 1736-45 above).—Bookseller's Note.

DUCAREL, A. C. The History and Antiquities of the Parish of Lambeth. London.

GUTCH, JOHN (Editor). Collectanea Curiosa; or, Miscellaneous Tracts, relating to the History and Antiquities of England and Ireland, the Universities of Oxford and Cambridge, and a Variety of other Subjects. Chiefly collected, and now first published from the MSS. of Archbishop Sancroft; given to the Bodleian Library by the late Bishop Tanner. 2 vols. Oxford.

> Reviewed *Gent. Mag.,* vol. 52, 298-99. Vol. I contains 74 tracts and vol. II, 49. Among them occur the names of Sir Walter Raleigh, Archbishop Ussher, Sir Edward Coke, etc. —From the review.

Reliquiae Galeanae. No. 2, pt. 1, of *Bibl. Topog. Brit.* 4to. London.

> Reviewed *Gent. Mag.*, vol. 51, 471. This consists of some of the unpublished papers of the antiquary Samuel Gale. Included is his tour through several parts of England in 1705 (revised by the author in 1730) in company with four friends—the Marquess, Viatorio, the Count, and Civiliano. They took in Oxford, Blenheim (then in process of building), Gloucester, Bristol, Bath, Stonehenge, Wilton House, Old and New Sarum, Portsmouth, Guildford, Hampton Court, Kensington, etc. Also published here are the correspondence of the antiquaries Stukeley, Knight, Chr. Hunter, Mortimer, and many others with Gale; the minutes of the Spalding Club; Gale's Historical Account of the Borough of North Allerton; and a Description of Scruton. In 1782 was published in the same series a third part of the *Reliquiae Galeanae.*

WARTON, THOMAS. The History of Kiddington. Oxford. (Privately printed.)

> 2nd edit. (this one for sale), 4to, London, 1782.
> The author of *The History of English Poetry* was also an eminent antiquary.—"The History of Kiddington is certainly an excellent specimen of parochial history."—Nichols, *Literary Anecdotes,* vol. VI, 181.

WORSLEY, SIR RICHARD. The History of the Isle of Wight. Large folding map, 32 engraved views, besides vignettes in the text. 4to. London.

> Walpole mentions this publication in a letter to Cole, June 16, 1781, but says that the views were "poorly done enough." Cole, in a letter of June 30, 1781, wishes that it had "been more ecclesiastical." Worsley was governor of the Isle of Wight. The volume is not regarded very highly.

1781-82 NASH, TREADWAY, F.A.S. Collections for the History of Worcestershire. Numerous plates. 2 vols. Fol. London.

> The rare Supplement was printed in 1791. This appeared with the two original volumes in 1799; an Index was added by J. Amphlett in 2 vols., 1894. The whole in 4 vols., fol., London, 1781-1895. This edition contained also an English translation of the Domesday Book relating to this county.
> Reviewed *Gent. Mag.*, vols. 51, 372-74, and 52, 398. At great expense and labor Nash has here arranged materials that have been collecting for nearly two hundred years by Thomas Habingdon (Abingdon) of Henlip, his son William, the editor of Dugdale's *Warwickshire,* and the late Bishop Lyttleton. The author admits that a county historian "is a dealer in small wares." This history of manors and descent of property is naturally limited in interest to the Proprietors or Heirs.—From the review. The work is praised by the reviewer for its industry.

1782 ANDERSON, JAMES. A Further Description of ancient Fortifications in the North of Scotland. In *Archaeologia,* vol. 6, 87. 4to. London.

CRAWFORD, GEORGE. The History of the Shire of Renfrew, containing a Genealogical Account of the Nobility and Gentry of the County, by George Crawford, and continued to the present Period by Wm. Semple. 4to. Paisley.

WARTON, THOMAS (Rector of Kiddington). Specimen of a Parochial History of Oxfordshire. London.

> 2nd edit., corrected and enlarged, 4to, London, 1783.
> Reviewed *Gent. Mag.*, vol. 52, 244-46, where considerable praise is given the work.

1782-83 THORPE, JOHN (of Hexley). Antiquities in Kent, hitherto undescribed. 2 pts. Plates. No. 6 of *Bibl. Topog. Brit.* London.

> Reviewed *Gent. Mag.*, vol. 53, 51-52 and 422-23.

1783   BLOMEFIELD, STEELE, FOULKES (and others). Collections towards the History and
        Antiquities of Bedfordshire, containing Puddington, Luton and Dunstaple. No.
        8 of *Bibl. Topog. Brit.* London.

   Additions were made in vol. IV, no. 26, of the same series.

        BROWN, J. Sketches of the History of the Parish of Stoke Newington. 1 plate and
        folding pedigree of Fleetwood. No. 9 of *Bibl. Topog. Brit.* London.

   Additions to this history were made in no. 14.

        Collections towards a Parochial History of Berkshire. No. 10 of *Bibl. Topog. Brit.*
        London.

        Extracts from the MS. Journal of Sir Simond d'Ewes. No. 15 of *Bibl. Topog. Brit.*
        London.

   Reviewed *Gent. Mag.*, vol. 53, 863. In addition to being member of Parliament (expelled
   1648), Sir Simon was also an antiquary and a Saxonist. His Anglo-Saxon Dictionary never
   got beyond the stage of manuscript.

        The History and Antiquities of the Parish of Great Coxwell, in the County of
        Berks. No. 13 of *Bibl. Topog. Brit.* London.

        A Short Account of Holyhead, in the Isle of Anglesey. No. 10 of *Bibl. Topog.
        Brit.* London.

1784   An Account of the Gentlemen's Society at Spalding: being an Introduction to the
        Reliquiae Galeanae. No. 20 of *Bibl. Topog. Brit.* London.

   Reviewed *Gent. Mag.*, vol. 54, 278-80; 353. This society, which called itself a "cell"
   to that of London, was established in 1710 to secure antiquities, natural history, improvements in arts and science in general against oblivion.—From the review.

        BLOUNT, THOMAS. Fragmenta Antiquitatis; or, Antient Tenures of Land, and
        Jocular Customs of some Manors. New edit., with Alterations, English Trans-
        lations, etc., with Notes by J. Beckwith. 8vo. York. See under 1679 above.

        COOPER, REV. OLIVER ST. JOHN. An Historical Account of the Parish of Wim-
        mington, in the County of Bedford. No. 29 of *Bibl. Topog. Brit.* London.

        DUNSCOMBE, JOHN. The History and Antiquities of the Two Parishes of Reculver
        and Herne, in the County of Kent. No. 17 of *Bibl. Topog. Brit.* London.

        PEGGE, SAMUEL. An Historical Account of that Venerable Monument of Antiq-
        uity, the Textus Roffensis; including Memoirs of the learned Saxonists Mr.
        William Elstob and his Sister. To which are added, Biographical Anecdotes of
        Mr. Johnson, Vicar of Cranbrook; and Extracts from the Registers of that
        Parish. No. 25 of *Bibl. Topog. Brit.* London.

   Reviewed *Gent. Mag.*, vol. 55, 42-44. Miss Elizabeth Elstob was a recognized authority
   in the early study of Old English, probably surpassing in scholarship any of the "learned
   ladies" of the late 18th century.

        S., M. Remarkable Antiquities in Jersey. In *Gent. Mag.*, vol. 54, 809-10. London.

   Nothing really remarkable is brought to light here.

1785-95 HUTCHINSON, WILLIAM. The History and Antiquities of the County Palatine of Durham. Numerous engravings of seats, portraits, Roman altars, arms and seals of the bishops, etc. 3 vols. Newcastle and Carlisle.

> Other editions in the next century. Vol. I appeared in 1785; vol. II in 1787; and the concluding volume in 1795 (also dated 1794).
> Vol. I gives the history of the province from early days under the druids, Romans, and Saxons; the state of religion; an account of the kingdoms of Northumbria, Bernicia, and Deira, etc., with the lives of the bishops of different places. Vols. II and III take up the city of Durham, its cathedral, churches, chapels, castle, parochial surveys, and the like. The work is arranged by parishes. It pays some attention to existing manufactures, canals, etc., but in the main it is concerned with antiquities. The basis of the text was the manuscript volumes—some twenty in number—left by Rev. Thomas Randall, pastor of the Free-School at Durham, at his death in 1775. He is said to have copied "literatim" every work found in Durham. This city produced an astonishing number of antiquaries.

1786 BOSWELL, HENRY. For views and representations of antiquities of England, see his *Description of a Collection of Picturesque Views,* under VIEWS.

HEARNE, THOMAS. For antiquities presented by means of views, see his *Antiquities of Great Britain Illustrated,* under VIEWS.

The History and Antiquities of the Parish of Lambeth, in the County of Surrey. Including Biographical Anecdotes of several Eminent Persons. Compiled from original Records, and other authentic Sources of Information. No. 39 of *Bibl. Topog. Brit.* London.

> Reviewed with commendation *Gent. Mag.,* vol. 56, 1061-62.

Remarks on the Progress of the Roman Army in Scotland, during the Sixth Campaign of Agricola, with a Plan and Description of the Camp at Raedykes. No. 36 of *Bibl. Topog. Brit.* London.

> Reviewed *Gent. Mag.,* vol. 56, 233-34. The reviewer caustically describes this as done by a Scotchman turned antiquary, and states that all it amounts to is that somebody conquered somebody.

SHARP, ARCHBISHOP. Observations on the Coinage of England, with his Letter to Mr. Thoresby, 1698-99. No. 35 of *Bibl. Topog. Brit.* London.

> Reviewed *Gent. Mag.,* vol. 56, 233. Thoresby's Museum of Numismatics was the first of its kind in England.

1786-88 GROSE, FRANCIS. Military Antiquities respecting a History of the English Army from the Conquest. Frontispiece and 76 plates of military costume (horse and foot), arms and armour, artillery pieces, "Infernal" machines, battering rams, the musketeer (showing 45 positions), pike exercises (33 positions), horse exercises, etc. 2 vols. 4to. London.

1786-91 BIGLAND, RALPH. Historical, Monumental, and Genealogical Collections relative to the County of Gloucester. Plates of churches, tombs, etc. 2 vols. Fol. London.

> The dating of this work and later issues is confusing. Apparently it began to appear in 1786, in numbers arranged by parishes, reaching the twentieth in 1791 and stopping with the parish of Newent. A continuation from the original papers of Bigland was issued in two volumes, with 34 plates, in 1791-92. Further continuations by Sir Thomas Phillipps were printed in 1798 by Phillipps at his private press. Two more volumes connected with it came out in 1819, one of 114 proof plates and unpublished plates, and the other a History

of the City of Gloucester by T. D. Fosbrooke, which aimed to supply the numerous deficiencies and to correct the errors of preceding accounts, and included also the original papers of Bigland.

Reviewed in various issues of *Gent. Mag.* As Bigland died in 1784, the work was put into print by his son. Gough, in a review, said of it: "This modest work (referring to the 1786 publication), which professes to be a little more than a Collection of Monumental Inscriptions, and 'rather a history of the Inhabitants of Gloucestershire, than of the Shire itself,' was begun about thirty years ago by the late Ralph Bigland, Esq., principally to obtain information relative to his profession (he was Clarenceux Herald)." It took in churchyards as well, the churches being therein printed more systematically than they have been for any other county.—"History from Marble," *Publ. Camden Soc.,* vol. 94.

1786-95   CORDINER, REV. CHARLES. Remarkable Ruins and Romantic Prospects of North Britain, with Ancient Monuments and Singular Subjects of Natural History. 32 plates dated 1784-85-86. 2 vols. 4to. London.

The engravings were done by Peter Mazell.

1786-96   GOUGH, RICHARD. Sepulchral Monuments in Great Britain, applied to Illustrate the History of Families, Manners, Habits, and Arts at the different Periods, from the Norman Conquest to the XVIIth Century, with Introductory Observations. Numerous copperplates. 2 vols. in 3. Fol. London.

The first volume appeared in 1786, the second in 1796. The work stopped with the 15th century. Vol. I was published without Gough's name, but the plate of his family arms was printed on the title page. "The object of this splendid and costly work is to fill up one of those voids in the study of our National Antiquities which P. Montfaucon accomplished, on a more extensive plan, for those of France—the illustration of national manners, habits, arts and taste, by those lighter records, . . . such as the arts of painting and sculpture afford.—From the review by Dr. Pegge, quoted by Nichols, *Literary Anecdotes,* vol. VI, 288. The review in *Gent. Mag.,* vol. 69, 585-86, states that here are some of the finest specimens of sepulchral monuments extant in this country. Of the 131 plates, 76 are by Schnebberlie, 24 by Carter, engraved by Basire, whose pupil William Blake was responsible for a few. In addition to a general view of sepulchres throughout the world, other subjects are shrines, characteristics of saints, epitaphs, inscriptions, letters, numerals, and dates, exemplifying the whole system of sepulture and memorials of mortality in Great Britain.

1787   COOPER, OLIVER ST. JOHN. Historical Account of the Parish of Odell. No. 44 of *Bibl. Topog. Brit.* London.

H., H. Inconsistencies of Modern Antiquarians. In *Gent. Mag.,* vol. 57, 49-53. London.

The writer criticizes severely the antiquaries Wallis and Hutchinson. The latter, he charges, was unable to read or write Latin and hence commits numerous errors in his Latin inscriptions. Gough, in his Preface to *Sepulchral Monuments,* has well castigated the inaccuracies of "our modern tourists" and describers of monuments.

1788   1. The Case of the Inhabitants of Croyden, 1673; with an Appendix to the History of the Town. 2. A List of the Manorial Houses which formerly belonged to the See of Canterbury. 3. A Description of Trimly Hospital, Guildford; and of Albury House. With 4. Brief Notes on Battersea, Chelsham, Nutfall, and Tatsfield, in the County of Surrey. No. 46 of *Bibl. Topog. Brit.* London.

Reviewed *Gent. Mag.,* vol. 58, 140. The first number of this miscellany contains an amusing account of the complaints the people of Croyden made against their vicar, who was charged with extortion and oppression, with pulling down the parsonage and selling the materials, with being inefficient in preaching in that he used printed sermons and nonsense, and with getting drunk and keeping a woman—all of which was a little excessive even among 18th century clergymen.

BROWN, PROFESSOR. The History and Antiquities of St. Rule's Chapel, in the Monastery of St. Andrews, in Scotland; with Remarks by Professor Brown. To which are added, 1. Riding of the Parliament of Scotland, in 1606 and 1681, and the Ceremonies observed in 1685. 2. The Statutes and Fees of the Order of the Thistle, etc. 3. The Suspension Lyon·King of Arms. 4. A particular Description of the Regalia of Scotland. No. 47 of *Bibl. Topog. Brit.* London.

> Reviewed *Gent. Mag.*, vol. 58, 240, with the remark that this volume shows that the editor of the series has extended his scheme to Scotland.

The History of the Town and County of Poole, compiled from Hutchinson's History of the County of Dorset . . . to which is added, A Supplement containing several curious and interesting Particulars. 8vo. Poole.

PRIDDEN, —. An Appendix to the Histories of Reculver and Herne; and Observations by Mr. Denne, on the Archiepiscopal Palace of Mayfield in Sussex. No. 45 of *Bibl. Topog. Brit.* London.

> Reviewed *Gent. Mag.*, vol. 58, 140. This miscellany offers particulars and drawings passed over in former accounts of Reculver, and some finds with reference to alterations of Canterbury Cathedral. See Dunscombe on Reculver under 1784 above.

THORKELIN, GRIMR JOHNSON. Fragments of English and Irish History in the Ninth and Tenth Centuries. Translated from the Original Icelandic, and illustrated with some Notes. No. 48 of *Bibl. Topog. Brit.* London.

WYNDHAM, HENRY PENRUDDOCKE. Wiltshire, extracted from Domesday Book: to which is added, A Translation of the Original into English; with an Index, in which are adapted the Modern Names to the Ancient; and with a Preface, in which is included a Plan for a general History of the County. 8vo. Salisbury.

> Reviewed *Gent. Mag.*, vol. 58, 726. A history of the County of Wilts has long been among the desiderata of British topography. Attempts at collections towards this end were made by Bishop Tanner. These, which are now probably preserved in the Bodleian Library, would make a good start.—From the review.

1789 BRAND, JOHN. The History and Antiquities of the Town, and County of Newcastle Upon Tyne, with Account of the Coal Trade. Illustrated with portraits, numerous folding engravings of buildings, monuments, coins, etc., by Fittler, and large map. 2 vols. 4to. London.

> An Index in a separate volume was added by William Dodd in 1881.
> Reviewed *Gent. Mag.*, vol. 59, 533. It is here described as an eminently satisfactory work. Brand was assisted by the Corporation of the city, which gave him access to valuable materials in the archives of the Corporation and elsewhere. It begins with the first walling of the city and building of the castle under William Rufus, and continues its fortunes down through the centuries. In the Appendix are found original deeds and records, description of the Roman Wall and stations, inscriptions, and other antiquities, a history of the town as incorporated from the first mention of it in Britain, account of the twelve Companies or Mysteries, the Corpus Christi Plays, historical events, the coal trade, etc. The work is a model in its treatment of local antiquities.

NICHOLS, JOHN. The History and Antiquities of Canonbury House at Islington, in the County of Middlesex: including Lives of the Priors of St. Bartholomew, of the Prebendaries and Vicars of Islington; with Biographical Anecdotes of such of them as have been of Eminence in the Literary World. 5 plates. No. 49 of *Bibl. Topog. Brit.* London.

> Reviewed *Gent. Mag.*, vol. 59, 339-40.

PILKINGTON, JAMES. For an account of the antiquities of Derbyshire, see his *A View of the Present State of Derbyshire,* under ANCIENT AND PRESENT STATE.

WARNER, RICHARD. Hampshire, extracted from the Domes-day Book, with an accurate English Translation. 4to. London.

1789-91 BRYDGES, SIR S. E., and S. SHAW. The Topographer, for the Years 1789, 1790, and 1791, containing a Variety of Original Articles, illustrative of Local History and Antiquities of England. Numerous engraved plates. 4 vols. 8vo. London.

> Vol. V, part 1 (all published), by Sir Thomas Phillipps, London, 1821.
> This gives special attention to seats and styles of architecture, monumental inscriptions, genealogies, and anecdotes of famous families, etc.

GROSE, FRANCIS. The Antiquities of Scotland. 100 engraved views. 2 vols. 4to and 8vo. London.

> 2nd edit., 2 vols., London, 1797.
> Captain Grose, of noted corpulence and redoubtable prowess with the bottle, was the "chield's amang you takin notes" against whom Burns in a delightful tribute warned his "Land o' Cakes, and brither Scots."
>
> > It's tauld he was a sodger bred,
> > And ane wad rather fa'n than fled;
> > But now he's quat the spurtle-blade
> > > And dog-skin wallet,
> > And taen the—Antiquarian trade,
> > > I think they call it.
>
> When Burns met Grose at the house of Captain Riddell, he proposed a drawing be made of Alloway Kirk, which the Captain said he would do if the poet would send some stories to go along with it. It has been suggested (Centenary edition of Burns) that Burns originally forwarded some prose stories and that the poem "Tam O'Shanter" was an afterthought. But before the *Antiquities* got published, the poem had already appeared in *The Edinburgh Magazine*, Mch., 1791.

1790 NICHOLS, JOHN. Collections towards the History and Antiquities of the Town and County of Leicester. 60 plates. Nos. 50 and 51 of *Bibl. Topog. Brit.* London.

> Reviewed *Gent. Mag.,* vol. 61, 156. The groundwork of this folio volume was the MS collections of the antiquary Mr. Peck, with augmentation by a brother in the same pursuit and the late Sir T. Cave. These were put into the hands of Nichols, the editor of *Bibliotheca Topographica Britannica,* who added observations taken from personal inspection made on summer trips.—From the review.

OLDFIELD, H. G., and R. R. DYSON. The History and Antiquities of the Parish of Tottenham High-Cross, in the County of Middlesex. Collected from authentic Records. With an Appendix, containing the Account of the said Town, drawn up by the Right Honourable Henry, last Lord Coleraine, printed from the Original MS. in the Bodleian Library at Oxford. 12mo. London.

> Reviewed *Gent. Mag.,* vol. 60, 1121-22. The subject is treated in the usual comprehensive manner, with a discussion of etymology, air, soil, rivers, woods, manors, churches, charitable foundations, benefactors, wells, bridges, etc. See also Bedwell, *Description of the Towne of Tottenham High-Cross,* under 1631, TOWNS.

POLWHELE, R. For his queries put to gentlemen and others on the history and antiquities for his *History of Devonshire,* see the *Gentleman's Magazine,* vol. 60, 1178-80. If all these questions were answered, few facts would escape the combing. For the latter work, see under 1794-98 below.

1791 Bartlett, Benjamin. Manduessen dum Romanorum: being the History and Antiquities of the Parish of Manceter, including the Hamlets of Hartshill, Old-bury and Atherstone, and also of the adjacent Parish of Ansley, in the County of Warwick. Enlarged and corrected, under the Inspection of several Gentlemen resident upon the Spot. Plates of views, pedigrees, antiquities, etc. 4to. London.

Collections toward the History and Antiquities of Elmeswell and Campsey Ash, in the County of Suffolk; and various additions to several of the Former Numbers. No. 52 of *Bibl. Topog. Brit.* London.

Reviewed *Gent. Mag.*, vol. 61, 359-60. With this number this series comes to a close. The publisher adds a grateful acknowledgement for the reception given these volumes.

Collinson, Rev. John. The History and Antiquities of the County of Somerset, collected from Authentic Records and an Actual Survey made by the late Edmund Rack. Adorned with a Map of the County and Engravings of Roman and other Reliques, Town-Seals, Baths, Churches and Gentlemen's Seats. 3 vols. 4to. Bath.

An Index of personal and place names and of things, edited by Rev. F. W. Weaver and Rev. E. H. Bates, including a Supplementary Index (alphabet and ordinary) to all the armorial bearings by Lt.-Col. Bramble, was brought out at Taunton, 1898.
Reviewed *Gent. Mag.*, vol. 63, 148-50, 236, 865. The reviewer is severe in his condemnation, asserting that the work is not considered to be up to the standard required of county historians in this era of advanced topographical research. His accounts of places like Wells, Glastonbury, and Hinton St. George, for instance, are inadequate. He is careless in his use of authorities or else ignorant of how to use them. He depends too much on printed works and his own assertions; he borrows even his descriptions of seats from that "universal tourist" Arthur Young.—It is true that he based his history on the standard antiquarian and historical works and so can claim little originality, but other critics have acknowledged his value and given him his due. For other strictures and a Supplement see below.

1794 D., R. Collinson's History and Antiquities of Somersetshire attacked in a Letter to the *Gentleman's Magazine*, vol. 64, 497-99.
Here the work is found deficient in antiquarian information and the errors pointed out in detail. On the other hand, the topographical part, so far as it relates to the face of the country, is well done, and the descriptions are lively and spirited, though a little touched with affectation.

R., J. B. Strictures on Collinson's History of Somersetshire. In *Gent. Mag.*, vol. 64, 1165.
This writer held back his criticism until after the death of the author and the sale of most of the volumes. In calling attention to the defects of Collinson, he has in mind doing a service to other county historians, by showing how exacting a science is the writing of county histories.

1939 Ward, F. Madeline (Editor). Supplement to Collinson's *History of Somerset*: Richard Locke, 18th Century Antiquary, Surveyor and Agriculturist. Extracts from Locke's Survey, with a short Biography by F. Madeline Ward, M.A. Foreword by Prof. R. B. Mowat, M.A. 4to. Taunton.
Mowat explains how this Survey by Locke supplements Collinson's *History*. Locke was an important figure in the agricultural development of the eighteenth century. He was also a member of the Friendly Society.

A Description of the Curious Monuments and Antiquities in the Island of St. Colman-Kill, also of Staffa, the rural Throne of King Fingal, etc., by a Gentleman who made the Tower of Europe, etc., and given to John M'Cormack to support a small Family. 8vo. London.

Reprinted, Dublin, 1792; Glasgow, 1798; Belfast, 1820.

GROSE, FRANCIS. The Antiquities of Wales. 70 engravings of views, castles, churches, towers, abbies, friaries, monasteries, etc. Fol. London.

A History of the County and City of Chester . . . With the Life of St. Werburgh, the Founder . . . of the Cathedral Church of Chester. With a ground Plan of the City and Suburbs of Chester. 8vo. Chester.

SCHNEBBERLIE, JACOB. The Antiquarian Museum. Illustrating the Antient Architecture, Painting, and Sculpture of Great Britain, from the Time of the Saxons to the Grecian and Roman Architecture by Inigo Jones in the Reign of King James I. Numerous plates. 4to. London.

> Reviewed *Gent. Mag.*, vol. 61, 156-57. This publication was projected by Carter (probably John). Schnebberlie the artist is well qualified to execute the project. At least four numbers a year are proposed, with four plates to each. Twelve numbers are to make a volume.—From the review. How far the work was carried out I do not know, but no. X was noticed in the *Gent. Mag.*, vol. 64, 247.—The plates and nearly all the stock were destroyed by fire at Nichols' printing office.—Maggs, no. 715.

WHALLEY, REV. PETER. The History and Antiquities of Northamptonshire. Compiled from the Manuscript Collections of the late learned Antiquary, John Bridges, Esq., by the Rev. Peter Whalley. Portrait of Bridges by Vertue, numerous engravings of buildings, coins, antiquities, etc., and Faden's four-sheet map. 2 vols. Fol. Oxford.

> Reviewed *Gent. Mag.*, vol. 61, 1128. The work is here commended. It was first projected in 1719 by John Bridges, of Barton Seagrave, near Kettering. He was a bencher of Lincoln's Inn, solicitor to the Customs, and commissioner of the same. He possessed an excellent collection of books, which were sold by auction after his death, and took twenty-seven days to dispose of. He had collected more than thirty volumes folio of transcripts. A small portion was published under subscription in numbers, about 1740. Adverse fortune stopped the work. The publication was resumed, the first volume appearing in 1762, and part of a second in 1769, but from then on it had to be postponed until the present.—From the review.

1792 ANDERSON, JAMES. An Account of the Antiquities in Scotland. With illustrations. In *The Bee*, vol. 7, 132-41, 181-89; vol. 8, 53-61, 94-104, 286-94, 330-33; vol. 9, 126-34, 211-16. 16mo. Edinburgh.

Caernarvonshire. A Sketch of its History and Antiquities, Mountains, and Productions. Intended as a Pocket-Companion to those who make the Tour of that Country. 12mo. London.

> Reviewed *Gent. Mag.*, vol. 62, 933-34. The reviewer allows the quotations he selects to do the damning for him.

Description of the Encampment on the Hill of Burnswork. Letter to the Society of Antiquaries of Scotland, 1785. In *Arch. Scot.* vol. 1, 124. 4to. Edinburgh.

The History of the Boroughs of Great Britain. 3 vols. 8vo. London. (So cited in Rowlands, *Cambrian Bibliog.*)

MACKENZIE, C. An Account of some Remains of Antiquity in the Island of Lewis, one of the Hebrides. Paper read 1783. In *Arch. Scot.*, vol. 1, 282. 4to. Edinburgh.

MOORE, JAMES. Monastic Remains and Ancient Castles in England and Wales, with Descriptions. 8vo. London.

RIDDELL, R. An Account of the Ancient Modes of Fortification in Scotland; in a Letter to Richard Gough, read Feb. 4, 1790. In *Archaeologia,* vol. 10, 99. 4to. London.

——————. Observations on Vitrified Fortifications in Galloway; in a Letter to Mr. Gough, read 11th Nov., 1790. In *Archaeologia,* vol. 10, 147. 4to. London.

1793 DOUGLAS, REV. JAMES. Nenia Britannica; or, A Sepulchral History of Great Britain; from the earliest Period to its general Conversion to Christianity. 36 large plates and numerous vignettes after Stothard, colored by hand and the vignettes in sepia. Fol. London.

> This valuable work includes a complete series of the British, Roman, and Saxon sepulchral rites and ceremonies, and descriptions of several hundred burial places and barrows with their contents, such as urns, swords, spearheads, daggers, knives, gems, bracelets, beads, gold and silver ornaments, brooches with precious stones, magical instruments, coins, etc. Douglas carried out systematic excavations in Kent, especially on Chatham Lines, from 1779 on.

LODGE, REV. JOHN. Introductory Sketches towards a Topographical History of the County of Hereford. 8vo. Kingston.

RIDDELL, R. Dissertation on Ancient Carved Stone Monuments in Dumfrieshire, etc. In *Mem. Phil. Soc.,* Manchester.

SHAW, REV. STEBBING. Proposals for publishing by Subscription the History and Antiquities of Staffordshire. Single sheet, fol. London.

> See Shaw under 1798 below.

URE, DAVID. The History of Rutherglen and East-Kilbride. Published with a View to promote the Study of Antiquity and Natural History. 21 plates. 4to. Glasgow.

1794 BUCHANAN, JOHN L. A Defence of the Scots Highlanders in General, and some Learned Characters in particular, with a New and Satisfactory Account of the Picts, Scots, Macs, Clans, etc. 8vo. London (?).

HUTCHINSON, WILLIAM. The History of the County of Cumberland and some Places adjacent, comprehending the local History of the County, its Antiquities, the Origin, Genealogy and Present State of the principal Families with biographical Notes, etc. 4to. Carlisle.

> Another edit., 2 vols., 4to, Carlisle (?), 1798.
> Reviewed *Gent. Mag.,* vol. 65, 50-52. In the description of Ullswater and the Lakes, there occur whole pages of poetry and prose excerpted from Gilpin and Dr. Brown; and in natural history, from Berkenhout, White's Selbourne, Pennant, Clarke, and the *Encyclopedia Britannica.* Only a small portion of original matter remains. The 1798 edition is reviewed in *Gent. Mag.,* vol. 68, 48, where it is alleged that the author seems more intent on getting out a book than on doing good writing.

SANDERS, REV. HENRY. The History and Antiquities of Shenstone, in the County of Staffordshire, illustrated with the Pedigrees of all the Families and Gentry both Antient and Modern of that Parish. 4to. London.

> Reviewed *Gent. Mag.,* vol. 64, 549-50. The author was vicar of Shenstone for thirteen years.

SHAW, REV. STEBBING. Mr. Shaw's Report of further Progress in Staffordshire. In *Gent. Mag.*, vol. 64, 1077-81. London.

This report deals with his researches for materials for his History of Staffordshire (published 1798).

SIMCO, —. Middlesex Monuments. Nos. 1 and 2 (all published). Plates. 4to. London.

1794-97 POLWHELE, RICHARD. The History of Devonshire. Map by Cary and numerous plates. 3 vols. Fol. Exeter.

Vol. II reviewed *Gent. Mag.*, vol. 64, 734. The second volume appeared before the first for reasons explained by the author. The work comes in for a hard basting by the reviewer, who finds it wanting in what is required of a county historian. It neglects to give references to original records; it contains many absurdities in comments and mistakes in derivation and descriptions. The topographical account is inflated in style. The history part is a compilation from Risdon, Westcott, Prince, Pole, and other antiquaries, who are for the most part already in print. Of twenty-four deaneries, 400 pages cover only nine. How are the remainder to be compressed in another volume? Like unfavorable criticism appeared from readers in the *Gentleman's Magazine* in ensuing numbers, as well as some defenses. But the attacks seem to have the best of it. There are some slight sections on agriculture, mining, manufactures, etc., down to 1790. Some doubts have been expressed whether the Cary map belonged to the original edition.

1795 ALBIN, JOHN. A New Correct, and much Improved History of the Isle of Wight, from the Earliest Times of Authentic Information to the Present Period: comprehending whatever is curious or worthy of Attention in Natural History; with its Civil, Ecclesiastical and Military State in the various Ages. Folding map. 8vo. Newport.

Reviewed *Gent. Mag.*, vol. 66, 220. The list of subjects treated in the various chapters runs through the category customary in local histories. This work will probably supersede the more costly one by Sir R. Worsley, 1781.—From the review.

POPE, LUKE. The History of the County of Middlesex; containing a general Description of it, its Rivers, and of the Churches from their Foundation, with the Patrons and Incumbents of each, the Antient Epitaphs and Monumental Inscriptions now to be found in the respective Churches, and the Endowments of the several Vicarages, also of St. Paul's Cathedral, and Waltham Abbey, with a List of the Bishops of London, from the Original Institution of that See, the Archdeacons, Deans, Prebends, etc. In the course of the Work will be an Account of the Royal Palaces, principal Seats, Royal Chaces and Manors. Vol. I. Published in Numbers of 40 pp. each. 4to. London.

Reviewed *Gent. Mag.*, vol. 65, 405-06; also 765. The reviewer doubts that the compiler can make six 4to volumes of this work. Preceding works have been contented with one volume. Doubts are also expressed of Pope's ability as a scholar when he speaks of the most authentic authors, but is silent on MS materials, which must be very extensive. Both in style and matter the work is inadequate.—From the review. Whether this history was carried out to completion I have been unable to discover.

WARNER, RICHARD. Collections for the History of Hampshire, and the Bishopric of Winchester, including the Isles of Wight, Jersey, Guernsey and Sarke, by D. Y., with the original Domesday of the County, and an accurate English Translation, containing an Account of this curious Record, a View of the Anglo-Saxon History and Form of Government, from the Reign of Alfred, together with a slight Sketch of the most material Alterations which the latter

underwent at the Period of the Conquest, to which is added, a Glossary explanatory of the obsolete Words. Map and numerous plates. 5 vols. in 3 (all published). 4to. Southampton.

> Reviewed *Gent. Mag.*, vol. 67, 44-47 (1797), which cites six volumes. The work is dedicated from no place under the initials of the author, May 26, 1795, to the Marquis of Hertford. It is an extensive mass of collections with little if anything new. It consists of compilations almost *verbal*, on the subject of Hampshire and the isles, from nearly every book mentioned. The plates are taken from Captain Grose, a dubious authority, and others. The History by Warner should have been done by a better hand.—From the review. One bookseller's note states that Warner did only the Introduction, which may be the historical part.

1795-1815 NICHOLS, JOHN. The History and Antiquities of the County of Leicester, compiled from the best and most Ancient Historians, Inquisitiones post mortem, and other valuable Records, in the Tower Rolls, Exchequer, Dutchy and Augmentation Offices; the Registers of the Diocese of Lincoln; the Chartularies and Registers of Religious Houses; the College of Arms; the British Museum; the Libraries of Oxford and Cambridge; and other Public and Private Repositories; including also Mr. Burton's Description of the County published in 1622; and the later Collections of Staveley, Carte, Peck, and Sir Thomas Cave. Portrait and hundreds of engravings of churches, seats, antiquities, pedigrees. 4 vols. in 8. Fol. London.

> Reviewed *Gent. Mag.*, vol. 65 (and later volumes), various pages. See also the *Annual Register*, 1796. In the *Gent. Mag.*, vol. 65, 185-89 and 220-23, Nichols makes a report on his progress, the sources investigated, collections obtained, and assistance received from different individuals. Portions of the work were destroyed in the disastrous fire on his printing premises.

1796 Essays by a Society of Gentlemen at Exeter. Exeter.

> Among the subjects discussed are British monuments in Devon, and the mythology and worship of the serpent.

PENNANT, THOMAS. The History of the Parishes of Whiteford and Holywell. 22 engraved plates. 4to. London.

> Reviewed *Gent. Mag.*, vol. 67, 499-501, where it is termed a valuable addition to British topography.

STRUTT, JOSEPH. A Complete View of the Dress and Habits of the People of England, from the Establishment of the Saxons in Britain to the Present Time. 143 engravings, from ancient illuminations arranged in chronological series. 2 vols. 4to. London.

WILLIAMS, DAVID. The History of Monmouthshire. Illustrated and ornamented by views of its principal landscapes, ruins and residences, by John Gardner, and with map. 4to. London.

> Reviewed *Gent. Mag.*, vol. 69, 586-87. The history is mixed with accounts of families and places, natural history, agriculture, etc. An Appendix of 78 numbers or essays deals with antique subjects and extracts from other writers. The 36 plates in aquatint are the principal merit of the book.—From the review.

1797 The Cambrian Register for the Year 1795. (Place?)

> This work is noticed under the year 1797 by the *Gent. Mag.*, vol. 67, 951. The work is to include a Sketch of the History of the Britons under five epochs; biography, antiquities, ancient laws, parochial history, topography, naval affairs, letters, Welsh Indians [*sic*], Welsh music and poetry, Cambrian oracles, sessions, occurrences, obituary, index. The project is well supported by the clergy and gentry.—From the review.

LANGLEY, THOMAS, M.A. The History and Antiquities of the Hundred of Des-
borough and Deanery of Wycombe, in Buckinghamshire; including the Borough
Towns of Wycombe and Marlow, and Sixteen Parishes. Folding map, plates,
pedigrees. 4to. London.

> Reviewed *Gent. Mag.*, vol. 67, 491. This work was announced by the author with
> "queries," *Gent. Mag.*, vol. 66, 736. The reviewer hopes that the author will undertake
> the remainder of the county, for which so little has been done in print, though much has
> been collected in manuscripts.

OWEN, REV. NICHOLAS. Carnarvonshire: a Sketch of its History, etc. 8vo. London.

SAVAGE, JAMES. An Historical Account of the Parish of Wressle in the East Riding of the County of York. 8vo. Howden.

WILSON, RT. REV. THOMAS (Bishop of Sodor and Man). History of the Isle of
Man. In his *Works,* vol. I. 8vo. Bath.

1798   DICEY, T. An Historical Account of the Island of Guernsey. Map and plates. 4to.
London.

ELLIS, SIR HENRY. The History and Antiquities of the Parishes of St. Leonard,
Shoreditch, and Liberty of Norton Folgate. 4to. London.

1798-99   HENSHALL, SAMUEL. Specimens and Parts, containing a History of the County
of Kent, and a Dissertation on the Laws from the Reign of Edward the Confessor to Edward the First . . . a History of South Britain, etc.; Domesday, or
an Actual Survey of South Britain by the Commissioners of William the Conqueror, faithfully translated, with Introductory Notes by S. Henshall and J.
Wilkinson, No. I (for Kent, Sussex, and Surrey). 2 vols. in 1. 4to. Privately
printed for the Author.

> This takes in the trade, population, shipping, etc., with a double-page map and large
> table of lands, their proprietors, occupants, etc., compiled from Domesday.

1798-1801   The Annual Hampshire Repository; or, Historical, Economical, and Literary Miscellany . . . comprising all Matters relative to the County, including
the Isle of Wight. Map and plates. 2 vols. 8vo. London (?).

SHAW, REV. STEBBING. The History and Antiquities of Staffordshire. Compiled
from the MSS. of Huntbach, Loxdale, Bishop Lyttleton, and other Collections
of Dr. Wilkes, the Rev. T. Feilde, etc., etc. Including Erdeswick's Survey of
the County, and the approved Parts of Dr. Plot's Natural History. The Whole
brought down to the Present Time; interspersed with Pedigrees, Anecdotes of
Families, Observations on Agriculture, Commerce, Mines and Manufactures,
illustrated with a very full and correct new Map of the County, and numerous
Plates. 2 vols. (all published). Fol. London.

> Reviewed *Gent. Mag.*, vol. 68, 957-59. This is a long awaited and valuable work, the
> excellent materials for which have been happily preserved for nearly two centuries, and
> fallen at last into good hands. It has a list of nearly 350 subscribers. The review notes some
> corrections. Shaw possessed a great fund of knowledge besides considerable skill in drawing.
> —Maggs, no. 505. The work was never finished.

1798-1821 FOWLER, W. Monumenta Antiqua: Representations of Tessellated Pavements, Stained Glass, and various Interesting Objects of Antiquity. 116 plates (81 colored). Atlas Fol. London.

> Only two sets of the complete series of 116 plates exist. Several of these cost as much as thirty-one shillings and six pence each. For graphic truthfulness and effect, these representations have never been equaled. The ingenious Mr. Fowler was originally a builder and architect on a limited scale. The difficulties he had to encounter in executing this work were almost insurmountable. He did all the work himself, even to the making of the paper, for he could get no papermaker to undertake it.—Bookseller's Note.

1799-1805 KING, EDWARD. Munimenta Antiqua: or, Observations on Antient Castles, including Remarks on the Whole Progress of Architecture, Ecclesiastical as well as Military, in Great Britain, and on the corresponding Changes in Manners, Laws, and Customs, tending both to illustrate Modern History, and to elucidate many interesting Passages in various Antient Classic Authors, with the Appendix, containing Answers to M. P. L. Dutens on the Invention of the Arch. 166 line engravings by Storer. 4 vols. Fol. London.

> An important and valuable historical work, illustrative of every county in the kingdom. —Maggs, no. 715.

1800 An Account of Certain Antiquities and other Curiosities in Saint Edmundsbury (in Suffolk), from an Ancient MS. found in the Ruins of the Cloacinium of the Abbey. 4to. Bury St. Edmunds. (11 pp.)

Antiquarian Society Tracts. 4to. London.

> Among these are 30 Engravings of old Inscriptions, ancient Snuff Boxes; Description of the Old Church of Melbourne, Derbyshire; Old MS; the government of a Nobleman's House; Antiquities found at Ribchester, Lancashire; Anglo-Norman Poetry; Fall of Stones at Stonehenge; Account of Inscriptions found on the Walls of an Apartment; Tower of London; On the History of Stone Pillars, Crosses, Crucifixions, etc.

Biographical and Antiquarian Collections for the Counties of Northants, Lancaster, Sussex, Salop, Gloucester, Herts, and Norfolk. 4to. London.

DALRYMPLE, SIR DAVID. Tracts relative to the History and Antiquities of Scotland. 4to. Edinburgh.

LYSONS, REV. DANIEL. An Historical Account of those Parishes in the County of Middlesex, which are not described in the Environs of London. 4to. London.

> See Lysons, *The Environs of London*, under 1792 and 1797, LONDON. The account of Hampton Palace is one of the prominent features of the present work. The author consulted local records and parochial registers as well as his brother clergymen. The plates show houses of mixed Gothic and Renaissance elements. The account is matter of fact aiming only to inform and to preserve memorials of the history of Middlesex County.

WHITAKER, T. D. An History of the Original Parish of Whalley, and Honor of Clitheroe, in the Counties of Lancaster and York, in Three Parts. Large folding map, 17 plates, and numerous pedigrees. 4to. Blackburn.

> Later editions appeared in the nineteenth century.

1804 HARINGTON, SIR JOHN. Nugae Antiquae, being a Miscellaneous Collection of Original Papers, in Prose and Verse; written during the Reigns of Henry VIII, Edward VI, Queen Mary, Elizabeth, and King James, by Sir John Harington,

Knt., and others who lived in these Times. Selected from the Authentic Remains, By the late Henry Harington, M.A., and Newly Arranged, with illustrative Notes by Thomas Park, F.S.A. 2 vols. 8vo. London.

Many of the letters provide descriptions and narratives of events.

1818   Miscellanea Scotica: A Collection of Tracts relating to the History, Antiquities, Topography, and Literature of Scotland. 4 vols. 12mo. Glasgow.

This is also listed under GENERAL REFERENCE as a basic repository for separate articles cited individually.

1821   AUBREY, JOHN. Aubrey's Collections for Wilts (North Wiltshire). Edited by Sir Thomas Phillipps. Pts. 1 and 2. 4to. London.

See Aubrey under 1862 below.

1822   DOW, REV. J. Remarks on the Ancient Weapon denominated the Celt. Paper read 1797. In *Arch. Scot.,* vol. 2, 199. 4to. Edinburgh.

1825   MERRICK, RICE. A Book of Glamorganshire Antiquities by R. M., 1578. Now first published by Sir Thomas Phillipps. Fol. London.

Edit. by J. A. Corbett, London, 1887.
Merrick was clerk of the peace of Glamorgan *ca.* 1584. His work gives valuable information upon administration in Wales. Corbett's edition gives lists of sheriffs to 1584 and prints part of Leland's Itinerary relating to this county.—Read, *Bibliog. Brit. Hist., Tudor Period.*

1826   BUCHANAN, R. (Editor). Scotia Rediviva: a Collection of Tracts illustrative of the History and Antiquities of Scotland. Vol. I (all published). 8vo. Edinburgh.

1836   TRACTS, Illustrative of the Traditionary and Historical Antiquities of Scotland. 8vo. Edinburgh (?).

Among them are The Roman Account of Britain and Ireland, in Answer to Father Innes, etc., by Alex Taitt, Remarks on Innes' Critical Essay on the Ancient Inhabitants, and History of Scotland during the Minority of King James.

1843-69   Collections for a History of the Shires of Aberdeen and Banff, and Illustrations of the Topography and Antiquities of the Shires of Aberdeen and Banff. 5 vols. 4to. *Publ. Spalding Club,* vol. 9. Aberdeen.

1848   Reliquiae Antiquae Scoticae, Illustrative of Civil and Ecclesiastical Affairs from Original MSS.; Letters, Forfar Witches, Household Inventories, etc. 8vo. Edinburgh (?).

1851-55   Origines Parochiales Scotiae: The Antiquities, Ecclesiastical and Territorial of the Parishes of Scotland. 3 vols. *Publ. Bann. Club,* no. 97. Edinburgh.

All three volumes were edited by Cosmo Innes with various assistants. Vol. I comprises the diocese of Glasgow; II, the dioceses of Argyll and the Isles; III, the dioceses of Ross and Caithness, with additions to those of Argyll and the Isles.

1860   A Brief Relation of the Isle of Anglesea, a curious Account of the State of that Island in the Seventeenth Century (1653). (Place?)

So cited by Rowlands, *Cambrian Bibliog.,* where it is stated that this work remained in manuscript until 1860, when an impression of only 26 copies was made by J. E. Adlard.

1862 AUBREY, JOHN. The Topographical Collections of John Aubrey. Corrected and enlarged by J. E. Jackson. *Publ. Wilts. Arch. and Nat. Hist. Soc.* Devizes.

1867 DINGLEY, THOMAS. History from Marble. Compiled in the Reign of Charles II. Printed in Photo-lithography by Vincent Brooks, from the Original. With an Introduction, Description, and Table of Contents by John Gough Nichols, F.S.A. *Publ. Camden Soc.*, vol. 94. London.

> Dingley was not mentioned by his literary or antiquarian contemporaries. The name is spelled both Dingley and Dineley. He traveled in France, the Low Countries, and Ireland. In 1684 he surveyed all the chief places in Wales. His *History from Marble* was in progress for several years. The materials were drawn from various counties, particularly Herefordshire and Wiltshire. Those from Bath and Oxford were mainly of his own collection. But additional matter he took over from Weever and from Dugdale's *History of St. Paul's* and from other printed books. The sketches of the funeral monuments and other drawings occupy about half the book.

1880-1918 Collections for a History of Staffordshire, edited by The William Salt Archaeological Society, from the Commencement in 1880 to 1918; together 38 vols. in 42. 8vo. Newcastle-on-Tyne.

1882 ORMERUD, GEORGE, F.R.S., and S.A. History of the County Palatine and City of Chester, compiled from Original Evidences in Public Offices, the Harleian and Cottonian MSS.; Collections of successive Antiquaries, and a Personal Survey of every Township in the County; with a Republication of King's *Vale Royal,* and Leycester's *Cheshire Antiquities*; New and Enlarged Edition, corrected throughout, by Thomas Helsby, of Lincoln's Inn. Portrait, colored maps, and numerous engravings of buildings, views, antiquities, arms, heraldic designs and many pedigrees. 3 vols. Fol. London.

> This, the 2nd edition, is the finest and most perfect of all our county histories.—Bookseller's Note.

1892 Court Book of the Barony of Urie in Kincardinshire, 1604-1747. Edit. with Notes and Introduction by D. G. Barron. *Publ. Scot. Hist. Soc.,* no. 12. Edinburgh.

> This is a contemporary record of social conditions and activities.

1920-29 Parochial Collections made by Anthony Wood and Richard Rawlinson. Edit. by F. N. Davis. 3 pts. *Oxford Record Society.* Oxford.

1931 LUCAS, JOHN. The History of Warton Parish (compiled about 1710-1740), now for the first Time published, and edited by J. R. Ford and J. A. Fuller-Maitland. 8vo. Kendal.

XVI

British, Roman, and Saxon Antiquities

(While a large number of works listed under HISTORY AND ANTIQUITIES include matter on the early inhabitants of Britain and their Roman and Saxon invaders, there were published many treatises which discussed specifically these phases of premedieval Britain. The classical training in vogue for so many centuries naturally turned the attention of scholars to the remains of Roman occupation, of which new traces kept turning up. Of particular interest were the northern Walls, on which some of the best work was done, Roman roads and military stations, camps and ports of Kent, identification of Roman sites with later place names, baths and villas, tessellated pavements, etc. Saxon barrows, urns, fortifications, and especially the White Horse in Berkshire, the manners and customs of the ancient Britons, who were at times derived from the Phoenicians, the alluring mystery of Stonehenge and the druids, the Picts and the "vitrified forts" of the Highlands—all occasioned prolific exercises of ingenious learning which were invariably countered with equally ingenious refutations. Under the ADDENDA to this section will be found an outline history of the interpretations evoked by Stonehenge and Avebury.)

1543 LHWYD, HUMPHREY. De Mona Druidum Insula Antiquitati suae restituta: Humph. Lludii Epistola ad Ortelium. 4to. London.

> So cited in Gough, *Anecdotes Brit. Topog.,* 607. Other dates given are 1570 (Rowlands, *Bibliog.,* where it is referred to as a poem); again, bound up with Lhwyd's treatise *De Armentario Romano,* and printed at the end of Sir John Price's *Historiae Brytannicae Defensio,* 4to, London, 1573 (see Price this date under HISTORY AND CHRONICLE); at the end of Ortelius' *Theatrum,* fol., Antwerp, 1592; annexed to William's edition of Lhwyd's *Commentarioli Britannicae Descriptionis Fragmentum* (see under 1572, HISTORY AND CHRONICLE), 4to, London, 1731.

1623 LISLE, WILLIAM. Saxon Monuments. London.

1655 JACOB, HENRY. De Origine Druidum. In his Delphi Phoenicizantes . . . Appenditur diatriba de Noae in Italiam adventu, ejusque nominibus ethnicis: nec non de origine Druidum, etc. Authore Edmundo Dickinsono. 16mo. Oxon.

> The work was published by Dickinson who had purloined Jacob's MS and disguised it with another style. See Watt, *Bibliotheca Britannica,* vol. II, 540.—Black, *List of Works relating to Druids and Druidism.*

JONES, INIGO. For his account of Stonehenge, see his *The Most Notable Antiquity of Great Britain,* under ADDENDA below.

> All the conjectures on Stonehenge and Avebury pertaining to this section are placed under the ADDENDA.

1658 BURTON, WILLIAM. A Commentary on Antoninus, his Itinerary, or Journies of the Roman Empire, so far as it concerneth Britain; wherein the First Foundation of our Cities, Lawes, and Government according to the Roman policy are clearly discovered, etc., a Work very Useful for all Historians, Antiquaries, Philologists, and more particularly for the Student of the Lawes. With a Chorographical Map of the Severall Stations; and Indexes to the Whole Work. Portrait by Hollar. Fol. London.

> According to Gough (*op. cit.,* 3-5), the text of this work was copied from the edition of the Itinerary printed at the end of Holinshed's *Description of Britain,* 1587, and reprinted in the English editions of Camden. It first appeared in print at Paris, 1512, edited by H. Stephens from a very old MS in the possession of Longolius. Dr. Robert Talbot,

treasurer of the church at Norwich, 1547, an eminent antiquary contemporary with Leland, was the first Englishman to illustrate it with various readings and notes, which were of great service to Camden. These were printed by Hearne with Stephens' text and the English names as fixed by Dr. Thomas Gale, at the end of the third volume of Leland's *Itinerary* (see under 1710-12, TOURS BY NATIVES), from a MS in the Bodleian Library which belonged to John Stow and is in his handwriting. In Campbell, *Political Survey*, vol. II, 250, it is stated that the above work was first printed at Florence in 1519. So much of it as pertains to Britain was published by Harrison at the close of his *Description of Britain*, 1587, from MSS. F. Jerom Surita put out an edition of the whole Itinerary, with learned annotations, at Cologne in 1600. Other 17th and 18th century editions are noted in the following pages as they occur. Two modern printings may be mentioned here: one dealing with the British section, by Rev. Canon Raven in *Antiquary*, vols. 36-40, 1900-04; and the other *Itineraria Romana*, edited by Otto Cuntz, Teubner, 1929.

This work is the most authentic of the records on the Roman roads. It is believed to have been compiled in the reign of Constantine the Great, though the exact date is in doubt. Very likely it was begun in one age and finished in the form it has reached us *ca.* A.D. 320. It is a geographical work containing the names of all the places and stations on the principal roads and crossroads of the Roman Empire, with their distances from each other in Roman miles, and was designed to serve mainly for the use of officers during their campaigns. It is usually ascribed to Marcus Aurelius Antoninus, but it more probably embodied the results of a survey originated by Julius Caesar. See Forbes, *Our Roman Highways*, and Brown, *Early Descriptions of Scotland*, 224, note.

1662 VAUGHAN, ROBERT. British Antiquities Revived; to which is added, The Pedigree of the Earl of Carbury, Lord President of Wales, with a Short Account of the Five Royal Tribes of Cambria. 4to. Oxford.

This was intended to end the controversy then subsisting over the primogeniture of the sons of Roderic, who, on the tripartition of Wales, gave the northern part to Anarawd, the southern to Cadel, and Powys to Merfyn.—Bookseller's Note.

1670 SHERINGHAM, ROBERT. De Anglorum Gentis Origine Disceptatio. London.

This was highly praised in its day as a scholarly investigation of the origin of the races which peopled the British Isles.—Eleanor Adams, *Old English Scholarship in England*.

1673 LANGHORNE, DANIEL. Elenchus Antiquitatum Albionensium, Britannorum, Scotorum, Danorum, Anglosaxonum, etc. Appendix. 2 vols. in 1. 8vo. London.

1676 GUIDOTT, THOMAS, M.D. For some plates of Roman antiquities, see his *Discourse of Bathe*, under SPAS.

SAMMES, AYLETT. Britannia Antiqua Illustrata: or, The Antiquities of Ancient Britain, derived from the Phoenicians, wherein the Original Trade of this Island is discovered; Names of Places, Officies, Dignities, Idolatry, Language, and Customs of the Primitive Inhabitants are clearly demonstrated, together with a Chronological History of this Kingdom, from the first Traditional Beginning, until the Year 800 A.D.; when the Name of Britain was changed into England, with the Antiquities of the Saxons, as well as Phoenicians, Greeks, and Romans. With plates. Fol. London.

This is called vol. I, but no more was published. It contains some curious etymologies, specimens of Runic and Anglo-Saxon fragments, and the Laws of King Ine in old and modern English. Sammes has been called an "impertinent pedant," who, according to Wood, never saw the books which he quoted. He asserted the Saxons to be of Getish extraction. See Adams, *op. cit.* See also this date under ADDENDA.

1678 C[UNNINGHAM], J[AMES]. An Essay upon the Inscriptions of Macduff's Crosse in Fyfe. 4to. Edinburgh.

Reprinted in *Tracts Illustrative of the Traditional and Historic Antiquities of Scotland*, 8vo, Edinburgh, 1836.

This gentleman has made intelligible this ancient Saxon inscription, very imperfectly given by Sir R. Sibbald from Balfour's papers, disguised under a Latin cover now extant only in various transcripts, none of which seems to have preserved the original character. Gordon says the form of this monument, which is now quite gone, is nowhere exhibited. There is a print of it prefixed to Sibbald's History.—Gough, 646, and note.

1685 STILLINGFLEET, EDWARD (Bishop). Origines Britannicae. London.

> Here the progress and proceedings of the Romans in Britain are learnedly and perspicuously treated.—Campbell, *Political Survey,* vol. II, 296. The author was the well-known popular preacher in London.

1693 SOMNER, WILLIAM. A Treatise of the Roman Ports and Forts in Kent, publish'd by James Brome, M.A., Rector of Cheriton, and Chaplain to the Cinque Ports; to which is prefixt the Life of Mr. Somner by White Kennett. Engraved portrait. 8vo. Oxford.

> Bishop Nicolson speaks of this as a valuable work rectifying a great many mistakes in Camden, Lambarde, Philipot, etc. Somner is best known as a Saxonist, whose *Dictionarium Saxonico-Latino-Anglicum,* 1659, aided materially in the study of Old English. His intimate acquaintance with Saxon manners and polity appears in his treatise of Gavel-kind, and his great improvement of Lambarde's code of their laws.

1694 ————. Julii Caesaris Portus Iccius Illustratus. 8vo. Oxford.

1700 LEIGH, CHARLES. For an account of British, Armenian, Greek, and Roman antiquities in Lancashire, Cheshire, etc., see his *The Natural History of Lancashire,* under NATURAL HISTORY.

1702 SACHEVERELL, WILLIAM. For an account of the Mona of Caesar and Tacitus, and of the ancient druids, see his *An Account of the Isle of Man,* the 1702 edition of the 1701 printing, under DESCRIPTIONS.

1706 MAULE, HENRY (of Melgum). The History of the Picts, containing an Account of their Original Language, Manners, Government, Religion, Bounds and Limits of their Kingdom, etc. 12mo. Edinburgh.

> Reprinted in *Miscellanea Scotica,* vol. 1, 8vo, Glasgow, 1818.

1707 SIBBALD, SIR ROBERT. Historical Enquiries concerning the Roman Monuments and Antiquities in the North Part of Britain called Scotland: in which there is an Account of the Roman Wall, Ports, Colonies, and Forts, Temples, Altars, Sepulchres, and Military Ways in that Country; and of the Roman Forces lodged there, from the Vestiges and Inscriptions yet remaining; and from the Urns, Medals, Measures, and Buckles and Arms, and such like Antiquities found there: with Copper Cuts of the most remarkable of them. Fol. Edinburgh.

> See Sibbald under 1711 below.

1709 GALE, ROGER (Editor). Antonini Iter Britanniarum Commentariis, ill. Thomae Gale, opus posthumum . . . Accessit Anonymi Ravennatis Britanniae Chorographia. Folding map and numerous engravings. 4to. London.

> Thomas Gale's notes on the Antonine Itinerary were revised, enlarged, and published after his death by his son Roger, who added the Ravenna Chorographia. This Itinerary has ever intrigued the interest of the antiquaries and historians, and well it might, for it is regarded as a document of the utmost importance in the study of Roman communication and military movements and identification of places (see under 1658 above). Supplementing it are the Peutinger *Tabula* and the *Geography* of the anonymous Ravenna. The *Tabula*

itineraria Peutingeria received its name from Konrad Peutinger (1465-1547), a friend of the Emperor Maximilian, who was one of the first to publish Roman inscriptions. The oldest existing copy was made by a monk of Colmar about 1265. A certain Konrad Celtes discovered it and brought it to the notice of the authorities, and it was given to Peutinger to publish (from Maggs, no. 693). It is really a map or chart of the world in Roman times, measuring in length 21 feet and in width 1 foot. It traces the military stations and the distances between them. The German editor of the Leipzig edition (1824) says it was drawn in the 3rd century A.D. The *Ravennatis anonymi Cosmographia et Guidonis Geographica* was compiled by an anonymous cosmographer of Ravenna, who seems to have flourished about 650 A.D. It likewise enumerates the Roman stations. A scholarly edition was put out by Moritz Pinder and Gustav Parthey, Berlin, 1860.—Gross, *The Sources and Literature of English History*.

1710-12 TALBOT, ROBERT. Annotationes in eam partem Itinerarii Antonini quae ad Britanniam pertinet. In Hearne's edition of Leland's *Itinerary*, vol. III, Oxford.

> Wood says of him, in his *Athenae Oxonienses*, that he was very much esteemed in his time and after, for his singular knowledge of the antiquities of England, and for his care in preserving and collecting ancient books and monuments decayed by time.—Quoted by Adams, *op. cit.*

1711 BATTELEY, JOHN, D.D. For an account of the ancient Rutupiae and Regelbium, with other cities and ports of Kent known to the Romans, see his *Antiquitates Rutupinae*, under ECCLESIASTICAL HISTORY AND ANTIQUITIES.

SIBBALD, SIR ROBERT. Conjectures concerning Roman Ports, Colonies, and Forts, in the Firths (of Forth and Tay) from their Vestiges and Antiquities found near them. In three Sections: the first concerning these upon the North Coast of Forth; the second concerning these upon the South Coast of Tay; the third concerning these upon the North Coast of Tay. Fol. Edinburgh.

————. Commentarius in Julii Agricolae expeditiones 3. 4. 5. 6. 7. in vita ejus, per C. Tacitum generum ejus, descriptas; & in Boreali Britanniae parte, quae Scotia dicitur, gestas: in quo, ex vestigiis castrorum & castellorum Romanorum, monumentisque antiquis ibi repertis, textus Taciti illustrantur. Fol. Edinburgh.

> To this is annexed Series Rerum a Romanis post avocatum Agricolam in Britannia boreali gestarum. With these essays Sibbald illustrated Roman antiquities in Scotland. The whole has the common title of Tractatus Varii. In his *Commentarius* Sibbald takes in the entire island, together with Ireland and the adjacent isles, not forgetting Thule. He made an actual survey of the scenes of action described by the Roman historians and described the monuments remaining. Mr. Gordon, however, charged him with wresting the genuine sense of Tacitus and other Roman writers, and contradicting the text, carrying people and stations from England to Scotland. See Gordon, *Iter Septentrionale*, pp. 43-46, where he uses an appendix to his 4th chapter to confute him.—Gough, 619-20. Scarcely any two editions of these printed pieces agree, it is said.

1712 HEARNE, THOMAS. A Discourse concerning the Stunsfield Tessellated Pavement, etc., discovered near Woodstock Jan. 25, 1711/12. Oxford.

> This was prefixed to vol. VIII of his edition of Leland's *Itinerary* (Oxford), with an exact drawing of it. His argument was attacked by John Pointer (see under 1713 below). The dispute arose over the figure on the pavement, which Pointer would have to be Bacchus and Hearne, Apollo. The latter writer refuted Pointer in his preface to Leland's *Collectanea*, 1715. The pavement was engraved by Vertue in 1712.—Gough, 398.

1713 POINTER, JOHN. An Account of a Roman Pavement, lately found at Stunsfield in Oxfordshire, prŏv'd to be 1400 Years Old. One plate. 8vo. Oxford.

> For the dispute over the figure in the pavement, see Hearne under 1712 above. Pointer was chaplain of Merton College in Oxford and rector of Slapton in Northamptonshire.

WOODWARD, JOHN. An Account of some Roman Urns, and other Antiquities, Lately Digg'd up near Bishopsgate. With Brief Reflections upon the Antient and Present State of London. In a Letter to Sir Christopher Wren. 8vo. London.

1716 L., J. A True (though Short) Account of the Antient Britons: in respect of their Descent, Qualities, Settlements, Country, Language, Learning, and Religion; with the Effigies of Llewelyn ap Gruffydd, the Last Prince of Wales of the British Blood. By J. L. a Cambro-Briton. 4to. London.

> One would conjecture that L. stands for Lloyd.

1718 BAXTER, WILLIAM. Glossarium Antiquitatum Britannicarum, sive Syllabus Etymologicus Antiquitatum veteris Britanniae atque Hiberniae temporibus Romanorum; accedunt Edvardi Luidii adversaria posthuma, cum notis MSS. M. C. Tutet; et Vita Gul. Baxter manuscripta. 8vo. London.

> 2nd edit., 8vo, London, 1733.
> Baxter was a Shropshire man, and from his skill in the old British language attempted to determine the geography by etymology, a method most uncertain, and which often misled Camden before him and others since. Lhwyd's work annexed represents the attempts of another etymologist in the same field.—Gough, 4.

1719 MUSGRAVE, DR. WILLIAM. Belgium Britannicum, in quo illius limites, fluvii, urbes, viae militares, populus, lingua, dii, monumenta, aliaque permulta clarius et uberius exponuntur Iscae Dunm. 8vo. Exeter.

> This is the title as given by Gough, 140, who states that the work deals with the state of the county of Devonshire under the Romans. The title cited by *DNB* runs: Antiquitates Britanno-Belgicae, praecipue Romanae figuris illustratae . . . quorum I de Belgico, Britannico, II de Geta Britannico, III de Julii Vitalis epitaphio cum Notis criticis H. Dodwelli. It is further stated that vol. II originally appeared in 1716, and III in 1711. And vol. IV quod tribus ante editis est appendix in 1720. To Musgrave, Belga meant the district from the Solent to near Henley, and from Cirencester to Bath and Porlock, thence back from Ilchester to the border of Hampshire.

1720 KEYSLER, J. G. Antiquitates Selectae, Septentrionales et Celticae. 19 folding and full-page engravings of Stonehenge, and other druidical and Celtic remains. 8vo. Hannoverae.

> The author was a Fellow of the Royal Society of London.

STUKELEY, DR. WILLIAM. An Account of a Roman Temple and other Antiquities, near Graham's Dyke, Scotland. 4to. London.

> This is the record of visits by Stukeley and Mr. Jelf, in the summer of 1720, to the Roman Wall between the Clyde and Forth. The course of the Wall is shown on a map, ten sculptured and inscribed stones are figured, and an elevation, plan, and section of Arthur's Oven are given.—Mitchell, *List of Travels*.

1723 ROWLANDS, HENRY. For much superfluous learning on the subject of druids and druidism, on the derivation of the inhabitants of Anglesey from the nations surviving the Deluge, and on the mixture of Hebrew and Celtic languages, see his *Mona Antiqua Restaurata*, under HISTORY AND ANTIQUITIES.

1724 POINTER, JOHN. Britannia Romana or, Roman Antiquities in Britain. 8vo. Oxford.

> Gough says that this pretends to give an account of Roman coins, roads, stations in Britain, and the Roman history of Oxford City and University; but his pompous title page produces nothing.—*Op. cit.*, 7.

STUKELEY, DR. WILLIAM. For an account of Roman antiquities in England and Scotland, see his *Itinerarium Curiosum,* under TOURS BY NATIVES.

1725 CHARLTON, WALTER. For his explanation of Stonehenge, see his *Chorea Gigantum,* under ADDENDA, this section.

A Discourse upon some Antiquities discovered near Conquest in Somersetshire, supposed to be the place where the Conquest of Britain, by the Romans, was completed. By an anonymous Author. Published by Thomas Hearne at the end of *Peter Langtoft's Chronicle.* Oxford. (See Langtoft under 1716-35, HISTORY AND CHRONICLE.)

1726 SALMON, NATHANIEL. Roman Stations in Britain, according to the Imperial Itinerary, upon Watling-Street, Ermine-Street, Ikening or Via ad Icianos, so far as any of these Roads lead through the following Counties, Norfolk, Suffolk, Cambridgeshire, Essex, Hertfordshire, Bedfordshire, Middlesex. 8vo. London.

> This was published anonymously. It and the following work were incorporated in his volume *New Survey of England,* 1731.

————. A Survey of the Roman Antiquities in some of the Midland Counties of England. London.

TOLAND, JOHN. A Specimen of the Critical History of the Celtic Religion and Learning: containing an Account of the Druids, or the Priests and Judges; of the Vaids, or the Diviners and Physicians, and of the Bards, or the Poets and Heralds of the Ancient Gauls, Britons, Irish, and Scots. With the History of Abaris the Hyperborean, Priest of the Sun, in Three Letters. . . . 8vo. London.

> Another edit., 8vo, London, 1740 (?) ; a new edit., with an abstract of Toland's life and writings and a copious index, by R[obert] Huddleston, 8vo, Montrose, 1814. (Huddleston's Notes occupy pp. 253-434.—Black, *List of Works relating to Druids and Druidism.*) Translated into German, by J. Ph. Cassel, 8vo, Braunschweig, 1763.

1729 INNES, THOMAS. A Critical Essay on the Ancient Inhabitants of the Northern Parts of Britain, or Scotland, with an Account of the Romans, the Britains [*sic*] betwixt the Walls, of the Caledonians or Picts, and particularly of the Scots, with Appendix of Ancient MS. Pieces. 2 folding plates. 2 vols. 8vo. London.

> This work, on which Innes' fame chiefly rests, was answered by Andrew Waddell in *Remarks,* etc. (see under 1733 below). Father Innes was born at Drumgask in Aboyne in 1662, but he spent most of his life at the Scots College in Paris, though he served for some years on the Scottish mission. This is a pioneer venture in scholarly historical investigation.

1730 WALLIS, STAMFORD. For a dissertation on Stonehenge, see under ADDENDA, this section.

1731 SALMON, NATHANIEL. For discussions of Roman military ways and the stations of the Itinerary of Antoninus, see his *New Survey of England,* under SURVEYS.

1732 HORSLEY, JOHN, M.A., F.R.S. Britannia Romana; or, The Roman Antiquities of Britain; in Three Books. The first contains the History of all the Roman Transactions in Britain, . . . The second, a Complete Collection of Roman

Inscriptions and Sculptures which have hitherto been discovered in Britain, . . . The third, the Roman Geography of Britain; in which are given the Originals of Ptolemy, Antonini Itinerarium, the Notitia, the anonymous Ravennas, and Peutinger's Table, so far as they relate to this Island. To which are added, a Chronological Table, and Indexes to the Inscriptions and Sculptures, also Geographical Indexes, both of the Latin and English Names of the Roman Places in Britain, and a General Index to the Work. The Whole illustrated with above an Hundred Copper Plates. Map. Fol. London.

To this dissenting minister at Morpeth in Northumberland, "still belongs the glory of having written the one exhaustive work on Roman Britain. For his period Horsley is as indispensable as Gibbon for his; and bearing in mind the difference between the extent of their fields, Horsley is Gibbon's equal." So writes R. G. Collingwood in *Journ. Rom. Stud.*, vol. 11. His great achievement was to fix the names of the Wall forts by comparing the lists of garrisons in the *Notitia Imperii* with those recorded in inscriptions—identifications so certain and obvious today that it is hard to see why they were a question to Horsley's contemporaries. With characteristic independence he decided against publication by subscription, the usual method for such costly books as his. Nor did he dedicate his work to any great nobleman of the day; instead he inscribed it to a scholarly recluse of his own church, Sir Richard Ellys, Bt., of Nocton near Lincoln. Horsley died before he saw it in print, but apparently everything had been prepared for the press. It set a standard of sober and methodical investigation, whose influence is still forward. He himself says that his practice was to be well assured from ocular demonstration where there were any visible remains or certain proofs of Roman settlements, and then to compare his findings with the records in the *Antonine Itinerary* and the *Notitia Imperii*. He was the first to point out that Hadrian's *Vallum* was shorter than the wall of Severus, owing to its being truncated at the ends. He had a thorough grasp of the system of mile-castles, knowing that there had been eighty-one in all. His error in making four turrets between each mile-castle instead of two is excusable, for there had been no such clearing with the spade as was done later by John Clayton. The collection of inscriptions, which he regarded as the core of his work, has been superseded by the Berlin *Corpus*. But as far as England is concerned, Horsley provided the solid foundation on which the later great work was reared. See Sir George MacDonald, "John Horsley, Scholar and Gentleman," and R. C. Bosanquet, "John Horsley and his Times" in *Archaeologia Aeliana*, 4th ser., vol. 10, 1933.

Few Roman remains have attracted more attention than the two Walls, the lower one stretching from the mouth of the Tyne to the Solway, and the upper one across the narrow isthmus between the indents of the Forth and the Clyde. Each was a complex system of forts, continuous rampart and ditch, military roads and outlying posts, planned with consummate skill and on an imperial scale. For an account of these and modern interpretations of features in dispute as well as historical corrections, see Collingwood and Myers, *Roman Britain and the English Settlements*, Oxford, 1937. For another work on the Walls, see John Warburton under 1753 below.

1733 [WADDELL, ANDREW]. Remarks on Mr. Innes's Critical Essay on the Antient Inhabitants of the Northern Parts of Scotland. 4to. Edinburgh.

See Innes under 1729 above.

1738 WISE, FRANCIS, B.D. A Letter to Dr. Mead concerning some Antiquities in Berkshire, particularly shewing that the White Horse, which gives its Name to the Vale, is a Monument of the West-Saxons, made in Memory of a Great Victory obtained over the Danes, A.D. 871. 2 engraved plates. 4to. Oxford.

This letter gave rise to much controversy, the nature of which is indicated below. In this Letter Wise touches upon the name of Berkshire, the Ickneild Street traced by him in this region, the Roman antiquities of Wantage, and other Roman and Saxon fortifications.

1740 RUSTICUS, P. The Impertinence and Imposture of Modern Antiquities Display'd, or, a Refutation of Mr. Wise's Letter to Dr. Mead, concerning the White Horse, and other Antiquities in Berkshire, in a Familiar Letter to a Friend. With a Preface by the Gentleman to whom this Letter was addressed. 4to. London.
Gough calls this a rude and silly animadversion. It was replied to in the following:

1741 [NORTH, GEORGE.] Answer to a Scandalous Libel, intitled The Impertinence and Imposture of Modern Antiquaries Display'd, etc. 4to. London.

1742 WISE, FRANCIS. Further Observations upon the White Horse and other Antiquities of Berkshire. With an Account of Whiteleaf-Cross in Buckinghamshire. As also of the Red Horse in Warwickshire, and some other Monuments of the same Kind. Plates. 4to. Oxford.

Wise here takes the Buckinghamshire cross to be a similar memorial of some victory not specified in history, gained probably by Alfred's son and successor, Edward the Elder, his father having changed the former national standard for this. The Red Horse Wise believes to be a monument of Sir Richard Nevil, the king-making Earl of Warwick.—Gough, 80-1.

1740 STUKELEY, DR. WILLIAM. For his account of Stonehenge, see under ADDENDA, this section.

1743 ————. For his account of Abury, see under ADDENDA, this section.

1746 RAUTHMELL, RICHARD. Antiquitates Bremetonacenses; or, the Roman Antiquities of Overborough; wherein Overborough is proved to be the Bremetonacae of Antoninus; the year when, and the Romans who erected this Station proved out of Tacitus; an Account of the Garrison there; also of the Idol who was tutelary Deity of Overborough; to which is added, a Description of as many Monuments of Antiquity as have been dug up or discovered there lately, tending to illustrate the History of that once famous Station. Plates. 4to. London.

Reprinted, with additions, 8vo, London (?), 1824.
The author was Perpetual Curate of Whitewell, in Bowland.—Some pertinent remarks are here delivered in most uncouth language. The author's explanation of an inscription on an altar found here was controverted by Mr. Pegge in *Gentleman's Magazine*, Sept., 1759, 407, who changed the name of the deity and the dedicator, in which last particular he was supported by another critic in the same Magazine for the following month, p. 451.—Gough, 235-36.

SMITH, G. For a map of the Roman wall (Tyne to Solway), see under MAPS.

1750 CLERK, SIR J. Dissertatio de Monumentis quibusdam Romanis, in boreali Magnae Britanniae parte detectis anno MDCCXXXI (in Middlebie parish, Dumfrieshire). Illustrations. 4to. Edinburgh.

For an account of Stonehenge, see this date under ADDENDA, this section.

1753 WARBURTON, JOHN (Somerset Herald). Vallum Romanum: or, the History and Antiquities of the Roman Wall, commonly called the Picts Wall, in Cumberland and Northumberland, built by Adrian and Severus, the Roman Emperors, seventy Miles in length, to keep out the Northern Picts and Scots. In Three Books, etc. Collected and abstracted from all Writers of the same Subject, as an Inducement to the young Nobility and Gentry of Great Britain to make the Tour of their native Country before they visit foreign Parts: to which are added, Two Letters from the Late honourable and learned Roger Gale to the Compiler, relating to the Antiquities in the North of England. The Whole illustrated with a Map of the Walls, military Ways and Stations laid down by a new geometrical Survey, and near 200 Sculptures on Copper Plate. 4to. London.

This is no more than Horsley's account of the walls (see under 1732 above) reprinted and all the inscriptions of each station thrown together, as a pocket companion for those who make the tour of the walls. The compiler, in company with Horsley, surveyed this county, of which he published a map in 1716, on three sheets, with the arms of the nobility

and gentry, and a great number of Roman altars and inscriptions. He caused a survey and plan of this wall and military ways to be made in 1715, to show the necessity of repairing the latter; but on the suppression of the rebellion of that year his scheme was no more thought of till the late rebellion revived it. An act was then passed in 1751 to make the road. Horsley, in his *Britannia Romana,* frequently charges Warburton with incorrectness in copying his map. Gordon, who spends the whole eighth chapter of his *Itinerarium Septentrionale* on this wall, complains of the great inaccuracy of Warburton's transcriptions. —Gough, 388-89. This was a dishonest work from a shady character. But it had a large sale. For his liftings from Horsley, he was pungently scored by George Allan, the Darlington antiquary, who wrote in his copy, "no more than Mr. Horsley's account of the Walls reprinted." Its virtue was its handy size, whereas others were too bulky to carry around. —Bosanquet, in *Archaeologia Aeliana,* 4th ser., vol. 10 (cited under Horsley above).

1754 BORLASE, WILLIAM. For an account of the druids, superstitions of the ancient Britons, etc., see his *Antiquities of Cornwall,* under HISTORY AND ANTIQUITIES.

COOKE, REV. WILLIAM. Enquiry into the Patriarchal and Druidical Religion, Temples, etc., particularly at Abiry, Stonehenge, etc. Plans. 4to. London.

> 2nd edit., 4to, London, 1755.
> This is said to be largely an abridgement of Stukeley, with the plates reduced in size from those in the latter's book.—Harrison, *Bibliog. of the Great Stone Monuments of Wiltshire.*

1757 STUKELEY, DR. WILLIAM. An Account of Richard of Cirencester, Monk of Westminster, and of his Works; with his Antient Map of Roman Britain; and the Itinerary thereof. Read at the Antiquarian Society, March 18, 1756. Folding map and plate. 4to. London.

> Richard lived about the end of the 14th century. He is called by Gough the Leland of his age. He searched all the monastic libraries, and compiled a history of the Anglo-Saxons, in five books, from the arrival of Hengist to Henry III. So much may be certificated from his Chronicles, for which see Giles, *Six Old English Chronicles,* under 1848, and the edition of his *Speculum,* Rolls Series, 1863-69. But the Itinerary was a forgery by Charles Bertram, an English teacher in the school for naval cadets, Copenhagen, who brought out between 1747 and 1757 an alleged transcript of a MS work by Richard of Cirencester, together with a copy of an ancient itinerary of Britain, in many places supplementing and correcting Antoninus. It imposed not only on Stukeley, who published his work, but also for many years later on most of the eminent English antiquaries. The imposture was exposed by B. B. Woodward in *Gentleman's Magazine,* 1866-67. Bertram furthered the credence of his forgery by publishing it with the histories of Gildas and Nennius. See *DNB* on Richard of Cirencester.

1758 STUKELEY, DR. WILLIAM. A Collection of Prints and Original Drawings, made by Wm. Stukeley, 1758, etc., many relating to the Druids, Caesar's Camp, called the Brill, at Pancras; Camp at Deal; Original Maps by Stukeley; Hounslow, Sheparton, Charing, Richborough, Kent Views; Roman Camps in various parts of Britain; Druid Temples; Druid Barrow; Original Appearance of Dover; upwards of 450 prints and drawings from Wm. Stukeley's library. 4 vols. 4to.

1763 Description of Kitts-Cotty-House, with illustrations. In *Gent. Mag.,* vol. 33, 248.

> This describes four huge stones—two as supports to a third, and the fourth placed at the back for a wall.

1766 STUKELEY, DR. WILLIAM. Dr. Stukeley's Account of several British Antiquities lately found near Chaleris, in the Isle of Ely. A Letter. In *Gent. Mag.,* vol. 36, 118-21. London.

1768 MACPHERSON, DR. JOHN (of Sleat). Dissertations on the Origin, Antiquities, Manners and Religion, Language, etc., of the Ancient Caledonians, Picts, and British and Irish Scots. 4to. London.

1769 PRICE, F. For reference to Stonehenge, see his *The Salisbury Guide,* under AIDS TO TRAVELERS.

STRANGE, JOHN. An Account of some Remains of Roman and other Antiquities in and near the County of Brecknock, in South Wales. London.
This was a paper read before the Society of Antiquaries, April 13 and 20, 1769.

1770 GARDEN, PROF. J. A Letter describing Stone Circles in Scotland. Read Dec. 4, 1766. In *Archaeologia,* vol. 1, 313. 4to. London.

1771 SMITH, DR. JOHN. For an account of Stonehenge, see his *Choir Gaur,* under ADDENDA, this section.

1773 Remains of a Druidic Work in the North of Scotland. In *Gent. Mag.,* vol. 43, 230-31. London.

1774 IVES, JOHN. Remarks upon the Garianonum of the Romans, the Site and Remains fixed and described. Map, plan, and south view of Garianonum, and 3 other plates. 8vo. London.

1774-76 STRUTT, JOSEPH. For a view of the manners, customs, arms, habits, etc., of the Anglo-Saxon period, see his *Horda Angel-Cynnan,* under HISTORY AND ANTIQUITIES.

1777 BROOKE, JOHN C. An Illustration of a Saxon Inscription on the Church of Kirkdale in Rydale, in the North Riding of the County of York. 4to. York (?).

1779 COLLINSON, REV. JOHN. The Beauties of British Antiquity, collected from the Writings of Esteemed Antiquarians. London.

Roman Urns, a Short Account of Three discovered in the West of Cornwall. 4to. (Place?)

1780 PRICE, J. E. A Description of the Roman Tessellated Pavement found in Bucklersbury. Plates and cuts. 4to. London.

SMITH, JOHN. Galic [*sic*] Antiquities: consisting of a History of the Druids, particularly those of Caledonia; a Dissertation on the Authenticity of the Poems of Ossian; and a Collection of Ancient Poems, translated from the Galic [*sic*] of Ullin, Orran, etc. 4to. Edinburgh.
The History makes a great pretense at learning, and the poetry is of the spawn of Macpherson.

1780-96 ANDERSON, PROF. JOHN. Monumenta Romani Imperii in Scotia, maxime vero inter Vestigia Valli auspiciis Antonini Pii Imperatoris a Fortha ad Glottam

perducti reperta, et in Academia Glasguensi adservata. Iconibus expressa. 32 plates of Roman remains in the Hunterian Museum. 4to. Glasgow.

1781   VINE, STEPHEN. Traces of a Roman Military Way through Suffolk, Surrey, and Kent. In *Gent. Mag.,* vol. 51, 306-07. London.

1784   PEGGE, SAMUEL. The Roman Roads, Ikenild Street, and Bath Way, described and investigated through the Country of the Coritani, or the County of Derby. To which is added, A Dissertation on the Coritani. No. 24 of *Bibl. Topog. Brit.* London.

> Reviewed *Gent. Mag.,* vol. 54, 767-68. The first part was printed but not published in 1768. Now it is reprinted, with Pegge's consent and improvements. The Dissertation annexed is also a republication.

1786   DOUGLAS, REV. JAMES. Two Dissertations on the Brass Instruments called Celts, and other Arms of the Ancients, found in this Island. No. 33 of *Bibl. Topog. Brit.* London.

> Reviewed *Gent. Mag.,* vol. 56, 150-52. The reviewer regards this work as dubious in learning and shaky in conclusions. A reply from Douglas to these strictures was printed in vol. 56, 245-48.

JAMESON, J. An Account of the Roman Camps of Battle Dyke and Haerfaulds. No. 36 of *Bibl. Topog. Brit.* London.

JOHNSTONE, REV. JAMES. Antiquitates Celto-Normanniae, containing the Chronicles of Man and the Isles. See this item under HISTORY AND CHRONICLE.

——————. Antiquitates Celto-Scandicae; Rerum Gestarum inter nationes Britannicarum Insularum et Gentes Septentrionales, from the Sagas. 4to. London.

Plan and Description of the Roman Camp at Dalginross, from a young Gentleman residing in the Neighbourhood.

1787   LYON, REV. JOHN. A Brief History of Dover Castle: or, a Description of Roman, Saxon, and Norman Fortifications, with a List of the Constables and Lord Wardens of the Cinque Ports. 8vo. Canterbury.

1787-88   ROOKE, HAYMAN. Some Account of the Brimham Rocks, in Yorkshire; an Account of the Remains of two Roman Villae discovered near Mansfield Woodhouse, Notts., in 1786; Observations on the Roman Road and Camps in the Neighbourhood of Mansfield Woodhouse. Plates. 4to. London.

1788   SHAND, CAPTAIN A. Some Observations on the Great Roman Road and adjacent Camps and Stations to the North of Graeme's Dyke. 4to. Perth.

1790   TYTLER, A. P. An Account of some Extraordinary Structures on the Tops of Hills in the Highlands; with Remarks on the Progress of the Arts among the Ancient Inhabitants of Scotland. In *Trans. Roy. Soc.,* vol. 2, 31. 4to. Edinburgh.

1792 MACKENZIE, C. An Account of some Remains of Antiquity in the Island of Lewis, one of the Hebrides. Paper read 1783. In *Arch. Scot.*, vol. 1, 282. 4to. Edinburgh.

WARNER, REV. RICHARD. An Attempt to ascertain the Situation of the Antient Clausentum, etc. (Observations on the Utility of provincial History, and Proposals for publishing the History of Hampshire). Map and vignette. 4to. London.

>   Reviewed *Gent. Mag.*, vol. 62, 1125. The author locates the place in question at Bittern Farm, about two and a half miles from Southampton as the spot where the Clausentum of Antoninus stood. Other antiquaries place it at or near Southampton.

1793 ANDERSON, PROFESSOR JOHN. Observations upon Roman Antiquities discovered between the Forth and Clyde. Illustrations. Appendix no. 4 to Roy's *Military Antiquities*. Fol. London. (See Roy this date below.)

>   Published separately, 4to, Edinburgh, 1880.
>   In Roy the article is dated 1773; in the separate issue, 1793. The two sets of engravings do not closely agree, that of the latter being the better of the two.

DOUGLAS, REV. JAMES. For a description of British, Roman, and Saxon sepulchral rites and ceremonies, and of the contents of burial places, see his *Nenia Britannica*, under HISTORY AND ANTIQUITIES.

ROY, WILLIAM, F.R.S., F.S.A. The Military Antiquities of the Romans in North Britain, and particularly of their Ancient System of Castramentation, illustrated from the Vestiges of the Camps of Agricola existing there, comprehending also a Treatise wherein the Ancient Geography of that Part of the Island is rectified, etc. 51 large plates. Fol. London.

>   Reviewed *Gent. Mag.*, vol. 63, 1021-23. This important work, published by the Society of Antiquaries of London, contains a history of Roman transactions from the arrival of Julius Caesar to the recall of Agricola and the coming of the Saxons in 449; the military institutions of the Roman militia, with a general description of North Britain, and commentary on the campaigns of Agricola. It also makes corrections to the geography of Richard of Cirencester. The author was the famous General Roy who opened up the Highlands with his military roads.

THROSBY, JOHN. Letter to the Earl of Leicester, on the recent Discovery of the Roman Cloaca, or Sewer, at Leicester; with some Thoughts on Jewry Wall. 8vo. Leicester.

1794 BUCHANAN, JOHN LANNE. A Defence of the Scots Highlanders in general . . . with a new and satisfactory Account of the Picts, Scots, Fingal, Ossian and his Poems. 8vo. London.

DESMOULINS, JACOB. Antiqua Restaurata. A Concise Historical Account of the Ancient Druids. Shewing their Civil and Religious Governments, Ceremonies, Groves, Derivations and Etymologies, Categorically deduced; With Biographical Sketches. To which will be annexed, The Animated Speech of Caractacus, when sent Captive to Rome. Also, the Remains of Druidical Antiquity, in England, Ireland, Scotland, Wales, and France; illustrated with Copious Remarks, the whole drawn from Sources of respectable Information, and by Permission

inscribed to the United Lodges of the Most noble and venerable Order of Druids. 8vo. London.

ROOKE, HAYMAN. An Account of some Druidical Remains, in Derbyshire. 4 plates. 4to. (Place?)

1795   POWNALL, GOV. THOMAS. Descriptions and Explanations of some Roman Antiquities dug up in the City of Bath, 1790; with an Engraving from Drawings made on the Spot. 4to. Bath.

> Reviewed *Gent. Mag.*, vol. 65, 495. These remains were described and different engravings published already in *Archaeologia*, vol. 10. For the numerous activities of Governor Pownall, see the Index to vol. II of this work.

1796   FOWLER, W. Engravings of the Principal Mosaic Pavements which have been discovered in the Course of the last and present Centuries in various Parts of Great Britain. Also, Engravings of several Subjects in Stained Glass in the Windows of the Cathedrals of York, Lincoln, etc. 51 colored plates, a dedication to Sir Joseph Banks, a dedication and pedigree to the series of the Earls of Chester, and 25 descriptive prospectuses, bound in 2 vols. Atlas Fol. Winterton.

1797   LYSONS, SAMUEL. An Account of the Roman Antiquities discovered at Woodchester, in the County of Gloucester. 40 plates, (mostly colored) including 3 colored aquatints of Woodchester. Fol. London.

> Reviewed *Annual Register,* vol. 40, 1798; and *Gent. Mag.,* vol. 67, 1033-34. By this time only the best is to be expected from Lysons, and here is no disappointment. This is a magnificent and elaborate publication. He describes the remains of a superb Roman villa at Woodchester, of which the first recorded mention occurred about a hundred years ago, when a small part of a mosaic pavement was brought to light. In December, 1793, Lysons undertook to rescue these noble fragments from oblivion. He explored the whole extent of the building and here gives the result of his researches.—From the review.

WARNER, REV. RICHARD. Roman Antiquities discovered at Bath. 14 woodcuts. 4to. Bath (?).

> Reviewed *Gent. Mag.,* vol. 67, 319. This is a superficial compilation and a disappointment to those who have been expecting for a long time a scientific account of these discoveries by Mr. Baldwin, the architect, who conducted the new works and improvements. Instead we get an enumeration of the nine Roman inscriptions fixed in the walls at the eastern end of the abbey church or preserved in the Guildhall. The explanation is not always to the point.—From the review.

1799   REYNOLDS, THOMAS. Iter Britanniarum; or that Part of the Itinerary of Antoninus which relates to Britain. Folding map showing Roman Britain according to Antoninus, Ptolemy, and the Discoveries of modern Times. 4to. Cambridge.

TOWNLEY, J. An Account of Antiquities discovered at Ribchester. From *Vetusta Monumenta.* 4 plates, with 12 pp. of descriptive text. Fol. London.

> Reviewed *Gent. Mag.,* vol. 70, 759. This account is in the form of a letter to the Rev. John Barns, M.A., Secretary to the Society of Antiquaries of London. The four plates here are the first of a new volume (the fourth) of *Vetusta Monumenta* published by the Society of Antiquaries. The first three plates are of a bronze helmet of finished workmanship found in 1796 in a hollow near the bend of the River Ribble on which stood the station called Ribchester. The author is wrong in ascribing religious association to the helmet, which was purely military.—From the review.

1800 GIBSON, K. A Comment upon part of the Fifth Journey of Antoninus through Britain, in which the Situation of Durocobrivae, the Seventh Station there mentioned, is shewn from the various Remains of Roman Antiquity, to have an undoubted claim to that Situation. 4to. London.

1822 CARDONNEL, ADAM DE. A Description of some Roman Ruins discovered at Inveresk. Paper read 1783. In *Arch. Scot.,* vol. 2, 287-88. 4to. Edinburgh.

DOW, REV. J. Remarks on the Ancient Weapon denominated the Celt. Paper read 1797. In *Arch. Scot.,* vol. 2, 199. Edinburgh.

GRANT, REV. MR. (of Boharm). Memoir concerning the Roman Progress in Scotland to the North of the Grampion Hills. Paper read 1787. In *Arch. Scot.,* vol. 2, 31. Edinburgh.

The author assumes Bertram's publication to be genuine (see Stukeley under 1757 above).

1840 KEMBLE, JOHN MITCHELL. On Anglo-Saxon Runes. 6 plates. In *Archaeologia,* vol. 28, 327-72. 4to. London.

This item and many of the following exemplify some outstanding modern research, toward which the preceding century had been fumbling. Kemble here gives probably the first intelligent reading of the runes on the Ruthwell Cross in Dumfriesshire.

1856 Inventorium Sepulchrale: an Account of some Antiquities dug up at Gilton, Kingston, Sibertswold, Barfriston, Beakesbourne, Chartham, and Grundale, from 1757 to 1773. Edited from the original MS. by C. Roach Smith. Portrait, 20 plates (7 colored), and numerous woodcuts. Printed for Subscribers only.

1892 LOWSON, GEORGE. The Roman Wall of Antoninus. *Publ. Nat. Hist. and Arch. Soc.,* vol. 14. 8vo. Stirling.

1893 Travels along the Roman Wall in Scotland, 1697. *Hist. MSS. Comm.,* 13th Report, App. pt. ii, p. 54. 8vo. London.

1898 IRELAND, DR. The Roman Wall of Antoninus. *Publ. Nat. Hist. and Arch. Soc.,* vol. 1. 8vo. Stirling.

This belongs to the Transactions of 1878-89, but is republished to complete the series.

1911 MACDONALD, GEORGE. The Roman Wall in Scotland. In *Brit. Arch. Assoc. Journal,* new ser., vol. 17, 77-78. London.

1912 COOK, ALBERT S. The Date of the Ruthwell and Bewcastle Crosses. In *Connecticut Acad. Arts and Sciences Trans.,* vol. 17, 213-361. New Haven.

ADDENDA — STONEHENGE

(The neolithic builders of Avebury and Stonehenge very likely knew what they were about when they hauled, dressed, and raised the stones for these megaliths, but the only traces of their intentions they left behind lie in the monuments themselves. As with the Sphinx, the only answer they give to man's unceasing questioning is silence and immobility. Perhaps Defoe was right in stating that about all one could say about them was that there they were. But the testimony of antiquaries and historians, of poets and travelers, from Henry of Huntingdon down to today, is that these stones, though dumb themselves, will not let man rest. The number of theories proposed probably runs over a thousand titles. For an interesting record of guesses, learned disquisitions, and archaeological studies, one is referred to W. Jerome Harrison, "A Bibliography of the Great Stone Monuments of Wiltshire—Stonehenge and Avebury," *The Wiltshire Archaeological and Natural History Magazine,* vol. 32, Devizes, 1901-02. Other authorities on modern findings are E. H. Stone, *The Stones of Stonehenge,* London, 1924, and Frank Stevens (curator of the Salisbury Museum), *Stonehenge Today and Yesterday,* London, 1933. The latter contains excellent summaries of modern answers to age-long questions. The following list of references represents only scanty pickings from fields already harvested. At any rate, they present something of the range of speculative interest on the part of Englishmen in the history of their past.)

516-70 (?)   GILDAS. De Excidio Britanniae (MS *ca.* 547; first printed 1525) has no reference to Stonehenge nor to the story of the massacre of the Britons by the Saxons.

673-735   BEDE. Historia Ecclesiastica Gentis Anglorum (first printed 1473) makes no mention of Stonehenge.

796   NENNIUS. Historia Britonum (MS *ca.* 796; first printed 1691) has nothing to say of Stonehenge.

(The Anglo-Saxon Chronicles say nothing of Stonehenge.)

1085   Domesday Book makes no mention of the monument.

1130   HENRY OF HUNTINGDON. Historia Anglorum (MS 1130; first printed 1596). This author is the first to mention Stonehenge by name and to describe it, referring to it as the second of the four wonders of England.

1139   GEOFFREY OF MONMOUTH. Historia Regum Britanniae (final MS; first printed 1504) relates the oldest known legend about the origin of the monument. His story connecting Aurelius and Merlin with Stonehenge remained current for almost five hundred years. According to him it was erected as a funeral monument for the four hundred or more Britons treacherously killed by Hengist and his Saxons. For a scholarly article on the legends and the core of truth embedded in Geoffrey's account, see Laura Hibbard Loomis, "Geoffrey of Monmouth and Stonehenge," *PMLA,* vol. XLV, June (1930).

Geoffrey was followed by Wace, Layamon, and Robert of Gloucester.

1187   GIRALDUS CAMBRENSIS. Topographia Hibernica mentions Stonehenge.

1363   HIGDEN, RANULF. Polychronicon (the date given is that of Higden's death; first printed by Caxton, 1482) speaks of it as the second marvel of England.

1372   Chronicle of Malmesbury contains an account.

1436   HARDYNG, JOHN. The Chronicle of John Hardyng (original form, the Lancastrian, ended with 1436; first printed by Grafton, 1543). This repeats the story of Geoffrey of Monmouth.

1534   VERGIL, POLYDORE. Historiae Anglicae. This historian considers Stonehenge to be the tomb of Aurelius Ambrosius.

1547   BORDE, ANDREW. Boke of the Introduction of Knowledge reckons it among the wonders of England. His statement runs, "Upon the plain of Salisbury is the Stonehenge . . . ."

1552   LELAND, JOHN. Commentarii de Scriptoribus Britannicis (the date is that of Leland's death). Leland brings Merlin back into the story.

1562   FOLKERZHEIMER, HERMAN. Letter to Josiah Simler (in *Zürich Letters*, printed 1845; see under latter date, TOURS BY FOREIGNERS). He visited Stonehenge while in England. He regarded it as a Roman trophy.

1575   F., R. Stonhing (Stonehenge), an engraving. See Taylor, *Tudor and Stuart Geography*.

1577   HARRISON, WILLIAM. An Historical Description of the Iland of Britaine. To Harrison it was one of the four wonders of England, the others being a strong wind from the Peak (in Derbyshire), Cheddar Hole, and the gathering of clouds that could be seen on certain hills westward, which empty their waters on certain districts.

1586   CAMDEN, WILLIAM. Britannia. Camden mentions Rollrich (Rollright) besides Stonehenge as the only monuments of their kind in England.

1588   SMITH, WILLIAM. Description of England (first printed 1879). Smith makes a slight departure from the vogue of wonders by naming this as one of the "seven wonders" of England. "This monument was set up by Aurelius Ambrose, King of Britains, about the year of our Lord 470, in remembrance of 460 barons & noblemen of the Britains that were there slayne by treason of the Saxons, in the daies of Vortiger his predecessor; the picture of which stones are after to bee seen in the description of Wiltshire."

1597-1607   WHITE, RICHARD. Historiarum Britanniae, etc. White opposes the theory then generally held that the stones of this monument were artificial.

1624   BOLTON, EDMUND. Nero Caesar. Here it is supposed that the work was the tomb of Boadicea, raised by her subjects.—Gough, 530.

1627   HAKEWELL, DR. GEORGE. An Apologie of the Power and Providence of God. Oxford. (Here the theory is that the stones were artificially compounded.)

SPEED, JOHN. Theatre of Great Britain. In his map of Wiltshire there is an engraving of Stonehenge in one corner, with a description under it.

1631   STOW, JOHN. Annales, or a General Chronicle of England. Stow follows the old tradition of making it a memorial of the Britons slain by the Saxons.

1645   BLAEU, JOANNES. Orbis Terrarum sive Atlas Novus, pt. IV, has a view of Stonehenge.

1655   FULLER, THOMAS. Church History of Britain, Bk. I, states that "it seems equally impossible that they (the stones of Stonehenge) were bred or brought hither."

JONES, INIGO. The most Notable Antiquity of Great Britain, vulgarly called Stoneheng, on Salisbury Plain, restored by Inigo Jones. Edit. by J. Webb. 6 folding plates and 3 woodcuts. Fol. London.

> Reprinted with portrait, and ten plates by Hollar and others, fol., London, 1725.
> This work was published three years after the death of Jones, with a preface by John Webb, his son-in-law, who doubtless edited the volume from "some few undigested notes." Webb published further works on the subject (see under 1665 below). The investigation of Stonehenge was a project set going by James I. Jones thus describes the circumstances giving rise to the enquiry: "King James, in his progress in the year 1620, being at Wilton, and discoursing of that antiquity, I was sent for by William, then Earl of Pembroke, and received there by his Majesty's commands to produce out of myne own practice in architecture and experience in antiquities abroad, what possibly I could discover concerning this of Stone-Henge." The illustrations show, however, that neither Jones nor Webb can have studied the monument closely. The book is important for being the first after Camden to bestow particular attention to the actual monument. There were but few copies printed, and most of these disappeared in the fire of London. Jones fancied the work to be a temple of Caelus built by the Romans—an opinion that was scornfully refuted by many succeeding writers.

1661   CHILDREY, JOSHUA. Britannica Baconica. 12mo. London.

> In his opinion the stones making up the monument are "Naturall stones," i.e., "consolidated of sand."

1663   CHARLETON, WALTER. Chorea Gigantum: or, the Most Famous Antiquity of Great Britain, vulgarly called Stone-Heng, standing on Salisbury Plain, restored to the Danes. 2 woodcuts of the Stones (one folding). 4to. London.

> Dedicated to King Charles II, with 2 pp. of verse by Sir Robert Howard, and two further pages by John Dryden, addressed to the author. The argument was that Stonehenge was erected by the Danes as a place of assembly and of inauguration of kings. Charleton had corresponded with the Danish antiquary Wormius, and from him had learned that similar monuments existed in Denmark.

1665   AUBREY, JOHN. Monumenta Britannica (MS). Here is given quite a long descriptive account of Stonehenge as it then stood.—Harrison, *Bibliography*.

WEBB, JOHN. A Vindication of Stone-Heng Restored: in which the Orders and Rules of Architecture observed by the Ancient Romans, are discussed. Together with the Customs and Manners of several Nations of the World in matters of Building of greatest Antiquity. As also an Historical Narration of the most memorable Actions of the Danes in England. Cuts. Fol. London.

> Jones, Charleton, and Webb were printed together in one volume, fol., London, 1725, with certain memoirs relating to the life of Jones, and his effigies by Hollar, Charleton's by Lambert, four views of Stonehenge, with above 20 other copper plates by Edw. Kirkall, and a complete index to the whole collection.

1667 SAMMES, AYLETT. Britannia Antiqua Illustrata. London.

> Gough speaks of him as an impertinent pedant who knew nothing about antiquities, nor (if we are to believe Wood, *Fasti*, vol. II, 207) ever heard of the books he quotes in this work, which was supposed to have been written by his uncle. The book contains a distinct chapter or "treatise of the antient monument called Stone-henge," in which he labors hard to no purpose to prove it a work of the Phoenicians, from whom he would derive all our antiquities.—*Op. cit.*, 530-31.

1668 PEPYS, SAMUEL. In his Diary for June, 1668, Pepys speaks of visiting Stone-henge, and finding it to be all that had been said about it. But of what use it was, was hard to tell.

1682 BURTON, RICHARD. Admirable Curiosities, Rarities, and Wonders in England, Scotland, and Ireland, etc. 8vo. London.

> This contains some allusions to Stonehenge. For the work see under DESCRIPTIONS.

1686 PLOT, DR. ROBERT. For an account of Stonehenge, which he attributes to the Britons, see his *The Natural History of Staffordshire*, under NATURAL HISTORY.

1695 GIBSON, EDMUND (Bishop). In his edition of Camden's *Britannia*, Gibson allows Stonehenge to be the work of the Britons.

1720 KEYSLER, J. G. Antiquitates Selectae. Hannover.

> Keysler gives the credit of this monument to the Danes or Saxons, illustrating with 19 folding and full-page engravings Stonehenge and other druidical and Celtic remains. He was the first to present to the antiquaries on the continent representations of these monuments.

1723 TWINING, REV. THOMAS. Avebury in Wiltshire. Folding plan. 4to. London. (36 pp.)

> Twining considers this vast megalith to be a Roman work erected by Vespasian and Julius Agricola, during their several commands in Britain. It is good to know that this, the largest and perhaps the oldest of such monuments in England, has lately been acquired for perpetuity by the National Trust of England. John Aubrey was the first who had any inkling of its true character and who showed it to the admiring Charles II. He declared this great stone circle to exceed Stonehenge in grandeur "as a cathedral does a parish church." Nearly three-quarters of a mile in circumference, it encloses two separate double circles and is itself encircled by an embankment rising nearly fifty feet above the original floor of a ditch dug some thousand years ago by neolithic "beaker folk" with picks and shovels made from the antlers and shoulder blades of the red deer. In Aubrey's time thirty-one out of a probable hundred outer stones were still standing; now there are only nine.—Quoted from account in the *Manchester Guardian Weekly*.

1725 GIBBONS, JOHN. In his Fool's Bolt Shotte at Stonage, published on p. 481 of Hearne's edition of Langtoft's *Chronicle*, Oxford, the author makes it to be an old British triumphal trophical temple, erected to Anaraith, goddess of victory, on the defeat of Divitiacus and his Belgae, by Stunning and his Ceangic giants. —Gough, 531. This explanation pushes even the Phoenicians a little hard.

1730 WALLIS, STAMFORD. Dissertation in Vindication of the Antiquity of Stonehenge, in Answer to the Treatise of Mr. Inigo Jones, Dr. Charleton, and all that have written upon that Subject. By a Clergyman living in the Neighbourhood. 8vo. Salisbury.

1740   STUKELEY, DR. WILLIAM. Stonehenge, a Temple Restored to the British Druids. Frontispiece and 35 full-page copperplates. Fol. London.

> Though far off in his conclusions, Stukeley gives us here the first full and careful description of the monument. He was a competent observer and a good draughtsman. He discovered the avenue and the adjoining cursus. On opening several barrows in the neighborhood, he found chippings from Stonehenge in one of them. He dated it about 400 B.C. —Harrison, *Bibliography*. If any man was born for the service of antiquity, it was Dr. Stukeley. Benet College, Cambridge, which boasted of having trained the great Parker to revive the study of antiquity with that of humanity in the 16th century, educated Stukeley in this, to trace our antiquities to their remotest origin. Furnished with extensive reading, favoured with extensive correspondence, he visited with unwearying assiduity the greatest part of the kingdom, taking drawings and admeasurements of the monuments on the spot. He revived the Society of Antiquaries, and suggested to Mr. Samuel Buck, his fellow traveler, the useful design of preserving so many of our antient buildings, which he and his brother have since so successfully executed (see Buck, 1727-40, under VIEWS). The application of his whole life produced a vast quantity of drawings and writings, which he proposed to digest into a work to be intitled: Patriarchal Christianity, or the Chronological History of the Origin and Progress of true Religion and Idolatry, in five Parts, etc. Of these only the descriptions of those two temples (Stonehenge and Avebury) were published. . . . In the spring of 1766 his vast collections, the labour of above fifty years, were dispersed by public auction at Essex House.—Gough, 533-34.

1743   STUKELEY, DR. WILLIAM. Abury, a Temple of the British Druids, with some others described. Wherein is a more particular Account of the First and Patriarchal Religion; and the Peopling the British Islands. Plates. Fol. London.

> The two works abridged by William Cooke, 4to, London, 1754-55. See below.
> Stukeley described this monument as a "serpentine temple." Avebury is said to be much older than Stonehenge.

1747   WOOD, JOHN. Choir Gaure, vulgarly called Stonehenge, on Salisbury Plain described, restored, and explained. In a Letter to the Right Hon. Edward, late Earl of Oxford and Mortimer. Illus. Oxford.

> Wood is of the opinion that this was a temple of the moon, erected by the druids about 100 years before Christ, and similar to that at Stanton Dru in Somersetshire. When Lord Oxford was at Bath in 1740, Wood, having hinted to him his opinion of this latter pile of stones, was ordered to take a correct plan of it, for his book of drawings of the like British antiquities. His dissertation on the British works at Bath and Stanton Dru were incorporated into his Description of Bath. He considers the antient works still remaining at Harptree on the north side of Mendip Hills between Stanton Dru and Okey on Exmore, at Stonehenge, and at Aubury, as four colleges of druids; the first of poets; the second, of extispices; the third, of divines and necromancers; the fourth, of philosophers, who were to draw down the gods from above.—Gough, 531.

1750   A Concise Account of the most famous Antiquity of Great Britain, vulgarly call'd Stone-Henge, and the Barrows round it, with Views, Plan, and Elevation. 12mo. London.

> Another edit., 16mo, Salisbury, 1767.
> This apparently, from the title of the later edition, embodies the ideas of Inigo Jones, Stukeley, and others.

1754-55   COOKE, WILLIAM, M.A. (Rector of Oldbury and Didmarton in Gloucestershire). An Enquiry into the Patriarchal and Druidical Religion, Temples, etc., being the Substance of Some Letters to Sir Hildebrand Jacobs, Bart., wherein the primaeval Institution and Universality of the Christian Scheme is manifested, the Principles of the Patriarchs and Druids are laid open, and shewn to correspond entirely with each other, and both with the Doctrines of Christianity; the earliest Antiquities of the British Islands are explained, and an Account given of the Sacred Structures of the Druids; particularly the stupendous Work

of Abiry, Stonehenge, etc., in Wiltshire, are minutely described; with an Introduction in Vindication of the several Hieroglyphical Figures described and exhibited in the Course of this Treatise. Illustrated with copper plates. 4to. London.

> This is the abridgement of the two works of Stukeley on Stonehenge and Avebury. The author was chaplain to the Earl of Suffolk.—The plates are the doctor's plans of Abury and Stonehenge contracted. Had the author been less infected with Hutchinsonianism, his book would have been a useful compilation.—Gough, 532-33.

1763 VERTUE, GEORGE. Diary. Edit. by Horace Walpole. London.

> In his diary are comments on Stonehenge, which he believed was erected by the Saxon heathens. Vertue was the famous engraver whose researches were used by Walpole for his *Anecdotes of Painting.*

1769 PRICE, F. For "An Accurate Account of Stonehenge," etc., see his *Salisbury Guide,* under AIDS TO TRAVELERS.

1770 SMITH, JOHN, M.D. Choir Gaur: the Grand Orrery of the Ancient Druids, commonly called Stonehenge, on Salisbury Plain, Astronomically Explained and Mathematically Proved to be a Temple erected for Observing the Motions of the Heavenly Bodies. 3 folding plates and 2 other plates. 4to. Salisbury.

> Reviewed *Gent. Mag.,* vol. 41, 30-31. This work has fifty pages of abstract of preceding theories of Stonehenge, fourteen more describing the present state of the stones, and his own theory. He associates them with astronomy, as did Wood, the architect of Bath. The outer circle of thirty stones and the twelve within represent the solar year of 360 days. The inner circle is the lunar month of twenty-nine days and twelve hours, of which six at the upper end of the circle exhibit the harvest and hunter's moon, rising six nights together with little variation. Next to this circle is a great ellipse of seven pairs of pillars with imposts on each pair for the seven planets. Within these, in a concentric ellipse, are twelve smaller single stones for the twelve signs of the Zodiac, with a thirteenth at the end for the Arch Druid's seat before the altar. The oval form represents the Creation when the Druids conceived "all Nature to spring from this egg of the earth, which they represent as proceeding from and formed by, the Deity, emblemized by a serpent." The name Choir Gaur he finds in Calasio's Hebrew Lexicon, Chor or Cor rendered Concilia Marina, which he confines here to Cancer, from the oval form of its shell resembling the Choir of a church. Gaur, in Irish, signifies Caper-he-goat. He supposes Stone Henge arose from the fall and poise of the great impost on the Trilithon, representing the sun, which *hangs* in equilibrium across the altar, moveable by hand.—From the review. In a leaf of some copies of this work, Dr. Smith explains that having settled at Boscombe, Wiltshire, as an Inoculator (for smallpox), he was so set on and molested by the inhabitants, that he took up the study of Stonehenge as a diversion.

1774-76 STRUTT, JOSEPH. In his *Compleat View of the Inhabitants of England,* Strutt expresses the opinion that Stonehenge is not a Danish structure but a place where public assemblies were held and where Druids met.—Harrison, *Bibliography.*

1776 A Description of Stonehenge, Abiry, etc.: With an Account of the Learning and Discipline of the Druids. 12mo. Salisbury.

> Another edit., Salisbury, 1788.

1779 COLLINSON, REV. JOHN. In his *Beauties of English Antiquity,* Collinson wisely concludes that "we have no history to determine at what time, or on what occasion, Stonehenge was erected."

1783 JOHNSON, SAMUEL. In a letter to Mrs. Thrale, Oct. 9, 1783, Johnson makes Stonehenge to be a druidical monument, at least 2,000 years old.

1789   GOUGH, RICHARD. In his edition of Camden's *Britannia,* Gough offers quite a long account of the monument. He associates it with the druids.

1795   EASTON, J. A Description of Stonehenge. Folding frontispiece. 12mo. Salisbury.

WANSEY, HENRY. His remarks on Stonehenge are printed in Easton's work.

1797   MATON, W. An Account of the Fall of Some of the Stones at Stonehenge. In *Archaeologia,* vol. 13, pp. 103-06. London.

1798   GILPIN, REV. WILLIAM. For his views on Stonehenge, see his *Observations on the Western Parts of England,* under TOURS BY NATIVES.

1799   TOWNSON, REV. THOMAS. For a mineralogical account of the stones at Stonehenge, see his *Tracts,* etc., under NATURAL HISTORY.

1799-1805   KING, EDWARD. Vol. I of his *Munimenta Antiqua* (see under HISTORY AND ANTIQUITIES) is given up to pre-Roman antiquities, for which he says he is much indebted to Stukeley. He calls Stonehenge an "antient British Structure."

1801   BRITTON, JOHN. In his *Beauties of Wiltshire,* he ascribes the monument to Romanized Britons.

1804   DAVIES, EDWARD. In his *Celtic Researches,* Davies connects the work with the Druids.

1807   INGRAM, REV. JAMES. In a lecture at Oxford, 1807, Ingram speaks of Stonehenge as a heathen burial place.—Harrison, *Bibliography.*

1819   HOARE, SIR RICHARD COLT. In his *Ancient Wiltshire,* Hoare holds that Stonehenge was built by the Celts from Gaul.—Harrison, *op. cit.*

1840   RICKMAN, JOHN. On the Antiquity of Abury and Stonehenge. Paper read June 13, 1839. In *Archaeologia,* vol. 28. London.

Here Stonehenge is described as a temple perfected after the Romans had established themselves in Britain. Caesar, for instance, does not mention it.

1848   HERBERT, A. Cyclops Christianus: or, An Argument to disprove the supposed Antiquity of the Stonehenge and other Megalithic Erections. London.

Notwithstanding his arguments, modern scholars have ventured to place its date around 1800 B.C. This list might be extended, but enough has been shown to demonstrate how far speculation can range from its mark and how ingeniously learning can be misapplied.

XVII

Ecclesiastical History and Antiquities

(The older histories and chronicles which record either the course of the church in Great Britain or the affairs of abbeys and monasteries, when they are admitted at all, are usually to be found under HISTORY AND CHRONICLE. This present section concerns itself rather with accounts of particular churches or religious institutions—their antiquities, monuments, descriptions of their condition, their ruins and remains, etc. Interest in such vestiges of their former glory and power widens with the spread of antiquarian studies in the seventeenth and eighteenth centuries. And after the appearance in 1656 of Dugdale's *History and Antiquities of Warwickshire,* few county historians left the subject out of account. The monasteries of Scotland had far less care taken of their histories and records than those of England. Dugdale could procure no more than the endowment charters of a few, and Nicolson had met with only four.)

1572 PARKER, MATTHEW. De Antiquitate Ecclesiae et Privilegiis Ecclesiae Cantuariensis cum Archiepiscopis ejusdem LXX Historia. London.

> Reprinted, fol., London, 1605; again, fol., London, 1729.

1600 CAMDEN, WILLIAM. Reges, Reginae, Nobiles, & alii in Ecclesia Collegiata B. Petri Westmonasterii sepulti, usque ad Annum reparatae Salutis 1600. 4to. London.

> Republished, with additions, London, 1603 and 1606.
> This is the first printed account of the church of Westminster. It is said to have been enlarged from a collection begun by J. Skelton the poet, probably when this abbey sheltered him from Wolsey's wrath; though perhaps he only amused himself in scribbling epitaphs for the great people there. Camden, for fear of offending Elizabeth, omitted the coronation chair brought from Scotland.—Gough, *Anecdotes of British Topography,* 268.

1614 HOLLAND, HENRY. Monvmenta Sepvlchraria Sancti Pavlii. The Monuments, Inscriptions, and Epitaphs, of Kings, Nobles, Bishops, and others, buried in the Cathedrall Church of St. Pavl, London. Untill this present Yeare of Grace, 1614. Together with the Foundation of the Church: and a Catalogue of all the Bishops of London, Neuer before, now with Authoritie, published. 4to. Londini.

> 2nd edit., with continuation to 1633, London, 1633.

1618 ARITHMAEUS, VALENTIN. For a book upon the monumental inscriptions in St. Paul's, see Arithmaeus under TOURS BY FOREIGNERS.

1631 WEEVER, JOHN. Ancient Funerall Monuments within the United Monarchie of Great Britaine, Ireland and the Ilands adjacent, with the Dissolved Monasteries therein contained: their Founders, and what Eminent Persons have been in the same interred, etc., composed by the Travels and Studie of John Weever. Portrait by Cecil, woodcuts in the text. Fol. London.

> Another edit., 4to, London, 1767. See below.
> This extraordinary collection of epitaphs and inscriptions is of the greatest use to antiquaries, historians and genealogists, above all because of the subsequent destruction of many of the monuments themselves.—Bookseller's Note. It contains an interesting Shakespeare allusion: being two lines from *Hamlet,* "Now get you to my lady's chamber and tell her, let her paint an inch thick, to this favour she must come."—Halliwell-Phillipps, *Memoranda on Hamlet,* p. 64, 1879. Weever, a native of Lancashire, educated

at Queen's College, Cambridge, emulous of the honor foreign nations had received from the publication of their monumental antiquities, traveled over most parts of England (and earlier over some parts of the continent with the same design in mind) and Scotland, to collect the funeral inscriptions of all the cathedral and parochial churches, but being much discouraged by the many malignant and avaricious defacements of those venerable remains, . . . he was on the point of suppressing all of his collections, had he not been encouraged by the most eminent antiquaries his contemporaries, who assisted him in finishing the first part of his book. It contains only the dioceses of Canterbury, Rochester, London, and Norwich and part of Lincoln to complete the County of Hereford. Wharton charges him with gross mistakes in the numerical letters and figures. He or those who examined the monuments for him appear not to have been able to read many of those printed imperfectly. To complete the work he solicited the public, but he died the next year.—Gough, 53-54.

> 1767 WEEVER, JOHN. Ancient Funerall Monuments within the United Monarchie of Great Britaine, Ireland, and the Islands adjacent; with the dissolved Monasteries, their Founders, and Eminent Persons interred in them; also the Deaths and Burial of certain of the Bloude Royall, Nobility, Gentrie, etc. With Historical Observations, Annotations, and brief Notes, extracted out of approved Authors, Records, Leidger Books, Charters, Rolls, etc. Portrait. 4to. London.

1639 USSERIUS, JACOBUS (Archbishop). Antiquitates Britannicae Ecclesiasticae. 4to. Dublinii. (1196 pp.)

1640 SOMNER, WILLIAM. For an account of the cathedral of Canterbury, see his *Antiquities of Canterbury,* under TOWNS.

1641 The Arminian Nunnery, or, A Briefe Description and Relation of the late erected Monasticall Place, called, The Arminian Nunnery, at Little Gidding in Huntingdonshire, humbly recommended unto the wise Consideration of this present Parliament. The Foundation is by a Company of Farrars at Gidding. 4to. London.

> Reprinted by Hearne at the end of Langtoft's *Chronicle,* Oxford, 1725.
> This was a Protestant nunnery. Connected with it was a remarkable family, which made much noise at the beginning of the Civil Wars, and was objected to by Laud as being affected to Popery.—Gough, 204-05.

1643 BEDE. For his *Ecclesiastical History of Britain,* see this date under 1473, HISTORY AND CHRONICLE.

1644 CULMER, RICHARD. Cathedrall Newes from Canterbury, shewing the Canterburian Cathedrall to bee in the Abbeylike corrupt and rotten Condition which calls for a speedy Reformation or Dissolution. Recorded and published by Richard Culmer. 4to. London.

1655 BROUGHTEN, RICHARD. Monastichon Britannicum, or, A Historicall Narration of the First Founding and Flourishinge State of the Ancient Monasteries, religious Rules, and Orders of Great Britaine, in the Times of the Britaines and primitive Church of the Saxons. Collected out of the most authentick Authors, Leiger Books, and MSS. By that learned Antiquary R. B. 8vo. London.

FULLER, THOMAS. Church History of Britain. Fol. London.

> Reprinted, 1837; 1842; a new edit., 6 vols., by J. S. Brewer, Oxford, 1868.
> Fuller writes of the great stones at Stonehenge that "it seems equally impossible that they were bred or brought hither." The ground itself is chalk; while such "voluminous Bulks" could be borne by no wain or wagon. "This hath put learned men on necessity to conceive them artificial stones, consolidated of sand."

1655-73 DUGDALE, SIR WILLIAM. Monasticon Anglicanum, sive pandectae Coenobi-
orum, Benedictinorum, Cluniacensium, Cisterciensium, Carthusianorum a
primordiis ad eorum usque Dissolutionem ex MSS., Codd., etc. 3 vols. (1st vol.
in 1655, 2nd in 1667, and 3rd in 1673). Engravings of ecclesiastical costumes,
cathedrals, etc., by Hollar and King. Fol. Londini.

> 2nd edit., improved, fol., 1682; translated into English by Wright, 3 vols. in 1, fol., 1693;
> in English by John Stevens, 3 vols., 1722-23; with large additions by Caley, Ellis, Bandinel,
> 8 vols., fol., 1817-30; a new edit. of this last, 6 vols. in 8, fol., 1846; the same, 6 vols. in 8,
> fol., 1849. See below.
> The value of this monumental work is attested by the numerous editions and reprints.
> It would seem that English antiquaries, by preserving the record of religious houses to later
> ages, were trying to make amends for their destruction, which in ruthlessness exceeded
> that accomplished anywhere on the continent. Concerning the proportion of credit due to
> the authors Dodsworth and Dugdale, Gough remarks that the collecting of material was
> chiefly the labor of the former, the latter being responsible for methodizing the deeds,
> correcting the press, and compiling the indexes. Dodsworth died in August, 1664, before
> a tenth part of the first volume was printed; and thereby lost no doubt the credit of the
> whole, which Dugdale gained by publishing it. The third volume appeared under Dug-
> dale's name alone; but it is not to be doubted that he was greatly indebted to Dodsworth's
> collection.—*Op. cit.*, 55-56. The work contains the foundation charters of the old monas-
> teries at their first erection. The publication was productive of many lawsuits, by the
> revival of old writings, and incensed the Puritans, who looked upon it as a preliminary
> step toward introducing popery.—Hotten, *Topography and Family History.* Dodsworth
> was an indefatigable collector of the antiquities of Yorkshire. 122 volumes in his own hand-
> writing, besides original MSS. which he obtained from several hands, making all together
> 162 volumes folio, were lodged in the Bodleian Library. General Fairfax had great regard
> for his gifts as well as for antiquities themselves. For instance, he preserved the fine
> windows of the York Cathedral, and when St. Mary's Tower, in which were lodged
> innumerable public and private records, was blown up during the siege of York, he gave
> money to the soldiers who could save scattered papers, many of which were deposited at
> Oxford. Fairfax died in 1671, but the MSS were not brought to Oxford until 1673, and
> then in wet weather. A month was spent in drying them on the leads of the school tower.
> —Gough, 543-44. For the relative credit due to Dodsworth and to Dugdale, see David
> Douglas, *English Scholars.*

1693 DUGDALE, SIR WILLIAM. Monasticon Anglicanum, or, The History of the Ancient
Abbies and other Monasteries, Hospitals, Cathedral and Collegiate Churches in
England and Wales, with divers French, Irish and Scotch Monasteries formerly
relating to England, collected and published in Latin, and now epitomized in
English. 15 plates of religious habits. 3 vols. in 1. Fol. London.

1718 ————. Monasticon Anglicanum: or, The History of the Ancient Abbies, Monasteries, Hospitals, Cathedral and Collegiate Churches, Irish and French Monasteries as did in any manner relate to those of England. First published in Latin
and now translated into English, to which was added, Exact Catalogues of the
Bishops of the Several Dioceses to the Year 1717, the whole corrected and supplied
with Additions by an eminent Hand [John Stevens]. Illustrated with plates
depicting religious costumes, etc. Fol. London.

1817-30 ————. Monasticon Anglicanum: A History of the Abbies and other Monas-
teries, Hospitals, Friaries, and Cathedral and Collegiate Churches, with their
Dependencies in England and Wales; also of all such Scotch, Irish and French
Monasteries as were in any manner connected with Religious Houses in England.
Originally published in Latin, etc. New Edition, enriched with a large Accession
of Materials now first printed from Leger Books, Chartularies, Rolls, etc.; the
History of each Religious Foundation in English being prefixed to its respective
Series of Latin Charters by John Caley, Henry Ellis and the Rev. Bulkeley
Bandinel. 250 large engravings by John Coney, numerous woodcuts of costumes,
etc. 8 vols. Fol. London.

> In this splendid edition, hundreds of Religious Houses, of which Dugdale knew
> nothing, have been introduced, and Accounts of very numerous Destroyed Mon-
> asteries.—Bookseller's Note.

1656 KING, DANIEL. The Cathedrall and Conventuall Churches of England and Wales,
orthographically delineated. Obl. 4to. London.

> Another edit., London, 1656.

1658   DUGDALE, SIR WILLIAM. The History of St. Paul's Cathedral in London, from its
         Foundation until these Times, extracted out of Original Charters, Records,
         Leiger-Books, and other Manuscripts. Portraits and plates of tombs and monu-
         ments by Hollar. Fol. London.

>   2nd edit., corrected and enlarged by its author, fol., London, 1716; another, with addi-
>   tions and continuation, fol., London, 1818. See below.
>   The plates in this work, by the most famous engraver in 17th century England, Wence-
>   laus Hollar, are of the greatest historical interest, for they are the only pictorial records
>   we possess of the interior and exterior of old St. Paul's—the beautiful cathedral which was
>   so sadly abused at the time of the Civil War and which was destroyed by the Great Fire of
>   London in 1666. The plates display also the ancient monuments, tombs, etc., with their
>   quaint and interesting inscriptions, armorial achievements, etc., which eight years later
>   were to disappear for good.—Bookseller's Note.

>   1716   DUGDALE, SIR WILLIAM. The History of St. Paul's Cathedrall in London, from its
>   Foundation; extracted out of Original Charters, Records, Leiger-Books, and other
>   Manuscripts: beautified with sundry Prospects of the old Fabrick; which was
>   destroyed by the Fire of that City in 1666. Also with Figures of the Tombs and
>   Monuments therein; which were all defaced in the late Rebellion. Whereunto is
>   added, A Continuation thereof, setting forth what was done in the Structure of
>   the New Church to the Year 1685. Likewise an Historical Account of the Northern
>   Cathedrals, and the Chief Collegiate Churches in the Province of York. 2nd edit.,
>   corrected and enlarged by the Author's own Hand. To which is prefixed his Life,
>   written by Himself. Portrait and numerous engravings. Fol. London.

>   1818   ————. The History of St. Paul's Cathedral, etc. Extracted out of Original
>   Charters, . . . With a Continuation and Additions, including the Republication
>   of Sir William Dugdale's Life from his own Manuscript, by Henry Ellis. Portrait
>   and plates in proof state, including the whole of Hollar's plates, carefully re-
>   engraved by Finden, and important series of plates illustrating the present struc-
>   ture. Fol. London.

1661   SOMNER, WILLIAM. For an account of the cathedral of Canterbury, see his *The
         Most Accurate History of the Ancient City and Famous Cathedral of Canter-
         bury,* under TOWNS.

1662   DARLEY, JOHN. The Glory of Chelsea-College Revived: where is declared its
         Original, Progress, and Design, for preserving and establishing the Church of
         Christ in its Purity, for maintaining the Protestant Religion against Jesuits,
         Papists, and all Popish Principles and Arguments, etc. By what Means this
         excellent work, of such incomparable Use and Publick Concernment hath been
         impeded and obstructed. 4to. London.

1663   HEGGE, ROBERT. The Legend of St. Cvthbert; with the Antiquities of the Church
         of Durham. 12mo. London.

>   This treatise as written by Hegge was called Saint Cvthbert; or, the Histories of his
>   Churches at Lindisfarne, Cvncacestre, and Dvnholme, and was composed in 1625 and 1626.
>   Richard Baddeley, private secretary to Morton, Bishop of Durham, printed a poor edition
>   of the work (that above) and suppressed the author's name. A very correct edition in 4to
>   by George Darlington appeared in 1777, and another by John B. Taylor at Sunderland in
>   1816.—*DNB.*

1671   SOUTHOUSE, THOMAS. Monasticon Favershamiense in agro Cantiano, or, A Sur-
         veigh of the Monastery of Faversham in the County of Kent; wherein its
         Barony and Right to sit in Parliament is discovered. Together with its Antient
         and Modern State described; as also its Founder and Benefactors remembered:
         To which is added, An Appendix of the Descent of King Stephen, by Thomas
         Philipot. 12mo. London.

1672 DAVIES, JOHN (of Kidwelly). The Antient Rites and Monuments of the Monastical & Cathedral Church of Durham, collected out of Antient Manuscripts about
the Time of the Suppression. 12mo. London.

> 2nd edit., edit. by Christopher Hunter, 12mo, Durham, 1733. See below.
> This seems to have been compiled about the end of the 16th century, by an eyewitness
> of all that passed at the time. Gough says that the description of the windows is dated
> Durham, 1733.—*Op. cit.*, 154.

> 1733 DAVIES, JOHN. The History of the Cathedral Church of Durham, as it was before
> the Dissolution of the Monastery; containing an Account of the Rites, Customs,
> and Ceremonies used therein: together with a particular Description of the fine
> Paintings in the Windows (by Prior Washington, prior from 1416 on), likewise
> the Translation of St. Cuthbert's body from Holy-Island, with the various Acci-
> dents that attended its Interment here; with an Appendix of divers Antiquities,
> collected from the best MSS. By Christopher Hunter. 12mo. Durham.

1680 A Book of the Valuations of all the Ecclesiastical Preferments in England and
Wales. 12mo. London.

1681 BERCHET, P. Monument of James Sharp, Archbishop of St. Andrews, in the
Cathedral Church of St. Andrews. (2 sheets.)

1682 KEEPE, HENRY. Monumenta Westmonasteriensia: or, An Historical Account of
the Original, Increase and Present State of St. Peter's, or the Abbey Church of
Westminster. With all the Epitaphs, Inscriptions, Coats of Arms, and Atchievements of Honour belonging to the Tombs and Grave-stones: together with the
Monuments themselves, faithfully digested and set forth. 8vo. London.

> All his merit lies in his faithful copies of the inscriptions; he intended a new edition of
> it in folio like Dugdale's St. Paul's, but he did not live to finish it.—Gough, 269.

1683 TAYLOUR, CHARLES (alias Henry Keepe). A True and Perfect Narrative of the
strange and unexpected Finding the Crucifix and Gold Chain of the pious Prince
St. Edward the King and Confessor, which was found after 620 years' Interment, and presented to his Most Sacred Majesty King James II. By Charles
Taylour (name assumed by Henry Keepe). 4to. London.

> Reprinted at the end of *The Antiquities of Westminster Abbey*, 1722.

1684 FISHER, PAYNE. The Tombes, Monuments, And Sepulchral Inscriptions Lately
Visible in St. Paul's Cathedral, And St. Faith's under it. Compleatly Rendred
in Latin and English, With Several Historical Discourses, On Sundry Persons
Intombed therein. A Work never yet performed by any Author Old or New. By
P. F. Student in Antiquities, Batchelor of Arts and heretofore One of His Late
Majesties Majors of Foot, To the late Honorable Sir Patricius Curwen c. Cumb.
Baronet. 4to. London.

> Fisher at this time was a prisoner in the Fleet and the dedication to Sir Roger
> L'Estrange was probably inspired by an expectation that Sir Roger would relieve his
> distresses. The inscriptions rendered had been destroyed in the Great Fire. The book
> therefore is of considerable archaeological interest. The funeral epitaphs include those of
> Sir Philip Sidney, John of Gaunt, John Donne, etc.—Robinson, no. 61.

1685 STILLINGFLEET, EDWARD, D.D. (Dean of St. Paul's). Origines Britannicae, or,
The Antiquities of the British Churches. With a Preface Concerning some pre-
tended Antiquities relating to Britain, in Vindication of the Bishop of St.
Asaph's. 4to. London.

1686 GUNTON, SIMON (Vicar of Pytchley, Northants). The History of the Church of Peterburgh (Peterborough), wherein the most remarkable Things concerning that Place from the first Foundation thereof, with other Passages of History, not unworthy Publick View, are represented, by S. G., and set forth by Symon Patrick (44th Bishop of Ely). 4 plates. Fol. London.

> During his boyhood Gunton took copies of the inscriptions on the monuments in Peterborough Cathedral, many of which were destroyed by the Parliamentary troops. He had also through his father's position unlimited access to the cathedral archives before they were in turn destroyed. Ten years after his death his collections, revised and augmented with an appendix of charters and privileges and a supplement, were published by Simon Patrick.—*DNB*, quoted from Bookseller's Note.

1695 TANNER, THOMAS (Bishop). Notitia Monastica: or, A Short Account of the Religious Houses in England and Wales. 5 plates with 200 human figures. 8vo. Oxford.

> Republished, fol., London, 1744; another edit., with additions, by J. Nasmith, Cambridge, 1787. See below.
> This excellent compendium was so well received that within twenty years it became extremely scarce. So at the request of his friends he set about revising and enlarging it in 1715. His duties as chancellor of Norwich prevented a close application to it, and his infirmities afterwards occasioned it to be left at his death very far from finished. It came out, however, thirty years later under the same title, published by his brother, John Tanner. This edition was completed and enlarged by the additions from the many collections and notes he had left as well as by notes of the new editor. The work is a valuable and comprehensive repository. The bishop was a tireless searcher into antiquities, and he left as many volumes and bundles of MS collections as filled seven carts on their removal from Norwich to Christ Church Library at Oxford. Among them were 300 volumes of MSS purchased by him of Bateman, the bookseller, who had bought them of Archbishop Sancroft's nephew, being mostly written by the Archbishop's own hand.—Gough, 57-8.

> > 1744 TANNER, THOMAS. Notitia Monastica, or, An Account of all the Abbies, Priories and Houses of Friars, Heretofore in England and Wales; and also of all the Colleges and Hospitals founded before A.D. MDXL. Portrait and plates. Fol. London.

> > 1787 ————. Notitia Monastica: or, An Account of all the Abbies, Priories, . . . And now reprinted, with many Additions, by James Nasmith, M.A., Rector of Shalwell, Cambridgeshire, . . . Fol. London.
> > > Reviewed *Gent. Mag.*, vol. 57, 619. A new edition was a need; but whether this is the one is in doubt. Some deviations in plan from the original are to be regretted. The new preface is kept distinct from the old, and that is to the good.—From the review.

1700 An Account of the Several Monasteries, Priories, etc., which were demolished in the Reign of King Henry VIII. 12mo. London.

1704 MONTEITH, R. An Theater of Mortality; of the illustrious Inscriptions extant upon the Several Monuments . . . within the Grayfriars Churchyard and other Churches and Burial-places within the City of Edinburgh and Suburbs. 4to. Edinburgh.

> 2nd edit., enlarged, 1713; reprinted, with new additions, 8vo, Glasgow, 1834; also 1850 and 1851. See below.

> > 1713 MONTEITH, R. An Theater of Mortality, or, A Farther Collection of Funeral Inscriptions over Scotland, all Englished. Edinburgh.

1705-06 BOWACK, JOHN. For a collection of church monuments in Middlesex, see his *Antiquities of Middlesex*, under HISTORY AND ANTIQUITIES.

1708-10 NEWCOURT, RICHARD. For his *Ecclesiastical Parochial History of London Diocese,* see under LONDON.

1708-14 COLLIER, JEREMY. For his *Ecclesiastical History of Great Britain,* see under HISTORY AND CHRONICLE.

1711 BATTELEY, JOHN, D.D. Antiquitates Rutupinae. Oxford.

> 2nd edit., with additions by his nephew Oliver Batteley, 4to, Oxford, 1745; translated into English with another title, London (?). See below.
> This consists of four Latin dialogues between the author and his two friends and brother chaplains, Dr. Henry Maurice and Henry Wharton, on the ancient state of the Island of Thanet.

> 1745 BATTELEY, DR. JOHN. Opera Posthuma—viz. Antiquitates Rutupinae et Antiquitates S. Edmundi Burgi ad Annum 1271 perductas. Plates. 4to. Oxford.
> What the author had ready for publication of his projected history of the Abbey of St. Edmundsbury, i.e., as far as the death of Henry III, 1272, was published by his nephew Oliver Batteley at the end of this second edition of the *Antiquitates Rutupinae,* with an Appendix, and a list of the abbots, continued by Sir James Burroughs, of Caius College, whose ichnography of the abbey church drawn in 1718 and a view of the abbot's palace in 1720, now entirely demolished, are also annexed.—Gough, 493.

CRULL, JODOCUS, M.D. The Antiquities of St. Peter's, or, The Abbey Church of Westminster: containing all the Inscriptions, Epitaphs, etc., upon the Tombs and Grave-stones: with the Lives, Marriages, and Issue of the most Eminent Personages therein reposited; and their Coats-of-Arms truly emblazoned, adorned with Draughts of the Tombs curiously engraven. 8vo. London.

> A Supplement was printed to this in 8vo, 1711; 2nd edit., 1715; 3rd, vol. I edit. by H. S., vol. II by J. R., 2 vols., 1722; 4th edit., 2 vols., 1741; 5th, 2 vols., 1742.

1712 BROWNE, SIR THOMAS. Repertorium: or, Some Account of the Tombs and Monuments in the Cathedral Church of Norwich, begun by Sir Thomas Browne, and continued from the Year 1680 to this present Time, illustrated with severall Copper Plates of the principal Monuments, etc., mostly at the Expence of the Nobility and Gentry of this County. 8vo. London.

> Among the posthumous works of Sir Thomas Browne, published from his papers in the possession of Owen Brigstock, Esq., F.R.S., was the above. To this are annexed "Antiquitates Capellae divi Johannis Evangelistae, hodie scholae regiae Norwicensis. Authore Joanne Burton. A. M. ejusdem ludi magistro"; communicated by his son, the Rev. Mr. Joshua Burton. At the end is a list of the dignitaries of this church, with large alterations and corrections, first published by Dean Prideaux, in a broad sheet.—Gough, 369.

STAVELY, THOMAS. The History of Churches in England; wherein are shewed the Time, Means, and Manner of Founding, Building, and Endowing of Churches, both Cathedral and Rural, with their Furniture and Appendages. 8vo. London.

> A useful essay on ecclesiastical antiquities. The author was a barrister, who spent the latter part of his life in the study of English history, and acquired the reputation of a diligent, judicious, and faithful antiquary.—Gough, 48.

1715 GALE, SAMUEL. The History and Antiquities of the Cathedral Church of Winchester, containing all the Inscriptions upon the Tombs and Monuments; with an Account of the Bishops, Priors, Deans, and Prebendaries; also the History of Hyde Abbey, begun by the Right Hon. Henry late Earl of Clarendon, and continued to this Time by Samuel Gale, Gent. Folding engravings. 8vo. London.

Another edit., London, 1723.
Gale, who was only the editor, was largely assisted by Cranley, registrar of this church, who supplied the Clarendonian MS with a continuation of the monumental inscriptions, and a series of the dignitaries; and Browne Willis furnished the Account of the priory and Hyde Abbey. The learned editor added an historical introduction concerning the ancient and present state of the church, the lands given to it, and the sale of them in the civil wars, and adorned the whole with several views of the church and monuments drawn by C. Woodfield, and engraved by Vandergucht.—Gough, 180 ff.

1716 FARRANT, HENRY. The True Copies of some Letters occasioned by the Demand for Dilapidations in the Archiepiscopal See of Canterbury. In 2 pts. 4to. London.

This called forth the following protest:

1717 A Letter to Mr. Archdeacon Tennison, detecting several Misrepresentations in his Pamphlet relating to the Demand for Dilapidations. 4to. London.
Gough says that the first was written by Henry Farrant, and refers to Aubrey's Survey (presumably his Natural History and Antiquities of Surrey, see under 1718, HISTORY AND ANTIQUITIES), vol. V, p. 273.—Op. cit., 502.

1717 ABINGDON (HABINGTON), THOMAS. The Antiquities of the Cathedral Church of Worcester, to which are added, The Antiquities of the Cathedral Churches of Chichester and Lichfield. 8vo. London.

Another edit., 1728. See below.
The above work was taken from his MS collections of the civil and ecclesiastical history of Worcestershire (see under 1893-99, SURVEYS). Other parts were utilized by Nash for his History of Worcestershire (see under 1781-82, HISTORY AND ANTIQUITIES). Habington, who died in 1647, published translations of Gildas in 1638 and 1642. Both he and his brother Edward were implicated in the Babington conspiracy of 1586, but while his brother was executed he escaped with imprisonment.

1728 ABINGDON, THOMAS. Antiquities of the Cathedral Church of Worcester, and of the Great Malvern Priory, Worcestershire; to which are added, Antiquities of the Cathedrals of Chichester and Lichfield, with an Appendix of Curious Original Papers. 8vo. London.

BURNET, GILBERT (Bishop). A Summary of all the Religious Houses in England and Wales, with their Titles and Valuations at the Time of their Dissolution, and a Calculation of what they might be worth at this Day; together with an Appendix concerning the several Religious Orders that prevailed in this Kingdom. 8vo. London.

This was ascribed to Burnet, who, however, died two years before it appeared.

RAWLINSON, RICHARD. The History and Antiquities of the City and Cathedral Church of Hereford: containing an Account of all the Inscriptions, Epitaphs, etc., upon the Tombs, Monuments, and Grave-stones: with Lists of the Principal Dignitaries; and an Appendix consisting of several valuable original Papers. 8vo. London.

Among other papers are the obits of several benefactors to this cathedral transcribed from folio, Missal secundum usum Hereford in Hearne's possession, written about the reign of Edward III, printed on vellum, 1502. The work is concluded with 71 charters, or grants of land to this church, from Bodleian MSS. Some years after it came out it was attacked in a most ungenerous manner by a member of this church in a very warm and angry preface to a sermon preached in Landaff Cathedral, fathering it upon Browne Willis, with some uncharitable reflections, which were answered in Willis' account of the church in a survey of the cathedrals, etc., where he disclaims all concern in the book.—Gough, 191 ff.

—————. The History and Antiquities of the Cathedral Church of Rochester, containing the local Statutes of that Church; the Inscriptions upon the Monuments, Tombs, and Grave-stones; an Account of the Bishops, Priors, and Archdeacons; an Appendix of monumental Inscriptions in the Church of Canterbury, supplementary to Mr. Somner's and Mr. Batteley's Accounts of that Church: some original Papers, relating to the Church and Diocese. 8vo. London.

> Republished, 8vo, London, 1723.
> This anonymous publication has been attributed by some to John Lewis, but it is now generally supposed to have been written by Rawlinson.—Bookseller's Note.

WILLIS, BROWNE. A Survey of the Cathedral Church of St. David's, and the Edifices belonging to it, as they stood in the Year 1715. To which are added, Some Memoirs relating thereto and the County adjacent, from a MS. wrote about the latter end of Queen Elizabeth's Reign. Together with an Account of Archbishops, Bishops, Precentors, Chancellors, Treasurers, and Archdeacons of the See of St. David's. Illustrated with Draughts and adapted to the said Historical Description. 8vo. London.

1717-19 LE NEVE, JOHN. Monumenta Anglicana: being Inscriptions on Monuments of eminent Persons since A.D. 1600, in every Part of England. 5 vols. 8vo. London.

> Another edit., 3 vols., 8vo, London, 1854.
> In a way Le Neve carried on Weever's design (see Weever, under 1631 above), but in a more dry, immethodical manner. These inscriptions run from 1600 to the end of the year 1718, "deduced into a series of time by way of annals." In the last volume but one, he added at the end of each year an obituary of memorable persons who died therein, whose epitaphs, if erected, were not come to hand; but this, on account of its uncertainty, was omitted in the rest.—Gough, 54. The volumes were not published chronologically.

1718 WILLIS, BROWNE. An History of the Mitred Parliamentary Abbies, and Conventual Cathedral Churches, shewing the Times of their respective Foundations, and what Alterations they have undergone. With some Descriptions of their Monuments, and Dimensions of their Buildings, etc.; a Catalogue of their Abbots, Priors, etc. Lists of the Principals of divers Monasteries; Numbers of the Monks at their Surrender, etc.; with an exact Account of those religious Men and Women, and chantry Priests, receiving Pensions throughout England and Wales, 1553. 2 vols. (the 2nd in 1719). 8vo. London.

—————. A Survey of the Cathedral Church of Landaff: containing the Inscriptions upon the Monuments, with an Account of the Bishops and other Dignitaries belonging to the same; what other Preferments they enjoy'd; and the Times of their Decease, Places of Burial, and Epitaphs. To which is subjoined, A Large Appendix of Records, and other curious Matter relating thereto. Adorned with Draughts of the said Church, in order to illustrate the Description thereof. 8vo. London.

> The accounts of St. David's (see above) and Landaff cathedrals were drawn up by Dr. Wm. Wotton, author of *Reflections on Antient and Modern Learning*, when he retired into Wales.—Gough, 599. Wotton will be remembered as one of the principals in the quarrel ridiculed by Swift in the *Battle of the Books*.

1719 KIP, JOHANNES, ——— COLLINS, and others. For views of all the Cathedrals in England and Wales and other ecclesiastical edifices, see under VIEWS.

1720   HEARNE, THOMAS. Textus Roffensis. Accedunt professionum antiquorum Angliae Episcoporum formulae, de canonica obedientia Archiepiscopis Cantuarien-
sibus praestanda, et L. Hutteni dissertatio, Anglice conscripta, de Antiquitati-
bus Oxoniensibus. E Codicibus MSS. descripsit, ediditque T. Hearnius. 8vo.
Oxford.

> This is the most venerable monument of antiquity belonging to the cathedral of Rochester.
> It was written by Bishop Ernulf, who died in 1124. See Thorpe under 1768 below.

Prospects of all the Cathedral and Collegiate Churches of England and Wales,
neatly engraved. Vues de toutes les Eglises Cathédrales et Collègiats d'Angleterre et de Galles. Obl. 12mo. London.

WILLIS, BROWNE. A Survey of the Cathedral Church of St. Asaph, and the Edifices belonging to it; together with an Account of all the Inscriptions on the
Monuments and Grave-stones; the History of the Bishops, Deans, and other
Dignitaries, as far as they have come to hand from Records, or are to be met
with in any printed History. To which is subjoined, A Large Appendix of Records, and other curious Matters relating to St. Asaph Church and Diocese.
Illustrated with Draughts of the Ichnography and Uprights of the said Cathedral. 8vo. London.

> This is the smallest cathedral in the Kingdom. Bishop Goldwell carried all the muni-
> ments of the church to Rome, except one register called Coch Asaph, which was lost in the
> Civil War. And Bishop Humphrey's Catalogue of Deans since 1500 sent to Wood was
> printed by Hearne at the end of Otterburn's *Chronicle*. See Gough, 604, note, and 605.

1721   WILLIS, BROWNE. A Survey of the Cathedral Church of Bangor; and the Edifices belonging to it. Containing an Account of all the Inscriptions on the Monuments and Grave-stones; The History of the Bishops, Deans, and other Dignitaries: Their several Preferments, Times of Decease, Burial and Epitaphs.
Together with a large Appendix of Records, and other curious Matters relative
to Bangor Church and Bishoprick: As namely, The Dedications of all Churches
and Chapels in the Diocese of Bangor; and Descriptions of Clynogfawr and
Bodowen Chapel. To which are also subjoined, Several Supplementary Additions and Records to the like History of St. Asaph Cathedral some time since
published; the Dedications of the Churches and Chapels in that Diocese; and
Descriptions of Gresford and Mould Churches. Illustrated with Draughts of the
Ichnography and Upright of Bangor Cathedral, View of Bodowen Chapel. 8vo.
London.

1722   HEARNE, THOMAS (Publisher). The History and Antiquities of Glastonbury. To
which are added, I. The Endowments and Orders of Sherington's Chantry,
founded in St. Paul's Church, London. II. Dr. Plot's Letter to the Earl of
Arlington concerning Thetford. To which Pieces (never before printed) a
Preface is prefixed, and an Appendix subjoined, by the Publisher Thomas
Hearne, M.A. 8vo. Oxford.

A Little Monument to the once famous Abbey and Borough of Glastonbury: or,
A Short Specimen of the History of that Ancient Monument and Town, giving
an Account of the Rise and Foundation of both. To which is added, The De-

scription of the remaining Ruins, and of such an Abbey as that of Glastonbury is supposed to have been: . . . Together with an Appendix, consisting of Characters and Instruments, to strengthen the Authority of what is related. Whereunto is annexed, The Life of King Arthur, who there lay buried, and was a considerable Benefactor to this Abbey. Collected out of our best Antiquaries and Historians, and finisht April the 28th, 1716.

STEVENS, JAMES. The History of the Antient Abbeys, Monasteries, Hospitals, Cathedral and Collegiate Churches, being two additional Volumes to Sir William Dugdale's Monasticon Anglicanum, containing the Original and first Establishments of all the religious Orders that ever were in Great Britain, being those treated of in the Monasticon Anglicanum, as also of the Franciscans, Dominicans, Carmelites, Augustinian Friars, . . . not spoken of by Sir W. Dugdale and Mr. Dodsworth, etc.; adorned with a considerable Number of Copperplates of the several Habits of the religious Orders, the Ichnographies of Cathedral and Collegiate Churches, and the Ruins of sacred Places destroyed or gone to Decay, and the Prospects of others still standing. 2 vols. Fol. London. (See Dugdale under 1655 above.)

Stevens was of the Romish communion and held a Captain's commission under James II in Ireland. He did much translating especially from the Spanish.

Summary of Christian Antiquities. London. (So cited in Ponton's Catalogue.)

1723 DART, JOHN. Westmonasterium, or, The History and Antiquities of St. Peter's, Westminster; together with the Lives of the Abbots and Deans: a Survey of the Church and Cloisters taken in 1723; and Westminster Abbey: a Poem by the Author. Engraved frontispiece, 7 plates, containing the Arms of 294 Subscribers and 144 engravings, besides numerous head and tail pieces. 2 vols. in 1. Fol. London.

Another edit., 2 vols. in 1, fol., London, 1742. See below.
For this pompous but very inaccurate work Dart had assistance from the Cotton Library, the church records, and the papers of Charles Batteley, who had begun something relative to these antiquities but left it unfinished at his death.—Gough, 270.

1742 DART, JOHN. Westmonasterium, or, The History and Antiquities of the Abbey Church of St. Peter's, Westminster, containing an Account of its Ancient and Modern Building, Endowments, Chapels, Altars, Reliques, Customs, Privileges, Forms of Government, &c.: with ye Copies of Ancient Saxon Charters, &c., and other Writings relating to it, with Lives of the Abbots, Deans, &c.: a Survey of the Church and Cloysters, taken in 1723, with the Monuments there, engraved by J. Cole. 2 vols. in 1. Fol. London.

RAWLINSON, RICHARD. The History and Antiquities of the Cathedral Church of Salisbury and the Abbey Church of Bath; A Vindication of the King's Sovereign Rights, Together with a Justification of His Royal Exercises thereof in all Causes, more particularly applyed to the King's Free Chapel and Church of Sarum, with Appendix. 2 vols. in 1. 8vo. London.

Another title of the same date, but with a variant wording:

RAWLINSON, RICHARD. The History and Antiquities of the Cathedral Church of Salisbury, containing, 1. All the monumental Inscriptions; 2. An Account of the respective Dignitaries; 3. A Catalogue of the several Missals, or Books of Divine Service, published before the Reformation for the Use of the Church at Sarum. 4. An Architectonical Account of Salisbury Cathedral, by Sir Christopher Wren, 1719. 8vo. London.

1724 THORESBY, RALPH. Vicaria Leodiensis: or, The History of the Church of Leedes in Yorkshire; containing an Account of learned Men, Bishops, and Writers who have been Vicars of that Populous Parish; with the Catalogues of their Works, printed and in MS.; to which are added, The Lives of several Archbishops of York, and other eminent Persons, Benefactors to that Church; with many other Things interspersed relating to the City and County of York. And Archbishop Thoresby's memorable Exposition of the Decalogue, Creed, and Lord's Prayer. With an Appendix of Original Records and MSS. 8vo. London.

> Thoresby was not without merit as an antiquary. He seems to have been well skilled in the Saxon language, and in general to have applied it happily in his etymologies. What antiquities came his way he gives a good account of, as well as some idea of the face of the country. His credulity and want of judgment in collecting his curiosities must be charged on the infancy of those pursuits in the age he lived in. Tradescant was the first English collector in a private rank; Thoresby the second.—Gough, 558. See Thoresby, *Ducatus Leodiensis*, under 1715, TOWNS.

1725 THOMAS, DR. WILLIAM. Antiquitates Prioratus majoris Malverne in Agro Wicciensi: cum Chartis originalibus easdem illustrantibus, ex registris Sedis Episcopalis Wigorniensis nunc primum editis. 8vo. London.

> There is an account of both the Benedictine priories founded at Malvern within a century of each other, in Abingdon's *Antiquities of Worcester* (see under 1717 above); the present account is a more particular one of the larger and older priory.—Gough, 541.

1726 DART, JOHN. The History and Antiquities of the Cathedral Church of Canterbury, and the once adjoining Monastery, containing an Account of its first Establishment, Buildings, Re-edifications, Repairs, Endowments, Benefactions, Chapels, Altars, Shrines, Reliques, Chauntries, Obits, Ornaments, Books, Jewels, Plate, Vestments, before the Dissolution of the Monastery, and the Manner of its Dissolution: a Survey of the present Church and Cloysters, Monuments, . . ; the Lives of the Archbishops, Priors, etc., of Christ Church; with an Account 'of learned Men there flourishing in their several Times; and an Appendix of antient Charters and Writings relating to the Church and Monastery. Fol. London.

> Another edit., fol., London, 1762.
> The volume on Canterbury, corresponding to that on Westminster, has all the monuments of the cathedral engraved.—*Publ. Camden Soc.,* vol. 94. Many views of the church and monuments were engraved by Cole, with epitaphs and translations. The plates fell into the hands of Hildyard, of York, who having likewise most of those of Drake's *History of York Cathedral* (1736), published them to the number of 117, with an abridgement of the two histories.—Gough, 215.

PARKINSON, ANTHONY (Franciscan). Collectanea Anglo-Minoritica; or, a Collection of Antiquities of the English Franciscans, or Friars Minors, commonly called Grey Friars: in two Parts, with an Appendix concerning the English Nuns of the Order of St. Clare. Compiled and collected by A. Parkinson. 4to. London.

1727 GIBSON, MATTHEW. View of the Ancient and Present State of the Churches of Door, Home-Lacy, and Hempsted, endow'd by Lord Viscount Scudamore, with some Memoirs of that Ancient Family, and an Appendix of Records and Letters relating to the same. Folding plate. 4to. London.

LEWIS, JOHN (Vicar of Mynstre, and Minister of Margate). The History of the Abbey and Church of Faversham, the adjoining Priory of Davington, and Maison Dieu of Ospringe, and Parish of Bocton subtus le Bleyne; to which is added, A Collection of Papers relating to the Abbey, etc., and of the Funeral Monuments, and other Antient Inscriptions in the several Churches of Faversham, Shelwich, Bocton under le Bleyne, Ospringe, Graveney, and Throwley; with the charitable Benefactions thereto given. 5 plates. 4to. London.

THOMAS, WILLIAM, D.D. A Survey of the Cathedral-Church of Worcester: with an Account of the Bishops thereof, from the Foundation of the See, to the Year 1600: also an Appendix of many original Papers and Records, never before printed. 4to. London.

> Another edit., 1736; republished, 1737.
> The views of the monuments are miserably executed; Abingdon's account of the painted window is inserted at large; also his survey of the monuments, with additions, and Heming's Chartulary digested in order of time. This work does Thomas least credit, although he was esteemed as an antiquary.—Gough, 539-40.

WILLIS, BROWNE. A Survey of the Cathedrals of York, Durham, Carlisle, Chester, Man, Lichfield, Hereford, Worcester, Gloucester, and Bristol, giving an Account of their Foundations, Builders, Antient Monuments and Inscriptions, Endowments, Alienations, Sales of Lands, Patronages: Dates of Consecration, Admission, Preferment, Deaths, Burials; and Epitaphs of the Archbishops, Bishops, Deans, Precentors, Chancellors, Treasurers, Archdeacons, and Prebendaries, in each Stall belonging to them, with an Account of all the Churches and Chapels in every Diocese, distinguished under their Proper Archdeaconries and Deaneries, the Patrons of them, to what Religious Houses impropriated and to what Saints many of them are dedicated. The Whole extracted from numerous Collections out of the Registers in the Tower and Rolls Chapel; and illustrated with 20 curious Draughts of the Ichnographies and Uprights of every Cathedral, newly taken to rectify the erroneous Representations of them in the Monasticon (Dugdale's) and other Authors. 3 vols. 4to. London.

> The works of Samuel Gale, Thos. Abingdon, Dr. Rawlinson, Aubrey, and Norden seem to have been drawn on for the volumes. For a continuation of this survey, see under 1730 below.
> Willis' intense love of antiquities seems to have been implanted in him in his rambles about the Abbey while a schoolboy at Westminster. He gave fifty-nine folio, forty-eight quarto, and five octavo MSS to the Bodleian.—Bookseller's Note.

1730 The Cathedral Church of Paul, Saint and Apostle, in London. The Dimensions and Curiosities of St. Paul's Cathedral, London. 8vo. London.

> Another edit., 12mo, London, 1750; again, 8vo, 1780.

GENT, THOMAS. For an account of the Cathedral of York, see his *Ancient and Modern History of the Famous City of York,* under TOWNS.

WILLIS, BROWNE. A Survey of the Cathedrals of Lincoln, Ely, Oxford, and Peterborough. 12 plates of the Ichnographies. 4to. London.

> This work and the volumes of 1727 were united in 1742 under such a title as would lead one to think that the thirteen remaining cathedrals therein mentioned had been surveyed as were the others. Whereas in their place we find only a list of the churches and chapels in the respective dioceses of the missing cathedrals. And these last were but incompletely

surveyed. The usefulness of these surveys is greatly lessened by the many errors occasioned either by haste and inaccuracy, or by the carelessness of the printers.—Gough, 49.

1742   A Survey of the Cathedrals of York, Durham, Carlisle, Chester, Man, Lichfield, Hereford, Worcester, etc. 3 vols. 8vo. London.

1732   LAMBERT, NICHOLAS. The History and Antiquities of Lincoln Cathedral, containing an Exact Copy of all the Antient Monumental Inscriptions there (163 in number) as they stood in 1641, most of which were soon after torn up or otherwise defaced; collected by Robert Sanderson, S.T.P. (afterwards Bishop of that church) and compared with and corrected by Sir. Wm. Dugdale's MS. Survey. Communicated by Nich. Lambert, LL.D., Fellow of St. Peter's, Cambridge. Inserted in Peck's *Desiderata Curiosa* (see under 1732, HISTORY AND ANTIQUITIES), vol. II, bk. viii, no. 1, with Notes and Additions by the Editor. (Dugdale's Survey was taken in 1641.)

1733   HUNTER, CHRISTOPHER. Durham Cathedral as it was before the Dissolution of the Monastery; containing an Account of the Rites, Customs, and Ceremonies used therein. Together with the Histories painted in the Windows. 8vo. Durham.

WILLIS, BROWNE. Parochiale Anglicanum: or, The Names of all the Churches and Chapels within the Dioceses of Canterbury, Rochester, London, Winchester, Chichester, etc. 4to. London.

See note to Willis under 1730 above.

1735   FARMER, J. The History of the Antient Town and once Famous Abbey of Waltham, from the Foundation to the Present Time: containing many curious Extracts from Records, Leger-books, Grants, Charters, Acts of Parliament, Approved Authors, and from Inscriptions on the Monuments in the Church; together with the Inquisition taken (17 Charles I, 1642) of the Perambulation of the Forest of Waltham, setting forth all and singular the Meers, Metes, Bounds, etc., of the said Forest: to which is added, The History of Abbies, abridged (from Fuller's *Church History*), from the Year 977 to their Dissolution, and down to the Reign of Queen Elizabeth. Illustrated with many curious Copperplates. By J. Farmer, of Waltham Abbey, Gent. 8vo. London.

This first appeared at the end of Fuller's *Church History* (see under 1665 above). It was written by him while he was a curate at Waltham, and republished this present date.

1736   DRAKE, FRANCIS. For an account of the cathedral of York, see his *Eboracum*, under TOWNS.

An abridgement of Drake's history of the church and Dart's description of Canterbury Cathedral, with the plates of each work, was published in 1755. See below.

1755   DRAKE, FRANCIS, and JOHN DART. An Accurate Description and History of the Metropolitan and Cathedral Churches of Canterbury and York, from their first Foundation to the Present Year. Illustrated with 117 Copperplates, consisting of different Views, Plans, Monuments, Antiquities, Arms, etc. With an Appendix of Monuments, erected after it went to the press. Fol. London.
2nd edit., with additions, York, 1768.

1742   LOGGON, J. The History of the Brotherhood of the Guild of the Holy Ghost, in the Chapel of the Holy Ghost, near Basingstoke, in Hampshire. 8vo. Reading.

1743 WIDMORE, RICHARD. An Enquiry into the Time of the first Foundation of Westminster Abbey, as discovered from the best Authorities now remaining, both printed and MS. To which is added, An Account of the Writers of the History of the Church. 4to. London.

1747 TOPHAM, JOHN. Some Account of the Collegiate Chapel of Saint Stephen, Westminster. 28 plates, with descriptions.

> This account is bound up with the volumes of *Vetusta Monumenta*. See the latter under HISTORY AND ANTIQUITIES, 1747-1904.

1748 KIRBY, JOHN. An Historical Account of the Twelve Prints of Monasteries, Castles, Antient Churches, and Monuments, in the County of Surrey, drawn by John Kirby and published by him. 8vo. Ipswich.

1750 SABIN, JOHN. A Description of the Collegiate Church and Choir of St. Mary in the Borough of Warwick. 8vo. Coventry. (The date given is approximate.)

1751 WIDMORE, RICHARD. An History of the Church of St. Peter, Westminster, commonly called Westminster Abbey, chiefly from Manuscript Authorities. Plate. 4to. London.

> In this work is inserted an Historical and Architectonic Account of it, and of the Repairs, in a letter from Sir Christopher Wren to Bishop Atterbury, principal commissioner for these repairs (about 1714), with additional notes by Widmore. The Wren letter was first published in the *Parentalia, or Memoirs of the Family of the Wrens*, London, 1750.—Gough, 270.

1753 The Historical Description of Westminster Abbey, published by Newbery. 12mo. London.

> Another edit., 8vo, London, 1761; again, 1778.
> Gough calls this a useful pocket companion to the abbey, its monuments and curiosities.

PRICE, FRANCIS. A Series of Particular Observations, made with great Diligence and Care, upon that admirable Structure, the Cathedral Church at Salisbury: calculated for the Use and Amusement of Gentlemen and other curious Persons, as well as for the Assistance of such Artists as may be enabled to form a right Judgment upon this or any other antient Structure, either in the Gothick or other Stile of Building. By Francis Price, Author of the British Carpenter [and Surveyor to this Cathedral]. 4to. London.

> To this is prefixed a translation of a Latin MS belonging to the bishops of Sarum, wrote by William de Wenda, praecentor at the removal from Old Sarum, and afterwards dean, giving an account of the building of the present church, and Pope Honorius' bulls for the same purpose.—Gough, 525.

1758 BURTON, JOHN, M.D. Monasticon Eboracense, and the Ecclesiastical History of Yorkshire, containing an Account of the first Introduction and Progress of Christianity in that Diocese until the End of William I's Reign, with a Description of the Situation, Fabric, Monuments, etc., Catalogues of all the Abbots, etc. Folding map and 2 plans. Fol. York.

> A second volume was intended, but never written, owing to the death of the author intervening.—Bookseller's Note. The doctor appears to have the greatest zeal for illustrating the antiquities of his native country, and his indefatigable researches were appreciated by others who have sent him collections.—Gough, 546.

1761   HOLE, W. The Ornaments of Churches considered, with a particular View to the late Decoration of the Parish Church of St. Margaret, Westminster [by Hole]; to which is subjoined, An Appendix, containing the History of the said Church; an Account of the Altar-Piece, and stained Glass Windows erected over it; a State of the Prosecution it has occasioned; and other Papers (by Thomas Wilson). 4to. Oxford.

1762   GENT, THOMAS. The most Delectable, Scriptural, and Pious History of the Famous and Magnificent Great Eastern Window (according to Beautiful Portraitures) in St. Peter's Cathedral, York: previous thereto is a Remarkable Account how the Ancient Churches were differently erected by two Famous Kings; the present built by Five Excellent Archbishops, one Extraordinary Bishop, with others: the Names of sepulchred Personages, and important Affairs worthy of Remembrance; a Book which might be styled The History of Histories. Succinctly treated of in Three Parts. Likewise is added, A Chronological Account of some eminent Personages there depicted, anciently remarkable for their Learning, Virtue, and Piety. Impressed for the Author, in St. Peter's Gate. Folding woodcut of the window and 626 other cuts in the letterpress, folding leaf with vignette view of York entitled "Pious Contemplations." 8vo. York.

   This window is 75 feet high and 32 broad, and contains, besides the tracery, 117 panes, each nearly a yard square. John Thornton, of Coventry, did it for fifty-six pounds in three years. He agreed for four shillings a week, and was to have 100 shillings a year, and ten pounds at the end for his care.—Gough, 552-53. Elsewhere Gough says that no city or town in the kingdom can boast of such a collection of paintings on glass as York. Above half of the twenty-three churches can show some good remains in the windows, and there are not above six or seven plain ones out of the sixty-seven in the minster (this was true in 1768).

1763   RUDDER, S. The History of Fairford Church in Gloucestershire. 8vo. Cirencester.
   Another edit., 8vo, 1777; again, 1780, 1785, and 1795.

1764   KEATE, GEORGE. The Ruins of Netley Abbey. 4to. London. (In verse.)
   Netley Abbey was the most besung ruin in the 18th century.

1765   DUMMER, T. The Ruins of Netley Abbey, with a Short Account of that Monastery. 4to. (Place?)

   For an account of St. Peter's Cathedral in Exeter, see *The Ancient History and Description of Exeter,* under TOWNS.

1767   SANDERSON, PATRICK. The Antiquities of the Abbey, or Cathedral Church of Durham; also a Particular Description of the County Palatine of Durham, compiled from the best Authorities and Original MSS. To which is added, The Succession of the Bishops, Deans, Archdeacons, and Prebends: the Bishop's Courts and his Officers; the Castles and Mansion Houses of the Nobility and Gentry; with other Particulars. 8vo. Newcastle-upon-Tyne.

   The description of the cathedral is the old one reprinted; that of the county taken from *Magna Britannia* (see Cox under 1720-31, SURVEYS), with no material additions.

1768   DRAKE, FRANCIS. An Accurate Description and History of the Cathedral and Metropolitan Church of St. Peter, York, from its first Foundation to the Present

Year. Illustrated with Copperplates, consisting of different Views, Plans, etc., and Translations of all Latin Epitaphs. To which are added, Catalogues of all the Archbishops, Deans, Subdeans, Chancellors, Treasurers, Precentors, and Succentors. 12mo. York.

2nd edit., with additions, 12mo, York, 1783; 3rd, with additions, 2 vols., York, 1790. This is a pocket-companion compiled from Drake (see under 1736 above and his *History and Antiquities of the City of York,* under 1736, TOWNS).

1769 THORPE, JOHN, M.D., F.R.S. Registrum Roffense: containing a curious and valuable Collection of all such Records, Charters, Grants, Feoffments, Endowments, Appropriations, and other Deeds and Instruments hitherto unpublished, as are necessary for illustrating the Ecclesiastical History and Antiquities of the Diocese, and Cathedral Church of Rochester; faithfully transcribed from the Originals in the Tower of London, the Chapel of the Rolls, etc., by John Thorpe, late of Rochester, and prepared for the Press by his Son John Thorpe. To which will be added, The Monumental Inscriptions in the several Churches within the Diocese; the Effigies of the Author elegantly engraved, together with some Account of his Life. Fol. London.

SWAINE, JOHN. Memoirs of Osney Abbey, near Oxford, collected from the most Authentic Authors. 8vo. London.

In the *Gent. Mag.,* vol. 41, 153, is "A Short Account of Osney-Abbey" with illustrations.

1771 BENTHAM, JAMES. History and Antiquities of the Conventual and Cathedral Church of Ely, from the Foundation of the Monastery A.D. 673 to the Year 1771. 4to. Cambridge.

2nd edit., 1812; with a Supplement by William Stevenson, 3 vols. in 2, Norwich, 1817. Noticed, with extracts, in the *Annual Register,* vol. 15, 130-33.

An Historical Account of the Antiquities in the Cathedral Church of St. Mary, Lincoln. 8vo. Lincoln.

2nd edit., 12mo, Lincoln, 1791.

1772 BURNBY, JOHN. An Historical Description of the Cathedral and Metropolitan Church of Christ, Canterbury: containing an Account of its Antiquities, and of its Accidents and Improvements, since the first Establishment. 8vo. Canterbury.

2nd edit., enlarged, Canterbury, 1783. See below.

1783 BURNBY, JOHN. Historical Description of the Metropolitical Church of Christ, Canterbury, with Observations on Gothic Architecture, and Lives of the Bishops from St. Augustine to the present Time. 8vo. Canterbury.

1774 Collectanea ad Statum Civilem et Ecclesiasticum Comitatus Dunelmensis spectantia, ex variis codicibus tam Manuscriptis, quam impressis, sine Ordine congesta, etc. 4to. Darlington.

FORBES, R. (Bishop of Caithness and Orkney). An Account of the Chapel of Roslin . . . built in 1446 by W. St. Clare, Prince of Orkney, etc. Inscribed to William St. Clare of Roslin. 12mo. Edinburgh.

Later edit., 8vo, 1782.

PRICE, FRANCIS. Description of that Admirable Structure, the Cathedral of Salisbury, with the Chapels, Monuments, Grave-Stones and their Inscriptions, to
which is prefixed an Account of Old Sarum. Copperplates. 4to. London.

> Reviewed and epitomized *Gent. Mag.,* vol. 45, May. The author is wanting in style but
> not in knowledge of the church. It contains a plea for the recognition of the Gothic style,
> which will be found to have its rules as well as the Grecian. He points out that it is not a
> question of which is better or preferable, but whether there is not sense and design in
> both, when scrutinized by the laws on which each is founded. This attitude marks a notable
> advance in the conception of Gothic architecture. For strictures on this work see *Gent.
> Mag.,* same volume and month. The contributor here states that in 1753 Francis Price
> published a Series of Observations on that cathedral, made from careful surveys of his
> own, when he was employed in its repairs. This book Baldwin reprinted, with little varia-
> tion in title and plates, but said nothing about the text. To mislead the reader further, he
> transposed some paragraphs and used *We* for *I.* He prefixed an account of Old Sarum,
> stolen from somebody else, and added a view of a city in Gaul.—From the review. Literary
> ethics in the 18th century were not of the highest.

WEST, THOMAS. The Antiquities of Furness, or, An Account of the Royal Abbey
of St. Mary's in the Vale of Nightshade, near Dalton in Furness. Folding map,
view, ground-plan, and a seal. 4to. London.

> Reviewed with epitome *Gent. Mag.,* vol. 44, 523-24. The abbey was founded July 7, 1127,
> by Stephen Earl of Morton and Bulloiges, afterwards king of England. The monks of
> this abbey were a filiation from the Cistercian monastery of Savigny, Normandy. West
> was a lay priest of the Society of Jesus, and afterwards a guide to the Lakes. He died
> in 1779.

1775 WATSON, S. Some Account of Cathedrals in Scotland. In *Gent. Mag.,* vol. 45,
165-66.

1776 ESSEX, JAMES. Some Observations on the Cathedral at Lincoln (relative to its
having been built by Free Masons). In *Archaeologia,* vol. 4. London.

1777 BELLAMY, D. The Present State of the Church of Petersham. 8vo. (Place?)

1778 An Historical Description of the Church Dedicated to St. Peter and St. Paul
in Bath, commonly called the Abbey. 12mo. Bath.

HUTCHINSON, WILLIAM. For a state of the churches under the Archdeaconry of
Northumberland, see his *View of Northumberland,* under DESCRIPTIONS.

TALBOT, THOMAS. A Treatise of the Abbey of Evesham, written, as it seemeth,
by some one of that House. Transcribed by that learned Antiquary, Mr. Thomas
Talbot, and out of Latin truly translated. In *Gent. Mag.,* vol. 48, 458-62.

> This treatise was sent to the *Gentleman's Magazine* by a Reader, who says that the MS
> was found among the papers of the late learned Mr. Francis Wise. Apparently it is here
> reproduced in full, with additions, carrying the story on to a later date. It gives a chrono-
> logical account of the fortunes of the abbey, founded in 709 by the Benedictines, and of its
> successive abbots. The abbey was immediately subordinate to the Pope, and the abbot a
> great Baron of Parliament.—From the review.

1779 CHARLTON, LIONEL. For an account of Whitby Abbey, see his *History of Whitby,*
under TOWNS.

RANDAL, THOMAS. A State of the Churches under the Archdeaconry of Northumberland and in Hexham Peculiar Jurisdiction, with the Succession of In-

cumbents. Extracted from the MS. of T. Randal and edited by Wm. Hutchinson. Appendix. 4to. Durham.

WARBURTON, JOHN. Some Account of the Alien Priories and of such Lands as They are known to have Possessed in England and Wales (from the MSS. of John Warburton). Edited by John Nichols, Andrew Ducarel, and Richard Gough. Map of Normandy and folding plates. 2 vols. 8vo. London.

1779 DUCAREL, ANDREW COLTEC. A Repertory of the Endowments of Vicarages in the Dioceses of Canterbury. In a volume containing 21 Tracts on Antiquities. 4to. London. (The date is approximate.)

1780 AYLOFFE, SIR JOSEPH. An Account of some Ancient Monuments in Westminster Abbey; read at the Society of Antiquaries, March, 12, 1778. Fol. London.

For an account of the abbey and abbots of Cirencester, see the *History and Antiquities of Cirencester,* under TOWNS.

CROFT, SIR HERBERT. The Abbey of Kilkhampton; or, Monumental Records for the Year 1780; . . . compiled with a View to ascertain with Precision the Manners which prevailed in Great Britain during the last Fifty Years of the Eighteenth Century. 2 pts. in 1 vol. 4to. London.

> Interesting satirical epitaphs on many of the best-known men and women of the time.— Bookseller's Note. Another 18th century hoax.

1781 An Account of the Cathedral of Lichfield, from its Foundation to the Present Time. 12mo. Lichfield.

For an account of St. Peter's Abbey, the cathedral church at Gloucester, see *History and Antiquities of Gloucester,* under TOWNS.

1782 A Concise History of the Cathedral Church of Peterborough; including the Death of Mary Queen of Scots at Fotheringay Castle, and her Interment in this Cathedral. 8vo. Peterborough.

> 2nd edit., 1786; again, 1800.

DUCAREL, ANDREW COLTEC. The History of the Royal and Collegiate Church of St. Katherine, near the Tower of London, from its Foundation in the Year 1273 to the Present Time. 16 plates. No. 5 of *Bibl. Topog. Brit.* 4to. London.

1783 DUCAREL, ANDREW COLTEC. For an account of the Church of Croydon, see his *Account of the Town . . . of Croydon,* under TOWNS.

GOUGH, RICHARD. The History of Croyland-Abbey, in the County of Lincoln. Folding and other plates. No. 11 of *Bibl. Topog. Brit.* London.

1784 ESSEX, JAMES (?). Mr. Essex's Observations of Croyland Abbey and Bridge; and other Additions to the History of the Abbey. No. 22 of *Bibl. Topog. Brit.* London.

1785   HUTCHINSON, WILLIAM. For an account of the churches and cathedrals of Durham, see his *History and Antiquities of the County Palatine of Durham*, under HISTORY AND ANTIQUITIES.

        OLDFIELD, H. G. A Description of the Church of Saint Giles at Camberwell. 4to. London.

1786   BACON, JOHN. Liber Regis, vel Thesaurus Rerum Ecclesiasticarum. With an Appendix and Alphabetical Index. 4to. London.

        GOUGH, RICHARD. The Font at Winchester Cathedral. 2 plates and 7 pp. of descriptive text. In *Vet. Mon.* Fol. London.

1786-96 GOUGH, RICHARD. For an account of sepulchral monuments, see his *Sepulchral Monuments in Great Britain*, under HISTORY AND ANTIQUITIES.

1787   The Antiquities of Tewkesbury Church, to which is added, Particulars of the Battle of Tewkesbury. 8vo. Tewkesbury.

        LYON, J. The History and Antiquities of St. Radigund's or Bradsole Abbey near Dover. No. 42 of *Bibl. Topog. Brit.* London.

        MARTINE, G. The History and Antiquities of St. Rule's Chapel in the Monastery of St. Andrews; with Remarks by Prof. Brown. To which are added, The Riding of the Parliament of Scotland, 1606, 1681; the Suspension of Lyon King of Arms; the Statutes of the Order of the Thistle; and a Description of the Regalia of Scotland. Illustrations. No. 47 of *Bibl. Topog. Brit.* London.

        RASTALL, WILLIAM D. For the antiquities of Southwell Church, see his *History and Antiquities of the Town . . . of Southwell*, under TOWNS.

1788   THORPE, JOHN. Custumale Roffense; from the Original MS. in the Archives of the Dean and Chapter of Rochester. To which are added, Memorials of the Cathedral Church; and some Account of the Remains of Churches, Chantries, etc., whose Instruments of Foundation and Endowment are, for the most part, contained in the "registrum Roffense;" with divers curious Pieces of Ecclesiastical Antiquity, hitherto unnoticed, in the said Diocese. The Whole intended as a Supplement to that Work. Illustrated with Copper-plates, from accurate Drawings, taken principally under the Editor's Inspections. By John Thorpe, of Bexley, M.A., F.R.A. Fol. London.

        Reviewed *Gent. Mag.*, vol. 58, 341-42. Thorpe and his father have done much for preserving the antiquities of Rochester Cathedral and other churches in Rochester diocese by publishing them in the *Registrum Roffense*. Shortly after that work appeared, Thorpe visited the remains of churches, chapels, or chantries in this diocese, which are now mouldering in ruins, for the purpose of preserving the remains of antiquity, chiefly ecclesiastical, such as fonts, doorways, brassplates, etc., which he took down with the aid of skilful draughtsmen. Many of these remains were never before sketched and were even unknown to Kentish historians. This is a valuable addition to our national antiquities.— From the review.

1789   GOUGH, RICHARD. Accounts of Beaufort, Wainflete and Fox Monuments in Winchester Cathedral. 6 plates with 25 pp. of descriptive text. In *Vet. Mon.* London.

1790 BARROW, —. Views and Descriptions of Churches in England. Fol. London.

Description of Woodbridge Church in the County of Suffolk. Fol. Woodbridge.

A Short Description of that Admirable Structure, the Cathedral Church of Salisbury. 12mo. Salisbury.

> See Price under 1774 above.

St. George's Chapel, Windsor. The Vault, Body and Monument of Edward IV in St. George's Chapel at Windsor Castle.—The Rood-Loft in the same Chapel. 3 plates, with 4 pp. of descriptive text. In *Vet. Mon.* London.

WELLS, D. A Description of Stalls discovered in Chatham Church. Kent. 2 plates, with 6 pp. of descriptive text. In *Vet. Mon.* London.

1791 Plans and Descriptions of the Cathedral at Lincoln. 2 plates, with 4 pp. of descriptive text. In *Vet. Mon.* London.

1792 An Account of the Two Famous Fonts at Ufford and Sudbury. 1 plate, with a leaf of descriptive text. In *Vet. Mon.* London.

CARLILE, RICHARD. The Antiquities of the Cathedral Church of Saint Mary, Carlisle, taken on the spot by Richard Carlile, with the finely executed original drawings and manuscript, in a folio volume.

> This work is also found with the date of 1795. Whether it reached the stage of publication is not clear. The drawings, which are in water-colors, number 50 in the 1792 text and 45 in that of 1795. They are said to be beautiful views of the church from different sides, and of incidents in the life of St. Anthony; also of the choir, stalls, tombs, and monuments.

DODSWORTH, WILLIAM. A Guide to the Cathedral Church of Salisbury, with a particular Account of late great Improvements made therein, under the Direction of James Wyatt. 8vo. Salisbury.

> 4th edit., 12mo, 1796; another, Salisbury, 1798.
> Reviewed *Gent. Mag.,* vol. 63, 444-46. The Guide gives an historical and descriptive account of this ancient structure, which has been selected from the best accounts published. The "late improvements" are described and an abridgement of the Lives of the Bishops of Sarum furnished. The principal alteration was the opening up of the Lady Chapel by removing a screen, which necessitated removing the chapels on either side of it, resulting in the destruction of external and internal uniformity of the building. This involved also doing away with some very material supports in the way of buttresses, walls, and columns, and reducing the windows to smaller size with total disregard of the glass. But it was asserted that this was done for the safety of the building. Monuments were also removed. On these changes, as on those of Lichfield, Durham, and others, there was a great conflict of opinion. The disreputable state into which the cathedrals had been allowed to lapse was a source of agony to the Gothicists of the time. Men like John Carter, who wrote some 200 letters to the *Gentleman's Magazine* in protest against the vandalism of "restorers," would prefer to allow them to sink gracefully into ruin than to have them mutilated by the ignorance of "improvers." Some of the Gothic work done by Wyatt was tolerable, but what was bad was terrible. For an account of Wyatt as architect see Anthony Dale, *James Wyatt, Architect,* Oxford, 1936.

1793 CLARKE, CHARLES. Observations on Episcopal Chairs and Stone Seats; as also on Piscinas and other Appendages to Altars still remaining in Chancels; with a Description of Chalk Church, in the Diocese of Rochester. Plates. 4to. London.

HEATH, CHARLES. A Descriptive Account of Tintern Abbey, Monmouthshire, selected from various Writers, . . . 8vo. Monmouth.

> An edition listed in *Gent. Mag.*, vol. 65, 411, for 1795. See below.
> The reviewer's comment is "More Guides and Compilations." An amusing description of Tintern Abbey is to be found in Torrington's *Diary*, vol. I, of how best to enjoy a visit to this famous ruin. He recommends a good hamper of food, a bottle of wine, a hermit and a harper. Wordsworth, by the way, was not sufficiently interested in antiquities at the time of his second tour to even mention the abbey.

> 1795 HEATH, CHARLES. Descriptive Account of Tintern Abbey, Monmouthshire, a Cistercian Monastery, founded in 1131, 662 years ago: selected from Grose, Gilpin, Shaw, Wheatley, and other esteemed Works. To which is subjoined, An Account of the Cistercian Order of Monks; an History of Monasticism, from their first Foundation in England till their Dissolution in the Reign of Henry VIII.

An Historical Account of Lincoln and the Cathedral. 8vo. Lincoln.

The History of the Cathedral Church at Chester, from its Foundation to the Present Time. 12mo. London.

NEWCOME, PETER. The History of the Ancient and Royal Foundation, called the Abbey of St. Alban, from the Founding thereof in 793 to its Dissolution in 1539, exhibiting the Life of each Abbot, and the Principal Events relating to the Monastery during his Rule and Government, with a Frontispiece, Plans and Map of the County. 2 pts. in 1 vol. 4to. London.

> Reprinted, 4to, London, 1795.

TODD, H. J. Some Account of the Deans of Canterbury, to which is added, A Catalogue of the MSS. in the Church Library. 8vo. Canterbury.

1794 PARSONS, P. (Minister of Wye). The Monuments and Painted Glass of upwards of 100 Churches in the Eastern Part of Kent, most of which were examined by the Editor in person, and the rest communicated by the resident Clergy; with an Appendix, containing Three Churches in other Counties, to which are added, A Small Collection of detached Epitaphs, with a few Notes on the Whole. 4to. Canterbury.

> Reviewed *Gent. Mag.*, vol. 64, 742-43. The author, being obliged to resort to horseback riding for his health, used the occasion for keeping himself at it by making these records of the churches. Of the hundred he lists he visited personally sixty-seven. Of the others he got accounts from some forty officiating clergymen. He was properly indignant over the neglect of so many beautiful monuments of antiquity, which were falling into ruin.—From the review. Nearly all copies of this work were destroyed in a fire at the printer's premises.

RIDDELL, R. Notices of Fonts in Scotland; in a Letter to Mr. Gough, read Jan. 31, 1793. In *Archaeologia*, vol. 11. 4to. London.

TINDAL, WILLIAM. The History and Antiquities of the Abbey and Borough of Evesham. Compiled chiefly from MSS. in the British Museum. 7 plates engraved by Roe. 4to. Evesham.

> Reviewed *Gent. Mag.*, vol. 64, 836. The author confesses himself to have been a mere novice in antique lore when he began, but it is evident that he became very well educated through his labors in the duties of a local historian. He starts with the etymology of the name and the foundation of the abbey, and passes on to an account of the abbots, revenues, and endowments, customs and internal regulations, site and the antiquities extant, description of the towns, its gardens, soil, air, public edifices, inhabitants, etc.—From the review. The author was chaplain of the Tower of London. He shot himself in the Tower in a fit of melancholy in 1804. The above work was highly praised by Horace Walpole.—Sotheran.

1795-1800 HALFPENNY, JOSEPH. Gothic Ornaments in the Cathedral Church of York; drawn and etched by Joseph Halfpenny, with 105 copperplate engravings. 20 parts. Fol. London (?).

> Reprinted with the same author's *Fragmenta Vetusta, or the Remains of Ancient Buildings in York,* with 34 copperplates, 1807. Reviewed *Gent. Mag.,* vol. 70, 759. It is called a beautiful work. Evidently Halfpenny evinces an appreciation of Gothic detail that was unusual for the time.

JACKSON, JOHN. The History and Antiquities of the Cathedral Church of Lichfield, chiefly compiled from Antient Authorities, MSS., and the Works of eminent Authors. 8vo. Lichfield.

> Reviewed *Gent. Mag.,* vol. 66, 50-51. Only when considered as a guide for a stranger does this work have merit. A county historian needs to give a fuller account. Lichfield Cathedral was the first to be seized by the Parliamentarian troops and was destined to total destruction. The restoration of it by Bishop Hackett is as complete as the havoc it sustained. The author failed to notice in its library the famous Gospel of St. Chad, the greatest curiosity of the place. The cathedral contains monuments to Johnson, Garrick, Locke, Mary Montague, Addison, and his father, the dean of the church.—From the review.

TOPHAM, JOHN. Some Account of the Collegiate Chapel of St. Stephen, Westminster: with Plans, Elevations, Sections, and Specimens of the Architecture and Ornaments of such Parts of it as are now remaining. By Order and at the Expence of the Society of Antiquaries. 28 plates, with descriptions. Fol. London.

> Reviewed *Gent. Mag.,* vol. 65, 503-04. The price of this was to be two guineas for a set of fourteen plates engraved by Basire from drawings by Carter, and eight sheets of Shakespeare press work. It was seemingly the start of a plan to engrave all the cathedrals and churches which have survived either the penury of chapters or the ignorance of the clerks of the works.—From the review.

1795-1813 TOPHAM, JOHN. Some Account of the Collegiate Chapel, Churches and Abbeys of St. Stephen's, Westminster, Exeter, Bath, Durham, Gloucester and St. Albans. Illustrations of the Plans, Elevations and Sections of those Buildings, by J. Topham and others. Nearly 100 plates. By the Society of Antiquaries. Fol. London.

> This was probably a continuation of the plan mentioned in the note to Topham preceding this item.

1796 BONNOR, THOMAS. For views of Gloucester Cathedral, see his *Perspective Itinerary,* under VIEWS.

JACKSON, JOHN. Historical Description of the Castle and Priory of Tutbury; with an Account of the Borough and Abbey of Burton-on-Trent. 8vo. London.

A Survey of the Present State of Aspeden Church, Herts., June 1793. 4to. London.

> Reviewed *Gent. Mag.,* vol. 66, 667. A superficial work; it fails to tell us of its situation, the description of the church is inaccurate, misinterpretations of antiquities and misspellings abound.—From the review.

1797 MARTINE, GEORGE. Reliquiae Divi Andreae; or, The State of the See of St. Andrews; containing An Account of the Rise, Advancement, and Revolutions of the See; with historical Memoirs of some of the most famous Prelates and Primates thereof. Plates. 4to. St. Andrews.

WILKINSON, ROBERT. Antique Remains from the Parish Church of St. Outwich, London; humbly dedicated to the Master, Wardens, and Court of Assistants of the Worshipful Company of Merchants-Tailors, Patrons of the said Church. 4to. London.

> Noticed in the *Gent. Mag.*, vol. 67, 316. The church was lately taken down to be rebuilt, but first the author engaged an artist to make drawings of the old building and its monuments, which were neatly engraved, together with a plan of the parish as it was in 1599, in 13 plates, with a text of particulars concerning the church and parish. It were well if every parish church of equal antiquity in London and the kingdom were as well treated by so good an artist.—From the review.

1798   BENTHAM, JAMES. The History of Gothic and Saxon Architecture in England exemplified. With Descriptions of the Cathedrals of Ely, Lincoln, Peterborough, Carlisle, Chester, Worcester, Wells, Exeter, and Rochester. Fol. London.

CARTER, JOHN. Plans, Elevations, Sections and Specimens of the Architecture and Ornaments of the Abbey Church of Bath. 10 plates engraved by Basire on copper, with some Account of the Abbey and descriptions. Soc. of Antiquaries. Fol. London.

ENGLEFIELD, SIR H. C. Some Account of the Abbey Church at Bath; illustrative of the Plans, Elevations, and Sections of that Building. Soc. of Antiquaries. Fol. London.

MILNER, JOHN. A Dissertation of the Modern Style of altering Ancient Cathedrals, as exemplified in the Cathedral of Salisbury. 4to. London.

MOORE, —. A List of the Principal Monasteries in Great Britain. 8vo. London.

1799   Descriptive Accounts of Tintern Abbey, Monmouthshire. 8vo. Chepstow.

SAVAGE, J. The History of Howden Church. 8vo. Howden. (35 pp.)

1800   A Companion in a Visit to Netley Abbey. 12mo. Southampton.

> The author may have been a John Bullar.

G., J. The Recent Alterations in Lichfield Cathedral. In *Gent. Mag.*, vol. 70, 16-18.

> These changes seem to have met with the approval of the writer. But evidently he was not a pure Gothicist.

1819   BUCHAN, P. Annals of Peterhead, from its Foundation to the Present Time. With curious Articles hitherto unpublished. Plates by the Author. 8vo. London.

1838   THOMSON, J. History of the Abbey of Aberbrothock; with Account of the Town, and History of the Ruins of the Monastery in 1742. 8vo. Arbroath.

1839   FERRERIUS, JOHN. Historia Abbatum de Kynlos: una cum Vita Thomae Chrystalli Abbatis. Edit. by James Patrick Muirhead. *Publ. Bann. Club,* no. 63. Edinburgh.

> Ferrerius was teacher to the monks of Kinloss, 1531-37.

1840   JOCELIN DE BRAKELONDA. For his chronicle of his monastery, see under HISTORY AND CHRONICLE.

1842 RAINE, DR. — (Editor). Description, or Briefe Declaration of all the Ancient Monuments, Rites, and Customes belongeing or beinge within the Monastical Church of Durham before the Suppression. Written in 1593. 8vo. London (?).

1847 Documents relative to the Foundation and Antiquities of the Collegiate Church of Middleham in the County of York. *Publ. Camden Soc.,* vol. 38. London.

1853 HULTON, W. A. (Editor). Documents relating to the Priory of Penwortham and other Possessions in Lancashire of the Abbey of Evesham. *Publ. Chetham Soc.,* vol. 30. Manchester.

1857 HATFIELD, THOMAS DE (Bishop of Durham). Bishop Hatfield's Survey of Durham; a Record of the Possessions of the See of Durham, made by Order of Thomas de Hatfield . . . With an Appendix of original Documents by the Rev. W. Greenwell. 8vo. London (?).

    This survey, made under the direction of Bishop Hatfield, was apparently completed about 1382.

1863-67 HART, WILLIAM H. (Editor). Historia et Cartularium Monasterii Sancti Petri Gloucestriae. 3 vols. Rolls Ser. London.

1864-68 The Priory of Hexham, its Chronicler, Endowments and Annals. Frontispiece and other illustrations. 2 vols. 8vo. London (?).

1872 GREENWELL, REV. W. (Editor). Feodarium Prioratus Dunelmensis. A Survey of the Estates of the Priory and Convent of Durham, compiled in the Fifteenth Century. Illustrated by the original Grants and other Evidences. 8vo. London (?).

1874 STUBBS, WILLIAM (Bishop). Memorials of St. Dunstan, Archbishop of Canterbury. Edit. by Bishop Stubbs. London.

1879 DEANS, W. The Old Church and Parish of Abbotrule, suppressed in 1777. *Trans. Hawick Arch. Soc.,* vol. 22. 4to. Hawick.

1880 SIMPSON, W. SPARROW, D.D., F.S.A. (Editor). Documents illustrating the History of St. Paul's Cathedral. Edit. for the most part from original Sources. *Publ. Camden Soc.,* vol. 26, n.s. London.

    Among the documents are Indulgences granted for building or repairing portions of the Cathedral 1201-1387; commemoration of Thomas of Lancaster, to whom much devotion was paid, though he was not liked by Edward II; Office of same, *ca.* 1322; prayers, collects, short chronicles of the cathedral, 1140-1341; list of Obits, petitions, accounts, Ballad on the Burning of the Cathedral, 1561; Poems on the Fire in St. Paul's, 27 Feb., 1698-99; Queries about the organ, *ca.* 1700; Paper relating to the dome, *ca.* 1708, etc.; and liturgical matters of interest to the antiquary.

1891 RICH-JONES, REV. W., and REV. W. D. MACRAY. Charters and Documents illustrating the History of the Cathedral City, and Dioceses of Salisbury in the Twelfth and Thirteenth Centuries. Rolls Series. London.

1893 BEVERIDGE, ERSKINE, LL.D. The Churchyard and Memorials of Crail, containing a full Description of the Epitaphs anterior to 1800; with some Account of the

other Antiquities of the Burgh. Privately printed. Autotype plates and other illustrations. 4to. Edinburgh.

1895 SIMPSON, W. SPARROW, D.D., F.S.A. (Editor). Visitations of Churches belonging to St. Paul's Cathedral in 1297 and 1458. Edit. from original MSS. *Publ. Camden Soc.,* vol. 55, n.s. London.

The first of the above visitations was undertaken in stormy times by the Dean of St. Paul's, Ralph de Baldock, afterwards Lord Chancellor of England, and a man of letters, author of a History of Great Britain from the earliest times down to his own—seen by Leland but now lost. He and his staff set out from London, Sept. 1297, to hold visitations of certain churches in Essex, Hertfordshire, and Middlesex. This inquiry occupied them from October through November. An earlier inventory which they carried with them served as a check against the present state of affairs. Their object was to note deficiencies —a chalice missing here, a comb lost there—to examine the fabric of the church and the burial grounds, doors, windows, ceilings, roofs, chapels, church and bell towers, bell ropes, etc. The inventories give a good idea of the furniture of ecclesiastical edifices of those days—altars, the pix, canopies over it, candelabras, relics, vessels for holy oil, ritual books, etc. The visitation of 1458 was conducted by the Dean William Say, one of the Privy Council of Edward IV in 1464. It lasted from July to October, 1458. This time matters of far greater social importance were taken note of, such as the probate of wills, cases of immorality, real and pretended marriages. Considerable immorality was found in places.

XVIII

Natural History

(The term Natural History as ordinarily understood would be confined to the organic world of growing things, but as used by the writers listed below as well as omitted it turns out to be extremely flexible. It is often combined with antiquities or with rarities and curiosities of nature and art, and in the text with topographical descriptions. Hospitality is extended to all manner of things—air, climate, mineral waters, metals and mining, rocks, fossils (which were soon to disturb the peace of *Genesis*), as well as to beasts, birds, fishes, insects, and plants. The work that was to stereotype the title and procedure was Dr. Plot's *Natural History of Oxfordshire* (1677), but preceding its publication numerous treatises on plant life had appeared, which by the researches of Ray and Willoughby had arrived at the status of a science. Herbals, which stood to botany much as alchemy did to chemistry, made their appearance in the century preceding. The range and character of investigations into other forms of natural history, which marked the intellectual life of the 17th and 18th centuries, may be gauged by a few samples of titles: Dr. Willoughby's three books on Ornithology (1676); Edwards' *A Natural History of English Song-Birds* (1737); John Moore's *Columbarian, or the Pigeon-House* (1765); Willoughby's *De Historia Piscium* (1686), and Ray's *Synopsis methodica avium et piscium* (1713); Martin Lister's *Historia conchyliorum* (1655) and his *Historiae animalium Angliae tres tractatus, unus de araneis*, etc. (1678); Ray's *Methodus insectorum* (1705); W. Derham's *A Natural History of Insects* (1724); Wm. Gould's *An Account of English Ants* (1747); Benj. Wilkes's *The English Moths and Butterflies* (1742); John Kay's *De canibus Britannicis* (1729); and Pennant's *British Zoology* (1763-66), of which the first part consisted of 24 plates of birds and one of the polecat! The natural history of inanimate objects may be exemplified by the following: Webster's *Metallographia, or History of Metals* (1671); Lister's *Attempt toward a Natural History of the Fossils of England* (1729); Benj. Allen's *The Natural History of the Chalybeat and Purging-Waters of England* (1699); Dr. Short's *The Natural, Experimental, and Medicinal History of the Mineral Waters of Derbyshire,* etc. (1734).

In the face of such confounding of genera what is the bibliographer to do? What I have based my selections on is in general the consideration whether this or that subject constituted a fixed and visible feature of the landscape, whether it was something that might be searched out by the traveler as an object to be looked at, and whether such a search might be the occasion of travel or description. Titles beginning with "The Natural History of," I have accepted unreservedly, though where the emphasis seemed to be on antiquities, I have usually placed them under HISTORY AND ANTIQUITIES. Other titles have been included as examples of the various interests engaging the attention of the intellectually curious.)

1470 DODOENS, REMBERT. A Niewe Herball, or Historie of Plants: wherein is contayned the whole Discourse and perfect Description of all sortes of Herbes and Plants: their diuers and sundry Kindes: their straunge Figures, Fashions, and Shapes: their Names, Natures, Operations, and Vertues; and that not onely of those whiche are here growyng in this our Countrie of Englande, but of all others also of forrayne Realmes, commonly used in Physicke; First set foorth in the Doutch or Almaigne Tongue, by that learned D. Rembert Dodoens, Physition to the Emperour: And nowe first translated out of French into English, by Henry Lyte, Esquyer. Numerous woodcuts. Fol. London.

Another edit., London, 1586.
Henry Lyte, the translator, was a student at Oxford, 1546, and celebrated as a botanist and archaeologist.—Bookseller's Note.

GLANVILLE, BARTHOLOMEW DE. Liber de Proprietatibus Rerum Bartholomei Anglici. Fol. Basel.

Translated into English by John de Trevisa and published by Wynkyn de Worde, London, *ca.* 1495. 2nd edit. of this, 4to, London, 1535.

The author, generally known as Bartholomew Anglicus, was a minorite friar who taught theology at Paris, probably in the second decade of the 13th century. His work was one of the earliest printed texts in English on natural history, and one of the most widely read books of medieval times. It was encyclopediac in character.—*DNB.*

1580 CHURCHYARD, THOMAS. The Wonders of Wiltshire and the Earthquake of Kent. London.

1629 JOHNSON, THOMAS. Iter Plantarum Investigationis ergo susceptum in agrum Cantianum Anno Dom. 1629 Julii 13. Ericetum Hamstedianum sive Plantarum ibi crescentium Observatio . . . . 4to. London.

Another edit., 8vo. London, 1632. See also Johnson under 1641 below.

1640 PARKINSON, JOHN. Theatrum Botanicum. The Theatre of Plants; or, A Herbal of large Extent; containing a more ample Exact History and Declaration of the Physicall Herbs and Plants. London.

1641 JOHNSON, THOMAS. Mercurii Botanici Pars Altera, sive Plantarum Gratia suscepti Itineris in Cambriam, sive Walliam, Descriptio, exhibens Reliquarum Stirpium Nostratium (quae in priore Parte non Enumerabantur) Catalogum. 8vo. London.

The first part was probably the *Theatrum Botanicum* listed under 1629 above. The present part is a collection of plants native to Wales. It also contains an account of the author's journey through Wales in search of rare plants, which was undertaken in company with Paul Sone and Edward Morgan. See Rowlands, *Cambrian Bibliog.,* for a note on this author and this work (in Welsh).

1656 BEALE, DR. JOHN. Herefordshire Orchards, a Pattern for all England. London.

The above was published in the form of a letter. There is another on the same subject printed 8vo in 1724. Herefordshire is under great obligations to this author, in whose family, natives of the county, a zeal for the plantation of orchards was hereditary. By these letters he so raised and extended their reputation, that within a few years the county gained some hundred thousands of pounds by it.—Gough, *Anecdotes of British Topography,* 193. Herefordshire's fruitful orchards are also celebrated in John Philip's poem, "Cyder" (1708).

TRADESCANT, JOHN. Musaeum Tradescantianum; or, A Collection of the Rarities preserved at South-Lambert, near London, by John Tradescant. 12mo. London.

Here is included an ample catalogue of Tradescant's plants, shrubs, and trees, in English and Latin, and a list of benefactors to this collection. These were sold to Ashmole, who afterwards gave them to Oxford University.—Gough, 426. This naturalist and his father were outstanding in their age for their zeal in collecting plants from abroad and domiciling them in England.

1660 PETTUS, SIR JOHN. Fodinae Regales; or, The History, Laws, and Places of the Chief Mines and Mineral Works in England, Wales, and the English Pale in Ireland. As also of the Mint and Money. Fol. London.

Another edit., fol., London, 1670.
"This rare work is very valuable for giving an account of the state of mining in England during the XVIIth Century."—Quoted by Robinson, no. 61.

RAY, JOHN. Catalogue of Plants about Cambridge, 1660. (Cited by Gough without place or date.)

This is the first book of this great master of the botanical science, which by exciting an attention in many to those neglected subjects revived the science, and laid the foundation for the study of botany among us.—Gough, 63. See Ray under 1670 below and also under 1673, WEST EUROPE, vol. I of this work.

1661   CHILDREY, JOSHUA. Britannia Baconica: or, The Natural Rarities of England, Scotland, and Wales, according as they are found in every Shire; historically related, according to the Precepts of the Lord Bacon. 8vo. London.

> The date of this first edition is given as 1660 in *DNB;* republished 1662. Translated into French, 12mo, Paris, 1667. See below.
> "His *Britannia Baconica* contains but little ornithology but is of importance as the earliest attempt at a systematic description of the Natural History of the whole of Great Britain. This work seems further to have inspired Robert Plot to write his *Natural History of Oxfordshire,* the forerunner of a long series of county natural histories by various authors."—Major Mullen's *Bibliography,* quoted by Bookseller.

> 1662   CHILDREY, JOSHUA. Britannia Baconica: or, The Natural Rarities of England, Scotland, & Wales . . . Historically related, according to the Precepts of the Lord Bacon . . . With Observations upon them, and Deductions from them, whereby divers Secrets in Nature are discovered, and some things hitherto reckoned Prodigies, are fain to confess the Cause whence they proceed. . . . 8vo. London.

> 1667   (In French.) Britannia Baconica: Histoire des Singularités naturelles d'Angleterre, d'Escosse, & du Province de Galles: raisonement qu'explique les causes naturelles des choses qui paroissent les plus singulières. Ce qui fait avec l'histoire naturelle d'Irland, que l'on a donné au public depuis peu, une histoire naturelle entière de tous les provinces & de tous les états que posséde de roy de la Grande Bretagne. Traduite de l'Anglois de Mr. Childrey par M. P. B. 12mo. Paris.

1666   MERRETT, CHRISTOPHER, M.D. Pinax Rerum Naturalium Britannicarum, continens Vegetabilia, Animalia, et Fossilia, in hac Insula reperta inchoatus. 8vo. London.

> 2nd edit., 8vo, London, 1667.
> "This, the first printed list of British birds, mentions about 170 species. Merrett, although a botanist primarily, has acquired a special interest in the eyes of British ornithologists on account of the list of British birds contained in his Pinax."—Major Mullen's *Bibliography,* quoted by Sotheran, Bookseller.

1670   RAY, DR. JOHN. Catalogus Plantarum Angliae, et Insularum adjacentium: tum indigenas, tum in Agris passim cultas complectens. In quo praeter Synonyma necessaria Facultates quoque summatim traduntur, una cum Observationibus & Experimentis novis Medicis & Physicis. 8vo. London.

> Republished, London, 1677.
> This work was the result of three journeys with his learned friends over the most part of England. The counties are arranged alphabetically with their plants. The second edition was in so great demand that he prepared a third, but meeting with some opposition from the bookseller who had the right to the copy, he published instead, in compliance with the solicitations of his friends, his *Methodus Plantarum Nova, brevitatis & perspicuitatis Causa synoptice in Tabulis exhibita, cum Notis Generum tum Summorum tum Subalternorum Characteristicis:* etc., 12mo, London, 1682. Likewise his *Fasciculus Stirpium Britannicarum post editum Catalogum Plantarum Angliae,* 8vo, London, 1688. Other editions of these and other works followed.

1677   PLOT, DR. ROBERT. The Natural History of Oxfordshire: being an Essay toward the Natural History of England. Map and 16 copperplates. Fol. Oxford.

> 2nd edit., with large additions and corrections, fol., Oxford, 1705, by his son-in-law, Mr. Burman, fellow of University College, who prefixed a short life of the author. Plot was also author of *Natural History of Staffordshire* (see under 1686 below).
> Plot was the first to attempt to describe the natural history of the counties of England. Apparently he had in mind the ambitious project of doing the whole of England, but he seemingly grew weary of the task after publishing those of Oxfordshire and Staffordshire. According to Gough, he set forth his plan of an intended journey through England to search for antiquities, etc., in a letter to Dr. Fell, then dean of Christ Church; the letter was published by Hearne, from a MS in the Bodleian Library, at the end of *Leland's Itinerary.* His scheme for illustrating the natural history of England was based on an excellent syllabus of inquiries. Plot's too easy admission of fables may be attributed to the credulous temper of the age. Still the work was quoted as an authority until the close of the 18th century, and in the accounts he gave of rare plants, he "has not been excelled," says Pulteney, "by any subsequent writer."—Quoted by Maggs, no. 577.

1682   BURTON, RICHARD. For some account of natural rarities in the British Isles, see his *Admirable Curiosities,* under DESCRIPTIONS.

1683   SUTHERLAND, JAMES. Hortus Medicus Edinburgensis. 8vo. Edinburgh.

> The author was overseer of Balfour's physic garden in Edinburgh. This work describes the garden. It had a second edition, the date of which I have not ascertained.

1684   SIBBALD, SIR ROBERT. Scotia Illustrata Sive Prodromus Historiae Naturalis In Quo Regionis natura, Incolarum Ingenia & Mores, Morbi iisque medendi Methodus, & Medicina Indigena accurate explicantur: Et Multiplices Naturae Partus in triplice ejus Regno, Vegetabili scilicet, Animali & Minerali per hancce Borealem Magnae Britanniae Partem, quae Antiquissimum Scotiae Regnum constituit undiquaque diffusi nunc primum in Lucem eruuntur, & varii eorum Usus, Medici praesertim & Mechanici, quos ad Vitae cum necessitatem, tum commoditatem praestant, cunctis perspicue exponuntur. . . . 22 copperplates. Fol. Edinburgh.

> This was the only edition with the Latin title. There seems to have been an English title of the same date. See below.
> Part 2 contains a catalogue of the plants in the medical garden at Edinburgh, of which Sibbald and Balfour were the founders. This work was to serve as an introduction to a more extensive volume, which was to have comprehended all that related to the ancient and present state of Scotland. Sibbald was physician to Charles II, and was chiefly instrumental in establishing the Royal College of Physicians in Edinburgh. See also his *Vindiciae Scotiae Illustratae* under 1710 below.

> 1684   SIBBALD, SIR ROBERT. Scotia Illustrata: Scotland Illustrated: or, An Introduction to the Natural History, in which are accurately described the Characteristics of the Country, the Character and Customs of the Inhabitants, the Diseases and the Method of Curing them, and the Medicinal Herbs of the Country, etc. 20 plates. Edinburgh.

1686   PLOT, DR. ROBERT. The Natural History of Staffordshire, by Robert Plot, Keeper of the Ashmolean Museum, and Professor of Chymistry in the University of Oxford. Fol. Oxford.

> The contents of this work are indicated by the following chapter headings: 1. Of the Heavens and Air; 2. Of the Waters; 3. Of the Earths; 4. Of Stones; 5. Of Formed Stones; 6. Of Plants; 7. Of Brutes; 8. Of Men and Women; 9. Of Arts; 10. Of Antiquities.—In the Epistle Dedicatory to his *History of Oxfordshire* (see under 1677 above), he seems to promise an account of other counties; but he closes his work, the result of nine years' study and travel, with a resolution to publish no more of these histories unless commanded by a power that he must not resist; meaning James II, whose approbation of his first *History* encouraged him to compile the present work, which was published by subscription of a penny a sheet, a penny a plate, and sixpence the map, amounting to ten or twelve shillings the copy.—Gough, 486. The Staffordshire squires often boasted of having "humbugged old Plot." He was said to be a witty man who liked good society, was intimate with Pepys and Evelyn, but his moral reputation left much to be desired.—Walters, *The English Antiquaries.*

1692   SIBBALD, SIR ROBERT. Phalainologia Nova, seu Observationes de rarioribus quibusdam Balaenis in Scotiae Littoribus nuper ejectis. 4to. Edinburgh.

> Another edit., London, 1773.

1694   LEIGH, CHARLES. Phthisiologia Lancastriensis, cui accessit Tentamen Philosophicum Mineralibus Aquis in eodem Comitatu Observatis. London.

> This volume formed the basis of the *Natural History of Lancashire and Cheshire.* See Leigh under 1700 below.

1697 SIBBALD, SIR ROBERT. Auctaria Musaei Balfouriani e museo Sibbaldiano; sive enumeratio & Descriptio Rerum Rariorum, tam Naturalium quam Artificialium, tam Domesticarum quam Exoticarum, quas Rob. Sibbaldus, M.D. eq. aur. Academiae Edinburgenae donavit; quae quasi manuductio brevis est ad Historiam Naturalem. 8vo. Edinburgh.

> Sir Andrew Balfour, M.D., made many interesting discoveries and observations on the natural history of Scotland, and left a noble collection of natural and artificial curiosities in the museum that bears his name at Edinburgh; to this his intimate friend and colleague Sir R. Sibbald made considerable additions. Later he published a catalogue of the whole under the above title.—Gough, 635.

1698 MACKWORTH, SIR HUMPHREY. The Adventurer, or, An Expedient for composing all Difference between the Partners of the Mine Estate of Sir Carberry Pryse, etc. Proposed by Sir Humphrey Mackworth. Fol. London.

> This is connected with the following item.

WALLER, W. Essay on the Value of the Mines late of Sir Carberry Price (in Wales), writ for the private Satisfaction of all the Partners. Writ by W. Waller, Gent., Steward of the said Mines. Privately printed.

1699 WALLER, W. An Account of the Cardiganshire Mines. (Place?) (So cited by Rowlands, *Cambrian Bibliog.*)

1700 COX, REV. THOMAS. For the natural histories of various counties, see his *Ecclesiastical and Natural History*, etc., under SURVEYS.

LEIGH, CHARLES. The Natural History of Lancashire, Cheshire, and the Peak of Derbyshire, with an Account of the British, Armenian, Greek and Roman Antiquities in those Parts. Portrait by Faithorne, double-page map, with outlines in color, 2 plates of coats-of-arms, 8 plates of coins, and 14 other plates of the natural history. Fol. Oxford.

> What he says of Derbyshire is trite, being only a trifling account of its wonders. Bishop Nicolson speaks of the work with contempt.—Gough, 233.

SHIERS, —. A Familiar Discourse, or Dialogue, concerning the Mine Adventurers, wherein Sir Humphrey Mackworth and other Welsh Gentlemen were concerned. To which is prefixed, An Abstract of the Present State of the Mines of Bwlch yr Yskair hir, etc. 12mo. London.

> Here is presented in full the lead and copper mines in Cardiganshire, the coal works in Morganshire, the melting works in various places.—Rowlands, *Cambrian Bibliog.* The litigation over the management of the affairs of the Mine Adventurers continued for some time, and brought to the press a number of pamphlets.

1707 HETON, THOMAS. Some Account of Mines, and the Advantages of them to this Kingdom, with an Appendix relating to the Mine Adventure in Wales. 4to. London.

> This refers to the mines in Cardiganshire. Campbell, in his *Political Survey* (1774), mentions a work by Heton called, Discourse on Mines of England. Select Essays on Commerce, Agriculture, Mines and Fisheries, but gives no date for it.

WALLER, WILLIAM. Some Account of Mines in Cardiganshire. Large folding map and 12 folding plates. 8vo. London.

Contents: Lead and Silver Mines of Bwlch yr eskir-hir; Lead and Copper Mines at Bwlchkaninogg; Lead and Silver Mines of Cwmsumblock; Great Lead and Silver Mines of Goginian; Lead and Silver Mines of Brinpica, etc.—From Bookseller's Note.

1709 ROBINSON, REV. THOMAS. An Essay towards a Natural History of Westmoreland and Cumberland, wherein is an Account of their several Minerall and Surface Productions; with some Directions how to discover Mines by the external and adjacent Strata, etc. To which is annexed, A Vindication of the Philosophical and Theological Paraphrase of the Mosaick System of the Creation. 2 pts. 8vo. London.

1710 SALMON, WILLIAM, M.D. The English Herbal, or History of Plants, Names, Greek, Latin and English Species, Place of Growth, Times of Flowering, Preparations, Florilegium, Culture, Management, etc., with exquisite Icons or Figures, etc. Hundreds of wood-cuts of flowers through the work. Fol. London.

SIBBALD, SIR ROBERT. Vindiciae Scotiae Illustratae, sive Prodromi Naturalis Historiae Scotiae, contra Prodromomastiges, sub Larva Libelli de Legibus Historiae Naturalis, Latentes. Fol. London.

This was annexed to his *Miscellanea Eruditae Antiquitatis* and reprinted 1739.

1711 ALLEN, BENJAMIN. The Natural History of the Mineral Waters of Great Britain. 8vo. London.

See Allen under 1699, SPAS.

1712 LLWYD, EDWARD. Letters from Mr. Edward Llwyd, Keeper of the Ashmolean Museum, Oxford, to Dr. Tancred Robinson, F.R.S. (containing several observations in natural history made in his travels through Wales). In *Phil. Trans.*, vol. 27, no. 334, 462-66; no. 335, 500-03. London.

MORTON, JOHN (Rector of Oxendon). The Natural History of Northamptonshire, with an Account of the Antiquities: also Transcript of Doomsday-Book, as far as it relates to that County. Folding map by John Harris, and 14 copperplates of shells, birds, fossils, etc. Fol. London.

This book deals largely with "figured fossils"; Pulteney praises the botanical part.— *DNB*, quoted by Sotheran, Bookseller. It is noticed in the *Journal des Scavans*, vol. II, 62, 1715.

1713 LLWYD, EDWARD. On the Natural History and Antiquities of Wales and Scotland. *Phil. Trans. Abr.*, vol. 6, 19. 4to. London.

1718 AUBREY, JOHN. Introduction towards a Natural History of Wiltshire. With other curious Miscellanies. London. (So cited in Straus's Handlist to his *Unspeakable Curll.*)

1718-19 AUBREY, JOHN. For the natural history of Surrey, see his *Natural History and Antiquities of the County of Surrey*, under HISTORY AND ANTIQUITIES.

1721 BRADLEY, RICHARD. A Philosophical Account of the Works of Nature, endeavouring to set forth the several gradations remarkable in the Mineral, Vegetable and

Animal Parts of Creation; also an Account of the State of Gardening, in Great Britain and other Parts of Europe; Improvement of Barren Ground, Propagating of Timber-Trees, Fruit-Trees, etc. Colored plates. 4to. London.

> Bradley was professor of botany at Cambridge, where he also lectured on Materia Medica.

1725 DOUGLAS, JAMES, M.D., F.R.S. Lilium Sarniense; or, A Description of the Guernsey Lilly: to which is added, The Botanical Dissection of the Coffee Berry: with Figures. Fol. London.

> The first account of this beautiful flower, a native of Japan and not of the island whose name it bears, is in James Cornutus' *Canadensium Plantarum, aliarumque nondum editarum Historia,* Paris, 1635, which, besides the plants of Canada, includes other curious ones the author met with. John Rea mentions the plant in his *Complete Florilege,* fol., London, 1665, and first gave it its present name, though that of Narcissus, or Lilio-narcissus Japonicus, is still the true botanical one. Succeeding botanists have barely mentioned it. Dr. Douglas has entered into a minute examination of it, and illustrated it with very particular and accurate draughts.—Gough, 613.

1729 MARTYN, J. An Account of some Observations relating to Natural History, made in a Journey to the Peak (of Derbyshire). In *Phil. Trans.,* no. 407. London.

1730 MILLER, PHILIP. Catalogus Plantarum Officinalium quae in Horto Botanico Chelseyano Aluntur. 8vo. London.

> Sir Hans Sloane gave the Apothecary's Company his physic garden, which they rented of him, on condiiton it should always be kept up, in evidence of which they were to present yearly to the Royal Society 50 plants grown there the preceding year, specifically distinct from each other, till they amounted to 2,000, to be carefully preserved by the Society.—Gough, 262.

1732 COKER, JOHN. For the natural history of Dorsetshire, see his *Survey of Dorsetshire,* under SURVEYS.

> This antiquary held a vicarage in Dorset 1576-79. He died in 1635(?). His Survey was not published, however, till 1732.

COWELL, JOHN. A True Account of the Aloe Americana or Africana, now in Blossom . . . Also Two Other Exotic Plants called the Sereus or Torch-Thistle. London.

DALE, SAMUEL. For an appendix on the natural history of the sea coast and country about Harwich, see his *History and Antiquities of Harwich,* etc., under TOWNS.

1734 SHORT, T. For a natural history of the earth's minerals and fossils, see Short this date under SPAS.

1737 A Natural History of English Song-Birds and such of the Foreign as are esteemed for their Singing. 24 plates. 8vo. London.

1738 DEERING, CHARLES. Catalogus Stirpium. A Catalogue of Plants naturally growing and commonly cultivated in divers Parts of England, more especially about Nottingham. 8vo. Nottingham.

1739 RAND, ISAACUS. Horti Medici Chelseiani Index Compendiarius exhibens Nomina Plantarum quas ad Rei Barbariae praecipue Materiae Medicae Scientiam promovendam ali curavit Societas Pharmacopaeorum Londinensium. 8vo. London.

1749 ALSTON, CAROLUS. Index Plantarum, praecipue Officinalium, quae, in Horto Medico Edinburgensi, a Carolo Alston, M. & B. P. Medicinae Studiosis Demonstrantur. 12mo. Edinburgh.

1750 HEATH, CAPTAIN ROBERT. For a natural history of the Islands of Scilly, see his *Natural and Historical Account of the Islands of Scilly,* under HISTORY AND ANTIQUITIES.

1751 HAYNES, JOHN. An Accurate Survey of the Botanic Garden at Chelsea, with the Elevation and Ichnography of the Green-House and Stoves, and an Explanation of the several Parts of the Gardens, shewing where the most Conspicuous Trees and Plants are disposed. Surveyed and delineated by John Haynes. London.

1754 OWEN, EDWARD. Observations on the Earths, Rocks, Stones and Minerals, for some Miles about Bristol, and on the Nature of the Hot-Well and the Virtues of its Waters. Engravings. 12mo. London.

1755 ELLIS, JOHN. Essay towards a Natural History of the Corallines, and other Marine Productions of the like Kind, commonly found on the Coasts of Great Britain and Ireland. With the Description of a large Marine Polype taken near the North Pole, by the Whale-fishers, in the Summer 1753. Frontispiece and 38 engravings (many folding), including Cuff's aquatic microscope. 4to. Printed for the Author.

> Ellis established his reputation as one of the most acute observers of his time by the publication of this *Essay.* The work was translated into French, 1756; and though his views were opposed by Dr. Job Baster and but imperfectly comprehended by Linnaeus, he established by it the animal nature of this group of organisms. In 1768 the Copley medal of the Royal Society was awarded to Ellis for these researches . . . . Linneaus termed him a "bright star of natural history" and "the main support of natural history in England."— *DNB,* quoted by Sotheran, Bookseller.

1756 Natural History of Kent (extract from a larger work). Map. 8vo. (Place?) (So cited in Bookseller's Catalogue.)

1757 BOTANISTA, DR. THEOPHILUS. Rural Beauties; or, The Natural History of the Four Following Counties, viz., Cornwall, Devonshire, Dorsetshire, and Somersetshire. With Additional Remarks by Theophilus Botanista, M.D. Folding map. Frontispiece. 12mo. London.

> Gough says this is a trifling book fit only for children. *Op. cit.,* 74.

1758 BORLASE, WILLIAM. The Natural History of Cornwall: the Air, Climate, Waters, Rivers, Lakes, Sea, and Tides, the Stones, Metals, Tin, and Mining, the Vegetables, Rare Birds, Fishes, Shells, Reptiles, and Quadrupeds; and of the Inhabitants, their Manners, Customs, etc. Folding map and 28 plates of views and examples of natural history. Fol. Oxford.

> This book is much scarcer than the *Antiquities of Cornwall* (see under 1754, HISTORY AND ANTIQUITIES), there having been only one edition of it.—Lowndes. The work includes

an account of the Stannaries and the processes of mining iron, copper, silver, lead, and gold, together with a relation of recent improvements in mining.

1759 ALBIN, ELEAZAR. Natural History of English Song-Birds and such of the Foreign as are brought over, with an Account of how to order the Canary-Birds in Breeding, etc. 21 colored copperplates. 8vo. London.

This may be another edition of the item listed under 1737 above.

1759-63 BOWEN, EMANUEL, and BENJAMIN MARTIN. The Natural History of England; or, A Description of each particular County, In regard to the curious Productions of Nature and Art. Illustrated by a Map of each County. 40 maps. 2 vols. 8vo. London.

These volumes formed part of *The General Magazine of Arts and Sciences* . . . by Martin.—Chubb, *The Printed Maps*. Martin was a scientific instrument maker.

1762 HUDSON, WILLIAM. Flora Anglica: exhibens Plantas per Regnum Britanniae. 8vo. London.

2nd edit., 8vo, London, 1778.

INCOLA. The Natural History of Sutton Coldfield. In *Gent. Mag.,* vol. 32, 401-04. London.

This article appeared in response to some queries printed in *Gent. Mag.,* vol. 25, asking for accounts of antiquities, etc., to be found in various counties.

1763 MARTYN, THOMAS. Plantae Cantabrigienses, or, A Catalogue of the Plants which grow wild in the County of Cambridge, disposed according to the System of Linnaeus. Herbationes Cantabrigienses, or, Directions to the Places where they may be found: comprehended in thirteen Botanical Excursions: to which are added, Lists of the more Rare Plants growing in many Parts of England and Wales. London.

The first of these consists of three columns, containing generical and marginal names from Linnaeus, J. Martyn, Ray, etc.—Gough, 96. See Ray under 1660 above.

1764 G., E. The Natural History of Sheffield. In *Gent. Mag.,* vol. 34, 157-61. London.

1766 PENNANT, THOMAS. British Zoology. Fol. London.

Another edit., fol., Augsburg, 1771. See below.
Pennant earned a well-deserved reputation as a naturalist among the scientists of his day, by his industry in correspondence as well as by his publications. He will be met with several times in the section TOURS BY NATIVES.

1771 PENNANT, THOMAS. Zoologia Britannica: Classis I. Quadrupeda; Classis II. Aves . . . Latinitate donavit Christophorus Theophilus de Murr. 61 large colored plates (11 of quadrupeds, and plates 1-50 of birds as in the English edition), by J. J. Ha¡d after P. Paillon, copied from Pennant's plates, with descriptions in Latin and French. Fol. Augsburg.

1767 BRANDER, GUSTAVUS. Fossilia Hantoniensia; or, Hampshire Fossils. 4to. London.

Of these curious fossil shells, collected out of the cliffs between Christ Church and Lymington, and presented to the British Museum by G. Brander, very few are known to be natives of our own, or indeed of any of the European shores; the greater part, upon a comparison with recent specimens, are wholly unknown to us. The copperplates are exact draughts, engraved from the originals, by the late Mr. Green. To the figures are annexed a scientific Latin description by Dr. Solander, (who is now composing a scientific catalogue of all the natural productions in the British Museum) and a prefatory account of phenomena in Latin and English.—Gough, 711.

1769 WALLIS, JOHN. The Natural History and Antiquities of Northumberland, and of
      so much of Durham as lies between the Tyne and Tweed; commonly called
      North Bishoprick. 2 vols. 4to. London.

1769-72 BERKENHOUT, JOHN, M.D. Outlines of the Natural History of Great Britain
      and Ireland, containing a Systematic Arrangement and Description of all the
      Animals, Vegetables, and Fossiles. 3 vols. 8vo. London.

>   2nd edit., called the *Synopsis of the Natural History*, 2 vols., 8vo, 1789; 3rd, 2 vols., 1795.
>   Dr. Berkenhout was the son of a Dutchman settled in Leeds, with a "deep knowledge
>   of natural history, botany, and chemistry."—*DNB*. His scientific career was varied by his
>   being sent in 1778 by the British Government as one of a commission to the new United
>   States Congress. He was thrown into prison at Philadelphia on the suspicion that he was
>   tampering with some leading citizens.—Sotheran.

1771 EDWARDS, —. The Natural History of the Isle of Wight. Extract from his "Ac-
      count of the Needles, in the Isle of Wight." In *Annual Register*, vol. 14, 82-83.

1772 LETTSOM, JOHN COAKLEY, M.D. The Naturalist's and Traveller's Companion, con-
      taining Instructions for Discovering and Preserving Objects of Natural
      History. Colored frontis. 8vo. London.

>   2nd edit., 8vo, London, 1774; another edit., with illus., 8vo, London, 1799.
>   This treats of the "Method of analysing Medicinal or Mineral Waters," "Method of
>   catching and preserving Insects," "Preserving Birds and other Animals," "Directions for
>   bringing over Seeds and Plants from distant Countries," "Experiments for discovering the
>   Contents of Air," etc.

1775 JENKINSON, JAMES. Description of British Plants, translated from the *Genera et
      Species Plantarum* of Linnaeus, to which is prefaced, An Etymological Dic-
      tionary, explaining the Principal Classes, Orders and Genera, and a Glossary.
      127 figures of plants, leaves, etc. London.

1775-77 LIGHTFOOT, J. Flora Scotica: the Native Plants of Scotland and the Hebrides.
      2 vols. 8vo. London.

>   Republished, 2 vols., 8vo, London, 1777; another edit., called the 2nd, 2 vols., 8vo,
>   London, 1792. See below.
>   It contains a full synonymy, and English, Scottish, and Gaelic names of the plants. The
>   cryptogramic plates are treated with a care and detail that was then unusual. In his work
>   Lightfoot was assisted by Dr. Hope of Edinburgh, Dr. Burgess, the Rev. Dr. John Stuart
>   of Luss, Dr. Parsons of Oxford, Sir Joseph Banks, Dr. Solander, and John Sibthorp.
>   Pennant prefixed a "Fauna Scotica," and to the second edition a life of the author.—G. S.
>   Boulger, quoted by Sotheran.
>
>>   1792 LIGHTFOOT, JOHN. Flora Scotica, or, A Systematic Arrangement, in the Linnaean
>>   Method, of the Native Plants of Scotland and the Hebrides. 2nd edit., with 35
>>   plates (5 of animals). 2 vols. 8vo. London.

1776 WITHERING, WILLIAM. A Botanical Arrangement of all Vegetables naturally
      growing in Great Britain. London.

>   2nd edit., 3 vols., 8vo, London, 1787-92; 3rd edit., 4 vols., 8vo, London, 1796.
>   The author was a physician, botanist, and mineralogist. He published in 1786 an account of
>   the foxglove, which he did much to introduce into the pharmacopoeia.—*DNB*.
>
>>   1787-92 WITHERING, WILLIAM. A Botanical Arrangement of British Plants, including a
>>   New Set of References to Figures. 2nd edit. Numerous plates. 3 vols. 8vo. London.

1777 JACOB, EDWARD. Plantae Favershamienses. A Catalogue of the more perfect
      Plants growing Spontaneously about Faversham. 8vo. London.

NIMMO, REV. WILLIAM. For the natural history of Stirlingshire, see his *General History of Stirlingshire,* under HISTORY AND ANTIQUITIES.

ROBSON, S. British Flora, containing the Select Names, Characters, Places of Growth, Duration and Time of Flowering of the Plants growing Wild in Great Britain. 8vo. York.

1777-98 CURTIS, WILLIAM. Flora Londinensis; or, Plates and Descriptions of such Plants as grow wild in the Environs of London, with their Places of Growth and Times of Flowering, their Several Names according to Linnaeus and other Authors, with a Particular Description of each Plant in Latin and English, their several Uses in Medicine, Agriculture, Rural Oeconomy, and other Arts. 434 full-page, hand-colored plates, vignettes, indices, etc. 5 vols. Fol. London.

1778 PRYCE, WILLIAM. Mineralogia Cornubiensis: a Treatise on Minerals, Mines and Mining, Theory, etc., of Strata, Fissures and Lodes, Methods of Discovering and Working of Tin, Copper, and Lead Mines, Cleansing, etc., their Products, Terms and Idioms of Miners, Account of the Steam Engine. Tables. Fol. London.

1786 HURTLEY, T. A Concise Account of some Natural Curiosities in the Environs of Malham, in Craven, Yorkshire, with Appendix containing a Pedigree of the Lambert Family. Copperplate engravings. 8vo. London.

1787 KLAPROTH, M. H. Observations relative to the Mineralogical and Chemical History of the Fossils of Cornwall. Translated from the German by J. G. Groscke. 8vo. London.

1787-96 CURTIS, WILLIAM. The Botanical Magazine, or Flower Garden Displayed, in which the most Ornamental Foreign Plants, cultivated in the Open Ground, the Green-House, and the Stove, will be accurately represented in their natural Colours, with the most approved Methods of Culture. 357 hand-colored plates. 10 vols. 8vo. Published by the Author.

1789 WHITE, REV. GILBERT. The Natural History and Antiquities of Selborne, in the County of Southampton. Frontispiece and 7 plates. 4to. London.

> Numerous editions in the 19th and 20th centuries. See below for that illustrated by Kearton, London, 1924.
> This work is rightly termed a classic among natural histories. The reviewer in *Gent. Mag.,* vol. 59, 60-62, could not help being pleased with the book. Loving, intimate observation down to the minutest detail was matched by a beautifully adequate description. Of his accuracy the statement has frequently been quoted that the number of mistakes recorded by White could be counted almost on the fingers of one hand.

> 1924 WHITE, REV. GILBERT. The Natural History of Selborne, with Notes by Richard Kearton, and 85 photographs, including many taken specially at Selborne by Cherry Kearton and Richard Kearton. 8vo. London.
> Many years ago Mr. Richard Kearton, the famous naturalist and photographer, edited and illustrated an edition of Gilbert White's great book on the natural history of a Hampshire village. Now, with fresh knowledge of greater experience, Mr. Kearton has done his work anew, and the present edition of the classic contains new photographs specially taken in the neighbourhood of Selborne, and including both bird studies and landscape. As is well known, there is no other naturalist photographer who can portray bird life with nature's own background so well as Mr. Kearton.—Bookseller's Note.

1790   BEWICK, THOMAS. General History of Quadrupeds. Woodcuts by Bewick. 8vo.
       Newcastle (?).

> 2nd edit., 8vo, Newcastle-upon-Tyne, 1791; 5th edit., 8vo, Newcastle-upon-Tyne, 1807.
> The text of this work was supplied by Beilby, to whom Bewick was apprenticed in 1767.
> Bewick was one of the best known artists in woodcut of his age, and was called upon
> frequently to illustrate various works besides those in natural history.

1790-1814   SOWERBY, JAMES. English Botany; or Coloured Figures of British Plants,
       with their essential Characters, Synonyms and Places of Growth, to which be
       added occasional Remarks, with the general Index. Over 2,500 colored plates.
       36 vols. 8vo. London.

1791   DARWIN, ERASMUS. The Botanic Garden. A Poem in Two Parts, with Philosoph-
       ical Notes. Plates. 4to. London.

> The inception of this poem, which is usually termed the worst poem in the English
> language, is too well known to students of English literature to be retold. Its notes show
> the author to have been an omnivorous reader in all fields of scientific studies of the day.
> How much Shelley owed to them has been brought to light by recent scholars.

1792   DONOVAN, E. The Natural History of British Insects, Periods of Transformation,
       Food, etc., and the History of Minute Insects. Colored plates. Vols. I-IV. 8vo.
       London.

1793   MILNE, C., and A. GORDON. Indigenous Botany: or, Habitations of English
       Plants, containing the Result of several Botanical Excursions, chiefly in Kent,
       Middlesex, and the adjacent Counties, in 1790, and 1792. 8vo. London.

1794   TAIT, REV. C. An Account of the Peat Mosses of Kincardine and Flanders in
       Perthshire. (Flanders in Stirlingshire; Kincardine in Fifeshire.) *Trans. Roy.
       Soc. Edinb.,* vol. 3, 226. 4to. Edinburgh.

1795   WARNER, RICHARD. For the natural history of the Isle of Wight, see his *History
       of the Isle of Wight,* under HISTORY AND ANTIQUITIES.

       WHITE, REV. GILBERT. A Naturalist's Calendar, with Observations in various
       Branches of Natural History; extracted from the Papers of the late Gilbert
       White. Colored plates. London.

1797   MATON, WILLIAM GEORGE. For a natural history of the western counties of Eng-
       land, see his *Observations,* etc., under DESCRIPTIONS.

       SALISBURY, W. Hortus Paddingtonensis: or, A Catalogue of Plants cultivated in
       the Garden of J. Symmons, Paddington-House. 8vo. London.

1798   ABBOT, CHARLES. Flora Bedfordiensis, comprehending such Plants as grow wild
       in the County of Bedford. 8vo. London (?).

       JAMESON, ROBERT. An Outline of the Mineralogy of the Shetland Islands and of
       the Island of Arran, with an Appendix containing Observations on Peat, Kelp,
       and Coal. Maps. 8vo. Edinburgh.

> Another edit., 2 vols., 4to, Edinburgh, 1800; also in 1813, with change of title to
> *Mineralogical Travels through the Hebrides.*

1799 TOWNSON, DR. THOMAS. Tracts, etc., in Natural History. 8vo. London.

> Here is found a mineralogical account of the stones of Stonehenge.—Harrison, *Bibliog. Account of The Great Stone Monuments,* etc.

1825 ATKINSON, STEPHEN. Discoverie and Historie of the Gold Mynes in Scotland, written in the Year 1619. *Publ. Bann. Club,* no. 14. Edinburgh.

1847 AUBREY, JOHN. The Natural History of Wiltshire. Edited and elucidated with Notes by John Britton. *Publ. Wiltshire Bibliog. Soc.* 4to. London.

XIX

Agriculture, Husbandry, Gardening

(One justification for including this section in the present volume is that many of the publications on agriculture, husbandry, and gardening were the outcome of tours undertaken specifically to investigate and report on the existing state of the countryside as well as on the changes being wrought on "the face of Britain" by the advancing march of applied science and practical experiment. Another is that they frequently contain descriptions of the topography, accounts of manners and customs, and itineraries. A third that can be adduced is that they extend the reader's acquaintance with facets of interest generally ignored in histories and literary studies. No other attempt has been made here than to fill out the contours of an activity that was of the utmost concern to the national life. The more curious will find other and more detailed lists in the *Cambridge Bibliography* (1942), W. Carew Hazlitt's *Gleanings in Old Garden Literature* (1887), Amherst's *A History of Gardening in England* (1896), Rohde's *Old English Gardening Books* (1924), and Blomfield's *The Formal Garden in England* (1901). Herbals have generally been omitted and likewise the "simple" garden. More attention has been paid to the domestic garden as one of the phases of husbandry (the term most often used), and to the pleasure or landscape garden, which was created for show and hence became the objective of tours. Though much of the purpose of draining the fens was to increase the acreage for tillage, yet the printed accounts of such endeavors are listed under the section CANALS, RIVERS, FEN DRAINAGE, since they had as much, if not more, to do with improving navigation.

That the Englishman has always loved the soil and its products may be put down as a national characteristic which is attested by numerous publications and the tendency towards scientific experimentation. The result was that by the 18th century Britain had far outstripped continental Europe in practically all branches of husbandry. By virtue of habit and political system, the English gentry felt free to spend much of its time managing its estates, and by temper was inclined to be hospitable to suggestions that promised to improve production and increase income. Whereas the impetus towards the ornamental garden came largely from abroad, the initiative towards advances in agriculture was native born. The steady progress in scientific agriculture made during the 18th century was as notable a sign of the times as was the industrial revolution. Modern practices were stimulated through the efforts of the Board of Agriculture, founded in 1793, to spread more widely the knowledge gained from the experiments of such far-seeing landowners as Bakewell, Coke, Townsend, Sir John Sinclair, president, and Arthur Young, secretary of the Board. Fairs and exhibits at which prizes were given, publication of reports contributed by various research workers and practical farmers to the *Annals of Agriculture* (1784-1815), and a complete survey by counties of the agricultural practice, together with observations on the means of improving it, were some of the enterprises sponsored by the Board. Other societies were also active in disseminating the new knowledge, such as the Bath and West of England Society for the Encouragement of Agriculture, Arts, Manufactures, and Commerce, which published its correspondence, letters, and papers in a total of fourteen volumes between 1780 and 1816. And Scotland, which had been reckoned among the most backward of nations, was now come to the very front rank.)

1523 FITZHERBERT, SIR ANTHONY. Here begynneth a Newe Tracte or Treatyse moost Profytable For All Husbande Men: and very frutefull for all other Persons to Rede. 4to. London.

Other edits., about 1525, 1532, 1537, 1546, 1548, 1560, 1562, 1576, 1598, 1767.—Rohde, *Old English Gardening Books*.
In Pinson's edition of Sir Anthony Fitzherbert's *Boke of Surveying*, printed in 1523, the above work is mentioned as having been already published. Its date cannot therefore be later than that year. The authorship by Sir Anthony is considered doubtful, and the Brit. Mus. Catalogue suggests that his elder brother John may have written it.—Amherst's *History of Gardening*. The question is fully discussed in Skeat's reprint of the Treatise for the English Dialect Society, 1882.

1557 TUSSER, THOMAS. A Hundreth Good Pointes of Husbandrie. London. (In verse.)

Of this several varying editions were issued between 1561 and 1571. It was enlarged to Five Hundreth Points in 1573. See below.

1573 TUSSER, THOMAS. Five Hundreth Points of Good Husbandry vnited to as many of Good Huswiferie, first deuised, & nowe lately augmented with diuerse approued Lessons concerning Hopps & Gardening and other needful Matters, together with an Abstract before euery Moneth, conteining the whole Effect of the sayd Moneth. . . . 4to. London.

 Reissued in 1576, 1577, final complete edit., 1580, and so on in 19 more editions up to 1848. Edit. by W. Payne and Sidney J. Herrtage for the Early English Dialect Society, 8vo, London, 1878.

1563 HYLL, THOMAS. A Most Briefe and Pleasaunt Treatyse, Teachynge howe to dress, sowe, and get a Garden, and what Propertyes also these few Herbes heare spoken of, haue to our Comodytie. With the Remedyes that may be vsed against such Beasts, Wormes, Flies and such lyke, that noy Gardens, gathered out of the principallest Authors in this Art. 8vo. London.

 2nd edit., with same title, London, 1590. The above is apparently not the first, for at the end of *The Profitable Arte of Gardening*, 1568, Hill speaks of it as being "encreased by me ye seconde tyme." For new title, see Hill under 1568 below.

 Hill was a Londoner of not much learning, as he himself confesses, but that he loved gardens is most evident. This book is said to be the earliest English garden work.

1568 HILL, THOMAS. The proffitable Arte of Gardening, now the third tyme set fourth: to whiche is added much necessary matter, and a number of Secrettes with the Phisick helpes belonging to eche Herbe, and that easie prepared. To this annexed two propre treatises, the one entituled The marueilous Gouernment, propertie, and benefite of the Bees, with the rare Secrets of the Honny and Waxe. And the other, The yerely Coniectures, meete for husbandmen to knowe. Englished by Thomas Hill, Londiner. Ars naturam adiuuans. London.

 Later edits., 1572, 1574, 1579, to which is added, A Treatise of the Art of Graffing and Planting of Trees; 1586, 1593, 1608.

 Hill is probably the same person as Didymus Mountain, author of *The Gardener's Labyrinth.*—Amherst, *op. cit.* See below under 1577.

1572 MASCALL, LEONARD. A Booke of the Arte and maner, howe to plant and graffe all sortes of trees, howe to set stones, and sowe Pepines to make wylde trees to graffe on, as also remedies and mediicnes [*sic*]. VVith diuers other newe practise, by one of the Abbey of Saint Vincent in Fraunce, . . . With an addition in the Ende of this booke, of certaine Dutch practises, set forth and Englished by Leonard Mascall. 4to. London.

 Other edits., 1575, 1582, 1592, 1596, 1656, London.

1574 SCOT, REYNOLDE. A Perfite platforme of a Hoppe Garden, and necessarie Instructions for the making and mayntenaunce thereof, with notes and rules for reformation of all abuses, commonly practised therein, very necessarie and expedient for all men to haue, which in any wise haue to doe with Hops. Now newly corrected and augmented. . . . London.

 Other edits., 1576, 1578. See also *The Countryman's Recreation,* under 1640 below.

1577 HERESBACHIUS, CONRADUS. Fovre Bookes of Husbandry, collected by M. Conradus Heresbachius, Councellour to the high and mightie Prince, the Duke of Cleue, containing the whole Art and Trade of Husbandry, Gardening, Graffing, and Planting, with the Antiquitie, and Commendation thereof. Newely Englished, and encreased by Barnaby Googe. 4to. London.

 Other edits., 1578, 1585, 1601, 1631, and 1658.

MOUNTAINE, DIDYMUS. The Gardeners Labyrinth: Containing a discourse of the Gardeners Life in the yearly trauels to be bestovved on his plot of earth, for the vse of a Garden: with instructions for the choise of Seedes, apte times for sowing, setting, planting, & watering, and the vessels and instruments seruing to that vse and purpose: Wherein are set forth diuers Herbes, Knottes and Mazes, cunningly handled for the beautifying of Gardens. Also the Physicke benefit of eche Herbe, Plant and Floure, . . . Gathered ovt of the best approved writers of Gardening, Husbandrie, and Physicke. 4to. London.

Other edits., 1586, 1594, 1608, 1652.

1592   A Short instruction very profitable and necessary, for al those that delight in gardening, to know the time and season when it is good to sow and replant all manner of Seedes. Whereunto is annexed diuers plots both for planting and grafting, for the better ease of Gardener. Translated out of French into English. 4to. London.

This little book contains 16 woodcuts in 4 gatherings, which are very similar to those in Thomas Hill's works. Some appear to be from the same blocks.—Amherst.

1594   PLATT, SIR HUGH. The Jewell House of Art and Nature. Conteining diuers rare and profitable Inuentions, together with sundry new experiments in the Art of Husbandry, Distillation, and Moulding. . . . 4to. London.

Sir Hugh Plat was supposed to be the most learned man of his time, in soils and manures. See Plat under 1608 below.

1597   The Orchard, and the Garden: containing certaine necessarie, secret, and ordinarie knowledges in Grafting and Gardening. Wherein are described sundry waies to graffe, and diuers proper new plots for the Garden. Gathered from the Dutch and French. Also to know the time and season, when it is good to sow and replant all manner of Seedes. London.

2nd edit., London, 1602.

1600   ESTIENNE, CHARLES, and JOHN LIEBAULT. Maison Rustique, or The Covntrie Farme. Compiled in the French tongue by Charles Steuens and Iohn Liebault Doctors of Physicke. And translated into English by Richard Svrflet Practititioner in Physicke. . . . Fol. London.

Other edits., 1606, 1616.
A scarce Elizabethan farming book, which contains some amazing remedies for diseases. —Bookseller's Note. Liebault was son-in-law of Estienne, the distinguished French physician. The above book was the most important of the early French treatises on agriculture and gardening; that it was popular is evidenced by the fact that it went through over 30 editions. For a description of its contents, see Rohde, *Old English Gardening Books*, 50 ff.

1603   GARDINER, RICHARD. Profitable Instrvctions for the Manvring, Sowing and Planting of Kitchin Gardens. Very profitable for the common wealth and greatly for the helpe and comfort of poore people. Gathered by Richard Gardiner of Shrewsberie. 4to. London.

This is said to be the 2nd edit. The 1st, according to Lowndes, appeared in 1599, but no copy of it has been traced.—Amherst.
This linen draper of Shrewsbury has the distinction of having written the only book devoted entirely to kitchen gardening in which the potato is not even mentioned. Although this plant aroused much interest when first introduced, and figured largely in Gerard's and Parkinson's Herbals, potatoes were not grown to any extent, and the working people did

not eat them for another two hundred years. He treats of cabbages, parsnips, turnips, lettuces, beans, onions, cucumbers, artichokes, and leeks. He was an enthusiast on the subject of carrots.—Rohde, 28 ff.

1604 N., F. The Frviterer's Secrets, containing Directions, of the due Time and Manners of gathering all Kinds of Fruit. 4to. London.

> Reprinted, with another title, London, 1608 and 1609. See below.

> 1609 The Husbandman's fruitfull Orchard. Shewing Divers rare new Secrets for the true Ordering of all Sortes of Fruite in their due Seasons. Also how your encrease and profite maie bee much more then heertofore, and yet your Charge and Labour the same. With the manner of gathering all kindes of fruite as wel stone-fruit as other, and how they are to be ordered in packing, carrying and conueying them by land or by water, then in separating or culling them into diuers sortes and lastlie in reseruing or laying them vp as may be for their best lasting and continuance. Neuer before published. 4to. London.
> Another edition of this, 4to, London, 1609.

1607 GEFFE, NICHOLAS (Translator). The perfect Use of Silk-Wormes, and their Benefit. With the exact Planting, and artificiall Handling of Mulberrie Trees whereby to nourish them, and the figures to know how to feed the Wormes, and to winde off the Silk . . . Done out of the French Originall of D'Oliuier de Serres Lord of Pradel into English, by Nicholas Geffe Esquire. With an Annexed Discourse of his owne, of the Meanes and Sufficiencie of England for to haue Aubundance of fine Silke by feeding of Silk-Wormes within the same. . . . 4to. London.

> For the interest in breeding silk worms in England and Virginia, see John Bonoeil under 1622, NORTH AMERICA, vol. II of this work.

1608 PLATT, SIR HUGH. Floraes Paradise, Beautified and adorned with sundry sorts of delicate fruites and flovvers, By the industrious Labour of H. P. Knight: With an offer of an English Antitdote, (beeing a present easie, and pleasing remedy in violent Feavers, and intermitting Agues) as also of some other rare inuentions, fitting the Times. Hijs Fruere, & expecta meliora. 8vo. London.

> Reissued as the *Garden of Eden*, 12mo, London, 1653; 4th edit., 12mo, London, 1654; again, 1659, 1660; 6th edit., 8vo, 1675. See below.
> Plat was probably the best known of early gardening authorities. He conducted horticultural and agricultural experiments in his gardens in St. Martin's Lane, and maintained correspondence on these subjects with experts all over the country. On soils and manures he was regarded highly, and for his inventions of mechanical sorts he was knighted by James I. See Rohde, 31 ff.

> 1653 PLAT, SIR HUGH. The Garden of Eden, or, An Accurate Description of all Flowers and Fruits now growing in England, with particular Rules how to advance their Nature and Growth, as well in Seeds and Herbs, as the secret ordering of Trees and Plants . . . As now published by the Authors own Manuscript. 12mo. London.
> The above work was rearranged from *Floraes Paradise* by Charles Bellingham, who claimed relationship with Plat.

> 1675 ————. The Garden of Eden . . . Sixth edition (containing the Second Part from his unpublished notes). 8vo. London.

1609 S., W. Instructions for the increasing of Mulberie Trees, and the breeding of Silk-wormes for the making of Silke in this Kingdome. Whereunto is annexed, His Maiesties Letters to the Lords Lieftenants . . . tending to that purpose. 4to. London.

1611 STANDISH, ARTHUR. The Commons' Complaint . . . first the generall Destruction amd Waste of Woods in this Kingdom. Also how to plant wood . . . The second Grievance the dearth of Victualls. Four Remedies, etc. London.

1612 C., R. An Olde Thrift newly revived . . . the Manner of planting, preserving, and husbanding yong Trees. . . . 4to. London.

1613 MARKHAM, GERVASE. The English Husbandman. The first Part: Contayning the Knowledge of the true Nature of euery Soyle within this Kingdome: how to Plow it; and the manner of the Plough, and other Instruments belonging thereto. Together with the Art of Planting, Grafting, and Gardening after our latest and rarest fashion. A worke neuer written before by any Author: and now newly compiled for the benefit of this Kingdome. 4to. London.

> The second book came out in 1614. Both enlarged by the author, in 3 pts., appeared again, 4to, London, 1635. See below.
> Markham was a versatile writer, who had the annoying habit of writing several books on the same subject, giving to each different titles, and reissuing old works with new titles. But all his works are lit up with his enthusiasm for his subject and are deserving of the popularity they won in Stuart days. Vivid pictures are afforded us, in the above work, of country life centered around the comfortable Jacobean house, with its orchards, squares, knots and mazes, fountains, and old fashioned names of flowers. See Rohde, 60 ff., and Blomfield, *The Formal Garden in England.*

> 1614 MARKHAM, GERVASE. The second Booke of the English Husbandman. Conteyning the ordering of the Kitchen Garden. 4to. London.

> 1635 MARKHAM, GERVASE. The English Husbandman, drawne into two Bookes, and each Book into two Parts. The First Part Contayning the knowledge of Husbandly Duties, . . . The Second Part Containing the Art of Planting, Grafting, and Gardening, the use of the Vines, the Hop garden and the Preservation of all sorts of Fruits, the Draught of all sorts of Knots, Mazes, and other Ornaments. Newly Reviewed, Corrected and Inlarged by the first Author, G. M. 4to. London.

STANDISH, ARTHUR. New Directions . . . for the planting of Timber and Firewood: with a neare Estimation what millions of Acres the Kingdome doth containe, what Acres is waste Grounds . . . London.

1617 LAWSON, WILLIAM. The Covntrie Hovswifes Garden. Containing Rules for Hearbes of common vse. Together With the Husbandry of Bees, Published with secrets, very necessary for euery Housewife. Together with diuers new knots for Gardens. . . . London.

> Other edits., 1623, 1626; also issued with separate title page but not separate pagination, with *A New Orchard and Garden,* 1631, 1638, 1648, 1656, 1660, 1668, 1683.
> The works of this enthusiast were often published together with those of his friend Markham. Lawson was a North Countryman, who wrote from his own experience with orchards and fruit trees. Not much is known of his life.

1618 ————. A New Orchard & Garden or The best way for planting, grafting, and to make any ground good, for a rich Orchard: Particularly in the North parts of England: generally for the whole Kingdome, as in Nature, reason, scituation and all probability, may and doth appeare. With the Country Housewifes Garden for hearbes of common vse. . . . 4to. London.

> Other edits: 2nd, 1623; 3rd, corrected and much enlarged, 4to, 1626; 1631, 1638, 1648, etc. Reprinted, London, 1927.

1625 BACON, FRANCIS (Viscount St. Albans). The Essayes or Covnsels, Civill and Morall, of Francis Lord Verulam Viscount St. Albans. New enlarged. 4to. London.

> This edition contains the essay "Of Gardens," which stands as a landmark in the history of the ornamental garden.

1626 SPEED, ADAM. Adam out of Eden. 8vo. London.

> Watt and Allibone give this date to the first edition, and treat the volume of 1659 as a reprint.—Amherst. See below.

> 1659 SPEED, ADAM. Adam out of Eden, or an abstract of divers excellent Experiments touching the advancement of Husbandry. 8vo. London.

1629 PARKINSON, JOHN. Paradisi in Sole Paradisus Terrestris. A Garden of all Sorts of Pleasant Flowers Which Our English Ayre will Permitt to be noursed up: with A Kitchen garden of all manner of herbes, rootes, & fruites, for meate or sause used with us, and An Orchard of all sorte of fruit bearing Trees and shrubbes fit for our Land together With the right orderinge, planting & preseruing of them and their uses & vertues. Collected by Iohn Parkinson Apothecary of London. Woodcut portrait aet. 62, and numerous full-page woodcuts of flowers, fruits, and vegetables. Fol. London.

> 2nd edit., much corrected and enlarged, fol., London, 1656; facsimile reprint of the 1629 edit., London, 1904.
> Nearly a thousand plants are described under the three heads enumerated in the title, and of these 780 are figured on 109 plates, the wood-blocks for which, many of them copied from Clusius and Lobel, were specially cut in England. The title is a pun on the author's surname. The work is dedicated to Queen Henrietta Maria. He was appointed apothecary to King James I, and on the publication of the above work obtained from Charles I the title of "Botanicus Regius Primarius."—*DNB*. The 2nd edit. has a woodcut frontispiece depicting the Garden of Eden.—This has been called the most lovable of garden books, and though he wrote a more learned work, *Theatrum Botanicum*, which remained the most complete treatise on plants until the time of Ray, it is the *Paradisus* that will keep Parkinson's name alive. See Rohde, 66 ff.

1638 MARKHAM, GERVASE. A Way To Get Wealth: Containing Sixe Principall Vocations or Callings, in which every good Husband or House-wife may lawfully imploy themselves. As

> i. The natures, ordering, curing, breeding, choice, use, and feeding of all sort of Cattell and Fowle, fit for the service of Man: As also the riding and dieting of Horses, either for warre or Pleasure.

> ii. The Knowledge, use, and laudable practise of all the recreations meete for a Gentleman.

> iii. The office of a Housewife, in Physicke, Surgery, extractions of Oiles, Banquets, Cookerie, ordering of Feasts, preserving of Wine, Concerves, Secrets, Distillations, Perfumes, ordering of Wooll, Hempe, Flaxe, Dying, use of Dayries, Malting, Brewing, Baking, and the profits of Oates.

> iv. The enrichment of the Weald of Kent.

> v. The husbanding, and enriching of all sorts of barren grounds making them equal with the most fruitfull, with the preservation of Swine, and a computation of Men and Cattels labours, etc.

> vi. The Making of Orchards, Planting and Grafting, the office of Gardening, and the ornaments, with the best husbanding of Bees.

> The first five Bookes gathered by G. M. The last by Master W. L. [William Lawson] for the benefit of Great Britain. The first time corrected and augmented by the Author. 4to. London.

> A compilation of some of Markham's works already issued separately.

1640 —————————. The Countryman's Recreation or the Art of Planting, Graffing, and Gardening, in three Bookes. The first declaring divers wayes of Planting and Graffing, and the best times of the Yeare, with divers Commodities and secrets herein how to Set or Plant with the Roote and without the Roote, how to sow or set Pepins or Curnels. . . . The second treateth of the Hop Garden, with necessary Instructions for the making and the maintenance thereof. . . . Whereunto is added, The Expert Gardener, Containing divers necessary and rare Secrets belonging to that Art . . . with divers new Inventions and Garden Knots, and also present Remedies to destroy Snailes, Canker-Worms, Moles, and all other Vermin which commonly breed in Gardens. 4to. London.

> Reprinted 1653, 1654. *The Expert Gardener* was also published separately in 1654.
> The above is a compilation of the works of Leonard Mascall (1572) and Reynolde Scot (1574). *The Expert Gardener*, with the exception of the title, is identical with *The Orchard and the Garden* (1597).—Rohde, Bibliography.

1645 HARTLIB, SAMUEL. A Discourse of Husbandrie used in Brabant and Flanders. 4to. London.

> 2nd edit., 1650; 3rd, corrected and enlarged, 1654. See Hartlib below under 1651.
> Hartlib was a Pole who settled in London early in the reign of Charles I.

1649 BLITH, WALTER. The English Improver, or, A New Survey of Husbandry. 4to. London.

> 3rd impression, 1652. See below.
> Blith combined writing on agriculture with soldiering under Cromwell as captain in the Parliamentary army.

> 1652 BLITH, WALTER. The English Improver Improved, or, The Survey of Husbandry Surveyed; discovering the Improvableness of all lands; some to be under a Double and Treble, others under a Five or Six Fould and many under a Tenn Fould, yea, some under a Twenty Fould Improvement; all clearly demonstrated from principles of Reason, Ingenuity, and late but most real Experiences and held forth at an inconsiderable Charge to the Profits accruing thereby, under Six Peeces of Improvement. 4to. London.

1651 HARTLIB, SAMUEL. Samuel Hartlib his Legacie; or an Enlargement of the Discourse of Husbandry used in Brabant and Flanders. . . . With Appendix. 4to. London.

> Other edits., 1652, 1655.
> This is a collection of letters on agriculture, probably by Cressy Dymock, Robert Child, Gabriel Plats, and others. They are in favor of increasing the number of nurseries and orchards, and argue that gardening would pay well if properly managed.—Amherst, 180. Other works by Hartlib follow below.

—————————. An Essay for the advancement of Husbandry-Learning; or Propositions for the erecting Colledge of Husbandry. . . . 4to. London.

—————————. The Reformed Husbandman, or a brief treatise of the errors, defects . . . of English Husbandrie. . . . 4to. London.

> This treatise is elsewhere attributed to Adam Speed. See Speed under 1626. It appears in Watts's *Bibliotheca* under both names.—Amherst.

1653 AUSTEN, RALPH. A Treatise of Fruit-Trees Shewing the manner of Graffing, Setting, Pruning, and Ordering of them in all respects: According to divers new and easy Rules of experience, gathered in ye space of twenty years. Whereby the value of Lands may be much improued, in a short time, by small cost and

little labour. Also discovering some dangerous Errors, both in ye Theory and Practise of ye Art of Planting Fruit-trees. With the Alimentall and Physicall vse of fruits. Together with the Spirituall vse of an Orchard: Held forth in divers Similitudes betweene Naturall and Spirituall Fruit-trees: according to Scripture and Experience. 4to. Oxford.

2nd edit., with addition of many new experiments, 4to, Oxford, 1657; another, to which was added, Observations upon Sir Francis Bacon's Natural History, also directions for planting wood, 4to, Oxford, 1665. For the *Observations* see under 1658 below.

This treatise was written to encourage more extensive cultivation than had been so far carried out in England. How great an interest was shown in this branch of husbandry in the seventeenth century can be gathered from the numerous titles listed in this section. Much attention was paid to grafting and to importing of fruit stock from France and the Lowlands, to picking and preserving, and to the improving of cider. By the middle of the century, Herefordshire and Worcestershire were already famous for the quality of their apples and cider. Austen wished to show that with equal care the northern part of England was capable of producing fruit as fine as that grown elsewhere. See Rhode, 76 ff.

BEALE, JOHN. A Treatise on Fruit Trees shewing their manner of Grafting, Pruning, and Ordering, of Cyder and Perry, of Vineyards, in England. 4to. Oxford.

To encourage the cultivation of the grape in England, John Rose, gardener to Charles II, used to advertise vines for sale "at reasonable prices." Beale went considerably farther by offering to give plants of vines to "cottagers," but they generally answered "churlishly that they would not be troubled with grapes"; when, however, he explained that in a few years their grapes would fetch a good price in the market, "they were soon of a more thankful mind."—Quoted from Amherst, 230.

1657 BEALE, JOHN. The Hereford Orchard; a pattern for the whole of England Written in an Epistolary Address to Samuel Hartlib Esq. 12mo. London.

1658 AUSTEN, RALPH. Observations upon some part of Sir Francis Bacon's Naturall History as it concernes Fruit-trees, Fruits, and Flowers: especially the Fifth, Sixth, and Seaventh Centuries. Improving the experiments mentioned, to the best Advantage. 4to. Oxford.

The 1st edition of the *Observations,* which was annexed to the 1665 edition of his *Treatise.* See Austen under 1653 above.

EVELYN, JOHN. The French Gardener; Instructing How to cultivate all Sorts of Fruit-Trees & Herbs for the Garden: Together with directions to dry and conserve them in their Natural: Six times printed in France and once in Holland. An Accomplished Piece. First Written by R. D. C. D. W. B. D. N. And now transplanted into English by Philocepos (i.e., John Evelyn). Illustrated with Sculptures. 8vo. London.

Other edits., 1669, 1672, 1675, 1695.

1660 SHARROCK, ROBERT. The History of the Propagation and Improvement of Vegetables, by the Concurrence of Art and Nature. 8vo. Oxford.

2nd edit., much enlarged, 8vo, Oxford, 1672; 3rd, 8vo, London, 1694.

1661 STEVENSON, M. The Twelve Moneths or, A pleasant and profitable discourse of every action, whether of Labour or Recreation, proper to each particular Moneth, branched into Directions relating to Husbandry, as Plowing, Sowing, Gardening, Planting, Transplanting, Plashing of Fences, felling of Timber, ordering of Cattle and Bees, and of Malt, As Also Of Recreation, as Hunting, Hawking, Fishing, Fowling, Coursing, Cock fighting. To which likewise is

added a necessary advice touching Physick, when it may, and when not be taken. Lastly, Every Moneth is shut up with an Epigrame. With the Fairs of every Month. London.

1664   BLAKE, STEPHEN. The Compleat Gardeners Practice, directing The Exact Way of Gardening, In three Parts. The Garden of Pleasure, the Physical Garden, the Kitchen Garden. How they are to be ordered for their best Situation and Improvement, with variety of Artificial Knots for the Beautifying of a Garden (all engraven in Copper) the choisest way for the Raising, Governing and Maintaining of all Plants cultivated in Gardens now in England. Being a plain Discourse how Herbs, Flowers and Trees according to Art and Nature may be propagated by Sowing, Setting, Planting, Replanting, Pruning; also Experience of Alteration of Sent, Colour and Taste, clearly reconciling as it treateth of each Herb and Flower in particular. . . .
>   Search the World, and there's not to be found
>   A Book so good as this for Garden ground.
4to. London.

EVELYN, JOHN. Kalendarium Hortense: or the Gard'ners Almanac, Directing What is to do Monethly throughout the Year and What Fruits and Flowers are in Prime. London.

According to Amherst's bibliography, the first edition of this work had been issued as part of the *Sylva* (see below), fol., 1664. Other edits., 1666, 1669, 1671, 1683, 1691, 1706.

——————. Sylva, or, A Discourse of Forest Trees . . . To which is annexed Pomona, or an Appendix concerning Fruit-Trees. . . . Fol. London.

4th edit., with additions, fol., London, 1706; later edits., 2 vols., 4to., London, 1776, and York, 1786. See below.
This work was written for the Royal Society, of which Evelyn was one of the founders, as an aid in planting trees in parks, woods, and forests; and shows intimate knowledge of the suitableness of various trees for specific purposes. In a later edition of the book, he mentions the depredations committed in his gardens at Say Court by the Muscovite Czar Peter the Great, who resided there in 1698. One surmises from his account that Peter must have romped over the place like a veritable Russian bear. At any rate, the damage done was estimated by Sir Christopher Wren, the King's Surveyor, to be 150 pounds; and it was recommended in the report to the Lords of the Treasury that Evelyn be reimbursed in this amount. See Amherst, 191.

1706   EVELYN, JOHN. Sylva, or, A Discourse of Forest Trees. With Terra, Pomona, Acataria [A Discourse of Sallets, 1699], and Kalendarium Hortense. Portrait by Nanteuil. Fol. London.

1786   ——————. Sylva, or, A Discourse of Forest-Trees, and the Propagation of Timber in his Majesty's Dominions. Notes by A. Hunter. Portrait and numerous plates. 2 vols. 4to. York.

FORSTER, JOHN. England's Happiness Increased, or, A Sure and easie Remedy against all succeeding Dear Years. By a Plantation of the roots called Potatoes, whereof (with the Addition of Wheat Flower) excellent good and wholesome Bread may be made, every year, eight or nine months together . . . Also By the Planting of these Roots, Ten Thousand Men in England and Wales, who know not how to Live, or what to do to get a Maintenance for their Families, may of One Acre of Ground, make Thirty Pounds per Annum. Published for the Good of the poorer Sort. 4to. London.

1665 HUGHES, WILLIAM. The Compleat Vineyard: or A most excellent Way for the Planting of Vines: Not onely according to the German and French way, but also long experimented in England. Wherein are set forth the whole circumstances necessary for the Planting a Vineyard, (viz.) The best Selection of the Soil; the scituation thereof; the best way for the Planting of your young Plants; the best time and manner of Proining, both the Stocks and Roots, the turning and translation of the ground, &c. With other things necessary to the Plant; and the fashion of your Wine-Presses; with the manner of Bruising and Pressing; and also how to advance our English Wines; never before Printed. 4to. London.

2nd edit., London, 1670.

1666 ROSE, JOHN. The English Vineyard Vindicated. . . . 8vo. London.

With a preface by Philocepos, i.e., John Evelyn. It was reissued in a third edition in 1675, as an appendix to Evelyn's *French Gardener.*—Amherst.

1669 WORLIDGE, JOHN. Systema Agriculturae, The Mystery of Husbandry Discovered; Wherein is Treated of the Several new and most advantageous Ways Of Tilling, Planting, Sowing, Manuring, Ordering, Improving All sorts of Gardens, Orchards, Meadow, Pastures, Corn-lands, Woods & Coppices. And of all Sorts of Fruits, Corn, Grain, Pulse, New Hays, Cattel, Fowl, Beasts, Bees, Silkworms, &c. With an Account of the several Instruments and Engines useful in this Profession. To which is added Kalendarium Rusticum; or, The Husbandmens Monethly Directions, Also The Prognostics of Death, Scarcity, Plenty, Sickness, Heat, Cold, Frost, Snow, Windes, Rain, Hail, Thunder, &c. And Dictionarium Rusticum: Or, The Interpretation of Rustick Terms. Published for the Common Good. The whole Work being of great Use and Advantage to all that delight in that most noble Practice. Fol. London.

Other edits., 1675, 1677, 1681, 1687.

1670 MEAGER, LEONARD. The English Gardener: or, a Sure Guide to young Planters and Gardeners. In three Parts. The First, Shewing the way and order of Planting and raising all sorts of Stocks, Fruit-trees and Shrubs, with the divers ways and manners of Ingrafting and Inoculating them in their several Seasons, Ordering, and Preservation. The Second, How to order the Kitchin-Garden, for all sorts of Herbs, Roots, and Sallads. The Third, The ordering of the Garden of Pleasure, with variety of Knots, and Wilderness-work after the best fashion, all Cut in Copper Plates; also the choicest and most approved ways for the raising all sorts of Flowers and their Seasons, with directions concerning Arbors, and Hedges in Gardens, . . . 24 copperplates of grafting implements, garden plans and mazes. 4to. London.

Numerous later edits.; 11th, with supplements, 4to, London, 1710; 12th, 1721.
This was one of the most popular early English books on gardening, which enjoyed an unbroken favor of 40 years. Meager was a working gardener employed by Philip Holmlan, of Warkworth, and although hampered by want of learning, managed to get published his experiments in the art of gardening.—Bookseller's Note. This author was much more old-fashioned than his contemporaries. His book gives a great deal of practical information about fruit and kitchen gardening.—Amherst, 227.

MOLLET, ANDREW. The Garden of Pleasure, Containing several Draughts of Gardens Both in Embroyder'd Ground-Works, Knotworks of Grass, as likewise in

Wildernesses, and others. With their Cuts in Copper. 40 plates of garden plans and ornamental designs (mostly double or folding) by J. V. (Jan van de?) Velde and W. Hardman. Fol. London.

> According to Rohde, only one copy is known. André Mollet was the son of Claude Mollet, gardener to Henry IV and Louis XIII, who introduced the Italian style of garden planning into France, and designed the gardens of the Tuilleries, Fontainebleau, and Saint-Germain. André Mollet became gardener to Christina, Queen of Sweden, to whom he dedicated his *Jardin de Plaisir,* published at Stockholm in 1651. He afterwards removed to London, and was appointed gardener to Charles II, to whom he dedicated the above work.—Bookseller's Note.

SMITH, CAPTAIN JOHN. England's Improvement Reviv'd: Digested into Six Books. In a Treatise of all manner of Husbandry and Trade by Land and Sea . . . discovering the ways of Improving Waste and Barren Grounds, Planting, Timber-trees, Ordering Cattel, with Observations about Sheep, Cows, Fowles, Bees, . . . 4to. London.

> 2nd edit., London, 1673.
> This "very practical" treatise is prefaced by a eulogistic notice from John Evelyn. It includes the author's former work on the Islands of Orkney and Shetland (see his *Trade and Fishing of Great Britain,* under 1662, ANCIENT AND PRESENT STATE).

1671 HUGHES, WILLIAM. The Flower-Garden. Shewing How all Flowers are to be ordered, the time of Flowering, the Taking up of the Plants, and the increasing of them by Layers of Sets, Slips, Cuttings, Seeds, etc. with other necessary Observations. To which may be added, The Compleat Vineyard, shewing how to plant and order Vines, by the same Author. 12mo. London.

1675 COTTON, CHARLES. The Planter's Manual: Being Instructions for the Raising, Planting, and Cultivating all sorts of Fruit-trees, whether Stone-fruits or Pepin-Fruits, with their Natures and Seasons. Very useful for such as are Curious in Planting and Grafting. 8vo. London.

> Cotton also published a "second part" of his friend Walton's *The Complete Angler.* He was the author of the poem *The Wonders of the Peak* (see under 1681, DESCRIPTIONS).

1676 AUSTEN, RALPH. A Dialogue, or, Familiar Discourse, and Conference betweene the Husbandman, and Fruit-Trees, in his Nurseries, Orchards, and Gardens. Wherein are discovered many usefull, and profitable Observations, and Experiments in Nature, in the Ordering of Fruit-Trees, for temporall profit; Improving also the same to higher ends and uses, in Spirituall Things, for the Good, and profit of all; both in the Church, and of the World . . . followed by quotations from the Bible. Oxford.

> This work differs from other dialogue treatises in that it is the only one in which the trees take part in the conversation. It begins with the query whether the trees speak English, Latin, Greek, or Hebrew, to which they answer that they speak all languages. The husbandman then asks them, since he is English, to speak in that language. From the specimens given in Rohde, it appears to be a very attractive volume. See Rohde, 82 ff.

COOK, MOSES. The manner of raising, ordering, and improving Forrest- [and Fruit-] trees. . . . 4to. London.

1677 BEALE, JOHN. Nurseries, Orchards, Profitable Gardens, and Vineyards Encouraged, The present Obstructions removed, and probable Expedients for the better Progress proposed; For the general benefit of his Majesties Dominions, and

more particularly of Cambridge, and the Champain-Countries, and Northern parts of England. In several Letters out of the Country, Directed to Henry Oldenburg, Esq., Secretary to the Royal Society. The first letter from Anthony Lawrence; All the rest from John Beale, D.D., and Fellow of the Royal Society. 4to. London.

WORLIDGE, JOHN. Systema Horticulturae: or, the Art of Gardening. In Three Books. The I. Treateth of the Excellency, Situation, Soil, Form, Walks, Arbours, Springs, Fountains, Water-works, Grottos, Statues, and other Magnificent Ornaments of Gardens, . . . with many necessary Rules, Precepts, and Directions, . . . The II Treateth of all sorts of Trees planted for Ornament or Shade, Winter Greens, Flower Trees, and Flowers that are usually propagated or preserv'd in the Gardens of the best Florists and the best ways and methods of Raising, Planting, and Improving them. The III Treateth of the Kitchin Garden, and of the great variety of Plants propagated for food & for any Culinary uses: Together with many general and particular Rules, Precepts, Observations, and Instructions for the making of Hot Beds, altering and enriching any sort of Garden Ground, watering, cleansing, and adapting all sorts of Earth to the various Plants that are usually planted therein. . . . 8vo. London.
2nd edit., 1682.

1679 STRANGEHOPES, SAMUEL. The Countrey-man's Guide to Good Husbandry. (The third part of A Book of Knowledge. In Three Parts. The First, Containing a brief Introduction to Astrology . . . The Second, A Treatise of Physick, the Anatomy of Man's Body, the Diseases incident to the Body of Man . . . The Third, The Countrey-man's Guide.) 8vo. London.

This little book contains a particularly good series of the crude woodcuts which must have been the delight of country firesides on winter evenings.—Bookseller's Note.

1681 LANGFORD, T. Plain and Full Instructions To raise all sorts of Fruit-Trees That prosper in England; In that Method and Order, that everything must be done in, to give all the advantage may be, to every Tree, as it is rising from its Seed, till it comes to it.· full Growth. Together with all necessary directions about those several ways of making Plantations, either of Wall-Fruit, or Dwarf-trees in Gardens, or large Standard-trees in Orchards or Fields. . . . 8vo. London.

1682 GILBERT, SAMUEL. The Florist's Vade Mecum. Being a Choice Collection of whatever is worthy Notice hath been Extant, for the Propagation, Raising, Planting, Increasing and Preserving the Rarest Flowers and Plants, that our Climate and skill (in Mixing, Making, and Meliorating, apted Soils to each Species) will perswade to live with us. With Several New Experiments for Raising New Varieties, for their most advantageous Management. In a more particular Method than ever yet published. To which is added, The Gardeners Almanack Remembring and Directing him what to do each Month throughout the Year, in both Orchard and Flower-Garden. 12mo. London.

Other edits., London, 1683, 1690, 1693, and, enlarged, 1702.
This work is characterized by Rohde, 84 ff., as one of the most charming books of the late 17th century on gardening. The author, who was a physician and a preacher, was a lover of irises and more particularly of auriculas, of which he states that he has the best

collection in the whole of England. In those days auricula enthusiasts paid as much as twenty pounds for a root. The astrological calendar Gilbert offers the reader is probably the latest to appear in a gardening book.

HOUGHTON, JOHN. A Collection of Letters for the Improvement of Husbandry and Trade. 4to. London.

These were issued in numbers from 1681 to 1682.—Amherst.

1683   REID, JOHN. The Scots Gard'ner in two parts, The First of Contriving and Planting Gardens, Orchards, Avenues, Groves: With new and profitable wayes of Levelling; and how to Measure and Divide Land. The Second of the Propagation & Improvement of Forrest and Fruit-Trees, Kitchen-Hearbes, Roots and Fruits: With some Physick Hearbs, Shrubs and Flowers. Appendix shewing how to use the Fruits of the Garden: Whereunto is annexed, The Gard'ners Kalendar. Published for the Climate of Scotland. 4to. Edinburgh.

Other edits., 1721, 1766.
This is the first book on Scotch gardening.—Rohde.

1684   HAINES, RICHARD. Aphorisms upon the new way of improving Cyder, or making Cyder-Royal . . . raising and planting of Apple-trees, . . . Fol. London.

1685   The Art of Pruning Fruit-Trees with an Explanation of some Words which Gardiners make use of in speaking of Trees. And a Tract of the Use of the Fruits of Trees, for preserving us in Health, or in Curing us when we are Sick. Translated from the French Original, set forth the last year by a Physician of Rochelle. 8vo. London.

BLAGRAVE, JOSEPH. The Epitomie of the Art of Husbandry. Comprizing all Necessary Directions for the Improvement of it, viz., Plowing, Sowing, Grafting, Ordering of Flowers, Herbs; Directions for the Use of the Angle; Ordering of Bees: Together with the Gentlemans Heroick Exercise; Discoursing of Horses, their Nature and Use, with their Diseases and Remedies: Of Oxen, Cows, Calves, Sheep, Hogs, with the Manner of Ordering of them, their Diseases and Remedies. Of the Nature of Marle, the best Way of Planting Clover Grass, Hops, Saffron, Liquorice, Hemp, &c. To which is Annexed by way of Appendix, a New Method of Planting Fruit-trees, and Improving of an Orchard. With Directions for Taking, Ordering, Teaching and Curing of Singing-Birds, and other useful Additions. 2 vols. 8vo. London.

[ELLIS, WILLIAM.] The Complete Planter & Ciderist or choice Collections and Observations for the propagating all manner of Fruit-Trees . . . By a Lover of Planting. 8vo. London.

The author's name does not appear in the book.—Amherst, 350.

1693   DE LA QUINTINYE. The Compleat Gard'ner; or Directions for Cultivating and Right Ordering of Fruit-Gardens and Kitchen-Gardens; with Divers Reflections on several Parts of Husbandry. In Six Books. By the famous Monsr. De La Quintinye, Chief director of all the Gardens of the French-King. To which is added His Treatise of Orange-Trees, with the Raising of Melons,

omitted in the French Editions. Made English by John Evelyn, Esquire, Illustrated with Copper Plates. 2 vols. Fol. London.

> Other edits., 1699, 1701, 1704, 1710.
> It was fitting that this magnificent work, perhaps the most beautiful book about kitchen gardening in any language, and one that was the standard authority in England on the subject, should have been translated by the most famous writer on gardens in England. It was probably to be found in every English country house. The translation was done to a faultless turn, and the personality and delightful precision of the original author was exquisitely preserved. De La Quintinye was for forty years in the service of Louis XIV, who created for him the important post of "Director General of the Fruit and Kitchen Gardens of all the Royal Houses." He twice visited England and twice resisted the attempts of Charles II to lure him into his own service. He was held in highest esteem by English gardeners, with most of whom he maintained correspondence.—Summarized from Rohde's description of the work, 87 ff.

1697 DONALDSON, JAMES. Husbandry Anatomized, or, Enquiry into the present manner of Tilling and Manuring the Ground in Scotland. Edinburgh.

MEAGER, LEONARD. The Mystery of Husbandry or Arable, Pasture, and Wood-Land Improved (from his own experience). To which is added The Countryman's Almanack. 12mo. London.

——————. The New Art of Gardening; with the Gardener's Almanack. 12mo. London.

1700 NOURSE, TIMOTHY. Campania Felix, or Discourses of the benefits and improvements of Husbandry. 8vo. London.

1703 LE BLOND, A. The Theory and Practice of Gardening, translated from the French by John James. 8vo. London.

> Other edits., London, 1712, 1728.

VAN OOSTEN, HENRY. The Dutch Gardener: or, the Compleat Florist. Containing, The most successful Method of Cultivating all sorts of Flowers: the Planting, Dressing, and Pruning of all Manner of Fruit Trees. Together with A particular Account of the nursing of Lemon and Orange Trees in Northern Climates. Written in Dutch by Henry Van Oosten, The Leyden Gardener. And made English. 8vo. London.

> 2nd edit., London, 1711.
> It is of interest to note that among the some 200 English translations from the Italian between 1547 and 1600, none deals with gardening. It was rather the Dutch and French manuals of gardening that had most to offer to the average English gentleman, not only in Tudor times but also throughout the seventeenth century.

1704 Dictionarium Rusticum et Urbanicum. A Dictionary of all sorts of County Affairs, trading, &c. 8vo. London.

1705 TEMPLE, SIR WILLIAM. Upon the Garden of Epicurus or of Gardening in the year 1685. London.

> This treatise on gardening, relating especially to his place at Sheen, where Temple found much comfort in ordering his gardens, was written in 1685, and published in the *Miscellaneous Works of Temple*, 1705 and 1720. Amherst suggests that it may have appeared in the edition of 1689. The tendency towards extravagantly large gardens in the formal style, due in part to the influence of Le Notre, whose hand was much in evidence at Versailles, was one that Temple deplored. His own grounds at Sheen were comparatively small but beautifully ordered. Those which he laid out later at the new Moor Park were fashioned in the Dutch style.

1706   D'AUXERRE, FRANCIS GENTIL-LOUIS LIGER. Le Jardinier Solitaire, The Solitary
         or Carthusian Gard'ner, being Dialogues Between a Gentleman and a Gardner.
         Containing The Method to make and Cultivate all Sorts of Gardens; with many
         New Experiments therein; and Reflections on the Culture of Trees. Written in
         French by Francis Gentil, Lay-Brother of the Order of the Carthusians, and
         above Thirty Years Gard'ner to the Charter-House at Paris. In Two Parts.
         Also The Compleat Florist: Or, The Universal Culture of Flowers, Trees and
         Shrubs; Proper to Imbellish Gardens; With the way of Raising all Sorts of
         Parterres, Greens, Knots, Porticoes, Columns and other Ornaments. The whole
         illustrated with many Cuts, and with the Fable and Moral of each Plant. . . .
         In Three Parts. Newly done into English. London.

> The above work was issued the same year with the title *The Retired Gard'ner. Being
> a Translation of Le Jardinier Solitaire,* etc. By George London and Henry Wise. London.—
> Rohde, 139.

1707   EVELYN, CHARLES. Ladies' Recreation; or the Pleasure and Profit of Gardening
         Improved. 8vo. London.

> Several later editions, with slightly varying titles. That of 1718 is called *Lady's Recrea-
> tion or the Art of Gardening farther Improved.*

         FLEETWOOD, WILLIAM (Bishop of St. Asaph and Ely). Curiosities of Nature and
         Art in Husbandry. 8vo. London.

> This celebrated divine, a favorite of Queen Anne, despite his Whiggism, was also skilled
> in antiquities.

         MORTIMER, JOHN. The Whole Art of Husbandry, or, the Way of Managing and
         Improving of Land; to which is added, The Countryman's Kalendar, what he
         is to do every Month in the Year. 8vo. London.

> Another edit., with Part II added, 8vo, London, 1712; in 2 vols., 8vo, Dublin, 1721;
> 6th edit., revised by his grandson, T. Mortimer, 1716-21 and 1761.

1712   ADDISON, JOSEPH. An Essay on the Pleasures of the Garden (in the *Spectator,*
         no. 477). London.

         JAMES, JOHN. Theory and Practice of Gardening, wherein is fully handled all that
         relates to Fine Gardens, commonly called Pleasure Gardens, containing Plans
         and general Dispositions of Gardens, new Designs of Parterres, Groves, Maizes,
         Arbor Work, etc., etc., with the manner of Laying out the Ground, the Method
         of Planting, and Raising all Plants, done from the French Original, printed at
         Paris, 1709. Numerous folding plates. 4to. London.

> Before long the formal garden of squares, knots, mazes, parterres, etc., was to give way
> to the so-called "natural garden," under the changes wrought by Kent and Bridgeman,
> as well as by the attacks of Addison and Pope.

1713   POPE, ALEXANDER. Essay on Verdant Sculpture (in the *Guardian,* no. 173). Lon-
         don.

> This essay contains Pope's famous skit on topiary work in gardens, which is always
> quoted in all works dealing with this subject.

1714   LAWRENCE, JOHN. The Clergyman's Recreation, shewing the Pleasure and Profit
         of the Art of Gardening. 8vo. London.

Other edits., 1715, 1716; 5th, 1717. This work appeared in 1718 bound up with *The Gentleman's Recreation* (1716) and *The Lady's Recreation* (1718), under the title of *Gardening Improved*.

1715 SWITZER, STEPHEN. The Nobleman, Gentleman and Gardener's Recreation. . . . 8vo. London.

> Republished enlarged as *Ichnographia Rustica,* 3 vols., 8vo., London, 1718; this last had a second edition, 1741. See below.
> Switzer explains the second title to mean "the general Designing and Distributing of County Seats into garden woods, Parks, Paddocks, etc.: which I call forest, or in more easie stile Rural gardening." He goes on to speak of "little walks and purling streams," "level easy walk of gravel or sand shaded over with Trees and running thro' a corn field or Pasture ground," etc. With him the garden was no longer an enclosure but was beginning to admit the park and the countryside. This definitely marks the beginning of the end of the formal garden. Switzer was a pupil of London and Wise, and professed himself to be an admirer of Pope's ideas on gardens. See Amherst, 245. Switzer was one of the best-educated writers on gardening and agriculture of his age. In his monthly periodical, *The Practical Husbandman and Planter,* he warmly defended Vergil's Georgics as an exposition of practical agriculture.—*DNB.*

> 1718 SWITZER, STEPHEN. Ichnographia Rustica: or, The Nobleman, Gentleman and Gardener's Recreation, containing Directions for the general Distribution of a Country Seat into Rural and Extensive Gardens, Parks, Paddocks, etc., and a General System of Agriculture. Numerous folding and other copperplate engravings. 3 vols. 8vo. London.

1716 STEVENSON, REV. HENRY. The Young Gardener's Director. 12mo. London.

————————. The Gentleman Farmer Instructed. 12mo. London.
> 6th edit., London, 1769.

1717 BRADLEY, RICHARD. New Improvements of Planting and Gardening, both Philosophical and Practical. Explaining the Motion of the Sap and Generation of Plants; with other Discoveries never before made Publick, for the Improvement of Forrest-Trees, Flower-Gardens, or Parterres; with a New Invention whereby more Designs of Garden Plotts may be made in an hour, than can be found in all the Books now extant. Likewise several rare Secrets for the Improvement of Fruit-Trees, Kitchen Gardens and Green-House Plants. Copperplates. 3 pts. in 1 vol. 8vo. London.
> 4th edit., with additions, 8vo, London, 1724; 6th, 1731.

CARPENTER, JOSEPH. The Retir'd Gardener, in Six Parts, the two first being Dialogues between a Gentleman and a Gardener; the last four Parts treat of the Manner of Planting and Cultivating most kinds of Flowers, Plants, Shrubs, etc. 8vo. London.

COLLINS, SAMUEL. Paradise Retrieved, or the Method of managing and improving Fruit Trees, with a Treatise on Melons and Cucumbers. 12 plates. 8vo. London.

JACOB, GILES. The Country Gentleman's Vade-Mecum. 12mo. London.

1718 BRADLEY, RICHARD. The Country Gentleman Farmer's Monthly Director. 3rd edit., with large additions. 8vo. London.

The 1st edition I have not noticed. Bradley, along with Miller, Fairchild, and Lawrence, was one of the most famous practical gardeners of this period. Though he was professor of botany at Cambridge from 1724 on, he was said to be ignorant of Greek and Latin. Nevertheless he was a prolific writer on natural history, gardening, and botany. He was much interested in the movement of sap, which he likened to the circulation of fluids in animal bodies, and in fertilization. The research of the scientists of the day was much assisted by the experiments of these practical gardeners.

1722 FAIRCHILD, THOMAS. The City Gardener. . . . 8vo. London.

Fairchild carried on many experiments in fertilization in his garden at Hoxton. He is mentioned by Bradley as one of the most skilful gardeners of his acquaintance. In the above work he lists various evergreens, trees, and flowers that both will and do thrive in London, despite the "smoke of the sea-coal." His name has been perpetuated in that part of London in which he lived by the "Fairchild Lecture," which, according to his will, is delivered annually in St. Leonard's, Shoreditch. He was a leading member of the Society of Gardeners. See Amherst, 252, 254.

1724 B(EALE), J(OHN). Herefordshire Orchards, a Pattern for all England. 8vo. London.

COOK, N. (Gardener to the Earl of Essex). The Manner of Raising, Ordering, and Improving Forest-Trees, with Directions how to Plant, Make, and Keep Woods, Walks, Avenues, Lawns, Hedges, etc. 4 plates. 8vo. London.

MacINTOSH, WILLIAM. A Treatise concerning the Manner of Fallowing the Ground, Raising of Grass Seeds, and Training of Lint and Hemp, for the Improvement of the Linnen-Manufactories in Scotland. 7 plates of looms. 8vo. Edinburgh.

MILLER, PHILIP. The Gardener's and Florist's Dictionary. London.

Other edits., 2 vols., 8vo, London, 1735; 3 vols., 1754; 11th edit., "adapted to the New Style," with a list of medicinal plants, 1757. This may be the same work as *The Gardener's Dictionary*, first published in 1731, and frequently republished and translated into French, German, and Dutch. See below under 1731.
Miller was the best-known member of the Society of Gardeners. His reputation as a gardener was sufficiently advanced to procure for him a recommendation from Sir Hans Sloane as keeper of the Chelsea Botanical Gardens.

1726 BRADLEY, RICHARD. A General Treatise of Husbandry and Gardening. Formerly published monthly, now methodized and digested. 2 vols. 8vo. London.

LAWRENCE, JOHN. A New System of Agriculture, being a Complete Body of Husbandry and Gardening in all parts of them. 3 plates. Fol. London.

Lawrence was an early advocate of enclosures.

1727 HOUGHTON, JOHN. Husbandry and Trade Improved: Being a Collection of Valuable Materials relating to Corn, Cattle, Coals, Hops, Wool, etc., Several sorts of Earth, Manures, etc. the Malting and Brewing Trades, etc. by J. Houghton; corrected and revised by R. Bradley. 4 vols. 8vo. London.

The author is said by *DNB* to have been the first writer to notice the potato as an agricultural vegetable.

J., S. The Vineyard; a Treatise shewing, I. The Nature and Method of Planting, Manuring, Cultivating, and Dressing of Vines in Foreign Parts. II. Proper Directions for Drawing, Pressing, Making, Keeping, Fining, and Curing all

Defects in the Wine. III. An Easy and Familiar Method of Planting and Raising Vines in England, to the greatest Perfection; illustrated with several useful
Examples. IV. New Experiments in Grafting, Budding, or Inoculating;
whereby all Sorts of Fruit may be much more improved than at present; particularly the Peach, Apricot, Nectarine, Plumb, etc. V. The best Manner of
Raising several sorts of compound Fruit, which have not yet been attempted in
England. 8vo. London.

> Another edit., 8vo, London, 1732.
> This work has been attributed to Bradley.

1728 BRADLEY, RICHARD. Dictionarium Botanicum, or, A Botanical Dictionary for the
use of the Curious in Husbandry and Gardening. 2 vols. 8vo. London.

> "A work never before attempted" (a common claim).

LANGLEY, BATTY. A Sure Method of Improving Estates, by Plantations of Oak,
Elm, Ash, Beech, and other Timber-trees, Coppice-Woods, etc. 4to. London.

> Langley was another of the "improvers" who wrecked stately avenues of trees, the
> work of the 17th-century planters, parterres, mazes, knots, etc., to make room for
> the landscape garden. He was one of the few architects of the new order who retained
> some feeling for the Gothic, though he earned well-deserved flaying which the Gothicists
> of the century laid upon him for his attempt to reduce Gothic to the rule of the "Five
> Orders."

——————————. New Principles of Gardening, or the laying-out and planting Parterres. 4to. London.

1729 BRADLEY, RICHARD. The Riches of a Hop Garden explained. 8vo. London.

LANGLEY, BATTY. Pomona, or the Fruit Garden illustrated. . . . Fol. London.

SWITZER, STEPHEN. A Compendious Method for raising of Italian Brocoli . . . .
and other Foreign Kitchen Vegetables, . . . 8vo. London.

> Another edit., 1735.

1730 COWELL, JOHN. The Curious and Profitable Gardener. 8vo. London.

1731 MILLER, PHILIP. The Gardener's Dictionary. Fol. London.

> 2nd edit., 1733; again, 2 vols., 8vo, London, 1735; 7th, fol., London, 1759. This work
> was many times republished, abridged, enlarged, and translated. See below.
> In the successive editions, Miller took advantage of increasing knowledge of botany
> and importations of foreign plants to keep his work up to date. From having followed
> Ray, in 1759 (the 7th edition) he turned to the system of classifying plants published in
> Linnaeus' first great work, *Genera Plantarum* (1737). Miller had met the Swedish botanist
> in 1736 when the latter was visiting England.

>> 1759 MILLER, PHILIP. The Gardener's Dictionary: containing the best and newest Methods
>> of Cultivating and Improving Kitchen, Fruit, Flower Garden, and Nursery; as
>> also for Performing the Practical Parts of Agriculture: including the Management
>> of Vineyards, with the Method of Making and Preserving the Wine, according
>> to the present Practice of the most skilful Vignerons in the several Wine
>> Countries in Europe. Together with Directions for propagating and improving
>> from real Practice and Experience, all Sorts of Timber Trees. Copperplates. Fol.
>> London.

1732 ELLIS, WILLIAM. Complete Modern Husbandry, containing the Practice of
Farming. . . . 2nd edit. 8vo. London.

——————. The Practical Farmer or Hertfordshire Husbandman. London.

An Essay concerning the best Methods of pruning Fruit Trees. . . . 8vo. London.

The Flower-Garden Displayed, in above Four Hundred Curious Representations of the Most Beautiful Flowers; regularly dispos'd in the respective Months of their Blossom, curiously engraved on Copper-Plates from the Designs of Mr. Furber and others, and coloured to the Life, with the Description and History of each Plant and the Method of their Culture; whether in Stoves, Green-Houses, Hot Beds, Glass-Cases, Open Borders, or against Walls. 12 plates colored. 4to. London.

> 2nd edit., with additions, 4to, London, 1734. See below.
> This book forms an accurate record of the principal cultivated flowers of the time.—Bookseller's Note.

> 1734   The Flower-Garden Displayed . . . to which is added, A Flower-Garden for Gentlemen and Ladies, being the Art of raising Flowers . . . also salleting, cucumbers, &c. as it is now practised by Sir Thomas More. Above 400 curious representations of the most beautiful Flowers. . . . 4to. London.

FURBER, ROBERT. Fruits for every month in the Year. 12 plates. 8vo. London.

The Great Improvement of Commons that are enclosed for the Advantage of Lords of the Manor, the Poor, and the Public, with Methods of enriching all Soils; and raising Timber. To ripen Fruit at all times of the year; an Improvement in raising Mushrooms, Cucumbers, &c. London.

MILLER, PHILIP. The Gardener's Kalendar. 8vo. London.

> Many later edits., the 13th, 1782.

The Nature and Method of Planting, Manuring, and Dieting a Vineyard. 8vo. London.

1733   ELLIS, WILLIAM. Chiltern and Vale Farming Explained, according to the latest Improvements (in ploughing, horse houghing, cereals, root crops, etc.). 8vo. London.

> Reprinted, 8vo, London, 1745.

1733-40   TULL, JETHRO. The New Horse-Houghing Husbandry, or an Essay on the Principles of Tillage and Vegetation. London.

> 3rd edit., corrected, 8vo, London, 1751. See below.
> These essays on agriculture and his invention of the drill, which in time came to supplant the wasteful method of sowing by hand, together with his advocacy of hoeing, won for Tull the appellation "father of modern husbandry." By the end of the century his principles were almost universally adopted.

> 1751   TULL, JETHRO. Horse Hoeing Husbandry: or, An Essay on the Principles of Vegetation and Tillage, whereby the Produce of the Land will be increased and the Expence Lessoned. Third Edition, carefully corrected. Folding plates. 8vo. London.

1738   ELLIS, WILLIAM. The Timber Tree Improved, or the best practical Methods of improving different Lands, with proper Timber. London.

1739 TROWELL, SAMUEL. A New Treatise of Husbandry, Gardening, and other Curious Matters relating to Country Affairs. 8vo. London.

1741 A New Method of Improving Cold, Wet, and Barren Lands, particularly Clayey Grounds, with the manner of burning Clay, Turf, and Molehills as practiced in North Britain. 7 plates. (Place?)

1743 BRACKEN, HENRY. The Traveller's Pocket Farrier; or, A Treatise upon the Distempers and Common Incidents happening to Horses upon a Journey. Being very useful for all Gentlemen and Tradesmen who are obliged to travel the Countries. London.

MAXWELL, ROBERT. Select Transactions of the Society of Improvers in Agriculture in Scotland; Agriculture, Manufactures, etc. Edinburgh.

1744 Adam's Luxury and Eve's Cookery, or the Kitchen Garden displayed. 8vo. London.

STEVENSON, H. The Gentleman's Gard'ner's Director. Being Instructions for Planting and Sowing, Trees or Seeds, for Profit or Pleasure. . . . 8vo. London.
Amherst, 358, cites the same title as by David Stephenson, under date of 1746.

Report on the Mosses, with the Methods of Agriculture practiced by Graeme of Ardgomry. 8vo. Edinburgh (?).

1747 BRADLEY, RICHARD. A Dictionary of Plants, their Description and Uses. 2 vols. 8vo. London.

CARWITHAM, J. The Compleat Florist. 100 colored plates of flowers. 8vo. London.

MAXWELL, ROBERT. The Practical Bee-Master: A Treatise on the Management of Bees without killing them. 8vo. Edinburgh.

TROWELL, SAMUEL. The Farmer's Instructor, or, The Husbandman and Gardener's Companion. Edit. by William Ellis. 8vo. London.

1749 JAMES, W., and J. MALCOLM. General View of the Agriculture of the County of Surrey, with Observations on the Means of its Improvement. Plates. 4to. London.
This is the first of those county surveys which in the last decade of the century were to embrace the whole of Britain.

1750 HALFPENNY, J. Rural Architecture in the Chinese Taste, Being Designs for the Decoration of Gardens, etc. 4 parts. London.
This is the first notice I have seen of a vogue which, after Sir William Chambers came on the scene, was to grow rapidly in popularity.

1751 WHITMIL, BENJAMIN. Kalendarium Universale, or the Gardener's Universal Calendar. 5th edit. 8vo. London.

1752   Attiret, J. D. An Account of the Emperor of China's Gardens at Pekin. Translated by Sir H. Beaumont, i.e., Joseph Spence. London.

1753   Coventry, Francis. Essay entitled Strictures on the Absurd Novelties introduced in Gardening, and a humorous description of Squire Mushroom's Villa (in the *World,* no. 15). London.

   Stafford, Hugh. A Treatise on Cyder-Making, founded on long Practice and Experience, with a Catalogue of Cyder-Apples of Character in Herefordshire and Devonshire, etc. To which is prefixed, A Dissertation on Cyder and Cyder Fruit. 4to. London.

1754   The Compleat Cyderman: or, The Present Practice of Raising Plantations of the best Cyder Apple and Perry Pear Trees, with the Improvement of their excellent Juices. London.
      See Ellis under 1757 below.

   Justice, James. The Scots Gardiner's Director; Instructions to those Gardiners, who make a Kitchen Garden and the Culture of Flowers their Business. 2 plates. 8vo. Edinburgh.
      Another edit., 8vo, London, 1764.

1756   Hale, Thomas. Complete Body of Husbandry: the Whole Business of the Farmer and Country Gentleman in Cultivating, Planting, and Stocking, with the most approved Methods. Numerous plates. 2 vols. Fol. London.

   Observations on the Methods of growing Wool in Scotland and Proposals for Improving it. 8vo. Edinburgh.

   Reid, John. The Scots Gardener for the Climate of Scotland, together with the Gardener's Kalendar, the Florist's Vade-Mecum, the Practical Beemaster. Edinburgh.

   Sheldrake, Timothy (the Elder). The Gardener's Best Companion in a Greenhouse. Fol. London.

1757   Bradley, Richard. A General Treatise of Agriculture both Philosophical and Practical, displaying the Arts of Husbandry and Gardening. 23 copperplates. 8vo. London.

   Ellis, William. The Complete Planter and Cyderist, or, A New Method of Planting Cyder-Apple and Perry-Pear Trees; and the most approved Ways of making Cyder, in Two Parts. The first treating of the Cultivation of Orchards. The second, of the various Ways of making Cyder and Perry as practiced in Devonshire and Herefordshire, etc., how to distil Cyder Spirits: with a Proposal for making a strong-bodied Cyder as a noble Antiscorbutic for the Navy. 8vo. London.

HALE, THOMAS. Eden, or, A Compleat Body of Gardening, containing plain and familiar Directions for raising the Products of a Garden. 60 large copperplate engravings of flowers, fruits, etc. Fol. London.
> This was compiled by Sir John Hill from the papers left by Hale.

HITT, THOMAS. A Treatise of Fruit Trees. 2nd edit. 8vo. London.

HOME, FRANCIS. Principles of Agriculture and Vegetation. 8vo. Edinburgh.

MAXWELL, ROBERT. The Practical Husbandman. London.

1758 BARNES, THOMAS. A New Method of Propagating Fruit Trees and Shrubs, confirmed by repeated and successful Experience. 8vo. London.
> Other edits., 1759 and 1762.

HANBURY, REV. WILLIAM. An Essay on Planting, and a scheme for making it conducive to the Glory of God. 8vo. Oxford.

MILLER, PHILIP. The Method of Cultivating Madder. . . . London.

1759 MILLS, JOHN. A Practical Treatise on Husbandry, translated from the French of Duhamel de Monceau. Plates. 4to. London.
NORTH, RICHARD. A Treatise on Grasses and the Norfolk Willow. 8vo. London.

1760 GRANT, SIR ARCHIBALD (of Monymusk). The Chief Obstacles to the Improvement of Land, and Introducing better Methods throughout Scotland. 8vo. Aberdeen.

The London Gardener. 8vo. London.

PULLEIN, SAMUEL. Observations towards a Method of preserving the Seeds of Plants in a State of Vegetation during long Voyages. 8vo. London.

1761 ROCQUE, BENJAMIN. A Treatise on Cultivating Lucerne, Methods found to Succeed, etc. 4to. London. (24 pp.)

1762 LIGHTOLER, T. The Gentleman and Farmer's Architecture: being Plans for Parsonage and Farm Houses, with Pineries, Greenhouses, etc. Plates. Fol. London.
> Another edit., 1766.

MILLS, JOHN. A New and Complete System of Practical Husbandry. 5 vols. 8vo. London.

Treatise of Agriculture: Vegetation, Tillage, Manures, and Soils. 2 folding plates. 8vo. Edinburgh.
> During the decades to follow Scotland was to make great advances in the art and science of agriculture and gardening, so that before the century closes, to have a Scotch gardener on the place was almost equal to possessing a patent of nobility.

1763 WHEELER, JAMES. The Botanist's and Gardener's New Dictionary, containing the Names, etc., of the several Plants, etc., cultivated in England, according to the System of Linnaeus, directing the Culture of each Plant, etc., also A Gardener's Calendar, and an Introduction to the Linnaean System of Botany. Plates. 8vo. London.

1764 The Complete Farmer; or, Dictionary of Husbandry. Publ. by David Henry. London (?).

HARTE, REV. WALTER. Essays on Husbandry, and a Treatise on Lucerne, by W. H., Canon of Windsor (1770). Plates. London.

JUSTICE, JAMES. The British Gardener's Director, chiefly adapted to the Climate of the Northern Countries: Directing the necessary Works in the Kitchen, Fruit and Pleasure Gardens, and in the Nursery, Green-House and Stove. 8vo. Edinburgh.

MILLER, PHILIP. The Elements of Agriculture, translated from the French of Duhamel de Monceau. 2 vols. London.

Museum Rusticum et Commerciale, . . . 6 vols. 8vo. London.

RANDALL, JOHN. The Semi-Virgilian Husbandry, deduced from various Experiments, or, An Essay towards a New Course of National Farming . . . with the Philosophy of Agriculture, exhibiting at Large, the Nutritive Principles derived from the Atmosphere. . . . 8vo. London.

SHENSTONE, WILLIAM. Unconnected Thoughts on Gardening, in Essays on Men and Manners. 3 vols. 8vo. London.

> Shenstone's garden at Leasowes was a much visited and admired place, and was generally recognized as a pattern for the "ferme ornée." It contained about everything that could be crowded into five acres.

1765 Foreign Essays on Agriculture . . . communicated for the Improvement of British Husbandry: Wool, Marling, Clover, Lucerne, Road Making, Cereals, etc. 8vo. London.

HADDINGTON, EARL OF. A Short Treatise on Forest Trees. London.

Museum Rustique et Commerciale—Observations on Some Papers (on Farming) in the Museum Rusticum, by a Gentleman. 8vo. London.

1766 LOCKE, JOHN. Observations upon the Growth and Culture of Vines and Olives, etc., from the Original MS. in the possession of the Earl of Shaftesbury. 8vo. London.

VARLEY, CHARLES. A Treatise on Agriculture, intitled the Yorkshire Farmer; also a Monthly Kalendar of Works to be done in Season throughout the Year. Numerous engraved plates. 2 vols. 8vo. Dublin.

1767 ABERCROMBIE, JOHN. Every Man his own Gardener. Being a New and much more Complete Gardener's Kalendar than anyone hitherto published. . . . 12mo. London.

> 6th edit., enlarged, 8vo, London, 1773; again, 1787 and 1800.
> This work has also the name of Thomas Mawe on the title page. Abercrombie published a long series of books on different phases of husbandry.

Complete Grazier, or, Gentleman and Farmer's Directory: Breeding Cattle, Sheep, Poultry, etc., by a Country Gentleman. 8vo. London.

GILES, JOHN. Ananas; or, A Treatise on the Pine Apple, etc. To which is added, The True Method of raising the finest Melons with the greatest Success, etc. 8vo. London.

The Rise and Progress of the present Taste in planting Parks, Pleasure Grounds, Gardens, etc., from the time of Henry VIII. to George II. In a poetic Epistle to the Right Hon. Charles, Lord Viscount Irwin. (Place?)

RUTTER, JAMES, and DANIEL CARTER. Modern Eden, or the Gardener's Universal Guide. . . . 8vo. London.

Select Essays on Husbandry: Cereals, Turnips, Carrots, Cattle, Tull vindicated, etc., with Experiments which have succeeded in Scotland. Plate. 8vo. Edinburgh.

YOUNG, ARTHUR. A Farmer's Letters to the People of England. 8vo. London.

> 3rd edit., enlarged and corrected, 2 vols., 8vo, London, 1771. See below.
> Young's words were soon to carry more weight than those of any other agriculturist in Europe. High and low sought his advice, from "Farmer George," as he was lampooned, down to the plain countryman. He made numerous tours throughout England and into Ireland and France, in the interest of agriculture. In the last-named country he was especially honored by the Duc de Liancourt (see Young under 1792, WEST EUROPE, vol. I). In 1793 he became secretary to the Board of Agriculture. His latter days were clouded over with a mental disorder.

> 1771 YOUNG, ARTHUR. A Farmer's Letters to the People of England, containing the Sentiments of a practical Husbandman on various Subjects of great Importance, particularly Exportation of Corn, Agriculture and Manufactures, State of the Poor, Price of Provisions, Timber and Planting, Emigration to the Colonies, etc.: to which is added, Sylvae, or Occasional Tracts on Husbandry, and Rural Economics. 3rd edit., corrected and enlarged. 2 vols. 8vo. London.

1768 MASON, GEORGE. An Essay on Design Gardening. 8vo. London.

WILDMAN, THOMAS. A Treatise on the Culture of Peach Trees, to which is added, A Treatise on the Management of Bees. London.

1769 BARRINGTON, THE HON. DAINES. On the Trees which are supposed to be Indigenous in Great Britain. London.

> Barrington was a man of many interests. For his tracts on the possibility of reaching the North Pole, see under 1774-75, ARCTIC, vol. II. He was a frequent correspondent of Gilbert White, the naturalist (see under 1789, NATURAL HISTORY), and Thomas Pennant, the traveler and zoologist.

GARTON, JAMES. The Practical Gardener and Gentleman's Directory for every Month in the Year, etc. 12mo. London.

POWELL, ANTHONY. The Royal Gardener, or complete Calendar of Gardening for every Month in the Year. 12mo. London.

Society of Gentlemen. The Complete Farmer; A General Dictionary of Husbandry, according to the Old and New Husbandry; to which is added, The Gardener's Kalendar. 28 plates. 4to. London.

WESTON, RICHARD. Tracts on Practical Agriculture and Gardening . . . to which is added, a Complete Chronological Catalogue of English Authors on Agriculture, Gardening, etc. 8vo. London.

> 2nd edit., greatly enlarged, 1773. Weston's name appears in this edition, but not in the first.—Amherst, 365.

1770 DOVE, JOHN. Strictures on Agriculture, wherein a Discovery of the Physical Course of Vegetation, of the Food of Plants, and the Rudiments of Tillage, is attempted. 12mo. London.

ELLIS, JOHN. Directions for bringing over Seeds and Plants from the East Indies and other distant Countries in a state of Vegetation. 4to. London.

The Farmer's Guide in Hiring and Stocking Farms. 2 vols. London.

MILLS, JOHN. The Natural and Chemical Elements of Agriculture, translated from the German of Gyllenborg. 12mo. London.

The Pocket Flower Gardener. 12mo. London.

The Pocket Kitchen Gardener. 12mo. London.

Rural Oeconomy, or Essays on the Practical Parts of Husbandry . . . to which is added, The Rural Socrates, being Memoirs of a Country Philosopher. 8vo. Dublin.

WHEATLEY (WHATLEY), THOMAS. Observations on Modern Gardening, illustrated by descriptions. 8vo. London.

> 5th edit., 1793.
> This Under-Secretary of State under Lord North, author of *Remarks on Shakespeare's Characters of Macbeth and Richard III,* was likewise interested in landscape gardening.

1771 DICKS, JOHN. The New Gardener's Dictionary, or the whole Art of Gardening fully and accurately displayed. Fol. London.

> An edition of 1769 is mentioned by Watt, *Bibliotheca.*—Amherst, 366.

MEADER, JAMES. The Modern Gardener or Universal Kalendar . . . from the Diary and MSS. of the late Mr. Flitt, corrected and improved by J. M. 12mo. London.

PETERS, MATTHEW. The Rational Farmer, or A Treatise on Agriculture and Tillage. 8vo. London.

> Among agricultural writers Peters had a high reputation.

—————. Rudiments and Observations on a New Vegetable System of Agriculture; Turnips, Cabbage, Cereals, Winter Feeding, etc. Plate. 8vo. London.

> The new practice of feeding turnips to cattle in winter time permitted the size of herds to be greatly increased.

YOUNG, ARTHUR. The Farmer's Kalendar: A Monthly Directory for Buying and Selling Live Stock, Arable Crops, etc., Farm Management and Economy. 8vo. London.

—————. For Young's Observations on agriculture made in his various tours throughout England, see under 1771 and later dates, TOURS.

1772 CHAMBERS, SIR WILLIAM. A Dissertation on Oriental Gardening. 4to. London.

> 2nd edit., London, 1773.
> This well-known architect, whose best work was Somerset House, in London, had published in the *Gentleman's Magazine*, May, 1757, an account of Chinese landscape gardens, the materials for which he had gathered on a trip to China in 1742-44. Therefore he was supposed to speak with authority. While the garden of emotions and the vogue of the exotic, in the second half of the century, was greatly strengthened by Chambers' publications and designs, yet his ideas on Chinese gardens were vigorously attacked, especially by William Mason, the poet, in his *The English Garden* (1757), and in his *Heroical Epistle to Sir William Chambers* (1773). Certainly the pagoda he erected in Kew Gardens must have tilted the eyebrows of Chinese visitors. After all, the principles ruling the English landscape gardening did not have to go far, except in the matter of Chinese bridges and pagodas, to meet those which governed Chinese art. As stated by a Chinese writer, Lien-tschen, they run: "The art of laying out gardens consists in an endeavour to combine cheerfulness of aspect, luxuriance of growth, shade, solitude, and repose, in such a manner that the senses may be deluded by an imitation of rural Nature."—Quoted by Amherst, 266. The same ideas may be found in Shenstone, Goldsmith, Wheatley, and others.

ST. PIERRE, LOUIS DE. The Art of Planting and Cultivating the Vine, etc., according to the most approved Methods in France. 12mo. London.

VARLO, C. A New System of Husbandry. 3 vols. 8vo. Winchester. (For the Author.)

1773 WESTON, RICHARD. The Gardner's and Planter's Calendar. Containing the Method of raising Timber-Trees, Fruit-Trees, and Quick for Hedges, etc. 8vo. London.

YOUNG, ARTHUR. Observations on the Present State of the Waste Lands of Great Britain. London.

> Young, who was an advocate for enclosure, proposes here to divert intending emigrants to America to settlement on the waste lands of England.

1774 GORDON, JAMES. The Planter's Florist and Gardener's Pocket Dictionary, adapted to Scotland, being a Practical Collection from the most approved Authors, relating to the above. Three Parts of Gardening, with Appendix. 8vo. Edinburgh.

YOUNG, ARTHUR. Political Arithmetic, containing Observations on the Present State of Great Britain; and the Principles of her Policy in the Encouragement of Agriculture . . . to which is added, A Memoir on the Corn Trade, by Governor Pownall. 8vo. London.

1775 BOUTCHER, WILLIAM. A Treatise on Forest Trees: Varieties, Culture, Disposition, . . . 4to. (For the Author.)

KENT, NATHANIEL. Hints to Gentlemen of Landed Property. Draining, Cattle, Grasses, Soil, Timber, Manures, etc. Folding Plates. 8vo. London.

RIDER, —. Rider's British Merlin for the Year 1775, with Notes on Husbandry, Fairs, Marts, High Roads. (Bound up with this is The Royal Kalendar, or Compleat and Correct Annual Register for the Year 1775.) 12mo. London.

> The 2nd item contains a list of the military and civil establishments, governors, law and revenue offices, etc., in America.—Bookseller's Note.

WARD, REV. SAMUEL. An Essay on the different Natural Situations of Gardens. 4to. London.

1776 HOME, HENRY (LORD KAMES). The Gentleman Farmer; an Attempt to Improve Agriculture on Rational Principles. 8vo. Edinburgh.

> Several later editions—the 6th in 1815.
> A valuable addition to agricultural knowledge.—*DNB*.

1777 HUNTER, A. Georgical Essays: Rise and Progress of Agriculture; Drill Sowing, Manures, . . . Folding plates. 8vo. York.

KENNEDY, JOHN. A Treatise upon Planting, Gardening, and the Management of the Hot-house. 2nd edit. enlarged. 2 vols. 8vo. London.

WILSON, WILLIAM. A Treatise on the Forcing of early Fruits, and the Management of Hot Walls. 12mo. London.

1778 ABERCOMBIE, JOHN. The Universal Gardener and Botanist, . . . 4to. London.

FORBES, FRANCIS. Improvement of Waste Lands: Wet, Moory Land; Peat Land; Propagating Oak and Timber on Waste Land. With Dissertation on Farms. 8vo. London.

1778-84 WIGHT, ALEXANDER. Present State of Husbandry in Scotland; extracted from Reports to the Commissioners of the Annexed Estates: Forfar, Aberdeenshire, East Lothian, etc. 4 vols. in 6. 8vo. Edinburgh (?).

1779 ELLIS, THOMAS (Gardener to the Bishop of London). The Gardener's Pocket Calendar. 12mo. London.

> An earlier edition is said to have been published anonymously in 1770.—Amherst, 368.

A General Dictionary of Husbandry, Planting, Gardening, and the Vegetable Part of the Materia Medica . . . selected from the best Authors by the Editors of the Farmers' Magazine. 2 vols. 8vo. Bath.

SPEECHLEY, WILLIAM. A Treatise on the Cultivation of the Pine Apple. 8vo. York.

1780 TRUSLER, JOHN. Practical Husbandry, or the Art of Farming, with Certainty of Gain. 8vo. London.

1781 FULLMER, SAMUEL. The Young Gardener's Best Companion for the Kitchen and Fruit Garden. 12mo. London.

1782 BAILEY, ALEXANDER M. Mechanical Machines and Implements of Husbandry, approved and adopted by the Society for the Encouragement of Arts, Manufactures and Commerce, and contained in their Repository in the Adelphi Buildings in the Strand, illustrated by a particular Description of each Instrument and Account of the several Discoveries and Improvements in Agriculture, Manufactures, Mechanics, Chemistry, and the Polite Arts, which have been promoted and encouraged by the Society, in different Parts of this Kingdom, and in the Colonies of America, corrected and revised by Alex. M. Bailey. 106 copperplates, with descriptions. 2 vols. in 1. Fol. London.

> This Society was an influential factor in the development of technical inventions. Its offer of 10,000 pounds for an accurate means of determining longitude was of long standing. It sponsored all sorts of agricultural improvements, cattle shows, ploughing matches, and farmers' clubs, and everywhere awarded medals to the winners, whether they were noblemen or farmers.

1783 The Experienced Bee-Keeper, containing an Essay on the Management of Bees: with many Experiments entirely new. Together with an improved Method of making Mead and a great Variety of other Wines with Honey. 8vo. London.

FALCONER, WILLIAM. An Historical View of the Taste for Gardening and Laying out Grounds among the Nations of Antiquity. 8vo. London.

GERARDIN, R. L. An Essay on Landscape, or the Means of Improving the Country round our Habitations. 8vo. London.

LAMBERT, J. The Countryman's Treasure: shewing the Nature, Causes and Cure to all Diseases incident to Cattle. Means of Prevention, a treatise on Coneys, Destruction of Vermin, . . . 12mo. London.

1784-1809 YOUNG, ARTHUR. Annals of Agriculture. 45 vols. 8vo. London.

> This valuable collection of papers on agriculture contains mention of a number of tours by Young and others. More or less introductory to this work, Young has given a running commentary on the American revolution and the effect of the loss of the American colonies on the agriculture of England. Farmers both practical and amateur contributed to these *Annals*, the most notable of whom was George III, who wrote under the pseudonym of Ralph Robinson.

1785 FELTON, SAMUEL. Miscellanies on Ancient and Modern Gardening, and on the Scenery of Nature. 8vo. London.

> Published anonymously.

MARSHALL, WILLIAM. Planting and Ornamental Gardening: a Practical Treatise. 8vo. London.

> 2nd edit., with additions and changes of title to *Planting and Rural Ornament*, 2 vols., 8vo, London, 1796.

WALPOLE, HORACE. Essay on Modern Gardening. 4to. Strawberry Hill.

This essay, written in 1770, was printed with a French translation on opposite pages done by the Duc de Nivernois. It is reprinted in vol. III of Walpole's *Anecdotes of Painting in England* (1876 edit.). After glancing at the garden of Eden, the Hanging Gardens of Babylon, the Garden of Alcinous in the *Odyssey*, Pliny's villas, etc., he takes up the English garden with Sir William Temple and from there on traces the changing vogues and various influences of different landscapists down through the century to his own time. He picks out Kent as the one who "leaped the fence, and saw that all nature was a garden," meaning thereby that Kent was the first (but not in fact) to extend the garden into the surrounding park or countryside by substituting for the wall or hedge a ditch or foss, commonly known as a "ha-ha." As the editor of Mason's *Satirical Poems,* Walpole would naturally turn up his nose at Sir William Chambers and the Chinese garden. And he is equally hard on the excesses of the modern landscape garden in other directions. This work has been edited by Isabel W. Urban Chase in her *Horace Walpole, Gardenist,* Princeton, 1944.

YOUNG, DAVID. National Improvements upon Agriculture. 8vo. Edinburgh.

1786 LE BROCQ, REV. PHILIP. A Description of certain Methods of Planting, Training, and Managing all kinds of Fruit Trees, Vines, . . . 8vo. London.

1787 HOME, JOHN. Rectified Report of Berwickshire Agriculture, Digested from the Communications of the County. Folding map. 8vo. Berwick.

MARSHALL, WILLIAM. The Rural Economy of Norfolk. Comprising the Management of Landed Estates, and the present Practice of Husbandry in that County. 2 vols. 8vo. London.

Reprinted, 2 vols., 8vo, London, 1795.
With this work Marshall starts his series of volumes on the rural economies of England, which let the light in on many a hidden corner of English life. In addition to his active interest in agriculture, he made studies in dialects.

————. The Rural Economy of Yorkshire, comprising the Management of Landed Estates, and the present Practice of Husbandry in the agricultural Districts of that County. 8vo. London.

2nd edit., 2 vols., 1796.

WINTER, GEORGE. A new and compendious System of Husbandry, containing the Mechanical, Chemical, and Philosophical Elements of Agriculture. 8vo. Bristol.

1788 Bath Society's Letters and Papers on Agriculture, Planting, etc. Vols. I-IV. 8vo. London.

See also Bath Society under 1799-1818 below.

YOUNG, DAVID. Agriculture, the Primary Interest of Britain. 8vo. Edinburgh.

1789 ADAM, JAMES. Practical Essays on Agriculture, containing an Account of Soils, and the Manner of correcting them; an Account of the Culture of all Field Plants; also on the Culture and Management of Grass Lands. 2 vols. 8vo. London.

ALTON, WILLIAM. Hortus Kewensis, or a Catalogue of the Plants cultivated in the Royal Botanic Garden at Kew. 3 vols. 8vo. London.

MARSHALL, WILLIAM. The Rural Economy of Gloucestershire, including its Dairy; together with the Dairy Management of North Wiltshire; and the Management of Orchards and Fruit Liquor in Herefordshire. 2 vols. Gloucester.

2nd edit., 2 vols., 8vo, London, 1796.

1790   BRULLES, —. Hints for the Management of Hot-beds, . . . 8vo. Bath.

MARSHALL, WILLIAM. The Rural Economy of the Midland Counties; including the Management of Livestock in Leicestershire and its Environs. 2 vols. 8vo. London.

2nd edit., 1796.
This contains brief accounts of all phases of husbandry—size of estates, management, roads, workmen, farmers, as well as actual methods of tilling the soil.

TAPLIN, WILLIAM. The Gentleman's Stable Directory, containing the System of Treatment and Cures for Horses. 2 vols. 8vo. London.

2nd edit., 2 vols., 1796. See below.

1796   TAPLIN, WILLIAM. The Gentleman's Stable Directory (containing valuable prescriptions, references to obsolete and dangerous practices, buying, selling, feeding, getting into condition, etc., and a supplement). 2 vols. 8vo. London.

FORSYTH, WILLIAM. Observations on the Diseases, Defects, and Injuries in all kinds of Fruit and Forest Trees, . . . 8vo. London.

NICHOLS, THOMAS. Observations on the Propagation and Management of Oak Trees in General; but more immediately applying to his Majesty's New-Forest in Hampshire, with a view of making that extensive Tract of Land more productive of Timber for the Use of the Navy. 8vo. Southampton. (42 pp.)

SOWERBY, JAMES. The Florist's Delight, . . . Fol. London.

1792   BOSWELL, GEORGE. A Treatise on Watering Meadows. 5 folding plates. 8vo. London.

MADDOCK, JAMES. Florist's Directory and Treatise on the Culture of Flowers, . . . 8vo. London.

1793   BAIRD, THOMAS. General View of the Agriculture of the County of Middlesex. 4to. London.

2nd and 3rd edits., same year.

CLARIDGE, JOHN. General View of the Agriculture of Dorset. 4to. London.

FULLARTON, COL. —. General View of the Agriculture of the County of Ayr, with Observations on the Means of its Improvement. Edinburgh.

MAXWELL, GEORGE. General View of the Agriculture of the County of Huntingdon. 4to. London.

ROBERTSON, GEORGE. General View of the Agriculture of the County of Mid-Lothian. Map. 4to. Edinburgh.
> 2nd edit., 8vo, Edinburgh, 1795.

STEELE, RICHARD. Essay upon Gardening, containing a Catalogue of Exotic Plants for the Stoves and Green-Houses of British Gardens. 3 folding plates. 4to. York.

STONE, THOMAS. General View of the Agriculture of the County of Huntingdon. 4to. London.

YOUNG, ARTHUR. General View of the Agriculture of the County of Sussex. 4to. London.

1794   AMOS, WILLIAM. The Theory and Practice of Drill Husbandry. 4to. London.

GIBSON, —. His description of truck gardens near London in 1691, preserved in *Archaeologia*, 1794, was reprinted by W. C. Hazlitt, in his *Gleanings in Old Garden Literature*, 1887. See this date under LONDON.

HAYES, SAMUEL. A Practical Treatise on Planting. 8vo. Dublin.

McPHAIL, JAMES. A Treatise on the Culture of the Cucumber, . . . 8vo. London.

MAUNSELL, WILLIAM. A Letter on the Culture of Potatoes from the Shoots. 8vo. London.

SHAW, JAMES. Plans, Elevations, Sections, Observations, and Explanations of Forcing Houses in Gardening. Fol. Whitby.

In this year 1794 began the series of county reports on agriculture issued by various authors for the Board of Agriculture. Since they all appear with practically the same title—General View of the Agriculture of the County of so-and-so, with Observations on the Means of its Improvement—they will be listed alphabetically under authors with the name of the county following. These surveys are catalogued in the British Museum under the heading of London Academies: Board of Agriculture.

> 1794   ANDERSON, JAMES. Aberdeen. 4to. London.
> > BAILEY, JOHN. Cumberland.
> > BAILEY, JOHN, and G. CULLEY. Northumberland.
> > > Another edit., with Cumberland and Westmoreland added, 8vo, Newcastle, 1797; another edit. of the original, Newcastle, 1800.
> > BEATSON, R. Fife.
> > BILLINGSLEY, J. Somerset.
> > > Reprinted, 8vo, Bath, and London, 1798.
> > > Reviewed *Gent. Mag.*, vol. 68, 966-67. The preface contains a plan for reprinting these surveys on a uniform model, as follows: Preliminary Observations. I. Geographical State and Circumstances. II. State of Property. III. Buildings. IV. Mode of Occupation. V. Implements. VI. Including Fences and Gates. VII. Arable Lands. VIII. Grass. IX. Gardens and Orchards. X. Woods and Plantations. XI. Wastes. XII. Improvements. XIII. Live Stock. XIV. Rural Economy.

(Author?) Salop. 4to. Brentford.

BOYS, JOHN. Kent. 4to. Brentford.
    Reprinted, 8vo, London, 1796.

BROWN, THOMAS. Derby. 4to. London.

BROWN, RENNIE, and SHIRREFF. West Riding of Yorkshire. 4to. London.
    Reprinted, 8vo, Edinburgh, 1799.

BUCHAN-HEPBURN, G. East Lothian. 4to. Edinburgh.

CLARK, JOHN. Brecknock. 4to. London.

————. Hereford.

————. Radnor.

CRUTCHLEY, J. Rutland.

DAVIS, RICHARD. Oxford.

————. Wilts. London.

DONALDSON, JAMES. Banff. Edinburgh.

————. Carse of Gowrie, Perth. London.

————. Elgin, including part of Strathspey, Invernesshire.

————. Nairn, East Coast of Invernesshire, and Dyke, Edenkellie, and Forres in Moray.

————. Northampton, with Appendix containing a Comparison between English and Scotch Systems of Husbandry. 4to. Edinburgh.

DRIVER, A., and W. Hants. 4to. London.

FOOT, PETER. Middlesex.

FOX, JOHN. Monmouth. 4to. Brentford.

FRASER, ROBERT. Cornwall. 4to. London.

————. Devon.

GRANGER, J. Durham.

GRIGGS, MESSRS. Essex.

HASSALL, C. Carmarthen.

————. Pembroke.

HERON, ROBERT. The Hebrides. 4to. Edinburgh.

HOLT, JOHN. Lancaster. London.
    Another edit., with Remarks of several Respectable Gentlemen and Farmers, 8vo, London, 1795.

JAMES, WILLIAM, and J. MALCOLM. Buckingham.

————. Surrey.

JOHNSTON, REV. T. Dumfries.

————. Selkirk.

————. Tweedale in Peebleshire.
    Reprinted, 1799.

KAY, GEORGE. North Wales.

KENT, NATHANIEL. Norfolk.
    Reprinted, with Additional Remarks by several Respectable Gentlemen and Farmers, 8vo, Norwich, 1796.

LEATHAM, ISAAC. East Riding of Yorkshire.

LLOYD, T. Cardigan.

LOWE, A. Berwick.
    2nd edit., 1798.

MARSHALL, WILLIAM. Central Highlands.

MARTIN, A. Renfrew.

MONK, JOHN. Leicester.

NAISMITH, JOHN. Clydesdale. 4to. Brentford.
  2nd edit., 8vo, Glasgow, 1798.

PEARCE, WILLIAM. Berkshire.

PITT, WILLIAM. Stafford.
  Reprinted, 8vo, London, 1796.

POMEROY, W. T. Worcestershire.

PRINGLE, A. Westmoreland. 4to. Edinburgh.

QUAYLE, BASIL. Isle of Man. London.

ROBERTSON, REV. J. Banff. 4to. Edinburgh.

————. Southern Districts of Perth. London.

ROBSON, JAMES. Argyll and Western Part of Invernesshire.

ROGER, REV. M. Angus (or Forfar). 4to. Edinburgh.

STONE, T. Lincoln. London.
  See Young, 1799, and Stone, 1800, below.

TROTTER, J. West Lothian. 4to. Edinburgh.

TUKE, JOHN. North Riding of Yorkshire. London.
  Another edit., 8vo, London, 1800.

TURNER, GEORGE. Gloucester.
  Reprinted same year.

URE, REV. D. Dumbarton.

————. Roxburgh.

VANCOUVER, CHARLES. Cambridge.

WEBSTER, J. Galloway, embracing Kirkcudbright and Wigton. Edinburgh.

WEDGE, JOHN. Warwick. London.

WEDGE, T. Chester.

YOUNG, ARTHUR. Suffolk.
  Another edit., 8vo, London, 1797.

1795 DONALDSON, JAMES. Kincardine (or the Mearns).

ERSKINE, J. F. Clackmannan, and some adjacent Parishes in Perth and Stirling. 4to. Edinburgh.

ROBERTSON, GEORGE. Kincardine. London.

————. Mid-Lothian. 8vo. Edinburgh.

SINCLAIR, SIR JOHN. Northern Counties and Islands of Scotland; including Cromarty, Ross, Sutherland, & Caithness, and the Islands of Orkney and Shetland.

VANCOUVER, CHARLES. Essex.

WALKER, D. Hertford.

1796 BELSCHES, R. Stirling. 4to. Edinburgh.

FOX, JOHN. Glamorgan. London.

1797 URE, REV. D. Kinross, including a Letter from W. Adam on Plantations. 4to. Edinburgh.

1798 DOUGLAS, R. Roxburgh and Selkirk. 8vo. Edinburgh.

MIDDLETON, J. Middlesex. 8vo. London.

SMITH, JOHN. Argyll. 8vo. Edinburgh.

SOME, R. Nottinghamshire. 8vo. London.

1799 ROBERTSON, JAMES. Perth. 8vo. Perth.

YOUNG, ARTHUR. Lincoln. 8vo. Lincoln.
  Reviewed *Gent. Mag.*, vol. 69, 322-23. The work is said to be disappointing in form, consisting of notes, which are of no value to the management of farms, the proper course of crops, etc. See Stone, following.

1800 STONE, THOMAS. A Review of the corrected Agricultural Survey of Lincolnshire by
Arthur Young. 8vo. London.

THOMSON, JOHN. Fife. 8vo. Edinburgh.

1795 BONNER, J. A New Plan for speedily increasing the Number of Bee Hives in Scotland (also England and America). 8vo. Edinburgh.

Report of the Board of Agriculture on the Culture and Use of Potatoes. Illustrations. 4to. London.

1796 MARSHALL, REV. CHARLES. Introduction to the Knowledge and Practice of Gardening; with Hints on Fish Ponds. 12mo. London.

   3rd edit., 1800.

MARSHALL, WILLIAM. Rural Economy of the West of England (Devonshire,
Somersetshire, Dorset, Cornwall). 2 vols. 8vo. London.

   Excerpts from this work are printed in Chope's *Early Tours in Devon and Cornwall,*
   Exeter, 1918.
   Marshall's account gives an excellent idea of how the humbler folk lived in those
   counties in 1796. He found the buildings to be largely of stone, which was plentiful in
   southwestern England, and the cottages to be more than usually comfortable. But the fare
   of the working class was much below par (his own term). Their drink consisted mainly of
   cider, and their food of barley bread and potatoes. The improvement in road making led
   to a big increase in travel by carriage. Land was being rented out to individuals from
   other parts of the kingdom rather than to the natives. The children of paupers, boys of
   seven and eight years of age, were let out to farmers till they became twenty-one. Work
   was done by ox teams, which were driven to tunes of a chanting boy. All sowing was done
   by hand. Cornwall turned out to be much better than he had expected: the soil and its
   cultivation were good, accommodations were superior, and the towns substantial and neat.
   Concerning North Devonshire, he concurs with the opinion of the inhabitants that it was
   "the richest, finest country in the world." Marshall's studies of rural England deserve far
   more attention than they receive from students of English life and literature in the
   eighteenth century.

1797 ASTLEY, FRANCIS DUCKENFIELD. A few minutes' Advice to Gentlemen of landed
Property, and the Admirers of Forest Scenery, . . . 12mo. Chester.

BUCKNAL, THOMAS SKIP DYOT. The Orchardist, . . . 8vo. London.

KNIGHT, THOMAS ANDREW. A Treatise on the Culture of the Apple and Pear, and
on the Manufacture of Cyder and Perry. 12mo. London.

NICOL, WALTER. The Scotch Forcing Gardener, . . . 5 copperplates. 8vo. Edinburgh.

   2nd edit., 8vo, Edinburgh, 1798. See below.

   1798 NICOL, WALTER. The Scotch Forcing and Kitchen Gardener, together with the
   Management of the Green House, Wall and Orchard Fruits. 5 folding plates. 8vo.
   Edinburgh.

1797-1806 Communications to the Board of Agriculture; on Subjects relating to the
Husbandry and Internal Improvements of the Country. Numerous plates. Vols.
I-V. 4to. London.

   2 vols. were published later.

1798 MARSHALL, WILLIAM. The Rural Economy of the Southern Counties, comprising Kent, Surrey, Essex, the Isle of Wight, the Chalk Hills of Wiltshire, Hampshire, etc., and including the Culture and Management of Hops in the District of Maidstone, Canterbury, and Farnham. 2 vols. 8vo. London.

ROBINSON, —. Forms of Stoves for Forcing Houses. 8vo. London.

1798-1817 Observations on the Means of Providing Naval Timber. Observations on the present State and future Prospects of the British Farmer, by Rusticus. Letters on the distressed State of Agriculturists by Robert Brown. And eight others, in one volume. London.

> War and weather, those unfathomable symbols of the ways of Providence, were to have their sport with the British farmer for the next eighteen years. From the year 1794, when the Board of Agriculture was beginning its surveys with the idea of improving husbandry, down to 1800, lean years followed each other in increasing severity. But war stimulated agriculture, which in turn fed the fever for enclosures, so that by 1815 hardly a common was left untilled or fen undrained. Speculation in land rose to dizzy heights, and the strain on means and credit was bound to break at the first disaster. The year 1810 saw a bounteous harvest; the year 1811 saw a promising harvest withered up by burning heat. The list of bankruptcies published in the gazettes might well be mistaken for war casualties. When peace came in 1815, she held in her hand, not an olive branch, but a sword, for there followed that curious anomaly of three abundant harvests in succession and a ruined class of farmers. Inflated agriculture broke under a superabundance that knocked the bottom out of prices. It is said that between 1814 and 1816 nearly a third of the country banks, numbering about 700, failed. Small wonder that "the distressed State of the Agriculturists" called for something to be done.

1799 MARSHALL, WILLIAM. Minutes, Experiments, etc., in the Southern Counties, with a Sketch of the Vale of London. 2 vols. 8vo. London.

1799-1816 Letters and Papers from the Correspondence of the Bath and West of England Agricultural Society. Culture of Potatoes, Rhubarb, Carrots, Turnips, Weaning and Rearing of Lambs, Managing Silk-Worms, Setting Wheat, Reclamation of Bogs, Nature of Sheep and Wool, Analysis of Soils, Manures, etc. By Arthur Young, James Anderson, and many others. 14 vols. 8vo. London.

1800 ANDERSON, JAMES. Essays Relating to Agriculture and Rural Affairs. Draining, Inclosures and Fences, Waste Lands and their Improvement, Obstacles to Agriculture in England, etc. 3 vols. 8vo. London.

1800-20 The Farmer's Magazine; a Periodical Work exclusively devoted to Agriculture and Rural Affairs. 20 vols. 8vo. Edinburgh.

> Of great historical value to the student of husbandry, and of social and economic conditions.—Bookseller's Note.

1825 ATKINSON, STEPHEN. The Discoverie and Historie of the Mynes in Scotland. (Place?)

> The MS is dated approximately 1625 by Taylor, Late Tudor and Early Stuart Geography.

1857 BEST, HENRY. Rural Economy in Yorkshire in 1641, being the Farming and Account Books of Henry Best, of Elmswell, in the East Riding of the County of York. Publ. Surtees Soc., vol. 33, Durham.

XX

Aids to Travelers

Roadbooks, Itineraries, Guides, Directories

(Since man must or will travel, he needs to know something of the routes to be traversed, the stages of his journey, and the actual distance he has gone and has yet to go. The development of such aids to travelers presents a fascinating story of supply attempting to overtake demand, which may be read in part in Fordham's *Road-Books and Itineraries* (1924). Here the barest outline must suffice. The account begins with the simple notation of military stations on a roll, like the *Peutinger Table*—which contains the oldest road map of any part of Britain—and similar Roman itineraries. These progress to records in book form of pilgrim routes to the Holy Land and other sacred shrines, and to road lists preserved in the chronicles of the fourteenth and fifteenth centuries, such as those in William of Worcester (1478), and printed in almanacs of the early sixteenth century. As the century of the Tudors advanced, the writers widened their scope to include lists of market and fair days and places, and, following in the footsteps of the French, books of the post roads for the benefit of the developing postal system. With Norden (1593), maps begin to assist the traveler by indicating how he may "spedilie find any place desired in the Mappe, and the Distance between Place and Place, without Compasses." It is with Ogilby's *Britannia* (1675) that the greatest step forward was taken. Here appears for the first time the familiar presentation of roads on strips (the ancestor of the modern automobile Blue Book), accurately measured according to the modern statute mile of 1760 yards, with detailed delineation of the terrain on either side of the road and with the distances from London to various towns. The usefulness of this system gave rise to a numerous progeny of portable roadbooks in strips "fit for the pocket of any gentleman." No marked advance was made in the eighteenth century until the publication of John Cary's *New Itinerary* (1798), which was characterized by new and exact measurements extending over 9,000 miles of roads. The nineteenth century saw the advent of the Murray Handbooks and finally the indispensable Baedeker, which eases the worries of the timid soul and anticipates every need of the traveler. As time went on, additional aids came into being in the shape of town and city Directories and Guides to cities, watering places, and gentlmen's seats, whose intent was to serve the sight-seer. One will notice in the titles of maps, from the beginning of the seventeenth century, the increasing number of crossroads incorporated as well as the habitual reference to distances between places. The bird's-eye view of cities of the sixteenth and seventeenth centuries must likewise have been of considerable help to a traveler in orienting himself.)

1568 Hubrighe, J. Almanack . . . with a Rule to knowe the Ebbes and Fluddes . . . also all the principal Faires and Martes., etc.

> Cited by Taylor, *Late Tudor and Early Stuart Geography*.

1571 Grafton, Richard. A little Treatise containing many proper Tables and Rules, etc. London.

> Cited by Taylor, *op. cit.* This contains a list of fairs.

1572 ————. For a list of fairs and highways, see his *Abridgement of the Chronicles of Englande*, under HISTORY AND CHRONICLE.

1575 Stow, John. For a list of fairs and tables of roads, see his *Summarie of the Chronicles of England*, under HISTORY AND CHRONICLE.

1576 Rowlands, Richard. The Post of the World (also known as The Post for Divers Partes of the Worlde). London.

The second title of the above, which is apparently found in only a few copies, runs: The Post for Diuers partes of the Worlde: to trauaile from one notable Citie vnto an other, with a Descripcion of the Antiquities of diuers famous Cities in Europe . . . The like not heretofore in English . . . Published by Richard Rowlands. The title of the copy in the British Museum runs: The Post of the World. Wherein is contayned the Antiquities and Originall of the most famous Cities in Europe. With their Trade and Traficke. With their Wayes and Distance of Myles, from country to country . . . A Booke right necessary and profitable, for all sortes of Persons, the like before this tyme not Imprinted. Both title pages carry the imprint of Thomas East, London, 1576. The roadbook portion consists of "The wayes and most vsed passages, from one notable citie to another, in *Germany, Bohemia, Hungaria, Polonia, Lyttaw,* and the low countries, with *Italy, Fraunce, England, Spagne, and Portingale."* The roads listed in England are the highways from Dover to London, Oxford to London, Bristol to London, Berwick to York, and St. David's to London. The fairs of England and Wales are set forth in chronological order, arranged by months. See Fordham, *Road-Books and Itineraries.* According to *DNB,* this work is a translation from the German. J. Williams suggests that the original German may have been *Kronn und Ausbundt aller Wegweiser* or an equivalent work.—*Guide to Printed Materials.* Rowlands also wróte under the pseudonym of Richard Verstegan (see Verstegan, *Restitution of Decayed Intelligence,* 1605, under HISTORY AND ANTIQUITIES).

1577   HOLINSHED, RAPHAEL. For a description of "Our Innes and Thorowfaires," see his *Chronicles,* bk. I, ch. xvi, under HISTORY AND CHRONICLE.

   In Harrison's *Description of England,* this is listed in Book III, ch. xvi. It is an account of the inns and hostelries of the period, with their customs and many curious warnings to travelers, and also a table of roads with distances in miles set out for each stage, described as "a Table of the best Thorowfaires and Townes of the greatest Travell of England." Twelve English roads are set forth and "certaine waies in Scotland, out of Reginald Wolfes his annotations."

1581   ADAMS, FRANK. Writing Tables with a Kalendar for xxiii yeres, etc. (With Tables of Roads).

   Cited by Taylor, *op. cit.*

1588   SMITH, WILLIAM. For a note on the roads listed in his *Particular Description of England,* see Smith under 1879 below.

1603   HOWE, EDWARD. For directions how to travel "from any notable towne in England to the Citie of London, or from London to any notable towne in the Realme," see his *Chronicle,* under HISTORY AND CHRONICLE.

1604   Proclamation of the certified distances between the various headlands round the English coast, entitled, "A Note of the Headlands of England as they beare one from another, agreeing with the Plot of the Description of the Countrey, with their severall Distances." Printed on the recto of a large folio sheet. With the engraved folding portulan map of England and Wales, light contemporary coloring, decorated with two compasses, the Royal Coat of Arms, and two scales. London.

1616   SINCERUS, IODOCUS. Itinerarium Galliae, ita accomodatum, ut eius ductu mediocri tempore tota Gallia obiri, Anglia et Belgium adiri possint; nec bis terve ad eadem loca rediri potest: notatis cuiusque loci, quas vocant deliciis. Lugduni.

1620   PROCTOR, THOMAS. A Profitable Work to this Whole Kingdom concerning the Mending of the Highways. London (?).

   Cited by Taylor, *op. cit.*

1625 NORDEN, JOHN. England An Intended Guyde, For English Travailers. Shewing in generall, how far one Citie, and Many Shire-Townes in England, are distant from other. Together, with the Shires in particular: and the Cheife Townes in every of them. With a generall Table, of the most of the principall Townes in Wales. Invented and Collected, by John Norden. 4to. London.

This has been called the first pocket companion for travelers. It is a series of tables, shaped in the triangular form that is still familiarly used for indicating distances from one place to another. The tables are based on the old British mile, which was employed to measure distances on roads before John Ogilby made his perambulation in the reign of Charles II. From then on, the measure of 1760 yards became the norm. These tables were compiled to go with Speed's recently completed set of county maps. See Norden under 1593, MAPS AND CHARTS.

1635 LANGEREN, JACOB VAN. A Direction for the English Traviller By which he shal be inabled to Coast about all England and Wales. And also to know how farre any Market or noteable Towne in any Shire lyeth one from an other and whether the same be East, West, North or South from ye Shire Towne. As also the distance betweene London and any other Shire or great Towne . . . Sold by Mathew Simons . . . Jacob van Langeren sculp. 39 plates and frontispiece (2 pp. of text). 4to. London.

Other edits., 1636; 3rd, 4to and 18mo, 1643; 1645, 1650; with change of title, 1657; 1662, 1668, 1677, 1680. See below.
The frontispiece of the first edition is a circular map of England. All the county maps are of "thumbnail" size, drawn to the scale of 10 miles to ¼ inch. The rivers constitute the chief feature of the maps, which otherwise are of no practical value.—Chubb, *Printed Maps in the Atlases of Great Britain and Ireland.*

1643 LANGEREN, JACOB VAN. A Direction for the English Traviller By which he shal be inabled to Coast about all England and Wales; by the help also of this Worke one may know (in what Parish, Village or Mansion House, soever he be in) what shires he is to passe through and which way he is to travell till he comes to his journies end. 37 engravings and 5 folding tables and maps. 4to. London.
For this edition all the former maps were erased and an entirely new set of maps on double the scale inserted. The first three editions are all extremely rare, no perfect copy of any being known.—Thorp, no. 518.

1657 ————. A Book of the Names of All Parishes, Market Towns, Villages, Hamlets, and smallest Places in England and Wales. Alphabetically set down, as they be in every Shire. With the Names of the Hundreds in which they are, and how many Towns there are in every Hundred . . . A Work very necessary for Traveilers, Quartermasters, Gatherers of Breefs, Strangers, Carriers, and Messengers with Letters, . . . 8vo. London.
This was published by both Simons and Jenner, in 1662 and 1668 by Jenner, and in 1677 by John Garret. It includes the impressions from the original plates by Langeren, as well as a printed list of places, together with the insertion of larger and more detailed though still very small maps of the counties.—See Fordham, *Road-Books and Itineraries.*

1636 TAYLOR, JOHN (the Water Poet). A Catalogue of Tavernes in tenne Shires about London. 12mo. London.

1637 ————. For a directory of inns and ordinaries, etc., in or near London, see his *Carriers Cosmographie,* under LONDON.

1638 LANGLEY, THOMAS. A New Almanacke and Prognostication, for . . . 1638 . . . Composed for the Meridian of Shrewsbury, and generally for the North-West parts of Great Britaine. . . . 8vo. London.

Amongst other matter this contains a table of the principal fairs of England and Wales on nine pages.—Quaritch, no. 592.

1640   HOLYOKE, F. The Rider's Dictionarie . . . with the Names of the chief Places and Towns in England, Scotland, and Ireland. 4to. London.

1653   The Kingdome of England and Principality of Wales exactly described . . . euery sheere and the small towns . . . in euery one of them. In Six Mappes. Portable for euery Mans use . . . Vsefull for all Gentlemen and Travellors . . . Described by one that trauailed through the whole Kingdome for it's purpose. Very large maps by Hollar, folded to oblong 8vo. London.

1655   PORTER, THOMAS. A New Booke of Mapps, Being a ready Guide or Direction for any Stranger, or other, 'who is to Travel in any part of the Common-wealth of England, Scotland, and Ireland. Wherein are, I. Alphabetical Tables shewing the Longitude and Latitude of all the Towns named in the said Maps; with easie and ready Directions how to find any of them. II. Tables of the Highwayes alphabetically methodized. III. Tables as easie as an Almanack, which may supply the Use thereof for 100 years, that is to say, from anno 1600 to 1700, and other useful Tables. 2 folding maps. 12mo. London.

> A very rudimentary roadbook, with the various routes arranged in small tables lettered successively. The highways shown for England and Wales number twenty-five, and the principal crossroads twelve. For Ireland roads are given, but for Scotland only an alphabetical table and no roads.—Fordham, "Itineraries," *The Library*, 4th Ser., vol. VI, no. 2, Sept. 1925.

1658   ANTONINUS. For the itinerary of Antoninus Augustus, see Wm. Burton, under BRITISH, ROMAN, AND SAXON ANTIQUITIES. In the same section see also Thomas Gale under 1709, Thomas Reynolds under 1709, Robt. Talbot under 1710-12, and K. Gibson under 1800.

> Though this work has to do with Roman roads and stations in Britain, it is listed under BRITISH, ROMAN, AND SAXON ANTIQUITIES, because its interest to editors and scholars was antiquarian.

1664   IRWIN, SIR CHRISTOPHER. Index locorum, nominum propriorum, gentilitiorum, vocumque difficiliorum quae in Latinis Scotorum historiïs occurrunt. 8vo. Edinburgh.

> This seems to have been reprinted, Edinburgh, 1682. See below.

> 1682 IRWINUS, CHRISTOPHORUS. Historiae Scotiae nomenclatura Latino-vernacula: multis flosculis, ex antiquis Albinorum monumentis, & lingua Galeciorum prisca decerptis, adspersa; in gratiam eorum qui Scotorum nomen & veritatis numen colunt, Christophorus Irwinus, abs Bon-Bosco, auspice summo numine, concinnavit; & Edinbruchii cal. Jan. 1682. imprimi curavit. 12mo. Edinburgh.

1665   GALLEN, T. Gallen, 1665; A New Almanack for the said year, containing the Lunations, Eclipses, Aspects of the Planets, etc., with directions to such as use Marts or Fairs, also to Travellers that Coast the Nation, etc. 16mo. London.

1675   MACE, THOMAS. Profit, Conveniency, and Pleasure, to the whole Nation. Being a short Rational Discourse, lately presented to His Majesty, concerning the High-Ways of England: Their Badness, the Causes thereof, . . . the impossibility of ever having them well-mended according to the old way of mending. But may most certainly be done, and for ever so maintained . . . substantially. . . . And so, that in the very depth of Winter there shall not be much Dirt, no Deep-

Cart-rutts, or High-ridges. . . . Printed for a Publick good in the Year 1675. 4to. London.

The author of this curious tract, which is written in prose and verse, was clerk to Trinity College Chapel, Cambridge, and one of the first musicians in psalmody of his time, 1676. At the end of the present tract is a curious, quaint advertisement of his "Musick's Monument," occupying seven pages. The book is very rare, only a few copies having been printed.—Bookseller's Note.

OGILBY, JOHN. Britannia: or an Illustration of the Kingdom of England and Dominion of Wales; By a Geographical and Historical Description of the principal Roads thereof. Actually admeasured and Delineated in a Century of Whole-Sheet Copper-Sculps. Accomodated with the Ichnography of the several Cities and Capital Towns; compleated by an accurate Account of the more remarkable Passages of Antiquity, with a novel Discourse of the present State, Vol. I (all published). Folding map of England and Wales, 100 engraved copperplates of road maps. Fol. London.

Ogilby's survey was utilized in roadbooks again and again, with varying titles, throughout this and the succeeding century. For the ordering of these various editions, one should consult Chubb, *Printed Maps,* and Fordham, *Road-Books and Itineraries.* Some indication of their variety and complexity is indicated below.

Another edit., with slight changes and a new title, reissued without the text, fol., London, 1675; an epitome called The English Traveller's Companion, by Ogilby and Morgan, 12mo, 1676, which ran through numerous editions, the 24th appearing in 1794; 2nd impression of the original 100 plates, with text, fol., 1698; the text alone reprinted, 8vo, 1699 (this again in 1711); the first reduction to pocket size of Ogilby's road maps, 1719; another form of this reduction engraved more delicately by Senex, 1719. Many of the titles listed for the 18th century below are variants of Ogilby.

Ogilby's upbringing was not well calculated to prepare him as a cartographer. His father had him bred as a dancing master. Lord Strafford engaged him to teach in his household and later made him Master of the Revels in Ireland, where he built a playhouse. The Irish rebellion of 1641 deprived him of fortune and occupation. Cambridge next became his residence and translations of Vergil and Homer, issued in pompous editions, together with editions of the Bible restored him to prosperity and enabled him to rebuild his theatre in Ireland. But the Great Fire of London brought him low again, though it proved to be a blessing in disguise, for it got him an appointment as cosmographer to the King and geographic printer. He published an atlas in several parts and planned to do a noble description of England in three volumes, of which only the first appeared; the second was to give a like view of cities, and the third a topographical description of the whole kingdom (see Gough, *Anecdotes of British Topography,* 35). His survey, which was carried out under order of Charles II, was planned to measure 40,000 miles of roads. Those he completed were engraved on strips, with six or seven to a plate. Only the main roads were traced, the crossroads being merely indicated. Villages and mansions were named on the maps, and in some cases the names of the owners were given. The spelling of place names often varies widely from that current today. For a standard of measurement he used the new distance of 1760 yards to a mile instead of the old standard of 2428 yards. The survey was regulated by a methodical perambulation and the distances calculated by the "great wheel," thus ensuring more accurate results.

1675 OGILBY, JOHN. Itinerarium Angliae: or, A Book of the Roads, Wherein are Contain'd The Principal Road-Ways Of His Majesty's Kingdom of England and Dominion of Wales: Actually Admeasured and Delineated in a Century of Whole-Sheet of Copper-Sculps., and Illustrated with the Ichnography of the several Cities and Capital Towns. . . . Fol. London.

1676 ————. The English Traveller's Companion, or, A Ready and Sure Guide from London to any of the principal Cities and Towns in England and Wales; containing all the grand Roads, with their Branches, and the Towns and Villages they pass through: to which is affixed the computed Distances from one to another, exhibited in five Tables, of a new and accurate Method. By a Lover of his Countrymen. 12mo. London.

1679 OGILBY, JOHN, and WILLIAM MORGAN. Mr. Ogilby's Pocket Book of Roads with the Computed & Measured Distances and the Distinction of Market and Post Townes. The 3rd Impression, To which is added, More Roads and Remarkable Places omitted in the Former, . . . By William Morgan. 8vo. London.

1699 OGILBY, JOHN. The Traveller's Guide, or, A Most Exact Description of the Roads
of England: being Mr. Ogilby's actual Survey and Mensuration by the great
Wheel, of the great Roads from London and all the considerable Cities and
Towns in England and Wales; together with the Cross-Roads from one City or
Eminent Town to another, . . . 8vo. London.

1678 SPELMAN, SIR HENRY. Villare Anglicum: or, a View of all the Cities, Towns, and
Villages in England, alphabetically composed, so that naming any town or place,
you may readily find in what Shire, Hundred, Rape, Wapentake, etc., it is in. . . .
8vo. London.

1680 ADAMS, J. Index Villaris, or, An Alphabetical Table of all the Cities, Market-
Towns, Parishes, Villages and Private Seats in England and Wales. Fol.
London.

2nd edit., to which is added a list of the nobility and their seats, fol., London, 1690; a
3rd, fol., 1700. See below.
Gough calls this the best book of its kind, which, however, is that of a gazetteer.

1700 ADAMS, J. Index Villaris, or An Exact Register, Alphabetically digested, of all the
Cities, Market Towns, Parishes, Villages, Private Seats of the King's Nobility and
Gentry, . . . with their Longitudes and Latitudes. Also the number of Parliament
Men, and a Catalogue of the Nobility and their several Seats against their Names,
and their Countries wherein scituated. Fitted to Adams' large Map of England and
Wales. Fol. London.

MORDEN, ROBERT. A Pocket Book of all the Counties of England and Wales:
Wherein are describ'd, the Chief Cities, Market-Towns and others; With the
Rivers and Roads from London. To which is added, a Compass, shewing the
bearing, and a Scale for the Distance of Places. There is also given the Length,
Breadth and Circumference of each County. The Latitude of each City or
Town, and its Distance from London. . . . 52 small outline maps of the counties.
8vo. London.

1750 MORDEN, ROBERT. A Brief Description of England and Wales; containing a particular
Account of each County; With its Antiquities, Curiosities, Situation, Figure,
Extent, Climate . . . As also, the Distance of each Market Town from London
. . . Very proper for Schools, to give Youth an Idea of Geography, and the Nature
of his own Country, and each County. 12mo. London.
This edition contains a reprint of the plates of 1680, an introduction of eight
pages, and 126 pages of letter press, divided into counties. Chubb, *op. cit.*

1681 PATERSON, JAMES. A Geographical Description of Scotland. With the Faires
largely inserted; As also, An Exact Table of Tides, and Table of the Latitude
and Longitude of the most remarkable Places in Scotland; with other useful
Notes, fit for every Man to know, either on Sea or Land. Exactly Calculated
and formed, for the Use of Travellers, Mariners, and others, who have any
Affairs or Merchandizing in this Kingdom of Scotland. Edinburgh.

2nd edit., 1685; 3rd, "much Corrected and Inlarged," 1687.
The 1st edition has 16 pages and the 2nd 24 pages. In the former the roads are merely
listed with their distances; in the latter, the roads are arranged in ordinary roadbook
form in two columns.

1682 H., W. The Infallible Guide to Travellers, or, Direct Independents, giving an
exact Account of the four principal Roads of England, beginning at the Standard at Cornhill . . . extending to the Seashore and branching to most of the
Cities . . . market-towns in England and Wales, . . . 12mo. London.

This work is closely associated with Ogilby's roadbook.—Fordham, *Road-Books and
Itineraries.*

1683 M., J. The Traveller's Guide, and the Country's Safety: Being a Declaration of the Laws of England against High-way-men, or Robbers upon the Road; what is necessary and requisite to be done by such persons as are robbed in order to the recovering their Damages; against whom they are to bring their Action, and the manner how it ought to be brought. Illustrated with a variety of Law Cases, Historical Remarks, Customs, Usages, Antiquities and Authentik Authorities. 12mo. London.

> This title suggests that the eighteenth century did not have a monopoly of "the Gentlemen of the Road."

1684 FORBES, JOHN (Publisher). The Whole Twenty-Two yearly Faires and Weekly Mercats of this ancient Kingdom of Scotland plainly set down, according to their severall Shyres, Cities, Towns, and Parish-Kirks, where they stand; as also the Noblemen and Gentlemens Names and Tytles, to whom they doe belong. 16mo. Aberdeen.

1689 GALLEN, T. Gallen, 1689. A Complete Pocket Almanack for the Year of Our Lord 1689. Containing in addition to the usual contents "the Fairs and Roads in England and Wales." 8vo. London.

1693 An Alphabetical Table of all the Cityes and Market-Townes in England and Wales: with the Counties they are in, the dayes of the Week they are kept on; with their Distance from London. Copperplates. London.

1695 CARR, WILLIAM. Traveller's Guide. 12mo. London.

1696 PLAYFORD, JOHN. Vade Mecum, or, The Necessary Companion, containing *inter alia* The Principal Roads in England. 6th edit. London.

1699 A Pocket Book of England and Wales; with Roads and Distances by Inspection. 12mo. London.

1705 OWEN, JOHN. Owen's New Book of Roads, or, A Description of the Roads of Great Britain. Folding map. 12mo. London.

> Owen's chief work was his *Britannia Depicta* (see under 1720 below).

1706 The Freemen of London's Necessary and Useful Companion, etc. See under LONDON.

1707 A List of the Several Charity Schools lately erected in the Cities of London and Westminster, and the respective Counties of England, Ireland, and Wales. Fol. London.

> This item, being so to speak an orphan, is placed here for lack of claim by any other section. One who is familiar with the widespread interest in Charity Schools in the reign of Queen Anne will readily appreciate the advantage offered by this list to a traveler intending to visit these institutions. Since no provision was made by the State to educate the children of the poor, these schools were established by philanthropic-minded individuals to enable the less fortunate classes to gain the rudiments of an education. At the close of Queen Anne's reign, some 5,000 boys and girls in the London area were taking advantage of this opportunity, and in the rest of the country the number rose to over 20,000. They were also furnished with decent clothing while at school and were apprenticed to some trade after leaving. It is no wonder that Mandeville's attack upon Charity Schools, in his *Fable of the Bees,* aroused resentment.

1708   HATTON, EDWARD. For a book "usefull, not only for Strangers but the Inhabitants," see his *A New View of London,* under LONDON.

>   The section LONDON contains many references to works intended as guides to visitors.

1709   An Useful Companion: or, A Help at Hand, being a Convenient Pocket Book. London.

>   This gives the "Rates fixed by Authority." Cited by John Ashton, *Social Life in the Reign of Queen Anne,* 358-59.

1710   A Brief Directory for those that would send their Letters to any part of England, Scotland, and Ireland. 4to. London.

1711   A Description of the Most Remarkable High-Ways, and whole known Fairs and Mercats in Scotland, With several other Remarkable Things: As also, A Description of the High-Ways from one Notable Town to another, over all England, and thereby how to Travel from any of them to the City of London. Edinburgh. (8 leaves).

1712   BERGIER, NICOLAS. The General History of the Highways in all Parts of the World, more particularly in Great Britain, Part I (all published). 8vo. London.

>   Only the first book was finished. It contained the manner of making highways used by the Carthaginians, Lacedaemonians, Romans, Peruvians, and all other nations, from the remotest antiquity to the above date. Only the last chapter deals with British Roman roads. —Gough, 6.

1713   For "An Appendix concerning the Posts, Markets, and Fairs," see *British Curiosities in Nature and Art,* under NATURAL HISTORY (1721 edition).

1715   TAYLOR, THOMAS. England Exactly Described, or, A Guide to Travellers: in a Compleat Sett of Mapps of all the Counties of England, being a Mapp for each County, where every Town and Village in each County is Perticularly Expressed with the Names and Limits of each Hundred, etc. Very usefull for all Gentlemen & Travellers, being made fitt for the Pocket. 41 uncolored maps. Obl. 4to. London.

>   2nd edit., with a map of Ireland, 8vo, London, 1716; again, 1730.
>   The maps of England are those issued in 1681 in Speed's *Maps Epitomiz'd,* except that the map of England is given instead of the map of Great Britain and Ireland, and in most cases the arms have been changed. The roads and distances are taken from Ogilby's survey. —Thorp, no. 518.

1718   Laws concerning Travelling. London. (237 pp.)

>   This treats of robbery, accidents, bad roads, innkeepers, bills of exchange, hackney coaches, chairs, carmen, and watermen in and about London, with tables and fares.—Cited by Morgan, *Bibliog. Brit. Hist.,* vol. III.

1719   GARDNER, THOMAS. A Pocket-Guide to The English Traveller: Being a Compleat Survey and Admeasurement of all the Principal Roads and most Considerable Cross-Roads in England and Wales. In One Hundred Copper-Plates. 4to. London.

>   The 100 strip maps of the roads are those of Ogilby's *Britannia* (see 1675 above) reduced to portable size. The author claims originality in "keeping the roads themselves, and every mile of them in view, with all the remarkable adjoining." He is doubtless right in stating that the *Britannia* is "Rather an Entertainment for a Traveller within Doors, than a Guide to him upon the Road," for the original is a folio.—Thorp, no. 518. The plates are more coarsely engraved than those of Senex of the same date.—Fordham, *op. cit.*

SENEX, JOHN. An Actual Survey of all the Principal Roads of England and Wales; Described by One Hundred Maps from Copper Plates. On which are delineated All the Cities, Towns, Villages, Churches, Houses, and Places of Note throughout each Road. As also, Directions to the Curious Traveller what is worth observing throughout his Journey; The whole described in the most easy and intelligible Manner. First perform'd and publish'd by John Ogilby, Esq.; And now improved, very much corrected, and made portable by John Senex. Vol. I. Containing all the Direct Roads . . . in 54 plates. Vol. II. Containing . . . Cross Roads . . . in 46 plates. Obl. 8vo. London.

Other edits., with change of title but with impressions of plates unaltered, obl. 8vo, 1742; a reissue of the strip maps of 1719, 1757; a similar edit., 1759; again, 1762; another edit. of the maps in Kitchin's *Post-Chaise Companion* (see Kitchin, 1769), 1769; with another change of title, 1775. A French and English version in parallel columns, with details of the plates rewritten in French, Paris, 1767. See below.

For Senex as a map maker see under 1714, MAPS. The reduced editions of Ogilby's *Britannia* were generally bound in leather and shaped so as to roll up and fit in the pocket. Senex's publications were continued, after his death in 1740, by his widow.

1757 SENEX, JOHN. The Roads through England delineated, or, Ogilby's Survey Revised, Improved, and Reduced to a Size portable for the Pocket. Obl. 8vo. London.

1775 JEFFERYS, THOMAS. Jefferys' Itinerary (see Jefferys this date below).

1767 (In French.) Nouvel Atlas d'Angleterre Divisé En ses 52 Comtés Avec toutes les Routes Levées Topographiquement par ordre de S. M. Britannique et les Plans des Villes et Portes de ce Royaume. 4to. Paris.
This has a second title in English and French. There is an earlier French edition, the date of which I have not ascertained. Its title runs:

Les Routes d'Ogilby par l'Angleterre. Revues, Corrigées, Augmentées, et Réduites, par Senex en 101 Cartes. Paris.

1720 J., G. Great Britain's Vademecum. 8vo. London.

OWEN, JOHN. Britannia Depicta, or, Ogilby Improv'd; Being a Correct Coppy of Mr. Ogilby's Actual Survey of all ye Direct and Principal Cross Roads in England and Wales: Wherein are exactly Delineated & Engraven All ye Cities, Towns, Villages, Churches, Seats, etc. scituate on or near the Roads, with their Respective Distances in Measured and Computed Miles. . . . To which are added, 1, A full & particular Description & Account of all the Cities, Borough-Towns, Towns-Corporate, etc., their Arms, Antiquity, Charters, Privileges, Trade, . . . with suitable Remarks on all places of Note drawn from the best Historians and Antiquaries. By Jno. Owen. . . . 2, The Arms of the Peers of this Realm, who derive their Titles from Places lying on, or near the Roads. 3, The Arms of all the Bishopricks & Deaneries, their Foundation, . . . 4, The Arms & a succinct Account of both Universities & their respective Colleges, . . . Lastly Particular & Correct Maps of all ye Counties of South Britain; with a summary Description of each County, its Circumference, Number of Acres, Boro' & Market Towns & Parishes, Air, Soil, Commodities, Manufactures, and what each Pays in ye Parish Aid, . . . 273 plates. 4to. London.

Many later editions: 2nd and 3rd retain the date of 1720; 4th, edit. by Emanuel Bowen the engraver, 1724; others, 1730, 1731, 1734, 1749, 1751, 1753, 1759, 1764. Strangely enough the one title runs through all the editions.

The plates containing the maps are numbered 1-273, printed on both sides of the sheet, and remain substantially unaltered from first to last.—Chubb, *op. cit.*

1721   S., H. The Traders' Dictionary: being an Historico-geographical Description of all the Cities, Towns, and most of the noted Villages in Great Britain; their Distances of Miles and Bearings from London; Market Days, Fairs, Lists of the Inns where the Stage-Coaches and Carriers put up in London, By H. S., A Lover of his Country. 2nd edit. 12mo. London.

1722   The Gentleman's Pocket Companion for Travelling into Foreign Parts: being a most Easy, Plain and Particular Description of the Roads from London to all the Capital Cities in Europe, with an Account of the Distances of Leagues or Miles from Place to Place, . . . with Three Dialogues in Six European Languages . . . to ask the way, etc. . . . Common Talke in an Inn. Folding maps. 8vo. London.

1729   For the Foreigner's Guide to London, see under LONDON.

1734   ROWE, JACOB. All Sorts of Wheel-Carriages Improved. Wherein it is plainly made appear, that a much less than usual Draught of Horses, etc., will be requir'd in Wagons, Carts, Coaches, and all other Wheel Vehicles, as likewise all Water-Mills, Wind-Mills and Horse-Mills. This method being found good in Practice, by the Trial of a Coach and Cart already made, shews of what great Advantage it may be put to all Farmers, Carriers, Masons, Miners, etc., and to the Publick in general, by saving them one half of the Expences they are now at in the Draught of these Vehicles, according to the common Method. Copperplates. 4to. London.

1735   BORDE, ANDREW. The Itinerary of England, or, The Peregrination of Doctor Boarde. London.

> See this work under TOURS BY NATIVES. It has a list of market towns, highways from London to Colchester and Orford, the compass of England round about by the towns on the sea coasts. It may therefore in part be classed as a guide.

KIRBY, JOHN. The Suffolk Traveller, or, A Journey through Suffolk; in which is inserted the true Distances in the Roads from Ipswich to every Market Town in Suffolk, and the same from Bury St. Edmund's. Likewise the Distance in the Roads from one Village to another; with Notes of Directions for Travellers, as what Churches and Gentlemen's Seats are passed by, and on which Side of the Road, and the Distance they are at from either of the said Towns; with a short historical Account of the Antiquities of every Market Town, Monasteries, Castles, etc., that were in former Time. 12mo. Ipswich.

> An improved edition was published by his sons, with alterations and additions, and folding map of the county, 1764. See below.
> This is no more than a compilation from other books by the publisher's friends. The new edition, though much improved beyond the former, is by no means equal to what might be done.—Gough, 491.

> 1764 KIRBY, JOHN. The Suffolk Traveller, first published by John Kirby, who took an actual Survey of the Whole Country in 1732, 1733, and 1734. 8vo. London.

1741   The Traveller's Pocket-Companion: or, A Compleat Description of the Roads in Tables of their Computed and Measured Distances, by an actual Survey and Mensuration, by the Wheel, from London to all the considerable Cities and

Towns in England and Wales; together with the Mail-Roads, and their several Stages, and the Cross-Roads. With Directions what Turnings are to be avoided in going or returning on Journeys, and Instructions for Riding Post. By a Person who has belonged to the Publick Office upwards of Twenty Years. With map "laid down in a manner that strangers may travel without any other Guide." Sq. 18mo. London.

This little roadbook professes to be the first adequate and correct guide for the English traveler, and contains a good deal of information as to postal arrangements and charges. —Bookseller's Note. The indebtedness to Ogilby is evident.

1742 POOLE, R., M.D. A Journey from London to France and Holland: or, The Traveller's Useful Vade-Mecum. Illustrated with folding Plan of Paris, folding map of London streets and engravings of French coins. Contains lists of Posts throughout the Kingdom of France, account of French money, etc. 8vo. London.

Universal Pocket Companion. A More Useful and Instructive Book than the like of the Kind. Plans, etc. London.

Included are accounts of the penny post, *ca.* 1740, and of the various stage coaches in England, with the fares, etc.—Bookseller's Note.

1745 COOPER, RICHARD. A Map of His Majesty's Roads from Edinburgh to Inverness, Fort Augustus, and Fort Williams, and of the Country adjacent thereto. 25½ × 19½ ins. (1 inch to 3½ miles.) London.

RUTHERFORD, ANDREW. Exact Plans of His Majesty's great Roads thro' the Highlands. 20¾ × 14 ins. (1 inch to 5 miles.) Cited by Gough, 626.

1748 KITCHIN, THOMAS. The Small English Atlas, being a New and Accurate Set of Maps of all the Counties in England and Wales, designed and engraved in a portable size for the Use of Travelers. 12mo. London.

SALMON, THOMAS. For a guide through the Universities of Oxford and Cambridge designed for foreigners, see under UNIVERSITIES.

1750 For distances of market towns from London, see *A Brief Description of England and Wales,* under DESCRIPTIONS.

A New Traveller's Guide through, or, A Compleat Map of South Britain, from the most accurate Surveys, the Distances between every Town on ye Roads are shewn in measured Miles. 23 × 20 ins. (No publisher's name or date.)

The Tradesman's and Traveller's Pocket Companion, or the Bath and Bristol Guide. 2nd edit. 12mo. Bath.

4th edit., 1760.

WHATLEY, STEPHEN. England's Gazetteer, or, An Accurate Description of the Cities, Towns, Villages of the Kingdom. 3 vols. 12mo. London.

The same title is given for 1751; two similar titles, of 1775 and 1779, are listed below. Perhaps they are later editions.

1775 The Complete Gazetteer of England and Wales; or, An Accurate Description of all the Cities, Towns, and Villages in the Kingdom, shewing their Situation, Manufactures, Trades, Markets, Fairs, Customs. With a descriptive Account of every County, etc. 2 vols. 12mo. London.

1778 England's Gazetteer; or, An Accurate Description of all the Cities, Towns, and Villages, in England and Wales. Shewing their Situations, Manufactures, Trades, Markets, Fairs, etc. 2 vols. 8vo. London.

1751 BRACKEN, HENRY. Bracken's Traveller's Pocket Farrier. London.

1752 An Exact List of all the Fairs in England and Wales, in Three Parts. London.

1753 The Bath and Bristol Guide. 12mo. Bath.

Proposals for the Effectual Amendment of the Roads, concerning the Wheels of all Carriages and the Method and Rules of Travelling of all Persons, by a Gentleman. 8vo. London.

This is bound up with the following item:

WICKHAM, M. The Utility and Advantages of Broad High Wheel-Carriages demonstrated Rationally and Mathematically. Folding plate. 8vo. London.

1756 DODSLEY, ROBERT and JAMES. A New and Accurate Description of the Present Great Roads and Cross Roads of England and Wales, with the several Branches leading out of them, and a Description of the several Towns thereon, divided into Four Parts, Western, Northern, Eastern and Southern: to which are added, The Ancient Roman Roads and Stations in Britain; some general Rules to know the Original of the Names of Places in England, a List of Mitred Abbots, and an Alphabetical List of Fairs regulated by the New Style. 12mo. London.

This leads through many ways long since disused, and differs in measurement from the milestones.—Gough, 37. The "New Style" refers to the change in the calendar made in 1751, in which eleven days were taken out of September and the beginning of the year shifted from March 25 to January 1.

Essay on the Present State of Publick Roads: Advantages of broad-wheeled Carriages to Trade, Travellers, etc. 8vo. London.

OWEN, WILLIAM. The Book of Fairs: An Authentic Account published by the King's Authority of all the Fairs in England and Wales, as they have been settled to be Held since the Alteration of the Stile, noting likewise the Commodities which each of said Fairs is remarkable for furnishing. 8vo. London.

6th edit., 8vo, 1770; "New edition," with title, Owen's New Book of Fairs, 12mo, 1783; also 1792.

1758 TUCKER, JOSIAH. Instructions for Travellers. Dublin.

This suggests topics for inquiry on the part of travelers, and gives corresponding information for England.—J. Williams, *op. cit.*

1759 BRICE, ANDREW. Grand Gazetteer, or Topographical Dictionary. Exeter.

This item also appears under the title *Geographical Dictionary,* 2 vols., fol., Exeter, 1760. A laborious compilation, now almost obsolete.—Lowndes, *Bibliographer's Manual.* The author was a printer in Exeter and the publisher of a newspaper there *ca.* 1715-63. He also put out a *History and Description of Exeter.*

OGILBY, JOHN, and WILLIAM MORGAN. The Traveller's Pocket-Book, or, Ogilby and Morgan's Book of the Roads improved and amended; containing, I. The Distances in measured Miles from London according to the new erected Mile-Stones, and an Account of the Seats near the Road Side. II. The Cross Roads in England and Wales. III. An Alphabetical List of all the Cities, Towns, and Villages, etc., with a whole Sheet Map of the Roads, etc. London.

> 2nd edit., sq. 24mo, London, 1761; 5th edit., corrected, with many additions, particularly Cross-Roads, 4to, 1770; sq. 12mo, 1771; same, 1775.
> This is doubtless Ogilby and Morgan's book of 1679 reworked. It seems to have been regarded as a new edition, because of the new method of measuring distances.

1760 FRENCH, JOHN. A Pocket Companion for Harrogate Spaw. 12mo. Halifax.

1761 BEAWES, WYNDHAM. Lex Mercatoria Rediviva: or, The Merchant's Directory. A Complete Guide for Traders, Captains, Insurers, Agents, with Account of our Trading Companies and Colonies, Duty of Consuls, the present general Traffick of the World, etc. Fol. London.

1762 The Book of Coach-Rates; or Hackney-Coach Directory. Describing above four thousand Fares . . . to which is added an Appendix; giving the Precise Length of most of the Principal Streets of London; together with the Rates of Chairmen, Watermen, and Carmen. 8vo. London.

The New Bath Guide, or Useful Pocket-Companion, giving an Account of its Antiquity, the Reality and Eminence of King Bladud, Description of the City, . . . with Life of Richard Nash. 2nd edit., enlarged. Portrait. 12mo. Bath.

> Other edits., 16mo, 1763; 1765, 1775, 1777, 1780, 1782, 1784, 1788, 1791, 1795, etc. See below.
> However much Bath may have owed its eminence as a resort to its antiquity and the virtues of its waters, it owed as deep a debt to the beneficent rule of Beau Nash and to the new planning of the town by the architects John Wood and his son, who rebuilt its streets in conformity with the dignity befitting a Queen of Spas. Its attractions were carried farther abroad through the numerous Guides to the place that were issued from this decade on, and travel thither was facilitated by improvements both in roads and carriages. Rival resorts soon caught on to the value of advertising, and Guides to this and that watering place became increasingly general throughout the remainder of the century.

1763 BENNETT, RICHARD. A New and Correct Post Map of the Great Cross Roads throughout England and Wales, with the measured Distances, engraved by Richard Bennett, with Views of the Sea Ports as before. 2 sheets. London.

> This also appeared on one sheet without the views.—Gough, 703.

BROWN, D. A Treatise upon Wheel Carriages.

> So cited in Turberville, *Johnson's England*, vol. I.

BROWNE, ISAAC HAWKINS. Observations on the State of the Highways. London.

> Reviewed in resumé *Gent. Mag.*, vol. 33, 234-38. These Observations, which preceded the presenting of the author's Bill, pointed out the inequalities of the laws governing the maintenance of highways and turnpikes. Apparently the latter were kept in a better condition.

HAWKINS, JOHN. Observations on the State of the Highways. London.

> There must be some relation or confusion between these two items.

Rocque, John. Rocque's Traveller's Assistant: being the most general and compleat Directory extant, to all the Post, Principal, and Cross Roads in England, Wales, Scotland, and Ireland; giving the true Names and exact Distances from the Standard in Cornhill for Great Britain; and from Dublin in Ireland, to all the several Cities, Towns, Villages, etc., in the Three Kingdoms. The Whole collected and computed in a new Manner, more clear and intelligible than any yet published. With Kitchin's engraved road-maps of England and Wales. 12mo. London.

> The work of Rocque, who was topographer to His Majesty, was highly esteemed for its excellent fidelity and accuracy.

1764   Considerations on the Acts of Parliament relative to Highways in Scotland and on the new Scheme of a Tax in Lieu of Statute Labour; altogether with an Abstract of these Acts and a Plan for a New General Act. Edinburgh.

> Statute labor was one of the feudal survivals in Scotland, and, though not so bad as the statute slavery in saltpans and coal mines, was one of the blots on national freedom so generally forgotten in histories today.

1765   Brown, D. Description of the Present Great Roads and the Principal Cross Roads. London.

1765-73   Hinton, John. The Universal Magazine of Knowledge and Pleasure. . . . London.

> This contains 39 plates of the roads of England and Wales, reduced from the 102 plates published by John Ogilby in his *Britannia*. The roads are shown in strips similar to those in John Owen's *Britannia Depicta* (see under 1720 above), but the plates are about four times larger. The names of the author and engraver are not given.—Chubb.

1766   Gore, J. The Liverpool Directory, For the Year 1766: Containing an Alphabetical List of the Merchants, Tradesmen, and Principal Inhabitants of the Town of Liverpool; with their respective Addresses. Also separate Lists of the Worshipfull the Mayor and Common Council: Officers of the Customs and Excise: Commissioners of the Dock: Light Houses: Watch, Lamps, and Scavengers: Stage Coaches, Wagons, and Carriers. . . . 8vo. Liverpool.

> Directories of Liverpool were issued also in 1769, 1773, 1774, 1777, 1781, 1783, 1790, 1796.
> Gore was both the bookseller and the compiler of this work. How a skeleton-like directory can take on the appearance of the full-bodied life of the city is revealed in an article on this directory and the succeeding one by G. Shaw, published in *Hist. Soc. Lancashire and Cheshire*, vol. 22, 1907.
> Since early editions of these directories appeared in small pamphlet form, only a few have come down to us. Gore intended his to be something more than a mere list of names· from the first it was a handbook of useful information. To each issue he added an appendix, which is full of historical interest. In the first issue this was limited to lists of the Corporation. In the next one was added a table of the Kings and Queens of England, etc. That of 1773 suggests that the sale was not very large, as he solicits encouragement, which must have come, for in 1774 came out another. Apparently, however, he found that annual issues were not wanted, for the next one did not appear until 1777, in which the appendix was enlarged to include lists of local bankers, churches, clergymen, Dissenting chapels and their ministers. The 1781 issue had lists of the local hospitals and the doctors attending, trustees of charities, and a list of streets. Down to 1790 Gore had been the sole publisher of these directories. But in that year a directory was put out by Charles Wosencroft, printer, who states in his Preface that a *correct* directory was needed. His attempt to push Gore out of the scene was not, however, successful, for the latter published one the same year, carefully revised with supplemental information. On the title pages of directories from 1774 on was the sentence "with the numbers as they are affixed to their houses"; on that of 1790 was added "(or ought to be)." (In 1766 the houses were numbered. The present system of identifying them with even numbers on one side and odd on the other was adopted in Liverpool in 1838.) The chief matter of interest for the historical student

in the 1790 edition lies in the appendix: there are recorded lists of mayors and bailiffs from 1625, recorders from 1577, and town clerks from 1568, members of Parliament, etc., and a full list of the "Names of the Streets, lanes, etc., within the Liberties of Liverpool, with the number of persons in each house." Gore's next directory came out in 1796, then 1800, and so on into the 19th century. The population of the city in 1766 was about 30,000, and the number of houses estimated was about 6,000. The phrase "principal inhabitants" in the title implies that not all were counted, but what was the hall-mark of respectability is not indicated. The classification of ranks and occupations lists 29 people as gentlemen, 188 as merchants, 16 as ministers, 22 as attorneys, 4 as physicians and 17 as surgeons, 7 as druggists, 6 as architects and surveyors, 13 as schoolmasters, 1 as French teacher, 4 as booksellers and stationers, 1 as portrait painter (not in *DNB*), 4 as pilots, 4 as boat builders, 24 as sail makers, rope makers, ship carpenters, and anchor smiths, 24 as potters and mugmen, 7 as sugar bakers, 3 as coal merchants, 1 as fishmonger, 38 as brewers (some of these innkeepers who brewed the ale they retailed), 24 as hotel and innkeepers, etc. Thus these dry bones take on flesh.

1767   The Beauties of England; or, A Comprehensive View of the chief Villages, Market-Towns and Cities, divided into the respective Counties, and intended as a Travelling Pocket Companion. 12mo. London.

The Great Roads of England. London. (Cited by Gough without date—so before 1768.)

HOMER, HENRY. An Enquiry into the Means of Preserving and Improving the Publick Roads of this Kingdom. With Observations on the probable Consequences of the present Plan. London.

KITCHIN, THOMAS. Kitchin's Post-Chaise Companion through England and Wales, containing all the Ancient and New Additional Roads, with every Topographical Detail relating thereto. 103 copperplates of strip maps. Obl. 8vo. London.

     Kitchin utilizes the maps of Senex's Survey of 1719, which in turn go back to Ogilby.

RUSSELL, ROBERT. A Description of Kent and Sussex; or, A View of all the Cities, Towns, and Villages in each County, Alphabetically Composed; so that naming any City, Town, or Village, you may readily find in what Lath or Rape they are in: to which is added, The Number of Parishes in each County, and what Cities and Borroughs return Parliament-Men; with an exact Account of all the Market-Towns in each County and what Days the Markets are kept. Written for the Use of his Countrymen. London.

     This "Index Villaris" is mentioned by Gough without date, and so appeared before 1768.

1768   Nomina Villarum Eboracensium; or, An Index of all the Towns and Villages in the County of York and County and City of York, Alphabetically Digested; shewing at one View what Riding, Wapentake, and Liberty, each Town and Village is situate; also the Borough-Towns, Parishes, and Chapelries; and the Market-Towns, with the Market and Fair Days, etc. 8vo. York.

     2nd edit., An Alphabetical Index of all the Towns, etc., (date?), York.

The Southampton Guide, or, An Account of the Antient and Present State of that Town. To which is added, A Description of the Isle of Wight, Netley Abbey, etc. 12mo. Southampton.

     2nd edit., 12mo, 1775; again in 1781, 1787, 1790, 1797.

1769   An Act of Parliament for repairing the Highways from Counter's ·Bridge, through Brentford and Hounslow, to the Powder Mills, Staines, and to Cranford Bridge (all in Middlesex), etc. Folding map. 8vo. Oxford.

>   Between 1700 and 1750, 400 Road Acts were passed by Parliament, and between 1751 and 1790, 1600 such Acts.—Trevelyan, *English Social History*, 382.

PRICE, F. The Salisbury Guide . . . to which is added, an Accurate Account of Stonehenge, etc. 12mo. Salisbury.

>   A popular Guide. 3rd edit., 1778; 19th, 1797.

1770   BOWLES, CARINGTON. Bowles's Britannia Depicta: or, Ogilby Improved. An actual Survey of all the Direct and Principal Cross Roads of England and Wales, shewing the Cities, Towns, Villages, Seats, etc., with Distances through each Road. Engraved by E. Bowen. 4to. London.

>   Bowles was one of the publishers of this work, which seems to have borrowed the title and perhaps the maps from that of John Owen (see under 1720 above).

The Margate Guide, containing a particular Account of Margate, . . . in a Letter to a Friend, with a short Description of the Isle of Thanet in general. Map of the Isle of Thanet and frontispiece of a bathing machine in its several positions. 8vo. London.

>   Other edits., 12mo, 1775; 1780, 1785. See below.

>   1775   The Margate Guide, containing a particular Account of Margate, new Buildings, Assemblies, Accomodations, Manner of Bathing, and remarkable Places in its Neighbourhood; with a short Description of the Isle of Thanet, and a Tide Table for Margate. Folding map and view of the bathing machine, etc. (one with a collapsible contrivance at the rear reaching to the sands and curtained from view). 8vo. Margate.

1771   List of Inns and Inn-Keepers in Scotland. In *Gent. Mag.*, vol. 41, 543-46. London.

>   After the name of each inn is placed a comment—good, excellent, bad, etc. The inns are located by the names of towns. This was intended as a supplement to Young's list of the same (not known to me). The compiler had in mind diverting some of the money spent in France and Germany to North Britain and the Highlands.

PATERSON, DANIEL. A New and Accurate Description of all the Direct and Principal Cross Roads in Great Britain . . . The Whole on a Plan far preferable to any Work of the Kind Extant. 8vo. London.

>   18 edits. of this from 1771 to 1829, with continuation by Moggs up to 1832. 2nd edit., 1772, in which mention is made of "a second part," *A Travelling Dictionary* (see below), usually bound up with the *Roads,* but also published separately; 12th edit., increased by matter taken from Cary's *New Itinerary* (see Cary, 1798, below), over which a lawsuit arose that ended in Cary's favor. Each edition gradually increased in size. See below.
>   Paterson entered the army service and rose from Captain to Lieut.-Colonel. In 1812 he became Lieut.-Governor of Quebec. His work was popular not only with the traveling public but also with the army, as by its use all the distances of military marches were calculated and charged in the public accounts. The 8th edition (1789) must have been in much request during the exciting days of the French Revolution.—*DNB*. See Fordham on Paterson, *The Library*, 4th Ser., vol. V, no. 4, March 1925.

>   1772   PATERSON, DANIEL. A New and Accurate Description of all the Direct and principal Cross Roads in Great Britain, containing, I. An Alphabetical List of all the Cities, Boroughs, Market and Sea-Port Towns, in England and Wales, with their Market Days. II. The Direct Roads from London to all the Cities, Towns, and remarkable Villages in England and Wales, with the Distances, and Accounts of the Seats of the Nobility and Gentry near the Road. III. The Cross Roads of England and Wales. IV. The Principal Direct and Cross Roads of Scotland. V. The Circuits of the Judges in England, never before published. The Whole on a

Plan far preferable to any Work of the Kind extant, by Daniel Paterson, Assistant to the Quarter-Master-General of His Majesty's Forces. 2nd edition, corrected, with the Addition of a Map, and other Improvements. 8vo. London.

The roadbook for Scotland was apparently published concurrently with his *Roads in Great Britain*. See below. With some issues of this 2nd edition was bound up his *Travelling Dictionary*.

PATERSON, DANIEL. A New and Accurate Description of all the Direct and Principal Cross Roads of Scotland. London.

6th edit., 1791, bound up with the 9th edit. of the *Roads in Great Britain*, 8vo, (1792).

Since the *Travelling Dictionary* is closely related to the roadbook, it is listed immediately below.

1772 PATERSON, DANIEL. A Travelling Dictionary, or, Alphabetical Tables of the Distances of all the principal Cities, Borough, Market and Sea-Port Towns in Great Britain from each other. 8vo. London.

This work ran through 8 edits. up to 1790. It was intended to be bound up with the roadbook.

SPENCER, NATHANIEL. For a guidebook in the form of a Description, see his *The Complete English Traveller*, under DESCRIPTIONS.

The author's real name was Robert Sanders.

1772 BEATNIFFE, RICHARD. The Norfolk Tour, or, Traveller's Pocket Companion: being a concise Description of all the principal Towns, Noblemen's and Gentlemen's Seats, and other remarkable Places in the County of Norfolk. 8vo. Norwich.

This was evidently a popular guidebook. 2nd edit., enlarged, Norwich, 1773; 3rd, Norwich, 1777; 4th, 12mo, 1786; 5th, 8vo, Norwich, 1795.

LETTSOM, J. C. The Naturalist's and Traveller's Companion. 8vo. London.

For description of this work, see under NATURAL HISTORY.

The New Bath Guide, or Useful Pocket Companion. 2nd edit. 12mo. Bath.

Other edits., Bath, 1776, 1779, 1791.

This may be related to the work with the same title listed under 1762 above; but it will be noticed that the later editions of each are of different dates.

RAFFALD, ELIZABETH. The Manchester Directory for the Year 1772. Containing an Alphabetical List of the Merchants, Tradesmen, and principal Inhabitants in the Town of Manchester, with the Situation of their Warehouses and Places of Abode. Also separate Lists of the City Tradesmen and their Warehouses in Manchester. The Officers of the Infirmary and Lunatic Hospital. The Officers of the Excise. The principal Whitsters, Stage Coaches, Waggons, and Carriers, with their Days of Coming in and Going out. The Vessels to and from Liverpool upon the old Navigation and Duke of Bridgewater's Canal, and their Agents. Manchester Bank and Insurance Office. His Majesty's Justices of the Peace in and near Manchester; and the Committee for the Detection and Prosecution of Felons and Receivers of Stolen or Embezzled Goods. 8vo. London.

2nd Directory of Manchester, 8vo, Manchester, 1773 (reprinted, Manchester, 1889); continued as a Directory for the Towns of Manchester and Salford, 12mo, Manchester, 1788; continued as Scholes's Directory for the same, 1794-97; continued as Banck's Manchester and Salford Directory, 12mo, Manchester, 1800. See below.

1773 RAFFALD, ELIZABETH. The Manchester Directory for 1773, designed for the Use of Persons of all Degrees, as well Natives as Foreigners. 8vo. Manchester.

1772-84   RIDER, ——. Rider's Merlin for the Years 1772, 1773, 1776, 1777, 1780, 1782, 1784, adorned with many delightful and useful Verities fitting all Capacities in the Islands of Great Britain's Monarchy, with Notes of Husbandry, Fairs, Marts, High Roads, and Tables for many Uses. 7 vols. 12mo. London.

> Each volume contains several pages dealing with America, and gives a list of the Military and Civil Establishments, Governors, Law and Revenue Officers, Agents, Staff of the Army, of each State.—Bookseller's Note.

1773   ARMSTRONG, CAPTAIN MOSTYN JOHN. A Companion to Capt. Armstrong and Son's Map of the Three Lothians, containing an Alphabetical Index of the Market Towns, Villages, and Churches; Nobility and Gentry's Seats, Castles and Ruins; Camps, Battles, Hills, etc. 8vo. London.

> See Armstrong this date under MAPS AND CHARTS.

BAYLEY, B. Observations on the General Highway and Turnpike Acts. London.

GRAY, THOMAS. The Traveller's Companion in a Tour through England and Wales: a Catalogue of the Antiquities, Houses, Parks, Plantations, Scenes, etc. London.

The Stranger's Assistant and Guide to Bath. 8vo. Bath.

1774   EASTON, J. The Salisbury Guide, an Account of Old and New Sarum, its Fairs, Markets, Trade, etc. 3rd edit. 12mo. Salisbury.

> 7th edit., 12mo, Salisbury, 1782; others, 1786, 1792, 1797, 1799, 1800.

WILLIAMSON, PETER. Williamson's Directory for the City of Edinburgh, Canongate, Leith, and Suburbs, from the 25th May 1773 to 25th May 1774, being the First Published. 12mo. Edinburgh.

> Later editions followed. Reproduced in exact facsimile, 12mo, Edinburgh, 1889.

1775   ARMSTRONG, CAPTAIN MOSTYN JOHN. A Companion to the Map of the County of Peebles, or Tweedale. 8vo. Edinburgh.

> For a guide to the County of Middlesex, see *A Description of the County of Middlesex*, under DESCRIPTIONS.

JEFFERYS, THOMAS. Jefferys' Itinerary, or, Traveller's Companion through England, Wales, and Part of Scotland. Maps of the roads on 104 plates. London.

> See Senex under 1719 above.

The Portsmouth Guide, or, A Description of the Ancient and Present State of the Place . . . with the Times of coming and going out of Machines, Waggons, Posts, etc. To which is added, Some Account of the Isle of Wight. Folding engraved view. 12mo. Portsmouth.

1776   ARMSTRONG, CAPTAIN MOSTYN JOHN. An Actual Survey of the Great Post-Roads between London and Edinburgh. 45 engraved plates of maps. 8vo. London.

> 2nd edit., London, 1783.

FISHER, THOMAS. The Kentish Traveller's Companion, in a descriptive View of the Towns, Villages, Buildings, and Antiquities on or near the Road from London to Margate, Dover, and Canterbury. 3 plates containing nine sections of maps. 12mo. Rochester and Canterbury.

> 2nd edit., 8vo, Rochester, 1779; 3rd, considerably enlarged, 8vo, Rochester, 1790; 4th, 12mo, Rochester, 1794.
> Reviewed *Gent. Mag.*, vol. 47, 34-35. As a Guide or Companion it is well spoken of. Instead of chapters, the book is divided into stages, the first ending at Dartford, the second at Rochester, the seventh at Dover, and the eighth at Canterbury. The author was a Rochester bookseller.

Highlands and North of Scotland Road-Book in 1776. 12 engraved sheets of roads from Edinburgh to Thurso and John o' Groats, to Perth, Inverness, Fort George, and cross roads in Ross, etc. 8vo. Edinburgh (?).

PATERSON, DANIEL. Paterson's British Itinerary: being a New and Accurate Delineation and Description of the Direct and principal Cross-Roads of Great Britain. 2nd edit. improved. 2 vols. 8vo. London.

> Another edit., 2 vols., 8vo, London, 1785. Other edits., 1796, 1803, and 1807. See Paterson under 1771 above.
> This survey is made up of engraved road maps in strips after the manner of Ogilby and Senex. In a note at the end of the Preface to the 1785 edition, Paterson informs us that he has withdrawn all his interest and connection from the other works of this sort. Apparently he intends to retain responsibility only for the first six editions of the *Roads*, 1771-74. While not distinguished for innovations, Paterson worked some improvements in style, arrangement, and matter along the lines pretty well established in the eighteenth century, and he did good service in this direction. Of his life very little is known.—Fordham, "Itineraries," *The Library*.

TAYLOR, GEORGE, and ANDREW SKINNER. Taylor and Skinner's Survey of the Great Post-Roads, Between London, Bath and Bristol. 12mo. London.

——————. Taylor and Skinner's Survey and Maps of the Roads of North Britain or Scotland. 61 large plates of the roads, with distances from Edinburgh, on a scale of 1 in. to the mile. Obl. fol. London.

> This was also published in reduced size, with title of The Traveller's Pocket-Book, or Abstract of, etc., 12mo, London. Other edits., 178 maps, 8vo, Edinburgh, *ca.* 1785; again, 8vo, London(?), *ca.* 1790, and 1800.
> The work was engraved after the plan of Ogilby's survey of England, by a variety of artists for the surveyors Taylor and Skinner, with a general map and index. In make-up it consists of three columns of roads with pretty full detail. The authors note that the military roads are kept in best repair. Traveling has become more commodious, and the spirit of improvement generally prevails throughout Scotland.—Fordham, *op. cit.*

1777 ARMSTRONG, CAPTAIN MOSTYN JOHN. Armstrong's Actual Survey of the Great Post Roads between London and Dover, With the Country Three Miles on each Side. Drawn on a Scale of Half an inch to a Mile. Maps and folding table of posting prices. 8vo. London.

> From the Preface to this book, it appears that Armstrong intended to publish a series of such works, one for each of the principal roads throughout England on the same plan and scale. But the volumes for the roads from London to Edinburgh and to Dover seemingly were the only ones that appeared.—Fordham, *Road-Books and Itineraries.*

The Birmingham Directory for the Year 1777. Birmingham.

> This was issued for other years as well, 1780 and 1800.

CRADOCK, JOSEPH. For an account of inns and roads, with directions to travelers, see his *Letters from Snowdon,* under TOURS BY NATIVES.

1778 BOWLES, CARINGTON. Bowles's New Travelling Map of England and Wales, exhibiting all the Direct and principal Cross Roads. Map outlined in color, measuring 24 × 21 ins. London.

> Another map, with the same title, but measuring 25 × 20½ ins., *ca.* 1780.

NASMITH, J. (Editor). Itineraria Symonis Simeonis et Wilhelmi de Worcestre, quibus accedit Tractatus de Metro; edidit J. Nasmith. 8vo. Cantab.

> Simon Simeon *fl.* 1322. He was a Franciscan monk who traveled considerably and is known only from his Itinerary of his travels. He set out from Ireland for Wales, where he met a minor friar Hugh, who became his companion in his journeys till his death just before reaching Jerusalem. From Wales he proceeded to London, and thence to France, Italy, Alexandria, and Jerusalem, of which he described the exterior. Here his manuscript ends. His remarks on foreign places are of more interest than those on England, which consist mainly of the places he passed through.—*DNB.* Walpole, in a letter to Wm. Cole, 21 May, 1778, says of this work, "I was not in the least amused with either Simon Simeon or William of Wyrcestre. If there was anything tolerable in either, it was the part omitted, or the part I did not read, which was the journey to Jerusalem, about which I have not the smallest curiosity." The Itinerary of William of Worcester is a record of his journeys in the summers of 1478 and 1480. It is a mass of undigested notes, of unequal importance, but interesting, if only as an anticipation of Leland's great work. His Survey of Bristol is of the greatest service to local topographers. He was secretary for many years to Sir John Falstolf.—*DNB.*

THICKNESSE, PHILIP. The New Prose Bath Guide, for the Year 1778. Dedicated to Lord N(orth). With a frontispiece characteristic of the Times. By the Author of A Year's Journey through France and Spain. 8vo. London.

> 2nd edit., 8vo, London, 1780 (?).
> Cited in *Gent. Mag.,* vol. 48, June, and an excerpt given in the September number of the same year. The author was a well-known traveler (see under 1777, WEST EUROPE, vol. I of this work). The present volume aims to help a visitor find his way about Bath, and to acquaint him with the people, the etiquette, the days of amusements for the healthy and the precautions to be taken by the sick with respect to bathing and drinking the hot waters. He gives an account of his sufferings from gall stones in the bladder. The title is apparently suggested by the currently popular skit on Bath, Anstey's *New Bath Guide.* See also under SPAS.

WEST, THOMAS. A Guide to the Lakes: Dedicated to the Lovers of Landscape Studies, and to All who have visited or intend to visit the Lakes in Cumberland, Westmoreland and Lancashire. By the Author of The Antiquities of Furness. 8vo. London.

> Edits., with revisions and enlargements, followed in 1780, 1784, 1789, 1793, 1796, 1799, etc.
> This work marks a notable shift from interest in roads, fairs, markets, antiquities to that in scenery and landscape. The growth of the latter interest is evidenced in the popularity of the book. The objective of the book, indicated in the title, is further amplified in its introductory paragraphs: to gratify the taste for scenery furnished in nature's highest tints; to show what refined art labors to imitate; to exhibit the pastoral and rural landscape, varied in all the "stiles, the soft, the rude, the romantic, and sublime." Then there is pointed out the improved condition of the roads, "much improved since Mr. Gray made his tour in 1765, and Mr. Pennant his in 1772." The intention is further to encourage the taste for visiting the lakes, by furnishing the traveler with a Guide, for which purpose there are laid down all the select stations and points of view noticed by those who have made the tour, verified by repeated observations, with remarks on the principal objects as they appeared from different stations, for the active as well as for the contemplative traveler. West owed much to Gray, Young, and Pennant, the earliest tourists to these regions. See Myra Reynolds, *Nature in English Poetry from Pope to Wordsworth,* ch. IV.

1779 BURLINGTON, CHARLES. The Modern Universal British Traveller; or, A New, Complete, and Accurate Tour through England, Wales, and Scotland, and the

neighbouring Islands, comprising all that is worthy of Observation in Great Britain. Maps, Views, etc. Fol. London.

> Reviewed *Gent. Mag.,* vol. 49, 198-99. The reviewer does not consider this to be a reliable work, and points out some gross errors. It is a topographical compilation arranged by counties. The text on England was done by Burlington; that on Wales by David Lewellyn Rees, Gent.; and the descriptions of Scotland by Alexander Murray, M.A. It was to appear in six penny numbers.

OWEN, JOHN. A New Book of Roads; or, A Description of the Roads of Great Britain. Being a Companion to Owen's Complete Book of Fairs. 2nd edit. 8vo. London.

> 4th edit., 1784; 7th, 1796, and later issues; combined with *New Book of Fairs,* 2 vols., 8vo, London, 1788. See below (and also under 1756 above).
> This is a roadbook without maps. What relation to William Owen is John Owen I have not been able to discover. The latter name is used by Fordham, "Itineraries."—*The Library.*

> 1788 OWEN, WILLIAM. New Book of Roads, or, A Description of the Roads of Great Britain; New Book of Fairs: a complete and authentic Account of all the Fairs in England and Wales; 5th edit., greatly improved. Folding roadmap of Great Britain. 2 vols. in 1. 8vo. London.

1780 BOWLES, CARINGTON. New Traveller's Guide through the principal Direct and Cross Roads of England and Wales, with the Distances from Town to Town in Measured Miles. A colored map 18½ × 14 ins., with the roads very clearly depicted, folded into square 12mo. London.

> See Bowles under 1778 above.

COOKE, A. For a traveling Guide, see his *Topographical and Statistical Description of the County of Essex,* under DESCRIPTIONS.

DALTON, W. H. The New and Complete English Traveller. Numerous engravings and maps. Fol. London.

> Listed also under DESCRIPTIONS.

HOPE, —. Hope's Curious and Comic Miscellaneous Works, started in his Walks. 8vo. Privately printed.

> This contains also *New Brighthelmstone Directory,* with a curious account of the bathing at Brighton.—Bookseller's Note.

SPRANGE, J. The Tunbridge Wells Guide, or, An Account of the Ancient and Present State of that Place. Folding plates. 8vo. Tunbridge Wells.

> Other edits., 1786, 1797, 1801. See below.

> 1786 SPRANGE, J. The Tunbridge Wells Guide; or, An Account of the Ancient and Present State of that Place, with a Description of Towns and Villages, Gentlemen's Seats, Foundries, Remains of Antiquity, etc., within Sixteen Miles. Numerous folding plates. 8vo. Tunbridge Wells.

The Winchester Guide: or, A Description of the Antiquities and Curiosities of that Ancient City. Copper plates. 12mo. Winton.

> Another edit., 8vo, Winton, 1796.

1781 BAILEY,—. Northern Directory, or Merchants' and Traders' Useful Companion for 1781, with the Cities of London, Westminster, Edinburgh, and Glasgow. 8vo. Warrington.

> The earliest known Directory of Glasgow.

BUTLER, WEEDEN (the Elder). The Cheltenham Guide; or, Useful Companion . . . to the Cheltenham Spa. 8vo. London.

The Cheltenham Guide: or, Memoirs of the B-N-R-D- Family continued; in a Series of Poetical Epistles. 5th edit. 8vo. London (?).
> This may be an imitation of Anstey's *New Bath Guide.*

A Complete List of all the Fairs in England and Wales fixed and moveable, as settled since the Alteration of the Stile. 8vo. London.

1782   BOWLES, CARINGTON. Bowles's Post-Chaise Companion; or, Travellers' Directory through England and Wales . . . a Survey of all the Direct and Principal Cross Roads. 200 strip maps. 2 vols. 12mo. London.

The Chester Guide; or, An Account of the Antient and Present State of that City. To which is added A Directory. 2nd edit. 12mo. Chester.
> 3rd edit., 1787; again, 1793, with a List of the Earls of Chester; another 1795; again, 1797.

A Description of the Towns and Villages on and adjoining the Great North Road from London to Bawtry. 8vo. London.

1783   AINSLIE, —. Ainslie's Travelling Map of Scotland, showing the Distances from one Stage to another. 23 × 21 ins. Edinburgh.

KITCHIN, THOMAS. The Traveller's Guide through England and Wales. Routes from Stage to Stage (with mileage). Direct Roads, Mansions, Castles, etc. Large map, 21½ × 25½ ins., showing the roads. 4to. London.
> This work includes "General Hints for the Management of Horses."

The Roads of Great Britain, with a Supplement for the Roads of Scotland, by Wm. M. Faden. 24 × 30 ins. London (?).
> Another issue for 1787.

TAIT, JOHN. John Tait's Directory for the City of Glasgow, Villages of Anderton, Calton and Gorbals, also for the Towns of Paisley, Greenock, Port-Glasgow, and Kilmarnock, for 1783-4. 8vo. Glasgow.
> Facsimile reprint, Glasgow, 1871.

The Windsor Guide, containing a Description of the Town and Castle. 12mo. London.
> Other edits., 1793, 1795, 1800, etc. See below.
>
> 1800   The Windsor Guide, containing a Description of the Town and Castle, the Lodges, Parks and Forests, the present State of the Paintings and Curiosities in the Royal Apartments, etc., to which is added, a Brief Account of Eton. Folding plate. 12mo. Windsor.

1783-1830   The Highways Book of the Township of Welburn in the North Riding of Yorkshire: from 1783 to 1830. 4to. London (?).
> This should never have been taken from the parish chest. It shows all the disbursements for the highways during nearly fifty years, and contains the signatures of the surveyors and principal inhabitants.—Bookseller's Note.

1784 BAILEY, —. Bailey's British Directory; or, Merchants' and Traders' Useful Companion for the Year 1784. 4 vols. 8vo. London.

CARY, JOHN. The Actual Survey of the Great Post Roads between London and Falmouth. 12mo. London.

> This is in the form of road strips. Probably in anticipation of his *New Itinerary*, Cary had published from as early as 1783 maps of London and environs, and other topographical works. His roadbooks are of considerable beauty, very finely engraved and colored by hand.—Fordham, *John Cary*.

The Newcastle and Gateshead Directory for 1782, 1783, and 1784. 12mo. Newcastle.

> The same for 1795, Newcastle. Reprinted in facsimile, Newcastle-upon-Tyne, 3 tables, 1889.

1785 HENINGTON, JOHN. The Merchant's Miscellany and Traveller's Complete Compendium, containing a mercantile State and public View of the County of Bedford for 1785. 8vo. Bedford.

Les Délices des Chateaux Royaux: or, a Pocket Companion to the Royal Palaces of Windsor, Kensington, Kew, etc. 12mo. Windsor.

A Pocket Vade-Mecum through Monmouthshire and Part of South Wales; containing a Description of the Counties of Monmouth, Glamorgan, Carmarthen, and Brecknock. 8vo. London.

> This contains descriptions of the views and an account of the antiquities, curiosities, etc.

WALLIS, JOHN. New Pocket Edition of the English Counties, or Travellers' Companion, in which are carefully laid down all the Direct and Cross Roads, Cities, Townes, Villages, Parks, Seats, and Rivers. General map of England and Wales and 43 county maps (all hand colored). 12mo. Apud Auctorem.

> Another edit., 12mo, London, 1800.
> A neatly executed pocket atlas of England and Wales. It was unknown to Watts, Lowndes, or Allibone. The counties, which happen to stretch parallel with the latitude, like Suffolk, Surrey, and Sussex, are maddeningly shown to be standing on end.—Sotheran, Catalogue.

The Weymouth Guide, exhibiting the Ancient and Present State of Weymouth and Melcombe Regis. 8vo. Weymouth.

> See John Harvey's *Guide* under 1788 below.

1786 Advice to a Young Rider, and Travelling Tradesman. (So listed in *Gent. Mag.*, vol. 56, 981.)

CARY, JOHN. Cary's Actual Survey of the Country Fifteen Miles round London. On a Scale of one inch to a mile. Wherein the Roads, Rivers, etc., . . . are distinguished . . . Preceded by a General Map of the Whole, to which is added, An Index of all the Names contained in the plates. 51 maps. 8vo. London.

> The fine engraving of the plates was done by Cary himself.

FADEN, WILLIAM. Faden's Map of the Roads of Great Britain. Shires outlined in color. 28 × 22½ ins. London.

MINSHULL, T. The Shrewsbury Guide, and Salopian Directory for 1786. Shrewsbury.

Tunbridge Wells Guide, with Descriptions of the Towns and Villages, Gentlemen's Seats, etc. Folding plates. 12mo. Tunbridge (?).

1787   For a guide to Eastbourne, see under TOWNS.

JONES, NATHANIEL. Directory or useful Pocket Companion for 1787 (Glasgow). 12mo. Glasgow.

> Reprinted, with an Introduction and Notes on old Glasgow celebrities, by "the Rambling Reporter," Glasgow, 1868.

KINCAID, ALEXANDER. The History of Edinburgh . . . by way of Guide to the City and Suburbs. To which is annexed, A Gazetteer of the County, embellished with a Plan of the Town, and a Map of the Environs. 8vo. Edinburgh.

> Listed also under TOWNS. See Kincaid under 1794 below.

MAVOR, REV. WILLIAM. Blenheim, a Poem. To which is added, A Blenheim Guide. Inscribed to their Graces the Duke and Duchess of Marlborough. Oxford.

> Reviewed *Gent. Mag.,* vol. 57, 166. The reviewer is of the opinion that the apology Gilpin makes for the architect Vanbrugh is worth more than "10,000 lines of poetical panegyric from the parson of the parish" (see Gilpin, *Observations on the Mountains and Lakes in Cumberland*). See also Mavor this date under TOWNS.

SCHOFIELD, JAMES. Historical and Descriptive Guide to Scarborough and its Environs. 8vo. York.

The Walker's Companion. (So listed in *Gent. Mag.,* vol. 57, 255.)

WILLIAMS, J. A Directory of Sheffield; including the Manufacturers of the adjacent Villages, etc. 8vo. Sheffield.

> Reprinted in facsimile, with an Introduction by S. O. Addy, Sheffield, 1889.
> This contains lists by occupations and in alphabetical order.—J. Williams, *op. cit.*

1788   England Described: or, The Traveller's Companion, containing whatever is curious in the several Counties, Cities, Boroughs, Market Towns and Villages of Note, in the Kingdom, etc., with an Appendix containing a Brief Account of Wales. 8vo. London.

The Hampshire Pocket Companion . . . for 1788. 8vo. Southampton.

HARVEY, JOHN. Harvey's Improved Weymouth Guide, containing a Description of Weymouth, Portland, Lulworth Castle, etc., with a List of the Members of Parliament for the Boroughs of Weymouth and Melcombe Regis, from the earliest Period, a List of Lodging Houses and a New Map of Weymouth. (This is bound up with the History of the Town and County of Poole, with a chronological List of Mayors, from 1490 to the present Time, 1788.) 8vo. Dorchester.

> Another edit., 8vo, Dorchester, 1800.

HOLME, EDWARD. A Directory for the Towns of Manchester and Salford for the Year 1788. 8vo. Manchester.

LOVE, JOHN. The New Weymouth Guide, or Useful Pocket Companion. 8vo. Weymouth.

OGDEN, JAMES. Radford's Directory for the Towns of Manchester and Salford for 1788. (Bound up with A Description of Manchester, by a Native, 1783.) Manchester.

The Worcester Directory. 12mo. Worcester.

1789 A Companion to the Leasowes, Hagley, and Enville; with a Sketch of Fisherwick. 8vo. London and Birmingham.

> These three famous gardens were also described by Heely, *Letters on the Beauties of Hagley, Envil, and the Leasowes,* under 1777, TOWNS.

The Itinerary of Part of Scotland. (So cited by Mitchell, *Scot. Topog.,* vol. II.)

PRIDE, THOMAS, and PHILIP LUCKOMBE. The Traveller's Companion, or New Itinerary of England and Wales, with Part of Scotland, arranged in the Manner of Copper Plates; being an Accurate and Complete View of the principal Roads in Great Britain: taken from Actual Surveys, wherein every Object worthy of Notice is pointed out: illustrated by two Maps. To which are annexed, The Circuits of the Judges, the Ports from which the Packets sail, and a copious Index, where the Market Days of each Town are particularlized. London.

> Reviewed *Gent. Mag.,* vol. 59, 634-35. Pride was a land surveyor for nearly forty years, and had occasion on his journeys to note the inaccuracies and deficiencies of all the Books of Roads extant. So he proposes to do one that will be both accurate and serviceable. But the work belies his pretensions in almost every respect, being as inaccurate and erroneous as those he condemns. He cites owners of houses who have been dead twenty years; misnames those who are living; while tolerably accurate in the roads he takes over from Rocque, he carries over in his other borrowings the errors of his originals. Tide tables for crossing washes are listed for only two places, and these cannot be relied on. The reviewer cannot be persuaded to recommend any one "Traveller's Guide," and this one least of all.

SHERIFF, JAMES. A Plan of the Present and Propos'd New Road lying between Wood Brook and the Pigeon House, on the Road from Birmingham to Bromsgrove. (Place?)

> The survey was made by Sheriff in 1786. It includes excellent plates.—Quoted.

SHIERCLIFF, E. The Bristol and Hot-Well Guide, or Useful Entertaining Pocket Companion. 8vo. Bristol.

> 2nd edit., corrected, Bristol, 1793. See below.

> 1793 SHIERCLIFF, E. The Bristol and Hot-Well Guide; containing an Historical Account of the Antient and Present State of that opulent City, also of the Hotwell: the Nature, Properties, and Effects of the Medicinal Water. To which is added, A Description of Clifton, Monuments of Antiquity, principal Seats, and Natural and other Curiosities in the adjacent Country. 2nd edit., corrected and enlarged to the present Time. Bristol.
> Reviewed *Gent. Mag.,* vol. 64, 63-64; 153-55. This was found to be a pleasant and useful Guide on a visit to Bristol the summer preceding. It contains almost everything a traveler needs to know, except an accurate plan of the town.

WARNER, R. A Companion in a Tour round Lymington; comprehending a Brief Account of that Place and its Environs, the New Forest, Isle of Wight, etc. 12mo. Southampton.

1790 BARFOOT, PETER, and JOHN WILKES. The Universal Directory of British Trade and Commerce, comprehending Lists of the Inhabitants of London, Westminster, and Southwark, and all the Cities, Towns, and principal Villages in England and Wales, with the Mails and other Coaches, Stage Waggons, Hoys, Packets, and Trading Vessels, etc. 8vo. London.

> See Barfoot, under 1793 below, and same date under LONDON.

BROSTER, J. The Chester Guide, giving an Account of its Antiquities, Buildings, Churches, Trade, etc., with a Directory. Folding plan. 12mo. Chester.

CARY, JOHN. Survey of the High Roads from London to Hampton Court, Bagshot, Oakingham, Binfield, Windsor, Maidenhead, High Wycombe, Amersham, Rickmansworth, Tring, St. Albans, Welwyn, Hertford, Ware, Bishops Stortford, Chipping Ongar, Chelmsford, Gravesend, Rochester, Maidstone, Tunbridge Wells, East Grinsted, Ryegate, Dorking, Guildford, Richmond. On a Scale of one Inch to a Mile. Folding general map, plan for explaining the different Trusts of the Turnpike Gates, and 80 road maps. 4to. Apud Auctorem. London.

> Later edits., 1799, 1801.
> Other citations of this work list only 40 maps, all hand colored. The maps cover a complete circle of all the roads leading out of London for a limited distance.—Thorp, no. 523. The minute details given render this one of the most attractive and interesting of Road Books. Houses on the open and closed roads, heaths, commons, parks, gentlemen's seats, inns, bridges, are all clearly denoted, with the names of the residents and exact situation of their houses, and points on the road from which they may be seen. As usual, the names of residents bring back the age to very life, such as on the High Wycombe Road, just beyond the 24th milestone. Gregory's *Mr. Burke,* cited by Sotheran.

————. Cary's Traveller's Companion: or, A Delineation of the Turnpike Roads of England and Wales; shewing the immediate Route to every Market and Borough Town throughout the Kingdom. Laid down from the best Authorities, on a New Set of County Maps. 8vo. London.

> This ran through at least twelve editions. It is not actually a roadbook, but a series of small county maps, with the roads specially distinguished upon them.—Fordham, *John Cary.*

CRUTTWELL, CLEMENT(?). Bath Guide. London.

Directions for the Junction of the Roads of England and Wales through all the Counties, with a List of Seats in each County. Fol. London. (n.d.)

> Cited in another catalogue as of *ca.* 1800.

HALL, J. New Margate and Ramsgate Guide. 8vo. London.

LUCKOMBE, PHILIP. England's Gazetteer; or, an Accurate Description of all the Cities, Towns, and Villages in the Kingdom. 3 vols. 12mo. London.

RYALL, J. The New Weymouth Guide, containing a Description of Weymouth, the Mineral Spring at Nottingham, etc. 8vo. Weymouth.

> 2nd edit., 12mo, Weymouth, 1790; another edit., 1798; again, 1800.

Wosencroft, Charles (Printer). The Liverpool Directory for the Year 1790. 18mo. Liverpool.

1791 Battle, R. G. Battle's Hull Directory for 1791. 12mo. Hull.

> Facsimile reprint, together with the appendix for 1792, including a Directory of Beverley, Hull, 1885.
> This contains lists of officials, bankers, merchants, vessels, time tables of coaches and boats, etc.—J. Williams.

Brown, T. A New and Accurate Travelling Map of Scotland. 21 × 17 ins., colored. Edinburgh.

> Another issue, Edinburgh, 1795.

1792 An Alphabetical Index of all the Towns, Villages, Hamlets, etc., in the County of York, and County of the City of York. 8vo. York.

Baker, James. A Picturesque Guide to the Local Beauties of Wales, and the Marches, interspersed with the most interesting Subjects of Antiquity in that Principality. By James Baker. Assisted by Gentlemen of great Scientific Learning and Knowledge. Vol. I. 4to. London.

> 2nd edit., with additions, 3 vols., Worcester, 1795.
> Reviewed *Gent. Mag.*, vol. 65, 409-10. The criticism runs to the effect that there seems to be no end to the multiplication of picturesque views or topographical accounts of this country. In this work the views are its chief merit, but the selection could have been improved. The depiction of seats may please the owner's vanity, but they are not of general interest. The descriptions are meager.

Caernarvonshire. For a guide book to this county, see this date under history and antiquities.

Cary, John. The Road from the New Port of Milford, To the New Passage of the Severn, and Gloucester. Plates. London.

> This was surveyed by C. Hassall and J. Williams in 1790. Cary engraved and published a set of plates for the survey.

The Gloucester Guide . . . containing Every Thing that is worthy of Observation in that Ancient City, Suburbs, etc. With a folding Table of the Posts to and from the City of Gloucester. Collected and arranged by a Citizen and Member of the University of Oxford. 12mo. London.

A New Guide to the City of Edinburgh, containing a Description of all the Public Buildings and a concise History of the City. Plan and illustrations. 12mo. Edinburgh.

> 3rd edit., 12mo, Edinburgh, 1797.

Plymouth Dock Guide, with a Description of the Towns and Villages surrounding it. 8vo. Plymouth Dock.

Robertson, Archibald. A Topographical Survey of the Great Road from London to Bath and Bristol, with Historical and Descriptive Accounts of the Country, Towns, Villages, and Gentlemen's Seats. Illus. by Perspective Views of the Most Select and Picturesque Scenery, and a map. 2 vols. 8vo. London.

An edit., 2 vols., 8vo, London, 1798.—Pinkerton, vol. XVII.
The map includes the country three miles on each side of the road. It is drawn on a scale of one inch to a mile. The plates are beautifully engraved and resemble Cary's work, but they carry no name.—Fordham.

Ross, C. The Traveller's Guide to Loch Lomond and its Environs. Map. 8vo. Paisley.

This work describes Paisley, Old Kirkpatrick, Dumbarton, Glenfruin, Loch and Ben Lomond, Loch Long, etc.—Mitchell, *Scot. Topog.*, vol. II.

Travellers' Directory through Scotland: Lists of all the Direct and Principal Cross Roads, shewing Towns, Post-Stages, etc. Folding map. 8vo. Edinburgh (?).

1793   IBBETSON, J. C., JOHN LAPORTE, and JOHN HASSALL. A Picturesque Guide to Bath, Bristol Hot-Wells, the River Avon and adjacent Country. Illustrated with a set of 16 views in aquatint, taken in the summer of 1792. 4to. London.

These charming views are a happy result of the collaboration of Ibbetson and Hassall (both friends of George Morland), the former adorning with interesting figures, cattle, etc., the fine landscapes of the latter.—Bookseller's Note.

L., G. C. Useful Instructions for Travellers. 8vo. London.

The New Bath Guide. Map and Portraits. 12mo. Bath.

The same, 1798. To identify the various Bath Guides and their later editions is difficult without an actual examination of the individual issues.

The Traveller's Companion from Holyhead to London. 12mo. London.

2nd edit., 8vo., London, 1796.

1793-94   AITCHISON, T. Edinburgh Directory, 1793-94, with a List of the Principal Inhabitants of Leith and its Neighbourhood. Map. 12mo. Edinburgh.

See Aitchison under 1800 below.

1794   CARY, JOHN. Itinerary, or, Accurate Delineation of the Great Roads both Direct and Cross, through England and Wales, and many of the Principal Roads in Scotland; with the Names of those Inns which supply Post Horses and Carriages; accompanied with a most extensive Selection of Noblemen and Gentlemen's Seats, a List of the Packet Boats, and their Time of Sailing, etc. Maps. 8vo. London.

Other edits. followed. See Cary, under 1798 below.

————. New Map of England and Wales, with Part of Scotland, in which are carefully laid down all the Direct and Principal Cross Roads, the Course of the Rivers and Navigable Canals. 80 large scale, colored maps, with a very extensive index. Apud Auctorem.

The Chichester Guide, containing an Account of the Antient and Present State of the City. 8vo. Chichester.

Later edits., 1795 and 1800. See below.

1800   The Chichester Guide, containing an Account of the Antient and Present State of the City, and the Fashionable and Elegant Watering-Place of Bognor. 8vo. Chichester.

CRAWFORD, —. Crawford's Description of Brighthelmstone and the adjacent Country, or, New Guide for Ladies and Gentlemen using that Place of Health and Amusement. 12mo. Brighthelmstone.

A Description of Buxton and the adjacent Country: or, The New Guide, for Ladies and Gentlemen, resorting to that Place of Health and Amusement; where, for the Convenience of the Public, His Grace the Duke of Devonshire has magnificently provided such very handsome and ample Accomodations. (Place?)

    Noticed in *Gent. Mag.,* vol. 64, 360. This Guide fulfills tolerably well the genuine needs of visitors to this place.

Eighty-four Acts of Parliament passed between 1724 and 1794, dealing with the Construction and Alterations of Roads throughout England. Fol. London.

KINCAID, ALEXANDER. The Traveller's Companion through the City of Edinburgh and Suburbs, with a Concise History and Description of the Public Buildings, etc. Engravings and plan. 8vo. Edinburgh.

    This may be the 2nd edit. of his *New Guide to the City of Edinburgh*; see Kincaid, under 1792 above.

The Liverpool Directory and Guide. Liverpool.

    Shaw says that this was taken from the *Universal British Directory of Trade, Commerce,* etc., 5 vols., London (see Barfoot, under 1790 above, and the *Universal Directory* below). The preliminary matter which the publisher of the *Directory* had taken from Gore (see Gore, under 1766 above) was omitted in the above *Liverpool Directory,* and the short history of the town rewritten. The volume was repaged and a title page added.—*History of the Liverpool Directories, 1766-1907.*

MATTHEWS, —. Matthews' New Bristol Directory, for the Year 1793-94. . . . Map. Bristol.

SCHOLES, —. Scholes' Manchester and Salford Directory, etc. 12mo. Manchester.

    2nd edit., Manchester, 1797. See Raffald, under 1772 above.
    This contains a "Short Sketch of the History of Manchester, first published in the Encyclopaedia Britannica."—Fishwick, *The Lancashire Library.*

STELL, J. The Hastings Guide, or, A Description of that Ancient Town and Port . . . By an Inhabitant. 8vo. London.

    2nd edit., 1797.

The Universal British Directory of Trade, Commerce, and Manufacture, comprising Lists of Inhabitants of London . . . and of all the Cities, etc., in England and Wales. 5 vols. 8vo. London.

WESTON, RICHARD. The Leicester Directory. 12mo. Loughborough.

1795 BOSWELL, EDWARD. The Civil Division of the County of Dorset methodically digested and arranged, with Lives of Magistrates, their Fees, and a complete Nomina Villarum. Map. 8vo. Sherborne.

The Cambrian Register, for the Year 1795. 8vo. London.

    The same for 1796 and later years.

1796 KENT, NATHANIEL. For his Directory of stage coaches, hackney coaches, inns, where carriers "put up and go out from," rates, etc., see Kent, under this date, LONDON.

PASQUIN, ANTHONY (i.e., John Williams). The New Brighton Guide, involving a Complete, Authentic, and Honourable Solution of the recent Mysteries of Carlton House, by Anthony Pasquin. 6th edit. 68 pp. And a Looking-Glass for the Royal Family, with Documents for English Ladies, and all Foreigners residing in London, being a Post-script to Brighton Guide, by John Williams, whose public Appelation is Anthony Pasquin. 36 pp. London.

> This satirist and miscellaneous writer became involved in libel suits, which he issued against Gifford, for his "Baviad and Maeviad," and against others as well. He edited the *Federalist* in New York City and died in Brooklyn.—*DNB*.

SOTHERAN, —. Sotheran's York Guide, including a Description of the Public Buildings, etc. 8vo. York.

> Another copy with a different title page was issued, York, 1799.

1797 CHEYNE, N. R. The Roads of Great Britain, with Tables of Distances. Edinburgh.

A Directory of Sheffield. 12mo. Sheffield.

> See Williams, under 1787 above.

HATFIELD, J. A New Scarborough Guide; containing Customs, Amusements, Lodging-houses, etc.; with miscellaneous Anecdotes, and other incidental Matter. By a Gentleman. 12mo. London.

> Noticed in *Gent. Mag.*, vol. 67, 952. As a rule the latest Guide to a place of fluctuating fortunes is generally the best. So with this one.

HEATH, CHARLES. For a guide to Bristol, see his second edition of *History*, etc., *of Bristol*, under 1794, TOWNS.

The Margate Guide; a descriptive Poem with Notes. Also, a general Account of Ramsgate, Broadstairs, etc. By an Inhabitant. 12mo. Margate.

M'NAYRE, JAMES. A Guide from Glasgow to some of the most Remarkable Scenes in the Highlands of Scotland and to the Falls of the Clyde. 8vo. Glasgow.

> This differs from the form of the ordinary tourist's guide, in that it consists of the impressions made on the author during his various journeys.—Mitchell, *List of Travels*.

Moss, W. The Liverpool Guide, including a Sketch of the Environs. 2nd edit. Folding map of the town. 8vo. Liverpool.

> 3rd edit., 1799.
> Noticed in *Gent. Mag.*, vol. 68, 1060, which considers it to be a useful manual, with a neat, well-executed map, though it could do with more detail about the environment.—Shaw points out that the principal manufactures are chiefly confined to what is necessary for the construction and equipment of ships, an observation that applies also to Gore's *Directory* of 1766.

The New Bristol Guide, containing its Antiquities . . . and other Particulars. Also improved and distinct Accounts of the Hotwells and Clifton. 12mo. Bristol.

> Another edit., 1799. See below.

1799 The New Bristol Guide, with Accounts of the Hotwells and Clifton, Biographies, Memoirs of Chatterton the Juvenile Poet, List of Bankers, Coaches, Posts, etc. 12mo. Bristol.

PRICE, JOHN. The Ludlow Guide, comprising an Account of the Antient and Modern State of that Town and Neighbourhood, with every necessary Information for the Stranger and Traveller. 2nd edit. 12mo. Ludlow.

3rd edit., Ludlow, 1798.
Noticed in *Gent. Mag.*, vol. 67, 771. Here it is called a most elegant publication. Price was also the author of a work on Leominster and Hereford (see Price, under 1795, TOWNS).

——————. The Worcestershire Guide and Worcestershire Royal Directory; containing . . . an historical Account of the principal Towns, Villages, Gentlemen's Seats, etc., in the County. 8vo. Worcester.

See also Price, under 1799 below.

1798 CARY, JOHN. New Itinerary, or An Accurate Delineation of the Great Roads, both Direct and Cross, throughout England and Wales, with many of the Principal Roads in Scotland, from an Actual Admeasurement made by Command of the Postmaster General and Superintendent of the Mail Coaches, with the Names of the Inns which supply Post Horses and Carriages, a most extensive Selection of Noblemen and Gentlemen's Seats, a List of Packet Boats, etc. Folding map of England and Wales. 8vo. London.

Several later editions in the following decade.
This was Cary's best known work, one which placed him at the head of all surveyors. How particular and minute was the information he supplied to travelers can be gathered from the instructions he gave to his numerous assistants in the actual surveys, which were probably done by the wheel: "to ascertain the whole of the turnings, branching or running out of the road he was surveying, and to note every object of the smallest importance, or that could be of use to the traveller, and the exact distance of one stationary object from another, wherever it could be in any degree useful; and to inform himself of the different seats which came within his observations as well as any other matter deserving notice."—Quoted by Jervis, *The World in Maps.*

Guide to the Castle and Town of Windsor. 8vo. Windsor.

This may be a variant of the Windsor Guide of 1783 above.

MOORE, JAMES. A List of the principal Castles and Monasteries in Great Britain. 8vo. London.

A New Guide to the City of Edinburgh, with 13 Views and a Plan of the City. Edinburgh.

RICHARDSON, T. A Guide to Loch Lomond, Loch Long, Loch Fine, and Inverary, with Maps from actual Surveys. With a concise Description of all the Towns, Villages, Gentlemen's Seats, etc., situated near these Roads. Maps and illustrations. 12mo. Glasgow.

The description is printed separately and consists of brief notices of the places passed through en route from Glasgow as the starting point. The author waxes lyrical over the view from Ben Lomond, and lays down the emotions one will experience as he turns his gaze from this feature to that. In this respect he is in accord with the vogue of using visual perception to awaken feelings as the object of tours. There is reference to the practice of landlords of peopling their estates with sheep and the consequent depopulation of men, and also to the remedy, as yet ineffective, of planting villages on the coast to encourage the fisheries. Maps accompany the text.

The Traveller's Guide, or, A Topographical Description of Scotland and the Islands belonging to it. Folding maps and illustrations. 8vo. Edinburgh.

Many later edits. followed.

1798-1800   MAVOR, REV. WILLIAM. The British Tourist, or Traveller's Pocket Companion through England, Wales, Scotland, and Ireland; comprehending the most celebrated Tours in the British Islands. 6 vols. 12mo. London.

This consists of condensed and partial accounts of tours already published. It was obviously intended to furnish prospective tourists with information and experience.

1799   A Companion in a Tour round Southampton, various Particulars of the New Forest, Lymington, Christchurch, etc., and the Isle of Wight. 8vo. Southampton.

EDWARD, —. The Bristol Guide. 12mo. Bristol (?).

GLASSE, G. H. The Margate New Guide. 12mo. Margate (?).

For a guide to Stratford-upon-Avon, see *A Brief Account of Stratford,* under TOWNS.

The Modern Universal Traveller, or a Complete and Accurate Tour through England, Wales and Scotland and neighbouring Islands. London.

MURRAY, THE HON. MRS. A Companion and Useful Guide to the Beauties of Scotland, to the Lakes of Westmoreland, Cumberland, and Lancashire; and to the Curiosities in the District of Craven in the West Riding of Yorkshire. To which is added, a More Particular Description of Scotland, especially that Part of it called the Highlands. 2 vols. 8vo. London.

PRICE, JOHN. The Worcester Guide, containing an Account of the Ancient and Present State of that City, etc. 8vo. Worcester.

See Price, under 1797 above.

1799-1820   Notes on Bridges and Roads in the Highlands. *Trans. High. Soc.,* Introductions to vols. 1-4. 8vo. Edinburgh.

1800   AITCHISON, T. Leith and Edinburgh Directory (separately), from July 1799 to July 1800. 12mo. Edinburgh.

BANCK, —. Banck's Manchester and Salford Directory, or Alphabetical List of Merchants, Manufacturers, and Principal Inhabitants, with the Numbers affixed to their Houses, etc. 12mo. Manchester.

See Raffald, *Manchester Guide,* under 1772 above.

BISSETT, JAMES. A Poetic Survey round Birmingham, with a Brief Description of the different Curiosities and Manufactories of the Place, intended as a Guide to Strangers, accompanied by a Plan of the Town and Magnificent Directory, comprising the Names, etc., of Professional Gentlemen, etc., of Birmingham. Engraved plates by Egerton and others. 8vo. Birmingham.

This gives useful notes on the residents and manufactories of the town as well as many engravings of old buildings now long removed.—Bookseller's Note.

BOTT, W. Description of Buxton. Description of Manchester. (Bound in one volume with a collection of other guides.)

BRIDGES, J. A Book of Fairs; or, a Guide to West-country Travellers. 8vo. London.

Brighton New Guide; or, a Description of Brighthelmstone, and the adjacent Country. 12mo. London.

The Cambrian Directory, or, Cursory Sketches of the Welsh Territories. With a chart. 8vo. Salisbury.

A Companion to the Isle of Wight. 2nd edit. 12mo. Newport.

A Companion to the Watering and Bathing Places of England. 12mo. London.

Among the places mentioned are Bognar, Brighton, Margate, Bath, Scarborough, etc.—Bookseller's Note.

COOKE, G. A. Cooke's Topography of Great Britain, or, British Traveller's Pocket Directory, containing a Complete Description of each County. 43 vols. Maps. London.

See under 1780, DESCRIPTIONS.

The Dover and Deal Directory and Guide, containing a concise Account of the Town, Harbour, Castle and Neighbourhood of Dover; also the Town of Deal. 8vo. Dover.

EDWARDS, J. Tables of Lineal Distances for Sussex. Plates. 4to. London.

FADEN, WILLIAM. Faden's Map of the Roads to accompany Paterson's Book. Counties outlined in color. 29 × 25 ins.

——————. Old Road Map of Great Britain. 30 × 15 ins.

HOUSMAN, JOHN. A Descriptive Tour and Guide to the Lakes, Caves, Mountains and other Natural Curiosities in Cumberland, Westmorland, Lancashire, and part of the West Riding of Yorkshire. 3 folding maps. 8vo. Carlisle.

See this title under DESCRIPTIONS.

MAVOR, REV. WILLIAM. A List of all the Cities, Boroughs, Market Towns, and remarkable Villages in England and Wales, etc. In Mavor's *British Tourists*. (See Mavor under 1798-1800 above.)

This includes the days on which markets are held and how far distant in measured miles from London the markets are.

The New Bristol Guide. Bristol.

Of little value except for the map.—J. Williams.

A New History of the City of Edinburgh . . . with a Description of all the principal Public Buildings. Engravings, map and plates. 8vo. Edinburgh.

Observations made in a Survey of the Road leading from Woodbridge to Debenham, through the several Parishes of Hasketon, Burgh, Clopton, Otley, etc. Fol. Woodbridge.

SMITH, C. Actual Survey of the Roads from London to Brighthelmstone through Ryegate, Crawley, and Cuckfield, also from London to Worthing, with a List of the Inns. Scale 1 inch to a mile. 27 colored maps. 12mo. London.

1803   Acts of Parliament for Making and Repairing Turnpike and High Roads within the County of Edinburgh, 1707-1803. Index. 8vo. Edinburgh.

1804   The Manchester Guide. A Brief Historical Description of the Towns of Manchester and Salford, the Public Buildings and Charitable and Literary Institutions. Illustrated by a Map, exhibiting the Improvements and Additions made since the Year 1770. 8vo. Manchester.

1829   For an Itinerary of King John's movements, see *Itinerarium Johannis Regis,* under TOURS BY NATIVES.

1882   WARE, SAMUEL. Life and Correspondence of the Late Samuel Ware. 8vo. London.

> Part of this work deals with such items as the cost of things, coaches, traveling companions, etc., of the late 18th century.

1883   GUILD, J. WYLLIE. Early Glasgow Directories. *Trans. Glasgow Arch. Soc.,* vol. 2, 199-203. Glasgow.

1883-84   Iter Oxoniense May 1710 (from near Boston, Lincolnshire). In *Reliquary,* vol. 24, 168-74. 8vo. London.

> This is mainly concerned with gentlemen's houses and antiquities.—Fussell, *Travel and Topography in the Eighteenth Century.*

1886   SKETCHLEY and ADAMS. Birmingham in 1770, Streets and Inhabitants, reprinted from Sketchley and Adams' *Tradesman's True Guide and Universal Directory* (by Samuel Timmins, F.S.A.). 4to. Birmingham.

1911   Anglia Wallia. *Arch. Cambr.,* vol. 11, 6th ser., 421-32.

> A contemporary description of roads, etc., of Wales, from Q. Rembr. Roll, 4th Eliz.—Read, *Bibliog. Brit. History, Tudor Period.*

1916   INGLIS, HARRY R. G. The Roads that led to Edinburgh. *Proc. Soc. Antiq. Scot.,* vol. 1, 18. 4to. Edinburgh.

1925   PATERSON, DANIEL. Paterson's Roads. See *The Library,* vol. 5, no. 4, 4th ser., March, 1925. London.

XXI
Maps and Charts

("It hath bin lately maintained in an Academicall Dispute, That the best Travailing is in maps and good Authours: because thereby a man may take a view of the state and manners of the whole world, and never mix with the corruptions of it. A pleasing opinion for literary prisoners, who may thus travell over the world, though confined to a dungeon."—Quoted from Profitable Instructions for Travellers (1633) by the *York Gate Catalogue.*

However diverse have been the attempts to represent the face of the earth pictorially, from the hand-drawn maps of the early ages down to the supreme achievements of aerial photography, there have persisted at least three constants—direction, orientation, and distance—with scale and physical features following close in attendance. It is not the intention of this foreword to chart the shifting courses of map makers in accommodating themselves to the needs of travelers and the increasing demands of new discoveries. The history of the improvements in answer to the questions, in what direction? where with reference to the known? and how far away lies the goal? may be read in many excellent authorities (e.g., Sir Herbert G. Fordham, *Maps, their History, Characteristics, and Uses;* W. W. Jervis, *The World in Maps;* J. W. Cameron, *Maps and Map-Work;* T. Chubb, *Printed Maps in the Atlases of Great Britain and Ireland,* Introduction, etc.). Neither does this section pretend to an exhaustive coverage of printed maps of Great Britain and Ireland, for such an effort would be largely a reproduction of the work of Chubb. What the following listing will provide, however, is an introduction to the landmarks of cartography as it moved away from the highly ornamental maps of the sixteenth and seventeenth centuries, with their waste spots populated by curious monsters of the deep—spouting whales, musical dolphins, none too seductive mermaids, ships in full sail, and the like—to the increasing complexity of interpreting, not only the lay of the land, relief, and contour, but also climate, vegetation, population, in fact, the whole economic life of a region. One will perceive the tenacity of the Ptolemaic tradition which did so much in advancing geography as well as in obstructing it. One will see the rise of the Dutch school of cartography and their century-long rule, and, on its decline, the emergence of an English school of engravers and publishers. And the vexed question of where to fix the prime meridian will appear solved at the close of the eighteenth century by the selection of Greenwich. In general maps become much more specific and varied in response to new interests born of the times, much more local, and naturally more accurate, though infinitely less pictorial and less interesting. Dullness reigns over all—until we come to John Cary, who knew how to combine beauty with accuracy.

The titles offered below represent but a small portion of the total output of maps of Great Britain. In other sections of this volume references to maps will be found on almost every page. Attention is called particularly to AIDS TO TRAVELERS, DESCRIPTIONS, and GEOGRAPHY. The notes appended to individual titles owe more than usual to the researches of expert students in this field, as is duly acknowledged on appropriate occasions. For world maps which include the British Isles, see MAPS AND ATLASES, vol. II of this work.)

1462 PTOLEMY, CLAUDIUS. Geographia. Maps. Bologna.

The above date has been questioned. If it is valid, then this Latin version of Ptolemy is the first printed edition of his *Geography.* If not, then the honor must fall to that printed at Vicenza in 1475, which, however, was unaccompanied by maps. The first one printed in Germany, that of Ulm in 1482, stands out as one of the finest books printed in Germany during the 15th century. It is also the first with woodcut maps. The edition of 1513, Strassburg, is called by Nordenskiöld "the first modern atlas of the world." One of its maps is printed in colors—black, red, and brown—and is therefore asserted to be the first map printed in colors. Its map of Great Britain entitles it to another first, being, according to Nordenskiöld, the first printed modern special map of that island. The edition of 1535, Lyons, is celebrated for its association with the trial and burning alive of Servetus (its editor) in 1553. The edition printed at Firenze, 1581 (?), is supposed to be the first book appearing with maps wholly engraved on copper. The Greek text, edited by Erasmus, was published at Basel, 1533. The great number of printings of this work point to the reverence accorded Ptolemy as a geographer, a reverence that perpetuated errors and slowed the progress of cartography all through the period of the Renaissance, although departures and corrections based on new discoveries were creeping in.

So far as is known, Ptolemy did not draw maps himself, but he furnished data for the compilation in atlas form of the maps that go under his name. Because he followed

Poseidonius instead of Erastothenes, he led future geographers into errors that lived on until as late as 1700. Perhaps the most curious example of his miscalculations was the bending of Scotland at right angles to the east, though he did avoid the mistake found in some early maps of separating Scotland from England by a strait. Against his slips may be set, however, his conception of the earth as a sphere and his use of lines of latitude and longitude as a means of constructing a trustworthy map of the inhabited world. And the terms latitude and longitude he was the first to use in their technical sense. See article "Ptolemy" in the *Encycl. Brit.,* 11th edit.; G. Schutte, "Ptolemy's Atlas—A Study of the Sources," *Scot. Geog. Mag.,* vol. 30, 55-57; Maggs, *A Catalogue of Atlases and Maps,* no. 693.

1528   BORDONE, BENEDETTO. Libro di Benedetto Bordone nel qual si ragiona de tutte l'Isole del Mondo con li lor nomi antichi & moderni, historie, fauole, & modi del loro vivere, & in qual parte del mare stanno, & in qual parallelo & clima giaccione. Fol. Vinegia.

This has 3 folding woodcut maps of Europe, Grecian Archipelago and the Aegean, and world map, and 105 smaller woodcut maps of celebrated islands or views of famous ports, including a plan of Mexico City. Maggs, no. 693. The map of Great Britain follows Ptolemy in bending Scotland to the east.

1533   ————. Isolaria. Fol. Venice.

This atlas contains a map entitled Inghilterra; tauolo secondo moderni, 5¼ × 5½ ins., which sometimes has been read as indicating a strait separating England and Scotland. English manuscript maps of the 13th, 14th, and 15th centuries also show Scotland to be an island by itself, an error that was corrected in the world map of Pierre Desceliers, of the Dieppe school of cartographers, 1546. See John E. Shearer, *Old Maps of Scotland.*

1546   GASTALDI, G. Britanniae insulae quae insula Angliae et Scotiae Regna continet cum Hibernia adjacente nova descriptio. Rome.

The map measures 21¼ × 15½ ins. The same title is given to the atlas published by Antonio Lafreri, Rome, 1558, and the map agrees entirely with that of Britain printed in the *Carte Nautiche di Battista Agnese dell' anno 1554.*—Quoted.

LILY, GEORGE. Map of the British Isles. Rome.

The author was the son of the famous grammarian William Lily. The map is an important one in the history of English cartography, for it is the earliest map of England drawn by an Englishman. Many "firsts," based on different points, have been claimed for various maps. Perhaps the earliest known engraved map of Great Britain is the one published by Pietro Coppo, which was recently discovered by Professor Roberto Almagio in the municipal library at Pirano, Istria. The first printed map of England and Wales, with parts of Scotland and Ireland is said to be that prepared by Sebastian Munster and included in his edition of Ptolemy dated 1540. Another noteworthy early map of the British Isles is the one printed by Mercator in 1564 (see following item). See Thiele, *Official Map Publications.*

1564   MERCATOR, GERHARD. Angliae, Scotiae et Hiberniae noua descriptio. Duisberg.

This map appeared in eight sheets, each 13¾ × 17¾ ins. The information for it was probably supplied by Camden and Llwyd. It was printed in facsimile by the Gesellschaft für Erdkunde zu Berlin, 1681. The original is a recent discovery. Five years later this geographer published his marine world map which embodied the well known "Mercator's projection," by which mariners could mark out their courses in straight lines. It differed from the ordinary portulan or chart of the practical navigator in that it was the work of a scholar who based his findings on careful research. See Mercator under 1595 below.

1569   LLWYD, HUMFREY. Map of England and Wales. London.

This has been called "the first modern map of England," as well as the first engraved map published in England. For comments on Llwyd, see under 1572, HISTORY AND CHRONICLE.

1570   ORTELIUS, ABRAHAM. Theatrum orbis terrarvm. 53 maps. Fol. Antwerp.

This famous *editio princeps* was known as the "XX Maii 1570" edition. Very likely this atlas with the date of 20 May 1570 was printed in a very limited number of copies.

Its excessive rarity made a reprint necessary in the same year.—Martinus Nijhoff, Catalogue no. 556. 3rd edit., Antwerp, 1571; editions appeared almost every year until the last one in 1612, and in various languages. 5 supplements were also published—1573, 1580, 1584, 1590, and 1595—which were annexed to successive editions. The titles ran through Theatrum, Speculum, and Epitome. After 1600 texts appeared in English.

Under no. 6 is listed Angliae, Scotiae, et Hiberniae, sive Britanniae: insularvm descriptio. With this atlas begins the study of modern cartography. Ortelius, second only to Mercator among the Dutch cartographers who were now to dominate the field of map making for many years, must have used his eyes to good purpose on his business travels. Early he became interested in collecting, mounting, and selling maps, and after his meeting with Mercator in 1560, definitely turned his attention to the study of scientific geography. His great work listed above exerted a profound influence on English geographers and map makers. His maps were not the result of his own surveys, but were a compilation from a large number of cartographers, to whom he made due acknowledgment. Among them was Humphrey Llwyd the Welshman. See Ortelius under 1602, GEOGRAPHY, vol. II of this work.

The use of the term Theatrum, meaning a display or show, invites a review of the terminology used at various times in designating collections of maps. The above title was selected by Speed (see under 1610 below), and in France by Bougereau in his *Theatre François,* Tours, 1594. Mercator, working on similar lines, chose the name Atlas for his collection (see under 1595 below), doubtless bearing in mind its mythological associations. Other terms used were Speculum (see Norden under 1593 below), Geographia, Cosmographia, and Chorographia. For single issues the word Map sufficed. Mappemonde indicated that the map was painted on cloth. Tabula was the name in use among the Romans, e.g., the much discussed *Tabula Peutingeria* (see Gale under 1709, BRITISH, ROMAN, AND SAXON ANTIQUITIES). Charts, i.e., Carta Nautica, designated maps for the sea as early as the 14th century, though the term did not become general until the 16th. Portulan was the name given by the navigators of the Mediterranean to the charts they made of that sea. Out of this mixture of terms, we have retained Map, Chart, and Atlas. See Fordham, *Maps, Their History, Characteristics and Uses.*

1572 PORCACCHI, TOMASO. L'Isole piu famose del Mondo. Fol. Venetia.

> This contains the map of the Hebrides and Orkneys, 4 × 5½ ins., with one of Scotland, 5½ × 4 ins.

1574 SAXTON, CHRISTOPHER. Maps of Oxfordshire, Buckinghamshire, and Berkshire in one map, and Norfolk. For the completed work see under 1579 below.

1578 LESLEY, JOHN (Bishop of Ross). Scotiae Regni antiquissimi nova et accurata descriptio; propria et hoc tempore usitata regionum et locorum nomina continens. Rome.

> This map, which is elliptical in shape, measuring 20½ × 15 ins., was abridged to a rectangular shape when used in his *De Origine, Moribus et rebus Gestis Scotorum* (see under HISTORY AND CHRONICLE). It has been regarded as the work of Lesley himself, but it has been pointed out that he got it from one of Britain by Jacopo Gastaldi in Rome, where his history was being printed.—Shearer, *op. cit.* On it were printed the royal arms and those of the bishops and some account of the country.

1579 ORTELIUS, ABRAHAM. Separate maps of the British Isles from Ortelius' *Theatrum* often appear in various years. See below.

> Angliae, Scotiae et Hiberniae, sive Britanniae, insularum descriptio. Map with the British arms in contemporary coloring. Obl. fol. Antwerp.
> Scotiae tabula. Map in colors. Obl. fol. Antwerp.
> Cambriae typus auctore Humfredo Lhuydo Denbigiense Cambrobritanno. Contemporary coloring. Obl. fol. Antwerp.

SAXTON, CHRISTOPHER. Maps of the Counties of England and Wales. 35 maps and a frontispiece portrait of Queen Elizabeth, surrounded by allegorical figures. Fol. London.

> For a description of Saxton's maps and the details of various editions, one should consult Chubb, *Printed Maps in the Atlases of Great Britain and Ireland.* The maps making up this atlas were published at different intervals from 1574 to 1578, and then were assembled in one collection as listed above. This original collection is very rare,

but a goodly number of later editions are extant. Individual maps were sold separately on local demand at various times. These maps were used by the editors of the 5th edition of Camden's *Britannia*, 1600, and were also printed in Speed's *Theatre of the Empire of Great Britain*, 1610, with some corrections. Mention may be made of the 1645 edition, as having been "newly revised, amended and reprinted." More important editions are: that with corrections and additions of the hundreds and roads, by Philip Lea, 1690; and that of 1699, which included many additions to keep up with the changes. The work was reproduced, London, 1936. See below.

This, the first set of county maps in the history of English cartography, is the starting point of a long series of such productions in the years to come. The survey was made under the patronage of Thomas Seckford, Master of the Requests to Queen Elizabeth, who procured Saxton a license to print maps for England or any county therein for ten years. The Queen herself was very much interested in the project, perhaps sensing in some vague way that the result would assist in the unification of the country by inducing a feeling of national pride. From the instructions sent in 1576 to all justices of the peace, mayors, etc., in Wales, Saxton was to be accorded the privilege of entry into "any tower, castle, high place or hill to view that country," and to see that "he may be accompanied by two or three honest men, such as do best know the country . . . do set forth a horseman that can speak both Welsh and English to safe conduct him to the market Towne" (quoted by Jervis, *op. cit.*). The surveys took him nine years to complete and, in the days when roads were few or none, must have turned out to be a "paineful peregrination." Saxton himself engraved only the Welsh counties and, in conjunction with one Nicholas Reynold, Herefordshire; the remaining counties were engraved by Dutchmen—Cornelius Hogius, Remigius Hogenbergius, Leonard Tervoort, Francis Scaterius, Augustine Ryther, and William Borough.—Gough, *Anecdotes Brit. Topog.*, 41. For topographical descriptions he must have utilized Leland's *Itinerary*, and is thought to have got assistance from Lambard, who from 1568 to 1577 was preparing a great "Topographical Dictionarie" of England (not published until 1730; see under DESCRIPTIONS). To the whole he prefixed the coats of arms of the nobility, a Latin catalogue of the cities, bishoprics, market towns, castles, parish churches, rivers, bridges, groves, forests, inclosures, and an index to the maps. Roads had to wait until Norden published his map of Middlesex, 1593.

1699 SAXTON, CHRISTOPHER. Saxton's County Maps of England and Wales; with many Additions, viz. The Hundreds, Lathes, Rapes, Wards, Wapentakes, Roads, and a great many Places in each Map: also several Symbols shewing the Bishopricks, Parliament Towns, Market Towns, etc. Then is added, The New Surveys of Middlesex, Essex, Kent, Hertfordshire, Surrey, Buckingham, Oxford, Cambridge, and twenty miles around London; the River Thames, Scotland and Ireland. London.

1583 NICOLAY, NICOLAS D'ARFEVILLE, SIEUR. For his map of Scotland, see his *La Navigation dv Roy d'Escosse Iaques Cinquiesme*, under TOURS BY FOREIGNERS.

D'Arfeville gives the impression that he made the map of Scotland during his stay in that country, but if so, it could not have been from personal observation. Probably it was compiled from information supplied by Alexander Lyndsay, who acted as pilot of the expedition. A reduced facsimile is printed in Shearer's *Old Maps of Scotland*.

SAXTON, CHRISTOPHER. "The large Map of England." London.

This large scale general map in twenty sheets, taken as a whole, measures 5½ feet in width and 4½ feet in height, and is on a scale of 7½ and 8 inches to a mile.—Quoted. Until within recent times it was thought that no copy of the original was extant, though it was known by later copies. But in 1930 a copy in its original state was discovered at Docking Hall in Norfolk. A comparison with later issues shows that the roads were absent from the former, that the Elizabethan ships in the coastal waters had been replaced by craft of the later period, and that the place names had been modernized. Most of the names printed on the county maps of the 1574-78 collection had been crowded in on this map. In addition, it is marked with the degrees and minutes of latitude and longitude on the margin. The earliest of the later copies appeared about 1688, probably done by Philip Lea. See Jervis, *op. cit.*

1584 WAGHENAER, LUCAS JANSZON. For the first proper marine atlas, see his *Spieghel der Zeevaerdt* (translated into English as *The Mariner's Mirrour*) under 1588, NAVIGATION II, vol. II of this work. This contains charts of southern and eastern coasts of England and of eastern Scotland.

1586 LLWYD, HUMPHREY. In Ortelius' Geography is an exact draught of the sea coast of Scotland by Humphrey Llwyd, dated Apr. 5, 1586.—Gough, *op. cit.*, 628.

WARNER, WILLIAM. Albion's England, or an Historical Map of the same Island. London.

> Reprinted, London, 1589.

1589 ADAMS, ROBERT. Expeditionis Hispanorum in Angliam nova descriptio anno 1588. 11 maps. 4to. London.

> This is a series of charts showing the course of the Spanish Armada around the British Isles. They were drawn and engraved by Robert Adams and published by Augustine Ryther. They were intended to accompany the *Discourse concerninge the Spanishe Fleete* by Petrucchio Ubaldini, London, 1590. They may also have inspired the tapestry hangings in the House of Lords representing the several engagements between the English and Spanish fleets. See Gough, 273.

1592 ORTELIUS, ABRAHAM. Scotiae Tabula. 18¾ × 14 ins. In contemporary coloring. Antwerp.

> This is probably a separate issue from the 1590 edition of his *Theatrum*.

1593 NORDEN, JOHN. Speculi Britanniae Pars: the Firste Parte, and Historical and Chorographical description of Middlesex. Wherein are also alphabeticallie set down the Names of the Cyties, Townes, Parishes, Hamlets, Howses of Name, etc. With Direction spedelie to find any Place desired in the Mappe, and the Distance between Place and Place, without Compasses, by the Travail and View of John Norden, anno 1593. London.

> Norden designed to publish a complete set of county maps for his *Speculum Britanniae,* but owing to lack of funds he was able to bring out only two counties, Middlesex, 1593, and Hertfordshire, 1598. These two were printed together in 1637 and again in 1723. Northamptonshire was written in 1610 but not published until 1720, and Cornwall not until 1728. Essex, written in 1594, appeared in print in 1840, edited by Sir Henry Ellis for the Camden Society. Kent and Surrey are said to be still extant in manuscript but as yet remain hidden. His maps of Hampshire, Hertfordshire, Kent, Middlesex, Surrey, and Sussex were printed on an enlarged scale with his name in the 5th edition of Camden's *Britannia,* an edition that for the first time contained maps. These same county maps were still more enlarged (with the exception of Kent), and with the addition of Cornwall, were inserted in Speed's *Theatre of the Empire of Great Britaine* (see under 1610 below). See Henry B. Wheatley, "Notes on Norden and his Map of London," *London Topographical Record Illustrated,* edited by T. Fairman Ordish, London, 1903. See also the interesting Introduction by Sir Henry Ellis in the Camden Society edition of Essex. See also under DESCRIPTIONS.
> Norden's maps differ from Saxton's by the insertion of roads, the first appearance of such a feature, and by the use of triangular tables of distances from town to town, a convenience still employed by railroad and transportation folders. Another distinguishing convenience is his use of grids with lines marked by letters and figures on the margins to facilitate the location of places.

1595 MERCATOR, GERHARD. Atlas, sive Cosmographicae Meditationes de Fabrica Mundi et Fabricati Figura. Fol. Duisburg.

> Place of imprint changed to Amsterdam in later editions, which offered an increasing variety of maps with texts in different languages. That edited by J. Hondius was augmented with 50 new maps, with the descriptive text done by Petrus Montanus; that of 1613 included 150 maps; and that of 1636 with the text in English by Henry Hexham, Amsterdam. Individual issues were common on the market. See below.
> In this atlas are combined the maps appearing in 1585 and in 1590. It includes the entire series of 16 maps of England and Wales dedicated to Queen Elizabeth, with others of northern Europe. No set so far issued can compare with these for detail.—Bookseller's Note. The atlas was placed on the *Index* by Rome. Mercator died in 1594. During the last years of his life he was assisted in the work by his son Rumold and Jodocus Hondius, another Dutch engraver and map maker, who acquired the business on the death of Rumold in 1600. Jodocus Hondius died in 1611 and was succeeded by his son Henrik and son-in-law Jan Janszon, who carried on the business of publishing maps under the firm name of "Jansonius."

1636   MERCATOR, GERHARD. Atlas, or a Geographical Description of the Regions, Countries, and Kingdomes of the World . . . translated by Henry Hexham. 2 vols. Fol. Amsterdam.

1599   KEERE, PIETER VAN DEN. A Collection of Maps of the Counties of England and Wales, and Maps of the Four Provinces of Ireland. Engraved by Peter Keer. Amsterdam (?).

> These maps were used in Camden's *Viri clarissimi Britanniae,* London, 1617; another edit., London, 1620; still others, 1627, 1630, 1646, 1662, 1666, 1676. See below.
> Van den Keere, or Keer as he is generally known, was one of the Low Country artists who helped to engrave the maps of Saxton. The above set is probably a reduced reproduction of the county maps of the latter.

> 1620   KAER, PETER. England, Wales, Scotland, and Ireland described. 65 maps. 8vo. (Place?)

1602   BERTIUS, P. Tabularum geographicarum contractarum libri quinque. 2nd edit. 8vo. Amsterdam.

> The maps of the British Isles are listed as: 1. Magna Britannia, 5 × 3½ ins. 2. Scotia, 3⅝₆ × 4¾ ins. 3. Scotia, Septentrionalis et Australis, each 3⅝₆ × 4⅞ ins.

1603   ORTELIUS, ABRAHAM. Abraham Ortelius, his Epitome of the Theatre of the World, nowe latlye since the Latine, Italian, Spanish and French Editions, renewed and augmented, the Mappes all newe grauen according to geographical Measure by Micheal [*sic*] Coignet, Mathematician of Antwerp, beeinge more exactlie set forth, and amplifyed with large Descriptions, than any done heere to fore. 124 maps. Obl. 24mo. London.

> The maps printed here are the same as those used by Coignet in his Latin edition of 1601. The text and maps differ from the English edition published by John Norton, London, 1602 (?).—Phillips, *A List of Geographical Atlases in the Library of Congress.*

1604   JAMES I. A Note of the Headlands of England as they beare one from another, agreeing with the Plot of the Description of the Countrey, with their severall Distances. Engraved portulan folding map of England and Wales, decorated with two compasses, the royal coat of arms, and two scales. Fol. London.

> This is a Proclamation of James I. It is a very rare sea chart of England drawn up by thirteen of the leading pilots, cosmographers, etc., whose names are given at the foot of the Proclamation, and who swore as to its accuracy before Sir Julius Caesar, Judge of the High Court of Admiralty.—Maggs, no. 693.

1608   PONT, TIMOTHY.

> Pont, an accomplished mathematician and a minister of the Church of Scotland, made the first topographical survey of Scotland about 1608. To insure accuracy and fidelity he traveled over the greater part of Scotland, even to the remotest districts, making sketches of the principal features and afterwards drafting them into regional maps. Before he had completed his task he died (somewhere between 1625 and 1630). King James I gave orders for their purchase from the heirs, but somehow they got "lost" and remained so for twenty years—some say in the Scottish Court of Chancery (one is reminded of *Bleak House*). Sir John Scot of Scots-Tarvet, who by the way was Director of the Chancery, persuaded Sir Robert Gordon of Straloch to prepare them for publication. With the aid of his son James Gordon he completed Pont's survey. The maps were taken over to Amsterdam for inclusion in the atlas of Willem Blaeu (see Blaeu under 1634-35). In addition to his maps, Pont had made notes on the monuments of antiquity and other curiosities, of which the most complete were those on the district of Cunningham. Gordon added further descriptions, as did others. Gordon also published an atlas at Amsterdam, 1648, in compliance with a request of Charles I. Two years later he is said to have brought out at Amsterdam another called *Theatrum Scotiae,* which was dedicated to Cromwell. Changed times, changed manners. Although it is generally stated that the Pont-Gordon maps first appeared in Blaeu's atlas in 1654, yet single maps attributed to Pont with the date 1638 have appeared in sales catalogues. The complexity of the Blaeu issues is difficult to unravel.

1610 SPEED, JOHN. The Theatre of the Empire of Great Britaine: Presenting an Exact Geography of the Kingdomes of England, Scotland, Ireland, and the Isles adjoining: with the Shires, Hundreds, Cities, and Shire-Townes, within ye Kingdome of England, divided and described by Iohn Speed. Fol. London.

Editions of this atlas continued to appear down into the 1770's. A few are singled out for mention. One in 1614; the 2nd Book containing the Principality of Wales, etc., 1616; a Latin edit., 1616; one with change in title and abridged, 1627; with the title *A Prospect of the most Famous Parts of the World*, etc., enlarged to the scope of a general atlas, 1631; others, 1642, 1662, 1666, 1676, etc. See below.

These maps, which measure 20 × 15 ins., were largely engraved by Jodocus Hondius, with the help of Abraham Goos, another Dutch cartographer. This Dutch handiwork is what mainly distinguishes Speed's maps from those of Saxton. Speed began his career as a tailor, a fact that impresses itself in his depiction of costumes on the figures ornamenting the margin of his maps. At an early period, however, he took up the study of antiquities. Seeing in him an apt student, Sir Faulk Freville took the youth under his patronage and thus freed him for the work that culminated in this collection of maps. Though obviously using Saxton for groundwork, Speed made some improvements, one of which was the division of the counties into hundreds. The chief attraction of his maps lies in their ornamentation, which consists of a great variety of conventionalized detail, such as, plans of cities, villages, hundreds, parks, moors, rivers, pictorial drawings of hills, figures with contemporary costumes, ornamental lettering, decorated borders and cartouches, coats of arms of prominent local families, etc. The text on the reverse side is generally drawn from Camden's *Britannia*. The maps appear to have been sold singly also, probably in response to large local demands. Some single issues are found which seem to antedate the publication of the atlas. See Jervis, *op. cit.*

1616 SPEED, JOHN. The Second Booke, Containing the Principality of Wales, Delivering an Exact Topographie of the Counties, Divisions of the Cantraves and Commotes, Description of the Cities and Shire Towns. With a Compendious Relation, of things most Memorable in every one of them performed. London.

This is the first general map of Wales. It is adorned with views of the four cathedrals and of various towns, Beaumaris, Carnarvon, Harlech, Cardigan, Denbigh, etc.

1616 ————. Theatrum Imperii Magnae Britanniae: Exactam Regnorum Angliae, Scotiae, Hiberniae et Insularum Adiacentium Geographiam ob oculos ponens: una cum Comitatibus, Centuriis, Urbibus et primariis Comitatum Oppidis, intra Regnum Angliae, divisis et descriptis. Opus nuper quidem a Johanne Spedo Cive Londiensi Anglice conscriptum; Nunc vero, a Philemone Hollando: apud Coventrianos Medicinae Doctore Latinitate donatum. 67 double page maps of various counties. Fol. London.

1627 ————. England, Wales, Scotland, and Ireland, described and abridged, with ye Historical Relation of things worthy memory, from a farr larger Volume Donne by John Speed. 63 maps. Obl. 8vo. London.

The reduced size of this volume makes it a pocket companion for travelers.

1630 ————. Map of the Kingdom of England, with a Catalogue of all the Shires, Cities, Bishopricks, Market Townes, Castles, Parishes, Rivers, Bridges, Chaces, Forrests and Parkes, described by Christopher Saxton, augmented by John Speed. 16 × 20 ins. Abraham Goos, Amsterdam.

1676 ————. The Theatre of the Empire of Great Britain, presenting an Exact Geography of the Kingdoms of England, Scotland, Ireland, and the Isles adjoyning: as also the Shires, Hundreds, Citys and Shire Townes within the Kingdom of England and Principality of Wales, devided and described, as also A Prospect of the most Famous Parts of the World, viz., Asia, Africa, Europe, America . . . New Edition, with many Additions never before extant (by Ed. Phillips). 96 engraved maps. Fol. London.

1612 WAGHENAER, LUCAS JANSZON. The Light of Navigation, wherein are . . . portrayed all the Coasts and Havens of the West, North, and East Seas. 4to. Amsterdam.

This is an English compilation, mostly taken from the *Spieghel der Zeevaerdt* (see under 1584 above.

1613   HOLE, WILLIAM. Maps of the English Counties (from Drayton's *Polyolbion*). 7¼ × 11¼ ins. London.

> For Drayton see under DESCRIPTIONS.—These are among the most curious and interesting of county maps. The details are not very full excepting as regards rivers, but the towns are decorated with curious mythological and symbolical figures illustrating historical events and local customs.—Bookseller's Note. Hole and Kip engraved the portraits and title page of maps for Camden's *Britannia*. Hole is known as the first to engrave music on copper plates. For Kip's *Britannia Illustrata* see under 1708, VIEWS.

1630   HONDIUS, HENRICUS. Nova totius terrarum orbis geographica ac hydrographica Tabula. Amsterdam.

> A finely decorative map in contemporary coloring, with portraits in the corners of Julius Caesar, Mercator, Ptolemy, and Hondius. It is a world map divided into two hemispheres. The intermediate spaces are filled in with various emblematical subjects. Size 21¼ × 15 ins. —Maggs, no. 693. What kind of representation it gives of the British Isles is not stated in the description.

JANSZON, JOHN. Provincae Lauden seu Lothien et Linlitouo (i.e., Lothian and Linlithgow). Colored map measuring 21 × 25 ins. Amsterdam (?).

> This is probably a single map from one of the Hondius-Mercator atlases, in the production of which Janszon assisted. After the death of Henrik Hondius in 1657, the business established by Mercator passed to the son-in-law of Hondius, Jan Janszon. The great work of the latter was his atlas in 4 vols. (see under 1646-49 below).

MERCATOR, GERHARD. Scotiae Regnum per Gerardum Mercatorum. Letterpress in Latin on the reverse of the sheet, which measures 17½ × 20½ ins. Amsterdam.

> This is probably one of the later issues of Mercator's *Scotiae Regnum*, Duisburg, 1595 (see Mercator under 1595 above), worked up perhaps by Janszon.

1631   BLAEU, WILLEM J. Appendix Theatri Ortelii et Atlantis Mercatoris. Amsterdam.

> This is the first of the series of Blaeu atlases which poured forth from one of the most famous presses of Holland.

1634-35   BLAEU, WILLEM J., and JOANNES. Theatrum orbis terrarum. 2 vols. Fol. Amsterdam.

> Numerous editions followed with volumes increasing in number up to 12 by 1663, and with texts varying in languages—Latin, Dutch, French, German, and Spanish. That of 1646 was printed in Latin, Dutch, French, and German. The Pont-Gordon maps of Scotland make up volume V (1654) of the 1646-55 edition. The contents of this volume are:
> 1. Insulae Albion et Hibernia cum minoribus adjacentibus (Ptolemy map). 14⅜ × 16¾ ins.
> 2. Scotia Antiqua, etc., by Robert Gordon. 15¾ × 13 ins.
> 3. Scotiae Regnum cum insulis adjacentibus by Robert Gordon. 15¾ × 13¼ ins.
> 4. 46 maps of parts of Scotland, each 15¾ × 13¼ ins.
> The 4th volume contains county maps of England and Wales. In this 1646-55 edition are included 403 maps; in the Spanish edition of 1659-72 (11 vols.), 547 colored maps. This issue was never completed owing to the fire which burned down the establishment in 1672.
> This famous printing and publishing house of Blaeu was the great rival of the other two eminent publishing houses, those of Hondius and Janszon. No sets of atlases ever appeared more sumptuously decorated. The title pages are works of art in themselves, and the maps must have appealed as much by their rich assortment of figures as by their representations of the known world. Ships, galleons, tritons, Neptunes, etc., in all their traditional grotesqueness and quaintness, lie scattered over the sea, and the land wastes are enlivened by the strange monsters that caught the fancy of medieval cartographers. Among the normal human figures of men, women, and children are touches of modernity, such as that of Tycho Brahe, Blaeu's old instructor, and in the Pont maps, women wearing wide-brimmed bonnets and men capped with feathered glengarries. See Jervis, *op. cit.*, 111. Willem Blaeu died in 1638 and was succeeded by his son Johannes, who continued and expanded the business. The culminating work of this house was probably the French edition of twelve volumes, 1667. The firms that meet the eye in the later decades of the century are the Visschers and their successor, Schenck.

1638 ROBERTS, LEWIS. The Merchants Mappe of Commerce; wherein the Universalle Manner and Matter of Trade, is compendiously handled . . . Necessary for all such as shall be imployed in the publique Affaires of Princes in forreigne Parts . . . and for all Merchants or their Factors that exercise the Art of Merchandizing in any Part of the Habitable World. Portrait of the Author by Glover. Folding world map and 4 full-page engraved maps of the continents in the text. Fol. London.

> This is one of the earliest English books to deal thoroughly and systematically with trade and commerce with other countries throughout the world.—Bookseller's Note.

1644 HOLLAR, WENCELAUS. Map of England and Wales. London.

> The scale used in this map is 5 miles to one inch. For Hollar's views of London, see under 1647 and 1664, LONDON.

1646-47 DUDLEY, SIR ROBERT (styled Duke of Northumberland and Earl of Warwick). Dell' arcano del mare . . . libri sei. 3 vols. in 2. Fol. Firenze.

> This 1st edition is rare. The author, son of the Earl of Leicester, was well qualified by education, travel, and possession of valuable new material through his experience as a seaman in the voyages of his brother-in-law, Henry Cavendish, for bringing out this sea atlas, which is regarded as of scientific value for its day. For the maps some of the English pilots are responsible.—Phillips, *Atlases in the Congressional Library*, vol. I.

1646-49 JANSSONIUS, JOANNES. Novus Atlas, sive Theatrum Orbis Terrarum: in quo Tabulae et Descriptiones omnium regionum totius universi accuratissime exhibentur. 4 vols. Fol. Amsterdam.

> An edit. with German title, 1649; with French title, 1652; and later editions down to 1724, which is a London issue or one sold in London, with French title.—Chubb, *op. cit.*
> These maps are compiled from many authors and re-imprinted. The descriptive text is printed on the back.

> (Vol. IV) Novus Atlas, sive Theatrum Orbis Terrarum: in quo Magna Britannia, seu Angliae et Scotiae nec non Hiberniae, Regna Exhibentur.
> This last contains 48 beautifully engraved maps in double page and 364 pages of text from Camden's *Britannia*. Part II exhibits Scotland and Ireland with 8 maps and a small amount of text.

1650 DANCKERTS, JUSTUS. Novissima et accuratissima totius Angliae, Scotiae, et Hiberniae Tabula. From his Atlas. Fol. Amsterdam. (19 × 22 ins.)

DE WIT, F. Maps of England and Wales. Colored. Amsterdam.

> The De Wits, unlike most Amsterdam firms, had a London imprint as well as one in Amsterdam. The publications of this firm, father and son, numbered, between the years 1648 and 1712, 380 land maps and 30 sea charts. No texts were printed on the reverse side—another depature from the common practice. Probably the maps were issued separately.—Phillips, *op. cit.*

VISSCHER, NICOLAUS. Regni Scotiae Tabula. Colored. Fol. Amsterdam.

> From this period on the Visscher family was the largest producer of maps in Amsterdam. Their atlases, which were very numerous, contained maps engraved by Ortelius, Blaeu, Sanson, and others. Their plates finally passed into the hands of Schenck.—Jervis.

1651 The False Brother, or, A New Map of Scotland, drawn by an English Pencil. 8vo. London.

> So cited in Bandinel. It reads suspiciously like a diatribe against the Scotch.

1653   GORDON, SIR ROBERT (of Straloch). Scotia Antiqua, qualis priscis temporibus, Romanis praesertim, cognita fuit, quam in lucem eruere conabatur Robertus Gordonus a Straloch. M.CVI.LIII. (20 × 24 ins.). Amsterdam (?).

This may be the map that was dedicated to Cromwell mentioned above under Pont, 1608.—In this Gordon has printed both the ancient and modern names of the counties and people, with annotations on Ptolemy's map. He has also given us a map of Albion and Ireland, entitled, Insulae Albion & Hibernia, cum minoribus adjacentibus, and a dissertation on Thule, where he explains what he thinks the Romans meant by the name. This opinion is much the same which Bertius presents in his Theatrum geographiae veteris, in which Ortelius's Britannicarum insularum typus is also found. There is a later description of our islands by Ortelius in Hornius.—Gough, 629.

JENNER, THOMAS. A Description and Plat of the Sea Coasts of England, from London, up all the River of Thames, all along the Coasts, to Newcastle and so to Edinburgh, all along Scotland, the Orchades, and Hitland, where the Dutch begin their Fishing. . . . With the Depth and Showlds about these Places . . . of the Tides and Courses of the streams. . . . Unto which is added, A List containing the Monethly Wages of all Officers, Seamen, and others serving in the States Ships at Sea . . . their Shares in Prizes, and relieving of the sick and wounded. . . . Usefull not only for Seamen and Marchants, but for all that desire to know where our Fleets lye, etc. As also: All those Parts over against us, as Norway, Denmarke, the Sound, Holland and Zealand. 2 folding maps, one showing the course of the Thames from London to the Sea. 4to. Printed by M. S. for Thomas Jenner. London.

1654   SANSON, NICOLAS. Cartes des Isles Britanniques. 14 maps. Fol. Paris.

Sanson was one of the most famous cartographers of France, in fact he was the founder of the French school. His work was carried on by his sons, Adrien and Guillaume down to the middle of the next century. Readers of Swift's account of Gulliver in Brobdingnag will recall the comparison with a Sanson atlas. His work is noted for its fine engraving.

1660   DANCKERTS (or DONCKER), HENRIK. De Zee-atlas ofte Water-waereld vertoonende alle de zee-kusten van het bekende deel des aerdbodems, met een generale Beschryving van dem. Fol. Amsterdam.

Many editions of this work followed, with texts in various languages. That of 1666 contained maps dated 1658, 1659, 1660, 1661, 1664, 1665. An English text appeared in Amsterdam, 1699, 1700. See below.

1699   DONCKER, HENRIK. The Lightningh Columne, or sea-mirrour, contaighningh the Sea-coasts of the Northern and Eastern (and) Western Navigation. . . . As alsoo the Situation of the northernly Countries, as Islands, . . . Old Greenland, Spitsbergen and Nova Zembla . . . With a brief Instruction of the Art of Navigation. 67 maps and a number of maps, figures, etc., in the text. Fol. Amsterdam.

DE WIT, FREDERICK. Atlas & Zee-Kaerten. 150 engraved decorative folding maps and charts in contemporary coloring. Fol. Amsterdam.

Another edit., Amsterdam, ca. 1690. These maps are ornamented with many small engravings of ships, naval battles, etc.

1662   BLAEU, JOHANNES. Atlas de l'Angleterre. 60 engraved double maps with arms and vignettes of the English and Welsh counties. Fol. Amsterdam.

The 1662 edition of Camden's Britannia was illustrated with general and county maps, 20 × 24 ins., provided by Blaeu. Another Blaeu atlas, Scotia et Hibernia, of the same date contains the maps of Scotland and Ireland, 54 double page in number.

1666 Goos, P. De Zee-atlas, ofte Water-weereld. Waer in vertoont werden alle de Zee-kusten van het bekende des aerd-bodems. 40 maps. Fol. Amsterdam.

> Another edit., with 2 charts added, one being of the Channel, Amsterdam, 1675; an edit. in French, Amsterdam, 1670; one in English, Amsterdam, 1667. See below.
> All of the maps are colored and decorated with coats of arms, costumes, emblematical figures, etc., and are said to be remarkably accurate.

> 1667 Goos, PETER. The Sea-Atlas or the Watter-World, Wherein are described all the Sea Coasts of the Knowne World. Very usefull and necessary for all Shipmasters, Pilots and Seamen, as allso for Marchants and Others. This Boock is printed and cut by Peter Goos, at Amsterdam. Fol. Amsterdam.
> This edition omits the preliminary text. Another edition appeared in 1668.

> 1670 ————. L'Atlas de la mer, ou monde aquaticque, representant toutes les costes maritimas de l'univers descouvertes et cognues. Très nécessaire et commode pour tous les pilotes, maistres de navire et merchants. 40 maps. Fol. Amsterdam.

1667 HOLLAR, WENCELAUS. Map of Great Britain, containing the Three Kingdoms of England, Scotland and Ireland, with the Principality of Wales, etc., as also an Addition of several of the chief Cities belonging to the said Kingdomes. Printed and published by J. Overton. London.

> This map consists of a single sheet. The views represent Edinburgh, plans of York, Dublin, Oxford, Cambridge, and London, and a prospect of the latter "as appearing in the time of its flames."

1671 A New Map of England, drawn according to the truest Descriptions and best Observations that have been made; with an Addition of the Highways and Roads from the chief Towns to London, never done before. 4 ft. × 3 ft. 3 ins. Also in sheets pasted on cloth and colored, with a roller and ledge. London.

SELLER, JOHN. The English Pilot; describing the Sea-Coasts, Capes, Head Lands, Soundings, Sands, Shoals, Rocks, and Dangers, the Bays, Roads, Harbours, Rivers, and Ports, etc., in most of the Known Parts of the World, etc. Fol. London.

> Another volume appeared in 1672. See Seller under 1675 and 1676-1701 below.

1672 ————. A New Chart of the Sea Coasts of England, Flanders, and Zealand and Holland, etc. Described by J. Seller. London.

1673 BLOME, RICHARD. Britannia, etc. For this work, which contained 50 maps copied from Speed, see under DESCRIPTIONS.

> In addition to the theft of the maps, there was a theft of the text from Camden's *Britannia*. Yet Blome had a high reputation as printer and compiler.

MORDEN, ROBERT. A New Map of England, in a Royal Sheet, containing the Adjacent Parts of Scotland, Ireland, France, Flanders, and Holland; shewing the True Situation and Distance of London from Edinburgh, Dublin, Paris, Maestricht, Antwerp, Amsterdam, etc.; with a Description of the Post-roads, and their several Branches from Town to Town. London.

> Though the influence of the Dutch school continued to affect map engraving, with Morden we come to a series of English map publishers whose names will appear again and again, viz., Ogilby, Morgan, Senex, Seller, Moll, Adair, who in the next century are followed by the Bowens, Kitchin, La Rocque, Jefferys, and Cary as the outstanding producers. From now on map producing continues to grow as a profitable enterprise, with, however, a corresponding loss of artistry and interest. Much dependence on Saxton, Norden, and Speed continues to be manifested, but in time cartography spurs itself to catch up with new discoveries.

A New Map of the Kingdome of England and Principality of Wales, taken out of J. S. [John Speed], printed and sold by J. Overton. London.

> This map presents 30 small views of the chief cities of England on the border.

1675   OGILBY, JOHN. Britannia. Fol. London.

> The many editions, adaptations, and reproductions of this "road book" shows that it completely and immediately satisfied the need of a map book "for gentlemen and travellers, being made fit for the pocket." For a description of some of these editions and an account of Ogilby, see under AIDS TO TRAVELERS.

The Royal Map of England and Wales: wherein you have a Description both of the whole in general; and of every County therein in particular. Together with the Ro(a)des and Highways. London.

SELLER, JOHN. Atlas Maritimus. London.

> This sea atlas, as well as many of his other maps, geographies, and charts, was taken from the Dutch publishers of like work. Seller was hydrographer to Charles II, who granted to this official the protection of the copyright of these charts and atlases, many of which, it is said, were printed from the Dutch plates with erasure of such marks as would betray their origin.—Jervis, 98.

1676   The Fifty-two Counties of England and Wales described in a Pack of Cards. In each Card you have a Map of the County, with the chief Towns and Rivers, a Compass for the Bearings, and a Scale for Mensuration. There is also given the Length, Breadth, and Circumference of each County; the Latitude of the Chief City, or Town, and its Distance from London, first the Reputed, and the Measured, Miles. As also the Road from London to each City or Town: with other Remarks. London.

> The use of cards to teach geography both local and general is indicated in a number of such titles.

HOLLAR, WENCELAUS. The Kingdom of England and Principality of Wales described in every one, useful for all Commanders and Quartering of Soldiers, in six maps and the title. London.

> These maps, commonly called the "Quartermasters' Maps," were compiled by order of Cromwell.

SPEED, JOHN. Map of Wiltshire, engraved by Jodocus Hondius. A colored copy with 17 coats of arms, a Plan of Salisbury, a view of Stonehenge. 20 × 15 ins. Text on back.

> This is listed here to show the persistence of the Speed tradition and to record its interest in Stonehenge.

1676-1701   SELLER, JOHN. The English Pilot, or The Coasting Pilot. Fol. London.

> According to Jervis, this is the rarest of English pilot books.

1680   A New Map of England, Scotland, and Ireland, with the Roads; and a Delineation of the Genealogy of the Kings thereof, from William the Conqueror; with an Alphabetical Table. London.

1680-83   PITT, MOSES. The English Atlas. Portraits and numerous double-page maps. 4 vols. Fol. London.

For details of these volumes, see under GEOGRAPHY, vol. II of this work. These maps were based mainly on Janszon's atlas. The geographical descriptions were generally the work of Bishop William Nicolson and Richard Peers, but Thomas Lane, Obadiah Walker, and Dr. Todd had compiled the first volume. The work was highly commended by Anthony à Wood, in whose *Athenae Oxonienses* an account of the various contributors is to be found. See *DNB*. The undertaking was too ambitious for the purse of Pitt, and the result was imprisonment for debt.

1681   BLOME, RICHARD. Speed's Maps Epitomiz'd: or the Maps of the Counties of England, Alphabetically placed. 8vo. London.

Here are 39 maps of the counties of England by Blome, engraved by Hollar and Richard Palmer. Some of the maps are of earlier date. Fordham, in his *Hertfordshire Maps,* states that these maps were first issued collectively by Thomas Taylor in *England Exactly Described,* 1671. See Chubb, *op. cit.*

1681-96   KEULEN, JOANNES VAN. De lichtende Zee-fakkel. 2 vols. Fol. Amsterdam.

This firm is spoken of as the oldest existing firm in Europe which had devoted itself to nautical works, being then over 200 years at the work (*Gent. Mag.,* for 1858). Prior to the beginning of the 18th century, England was almost entirely dependent on the Dutch for sea charts and directions by which their ships were navigated. Their Great and Little Sea Torch was copied from Van Keulen's great work.—Phillips, *op. cit.,* vol. III.

1683   SIBBALD, SIR ROBERT. An Account of the Scottish Atlas, or the Description of Scotland Ancient and Modern. Fol. Edinburgh.

1686   GREENE, ROBERT. A New Map of Scotland, with the Roads. Engraved map outlined in colors. 21½ × 18 ins. London.

MORDEN, ROBERT. A Map containing the Towns, Villages, Gentlemen's Houses, Roads, Rivers, and other Remarks, for twenty Miles round London. London.

1687   GORDON, SIR ROBERT. A New Map of Scotland, made by R. Gordon, corrected and improved by R. Morden: to which is added, Alphabetical Tables for the ready finding out any Place in the Map. London.

1688   ADAIR, JOHN. Small Atlas of Scotland. Paris.

Adair was the most prominent surveyor and mapper of Scotland. His chief work, the *Survey of the Scottish Coasts,* is listed under 1703 below.

————. The Turnings of the River Forth, with the adjacent County of Clackmannan and Part of Stirlingshire. (Place?)

This may be an extract from his atlas of this date.

LEA, PHILIP. The Shires of England and Wales described by C. Saxton, being the best and most original Mapps, with many Additions, and Corrections, viz. the Hundreds, Roads, etc., by Philip Lea: also the New Surveys of Ogilby, Seller, etc. Sold by Philip, Globemaker. Fol. London.

This title is taken from Gough, *op. cit.,* 702, who adds that the map of Ireland is abridged from Petty, and that of Scotland from Camden.—This is thought to represent impressions from the plates of a large general map of England and Wales by Saxton about 1583 (see Saxton under this date above), much cut and amended. Saxton's Elizabethan ships are erased and those of the 17th century substituted, a new decorative title is added, and other features changed or removed. Lea added also a network of roads taken from Ogilby's *Britannia* of 1675 (see under 1675 above). This Lea version continued to be reprinted until the middle of the 18th century. How powerful an influence was exerted by the original Saxton general map is demonstrated by the fact that an examination of

Hollar's "Quartermasters' Map" (1676 above) proves the latter to be an exact copy of Saxton. Garrett reissued this map in 1688, and it appears again in 1752, published by John Rocque.—Jervis, 105.

1689   SANSON, NICOLAS. Atlas nouveau. Fol. Paris.

Other editions appeared for some time to come. The map of Scotland, Le Royaume d'Ecosse, measures 33¼ × 22⅝ ins.

1690   ADAMS, JOHN. Mr. Adams' Map of England, contracted and made portable for the Pocket without folding; containing all Cities and Towns, with the Roads from Town to Town; and the reputed Miles between them given by Inspection without Scale or Compass: to which is added, Alphabetical Tables of the Names of the Towns, the Countreys in which they are, their Distance from London, and their Market Days. London.

According to *DNB,* Adams published a map of England in 1677. The above may be a portable edition of that work. The same authority says that it was revised in 1693. The title of the 1690 item was taken from Arber, *Term Catalogues,* vol. II, 322. See Adams under 1680, AIDS TO TRAVELERS.

CORONELLI, VINCENZO MARIA. Atlante Veneto, nel quale si contiene la Descrittione Geografica, Storica, Sacra, Profana, e Politica, degl' Imperii, Regni, Provincie, e Stati dell' Universo. Engraved title, many plates of numerous navigational, astronomical and surveying instruments; 4 plates of astronomical and geographical diagrams, the Hemisphere as known to the Ancients; the eastern Planisphere as known to Coronelli; the western Planisphere; series of 65 engraved double-page maps, numbered 9-74, of European countries, commencing with the British Isles: Vol. I. Vol. II contains 69 maps, of which the first 37 complete the European section. 2 vols. Fol. Venice.

This atlas is sometimes found in one volume, sometimes in two. Coronelli won the highest respect from his contemporaries for his achievements in the science of geography. He founded in 1680 the first geographical society, to which he gave the name Academia Cosmografo degli Argonauti. Its membership came to include men of distinction in all branches of learning and in all stations of rank. The publications issuing from its press all bore the Argonautic emblem—a ship on a terrestial globe with the motto "Plus Ultra."— Maggs, no. 693. In 1696-97 was published his *Isolario dell' Atlante Veneto,* which includes the British Isles.

A New Map for the Kingdom of Scotland, divided into the North and South Parts; subdivided into Countys, Vice-countys, Provinces, Governments, Lordships, and Islands: with all Cities, Towns, Rivers, Bridges, etc. London (?).

(This year saw atlases from the presses of Valk and Schenck and of Visscher, from which individual general and local maps of the British Isles were sold separately. Place of imprint was Amsterdam.)

1693   COLLINS, CAPTAIN GREENVILLE. Great Britain's Coasting Pilot, the first Part; being a New and Exact Survey of the Coast of England, from the River of Thames to the westward, with the Islands of Scilly, and from thence to Carlisle, describing all the Harbours, Rivers, Bays, Roads, Rocks, Sands, Buoys, Beacons, Sea Marks, Depth of Water, Latitudes, Bearings, and Distances from Place to Place, the Setting and Flowing of the Tides, with Directions for the Knowing of any Place, and how to harbour a Ship with Safety, with Directions for coming into the Channel between England and France. The Second Part: is a Survey of the

Sea-Coast of England and Scotland from the Thames to the Northward, with the Islands of Orkney and Shetland, etc. Numerous large maps measuring 21 × 17 ins. Fol. London.

Many editions followed, some of which are dated 1738, 1744, 1749, 1760, this last with 50 engraved charts, mostly folding, introducing views of towns, ships, historical events, etc.; 1781. The titles of all these read very much alike.

Collins, who was hydrographer to King William and Queen Mary, published these charts from actual surveys, and thus helped to free English seamen from the long dependence on Dutch publications of this kind.

1695   SELLER, JOHN. Anglia Contracta, or, A Description of the Kingdom of England and Principality of Wales in Several New Mapps of all the Countyes therein Contained. Portrait of King William and Queen Mary and 66 colored maps on copperplates. 8vo. London.

2nd edit. in Camden's *Britannia Abridg'd,* with improvements and continuations, 2 vols., 8vo, London, 1701 (included are a Traveling Map of England and a Mapp of the Ecclesiastical Divisions of England, with some of the Islands); 3rd edit., in *The History of England,* uses the 66 maps of the 1695 edit., with Map of Ireland added; the County Maps reprinted with some corrections in the *Supplement to the Antiquities of England and Wales* (see Grose under 1783-87, HISTORY AND ANTIQUITIES).

Seven of the maps are designed for a special purpose. These with the county maps of England are each accompanied by a page of text showing the various divisions of the county. The Welsh maps have no text.—Chubb, *op. cit.*

1696   JAILLOT, H. Les Isles Britanniques . . . Angleterre, Escosse et Irlande. Map 20¼ × 25 ins. Paris.

The Jaillots were in the line of eminent cartographers of the French school.

A New Map of the Kingdoms of England, representing Cities, Market Towns and Roads. Outlines and vignette title in contemporary coloring. 24½ × 20¼ ins. London.

VISSCHER, NICOLAUS. General Map of Scotland (including the Orkneys and Hebrides). 20 × 24¾ ins. Outlines, vignette title, and arms in contemporary coloring. Amsterdam.

On the reverse of the sheet is an alphabetical table of towns, villages, etc.

1700   ADAIR, JAMES. Mapp of Straithern, Stormount, and Cars of Gowrie, with Rivers Tay and Yern, survey'd by J. Adair. Edinburgh (?).

Probably a single issue from an atlas.

ALLARD, —. Map of Great Britain and Ireland (with inset of the Orkneys). Outlined in contemporary coloring. 21½ × 24¾ ins. Amsterdam.

BROWNE, CHRISTOPHER. A New Mapp of Scotland, the Western, Orkney, and Shetland Islands; begun by Appointment of Robert Morden, finished at ye Charge and by Direction of Chris. Browne. Dedicated to Queen Anne. 21¾ × 18 ins. London.

DISTON, JOHN. The Seaman's Guide, comprising the Courses by the Compass, and Distances from Place to Place round Great Britain and Ireland, France, Holland, Norway, etc. Liverpool.

THORNTON, J. Atlas Maritimus, or, the Sea Atlas, being a Book of Maritime Charts, describing the Coasts, Capes, Headlands, Sands, Shoals, Rocks, Dangers, etc. With the True Course and Distances from one Place to Anot(her), etc. 23 maps. London.

No. 5. A Chart of England, Scotland, France, and Ireland.
No. 6. A Large Chart of the Channell describing the Sands, Shoals, Depth of Water and Anchorage on the Coasts of England and France.

VALK, G. Maps of Great Britain (from his Atlas with text in Latin). Amsterdam. (Maps measure 21¼ × 25 ins.)

Separate issues of various localities are advertised.

1701   MORDEN, ROBERT. The New Description and State of England, containing the Maps of the Counties of England and Wales, in Fifty Three Copper-Plates, Newly Design'd . . . by the best Artists. 8vo. London.

2nd edit., with new maps added, London, 1704; another edit., in *Magna Britannia*, 1758. In between there were other editions.
A lot of miscellaneous information on the inhabitants, towns, cathedrals, lists of peers, lord lieutenants, army and navy officers, etc., is included.

1703   ADAIR, JOHN. A Description of the Sea Coasts and Islands of Scotland; with large and exact Maps for the Use of Seamen. Part I (all published). Fol. Edinburgh.

1. A True and Exact Hydrographical Description of the Sea-Coast and Isles of Scotland, made in a Voyage round the same, by that great and mighty Prince James the 5th; published at Paris by Nicolay Dauphinois, etc., Chief Cosmographer to the French King, anno 1583; and at Edinburgh by John Adair, F.R.S., anno 1688. 15 × 11¼ ins. (For Nicolay see under 1583, TOURS BY FOREIGNERS.)
2. Holy Island, Fairn Islands, with the many Rocks and Hazards that ly scattered in that sea: and the Coast from Sunderland Point in England to St. Abb's Head in Scotland, surveyed and navigated by John Adair, Geographer for Scotland. 13½ × 18 ins.; 2000 passus.
3. The Frith of Forth, from the Intry to the Queensferry, with all the Islands, Rocks, Sands, etc., surveyed by John Adair. 17½ × 25½ ins.
4. The Frith and River of Tay, with all the Rocks, Sands, Shoals, etc., surveyed by John Adair. 16½ × 25 ins.
5. The Town and Water of Montrose with the neighboring Country and Coast from the Redhead to the North Water; surveyed and navigated by John Adair. 18 × 12 ins.

1708   MORDEN, ROBERT (and H. Moll). Fifty-Six New and Accurate Maps of Great Britain, Ireland and Wales, with all the Direct and Cross Roads exactly traced in the Maps, which are more full and exact than any extant, having all the Cities, Parliament and Market Towns, Villages, Hundreds . . . distinguished, begun by Mr. Morden, enlarged by Mr. Moll. 12 × 8 ins. London.

A work with practically the same title advertised as "Rolled up for the Pocket" published the same year.

1709   A New and Exact Map of Great Britain; according to the latest and best Observations. Printed on a sheet of fine Elephant Paper; describing the Roads and Distance in Miles from Place to Place: it being the best and fullest Map yet Extant. London.

1710   HOMANN, J. B. Atlas. Fol. Nürnberg.

Many editions were published by Homann and his heirs down to 1780, with various titles in Latin, Dutch, German, and English. The British Isles are noted as follows:
1. Magna Britannia complectens Angliae, Scotiae, et Hyberniae Regna. 18¼ × 21½ ins.
2. Magnae Britanniae pars septentrionalis . . . Regna Scotiae. 21¾ × 18¼ ins.

MOLL, HERMAN. Map of England and Wales. Colored, with engraved list of all towns and their positions. 40 × 24 ins. London.

> Moll was one of the most tireless producers of maps and geographies of this period. A native of Holland, he brought over with him much of the artistic feeling for beauty in ornamentation characterizing the Dutch school of cartography. In coloring and composition, in employment of quaint figures and depiction of scenes, he stands up well with the best. Somewhat unique is his insertion of legends in vacant places on his maps. Some of his maps measure four by three feet in size. For his geographical works see under 1701 and 1711-17, GEOGRAPHY. Other productions of maps follow below.

SIBBALD, SIR ROBERT. A Catalogue of Maps and Prospects, with figures of the ancient monuments of Scotland, is to be found in his *Account of the Writers, Antient and Modern, Printed and MSS.,* etc., under GENERAL REFERENCE.

WALTON AND MORDEN. A New Map Containing All the Cities, Market Townes in England and Wales. Counties outlined in color. 25 × 21¼ ins. London.

1711 MONTEITH, R. The Description of the Isles of Orkney and Zetland: with Mapps of them done from Observations of the Learned Men who lived in these Isles. Published by Sir Robert Sibbald. Fol. Edinburgh.

1712 PRICE, CHARLES. A Correct Map of South Britain. London.

1714 MOLL, HERMAN. Map of England, Scotland, Wales, and Half of Ireland, as at the Union (1707). In colors. 39 × 24 ins. London.

——————. Map of the North Part of Great Britain called Scotland. 11 engraved inset views of Edinburgh, Aberdeen, Glasgow, St. Andrews, etc. With many Remarks not extant on any map. 25¾ × 41 ins. London.

> Reprinted by Shearer, showing the "King's Roads," 21 × 35 ins., 4to, London (?), 1896.
> No roads were shown on this first edition, but after Gen. Wade had put through some in 1725 and later, an edition was published which included the roads and bore the date of the old edition, 1714. The views of the cities on the sides were taken from Slezer's *Views of Scotland* (see under 1693, VIEWS). The Remarks give full details of fish caught in the sea, make mention of birds, fowl, etc. Loch Lomond is made the scene of marvels that earlier were credited to Loch Tay.—Shearer, *Old Maps of Scotland.* For the Scottish atlas see under 1725 below.

SENEX, JOHN. A New Map of Great Britain, corrected from the Observations communicated to the Royal Society at London. Engraved colored map decorated with small ships. 24 × 37 ins. London.

> Senex was another member of the English group of cartographers and geographers who kept their presses busy pouring forth maps and charts, atlases, and geographies in a vain endeavor to catch up with travel and exploration.

WILLDAY, GEORGE. Atlas. A series of 24 large folding maps in color. Fol. London.

> In addition to other countries, this includes Great Britain and Ireland, England and Wales.

1715 TAYLOR, THOMAS. For a complete set of maps of the English counties, see his *England Exactly Described,* under AIDS TO TRAVELERS.

1719 MOLL, HERMAN. A Catalogue of a New and Compleat Atlas, or, A Set of 27 Two-sheet (colored) Maps. Views of towns, forts, etc. Fol. London.

1720   Britannia prout divisa fuit temporibus Anglo-Saxonum praesertim durante illorum Heptarchia. Engraved compartment borders of incidents in English history. 16½ × 20¾ ins. London. (The date is approximate.)

OWEN, JOHN. For a survey of all the roads in maps, see his *Britannia Depicta,* under AIDS TO TRAVELERS.

SENEX, JOHN. New Map of England. Counties outlined in colors. 21 × 24 ins. London.

1720-31   COX, REV. THOMAS. For a map of each county in Great Britain and Ireland, see his *Magna Britannia et Hibernia,* under SURVEYS.

1721   SENEX, JOHN. A New General Atlas. Fol. London.
The map of Scotland is based on Gordon's, revised and improved. 21⅛ × 17¾ ins.

1722   JOHNSTON, ANDREW. A New Map of the North Part of Scotland. London.
This includes the south part as well; it is taken from Gibson's edition of Camden's *Britannia.* Each measures 13⅝ × 17⅝ ins.

1723   The English Pilot, Part II, Describing the Sea Coasts, Capes, Headlands, Soundings, Rocks, Bays, Roads, etc., to the Northern Navigation, with many other Things belonging to Navigation, describing the North Coast of England, and Scotland, with the Isles of Orkney, Shetland, Lewis, Farre, Iceland, etc. Large folding charts and numerous woodcuts in the text. Fol. London.
The similarity of this title to that listed under Seller, 1671-72, NAVIGATION II, vol. II of this work, suggests that it may be attributed to Seller. John Thornton also issued sea atlases bearing the title of *The English Pilot.* See under 1703 and 1730, same reference. See also under 1752 below.

1724   BADESLADE, THOMAS. Chorographia Britanniae, or a Set of Maps of all the Counties in England and Wales; to which are prefixed an accurate Chart of the Sea Coast, etc., a Map of England and Wales as divided into Counties, with the Names of the Cities and County Towns, . . . a Map of the Roads from London to all Parts of South Britain, with Tables shewing the Distance of each City and Town on the Road from the Metropolis, both in computed and measured Miles. . . . This Collection was first drawn and compiled into a Pocket-Book by Order and for the Use of his late Majesty King George I by Thomas Badeslade, Surveyor and Engineer, and now neatly engraved by W. H. Toms. 12mo. London.
Another edit., with 46 maps, double page, obl. 8vo, London, 1742; reprinted 1742; another edit., called *A New Set of Maps,* a reprint, 1742; 2nd edit., *A New Set of Maps,* 1745. This last edition adds the Rates of Hackney Coaches, Chairmen, and Watermen, etc.

1725-30   MOLL, HERMAN. A Set of Thirty-Six New and Correct Maps of Scotland divided into its Shires. Obl. fol. London. (36 maps.)
This is the first complete county atlas of Scotland.—Shearer, *op. cit.,* 44. Another edit., London, 1745.

1726   MACKAY, JOHN. A Map of South Scotland and North England, showing the Situations of Roman Camps, Forts, and Walls, between the Tay in Scotland and Tyne in England. 17¼ × 19 ins. In Gordon's *Itinerarium Septentrionale* (see this date under TOURS BY NATIVES).

1730 KEULEN, JOANNES VAN. Atlas of Charts for Navigation of the British Isles. Series of 22 engraved folding portulan charts, in contemporary coloring, with titles in English, Dutch, and occasionally French. Fol. Amsterdam.

These include the coasts of Ireland and extend up to the Shetlands.

1733 BRUCE, ALEXANDER. A Plan of Loch Sunart, etc., become famous by the Greatest National Improvement this Age has produced, survey'd, etc., by Alex. Bruce. 20 × 27 ins. London (?).

An interesting map with copious and curious information on sailing the Loch, on the Lead Mines of Morvern, Glendow, Strontian, worked by the York Building Company, with plan of their buildings, etc.—Bookseller's Note.

1734 BEARHOPE, A. A Map of Such Part of his Grace the Duke of Argyle's Heritable Dukedom, and Justiciary Territories, Islands, Superiorities, and Jurisdictions, as lye contiguous upon the Western Coast of North Britain, within the now United Shyres of Inverary and Dunbarton: Extent and Situation described accurately without actual Survey, etc., by A. Bearhope, Gardener to Murray of Stanhope, which is the Foundation of this Map, by J. Cowley. A valuable Map showing the old Boundaries on the West. 30 × 23 ins. (Place?)

COWLEY, J. A New Map of North Britain with the Islands thereunto belonging, done from some late Surveys of Part of the East and West Coasts, and from modern Accounts of the Country, and other Authorities mentioned in the Explanation annexed. 21 × 14 ins. London.

—————————. Display of the Coasting Lines of Six Several Maps of North Britain shewing disagreement among Geographers, etc., and their Extent, drawn from the Originals and laid down by one and the same Scale from their Bearings, etc., from Ardnamurchan on the West. 25 × 20 ins. London.

1737 PACKE, DR. CHRISTOPHER. For his *Anchographia* ("a curious performance"), see his *Dissertation upon the Surface of the Earth,* under DESCRIPTIONS.

1737-72 BELLIN, J. N. (and others). L'hydrographie françoise, recueil des cartes générales et particulières qui ont été faites pour le service des vaisseaux du roy. 2 vols. Fol. Paris.

Of this work numerous editions appeared. The parts dealing with Great Britain are:
1. Carte réduite des Isles Britanniques. 33⅝ × 20½ ins.
2. Carte réduite des Isles Britanniques, troisième feuille; partie méridionale de l'Ecosse. 21 × 33 ins.
3. Carte réduite des Isles Britanniques, quatrième feuille; partie septentrionale de l'Ecosse. 21 × 33 ins.

1738 FEARON, S. and J. EYES. For a sailing chart see *A Description of the Sea-coast of England and Wales,* under DESCRIPTIONS.

1740 AVERY, DAVID. A Chart of the Entrance of the Rivers Thames and Medway and Places adjacent, with the Floating Light at the Nore Sand; surveyed by Capt. John Mitchell, engraved by Toms and dedicated to Sir Charles Wager, by David Avery. London (?).

The date is a guess. Sir Charles Wager was First Lord of the Admiralty 1733-42 and died 1743.

1742   Chorographia Britanniae, or, A Set of Maps of all the Counties of England and
        Wales: to which is prefixed Charts of Sea Coast, Royal Docks, Harbours, etc.,
        Roads from London to the South, and Distances, etc. Maps of the various Cross
        Roads with Distances and a general Index to the whole. 8vo. London.

1744   BRYCE, REV. ALEXANDER. A Map of the North Coast of Britain from Row Stoir of
        Assynt to Wick in Caithness, by a Geometrical Survey; with the Harbours,
        Rocks, and an Account of the Tides in the Pentland Firth, done at the Desire of
        the Philosophical Society at Edinburgh. 19 × 26½ ins. Edinburgh.

        The Rev. Bryce was well known in his day as a mathematician and had some local fame
        as a poet.—In the above map he used Edinburgh as the meridian, which he had calculated by
        observations and instruments.—Quoted.

1745   ADAIR, JOHN. A Compleat and Exact Map of the Lothians, containing the Shires of
        Edinburgh, Haddington, and Linlithgow. Completed by R. Cooper. Edinburgh.

        In 1743 Adair made a map of the West Lothians, which was engraved with castles and
        mansion houses with grounds. In this the houses, trees, rivers, hills are all shown, with dotted
        lines.—Shearer, 66.

        DODSLEY, ROBERT, and J. COWLEY. A New Sett of Pocket Mapps of all the Counties
        of England and Wales. Shewing, The Situation of all the Cities, Boroughs,
        Market-Towns, and most considerable Villages, with the Distances between each.
        Also the Rivers and Roads both direct and across. Together with A Separate
        Mapp of England, A Plan of the Roads, and a Chart of the Channel. 4to. London.

        ELPHINSTONE, JOHN. A New and Correct Mercator's Map of North Britain copied
        from the latest Surveys and Maps, with Observations, by John Elphinstone, esq;
        principal Engineer. Edinburgh or London (?).

        This first attempt to settle the geography of Scotland was severely criticized by Mr.
        Jefferys, who proposed to engrave on one sheet of imperial paper a new map of Scotland,
        correctly drawn from Adair's and other later surveys, divided into the proper shires as they
        return members to Parliament . . . with the cities and parliament boroughs, presbyteries, etc.
        Jefferys' criticism was based on the contention that the projection of a land map should
        certainly be drawn according to the gradual declension of the meridian, not on Mercator's
        projection, which was designed merely for sea charts. In consequence the whole surface of
        Scotland was distorted, and the geography needlessly confused. The longitudes from Fero and
        Paris were both computed wrong: the former a degree too much, and the latter a degree too
        little. Using the longitude of Paris was a gross absurdity in a map representing part of an
        island where London was the metropolis.—From Jefferys Proposals, quoted by Gough, *op.
        cit.*, 631, and note. This was a greatly improved map of Scotland. When the Jacobite
        Rebellion broke out in July of this year, this map was utilized by both sides. When it became
        apparent that it was defective, the government sent Wm. Edgar out with the troops to survey
        Perthshire and Inverness. The result was a more accurate map.

1746   Extract from a Letter giving an Account of a Survey of the North West Coast of
        England in August 1746. In *Gent. Mag.,* vol. 16. London.

        KITCHIN, THOMAS. Geographia Scotiae; being a New and Correct Map of all the
        Counties and Islands in the Kingdom of Scotland; containing the Universities,
        Cities, Presbytery and Market Towns, Rivers, Lochs, Roads, etc. With a General
        Map of the whole Kingdom, from the latest Observations. 4to. London.

        Another edit., 12mo, 1756.
        Kitchin was a prolific publisher and map maker. His name will be found frequently linked
        with those of the Bowens, Jefferys, and others of the period.

SMITH, G. A Map of the Wall erected by the antient Romans to guard the Isthmus between the North and South Britain (Tyne to Solway) . . . exhibiting also the Rout of the Rebels in three Columns from Dalkeith to Carlisle, and of their Flight back from that City, as laid before his Royal Highness the Duke of Cumberland. Inset of the west prospect of the Castle of Carlisle. 13¼ × 17¼ ins. London.

This "flight" was the backward retreat of Bonnie Prince Charlie from England into Scotland.

WILLDEY, T. A Map of the King's Roads made by His Excellency General Wade in the Highlands of Scotland, from Stirling to Inverness, with the adjacent countries, etc. Dedicated to General Hawley. 17⅝ × 14¾ ins. Scale 5 miles to one inch. London.

Dated Jan. 4, 1746. Yet it shows details of the battle of Culloden, which was fought April 16, 1746.

1747 FINLAYSON, JOHN. A General Map of Great Britain, wherein are delineated the military Operations in that Island during the Years 1745 and 1746, even the secret Routes of the Prince Charles Edward after the Battle of Culloden until his Escape to France. Illustrated by an authentic Abstract of that interesting Piece of History, and an Exact Chronological Table. 38 × 26⅜ ins. London.

MOLL, HERMAN. A Set of Fifty New and Correct Maps of England and Wales, etc. London.

See Fordham, *Hertfordshire Maps.*

1747-60 KITCHIN, THOMAS. A series of 56 maps of the counties of England and Wales appeared from 1747-60 in the *London Magazine: or, Gentleman's Monthly Intelligencer.* London.

1747-66 BOWEN, EMANUEL, THOMAS KITCHIN, and R. W. SEALE. A series of 51 maps of counties of England and Wales appeared in *The Universal Magazine of Knowledge and Pleasure* . . . published Monthly according to Act of Parliament. London.

For a second series see under 1791-97. Speaking of the work of Bowen and Kitchin, Gough asserts that, notwithstanding declaration to the contrary that their maps are framed from actual new surveys, there is scarce a single one which does not abound with faults: and a set of correct maps remains to be hoped for from the encouragement given to the abilities and industry of Mr. Taylor.—*Op. cit.,* 46.

1748 Hydrographical Survey of the Coast of Wales. (So cited by Rowlands, *Cambrian Bibliography,* who states in another place that the name of this work is: Plans of the Harbours, Bars, Bays, and Roads in St. George's Channel.) See following item.

MORRIS, LEWIS. Plans of the Harbours, Bays, and Roads in St. George's Channel, lately surveyed under the Direction of the Lords of Admiralty, and now published with their Permission: with an Appendix concerning the Improvements that might be made in the several Harbours, etc., for the better securing the Navigation on those parts: together with a short Account of the Trade and Manufactures on the Coast. 4to. London.

OSBORNE, THOMAS. Geographia Magnae Britanniae. Or, Correct Maps of all the Counties in England, Scotland, and Wales; with the General ones of both Kingdoms, and of the several Adjacent Islands: Each Map expressing the Cities, Boroughs, Market and Presbytery Towns, Villages, Roads and Rivers; with the Number of Members sent to Parliament. 8vo. London. (63 maps of the counties.)

Another edit., London, 1750.

MARTYN, THOMAS. A New and Accurate Map of the County of Cornwall, from an actual Survey; containing a Map of the Scilly Isles inset, the arms of the Nobility and Gentry (about 150 in number), with other decoration. London.

A complete index was added to the map, with an account of the Archdeaconry of Cornwall, in 1816.

1749   BOWEN, EMANUEL. The Map of Norfolk, divided into Hundreds and drawn from Surveys, shewing what Parishes are Rectories, and what Vicarages, where Charity Schools have been erected, etc. 22 × 29½ ins. London.

This Bowen was map engraver to George II and Louis XV.

KITCHIN, THOMAS, and THOMAS JEFFERYS. The Small English Atlas, being A New and Accurate Set of Maps of all the Counties in England and Wales. 4to. London.

Other edits., 1751, 1785, and 1800.
This contains 49 maps, of which two describe England and Wales. On the bottom of each plate are the fairs, market days, members returned to Parliament, etc.

WARBURTON, JOHN. A New Map of Essex by Actual Survey and Dimensuration, with the Coats of Arms and Seats of the Nobility and Gentry, together with the Courses of the Several Roman Ways, and the Stations thereon, the Present Roads, Rivers, Rivulets, etc. On 2 sheets of imperial atlas. London.

Warburton was Somerset herald of arms and fellow of the Royal Society.

——————. A New and Correct Map of the County of York, in all its Divisions, by Actual Survey and Dimensuration: with the Arms and Seats of the Nobility and Gentry, the Distances in Miles and Furlongs between each of the Market Towns, the Courses of the Several Roman Ways, Present Roads, Rivers, Rivulets, Churches, Castles, Religious Houses, Ancient Baronies, Forests, Chaces, Parks, Woods, Mountains, Lakes, Fields of Battle, Collieries, Copper Mines, and Lead Mines, Allom Works, or other Minerals, Sea-Coasts, Rocks, Shoals, etc. London (?).

This work is cited by Gough, 579, without date or place.

1749-55   BOWEN, EMANUEL, and THOMAS KITCHIN. The Large English Atlas. Fol. London.

Whether these maps were published in atlas form before 1760 is a question. In this last named edition the title is given in full as *The Large English Atlas,* etc. See 1760 below. There were four editions, with change in imprint only, viz., 1760; 1763, with maps about the same; another, 1777; and again, 1785. A newly prepared edition by R. Sayer, with several new maps, 1787.—Chubb.

1760   ——————. The Large English Atlas: or, A New Set of Maps of all the Counties in England and Wales. Drawn from the Several Surveys which have hitherto been published, Laid down on a large Scale, And containing all the Cities, Towns, Villages, and Churches, . . . many Noblemen's and Gentlemen's Seats, etc., etc. Each

Map is Illustrated With a General Description of the County, its Cities . . . the Number of Members Returned to Parliament, . . . And Historical Extracts relative to the Trade, Manufactures, and Government of the Cities and Principal Towns, and the Present State of their Inhabitants, etc. Fol. London.

This is the second issue of the maps and perhaps the first edition of *The Large English Atlas*. See Bowen and Kitchin under 1762 below.

1750   BOWEN, EMANUEL. An Improved Map of Sqmerset divided into its Hundreds . . . with Historical Extracts relative to its Natural Produce, Trade, Manufactures, etc., With the Ichnography of Bath. 27½ × 20⅞ ins. London.

DICKINSON, J. A New and Correct Map of the South Part of the County of York by actual Survey, shewing the true Situation of the several Towns, Noblemen and Gentlemen's Seats, the Courses of the several Rivers and Rivulets, present Roads, Castles, antient Abbies and Priories, Woods, Hills, Lakes, Collieries and other Minerals. Taken at the Cost of the most Hon. Thomas Marquis of Rockingham, . . . for the Marquis's Use, and not to be sold.

DORRET, JAMES. A General Map of Scotland and Islands thereto belonging, from new Surveys; the Shires properly divided, the Forts lately erected and Roads of Communication or Military Ways . . . the Times when and the Place where the most Remarkable Battles have been fought, etc. 69½ × 51¾ ins. (Place?)

The first really good map of Scotland.—Quoted.

MACKENZIE, MURDOCH. Orcades: or, A Geographic and Hydrographic Survey of the Orkneys and Lewis Islands, in eight Maps, exhibiting the Rocks, Shoals, Soundings, Quality of the Bottom, Diversities of the Coast, Flowings and Settings of the Tides, and distant Views of the Land: Also an Account of the Orkney Islands, the Manner of taking a Survey, the State of the Tides, and a Particular Description of the Rocks, Shoals, Channels, Harbours, Anchoring Places, the Directions, Irregularities, and Velocities of the several Streams of Tide round each Island. Interspersed with suitable Observations for Sailors. Fol. London.

An edit., Dublin, 1785. See Mackenzie under following item and under 1776 below.

1751-71   MACKENZIE, MURDOCH. Charts of the West Coast of Great Britain, and the Coast of Ireland, surveyed 1751-71. London.

This contains 18 charts on the scale of one mile to one inch. Chart no. 19 is a general chart. Nautical descriptions accompany the collection.

Mackenzie was employed as surveyor to the Admiralty. Before 1740 he was working in the Orkney and Shetland Islands, and between 1750 and 1760 he was engaged in surveying the Irish Coast and West Coast of Scotland, and on similar work in other parts. The results of his labors were published in his atlas of 1776.

1752   The English Pilot (Part I) for the Southern Navigation: describing the Sea-Coasts, Capes, Headlands, Bays, Roads, Harbours, Rivers and Ports. Together with the Soundings, Sands, Rocks, and Dangers on the Coast of England, Scotland, Ireland, Holland, Flanders, Spain, Portugal, to the Streights-Mouth; etc. 22 engraved folding charts, and a great many woodcuts in the text of coastal silhouettes, etc. Fol. London.

As Part II was published in 1723, the present work would seem to belong to an earlier date than 1752. Part III has been advertised as of 1736, and Part V as of 1744. See under 1723 above.

1753   ROCQUE, JOHN. The Small British Atlas: Being a New Set of Maps of all the Counties of England and Wales: To which is added, A General Map, with Tables of Length, Breadth, Area. . . . Likewise a Parliamentary Map of England, with Tables of the Produce of the Land-Tax, etc. 54 maps. Obl. 4to. London.

> Another edit., 1762; also 1764; reprinted 1769.
> These maps were first issued in the *English Traveller*, 1746 (see Simpson under AIDS TO TRAVELERS). They resemble those found in *The Small English Atlas of Kitchin* (see under 1749). The title appears in both English and French. The reprint of 1769 is found in Russell and Price, *England Displayed* (see this date under DESCRIPTIONS).

1754-1804   Ordnance Survey of the Various Counties of England and Wales, a Collection of 39 maps of the Counties, each on several sheets. London.

> The earliest map of this collection was that of Middlesex by Rocque. The others followed at varying intervals done by a variety of editors. What this Ordnance Survey entailed in preparation I cannot tell, but it is not to be confused with the scientific survey begun in 1784 (see this date below).

1755   BERTRAM, CHARLES J. Mappa Britanniae faciei Romanae secundum fidem monumentorum perveterum depicta. 15⅛ × 12⅞ ins. Copenhagen.

> For Bertram and his forgery of Richard of Cirencester, see Stukeley under 1757, BRITISH, ROMAN, AND SAXON ANTIQUITIES.

1759   GIBSON, JOHN. New and Accurate Maps of the Counties of England and Wales. Drawn from the latest Surveys. 24mo. London.

> Another edit., with 53 maps and a descriptive note to each map, 12mo, London, 1770; again, 1779.

1760   PRESTON, CAPTAIN T. A Chart of Zetland or Shetland, surveyed and engraved by Captain Thomas Preston in the Years 1743 and 1744. 26 × 17 ins. London.

> Of this there were later editions.

ROCQUE, JOHN. A Map of England and Wales, in 2 Parts. Drawn from the most accurate Surveys, containing all the Cities, Boroughs, Market Towns and Villages, in which are included all the Improvements and Observations both Astronomical and Topographical which have been made by the Members of the Royal Society and others down to the Present Year, the Whole corrected and improved by John Rocque. 22¾ × 38¾ ins. London.

1761   ROCQUE, JOHN. Topographical Survey of the County of Berks, in Eighteen Sheets, with the Royal Palace of Windsor, Seats, Towns, Villages, Main and Cross Roads, Bridle Ways, Pales, Hedges, Commons, Greens, etc., belonging to each Parish, with a Geographical and Historical Index. Atlas fol. London.

> Reissued in reduced form, with plan of the City of Oxford, 26 × 17 ins., 8vo, 1762.

1762   BOWEN, EMANUEL, and THOMAS KITCHIN. The Royal English Atlas: being a New and Accurate Set of Maps of all the Counties of South Britain, Drawn from Surveys . . . and exhibiting all the Cities, Towns, etc. Particularly Distinguishing More Fully and Accurately the Church Livings, Than any other Maps hitherto Published. Adorned with Views of all the Cathedrals; and a concise Description of each Diocese: illustrated with Historical Extracts . . . to the whole is prefix'd, A General Map of England and Wales, . . . all the Direct and Principal Cross Roads. 44 maps. Fol. London.

Another edit., 1778; again 1780. See Bowen under 1794 below.

The maps in this collection closely resemble those in *The Large English Atlas* (see Bowen under 1749-55 above), and the historical notes and views of the cathedrals are practically the same as those in that atlas.—Chubb.

ROCQUE, JOHN. A Topographical Map of the Country of Surrey, in Eight Sheets, to a Scale of two inches to a mile: in which are expressed, all the Main and Cross Roads, Lanes, Paths, Walls, Pales, Hedges, Hills, Valleys, Rivers, Brooks, Ponds, Bridges, Mills, Woods, Heaths, Commons, Parks, Churches, Noblemen and Gentlemen's Seats, Houses, Gardens, Cottages, etc. London.

A map on so enlarged a scale must be a delight to pore over. This was reprinted on a three-quarters' reduced scale, on nine sheets, with a preface by R. L. Atkinson, fol., Guildford, 1931.

1763 BONNE, M. Petit Neptune Anglois, ou carte marine des costes d'Angleterre, d'Ecosse, et d'Irlande. Paris.

BOWEN, EMANUEL, THOMAS KITCHIN (and others). The Large English Atlas, etc. Fol. London.

The first edition of this atlas, 1760, is described above under Bowen, 1749-55. The present edition contained 47 maps; the Royal Atlas had only 44 and a general one of England, which was described as to be had singly at one shilling, and the others at one shilling six pence. Bowen, reduced by family extravagances and almost blind through age, had begun to engrave them on a long quarto, in eighteen-penny numbers of three maps each; but dying before he had finished three or four numbers, he left them to be continued by his son,—Gough, 703.

LAURIE, J. A Map of the County Midlothian or Shire of Edinburgh, from an actual Survey. 4 Sheets, each 10 × 14 ins. Edinburgh.

1764 KITCHIN, THOMAS. For 54 maps of the counties of England, see his *England Illustrated,* under DESCRIPTIONS. The maps are clearly engraved, though too small to hold detail. They were reissued without change in his *English Atlas* of 1770.— Chubb.

1765 DONN, BENJAMIN. A Map of the County of Devon with the City and County of Exeter delineated from an Actual Survey, on Twelve Sheets of imperial Paper, the scale an inch to a mile, by Benjamin Donn, Teacher of the Mathematics, etc., late of Bideford, now of the City of Bristol, engraved by Thomas Jefferys, Geographer to His Majesty; to which is prefixed a General View of the County on one Sheet, with Indexes of the Parishes, Seats, etc., for the Reader finding them on the large Map. Colored throughout. Fol. London.

At the corners are plans of the town and citadel of Plymouth, of Stoke Town, Plymouth Dock, and the city and suburbs of Exeter.

1766 DURY, ANDREW, and J. ANDREWS. A Topographical Map of Hartfordshire, from an Actual Survey. Scale one mile to two ins. Printed in colors on 9 large double-page sheets, together with a key map and large-scale plans of Hertford and St. Albans. Fol. London.

ELLIS, JOHN. Ellis's English Atlas: or, A Compleat Chorography of England and Wales: in Fifty Maps Containing more Particulars than any other Collection of the same Kind. The Whole Calculated for the Use of Travellers, Academies, and

of all those who desire to Improve in the Knowledge of their Country. From the latest Surveys of the several Counties, engraved by and under the Direction of J. Ellis. Obl. 8vo. London.

> Another edit. dated 1766, with the addition of 4 maps, viz., Of the Rivers of England and Wales, of 25 Miles of the Country round London, of the Island of Jersey, and of Guernsey, Sark, Alderney, and Burhou (may have been published later) ; another edit., with a Modern Map of the Post Roads of England and Wales (not in previous issues) ; another, 1773 ; another, 1777, with corrections in imprint.—Chubb.

1767   BOWEN, EMANUEL and THOMAS. Atlas Anglicanus, Or, A Complete Sett of Maps of the Counties of South Britain; Divided into their Hundreds, Wapentakes, Wards, Rapes, Lathes, etc. . . . Describing also the Church Livings . . . With various Improvements, not inserted in any other Sett of Half Sheet Maps extant . . . By the late Emanuel Bowen, Geographer to His Majesty George II, and Thomas Bowen. 45 maps with numerous historical notes. Fol. London.

> The maps were reissued, with new titles, by Carington Bowles in Bowles' *New Medium Atlas,* London, 1785. Another edit., 1777.

1769   ANDREWS, J., A. DURY, and W. HERBERT. A Topographical Map of the County of Kent, on a Scale of Two Inches to a Mile, from an Actual Survey, showing Roads, Lanes, Churches, Gentlemen's Seats, Hills, Rivers, Cottages and Everything Remarkable in the County, comprising 25 double folio sheets, including a smaller Scale Key Map, a Chart of the Coast and a detailed Plan, 300 feet to the inch, of the City of Canterbury, the Boundaries of the Hundreds shown in colour. 26 engraved maps, 25 × 19 ins. Fol. London.

> This is the largest scale map of Kent hitherto issued and is remarkably full of details.— Quoted. This county map, like that of Devon by Donn (see under 1765) and others of the same kind, was an answer to the offer of bounties and premiums made by the Society of Arts (founded 1754) for large-scale maps on the proportion of one or two inches to the mile. These were issued separately but probably found their way into atlases.

ARMSTRONG, ANDREW. Ordnance Survey Map of Northumberland. London.

JEFFERYS, THOMAS. The County of Oxford, surveyed 1766 and 1767, and engraved by Thomas Jefferys, 1768. Colored, folded to 4to. London.

KITCHIN, THOMAS. Kitchin's Pocket Atlas, of the Counties of South Britain or England and Wales, Drawn to one Scale. By which the true Proportion they bear severally to each other may be easily ascertained with the Measured Distances from London by the nearest Roads annexed, to all the Cities, Boroughs, etc. Being the first Set of Counties ever Published on this Plan. Obl. 8vo. London.

> A very rare and apparently unknown atlas, of which a copy is extant in the Cambridge University Library. Maps are very similar to those engraved by Kitchin and issued in his *England Illustrated.*—Chubb.

1769-74   JEFFERYS, THOMAS, THOMAS DONALD, and ANDREW ARMSTRONG. A Series of 23 double-page colored maps of the Counties of Durham, Northumberland, and Westmoreland. Fol. London.

1770   BOWLES, J. Atlas. (Maps by J. Palairet.) Fol. London.

> 1. Great Britain and Ireland, 25½ × 20½ ins.
> 2. Scotland (based on Dorret's survey), 21 × 19⅛ ins.

JEFFERYS, THOMAS. Ordnance Surve y Map of Westmoreland. Large folding map on 3 sheets, with the contours displayed in detail. 36½ × 42 ins. London.

KITCHIN, THOMAS. Kitchin's English Atlas: or, A Compleat Set of Maps of all the Counties of England and Wales. Containing all the Cities, Towns, Parishes . . . and in general, every other Particular that is usually sought for, or to be found, in Maps. 54 maps. 4to. London.

> The maps are precisely the same as those issued in *England Illustrated*. (See under 1764.)

STOBIE, MATTHEW. A New and Accurate Map of Roxburghshire or Teviotdale, by Matthew Stobie, Land Surveyor, on a large scale, showing all the old roads, houses, etc., with inset of East Point of County with Cheviot Hill. In 4 sheets, each 19¾ × 18¼ ins. London.

1771 JEFFERYS, THOMAS. Ordnance Survey Map of the County of York. Engraved on 20 double sheets, including key-map, plans of York, Hull, Sheffield, Ripon and Leeds, and views of Fountains Abbey and Middleham Castle. Fol. London.

1772-74 CHAPMAN, JOHN. A Map of the County of Essex, from an Actual Survey taken in MD.CC.LXXII.-III.-IV. by John Chapman and Peter André, on 25 double pages, 28 × 21 ins. Colored throughout, with double-page title depicting a picturesque view, etc. Atlas folio. London.

1773 AINSLIE, JOHN. A Map of Selkirkshire or Ettrick Forest, from a Survey taken in 1772. 25¾ × 25 ins. Edinburgh.

ARMSTRONG, CAPTAIN MOSTYN JOHN. A Scotch Atlas, Divided into Counties. 32 maps, colored. 4to. London.

ROSS, C. A Map of the Shire of Lanark, taken from an actual Survey. 4 sheets, each 22½ × 18 ins. Edinburgh (?).

1774 BUCK, SAMUEL and NATHANIEL. The Index Map to Buck's Antiquities of every City, Town, Castle, Abbey, etc. 15½ × 18 ins. London.
> See Buck under 1727-40, VIEWS.

1775 AINSLIE, JOHN. The Counties of Fife and Kinross, with the Rivers Forth and Tay. 39 × 40 ins. Edinburgh and London.

JEFFERYS, THOMAS. A New and Correct Map of England and Ireland, containing the Cities, Towns, Castles, etc. 60 × 46 ins. London.

1776 EDGAR, W. Map of Breadalbane. Edinburgh.
> Edgar was employed by the Government to go with the troops in the Rebellion of the '45 and survey Perthshire and Invernesshire. An improved map was the result.

GARDEN, W. A Map of Kincardinshire, drawn from a Survey taken anno 1774. 30 × 28¾ ins. London.

MACKENZIE, MURDOCH. A Maritime Survey of Ireland and the West of Great Britain; taken by Order of the Right Hon. The Lords Commissioners of Admiralty. Accompanied with a Book of nautical Descriptions and Directions to each volume. 2 vols. Fol. London.

> Vol. I contains the maritime survey of Ireland in 28 charts, and views of the land taken at sea. Vol. II contains the west coast of Great Britain, from Bristol Channel to Cape Wrath, the northwest point of Scotland, in 31 charts, exhibiting the tides, rocks, shoals, sand banks, etc. While the title states that Mackenzie was surveyor to the Admiralty, actually he was superseded in this position by his nephew, Murdoch Mackenzie the Younger, in 1771.— Maggs, no. 693.

TAYLOR, GEORGE, and ANDREW SKINNER. For their survey and map of the roads of North Britain, or Scotland, see their *Survey of the Great Post-Roads,* under AIDS TO TRAVELERS.

1777   ARMSTRONG, CAPTAIN MOSTYN JOHN. A Scotch Atlas; or, Description of the Kingdom of Scotland: divided into Counties, with the Subdivisions of Sheriffdoms. 4to. London.

BOWEN, EMANUEL and THOMAS. An Accurate Map of the County of Surrey, divided into Hundreds. A colored map on the scale of 12 miles to 5½ ins., measuring 20 × 17½ ins. London.

> During the '70's a number of single issues of the various counties, described as in the above, appeared.

1778-91   A series of 15 double-page colored maps of the counties of Derbyshire, Lincolnshire, and Nottinghamshire, by Burdett and Kitchin, Armstrong and Chapman were published during these years.

1780   BOWEN, EMANUEL. Accurate Map of Northamptonshire, divided into its Hundreds. Descriptive text. 28 × 22 ins. London.

> The other counties were also issued separately.

BOWLES, CARRINGTON (or THOMAS KITCHIN). New and Complete Map of Scotland and the Islands, showing early Forts, Military Roads, Seats, etc. Border decorated with ships around the Coast. Outlines colored. 4 sheets in 2 sections, each 23 × 39 ins. London. (Date is approximate.)

——————. A New Topographical Chart of the English Channel and its Environs (the Maritime Provinces of France, Flanders, etc). In colors. 19 × 26½ ins. London.

DORRET, JAMES. A Correct Map of Scotland. Outlines colored. 30 × 23 ins. London.

1781   A Chart of the East Coast of North Britain (Firth of Forth and Pentland Firth). Leith.

Two Charts of the Forfar, Aberdeen, Murray Firth, and Caithness Coasts, etc. 21 × 29 ins. London.

1782 DURY, ANDREW, and J. ANDREWS. A Topographical Map of Hartfordshire, from an Actual Survey, in which is expressed all the Roads, Lanes, Churches, Noblemen and Gentlemen's Seats, together with the Division of the Parishes. 10 sheets (all colored). W. Faden. London.

Faden is frequently met with as the publisher of a large number of charts and atlases.

KNOX, J. A Commercial Map of Scotland, with the Roads, Stages, and Distances. 27¼ × 20⅞ ins. London.

Other editions followed.

MASTERS, —, and — DAY. The Ordnance Survey Map of Somerset. Large map on 9 sheets. London.

1782-90 LODGE, JOHN. The Political Magazine and Parliamentary, Naval, Military and Literary Journal. 8vo. London.

This contains 45 clearly engraved maps of England, Scotland, Ireland, and the 42 English counties, engraved by Lodge. Another edition, 1795, reprints the above maps but removes all traces of the engraver's name and the name of the magazine.—Chubb.

1783 DORRET, JAMES. A General Map of Scotland and Islands thereto belonging, from New Surveys, the Shires properly divided, etc., Forts lately erected, old Roads of Communication, Military Ways, Memorable Battles, Camps, Forts, Seats of Nobility, etc. 6 feet by 4½ feet. London.

HODGKINSON, J. Ordnance Survey Map of Suffolk. Large folding map in 4to. London.

STOBIE, J. Map of the Counties of Perth and Clackmannan, survey'd by Stobie, 1783, with inset views of Athole House, Taymouth, Dunkeld, Balgowan, Perth, Keir, old roads, etc. London.

This came out in 9 sheets, each 21 × 23 ins.

1783-88 CROSTHWAITE, P. Plans of the Lakes of Lancashire, Cumberland, and Westmoreland, with a short Description to each Map. (Place?)

Another edit., 8vo, London, 1794.
The only title given is on the maps, which include views of churches, houses, Roman remains, etc. The author describes himself as "Admiral at Keswick Regatta, who keeps the Museum at Keswick, and is Guide, Pilot, Geographer, and Hydrographer to the Nobility and Gentry who make the Tour of the Lakes." The plans were probably first issued separately.—Fishwick, *The Lancashire Library.*

1784 CHANDLER, J., and S. A. ARNOLD. Eleven Charts of the Coasts of Great Britain and Ireland, the British Channel, etc. Fol. London.

Other editions followed.

ORDNANCE SURVEY.

The foundation for this elaborate undertaking seems to have been laid in the military surveys of Scotland initiated by Major Gen. Watson after the battle of Culloden (1746) and carried out by Lieut. (later General) Wm. Roy. In 1784 Roy measured a base line of 27,404 feet on Hounslow Heath. By 1849 six other base lines had been established, and in 1858 the triangulation was completed. Meanwhile the detail survey was got under way in 1791, but the first map to contain these measurements did not appear until 1801. The plans as first conceived were modified as the work went on during the 19th century. It was originally

determined that a map sufficiently accurate could be made on a scale of one mile to one inch, i.e., 1:62,360. For town plans larger scales were adopted. A one-inch scale map for the whole kingdom, covering 697 sheets, was completed by 1890. On the whole, these maps, with rare exceptions, are considered to be more accurate than similar maps produced by other governments. For an interesting account of the progress of this survey, see Jervis, *op. cit.,* ch. X. It seems strange that maps based on triangulation were so late in making their appearance, for as early as 1615 a Dutch geometer, Willibrand Snellius, had worked out the problem, to be followed more accurately by the French Academy of Science, founded in 1666. See Chubb, Introduction.

1785   BOWLES, CARRINGTON. The New Medium Atlas; or, A Complete Set of Maps of the Counties of England and Wales; divided into their respective Hundreds, Wapentakes, Wards, Rapes, Lathes, etc. 44 colored maps, with titles engraved on circular or oval panels. 4to. London.

> These maps are reissues of those by Emanuel and Thomas Bowen published by Kitchin in *Atlas Anglicanus.*—Thorp, no. 523.

————. Bowles's Pocket Atlas of the Counties of South Britain or England and Wales, Drawn to one Scale: by which the True Proportion they severally bear to each other may be easily ascertained, with the Measured Distances from London by the nearest Roads, annexed, to all the Cities, Boroughs and Market Towns in the Kingdom. Being the only Set of Counties, ever Published on this Plan. 57 maps. 8vo. London.

> For the same title and the same claim, see Kitchin under 1769 above.

TAYLOR, GEORGE, and ANDREW SKINNER. For a collection of 178 maps, see their *Survey of the Roads of Scotland,* under AIDS TO TRAVELERS.

Thames. A Correct Chart of all the Channels between the Nore and the Downs, and likewise between the Nore and Orfordness, collected from the latest and best Observations. A finely drawn MS chart of the Thames Estuary from the Downs to the Coast of Suffolk. 22 × 33 ins. Dated 1785.—Maggs, no. 693.

WALTER, J., and J. GORDON. A Commercial Map of Scotland, showing the Islands and Lakes comprising the great Theatre of the Fisheries, the proposed Canals, etc. London and Edinburgh.

1786   ANDREWS, JOHN. A New Physical, Historical, and Political Map of England and Wales, from Actual Surveys and Astronomical Observations of the Royal Society. Colored map measuring 63½ × 54¼ ins. London.

> "As there is no general Map of England and Wales of essential service to Military information, in order to render this the more serviceable, the Author has endeavour'd by representing the great ranges of Mountains, Hills and High Lands, which bound the Rivers to point out the extent of the Vallies and Low Lands by Number, which, as it will give a View of the Grounds proper for Encampments, he flatters himself will not prove unacceptable to Gentlemen of the Army."—Advertisement, quoted by Bookseller.

BOSWELL, HENRY. For a complete set of county maps, see his *Picturesque Views of the Antiquities,* etc., under VIEWS.

TAYLOR, I. Ordnance Survey Map of Hereford. On 4 sheets. London.

1787   CARY, JOHN. Cary's New and Correct English Atlas: being a New Set of County Maps from Actual Surveys. Exhibiting all the Direct and Principal Cross Roads, Cities, Towns, and most considerable Villages, Parks, Rivers, Navigable Canals, etc. Preceded by a General Map of South Britain, shewing the Connexion of one Map with another; also a General Description of each County, and Directions for the Junction of the Roads from one County to another. 46 maps, each with a page of descriptive text. Index. 4to. London.

> Another edit., 1793; reissued this same year, and a further reissue of this 1793 edition the same year; and so on to 1831. All in all, a total of eight reissues appeared by 1831.
> With Cary a new luminary in the art and science of cartography appears on the scene. What Saxton, Norden, and Speed were to the 16th and early 17th centuries, Seller, Morden, and Senex to the latter part of the 17th century, Bowen, Kitchin, and Jefferys to the middle of the 18th, John Cary was to the closing years of the 18th century, and even to modern times. A more prolific map maker never put graver to copper. According to Fordham (*John Cary, Engraver, Map, Chart and Print Seller and Globe Maker,* 1925), if sheets separately engraved were counted, his total productions might tally a thousand. Yet he has scarcely been noticed by biographers; the *DNB* passes him up entirely. Of his life little is known. Probably more is related in Fordham's Introduction to the above mentioned work than is to be found anywhere else. His entire output includes geographies, canal plans, road maps, itineraries, geological maps, works on astronomy, globes, together with atlases and maps proper. In addition to his merit in producing accurate and artistic maps, he is credited with being the first to establish the meridian of Greenwich as zero longitude. In every way he was superior to his contemporaries and to most of his predecessors. For an extensive and seemingly complete bibliography of his publications, see Fordham, *op. cit.,* which gives also descriptions of the items.

    SAYER, ROBERT. An English Atlas, or, A Concise View of England and Wales; Divided into Counties, and its Subdivisions into Hundreds, etc. Describing their Situation, Extent, Boundaries, Circumference, Soil, Product, Chief Rivers and Principal Great and Bye Roads; with a Chart of the Distances between the Cities and Chief Towns. Together with a Description of the Situation of the most venerable Antiquities whether Ruins of Castles, Palaces, or Monasteries, . . . On Fifty-Two Copper Plates. 4to. London.

> These maps are reprints of those by Kitchin and Jefferys in *The Small English Atlas,* 1749. A page or two of text accompanies each county map.—Chubb. As far as titles go, this period of map publication offers but a dreary repetition of copies of copies, which often get farther away from fidelity to fact. The maps are sometimes named after the engraver, sometimes after the publisher, and sometimes after the surveyor. Hence ensues the difficulty of identifying various issues.

    TUKE, JOHN. Map of Yorkshire. London.

> This map, which is well engraved and filled with detail, is mainly based on Jefferys' map of Yorkshire published in 1775. The latter remained the standard map of this county until it was superseded by Cary's of 1790. Coming between two notable publications, Tuke's map had little influence.—Quoted from *Torrington's Diary,* vol. III, note by editor, 176.

1789   AINSLIE, JOHN. Map of Scotland, containing Tables of Mountain Heights, Distances, etc., Drawn and engraved from a Series of Angles and Astronomical Observations. 72 × 65 ins. Edinburgh.

> Another edit., Edinburgh, 1800.
> This map is a great improvement on previous maps of Scotland. It gives much detail on the physical features of the country. By using special types it distinguishes the various objects marked, such as the borough towns which send members to Parliament from the market towns, the different remains of Roman antiquity, such as Roman roads, camps, country roads, military roads, turnpike roads, etc.—Shearer.

    RICHARDSON, T., W. KING (and others). A Plan of His Majesty's Forest called the New Forest in the County of Southampton, laid down from Surveys engraved and published by W. Faden. 9 colored double-page maps. Fol. London.

1790 FADEN, W. Atlas. Fol. London.

> ROY, GENERAL WM. Map of Scotland from the Topographical Survey by Gen. Roy.
> 2 sheets, measuring 39 × 44 ins. London.
>
>> Through the cartographic work of Gen. Roy, map making in England was lifted up to the
>> status of a science under the control of government authority. His training in this field began
>> with his completion of the military survey of Scotland initiated by Gen. Watson, and when
>> the French and British governments agreed on the project of connecting the observatories of
>> Paris and Greenwich geodetically, Roy was provided with the opportunity long sought to
>> execute the first really systematic triangulation in Great Britain. His first base was estab-
>> lished at Hounslow Heath. In 1787 formal triangulation was started in cooperation with the
>> French efforts, and thus the work was carried on under the name of the Ordnance Survey
>> (see under 1784 above). See Thiele, *Official Map Publications;* Inglis, *The Early Maps of
>> Scotland, with an Account of the Ordnance Survey.*

1791 HARRISON, JOHN. Maps of the English Counties with the Subdivisions of Hun-
      dreds, Wapontakes, Lathes, Wards, etc. To which are added, Two Folio Pages of
      Letter-Press, to face each Map; descriptive of the Extent, Boundaries, Rivers,
      Lakes, Canals, Soil, Mines, Minerals, curious Plants, Husbandry, and every
      Curiosity that is nearly connected with the Maps. 38 plates of maps of counties of
      England and North and South Wales. Obl. fol. London.

> Another edit., London, 1792.

> HOOPER, S. An Index Map to the Antiquities of Scotland, showing the Situation of
> every Building described in Grose's *Antiquities.* 16¾ × 14 ins. London.
>
>> For Grose's *Antiquities of Scotland,* see under 1789-91, HISTORY AND ANTIQUITIES.

> MILNE, THOMAS. Map of Hampshire, or the County of Southampton, including
> the Isle of Wight, surveyed by Thomas Milne, 1788-90, executed and published
> by W. Faden. Colored with inset plans of Winchester and Southampton. 58 × 55
> ins. London.

> ――――――. Ordnance Survey of Hants. Large folding map in 6 sheets. London.

1791-97   BAKER, BENJAMIN. The Universal Magazine of Knowledge and Pleasure. . . .
          8vo. London.

> This contains a second series of county maps issued in the *Universal Magazine.* See
> 1747-66 above for the first series.

1792 DOWNIE, MURDO. The New Pilot for the East Coast of Scotland; giving a particu-
      lar Account of the Tides, a Description of the Fishing Banks, and Appearance of
      the Land from the Sea; also, a Description of all the Rocks, Sands, Shoals, Chan-
      nels, Creeks, Bays, Harbours, etc. With Directions for conducting Ships in every
      Situation along this Coast. 4to. London.

> This "New Pilot" was written partly as the handbook to a series of four large charts pre-
> pared by Murdo Downie from actual surveys.—Maggs, no. 742.

> The New Pilot for the East Coast of Scotland; a true and correct Chart from St.
> Abb's Head to the Red Head, up to Edinburgh Firth, etc. Edinburgh (?).

1793 CARY, JOHN. A New and Correct English Atlas: a new Set of County Maps, from
      actual Surveys, exhibiting all the Direct and principal Cross Roads, Cities, Towns,

and most considerable Villages, Parks, Rivers, Navigable Canals, etc., with Description of each County, and Directions for the Junction of the Roads from one County to another. 47 double maps, with the roads and boundaries colored. 4to. London.

This is an edition of his atlas of 1787. Its scale is 10 miles to an inch and a half.

CLARKE, JAMES. Plans of the Lakes in Cumberland, Westmorland and Lancashire, with an Accurate Survey of the Roads leading to them from Penrith, Keswick, etc. 12 large-scale folding maps of the district. 4to. London.

EVANS, J. Ordnance Survey Map of North Wales. London.

YATES, G. Ordnance Survey Map of Warwick. London.

1794 CAMPBELL, LIEUT. A New and Correct Map of Scotland or North Britain, with all the Post and Military Roads, Divisions, etc., drawn from the most approved Surveys, illustrated with many additional and regulated with latest Astronomical Observations, Insets of the Orkneys and road distances from Edinburgh. In two Parts, each 24½ × 4¼ ins. London.

This map bears a resemblance to that of Bowles, 1735. It may have been the work of a lieutenant in the Navy, for it notes sandbanks and dangerous rocks. A number of battlefields are indicated, with some errors in dates and spelling.—Shearer.

CARY, JOHN. A New Map of England and Wales, with Part of Scotland. On which are carefully laid down All the Direct and Principal Cross Roads, the Course of the Rivers and Navigable Canals, Cities, Market and Borough Towns, Parishes and most considerable Hamlets, Parks, Forests, etc. Delineated from Actual Surveys; and materially assisted from Authentic Documents Liberally supplied by the Right Honourable the Post Masters General. Scale 5 miles to one inch. 4to. London.

Several editions, issues, and impressions appeared in the next century; a reduced edition, 15 miles to the inch, London, 1796.
The map is engraved on 81 sheets, and extends far enough north to include Edinburgh, Stirling, and Glasgow. The old meridian of London (St. Paul's Cathedral) used by Englishmen since its introduction by Seller in 1676 was discarded for the first time in favor of Greenwich. For a complete description of the map, see Fordham, *John Cary*. It was reviewed in *Gent. Mag.*, vol. 65, 671.

HUDDART, CAPT. J. A New Hydrographical Survey (made in 1789) of the Northeast of Ireland, and the West Coast of Scotland, from Tory Island to Cape Wrath, including the Western Islands; in 3 sheets. For the British Society for the Encouragement of Fishery. 52½ × 28¼ ins. Edinburgh.

KITCHIN, THOMAS. A General Map of England and Wales, divided into its Counties, corrected from the best Surveys and Astronomical Observations. 25 × 21¼ ins. London.

LAURIE AND WHITTLE (Publishers). A New Hydrographical Survey of the Firth of Forth, called also the South Firth or Edinburgh Firth, from the Entrance to Queensferry. London.

1795 BOWLES, CARRINGTON. Scotland laid down from the Survey of Dorret. Colored. 21 × 20 ins. London.

> See Dorret under 1780 above.

BROWN, THOMAS. A New and Correct Map of Scotland, dedicated to the Highland Society, with all the old Roads shewn very clearly. London (?).

GARDNER, W., and T. YEAKELL. A Topographical Map of the County of Sussex, divided into Rapes, Deaneries, and Hundreds, begun by W. Gardner and T. Yeakell, and completed by Thomas Gream. In 4 sections, each 30 × 19 ins. Scale one mile to an inch. Fol. London.

TAYLOR, I. Ordnance Survey Map of Dorset, on 6 sheets. London.

1795-97 Agricultural Maps of Midlothian, Selkirk, and Roxburghshire. Edinburgh (?).

1795-1808 CARY, JOHN. Inland Navigation; or Select Plans of the Several Navigable Canals, throughout Great Britain: Accompanied with Abstracts of the different Acts of Parliament relative to them; likewise the Width, Depth, Length, and Number of Locks on each; with the principal Articles of Carriage, etc. 4to. London.

1796 AINSLIE, JOHN. Map of Scotland, surveyed by John Ainslie, 1796, showing old Estates and Owners, old Roads, etc. Large scale. London.

CLARK, HENRY. Maps and Surveys of the Several Farms in the Parish of Seasoncote in the County of Gloucester, the Property of Colonel Cockerell. Surveyed in 1796 by Henry Clark. Fol. London.

MACPHERSON, D. An Historical Map of Scotland with the north Part of England, adapted to the Year 1400, and constructed from the most authentic Materials attainable. 4to. London.

> This map, which measures 14¼ × 12½ ins., is printed in *Geographical Illustrations of Scottish History* (see Macpherson under 1797, GEOGRAPHY). On the title a figure points a hand to Scotland, and at the side is printed:
> "There Roman eagles fled from conquering foes,
> The rugged rock, the barren desert smil'd;
> For I, and loose-rob'd Freedom, walked the wild."
> —Quoted from Shearer.

1797 ANDREWS, JOHN. Historical Atlas of England; physical, political, astronomical, civil and ecclesiastical, biographical, naval, parliamentary, and geographical; ancient and modern; from the Deluge to the Present Time. In which are described its Minerals, Curiosities, Inland Fisheries and Navigation, Commerce, Peerages, . . . Interspersed with geographical Notes and Dates for the Curious, and Explanations to each Map, in order to enable Persons of every Rank to read, with Advantage, the Natural History, Antiquities, Belles Lettres, and Geography of this Country, etc. Edinburgh.

BLACKADDER, J. Map of Berwickshire, from Actual Survey. 2 sheets, each 26 × 19½ ins. Edinburgh and London.

CARY, JOHN. A New Map of the County of Oxford, from an Actual Survey; on which are delineated the Course of the Rivers and Roads, Parks, Gentlemen's Seats, Heaths, Woods, Forests, Commons, etc. By Richard Davis of Lewknor, Topographer to his Majesty. Engraved by John Cary. 16 sheets; scale ½ mile to one inch. With key map. Fol. London.

> The sheets are so engraved so as to enable one to put them together as one map. Sheets 13 and 14 are filled with a large scale inset plan of Oxford, extending to parts of sheets 9 and 10. The map is filled with the usual detail of county maps. For a complete description of the map, see Fordham, *John Cary*.

EVAN, JOHN. Map of North Wales, inscribed to Sir Watkin Williams Wynn by John Evan. 26 × 30 ins. London.

1797-99   HEATHER, W. Chart of the English Channel. Also River Thames, the Downs, Spithead, Plymouth, Falmouth, Atlantic North and South, Southern Africa, Indian Ocean, Eastern Straits. 74 × 32 ins. Atlas fol. London.

1798   Chart of the East Coast of England and Scotland, from the Humber to Aberdeen. Heather's Navigation Warehouse. London.

TUKE, J. Map of Ninety Miles by Seventy-five in which Chesterfield is the Centre, comprising Derby, Nottingham, etc. 25¾ × 32 ins. Colored. London.

1799   A General Map of Scotland, distinguishing the Lowland, Highland, and Intermediate Districts . . . for the Report to the House of Commons respecting the Distilleries in Scotland. 21⅝ × 18 ins. London.

GREAM, THOMAS. A Topographical Map of the County of Sussex, reduced from the large Survey in four sheets by Thomas Gream. London.

> For the large map see Gardner, under 1795 above.

YATES, GEORGE. A Map of the County of Glamorgan; from an Actual Survey, made by George Yates of Liverpool. On which are delineated the Courses of the Rivers, and Navigable Canals; with the Roads, Parks, Gentlemen's Seats, Castles, Woods, etc. In 4 sheets, drawn on the meridian of London. Published by J. Cary. London.

1800   (Maps of the various counties called Ordnance Surveys continued to appear during this decade.)

LIZARS, —. Map of the Scenery of the Grampian Mountains. Colored. 18 × 18 ins. London (?).

1870   LOWER, MARK ANTHONY. A Survey of the Coast of Sussex, made in 1587, with a View to its Defence against Foreign Invasion, and especially against the Spanish Armada. Edit. with Notes, by Mark Anthony Lower, M.A., F.S.A. With 5 maps and facsimile reproduction of the old text. Obl. fol. Lewes.

1871 BULLOCK, HENRY. Map or Plan of the West Border Land, the "Debateable Land," showing the Border Line proposed and agreed on, Sept. 24, 1552. 23 × 17 ins. Original MS. in Public Record Office, London. Fol. London.

1876 PONT, TIMOTHY. Cuninghame, Topographized, 1604-08. With Continuations and Illustrative Notices by Jas. Dobie. Numerous illustrations and early folding map. 4to. London.

> The district of Cuninghame was the most fully described district of all those he surveyed. Pont's maps appeareɛ in Blaeu's *Atlas*, 1654, as revised by Robert Gordon. See Pont under 1608 above.

1885 BRADLEY, HENRY. Ptolemy's Geography of the British Isles. In *Archaeologia,* vol. 48, 379-96. London.

> The author reconstructs the map of Britain from the information supplied by Ptolemy in the way of a table of latitudes and longitudes. The projection employed is that of Ptolemy, i.e., a projection in which the meridians and parallels are represented by straight lines at right angles to each other. This would allow the proportions in length between the degree of latitude and that of longitude to be correct for the middle parallel of the map. Of course, the attempt resulted in the well-known twist of Scotland to the east, which all Ptolemaic maps exhibited. Bradley presents an original theory for the cause of this error. Ptolemy's degree of longitude was measured from the western extremity of the known world, i.e., from the Fortunate Isles, and his degree of latitude from the equator. He divided his degrees into twelfths, not minutes. The terms latitude and longitude, referring to the breadth and length of the known world, seemed to be his own invention. The distances in longitude were obtained, not from astronomical observations, but from reductions of itinerary distances. Since his estimate of the globe's circumference was one-sixth too small, his regular measurements must be reduced in this proportion, so that one of his degrees would correspond to 50 minutes of our measure. And since he made the latitude of the south coast of England two degrees too high, the rectification would make his degree 48 minutes.

1887 NORDEN, JOHN. John Norden's Map of Essex, by William Cole. In *Essex Naturalist,* vol. 1. 8vo. Buckhurst Hill.

1892 EDGAR, W. A Map of Stirlingshire, from a Survey in 1745 (showing the Roman Wall, etc., and the Canal), with Plans of the Battles of Falkirk and Bannockburn. Facs. by John E. Shearer of Stirling. 16¼ × 23½ ins. Stirling (?).

> This map was used in Nimmo's *History of Stirlingshire,* 1777.

1907 GILLOW, JOHN. Lord Burghley's Map of Lancashire in 1590. Privately printed, Catholic Record Society. Facs. London (?).

1923 COWAN, WILLIAM. The Maps of Edinburgh, 1544-1851. 4to. Edinburgh.

1928 PARIS, MATTHEW. Four Maps of Great Britain, designed by Matthew Paris about A.D. 1250. Reproduced from three MSS. in the British Museum and one at Corpus Christi College, Cambridge. With 4 colored facsimile reproductions. Fol. British Museum, London.

> High praise has been bestowed on this medieval chronicler for the scholarly quality of his maps, which fell short in that they were not the result of practical observation. Of his productions in this field there are six maps extant. The map of England, of which there are four copies, is the best in execution and detail, as well as the most interesting. It has been pointed out that for the first time in North European maps, the north appears at the top of the map. "This was a victory for science and for the compass." But Scotland appears as an island in itself, being joined at Stirling by a wide bridge. And the influence of Ptolemy is still evident

in that this country has a slight twist to the east. The map may have been drawn as it was for the purpose of inducing travelers going from Dover to Durham to pass through St. Albans, for these places are set in a straight line running north and south. In its hydrography the map is fairly accurate in placing of rivers, although the Thames is made to empty on the south coast. For further description, see Jervis, *op. cit.*

1933 Reproductions of Early Engraved Maps. English County Maps in the Collection of the Royal Geographical Society. With an Introduction and Notes by Edward Heawood. 31 maps. Fol. Published for the Royal Geographical Society. London.

1934 LYNAM, EDWARD. The Map of the British Isles of 1546. (Described) by Edward Lynam. Photostatic reproduction in 2 sheets. 4to. London.

This is a facsimile of the first separately engraved map of the British Isles by George Lily (see under 1546 above).

XXII

Letters, Diaries, Memoirs

("Private Records are remnants of history which casually escaped shipwreck of time."— Bacon. Intimate letters which convey the interchange of soul with soul are valued for their glimpses into human nature. Those which reveal the thought and spirit of an age, the stamp and character of the times, add to our historical knowledge. And even those which merely retail the gossip of the day build up in our minds a more complete picture of the way people lived. But not all communications that label themselves letters belong to the category of correspondence. Many a traveler, under the pretense of pressure from friends, published the narrative of his journeyings in the disguise of letters, partly no doubt to establish an informal attitude towards his material and partly to screen himself from attack, should his remarks about people and places cause offense, by the plea that what he wrote was not meant for publication. These naturally fall under the classification of TOURS. Those which are frankly topographical are entered under DESCRIPTIONS. Then there is the group of borderline cases which baffle exact definition. If they are found to be put in the wrong company, they are but paying the penalty for not declaring themselves more openly. Letters which have the unchallenged right to inclusion in this section are those in which narratives of travel or passages of description are but incidental to the main purpose of the message. The same difficulties attend the ordering of diaries and memoirs. Bringing these to light is one of the main literary sports of our day. Extended lists of this latter form of literature are to be found in various sections of the *Cambridge Bibliography*.)

1588 LEIGH, RICHARD. The Copie of a Letter sent out of England to Don Bernardin Mendoza Ambassador in France for the King of Spaine, declaring the State of England. (With separate title page) Certaine Advertisements out of Ireland, concerning the Losses and Distresses Happened to the Spanish Navie. . . . 4to. London.

> It is thought by some that Shakespeare may have had a hand in the printing of this work.— Bookseller's Note.

1594 NORRIS, SIR JOHN. A Diurnal of al that Sir John Norreis hath doone since his Last Ariuall in Britaine at the end of February 1591-92. Also of the Taking in of the Porte by Croyzon, and the Names of such Captaines Gentlemen and others that were slaine and hurte in his Seruice, 1594. 4to. London. (8 leaves.)

> The *Short-Title Catalogue* mentions only one copy. Sir John Norris' military career was a highly varied and interesting one, the details of which are very fully stated in *DNB*. He was less successful as a diplomat in Ireland, and is said to have died of a broken heart, owing to the Queen's disregard of his twenty-six years' service.—Bookseller's Note.

1643 THREE LETTERS. The First from an Officer in His Majesties Army to a Gentleman in Gloucestershire, upon occasion of certain Queries scattered about that Country; The Second a Letter from a grave Gentleman once a Member of the House of Commons, to his Friend in London, concerning the Reason why he left the House, and concerning the Late Treaty; etc. 4to. Oxford.

1645-55 HOWELL, JAMES. Epistolae Ho-Elianae: Familiar Letters, Domestic and Forren, divided into sundry Sections, partly Historicall, Politicall, Philosophicall. 8vo. London.

> The 1st vol. appeared in 1645; the 2nd in 1647; the 3rd in 1650; and the collected edition in 1655. Modern reprint, by Joseph Jacobs, London, 1892; another with an Introduction by Agnes Repplier, Boston, 1907.
> These letters were written for the most part in the Fleet prison where Howell had been confined as a Royalist, and were addressed to imaginary correspondents. They partake of the nature of articles on affairs rather than of private correspondence. See Howell this date under WEST EUROPE, vol. I of this work.

1647 EVELYN, JOHN. For his Character of England, as it was lately presented in a Letter, see under DESCRIPTIONS.

1671 POWELL, VAVASOR. The Life and Death of Vavasor Powell. 12mo. (Place?)

This contains Powell's autobiography. The editor is thought to have been Edward Bagshaw the Younger, a Baptist evangelist in Wales in the 17th century.—Davies, *Bibliog. Brit. Hist., Stuart Period.*

1683 MELVILLE, SIR JAMES. Memoirs of his Own Life, 1549-1593. By George Scott. London.

Edit. by Thomas Thomson, *Publ. Bann. Club*, no. 18, Edinburgh, 1827; and *Publ. Maitland Club*, vol. 21, Edinburgh, 1827; edit. by A. F. Steuart, London, 1929.
The manuscript of this autobiography was discovered in 1660. Sir James spent his youth as a page to Mary Queen of Scots and naturally in his later days attempted to further her interests. During the minority of James VI he was employed in various diplomatic missions.

1691 CAMDEN, WILLIAM (and others). Gulielmi Camdeni, et Illustrium Virorum ad G. Camdenum Epistolae. Cum appendice varii Argumenti. Accesserunt Annalium Regni Regis Jacobi I. Apparatus et Commentarius de Antiquitate, Dignitate et Officio Comitis Marescalli Angliae. With Life of Camden by T. Smith. Portrait. 4to. London.

1694 Fox, GEORGE. A Journal, or, Historical Account of the Life, Travels, Sufferings, Christian Experiences, and Labour of Love in the Work of the Ministry of . . . George Fox. Fol. London.

Fox is naturally more concerned with recording the state of religious opinion than that of the countryside. The account is not utterly bare of comment on places. Fox visited Scotland in 1657.

1707 DUNOIS, COUNTESS OF. Memoirs of the Court of England, in Two Parts, now made English, to which is added, The Lady's Pacquet of Letters, taken from her by a French Privateer in her Passage to Holland, Suppos'd to be written by several Men of Quality, brought over from St. Malo's by an English Officer. 8vo. London.

Revised edit., by G. D. Gilbert, London, 1913. See below.
The full name of this adventuring lady was Marie-Catherine Jumelle de Berneville, Comtesse d'Aulnoy. For her travels, see under 1691, WEST EUROPE, vol. I of this work.

1913 D'AULNOY, MARIE CATHERINE, BARONNE. Memoirs of the Court of England in 1675. Translated by Mrs. W. H.·Arthur; revised edition, by G. D. Gilbert. 16 portraits. 8vo. London.

1710 DAVIES, RICHARD. An Account of the Convincement, Exercises, Services, and Travels of . . . Richard Davies, with some Relation of ancient Friends and the spreading of the Truth in North-Wales. 12mo. London.

7th edit., London, 1844.
This is said to be an interesting autobiography.

1717 ASHMOLE, ELIAS. Memoirs of the Life of that learned Antiquary Elias Ashmole drawn up by Himself by Way of Diary, with an Appendix of original Letters. Edit. by C. Burman. 12mo. London.

Reprinted in *The Lives of those Eminent Antiquarians, Elias Ashmole and William Lilly*, 8vo, London, 1774.
His chief work was the *Antiquities of Berkshire;* see under 1719, HISTORY AND ANTIQUITIES.

1718   RAY, JOHN. Philosophical Letters between John Ray and his Correspondents, with those of Francis Willoughby. Published by Derham. 8vo. London.

> For the travels and works of these famous botanists, Ray and Willoughby, see under 1673, WEST EUROPE, vol. I of this work.

1719   RAMKINS, MAJOR ALEXANDER. The Memoirs of Major Alexander Ramkins, A Highland-Officer, Now in Prison at Avignon. Being an Account of Several remarkable Adventures during about twenty-eight Years Service in Scotland, Germany, Italy, Flanders, and Ireland; exhibiting a very agreeable and instructive Lesson of Human Life, both in a Publick and Private Capacity, in several pleasant instances of his Amours, Gallantry, Oeconomy, etc. 8vo. London.

> An edit. printed, 8vo, Cork, 1741.
> There were two issues of this remarkable book, of which the above is the first. The second has a canceled title page dated 1720. Between the publication of the two issues Ramkins died in prison at Avignon, where he had been thrown on account of his wife's debts. He had an extremely exciting and picturesque career, as an adherent of James II, to whose cause he remained steadfast, despite many offers from the English Government to change sides. His account is marked by understatement rather than by overstatement.—*DNB.*

1720   GRATTON, JOHN. A Journal of the Life of that ancient Servant of Christ, John Gratton, giving an Account of his Exercises when Young, also of his Labours, Travels, and Sufferings. London.

> Frequently reprinted in the following decades.

1733   VOLTAIRE, FRANCOIS AROUET DE. For his letters on the English Nation, see under TOURS BY FOREIGNERS.

1734   RERESBY, SIR JOHN. Memoirs of Sir John Reresby, Bart., and late Governor of York, containing several Private and Remarkable Transactions, from the Restoration to the Revolution. From his Original Manuscript. London.

> A reimpression, 1735; the *Memoirs* with the *Travels* added, London, 1813; the *Memoirs,* edit. from the original MS, by James J. Cartwright, London, 1875 (with matter restored which had been omitted from the 1st edition); edit. by Albert Ivatt, M.A., for Dryden House Series, London, 1904.
> The *Memoirs* end abruptly in May, 1689, a few days before the writer's death. His support of the House of Stuart led to an increase in fortune and appointments after the Restoration, such as that of the governorship of York in 1682. On this occasion he showed himself to be a magnificent entertainer. He records that on Dec. 30 he had in to dinner eighteen gentlemen and their wives; on Jan. 1, sixteen more gentlemen, on Jan. 3, twenty others, on the 4th, twelve of the neighboring clergy, and on the 6th, seven gentlemen and tradesmen from various places. For music "I had two violins and a bass from Doncaster that wore my livery, and that played well for the country; two bagpipes for the common people; a trumpeter and a drummer. The expense of the liquor both of wine and others was considerable, as well as other provisions; and my friends appeared well satisfied." The *Memoirs* also go into details of the management of his estate and of his experiences as J. P., and offer comments on the politics of the day.

1736   KELLY, REV. GEORGE. The Memoirs of the Life, Travels, and Transactions of the Rev. Mr. George Kelly, from his Birth to his Escape from Imprisonment out of the Tower of London. London.

1739   CARTE, THOMAS. Collection of Original Letters and Papers concerning the Affairs of England, 1641-60, from the Ormonde Papers. 2 vols. 8vo. London.

STRAFFORD, (Thomas Wentworth) EARL OF. Letters and Despatches, with an Essay towards his Life, by Sir George Radcliffe, collected by W. Knowles. 2 vols. Fol. London.

> Another edit., 2 vols., fol., Dublin, 1740.
> In 1631 Strafford was appointed Lord Deputy of Ireland, where he made an evil name for himself among the Irish for his ruthless administration of affairs. In 1641 he was executed for treason.

1748 PILKINGTON, LAETITIA. Memoirs of Laetitia Pilkington. London.

> Reprinted Peter Hoey, Dublin, 1923.
> Her account of her early association with Dean Swift, if reliable, makes this work an important source for material on Swift's life in Dublin. Her narrative of her life in London, where she tried to maintain a sort of respectability, shows the difficulties besetting a lady trying to keep her head above water and her virtue above reproach. Especially amusing is the story of how she attempted to "make a touch" on Sir Hans Sloane, the celebrated naturalist and physician. But her poetry, with which she is generous, is her most grievous sin with the modern reader.

1750 Copy of a Letter from a Gentleman in London to his Friend at Bath. 8vo. Bath. (8 pp.)

> From the bookseller's note, one guesses that this had something to do with the case of one John Fraser, and extraordinary narratives of cruelties.

1763 VERTUE, GEORGE. Diary of George Vertue. Edit. by Horace Walpole. London.

> 2nd edit., 12mo, London, 1786.
> This famous engraver (1684-1756) can stand on his own merits, but he has been pushed farther into fame by the exertions of Walpole, who both edited the above diary and utilized his collections in the *Anecdotes of Painting*. Vertue became official engraver to the Society of Antiquaries in 1717 and served in this office till his death.

1764 PSALMANAZAR, GEORGE. Memoirs. Written by Himself. 8vo. London.

> This most remarkable confession, touched by a sincere contrition for imposing on the credulity of the English public through his *History of Formosa* (1705), well deserves a modern reprinting. What he tells us of his life in this volume still leaves his origin and name a mystery. There is a pleasant essay on him by Robt. Bracey, O.P., "George Psalmanazar, Impostor and Penitent," in *Eighteenth Century Studies*, Oxford, 1925.

1767 Tunbridge Epistles from Lady Margaret to the Countess of B. 4to. London (?).

> This is written in imitation of the *Bath Guide* (see Anstey, *The New Bath Guide*, under 1766, TOWNS).—Gough, *Anecdotes of British Topography*, 1715.

YOUNG, ARTHUR. For his *Farmer's Letters to the People of England*, see under AGRICULTURE.

1771 DALRYMPLE, SIR JOHN. Memoirs of Great Britain and Ireland from 1681 to 1692. With a large Appendix. 2 vols. 4to. London.

1772 For Letters concerning the Present State of England, see under ANCIENT AND PRESENT STATE.

1774 LOCH, D. His letters on the trade and manufactures of Scotland are listed under ANCIENT AND PRESENT STATE.

1777   ANDERSON, J. His observations on the means of exciting a spirit of national indus-
dustry are listed under ANCIENT AND PRESENT STATE.

1784   DODINGTON, GEORGE BUBB. The Diary of the Late George Bubb Dodington, Baron
of Melcombe Regis: From March 8, 1749, to February 6, 1761. With an Appendix containing some Curious and Interesting Papers, which are either referred
to, or alluded to, in the Diary. New edit. by Henry Penruddocke Wyndham. 8vo.
Salisbury.

> At his death in 1762, Dodington (who had assumed this name on accession to his uncle's
> estate) bequeathed his own property to his cousin, Thomas Wyndham of Hammersmith. He
> in turn, on his death in 1777, left to the present editor his books and political papers and
> poems, to be published as the editor thought fit. The diary was evidently written with an eye
> to publication, as it was copied clean in a final form from rough drafts. Dodington evidently
> intended it to be an apology for his political conduct, which is often regarded as synonymous
> with timeserving. His attachment to the party of Prince Frederick and opposition to Sir
> Robert Walpole seem, on the whole, to have been fairly constant. The diary is nearly all
> concerned with politics.

1786   DOWSING, WILLIAM. The Journal of William Dowsing, of Stratford, Parliamentary
Visitor, appointed under a Warrant from the Earl of Manchester, for Demolishing
the Superstitious Pictures and Ornaments of Churches, etc., within the County
of Suffolk, in the Years 1643-44. 4to. Woodbridge.

> Here is one name at least to be included in the anathema to be pronounced against ravagers
> of art among the Puritans.

1787-1823   PASTON LETTERS. Original Letters written during the Reigns of Henry VI,
Edward IV, and Richard III, by various Persons of Rank and Consequence.
With Notes by John Fenn. 5 vols. 4to. London.

> 2nd edit., 1787; a new edit., which contained upwards of 500 letters till then un-
> published, edited by J. Gairdner, 3 vols., 12mo, London, 1872-75; reprint of this last, with
> additions in a supplement, 4 vols., 8vo, London, 1900; new complete Library Edition, edited
> with Notes and Introduction, by J. Gairdner, 7 vols., London, 1904; a reprint of the 1872-75
> edit., 4 vols., Edinburgh, 1910.
> These letters, which run from 1422 to 1509, have become a household word among students
> of the 15th century. Few collections offer such intimate glimpses into the daily life of the
> period as do these.

1788   BORUWLASKI, JOSEPH. Memoirs of the Celebrated Dwarf, Joseph Boruwlaski, a
Polish Gentleman; containing a Faithful and Curious Account of his Birth, Edu-
cation, Marriage, Travels and Voyages written by Himself. Translated from the
French by Mr. Des Carrieres. 8vo. London.

> For notes concerning his career and his residence in England, see this date, CONTINENTAL
> EUROPE, vol. I of this work.

PIOZZI, MRS. H. L. Letters of Dr. Johnson. 2 vols. 8vo. London.

> While on a visit to the western part of England, Johnson stayed at Heale House, and from
> here he made a trip with Mr. Bowles to Stonehenge. His unimpressive account of this monu-
> ment should be compared with what he had to say in his Journey to the Western Islands of
> Scotland about the antiquities of Iona.

1791   LACKINGTON, JAMES (Bookseller). Memoirs of the First Forty-Five Years of the
Life of James Lackington, the present Bookseller in Chiswell Street, Moorsfield,
London. Written by Himself in Forty-six Letters to a Friend. 8vo. London.

A new edit., 8vo, London, 1792; again 1795.

In his roaming over the country in his younger days searching for work, and in his settlement in London as the first dealer in second-hand books, he collects material for many interesting descriptions of places and inns. After he had successfully established himself and become affluent, he made many trips to the north of England and into Scotland. His recantation of Methodism and attacks upon the sincerity and purity of its followers are amusing enough. The state of the bookselling business in London is well illuminated. Lackington began business as a bookseller with five pounds, and at the time of writing these memoirs he was selling 100,000 volumes annually. The work was dedicated to the public, and to respectable and sordid booksellers.

1792   CREECH, WILLIAM. For his letters on Edinburgh, see under TOWNS.

1793   NAPIER, ARCHIBALD (LORD). Memoirs of Archibald, First Lord Napier; written by Himself. Published from the original Manuscript in the Possession of the present Lord Napier. 4to. Edinburgh.

PENNANT, THOMAS. For his literary life written by himself, see under GENERAL REFERENCE.

1798   BIRREL, ROBERT. Diary of Robert Birrel, 1532-1605. In *Fragments of Scottish History*, by J. C. Dalyell. Edinburgh.

This is the diary of an Edinburgh burgess of no apparent party. He touches briefly and without comment on all important events and some minor ones.—Read, *Bibliog. Brit. Hist.*

1805   Correspondence between Frances, Countess of Hartford, afterwards Duchess of Somerset, and Henrietta Louisa, Countess of Pomfret (1738 and 1741). Edit. with Prefatory Memoir, by Wm. Bungley. Portrait. 3 vols. 8vo. London.

TRUSLER, REV. JOHN. Memoirs by Himself. Bath.

This eccentric divine, literary compiler, medico, bookseller, and what not, is best remembered for his *Hogarth Moralized*.

1807   GRANT, MRS. ANNE. Letters from the Mountains, being the real Correspondence of a Lady between 1773 and 1807. 3 vols. 8vo. London.

This has been reprinted. "Her letters from the Mountains . . . are among the most interesting collections of real letters that have lately been given to the public, and being indebted for no part of their interest to the celebrity of the names they contain or the importance of the events they narrate."—Lord Jeffrey (quoted). The author was well known in the United States for her *Memoirs of an American Lady*. She came to America with her husband, a British officer, in 1758.

1813   AUBREY, JOHN. Letters written by Eminent Persons in the Seventeenth and Eighteenth Centuries (from the originals in the Bodleian Library, etc.) : to which are added, Hearne's Journeys to Reading, and to Whaddon Hall, the Seat of Browne Willis, Esq.; and Lives of Eminent Men. 3 vols. 8vo. London.

This biographer of noted personages lived from 1626 to 1697. For his antiquarian work, see his *The Natural History and Antiquities of the County of Surrey*, under 1718-19, HISTORY AND ANTIQUITIES.

1814   ROBERTS, BARRE CHARLES. Letters and Miscellaneous Papers, with a Memoir of his Life, by G. C. Bedford. Portrait. 4to. London.

Roberts was a student of Christ Church, Oxford, and an ingenious young medallist. He died 1810. This work contains Note on Oseney Abbey, Note on Boxley Abbey, Kent, Letter on Mitred Abbots, Collections relating to Monasteries, Churches, and other Antiquities.— Bookseller's Note.

1818   HOWARD, JOHN. Memoirs of the Public and Private Life of John Howard (1726?-90), from his Diary and Letters. London.

> For the *State of the Prisons* of this noted prison reformer, see under 1777, WEST EUROPE, vol. I of this work.

1818-19   EVELYN, JOHN. Memoirs Illustrative of the Life and Writings of John Evelyn, comprising his Diary from the Year 1641 to 1705-06, and a Selection of his Familiar Letters. Edit. by William Bray. 4to. London.

> Edit. by William Upcott, London, 1827; edit. from original MSS at Wotton, by Wm. Bray, 4 vols., 1850-52; new edit., enlarged, 1857; edit. by Henry Wheatley, with Life, 4 vols., London, 1879; Everyman's Library, 2 vols., London, 1907.
> This journal ran from 1641 to the end of 1697, when it was carried on in a smaller book till within about three weeks of Evelyn's death, Feb. 27, 1705/6. Together with Pepy's diary, it is an indispensable source for material on life in London and on the makers of history.

1822   MALTRAVERS, SIR RICHARD. Life and Opinions of Sir Richard Maltravers. 2 vols. 8vo. London.

> This book offers much of interest in the way of comments on the social and economic history of the 17th century.—Bookseller's Note. (Not in *DNB*.)

1824-46   ELLIS, SIR HENRY. Original Letters, Illustrative of English History, including numerous Royal Letters from Autographs in the British Museum, the State Papers Office, and other Collections. Notes and illustrations, portraits and facsimiles. 11 vols. 8vo and 4to. London.

> This work appeared in three series: 1st, 3 vols., 1824-26; 2nd, 4 vols., 1727; 3rd, 4 vols., 1846. See also his *Original Letters of Eminent Literary Men,* under 1843 below.
> Ellis was principal librarian of the British Museum, but was virtually superseded in 1836 because of his unprogressive methods.—*DNB.*

1825   PEPYS, SAMUEL. Memoirs. Comprising his Diary from 1659 to 1660, deciphered by the Rev. John Smith, A.B., of St. John's College, Cambridge, from the Original Short-Hand MS. in the Pepsyian Library, and a Selection from his Private Correspondence. Edit. by Lord Braybrooke. 2 vols. 4to. London.

> Modern edit., by H. B. Wheatley, with portrait and illustrations, 10 vols., 1917-18; with the 3 vols. of Correspondence, 1926-29, together 13 vols., 8vo, London, 1917-29.
> A totally unexpurgated edition of this most famous of English diaries will probably have to wait for a more robust generation. Without this diary we should be infinitely the poorer in our knowledge of Restoration London. Many of its phrases have become household words.

1827   DUGDALE, SIR WILLIAM. The Life, Diary (1643-86), and Correspondence (1635-86) of Sir William Dugdale. Edit. by W. Hamper. 4to. London.

> The most representative work of this antiquary is his *Antiquities of Warwickshire.* See under 1656, HISTORY AND ANTIQUITIES.

WESLEY, JOHN. Journal. 21 Parts. 1739-91. 4 vols. London.

> *A Selection from his Journals,* London, 1890; *Journal* edit. by Nehemiah Curnock (and others), 8 vols., London, 1909-16; *Journal* edit. by Nora Ratcliff, London, 1940.
> The journal of this tireless evangelist was made up from his diaries, which opened in 1725 and ran till his death in 1791. The journal proper he began to write when he went to Georgia. This he sent in manuscript back to England to be read by his friends at home. For an account of its history, see T. B. Shepherd, *Methodism and the Literature of the Eighteenth Century,* London, 1940.

1828   BECKINGTON, THOMAS. The Journal of Thomas Beckington by one of the Suite of Thomas Beckington, afterwards Bishop of Bath and Wells, During an Embassy to Negociate a Marriage between Henry VI and a Daughter of the Count of

Armagnac, A.D. 1442. With Notes and Illustrations by Nicholas Harris Nicolas. 8vo. London.

1829 CALAMY, EDMUND. An Historical Account of my Own Life with some Reflections on the Times I have lived in, 1671-1731. Edit. by J. T. Rutt. 2 vols. London.

> The author came of a line of Edmund Calamys, all of whom were dissenting ministers. He visited Scotland in 1709 and was made a D.D. of Edinburgh, Aberdeen, and Glasgow. He made a further trip in 1713 to the west of England. In addition to the autobiography above, he published sermons and biographies.

MELVILL, JAMES. The Diary of Mr. James Melvill, 1556-1601. Edit. by G. R. Kinloch. *Publ. Bann. Club,* no. 34, 4to. Edinburgh. Also edit. by Robert Pitcairn, *Publ. Wodrow Soc.,* vol. 3. Edinburgh. (The latter contains a continuation.)

> This diary is of importance for the ecclesiastical and political history of James VI's reign.

TURNER, SIR JAMES. Memoirs of his own Life and Times, by Sir James Turner, MDCXXXII-MDCLXX, from the original Manuscript. Edit. by Thomas Thomson. *Publ. Bann. Club,* no. 28. Edinburgh.

> Turner took part in the Scottish campaign in England in 1645, in Hamilton's expedition thither in 1645, and in Charles II's march to Worcester in 1650. He also suppressed the Pentland rising in 1666. His memoirs are important for these events.—Terry, *A Catalogue of the Publications of Scottish Clubs.*

1830 LAMONT, JOHN. The Diary of Mr. John Lamont of Newton, 1649-71. *Publ. Maitland Club,* vol. 7. 4to. Edinburgh.

THORESBY, RALPH. The Diary of Ralph Thoresby, F.R.S., Author of the Topography of Leeds (1677-1724). Now first published from the original Manuscript. By the Rev. Joseph Hunter, F.S.A. 2 vols. 8vo. London.

> To this was added, Letters of Eminent Men addressed to Ralph Thoresby, now first published from the Originals, 2 vols. (making 4 vols. in all), London, 1832.
> Thoresby was born at Leeds, the son of a merchant in the wool trade, to which business he succeeded on his father's death. To prepare his son for the position, the father sent him to the house of a relative in London, where this diary begins. It records his life, studies, literary friendships, religious history, temporal concerns, etc. He began to prepare for his *Topography of Leeds* (see under 1715, TOWNS) in 1690. He was made a fellow of the Royal Society in 1697, and in 1704 retired from business to devote himself to his museum of coins, prints, autographs, etc., which his father had begun, and to further his literary pursuits and religious duties. He contributed to many antiquarian and topographical works; for instance, nearly the whole of the additions to Bishop Gibson's edition of Camden's *Britannia* was the work of Thoresby. Many entries in his diary are mere recordings of his movements, his going to church where somebody preached, his reading, etc., but as he gets older the antiquarian tours and interests assume more importance. He tells of the tours he made with his friend the Rev. Mr. Kirk, examining churches, barrows, finds, remains, and somewhat of the road, the places visited, and personages of the country. When in London in the winter of 1709, he seemed to get around mostly by walking. He sought out all the museums and curiosities as well as the sights, and extended his acquaintance among the learned, such as Strype, Wren, Hickes, Sloane, Wyatt, etc. His return trip was memorable for the hazards encountered on roads blocked by ice and snow. His coach was overturned four times near Lincoln and no guides were to be had. While travelers in the earlier centuries must have expected such things, still they could not have found them any more agreeable on that account. His last entry in his diary is on Sept. 12, 1724. The letters included in the additional volumes were written by Sloane, Gibson, Kennett, Vertue, Hearne, and others.

1832 GENT, THOMAS. The Life of Thomas Gent, written by Himself. Edit. by J. Hunter. 8vo. (Place?)

> For an account of this industrious historian of York, see under 1730, TOWNS.

TOOKE, JOHN HORNE. Memoirs of John Horne Tooke, interspersed with Original Documents, by Alexander Stephens. 2 vols. 8vo. London.

> Tooke led a stormy political life as a Wilkes agitator, and as a member of the "Constitutional Society," and the like. He was among those tried for treason in 1794 and was acquitted along with Hardy, Holcroft, Thelwall, and others. His *Diversions of Purley* have given him a philological reputation.

1833 JAFFRAY, ALEXANDER. The Diary of Alexander Jaffray, Provost of Aberdeen, one of the Scottish Commissioners to King Charles II, and a Member of Cromwell's Parliament; To which are added Particulars of his subsequent Life, given in connexion with Memoirs of the Rise, Progress, and Persecution of the People called Quakers in the North of Scotland; among whom he became one of the earliest Members. By John Barclay. 8vo. London.

> 3rd edit., issued uniformly with the Spalding Club volumes, Aberdeen, 1856.

1834 BETOUN, JAMES. Private Letters to James Betoun, Archbishop of Glasgow, while Ambassador at the Court of France, principally from his Servants in Scotland. Dated 1569-88. *Misc. Papers Maitland Club,* vol. 26, iii. Glasgow.

> The more familiar spelling of the name is Beaton or Bethune. In addition to high ecclesiastical preferments, he held the office of regent during the minority of James V.

Letter from John, Son of King Henry IV, relative to the State of the Castles of Berwick, Jedburgh, and Fastcastle. *Publ. Maitland Club,* vol. 28, xxxvi. Glasgow.

1836 WRAXALL, SIR NATHANIEL. Historical and Posthumous Memoirs, 1772-84. Together, 6 vols. 8vo. London.

> Edit., with Notes and additional chapters from MSS, by H. B. Wheatley, 5 vols., London, 1884.
> These memoirs practically comprise an encyclopedia of famous Europeans and Englishmen whom the author met and discoursed about. They provide interesting reading and a valuable source of biographical and historical information. For the *Historical Memoirs* alone see under 1815, WEST EUROPE, vol. I of this work.

1837 MONTAGU, LADY MARY WORTLEY. Letters and Works. Edit. by Lord Wharncliffe. 3 vols. London.

> An edit., with additions, by W. Moy Thomas, 2 vols., London, 1861; 3rd edit., with additions and corrections, by W. Moy Thomas, 2 vols., London, 1893.
> For her letters written during her travels on the Continent and to Constantinople, see under 1763, NEAR EAST, vol. I of this work.

1838 TELFORD, THOMAS. The Life of Thomas Telford, Civil Engineer, written by Himself, containing a descriptive Narrative of his Professional Labours, with a Folio Atlas of Copper Plates. Edit. by John Rockman, one of his Executors. 4to. London.

> This volume contains many reports of surveys which may be regarded as travel accounts. They are full of valuable information about Scotland in the beginning of the century. The references are chiefly to the northern parts and to the Highlands.—Mitchell, *List of Travels.* His most famous engineering achievement was the construction of the Caledonian Canal, from Inverness to Fort Williams, a picturesque but expensive undertaking, which cost more than it has returned. His many triumphs in canal, harbor, road, and bridge work point him out as the greatest benefactor to communications that Great Britain can name.

1841 BISSET, REV. JOHN. Extracts from the Diary of the Rev. John Bisset, Minister at Aberdeen, MDCCXLVI. *Misc. Spalding Club,* vol. 3, no. viii. 4to. Aberdeen.

> This touches on the Rising of the '45.

PEAKE, RICHARD B. Memoirs of the Colman Family, including their Correspondence with the Most Distinguished Personages of their Time. 2 vols. 8vo. London.

This work is important for the history of the London stage and the theatrical fortunes of Colman, Sr., and Colman, Jr. But its pertinence to this work lies in the accounts of tours to various parts of the country.

SMITH, ABIGAIL (ADAMS). The Journal and Correspondence of Miss Adams, daughter of John Adams, . . . Written in France and England in 1785. Edited by her Daughter. New York.

1841-42 BAILLIE, ROBERT, M.A. The Letters and Journals of Robert Baillie, M.A., Principal of the University of Glasgow, MDCXXXVII-MDCLXII. 3 vols. *Publ. Bann. Club,* no. 73. Edinburgh. (Edit. by David Laing.)

1842 BOWES, R. The Correspondence of R. Bowes, Esq., Elizabeth's Ambassador to Scotland. *Publ. Surtees Soc.,* vol. 14. Durham.

This acquaints one with Scottish names, personages, and places, diplomatic and historical matters, but it has little to say about travel or places.

CAMERON, SIR EWEN. Memoirs of the Sir Ewen Cameron of Locheill, Chief of the Clan Cameron. With an introductory Account of the History and Antiquities of that Family and of the neighbouring Clans. *Publ. Abbotsford Club,* vol. 4. Edinburgh.

Edit. by James Macknight. Sir Ewen's long life covered the years 1629-1719. He fought for Charles I and also for the Pretender. The memoirs were written by his son-in-law, John Drummond, of Balhady, in 1733. The appendix contains a "Memoir concerning the State of the Highlands in 1716," ascribed to Simon, Lord Lovat; and a portrait of Sir Ewen. The work was also printed in *Publ. Maitland Club,* vol. 59.—Terry, *Catalogue Publ. Scot. Clubs.*

CURWEN, S. Journals and Letters during his Period as an American Refugee in England, 1775-84, with Biographical Notices of American Loyalists and other Eminent Persons by E. A. Ward. 8vo. London.

Another edit., 8vo, London, 1864.

DEE, DR. JOHN. The Private Diary of Dr. John Dee, and the Catalogue of his Library of MSS. from the Original MSS. in the Ashmolean Museum at Oxford, and Trinity College Library, Cambridge. Edit. by James Orchard Halliwell, Esq., F.R.S. *Publ. Camden Soc.,* vol. 19. London.

This diary was written on the margins of old almanacs. The catalogue was made by himself before his house was plundered by the mob. The diary seems to confirm the character of him given by D'Israeli in his *Amenities of Literature,* as a scientist getting lost in the occult. It runs from Aug. 25, 1554, to Jan. 19, 1601. Many particulars of his life are recounted —what he bought and how much he paid, his kidney troubles, his counsels with learned men on the passage to the Northwest, charts and rutters, astrological performances, strange rappings in his bedroom, his dreams, etc.

1842-46 D'ARBLAY, MADAME. The Diary and Letters of Madame D'Arblay (1778-1840). Edit. by her Niece Mrs. C. Barrett. London.

New edit. by W. G. Ward, prefaced by Lord Macaulay's Essay, 3 vols., London, 1890; edit. by C. Barrett and Austin Dobson, 6 vols., 1904; the Ward edit., 3 vols., 1927.

Only a portion of the diary and the voluminous correspondence of the writer was utilized in the first edition. The selection was made by both Madame D'Arblay and the editor, Mrs. Barrett. The later editions were based on this selection. When Fanny Burney opened this diary, she was enjoying the sensation of being a popular but anonymous author of her first

novel, *Evelina,* and she records her amusement at the guesses floating around on the author-ship. From her two diaries the reader gets a close acquaintanceship with a charming, humorous personality, as well as with most people worth knowing in the latter half of the 18th century. At times, however, one would like to give her a good shake to startle her out of the everlasting decorum considered proper to a "female" of the period. Her descriptions of the household of George III and of the French refugees, one of whom she married, take us into the larger fields of public life. But—to fall back on the much-mouthed phrase—the diary is too well known to need description. For her *Early Diary,* see under 1889 below.

1843 CARTWRIGHT, DR. THOMAS. The Diary of Dr. Thomas Cartwright, Bishop of Chester, Commencing at the Time of his Elevation to that See, August 1686, and terminating with the Visitation of St. Mary Magdalene College, Oxford, October, 1687. Now first printed from the Original MS. in the Possession of the Rev. Joseph Hunter, F.S.A. *Publ. Camden Soc.,* vol. 22. London.

   Bishop Cartwright was handled right roughly by Wood, Burnet, and Richardson for his subservience to James II. He seems to have been a forward, pushing man in his own interests, rising from job to job in church preferments. He followed James II from France to Ireland and died there March 12, 1688. The diary is merely a recital of occurrences, many of no importance, written down hastily from day to day, as though they were useful memoranda to refer to. Seldom is an opinion expressed or a point of view indicated. For a Protestant bishop to be in close communication with Roman Catholics of his time naturally aroused ire. He evidently spent much time in visiting and dining out.

   ELLIS, SIR HENRY. Original Letters of Eminent Literary Men of the 16th, 17th and 18th Centuries, with Notes and Illustrations by Sir Henry Ellis, K.H., F.R.S. *Publ. Camden Soc.,* vol. 23. London.

   Among the writers illustrated are antiquaries, naturalists, scientists, literary folk, such as Camden, Sir Robert Cotton, Sir Symond D'Ewes, John Ray, Wheloc, Edmund Gibson, Humfrey Wanley, George Hickes, Swift, etc. The letters are valuable for the interchange of information on publications, books, the virtues and shortcomings of fellow workers, antiqui-ties, natural history, and scientific progress.

   ERSKINE, JAMES (of Grange). Extracts from the Diary of a Senator of the College of Justice, from 1717-18. Edit. with Memoir and Notes by James Maidment. 8vo. London. (Only 24 copies printed.)

   In this work will be found a very interesting account of the abduction of Lady Grange.—Bookseller's Note. For a reference to this belated stone-age act, see Martin Martin under 1698, TOURS BY NATIVES.

   FOTHERGILL, SAMUEL. Memoirs of the Life and Gospel Labours of Samuel Fother-gill, with Selections from his Correspondence; also an Account of the Life and Travels of his Father, John Fothergill, and Notices of some of his Desendants. 8vo. Liverpool.

   The author of the above was George Crossfield, who wrote also *The Calendar Flora for the Year 1809.* Samuel Fothergill composed several Friends' Books, Sermons, etc. He died at Warrington in 1772.—Fishwick, *The Lancashire Library.*

   TAYLOR, WILLIAM (of Norwich). Memoir of the Life and Writings of William Taylor of Norwich (1765-1836): Correspondence with Southey, Scott, Cole-ridge, etc. 2 vols. 8vo. London.

1845 JAMES, EARL OF PERTH. Letters from James, Earl of Perth, Lord Chancellor of Scotland to his Sister, the Countess of Errol, and other Members of his Family. Edit. by William Jerdan, M.R.S.L. *Publ. Camden Soc.,* vol. 33. London.

   The writer belonged to the ancient Scottish house of Drummond, and was related to the royal house of Stuart. He embraced Catholicism when James II came to the throne, and was

created Duke of Perth and Knight of the Garter by the king. He died at the age of 68, in 1716. His letters date from Dec. 29, 1688, when he attempted to flee Scotland, to April 1, 1696. He was detained a prisoner till in August, 1693, when he gave bond to leave the kingdom. His travels abroad are here related in a simple, familiar style. He visited the Low Countries, Antwerp, Brussels, Venice, Rome, etc., and notes down in his letters the sights seen and people met.

1848 ASSHETON, NICHOLAS. The Journal of Nicholas Assheton of Downham, in the County of Lancaster, Esq., for part of the Year 1617 and part of the Year following. Interspersed with Notes from the Life of his Contemporary John Bruen, Stapelford, in the County of Chester, Esq. Edit. by Rev. F. R. Raines, M.A., F.S.A. *Publ. Chetham Soc.,* vol. 14. Manchester.

This deals with the interests of a sportsman.

HERVEY, JOHN (Lord). Memoirs of the Reign of King George II. Edit. by J. W. Croker. 2 vols. London.

This, the first edition, has always been known to be incomplete. An edition with new matter, by Romney Sedgwick, 3 vols., London, 1931. See below.

1931 HERVEY, JOHN (Lord). Some Materials towards Memoirs of the Reign of King George II. Printed from a copy of the original Manuscript in the Royal Archives at Windsor Castle; and from the original Manuscript at Ickworth. Edit. by Romney Sedgwick. 5 collotype plates. 3 vols. 8vo. London.

Some parts of these memoirs were deemed so totally and permanently unfit for publication that they were not merely withheld, but removed from the MS and burned. Croker, the editor of the first edition, had never seen these passages and was permitted only in guarded terms to refer to their nature and existence. He did not mention that before they were destroyed a copy of the original MS had been made by a previous owner, and that he had unsuccessfully tried to trace and recover it. Yet it existed, and after a disappearance of over a century was returned to the Archives at Windsor Castle among the papers of George III and George IV. The edition above, issued by the King's Printers, contains about a hundred pages of entirely new matter, consisting of passages removed from the original MS and a hitherto unpublished "Account of my own Constitution and Illness" by Lord Hervey. —From Notice of Book.

MACHYN, HENRY. The Diary of Henry Machyn, Citizen and Merchant-Taylor of London, 1550-1563. Edit. by J. Gough Nichols. *Publ. Camden Soc.,* vol. 42. London.

The best passages of this diary have already been printed by Strype. Machyn was a citizen of London of no great education or knowledge of state affairs, but was representative of the opinions and sentiments of his fellow Londoners in their biases and interpretations. As a spectator and citizen he witnessed and recorded many strange sights, for the times were eventful and full of change. He gives numerous accounts of pageants, holiday-making, the Lord Mayor's day, the gay doings of May or mummeries of Christmas time. His business of furnishing funeral trappings naturally explains his interest in deaths. He gives little of his personal affairs but much of what passed by, who was hanged for what, the press of crowds at a fair where the victuals and drinks gave out too early, the movements of notabilities from place to place, who rode in the Fishmongers' Procession, the funeral of Stephen Warner, Bishop of Winchester, etc. The diary closes at a time when the plague was prevalent in London. Perhaps the author fell a victim to it.—From the Preface and the text.

YONG, WALTER. The Diary of Walter Yong, Esq., Justice of the Peace, and M.P. for Nornton. Written at Colyton and Axminster, County of Devon, from 1604 to 1628. Edit. by George Roberts. *Publ. Camden Soc.,* vol. 41. London.

The writer was a barrister-at-law and one of the justices of the commission from the County of Devon. He was also sheriff of Devon, 1628, and a member of parliament returned from Nornton till his death in 1649. Though a Puritan, he remained within the church to assist in her reform. The diary gives a good sample of the information available to a man of his station and condition. It begins in 1604, the year of the great pestilence in London, in which 3000 people died weekly. This was followed by a drought, then by the Gunpowder Plot against the king, queen, and clergy, intrigues of the Jesuits, bills against the recusants, etc.

Sad days these. Historic events abroad and domestic affairs are noted, such as the near drowning of King James I, January 1621/2, when he was thrown from his horse head downwards into the ice-covered pond which he had with great difficulty just crossed; the coming ashore of a stranded whale; the three clouds in the air that exploded; the attempts to revive the manufactures of the west of England; the big wind of Aug. 19, 1622; the letters of mark granted against the "Dunkirkers," etc. Such items are sandwiched in between mere records of factual historic events.

1849   NEWCOME, REV. HENRY. The Diary of the Rev. Henry Newcome, from Sept. 30, 1661, to Sept. 29, 1663. Edit. by Thomas Heywood, Esq., F.S.A. *Publ. Chetham Soc.,* vol. 18. 4to. Manchester.

> See Newcome, *Autobiography,* under 1852 below.

1850   CHARLES V (Emperor). The Correspondence of Charles V and his Ambassadors to England and France, with a Connecting Narrative and Itinerary, 1519-51. By W. Bradford. 8vo. London.

1852   NEWCOME, REV. HENRY. The Autobiography of Henry Newcome, M.A. Edit. by Richard Parkinson, D.D., F.S.A. *Publ. Chetham Soc.,* vol. 26. Manchester.

> The period covered runs from 1627 to 1670.

SURTEES, ROBERT. Memoir of Robert Surtees. . . . New Edition, with Additions by the Rev. J. Raine. Portrait. 8vo. London.

> This is the historian of Durham after whom the Surtees Society was named.

1853   BOHUN, EDMUND. Diary and Autobiography. Edit. by S. Wilton Rix. Privately printed at Beccles. Facsimiles. 4to.

> This is the narrative of the life of the Licenser of the Press in the reign of William and Mary, and subsequently Chief Justice of South Carolina. The diary extends from 1676 to 1696.—Bookseller's Note.

TASWELL, WILLIAM, D.D. The Autobiography and Anecdotes of William Taswell, Rector of Bermondey . . . A.D. 1651 to 1682. Edit. by George Percy Elliott, Esq. *Camden Misc.,* vol. II, *Publ. Camden Soc.,* vol. 55. London.

> This work was originally written in Latin but was preserved in a translation made by a grandson of the author, the Rev. Henry Taswell. It gives some particulars of the Great Fire of London, in which his own house was concerned. He recounts a trip to the Isle of Wight and the dangerous plight he and his companions found themselves in. He tells of affairs at Oxford in which he figured as disputant, and also of ecclesiastical politics.

1854   BYROM, JOHN. The Private Journal and Literary Remains of John Byrom. Edit. by Richard Parkinson, D.D., F.S.A., Principal of Saint Bees College and Canon of Manchester. 4 vols. *Publ. Chetham Soc.,* vols. 32, 34, 40, 44. Manchester.

1855   LESLEY, JOHN (Bishop). The Diary of John Lesley, Bishop of Ross, April 11 to October 16, 1571. *Misc.,* vol. III, *Publ. Bann. Club,* no. 19b. Edinburgh.

> This concerns his embassy to England in behalf of Mary, Queen of Scots.

1856   BROWN, GEORGE. The Diary of George Brown, Merchant in Glasgow, 1745-53. 4to. Glasgow.

Letters from Roundhead Officers, written from Scotland, and chiefly addressed to Captain Adam Baynes, July MDCL-MDCLX. Edit. by John Yonge Akerman. *Publ. Bann. Club,* no. 101. Edinburgh.

> Baynes was a member of the Army and Admiralty Committee under the Commonwealth. —Terry, *op. cit.*

WATSON, ELKANAH. Men and Times of the Revolution; or, Memoirs of Elkanah Watson, including Journals of Travels in Europe and America, from 1777 to 1842, with his Correspondence with Public Men and Reminiscences and Incidents of the Revolution. Edit. by his Son, Winslow C. Watson. London.

1857 BYROM, ELIZABETH. The Journal of Elizabeth Byrom in 1745. Edit. by Richard Parkinson, D.D., F.S.A. Reprinted from vol. II, pt. ii, of the Remains of John Byrom. *Publ. Chetham Soc.* (no volume no.). Manchester.

DAVIES, REV. ROWLAND. The Journal of the Very Rev. Rowland Davies, LL.D., Dean of Ross (afterwards Dean of Cork), from March 8, 1688-89, to Sept. 28, 1691. Edit. with Notes and Appendix and some Account of the Author and his Family, by Richard Caulfield, B.A. *Publ. Camden Soc.,* vol. 68. London.

> The landing of King James II in Ireland, March, 1689, sent many Protestants scurrying to England, among them the author. After many efforts to obtain employment, he was finally appointed to a lectureship at Great Yarmouth by the Corporation of the town. Later he became chaplain to a regiment in Ireland and as such followed the fortunes of war at the battle of the Boyne, the siege of Limerick, and so on throughout the campaign of William III. Rewards followed, the highest of which was the Deanship of Cork. His journal gives some curious details of London and Yarmouth, but on the whole little glimpse of his personality appears. On the other hand, he widens our range of acquaintances. The narrative of the campaign in Ireland is disappointing on account of its matter-of-factness.

LUTTRELL, NARCISSUS. A Brief Historical Relation of State Affairs, from September, 1678, to April, 1714. 6 vols. 8vo. London.

> This extremely curious and interesting diary of a most extraordinary man, during the reigns of Charles II, James II, William III, and Queen Anne, is now first printed from the original manuscripts in seventeen volumes in the library of All Souls' College, Oxford. There is a copious index.—Bookseller's Note. The author was annalist and bibliographer, who collected valuable manuscripts and fugitive poetical pieces, etc.—*DNB.*

1859 SYMONDS, COL. RICHARD. Diary of the Marches of the Royal Army during the Great Civil War. Edit. from the Original MS. in the British Museum, by Charles Edward Long, M.A. *Publ. Camden Soc.,* vol. 74. London.

> The author joined the royalist army at the beginning of the civil strife between Charles I and the Parliamentarians. He was never without his notebook in which he recorded as much antiquarian lore as he could cram into it. Between these jottings on his main interest the King marched hither and thither. His account of the war is very impersonal. His diary was frequently referred to and even in part transcribed by county historians, e.g., Shaw in his *Staffordshire,* Hutchins in his *Dorsetshire,* Nichols in his *Leicestershire,* Lysons, etc. It is also mentioned several times by Walpole in his *Anecdotes of Painting.* The volume takes in the years 1644 and 1645.—From Introduction.

1861 SOMERVILLE, THOMAS (Minister of Jedburgh). My own Life and Times, 1741-1814. 8vo. London.

1863 BRODIE, ALEXANDER. The Diary of Alexander Brodie of Brodie, MDCLII-MDCLXXX, and of his Son, James Brodie of Brodie, MDCLXXX-MDCLXXXV. Consisting of Extracts from the existing MSS. and a Republi-

cation of the Volume printed at Edinburgh in the Year 1740. Edit. by David Laing. *Publ. Spalding Club,* vol. 33. 4to. Aberdeen.

This has value for the Cromwellian period and that of the post-Restoration.

1867   BARNES, AMBROSE. The Diary of Ambrose Barnes, an Alderman of Newcastle-on-Tyne in the 17th Century. *Publ. Surtees Soc.,* vol. 50. Durham.

1868   R————, ALEXANDER. The Journal of a Soldier in the Earl of Eglinton's Troop of Horse, 1689. *Trans. Glasgow Arch. Soc.,* vol. 1, 39. Glasgow.

1869   HEARNE, THOMAS. Reliquiae Hearnianae: The Remains of Thomas Hearne, M.A., of Edmund Hall (Oxford), being Extracts from his MS. Diaries, collected, with a few Notes by P. Bliss. 2nd edit. 3 vols. London.

Here is life at Oxford at the beginning of the 18th century as seen through the eyes of this peppery antiquary and highflying, nonjuring Tory clergyman. His contemporaries come in for a plenteous castigating. It is full of bibliographical and antiquarian information.

1870   BORDE (BOORDE), ANDREW. Letter to Thomas Cromwell, 1536. In his *Introduction of Knowledge.* E.E.T.S. London.

This was also printed in Ellis' *Original Letters Illustrative of English History,* vol. II, 303, 1827.

PRYME, ABRAHAM DE LA. A Diary of my own Life, containing an Account of the most considerable Things that have happen'd therein. *Publ. Surtees Soc.,* vol. 54. Durham.

Born in 1671, he begins his diary in 1685. He belonged to the group of Dutch who left Flanders and settled in the Fen district. He attended Cambridge, got ordained and obtained a curacy, and later various other livings. He became interested in topography and antiquities, and reported many finds from casual diggings done here and there in the course of husbandry or construction. Often skeletons, some with valuable jewelry, specimens of dress, and ornaments of olden times came to light. He reports also on old churches in ruins and otherwise, ecclesiastical monuments, coins, inscriptions, foundations, castles, the damage done by Cromwell's troopers, especially to stained glass windows, etc. Notice is taken of the new coinage and the troubles it caused, of the dislike of the Quakers, who must have been obnoxious if the diarist is telling the facts without bias. Synthetic wine seems to have been known in his day. His opinion of the House of Commons makes that body to be a parcel of rogues. He has much to say of the Fens, the drainage, floods, and the weather. The winter of 1697-98 was especially severe, amounting to six winters in one. Throughout his diary, which runs on into 1700, his personality constantly emerges above his narrative.

1872-75   PASTON LETTERS. This edition, in 3 vols., is the starting point of the later editions, and so is referred to here, in case the reader forgets that it first appeared in 1787. See this date for full account of various printings.

1873   TYLDESLEY, THOMAS. The Tyldesley Diary. Personal Records of Thomas Tyldesley (grandson of Sir Thomas Tyldesley the Royalist) during the Years 1712-14, with Introduction, Notes, and Index. By Joseph Gillow and Anthony Hewitson. Illus. Map of Lancashire. 4to. Preston.

The life of this diarist ran from 1657 to 1715. He was a Roman Catholic and a loyal supporter of the Pretender James. Foxhall, Blackpool, was his favorite residence. His diary gives an interesting account of the life of a country gentleman of that period.

WILLOUGHBY, LADY. So much of the Diary of Lady Willoughby as relates to her Domestic History, and to the Eventful Period of the Reign of Charles the First, the Protectorate, and the Restoration. 8vo. London.

1877-86 Yorkshire Diaries and Autobiographies in the 17th and 18th Centuries. *Publ. Surtees Soc.*, vols. 65 (1877) and 77 (1886). Durham.

1880 BLUNDELL, SQUIRE. Crosby Records: A Cavalier's Notebook: being the Notes, Anecdotes and Observations of Squire Blundell, of Crosby, 1642. Edit. with Introductory Chapters by T. Ellison Gibson. Facsimiles. 8vo. London.

1882 TWINING, LOUISA. Recreations and Studies of a Country Clergyman of the Eighteenth Century. London.

> Here are interesting letters on travel, music, news, books, actors, and some politics.—J. Williams, *Printed Materials*. The subject was Thomas Twining, the well-known translator of Aristotle's *Poetics*. He was a musician as well as a linguist.

1882-85 STUKELEY, REV. WILLIAM. Family Memoirs of Rev. W. Stukeley, Diaries and Letters; Extracts from Letters and Diaries. Edit. by Lukis. 3 vols. *Publ. Surtees Soc.*, vols. 73 (1882), 76 (1883), and 80 (1885). Durham.

> These memoirs contain some hundreds of letters and notes which passed between Stukeley and the Gales.—Harrison, *Bibliography of the Great Stone Monuments of Wiltshire*. Vol. I contains Commentaries, Autobiography, Commonplace Book, Correspondence, Astronomical Observations. Vol. II, Antiquities of various Counties; Diaries and Letters. Vol. III, Extracts from Letters and Diaries. The life of this celebrated antiquary is here well laid out before us.

1884 BURTON, DR. The Genuine and True Journal of the most miraculous Escape of the Young Chevalier, from Culloden to his last Landing in France. By an Englishman (Dr. Burton). Privately printed. Edinburgh.

WOODWORTH, JONATHAN. Letters from a Lancashire Student at Glasgow University. During the Rebellion of 1715. 8vo. Privately printed.

1885 HEPBURN, REV. THOMAS (Of Birsay). A Letter to a Gentleman [George Paton] from his Friend in Orkney (written in 1757), containing the True Causes of the Poverty of that Country, attributed to Rev. Thomas Hepburn. 8vo. Edinburgh.

1886 DARLING, WILLIAM. The Journal of William Darling, at the Brownsman and Longstone Lighthouses, Farne Islands, from the Year 1795 to 1860. 8vo. London.

> It was his daughter, Grace Darling, who has made this name remembered by her rescue of four men and a woman from a wrecked steamboat in 1838.

LEYBURN, GEORGE. The Memoirs of George Leyburn. Being a Journal of his Agency for Prince Charles in Ireland in the Year 1647. *Publ. Clarendon Hist. Soc.*, no. 10. Edinburgh.

1887 CUNNINGHAM, WILLIAM. The Diary and general Expenditure Book of William Cunningham of Craigends, Commissioner to the Convention of Estates and Member of Parliament for Renfrewshire, kept chiefly from 1673 to 1680. Edit. from the Original MS. by the Rev. James Dodds, D.D., Glasgow, F.S.A. Scot. *Publ. Scot. Hist. Soc.*, no. 2. Edinburgh.

> Domestic life, manners, and the state of agriculture come to light in this work.

WAUS, SIR PATRICK. The Correspondence of Sir Patrick Waus of Barnbarroch, Knight, Parson of Wigton; first Almoner to the Queen; Senator of the College

of Justice; Lord of Council, and Ambassador to Denmark. Edit. from the original Documents by Robert Vans Agnew, F.S.A. Scot. *Publ. Ayrshire and Galloway Arch. Soc.,* vol. 14. 8vo. Edinburgh.

This is in two parts, the first dealing with the years 1540-1584; the second, 1584-1597.

1888 OSBORNE, DOROTHY. Letters to Sir William Temple, 1652-54. Edit. by Edward Abbott Parry. 8vo. London.

This lady became the wife of Sir William Temple.

RADCLIFFE, RICHARD (of Queen's College). Letters of Richard Radcliffe and John James, 1755-83, on Personal and University Life. Edit. by M. Evans. *Publ. Oxford Hist. Soc.,* vol. 9. Oxford.

1889 BURNEY, FRANCES. The Early Diary of Frances Burney, 1768-78. Edit. by Annie Raine Ellis. London.

New and revised edit., 2 vols., 8vo, London, 1907. This contains also a Selection from her Correspondence and from the Journals of her Sisters, Susan and Charlotte.
Since this diary was not intended to see the light of publication and was addressed to "Nobody," it became the repository of her secrets and the confidant to which she flew when in need of unburdening herself. It, together with her later diary (see Madame D'Arblay under 1842-46 above), introduces us to the England of the second half of the 18th century as few other volumes can do.

FORBES, DUNCAN (Lord Advocate and Lord President).

A Longish Letter from "Invernesse, 8 April 1715," to John M'Farlane, W.S., Edinburgh, giving an account of a Journey or Ride from Edinburgh to Culloden by Pettycur, Coupar, Dundee, Fettercairn, Innes House, Elgin, etc. This account is taken from the Pitfirrane MSS and is given in Appendix no. II of *Major Fraser's Manuscript,* vol. II, 159 (see this last under this date, TOURS BY NATIVES). There is much reference in this Letter to brandy, wine and ale, but none to whiskey.

MILL, REV. JOHN. The Diary of the Rev. John Mill (minister of the parishes of Dunrossness, Sandwick, and Cunningsburgh in Shetland), 1740-1803, with Selections from Local Records and Original Documents relating to the District. Edit., with Introduction and Notes, by Gilbert Goudie. Illus. *Publ. Scot. Hist. Soc.,* no. 5. Edinburgh.

Social and church life, economic conditions on the islands, shipwrecks, courts, Paul Jones, etc., make up the content of the above.

1890 MACKINTOSH, CHARLES FRASER (Editor). Letters of Two Centuries chiefly connected with Inverness and the Highlands, from 1616 to 1815. Edit. with introductory and explanatory Remarks to each. Inverness.

PATRICK, FIRST EARL OF STRATHMORE. The Book of Records: a Diary written by Patrick, first Earl of Strathmore, and other Documents relating to Glamis Castle, 1684-1689. Edit. from the Original MSS. at Glamis, with Introduction and Notes, by A. H. Millar, F.S.A. Scot. 3 plates. Portrait of the Earl. *Publ. Scot. Hist. Soc.,* no. 9. Edinburgh.

1891 WALPOLE, HORACE. Letters. Edit. by Peter Cunningham. 9 vols. London.

An edit. by Mrs. Paget Toynbee, 16 vols., with Supplement, 3 vols., 8vo, London, 1903-25; another by Peter Cunningham, the Library Edition, 9 vols., 8vo, London, 1906; the Yale Edition, edit. by W. S. Lewis, 14 vols., 4to, New Haven (in progress). See below.

These constitute the three main editions of this record of 18th century society in all its cultural aspects.

1903-25 WALPOLE, HORACE. Letters of Horace Walpole, fourth Earl of Orford. Chronologically arranged and edited with Notes and Indices by Mrs. Paget Toynbee. 16 vols. Supplement, 3 vols. Portraits and facsimiles. 8vo. London.
> This edition contains many letters not printed in former editions.

1937-44 WALPOLE, HORACE. Correspondencè. Edited by W. S. Lewis (in progress). Yale University Press. New Haven.
> By 1948 14 volumes had been issued. For the first time one gets in this edition not only hosts of letters hitherto unpublished but also the other side of the correspondence—an ideal arrangement rarely met with. The letters are also grouped according to correspondents. The text is accompanied bountifully by explanatory notes. Vols. I and II are taken up with the exchange between the Rev. Wm. Cole, the antiquary, and Walpole, and are almost wholly concerned, aside from complaints of gout and other ailments, with antiquarian matters. Hence these are highly relevant to the section HISTORY AND ANTIQUITIES.

1892 HONNYWELL, WILLIAM. A Devonshire Yeoman's Diary. Communicated by F. J. Snell. In *Antiquary,* vols. 26, 254-59; and 27, 214-16. London.

> A Devonshire newspaper, the *Western Times,* beginning with the issue of Oct. 30, 1832, printed a good part of this diary, but left off abruptly without completing the work. The above reprinting gives most of what the newspaper had published and supplies the omissions. The writer, a Devonshire yeoman, opens his diary on Jan. 16, 1596, making only a few entries the first year but increasing these as time went on. The last entry is dated in 1614, the year of his death. The diary gives a good idea of certain phases of life in Elizabethan days as it was passed in the country by a man of business—the nature of his domestic economy, his duties, obligations, work, prices of commodities, debts owed and owing, etc. His amusements were apparently confined to bowling, at which he enjoyed winning money. He made a trip to London, but what he saw en route or in the colorful metropolis he leaves out of the story.

1893 TURNBULL, REV. GEORGE. The Diary of the Rev. George Turnbull, Minister of Alloa'and Tyningham, 1657-1704. Edit. by Rev. Robert Paul. In *Miscellany,* vol. I; *Publ. Scot. Hist. Soc.,* no. 15. Edinburgh.

> The writer was a Scotch Covenanting minister who experienced exile in Holland and France for his faith until the Indulgences proclaimed by James II enabled him to return home. The early portion of the diary is written in retrospect, beginning with his birth in 1657 and relating his education and training, his travels in France and Holland, etc. The greater part is the record of his administrations as a preacher, in which he was as assiduous as Wesley. The account presents a vivid story of the struggles of the Scotch Presbyterians against Episcopacy and their constancy in maintaining their faith in those troubled times. There are many references to domestic affairs, sickness in the family, the crops and the weather.

1895 BLUNDELL, NICHOLAS. Selections from the Diary of Nicholas Blundell, Esq., from 1702-28. Edit. by Rev. T. Ellison Gibson. Frontispiece, facsimile, and plate. 4to. Liverpool.

ELIOT, JOHN. The Papers of John Eliot, Merchant, 1735-1813; His Journeys, Journals, etc. Edit. by E. Howard. 4to. London.

1895-96 ALLARDYCE, COL. JAMES (Editor). Historical Papers relating to the Jacobite Period, 1699-1750. 2 vols. *Publ. New Spalding Club,* vols. 14 and 16. Aberdeen.

> Vol. I contains materials relating to the Risings of 1715 and 1745, and reports on the state of the Highlands, by Marshall George Wade and Duncan Forbes of Culloden. There are portraits of the Old Chevalier, Prince Charles Edward, Lord Lewis Gordon, the Earl of Kilmarnock, and Lord Balmerino. Vol. II contains depositions against the Jacobite prisoners in 1746, and portraits.—Terry, *op. cit.*

1896   BICKLEY, FRANCIS B. Letters relating to Scotland, January, 1650. From Originals in the British Museum. *Engl. Hist. Rev.,* vol. 11, 112-17. 8vo. London.

BULSTRODE, SIR RICHARD. The Bulstrode Papers. Vol. I (1667-1675). 8vo. London.

> Sir Richard Bulstrode, author, soldier, was one of the best known diplomatists of his time. In 1673 he was appointed agent at the Court of Brussels, receiving the honor of knighthood on his return to England in 1675. A few months later he went back to Brussels as Resident, and after the accession of James II, he received the title of Envoy. He remained at Brussels until the Revolution, when he followed James to St. Germain, where he died in 1711 at the age of 101 years.
>
> The papers listed above consist of communications made to him from England in the form of news letters giving almost daily the most minute details of everything going on at court and in the country. They may be looked on as more or less a companion to and a continuation of Pepys' *Diary.*—Bookseller's Note.

GIBBON, EDWARD. Private Letters of Edward Gibbon (1753-1794), with an Introduction by the Earl of Sheffield, edit. by R. E. Prothero. 2 vols. 8vo. London.

> See Gibbon's *Memoirs* under 1900 below.

1896-1911   JOHNSTON, SIR ARCHIBALD. The Diary of Sir Archibald Johnston of Wariston, 1632-39. Edit. by Sir George M. Paul and J. R. N. MacPhail. Portrait and facsimile. 2 vols. *Publ. Scot. Hist. Soc.,* no. 26. Edinburgh.

> Vol. I contains Johnston's Diary. Vol. II, Johnston's Diary. Preservations of the Honours of Scotland, 1651-52. Lord Mar's Legacies, 1722-27. Letters concerning Highland affairs in the 18th century by Mrs. Grant of Laggan.

1897   DICK, SIR ALEXANDER. Curiosities of a Scots Charta Chest, 1600-1800, with the Travels and Memoranda of Sir Alexander Dick, Bart., (of Prestonfield, Midlothian), writtten by Himself. Edit. and arranged by Hon. Mrs. Atholl Forbes. 7 portraits, etc., 13 facs. of letters, receipts, etc. 4to. Edinburgh.

1898   BROWN, THOMAS. The Diary of Thomas Brown, Writer in Kirkwall (Orkney), 1675-1693. Edit., with Preface and Notes, by A. Francis Steuart. Facsimile. 8vo. Kirkwall.

WEDDERBURNE, DAVID. The Compt Buik of David Wedderburne, merchant of Dundee, 1589-1630, together with the Shipping Lists of Dundee, 1580-1618. Edit. from the Original MSS., with Introduction and Notes, by A. H. Millar, F.S.A. Scot. *Publ. Scot. Hist. Soc.,* no. 28. Edinburgh.

> From this one may obtain some idea of Scottish commerce during the time of James VI.

YOUNG, ARTHUR. The Autobiography of Arthur Young, with Selections from his Correspondence. Edit. by M. Betham-Edwards. Illus. London.

> For Young's travels in France see under 1792, WEST EUROPE, vol. I of this work. For his excursions in England in the interests of agriculture, see various dates from 1768 on, under TOURS BY NATIVES. The autobiography above gives an intimate insight into the temperament of the most famous agriculturist in Europe; his interest in philanthropy, literature, friends, travels; and his morbid preoccupation with his mental condition. It was previously published as a Prefix to his *Travels in France.*

1899   POWYS, MRS. PHILIP LYBBE. Passages from the Diaries of Mrs. Philip Lybbe Powys (née Caroline Girle) of Hardwick House (Oxon.), 1756-1808: Descriptions of Country Seats, Towns, Manufactures, Amusements, etc. Edit., with Introduction and Notes, by Emily Climenson. Portrait. 8vo. London.

1900 BOWLES, GEORGE. The Diary of a Journey from the South of Ireland in 1761 and 1762. In *Antiquary,* vol. 36, 203-06; 342-46; 366-70. London.

> The author was born in Ireland and was educated for the medical profession, but changing his plans, he entered the army. To get his commission he made the journey related here. The time covers a period of four and a half months. His route took him from the Cove of Cork to Bristol and thence to London, which he reached shortly after the marriage and coronation of George III. He got his commission in the 100th. Foot, went to York, and then was sent to Jersey. On his return to London, he exchanged into another regiment, got a leave of absence, and made a visit to Ireland for two months, after which he returned to London. He gives us considerable information on the manner of traveling, only too rare in most accounts of like nature, as well as the means of intercommunication between the two Islands. He also records quite amply what came under his notice.

GIBBON, EDWARD. Memoirs of his Life, with Various Observations and Excursions by Himself. Edit. by George B. Hill. 8vo. London.

> This is of great interest and value for the insight it reveals into a mind so richly stored with reading and keen in observation.

GRAY, THOMAS, and WILLIAM MASON. Letters of Gray, including the Correspondence of Gray and Mason. Edit. by D. C. Tovey. 3 vols. 8vo. London.

> This has been superseded by the better and fuller edition by Toynbee and Whibley. See below.

> 1935 GRAY, THOMAS. Correspondence of Thomas Gray. Edit. by P. Toynbee and L. Whibley. 3 vols. Oxford.
> > It is in Gray's letters that we get his accounts of his tours in Scotland and the Lake District, which are so important for the history of the taste for scenery in the latter half of the 18th century.

LAUDER, SIR JOHN. Journals of Sir John Lauder, Lord Fountainhall, with his Observations on Public Affairs and other Memoranda, 1665-1676. Edit., with Introduction and Notes, by Donald Crawford, Sheriff of Aberdeen, Kincardine, and Banff. 4 plates. *Publ. Scot. Hist. Soc.,* no. 36. Edinburgh.

> This includes his journal in France, 1665-67; his notes of journeys to London and Oxford, and in Scotland, 1667-70; a chronicle of events connected with the Court of Session, 1668-76; observations on public affairs, 1669-70; accounts for 1670-75; and a catalogue of books, 1667-79; a portrait of Fountainhall, his wife, his father (Sir John Lauder), and Sir Andrew Ramsay (Lord Abbotshall).

1901 The Beneden Letters. London, Country, and Abroad, 1753-1802. Edit. by Charles F. Hardy. London.

> This consists chiefly of the correspondence of Richard Waite Cox, of the Sick and Hurt Office in the Tower, to his friend Wm. Ward, with some others. It gives interesting sidelights on home affairs and political incidents and personages. See Book II, 154-178, for the impressions of London and the country imparted by a young French tutor, Jean de Caulier, to Birch and later to Lt. Gen. Fitsroy.

HAY, ANDREW. The Diary of Andrew Hay of Craignethan, 1659-1660. Edit., with Introduction and Notes, by Alexander George Reid, F.S.A. Scot. *Publ. Scot. Hist. Soc.,* no. 39. Edinburgh.

> This is the diary of a Covenanting Scottish gentleman, with interesting glimpses of the daily life of such a character.

1901-35 NICOLSON, WILLIAM (Bishop of Carlisle and Archb. of Cashel). Bishop Nicolson's Diary. Edit., with Notes, by Bishop Ware and R. G. Collingwood. Printed in part in *Trans. Cumberland and Westmoreland Antiq. and Arch. Soc.,* n.s., vols. 1-5 (1901-05), and 35 (1935). Kendal.

These diaries run from Jan. 1, 1683, to Dec. 31, 1725. The records of a man so notable in the ecclesiastical and political life of the day and so ardent in his pursuit of antiquarian and historical subjects are bound to be of great interest. Apparently he had no intention of publishing his diaries, as many of the entries are mere phrases, or brief chronicles of daily happenings, records of visits from innumerable people and of his own visits in return. But others describing the journeys he had to make are of more length; in them he sets down ample observations on sights, relics, curiosities. He was in London after the battle of Blenheim and saw the standards taken on that day. He visited Hadrian's Wall to see a Roman inscription at Cambeck Hill. He is also concerned with personal matters relative to his health, his ailments and their remedies. It is of interest to know that bishops had the power to grant licenses to practice medicine, surgery, and midwifery. Of his parochial business one learns little, but much of botany, history, and archaeology. What is unusual in an Englishman is his knowledge of German, which he had acquired from a visit to Germany. Some of his opening entries are in this language.

1904   COCKBURN, JOHN. Letters of John Cockburn of Ormiston to his Gardener, 1727-44. Edit., with Introduction and Notes, by James Colville, M.A., D.Sc. (Edinburgh), author of *Byways of History. Publ. Scot. Hist. Soc.,* no. 45. Edinburgh.

These letters throw light on the rise of modern agriculture in Scotland, as well as on the social development of the country gentleman.—Terry, *op. cit.*

1905   BROWNE, BENJAMIN. Letters from a Westmorland Man in London to his Father, 1719-34. Communicated by S. H. Scott. In *Antiquary,* vol. 41, 328-32; 379-83. London.

These letters were written by a son of a substantial "statesman." He had gone up to London as clerk to a lawyer in the Temple. And he proved to be a dutiful and conscientious son. The first letter describes his journey to London and is dated June 16, 1719. Many of them deal with clothes, wigs, bags, boots, etc. Some deal with his hours of work, his visits, and his purchase of a violin. Those of later years are written at greater intervals and are more wanting in detail. By the time he left for Troutbeck in 1736, he was a man of substance, a widower, and again a married man. At home he took over his father's farm, bought a house near his old home, with his father taking rooms in the house for himself. Both died in 1748.

1906   MACDONALD, JOHN. Autobiographical Journal of John Macdonald, Schoolmaster and Soldier, 1770-1830. Edit., with Introduction, Illustrations, and Notes, by Angus Mackay. 8vo. Edinburgh.

This is a short but interesting journal, the greater part of which deals with his soldiering, especially at the siege of Gibraltar, then held by Gen. Elliot, which began June 21, 1779. The part dealing with his career as a schoolmaster in the Highlands of Scotland, in the parish of Tongue, the country of the Mackay clan, runs from 1796 on. In the Introduction he gives an account of the efforts made to "civilize" the Highlands, particularly under the direction of the Society for Propagating Christian Knowledge.

WEDGWOOD, JOSIAH. The Correspondence of Josiah Wedgwood, 1781-94. With an Appendix containing some Letters on Canal and Bentley's Pamphlet on Inland Navigation. Edit. by Katherine Eufemia, Lady Farrer. London.

It was decidedly to the interest of this great potter to secure better means of transportation for his wares.

1907   POWELL, W. Diary, 1603-54. Edit. by J. A. Bradney. Portrait. Bristol.

This has value for the local history of Monmouthshire.—Davies, *Bibliog. Brit. Hist.*

WOTTON, SIR HENRY. Life and Letters. Edit. by L. P. Smith. Oxford.

Wotton was agent and secretary to the Earl of Essex, 1595, and collector of intelligence for his master; ambassador at the Court of Venice at various periods from 1604 to 1624; he also served on diplomatic missions to the Hague, France, and Vienna. He left works on architecture and his *Reliquiae Wottoniae,* first published 1651.—*DNB.*

1908 BELLINGHAM, THOMAS. Diary of Thomas Bellingham, An Officer under William III. Complete Transcript and Notes by Anthony Hewitson. Portrait and illustrations. 8vo. Preston.

ELIZABETH, LADY HOLLAND. The Journal of Elizabeth, Lady Holland, 1791-1811. Edit. by the Earl of Ilchester, with illustrations. 2 vols. London.

JOSSELIN, RALPH (Minister). The Diary of the Rev. Ralph Josselin, 1616-1683. Edit. by E. Hockliffe, for the Royal Historical Society. *Publ. Camden Soc.*, 3rd ser., vol. 15. London.

> The writer was vicar of Earles Colne, where he spent most of his life, from 1640 to 1683. The early years of the diary had daily entries, falling off in 1644 to weekly entries. He was a pious man, with a mind for business. He saw to it that he made profits from his farm and his lendings, his salary as schoolmaster, and his income from his post as chaplain to Col. Harlokenden's regiment, so that he was much better off for money than most clergymen. The daily concerns of his profession as vicar and as farmer tell something of how life went on in a small inland town. He was always finding God's mercy pointing its finger at him.—From the Introduction.

1910 BROADLEY, A. M. Doctor Johnson and Mrs. Thrale; Including Mrs. Thrale's Unpublished Journal of the Welsh Tour made in 1774 and much hitherto Unpublished Correspondence of the Streatham Coterie. With an Introductory Essay by Thomas Seccombe. Numerous Illustrations from contemporary portraits, etc., including one in color and one in photogravure. 8vo. London.

Six North Country Diaries. Edit. by John C. Hodgson. *Publ. Surtees Soc.*, vol. 118, I. Durham.

> A second volume was published in 1914 with additional diaries. The separate items are listed below.

1. ASTON, JOHN. The Journal of John Aston.
   > This is the most important one of the six. Aston was attached to the suite of Charles I on his expedition through the counties of York, Durham, and Northumberland in the First Bishops' War, 1639. The countryside appeared desolated and poverty-stricken. Berwick was much run down. The people of York were fond of shows, were affable and hospitable but vainglorious. The discipline and training of the Royalist troops were decidedly lax. Durham was "the London (as it were) of the North Parts." A visit to the Scottish camp revealed Highlanders garbed in the kilts, "well timbred men," with bagpipes, swords, targes, dirks, bows and arrows, and a few muskets. A treaty was signed and the Scotch army was disbanded.

2. SANDERSON, CHRISTOPHER. Selections from the Diary of Christopher Sanderson.
   > Only selections are given here because the Diary and Pedigree were printed by F. C. Beazley (from another MS) in the *Genealogist*, vol. 22, 1906. The writer was the son of a substantial haberdasher. He became justice of the peace for the county of Durham and purchased an estate at Eggleston in 1659. Three marriages and a numerous progeny fell to his lot. His diary reports only events of public interest, mere entries of dates and their transactions.

3. BEE, REV. NICHOLAS. The Diary of the Rev. Nicholas Bee.
   > The writer, a native of the City of Durham, was bred a Skinner and Glover. He may have once kept an ale house and have done some brewing. His business failed to prosper, and at the age of 65 be became an out-pensioner of the Hospital of Sherburn-House. His diary is largely limited to entries of disasters and remarkable events, such as dreadful storms, floods, blazing stars (Aug. 15, 1682), cruel murders by a boy of two girls, beheadings, quarterings, instances of people standing in the pillory, fires, the case of Christopher Maskall who was "so drunk he spew'd all his clothes and hatt, cravat, and lay all night in the entry," the death of Charles II, the case of Thomas Bell and Frances Kirkley, who were married 16 June, 1690, and said Frances a mother by 29 June, etc.

4. THOMLINSON, JOHN. The Diary of John Thomlinson.

This is here printed for the first time. The writer, born in 1692, was a native of Cumberland, who attended Cambridge, was ordained a deacon, became curate of Rothbury, and then drifted down to Leicestershire, where he was presented with a rectory. His diary opens July 24, 1717, and closes in 1722. There is an apparent fondness for curious anecdotes, some of them being very curious! The record, which is chiefly concerned with social and clerical life, makes on the whole very interesting reading. Evidently he was not a Puritan. The clergy of Cumberland, however, are represented as being near vicious.

5. GYLL, THOMAS. The Diary of Thomas Gyll.

Born in 1700 to a patrimonial estate, Gyll attended Cambridge and Lincoln's Inn in 1718-19, and was called to the bar in 1725, where he practiced with ability and integrity. In 1733 he was made solicitor-general for the city of Durham. His leisure showed his interests to be history, archaeology, and the fine arts. His entries, which are very brief, begin Feb. 24, 1748, and consist mainly of notices of deaths, with a few interruptions of local matters, such as the painting of the organ in the church, lightning striking and shattering the stonework of the spire of Darlington church, of a high wind Oct. 6, 1756. Among the deaths he records is that of the Rev. Joseph Spence, the reporter of Pope's anecdotes, on Aug. 20, 1768, who was said to have fallen into a pond and drowned.

6. BROWN, NICHOLAS. The Diary of Nicholas Brown.

The writer was an attorney in Alnwick and coroner for Northumberland. His entries, which are brief, deal with sundry affairs, with deaths predominating, among which he notes that of the Rev. Dodd, June, 1777, hanged for forgery after Dr. Johnson had vainly interposed with his noble plea for life. Other things entered are fires, fasts, setting rents, parliamentary actions, a few births, the new furniture put into the church, the seat of the Duke of Northumberland, the Alnwick races, bad weather, the winter of 1790 being noted as the worst ever experienced, cock fights, of which he seemed to be fond, the shyness marking the relations of Burke and Sheridan in their speeches in the House of Commons, etc.

MILLER, SANDERSON. An Eighteenth Century Correspondence: Being the Letters of Deane Swift, William Pitt, the Lytteltons and Grenvilles, Lord Dacre, Robert Nugent, Charles Jenkinson, the Earls of Guilford, Coventry, and Hardwicke, Sir Edward Turner, Mr. Talbot of Lacock, and Others, to Sanderson Miller, Esq., of Radway Grange. Edit. by Lilian Dickins and Mary Stanton. Illustrations and portraits. 8vo. London.

If there was a man to be envied it was the recipient of these letters, for few men could command for so long a period an unbroken set of friendships with personages of the first quality in rank and virtue. Surely no man was ever so beset with invitations to visits, or so much sought after. What he is like depends entirely on the testimony of these letters, for we are offered no direct look at his mind. These letters were selected and arranged by Miller himself and passed on to his descendants until they appeared in print as above. Miller was in great demand in his day as an architect, being regarded particularly as a specialist in the Gothic style, in which he perpetrated many monstrosities, not even sparing his own lovely Tudor mansion. Among students of the "Tides of Taste" of the 18th century, he will be remembered for Hagley House, the seat of Lord Lyttelton.

WALPOLE, HORACE. Last Journals. During the Reign of George III, from 1771-83. With Notes by Dr. Doran. Edit., with an Introduction, by A. F. Steuart. And containing numerous portraits reproduced from contemporary pictures. 2 vols. 8vo. London.

1912   The Seafield Correspondence, from 1685 to 1708. Edit. by James Grant. Portrait. Edinburgh.

For further correspondence, see under 1915 below.

STEPHENS, JOHN. The Journal of John Stephens. Edit. by H. H. Murray. Oxford.

WILLIAMSON, LIEUT.-GEN. ADAM. The Official Diary of Lieut.-Gen. Adam Wil-

liamson, Deputy-Lieutenant of the Tower of London, 1722-47. Edit. by John Charles Fox, F.R.H. *Publ. Camden Soc.,* 3rd ser., vol. 22. London.

The chief officers of the Tower in his lifetime were the Constable, who was supreme in command, the Deputy-Lieutenant, and Mayor. The Deputy-Lieutenant was the resident governor, though he usually got leave of absence for a good part of the year. Williamson was a staunch Hanoverian, a bitter enemy to all Papists, and a personal friend of George II. He was honest and capable, but arbitrary and bigoted, and wanting in tact. The diary illustrates well what it was like to be a prisoner in the Tower as well as what took up the time of the Deputy. We meet several famous figures, among them Bishop Atterbury, "who was the worst man I ever had to do with in my life," says Williamson. The Rebellion of the '45 brought at its conclusion many notable personages into confinement, such as Murray of Broughton, Alaister Macdonald, Lord Balmerino, the Earl of Traquair, and the old fox Simon, Lord Lovat, who being destitute, was assisted financially by Williamson.—From the Introduction.

1914 CRAVEN, ELIZABETH (Baroness). The Original Memoirs of Elizabeth Baroness Craven, afterwards Margravine of Anspach and Bayreuth and Princess Berkeley of the Holy Roman Empire, 1750-1828. Edit., with Notes and a Biographical and Historical Introduction, by A. M. Broadley and Lewis Melville. 48 Illustrations. 2 vols. 8vo. London.

Her journey to Constantinople is listed under 1789, WEST EUROPE, vol. I of this work.

North Country Diaries. Edit. by John C. Hodgson. *Publ. Surtees Soc.,* vol. 124, II. Durham.

Selected for notation are those of Sir William Brereton, Bishop Pococke, John Dawson, Bishop Warburton. See following.

1. BRERETON, SIR WILLIAM. Journal of Sir William Brereton, 1635.
   This has been printed in *Publ. Chetham Soc.,* vol. 1, 1844, and in Richardson's *Imprints and Reprints of Rare Tracts,* 1844. These last are rare. The writer was educated at Oxford, admitted to Gray's Inn 1623, and made a baronet in 1627, along with other honors. In the Civil War he was a Parliamentarian. His diary, which begins June 11, 1635, is interesting for its record of his ride from his home in Cheshire through Yorkshire, Durham, Northumberland to Edinburgh, Glasgow, Port Patrick to Ireland, where he spent twenty days, to Bristol and back home, where he arrived in August, 1635. His descriptions of towns and districts are of value, such as that of Durham and its Minster, which was well kept up (unlike the majority of cathedrals in the 17th and 18th centuries). Newcastle was the fairest and richest town in England, being inferior only to London. Berwick was decayed, with little or no shipping, as the harbor was too shallow. In Edinburgh he praised the High Street and the air of the place, but otherwise everything else was "sluttish" and "nasty"—favorite epithets for things Scottish. The description of the rights of the Scottish Church government and its penalties for derelictions—especially fornication, adultery, and going "fromwards" the church on Sundays—and of the communion service is interesting and noteworthy. He was less offended with Glasgow, which was a much cleaner city. The trip across the Irish Channel was a trying one because of too many horses and too few sailors.

2. POCOCKE, RICHARD (Bishop of Meath). Northern Journeys of Bishop Richard Pococke.
   The journals of this restless bishop recounting his travels in England and Wales were printed in the *Publ. Camden Soc.,* vols. 42 and 44; those in Scotland in *Publ. Scot. Hist. Soc.,* no. 1, 1887. The letters here edited relate his travels in the north of England in 1760 and are printed for the first time. His travels take him through Durham, Cumberland, and Northumberland. His interest lies in antiquarian and historical remains; *e.g.,* he discusses the site of the field of the Battle of Otterburne made famous by the ballad of that name (fought in 1388 between the Douglas and Percy), and notes that this is not the same as the battle of Chevy Chase. His itinerary is well indicated and can be followed on the map. The narrative is plain and prosy.

3. DAWSON, JOHN. The Diary of John Dawson of Brinton.
   The writer matriculated at Oxford, March 17, 1746, and was already entered at Gray's Inn. When the Northumberland Militia was first enrolled in 1759, in accordance with an Act of Parliament, Dawson was appointed captain of a Tynedale company. The diary is pretty much concerned with the doings of the militia during 1761, the riots against the Act, the shootings and trials. The entries are brief and impersonal.

4. WARBURTON, WILLIAM (Bishop). Two letters of Bishop Warburton, addressed to Ralph Allen, Prior Park.

Both of these letters are short. The first describes Durham, where he has been spending a week, with nothing to do but eat from morning to night. It is dated May 30, 1755. The second is also from Durham dated July 27, 1756. It is largely an amusing diatribe against a fellow clergyman, Dr. James Lesley, Prebendary of Durham, who had been made bishop of Limerick.

1915 PARRY, ROBERT. Diary of Robert Parry, 1539-1613. *Publ. Arch. Cambrensis,* 6th ser., vol. 15, 109-39. London.

Seafield Correspondence. Letters relating to Scotland in the Reign of Queen Anne. Edit. by Prof. P. Hume Brown. 8vo. Edinburgh (?).

The Stiffkey Papers: The Official Papers of Sir Nathaniel Bacon, of Stiffkey, Norfolk, as Justice of the Peace, 1580-1620. Selected and edit. by H. W. Saunders, M.A. *Publ. Camden Soc.,* 3rd ser., vol. 36. London.

These papers dealing with Bacon as Commissioner of Sewers tell us much of conditions of towns, piers, harbors, encroachments of the sea, dykes, etc.

1917 MINET, WILLIAM. Extracts from the Letter-Book of a Dover Merchant, 1737-41. In *Archaeologia Cantiana,* vol. 32. London.

These letters belong to a Dover merchant of the 18th century, Isaac Minet, a native of Calais who left France on account of the Revocation of the Edict of Nantes. He settled in Dover where he developed a general merchant's and ship-agency business that later grew into a bank. The letter-book that has survived from this firm's accounts of inland transactions is vol. 20. It points out the decay of the Cinque Ports and the conditions that made Dover a port of refuge and ship repair. It describes the cross channel traffic, the times of sailing and the conditions governing departure, the state of the bar, the landing of passengers, the absence of any connecting services with London, the difficulties of the passage during the war with Spain in 1738 and 1740, the resort to the packet boats which never entered the harbor of Dover but lay outside in the roads and so escaped the order forbidding boats to leave the harbor. The operations of the press gangs, the plundering of wrecked ships, the silting up of the harbor, the mistakes of the pilots handling the ships, etc.—all are matters of interest to this merchant, whose business lay with ships and shipping. He was also agent for the Dutch East India Company. The editor works in a running commentary with these letters.

1918 PETT, PHINEAS. The Autobiography of Phineas Pett. Edit. by W. G. Perrin. *Publ. Navy Records Soc.,* vol. 51. London.

This story of the life of a master shipwright in the time of King James I is of much interest. The entries seem to corroborate the charges of corruption in the navy at this time. It is to be suspected that Pett was not above making a little on the side by misappropriating materials for his own use They give us some account of the launchings of ships, among them that of the famous *Sovereign of the Seas.*

1919 STONE, NICHOLAS. Diary. *Publ. Walpole Soc.,* vol. for 1918-19. London.

Stone (1586-1647) worked as a mason and architect under Inigo Jones and at other projects. He is best known for his tombs, including that of Bodley at Oxford and that of Donne at St. Paul's, London.—*DNB.*

1920 FELL, SARAH. The Household Account Book of Sarah Fell of Swarthmoor Hall. Edit. by N. Penney, F.S.A. 8vo. Cambridge.

This gives a complete account of the domestic economy of a large middle-class household in the days of Charles II, and some information on the general conditions of the district. It is largely occupied with the working of the farm, markets, and a detailed record of prices. Entries about the activities of the Quakers are numerous.—Bookseller's Note.

Viscount Percival, Earl of Egmont. Diary of Viscount Percival Afterwards First Earl of Egmont. Vol. I, 1730-33; vol. II, 1734-38; vol. III, 1739-47. Edit. by R. A. Roberts. *Hist. MSS. Comm.,* Report no. 63. London.

> The diary is ample in detail and the entries are regular until near the close. The writer was a man of taste, fond of music, versed in travel, and a political supporter of Walpole's administration, but in no sense a "yes man." His comments form an excellent supplement to the history of the times and its political exigencies. The work is also rich in miscellaneous information. The last two volumes are deeply concerned with his trusteeship of the Oglethorpe colony of Georgia.

1921-25   Hickey, William. The Memoirs of William Hickey, 1749-1809. Edit. by Alfred Spencer. 4 vols. London and New York.

> These memoirs make delightful reading in the life of a gay young blade of London, who is full of zest for amusement but not wholly given over to play. The period he spent in India, especially at Calcutta, is very informing on the way of life led by a civil servant in the employ of the East India Company.

1922   Ridpath, Rev. George. The Diary of Rev. George Ridpath, Minister of Stitchel, 1755-61. Edit. by Sir J. Balfour Paul. *Publ. Scot. Hist. Soc.,* no. 12, 3rd ser. Edinburgh.

1922-27   Farington, Joseph. The Farington Diary (1793-1821). Edit. by James Greig. Numerous illustrations. 8 vols. London.

> The painter Farington was an accepted member of society and as such had entry to practically any house. His diary records an endless round of visits, anecdotes of prominent folk, and naturally of the inner workings of the Royal Academy of Painters, of which he was an influential member. He did much illustration for "views of gentlemen's seats."

1924   Wyndham, Maud (Editor). Chronicles of the Eighteenth Century: Founded on the Correspondence of Sir Thomas Lyttelton and his Family. 2 vols. London.

> This offers much information on the careers of various members of the Lyttelton family, their places in politics and intellectual activities of the 18th century.

1925   Newton, Lady (of the Legh's). The Lyme Letters, 1660-1760. Portraits. London.

> These letters are concerned with the domestic and social life of the Leghs of Lyme House.

Turner, T. Diary of T. Turner (of East Hoathly), 1754-65. Edit. by Florence S. Turner (Mrs. Chas. Lamb, great-great-granddaughter of the diarist), with an Introduction by J. B. Priestley. Facs. frontispiece and 3 other illus. 8vo. London.

1925-26   Fugger News-Letters. A Selection of unpublished Letters from the House of Fugger from 1568 to 1605. Edit. by V. von Klarwill, translated by L. S. R. Byrne. Illustrations. 2nd ser. London.

> These refer especially to Queen Elizabeth and English affairs. The great banking house of Fugger was outstanding in the 16th century.

1926   Sibbald, Susan. The Memoirs of Susan Sibbald, 1783-1812. Edit. by her greatgrandson, Francis Paget Hett. 40 illus. 8vo. London.

1926-31   Woodforde, Rev. James (Parson). The Diary of a Country Parson, 1758-1802. Edit. by J. Berésford. Portraits and other illus. 5 vols. Oxford.

> This is easily the outstanding diary of the 18th century for its day by day account of how life was lived in the jurisdiction of a country rector during the second half of the century. "The drums and tramplings of three conquests" beat in vain against the ears of these self-

contained folk of the inland counties. Even in Norfolk county the great event was dinner at the Squire's house or the trip to Norwich. The news of the deaths of rulers of France during the Terror evoked only a passing comment of horror. The making of beer, the annual dinners to the poor old men of the parish, the cultivation of his glebe, the games of whist, the rotation dinners, the weather, the menus which shock the moderns with their profuseness of various courses of meats, the prices of objects bought, etc., fill these pages to the utter exclusion of politics and state affairs. For half a century the parson makes the reader his guest, who departs for the sole reason that his host has departed this life. The editor confesses to have omitted much from even these five volumes, but hopes sometime to make good the omission.

1927 ASHMOLE, ELIAS. The Diary and Will of Elias Ashmole, edited and extended from the original manuscripts by R. T. Gunther. 8vo. Oxford.

GRAY, A. The Papers and Diaries of a York Family, 1764-1839. London.

1928 KLARWILL, VICTOR VON (Editor). Queen Elizabeth and Some Foreigners, being a Series of hitherto unpublished Letters from the Archives of the Hapsburg Family. Edit., with Introduction by Victor von Klarwill, translated by T. S. Nash. Illus. 8vo. London.

> Not only the Letters but also the Introduction make vivid the life of England during the reign of Elizabeth. I am much indebted to this work for material on foreigners in England.

TEMPLE, REV. W. J. The Diaries of W. J. Temple, 1780-96. Edit. with Memoir by Lewis Bettany. Oxford.

> Boswellians are grateful to Temple for being the occasion of so many letters from the biographer.

1930 BROCKBANK, REV. THOMAS. The Diary and Letter Book of the Rev. Thomas Brockbank, 1671-1709. Edit. by Richard Trappes-Lomax. *Publ. Chetham Soc.,* n.s. vol. 89. Manchester.

> The diarist was quite a model for this form of literature in that he kept a detailed account of his doings, recording everything of domestic interest and also many things of public notice in connection with James II and the Papists. But the main value of the work lies in the domestic realm: how people lived in certain circumstances, the household intimacies, entanglements with relatives, what was eaten, what things cost, how one was educated at Oxford, what kind of meals were served at inns, etc. He was apparently ambitious to get on, to make money, and to secure good living. Though a clergyman, or perhaps because he was, he tends to be something of a sycophant. His comments on what he sees on his travels reveal very personal reactions, and make good what is omitted in the accounts of the average tourist. In London he visits the Tower and enumerates its contents, admires London Bridge and wonders how it stands, and goes through Bedlam. He also attended the theatre, where he saw "Pastor Fido" acted entirely by women. The music between acts he thought to be very fine. He was appointed vicar of Cartmel, in northern Lancashire, in 1706, and there spent the rest of his life till his death in 1732.

HOBY, LADY MARGARET. The Diary of Lady Margaret Hoby, 1599-1605. Edit. by Dorothy M. Meade. Illustrated with 8 full-page plates from contemporary sources. 8vo. London.

> This journal, which is here printed for the first time, is the earliest known diary written by an English woman. It casts a welcome illumination on the domestic life of a serious-minded woman in the days of Queen Elizabeth. The Introduction gives an informing discussion of the relation of the diary to the general education and position of women at this period.

SCOTT, J. B. (of Bungay). An Englishman at Home and Abroad, 1792-1828, with Some Recollections of Napoleon: being Extracts from the Diaries of J. B. Scott of Bungay, Suffolk. Appendix and 12 illus. Edit. by Ethel Mann. 8vo. London.

VERNEY LETTERS. The Verney Letters of the 18th Century from the MSS. at Claydon House. Edit. by M. Maria, Lady Verney. Portrait and pedigrees. 2 vols. 8vo. London.

WINDHAM, WILLIAM. The Early Life and Diaries of William Windham (1750-85). Edit. by Robert Wyndham Ketton-Crem. 8vo. London.

Windham is the statesman who assisted Burke in the prosecution of Warren Hastings and thus brought grief to Fanny Burney. The work goes over the story of his early life from 1750 to 1785, and includes his diaries of visits to Ireland, to his English friends, of his tours in England and his balloon ascension.

1931 HOLBERG, LUDWIG. Memoirs. *Bodleian Quarterly Record,* vol. 3. Oxford.

This great Norwegian dramatist visited England in 1706. His experiences in London and Oxford are of great interest. For a full exposition of the interaction between him and England, see Olsvig, *Holberg og England,* under GENERAL REFERENCE.

THE PUREFOY LETTERS. The Purefoy Letters, 1735-53, selected from the Letter-Books of Mrs. Purefoy and her Son Henry (of Shalstone, near Buckingham). Edit. by G. Eland. Illustrated with 28 full-page plates of portraits, furniture, facsimiles, etc. Index, pedigree tables and map. 2 vols. 8vo. London.

These selections are arranged according to subject and cover all the working details of a household "in a secluded parish when traveling was difficult and the danger and haunting fear of small-pox was never long absent." The sections include Sport, Purlieu Hunting, visits for Holiday and Health, Newspapers and other Reading, Management of the Estate, Housekeeping, etc. Of considerable interest is the widespread investing in lotteries. Evidently the dangers of the road and infrequency of means of carriage made great demands on the courtesies of friends in those days, and called for expansive hospitality.

WHITE, GILBERT. The Journals of Gilbert White. Edit. by Walter Johnson. London.

These journals cover the years 1768-93, and contain much that relates to natural history. For his *Natural History of Selborne,* see under 1789, NATURAL HISTORY.

1932 SIBBALD, SIR ROBERT. The Memoirs of Sir Robert Sibbald, 1641-1722. Edit., with an Introduction, by F. Paget Hett. Portrait and facsimile. 4to. London.

Sibbald appears as the author of many works under HISTORY AND ANTIQUITIES. He was the founder of the Royal College of Physicians, Edinburgh.

1933 OXINDEN, HENRY. The Oxinden Letters, 1607-42, Being the Correspondence of Henry Oxinden and his Circle. Edit., with an Introduction and Notes, by Dorothy Gardiner. Illustrated with 13 full-page plates from contemporary sources. 8vo. London.

The Oxindens, like the Pastons, belonged to the old squirearchy. Henry Oxinden hoarded his letters, even the rough-draft replies. In the foreground is the county of Kent, and in the background is unrestful England. Rumor is rife—of the bishops on bob-tailed nags riding to Parliament, of Strafford on the scaffold, of Pym's great speech in the Commons, of King Charles in Canterbury climbing Bell Harry Tower. Romance has its place in Henry Oxinden's courtship of a yeoman's daughter.—Heffer & Sons Catalogue.

ROGERS, RICHARD, and SAMUEL WARD. Two Elizabethan Puritan Diaries by Richard Rogers and Samuel Ward. Edit., with Introduction, by M. M. Knappen. *Amer. Soc. Church Hist.* Chicago.

1934 MORRIS, CLAVER, M.D. The Diary of a West Country Physician, A.D. 1684-1726. Edit. by Edmund Hobhouse, M.D. London.

This physician, who lived in Wells, offers us some curious remedies for ailments. But his chief interest seems to lie in his music club, which met regularly to play for its own amusement, though to our regret he never tells us the names of the pieces played. He himself performed on several instruments and could sing as well. Other concerns are his beer, cider, and wine, and his relations with his neighbors.

1934-38   BYNG, HON. JOHN (Viscount Torrington). The Torrington Diaries (1781-94). For an account of these diaries, see under this date, TOURS BY NATIVES.

1935   The Wynne Diaries, 1789-98. Edit. by Anne Premantle. Illustrations. 2 vols. Oxford.

1936   PLAXTON, REV. GEORGE. Letters of the Rev. George Plaxton, M.A., Rector of Barwick-in-Elmet, 1706-10. Edit. by Miss E. M. Walker. *Publ. Thoresby Soc., Misc.,* vol. 37, pt. 1, 30-104. Leeds.

The letters published here are additional to those which the Thoresby Society had already printed. Plaxton is a good example of the Tory parson of the better class. He had a genius for friendship, and his letters, too individual to give a sharp picture of contemporary life, reveal an interesting and lovable character. Hearne described him as a good scholar and one that loved antiquities. Thoresby mentions the fact that Plaxton had planned to write a history of Barwick, but never completed the design. He tells us little of the countryside or even of his antiquarian studies, but he sets down frankly what he read, liked or disliked, and what he thought on various subjects. He had a turn for phrasing that at times approached the conceit, which led him to refer to his friends and correspondents by nicknames. One of his letters on bearbaiting is richly humorous with its description in the dialect of the sport. Whether he approved is difficult to get at; perhaps his advice was all spoofing. "Pray, turn on good Doggs, such as will chawle with him, for if he be not soundly Lugg'd, and mumbled, he will over run the country, and eat up all our honey." One of his statements could well refer to present times: "Had not the weather been as Mysty & dark as the Times, and the Ways as dangerous as the Politiques of the age," etc. These were the days of the War of the Spanish Succession (1710) and the French were then the enemy. He remarks that "nothing were more uncertain & contradictory than the News and Advices." His favorite poem was *Hudibras,* which tells us something of his temper.—From the Editor's Introduction.

1937   GIRALDUS CAMBRENSIS. Autobiography. Edit. and Translated by H. E. Butler. 8vo. London.

KNYVETON, JOHN. The Diary of a Surgeon in the Year 1751-52. By John Knyveton. Licentiate of the Society of Apothecaries; Doctor of Medicine of the University of Aberdeen; Teacher of Midwifery in the Infirmary Hall; Surgeon's Mate, H.M.S. Lancaster. Edit. by Ernest Gray. Illustrations (from contemporary sources). London.

The first half of this diary deals with the writer's apprenticeship period learning surgery through attending Dr. Urquhart's operations at the Infirmary, and with the study of Materia Medica. The second takes up his career as surgeon's mate on board the Ship of Navy *Lancaster.* This account of life on board a navy ship, in battles, cruises, and at ports, is as absorbing as that of *Roderick Random.* He was left on a small island in the West Indies to look after the numerous cases of yellow fever till the return of the ship. By that time he contracted the disease himself. The book, with its descriptions of operations performed without anaesthetics, makes one devoutly thankful that one was not born until after the advent of Dr. Morton.

MARLAY LETTERS. The Marlay Letters, 1778-1820. Edit. by R. Warwick Bond. Illustrated with 8 plates and 7 pedigrees. London.

This is a selection from the mass of family letters bequeathed to Prof. Bond by the late Mr. Charles Brinsley Marlay, around whose grandmother—Lady Charleville, wife of the first Earl of the second Charleville creation, a woman of marked wit and of high intelligence— the correspondence centers. They acquaint us intimately with the Anglo-Irish landholding families of Dawson, Tisdall, Bury, and Marlay; their preoccupation with their estates and

with Irish politics; their adventures in horsecropping and in keeping within their allowances at Oxford. After the Union (1801), Lord and Lady Charleville were much in London, where Lady Charleville's social and intellectual gifts attracted shoals of letters from a great variety of correspondents.—Bookseller's Note.

1939 CHAMBERLAIN, JOHN. The Letters of John Chamberlain. An Intimate Record of Life and Happenings in England during the Elizabethan and Jacobean Eras. Edit., with an Introduction, by Norman Egbert McClure. *Publ. American Philosophical Soc*. Philadelphia.

The publishers' announcement of this work states that Chamberlain (1554-1628) is perhaps the most interesting letter writer of his period. Not only the political drama as it was played by the great, but also the life as it was lived by the ordinary citizen is presented in his letters. Here we have the many-sided life of Elizabethan and Jacobean London.

PEMBROKE, HENRY, 10TH EARL OF. Letters and Diaries of Henry, Tenth Earl of Pembroke, and his Circle (1734-80). 12 illus. London.

RYDER, DUDLEY. The Diary of Dudley Ryder, 1715-16. Transcribed from shorthand and Edited by William Matthews. London.

This diary covers eighteen months of his young manhood, when he was a law student at the Middle Temple. Other journals were kept in later years. The above was written in shorthand, which had become popular by this time, and apparently was meant to serve as a mentor to himself, for here he could put down his shortcomings, his hopes and failures, his self-analysis without fear of being exposed to laughter. He was a man who greatly desired to be admired, but nature had withheld from him those qualities that win admiration. Studiousness, substantial intellectuality, and rectitude in his profession were his, and they brought him to high honor, for he became at the last Chief Justice and Lord Ryder, Baron Ryder of Harroby. But he seems to have made no great stir in the world of his day. He had many acquaintances but few friends, and he himself fails to win the affection of the reader of his diary. Our enjoyment of his records are probably not what he would have intended, viz., the pictures of London life of 1715-16.

1940 HAMPDEN, JOHN (Compiler). An Eighteenth Century Journal. Illustrations. 8vo. London.

This most entertaining diary records day by day the events of the years 1774, 1775, and 1776, when George III was almost dictator as well as king, and the American colonies were establishing their independence; when Sheridan, Johnson, Garrick, Reynolds, Burke, J. C. Bach, and Wesley were at the height of their fame, when Howard was initiating prison reform and Watt was developing his steam engine.—Bookseller's Note.

1941 (?) BRADSTREET, DUDLEY. The Life and Uncommon Adventures of Captain Dudley Bradstreet. Edit. by G. S. Taylor, with a Foreword by E. H. W. Meyerstein. London.

The cynically candid confessions of an 18th century soldier of fortune, born in Tipperary in 1711, are here presented. In early youth he became a trooper, then a linen draper, then a brewer, and later a spy in the service of the Dukes of Newcastle and Cumberland during the '45 Rebellion. His autobiography gives vivid accounts of Prince Charles Edward and his army. The frank story of his vicissitudes makes very entertaining reading, for he certainly possesses the art of telling a plain story.—Bookseller's Note. No date of publication is given in the reference, but its appearance is recent.

BULKELEY, WILLIAM. Mr. Bulkeley and the Pirate. A Welsh Diarist of the Eighteenth Century. Edit. by B. Dew Roberts. Illustrations. 8vo. Oxford.

The diarist lived in a lonely part of the Isle of Anglesey. He reveals himself to be a hot-tempered Welsh gentleman, much concerned with receiving his dues, being engaged as a result in numerous lawsuits and difficulties with his family and relatives. The sympathy of the reader goes out to him nevertheless, especially in his closing years. What life was like in Wales during this period has all too rarely been presented. The two volumes of MS diaries cover the periods of March, 1736, to June, 1743, and August, 1747, to September, 1760, with a later month.

1942 THRALE, MRS. HESTER LYNCH. Thraliana. The Diary of Mrs. Hester Lynch Thrale (later Mrs. Piozzi), 1776-1809. Edit. by Miss Katherine C. Balderston. 2 vols. 8vo. London.

> In addition to furnishing much information on Johnson, these volumes, which here publish the Thraliana in full, bring to view the social currents of the century as well as the literary movements. The material was obtained from the Huntington Library.

XXIII
General Reference Works

(The following list of general references could have been extended indefinitely, but to lengthen it unduly would be but a parade of vanity. Many of them contain bibliographies which supplied titles to the foregoing sections, and many are the sources of the notes appended to various items. No doubt the catalogue of local and county historical and archaeological societies is much larger than the sum total cited here. But some of these are defunct and others are so scarce and so restricted in their run that to locate and identify them with the proper bibliographical data would call for a long extension of life's term. A complete set of such publications housed and catalogued in some given library is greatly to be desired, but its realization is far from probable. The more important sets, however, are readily accessible. Where I have no knowledge to the contrary, I have indicated by a dash following the date of initial publication my supposition that the society is still active. Here again, owing to the lack of centralized information, my inferences are subject to correction. The section GENERAL REFERENCES in vol. II of this work will furnish additional mention of secondary sources.)

Abbotsford Club. Publications. Edinburgh, 1833-1865.

This club was founded in Edinburgh in 1833 for the "printing of miscellaneous pieces, illustrative of history, literature, and antiquities." Its secretary announced in 1866 that it had "reached its termination."—Terry, *A Catalogue of Scottish Historical and Kindred Clubs.*

ABELL, F. Prisoners of War in Great Britain, 1756-1815; A Record of their Lives, their Romance and their Sufferings. 8vo. Oxford, 1914.

ABRAHAM, J. J. Lettsom, his Life, Times, Friends and Descendants. 145 plates and illustrations. 4to. London, 1933.

This is a study of medical and social life in the London of the Third George, woven round the central figure of John Coakley Lettsom, the celebrated Quaker physician, philanthropist, and man of letters, who died in the year of Waterloo.—Bookseller's Note.

ADAMS, ELEANOR N. Old English Scholarship in England, 1566-1800. New Haven, 1917.

This acquaints one with the band of "Saxonists" who pioneered in the study of Old English. The work was utilized in the present volume for elucidating biographical and literary facts relative to antiquaries.

ADY, CELIA MARY. Aeneas Sylvius Piccolomini. London, 1913.

AIKIN, JOHN, M.D. A View of the Life, Travels and Philanthropic Labours of the Late John Howard, Esq., LL.D., F.R.S. 12mo. London, 1794.

This is a short memoir by a friend and literary executor of this great prison reformer, who "Has been the happy instrument of preserving female prisoners from an infamous and indecent outrage."

AITLEN, G. A. (Editor). Later Stuart Tracts. 8vo. London, 1903.

ALDIN, CECIL. Romance of the Road. Numerous plates and a large map of the London mail-coach roads in color, and many illustrations in black and white. 4to. London, 1933.

Mr. Aldin has taken each of the famous mail-coach roads radiating from London—the Great North, the Great West, etc., and has described them both in word and in picture. Of particular interest are the diagrammatical maps and charming drawings by the author-artist.—Bookseller's Note.

ALEXANDER, WILLIAM. Notes and Sketches illustrative of Northern Rural Life in the Eighteenth Century. 12mo. London, 1877.

ALLARDYCE, A. Scotland and Scotsmen in the Eighteenth Century, from the MSS. of John Ramsay of Ochtertyre. 2 vols. 8vo. Edinburgh and London, 1888.

ALLEN, R. J. The Clubs of Augustan London. Cambridge (Mass.), 1933.

AMHERST, HON. ALICIA. A History of Gardening in England. Numerous illustrations. London, 1896.

> This is an excellent story of landscape and domestic gardening in England, from the earliest times down to the present. Quotations are plenteous and documentation thorough. The surveys of Wimbledon and Theobalds by order of Parliament are transcribed from the MS in the Record Office. A very full bibliography of books on gardening, agriculture, and natural history is included. This work was freely drawn upon for obtaining titles and for checking publication data.

ANDERSON, R. M. C. The Roads of England, Being a Review of the Roads, of Travellers and Traffic in England from the Days of the ancient Trackways to the modern Motoring Era. London, 1932.

ANDREWS, MICHAEL CORBETT. The British Isles in the Nautical Charts of the XIVth and XVth Centuries. In *Geog. Journal,* vol. 68. London, 1926.

Anglesey Antiquarian Society and Field Club. Transactions. Llangefni, 1913—.

Annals of Archaeology and Anthropology, issued by the Institute of Archaeology, University of Liverpool, edit. by J. L. Myres and others. Vols. 1-6 in 3. 4to. Liverpool, 1908-14.

Annual Hampshire Repository, or Historical, Economical and Literary Miscellany. Colored folding flower plate and 2 engraved plates. Vol. 1 (all published). London(?), 1799.

Annual Register (founded and edited by Burke). London, 1758-1862; n. s. 1863-1919; 1920—.

> This periodical reviewed books, but since it was an annual production it could not give space to many books. In its critical method it followed the usual pattern of 18th century reviews, being generally more commendatory than critical and depending generously upon quotations to take the place of comment. An index for the years 1758-1819 appeared in 1819.

ANSTEY, REV. H. (Editor). Munimenta Academica, or, Documents illustrative of Academical Life and Studies at Oxford. 2 vols. London(?), 1868.

Antiquaries Journal, being the Journal of the Society of Antiquaries of London. Lavishly illustrated with photographs, plans, etc. 8vo. London, 1921—.

> This Journal is a continuation of the *Proceedings* of the Society. See Society of Antiquaries of London below.

The Antiquary: A Magazine devoted to the Study of the Past. Edit. by E. Walford, with contributions by Gomme, Lambert, Andrews, Wright and others. Numerous maps, plans, illustrations, facsimiles, etc. 51 vols. 4to. London, 1880-1915.

Antiquity: A Quarterly Review of Archaeology. Edit. by O. G. S. Crawford. Illustrated. London, 1927—.

The subjects discussed range from prehistoric agriculture in Britain, place names, archaeology to Spengler and historical cycles.

Archaeologia: or, Miscellaneous Tracts relating to Antiquity, published by the Society of Antiquaries of London. 4to. London, 1770—.

By 1937 84 volumes had been published, profusely illustrated with engravings. An Index to the first fifty volumes has also been printed. This is one of the most important archaeological journals with a roll of distinguished contributors from its beginning down to the present that can scarce be paralleled anywhere.

Archaeologia Aeliana: Publication of the Society of Antiquaries of Newcastle-upon-Tyne. 63 vols. (by 1935). Illustrated. Newcastle, 1822—.

This series contains much rare information on Roman antiquities, including the Roman Wall, prehistoric and pre-Conquest remains, religious houses, biography, genealogy, family history, heraldry, and the like.

Archaeologia Cambrensis: the Journal of the Cambrian Archaeological Association. 8vo. London, 1846—.

This journal records the antiquities of Wales and the Marches. The successive volumes are grouped into a number of series, and an Index to the first five has been issued in two volumes. In addition extra volumes have been printed.

Archaeologia Cantiana: Transactions of the Kent Archaeological Society. Numerous illustrations in color and on wood, maps, etc. 8vo. London, 1858—.

Few counties are richer in archaeological remains than Kent, which has registered in various forms the passage of men from the continent to England from the remotest times. Among its contributors are men honored in history, folklore, architecture, and antiquities.

Archaeologia Scotica: or, Transactions of the Society of Antiquaries of Scotland. 5 vols. With W. Smellie's Account of the Institution and Progress of the Society, 6 vols. 4to. Edinburgh, 1792-1890-1900. See Society of Antiquaries of Scotland below.

Archaeological and Historical Collections relating to the County of Renfrew: Parish of Lochwinnoch, Charters, Documents, Sculptured Stones, etc. Illustrated. 2 vols. 4to. Renfrew, 1885.

Archaeological Journal of the British Archaeological Association for the Encouragement of Researches into the Arts and Monuments of the Early and Middle Ages. Numerous illustrations. 8vo. London, 1845—.

Archaeological Magazine of Bristol, Bath, South-Wales and the South-Western Counties. Edit. by T. H. Sealy. Illustrated. 8vo. Bristol, 1843—.

Architectural, Archaeological and Historic Society of Chester and North Wales. Journal. Chester, 1857—.

For the years 1887-97 it was called Journal of the Chester Archaeological and Historic Society; now it is the Journal of the Architectural and Historic Society of Chester and North Wales.

Architectural and Archaeological Society for the County of Buckingham. Records of Buckingham. Aylesbury, 1858—.

Architectural and Archaeological Society of Durham and Northumberland. Transactions. Sunderland, 1870—.

Ascoli, Georges. La Grande-Bretagne devant L'Opinion Française. 2 vols. Paris.

See Livre II, ch. i-vi, for generalized accounts of French travelers to England—their experiences, the inns, London and its sights, the universities, physical appearance of Englishmen, habits, government, religion, the countryside, etc. The period is limited to the 17th century.

Ashmole, Elias, and William Lilly. The Lives of . . . written by Themselves. . . . Lilly's Life and Death of Charles the First . . . With Several Occasional Letters, By Charles Burman. 8vo. London, 1774.

Ashton, John. Social Life in the Reign of Queen Anne. London, 1883.

This household volume of the social life in Queen Anne's day contains many references to contemporary descriptions and accounts of England and London, with now and then liberal excerpts from these sources.

Atkinson, D. H. Ralph Thoresby the Topographer; His Town and Times. 2 vols. 8vo. Leeds, 1885.

These volumes draw freely on Thoresby's diary and letters, interpreted by editorial comments. The work will enlarge the reader's acquaintance with the worthies of the early 18th and late 17th centuries.

Aubin, Robert Arnold. Topographical Poetry in the Eighteenth Century (1640-1840). New York, 1936.

This survey of the poetry of places, hills, seats, towns, sea, etc., seems to have been done so thoroughly that it may well serve as a standard work of reference. It must have cost the author much dreary reading. It includes copious notes referring to sources and a very full bibliography of poems arranged according to the classification adopted. Apparently the popularity of topographical poetry allowed few spots of English ground to escape being commemorated in verse.

Aubrey, John. Brief Lives, chiefly of Contemporaries, set down by John Aubrey, between the Years 1669 and 1695. Edit. from the Author's MSS. by Andrew Clark. With Facsimiles, frontispieces. 2 vols. 8vo. Oxford, 1898.

Aungervyle Society. Publications. Edinburgh, 1881-88.

This society was founded in Edinburgh in 1881 for "the reprint of rare or curious pamphlets, tracts, articles, etc., interesting from either a literary, historical, or antiquarian point of view." —Terry, *op. cit.*

Aurner, Nellie Slayton. Caxton Mirrour of Fifteenth Century Letters. A Study of the Literature of the First English Press. Boston and New York, 1926.

Ayrshire and Galloway Archaeological Association. Archaeological and Historical Collections relating to Ayrshire and Galloway. Edinburgh, 1878-94.

This society was founded in Ayr in 1877 as the Ayrshire and Wigtonshire Archaeological Association "to preserve some record of the various prehistoric and medieval remains of antiquity in Ayrshire and Wigtonshire . . . and other matter relating to the history and topography of the counties, which would be of great interest and value to print." Its name was changed in 1885 to that recorded above, and it ceased to exist in 1897.—Terry.

BADDAM, BENJAMIN (Printer). Memoirs of the Royal Society, being a new Abridgement of the Philosophical Transactions, giving an Account of the Undertakings, Studies, and Labours of the learned and ingenious in many considerable Parts of the World, from the first Institution of that illustrious Society in the Year 1665, under their Royal Founder King Charles II. to the Year 1735 inclusive. Disposed under general Heads, with a Translation of the Latin Tracts from their Originals: the whole regularly abridged, the Order of Time observed, the theoretical Parts applied to practical Uses, and an Explanation of the Terms of Art as they occur in the Course of the Work: being a Work of general Use to the Public, and worthy the Perusal of all Mathematicians, Artificers, Tradesmen, etc., for their Improvement in various Branches of Business. Illustrated with copper plates. 8 vols. 8vo. London, 1738.

BAIN, MARGARET I. Les Voyageurs Français en Ecosse 1770-1830, et Leurs Curiosités Intellectuelles. Bibliothèque de la Revue de Littérature Comparé. Tome 79. Paris, 1931.

BALE, JOHN. Anecdota Oxoniensia. Index Britanniae Scriptorum quos ex variis Biblithecis non parvo labore collegit Ionnes Baleus, cum aliis. . . . Edit. by Reginald Lane Poole, with the Help of Mary Bateson. 4to. Oxford, 1902.

BALLANTYRE, ARCHIBALD. Voltaire's Visit to England 1726-1729. London, 1919.

This quotes largely from his letters, some of which have not appeared in any of Voltaire's works. The extracts are connected by a running commentary which serves to round out the figure of the man, his relations with Englishmen of letters, and his movements.

BALLARD, A. The Domesday Inquest. Illustrations. Antiquary's Books Series. London, 1906.

BALLINGALL, G. W. Historical Collections regarding the Royal Burgh and the Parish of Kinghorn. Kirkaldy, 1893.

Banffshire Field Club. Publications. 12mo. Banff, 1880—.

This club was founded in Banff in 1880 "for the purpose of promoting scientific study and investigation generally, and especially for the exploration of the district with reference to certain natural sciences, archaeology, etc."—Terry.

Bannatyne Club. Publications. 4to (usually). Edinburgh, 1823-61.

Founded in Edinburgh in 1825 for the "printing and publication of works illustrative of the history, literature, and antiquities of Scotland."—Terry. It was dissolved in 1861 but not before it had rescued from hiding places many valuable antiquarian and historical documents. For the *Miscellany* see following.

Bannatyne Miscellany. Vol. I edit. by Scott; vols. II and III by David Laing. Edinburgh, 1827-55.

Here are printed various documents from the 16th century.

BARBEAU, A. Une ville d'eaux anglaise au XVIIIe siècle. La société élégante et lit-téraire à Bath sous la Reine Anne et sous les Georges. London (?), 1904.

> An English title is to be noted below:
> BARBEAU, A. Life and Letters at Bath in the 18th Century, with a preface by Austin Dobson. Edition de luxe, limited to 100 copies, illustrated. 8vo. London, 1904.

BARTHOLOMEW, JOHN GEORGE. The Survey Atlas of England and Wales. Part VII. The Cartography of England and Wales from the earliest Time to the present Date. Fol. Edinburgh, 1903.

> Another edit, Edinburgh, 1939.

BASCHET, —. La diplomatie vénétienne. (Cited by Rye, *England as Seen by Foreigners,* 266.)

> Evidently the work contains something about Venetian Relations sent from England to Venice. Among them seems to be the Report of Giovanni Micheli, ambassador in England during the reign of Queen Mary, which was presented to the Senate on the ambassador's return in 1557. Of this there is an abridged translation by Sir Henry Ellis, published in his *Original Letters Illustrative of English History,* 2nd ser., vol. 2, 1827 (see Ellis under 1824-46, LETTERS, DIARIES, MEMOIRS).

BASTIDE, CHARLES. Anglais et Français du XVIIe siècle. 8vo. Paris, 1912.

> Trans. into English, New York, 1914. See below.
> (In English.) The Anglo-French Entente in the Seventeenth Century. New York, 1914.

BATES, E. S. Touring in 1600: A Study in the Development of Travel as a Means of Education. Illustrations from contemporary sources. 8vo. Boston, 1911.

> Though this interesting, lively account deals largely with travel abroad, it contains much that is pertinent to travel at home. A bibliography of travel accounts is included.

Bath Natural History and Antiquarian Field Club. Proceedings. Bath, 1867—.

Bath and West of England Agricultural Society for the Encouragement of Agriculture, Arts, Manufactures, and Commerce. 14 vols. London, 1780-1816; 1853—.

> These volumes include publications on all phases of husbandry.

BAYNE-POWELL, ROSAMUND. Eighteenth Century London Life. 14 illustrations from contemporary sources. 8vo. London, 1937.

—————. English Country Life in the Eighteenth Century. Illustrations. London, 1933.

> These two volumes make very interesting reading and bring to light, especially the latter volume, many curious facts concerning everyday life of the times.

BEALES, H. L. Travel and Communications. In Turberville's *Johnson's England,* vol. I, 125-59. Oxford, 1933.

BEATTY, J. M., and J. R. The English Lake District before Wordsworth. In *South Atlantic Quarterly,* vol. 22, 331-44. Durham, N.C., 1923.

BECKMANN, J. Literatur der älteren Reisebeschreibungen. 2 vols. Göttingen, 1809.

Here are listed as many as nineteen different works on the art of traveling published in Germany in the last half of the 16th and beginning of the 17th centuries. These are all written in Latin, and their popularity among German and other travelers is shown by their repeated printings.—Quoted.

Bedfordshire Notes and Queries. 3 vols. Bedford, 1886-93.

BELLOC, HILAIRE. The Highway and its Vehicles. Edit. by Geoffrey Holme. 100 full-page plates, including 24 in color. In *The Studio*. London, 1926.

BENNETT, H. S. Life on the English Manor. A Study of Peasant Conditions, 1150-1400. 6 plates and 4 woodcuts in text. Cambridge, 1937.

This presents a convincing picture of the common lot of the working man during the 12th, 13th, and 14th centuries, composed from many contemporary documents.

BERESFORD, JOHN (Editor). Mr. Du Quesne and Other Essays. 6 illustrations. 8vo. Oxford, 1932.

Readers of Parson Woodforde's Diary will have already met this good neighbor of the Parson. Besides widening one's acquaintance with a man well worth knowing intimately, a descendant of the famous French Admiral, the essay reveals much of interest in Norfolk country life.—From Announcement of the work.

Berkshire Archaeological and Architectural Society. Journal. Reading, 1889—.

Later this became the *Berkshire Archaeological Journal;* and from 1895 on, the *Berkshire, Buckinghamshire, and Oxfordshire Journal.*

Berkshire Notes and Queries. Vol. I, pts. 1-3. London, 1890-91. (Defunct.)

BERNOULLI, JOHANN. Sammlung kurzer Reisebeschreibungen. 16 vols. Berlin, 1781-85.

BESANT, WALTER. A Survey of London. 10 vols. London, 1902-12.

In addition to this well-known and massive survey, Besant published other works on various districts of the metropolis, such as: Westminster, 1895; South London, 1899; East London, 1901.

Bibliographical Society. Papers. A complete set from the beginning to 1937 numbered 30 vols. 4to. London, 1892—.

This is one of the foremost societies devoted to bibliographical activity. An index of its papers and of those issued by the Library Association was published by G. W. Cole, covering the years 1877-1932.

Bibliotheca Gloucestrensis: A Collection of Scarce and Curious Tracts, relating to the County and City of Gloucester; Illustrative of and Published during the Civil War. Edit. by J. Washbourne. 4to. Gloucester, 1823.

The three parts were published in one volume in 1825.

Birmingham and Midland Institute. Archaeological Section, Transactions. Midland Record Society. Transactions. 6 vols. Birmingham, 1897-1902.

BLADES, WILLIAM. Life and Typography of William Caxton. London, 1861-63.

2nd edit., with title of *Biography and Typography of William Caxton,* London, 1882.

BLEW, WILLIAM C. A. Brighton and its Coaches: A History of the London and Brighton Road, with some Account of the Provincial Coaches that have run from Brighton. 20 illustrations from original water color drawings by J. and G. Temple. 8vo. London, 1894.

BLOMFIELD, REGINALD. The Formal Garden in England. Illustrations by F. Inigo Thomas. 8vo. London, 1901.

> This contains a bibliography of early works on the formal garden. Blomfield here puts up a noble defense of the formal garden against the attacks from the proponents of the "natural garden," which quite inclines one to fall in with his views.

————. A History of Renaissance Architecture in England, 1500-1800. 2 vols. 8vo. London, 1897.

> An abridgment of this was published under the title of *A Short History*, etc., London, 1900.

BOARDMAN, JAMES. Liverpool Table Talk a Hundred Years Ago, or A History of Gore's Directory, with Anecdotes illustrative of the Period of its first Publication in 1766, in a Letter to the Members of the Historic Society of Lancashire and Cheshire. To which is added, A Continuation of the same Subject and a Map of the Town in 1650. 12mo. Liverpool, 1871.

> The first edition of this came out in pamphlet form in 1856. For Gore's *Directory of Liverpool*, see Gore under 1766, AIDS TO TRAVELERS.

BOASE, G. C. Collectanea Cornubiensia: A Collection of Biographical and Topographical Notes relating to Cornwall. Truro, 1890.

Book of the Old Edinburgh Club. Complete set from the Commencement, 1909 to 1938, 22 vols. Edinburgh(?), 1909-38.

> This contains contributions on all aspects of Old Edinburgh life, buildings, trade, etc., by Geddie, W. Cowan, Moir Bryce, Hannay, Boog Watson, and others, with many illustrations and maps.—Bookseller's Note.

BOSANQUET, R. C. John Horsley and his Times. In *Archaeologia Aeliana*, 4th ser., vol. 10. Society of Antiquaries of Newcastle-upon Tyne. Newcastle, 1933.

> This essay discloses to the modern reader the world of learning among the gentry and ministry of the North of England in the 18th century, and the changes in agriculture, sentiment, and outside contacts. See Horsley under Sir George MacDonald below.

BOULTING, WILLIAM. Giordano Bruno. His Life, Thought, and Martyrdom. 8vo. London, 1914.

> Chapter VIII deals with his visit to Oxford; IX with his stay in England; X with his impressions of Elizabethan England.

BOULTON, W. B. The Amusements of Old London. Being a Survey of the Sports and Pastimes, Tea Gardens, Parks, Playhouses, etc., of the People of London, from the Seventeenth to the Nineteenth Century. 12 full-page colored plates. 2 vols. 4to. London, 1901.

BOYNTON, PERCY H. London in English Literature. Chicago, 1913.

> This sketches the London of Chaucer, Shakespeare, Milton, Dryden, Addison, Johnson, Lamb and Byron, Dickens; and Victorian and contemporary London.

Bradford Historical and Antiquarian Society. The Antiquary. Bradford, 1881—.

BRETT-JAMES, NORMAN G. The Growth of Stuart London. With a Foreword by Sir Charles H. Collett, Bart., Lord Mayor of London in 1933-34. London, 1935.

London's growth is here treated from many viewpoints: trade, court, prosperity, foreigners, plague, fire and war, direction of growth westward and eastward, with maps drawn by the author, showing London as a whole in 1603, 1660, 1702. What would be incomprehensible to the modern Chamber of Commerce were the attempts made by the guilds and livery companies to check the city's expansion. A bibliography is included.

Bristol and Gloucestershire Archaeological Society. Transactions. 61 vols., with additional volumes, 69. 8vo. Gloucester, 1876—.

Among the additional volumes is one by T. H. Chubb, *Descriptive Catalogue of the Printed Maps of Gloucestershire, 1577-1911*, 1912. General Indexes to vols. of 1876-1917 appeared in 3 vols.

British Archaeological Association for the Encouragement and Prosecution of Researches into the Arts and Monuments of the Early and Middle Ages. Journal. (A complete set from its beginning in 1843 to 1917, with General Indexes to 1896.) Numerous plates. 77 vols. 8vo. London, 1846-1917.

BROOKE, RICHARD, F.S.A. Liverpool as it was during the last Quarter of the Eighteenth Century, 1755 to 1800. 8vo. Liverpool, 1853.

BROWN, HUME. Early Travellers in Scotland. Edit. by Hume Brown. 8vo. Edinburgh, 1891.

This is an extremely valuable and interesting source book. The travelers selected range from Edward I (1295) to Thomas Morer (1689). The editor points out the usefulness of these accounts in bringing before us a consciously emerging nationality. Even to the close of the 17th century, Scotland was still a kind of *terra incognita*, which men thought of as a half mythical country, where strange things existed which it would not be logical to look for elsewhere. The remoteness of the country from the main traveled routes and the tall tales of the early Scottish chroniclers, particularly those of Boece, whose history served Europe as a guide book, were responsible for the existence and persistence of the wildest legends which would scarcely be acceptable even in that period except for the fact that they were told of Scotland. Down to 1700 many notable European visitors found their way to Scotland, but few of them made any personal observations. The much traveled Georg von Ehingen, who was so royally treated, left hardly a dozen lines on his visit; the poet Ronsard who accompanied James V on his return from France; the charlatan genius Cardan who went thither to minister medically to Archbishop John Hamilton in 1552; the courtly Brantôme, who came in the train of Mary Queen of Scots and who wrote her life — all these have nothing to say of the country; the younger Scaliger who paid a flying visit in 1566 makes only a few casual remarks; the most famous poet of the day, Du Bartas, the idol of James VI, is remembered for his visit by a passage in James Melville's *Diary*; and what would one not give to have a record from Ben Jonson himself of what he saw and thought. English visitors from the 17th century on were more willing to commemorate their travels and impressions.—Summarized from Brown's Introduction. In various foregoing sections the accounts of the travelers recorded by Brown are listed with appropriate notes.

————. Scotland before 1700 from Contemporary Documents. Edit. by Hume Brown. 2 maps. 8vo. Edinburgh, 1893.

The individual selections are mainly extracts from larger descriptions culled from an ample variety of sources, and are generously documented with notes identifying places in their modern nomenclature. Each of these selections is separately listed in the foregoing sections accompanied with notes drawn mainly from the editor. The Introduction summarizes the progress made by Scotland during the period delimited, showing how much better off the Scotch peasant was than the French, and how solicitous the authorities were becoming over the morals and well being of the populace. This volume forms a sequence to the preceding. The unflattering account generally mouthed by the travelers there listed is somewhat offset by the records and descriptions printed in the present volume, which suggest that Scotland was enjoying a comparatively appreciable degree of prosperity and comfort.

—————. Scotland in the Time of Queen Mary: Town and Country Life, Trade, etc. 8vo. Edinburgh, 1904.

BROWN, RAWDON (Editor). Calendar of State Papers relating to English Affairs, existing in the Archives and Collections of Venice, and other Libraries of Northern Italy. Vol. III, edit. by Rawdon Brown. 8vo. London, 1869.

Buckinghamshire Miscellany: A Series of Concise and Interesting Articles illustrative of the History, Topography and Archaeology of the County of Bucks. Edit. by R. Gibbs. 4to. Aylesbury, 1891.

Buckinghamshire, Records of: Papers and Notes on the History, Antiquities and Architecture of the County. Illustrations. 10 vols. Aylesbury, 1858-1910.

Bury and West Suffolk Archaeological Institute. Proceedings. Ipswich (for vol. 1). See Suffolk Institute of Archaeology and Natural History.

BUTLER, REV. D. George Fox in Scotland. Edinburgh, 1913.

Bygones relating to Wales and the Border Counties. Oswesley, 1871—. Index to vols. 1-8, 1871-85. Brierley, 1887.

Caermarthenshire Notes and Miscellany for Southwest Wales. 3 vols. Llanelly, 1889-91.

> The name was changed in 1892 to *Caermarthenshire Miscellany and Notes and Queries for South Wales*. Only one volume was published.

Cambrian Institute. The Cambrian Journal. 11 vols. London, 1854-64.

Cambridge Antiquarian Society. Publications (Quarto Series). Nos. 1-15. Cambridge, 1840-59.

> The New Series, Nos. 1-54 (in both octavo and quarto) run from 1851 to 1939. An Index appeared in 1898. The contributions came from the pens of the best known Cambridge antiquaries of the time.

Cambridge and Huntingdon Archaeological Society. Transactions. Ely, 1904—.

Camden Society. Publications. 4to. London, 1838-19—.

> From 1898 on this series of publications has been edited for the Royal Historical Society. Through it have been made accessible to the public many valuable works on the civil, ecclesiastical, and literary history of Great Britain.

CAMERON, J. W. Maps and Map-Work. London, 1932.

CAMPBELL, DUNCAN. Giraldus Cambrensis. In *Trans. Gaelic Soc. of Inverness,* vol. 20. Inverness, 1897.

> This offers an analysis of Giraldus' life, his *Topography of Ireland* and his *Itinerary,* his character, the reliability of his remarks, etc.

Cambridge History of English Literature. Edited by A. W. Ward and A. R. Waller. 14 vols. New York, 1907-1917.

See vol. III, ch. 15, for accounts of antiquaries. The bibliographies supplied in these volumes have been superseded by the *Cambridge Bibliography* (see under BIBLIOGRAPHIES).

Cardiganshire Antiquarian and Archaeological Record. Transactions. Aberystwyth, 1909—.

Carmarthenshire Antiquarian Society and Field Club. Transactions. Carmarthen, 1905—.

CARTERET, J. GRAND. La Montagne à travers les âges. 2 vols. 4to. Grenoble.

This concerns the interest in mountain scenery during the 18th century and the Romantic Period.

CHAMBERS, ROBERT. Domestic Annals of Scotland from the Reformation to the Revolution (vols. I-II); Domestic Annals to the Rebellion of 1745 (vol. III). 3rd edit., 3 vols. Edinburgh and London, 1874. (See Chambers under 1858, HISTORY AND CHRONICLES.)

CHANCELLOR, E. BERESFORD. The Eighteenth Century in London. An Account of its Social Life and Arts. Numerous illustrations. 4to. London, 1920.

Other surveys of London by Chancellor are listed below.
History of London Squares, 1907.
Knightsbridge and Belgravia, 1909.
Annals of Fleet Street, 1912.
Annals of the Strand, 1912.
Annals of St. James' Street, 1922.
Pleasure Haunts of London During Four Centuries, 1925.
The West End of Yesterday and Today, 1926.
Wanderings in Marylebone, 1926.
London's Latin Quarter, 1930.
The Romance of Soho, 1931.

Chetham Society. Remains Historical and Literary, connected with the Palatine Counties of Lancashire and Cheshire. 4to. Manchester, 1840—.

The publications of this society are very important for local histories, wills, inventories, biographies, bibliographies, family histories, and reprints of rare works, historical and topographical.

CHOPE, E. PEARSE (Editor). Early Tours in Devon and Cornwall. Illustrations and Notes. 8vo. Exeter, 1918.

This contains excerpts from eleven tours, beginning with John Leland and coming down to Espriella (Southey) in 1802. The notes deal with place identifications, genealogies, and family histories.

COATS, R. H. Travellers' Tales of Scotland: Ben Jonson, Defoe, Goldsmith, Johnson, etc. London, 1913.

CODRINGTON, THOMAS. Early Britain: Roman Roads in Britain. Chart in pocket. 12mo. London, 1905.

COLE, G. D. H. Persons and Periods. London, 1938.

> See chapters: Defoe's England; Town Life in the Eighteenth Century; London—One-Fifth of England; Roads, Rivers, and Canals.

COLE, G. D. H., and RAYMOND POSTGATE. The British Common People, 1746-1938. 8vo. New York, 1939.

> See chapters II and III: A Journey Through England in 1746; and IV: Eighteenth Century London.

COLLIER, JEREMY. Historical Dictionary of England and Wales, in Three Parts. A Geographical Dictionary; a Dictionary of most Memorable Persons; a Political Dictionary of the Government of England. Engraved map. 12mo. London, 1692.

> 2nd edit., revised to 1688, 2 vols., 1701; a Supplement together with a Continuation, 1705; Appendix, 1721.

COLVIN, IAN D. The Germans in England, 1066-1598. With a map of the Hanseatic League. 8vo. London, 1915.

COOPER, WILLIAM DURANT, F.S.A. Lists of the Foreign Protestants, and Aliens resident in England, 1618-1688. From the Returns in the State Paper Office. *Publ. Camden Soc.,* vol. 82. London, 1862.

> The influx of refugees into England from France and Holland to escape persecutions disturbed the vested interests of the trades at home, and complaints were made, especially by the London companies, that the foreigners profited unduly by escaping certain duties and customs, that they devised many trades unknown before, used up the available places of residence, engrossed the French and Dutch trade, lived more cheaply, sold more cheaply, etc. Commissions were appointed from time to time to investigate and make returns of foreigners, where they came from, where they lived, etc. The returns of 1621 did not help the complainants much and they renewed their charges. Proposals were made for yearly censuses in July, 1621. The returns of March, 1621, and of April and June, 1622, are the ones printed here.—From the Introduction.

COULTON, G. G. Froissart Chronicler of European Chivalry: Froissart and his Times. 8 colored reproductions of miniatures and many smaller illustrations. 4to. London, 1931.

————. Life in the Middle Ages. 4 vols. Cambridge, 1928-30.

> The original edition was published in 1 vol., 1910. This is a source book of selections drawn from six different languages, with a few from MSS. Its subjects comprise religion, folklore, superstitions, chronicles, science and art, men and manners, monks, friars, and nuns.

————. Scottish Abbeys and Social Life: Monk and Peasant, Housekeeping, Revenues, Rules, etc. 8vo. London, 1933.

————. Social Life in Great Britain from the Conquest to the Reformation. Cambridge, 1919.

> This is a compilation of a rare assemblage of extracts (all translated) from all sorts of works belonging to medieval times. Of special interest to this present volume are the sections offering extracts on Wayfaring and Foreign Travel.

County Histories of Scotland. 7 vols. (all published). Numerous folding maps, bibliographies, and indices. 8vo. Edinburgh, 1896-1900.

> This set contains: Munro, Prehistoric Scotland; Mackay, Fife and Kinross; Maxwell, Dumfries and Galloway; Rampini, Moray and Nairn; Douglas, Roxburghe, Selkirk, and Peebles; Watts, Aberdeen and Banff.

COURTOIS, L. J. Le séjour de Jean-Jacques Rousseau en Angleterre (1766-67). Lettres et documents inédits. With a genealogical table. 8vo. Lausanne, 1911.

COUTTS, J. A History of the University of Glasgow from its Foundation in 1451 to 1909. Portraits. 4to. Glasgow, 1909.

COX, J. C., and A. HARVEY. English Church Furniture. Illustrations. In Antiquary's Book Series. 8vo. London, 1907.

CRAIK, SIR HENRY. A Century of Scottish History from the Days before the '45, to those within living Memory. 2 vols. 8vo. London, 1901.

This contains an interesting comparison between Johnson and Pennant as travelers in Scotland.

CROSS, W. R. Dutch Cartographers of the Seventeenth Century. In *Geographical Review*, vol. 5, 66-70. London, 1918.

Cumberland and Westmoreland Antiquarian and Archaeological Society. Transactions. Vols. 1-16, 1874-1900; new ser., beginning 1901, with volume published annually. Kendal, 1874—.

CUMING, E. D. Coaching Days and Ways. Illustrations by G. D. Armour. 8vo. London, n.d.

CUST, MRS. HENRY. Gentlemen Errant. Being the Journeys and Adventures of Four Noblemen in Europe during the Fifteenth and Sixteenth Centuries. London, 1909.

These narratives concern the adventures and "wanderings" of Lev, Lord of Rozmital and Blatna; the "exploits and hazards" of Wilwolt of Schaumburg; the "Early Life and Vicissitudes" of Frederick II, Elector Palatine of the Rhine; and the "Curious Fortunes" of Hans von Schweinichen at the Court of Duke Heinrich XI of Liegnitz in Silesia. The original narratives are here rewritten with an unflagging verve, with many quotations from their sources. Illustrative historical notes and a bibliography are included. These narratives will be found entered in their proper places in the section TOURS BY FOREIGNERS.

Cymmrodorion Society. Y Cymmrodor. London, 1877—. Transactions. London, 1892. Cymmrodorion Record Series. London, 1892—.

An Index to these publications down to 1912, by G. O. Williams, appeared in the Transactions, session 1911-12, as a supplement. 44 vols. (by 1935).

DANIELS, W. M. Saint-Evremond et l'Angleterre. Versailles, 1907.

DARBY, H. C. The Draining of the Fens. Appendices, Bibliography of Sources of Records, Books, and Pamphlets, and Maps and Illustrations. Cambridge, 1940.

This book takes up the story, from the 16th century down to the present, of the difficulties attending the various attempts at draining the Fens. In addition to the natural obstacles—the outfalls, embankments, drains, sluices, tidal silting, land floods, inundations, river beds getting raised to a level higher than the bordering country—further complications arose from changes in the commissions appointed, from the conflicting interests of fenmen, proprietors, farmers, fishermen, from the fear voiced by towns of losing their navigable highway and thereby their prosperity. From the Crown down to the humblest fenman, fisherman, or poacher, the condition of the Fens was of the utmost importance, a matter of wealth or beggary.

————————, (Editor). Historical Geography of England down to 1800. London, 1936.

> This consists of fourteen essays of collective authorship which view the changing history of England as conditioned by geography and geology. Among the contributors are some of the foremost names in these sciences.

DARK, SIDNEY. London Town. New York, n.d.

> This is a popular, readable sketch of the chief landmarks of London, past and present. It is somewhat marred, however, by some needless errors of fact.

DARWIN, BERNARD. John Gully and His Times. 4 plates from contemporary sources. London, 1935.

> Roistering times they were through which John Gully passed from the inn near Bristol via the prize ring and the turf, to his country mansion and a seat in Parliament. John Gully was an outstanding figure among his contemporaries, many of whom have almost become legendary for their prowess in the prize ring and on the race course, as gamblers and participators in fantastic wagers. Here are queer stories of Newmarket and Doncaster, of fighters, of owners and the hangers-on of the turf; of fortunes won—and lost—by the "sportsmen" of two hundred years ago.—Bookseller's Note.

DAVIES, MYLES. Athenae Britannicae, or a Critical History of the Oxford and Cambridge Writers and Writings. London, 1715.

> This bibliographer became a priest in 1688 and worked as a missioner in Worcestershire and nearby counties. He recanted in 1705. He hawked about his works in person.—DNB.

DAVIES, RANDALL. English Society of the Eighteenth Century in Contemporary Art. 4 colored illustrations and 33 monochromes. London, 1907.

Derbyshire Archaeological and Natural History Society. Journal, 47 vols. (by 1926). London, 1878—.

Devon Notes and Queries: A Quarterly Journal devoted to the Local History, Biography, and Antiquities of the County of Devon and Cornwall. Edit. by P. F. S. and J. S. Amery, J. B. Rowe, and later by H. R. Watkins and T. P. Chope. Numerous illustrations. Vols. 1-16 and 15 supplemental vols. (by 1931). Exeter, 1900—.

DIBDIN, REV. THOMAS B. A Bibliographical, Antiquarian and Picturesque Tour in the Northern Counties of England and Scotland. 42 plates of portraits, views, facsimiles, etc., and numerous illustrations in the text. 8vo. London, 1838.

————————. Typographical Antiquities; or, the History of Printing in England, Scotland and Ireland; containing Memoirs of our Ancient Printers, and a Register of the Books printed by them. Begun by Joseph Ames, considerably augmented by William Herbert, and now greatly enlarged with copious Notes and Illustrated with appropriate Engravings; Comprehending the History of English Literature, and a View of the Progress of the Art of Engraving, in Great Britain. With Full-Page Engraved Portraits and Many Facsimiles of Titles, Pages, Printers' devices, and Engravings. 4 vols. 4to. London, 1810-1819.

> This work is well known as a landmark in the history of English typography.

DOBSON, AUSTIN. A Day at Strawberry Hill. In *Eighteenth Century Vignettes,* vol. I, 151 ff. Oxford Classics Edition. London. 1906.

> By describing how one would spend the day here, Dobson reveals what made Strawberry Hill the pilgrimage of curious visitors.

Documents relative to the Reception at Edinburgh of the Kings and Queens of Scotland, 1561-1650. Edinburgh, 1832.

> These selections illustrate the ceremonies and official duties printed *in extenso* from the register of the Privy Council and the records of Edinburgh.—Read, *A Bibliography of British History, Tudor Period.*

DONALDSON, JOHN. Agricultural Biography: containing a Notice of the Life and Writings of the British Authors on Agriculture, from the Earliest Date in 1480 to the Present Time. London (?), 1854.

DORAN, DR. London in the Jacobite Times: Spies, Trials, etc. 2 vols. 8vo. London, 1877.

Dorset Natural History and Antiquarian Field Club. Proceedings. Sherborne, 1877—.

DOVE, P. EDWARD (Editor). Domesday Studies, 1086-1886: Being the Papers read at the Meetings of the Domesday Commemoration, 1886. With a Bibliography of Domesday Book and Accounts of the MSS. and Printed Books exhibited at the Public Record Office and at the British Museum. 2 vols. 4to. London, 1888.

> The first essay by Stuart Moore sets forth the nature of the original Domesday inquiry and justifies its purpose as leading to a more equitable system and basis of taxation than had hitherto prevailed. Its chief question seems to have been what was the extent of cultivatable land in each estate as determined by teams. This also involved pasturage needed for the teams. Its intention was not to list every man's pig or cow, but only those that went with the estate and thus marked its value. Domesday Book has a great interest for antiquaries and besides makes a slight contribution to the topography of England.

Dugdale Society. Publications. 14 vols. (by 1936). 4to. Oxford, 1921—.

> The volumes comprise Minutes and Accounts of Corporation of Stratford-on-Avon, and other Records, 1553-1629; Records of King Edward's School, Birmingham; Lay Subsidy Roll for Warwickshire of Edward III; Abstract of Bailiff's Accounts of Monastic and other Estates in the County of Warwick; etc.

Dumfriesshire and Galloway Natural History and Antiquarian Society. Dumfries, 1862—.

> This society was founded in Dumfries in 1862 "to secure a more frequent interchange of thought and opinion among those who cultivate natural histories and antiquities." The society ceased to meet in 1875, but in 1876 it was reconstituted with a slight change in name.—Terry.

DUNCUMB, J. Collection towards the History and Antiquities of the County of Hereford. 2 vols., with index. London, 1804-40.

> Additions and Continuations were printed in 1882, 1886, 1892 by others.

Durham and Northumberland Architectural and Archaeological Society. Transactions. Sunderland, 1863—.

The East Anglian: or, Notes and Queries on Subjects connected with the Counties of Suffolk, Cambridge, Essex, and Norfolk. Edit. by Samuel Tymms for the first series of 4 vols.; new ser., 13 vols. (by 1910). Plates. 8vo. Lowestoft, 1864-1910.

> Complete sets of the first series are difficult to obtain, as the stock was destroyed by fire in 1874. These volumes contain several articles by Edward Fitzgerald.—Bookseller's Note.

East Hertfordshire Archaeological Society, Transactions. Hertford, 1901—.

East Riding Antiquarian Society. Transactions. Hull, 1873—.

EDEN, SIR WILLIAM. The State of the Poor: or, An History of the Labouring Classes in England, from the Conquest to the Present Period . . . With a large Appendix containing a Comparative and Chronological Table of the Prices of Labour, of Provisions, and of other Commodities. 3 vols. 4to. London, 1797.

> This work is an indispensable source book for the history of the lower classes in England. It appeared in an abridged form, edited by A. G. L. Rogers, London, 1928.

Edinburgh Bibliographical Society. Publications. 8 vols. (by 1907). 4to. Edinburgh, 1896—.

> This society was founded in 1890 for "the discussion and elucidation of questions connected with books, more especially Scottish," "the compilation of special lists with a view to the formation of a complete Scottish Bibliography," and "the occasional issue of selected papers, reprints, and facsimiles."—Terry. Vol. VII contains lists of books printed in Scotland before 1700, by H. G. Aldis. See under BIBLIOGRAPHIES.

ELIAS, C. F. Dr. Samuel Johnson as Traveller. An Address read before the Liverpool Philomathic Society at the Opening of the One Hundred and Third Session, Oct. 5, 1927. 8vo. Liverpool, 1927.

> Elias was president of the society at the time. His address puts forth the claim that Johnson was one of the greatest travelers of his age. It examines his record on a strictly geographical basis, pointing out the various places he visited, and citing among his qualifications as a traveler his powers of observation and physical endurance. It describes his Welsh tour, with citations of passages from his journal; likewise the French tour. It calls attention to the imaginative descriptions of Abyssinia in *Rasselas,* etc.

ELLIS, SIR HENRY. General Introduction to Domesday Book, accompanied by Indexes of the Tenants in Chief, and under Tenants at the Time of the Survey, as well as of the Holders of Lands mentioned in Domesday Anterior to the Formation of that Record, with an Abstract of the Population of England at the Close of the Reign of William the Conqueror, illustrated by Notes and Comments. 2 vols. 8vo. London, 1833.

ELSASSER, ROBERT. Über die politischen Bildungsreisen der Deutschen nach England. Heidelberg, 1917.

English Historical Review. London, 1886—.

> Here are to be found scholarly articles on all phases of English history and antiquities.

Essex Archaeological Society. Transactions. Indexes. Colchester, 1858—.

Essex Historical Monuments (Commission on). An Inventory of Ancient Monuments. Vol. I, North-West; vol. II, Central and South-West. Map and numerous plates. 4to. London (?), 1916-21.

EVANS, E. V. Andrew Boorde and the Welsh People. In *Y Cymmrodor,* vol. 29, 44-55. London, 1919.

Essays, by a Society of Gentlemen, at Exeter. Vol. I in 2 parts. 8vo. Exeter, 1796.

These are papers that were read at some of the first meetings of a Society formed at Exeter, June 28, 1792. The subjects covered included one or two of local interest.—Bookseller's Note.

FABRI, JOHANNES ERNST F. Neues Geographisches Magazin. Dessau und Leipzig, 1785-87.

This work was a successor to his *Geographisches Magazin,* 4 vols., 1783-85.

Fenland Notes and Queries: A Quarterly Antiquarian Journal for the Fenland, in the Counties of Huntingdon, Cambridge, Lincoln, Northampton, Norfolk, and Suffolk. Edit. by W. H. B. Saunders and W. B. Sweeting. Maps and plans. Peterborough, 1889—.

FISHER, J. Wales in the Time of Queen Elizabeth. In *Archaeologia Cambrensis,* 6th ser., vol. 15. 237-48. London, 1915.

This prints *in extenso* an anonymous tract, *De presenti Statu totius Walliae.*—Read, *op. cit.*

FISHER, THOMAS. Collections, Historical, Genealogical and Topographical for Bedfordshire. London, 1812-36.

FISHWICK, HENRY. Lancashire in the Times of Elizabeth. In *Trans. Roy. Hist. Soc.,* vol. 6, 183-200. London, 1877.

Flint Historical Society. Publications. Prestatyn, 1911—.

FLOWER, R. Laurence Nowell and the Discovery of England in Tudor Times. London, 1935.

Nowell returned to England from abroad after the accession of Elizabeth, who preferred him to the deanship of Lichfield. He was a diligent student of antiquities and left manuscripts on Anglo-Saxon.—*DNB.*

FORBES, J. The Social Condition of Scotland during the Fifteenth and Sixteenth Centuries, illustrated by Extracts from the Burgh Records of the City of Aberdeen. Social Science Association, 1863. 8vo. Aberdeen, 1863.

FORBES, URQUHART A., and ARNOLD C. BURMESTER. Our Roman Highways. London, 1904.

This offers an historical treatment of the Roman highway system in Britain and discusses the *Itinerary of Antoninus* as far as it relates to Britain. Appendices furnish the names of places in Britain mentioned in Ptolemy's *Geography;* the *Diaphragmata* of Richard of Cirencester is compared with the *Itinerary of Antoninus;* the *Notitia Imperii* is examined with reference to the Military Stations on the Saxon Shore and along the Roman Wall; the Stations marked in the *Peutingerian Table* (British) are compared with the corresponding portions of Antonine's *Itinerary;* and the list of Roman towns and of some of the Roman camps in various English counties and Welsh and Scottish counties determined.

FORDHAM, SIR HERBERT GEORGE. Christopher Saxton of Dunningley, his Life and Work. In *Thoresby Society Miscellany,* vol. 28. Leeds, 1928.

—————. The Earliest Tables of the Highways of England and Wales, 1541-61. In *The Library,* 4th ser., vol. 8, no. iii. London, 1927.

The Road Tables printed in Grafton's *Abridgement of the Chronicles of Englande* (1570) and his *A Little Treatise* (1571) have been commonly accepted as the first known examples of road tables for England and Wales. But Fordham has discovered a still earlier set of such productions, namely, some thin little books gathered up under "England—Appendix" in the Bibliographical Society's *Short Title Catalogue of Books printed in England, Scotland and Ireland, 1475-1640,* recently issued. The titles of these booklets are: *The Chronicle of yeres* (the same work with title slightly altered, *A breuiat Chronicle*), which contains tables of the roads of England and Wales during a period of at least twenty years, 1541 to 1561. The list is no doubt incomplete. From 1541 the title reads *Cronicle of yeres* through 1543, 1544, 1550, 1552; then *A breuiat Chronicle,* 1553; *A breuyat Chronicle,* 1555, 1556; *A Breviat Chronicle,* 1559, 1560; *A briefe Cronicle,* 1561. The pages vary from 4½ to 7, and the place of imprint is London, except for the 1552, 1553 editions, where it is Canterbury. Throughout the whole series nine principal thoroughfares are mentioned: Walsingham to London; Berwick to York and London; Cockermouth to Lancaster and London; Yarmouth to Colchester and London; Carnarvon to Chester and London; Dover to London; Saint Burien to London; Bristol to London; Saint David's to London. Fordham attributes the very beginning of these English roadbooks in their most elementary form to the year 1541. No road tables are found in *A lytell short Cronycle* printed by Wynkyn de Worde in 1530. In the *Cronycles of Englande,* of Caxton, de Worde, and Julyan Notary, there is found from 1498-1528, in the section the Description of England, a chapter entitled "Of the kynges hye wayes and stretes," which gives a short general description of four roads, The Fossway, Watling Street, Ermin Street, and the Icknield Way. This description seems to occur first in de Worde's *St. Albans Chronicle,* 1498. The selection of the nine roads of 1541 should be traceable to the royal proclamations setting out the posts, and establishing the official postal service, but none of these early proclamations have survived. The nine roads plotted on the map show that they served the needs of the time in transportation and communication.

—————. An Itinerary of the Sixteenth Century (Jean Bernard). London (?), 1910.

—————. John Ogilby (1600-1676) His *Britannia,* and the British Itineraries of the Eighteenth Century. In *The Library,* 4th ser., vol. 6, 157-178. 4to. London, 1926.

This gives an historical account of his work, its importance, and a description of its contents.

—————. Notable Surveyors of the Sixteenth, Seventeenth, and Eighteenth Centuries and their Work. A Study in the History of Cartography. Cambridge, 1929.

—————. Notes on British and Irish Itineraries and Road-Books. Tract 4, 34 pp. 8vo. Hertford, 1912.

This is a paper that was read for the Geographical Section at the meeting of the British Association for the Advancement of Science, held at Dundee, Sept., 1912.

—————. Paterson's Roads: Daniel Paterson, His Maps and Itineraries. In *The Library,* 4th ser., vol. 5, no. iv. London, 1925.

—————. The Road-Books of Wales, With a Catalogue, 1775-1850. In *Arch. Camb.,* vol. 80. 8vo. London, 1927.

—————. Saxton's General Map of England and Wales. In *Geographical Journal,* vol. 67. London, 1926.

——————. Studies in Carto-Bibliography, British and French, and in the Bibliography of Itineraries and Road-Books. 8vo. Oxford, 1914.

This excellent survey of the development of mapping and of roadbooks places individuals and their work in their relation to each other.

FORSTER, GEORG. Sämmtlichte Schriften. 9 vols. in 5. Leipzig, 1843.

There are numerous references to the Forsters, their voyages, descriptions, and position among travelers, in the foregoing sections and in the two preceding volumes of the present work.

FORSTER, JOHANN REINHOLD. Magazin von merkwürdigen neuen Reisebeschreibungen, aus fremden Sprachen übersetzt. 3 vols. Berlin, 1790—.

FOSBROKE, T. D. The Tourist's Grammar, or Rules relating to the Scenery and Antiquities incident to Travellers, and including an Epitome of Gilpin's Principles of the Picturesque. 8vo. London, 1826.

The title of this work suggests how a "picturesque" traveler should regulate his reactions to scenery.

FRANTZ, R. W. The English Traveller and the Movement of Ideas, 1660-1732. *University of Nebraska Studies,* vols. 32-33. Lincoln, Neb., 1934.

This discusses the effect of travelers' accounts on trends of thought—religious, moral, philosophical, and scientific. It is richly documented and supplemented with a bibliography.

FUSSELL, C. E. Travel and Topography in Eighteenth Century England. In *The Library,* 4th ser., vol. 10. London, 1929.

Gaelic Society of Glasgow. Transactions. 3 vols. Glasgow, 1887-1908.

Founded for the elucidation of Celtic antiquities.

Gaelic Society of Inverness. Transactions. 36 vols. (by 1941). Inverness, 1872—.

This society was formed in 1871 for, *inter alia,* "the rescuing from oblivion of Celtic poetry, traditions, legends, books, manuscripts, . . . bearing upon the genius, the literature of the Highlands and Highland people." And in the fulfillment of this objective the society has been most diligent. The contents of the volumes consist of selected papers read at the several meetings held each year, and cover in subject inedited poetry, folklore, traditions, antiquities, Ossianic matter, charter chests, personalities, historical events, literary questions, Highland education, the state of the language, etc. Many of the articles are in Gaelic.

GAUNT, W. English Rural Life in the Eighteenth Century, with a Foreword by C. Reginald Grundy. 15 full-page illustrations in color and 18 in half-tone, reproduced from the works of Bigg, Gainsborough, Girtin, Ibbetson, Morland, Rowlandson, Singleton, James Ward, Westall, Woodforde, and others. 4to. London, 1925.

This fascinating work on the social history of 18th century England reproduces with its charming illustrations both idealistically and realistically the rural life of the time.

Gentleman's Magazine. With many hundreds of portraits, views, and other woodcuts. 223 vols., and Index from 1731 to 1818, 5 vols. Together 228 vols. 8vo. 1731-1868. Entirely new series, 1868-1907. London.

For nearly a century and a half this famous periodical has served as an outlet for whatever was on the mind of Englishmen who had an itch for writing. As a work of reference it is invaluable, especially for such subjects as pertain to local history, family history, historical events, literature, biography, architecture, antiquities, and archaeology. Other useful features

are its monthly lists of births, marriages, and deaths; its running schedule of historical and political happenings; and its lists of new books and reviews, to which this present work is much indebted. For a "classified collection of the chief contents," see G. L. Gomme below.

Geographical Journal of the Royal Geographical Society (includes Proceedings of the Royal Geographical Society, formerly published separately). General Index to vols. 1-20, 1906; vols. 21-40, 1923; vols. 41-50, 1930; vols. 51-80, 1935. Many hundreds of illustrations, comprising plates from photographs, folding colored maps, etc. 8vo. London, 1893—.

Geographical Magazine. London, 1935—.

GEORGE, DOROTHY. London Life in the Eighteenth Century. 8 illustrations. Appendices and bibliography. London, 1925.

> The life of the London poor and the working class and the various public and private acts designed to alleviate the misery of their existence, as here portrayed, make sad reading.

GIBSON, JOHN. The Universal Museum, or, Gentleman's and Ladies' Polite Magazine of History, Politics and Literature, 1763-64, and the Universal Museum and Complete Magazine. . . . Published by J. Payne. London, 1765-69.

> Vols. 2 and 3 of the first series and 1-5 of the second series of the *Universal Museum* contain maps of England, chiefly by Gibson. The British Museum has nine volumes of this magazine, the last dated 1770. It was probably discontinued that year.—Chubb, *Printed Maps.*

GILBEY, WALTER. Early Carriages and Roads. London, 1903.

Glasgow Archaeological Society. Transactions. Numerous plates, plans, and other illustrations. Glasgow, 1857—.

> Vol. I of the new series is dated 1881. This society was founded in 1856 for "the encouragement of the study of archaeology generally, and more particularly in Glasgow and the West of Scotland."—Terry.

Gloucestershire Notes and Queries. Edit. by Beaver H. Blacker, W. P. Phillimore, and S. J. Madge. 9 vols. (by 1902). London, 1881—.

GODLEY, ALFRED D. Oxford in the Eighteenth Century. Illustrations. New York, 1909.

> The lack of intellectual curiosity and the existence of professorial indifference, antiquated systems of examination, and student dissipation herein described seem to bear out Gibbon's charges against the university.

GOMME, G. L. A Classified Collection of the Chief Contents of the Gentleman's Magazine, from 1731 to 1868. 30 vols. London, 1883-1902.

> The classification runs as follows:
> Archaeology, 2 vols.
> Architectural Antiquities, 2 vols.
> Bibliographical Notes.
> Dialects, Proverbs, Word Lore.
> Ecclesiology.
> English Topography, 17 vols.
> English Traditional Lore, etc.
> Literary Curiosities and Notes.
> Manners and Customs.
> Popular Superstitions.
> Romano-British Remains, 2 vols.

—————. Literature of Local Institutions. Book-Lover's Library. 8vo. London, 1884.

GOUGH, RICHARD. Anecdotes of British Topography: or, An Historical Account of what has been done for Illustrating the Topographical Antiquities of Great Britain and Ireland. 4to. London, 1768.

> 2nd edit., corrected and enlarged, 2 vols., London, 1780.
> This work is also listed under DESCRIPTIONS. Its titles and comments have been drawn on very generously in these present volumes. Many of his statements were corrected in the second edition, as well as new titles entered; but it was not my good fortune to secure possession of this edition.

GRAHAM, H. G. The Social Life of Scotland in the Eighteenth Century. 2 vols. 8vo. London, 1899.

GRANT, I. F. Economic History of Scotland, 11th to the 19th Century. London, 1934.

—————. Everyday Life in Old Scotland to the Nineteenth Century: Changes in Farming; Old Trades, etc. 3 vols. London, 1931-32.

—————. Everyday Life on an Old Highland Farm, 1769-1782 (Invernesshire). London, 1924.

> A very fascinating account of how life was conducted in the Highlands under conditions peculiar to the country and its traditions.

—————. Social and Economic Development of Scotland before 1603: Norman and Gaelic Influences, Agriculture, Gild Merchant, Fisheries, Foreign Trade and Craftsmen, Highlands, etc. 8vo. London.

GRANT, MARY ANN. Sketches of Life and Manners, with Delineation of Scenery in England, Scotland and Ireland. 2 vols. London, 1811.

GRAY, HOWARD L. Greek Visitors to England in 1455-56. In *Haskins Anniversary Essays in Medieval History,* edit. by Charles H. Taylor and John L. Moritz. Boston, 1929.

GUNTHER, R. T. Early English Botanists and their Gardens, based on unpublished Writings of Goodyer, Tradescant, and Others. 9 plates and 21 other illustrations. Oxford, 1922.

Halifax Antiquarian Society. Papers. Halifax, 1901—.

HALL, E. F. Gerardus Mercator: Life and Works. In *Journal of American Geographical Society,* vol. 10. New York, 1878.

HALL, HUBERT. Welsh Local Records: Details and Classified Topographical List. In *Trans. Cymmrodorion Soc.,* session 1914-15, 16-42. London.

Hampshire Antiquary and Naturalist; on Local Notes and Queries, etc., of the Hampshire Field Club. London, 1891—.

Hampstead Antiquarian and Historical Society. Transactions. Plates. London, 1898—.

HAMMOND, J. L. and BARBARA. The Town Labourer, 1760-1832. London, 1917.

This is one of the most widely consulted sources dealing with the economic life and intellectual attitudes toward the new industrial conditions.

HANTZSCH, VICTOR. Deutsche Reisende des 16ten Jahrhunderts. Pt. 4 of vol. I of Leipziger Studien aus dem Gebiet der Geschichte. Leipzig.

This furnishes brief notices of many typical adventurers of German blood all over the world in the 16th century.—Bates, Touring in 1600.

Harleian Collection. Some Account of the Harleian Collection of Manuscripts now in the British Museum. From the Preface to the new Index to that Collection, most judiciously compiled by Mr. Astle. In Annual Register, vol. 6, 140-55. London, 1763.

This gives a fair resumé of the contents of this collection formed by Robert Harley, Earl of Oxford, and continued by his son, who died 1741. At that time it comprised 8,000 volumes, many loose papers bound up in volumes, 40,000 original rolls, charters, letters patent, grants, etc. Every science was represented in its manuscripts, as well as topography, descriptions, and antiquities of Britain.

Harleian Miscellany, or, A Collection of Scarce, Curious and Entertaining Pamphlets and Tracts found in the late Earl of Oxford's Library, with Historical, Political and Critical Notes and an Index. 8 vols. 4to. London, 1744-46.

Another edit., with additional notes, 10 vols., London, 1808-13.

HARPER, CHARLES. The English Roads: A Series of Anecdotal and Pictorial Narratives of our Historic Roads, revised and largely rewritten; fully illustrated by the author from old time prints and pictures. (Reprints of Mr. Harper's famous histories of the coach roads of England in a compact and happy form for motorists, pedestrians and cyclists. Each volume has been revised and rewritten by the author, and, in many cases, contains entirely new pictures.) 20 vols. London, 1922.

These volumes are listed under their original dates of publication:
The Brighton Road, 1892.
The Portsmouth Road, 1895.
The Dover Road, 1895.
The Bath Road, 1899.
The Exeter Road, 1899.
The Norwich Road, 1901.
The Great North Road, 2 vols., 1901.
The Cambridge, Ely and King's Lynn Road, 1902.
The Holyhead Road, 2 vols., 1902.
The Newmarket, Bury, Thetford and Cromer Road, 1904.
The Oxford, Gloucester and Milford Haven Road, 2 vols., 1905.
The Manchester and Glasgow Road, 2 vols., 1907.
South Devon Coast, 1907.
Somerset Coast, 1909.
Thames Valley Villages, 2 vols., 1910.

—————. The Old Inns of Old England: A Picturesque Account of the Ancient and Storied Hostelries of our Country. 2 vols. London, 1906.

————. The Stage Coach and Mail in Days of Yore. 2 vols. London, 1903.

HARRISON, G. B. The Elizabethan Journals. Being a Record of those Things most Talked of During the Years 1591-1603. 3 vols. in 1. An Elizabethan Journal, 1591-94 (1928); A Second Elizabethan Journal, 1595-98 (1931); A Last Elizabethan Journal, 1599-1603 (1933). New York and London, 1928-1933.

These are given in the Elizabethan accent as a diary of happenings of every conceivable sort, gathered by the author from a vast ranging through sources. It is of absorbing interest as a record of what was talked of and done in Shakespeare's England.

————. A Jacobean Journal, being a Record of those Things most Talked of During the Years 1603-1606. London, 1940.

This is a sequel to the Elizabethan Journals. Among the events recorded are the accession of King James I, the great plague of 1603 and its horrors, the first voyage to the East Indies, the trial of Raleigh, along with innumerable lesser happenings, such as murders and mysteries, court and city scandals; mention is also made of books and sermons.

HARTLEY, DOROTHY, and M. E. ELLIOT. The Life and Work of the People of England. Illustrated from contemporary prints. 6 vols. 4to. London, 1926-1931.

The titles of the separate volumes are:
Eleventh to the Thirteenth Century, 1000-1300. 1931.
Fourteenth Century. 1928.
Fifteenth Century. 1925.
Sixteenth Century. 1926.
Seventeenth Century. 1928.
Eighteenth Century. 1931.

HARTMANN, CYRIL H. The Story of the Roads. London, 1927.

Hawick Archaeological Society. Publications. Hawick, 1863—.

This society was founded in 1856 for "the dissemination of antiquarian knowledge among its members, the elucidation and preservation of the antiquities of the surrounding district, and the formation of a museum." It began to publish in 1863. There were no publications for 1886, 1887, and 1891-97 inclusive.—Terry.

HAZLITT, W. CAREW. Gleanings in Old Garden Literature. London, 1887.

This contains many charming essays on little-known and out-of-the-way subjects connected with gardening, both domestic and landscape. One of the essays lets us know how London was supplied with garden truck.

HEAPE, R. GRUNDY. Georgian York. A Sketch of Life in Hanoverian England. Numerous illustrations. 4to. London, 1937.

HEARNE, THOMAS. Collections (Diaries, etc.), 1705-35. Edit. by C. E. Doble and H. E. Salter. 11 vols. *Publ. Oxford Hist. Soc.* Oxford, 1885-1918.

For list of Hearne's publications, see also *Camb. Bibliog.,* vol. II, 873.

HEAWOOD, EDWARD. Some Early County Maps. In *Geographical Journal,* vols. 68 and 69. London, 1926-27.

HEMMEON, J. C. The History of the British Post Office. London, 1912.

HENDERSON, T. F. Old World Scotland: Glimpses of its Modes and Manners. London, 1893.

Highways and Byways Series (of counties in England and Wales). Described by foremost authors, and illustrated by Hugh Thomson, Joseph Pennell, F. L Griggs, and other artists. 23 vols. 8vo. London, 1910-23.

> The text describes places as they are with many references to the past. The pen and ink drawings happily supplement the descriptions.

HILL, GEORGE BIRKBECK. In the Footsteps of Dr. Johnson in Scotland. Illustrations. 4to. London, 1890.

> This contains a lengthy introduction on Johnson's travels and a bibliography of travelers. To what Dr. Johnson did see Dr. Hill adds what he did not see. The illustrations show sites both as they were and as they are.

HIND, A. M. Wencelaus Hollar and his Views of London and Windsor in the Seventeenth Century. Frontispiece and 96 illustrations on 65 plates. 4to. London, 1922.

> Through the maps and drawings of London here reproduced we can appreciate what we owe to this Czech artist in helping us to know the London of both before and after the Great Fire.

HINDLEY, CHARLES (Editor). The Old Book Collector's Miscellany. 3 vols. 4to. London, 1873.

> This contains reprints of some of the tracts by John Taylor the Water Poet.

Historic Society of Lancashire and Cheshire. Proceedings and Papers. (Volumes issued annually.) Liverpool, 1849—.

> From 1855 on, its publications were known as Transactions. By 1939 the number of volumes should total 90.

Historical Manuscripts Commission. Reports 1-221 (by 1938). London, 1870—.

> The Royal Commission on Historical Manuscripts was first appointed in 1869. Its duty was to inquire what papers and manuscripts belonging to private families and institutions were extant which would be useful in elucidating history, constitutional law, science and general literature, and which would be made accessible to the student. Its first report in 1870 revealed a great wealth of material awaiting the editor. Such a vast accumulation of records obviously would be an amorphous mass without some shaping of its contents. Accordingly Guide No. I (Topographical) was published in 1914 as Report 17, and a Guide to Persons, Part II, in two volumes appeared in 1935-38, as Report 63.

Historical Monuments Commission: An Inventory of Ancient Monuments. 14 vols. (by 1932). London, 1912—.

> The regions covered by 1932 are as follows:
> Buckinghamshire. Maps and numerous plates and other illustrations. 2 vols. 4to.
> Herefordshire. 2 maps, etc. 3 vols. 1931-32.
> Hertfordshire. Folding map, 45 plates, etc. 1911.
> Huntingdonshire. Folding map and many plates. 1926.
> London: Westminster Abbey; West London; Roman London; the City; East London. Maps, and many illustrations. 5 vols. 1924-30.
> Wales and Monmouthshire. County Denbigh. Fol. 3 maps and 78 illustrations. 1914.
> Pembrokeshire. Over 300 illustrations from photographs, maps, etc. Fol. 1925.

Historical Society of West Wales. Historical Records published annually. Carmarthen, 1910—.

HODGKIN, R. H. History of the Anglo-Saxons. London, 1935.

> This is said to supersede all earlier general works on the subject.

HODGSON, J. C., M.A. William Hutchinson, F.S.A., The Historian of Three Counties. In *Arch. Aeliana,* n.s., vol. 12. Newcastle-upon-Tyne, 1916.

This gives an account of the historian's antecedents, his marriage, his friendship with George Allen, who had been making collections for a history of Durham county, which he turned over to Hutchinson. In addition to his county histories and *Excursion to the Lakes of Westmoreland,* Hutchinson was the author of some novels of a Walpolesque sort and likewise of tragedies and poetry.

Home Counties Magazine. See Middlesex and Hertfordshire Notes and Queries below.

HOWIE, J. Biographia Scotiana: or, Scots Worthies. 8vo. Glasgow, 1775.

Later edit., 1781, followed by others.

HUDDESFORD, WILLIAM. The Lives of Leland, Hearne, and Anthony Wood. 2 vols. London, 1772.

The author was keeper of the Ashmolean Library, 1755-72.

Huguenot Society of London. Proceedings. London, 1886—.

This deals with the many Protestant sects in England and France besides the Huguenots. It contains also articles of historical and antiquarian interest.

Hunterian Club Publications. Being Reprints of the Works of the Scottish Writers of Elizabethan Times. 68 nos. 4to. London, 1872-1902.

The contents include: Works of Thomas Lodge, Samuel Rowlands, Alexander Garden, Patrick Hannay, Alex. Craig; Sir Thomas Overburie's Vision; the Bannatyne Manuscript and Club Reports.

HURST, HERBERT. Oxford Topography; An Essay . . . forming a companion volume to the port-folio containing Agas's Map (1578-88) and other Old Plans of Oxford, with Index by George Parker. In *Publ. Oxford Hist. Soc.,* vol. 39. Oxford, 1899.

HUSSEY, CHRISTOPHER. The Picturesque: A Study in a Point of View. Illustrations. London, 1927.

See the chapter on Picturesque Travel.

HUTCHINGS, W. W. London Town Past and Present. Numerous illustrations from old prints and modern views. 2 vols. 4to. London, 1909.

Imago Mundi. A Periodical Review of Early Cartography, edit. by Leo Bagrow and E. Lynam (Jahrbuch der Alten Kartographie). Plates, maps, Drawings in the text, etc. London and Berlin, 1935—.

INGLIS, HARRY R. C., JOHN MATHIESON, C. B. BOOG WATSON. The Early Maps of Scotland. With an Account of the Ordnance Survey. *Publ. Roy. Scot. Geog. Soc.* Edinburgh, 1934.

Reproductions of some of the famous old maps are included. The authors point out that some of the variations in the maps were due to different scales used for measuring distance. The earlier maps figured on a scale of 48 to 50 miles to one degree. Later the English "computed" mile was put at 60 miles to one degree, while the Scotch mile remained at the older

reckoning. The old British mile of 2,428 yards, referred to as the "computed" mile, was used in nearly all measurements and itineraries of Scotland, until the "measured" turnpike roads came into being in the middle of the 18th century. The Scottish mile proper, called the "Scots" mile, was 1,984 yards in length, and the English mile, called the "measured" mile was 1,760 yards. As the latitude and longitude of the chief points of Scotland were not settled till about 1750, the scales are of little value because of the consequent distortions. The account as a whole provides a variety of interesting facts concerning the development towards an accurate delineation of the face of Scotland from Ptolemy down to the Ordnance Survey.

INNES, COSMO. Origines Parochiales Scotiae: The Antiquities, Ecclesiastical and Territorial, of the Parishes in Scotland, edit. by Cosmo Innes, assisted by Rev. W. Anderson, Messrs. Jas. Robertson, J. B. Brichan, and J. M'Nab. Map. 2 vols. in 3. 4to. Edinburgh, 1850-55.

—————. Scotch Topography and Statistics (a review of the Old and New Statistical Accounts of Scotland, with the history of Scottish topography). In *Quart. Rev.*, vol. 82, 342 ff. London, 1848. (Also published separately.)

Iona Club. Publications. Edinburgh, 1847—.

> This club was founded in Edinburgh in 1833 "to investigate and illustrate the history, antiquities, and early literature of the Highlands of Scotland, etc. The club was suspended in 1838 until a more general desire should be expressed for its continuance." Its single volume was subsequently published.—Terry. In a way its place has been taken by the Gaelic Society of Inverness. The title of the one volume is:
> Collectanea De Rebus Albanicis, consisting of original Papers and Documents relating to the History of the Highlands and Islands of Scotland. Iona Club, vol. 1. Edinburgh, 1847.
> These papers deal mainly with affairs of the 16th century.

IRVING, W. H. John Gay's London. Numerous illustrations and map. Harvard University Press, 1928.

JACKMAN, W. T. The Development of Transportation in Modern England. 2 vols. London, 1916.

> This includes a full bibliography of printed and MS material. It is regarded as a most careful survey of the history of inland transportation.

JERVIS, W. W. The World in Maps. A Study in Map Evolution. Illustrations in black and white and 24 pp. of maps in color. London, 1938.

> This is an excellent introduction to the history of the subject. It has proved to be very useful to the section MAPS AND CHARTS.

JONES, WILLIAM POWELL. Thomas Gray, Scholar. The True Tragedy of an Eighteenth-Century Gentleman. Harvard University Press, 1937.

> This volume is a demonstration of how a scholar should be treated by a scholar. It deepens almost to the point of anguish the regret that the most learned man in England should have left so little behind in print of the far-ranging and thorough investigations remaining only in notebooks. From the analysis of these notebooks, one gets the impression that the poet had taken the whole field of knowledge for his province. The portions dealing with Gray as a traveler have special significance for this present work.

JUSSERAND, J. English Wayfaring Life in the Middle Ages (14th century). Translated by Lucy Toulmin Smith. Numerous illustrations. London, 1901.

—————. A French Ambassador at the Court of Charles II: le comte de Cominges, from his Unpublished Correspondence. London, 1932.

KELLY, JOHN ALEXANDER. England and the Englishman in German Literature of the Eighteenth Century. New York, 1921.

> The author makes clear that the number of Germans who found their way to Britain in the 18th century is something to wonder at. Descriptions of travel, according to J. R. Forster, had become a *Modelekture*. According to Nugent *(The Grand Tour)*, it was the Germans who set the pace for globe-trotting in those days. And according to Schaible (see below for title), England had always attracted the Germans, who somehow felt very much at home there as if that land were their adopted country. About the middle of the 18th century, it is estimated that four to five thousand Germans were in London, and by the end of the period the number had risen to six thousand. Unlike Englishmen as travelers, most of them seem to have read up on the country before they set foot on it. The chief attraction in English culture seems to have been English literature, theater, and politics. A valuable bibliography is included in the above work.

————. German Visitors to English Theaters in the Eighteenth Century. Princeton University Press, 1936.

> This volume is an interesting and useful discussion of those German visitors to England who were concerned with the world of the theater. It is a study of the impact of English culture upon Germany of the 18th century. From Lessing onwards attention was being turned away from France as the center of the polite arts to England, until the close of the century saw the swing back to France. The student of the English theater of the days of Garrick gains almost as much knowledge of plays, performers, presentation, music, opera, and the like, from a reading of these German travelers as from domestic accounts. The bibliography and observations of the writer have been of great help to the section TOURS BY FOREIGNERS.

Kentish Note Book: A Half Yearly Magazine of Notes, Queries and Replies on Subjects connected with the County of Kent. Edit. by G. O. Howell. 1 vol. Gravesend, 1889-91.

Kentish Register and Monthly Miscellany. Views of Country Seats. Vol. 3, Jan. to Dec. Canterbury, 1795.

KING, WILLIAM. Original Works . . . Now first collected into three Volumes: with Historical Notes, and Memoirs of the Author (by John Nichols). Portrait and a few woodcuts. 3 vols. London, 1776.

KLARWILL, VICTOR VON. Queen Elizabeth and Some Foreigners. London, 1928.

> For a description of this work, see Klarwill this date under TOURS BY FOREIGNERS. Its Introduction provides much curious information on Tudor England in the days of Elizabeth.

LAMBERT, R. L. (Editor). The Grand Tour—A Journey in the Track of the Age of Aristocracy. Conducted by Mona Wilson, Douglas Woodruff, Edmund Blunden, Janet Adams Smith, Richard Pyke, Sacheverell Sitwell, Malcolm Letts, and edited by R. L. Lambert. Illustrations from contemporary sources. New York, 1937.

> The list of noted contributors promises to make this book readable. While its object is to take the reader abroad as if he were one of the conducted youth, yet it is not without interest for the traveler in England.

Lancashire and Cheshire Antiquarian Notes. Reprinted from the Leigh Chronicle and including Selections from "Sketches in Local History" in the Preston Guardian, by W. A. Abram. Edit. by Wm. Duncombe Pink. 2 vols. 4to. Leigh, 1885-86.

Lancashire and Cheshire Antiquarian Society. Transactions. 53 vols. (by 1938). Manchester, 1884—.

LEE, SIDNEY. Stratford upon Avon, from the Earliest Times to the Death of Shakespeare. London, 1885.

> Reprinted, 1907.

Leicestershire Archaeological Society. Transactions. Leicester, 1862—.

> Vols. 11 to 18 contain the very valuable series of Manorial Histories (1917-34).—Bookseller's Note.

Leicestershire and Rutland Notes and Queries and Antiquarian Gleaner. An Illustrated Quarterly Magazine. Edit. by J. and T. Spencer. Illustrated. 3 vols. Leicester, 1889-95.

LELAND, JOHN. Commentarii de scriptoribus Britannicis. Edit. by Thomas Hearne. 1709.

LETTS, MALCOLM. As the Foreigner Sees Us. Illustrated with 16 contemporary plates. London, 1936.

> This is "a reconstruction of the British Isles, customs, travel, amusements and living from 1500 to 1830, the beginning of steam transport, in the actual words of travellers who left experiences on record when visiting us. . . . Each century brings its own peculiarities to light and due recognition is paid to individuals and occurrences taking the traveller's fancy."— From the Announcement of the Bookseller (Maggs).

The Library: A Magazine of Bibliography and Literature. Edit. by J. Y. W. McAlister, F.S.A. Vols. 1-10, 1889-1898: Organ of the Library Association. 2nd series, vols. 1-10, 1899-1909: A Quarterly Review of Bibliography and Library Lore. 3rd series, vols. 1-10, 1910-1919, edit. by J. McAlister and Alfred Pollard. 4th series, vols. 1-18, 1920-1938: *Transactions of the Bibliographical Society.* Edit. by Alfred Pollard. London, 1889—.

Lincolnshire Notes and Queries. Edit. by E. L. Grange and J. C. Hudson. Horncastle, 1889—.

Literary and Antiquarian Society of Perth. Transactions. Perth, 1827.

Literary and Scientific Association of Elgin. Publications. 3 vols. Elgin, 1858-61.

> Founded in 1836 for "the study of literature, ancient history, antiquities, archaeology, geology, botany, and natural history."—Terry.

Liverpool Welsh National Society. Transactions. Liverpool, 1885—.

LOCKITT, C. H. Relations of French and English Society, 1763-93. London, 1920.

> The book presents the contrasts in manners, tastes, and ideas; the vogue of sentimentalism, lists of visitors, and a bibliography. The visit of Garrick to Paris brought home to the French acting profession the difference in the regard which the respective countries bestowed upon actors.

London and Middlesex Archaeological Society. Transactions. London, 1860—.

London Society of Antiquaries. Proceedings (later Journal). London.

> As early as 1572 a society was formed by Bishop Matthew Parker, Sir Robert Cotton, William Camden, etc., for preserving the remains of antiquities. It existed until 1604, when, suspected of being political in aims, it was abolished by King James I. The papers read at the meetings were preserved in the Cottonian Library. They were later printed by Thos. Hearne in 1720 as *A Collection of Curious Discourses* (see Hearne under 1720, HISTORY AND ANTIQUITIES). In 1707 a number of English antiquaries began to hold regular meetings for discussion of their hobby, and in 1717 a Society of Antiquaries was formally constituted, receiving a charter from George II in 1751. In 1780 George III granted the Society apartments in Somerset House. Now it resides at Burlington House, Piccadilly. The society is governed by a council of twenty and a president ex officio, and a trustee of the British Museum.

London Topographical Society. Publications. London, 1900—.

> The name Record was first used for its publications. The object of the society is the publication of maps, views, and plans of different periods and of all parts of the city and county of London, together with the publication of documents and data of all kinds illustrating the history of London.

LONG, GEORGE. English Inns and Road-Houses. Illustrated with 234 photographs taken by the Author. Oxford, 1937.

> The author traveled many thousands of miles in search of the oldest inn, the most beautiful inn, and the inn with a story. He visited the old monkish inns and pilgrims' hostels; he sought out those romantic houses which were the resorts of highwaymen and smugglers, and those where murders were committed or ghosts were reputed to walk. He made a pilgrimage to the Scottish inns and to the literary inns which were frequented by great poets and writers in the past.—From Blackwell's Announcement of the work.

LONG, WILLIAM. Stonehenge and its Barrows. In the *Wilts. Arch. and Nat. Hist. Mag.*, vol. 16, nos. 46-47. Devizes, 1876.

> This gives an historical account of the notices of Stonehenge from the earliest times down to the date of Sir R. C. Hoare's *Ancient Wilts*, 1812. It was freely used in the section BRITISH, ROMAN, AND SAXON ANTIQUITIES, Appendix.

MACARTNEY, MERVYN. English Houses and Gardens in the Seventeenth and Eighteenth Centuries: a Series of Bird's Eye Views reproduced from Contemporary Engravings by Kip, Badeslade, Harris, and others, with descriptive Notes by Mervyn Macartney. 61 plates. London, 1908.

MACDONALD, DONALD. Agricultural Writers from Sir Walter of Henley to Arthur Young, 1200-1800. With reproductions in facsimile from their actual writings, enlarged and revised. To which is added an exhaustive bilbiography (25 pp.). London, 1908.

MACDONALD, SIR GEORGE. General William Roy and his Military Antiquities of the Romans in North Britain. Society of Antiquaries. London, 1917.

——————. John Horsley, Scholar and Gentleman. In *Archaeologia Aeliana,* 4th ser., vol. 10. Society of Antiquaries of Newcastle-Upon-Tyne. Newcastle, 1933.

> This excellent essay evaluates the performance of Horsley in his studies of the Roman Wall and substantiates the claim made for its scholarly accuracy and permanence. See the essay on Horsley by R. C. Bosanquet, in the same publication.

——————. The Roman Wall in Scotland. 2nd edit. Oxford, 1934.

> This is regarded as definitive. It has value also for its references to earlier literature on the subject.

MacFarlane, Walter. Geographical Collections relating to Scotland made by Walter MacFarlane. Edit. from MacFarlane's Transcript in the Advocates' Library by Sir Arthur Mitchell, K.C.B., M.A., M.D., LL.D. 3 vols. *Publ. Scot. Hist. Soc.*, nos. 51-53. Edinburgh, 1906-08.

> The first two volumes deal with Carrick, Forfarshire, Galloway, Buchan, the Highlands, Dumbartonshire, Renfrewshire, Aberdeenshire. The descriptions contained herein, which vary in length and are often anonymous, belong mostly to the 16th and 17th centuries, and are derived from Sir Robert Sibbald's collections. Of many of them Robert Gordon of Straloch was the author. The third volume contains a variety of matter relating to antiquity, topography, and geography. Among them is Jo. Ben's *Description of Orkney*, written in 1529, and papers on minerals, horticulture, malting, etc., a description of the Western Isles, and genealogies of the chief clans of the Isles by Dean Monro, and notes on several of the sheriffdoms.

Mackenzie, William C. The History of the Outer Hebrides. 8vo. Paisley, 1903.

MacPhail, J. R. N. Highland Papers. 3 vols. *Publ. Scot. Hist. Soc.*, 2nd ser., nos. 5, 11, 20. Edinburgh, 1914-20.

> These papers are taken from Gregory's collection for his *History of the Western Isles*. Vol. 1 includes papers relating to the murder of the Laird of Calder, 1591-96; vol. 2 includes documents relating to the Euill Troubles of the Lewes, 1566-76.—Read, *Bibliog. Brit. History*.

MacWilliam, N. French Impressions of English Character (1663-95). In *French Quarterly*. London and New York, 1920.

Maidment, James. Excerpta Scotica (a Miscellany of 16th century papers). Edinburgh, 1825.

Maitland Club. Publications. Glasgow, 1829-59.

> This club was founded at Glasgow in 1828 "to print works illustrative of the antiquities, history and literature of Scotland." It ceased publishing in 1859. Among its publications are four volumes of the *Miscellany of the Maitland Club*, Edinburgh, 1833-47.

Malcolm, J. P. Anecdotes of the Manners and Customs of London during the Eighteenth Century: including the Charities, Depravities, Dresses, and Amusements of the Citizens of London during that period. With a Review of the State of Society in 1807. 45 engravings, with the costume plates colored. 2nd edit. 8vo. London, 1810.

—————. Lives of Topographers and Antiquaries who have written concerning the Antiquities of England, with Portraits of the Authors, and a complete List of their Works, so far as they relate to the Topography of this Kingdom. 4to. London, 1815.

> Among the antiquaries treated are Ashmole, Dart, Gent, Lambarde, Stow, Wood, etc.

Mansfield, William Murray (Lord). The Thistle: Examine of the Prejudice of Englishmen to the Scotch Nation. London, 1746.

Manx Society. Publications. Douglas, Isle of Man, 1859-93.

MARSHALL, DOROTHY. The English Poor in the Eighteenth Century. A Study in Social and Administrative History. London, 1926.

This is a very valuable survey of the state of the poor, the various administrative acts attempting to cope with the problem, the condition and failure of workhouses as a solution, and the general attitude of the more fortunate classes towards the submerged population.

MARTIN, WILLIAM. Early Maps of London. Papers contributed to the London and Middlesex Archaeological Society. London, 1916-19.

—————. The Interpretation of Maps of the Sixteenth and Seventeenth Centuries. In *The South-Eastern Naturalist*. London, 1910.

MATHESON, P. E. German Visitors to England, 1770-1795, and their Impressions. The Taylorean Lecture for 1930. Oxford, 1930.

This discusses four visitors—Carl Philipp Moritz, Dr. G. F. A. Wendeborn, Johann Wilhelm von Archenholz, and G. Christopher Lichtenberg. These all appear in the section TOURS BY FOREIGNERS.

MATHEW, DAVID. The Celtic Peoples and Renaissance Europe. A Study of Celtic and Spanish Influences on Elizabethan History. London, 1933.

The discussion of Irish and Welsh history and social life is pertinent to this present work.

MAYOR, J. E. B. (Editor). Cambridge under Queen Anne: illustrated by a Memoir of Bonwicke and Diaries of Burman and Uffenbach. 8vo. London, 1911.

Memoirs of the Literary and Philosophical Society of Manchester. 8vo. London, 1785—.

The place of imprint was later changed to Manchester. These volumes were published regularly up to 1875 [and perhaps later], and contain many articles on Lancashire. Fishwick, *The Lancashire Library*.

METEYARD, ELIZA. The Life of Josiah Wedgwood, from his Private Correspondence and Family Papers, with an Introductory Sketch of the Art of Pottery in England. Numerous illustrations. 2 vols. London, 1865.

From these volumes one learns much of the difficulties attending transportation of wares, the early struggles in getting the Duke of Bridgewater's Canal under way, and the experimentation carried on by Wedgwood in his search for suitable clays.

MICHEL, FRANCISQUE. Les Ecossais en France—Les Français en Ecosse. 2 vols. Londres, 1862.

The interchange of visitors and the cultural relations existing between Scotland and France over long periods of time are well impressed upon the reader of these volumes.

Middlesex and Hertfordshire Notes and Queries. London, 1895—.

This publication became the Home Counties Magazine after 1898. See below.
The Home Counties Magazine devoted to the Topography of London, Middlesex, Essex, Herts, Bucks, Berks, Surrey, and Kent. Edit. by W. J. Hardy. Numerous maps, plates and illustrations. Index to vols. 1-10. 8vo. London, 1899—.

Midland Antiquary. 4 vols. Birmingham, 1882-87.

Miscellanea Scotica: A Collection of Tracts relating to the History, Antiquities, Topography and Literature of Scotland. 24 vols. in 4. 8vo. Glasgow, 1818-20.

MOFFIT, LOUIS W. England on the Eve of the Industrial Revolution. A Study of Economic and Social Conditions from 1740 to 1760, with special Reference to Lancashire. 2 maps. 8vo. London, 1926.

MOORE, EDWARD. Various Views of Human Nature, taken from Life and Manners, chiefly in England. 2 vols. 8vo. London, 1796.

MORISON, REV. RODERICK. Clerical Life on the West Coast. Vol. 6 of *Publ. Northern Assoc.*, vol. II, pt. 1. Inverness, 1893.
> This contains 18th century extracts form the records of the Presbytery of Locharron.

MORRICE, J. C. Wales in the Seventeenth Century, its Literature and Men of Letters and Action. 8vo. Bangor, 1918.
> This is mainly biographical and bibliographical.—Read.

MOWAT, R. B. Americans in England (from Franklin to Page). Boston, 1935.

————. Jean-Jacques Rousseau. A Biography. London, 1938.
> Cited here for its discussion of Rousseau's stay in England.

MUNCKER, FRANTZ. Anschauungen vom englischen Staat und Volk in der deutschen Literatur der letzten vier Jahrhunderte. 2 Th. München, 1925.
> Kelly states that this admirable study discusses all tourists to England who held an important position in the history of German literature.

MURRAY, JAMES. Life in Scotland a Hundred Years Ago, as Reflected in the Old Statistical Account of Scotland, 1791-99. 8vo. Paisley, 1900.
> 2nd edit., enlarged, 1905.
> For this Statistical Account of Scotland, see Sinclair under 1791, SURVEYS.

Museum Rusticum et Commerciale, or, Select Papers on Agriculture, Commerce, Arts, and Manufactures, by Gentlemen engaged in these Pursuits. Plates. 6 vols. 8vo. London, 1764-66.
> These were revised by members of the Society for the Encouragement of Arts, and Manufactures, and Commerce—the forerunner of the Board of Agriculture.—Bookseller's Note.

National MSS. of Scotland. Facsimiles of the Book of Deir, Charters from 1094, Letters, Royal Precepts and Confirmations, etc. Reproduced by Sir H. James. 3 vols. Fol. London, 1867-71.

National MSS., from William the Conqueror to Queen Anne. Facsimiles of hundreds of important and characteristic historical documents with translation and notes, by W. B. Sanders. 4 vols. Fol. London, 1865-68.

NEVINS, J. B. A Picture of Wales during the Tudor Period. Liverpool, 1893.
> This quotes at length from contemporary sources. —Read,

Newcastle Reprints of Rare Tracts and Imprints of Antient Manuscripts, etc., chiefly illustrative of the History of the Northern Counties, printed at the Press of M. A. Richardson. 61 tracts bound in 7 vols. 8vo. Newcastle, 1843-49.

These are sometimes found listed under Richardson's name. Most of these tracts concern the Newcastle of the middle of the 17th century.

Newcastle-upon-Tyne Society of Antiquaries. Proceedings. 8vo. Several series. South Shields (later Kendal), 1855—.

Extra publications were issued from time to time.

Newcastle Typographical Society. Publications: A Collection of about 113 Pamphlets on a Variety of Subjects, many being Reprints of Rare Pieces. . . . Illustrated with woodcuts (many by the Bewicks), including portraits and other engravings. 12 vols. 8vo. Newcastle, 1817-43.

The items are arranged as follows: Biographical, 3 vols.; Historical, 2 vols.; Poetical, 3 vols.; Miscellaneous, 2 vols.; Numismatic, 1 vol.; Typographical, 1 vol. If the term "miscellaneous" has a superlative, it could most appropriately be applied to this collection.

New Club. Publications. Paisley, 1877—.

Founded in Paisley in 1877 "to print in a uniform and handsome manner a series of works illustrative of the antiquities, history, literature, poetry, bibliography, and topography of Scotland of former times." Occasional volumes are still issued to surviving members. —Terry.

NICHOLAS, SIR N. H. A Description of the Contents, Objects, and Uses of the various Works printed by Authority of the Record Commission. London, 1831.

NICHOLS, JOHN. Biographical and Literary Anecdotes of William Bowyer, Printer, and of many of his Learned Friends, containing an incidental View of the Progress and Advancement of Literature in this Kingdom from the Beginning of the present Century to the End of the Year 1777. Portrait. London, 1782.

William Bowyer the Younger (1699-1777) was the most learned printer of his age. In 1736 he was appointed printer to the Society of Antiquaries, to which he made several valuable contributions, including "A dissertation on the Gule or Yule of our Saxon Ancestors," and "The Inscription on Vitellius at Bath."—Quoted. For Nichols' *Literary Ancedotes of the Eighteenth Century*, see under GENERAL REFERENCE, vol. II of this work.

——————. The Progresses, Processions, and Magnificent Festivities of King James I, his Royal Consort and Family. 4 vols. London, 1828.

This work records forty masques and entertainments and ten pageants, and suggests that James's career was one lifelong pageant. The notes are rich in information on houses, itineraries, and castes. Many of the houses enumerated are long since destroyed.

NICOLSON, WILLIAM (Bishop). English, Scotch, and Irish Historical Libraries, a short View and Character of Most of our Historians in Print and MS., Records, Law Books, etc. 3rd enlarged edition. Fol. London, 1736.

A later edit., 4to, London, 1776.

NORDENSKIÖLD, A. E. Periplus—An Essay on the Early History of Cartography. Stockholm, 1897. (See this volume under GENERAL REFERENCE, vol. II of this work.)

Norfolk Antiquarian Miscellany. 3 vols. Norwich, 1872-87.

Norfolk and Norwich Archaeological Society. Norfolk Archaeology. Miscellaneous

Tracts relating to the Antiquities of the County of Norfolk. Illustrated. 8vo. Norwich, 1847—.

Extra volumes are issued from time to time.

Northamptonshire Notes and Queries. Northampton, 1884—.

This ceased publishing in 1896, but resumed in 1905.

Northern Association of Literary and Scientific Societies. Elgin, 1888-89.

Founded in Elgin in 1887 for "the promotion of joint action in literary and scientific work by the various societies joining it . . . in the counties of Aberdeen, Banff, Elgin, Nairn, Inverness, Ross, Sutherland, Cromarty, Caithness, and Orkney and Shetland." It issued no publications after 1889. Papers read at its meetings subsequent to that date may be found in the *Transactions of the Buchan and Inverness Field Club.*—Terry.

Northern Notes and Queries, or the Scottish Antiquary. Edit. by A. W. Cornelius Hallen. Illustrated. Edinburgh, 1886—.

North Oxford Archaeological and Natural History Society. Banbury, 1856—.

The name changed since 1888 to Oxfordshire Archaeological Society.

Notes and Queries: A Medium of Intercommunication for Literary Men, Artists, Antiquaries, etc. 4 vols. of Indexes to 1935. London, 1849—.

This greatest repository of questions and answers contains probably a more heterogeneous collection of "lost and found" facts than has ever been gathered together anywhere else.

Notes and Queries for Somerset and Dorset. Edit. by Hugh Norris and C. H. Mayo. Sherborne, 1890—.

Nottinghamshire and Derbyshire Notes and Queries. Derby, 1892—.

Nugae Scoticae. Miscellaneous Papers illustrative of Scottish Affairs, 1535-1781. By James Maidment, G. R. Kinloch, and Charles Baxter. Edinburgh, 1829.

This contains notices of early drama in Scotland.

Old-Lore Miscellany of Orkney, Shetland, Caithness and Sutherland. Edit. by A. W. Johnston. Vols. 1-4. 12mo. London, 1907-11.

See the Viking Club below.

OLSVIG, VELJAM. Holberg og England (1706-40). Kristiania, 1913.

This gives an account of Holberg's stay in England, with special reference to London and Oxford. It contains also an appraisal of the chief intellects of the day, a description of the dramatist's relations with the men he met, an analysis of the literature of the early 18th century, etc.

ORDISH, T. FAIRMAN. Shakespeare's London. A Study of London in the Reign of Queen Elizabeth. Illustrations. 8vo. London, 1897.

Orkney Antiquarian Society. Proceedings. Illustrations. 13 vols. (by 1935). 4to. London, 1922—.

Oxford Historical Society. Publications. Oxford, 1885—.

This series of publications presents an imposing array of notable works on Oxford—his-

tory, antiquities, books from the press, registers, deeds, cartularies, Parliamentary enactments, ecclesiastical connections, plans, views, maps, memorials, etc., with numerous illustrations. By 1939 vols. 1-101 and two volumes of the new series had appeared.

PAGE, WILLIS. London, Its Origin and Development. Boston, 1923.

PALMER, A. N. Towns, Fields, and Folk of Wrexham in the Time of James the First. Wrexham, 1883.

> This is based on Norden's Survey, parish registers, and family papers. —Davies, *Bibliog. Brit. Hist.*

PALMER, W. M. William Cole of Milton. 75 illustrations. 8vo. Cambridge, 1935.

> The life of Cole, the antiquary and correspondent of Horace Walpole, his interest in local history, and his writings are here set forth. Also described are his habits, his house at Milton, his diary, his library, and his parochial antiquities. The first two volumes of the Yale edition of the Walpole correspondence are given up to the interchange of letters between the two amateurs.

PARKES, JOAN. Travel in England in the Seventeenth Century: roads, land and water travel, inns, highwaymen, etc. 46 illustrations from contemporary plates and map (1689). 8vo. Oxford.

> This work is an admirable contribution to the social setting of the times.

PASQUET, D. La Découverte de l'Angleterre au XVIIIᵉ siècle. In Revue de Paris, 15 Dec. Paris, 1920.

> This is a delightful article on how England, and especially London, appeared and appealed to French travelers of the 18th century. It is based chiefly on Voltaire, Grossley, Madame du Bocage, Mirabeau, etc. The writer points out that Voltaire may be said to have revealed England to France with his *Lettres Philosophiques*. Henceforth one accepted the generalization that the English were a nation of philosophers, that England was the classic land of liberty, that their literature was unequalled, but original and powerful, that they had a genius for commerce, that they honored men of letters as these should be honored, etc.

PAUL, J. B. Edinburgh in 1544 and Hertford's Invasion. In *Scot. Hist. Review,* vol. 8, 113-32. Edinburgh, 1910.

PEARSON, C. H. Historical Maps of England, during the First Thirteen Centuries, with descriptive Text. 2nd edit. Fol. London, 1870.

PENDRILL, C. London Life in the Fourteenth Century. Illustrations. 8vo. London, 1925.

PENNANT, THOMAS. The Literary Life of Thomas Pennant, by Himself. Portrait and plate. 4to. London, 1793.

> Reviewed *Gent. Mag.,* vol. 63, 549. A few years earlier Pennant had distributed among his friends a list of his works, which he called "Catalogue of My Works, 1786," in four quarto pamphlets. It shows what an active literary and pedestrian life he had led, traveling over Great Britain, France, Holland, and working in antiquarian pursuits as well as in zoology. He corresponded with numerous scientists, travelers, and antiquaries. In addition to his two tours of Scotland and the Hebrides, he made one of the Isle of Man, the notes of which were lost. His tours were translated into German and French, in the *Nouveau Recueil des Voyages.* He also promoted the work of others, such as Dr. Forster's translation of the travels of Peter Kalm, the travels of Osbeck, of Bossu, Gough's edition of Camden's *Britannia,* Cordiner's *Antiquities and Scenery of Scotland.* He wrote many articles on social and economic affairs, and published works on zoology, which he called "imaginary Tours to the Southern Climate." He was admitted to several foreign and domestic societies. His account of his publications assists in straightening out the complicated dating of his works, wherein printing of new travels overlapped the issuance of second editions of earlier travels.

Penzance Natural History and Antiquarian Society. Transactions. 3 vols. Penzance, 1851-66.

PETRIE, SIR CHARLES. Travelling in Bygone England. In *Cornhill Magazine,* vol. 157, 791-802. London, 1938.

PHILLIPSTHAL, ROBERT. Deutsche Reisende des XVIII Jahrhunderts in England. In *Festschrift zum 13. Allgemeinen Deutschen Neuphilologentage.* Hannover, 1908.

PITS, JOHN. Relationum Historicarum de Rebus Anglicis Tomus Primus. Vol. I (all published). 4to. Paris, 1619.

> This is a rare source of information on English Roman Catholic writers subsequent to the Reformation. It is frequently referred to in the *Dictionary of National Biography.* The book is divided into four parts. The first includes an account of Oxford and Cambridge universities; the second, short lives of three hundred English writers; the third, a list of books, of which the authors are unknown; and the fourth, fifteen alphabetical indices.— Quoted from Robinson's Catalogue.

POLLARD, A. F. (Editor). Tudor Tracts, 1532-1588. London, 1902.

PONS, E. Le Voyage Genre littéraire au XVIIIᵉ Siècle. Strasbourg, 1926.

PONSOBY, ARTHUR. English Diaries: a Review of English Diaries from the Sixteenth to the Twentieth Century, with an Introduction on Diary Writing. London, 1923.

————. More English Diaries from the Sixteenth to the Nineteenth Century. London, 1927.

————. Scottish and Irish Diaries from the Sixteenth to the Nineteenth Century. With an Introduction. London, 1927.

> These volumes have established the editor as an authority on the subject. Extracts from diaries and comments interweaving them, together with an illuminating essay on diary writing, are the substance of the volumes. They should make addicts to the reading, if not to the writing, of diaries.

Powysland Club. Collections, Historical and Archaeological, relating to Montgomeryshire and its Borders. London, 1868—.

PRATT, E. A. History of Inland Transport. In Turberville, *Johnson's England,* vol. I. London, 1933.

Prehistoric Society of East Anglia. Proceedings. Vol. I (all published?) Illustrations. London, 1908-14.

> This contains articles on flint implements, stone age, local discoveries, etc., by Moir, Sturge, Underwood, Haward, and others.

PRINCE, JOHN. Danmonii orientales illustres, or, The Worthies of Devon. Fol. Exeter, 1701.

> This contains the lives of the most celebrated natives of this county. The undeserved ill-success of this laborious compilation discouraged Prince from venturing his second volume,

which he had already prepared for the press.—Gough, 140. It provides information on the works of various historians and antiquaries.

QUENNELL, MARJORIE, and C. H. B. "Everyday Life" Series. 4 vols. London, 1922-26.

> The titles in this series run as follows:
> I Everyday Life in the Old Stone Age. 128 pp., including 70 illustrations and a colored frontispiece from the authors' drawings.
> II Everyday Life In the New Stone, Bronze and Early Iron Ages. 144 pp., with 90 original illustrations, from the authors' drawings, of household life, agriculture, pottery, weapons, etc.
> III Everyday Life in Roman Britain. 128 pp., with over 100 original drawings from the authors' pens of camps, villas, ships, chariots, monments, costume, military, etc.
> IV Life in Anglo-Saxon, Viking and Norman Times. 128 pp., with illustrations of ships, cooking, metalwork, pottery, etc.

—————. "A History of Everyday Things" Series. 4 vols. London, 1918-34.

> The titles in this series run:
> I Everyday Things in England, 1066-1499. Illustrations.
> II Everyday Things in England, 1500-1799. Illustrations.
> III Everyday Things in England, 1733-1851. Illustrations.
> IV Everyday Things in England, 1851-1934. Illustrations.
> Both series have been printed in revised editions, New York.
> The above volumes practically reconstruct life as it was lived from day to day, much as a scientifically arranged museum would do. The charming pen drawings enhance enormously the value of the text.

RAINE, J. (Editor). The Historians of the Church of York and its Archbishops. 3 vols. London, 1879-94.

RAMSAY, J. (of Ochtertyre). Scotland and Scotsmen in the Eighteenth Century. 2 vols. Edinburgh and London, 1888.

Record and State Paper Commissioners and other Works relating to the Public Records. Publications. London, 1801—.

> This monumental series of publications is well known to every student of English history, particularly the State Papers, the various Rolls, the Calendars, the Chronicles and Memorials. A good listing of these Record Publications is printed in Quaritch, *A Catalogue of Books*, no. 480, 1934. Here and there are also to be found accounts of tours, which are recorded in the section TOURS BY NATIVES.

Record Society for Publication of Original Documents relating to Lancashire and Cheshire. London, 1879—.

REINHARD, W. Zur Entwicklung des Kartenbildes der Britischen Inseln bis auf Merkator . . . 1654. (Place?), 1909.

Reliquary: Quarterly Archaeological Journal and Review. London, 1860—.

> Since January, 1895, the title runs:
> The Reliquary and Illustrated Archaeologist. A Quarterly Journal and Review, devoted to the study of the early Pagan and Christian Antiquities of Great Britain, etc. Edit. by J. Romilly Allen. New Series. London, 1895—.

REYNOLDS, MYRA. The Treatment of Nature in English Poetry between Pope and Wordsworth. Chicago, 1909.

> The discussion of some of the travelers and their attitudes toward nature has been utilized in this work from time to time.

RICHARDSON, A. E. The English Inn Past and Present: A Review of its History and Social Life, treating of Medieval, Tudor, Georgian, and Later Times, London Interiors, the Small Tavern Signs, the Road Coach Travel, suggested Tours, etc., with about 200 illustrations, including pictures by Rowlandson, Hogarth, James Pollard, Morland, and Aiken. London, 1925.

——————. Georgian England. A Survey of Social Life, Trades, Industries, and Art, 1700-1821. Illustrations. 4to. London, 1931.

——————. The Old Inns of England. 132 plates from photographs, and many illustrations in the text. New York and London, 1935.

ROBERTS, R. A. The Public Records relating to Wales. In *Y Cymmrodor,* vol. 10, 157-206. London, 1890.

ROHDE, ELEANOUR. Old English Gardening Books. Illustrations. London, 1924.

> The subject is treated with loving care. The text is as charming as the numerous quotations sprinkled in.

Rolls Series: Rerum Britannicarum Medii Aevi Scriptores; or, Chronicles and Memorials of Great Britain and Ireland during the Middle Ages. Published by the Authority of H. M.'s Treasury under the Direction of the Master of the Rolls. 253 vols. 8vo. London, 1858-1911.

> A large number of these volumes will be found listed under their dates in the section HISTORY AND CHRONICLE.

Ross, A. Early Travels in Scotland. In *Trans. Gaelic Soc. Inverness,* vol. 23. Inverness, 1902.

> This is mainly concerned with travelers from 1295 to 1689, and draws largely from Hume Brown's *Early Travellers.*

Roxburghe Club. Publications. London, 1814——.

> "The Roxburghe Club is the oldest existing society of bibliophiles in Great Britain and probably in the world. It is also the parent of those publishing societies which have done so much in this country for history, letters, antiquity, and other branches of literature and art. It was founded in 1812 by the exertions of the Rev. Thomas Dibdin. . . . In 1804 John, 3rd Duke of Roxburghe died, and eight years later his books were sold for £23,000. The Valdarfer Boccaccio of 1471, gem of the collection, was to come under the hammer on 17 June, 1812, and to celebrate its sale Dibdin determined to assemble at dinner a party of bibliophiles, many of whom had partaken in the auction. . . . The Boccaccio was bought by Lord Blandford for the then stupendous sum of £2,260, and in the evening eighteen gentlemen, all more or less interested in books, dined in Waterloo Place. . . . At this gathering the Roxburghe Club was founded."—Extract from Viscount Mersey's Introduction to no. 188 of the Club's Publications, quoted by Quaritch, Cat. no. 522.

Royal Archaeological Institute of Great Britain and Ireland. Archaeological Journal. London, 1845——.

> An Index of vols. 1-25 published, 1878.

Royal Historical Society. Transactions. 66 vols. (by 1940). 8vo. London, 1874——.

> The list of contributors to these volumes includes many of the foremost historians and antiquaries of Great Britain.

Royal Society. Philosophical Transactions of the Royal Society of London. Vols. 1—A237 and B228, with General Indexes to vols. 1-120 (extra vols. of 1878 and the Report of the Eruption of Krakatoa). London, 1665-1939.

To be included with these are the volumes published by R. Hooke, 1679-82, the years when the *Philosophical Transactions* were temporarily suspended. They are called the *Philosophical Collections.* For the various classifications of the volumes, see the *Union List of Serials.*

Royal Society of London. Proceedings. 187 vols. (by 1935). 8vo. London, 1800—.

RYE, WILLIAM BRENCHLEY. England as Seen by Foreigners in the Days of Elizabeth and James I, comprising Translations of the Journals of the two Dukes of Wirtemberg in 1592 and 1610; both illustrative of Shakespeare, etc. Introduction and Notes. 7 portraits and etchings, and a bibliography. 4to. London, 1865.

In addition to these two main journals, the work includes other briefer accounts of German visitors. It contains a great wealth of information on personalities and places of Elizabethan England. The present volume has drawn freely upon its offerings.

St. Albans Architectural and Archaeological Society. Transactions. St. Albans, 1885—.

Since 1895 the name has been changed to St. Albans and Hertfordshire Architectural and Archaeological Society.

SALAMAN, MALCOLM C. The Old Engravers of England. 8vo. London, 1906.

This is an account and appraisal of the work of such important engravers as John Payne, Thomas Cockson, William Faithorne, Wencelaus Hollar, David Loggan, John Smith, George White, John Faber, James Watson, Valentine Green, James Basire, William Blake, etc. Many of these names are met with on the title pages of works cited in the foregoing sections.

SALTER, EMMA GURNEY. Tudor England Through Venetian Eyes. London, 1930.

The work summarizes the views of the Venetian ambassadors and secretaries of Tudor England as set down in their *Relations* and *Despatches,* which were presented to the Senate at Venice. An immense amount of information is distilled by the author from these works, and reveals what the student may expect to find concerning England from these astute observers. A list of the ambassadors and their dates between 1496 and 1558 is given, together with the contents of their reports, their manner of communication, and the ups and downs of English and Venetian commercial and diplomatic interactions. A number of these *Relations* were published by the Camden Society and are recorded under TOURS BY FOREIGNERS.

SCHAIBLE, KARL HEINRICH. Geschichte der Deutschen von den ersten germanischen Ansiedlungen in Britannien bis zum Ende des 18. Jahrhunderts. Strassburg, 1885.

This is an investigation of the presence of Germans in England and the attractions of the country for them.

SCHUTTE, G. Ptolemy's Atlas—A Study of its Sources. In *Scot. Geog. Mag.,* vol. 30, 55-57. Edinburgh, 1914.

Scotia Rediviva. A Collection of Tracts illustrative of the History and Antiquities of Scotland. Vol. I (all published). Edinburgh, 1826.

Later edit., with slight change in title, Edinburgh, 1836.

SCOTT, SIR WALTER. The Border Antiquities of England and Scotland: comprising Specimens of Architecture and Sculpture, and other Vestiges of Former Ages. 2 vols. 4to. London, 1814-17.

—————. The Secret History of the Court of James the First. 2 vols. Edinburgh, 1811.

> Among the items is A Perfect Description of the People and Country of Scotland (1659).

Scottish Antiquary. See *Northern Notes and Queries* above.

Scottish Burgh Records Society. Publications. Comprising the Records and Laws of the Burghs, and other Contemporary Documents from the earliest Period, edited with Prefaces, Notes, and Glossaries, by Cosmo Innes, J. D. Marwick, and John Stuart. Facsimiles and plans. 4to. Edinburgh and Glasgow, 1868—.

> These old Records of the Burghs of Scotland are highly valuable for the light they throw upon national life and manners, national institutions, and social progress.

Scottish Ecclesiological Society. Transactions. Comprising (up to 1937) Three Sections: *Aberdeen* (1887-1901), *Glasgow* (1895-1901), continued by the *Scottish Ecclesiological Society* to 1937. Also the *Rathan Manual* and *Aberdeen-Glasgow Special Issue*. Glasgow, 1887—.

> This society was founded in 1903, on the union of the Aberdeen and Glasgow Ecclesiological Societies, "for the study of the principles of Christian worship and of Church architecture and the allied arts which minister thereto."—Terry.

Scottish Geographical Magazine. Edinburgh, 1885—.

Scottish Historical Review. Contributions on special Periods of Scottish History and Economics by leading Historians. Edinburgh, 1903-28.

> This is a new series of the *Scottish Antiquary* begun in 1886. See *Northern Notes and Queries* above. A proposal to resume publication has recently appeared.

Scottish History Society. Publications. Edinburgh, 1887—.

> This society was instituted "for the discovery and printing, under selected editorship, of unpublished documents illustrative of the civil, religious, and social history of Scotland," and it has nobly carried out its purpose with an impressive array of volumes to its credit (115 nos. by 1940).

Scottish Notes and Queries. Contributions on Scottish History, Antiquities, Family History, Biography, etc. Edinburgh, 1887—.

Scottish Text Society. Publications. Edinburgh, 1884—.

> This society was founded in Edinburgh in 1882 "for the purpose of printing and editing texts in early and middle Scots." To date (1944) the volumes number 90. In range, style, and scholarship and purpose, the series corresponds to the publications of the Early English Text Society.

SEARLE, MARK. Turnpikes and Toll-Bars. Compiled by Mark Searle. Special Introduction by the Right Hon. the Earl of Birkenhead. 12 colored plates and 515 other illustrations. 2 vols. 4to. London.

> The illustrations are for the most part reproduced from old prints and broadsides. This is the only work dealing with this fascinating and neglected subject. Every phase of the turnpike period is covered.—Bookseller's Note.

SEARLE, W. G. Ingulf and the Historia Croylandensis. An Investigation attempted. 8vo. Cambridge, 1894.

> See Ingulph under Savile, 1596, HISTORY AND CHRONICLE.

SHAW, GEORGE T. The History of the Liverpool Directories, 1766-1907. *Publ. Hist. Soc. Lancashire and Cheshire,* n.s., vol. 22. Liverpool, 1907.

> The writer points out that 18th century directories of the city did not list the inhabitants under the names of the streets. He proposes to do this for that of 1766. He analyzes the professions and trades in existence then, follows the course of later directories, notes the inclusion of additional matter, such as the history of the town in that of 1794, the advertisement of facilities for sea bathing, the fact that Liverpool has passed Bristol, etc.

――――――. Liverpool's Second Directory, 1767. In *Publ. Hist. Soc. Lancashire and Cheshire,* n.s., vol. 42. Liverpool, 1926.

SHEARER, JOHN E. Old Maps and Map Makers of Scotland, with 10 facsimiles from Original Early Maps with Historical and Descriptive Account. 4to. Stirling, 1905.

> This work furnished data for many items in MAPS AND CHARTS.

SHEARS, F. S. Froissart, Chronicler and Poet. The first Biography in English of the great Fourteenth Century Chronicler. Illustrations. London, 1930.

> This describes his travels in England, Scotland, and Europe, with chapters on his outlook on life and his attitude to different classes and nations, with notes, bibliography, and index. —Bookseller's Announcement.

SHELDON, GILBERT. From Trackway to Turnpike. London, 1928.

Shropshire Archaeological Society. Transactions. Numerous plates and text-illustrations. 8vo. Shrewsbury, 1878——.

Shropshire Notes and Queries. Shrewsbury, 1886——.

SIBBALD, SIR ROBERT. An Account of the Writers Antient and Modern, printed and MS. which treat of the Description of North Britain, called Scotland, as it was of old, and is now at present, with a Catalogue of the Maps, and Prospects, and Figures of the Antient Monuments thereof, such as have come to his hands, in several Languages. Fol. Edinburgh, 1710.

> Sibbald first broke the ice, as he himself says, in the way of writing the antiquities of his country. —Gough, *op. cit.*

SIMPSON, J. Antiquarian Notices of Syphilis in Scotland in the 15th and 16th Centuries. 8vo. London, n.d.

SIMS, R. Manual for the Genealogist, Topographer, Antiquary, and Legal Professor. London, 1856.

SINCLAIR, J. An Account of the Origin of the Board of Agriculture and its Progress for Three Years after its Establishment. London, 1793.

SKENE, WILLIAM FORBES. Celtic Scotland: A History of Ancient Alban. 3 vols. Edinburgh, 1876-80.

> This was an ambitious work in its day, but modern scholarship has found much to correct in it.

SKINNER, REV. J. Annals of Scottish Episcopacy from 1788-1816, with a Biographical Memoir of the Rt. Rev. J. Skinner Primus. 8vo. Edinburgh, 1818.

SMITH, C. FELL. Eighteenth Century Travels. In *Essex Review,* vol. 36, 113-120. Chelmsford (now at Colchester), 1927.

SMITH, C. R. Collectanea Antiqua. Etchings and Notices of Ancient Remains, illustrative of the Habits, Customs and History of Past Ages. Numerous drawings. 7 vols. 8vo. London, 1848-80.

> A vast storehouse of valuable papers on the history of the Southern counties.—Quaritch, no. 529.

SMITH, D. C. The Historians of Perth, and other Local Topographical Writers, up to the End of the Nineteenth Century. Portraits. 4to. Perth, 1906.

SMITH, EDWARD. Foreign Visitors in England and what they have thought of us; being some Notes on their Books and their Opinions during the last Three Centuries. London, 1889.

> This discusses chiefly the visitors of the 17th and 18th centuries, with references to diarists of later generations. A bibliography and descriptive notes make it a useful book.

SMITH, J. T. Nollekins and his Times. 2 vols. London, 1828.

> Also published in the Oxford Classics series, 1929.
> In an age of eccentric characters, the sculptor Nollekins could rate as high as any in superlatives. Of him one might say he was the dirtiest, stingiest (outside of Mrs. Nollekins), most ignorant, contrivingest, and so on, of geniuses that ever walked the streets of London. On the other hand he knew more of antiquarian history of houses, standing or demolished, than any man in London. He died, as is proper for a miser, worth £200,000. His biographer Smith was his pupil and assistant, later keeper of prints and drawings in the British Museum.

Society of Antiquaries of London. Proceedings. Plates and woodcuts. 8vo. London, 1843—.

> The *Proceedings* became the *Journal* from 1921 on.

Society of Antiquaries of Scotland. Archaeologia Scotica; or, Transactions and Historical Account of the Society of Antiquaries of Scotland. Maps and plates of ancient Remains, Inscriptions, etc. 5 vols. (1792-1890); added volume, W. Snellie's Account of the Institution and Progress of the Society, 1900. Edinburgh, 1792-1890.

> No more volumes with the above title appeared after 1890. The society was founded in 1780 by the Earl of Buchan. It collected quite a museum of curiosities, the list of which was published. This museum developed into a large national institution housed in Edinburgh. Another set of publications seems to have grown up taking the place of the *Archaeologia.* See below.

Society of Antiquaries of Scotland. Proceedings. 75 vols. (by 1938). Indices to vols. 1-48 and library catalogue. 8vo and 4to. Edinburgh, 1851—.

Society for the Encouragement of Arts, Manufactures, and Commerce. Transactions, 55 vols., with Index of Vols. 1-40. Large number of plates. 8vo. London, 1783-1845.

> A large proportion of the articles deal with agriculture and the advantages of new methods and machinery then being introduced.

Society in Scotland for the Propagating Christian Knowledge. An Account of, from its Commencement in 1709. In which is included, The Present State of the Highlands and Islands of Scotland with regard to Religion. Together with some Account of the Society's Missionaries for converting the Native Indians of America. 4to. Edinburgh, 1774.

Somers' Tracts. A Collection of Scarce and Vauable Tracts, on the Most Interesting and Entertaining Subjects, but chiefly such as relate to the History and Constitution of these Kingdoms. Selected from an Infinite Number in Print and in Manuscript, in the Royal, Cotton, Sion, and other Public, as well as Private Libraries, particularly that of the Late Lord Somers. 2nd edit., revised, augmented, and arranged by Walter Scott. 13 vols. London, 1809-15.

Somerset Archaeological and Natural History Society. Proceedings. Vols. 1-85 (by 1940). Indexes to vols. 1-40. Illustrations. Taunton, 1851—.

SOUTHEY, ROBERT. On the Accounts of England by Foreign Travellers. *Essays,* vol. I, no. vi, 251-325. London, 1832.

In this lengthy survey of French opinion Southey shows from liberal quotations that the French generally were hostile to England.

Spalding Club. Miscellany, edit. by Dr. Stuart. 5 vols. Aberdeen, 1841-52.

This club was founded in Aberdeen in 1839 "for the printing of the historical, ecclesiastical, genealogical, typographical, and literary remains of the north-eastern counties of Scotland." It was dissolved in 1870. For the New Spalding Club see below. During its brief existence the club published a vast amount of rare and valuable materials relating to the history of Scotland, which are found nowhere else.

New Spalding Club. Proceedings. Aberdeen, 1887—.

This club was founded in 1886 "to promote the study of history, topography, and archaeology of the north-eastern counties of Scotland, and to print the works illustrative thereof."

SPILLER, ROBERT E. The American in England During the First Half Century of Independence. New York, 1926.

The material is arranged under general headings, such as: Travel by Sea and Land, Students, Artists, Envoys, Practical Tourists, Philanthropic Travellers, Literary Men, Critics, etc. The great majority of the travelers belong to the early 19th century. Quotations from their writings are freely used to allow the visitors to speak for themselves. What the Americans saw, whom they met, how they were received as Americans, and their different reactions as Americans naturally varied with their individualities, their training, their business, and their objectives. A bibliography of the material used is appended.

SPOTTISWOODE, JOHN (Archbishop of St. Andrews). The History of the Church of Scotland. 3 vols. *Publ. Bann. Club.,* no. 93. Edinburgh, 1850.

Vol.1 was edited by Bishop Michael Russell; vols. 2 and 3 by Mark Napier. See also *Publ. Spottiswoode Soc.,* vol. 6 (1851).

Spottiswoode Society. Publications. Edinburgh, 1843-51.

This society was founded in Edinburgh in 1843 for "the revival and publication of the acknowledged works of the bishops, clergy, and laity of the Episcopal Church of Scotland, and rare, authentic, and curious MSS, pamphlets, and other works, illustrative of the civil and ecclesiastical history of Scotland." Publications ceased with 1851.

Staffordshire Record Society. See William Salt Archaeology Society below.

STANLEY, ARTHUR. The Golden Road—An Anthology of Travel. Selected and arranged by Arthur Stanley. Illustrated by Phyllis Bray. 8vo. London, 1938.

> This contains selections from Homer to airplane travels of the present day. The selections are usually short, but they make pleasant reading.

STEVENS, FRANK (Curator of the Salisbury Museum). Stonehenge Today and Yesterday. Plans and illustrations. London, 1933.

> This is an excellent survey of the questions raised by this intriguing monument of the late Stone Age and the modern answers attempted. Unfortunately for the curious reader it is out of print.

STEVENSON, E. L. Willem Janzoon Blaeu (1571-1638). A Sketch of his Life and Work. New York, 1914.

Stirling Field Club (after 1882, The Stirling Natural History and Archaeological Society). Publications. Stirling, 1878—.

> Founded in 1878 as the Stirling Field Club "to explore the district for the purpose of inquiring into its geology, botany, natural history and archaeology."

STILLIE, J. Tracts illustrative of the Traditionary and Historical Antiquities of Scotland. Portrait. Edinburgh, 1836.

STONE, E. H. The Stones of Stonehenge, a full Description of the Structure and of its Outworks. 36 plates, plans, and diagrams. 4to. London, 1924.

STRAUS, RALPH. Carriages and Coaches. Their History and their Evolution. 46 illustrations. London, 1912.

STRETTON, GRACE. Aspects of Medieval Travel. *Publ. Roy. Hist. Soc.,* 4th ser., vol. 8. London, 1924.

STUART, JOHN. Documents relating to Orkney and Shetland, 1438-1563. *Misc. Spalding Club,* vol. 5. Aberdeen, 1852.

Suffolk. A Collection of Miscellaneous Papers, Political, Topographical, Parochial, etc., relating to the County of Suffolk. 4to and fol. London (?), 1756-1825.

Suffolk Green Books. Parish Register of Ickworth, Denham, Whelnatham, Bury St. Edmunds, 3 vols.; Shotley, 2 vols.; Rushbrook, Wordwell, etc.; Suffolk in 1327, 1524, 1568; Journals of Hon. Will. Hervey, 1755-1811; Diary and Letter Books of John Hervey, 4 vols.; Dictionary of Herveys of all the Counties, 1040-1500, 5 vols. 29 vols. 4to. London (?), 1894-1929.

Suffolk Institute of Archaeology and Natural History. Proceedings. Bury St. Edmunds, 1853—.

> Vol. 1 was called Proceedings of the Bury and West Suffolk Archaeological Society. Some of the issues bear the imprint of Ipswich.

SUMNER, JOHN. William Hutton, The Birmingham Historian (1723-1815). *Trans. Worcestershire Arch. Soc.,* n.s., vols. 5-6. Worcester, 1927-29.

Hutton was known as the Birmingham historian because of his *History of Derby,* which is still a standard work of reference. The above account runs over his life and its accomplishments, drawing in part from his autobiography, which must be a charming work as well as highly informing on the character of a remarkable man and on the social and economic life of the last half of the 18th century. From depths of poverty as a child working in the silk mills twelve hours a day, then a runaway apprentice subsisting on next to nothing—he rose to be Commissioner of the Court of Requests, followed by other public employments as historian, antiquary, and writer. A tireless traveler, he walked the length of the Roman Wall from Carlisle to Newcastle and back at the age of 79 years. He died in his 92nd year. His houses were burned in the Birmingham riots that destroyed Priestley's.

Surrey Archaeological Society. Collections relating to the History and Antiquities of the County. Numerous illustrations. Indexes and extra volumes. 53 vols. (by 1941). London, 1858—.

Surtees Society. Publications. 142 vols. (by 1937). Durham, 1835—.

The range and output of this society have been enormous—wills, deeds, correspondence, diaries, monkish chronicles, inventories, charters, registers and rolls, heraldic visitations, lives, etc. The series is of the utmost value to the historian, antiquary, and student of literature and social conditions.

Sussex Archaeological Society. Collections, relating to the History and Antiquities of the County. 74 vols., with General Index to vols. 1-25 (by 1932). Brighton, Lewes, London, 1848—.

Sussex Notes and Queries. Devoted to the Antiquities, Family History, Place Names, Folk-Lore, etc., being a Quarterly Journal of the Sussex Archaeological Society. Lewes, 1926—.

Sutherland Association of Edinburgh. Publications. Edinburgh, 1866—.

This association was founded in 1866 to, among other things, "publish a series of short essays, bearing on the history, folklore, topography, and antiquities of the county." There is also a Glasgow-Sutherlandshire Association, founded in 1857, "for the study and preservation of the literature, history, and traditions of the county."—Terry.

SYDNEY, WILLIAM CONNOR. England and the English in the Eighteenth Century. 2 vols. London, 1892.

See chap. XI, vol. 2, Roads and Travelling; and chap. XII, Favorite Health Resorts.

TAYLOR, E. G. R. Tudor Geography 1485-1583. With bibliography of early Tudor works on Geography. 16 plates. 8vo. London, 1930.

—————. Late Tudor and Early Stuart Geography 1583-1650. A Sequel to Tudor Geography. Bibliography. London, 1934.

The texts and bibliographies of these two works are extremely valuable for their completeness and accurate scholarship.

THOM, WALTER. Pedestrianism; or, An Account of the Performances of Celebrated Pedestrians during the last and present Century, with full Account of Captain Barclay's Public and Private Matches. Full length portrait of Capt. Barclay in walking dress. Aberdeen, 1813.

THOMS, W. J. (Editor). Anecdotes and Traditions, illustrative of Early English

History and Literature, from various Sources. *Publ. Camden Soc.,* vol. 5, London, 1839.

THOMSON, G. S. Life in a Noble Household, 1641-1700. London, 1937.

THORESBY, RALPH. Letters of Eminent Men addressed to Ralph Thoresby, F.R.S., now first published from the Originals. 2 vols. London, 1832.

> These contain much that relates to antiquities, which was the absorbing hobby of Thoresby.

Thoresby Society. Publications. 38 vols. (by 1937). Leeds, 1891—.

> The papers here printed are chiefly concerned with the Leeds district, its antiquities, history, topography, and manufactures.

Thoroton Society. Transactions. 42 vols. (by 1939). Nottingham, 1897—.

> This is an antiquarian society for Nottinghamshire.

TOMBS, R. C. The Bristol Royal Mail. London, 1899.

——————. The King's Post. London, 1905.

TOVEY, D. C. Gray and His Friends. Cambridge, 1890.

> Pertinent to this work where the correspondence concerns Gray's comments on landscape.

TRAILL, HENRY D. Social England. A Record of Progress of the People in Religion, Laws, Learning, Arts, Literature, and Manners from the Earliest Times to the Present Day. Numerous illustrations. 6 vols. London, 1902-04.

> Valuable also for its bibliographies.

Tunbrigialia, or, Tunbridge Miscellanies. London, 1737, 1738, and 1739.

TURBERVILLE, A. S. English Men and Manners in the Eighteenth Century. Illustrations from contemporary prints. 2nd edit. Oxford, 1929.

> An excellent handbook to the 18th century. Bibliographies are appended to the end of chapters.

——————. (General Editor). Johnson's England, an Account of the Life and Manners of his Age. 2 vols. Oxford, 1933.

> This is a collaborative work. See "Travel and Communications," by H. L. Beales, vol. I, ch. vi.

TURNER, J. HORSFALL.. Halifax Books and Authors, a Series of Articles on the Books written by Natives and Residents, Ancient and Modern, of the Parish of Halifax, with Notices of their Authors and Local Printers; comprising Materials for the Local and Literary History, etc. 4to. Privately Printed, 1906.

URQUHART, SIR THOMAS. Tracts of the Learned and Celebrated Antiquarian Sir Thomas Urquhart of Cromarty. 12mo. Edinburgh, 1774.

URZIDIL, J. Hollar: A Czech Emigré in England. Translated by Paul Selver. 30 illustrations. 4to. London, 1942.

Viking Club. Publications. London, 1892—.

This club was founded in 1892 as the Orkney, Shetland and Northern Society to deal with "subjects connected with northern history, literature, music, art, archaeology, language, folklore, anthropology and other matters."—Terry. It has also taken as its province Viking culture and invasions, Celtic history and antiquities, etc.

WALPOLE, HORACE. Walpole's England as his Letters Picture It. Edit. by A. B. Mason. London, 1930.

—————. Anecdotes of Painting. Edit. by Ralph N. Wornum. 3 vols. London, 1876.

Included is his famous "Essay on Gardening."

WALPOLE SOCIETY. Publications (annual). Numerous plates. 4to. London, 1911—.

This society was founded in April, 1911, to promote the study of British art.

WALTERS, H. B. The English Antiquaries of the Sixteenth, Seventeenth, and Eighteenth Centuries. Portraits. London, 1934.

The Introduction points out that the Greek and Roman historians were not devoid of antiquarian interests, but that the medieval chroniclers paid no attention to topography or the past history of buildings and the like. Not until the advent of Leland do we have in England any attempts to record the antiquities of the country. The book is then devoted to the lives of the chief antiquaries, all of whom are listed somewhere in the foregoing sections, such as Leland, Stow, Camden, Dugdale, Habingdon, Aubrey, Wood, Plot, Hearne, Stukeley, Willis, Bridges, Hutchins, Morant, Bray, Gough, Lysons (the two), Nash, Prattington, Cole, and Hasted.

WARD, J. The Roman Era in Britain. Illustrations. The Antiquary's Books Series. London, 1911.

WARRACK, JOHN. Domestic Life in Scotland, 1488-1688. A Sketch of the Development of Furniture and Household Custom. Rhind Lectures in Archaeology, 1919-20. 16 illustrations. London, 1920.

Warwickshire Antiquarian Magazine. 8 pts. Warwick, 1859-77.

WEBB, S. and B. English Local Government: The Story of the King's Highway. London, 1920.

Cited in Turberville, *Johnson's England*, vol. I, as primarily a study in road administration, with helpful references to contemporary sources.

Welsh Bibliographical Society. Journal. Carmarthen, 1910—.

Western Antiquary, or, Notebook for Devon, Cornwall and Somerset. Edit. by W. H. K. Wright. Illustrations and pedigrees. 12 vols. and Supplement. Plymouth, 1882-95.

WHARTON, HENRY. Anglia Sacra (Lives of the English prelates to 1540). London, 1691.

Wharton left behind him large MS collections.

WHEATLEY, HENRY B. Hogarth's London. Illustrated from Hogarth. London, 1909.

——————. Notes on Norden and his Map of London. In *London Topographical Record Illustrated,* of the London Topographical Soc., vol. 2. Reprinted from the *Trans. New Shakespeare Soc.* London, 1903.

WILLAN, T. River Navigation in England, 1600-1750. Maps. Oxford, 1936.

William Salt Archaeological Society. Collections for a History of Staffordshire. Birmingham, 1880—.

> The name was changed to The Staffordshire Record Society with the 1934 volume. Beginning 1910, the society stopped numbering its volumes. The subject matter is rather records than archaeology.

WILLIAMS, CLARE. Thomas Platter in England. London, 1937.

> See Platter under 1929, TOURS BY FOREIGNERS. The Introduction to this work provided me with much valuable material.

WILLIAMS, E. R. Some Studies in Elizabethan Wales. Newtown, 1924 (?).

> Popular treatment, with much relating to the sea and piracy.—Read.

WILLIAMS, J. Records of Denbigh and its Lordship. Vol. 1 (all published). Wrexham.

> This contains valuable material of more than local interest.—Read.

WILSON, DANIEL. Memorials of Edinburgh in the Olden Time. Full-page engravings and other illustrations. 2 vols. 4to. Edinburgh, 1848.

WILSON, THOMAS. Archaeological Dictionary. 8vo. London, 1783.

Wiltshire Archaeological and Natural History Magazine (published under the Direction of the Society of the same name). Extra volumes and Indexes. Numerous illustrations. Devizes, 1854—.

> Wiltshire is especially full of fascinating remains of local history. Its wonderful prehistoric antiquities, its ecclesiastical and domestic architecture, its varied history, and the natural history of its rolling downs, all combine to make the present work one of the most interesting of its class.—Quoted.

Wiltshire Notes and Queries. An Illustrated Quarterly, Antiquarian and Genealogical Magazine. Plates and illustrations. 4 vols. Devizes, 1893-1904.

WINSTANLEY, D. A. The University of Cambridge in the Eighteenth Century. Portraits. Cambridge, 1922.

Wodrow Society. Publications. Edinburgh, 1841-50.

> This society was founded in Edinburgh in 1841 "for the publication of the works of the fathers and early writers of the Reformed Church of Scotland." It ceased publishing in 1850.

WOOD, ANTHONY A. Athenae Oxonienses, an Exact History of all the Writers and Bishops who have had their Education in the Most Ancient and Famous University of Oxford, with the Fasti or Annals. 2 vols. Fol. Oxford, 1691/92.

> This famous work did not turn out to be exactly what was expected. "An inscription dated Oxon, July 31, 1693, runs as following: On the 29th Instant Anthony a Wood (author of

this book) was condemn'd in the Chancellor's court of the University of Oxford for having written and publish'd in the 2nd vol. of his book entitled Athenae Oxonienses divers infamous libels agth the right Honble Robt late Earl of Clarendon . . . And was therefore banish'd the sd University, untill such time as he shall subscribe such a publick recantation as the Judge of the court shall approve of, and give security not to offend in the like nature for the future. And his said book was therefore also decree'd to be burnt before the publick Theatre and on this day it was burnt accordingly."—Quoted from Bookseller's Note.

—————. Life and Times of Anthony Wood, Antiquary, of Oxford, 1632-1695, described by Himself, Collected from his Diaries and other Papers. Edit. by Rev. Andrew Clark. 5 vols. *Publ. Oxford Hist. Soc.,* vols. 19, 21, 26, 30, 40. Oxford, 1891-1900.

WOOD, L. S., and H. L. BURROWS. The Town in Literature. Source Book of London. London, 1925.

Worcestershire Archaeological Society. Transactions. Worcester, 1923—.

Worcestershire Historical Society. Publications. Worcester, 1893—.

> This contains registers, diaries, county records, and other various documents. It was directed toward a history of the county of Worcester.

WORDSWORTH, REV. CHRISTOPHER. Social Life at the English Universities in the Eighteenth Century. Cambridge, 1877.

WROTH, WARWICK. London Pleasure Gardens of the Eighteenth Century. 62 illustrations. London, 1896.

Yorkshire Archaeological and Topographical Association. Journal. Numerous plates, plans, maps, and other illustrations. 35 vols. (by 1943). London, 1869—.

> Since 1893 the name used was Yorkshire Archaeological Society. For the Record Series see following:
> —————. Record Series. 109 vols. (by 1945), including the three Extra Series volumes. Worksop, 1885—.
> This series was intended to be a contribution towards the history and antiquities of the county. It prints such matter as Yorkshire Deeds and Fines, Beverley Records, Early Charters, Wakefield Manor Book, Yorkshire Maps, etc.

Yorkshire County Magazine. Bingley, 1891—.

> With this periodical was incorporated the Yorkshire Notes and Queries and Folklore Journal, which ran from 1885 to 1890.

XXIV

Bibliographies

(In addition to the following list of references, one will find the section BIBLIOGRAPHIES of vol. II to contain many titles that bear on Great Britain. Likewise under the section GENERAL REFERENCE of the present volume are cited works which append bibliographies, some of which are quoted in cross reference. My indebtedness to sales catalogues has been acknowledged in vol. II. One needs to consult also the well-night exhaustive *Cambridge Bibliography* [4 vols., Cambridge, 1941], both for supplementing and for checking this present work. For other bibliographical data the *Bibliographical Guide to English Studies* compiled by Tom Peete Cross [8th edition, Chicago, 1943] will be found useful.)

Advocates Library (now the National Library of Scotland). Catalogue of Printed Books in the Advocates' Library. Complete set with the two supplementary volumes. 7 vols. in 9. 4to. Edinburgh, 1867-79.

AKERMAN, J. Y. Archaeological Index to Remains of Antiquity of the Celtic, Romano-British, and Anglo-Saxon Periods. 19 plates. 8vo. London, 1847.

ALDIS, H. G. A List of Books Printed in Scotland before 1700, including those printed forth of the Realm for Scottish Booksellers, with brief Notes on the Printers and Stationers. Printed for the Edinburgh Bibliographical Society, no. 6. 4to. Edinburgh, 1904.

ALLEN, JOHN. Bibliotheca Herefordiensis; or, A Descriptive Catalogue of Books, Pamphlets, Maps, Prints, etc., relating to the County of Hereford. 8vo. Hereford, 1821.

ALLIBONE, S. A. Critical Dictionary of English Literature, and British and American Authors, with Indexes of Subjects. 3 vols.; Supplement, 2 vols., by J. F. Kirk. 5 vols. 8vo. London, 1877-91.

AMHERST, HON. ALICIA. For a comprehensive bibliography of works on gardening, both domestic and ornamental, as well as on agriculture, see her *A History of Gardening in England,* under GENERAL REFERENCE.

ANDERSON, J. P. The Book of British Topography; a Classified Catalogue of the Topographical Works in the Library of the British Museum relating to Great Britain and Ireland. 8vo. London, 1881.

This is a very useful and, for its date, comprehensive collection of references. It has provided this volume with many items.

ANDERSON, P. J. A Bibliography of Invernesshire. *Aberdeen University Bulletin,* nos. 10-15. Aberdeen, 1914-16.

————. Collections towards a Bibliography of the Universities of Aberdeen. 7 plates. *Publ. Edinburgh Bibliog. Soc.,* no. 8. Edinburgh, 1907.

ANDERSON, R. Bibliography of Buchan. In Pratt's *Buchan* (4th edit.). Aberdeen, 1901.

ANDERSON and MACK. Sale Catalogue of an Extensive Collection of Books, being the greater portion of the general Library of John Fenwick: Comprising . . . topography and county histories, biography, heraldry, many rare local works, etc., illustrated by Bewick, etc., sold Sept. 25th, 1865. 8vo. Newcastle-on-Tyne, 1865.

ARBER, EDWARD. A List of 837 London Publishers between 1553 and 1640 A.D., being a Master Key to English Bibliography during a Period in which almost all authorized Books were printed in the Metropolis. 32 pp. 4to. Birmingham, 1890.

————. The Term Catalogues, 1668-1709. Contemporary Bibliography of English Literature. Edit. from the Rare Quarterly Lists Issued by the Booksellers, with Title Index, Glossary, Notes, etc. 3 vols. 4to. London, 1903.

As all students know, this work is as indispensable for the second half of the 17th century as the *Stationers' Register* is for the earlier half.

Archaeologia. An Index to Archaeologia or Miscellaneous Tracts relating to Antiquity, from vol. 1 to vol. 50 inclusive. Edit. by M. Stephenson. 4to. London, 1889.

AUSTIN, ROLAND. A Catalogue of the Gloucestershire Collection, Books, Pamphlets and Documents in the Gloucester Public Library relating to the County, Cities, Towns and Villages of Gloucestershire. Plates. 4to. Gloucester, 1928.

BAIKIE, W. List of Books and Manuscripts relating to Orkney and Zetland. London, 1847.

BALE, JOHN. Index Britanniae scriptorum quos ex variis bibliothecis non parvo labore collegit Ioannes Baleus cum aliis. Edit. by Reginald L. Poole and Mary Bateson. Oxford, 1902.

————. Scriptorum illustrium majoris Brytanniae, quam nunc Angliam & Scotiam uocant: Catalogus . . . Autore Ionne Baleo. 4to. Basileae, 1557.

BALLEN, DOROTHY. A Bibliography of Road-Making and Roads in the United Kingdom. Introduction by Sir George Gibb. London, 1914.

BANDINEL, B. A Catalogue of Books relating to British Topography, etc. (see Richard Gough below).

BARTHOLOMEW, A. T. A Catalogue of Books and Papers on the University, Town and County, bequeathed to the University of Cambridge by J. W. Clark. 8vo. Cambridge, 1912.

BAXTER, J. H. Collections towards a Bibliography of St. Andrews. St. Andrews, 1926.

BENTHAM, W. A Catalogue of the Valuable Topographical, Law and Miscellaneous Library of the late William Bentham . . . Sold by Auction to Mr. Evans . . . March 25 and ten following Days. London, 1838.

BEVERIDGE, ERSKINE. A Bibliography of Books relating to Dunfermline and the West of Fife, including Publications of Writers connected with the Districts. *Publ. Edinb. Bibliog. Soc.,* no. 5. 4to. Dunfermline, 1901.

A Bibliography of Published Works on the Municipal History of Wales and the Border, with special Reference to published Records. *Bull. of Celtic Studies* (Univ. of Wales), vol. II, pt. iv, with Addenda, vol. III, pt. i. Aberystwyth, 1925.

A Bibliography of Worcestershire. 4 pts. Oxford, 1898.

Bibliotheca Brandiana. A Catalogue of the unique, scarce, rare, curious and numerous Collections of Works on Antiquity, Topography, and Decayed Intelligence of Great Britain and Ireland, early Poetry, Classics, Belles Lettres and Miscellaneous, etc., being the entire Library of the late Rev. John Brand, sold by Auction by Mr. Stewart, May 6, and thirty-six following Days. 8vo. London, 1807.

> Brand is best remembered for his *Popular Antiquities.* He was one of the band of eminent antiquaries distinguishing the latter half of the 18th century, including Gough, Gutch, Grose, and Nichols.

Bibliotheca Bryantiana. A Catalogue of the . . . Topographical, Historical, and Scarce Collection . . . of County and other Histories, being the entire Library of William Bryant. 8vo. London, 1807. (A sales catalogue.)

Bibliotheca Celtica. A Register of Publications relating to Wales and the Celtic Peoples and Language, published by the National Library of Wales. Aberystwyth, 1909 (in progress).

Bibliotheca Harleiana. A Catalogue of the Harleian Library. 3 vols. 8vo. London, 1743.

> Johnson wrote the "Account," "The Proposals for Printing the Harleian Miscellany," and probably the Preface to vol. III.

Bibliotheca Scotica. A Catalogue of Books (4,483 annotated items) relating to Scotland offered by John Smith & Son. Glasgow, 1926.

BLACK, G. F. Bulletin of the New York Public Library, vol. 14. 8vo. New York, 1910.

> This contains full bibliographies of books in the Library relating to Genealogy, Local History, and Topography of Britain; together with many articles and notes.

——————. A List of Works relating to Druids and Druidism in the New York Public Library, vol. 24, no. 1. New York, 1920.

——————. A List of Works on Scotland in the New York Public Library, vol. 18. New York, 1916.

> Reprinted with additions from the *Bulletin of New York Public Library,* vol. 18, 1919.
> This includes sections on Bibliography, Periodicals, Transactions, Public Documents, Anthropology, History and Descriptions, Economics, Geology, etc. It is a valuable and very extensive collection of titles.

BLOCK, ANDREW. Key Books of British Authors,' 1600-1932. 8vo. London, 1933.

> A bird's-eye view of the field of English literature from 1600 to 1932, giving the first editions of all books which can be called key books by reason of either public demand or importance. In each case the date, the number of volumes, whether the work is illustrated, where and by whom published, and size are given. In addition there are one or more critiques or notices, either by a contemporary journal or author or by an eminent writer.—Bookseller's Note.

BLOMFIELD, REGINALD. For a bibliography of works on gardens, see his *The Formal Garden in England*, App. III, under GENERAL REFERENCE.

BLOOM, J. HARVEY. Early English Tracts, Pamphlets, and Printed Sheets (1473-1650), concerning the Counties of Suffolk (vol. I), Leicestershire, Staffordshire, Warwickshire and Worcestershire (vol. II). With full bibliographical descriptions of upwards of 3,300 titles and 14 facsimiles of title pages, initial letters, etc. 2 vols. 8vo. London, 1922-23.

BOASE, G. C., and W. P. COURTNEY. Bibliotheca Cornubiensis, a Comprehensive Catalogue of Works in any way relating to Cornwall, and Cornishmen, with interesting and useful Biographical Memoranda, etc. 3 vols. 4to. London, 1874-82.

BOWES, ROBERT. A Catalogue of Books printed at or relating to the University, Town and County of Cambridge, 1521-1893, with Bibliographical and Biographical Notes. 98 illustrations of woodcut initials and ornaments. 8vo. Cambridge, 1894.

BOYNE, W. The Yorkshire Library, a Bibliographical Account of Books on Topography, Tracts of the XVIth Century, Biography, Spaws, Geology, Botany, Maps, Views, Portraits and Miscellaneous Literature, relating to the County of York, with Collations and Notes on the Books and Authors. 4to. London, 1869.

> Of this valuable work only 150 copies were printed.

BRITISH MUSEUM. A Catalogue of the MS. Maps, Charts, and Plans, and of the Topographical Drawings in the British Museum. 2 vols. 8vo. London, 1844.

——————. A Catalogue of Maps, Prints, Drawings, etc., forming the Geographical and Topographical Collection attached to the Library of George III. 2 vols. 8vo. London, 1829.

Britwell Handlist. A Short Title Catalogue of the principal Volumes to the Year 1800 formerly in the Library of Britwell Court . . . 62 plates of facsimiles. 2 vols. 4to. London, (Quaritch), 1933.

> Many titles of voyages and travels are to be found in this library, which belonged to S. Christie-Miller.

Brown, P. Hume. For a bibliography of Scottish history, see his *History of Scotland,* 3 vols., 8vo. Cambridge, 1911.

Brunet, J. C. Manuel du Libraire, etc. 5th edit., vol. VI: Catalogue raisonné:— Isles Britannique: Histoire générale et particuliére de l'Ecosse. Supplement. Paris, 1878-80.

Burton, J. R., and F. S. Pearson. A Bibliography of Worcestershire. 2 vols. *Publ. Worcestershire Hist. Soc.,* vol 9. Worcester, 1898-1903.

Butler, G. S. Topographica Sussexiana; an Attempt towards forming a List of various Publications relating to the County of Sussex, vols. 15-18. Continued to 1882 by F. E. Sawyer. *Sussex Arch. Soc. Coll.,* vols. 32-33. London, 1863-82.

Cambridge Bibliography of English Literature. Edit. by F. W. Bateson. 4 vols. 8vo. Cambridge, 1941.

> This massive work, in preparation for some twenty years, is the first attempt since Watt's *Bibliotheca Britannica* (1824) to bring the whole of English literature within the bounds of a single work of reference. It records as far as possible, in chronological order, the authors, titles and editions, with relevant critical publications, of all the writings in book form that possess some literary interest, written by natives of what is now the British Empire, up to the year 1900. Newspapers and magazines have been recorded more fully than in any previous publication, and no type of written matter has been neglected.—Quoted from the Announcement of the work. Vol. IV contains the index to the whole. The list of contributors numbers over two hundred, half of whom are scholars from the United States. The sections on travel literature, letters and memoirs, and social conditions are especially pertinent to the student of travel and geographical literature. The value of this bibliography is immense; yet even it at times will disappoint the searcher for a date of a first edition or the place of publication of some little known work or even a mention of some given title. The editors are generous in their recognition of other publications.

Cambridge History of English Literature. For bibliographies see at back of each volume.

Cambridge Modern History. Planned by the late Lord Acton. Edit. by A. W. Ward. 13 vols. and atlas. New York, 1902-12.

> Bibliographies will be found at the back of each volume.

Camden Society Publications. Descriptive Catalogue of First Series (105 vols.) by J. G. Nichols. London, 1862.

> 2nd edit., 1872. In 1897 the Publications of the Camden Society became the Camden Series of the Royal Historical Society.

Cash, C. G. A Catalogue of the Maps of Scotland. In Mitchell, *Scottish Topography,* vol. II. Edinburgh, 1917. (See Mitchell below.)

A Catalogue of Books printed at or relating to the University, Town and County of Cambridge. Cambridge (?), 1844.

A Catalogue of Five Hundred Celebrated Authors of Great Britain Now Living. The Whole arranged in Alphabetical Order; and including a Complete List of their Publications, with Occasional Strictures, and Anecdotes of their lives. London, 1788.

CHUBB, THOMAS. A Descriptive Catalogue of the Printed Maps of Wiltshire from 1576 to 1885. Reprinted from *Wilts. Arch. Mag.* 8vo. Devizes, 1911.

—————. The Printed Maps in the Atlases of Great Britain and Ireland. A Bibliography, 1579-1870. With an Introduction by F. P. Sprent of the Map Room, and biographical Notes on the Map Makers, Engravers and Publishers by T. Chubb, assisted by J. S. Skells and H. Beharrell. Numerous facsimiles. 4to. London, 1927.

> This bibliography, which represents a lifetime research among the maps of the British Museum, is the only one of its kind that has so far attempted to organize the contents of the atlases of Great Britain and Ireland. It contains particulars of all the known atlases of these countries and descriptions of the successive editions. With it as a reference, one can go a long ways towards identifying unattached maps of the counties of Great Britain and Ireland.

CLAVELL, ROBERT. A Catalogue of the Books printed in England since the Dreadful Fire of London in 1666 to the end of Michaelmas Term, 1695. With an Abstract of the General Bills of Mortality since 1660. Fol. London, 1696.

> The contents are classified under the headings: Physick and Chyrurgery, Books Mathematical (including Navigation, Merchandise, Globes, Maps, Charts, Shorthand), Cookery, Husbandry, Gardening, Poetry, Plays, Music-Books, School-Books, etc.—Robinson, no. 63.

COCK, WILLIAM F. Kentish Bibliographical Notes. In *Arch. Cantiana,* vol. 41, London, 1929.

> This contains items that have turned up since 1837 and consequently are not included in John Russell Smith's *Bibliotheca Cantiana,* which practically brought up to date Gough's *Topographical Survey.*

A Compleat Catalogue of Modern Books, published from the Beginning of this Century (18th), to this Present Time (1766). Cited in *Gent. Mag.,* vol. 36, July.

COOKE, JOSEPH. Bibliotheca Cestriensis: a Catalogue of Books, Maps, Plates relating to Chester and Lists of Newspapers, Coins, Inclosure Awards, etc. With many views of the country seats of the county. Fol. Warrington, 1904.

CORNS, A. R. Bibliotheca Lincolniensis. A Catalogue of the Books, Pamphlets, etc., relating to the City and County of Lincoln, preserved in the Reference Department of the City of Lincoln Public Library. Lincoln, 1904.

CORRIE, JOHN. Sale Catalogue of the very Important and Valuable Library of John Corrie: comprising many Works of high Distinction and Rarity . . . forming a fine series of the works of our County Historians . . . and many other rare and curious Books in History, Topography, and Archaeology, sold by Sotheby, 20th April, 1863.

County History of Scotland Series. Bibliographies in each volume. Edinburgh, 1896-1900. (See under GENERAL REFERENCE.)

CRACE, F. G. A Catalogue of Maps, Plans and Views of London. London, 1878.

CROSS, TOM PEETE. A Bibliographical Guide to English Studies compiled by Tom Peete Cross. 8th edit., revised with an Index. University of Chicago Press. Chicago, 1943.

> The successive editions since 1919 bear witness to the usefulness of this *Guide*. While professedly intended to serve graduate students in English, it offers aid to researchers in most of the broad fields of humanistic investigations. In admirably arranged sections it directs the student with the least possible waste of time to the primary sources of research, such as bibliographies, catalogues, union lists, libraries, etc.

CUBBON, WILLIAM T. A Bibliographical Account of Works relating to the Isle of Man, with biographical Memoranda and copious literary References. 2 vols. (Vol. I, 1933; vol. II, 1937.) Oxford, 1933-37.

> This account includes sections on poetry, drama, prose fiction, and complete bibliographies of T. S. Brown and Hall Caine. Both volumes are fully indexed.

CUNNINGTON, AUGUSTUS. A Catalogue of Books, Maps, and Manuscripts, relating to or connected with the County of Essex, and collected by Augustus Cunnington. A Contribution towards the Bibliography of the County. Braintree, 1902.

> The work is almost valueless for this subject.—J. Williams, *Guide to the Printed Materials*.

CURSITER, JAMES W. A List of Books and Pamphlets Relating to Orkney and Shetland, with Notes of those by Local Authors. 8vo. Kirkwall, 1894.

DANIELL, W. V., and F. J. NEILD (Compilers). Manual of British Topography: a Catalogue of County and Local Histories, Pamphlets, Views, Drawings, Maps, etc., connected with and illustrating the principal Localities in the United Kingdom. 12 portraits and views from early copper plates. 8vo. London, 1909.

> The plates are of considerable interest. The bibliography is arranged by counties.

DAVIDSON, JAMES. Bibliotheca Devoniensis: a Catalogue of the Printed Books relating to the County of Devon. Supplement, 1862. Exeter, 1852.

> A useful work arranged by topics.—J. Williams, *op. cit.*

DAVIES, GODFREY. Bibliography of British History. Stuart Period, 1603-1714. Issued under the Direction of the Royal Historical Society and the American Historical Association. 8vo. London, 1928.

> The grouping of the items under comprehensive headings and the Index of authors' names with abbreviated titles of their works immediately below make this an extremely usable work. The value of the work for students of history, economics, social conditions, and literature is immense. The section on Voyages and Travels, by E. A. Benians, contains a representative bibliography of collections of voyages and of individual voyages abroad. See Conyers Read below.

DEE, JOHN. Private Diary and Catalogue of his Library and MSS. Notes by J. O. Hallwell. 4to. *Publ. Camden Soc.*, vol. 19. London, 1842.

DOUGLAS, SIR GEORGE. List of Books relating to or published in the Counties of Roxburgh, Selkirk, and Peebles. Pp. 433-472 of his *History of the Border Counties*. 8vo. Edinburgh, 1899.

> The bibliography was compiled by J. Sinton, and was also issued separately.

Duff, E. G. Fifteenth Century Books. A Bibliography of Books and Documents printed in England and of Books for the English Market printed abroad. 53 plates of facsimiles. 4to. Printed for the Bibliographical Society, London, 1917.

This valuable bibliography gives the collation and ownership of over 400 books.

East India Company. Catalogue of the Library of the East India Company. London, 1845.

Edinburgh Bibliographical Society. Publications. 15 vols. (all published). 1890-1935. Transactions. Vols. I and II. 1896-1941. 17 vols. in all. 4to and 8vo, with numerous facsimiles. Edinburgh, 1890-1941.

The following volumes are selected for listing:
Vol. II.   Bibliography of Works relating to Mary Queen of Scots, 1544-1700. By John Scott.
Vol. V.   Bibliography of Works relating to Dunfermline and the West of Fife, including Publications of Writers connected with the District. By Erskine Beveridge. Dunfermline, privately printed, 1901.
Vol. VII.   List of Books printed in Scotland before 1700. By H. G. Aldis. 1904.
Vol. VIII. Collections towards a Bibliography of the Universities of Aberdeen. By. P. J. Anderson.
Vol. XIII. A List of Fifteenth Century Books in the University Library of Aberdeen. 1925.

Engelmann, W. Bibliotheca Geographica: Verzeichnis der seit der Mitte des vorigen Jahrhunderts bis zu Ende des Jahres 1856 in Deutschland erschienen Werke über Geographie und Reisen. Leipzig, 1858.

English Historical Review. General Index of Articles, Notes, Documents and selected Reviews of Books in the *English Historical Review*. Vols. 1-20, 1866-1905; 21-30, 1906-15. 2 vols. London, 1906-1916.

Farmer, Rev. Richard. Bibliotheca Farmeriana. Catalogue of the Curious, Valuable and Extensive Library in Print and MSS. of the Rev. Richard Farmer, comprehending . . . a fine collection of English History, Antiquities and Topography, including all the old Chronicles, etc. Sold by Mr. King, 7th May, 1798. 8vo. London, 1798.

Firth, C. H. Stuart Tracts, 1603-1693. A Bibliography. 8vo. London, 1902.

Fishwick, Lieut.-Col. Henry, F.S.A. The Lancashire Library. A Bibliographical Account of Books on Topography, Biography, History, Science, and Miscellaneous Literature relating to the County Palatine, including an Account of Lancashire Tracts, Pamphlets, and Sermons printed before the Year 1720. With Collations, and Bibliographical, Critical, and Biographical Notes on the Books and Authors. London, 1875.

Most of the works contained in the above treat of the Nineteenth Century. Tracts and pamphlets of a date between 1720 and 1800 are generally omitted.

Fitch, W. S. Catalogue of a . . . Collection of Printed Books and MSS. illustrative of the History of the County of Suffolk, formed by W. S. Fitch, of Ipswich. 8vo. London, 1855.

FORDHAM, SIR HERBERT GEORGE. Cambridgeshire Maps: a Descriptive Catalogue of the Maps of the County and of the Great Level of the Fens, 1579-1900. Cambridge, 1908.

—————. Descriptive Catalogue of Maps. In *Trans. Bibliog. Soc.*, vol. 11. 4to. London, 1914.

—————. Descriptive List of the Maps of the Great Level of the Fens, 1604-1900. In *Itineraries and Road-Books, Studies in Carto-Bibliography*. Cambridge, 1914.

—————. Hand List of Catalogues and Works of Reference Relating to Carto-Bibliography and Kindred Subjects for Great Britain and Ireland, 1720-1927. 8vo. Cambridge, 1928.

—————. Hertfordshire Maps: a Descriptive Catalogue of the Maps of the County of Hertfordshire, 1579-1900. 8 plates and other illustrations. 4to. Hertford, 1907.

A Supplement was added in 1914.

—————. John Cary, Engraver, Map, Chart and Print Seller, and Globe Maker, 1754 to 1835: a Bibliography with notes. 4to. Cambridge, 1925.

—————. The Road-Books and Itineraries of Great Britain, 1570-1850. A Catalogue, with an Introduction and a Bibliography. 4to. Cambridge, 1924.

FREEMANTLE, W. T. A Bibliography of Sheffield and Vicinity. Section I, to the End of 1700. Upwards of 60 engraved plates, facsimiles of title pages, etc. 4to. Sheffield, 1911.

FUSSELL, C. E. The Exploration of England: a Select Bibliography of Travel and Topography, 1570-1815. 8vo. London, 1935.

This is a very useful selection, with annotations here and there indicating value, editions, and later printings.

—————. Travel and Topography in Seventeenth Century England. A Bibliography of Sources for Social and Economic History. In *The Library*, 4th ser., vol. 13, Dec., 1932. London, 1932.

A short introduction sets forth the general character of travel books in this period, pointing out the growth of interest in national antiquities, and in the increasing trade connected with various localities.

Garden Books. For a list of books on gardening, see *Gent. Mag.*, vol. 76, pt. I, 1100-1103; pt. II, 997-999, 1806.

General Index to the *Wiltshire Arch. and Nat. Hist. Mag.*, vols. 1-32. (Date not ascertained.) Devizes.

GILBERT, H. M., and G. N. GODWIN. Bibliotheca Hantoniensis: An Attempt at a Bibliography of Hampshire. Southampton, 1872.

> Another edit., with additional List of Hampshire newspapers, by F. E. Edwards, Southampton, 1891.

GIUSSEPPI, M. S. A Guide to the Manuscripts preserved in the Public Records Office. 2 vols: vol. I, Legal Records; vol. II, State Papers, etc. 8vo. London, 1923.

GODDARD, CANON E. H. Wiltshire Bibliography: A Catalogue of Printed Books, Pamphlets and Articles bearing on the History, Topography and Natural History of the County. 8vo. Wilts, 1929.

GOMME, G. L. Index of Archaeological Papers of the Royal Society, 1665-1890. 8vo. London, 1907.

> This index stops where the Annual Index published by the Congress of Archaeological Societies begins, and there is thus a continuous index from the first publications in the Philosophical Transactions of the Royal Society down to the present time.—Quoted by Bookseller.

GOSS, C. W. F. The London Directories, 1677-1855: A Bibliography with Notes on their Origin and Development. 8vo. London, 1932.

GOUGH, HENRY. Bibliotheca Buckinghamiensis: A List of Books relating to the County of Buckingham. Aylesbury, 1890.

> This is arranged by general lists and local lists, and includes local newspapers and local acts of Parliament.

GOUGH, RICHARD. A Catalogue of Books relating to British Topography, and Saxon and Northern Literature, bequeathed to the Bodleian Library in the year 1799, by Richard Gough. 4to. Oxford, 1814.

> This catalogue of Gough's library was arranged by B. Bandinel on the plan used by Gough in his *British Topography* (1780), according to counties, and where practicable, according to chronology. It contains a full index of names.

————. For early catalogues, with descriptions of their nature, on books, coins, medals, marbles, etc., see Gough, *Anecdotes of British Topography* (which is a descriptive bibliography in itself of the topography of Great Britain and Ireland), 417-426. London, 1768.

GRAY, HENRY. Reference Catalogue of British Topography and Family History offered for Sale. 8vo. London, 1887.

> The titles are abbreviated and usually want the place of publication.

GREEN, EMANUEL. Bibliotheca Somersetensis: A Catalogue of Books, Pamphlets, Single Sheets, and Broadsides, in some way connected with the County of Somerset. 3 vols. 4to. Taunton, 1902.

GROAT, A. G. For a bibliography of Orkney and Shetland, see his *Thoughts on Orkney and Shetland*, Edinburgh, 1831.

GROSS, CHARLES. The Sources and Literature of English History, From earliest Times to about 1485. 8vo. London, 1900.

This work was of great help in determining dates, editions, places of publication, and contents of items in the section HISTORY AND CHRONICLE.

HAILSTONE, EDWARD. Catalogue of a Collection of Historical and Topographical Works and Civil War Tracts relating to Yorkshire. Tracts concerning Sir Thomas Fairfax. Also Sermons and other Works connected with the County. In the Library of Sir Edward Hailstone. York (?), 1858.

Only fifty copies were printed for private circulation.—Bookseller's Note.

HALKETT, SAMUEL, and JOHN LAING. Dictionary of the Anonymous and Pseudonymous Literature of Great Britain. 4 vols. 4to. London, 1882-88.

A new and enlarged edit., 6 vols., London, 1926.

HARDY, SIR T. D. A Descriptive Catalogue of Materials relating to the History of Great Britain and Ireland to the End of the Reign of Henry VII. Edit. by Sir T. D. Hardy. 3 vols. in 4. London, 1862-71.

Harleian Collection. The Catalogue of the Harleian Collection of MSS. purchased by Authority of Parliament for the Use of the Publick, and preserved there (i. e., British Museum). 2 vols. Fol. London, 1753.

The same title appeared under date of 1759; the Preface and Index were added by Thomas Astle, 1762.
This catalogue was begun by Wanley, librarian to the Earls Robert and his son Edward Harley, who gave a particular abstract of each article and added literary anecdotes, as far as he had proceeded with the project. After his death in 1726, the job was continued by Casleu, who followed in some measure the plan initiated by Wanley. He was succeeded by Hocker, the deputy-keeper of the Tower Records, and his work was carried to completion by the librarians of the Museum. Lord Oxford's books were bought by Thomas Osborne, who published a catalogue of them by subscription in twelve numbers, at a shilling each, or four volumes, 8vo, at ten shillings. It was called *Bibliothecae Harleianae catalogus in locos communes distributus, cum indice autorum.* The most interesting pamphlets were reduced to eight quarto volumes called the *Harleian Miscellany*, with historical, political, and critical notes, a table of contents, and an alphabetical index, first published in weekly numbers. At the end of each was added *A Copious and Exact Catalogue of Pamphlets in the Harleian Library*, which gave a short account of their contents, arranged numerically that buyers might apply for the publication of any particular one. Lord Oxford's library filled thirteen handsome chambers and two large galleries.—Gough, *Anecdotes Brit. Topog.*, 332-33.

HARRISON, WILLIAM. A Bibliographical Account of Works relating to the Isle of Man. *Publ. Manx Soc.*, vol. 8. Douglas, 1876.

HARRISON, W. JEROME, F.G.S. A Bibliography of the Great Stone Monuments of Wiltshire—Stonehenge and Avebury: With other References. *Publ. Wiltshire Arch. and Nat. Hist. Mag.*, vol. 32. Devizes, 1901-02.

This is arranged alphabetically under the authors, with brief abstracts of the works listed, when possible, in the author's own words. It constitutes an interesting record of guesses, learned disquisitions, and archaeological studies.

HAWKES, A. J. A Bibliography of All Books Printed in Lancashire to the Year 1800. 8vo. Wigan, 1925.

HEARNE, THOMAS. Bibliotheca Hearniana. In *Remains of Thomas Hearne,* vol. III, App. xvii, 272 ff. (see under Hearne, 1869, LETTERS, DIARIES, MEMOIRS).

> Here are printed excerpts from Hearne's autograph Catalogue of his books, made with reference to the history and antiquities of Britain, "which by the aid of his books and his own researches elsewhere, he had so diligently illustrated."

HIND, JAMES PITCAIRN. Carlisle Public Library: Bibliotheca Jacksoniana. Kendal, 1909.

> This is a dictionary catalogue of books referring to Westmoreland, Cumberland, and northern Lancashire.

Historical MSS. Commission. Guide to the reports of the Historical Manuscripts Commission, 1870-1911. Part I, Topographical. Part II, 2 vols., Index of Persons. London, 1935-38.

HOARE, SIR R. C. A Catalogue of Books relating to the History and Topography of England, Wales, Scotland, and Ireland, compiled from his Library at Stourhead, in Wiltshire. 8vo. London, 1815.

HOTTEN, J. C. A Bibliographical Account of nearly 1,500 curious and Rare Books, Tracts, MSS., and Engravings relating to the History and Topography of Yorkshire, collected by Mr. Hotten, with Numerous Descriptive Notes, Literary Anecdotes, etc. London, 1863.

————. A Hand-Book to the Topography and Family History of England and Wales: being a Descriptive Account of 20,000 most Curious and Rare Books, old Tracts, Ancient MSS., Engravings, and privately printed Family Papers, etc. London, 1863.

HUDDESFORD, WILLIAM (Keeper of the Museum). Catalogus librorum manuscriptorum viri clarissimi Antonii a Wood; being a minute Catalogue of each particular contained in the MS. Collections of Anthony a Wood deposited in the Ashmolean Museum at Oxford. 8vo. Oxford, 1761.

HUMPHREYS, ARTHUR L. A Handbook to County Bibliography: Being a Bibliography of Bibliographies relating to the Counties and Towns of Great Britain and Ireland. 4to. London, 1917.

> A full index of authors is included.

Hunterian Museum. Topographical Index to the Fifteenth and Sixteenth Century Printed Books, by D. Baird Smith. Fol. Glasgow, 1930.

HYETT, FRANCIS ADAMS, and WILLIAM BAZELEY. The Bibliographer's Manual of Gloucestershire Literature; being a Classified Catalogue of Books, Pamphlets, Broadsides, and other Printed Matter relating to the County of Gloucester or to the City of Bristol, with descriptive and explanatory Notes. Illustrations. 3 vols. Gloucester, 1895-97.

> A Supplement by Francis Adams Hyett and Roland Austin was published in 2 vols., Gloucester, 1915-16.
> Some of the contents are annotated at length. The work includes biographical and genealogical literature, books dealing with wool, etc., and many references to prisons and lunatic asylums.

INGLIS, HARRY G. R. (and others). The Early Maps of Scotland, with an Account of the Ordnance Survey. *Royal Geog. Soc.* Edinburgh, 1934. (See this work under GENERAL REFERENCE.)

JENKINS, R. T., WILLIAM REES (and others). A Bibliography of the History of Wales. Cardiff, 1931.

JOHNSTONE, J. F. K. A Concise Bibliography of the City of Aberdeen. *Publ. Hist. Assoc. Scotland,* vol. 3. Aberdeen(?), 1913.

——————. A Concise Bibliography of the History, etc., of the Shires of Aberdeen, Banff, and Kincardine. *Aberdeen Univ. Studies,* vol. 66. 8vo. Aberdeen, 1914.

JOHNSTONE, J. F. K., and A. W. ROBERTSON. Bibliographia Aberdonensis. An Account of Books relating to or printed in Aberdeen, Banff or Kincardine Shires or by Natives and Graduates of Aberdeen University, from 1472 to 1700. General Index and Index of Locations. 64 facsimiles. 2 vols. 4to. *Publ. Third Spalding Club.* Aberdeen, 1929-30.

LAING, DAVID. Sale Catalogue of the Third Portion of the Extensive and Valuable Library of David Laing: comprising an extraordinary Collection of works, by Scottish writers, or relating to Scotland, including writings of eminent divines, historians, topographers, etc. Sold by Sotheby, 20th July, 1880, etc. 3 vols. in 1. 8vo. London, 1880.

LANSON, GUSTAVE. Manuel Bibliographie de la littérature Française moderne, xvi, xvii, xviii et xix siècles. Nouvelle édition, revue et augmentée. 2 vols. 8vo. Paris, 1921—.

LAWLEY, GEORGE. The Bibliography of Wolverhampton (including the Townships of the Parliamentary Borough). A Record of local Books, Authors, and Booksellers, etc. Bilston, 1890.

LLOYD, H. W. Welsh Books printed abroad in the Sixteenth and Seventeenth Centuries and their Authors. *Y Cymmrodor,* vol. 4, 25-69. London, 1881.

LOWNDES, W. T. The Bibliographer's Manual of English Literature, containing an Account of Rare, Curious, and Useful Books, published in or relating to Great Britain and Ireland, from the Invention of Printing, with Bibliographical and Critical Notices, Collations of the rarer Articles, and the Prices at which they have been sold. A New Edition, revised, corrected, and enlarged; with an Appendix relating to the books of Literary and Scientific Societies. By Henry G. Bohn. 4 vols. 8vo. London, 1871.

 The first edition of this essential reference book came out in 1834; enlarged to 11 volumes in 1857-65.

LYELL, A. H. A Bibliographical List descriptive of Romano-British Architectural Remains in Great Britain. 8vo. Cambridge, 1912.

MACKAY, AENEAS, J. G. A List of Books relating to Fife and Kinross. *Publ. Edinb. Bibliog. Soc.,* no. 3, 1-30; no. 4, 117-48. Edinburgh, 1896 and 1899.

McDONALD, DONALD. Agricultural Writers from Sir Walter of Henley to Arthur Young, 1200-1800. Reproductions in facsimile and Extracts from their actual Writings. . . . Illus. 8vo. London, 1908.

> This contains an extensive bibliography of writers on agriculture, chronologically arranged, accompanied at times with a note on a particular author.

MADAN, FALCONER. Oxford Books: A Bibliography of Printed Works relating to the University or City of Oxford, or printed or published there. With Appendixes, Annals, and Illustrations. 3 vols. 8vo. Oxford, 1895-1931.

> Vol. I (1895), The Early Oxford Press, 1468-1640; vol. II (1912), Oxford Literature, 1450-1640 and 1641-1650; vol. III (1931), Oxford Literature, 1651-1680.

MANTOUX, PAUL. The Industrial Revolution in the Eighteenth Century. Revised edition. Translated from the French by Marjorie Vernon. London, 1929.

> This contains a bibliography of Descriptions, Social, Economic, etc., of England.

MATHESON, CYRIL. A Catalogue of the Publications of Scottish historical and kindred Clubs and Societies and of Papers relative to Scottish History issued by H. M. Stationery Office, including Reports of the Royal Commission on historical MSS., 1903-27, with Subject Index. Aberdeen, 1928.

> This is a continuation of Terry (see below).

MATY, P. H. A General Index to the Philosophical Transactions, to the End of the 70th Volume. 4to. London, 1787.

MAYO, CHARLES HERBERT. A Bibliotheca Dorsetiensis, being a carefully compiled Account of Printed Books and Pamphlets relating to the History and Topography of the County of Dorset. London, 1885.

> This is arranged by topics. It includes a list of newspapers with the names of printers and often a statement of their politics, together with Acts of Parliament for roads, canals, railroads, and maps. It is a valuable work.—J. Williams.

MILL, HUGH ROBERT. Catalogue of the Library of the Royal Geographical Society, containing the titles of all works up to December 1893. 8vo. London, 1895.

> In App. I are listed collections of voyages with detail of contents. The work has a general author's Catalogue alphabetically arranged.

MILNES, ALEXANDER TAYLOR. A Bibliography of Books and Articles on the History of Great Britain from *ca.* 450 A.D. to 1914, published during the Year 1934. With an Appendix containing a Select List of Publications in 1934 on British History since 1914. 2 vols. 8vo. *Publ. Royal Hist. Soc.* London, 1934.

> A volume listing works for 1935 published in 1939; for 1936 in 1940. Titles are grouped in sections. The English Local History Section contains articles from periodicals on antiquities and books. Voyages are listed under Maritime History and Exploration.

Minet Library. A Catalogue of Works relating to Surrey in the Minet Library, Camberwell. London, 1901.

> A Supplement appeared in 1923.

MITCHELL, SIR ARTHUR. A List of Travels and Tours in Scotland, 1296-1900. *Proc. Soc. Antiq. Scot.*, vols. 35, 39, 44. Edinburgh, 1902-10.

Vol. 35 was reprinted in book form, Edinburgh, 1902.
The arrangement of the items is by date of the tour, not by that of publication. Many annotations explaining the circumstances of the journey and of publication increase the usefulness of this very full account of travel in Scotland.

MITCHELL, SIR ARTHUR, and C. G. CASH. A Contribution to the Bibliography of Scottish Topography. 2 vols. *Publ. Scot. Hist. Soc.*, nos. 14-15, 2nd ser. Edinburgh, 1917.

Section headings include Antiquities, Bibliographies, Communications, Maps, Natural History, Tours, Views, Universities, Industries, etc. The whole makes up quite an exhaustive catalogue of books, papers, maps, etc., dealing with Scottish topography in the widest sense of the word.

MORGAN, WILLIAM THOMAS. A Bibliography of British History, 1700-1715. With special Reference to the Reign of Queen Anne. 5 vols. *University of Indiana Studies.* Bloomington, Ind., 1934-42.

This lists a most generous array of bibliographical aids, which are as useful to the student of literature as to the student of history. It is especially rich in its references to the drama of the period. Other forms of publications included are Pamphlets, Memoirs, Correspondence, Autobiographies, Diaries, Journals, and secondary aids. How voluminously this age expressed itself in pamphlets is evidenced by the fact that these ephemera occupy nearly all of the first two volumes. Vol. IV provides information on MS sources in the chief archives of London and many continental countries. Vol. V adds supplementary items to vols. I-III. A copious index to the whole brings order into this huge work.

MOWAT, JOHN. The Bibliography of Caithness. 8vo. Glasgow, 1909.

—————. A List of Books and Pamphlets relating to the North of Scotland, with special Reference to Caithness and Sutherland. *Viking Club. Misc.*, vols. II, 238; III, 49, 170, 224; IV, 15, 99, 151, 201; V, 38, 82, 159. London, 1909-12.

This was also published in the *Old-Lore Misc. of Orkney, Shetland, Caithness, and Sutherland*, vols. 2-5, 8vo, London, 1909-12.

New York Public Library. A List of Works relating to British General and Local History in the New York Library. Bulletin, no. XIV. New York, 1910.

NICHOLS, C. L. A Bibliography of Worcestershire. Worcester, 1899.

NICOLSON, W. (Bishop of Carlisle). The Scottish Historical Library, containing a Short View and Character of most of the Writers, Records, Registers, etc., to 1603, which may be serviceable to the Undertakers of a General History of Scotland down to the Union. 8vo. London, 1702.

This contains also a "Vocabulary of the Irish Dialect."

NORRIS, H. E. A Catalogue of the Huntingdonshire Books collected by H. E. Norris. Cirencester, 1895.

OWEN, EDWARD. A Catalogue of the MSS. relating to Wales in the British Museum. 4 pts. *Cymmrodorion Record Series*, vol. 4. London, 1900-22.

A valuable reference work. The MSS are fully described and calendared.—Read, *Bibliog. Brit. Hist., Tudor Period.*

Oxford. A Catalogue of the Printed Books in the Library of Merton College. 8vo. Oxford, 1880.

PEDDIE, R. A. A Subject Index of Books published up to and including 1800. 2 vols. 8vo. London, 1933-35.

> The two series contain 100,000 entries arranged under 10,000 headings.—Bookseller's Note.

PERRY, WILLIAM. Bibliotheca Norfolciana, sive catalogus librorum, manuscriptorum et impressorum in omni arte et lingua, quos illustriss. princeps Henricus dux Norfolciae, etc., Regiae Societati Londienensi pro scientia naturali promovenda donavit. 4to. London, 1681.

> This valuable library, a great part of which came out of that of Matthew Corvinus, King of Hungary, at Buda, belonged to Bilibaldus Pirkeimerus, counselor to Charles V. Of his heirs it was purchased by the celebrated Earl of Arundel, whose grandson, Henry Duke of Norfolk, presented it to this Society. It received many later additions.—Gough, 327.

PETHERICK, EDWARD AUGUSTUS. A Catalogue of the York Gate Library formed by Mr. S. Silver. An Index to the Literature of Geography, Maritime and Inland Discovery, Commerce and Colonisation. 2nd edit. London, 1886.

> This contains extensive lists of voyages and circumnavigations, along with travels over the Continent and in the Colonies.

PINKERTON, JOHN. A General Collection . . . of Voyages and Travels in all Parts of the World. 17 vols. 4to. London, 1808-14.

> See vol. 17 for a very ample bibliography, which, however, must constantly be checked for inaccuracies. For a description of this collection, see under COLLECTIONS, Addenda I (vol. I of this work).

POLLARD, A. W. A Short-Title Catalogue of Books printed in France and of French Books printed in other Countries from 1470 to 1600, now in the British Museum. 8vo. London, 1924.

POLLARD, A. W., and G. R. REDGRAVE. A Short-Title Catalogue of Books printed in England, Scotland, and Ireland, and of English Books printed abroad, 1475-1640. 4to. London, 1926. (See under BIBLIOGRAPHIES, vol. II of this work.)

QUARITCH, BERNARD. General Catalogue of Books, with General Index. 16 vols. 8vo. London, 1880-92.

QUINTON, JOHN. Bibliotheca Norfolciensis: A Catalogue of . . . Works relating to Norfolk in the Library of J. J. Colman. Norwich, 1896.

READ, CONYERS. A Bibliography of British History: Tudor Period, 1485-1603. Oxford, 1933.

> This contains lists of works both contemporary and modern on Discovery, Exploration, and Colonization; of Local Histories of Individual Counties, etc.; and of works on England, Scotland, and Ireland. The evaluation of various items is of great assistance to the student.

ROBERTSON, A. W. A Hand-List of Bibliography of the Shires of Aberdeen, Banff, and Kincardine. *Publ. New Spalding Club*, vol. 11A. 8vo. Aberdeen, 1893.

ROWLANDS, REV. WILLIAM. Cambrian Bibliography: containing an Account of the Books printed in the Welsh Language, or relating to Wales, from the Year 1546 to the end of the Eighteenth Century; with Biographical Notices. Edit. and enlarged by the Rev. D. Silvan Evans, B.D. Llanidloes, 1869.

> This valuable work of reference has to be checked for accuracy in datings and editions. Unfortunately for the great majority of readers, the notes relating to the books and authors listed are in Welsh.

Royal Commission on Historical Monuments in Wales: *Inventories*. London, 1911.

Royal Historical Society and Camden Society. List and Index of the Publications of the Royal Historical Society, 1871-1924, and of the Camden Society, 1840-97. Edit. by H. Hall. London, 1925.

RYE, WALTER. An Index to Norfolk Topography. *Publ. Index Soc.* London, 1881; Supplement, Norwich, 1896.

RYE, WILLIAM B. For a bibliography of foreign visitors to England, see his *England as Seen by Foreigners,* under GENERAL REFERENCE.

RYLANDS, JOHN. Catalogue of the Printed Books and Manuscripts (in the John Rylands Library). 3 vols. Fol. Manchester, 1899.

> This is one of England's greatest libraries, formerly that of Lord Spencer at Althorp. It was purchased *en bloc* for nearly $1,250,000 and became the basis for the Rylands Library in Manchester. It was described by T. F. Dibdin, in his *Bibliotheca Spenceriana*. It has been added to with excellent judgment by the several librarians who have guided its destinies since its foundation in 1899 and is today one of England's richest storehouses of books.— Bookseller's Note.

SCOTT, SIR WALTER. Catalogue of the Library at Abbotsford. *Publ. Bann. Club,* no. 60. Edinburgh, 1838; *Publ. Maitland Club,* vol. 45. Edinburgh, 1838.

> This catalogue was prepared by J. G. Cochrane, and was presented by Major Sir Walter Scott.

Scottish Historical Review. Index to vols. 1-12, 1904-16. By A. Mill. 8vo. Glasgow, 1918.

SHUM, F. A Catalogue of Bath Books, being various Works on the Hot Mineral Springs of Bath from the 16th to the 20th Century, and a List of Books, Pamphlets, and Tracts. 4to. Bath, 1913.

SIBBALD, SIR ROBERT. A List of Books in the Latin Advertisement of his projected Atlas and Description of Scotland. Fol. Edinburgh, 1683.

SIMMS, RUPERT. Bibliotheca Staffordiensis; or, A Bibliographical Account of Books and other Printed Matter, relating to—printed or published in—or written by a native Resident, or Person deriving a Title from—any Portion of the County of Stafford; giving a full Collation and Biographical Notices of Authors and Printers, together with as full a List as possible of Prints, Engravings, Etchings, etc., of any Part thereof and Portraits of Persons so connected, compiled by Rupert Simms. 8vo. Litchfield, 1894.

SINKER, ROBERT. A Catalogue of the English Books printed before 1601 in Trinity College Library, Cambridge. 8vo. Cambridge, 1885.

SINTON, J. Bibliography of Works relating to or published in Hawick; with an Appendix containing a List of Hawick Newspapers, local Maps, and Music. *Trans. Hawick Arch. Soc.,* vol. 40 (also published separately). Hawick, 1908.

SKENE, GEORGE. A Catalogue of the extensive Library of George Skene (formed in the 17th and 18th centuries), comprising a large Number of old Books, Pamphlets, and Collections on the Ecclesiastical and Civil History of Scotland, Scottish Poetry, Heraldry, Antiquities, etc., scarce Books and Tracts on America, English Affairs in the 17th and 18th Centuries . . . scarce Plays and Poetical Pamphlets, Tracts on Trade, Commerce, Navigation, etc. Which will be sold by Auction . . . Jan. 1898. 8vo. London, 1898.

SLEZER, JOHN. A Bibliography of Slezer's *Theatrum Scotiae.* By James Cameron. With an analytical Table of the Plates by W. Johnston. *Publ. Edinb. Bibl. Soc.,* no. 3, 141-47. 8vo. Edinburgh, 1899.

   For Slezer see under 1693, VIEWS.

SMITH, EDWARD. For a bibliography of foreign travelers, see his *Foreign Visitors,* under GENERAL REFERENCE.

SMITH, JOHN RUSSELL. Bibliotheca Cantiana: a Bibliographical Account of what has been published on the History, Topography, Antiquities, Customs, and Family History of the County of Kent. 2 facsimiles. 12mo. London, 1837.

SMITH, JOHN, and SON. Bibliotheca Scotica; A Catalogue of Books relating to Scotland, with Foreword by Lauchlan MacLean Watt. 16 portraits. 8vo. Glasgow, 1926.

   This is a very extensive bibliography.

Society of Antiquaries of London. The Printed Books in the Library of the Society of Antiquaries of London, 1887, with Supplement to 1899, in one volume. London, 1887-99.

SPARGO, JOHN WEBSTER. A Bibliographical Manual for Students of the Language and Literature of England and the United States. A Short Title List. 2nd edit. Chicago, 1941.

   Pertinent to this present work are sections I, II, III, IV A, VI, XIII B 2, XIV A 1, 2, 3, XV B, C, XX, D 1, 2, and E.

SPARKE, A. Bibliographia Boltoniensis, being a Bibliography, with Biographical Details of Bolton Authors and the Books written by them from 1550 to 1912, Books about Bolton, and those printed and published in the Town since 1785. 4to. Manchester, 1913.

STANSFIELD, JOHN. A Catalogue of the Library collected by John Stansfield, Leeds, Comprising a Complete Series of County Histories, Local Topographies, Heraldic, etc., Publications. 8vo. Privately printed, 1882.

Stourhead Library. A Catalogue of the Library removed from Stourhead comprising a choice collection of British Topography, Prints, Water-Colour Drawings, etc. Sold by Sotheby, 30th July, 1883. London, 1883.

STRAUS, RALPH. For a full list of the books published by Edmund Curll, see his *The Unspeakable Curll*, London, 1927.

> The Handlist of Curll's books, begins with 1706 and closes with 1748. Straus explains the great difficulties involved in making an exact list of Curll's publications.

SUTTON, A. Bibliotheca Lancastrensis. Manchester, 1898.

Syon Monastery. Bibliothecae Sionensis Catalogi Pars Altera, omium auctorum Nomina et rerum praecipuarum capita; accedit Historia Collegii et Bibliothecae Anglice scripta. Fol. Londini, 1724.

TAYLOR, E. G. R. Tudor Geography, 1485-1583. London, 1930. Late Tudor and Early Stuart Geography, 1583-1650, a Sequel to Tudor Geography. London, 1934.

> The bibliographies of these works run to some 2,000 items, which range from drainage plans to reports of earthquakes, from atlases and travel collections to pamphlets on trade. Maps and plans are listed separately in the Index. MS material is also included. A third volume has been promised.

TAYLOR, JOHN. Bibliotheca Northantonensis: a Bibliographical Account of what has been written, or printed, relating to the History, Topography, Antiquities, Family History, Customs, etc., of Northamptonshire, including a List of Worthies and Authors and their Works. Northampton, 1869.

> Of this volume there are said to be only six copies, including those in the libraries of Northampton, Peterborough, and Ketting. 25,000 items are listed therein.—J. Williams.

TERRY, CHARLES SANFORD, M.A. A Catalogue of the Publications of Scottish Historical and Kindred Clubs and Societies, And of the Volumes relative to Scottish History issued by His Majesty's Stationery Office, 1780-1908. With a Subject-Index. 4to. Glasgow, 1909. (See Matheson above.)

> This is especially valuable for the researcher into Scottish antiquities. The articles appearing in the Miscellanies are listed separately by their titles. A short account of the various societies is prefixed to each group.

THIELE, WALTER. Official Map Publications: An Historical Sketch, and a Bibliographical Hand-Book of current Maps and Mapping Services in the United States, Canada, Latin America, France, Great Britain, Germany, and certain other Countries. By Walter Thiele under the direction of A. F. Kuhlman. *Publ. American Library Assoc.* 4to. Chicago, 1938.

> This constitutes an extremely useful survey of the progress in geography as explained by maps as well as of the development of the process and progress of map making from ancient times to the present. It is excellently documented with footnote references to authorities, biographies, and other works of both a general and a specific nature. For a brief survey amply supplemented by references to authorities, it is almost unsurpassed.

TOBIN, JAMES E. Eighteenth Century Literature and its Cultural Background. A Bibliography. Fordham University Press. New York, 1939.

See sections Historical Background for Agriculture, Travel Books, and Foreign Opinion and Social Thought.

TODD, ROBERT. Roads and Roadmaking: a Catalogue of Works on Roads, Roadmaking and Travelling in Great Britain, in the Library of Robert Todd, Esq., Hadley Green, Barnet. 8vo. London (?), 1913. (26 pp.)

TRAILL, HENRY D. For bibliographies see his *Social England,* under GENERAL REFERENCE.

TURNBULL, W. B. D. D. A Catalogue of the Extensive and Valuable Library of W. B. D. D. Turnbull: comprising some of the most important County Histories and other Topographical Works . . . privately printed. Sold 27th Nov., 1863. London, 1863.

Union Catalogue of the Periodical Publications in the University Libraries of the British Isles with their respective holdings, excluding titles in the World List of Scientific Periodicals, 1934. Compiled by Marion G. Roupell, under the direction of L. Newcombe, J. Wilks, W. Bonser, B. M. Headicar, Editorial Board. 4to. London, 1937.

Union List of Serials in the Libraries of the United States and Canada. New York, 1927.

Supplements to this work were added from time to time. In 1943 it was reissued with the inclusion of more than 600 libraries.

University College of Wales (Aberystwyth). A Catalogue of (1) Welsh Books, (2) Books relating to Wales, (3) Books written by Welshmen, (4) Books relating to Celtic Literature. Aberystwyth, 1897.

An unclassified but alphabetically arranged list.

UPCOTT, W. A Bibliographical Account of the principal Works relating to English Topography. 2 plates. 3 vols. 8vo. London, 1818.

A large paper edition was also issued the same year.

UPCOTT, W., and JOHN RUSSELL SMITH. A Catalogue of Ten Thousand Tracts and Pamphlets and Fifty Thousand Prints and Drawings, illustrating the Topography and Antiquities of England, Wales, Scotland and Ireland, collected by Wm. Upcott and John Russell Smith, now offered for sale by Alfred Russell Smith. 8vo. London, 1878.

WARD, JAMES. A Descriptive Catalogue of Books relating to Nottinghamshire in the Library of James Ward; with the Supplement. 2 vols. 8vo. Privately printed, Nottingham, 1892-98.

WASBOURN, JOHN. Bibliotheca Gloucestrensis: A Collection of scarce and curious Tracts, relating to the County and City of Gloucester; illustrative of and published during the Civil War, with an Historical Introduction, Notes, and an Appendix. Map and plates. 4to. Gloucester, 1825.

WATT, ROBERT. Bibliotheca Britannica; a General Index to British and Foreign Literature in two parts, Authors and Subjects. 4 vols. 4to. London, 1824.

> Up to the publication of the *Cambridge Bibliography*, this work was one of the handiest tools of the librarian and bibliographer.

WHEELER, H. A. A Short Catalogue of Books printed in England and English Books printed abroad, before 1641, in the Library of Wadham College. Biographical Introduction by J. C. Squire. 8vo. London, 1929.

WHITAKER, HAROLD (Editor). A Descriptive List of the Printed Maps of Yorkshire and its Ridings, 1577-1900. *Publ. Yorkshire Arch. Soc.,* Record Series, vol. 76. Leeds, 1933.

> The titles are followed by descriptions of maps in their technical make-up, and their historical relations to makers, predecessors, and prototypes, with reproductions of some of them. The Introduction presents interesting material for the history of map making.

WILLIAMS, JUDITH BLOW. A Guide to the Printed Materials for English Social and Economic History, 1750-1850. 2 vols. *Records of Civilization Series; Sources and Studies.* Columbia University Press. New York, 1926.

> This is a selective, annotated bibliography, including all aspects of social and economic life. It is of great value to the student of the period, especially of its economic conditions. Section IX deals with Travel, and section X with Local History.

WINSOR, JUSTIN. Bibliography of Ptolemy's Geography. Cambridge (Mass.), 1884.

WOODWARD, SAMUEL. The Norfolk Topographer's Manual, being a Catalogue of the Books, and Engravings published in relation to the County, by Mr. Samuel Woodward, the whole revised and augmented by W. C. Ewing; with a Catalogue of the Drawings, Prints, and Deeds collected for the County History and Antiquities, by Dawson Turner; also Lists of the MSS. and Drawings relating to Norfolk in the British Museum. 8vo. London, 1842.

WORRALL, JOHN. Bibliotheca Topographica Anglicana; or, A New and Compleat Catalogue of All the Books extant relating to the Antiquity, Description, and the Natural History of England, the Counties thereof, etc., to the Present Year 1736, Alphabetically digested in an easy Method; giving an Account of their various Editions, Dates, and Prices, and wherein they differ. 12mo. London, 1736.

WORTH, R. N. The Three Towns Bibliotheca; A Catalogue of Books, Pamphlets, Papers, etc., written by Natives thereof; published therein; or relating thereto; with Brief Biographical Notices of the Principal Authors. Reprinted from the *Transactions of the Plymouth Institution.* Plymouth, 1872.

> This contains notices about shipping, harbors, fisheries, etc., connected with Plymouth, Devenport, Stonehouse.—J. Williams.

Year Book of the Scientific and Learned Societies of Great Britain and Ireland. 16 vols. London, 1884-99.

> This was issued annually. It contains, however, many capricious omissions of societies. For these local societies see also the Catalogue of the British Museum under "Academies." See likewise G. L. Gomme, *Index of Archaeological Papers* for the period 1891-98, published under the Direction of the Congress of Archaeological Societies, London, 1899.—Gross, *The Sources and Literature of English History.*

"Z., A." A List of Works respecting the Islands of Orkney and Shetland, forming a Series of Donations to the Society of Antiquaries of Scotland, by "A. Z." *Publ. Arch. Scot.,* vol. 3. 4to. Edinburgh, 1831.

Index of Personal Names

(The personal names listed in this index are chiefly confined to those mentioned in the main titles, whether authors, editors, agents, engravers, or mappers. Additional listings from the notes include those persons who in some way are tied up with the subject matter or the production of a given work. Names that head the main titles are starred; when these occur elsewhere, their page numbers follow a semicolon. The sections GENERAL REFERENCE and BIBLIOGRAPHIES are omitted, since their alphabetical arrangement in itself constitutes an index. To assist in identification, initials are expanded and the first names added whenever this information is obtainable.)

*Roberts, Henry, 238
Roberts, J., 146
Roberts, J., 268
*Roberts, Lewis, 579
Roberts, R. A., 633
Roberts, S. C., 121
Robertson, —, 181
*Robertson, Archibald, 224, 563
*Robertson, David, 40
Robertson, George, 144
*Robertson, George, 532; 534
Robertson, Rev. J., 534
*Robertson, James, 60
*Robertson, Joseph, 162
Robertson, Lord, 55
Robertson, Mysie E. I., 120
Robertson, W., 163
*Robertson, William, 393, 394
*Robinson, —, 536
Robinson, James, 59
*Robinson, Dr. Nicholas, 22, 143; 304
Robinson, Ralph (pseud. George III), 529
*Robinson, T., 224
Robinson, Dr. Tancred, 494
*Robinson, Rev. Thomas, 494
Robson, James, 534
*Robson, S., 499
Roche, J., 81
*Roche, Sophie von la, 102; 105
*Rochefort, Jorevin de, 84
*Rochefoucauld, François de la, 121
Rockingham, Thomas, Marquis, 593
Rockman, John, 616
*Rocque, Benjamin, 523
*Rocque, John, 148, 199, 202, 206, 265, 266, 267, 270, 273, 358, 550, 594, 595; 271, 584
*Rodenhurst, T., 216
Roderick (the Imposter), 10
Rodocanachi, Emmanuel, 117
*Roe, F. C., 120
Roger of Hovenden, 385, 398, 401
Roger of Wendover, 396, 399, 402
Roger, Rev. M., 534
*Rogers, B., 182
*Rogers, N., 410
*Rogers, R. (pseud.), 9
*Rogers, Richard, 635
*Rohan, Henri, Duc de, 80
Rokewode, Gage, 397
*Roland de la Platière, Jean Marie, 107
*Rolewinck, W., 373
*Rolles, —, 245
*Rolt, Richard, 148
*Rooke, Major H., 353
*Rooke, Hayman, 157, 229, 230, 353, 452, 454; 217
Rooker, M. A., 176
*Rose, John, 511
Ross, Alexander, 37
*Ross, C., 564, 597
Ross, John (Joannis Rossi), 391
*Rosse, Guilio Raviglio, 71
*Rouse, Lewis, M.D., 313
*Rousseau, Jean-Jacques, 119, 122
*Rover, William, 19
*Row, John, 397
*Rowe, Jacob, 546
*Rowlands, Rev. Henry, 413, 446
*Rowlands, Richard, 537
*Rowlandson, Thomas, 32, 37, 193
Rownley, Col., 210
*Rowze, Lodowick, M.D., 307; 315
*Roy, Gen. William, 453, 602; 599
*Rudder, Samuel, 215, 420, 426, 478
Rudyard, John, 338
*Russell, P., 152
*Russell, Robert, 551
"Rusticus," 536
"Rusticus," P., 448
*Rutherford, Andrew, 547
*Rutledge, Jean Jacques, 94
*Rutter, James, 525
*Rutter, Jonathan, 318
*Ryall, J., 322, 562
*Ryder. Dudley, 637
*Rye, William B., 289; 113
*Ryland, I., 176
*Rymer, James, 214
Rymsdyk, Andrew, 425
Rymsdyk, John, 425
Ryther, Augustine, 264, 574

*S., G. (Saint Gellais), Monsieur de, 88
*S., H., 546
S., M., 32
*S., R., 328
*S., W., 505
*Sabin, John, 477
*Sacheverell, William, 11, 141, 444
*S—cy, 252
*Sagitarii, T. Ulysses Saxonicus, 78
St. Clare, William, Prince of Orkney, 479
St. Cuthbert, 466
*St. Dunstan, 401; 487
St. Werburgh, 434
S. Wilfrid, 389
*Saint Fond, Faujas de. 103
St. Pierre, Louis de, 527
Salabert, —, 130
*Saladin, C., 107
*Salisbury, W., 500
*Salmon, Nathaniel, 357, 411, 413, 415, 416, 447; 409
*Salmon, Thomas, 299, 300, 547; 301
*Salmon, William, M.D., 494
*Salter, Gurney, 120
Salter, Rev. H .E., 363
*Sammes, Aylett, 443, 455
Samson, (Abbot), 397
*Sancroft, William (Archbishop), 426
*Sandby, Paul, 176, 177; 174
*Sanders, Rev. Henry, 435
*Sanders, John, 55
Sanderson, Christopher, 629
*Sanderson, Patrick, 478
Sanderson, Robert (Bishop), 476
*Sandford, Francis, 250
Sandford, John, 304
*Sandys, George, 140; 138
Sanson, Adrian and Guillaume, 580
*Sanson, Nicolas, 580, 584; 579
Saunders, H. W., 632
Saunders, Robert, 152
*Saunders, Samuel, 215
*Saunders, William, M.D., 324
*Saussure, César de, 118
*Savage, Henry, 295
*Savage, James, 438, 486
*Savage, Richard, 200
*Savaux, Alexander de, 200
*Savile, Sir Henry, 385; 383
Savile, Sir George, 102
*Savorgnano, Mario, 114
*Saxton, Christopher, 573f.; 130, 132, 576, 577, 581, 583, 584, 601
Say, William (Dean), 488
*Sayer, Robert, 279, 601; 267, 592
*Scaliger, Joseph Justus, 90
Scaterius, Francis, 574
*Schaeffer, Jacob Chr. Gottlieb, 105
Schaschek, —, 72
*Schedel, Hartmann, 68
*Scheidt, Hieronymus, 77
Schenck, —, 578, 579, 584
Schlossberger, August, 113
*Schmeisser, Johann Godfr., 323
*Schnebberlie, Jacob, 190, 434; 222, 430
*Scholes, —, 565; 553
*Schofield, James, 560
*Schön, Theodor von, 115
*Schütz. Friedrich Wilhelm von, 105
Scot, John, 294
Scot, Sir John, 576
*Scot, Reynolde, 503; 508
*Scotin, Gerard, 174
*Scott, Mrs. George, 150
Scott, H. S., 628
*Scott, James, 361
*Scott, J. B., 64, 634
Scott, John, 112
*Scott, Robert, 183; 181, 182
Scott, Samuel, 29, 271
Scott, Sir Walter, 9, 146, 618
*Scribo, J., 329
Scudamore, Lord (John, 1st Viscount?), 388, 474
*Seacom(b)e, John, 148, 417; 37
*Seale, R .W., 591
Seamor (Seymour), Edward, Baron Beauchamp, 132
Seaton, Ethel, 117
Seccombe, Thomas, 629
Seckford, Thomas, 571